*Other Books by Edgar Johnson*

NOVELS

Unweave a Rainbow: A Sentimental Fantasy

The Praying Mantis

CRITICISM

One Mighty Torrent: The Drama of Biography

BIOGRAPHY

Charles Dickens: His Tragedy and Triumph

The Heart of Charles Dickens: His Letters to

Angela Burdett-Coutts

ANTHOLOGIES

A Treasury of Biography

A Treasury of Satire

The Dickens Theatrical Reader (with Eleanor Johnson)

# SIR WALTER SCOTT

## *The Great Unknown*

IN TWO VOLUMES

VOLUME I

# Edgar Johnson

# SIR WALTER SCOTT

*The Great Unknown*

*The Macmillan Company*

The Macmillan Company
866 Third Avenue, New York, N.Y. 10022
Collier-Macmillan Canada Ltd., Toronto, Ontario

*Library of Congress Catalog Card Number: 75-84431*

FIRST PRINTING

*Printed in the United States of America*

*To Eleanor*

AGAIN AND ALWAYS

# ACKNOWLEDGMENTS

No book such as this is written without the aid of scores, even hundreds, of helpers—research libraries and their custodians, scholars, dealers in rare books and manuscripts, bibliophiles and collectors. It is with many warm memories that I now thank both these institutions and the individual men and women who have given me of their knowledge and allowed me to use materials in their possession.

First should come the National Library of Scotland, not only one of the great libraries of the world but one of the richest repositories of Scott manuscripts and autograph letters. During the many months I worked there in a quiet room reserved for me I was aided in every conceivable way by Dr. William Beattie, the director, Mr. W. Park, the curator of manuscripts, and the entire staff of the library. I am deeply grateful.

At the University of Edinburgh, too, I received generous help from Mr. Charles Stuart, the secretary of the university, Mr. William Lindsay Renwick, the Regius Professor of English, and Professor David Murison, of the School of Scottish Studies, where I had an office in an eighteenth-century building immediately adjacent to Scott's boyhood home. In later visits to the university I received much assistance from the late Professor John Butt, who invited me to give the Sir Walter Scott Lectures at the University in 1966, from my friend K. J. Fielding, George Saintsbury Professor of English, and from Professor John MacQueen.

The university library extended me unstinting cooperation. Above all, I owe an overwhelming debt of gratitude to Dr. James C. Corson, the author of the monumental *Bibliography of Sir Walter Scott, 1797–*

*1940*, formerly deputy librarian, who aided me with unsurpassed generosity. Throughout my entire stay in Edinburgh he tirelessly answered my questions, and since then he has continued to respond to written inquires, has read a very great deal of this book in manuscript, and shared with me, in the most detailed and valuable comments, his vast knowledge of Scott and early nineteenth-century Scotland.

Other institutions in Edinburgh from whose resources I profited were the Signet Library, the Edinburgh Public Library, Her Majesty's Register House, the National Portrait Gallery, the Edinburgh High School, and the Edinburgh Academy. I have also had the advantage of seeing letters and other records in the Selkirk Sheriff Court, the Jedburgh Courthouse, and Queen Mary's House in Jedburgh, and of detailed inspections of Melrose Abbey, Dryburgh Abbey, Jedburgh Abbey, and Kelso Abbey. I wish to thank their custodians for their courtesy.

Mrs. Patricia Maxwell-Scott and Miss Jean Maxwell-Scott, Scott's great-great-great-granddaughters, invited my wife and me to Abbotsford, showed us the main rooms of that splendid dwelling, and allowed me to spend hours in Scott's great library, which is still preserved intact. The Reverend Mr. Ian Simpson, the owner of Scott's boyhood home at 25 George Square, also invited us there, and the occupants of 39 Castle Street, Scott's Edinburgh home from 1800 to 1826, showed us his former living rooms.

In the United States the greatest repository of Scott manuscripts, letters, and first editions is the Pierpont Morgan Library. Mr. Frederick W. Adams, Jr., the director, Mr. Herbert Cahoon, the curator of manuscripts, and Dr. Curt F. Buhler all gave me the friendliest aid in exploring its resources. I have profited from the valuable Scott letters and memorabilia in the Berg Collection of the New York Public Library, and owe a debt of gratitude to the late Dr. John W. Gordan, the curator, and to his successor, Mrs. Lola Szladits. In the New York Public Library I have also received invaluable aid from the manuscript division and the rare book room. Another large debt is to the Fales Library of New York University. Much of this collection was made available to me by the kindness of the late Commodore De Coursey Fales when it was still his own private library; since then I have had free access to it through the courtesy of Dr. Charles F. Gosnell, director of the libraries of New York University, and of Dr. Joel Egerer, former curator of the Fales Library.

Many other institutions and libraries and their custodians allowed me to use their materials. Among them I should especially name, with my thanks, the Boston Athenaeum, the Boston Public Library, the British Museum, the Library of the University of Chicago, the Folger

Shakespeare Library, the Houghton Library and the Harry Elkins Widener Library of Harvard University, the Library of the University of Hawaii, the Henry E. Huntington Library and Art Gallery, the Library of Wadham College, Oxford, the Carl Pforzheimer Collection and its curator, Dr. Donald Reiman, the Parrish Collection of Princeton University, the Library of the University of Rochester, and the Forster Collection of the Victoria and Albert Museum. The British Meteorological Office and the United States Naval Observatory also gave me useful information about the weather on the date of the dying Scott's arrival in London on June 13, 1832.

I should fail in gratitude to the City College Library of the City University of New York if I did not acknowledge the loan of numerous books that aided my work and the frequent bibliographical assistance of the library staff, especially the librarian, Dr. Bernard Kreissman—himself a distinguished Scott scholar—and Mrs. Alice Scanlan, Mr. Joseph R. Dunlap, Mr. James Troy Petrie, Mr. Frederick Driscoll, and one former member of that staff, Mr. Martin Kuhn.

Numbers of dealers in autograph letters and rare books have given me access to their materials, among them Maggs Brothers of London, James Thin of Edinburgh, Charles J. Sawyer of London, the late Colonel James F. Drake, the City Book Auction, the Rosenbach Company and John Fleming, and David Kirschenbaum of the Carnegie Book Shop. I wish to thank them for their cooperation and courtesy.

Many private collectors have been generous with their aid. Foremost among them I should thank His Grace the Duke of Buccleuch and Queensberry, who invited my wife and me to Bowhill and allowed me to transcribe without restriction the Scott autograph letters both there and at Dalkeith Palace. The late Mr. Donald F. Hyde and Mrs. Mary Hyde, of Somerville, New Jersey, cordially invited me to visit them and transcribe the Scott letters in their library. Mrs. Alfred Castle of Honolulu, Mr. Henry Lemle of New York, and the late Dr. Frank Pleadwell of Honolulu made available to me the Scott letters and other rare items in their collections.

Countless scholars have aided me with their knowledge and counsel. Professor Sir Herbert J. C. Grierson died while I was barely beginning my work, but not before he had sent me a warm letter of information and friendly encouragement. And all Scott scholars are in his debt for his edition of *The Letters of Sir Walter Scott*, his pioneering effort, in his *Sir Walter Scott, Bart*, to disentangle some of the confusions of the biographical record, and the huge mass of material, now deposited in the National Library of Scotland, that he collected in the course of his work on the letters.

My colleague Professor Coleman O. Parsons lent me the manuscript of his valuable book *Witchcraft and Demonology in Scott's Fiction* before its publication and gave me copies of all his numerous and useful articles and monographs on Scott. Professor Francis Russell Hart of the University of Virginia gave me a xerox copy of his illuminating study of Lockhart's *Life of Scott*, and I have further profited from conversation and correspondence with him about Scott and Lockhart as well as from the penetrating literary criticism in his *Scott's Novels: The Plotting of Historical Survival.* Professor Paul Ochojski of Seton Hall College gave me a typescript of his doctoral dissertation on the relations between Scott and the German romantics. I have profited from correspondence with Mrs. Elizabeth Dexter, of Belmont, Massachusetts, and she has also given me photostats of letters she has discovered. Mr. Marryat R. Dobie has presented to me the notes of a lecture on the *Chronicles of the Canongate* that I had the pleasure of hearing in Edinburgh. Professor Frederick W. Hilles of Yale University allowed me to use the proof sheets, in his possession, of Lockhart's *Life of Scott*.

Among other scholars and writers who have helped me in various ways with suggestions or information are Mr. W. R. Aitkin, the librarian of the Perth and Kinross County libraries, Mr. Benjamin Bromberg, Professor David Daiches of the University of Sussex, Miss Anne Miller Downes, Professor Charles Duffy of the University of Akron, Professor George Ford of the University of Rochester, Professor Leo Gershoy of New York University, Professor Gordon Haight of Yale University, the late Professor James T. Hillhouse of the University of Minnesota, Professor Ian Jack of Pembroke College, Cambridge University, Professor Edward Lecomte of the State University of New York, Miss Marian Lochhead, Mr. T. P. MacDonald, Sheriff of the County of Mid-Lothian, Mr. Carr Hepburn Miller of Perth, the late Dr. John Oliver of Edinburgh, Professor John Henry Raleigh of the University of California, Mr. George Reavey of New York, Professor John D. Rosenberg of Columbia University, Dr. Gregg M. Sinclair, president emeritus of the University of Hawaii, Professor Lionel Stevenson of Duke University, the late Professor Chauncey Tinker of Yale University, and Dr. G. A. M. Wood, as well as my colleagues Professor Morton Cohen, Professor Robert Hennion, and Professor John Connop Thirlwall, and my former colleague Professor Maximilian Graff Walten.

I am indebted to the United States Educational Commission for a grant as a Senior Research Scholar to the University of Edinburgh in 1956. The John Simon Guggenheim Memorial Foundation awarded me two fellowships, one in 1956–57 and another in 1966–67, to aid my work on this biography. I wish to voice my deepest thanks to Dr. Henry Allen Moe, president emeritus of the foundation, to Dr. Gordon

N. Ray, his successor as president, and to Mr. James F. Mathias, for all their aid. I am also grateful to the Corporation of Yaddo and to Mrs. Elizabeth Ames, the director, for three visits to Yaddo, during which I was able to accomplish encouragingly large amounts of the writing.

Parts of the book, though often in greatly modified forms, have appeared in a number of journals and other publications or have been delivered as lectures that are ultimately to appear in print. The entire chapter "Sceptered Kings and Laureled Conquerors" was published in *Nineteenth-Century Fiction*, Volume 17, No. 4, on the invitation of its editor, the late Professor Bradford A. Booth. I have drawn heavily from my introduction to *Rob Roy* in the Riverside Editions and from my introduction to *Waverley* for the New American Library for my critical sections on those two novels. The foundations of still other critical sections were originally read as papers before meetings of the Modern Language Association and published in the *Victorian Newsletter* under the editorship of Dean William E. Buckler of New York University, and given as lectures at the University of Sussex and at Cambridge University. Parts of the concluding section of my last critical chapter, "In Their Orbits Like Stars," were delivered as the Sir Walter Scott Lectures at the University of Edinburgh in April, 1966, and are to appear in their original form in a collected volume of those lectures.

My last and deepest debt is to my wife, Eleanor Johnson, who has been my helper, fellow researcher, editorial assistant, secretary, and critic throughout all the years both of research and writing. No less than was true of the labor on my life of Dickens, there is no aspect of the character of Scott and his associates, no critical judgment that I have formed of his writings, that has not been clarified in my mind by discussion with her. If I could think of any greater tribute than I have already paid to her devotion it would still hardly do her justice. I can therefore only repeat what I have said once before: "She has not only typed my manuscript in its numerous redrafts, but given the most detailed criticism to its style and structure. Every chapter, every page, almost every paragraph is in some way the better for her painstaking thought. But her influence extends far beyond the purely editorial realm. Her belief in me and in this book have sustained me in my work from its beginning to this moment of completion."

EDGAR JOHNSON

*The City College of the City
   University of New York*

# CONTENTS

PART SIX

## The Great Unknown (1816–1821)

**END OF VOLUME I**

PART SEVEN

## *Fame's Trumpet Sounding Loud (1821–1825)*

PART EIGHT

## *The Wand Shivered (1825–1829)*

Contents

PART NINE

## On Comes the Flood (1829–1831)

PART TEN

## Remeid Is None (1831–1832)

# ILLUSTRATIONS

[ *following page 388* ]

# PREFACE

THERE has been no satisfactory biography of Scott. Though the *Memoirs of Sir Walter Scott* by his son-in-law John Gibson Lockhart are impressive in narrative artistry and are written out of intimate personal association, the work is seriously distorted by misunderstanding and bias and riddled by misstatements extending even beyond ignorance of the facts to deliberate invention and falsification.

Close as Lockhart was to Scott, there were, inevitably, many records that were not accessible to him. And Lockhart had no such ideal of biographical precision as animated Boswell. He misplaced events by weeks, months, even years. He inaccurately transcribed documents before his very eyes. Far from being willing, like Boswell, to conduct a correspondence to verify a date or make a journey to authenticate a fact, Lockhart sometimes seemed unwilling to walk across a room to open a desk drawer. "What does it matter?" he would ask. His love of caricature led him to draw cruelly distorted pictures of Constable, the two Ballantynes, and James Hogg. The novelist in Lockhart impelled him to blur and suppress facts inconvenient to the impression he wished to make and to embellish his story with occasional dramatic fictions.

My own aim, nevertheless, has not been to confute Lockhart; it is above all to paint a revealing and truthful portrait of Scott. I have tried to make my narrative as accurate as possible and have corrected many previous errors of fact, but only in special circumstances have I indicated in the text the sources of such mistakes. If the reader is interested in these, he will find them in the Notes documenting the facts.

Most of Scott's later biographers, perhaps intimidated by Lockhart's seeming authority and the sheer bulk of his almost 900,000 words, instead of going to the original sources, have been content to hew their own narratives from the quarry of Lockhart's seven enormous volumes. (Two exceptions were S. Fowler Wright's *Life* in 1932 and Professor Grierson's in 1938, but many of the records were unavailable to Wright, and Grierson conceived his own work less as an independent literary entity than as a corrective supplement to Lockhart. And since then the documentary record has been swelling for another thirty years.) The time is therefore ripe, in the light of the evidence that Lockhart suppressed, distorted, or was unaware of, that Scott's personality be reevaluated, and that his eminence as a creative artist, an outstanding pioneer in the history of the novel, a seminal force in nineteenth-century literature, and a great interpreter of human life and character be portrayed and analyzed.

The bulk of available material is almost staggering and includes much that Lockhart could not possibly have known. There are volumes of reminiscences, memoirs, journals, and diaries, and countless works of literary criticism that have been published over the past 170 years —a mass of data of which the listing to the year 1940 alone runs to almost three thousand items and occupies four hundred pages of Dr. James C. Corson's great *Bibliography of Sir Walter Scott 1797–1940*. There are the twelve stout volumes of Scott's letters edited by Sir Herbert J. C. Grierson in 1932–1938, containing in the neighborhood of 4200 letters to 433 correspondents. And there are many Scott manuscript letters, some of which Professor Grierson published only in part or not at all, and many more which he did not see, which on the same scale might easily fill another six volumes. There is the huge Walpole Collection of letters written *to* Scott between 1796 and 1832 —some 6000 letters by more than 1600 correspondents. There are the papers of Scott's father and the Scott family, the Lockhart papers, the Constable papers, the Ballantyne papers, and the papers and Sederunt Books of the trustees of James Ballantyne and Company. All these, together with first editions and other materials, have been accumulating over the decades in university and research libraries and in the hands of dealers and private collectors.

Reading this mass of evidence, weighing, accepting, rejecting, reflecting upon it, is the foundation of the biographer's task. I have made no endeavor to record items that I have examined and discarded as useless, but any reader curious to know those that I have drawn upon as sources of information can obtain an idea of them from the Acknowledgments, Notes, and Bibliography.

Many of the letters and other documents quoted are taken from unpublished manuscripts, and those from printed sources have been checked wherever possible with the manuscript originals and, if necessary, corrected from them. They are transcribed unaltered, with two exceptions: to avoid confusion I have italicized the titles of books, and when an absence of punctuation obscured meaning I have supplied the minimum needed for intelligibility. Eccentricities of punctuation I have preserved; and with neither Scott nor his correspondents have I taken it upon myself to mend their syntax, to correct their grammar, or to rationalize their spelling. In quotations I retain their renderings of Gaelic words and phrases, though in my own text I conform to the usage of modern Gaelic scholars. Quotations in Scottish dialect are also given as each of the writers spelled them.

A word about money. The purchasing value of the pound throughout the sixty-one years of Scott's lifetime was much greater than that of 1970, but of course it was no more stationary during that period than it has been during the past sixty years. Between 1770 and 1830 rents rose five- or six-fold. Money wages for skilled workers doubled between 1760 and 1790 and rose another 50 per cent by 1830; during the same period the price of meat doubled, though that of wheat, barley, and oats rose only about 30 per cent. Machine-made articles often cost considerably more than those made by handicraftsmen, and both were relatively more expensive than food. The guinea and a half to two guineas for which Scott's novels sold, for example, rendered them a luxury out of reach for all except a very small segment of the population.

Facts such as these make economic historians understandably reluctant to give any simple index to the value of the pound in the late eighteenth and early nineteenth centuries as compared with the present. Nevertheless readers will feel the need of some rough guide. If all the qualifications suggested above are kept in mind, it should not be misleading to say that all monetary figures should be multiplied by between six and eight to obtain an approximate idea of their current purchasing value. One pound, therefore, would equal a little less than $15–$20 in 1970 United States currency. Thus, Scott's £300 salary as sheriff of Selkirkshire would be the equivalent of about $4500 to $6000. There figures make it possible to realize the astounding, the almost Hollywoodian, sums that publishers were willing to pay for Scott's novels.

Of Scott's personality I need say nothing in this preface; I have tried to portray him in the body of the book. I should note merely that I have adhered strictly to the recorded evidence and allowed myself no fictional embellishments, not even of the weather. When the facts were unknown, I have said so; when more than one interpretation of them was possible I have presented them all; when one version seemed to me more convincing than the others I have given that one in my narrative but presented the others in the notes together with my reasons for doubting them. For all factual statements whatsoever I have fully indicated my sources.

Let me end with a few words about the aim of the critical sections and the critical chapters of this book. I have sought neither to observe a slavish traditionalism of judgment nor to startle by paradox and iconoclasm. I make no attempt to pretend that pineapples grow on Scottish pinetrees; I do not ignore the heather that clothes the hills. I have often drawn upon the critical perceptions of my predecessors: so many learned and sensitive readers over the years could hardly have failed to say much that was penetrating and true. When I have quoted them I have made due acknowledgment. Even beyond this, however, there must be places where I have unconsciously drawn from them or echoed them and must beg forgiveness if there are such debts for which I have failed to voice my thanks.

But criticism can never claim, even collectively, to have said the last word, nor can anyone do so. A work of art reveals new meanings as it is seen in changing lights, from different angles, or under new cultural circumstances. The Shakespeare of Samuel Johnson does not cease to be true because of the Shakespeare of Dover Wilson; they coexist, and our awareness of their richness is deepened by the multiple sensibilities that interpret them for us. What I have tried to do is to approach each of Scott's works with a candid mind, and to clarify as I reflected upon it what seems to me its measure of success and failure and its significant achievement. So seen, Scott emerges as one of the greatest writers of the nineteenth century and one of the great figures in English literature.

                                                                    E. J.

# INTRODUCTION

No Scottish name is more widely known than that of Walter Scott. With Robert Bruce, with Robert Burns, with Mary Queen of Scots, it is among those that have echoed throughout the world. His country's name and fame, her bloody and heroic past, Scott celebrated to mankind. All save one of his major poems, twenty-two of his thirty-two works of prose fiction, have their scene in his native land and are filled with Scottish song and story, Scottish lakes and mountains and glens, Scottish men and women. Appropriately, he who gave such luster to Scotland derives his very name from the land he loved.

But fame so widely diffused nearly always melts into the mists of legend. Robert Bruce becomes a folk-hero, the unthroned king learning patience from the spider; Burns becomes the peasant poet, drinking, wenching, creating immortal lyrics, but dying in misery; Mary, the lovely and unhappy queen dethroned by tumultuous nobles and stern fanatics and losing her life beneath the headman's ax. Among these fabled beings Scott looms as a classical victim of tragic fate—the gloriously successful author, showered with renown and gold, then suddenly struck down in the peak of pride, overwhelmed beneath a mass of mysterious debt, killing himself with the gigantic toil of discharging these liabilities.

How much of the legend is truth? Was Scott a victim of fate, or did he provoke his own catastrophe? Was he an unworldly poet living in a realm of dream, deceived by dishonest publishers and bungling agents? Was he an ambitious materialist goaded by visions of wealth and the hope of founding a lordly dynasty? Was he a flatterer of kings and a sycophant of the aristocracy, or did he weigh plowmen and princes in the same balance and treat all men as brothers? Had he any standards other than those of convention and propriety? Did his life embody any ideals of character and conduct? Was it anything more than a melodrama of grandiose worldly triumph crashing down into disaster?

The problem is more complex than that of merely disentangling the man from the coil of myth that time has woven around him. Even among his contemporaries, who saw him close at hand, there was no one ringing and unanimous judgment. For some, among them his son-in-law John Gibson Lockhart, he was with only a few reluctant qualifications "A GREAT AND GOOD MAN";—in Lockhart's life of him, writes Andrew Lang, "the defects are blazoned by the intense light of genius and goodness." But for others, among them Thomas Carlyle, Scott was not a great man at all; "his ambitions were worldly," and his work, empty of all message, had no other aim than to make the world "simply pay him for the books he kept writing." The dispute has gone on to the present, idolators and iconoclasts ranged in opposing bands. Even more than in the days when Scott was the anonymous "Author of *Waverley*," and curiosity was rampant about the identity of "the Great Unknown," he remains the Great Unknown, the very outlines of his character in controversy.

As of the man, so of his work. There are readers for whom its sheer bulk and range have been too frightening to tackle. Meticulous critics, not always utterly without reason, have picked flaws in his style and structure. To many he has been predominantly a creator of colorful historical thrillers, filled with a pageantry of tournaments, clashing warriors, and courtly spectacles against a background of battlements and donjon keeps. These readers have found in his work no interpretation of life, no grappling with its real problems, but only a picturesquely romanticized view of the world. They have not seen that his thought was rooted in the eighteenth century within which he was born and that his judgments everywhere are a logical development of its commonsense rationalism. They have failed to observe that his paramount concern is the influence of men's environment on their characters and behavior, that his vision is primarily realistic and disillusioned, and his philosophy of life fundamentally stoic. In his work then, as well as in his life, Scott is still the Great Unknown. What was he really like, both as man and as writer? How was he shaped by the Scotland and the Edinburgh that saw his birth almost two hundred years ago?

                                                                    E. J.

# PART ONE

*Heir and Heritage*

1 7 7 1 – 1 7 8 3

# 1

## The College Wynd

### ( 1 7 7 1 – 1 7 7 3 )

In 1771, EDINBURGH still clung to its ridge of rock. From Holyrood
House, the palace of the Scottish kings, whose candle-snuffer turrets
lay within the morning shadow of Arthur's Seat, the old town stretched
like Leviathan more than a mile up to the gray walls and bartizans of
the Castle, girdling its basalt crag and gilded by the rays of the setting
sun. Along the humped backbone of the city, climbing to the Castle
Esplanade, the Canongate merged into the High Street and the Lawnmarket, crowded jumbles of stone buildings piling up to twelve stories
in height and thrusting their chimney pots and gables to the sky. Most
of the town's sixty thousand inhabitants[1] lived in these lofty tenements,
well-to-do families occupying an entire floor on the upper levels, the poor
crowded into rooms on the lower floors, burrowing into cellars and basements, or tucked away in the garrets.

Between the densely packed structures, plunging down the steep
sides of the hill both north and south, descended narrow foot-passages
called wynds and huddles of dark courtyards and blind alleys called closes,
where doorways clustered around entries to the common stairs and pigs
rooted in refuse piles. Southward the houses tumbled away to the Grassmarket and the cramped roadway of the Cowgate, and then climbed the
opposite slope to the low-roofed quadrangles of the old College. Here
a dismal lane called the College Wynd struggled up to the College Gateway, a handsome portico with a richly ornamented architrave. Despite
its sunless gloom, the Wynd was favored as a residence by members of
the gentry, professional men, and many of the professors of the College.
At the top of its sharp ascent, in a building just west of the Gateway,

which also housed Dr. Joseph Black, the famed discoverer of latent heat, dwelt the family of a legal practitioner named Walter Scott.[2]

Here, in their third-floor flat, on August 15, 1771, was born a flaxen-haired infant whom his parents christened Walter. He was their ninth child, but five of his brothers and sisters had died in babyhood or early childhood. At the time of Walter's birth there were three other children—Robert, who was eight, John, almost four, and Barbara, who was to die when her baby brother was five months old. The Scotts were a stubborn race: three of the children who had died in infancy had borne the names of Robert, John, and Walter, and the following year the parents were to name another infant Anne after her mother, whose first namesake had died in 1767.[3]

When the second son to bear his name was born, Mr. Scott was a pale, grave-faced gentleman of forty-two. Walter was a name that had been borne by generations of Scotts since the fifteenth century. From the tenth century on, their ancestors appear in Scottish history, a turbulent Border clan fierce in forays against the Southron, and wild in feuds, sheep stealing, and cattle reiving. They are chronicled among those who fought in the medieval battle of Halidon Hill and in the disastrous defeats of Flodden and Pinkie. Their numerous branches ranged in station from small landowners up to the great ducal house of Buccleuch. Eldest son of a junior offshoot of the clan, the senior Walter Scott was the first of his family to live in Edinburgh and follow a learned profession.

His father, Robert Scott, was a prosperous sheep farmer at Sandy-knowe, near Kelso. The wealthy peers and bellicose lairds of Berwick, Roxburgh, and Dumfries were, he observed, a litigious lot; he shrewdly calculated that a Borderer in the legal profession ought to do exceedingly well. Accordingly he determined that his oldest son should become a Writer to the Signet, a superior order of solicitors peculiar to Scotland, among whose privileges was that of appearing before the Court of Session, the supreme civil court of the kingdom. The youth was apprenticed to James Pringle of Bowland, and proved able and conscientious. Later he was employed, and then presently taken into partnership, by a writer named George Chalmers.[4]

Young Mr. Scott was a strange lawyer. Although his strict Calvinism made him more enthusiastic about church history than jurisprudence, he was an earnest law student. Perhaps the same bent that found excitement in the mazes of ecclesiastical contention gave fascination to the intricacies of abstruse feudal tenures. He became an expert conveyancer. Conscience and combativeness mingled in his devotion to the causes of his clients. His moral probity identified their welfare with his own; his Border blood easily boiled in their behalf. But he was incapable of chicanery and as unsuspicious of knavery as Sterne's Uncle Toby. Some of his clients he exasperated by assuming that their sense of duty was as lofty as his own and paying out to an old mother or a helpess aunt money they had intended for betting or the bottle. Others came to owe him thousands of pounds and rewarded him with lawsuits or declarations of bankruptcy. Those who wanted to slide out of obligations found that his peppery artlessness made it easy to blame him for a disagreement. He prospered, but many of his clients made more money out of him than he did out of them.

His rigidity of principle was unbending. Even in his youth his schoolfellows had found it impossible to seduce or shame him into the mildest forms of roistering. As a man, during a time when judges sometimes reeled onto the bench after a night's debauch, his habits remained severely abstemious. Not that he was a teetotaler; on festive occasions he heartily enjoyed a social glass of wine. But more than the pleasures of company or the table he liked to take his black knee-breeches and snowy ruffles into his own solitary room and sit poring over a folio volume of John Knox or Spottiswoode's *History of the Church and State of Scotland.*[5]

His Sabbatarianism was inflexible. Once a rich farmer of Haddington came to Edinburgh on a Sunday demanding to see some papers dealing with a process in which Mr. Scott was his agent. The man of law asked if a weekday would not do. The farmer insisted. Mr. Scott handed over all the documents in the file to his client, remarking dryly that it was not his habit to do business on the Sabbath but that it would be no task to find lawyers in Edinburgh who would not share his objection.[6] Despite such unaccommodating scruples, Mr. Scott's business grew.

In April, 1758, within little more than a month of his twenty-ninth birthday, he married. His bride was Anne Rutherford, eldest daughter of Dr. John Rutherford, professor of medicine in the University of Edinburgh. On her father's side she too came of an old Border family, which could claim descent from many a medieval warrior and distinguished outlaw, among them, according to family legend, that "Outlaw Murray" celebrated in a ballad of the time of James V. Her mother's family traced their line to an eleventh-century Edulf de Swinton and bore within their veins the blood of the haughty earls of Douglas; a Sir John Swinton had fought at the battle of Otterburn. Dr. Rutherford was a pupil of the illustrious Boerhaave, who as professor of medicine at Leiden had introduced modern methods of clinical instruction.[7]

At the time of her marriage, Anne Rutherford was already twenty-six years of age. Not pretty and short in stature, she was lively in mind. At the select boarding school of Miss Euphemia Sinclair she had learned not only the needle and the account book but correctness in speech and writing and something of history and belles-lettres. She delighted in ballads, folk tales and old lore, and genealogy. Together with many other young ladies of the gentry and nobility she was sent on to be "finished off" by the Honorable Mrs. Ogilvie, "supposed to be the *best-*

*bred* woman in Scotland," who taught a code of manners so unbending that not even in extreme old age would Anne Scott allow her back to rest against a chair.[8]

The newly married couple set up housekeeping in a lofty upper story of Anchor Close, a narrow ravine of a passage descending steeply from the High Street to the hollow where the Nor' Loch and its muddy waters still extended east all the way from below the Castle escarpments to the dam at Halkerston's Wynd.[9] Only a few yards down the alley, to the left, was the famous tavern of Dawney Douglas, with its dark fiery pandemonium of a kitchen and its handsomely paneled Crown Room, where advocates, writers, and judges caroused nightly on tripe, rizzared haddocks, and minced collops washed down with ale or claret followed by whiskey or brandy punch.[10] In Anchor Close, between 1759 and 1766, Mrs. Scott bore the five children who died at such early ages, and here in 1763 was born Robert, the oldest brother whom little Walter knew.[11]

For all the babies arriving every year or two, Anne Scott, more sociable than her husband, enjoyed entertaining friends around the tea table or having them drop in for an evening of reading and conversation. "How my heart would jump," wrote one of them who had gone to America, "were I to find myself set down in Anchor Close, or supposing I were to come slyly some evening and catch you reading a paper by Mr. Spectator in the Drawing room." Another mentions being interrupted in their reading "by a train of fine ladies who bounced in upon us—I am persuaded were I constantly living in your house I should be ready to cry out:

> Shut, shut the door, good John, fatigu'd I said,
> Tye up the knocker, say I'm sick or dead

for there is no resting a moment—but you Madam have been formed for society."[12] Friendly, sagacious, good-humored, she drew people about her. Presently she prevailed so far over her straitlaced husband as sometimes even to go to the theater. "Your being turned fine lady," wrote her sister from India, "and gadding about to plays delights me."[13]

Around 1767–68 the family moved to the College Wynd, where in succession were born John in 1768, Walter in 1771, and their sister Anne in 1772. Wattie, as he was called, was an unusually lively and robust child, though he narrowly escaped contracting consumption from his first nurse, who had concealed her illness. She went privately, however, to consult their neighbor Dr. Black, who warned Mr. Scott of the danger, so that she was dismissed. The child's second nurse, Lizzie Cranston, was a strapping peasant who lived near the Grange, a southern suburb, and supplied the family with eggs. Under her care he grew plump and vigorous, running about incessantly from morning till night.[14]

One evening, when he was eighteen months old, made fractious by teething, he resisted being put to bed, and had to be chased around and around the room before he was cornered. Next morning he had a fever, which was blamed on the cutting of his teeth. The fourth morning, while he was being bathed, his right leg was observed to be powerless. His grandfather and several other doctors found no dislocation or sprain; they tried in vain all the usual remedies, including blistering. The disease, not yet recognized at that time, was infantile paralysis. Dr. Rutherford sensibly suggested that the child be sent to his other grandfather's farm to try the effect of fresh air and outdoor exertion. From the dark and dirt of the College Wynd, in the spring of 1773, little Wattie was taken to his grandfather Robert Scott's home at Sandyknowe. Its swelling hills and wind-blown vistas were his earliest memories.[15]

## 2

---

# *Peel Tower and Time Past*

# *( 1 7 7 3 – 1 7 7 5 )*

THE FARM OF SANDYKNOWE lay some distance from the tiny thatched village of Smailholm, a little over thirty miles southeast of Edinburgh in Roxburghshire. To take care of Wattie his mother sent a maid, that he might be no trouble to the two grandparents: Robert Scott was in his sixty-eighth year and failing in health, and Barbara Scott only a little younger. The household also included the child's Aunt Jenny, his father's oldest sister, now forty years of age, and an elderly housekeeper named Alison Wilson, as well as the domestic servants and farm laborers.[1]

All kinds of stimulants, among them various folk-remedies, were tried to overcome Wattie's lameness. Whenever a sheep was killed for the use of the family, the child was stripped and wrapped in the skin, warm from the flayed carcass of the animal. Years later he still remembered how he lay upon the floor of the little parlor "in this Tartar-like habiliment . . . while my grandfather, a venerable old man with white hair, used every excitement to make me try to crawl." Sometimes his grandfather's second cousin, Sir George MacDougal of Makerston, joined these efforts. Kneeling on the floor, in his old uniform as a colonel of the Greys, with a small cocked hat, embroidered scarlet waistcoat, and light-colored coat, he dragged his fat watch across the carpet to tempt the child to creep after it.[2]

On sunny days, warmly wrapped, Wattie would be carried out on the shoulders of "Auld Sandy Ormiston," the cow bailie, or of one of the ewe milkers, or cradled in the arms of his mother's maidservant, sometimes to be laid in the green meadow among the quietly browsing sheep, sometimes deposited at the foot of the old peel tower whose beetling crag was only a bowshot from the farmhouse.[3] These daily airings almost cost him his life. The maid, a town girl, had left behind her in Edinburgh a lover who had possibly taken more than her heart. Lonely in the country-side and grieving for her absent sweetheart, she contracted a hatred for her infant charge as the cause of her unhappiness and began to feel deli-rious temptations to carry him up to the crag, cut his throat with her scissors, and bury him in the bog at its foot. Some impulse moved her to confess these urgings to old Alison Wilson, who at once took posses-sion of the child and saw that the girl was dismissed and sent back to town, where she later, in fact, was adjudged a lunatic.[4]

Wattie was soon a favorite among the help. One of the house servants named Tibby Hunter described him as "a sweet-tempered bairn, a dar-ling with all about the house." The ewe milkers, she said, delighted to carry him on their backs; and he was "very gleg [quick] at the uptake, and soon kenned every sheep and lamb by the headmark." Lying upon the velvet green tufts and rolling about on the grass among the flocks, he came to feel a fellowship with these patient animals and an affection that lasted throughout his life.[5]

The surrounding landscape too was sinking into his awareness. Over the ruined wall or rough crag behind him there clambered honeysuckle or yellow and orange wallflower.[6] Nearby was his grandfather's house, a gabled building of gray stone, with chimneys rising above the thatch at each end and a lower addition at one of them. The open entrance door in the center of the long wall was flanked by a bright window on each side.[7] All about were hilly meadows and furrows, rounded, dinted, rising, slanting, with stone dikes climbing straight up the slopes and disappear-ing over their summits, while dappled cloud-shadows rippled over the swelling yellows and greens of fields and the darker emerald of trees.[8]

Smailholm commanded a magnificent prospect of the wide country-side. The ridge upon which it was located rose between the valleys of the Leader and the Eden, coming down from the north to mingle their waters with the silver floods of the sharply meandering Tweed. Looking north, the child could see the dun slopes of the Lammermuir Hills and the heights of Lauderdale and, nearer at hand, the thick woods of Meller-stain. Eastward, beyond Kelso, bosomed in trees, extended the level country bounded by Flodden spur and the blue Cheviots. And over to the west, beyond the broomy Cowdenknowes, the purple heights of the Eildons raised against the sky the three peaks into which they were supposed to have been cleft by one of Wattie's own ancestors, the wizard Michael Scot.[9]

All this Border country was haunted and historic ground. Within those Eildon Hills, the child was told, Thomas the Rhymer, whose home had been in nearby Ercildoune, had been imprisoned by the Queen of the Fairies. At sunset their lengthening shadows bathed the blue-gray ruins of Melrose Abbey, within whose chapel lies the wizard's tomb. Farther down the Tweed, in a smooth and lazy loop of the river, glowed the pink-ish orange sandstone of Dryburgh Abbey, embowered among the dark green of its ancient yews. A little farther still, almost facing each other across the stream, were Mertoun, the seat of the Scotts of Harden, and Lessudden, the home of the Scotts of Raeburn, elder branches of the great Scott clan to which Wattie's family belonged. Not far to the south was Lilliard's Edge, named for a Scottish maiden heroine who had fought and died there in the battle of Ancrum Moor. From a rocky eminence four miles north of Smailholm frowned the blackened ruins of Hume Castle, a thirteenth-century fortress captured and destroyed by Cromwell in 1651. All those about Wattie, the cow bailie and the ewe milkers, the housekeeper and the maids, were steeped in the fairy legends and historic tales of that ancient countryside, and from them he eagerly absorbed these stories of wizardry, romance, and war.

Above the very meadow in which the child lay, on an almost per-pendicular crag, rose the Tower of Sandyknowe, its square and massive shape reflected in the deep loch bordering the morass below.[10] It was built of broken whinstone, with door frames of blood red sandstone, and its summit, to which he was sometimes carried to gaze over the country-side, towered sixty feet above its base. Through walls nine feet thick he passed into a dimly lit arched vault and then up a wheel stair to the great hall with its huge fireplace and wooden ceiling. From here the stairway spiraled to another chamber, and above it to yet another, vaulted with rough stones, and then at last to the bartizans of the roof looking west and east over the wide expanse.[11]

Every morning, when Wattie saw Sandy Ormiston, he clamored to be set astride the old man's shoulders and taken outdoors.

> Here was poetic impulse given
> By the green hill and clear blue heaven.[12]

When the little boy was to be carried home again, the cow bailie blew a special note on his whistle to tell the maidservants in the house below. One day Wattie was forgotten among the knolls when a thunderstorm came on. Suddenly remembering him, his Aunt Jenny ran out to bring him in, and found the child lying on his back, clapping his hands at every bright flash, and crying out, "Bonny! Bonny!"[13]

On stormy or wintry days, when he could not go out, Aunt Jenny would read aloud. A visitor on one of these occasions remembered the family scene: "Old Mrs. Scott sitting, with her spinning-wheel, at one side of the fire, in a *clean clean* parlor; the grandfather, a good deal failed, in his elbow-chair opposite; and the little boy lying on the carpet at the old man's feet, listening to the Bible or whatever good book Miss Jenny was reading to them."[14] Among a few old volumes that lay in a window seat were two that speedily became Wattie's favorites, *Auto-mathes* and Allan Ramsay's *Tea-Table Miscellany*.[15] From these his quick memory soon enabled him to pipe long passages in the lisp that marked his speech. In the latter volume, years afterward, he wrote: "This book belonged to my grandfather, Robert Scott, and out of it I was taught Hardiknute by heart before I could read the ballad myself. It was the first poem I ever learnt—the last I shall ever forget."[16]

So unbounded became his love of this ballad that he was soon shouting it out on all occasions. Once the minister of the parish, Dr. Alexander Duncan, who had come in for a sedate chat, sat exasperated under the bombardment, a tall emaciated figure, his legs cased in clasped gambadoes, his face as long as Don Quixote's, and at last protested in despair: "One may as well speak in the face of a cannon as where that child is!" But for all his faint acidity, the goodhearted minister was no more able than any of the family to remain annoyed by the precocious blue-eyed child.[17] As Scott was to write in later years:

> I was wayward, bold and wild,
> A self-willed imp, a grandame's child.
> But half a plague and half a jest,
> Was still endured, beloved, caressed.[18]

His grandmother, in whose childhood the old days of Border warfare between the English and the Scots were still living memories, told him many a tale of its wild heroes—Wight Willie of Aikwood, Jamie Telfer of the Fair Dodhead, and, of later date, the famous Deil of Littledean, who had married her grandmother's sister—all of them merry men like Robin Hood and Little John.[19] Her own forebears were of a loftier strain. Her ancient Berwickshire family, the Haliburtons of Newmains, named among their ancestry the Regent Albany, the Earls of Ross, and the Mertouns, and ranged through Sinclairs, Pringles, Erskines, Campbells, and the Rutherfords from whom Wattie's maternal grandfather was descended. The patrimony of the Haliburtons included the lands of Dryburgh and its ruined Abbey. Barbara Scott's brother Robert Haliburton, however, was a weak, foolish man who, without business sense, engaged in trade and went bankrupt. Wattie's father bid five thousand pounds for the estate, but Robert Scott dissuaded him from offering more. Thus the lands passed out of the family, although they later acquired the right of burial in the Abbey.[20]

On Robert Scott's side, Wattie's ancestors were a rough lot who had stolen cattle and burned castles with the best of them. From both his grandparents he learned the saga of their deeds. Auld Wat of Harden, Robert Scott's great-great-grandfather, had been a famed marauder whose ruined castle still towered high above the elms of a precipitous glen where the river Borthwick poured its red flood through western Teviot-dale. To this wild retreat in 1567 he had brought his bride, Mary Scott, the beautiful "Flower of Yarrow" who lives in Scottish song.[21]

When the last bullock stolen from English pastures had been eaten, the child was told, the Flower of Yarrow would place on the table a dish with a pair of clean spurs. This "Feast of Spurs" was a hint to ride forth and forage their next dinner. Once when the cowherd was driving the cattle to pasture, Auld Wat heard him call to goad out Harden's cow. "Harden's *cow!*" echoed the affronted chieftain. "Is it come to that pass? By my faith they shall soon say Harden's *kye* [cows]." Sounding his bugle, he set forth with his band, and next day returned with "a bow of kye, and a bassen'd [brindled] *bull*." But he had been forced to leave behind a large haystack because he had no cart to haul it in. "By my saul," he exclaimed, "had ye but four feet ye should not stand lang there."[22]

Auld Wat's heir, William, had been knighted by James VI but was later extortionately fined by Cromwell for his loyalty to Charles I. His youth had been one of furious clan warfare. One story about him which Wattie enormously enjoyed told how, in a foray against the lands of Sir Gideon Murray of Elibank, the treasurer-depute of Scotland, he was overpowered and brought in shackles before that baron. The angry laird was hot to hang his captive at once on the "doomtree" outside the castle gate. "What!" exclaimed his lady. "Hang the handsome young Knight of Harden when I have three ill-favoured daughters unmarried!" Sir Gideon saw the point: young Harden was given his choice of death or marrying the ugliest of them, known as "Meikle-mouthed Meg." The prisoner had three days to make up his mind; not until the rope was around his neck did he agree to save his life by accepting the marriage noose instead. A wedding contract was at once drawn up on the parchment of a drum. Wattie could picture it all hilariously—the unwilling bridegroom, the gleeful bride agape with wide-mouthed grin[23]—and later he cheerfully concluded that he himself had inherited some of his great-great-great-grandmother's amplitude of mouth.[24]

Their third son, Walter Scott, became the first Laird of Raeburn, and married Isobel, a daughter of the ancient Roxburghshire family, the MacDougals of Makerstoun. Although all the rest of their family were cavaliers and supporters of Charles I, these two surprisingly turned Whigs and later Quakers. After the Restoration, this Scott of Raeburn was imprisoned, first at Edinburgh in 1665, then at Jedburgh, by order of the Privy Council. On the petition of his elder brother, Sir William Scott of Harden, his children were taken away from him and a heavy sum levied annually against his estate for their education. The elder of his two sons—once again a William—was the progenitor of all the later Scotts of Raeburn. The second, who was named Walter, was Wattie's great-grandfather.[25]

Thanks, perhaps, to the discipline of the Privy Council, both brothers became devout Tories. The elder died in 1699, and his son was killed at the age of twenty-one. The younger brother, Walter, became, as the old Scots law phrase has it, "Tutor of Raeburn," that is, guardian to his infant grandnephew. The Tutor of Raeburn married Jean Campbell of Silvercraigs, thereby relating his descendants to the famous Highland Clan of Campbell, the Sliochd nan Diarmid, or sons of Dermot, whose chiefs were the Dukes of Argyll.

Wattie was fascinated by a picturesque detail in this ancestor's story. So fierce was his devotion to the Stuart kings that when James fled in 1688, he swore never to touch razor or scissors to his beard until the banished dynasty was restored to the throne. The luxuriant growth that gradually came to cover his breast led to his being called "Beardie," but he almost lost both his beard and his neck by intriguing and taking arms in the uprising of 1715. His fortune he did lose, though his distant kinswoman Anne, Duchess of Buccleuch and Monmouth, pleaded successfully for his life. Thenceforth Beardie lived in high-minded and long-bearded poverty upon the little property his wife had brought in dowry and a small allowance for managing his grandnephew's estate.[26]

Beardie's eldest son emigrated to America, where his family became extinct in the male line. His second son, Wattie's grandfather Robert, was brought up to be a sailor. But on his very first voyage he was shipwrecked off Dundee and took a violent distaste to the sea. Old Beardie was infuriated; when Robert refused to yield, he quarreled fiercely with his son and cast him off. Robert, who had his own share of Beardie's obstinacy and temper, turned Whig on the spot. Deciding to set up as a sheep farmer, he leased Sandyknowe from his kinsman, Scott of Harden. An old shepherd named Hogg lent him his life savings of £30 to stock the farm. With this sum, master and man set off to buy their sheep at Whitsun-Tryste, a fair near Wooler in Northumberland.

At the fair the shepherd went from drove to drove till he found a good flock, and then hastened to locate Robert and have him conclude the bargain. What was his surprise to see him galloping a mettled hunter about the racecourse and to learn that he had spent their entire capital on this animal! "Moses's bargain of green spectacles did not strike more dismay into the Vicar of Wakefield's family," Scott wrote years later, "than my grandfather's rashness into the poor old shepherd." They returned to Sandyknowe without any sheep, but a few days later Robert Scott rode the horse to hounds and displayed the animal so well at the hunt that he sold it for double what it had cost. Now stocking the farm, he began a prosperous career. He expanded his operations into the cattle trade between the Highlands of Scotland and the leading counties of England and made a tidy fortune by his droving transactions.[27]

His grandson delighted to hear these stories of his freebooting ancestors and of Robert Scott's own youthful adventures. Among the tales the old man loved to tell, his face "brightened in the evening fire," was one of a wild encounter with a gang of gypsies. Riding over Charterhouse Moor, he found himself surrounded by a large band who were carousing in a bushy hollow. They seized his bridle with shouts of welcome. They had often dined at his expense, they guffawed; now he must share their cheer. Robert Scott felt a little alarmed, for he had rather a large sum of money on him and gypsies had a sinister reputation for being willing to slit a man's throat for a few guineas. He put a bold face on it, however, and sat down to a feast of game, pigs, and poultry plundered from the surrounding countryside. The mirth around the fire "grew fast and furious," but in the deepening darkness, at a hint from some of the older gypsies, he suddenly leaped on his horse and galloped away from his entertainers.[28]

Gypsy stories were often in Robert Scott's mouth, many of them reminiscences of Jean Gordon, their queen. A farmer of Yetholm who had often been generous to her found himself benighted in the Cheviots and seeing a glimmer of light in a deserted barn, entered to her joyful shout of welcome: "Eh, sirs! The winsome gudeman of Lochside!" A feast for ten or twelve was preparing, but before the men returned, she made her guest put his gold in her custody, keeping just a few shillings in his pocket lest it look suspicious that he was traveling penniless. When the gang came in, the farmer was supposed to be sleeping, but he heard their stifled whispers and light footsteps by his bed of straw and knew they were rummaging his clothes. They decided that the smallness of the booty made it not worth stealing, and at dawn Jean roused him while the others were still in a drunken slumber and sent him on his way with his gold, refusing to accept so much as a single guinea.

Jean was a staunch Jacobite, and after the Pretender's desperate attempt on the throne in the '45, when Carlisle had tamely surrendered to the Highlanders, she was ducked to death by a mob there as a penalty for her zeal. A robust woman, she struggled vigorously with her murderers, and as often as she got her head above water continued to shout her loyalty to the Young Pretender: "Charlie yet! Charlie yet!" Wattie wept piteously over the fate of Jean Gordon. In later years he remembered having once seen her granddaughter Madge Gordon. And just as Dr. Johnson retained "a shadowy recollection of Queen Anne as a stately lady in black, adorned with diamonds," so his memory was "haunted by a solemn remembrance of a woman of more than female height, dressed in a long red cloak," who gave him an apple.[29]

Another female wanderer came to Robert Scott's door, probably before Wattie's time, but the child heard and long remembered her story. Arriving on a cold evening, she made mute signs, begging food and shelter for the night. Next morning the country was blanketed in snow, and she was allowed to remain. By the time the weather grew milder, the dumb woman had learned to tell them by signs that she would like to stay and earn her keep by working at the wheel.

After she had been a member of the household for some three years, while all the family except Dumb Lizzie were at church one Sunday, a shepherd boy who was supposed to be watching his flock on the lea slunk into the house. In the kitchen, believing himself unobserved, he put out his hand to take something that tempted him. The dumb woman came upon him suddenly, and, surprised, exclaimed in loud Scotch, "Ah, you little deevil's limb!" Terrified, the boy fled to the church with news of the miracle. When the family returned, however, they found Lizzie mute as before, denying the boy's story with headshakes and signs. They laid traps for her, without success; even at guns suddenly fired behind her back she never so much as started. But tired at last of all this distrust, Lizzie one morning disappeared as she had come. She was reported on the other side of the English border, speaking perfectly, and the shepherd always insisted, even in manhood, that he had told the truth.[30]

But all of Wattie's days were not passed drinking in such tales of his ancestors and days gone by, or in tumbling about outdoors among the hills surrounding Smailholm Tower. Some time after his arrival at Sandyknowe his aunt began teaching him to read. At first he rebelled against the confining task and seized every chance to join Sandy Ormiston in the meadows. But "Miss Jenny was a grand hand at keeping him to the bit," said Tibby Hunter, "and by degrees he came to read brawly." One of the first books of verse that fell into his hands was a small dark quarto dated 1688, a rhyming chronicle-history of his own family, by one Walter Scot of Satchells, an impoverished member of the clan. Describing himself on his title page as

> Captain Walter Scot, an old Souldier and no Scholler
> And one that can write nane
> But just the Letters of his Name,

Satchells goes on, in a jingling epistle to the Laird of Raeburn, to hint that his more fortunate kinsman, who enjoys so many fat *fleeces*, might bestow upon the poor author some of King James's *broad pieces*. Coming upon a copy of this volume again in 1818, Scott exclaimed, "I mind *spelling* these lines."

From Satchells he learned more about the Scotts of old, among them two who had contended successfully against physical defects like his own. The first of these, according to Satchells, was a son of a thirteenth-century Buccleuch who was Warden of the Border:

> A son he had at that same tide,
> Which was so lame could neither run nor ride.
> John, this lame son, if my author speak true,
> He sent him to Mungo's in Glasgu. . . .

This John the Lamiter was the founder of the branch of the Scotts of Sinton and Harden. From him there descended, in the sixth generation, William Boltfoot:

> The Laird and Lady of Harden
> Betwixt them procreat was a son
> Called William Boltfoot of Harden—

The next line Wattie always declaimed with proud emphasis:

> *He did survive to be a* MAN.

Boltfoot not only grew to manhood; despite his infirmity he became one of the "prowest knights" of them all, a fearless horseman, dreaded spearsman:

> To take the foord he aye was first,
>   Unless the English loons were near;
> Plunge vassal than, plunge horse and van,
>   Auld Boltfoot rides into the rear.

John the Lamiter and William Boltfoot were glorious portents that even a little lame boy might triumph over his handicap. "From childhood's earliest hour," Scott wrote in his last years, "I have rebelled against external circumstances."[31]

In the country air of Sandyknowe, Wattie had grown strong enough so that he could stand again, even limp about with a slow jerk, supported by a sort of crutch. His improvement encouraged hopes that his lameness might be cured, and Dr. Andrew Wilson, the Kelso physician chosen by his grandfather Rutherford to look after him, suggested that electrical treatment might help. Would the little boy, Dr. Wilson asked, let the current run through his shrunken leg? Frightening as the idea was, the child felt desperately eager to walk. The doctor's wife had won his heart; he agreed to sit on her knee and be electrified.

They drove along the dirt road into Kelso, with its great open square almost like a French provincial town. At the doctor's, Mrs. Wilson sat in an armchair beside a brass-handled mahogany tea table, with Wattie in her lap. While the powerful current was being regulated, it took a strange leap and knocked a wedge out of the end of the table opposite where they sat. But three-year-old Wattie refused to be terrified. Flinging out one arm, his whole face alive, in a heroic lisp he heartened himself with opening verses of Hardiknute:

> "Th-tately th-tepped he Eatht the La-and,
> "Th-tately th-tepped he Wetht!"

Noting that the lisp might prove embarrassing later, Dr. Wilson corrected it with a touch of his lancet to the tongue. Years later, when Sir Walter and Lady Scott met Dr. Wilson at the dinner table of Sir Alexander Don of Newton Don, the doctor reminded him of this service. "Docteur!" exclaimed Lady Scott, in the French accent she never lost, "What is that you have done? You have set a tongue agoing that has never stopped since!"[32]

Whether stimulated by the electricity or not, the child's leg did grow stronger. Gradually he became able to hobble briskly about, aided by a staff something between a crutch and a cane. Presently, plying this small staff, he could even run, tapping across the kitchen floor, chasing over the fields after Sandy Ormiston and the sheep, or stumping up the crag to the base of the peel tower. Although the leg was still much shrunken and contracted, Wattie was growing into a high-spirited and healthy little boy.[33]

At the end of January, 1775, when he was in his fourth year, his grandfather Robert died. The curious child watched Aunt Jenny writing the funeral letters and sealing them with black wax; and remembered all the ceremonial of the burial procession as it left Sandyknowe.[34]

The little boy who had known the free hills and green fields was now brought back to the gray stone streets and close quarters of Edinburgh. Though he may have seen his brothers on occasional visits, at Sandyknowe he had been a petted only child. The crippled child, to whom stairs were a painful climb, had no idea of what it would be to live with two older brothers racing and stamping up and down the steps of a full house.

# 3

## *A Virtuoso Like Me*

### *( 1 7 7 5 – 1 7 7 8 )*

THE FAMILY NOW LIVED in a spacious house of their own in George Square. This was a new residential development of private homes beginning to rise south of the Flodden Wall that confined the crowded seventeenth-century buildings of the Old Town. Edinburgh was bursting its bounds, the gentry and comfortable middle class deserting their tall flats and dark tenements for lighter and more spacious quarters. James Brown, a builder and architect, had already put up the private dwellings of Brown's Square opposite Greyfriars' Church, just within the Bristo Port, which was originally one of the old fortified gateways in the Flodden Wall defending the town. More recently he had acquired the site of George Square, a large area formerly the park of Ross House.[1] Mr. Walter Scott was doing well in his profession—old Mr. Chalmers had retired, leaving him the sole head of the firm. He was one of the first to contract for the erection of a dwelling with cellars and coach house on the west side of the new square.

Although its inhabitants numbered other professional men like himself, the prospering Writer to the Signet found himself a neighbor to some of the first families of Edinburgh. On the north row lived the Countess of Sutherland, Lord Braxfield, the Justice-Clerk of the Court, and Henry Dundas, already a growing power in politics and destined as a member of Pitt's cabinet to become virtually the ruler of Scotland and to be elevated to the peerage as Lord Melville. On the east row lived Sir George MacDougal of Makerstoun, whom Wattie had known at Sandyknowe, and, later, on the south row, Dr. Adam, the rector of the Edinburgh High School. On the west row, next door to Mr. Scott's house, was the Honorable Henry Erskine's, and next to that the home of James Brown, the builder.[2]

Mr. Scott had other reasons for moving to George Square than his rising position in the world. Six of his children had died in Anchor Close and the College Wynd, and although Robert and John seemed vigorous, the suspicion was gaining ground in men's minds that bad air and poor sanitation had some connection with ill health. The Scotts now had a baby daughter, Anne, and there was another child on the way. The land on George Square was therefore bought (subject to an annual "feu" of £5 14s, a procedure still customary in Scottish land purchases), and the building of the house begun. The first payment was made on Whitsunday, 1773, and the family moving probably took place sometime in 1774.[3] When Wattie came home after his grandfather's death, they could hardly have been there for more than a year.

He had no memories of the crowded old College Wynd with which to compare the Square's gently sloping central space of green and its three-story houses whose great blocks of freestone and whinstone made checkered patterns of gray and pale honey-color. His father's house, No. 25, was almost at the southwest corner near the Meadow which, once a lake with swampy shores, had been drained and was now a park. Like the other houses, No. 25 had a basement behind an iron-railed area, with three steps rising to a wide brass-knockered door flanked by Ionic columns. To the left of the doorway were two twelve-paned windows, with corresponding windows on the next two floors above them and the entrance, and little dormers in the slanting attic.

Indoors, the child found himself in a fine square hall with a graceful mahogany-railed staircase. There was also a drawing room and a dining room with deep paneled window-recesses, white-painted wainscoting, and Adam fireplaces, as well as a study for Mr. Scott, a basement kitchen, and the bedrooms needed for a growing family. Perhaps because of his lameness, Wattie slept in his mother's dressing room, although he sturdily stumped up and down the stairs exploring all the house. Its rear windows looked out on a little green garden of its own, and from the upper stories, over the lime trees of the Middle Meadow Walk, behind the house, he could see glorious expanses of greensward and venerable trees extending to the slopes of Bruntsfield Links and Merchiston, with the blue Pentlands rising in the distance. Outside the drawing-room windows the green of the Square, in which some of the residents pastured a few sheep and cows, extended some eighth of a mile to the houses that were still being erected on the east.[4]

But Wattie was not long confined to the house. Soon he was running in and out, visiting the next-door neighbors, the Henry Erskines, who rented Mr. Scott's stable for the black horses they used to draw their yellow carriage. He pestered Mrs. Erskine with so many questions that she impatiently called him "that silly tiresome boy." Once he ran up to her husband to ask, "Mr. Erskine, did you ever seen a whim-wham fastened to a goosey's bido?," the last word being a childish mispronunciation for bridle. (A whim-wham was a little rosette made of colored rags, and the expression "a whim-wham for a goose's bridle," the common rejoinder of an exasperated needlewoman teased with queries about what she was making.)[5]

With his brothers, too, Wattie began to see something of the world outside their home. His sister Anne was a toddler of two, and Tom, less than a year old, was still in his cradle. But Robert was a boisterous boy of twelve and John was eight;[6] with them, although in charge of a nurse, he played in the Square and the nearby Meadow. From outside, more could be seen of the other houses, some of them with gracefully curved fanlights over their doors, some with bow windows or delicately traceried wheel-windows. To the north the Square was partly open, giving a glimpse of Ross House and its flanking wings surrounded by spacious gardens. On the south there were as yet no buildings to shut out the trees and grass of the Meadow, whose rural greenery rose in slow stages to the gentle uplands of Grange.[7]

The solitary child at Sandyknowe had had no other children racing ahead of him to make him sharply aware of his lameness. But now it was painfully driven home to him. "There is the stile at which I can recollect a cross child's-maid upbraiding me with my infirmity as she lifted me coarsely and carelessly over the flinty steps which my brothers traversed with shout and bound. I remember the *suppressed bitterness* of the moment, and, conscious of my own infirmity, the envy with which I regarded the easy movements and elastic steps of my more happily formed brethren."[8] Again he rebelled against external circumstance, but perhaps the memories of John the Lamiter and William Boltfoot strengthened him against heartburning. What they had done he could do!

Probably the sight of his little limping figure toiling along after his leaping brothers led his parents to consider a suggestion from Dr. Wilson that the waters of Bath might aid his lameness. Dr. Rutherford must have been consulted, but there is no evidence of whether he felt hopeful or not. Affectionate Aunt Jenny agreed to take the child under her care, and early in the summer of 1775 she and Wattie started on their journey. They went to London by sea, sailing from the bustling Port of Leith in the *Buccleuch*, Captain Beatson, master.[9] As the vessel made its way out into the blue waters of the Firth of Forth, with the little island of Inchcolm slipping by to port, Wattie had his first sight of the Kingdom of Fife and, misty on the northern horizon, the violet of the Sidlaw Hills. Some twelve hours later, close on the starboard side, loomed the Bass Rock humping up huge and precipitous a craggy three hundred and fifty feet above the fierce spray of the German Ocean, and, on the coastline, crowning their cliff, the massive ruins of Tantallon Castle. Still farther down the rounding shores, when East Lothian gave way to Berwickshire, Fast Castle loured over the waves tearing at its rocky base; and, by the second day, when Scotland had been left behind for Northumberland, the dark red walls of Holy Island rose out of the sea.

The Leith packet took twelve days to make the voyage to London. In the crowded quarters of the little coastwise vessel the child shared a bed with a Scottish lady who thirty-six years later boasted that she "had once been Walter Scott's bedfellow" and remembered him as "the drollest-looking, odd entertaining urchin that ever was seen." The other voyagers also found Wattie fun. Once they persuaded him to shoot a pea gun at one of them. To the child's horror the man fell flat and motionless upon the deck. But when Wattie began to weep, miraculously the dead man leaped back to life.[10]

In London, Aunt Jenny took the little boy to see Westminster Abbey, the cruel old Tower, and other sights, which remained so vividly in his mind's eye that twenty-four years later, on his second visit, he was astounded by the accuracy of his memories. In Bath the child was delighted by the splendors of a toy shop near the Orange Grove and by the beauties of the Parade, with the river Avon winding around it, and the cattle lowing on the hills opposite the town. Among its Palladian squares and crescents he was subjected to the usual discipline of bathing in and drinking its waters. For some three months he had reading lessons at a dame-school near their lodgings, but the rest of his progress was made under the supervision of his aunt.[11]

His imagination, always struck by the dramatic and colorful, was strongly taken by two ballads sung to him by an Irish maidservant. The first of these, a variant of "The Outlandish Knight," concerned the daughter of a King of Ireland persuaded to ride off with her Scottish lover, Sir Malcolm. He takes her to a lonely place above the raging waves of the sea, where he tells her she must drown as have six other king's daughters before her.

> "Strip off, strip off that comely garb!"
>     That Knight did her command,
> "For surely it is too costly
>     "To rot on the salt sea sand."

After pleading in vain for her life, she begs him to turn his back while she strips off her clothes:

> "By all good saints do this Sir Knight
>     "Whilst off my dress I fling,
> "To spy a maid in such a state
>     "It is no knightly thing."

He yields to her prayer, upon which she seizes him from behind and pushes him to his death in the brine below.

The other ballad, a version of "Lammikin," filled Wattie with horror. It was about a mason named Lankin, who, not being paid for building

Lord Blakeney's castle, is admitted during its owner's absence by a treacherous nurse. The lady of the castle has locked herself within her chamber, but Lankin pierces her baby with a silver bodkin to make it cry.

"Oh nurse! oh nurse!
"How fast you do sleep
"Don't you hear my pretty baby
"Crying out its last weep?"

The old hag replies:

"I've fed him with the breast milk
"I've fed him with the pap
"I pray you fair lady
"To dandle him in your lap."

The mother is thus lured from her room and, despite her pleas, is slain by the relentless Lankin; but Lord Blakeney returns in time to prevent the murderer's escape and hangs him high from the castle walls.[12]

After Wattie and his aunt had been a while at Bath, they were joined by his uncle, Captain Robert Scott, home on leave from India. The Captain took his little nephew to his first play. Breathless anticipation filled the child as he looked about the brilliantly lighted theater filled with crowds of spectators, listened to the music of the orchestra, and glued his eyes to the wide and mystic curtain, whose dusky undulations now and again parted slightly and gave a glimpse of the spangles of a sandaled foot or the glitter of some gaudy form. As he watched it rise slowly, it seemed to disclose, as if by sorcery, a new world where dwelt a supernatural race of beings whose language was poetry, all of whose behavior seemed calculated to intensify emotion, "to melt with sorrow, overpower with terror, astonish with the marvellous, or convulse with irresistible laughter."[13]

The play was *As You Like It*, and the solitary child, who had so far lived with his brothers only for brief intervals, was scandalized by the quarrel between Oliver and Orlando. "A'n't they brothers?" he screamed. But soon he was caught up in all the enchantment of the Forest of Arden, joining in the thunder of applause by clapping his own tiny hands, and adding to the roars of the audience his own cries of delight. At last came the descending curtain, the sinking lights, the dispersing crowd, and the vain longing that the music would again sound, the magic curtain rise once more, and the enchanting dream recommence.[14]

Kind Uncle Robert served his small nephew in still another way. Somehow the child had found in himself a superstitious fear of statuary. He was especially terrified by the carved angels ascending and descending Jacob's Ladder on the turrets flanking the west window of the town's

Abbey Church. Gently the Captain coaxed him to draw nearer to a statue of Neptune that guarded the Avon where a pleasure boat crossed the river to Spring Gardens, until he could at last touch it without dread and his tremors were melted away.[15]

In May, 1776, toward the end of the little boy's stay, there arrived in Bath the Reverend Mr. John Home, then famous as the author of the poetic tragedy *Douglas*, with his friend and kinsman David Hume. Many among the more straitlaced Scots were outraged at an ordained minister of the Gospel writing for the stage, and perhaps no less so at his remaining on friendly terms with the skeptical philosopher, but Miss Jenny's faith did not force her to share their prejudice. The aged clergyman paid a good deal of kindly attention to his countrywoman, and his wife often took Wattie in her carriage when she went for an airing on the Downs. This venerable man had actually written a stage play!—like that exciting performance Wattie had recently seen, but made out of one of those ballad legends he had drunk in from his grandmother's lips at Sandyknowe. The child felt blissfully awed.[16]

Although Wattie continued to grow, and was becoming strong, the waters of Bath did not help his leg. In the summer of 1776, therefore, after a year in the south, he was brought back to Edinburgh, returning with an English accent. There was now another little brother, named Daniel, in the household at George Square, but it was his two elder brothers, not this infant or Anne and Tom, the other two tiny inhabitants of the nursery, who impressed the five-year-old child. Smashing his disbelief in the wrangle between Orlando and Oliver, "a very few weeks' residence at home," he wrote later, "convinced me that a quarrel between brothers was a very natural event." Robert's bold and haughty disposition sometimes made him a capricious tyrant to his younger brothers, but John, only four years his junior, fought back, and even Wattie rebelled.[17]

But soon Wattie was sent again to Sandyknowe. His grandmother was still running the farm, aided by her son Thomas Scott, who lived at Crailing as factor, or land steward, for an estate there. Possibly it was at this time that the child stayed for a while at Lessudden, the home of Walter Scott of Raeburn, whose wife, Jean, was a younger sister of his father's. The Laird of Raeburn was a harsh, rough fellow whom the child quickly came to detest. A large pigeon-house on the estate was being destroyed by starlings, who were caught in their nests, put in bags, and drowned. But the servants gave one to Wattie, which he was just beginning to tame when the brute of a Laird seized it and wrung its neck. The child, just escaped from a bullying elder brother, flew at the man's throat like a wildcat and was torn from him with no little difficulty. From that time on the two never got on with each other.[18]

But his aunt, known in the old Scottish usage as Lady Raeburn, Wattie immediately loved. He long remembered sitting by an old oak table and hearing her read from a volume entitled *The Voyages, Dangerous Adventures, and Imminent Escapes of Captain Richard Falconer*, who was supposed to have lived among the Indians of America, married an Indian wife, and made a thrilling escape from the Island of Dominico. Wattie's feelings were intensely harrowed by "the lamentable catastrophe of the ship's departing without Captain Falconer, in consequence of the whole party making free with lime-punch on the eve of its being launched."[19]

Among the breezy hills of Sandyknowe the child's world grew day by day. The American Revolution had broken out, and on his Uncle Thomas's weekly visits to the farm Wattie plied him anxiously for news of General Washington's defeat. Despite his longing for the success of the armies of George III in America, the family stories about Beardie and the songs and tales of the sufferings and heroism of the Jacobites also imbued him with a romantic feeling for the dethroned Stuarts. The cruel executions at Carlisle and in the Highlands after the battle of Culloden, in which some of his own family had fallen, made him hate the name of the Duke of Cumberland with a more than infant hatred. Another of his father's sisters, his aunt Barbara, was married to a farmer of Yetbyre named William Curle, who had seen some of these executions and curdled Wattie's blood with their horrors.[20]

Gruesome tales always filled him with a shuddering terror, sometimes more than could be borne. Once, after he had been put to bed in the nursery, two of the servant girls sat down before the embers of the fire, and one started telling a dismal ghost story. The child began to fear that he guessed the ghastly things that were to come. He wanted to listen, he shrank from hearing; curiosity was almost overpowering, but he knew that if he continued to hear on he should be terrified for the remainder of the night. With a mighty effort, he buried his head in the bedclothes so that he might not hear another word.[21]

In the long winter days he was now becoming a voracious reader. Josephus's *Wars of the Jews*, another of the old volumes lying about the farm, was one of his favorites. The Reverend Dr. Duncan had in his youth been chaplain to the family of Lord Marchmont; and when the old clergyman visited the farm, the child would listen to his familiar talk of Alexander Pope, whom he had seen, and other great literary figures whose lives reached back into the Augustan days of Queen Anne. "Your son Walter is very well," Dr. Duncan wrote his parents, "he has really great natural endowments . . ." The boy's progress grew precociously rapid.[22]

Although the waters of Bath had failed, the following summer it was thought that sea bathing might help his lame leg. Faithful Miss Jenny took him in charge again, this time to the little village of Prestonpans, on the sheltered southern coast of the Firth of Forth. Here they lodged in the house of a Mr. Warroch, of which the large gate, a black arch facing the sea, seemed to Wattie's childish eyes a monument of dignity. On weekdays he bathed in the salt water, and played on the links that ran along the shore, arranging shells on the turf and swimming small skiffs in the pools. There was a little girl (Jean Dalrymple, daughter of Lord Westhall, one of the judges of the Court of Session) whom Wattie thought adorably pretty, and "whom I laughed and romped with," he wrote later, "and loved as children love." He remembered also a garden under an old tower where he used to cram himself with gooseberries, and a childish fear that the minstrel Blind Harry's specter of Fawdon might show its headless trunk at one of the windows. And on Sundays, in the village church, he would yawn under the sermons of a Dr. M'Cormick, whose eloquence was afflictingly dull.[23]

Though his aunt Miss Jenny was now forty-three, she was still a beautiful woman, with a gentle good-breeding given piquancy by an occasional sharpness of utterance. She had an admirer, George Constable, an old friend of Wattie's father, bred to the law but now retired upon his property. A good-tempered man of considerable learning and wit, he had a droll, subacid humor and some of the oddities of an old bachelor. Following her to Prestonpans, he dangled in Miss Jenny's wake, courting her, as the child dimly realized, in a timid way. The middle-aged suitor was naturally kind to his lady's little nephew. On the beach where the fishermen dried their nets he sauntered hand in hand with the child, telling him wild stories of shipwrecked mariners and escapes over cliffs. At Bath, when he went to his first play, Wattie had discovered that there was a mighty magician named Shakespeare; now from George Constable he learned about Falstaff and Hotspur and other characters in the plays. No one knows how long after this it was before the child began drinking in great draughts from the dramas, but he steeped himself in them from an early age.[24]

At Prestonpans, there was also a retired half-pay ensign named Dalgetty, a veteran of the German wars, who was given the courtesy title of Captain. The old gentleman pacing what he called the Parade, the open space beside the shore, found in the child a more eager audience than he did among adults for tales of his military feats and old campaigns. With the veteran, Wattie explored the field where Cope's troops had been slaughtered in 1745, the thorn tree that marked the center of the battle, and the very spot where Colonel Gardiner was slain by the stroke of a Highland scythe. The man and the child often talked, too, about the war raging in America, and Captain Dalgetty was jubilantly sure that General Burgoyne's expedition, striking down from Canada and joining forces with the army of Lord Howe, would break the back of the rebellion. But Wattie, looking at a map of North America, was struck by the rugged country of forests and lakes and voiced some doubts that Burgoyne would arrive at his goal. The veteran derided these ignorant objections. When the news of the disastrous defeat at Saratoga on October 17 reached them, the triumph of the child somewhat jolted their intimacy.[25]

In the middle of November Wattie was back in George Square for a brief time, and then returned to Sandyknowe. Here his Uncle Thomas observed that, though he still limped, he was growing into robust health. He gave the boy a dwarf Shetland pony, hardly larger than a big Newfoundland dog. Wattie named the animal Marion and soon learned to sit her so well that he alarmed his Aunt Jenny by cantering over the rocky places about the peel tower. The little creature was so tame that she ate from the boy's hand and even walked into his grandmother's house. Once, probably with Uncle Thomas, he rode across the border into Northumberland, "a little boy on a little pony," to the neighborhood of Otterburn, but his uncle was too cautious to let him explore the rough ground of the battlefield as he wanted to do.

Sometimes now on his weekly visit to the farm Uncle Thomas brought his daughters as playmates for Wattie—Jane, who was the elder of the two, and Barbara, who was just about his little nephew's age. At times Wattie must also have ridden into Kelso, for one of Dr. Wilson's daughters remembered playing with him and his cousin Barbara under a great tree in the grass walks of an old garden. He hardly needed to use his crutch any more, and sometimes while the little girls ran about he chased after them, throwing his stick at them when he fell behind. The doctor's daughter well recalled her terror in fleeing from him, with his limp and long staff. "Ah, Jeany, Jeany," Scott said to her years later, "many a time you and me played boglie round that tree!"[26]

He had mingled so little with other boys that he had none of their scorn for girls and their games. In an attic room whose south window projected through the eaves, up a steep flight of stairs, was a "doll room," where he joined them dressing dolls. Only, he insisted, *his* dolls should all be *boys*. The lady dolls were of all sizes, made of fine linen stuffed with bran, their faces painted, and their hair garnered from Jeany's and Cousin Barbara's own ringlets. Wattie's dolls, something over three inches long, had features drawn in pen and ink, and were clad in pale blue cotton with a design in darker blue, taken from one of Barbara's frocks. When the dolls were not being played with, they sat in a row beside the window, a great array of ladies, one in a mob-cap and apron, and a smaller row of boys.[27]

Wattie's growing strength convinced his father that he should now return to Edinburgh and be entered in school. Though for a child of his years he had made astounding strides in intellectual development, there were many things that neither Aunt Jenny nor his Uncle Thomas could teach him. Probably early in 1778 he joined his brothers and his sister Anne in George Square, not this time as a visitor from the country, but as a permanent member of the household.[28] Two stories dating from his previous brief sojourn there, in November, reveal the qualities of mind and feeling already flowering in this six-year-old.

He had been taken to see his maternal grandmother's sister, Mrs. Keith of Ravelston, at Ravelston House, in the countryside just west of Edinburgh. The picturesque old mansion was surrounded by venerable gardens with massive hedges of yew and holly. At their gate a lady paying a call on his great aunt saw the child with an attending servant. A beggar had just been given a few pence, and the servant sententiously told Wattie he should be thankful to Providence for placing him above such miserable want. The little boy looked up, with a half-wistful, half-incredulous expression, and said, "*Homer* was a beggar!" "How do you know that?" "Why, don't you remember that

> Seven Roman cities strove for Homer dead,
> Through which the living Homer begged his bread?"

The lady smiled at the "*Roman* cities" but observed how imagination filled the gap of memory.[29]

The other story was told by Alison Cockburn, author of a variation of the old lyric "The Flowers of the Forest." She was distantly related to Wattie's mother—she had been born a Rutherford of Fairnalie, in Selkirkshire—and was staying at Ravelston. "I last night supped in Mr. Walter Scott's," she wrote in a letter. "He has the most extraordinary genius of a boy I ever saw. He was reading a poem to his mother when I went in. I made him read on; it was the description of a shipwreck. His passion rose with the storm. He lifted his eyes and hands. 'There's the mast gone,' says he; 'crash it goes!—they will all perish!' After his agitation, he turns to me. 'This is too melancholy,' says he; 'I had better read you something more amusing.' I preferred a little chat, and asked him his opinion of Milton and other books he was reading . . . One of his observations was, 'How strange it is that Adam, just new come into the world, should know everything—that must be the poet's fancy,' says he. But when he was told he was created perfect by God, he instantly yielded.

"When taken to bed last night, he told his aunt he liked that lady. 'What lady?' says she. 'Why, Mrs. Cockburn; for I think she is a virtuoso like myself.' 'Dear Walter,' says Aunt Jenny, 'what is a virtuoso?' 'Don't ye know? Why, it's one who wishes and will know everything.' Now, sir, you will think this a very silly story. Pray, what age do you suppose this boy to be? Name it now, before I tell you. Why, twelve or fourteen. No such thing; he is not quite six years old. He has a lame leg, for which he was a year at Bath, and has acquired the perfect English accent, which he has not lost since he came, and he reads like a Garrick."[30]

In only one thing was Mrs. Cockburn mistaken: Wattie was three months past his sixth birthday. As for the lingering traces of an English accent, he lost them later and came to speak in a tone and accent broadly Scotch, with the *burr* of the Border counties.[31] But otherwise her astonished wonder at the child virtuoso was entirely justified. Indeed, we might find his precocity incredible if we did not remember John Stuart Mill starting Greek at three and the youthful Macaulay with a book in one hand and a piece of bread and butter in the other at about the same age when Wattie also began to read. Staid Mr. Walter Scott and his wife might well have shared Mrs. Cockburn's belief that they had a young genius in their lame small boy.

More, the great roots of his character and sensibility were already deep and strong. Knotted into the soil of that Border country from which he drew his first memories, they were anchored in its land, those steeply slanting fields and meadows with sheep grazing amid rugged outcroppings of scaur and crag, those deep glens with their brown streams glinting in the shade and sunlight of oak and birch and fir. And no less than from the Scottish soil, those roots of feeling drew their nourishment from the Scottish past, tales of Thomas of Ercildoune, the wizard Michael Scot, Wight Willie of Aikwood, Jamie Telfer of the Fair Dodhead, the gray ruins of Melrose Abbey and the orange stones of Dryburgh, the sufferings of the Covenanters, the heroic deeds done in the Stuart cause, and even paradoxically, loyalty to the reigning English dynasty when challenged by rebellion in America.

Deeply entwined with the glamor of the storied past was that of his own wild clan, the stout maraudings of Auld Wat of Harden, the poetry of the Flower of Yarrow, the grim humor of the Feast of Spurs, the comedy of Meikle-mouthed Meg, the armed clatter of those ancestors who had fought at Halidon Hill, Pinkie, Otterburn, and Flodden, and in the '15 and '45, the quixotic devotion of old Beardie to the King over the water. In their doings resounded the same trumpet-note that stirred his soul in the ballads of Hardiknute and "The Hunting of the Cheviot"; and from that it was but a leap of the heart to Shakespeare and Milton.

To the child who had seen so little of other children and who had lain so many hours beneath the deserted peel tower at Smailholm, solitude was not lonely and imagination was companionship. He would soon learn to adjust himself to the rough give-and-take of association with other boys; would come to know the warmth of good fellowship and the deep love of friendship, of wife, of children. But in the profoundest recesses of his being he was always to find his surest resources within himself, bearing his sorest griefs in silence, rising on the wings of his loftiest exaltations not lonely but alone.

In great degree this girding-up of his emotional life within himself was the expression of a stoical pride engendered by the handicap of his lame leg. His parents, to be sure, unlike Byron's hysterical mother, were not of a kind to taunt him by calling him a deformed brat. There would have been others who were not so nice—jibes from other boys, who are not conspicuously gentle. We hear just once, no more, of a child's suppressed bitterness when a coarse maid upbraided his infirmity. But there was a strength within that small child that conquered self-pity. He rebelled against circumstance, not by morbid resentment of his misfortune, but with a determination to surmount it. Were not John the Lamiter and William Boltfoot among his own forebears? He too would be a MAN.

4

---

# *Limping Gamecock*

## *( 1 7 7 8 – 1 7 8 0 )*

THE CHATTERING MONKEY of a child who had been the indulged darling of his aunt and grandmother now had to fit into the large George Square family. He did not find the change easy. His brother Tom and little Dan, to be sure, were hardly more than babies, and his sister Anne, a year his junior, was a dreamy small girl in delicate health. But John and Robert were no more disposed than most boys to be gentle even to a younger brother with a lame leg. Robert was ambitious to be a naval officer and bullied his brothers with forecastle violence. Although he was often kind, and won Wattie's love by singing songs to him or telling him stories of bold adventures and narrow escapes, when he was in an evil temper he cuffed and kicked without mercy.[1] The rough boy-world in which Wattie found himself filled the sensitive child with agonies of heartburning and humiliation.[2]

His father, now almost fifty years of age, was an awe-inspiring figure, in solemn black or snuff color, with knee-breeches and snowy ruffles, his grave handsome face wearing an expression of faint anxiety. He was sweet tempered but austere; though he could laugh, he seldom gave way to high spirits. At dinner, if anyone remarked that the soup was good, he would taste it again, say, "Yes, too good, bairns," and dash a tumbler of cold water into his plate.[3] His rigid Presbyterianism made Sundays a nightmare for the children. Twice on every funereal Sabbath the family and the servants attended services at the old Greyfriars' Church. No amusements were allowed during the solemn day except for a few books of a devotional flavor, like *Pilgrim's Progress*, Rowe's *Letters*, and Gesner's *Death of Abel*.[4] Sunday dinner was always the same—sheep's head broth, and then the sheep's head itself, boiled the day before, so that the servants would have little to do on the Lord's Day. On Sunday evening, in the darkened drawing room, Mr. Scott read aloud a long, gloomy sermon, then another long, gloomy sermon, then a third as gloomy as it was long. The children struggled to keep awake, and six-year-old Wattie invariably found his eyelids closing. Afterwards, Mr. Scott examined both the servants and the children on all the sermons to which they had been subjected, as well as on the catechism. Still to be endured was an interminable succession of prayers. To a child the ordeal seemed endless.[5]

Although Mrs. Scott was as sincerely devout as her husband, she did not share his austerity. With a happy nature she had an outgiving heart and made a special pet of her little lame child, calling him "Wattie, my lamb." She loved poetry and works of imagination and recalled a great store of the ballads and folk tales he had come to love. She could tell exciting stories of Scotland's past and all the connections of its great families, and she herself stretched the boy's heart into actual contact with that glowing past. In her girlhood she had even known and talked with an old man who claimed to remember the battle of Dunbar in 1650 and the entry of Cromwell's army into Edinburgh.[6]

Wattie spent long affectionate hours curled up by her side reading aloud to her. One of their great favorites was Pope's translation of Homer, she making him dwell on those parts that expressed noble feelings, he exulting in the scenes of battle, blood, and tumult.[7] Almost without intending it, Wattie got by heart the passages that pleased him most. These he often recited aloud, both to himself and to others, but more often when he was alone, for he had observed that some of his auditors smiled, and he shrank from ridicule.[8] No doubt there were visitors who found him quaintly old for his years. Once at a tea party in his mother's drawing room, a lady complained of the heavy rains that had spoiled the whole of a visit she had made to the Highlands. Wattie looked up from under the table beneath which he was crouching. "That's Caledonia," he explained, "weeping for the poverty of her soil."[9]

After an early supper he would be put to bed. But in his mother's dressing room, where he slept, he found some odd volumes of Shakespeare, and could not resist their temptation. Huddled in his nightshirt, reading by the light of the fire, he was caught up in the rapture of the great music. On and on went the incantation—until, suddenly, the bustle of the grownups rising from the table in the dining room below warned him that it was time to scramble back beneath the covers where he was supposed to have been sleeping since nine o'clock.[10]

In school studies, however, including Latin, Wattie was not so advanced as he was in Shakespeare, Milton, and Homer. And Latin, above all, was the central study of the Edinburgh High School, which carried its pupils all the way from their earliest school days till they were ready for college. Consequently, to prepare for his admission to the High

School, Wattie was sent to a little private school just north of George Square, in Bristo Port, kept by a Mr. Leechman. But this did not prove as satisfactory as his parents had hoped, so they had him taught at home by a young man named James French, who afterwards became the minister of East Kilbride in Lanarkshire.[11] Wattie was also given some lessons in reading aloud, to acquire accuracy in pronunciation and appropriateness in expression, first from a Mr. Stalker and later from the Reverend Mr. Cleeve.[12]

When his daily tasks were over, if his mother was busy with her domestic duties, he would lie reading on the carpet in the drawing room, while the other boys were playing in the Square. His uncle Captain Robert Scott on one occasion asked him if he wouldn't rather be outside enjoying himself with them. "No, uncle," the child answered, "you cannot think how ignorant those boys are; I am much happier here reading my book." Another time Captain Scott found him reading *Tristram Shandy.* "Walter," he inquired, "do you understand that book?" "No, and I don't think the author intended it should be understood."[13]

Wattie was happy enough, though, when his mother took him with her in the coach for an airing. Beyond the High Street, they drove across the North Bridge, then only half a dozen years old, whose stone arches flung themselves over the hollow of the Nor' Loch. To their left the long narrow sheet of water still extended to the great scarped rock of the Castle; to the right rose the improbable volcanic heights of Arthur's Seat and the Salisbury Crags and, beyond the sloping land across the bridge, the humped shoulder of the Calton Hill.[14]

Some ten years before, Edinburgh had extended its Royalty to include a considerable area on this side of the little valley, and a young architect named James Craig had drawn a spacious plan for the New Town, north of the Loch. Here, around the new St. Andrew Square, Princes Street, George Street, and Hanover Street, blocks of houses were now beginning to appear among the rough whin and yellow broom of fields in which snipe, hare, and partridge once were shot. But the two miles between here and the Port of Leith, now solid with stone buildings, were then largely rural, market gardens and meadows, dotted with isolated villages.[15]

At the far end of the Bridge, where a road named the Lang Dykes was joined by another coming from the villages of Silvermills and Canonmills, Leith Walk curved in a rough bad road down toward the wharves and masts of the Port. This was probably the very route on which Wattie had been taken three years before to embark on his voyage to London. But this time the houses they had just passed in the New Town suggested a daring thought to his mind. "Mama, I should not be surprised if this road were yet to have houses built along it, all the way from Edinburgh to Leith." His mother scolded him for his forwardness in talking such nonsense. "What could be more absurd than your remark today in the coach! To think of Edinburgh and Leith ever being joined together!"[16]

Late in August of this very summer of 1778 while the American War still raged on, John Paul Jones sailed up the Firth of Forth in three small vessels, past the island of Inchkeith, and threatened Leith itself. The rattle of the warning drums awakened George Square at eight in the morning, and Mrs. Scott thought that the piratical invaders had landed. Alarm was great; Edinburgh had only three companies of troops under arms.[17]

One of Mr. Scott's Highland clients, Alexander Stewart of Invernahyle, an enthusiastic Jacobite who had fought for the Stuarts both in 1715 and 1745, now fierily rallied to the defense of King George against the American rebels. To the frightened city magistrates he offered to collect as many Highlanders as might be needed to cut off, among the high houses and narrow lanes, any of the pirate crew that ventured ashore in quest of plunder. The old war-horse champed at the bit to go into action, exultant "in the prospect of drawing his claymore once more before he died."[18]

Wattie hung breathless on his tales of the bloody exploits of his youth. "O, Inver," he asked in an earnest small voice, "were you ever afraid?" "Troth, Gurdie mavourneen," he replied, "the first time I gaed into action when I saw the red coats' ranks opposite to us and our people put their bonnets over their een and set forward like bulls driving each other on and beginning to fire their guns and draw their broadswords, I would have given any man a thousand merks to insure me I wadna' run away."[19]

But the dauntless old Trojan was offered no occasion now to display his valor: powerful west winds forced the American commander out into the open sea again.[20] Here, on the twenty-third of September, off Flamborough Head, Jones won a desperate victory over two men-of-war, swarming onto the British *Serapis* from his own sinking flagship, the *Bonhomme Richard*. These stirring events sharpened Robert Scott's eagerness for a naval career. His mother, hoping to discourage this ambition, invited to the house a Captain James Watson, with instructions to tell such tales of hardship as might disgust him with a seafaring life. The more Captain Watson dilated, however, upon disastrous chances and distressful strokes, the more fascinated were the young midshipman-to-be and the small brother who hung spellbound by his side.[21]

Wattie had now ceased to sleep in his mother's dressing room. Since he was only seven years old, however, a youthful maidservant named Becky, a girl of fifteen, shared his bedroom and could look after him if he was ill or suffered from bad dreams at night. Becky was a pious girl, a member of the Burgher secession, devout in her religious observances. Once, when a meteoric ball of fire shot over Warrender's

Park and someone asked her whereabouts, Wattie solemnly replied, "Becky would be at her prayers." The girl and the little boy became very fond of each other.[22]

In October, 1779, Wattie was sent to the High School and entered in Mr. Luke Fraser's second year class.[23] He was a full year younger than most of the eighty or so boys. There were three other masters, Mr. Trench, Mr. Nicol, and Mr. Cruikshank, teaching under the Rector, Dr. Alexander Adam.[24] Usually the boys studied with the same master through the fourth year and then went on for the next two years into the Rector's class. Wattie's brother Robert had entered the school at the age of eight but two years before had left school after a single year in Dr. Adam's class; John, although three years older than Wattie, was only a year ahead of him in the school.[25]

His fellow students, Wattie found, were not only older than he was but knew more Latin. This placed him at a double disadvantage. The boys were seated in the classroom in the order of their attainment, from the idlest dullard at the far end of the back bench to the head boy, or *dux*, at the front. Even a bright child, in a class for which he was not quite ready, would take some time to force his way to the standing his abilities merited. Meanwhile, surrounded by older and more mediocre youngsters satisfied to scramble through their lessons with no more labor than would avoid punishment, he was in danger of using his brains merely to hold his own with them.[26]

Mr. Fraser was a conscientious teacher, kindly disposed to his lame pupil. But, mainly a grammatical drill-master, he did not fire historical curiosity or poetic imagination. The boy's exertions for some time, therefore, as Scott recalled in later years, "were desultory and little to be depended on." "I glanced like a meteor from one end of the class to the other, and commonly disgusted my kind master as much by negligence and frivolity, as I occasionally pleased him by flashes of intellect and talent." Gradually, though, Wattie's quick wits and keen memory enabled him without much work to make his way to about the middle of the class. With this position, as Scott said, "I was the better contented that it chanced to be near the fire." After the first winter the boy settled down for the most part to a place between the seventh and the fifteenth from the top.[27]

Even so, his abilities attracted attention. "What I hear from all quarters, of little Wattie's genius," Mrs. Russell wrote his mother from Madras, "is astonishing, and assures me I shall one day have some vanity in being his Aunt."[28] Gradually his competitive ambition was fired. One boy, who sat at the top of the bench, he could not supplant; day after day he kept his place, let Wattie do what he would. At last he observed that whenever his rival was asked a question he fumbled with a button at the bottom of his waistcoat. This suggested a sly scheme. Surreptitiously Wattie cut off the button with a knife and waited anxiously to see if his trick would succeed. The boy was questioned; his finger sought the button; it was not there. In consternation he looked down, became confused, speechless, and Wattie triumphantly took his place. His conscience smote him for this trick, all the more because the boy never suspected the author of his fall and never regained his place.[29]

Wattie speedily became popular among his schoolmates. He was determined that, despite his lameness, nobody should patronize him or push him about. Barely had he made his first appearance in the High School Yards, as the playground was called, than he found himself embroiled in a dispute with one of the boys. Tauntingly, this youngster remarked that "there was no use to hargle-bargle with a cripple"; Wattie stoutly replied that "if he might fight *mounted*, he would try his hand with any one of his inches." An older boy suggested that the two little lads might be lashed front to front on a deal board. This was promptly done, they began flailing away at each other, and Wattie received his first bloody nose, "in an attitude," Scott said in later years, "which would have entitled me, in the blessed days of personal cognizances, to assume that of a *lioncel seiant gules*. My pugilistic trophies here," he added, "were all the results of such *sittings in banco*."[30]

The courage of this limping little gamecock lifted him into high esteem. The boys quickly found out that he was good-natured, too, and, although sometimes negligent of his own work, always ready to aid another. His flow of imagination also won admirers. In the winter play-hours when icy rain or sleet made outdoor exercise impossible, his stories, told around the fireside of Lucky Brown, a neighboring sweet-seller, always drew an eager circle of listeners. He soon commanded a staunch group of friends and adherents, "stout of hand and heart, though somewhat dull of head—the very tools for raising a hero to eminence. So, on the whole, I made a brighter figure in the *yards* than in the *class*."[31]

Now that he was a schoolboy, stumping every day the half mile from George Square, Wattie began to grow acquainted with the town. The High School was located near the end of the crowded and clamorous Cowgate, southwest of the Cowgate Port. At this point, quiet green gardens sloped gently down to the South Backs of the Canongate, along which Wattie could ramble on to the great open rectangle before the Italianate façade of Holyrood Palace. Here the Canongate began ascending the hill, and he could watch the coaches from the south clattering into the close of the White Horse, with its two outside staircases.[32]

All the narrow Canongate was noisy with schoolboys in round black hats and coats of blue, green, and scarlet, chasing one another and dodging an occasional sedan chair. Through the tunneled entries of the closes drying shifts and petticoats fluttered on the ends of poles projecting from upper windows. Corduroyed men from Gilmerton bawled coals or yellow sand. Red-jacketed water-carriers jostled sooty men with their bags. Pigs roamed and rooted in piles of refuse, and Wattie might have seen some bare-legged little girl (like the young hoyden who grew up to become the beautiful Duchess of Gordon) riding playfully on a sow while a small companion lustily thumped the grunting animal with a stick. "I myself remember some now very fine Scotch ladies," wrote a friend of Scott's, "who used to scud about without stockings when they were past fifteen."[33]

As Wattie climbed the street, he would pass on his right the strangely curving gables of the Canongate Church and the turreted steeple of the Canongate Tolbooth where the tolls were collected. Farther along on the left came Moray House, with its semioctagon tower and corbeled balcony. Beneath this very balcony in 1650, Wattie was told, had rumbled the hangman's tumbril bearing the heroic Montrose to his doom, and through its windows the family of the Marquis of Argyll had stepped out from a wedding banquet to exult over their fallen foe. One last detail in the story made the boy's heart swell with horror: in their hatred the Marchioness and her daughters leaned over the balustrade and, as Scott put it even years later, with a vibration of loathing in the words, "They spat upon his sacred head—the bitches!"[34]

Not far beyond Moray House, in the Playhouse Close, were the theater and another inn named Boyd's, and at the top of the Canongate the Netherbow Port, although its portcullised tower had been torn down before Wattie was born. Here St. Mary's Wynd descended to the Red Lion Inn at its foot, and here the wide High Street began its steep ascent past the ashlar-masonry house in which John Knox had breathed his last. Running downhill on the left to the Cowgate and the High School Yards was Hyndford's Close, midway in which, surrounded by its own garden, stood the turreted mansion of Wattie's grandfather. Dr. Rutherford had died in 1779, but his children by a second marriage still occupied the dwelling, and instead of going home from school at noon the boy went there to lunch, climbing its cramped inside stair.[35] His grandfather had also owned the building next door, and when he sold it, Wattie learned, had reserved what Scots Law called a *servitude*, the right when anyone died in his own house to carry the coffin through a closed private door down the wider staircase of its neighbor.[36]

The doctor's own burial may well have been the first at which this grim stipulation was invoked, but although it awed Wattie's imagination it did not darken his visits. He spent many happy lunch hours with his uncle, Dr. Daniel Rutherford, who was professor of botany at the University, and his young aunt, Miss Christian Rutherford, a girl of sixteen, who seemed to him more like a delightful sister than an aunt.[37] Miss Chritty, as he learned to call her, with her warm-heartedness and love of laughter, became a beloved confidante of her gifted little nephew.

One dim inner room of the house Wattie found strange and exotic. It had an old harpsichord and a tall India screen with a painted Harlequin and Columbine. The harpsichord had tinkled to the fingers of Miss Chritty's sister Jeany and her friend Lady Anne Lindsay, whose mother, the Countess of Balcarres lived on an upper floor off the same narrow stair.[38] But Miss Jeany had married Colonel William Russell a few years earlier and sailed away to Madras with her husband, and Lady Anne, too, was now married and living in England. Jeany had told her about this "little fellow," who, she said, "had more genius and mind than any young creature of his age she had ever seen," and sometimes he was taken upstairs to visit the old Countess.

As Wattie grew older his explorations widened. Beyond John Knox's house and the nest of wooden-fronted houses that followed, the High Street leveled off a little at the point where the Tron Kirk thrust its tall wooden steeple skyward. Here were the open-air markets, a bedlam of booths and stalls, shrill with gin-smelling old women on stools behind tables of fruit or heaps of vegetables piled on the ground. Opposite was the Flesh Market, bloody with joints of meat, and farther along, on the south side of the street, Fish Market Close, a steep, stinking ravine down which the fish were dragged to be sold unwashed from scaly and tottering wooden tables.

A small boy would have to dodge among jostling crowds of housewives, servants, gentlemen in silver-buckled shoes, and ladies in billowing skirts. Barbers with their hair-dressing materials darted from doorway to doorway, and clerks, wiping their mouths, emerged from Fortune's Tavern in the Stamp Office Close. Jawing with each other around the coffee houses lounged the caddies, ragamuffin public messengers who knew how to find everyone of importance in Edinburgh, and who ferreted out in twenty-four hours everything to be known about any stranger. Here and there stalked one of the City Guard, in rusty red uniform and black knee-boots, carrying his Lochaber ax with its curved blade at the top of a long staff.

Still going uphill, the boy would come upon the Guardhouse, a low ugly building dumped into the very middle of the High Street and looking to him like "a long black snail" crawling up the street. Its evil-smelling "black hole,"[39] he learned, had a bad name even among the drunken bucks and loose women of the town. Next, on the right, behind an arcaded courtyard, rose the Royal Exchange with its Corinthian pilasters, and, a few steps farther and again in the middle of the way, stood Creech's bookshop, a haunt for literary loungers and antiquaries poring over dusty folios. This formed the east end of the Luckenbooths, the enclosed shops (literally "locked booths"), behind whose small-paned glittering windows the watchmakers and jewelers displayed their wares to country couples buying silver spoons while goldsmiths in scarlet cloaks paced sedately past. Beyond loomed the melancholy walls of the Tolbooth, the old jail, with its black stanchioned windows and turnpike stair.

If Wattie turned to the left he would find himself in the Krames, a crooked alley squeezed between the Luckenbooths and the Tolbooth on one side and the fourteenth-century Kirk of St. Giles on the other. Plastered into every coign and buttress angle of the church were the wooden booths of hosiers, glovers, mercers, hatters, milliners, and drapers. Massive above the crowded strident passage rose the church tower with its strange open-work crown of eight buttresses joining in a pinnacle that pricked the sky. Wandering into the cavernous darkness of the church, beneath its pointed arches, Wattie could re-create the very scene of Jenny Geddes, the market woman, throwing her footstool at the head of the clergyman who tried to read from Archbishop Laud's prayer-book.

Behind the jumbled mass of St. Giles opened out Parliament Square, with the Gothic façade of Parliament House, grave in gray stone, extending its handsome balconies and ornamented doors and windows around two sides. No longer the seat of government since the Union with England in 1707, it was now the home of the Court of Session. Both the Square and the Outer House, a spacious hall with a carved oaken roof, were constantly thronged with lawyers and litigants.[40] Here the boy would see gowned advocates, some in wigs, some bareheaded, striding the stone floor or standing in knots telling stories, and disconsolate farmers, in clouted shoes and coats of gray or cerulean blue, anxiously clutching their staffs in horny ungloved hands. Solicitors, agents, and men of business darted about the bars where cases were being pleaded, the wigged Lords of Session sitting amid the uproar calm as statues in their gowns of purple cloth faced with crimson silk.[41]

Outdoors again, the boy would find the High Street broadening still more into the Lawnmarket, at the far end of which extended Castle Hill Walk and the jagged fortifications of the Castle. From here the West Bow, a chaos of sculptured dovecot gables projecting over the shops of coppersmiths and pewterers, zigzagged precipitously to the bustle of the Grassmarket below. Wattie knew, like every schoolboy, that it was down this sharp descent in 1736 that rioters had dragged Captain John Porteous; he could picture the glaring torches in the darkness, the silent surge of the mob, and at the eastern end of the open space the body of the victim jerking from its rope above the huge red sandstone block of the gallows.

The scene around him now was one of cheerful bustle. This was where travelers from Glasgow and the west of Scotland came into Edinburgh, by the West Port, through the neighing and bellowing of the Cattle Market. Maids in pattens clicked on the cobbles, children played in gutters among the manure heaps, fisherwomen cried caller haddies from Newhaven, and piemen rang their bells. Above the tumult the White Hart Inn reared its five stories under the looming Castle Rock. And by the twisting climb of Candlemakers Row, past Grey-friars' Church and the bowling green opposite, and through Bristo Port, it was only a quarter of a mile home to the green quiet of George Square.

Thus roaming the streets and wynds, sometimes alone, sometimes among a chattering band of other schoolboys, Wattie steeped himself in all the colorful present and dramatic past of his native town. When he was still too young to be more than an onlooker, he had trailed along to Blackfriars' Wynd after some of the wild older boys and seen them stone the windows of a strumpet who had struck one of them. The scarlet-clad Town Guard had sailed in through a shower of rocks and seized some dozen of the ringleaders, while Wattie dived to safety under the stall and petticoat of an old applewoman.[42] But it was not long before he made one of the excited garrison of youngsters who during the winter season would sometimes man the Cowgate Port, clambering to the top of its fortified walls, and defend their possession against the Town Guard with thick bombardments of snowballs.[43]

Climbing the old Flodden Walls, which partly encircled the city, was another great "ploy"—a sport or pastime—among the boys, creep-ing up by finger- and toe-holds between the joints of the rough masonry. Wattie's lame leg made such an exploit no easy job for him, but he re-fused to be daunted. Before he finished High School he became one of the boldest and nimblest climbers. He successfully tackled the dangerous Cat's Neck on Salisbury Crags. And he was even among those daring enough to conquer "the kittle nine steps," a dizzy passage where the black granite western verge of the Castle Rock towered almost two hundred feet, and whose footholds, few and far between, might have vanquished an Alpine chamois-hunter.[44]

Street fights called "bickers" broke out constantly between boys from one square or district and their neighbors and were almost a weekly warfare between the boys attending the High School and those of humbler parentage. More a kind of violent play than any malice or ill will, these brawls were fought with a vigor of sticks and stones and fisticuffs.[45] The youngsters dwelling in George Square, who had to make their way daily through the poorer quarter of Bristo Street, Potter Row, and Cross Causeway, were involved in such unending hostilities with the hardy lads who lived there that they formed themselves into a com-pany, to which the Countess of Sutherland, who resided on the north side of the Square, gave a handsome set of colors.[46] Many were the skirmishes of these two bands, and many the bruised rib and bloodied head, one group charging while the other tried to stand its ground, the battle sometimes surging backward and forward over two or three blocks of houses for an entire evening, with older brothers and servants joining the fray.

Wattie and his companions came to recognize some of their regular opponents well. Their principal leader, always first in the charge and last to retreat, was a blue-eyed boy of thirteen or fourteen, with long flaxen hair. His arms, legs, and feet were always bare, but he wore a pair of old green livery breeches, from which he was known as Green-Breeks. Once he "headed a charge so rapid and furious that all fled before him. He was several paces before his comrades, and had actually laid his hands on the patrician standard" when one of Wattie's party who had gotten possession of an old *couteau de chasse*, or light saber, struck Green-Breeks over the head and cut him down.[47]

Terrified, both bands fled in opposite directions. Poor Green-Breeks, "his bright hair plentifully dabbled in blood," was taken to the Infirmary by a watchman. The victors swore one another to secrecy and flung the bloody sword into a ditch in the Meadow, but the remorse and apprehension of the boy who had wielded it were beyond all bounds. Green-Breeks's wound, however, turned out to be trifling, and no argument could make him reveal who had struck the blow. When he recovered, Wattie and his brothers got in touch with him through a gingerbread baker, offering him in appreciation a small sum of "smart-money." The heroic Green-Breeks refused it, saying that he wouldn't sell his blood but that he wouldn't be an informer. That was "clam"—base, or mean. They finally persuaded him to accept a pound of snuff for the old aunt or grandmother with whom he lived. The two bands did not become friends, "for the bickers were more agreeable to both parties than any more pacific amusement," but henceforth they fought "under mutual assurances of the highest consideration."[48]

# 5

---

# *From Dreamer to Doer*

# *( 1780–1783 )*

WATTIE'S OLDER BROTHER John had in 1780 advanced into the the Rector's class, and that same autumn Tom entered the High School.[1] The oldest brother, Robert, was no longer in Edinburgh; instead of completing his course of studies there he had first gone to a boarding school at Dumfries, and later, still insisting on a naval career, to the academy from which youthful aspirants to the service were inducted into their first berths.[2] On his way to London at the end of May, 1779, he had stopped at York and seen the Minster and the town, and on September 23, a proud midshipman, he boarded the frigate *Greyhound*.[3]

Anne was a child of misfortune. When she was only six years old, while she was alone in a room, her cap had taken fire; before the flames could be put out her head had been dreadfully scorched. She recovered only after a long and dangerous illness. She was often ailing, and even the slightest cold made her face swell painfully. At the age of eight and again at nine she had further accidents. The iron-railed gate into the center of George Square was blown shut upon her fingers and her hand was cruelly mangled. And she nearly drowned falling into a pond or old quarry-hole in Brown's Park, just south of the Square. She was an affectionate and intelligent little girl, but her accidents and illnesses generated nervous uncertainties of temper that led her to withdraw much into a world of her own dreams.[4]

Nevertheless, Anne joined her brothers in some of their more imaginative pastimes. Encouraged by their mother, they shared happy evening hours in the family circle while Wattie read aloud from the plays of Shakespeare and from *The Arabian Nights*. More surprisingly, Mr. Scott, despite his Calvinist principles, allowed the children to get up private theatricals in the dining room with their friends after the day's lessons were over. Wattie not only was principal actor but took charge as stage manager. In *Jane Shore*, a family favorite, he acted Hastings and Anne played Alicia. As the deformed Gloucester in *Richard III*, he cheerfully observed that his limp "would do well enough to represent the hump,"[5] and declaimed with enormous gusto Richard's soliloquy upon his whirlwind courtship of the Lady Anne, working up to a climax of derisive exultation over his triumph in making her look with favor —"on me, that halt and am misshapen thus!"[6]

At Christmas and Hogmanay—the Scottish New Year's Eve—in accordance with ancient custom, Wattie and his brothers joined the bands of children who roamed the snowy streets from door to door, acting crude traditional versions of the old mystery plays, like the Christmas Mummers of England. Called Guisards, or maskers (though often their disguise was only a white shirt and smutted cheeks), these holiday troupes did St. George and the Dragon, or a patriotic play in which Alexander the Great found Scotland altogether a tougher job to conquer than the rest of the world. Sometimes they were the Nine Worthies, or characters from Scripture, or, again, the Apostles, St. Peter with his keys, St. Paul with a sword, and Judas Iscariot with a bag in which the neighbors were supposed to deposit gifts of plum cake. After a round of such performances in the tingling air, they trooped home with red cheeks to Christmas cheer and the glow of fires roaring up the chimneys: even in Presbyterian Scotland the season was festal with savory goose, plum pudding, and wassail in brown bowls.[7]

The children took no such joy in music as they did in play-acting. Although their father played the violoncello, drawing a melodious baritone from the entrails of his instrument at gentlemen's concerts, none of them except the absent Robert had either voice or ear. Mr. Scott engaged a music master, Alexander Campbell, the editor of *Albyn's Anthology*, to give them singing lessons, and their mother was eager that they should at least learn psalmody, but their sessions with their unhappy teacher were disasters of cacophony. Their neighbor Lady Cumming sent to beg that they might not all be flogged at the same hour; though she had no doubt, she said, that the punishment was deserved, the noise was dreadful. The unhappy musician, who was fond of Wattie, would not allow that he had a bad ear but insisted that he did not choose to learn.[8]

If they were not musical, however, the youngsters dearly loved listening to stories, many of which reappeared in Scott's writings years later. One which they heard from their father's manservant, a Highlander named John M'Kinlay, gave him the germ of *Guy Mannering*. It was a tale of a traveler in Galloway who toward nightfall was given shelter in a country house just as its lady was about to bear her first child. A learned astrologer, he cast the infant's horoscope, which foretold some unhallowed danger on the boy's twenty-first birthday. The years passed; as the fatal time approached, the youth fell beneath the power of a dark suggestion that he take his own life. In desperation the father sent him on a long journey to the astrologer's house. There the sage fortified him with a Bible and left him alone to resist the final assault. It came in the shape of a swarm of demons, and finally the Author of Evil himself appeared, urging that the young man had sinned beyond redemption and should destroy himself. Almost overwhelmed by despair, the victim still resisted, though the satanic power somehow rendered him unable to articulate the name of God. But at last he raised the Bible, asserting his faith in its assurances. As he spoke, the clock struck the hour with which his birthday ended, and with a yell the defeated fiend vanished.[9]

Another inexhaustible source of stories was Mrs. Scott's maiden aunt, Miss Margaret Swinton, who lived with one old maidservant in a small house in Clark Street, not far from George Square.[10] In and out of her little parlor, with its projecting lattice windows, the children were constantly trooping, from John, now a gangling thirteen, down to laughing Tom and little Dan, who was almost six. At her spinning wheel, or working a stocking, the old lady received them, in a chocolate-colored silk gown with ruffles of Mechlin lace, black silk mittens, and a cap of spotless cambric on her head, and spun out mysterious or heroic legends for them while her fingers plied their task.[11]

One that enthralled Wattie and that his memory called up in later years was about an Italian necromancer. In a magic mirror he shows a lady a vision of her husband who had deserted her. As he is going through a ceremony of marriage in a foreign land a military officer furiously rushes upon him with drawn sword.[12] Then there was the story of one of Aunt Margaret's own ancestors, a gigantic warrior who had died at the battle of Halidon Hill. The Swintons were then engaged in a bloody feud with the powerful Gordon family, whose chief had been slain by the knight of Swinton. But when the young Gordon heard Swinton volunteer to charge the English archers with his cavalry, he knelt down before the foe of his clan. "I have not yet been knighted," he said. "and never can I take the honour from the hand of a truer, more loyal, more valiant leader, than he who slew my father: grant me the boon I ask, and I unite my forces to yours, that we may live and die together." His feudal enemy became his godfather in chivalry, and the two fell together on the field of battle. But while the fight lasted the old giant guarded the young man's life more than his own, and in death his body lay stretched over that of the Gordon.[13]

With the macabre streak that ran through some of her stories, Aunt Margaret combined strong nerves. Among her fancies was reading alone in her chamber by the light of a taper fixed in a candlestick she had made out of a human skull. One night this object, after performing some odd circles on the chimney piece, leaped to the floor and began rolling about the apartment. She calmly went to the next room for another light, and returned to solve the mystery. She found that within her *memento mori* had crawled a rat, whose struggles had produced its strange gyrations.[14]

When Wattie or any of the other children were ill, Aunt Margaret was constant in attendance, her kind face, beneath its combed-back white hair, bent over their bedsides. These affectionate ministrations made the manner of her death peculiarly dreadful to them. The servant who had been attached to her for half a lifetime suddenly went insane, hacked her mistress to death with a coal ax, and rushed into the street with the bloody weapon, screaming aloud the deed she had just done. Wattie had sickened with terror at some of the ballads he had heard, like that of Lankin stabbing the baby to death with a silver bodkin and then slaying its mother; he had not previously had brought home to him that such things did indeed happen in life, not only in legend. For the nine-year-old boy this slaughter of his great-aunt awakened, he later said, "the first images of horror that the scenes of real life stamped upon my mind."[15]

The following October Wattie's class, according to the usual routine of the High School, came under the instruction of the Rector. Although Mr. Fraser had been a pedestrian teacher, he had drilled his pupils well in the rudiments of Latin, and Wattie had fairly well mastered its difficulties.[16] Dr. Adam made what had been a burdensome task into enjoyment. He was a progressive teacher; his *Principles of Latin and English Grammar* had bought down upon his head a storm of abuse because it was written in English instead of Latin. Some years later, the Doctor, whose ideas of republics were derived from Athens and Rome (and whose experience of the Town Council of Edinburgh had given him no reverential feelings about existing authorities), horrified respectable opinion by defending the French Revolution.[17]

In other ways Dr. Adam was, rather contradictorily, a stickler for old fashions. Boys, he said dogmatically, should wear cocked hats, wide-skirted coats, breeches with stockings, and buckled shoes. "If you see a boy with a round hat, tied shoes, and a short coat like a groom, that is a bad boy—mark that boy in after life, and you will see how he will turn out!"[18] Despite these dire predictions, throughout the fifty years he headed the school the Doctor took the greatest pleasure in the later careers of some of his round-hatted, short-coated boys, never failing to plume himself with innocent vanity upon their triumphs as the fruit of his instructions.[19]

Severe in his censure when he thought them inattentive, the good Doctor enthusiastically fanned to a flame whatever sparks of sensitivity to literature he found in them. Wattie's heart swelled with pride when the Rector said that although many others "understood the Latin better,

*Gaulterus Scott* was behind few in following and enjoying the author's meaning." He began to feel the beauties of the language, "gathering grapes from thistles." He saw that the Doctor expected him to do well, and felt honor-bound to vindicate his master's high opinion. So encouraged, the boy even tried his hand at making some translations of Horace and Virgil into English verse.[20]

One of these, written in a childish scrawl at the age of ten or eleven, his mother preserved in a folder that she inscribed, "My Walter's first lines, 1782":

> In awful ruins Aetna thunders nigh,
> And sends in pitchy whirlwinds to the sky
> Black clouds of smoke, which, still as they aspire,
> From their dark sides there bursts the glowing fire;
> At other times huge balls of fire are toss'd,
> That lick the stars, and in the smoke are lost:
> Sometimes the mount, with vast convulsions torn,
> Emits huge rocks, which instantly are borne
> With loud explosions to the starry skies,
> The stones made liquid as the huge mass flies,
> Then back again with greater weight recoils,
> While Aetna thundering from the bottom boils.

These lines were judged the second best on the subject, Wattie's boyhood and lifelong friend Colin Mackenzie winning pride of place over him.[21]

Before coming under the tutelage of Dr. Adam, Wattie had spent an hour daily at a small seminary where a Mr. Morton taught writing and arithmetic, subjects not included in the High School curriculum, which was primarily concerned with Latin. One of the little girls among his fellow pupils remembered the odd humor with which the boy called inking his pen "sending his doggie to the mill," and was awed by his stories of what he called his "visions," misty but radiant images of the glories of Paradise which came to him when he was lying alone on the floor or sofa.[22] But now Mr. Scott withdrew Wattie from this little school and engaged a private tutor for his children.[23]

The tutor was a solemn young divinity student named James Mitchell, who, in addition to teaching the others, continued Wattie's lessons in writing and arithmetic, taught him French, and helped him study his themes in the classics.[24] Mitchell found Wattie's mind quick, his memory tenacious, his application diligent. His example stimulated his brothers, and the young man and the boy came to feel less like master and pupil than like friend and companion.[25] From Mitchell, who was fanatically devoted to the Kirk, Wattie acquired some knowledge of church history, especially the early history of the Church of Scotland and the wars and sufferings of the Covenanters.[26]

Despite the straitness of his views, the tutor was no tyrant and allowed his pupil to dispute with him. Wattie, "with a head on fire for Chivalry," was a Cavalier; Mitchell was a Roundhead. "I was a Tory," Scott said, "and he was a Whig. I hated Presbyterianism, and admired Montrose with his victorious Highlanders; he liked the Presbyterian Ulysses, the dark and politic Argyle." The boy argued from the amorphous feeling that the Cavaliers were the gentlemanly side; the tutor from the conviction that the Roundheads were the right side.[27] But there was no anger in their contentions: only once did Mitchell have to threaten punishment for unruliness, and then the child disarmed him by leaping up and affectionately flinging his arms around the tutor's neck.[28]

The Sunday devotions of the Scott family gave a good deal more pleasure to the young man than they did to the children. To see the whole family, down to the last servant, attending the old Greyfriars' Church was for the pious Mitchell "a sight so amiable and exemplary as often to excite in my breast a glow of heartfelt satisfaction." He loved being called upon to perform the part of chaplain when they assembled in the drawing room on Sunday evenings, and warmly approved the rigorous catechism they were obliged to undergo.[29] But one phenomenon baffled him: that although Wattie always fell asleep during the sermon, he was better than any of the other children at passing examination on its contents. "The only way I could account for this," said the puzzled tutor, "was that when he heard the text, and divisions of the subject, his good sense, memory, and genius supplied the thoughts which would occur to the preacher."[30]

In still other ways his young charge made a strong impression on the tutor. One day Wattie told him he had found a half-guinea piece in the High School Yards. Looking about, he saw a rustic who, he thought, might have dropped it. He asked the man if he missed anything; the fellow searched his pockets and then said he had lost half a guinea. The boy then handed him the coin. "In this transaction," the tutor comments rather heavily, "his ingenuity in finding out the proper owner, and his integrity in restoring the property, met my most cordial approbation."[31]

At school, under Dr. Adam, Wattie was now reading Cicero, Livy, and Sallust, in prose; and, in verse, Virgil, Horace, and Terence.[32] Although he attained no high place, his quick memory often helped him. The Doctor "would constantly refer to him for dates, the particulars of battles, and other remarkable events alluded to in Horace, or whatever author the boys were reading, and used to call him the historian of the class."[33] Once he made a great leap in rank, when a dolt of a boy boggled at the preposition *cum*. "What part of speech is with?" asked the Rector. "A substantive," replied the dunce. After a pause, Dr. Adam asked the *dux*, "Is *with* ever a substantive?" The head boy could not answer; the Rector went down the class, all of whom were baffled and silent, until he reached Wattie, on this occasion eighteenth or twentieth. Instantly Wattie quoted: "And Samson said unto Delilah, If they bind me with seven green *withs* that were never dried, then shall I be weak, and as another man."[34]

Another time, chance gave him the opportunity of distinguishing himself. The Earl of Buchan, a foolish, self-important man of forty, took into his head the pompous caprice of paying a visit of inspection to the High School and examining the Rector's class. Some deference for his rank, perhaps, induced Dr. Adam to endure this impertinence. Wattie, in disgrace at the moment for some aggravated case of negligence, was seated on a low bench. But desirous of showing off the abilities of his pupils, Dr. Adam called upon him to recite a passage from the *Aeneid*. It was the apparition of Hector's ghost, which he rendered with such spirit and feeling that the eminent stranger—as the boy took him to be—applauded him warmly. Wattie glowed with pride at his praise.[35]

Two more of his boyish attempts at poetry, written before he was twelve, were preserved by Dr. Adam.[36] One was entitled "On the Setting Sun," the other, "On a Thunderstorm":

> Loud o'er my head though awful thunders roll,
> And vivid lightnings flash from pole to pole,
> Yet 'tis thy voice, my God, that bids them fly,
> Thy arm directs those lightnings through the sky.
> Then let the good thy mighty name revere,
> And hardened sinners thy just vengeance fear.

Readers today will find them more piety than poetry, but Wattie was proud of these effusions and mightily indignant when the blue-buskined wife of an apothecary claimed they had been copied from an old magazine.

"I never forgave the imputation, and even now I acknowledge some resentment against the poor woman's memory. She indeed accused me unjustly when she said I had stolen my poem ready made; but as I had, like most premature poets, copied all the words and ideas of which my verses consisted, she was so far right. I made one or two faint attempts at verse after I had undergone this sort of daw-plucking at the hands of the apothecary's wife, but some friend or other always advised me to put my verses in the fire; and, like Dorax in the play, I submitted, though with a swelling heart."[37]

All his pupils admired Dr. Adam, but his encouragement made Wattie deeply devoted. When one of the masters, Mr. Nicol, supported by the Town Council, embarked on a quarrel with the Doctor and insulted his person and authority, Wattie was bitterly indignant. Nicol was an excellent classical scholar and a witty drinking companion, but a sot and inhumanly cruel to his pupils. He may have been the schoolmaster who, while punishing Wattie, struck him to the ground and then apologized by saying that he did not know his own strength—which Wattie accepted as a perfectly rational excuse. Nicol carried his feud with the Rector to the point of physical violence, waylaying and knocking him down in the High School Wynd one dark night. Dr. Adam's boys were outraged, and when he conducted one of his periodic examinations of Mr. Nicol's class, they conspired under Wattie's leadership to express their feelings. On this occasion, according to custom, Mr. Nicol substituted in the Rector's class. The lesson was that passage of the *Aeneid* in which the Queen of Carthage questions her court about the stranger who has come into her domain:

> Quis novus hic nostris successit sedibus hospes?
>
> (What new visitor approaches our throne?)

Wattie wrote this line on a sheet of paper, changing *novus* to *vanus*, which alters the meaning to "vain intruder"; this he surreptitiously pinned on the master's coattail, raising a laugh of ridicule against him throughout the school.[38]

Among his schoolmates at this time Wattie's closest friend was a boy named John Irving.[39] The two became constant companions. Every Saturday, and even more often during vacations, they took long walks to solitary places like Arthur's Seat, Salisbury Crags, Blackford Hill, or the Braid Hills, clambering up the rocks to some inaccessible nook sheltered from the wind. Sometimes the two got into places from which they found it hard to move either up or down, and there were times when John thought he would have to fetch a ladder to extricate his friend; but somehow Wattie always found it possible to scramble his way to the top and to descend.[40]

From the rocky height of Arthur's Seat they could look down over the city, from Holyrood, almost beneath their feet, to the ramparts of the Castle, or gaze over the undulating landscape to the silvery waters of the Firth and, far beyond, to the purple Sidlaw hills. Snug and alone in a cranny of the rocks, they brought out three or four volumes borrowed from the lending library above Creech's bookshop on the High Street.[41] Their favorites were romances of knight errantry, *The Castle of Otranto*, Spenser, Boiardo, and Ariosto. Wattie read faster than his companion and every two pages had to wait before turning the leaf. John forgot most of what he read but was astonished to discover that in spite of Wattie's speed he remained master of it all and even months afterwards could repeat whole pages that had pleased him. From these orgies of reading they were presently inspired to make up and tell each other interminable tales filled with battles, giants, and enchantments, wildly founded on Arthurian romance, the paladins of Charlemagne, the poets and Gothic novels they had gulped down, and all the ballads and fairy tales that mingled fantastically in their memories.[42]

The time was now drawing near when the two boys would be graduated from the High School. James Mitchell had already taken his departure from the Scott household. "When it was understood I was to leave the family," he wrote, "Master Walter told me that he had a small present to give me to be kept as a memorandum of his friendship, and that it was of little value: 'But you know, Mr. Mitchell,' said he, 'that presents are not to be estimated according to their intrinsic value, but according to the intention of the donor.' This was his Adam's *Grammar*, which had seen hard service in its day, and had many animals and inscriptions on its margins."[43]

Although Mr. Mitchell's pupil had no doubt gained a great deal from his earnest tutor, and still more from Dr. Adam, and even from the dry ministrations of Mr. Fraser, there can be no question that what he was already teaching himself was to prove the most valuable. The intervals of his school hours were always being filled with books of history, voyages, and travels, besides the ballads, poems, plays, fairy tales, Eastern stories, and romances he had devoured.[44] His uncle, Dr. Rutherford, good-humoredly remonstrated with him for reading at breakfast. He also read in bed, or lying on his back on the carpet, surrounded by books, "his lame leg resting upon his left thigh and the book he was reading laid upon the lame foot as on a reading desk."[45]

"I left the High School," Scott recalled later, ". . . with a great quantity of general information, ill arranged, indeed, and collected without system, yet deeply impressed upon my mind; readily assorted by my power of connexion and memory, and gilded, if I may be permitted to say so, by a vivid and active imagination. . . . I waded into the stream like a blind man into a ford, without the power of searching my way, unless by groping for it. My appetite for books was as ample and undiscriminating as it was indefatigable and I since have had too frequently reason to repeat that few ever read so much, and to so little purpose."[46]

But the boy's education was not confined to books. He had taken his place in the active life of Edinburgh. The indulged child from the farm at Sandyknowe had learned the give-and-take of a family of children. He traded bloody noses in the High School Yards, mingled red-cheeked in the thick of snowball fights, climbed the Flodden Wall, scaled the Kittle Nine Steps of the Castle Rock and even the heights of Arthur's Seat. He roamed Edinburgh's streets, soaking up their atmosphere and color, went from door to door with the Guisards at Christmas. He fought panting against Green-Breeks and his band in the battle of Cross Causeway. He grew strong and healthy, an indefatigable walker, his quick hobble aided by a stout stick. He became a doer and a laugher as well as a dreamer drenched in the storied scene of his native land.

# PART TWO

## *Makin' Himsell A' the Time*

### 1 7 8 3 – 1 7 9 6

# 1

## The Delilahs of the Imagination

### ( 1 7 8 3 – 1 7 8 8 )

DURING HIS LAST YEAR in Dr. Adam's class Walter had shot up so rapidly that he had outgrown his strength. Instead of sending him directly to college, therefore, Mr. Scott decided that he should spend half a year in Kelso with his Aunt Jenny.[1] His grandmother was now dead, and Miss Jenny dwelt in a house belonging to his father, just east of the churchyard.[2] Besides an old maidservant, Walter's cousin Barbara, with whom he had played dolls in his childhood, now lived with Miss Jenny as her companion.[3]

In this peaceful retreat the boy's time was his own, except that he was expected to keep up his Latin by spending four hours a day at the Kelso Grammar School. The master, Mr. Lancelot Whale, was an absent-minded, grotesque, enormous figure nearly seven feet tall. Despite being something of a humorist himself, he was driven frantic by the inevitable puns his pupils made upon his name—calling him an odd fish, slyly alluding to Jonah, and nicknaming his son the Prince of Whales. But he was an able Latin scholar, delighted at the chance to escape from rudimentary drill and read Tacitus and Persius with a student beginning to understand them. Walter suspected that some of the time devoted to him represented a neglect of Mr. Whale's regular pupils, but he himself made rapid progress. In return he acted as an assistant to the enthusiastic pedagogue and heard the recitations of the lower classes. At the public examination he spouted from the *Life of Agricola* the speech of the Caledonian chieftain Galgacus, which was no less appreciated by the audience, he says, because "few of them probably understood one word of it."[4]

On the form next to his sat a slim dark-haired boy, about a year older than Walter, named James Ballantyne.[5] His father was a local merchant; his mother the daughter of a former classical master at the Edinburgh High School who had later become the Rector of the Dalkeith Grammar School.[6] The two boys soon became friends. When Walter had mastered his lesson for the day, James recorded, "I alas being still sadly to seek in mine, he used to whisper to me, 'Come, slink over beside me, Jamie, and I'll tell you a story.'" After school the two walked along the banks of the Tweed together, Walter continuing in an inexhaustible flow. Through all the connections that were to intertwine their fortunes in later years, and indeed to the very end of his life, James thought him "the best story-teller I had ever heard, either then or since."[7]

Another schoolfellow was a boy named Robert Waldie, whose widowed mother, a Quaker, possessed a small but well-selected library.[8] "This the kind old lady permitted me to rummage at pleasure," Walter remembered, "and carry home what volumes I chose, on condition that I should take, at the same time, some of the tracts printed for encouraging and extending the doctrines of her own sect." She did not ask him to agree to read them, "being but too justly afraid of involving me in a breach of promise"; she merely wanted them available if whim or curiosity moved him.[9]

Spinning a tale for James Ballantyne, or running out of Mrs. Waldie's house on the Bridge Street with a book tucked under his arm, Walter was at the same time keenly drinking in his surroundings. He always felt Kelso "the most beautiful if not the most romantic village in Scotland."[10] The site of the Grammar School had once been the nave of the old Abbey, and the building stood within the shadow of its square Norman towers, now in gray and moldering ruin. The great market square, where James's father had his shop, throbbed with memories of the past: here the rebel forces had proclaimed James VIII as King in 1715, here Prince Charles Edward had stayed two nights on his northward retreat in 1745, here Queen Mary had slept for two nights in 1566.[11]

Kelso's resources included a circulating library "of ancient standing" and a subscription library where current books could be obtained. From their shelves Walter borrowed the novels of Richardson, Fielding, and Smollett, and of Henry Mackenzie, remembered today mainly as the author of *The Man of Feeling*.[12] Exciting also was Tasso's *Jerusalem Delivered*, even in the flatness of Hoole's translation, whose verses Scott later dismissed as "absolute dish washings."[13] The greatest revelation of all, however, was Percy's *Reliques of Ancient English Poetry*. What was Walter's delight to find that very ballad lore which had held him captive in his Sandyknowe infancy, and which "still continued in secret the Delilah of my imagination, considered as the subject of sober research, grave commentary, and apt illustration," by an editor of poetic genius! To find his own enthusiasm so confirmed was breathtaking.[14]

"The very grass sod seat," he wrote, years later, to Bishop Percy himself, "to which . . . I retreated from my playfellows to devour the works of the ancient Minstrels, is still fresh and dear to my memory." Beneath a huge plane tree, in the ruins of what had been a old-fashioned arbor in Miss Jenny's garden, "The summer day sped onward so fast, that notwithstanding the sharp appetite of thirteen, I forgot the hour of dinner, was sought for with anxiety, and was still found entranced in my intellectual banquet." (In fact he was not thirteen but twelve.) "To read and to remember was in this instance the same thing, and henceforth I overwhelmed my schoolfellows, and all who would harken to me, with tragical recitations from the ballads of Bishop Percy." With the first few shillings he could scrape together he bought his own copy of the thrilling volumes, and read and reread them with exaltation.[15]

No doubt as he lost himself in the ballad of Sir Patrick Spens or Chevy Chase the magic was enhanced by the loveliness of the surrounding scene. Speading over seven or eight acres, the garden of his aunt's home sloped gently down to the rippling Tweed. It had been laid out early in the eighteenth century, with long straight walks between tall hedges of yew and hornbeam, parterres of bright flowers, thickets of blossoming shrubs, and fine ornamental trees. There was a banqueting house; there were wildernesses and seats and trellis walks. There was an orchard filled with fruit trees, and an arbor, and a bower approached "through a little maze of contorted walks, calling itself a labyrinth." In the center of this bower was the plane tree, "a splendid platanus, or Oriental plane," says Scott, "—a huge hill of leaves—one of the noblest specimens of that regularly beautiful tree which [I] remember to have seen."[16]

The beauty of landscape that had insensibly melted into his heart when as a small child he lay among the quiet sheep at the foot of Smailholm tower now flowered into an enchantment with which mingled his feeling for the way the world of nature was steeped in the deeds and emotions of the human past. The meeting of those two lovely rivers, the Tweed and the Teviot, their green banks clustered with trees; the ancient Abbey of Kelso rising from its massive arches to the delicately shafted triforium and soaring clerestory; the venerable ash trees flecking with shadow the heavy masonry foundations of the ruined fortress of Roxburgh; the terraces and sweeping lawns of Fleurs Castle—all harmonized for him into a single whole, not merely concord but unison, tinged with reverence, "which at times," he said, "made my heart feel too big for its bosom." "The love of natural beauty, more especially when combined with ancient ruins, or remains of our fathers' piety or splendour, became with me an insatiable passion."[17]

From these scenes Walter was recalled home in November, 1783, and enrolled in Edinburgh College. It is probable that about this time his oldest brother, Robert, was home for a brief period. He had fought under Rodney in the great naval victory at Martinique on April 12, 1782.

Walter hung enthralled upon his stories of Rodney's battles and the haunted Keys of the West Indies.[18] But the Peace of Paris in September had cut off Robert's hopes of promotion, and he was resigning to take service in the East India Company. He obtained appointment as fourth mate on the *Neptune*, sailing for Bombay in February, 1784. A little less than three years later, as third mate of the *Rodney*, at the age of twenty-three, Robert died on a voyage from Madeira to Bengal and was buried at sea some thousand miles south of Ceylon.[19]

When Walter returned from Kelso he was only a few months past his twelfth birthday, and a year or two younger than most of his fellow students in the College.[20] Its buildings stood on the same site where now extends the great classical University structure designed by William Playfair. But in 1783 the College was still a huddled warren of small courts and dingy classrooms. Here the boy took Latin under Professor Hill and began the study of Greek with Professor Dalzell. Unhappily for Walter's Latin, Hill, though a good scholar and a good-natured man much liked by his students, was a dull teacher and a lax disciplinarian.[21] His classroom was a rowdy place of unchecked idleness and disrespectful mirth.[22] Walter joined the fun, and in the turmoil "speedily lost much of what I had learned under Adam and Whale."[23] Professor Dalzell held the reins of authority more tightly, and was an enthusiast of classical learning, deeply concerned for the progress of his students. When he spoke about Aeschylus or Periclean Athens in his slow, soft voice, he inspired his students "with a vague but sincere ambition of literature, and with delicious dreams of virtue and poetry." But he could not arouse these passive vessels to active labor, and in a classroom crowded with no fewer than seventy-four students his task was almost impossible.[24]

Some of the boys, like Walter, did not know even the letters of the Greek alphabet. It was impracticable to drill so large a group, hopeless to teach them by lecturing.[25] Those who had acquired some smattering of Greek before they came to College might make progress; those who had none, unless they toiled desperately, fell behind. Finding himself far inferior to most of the other students, Walter took refuge in professing contempt for the language and a determination not to learn it. He speedily became known as the "Greek Blockhead," which only fortified his obstinacy.[26]

A fellow student named Thomas Archibald, himself a superior Greek scholar, tried to make Walter see the foolishness of his conduct, generously offering to coach him until he caught up with the foremost in the class.[27] Archibald was the son of a sheep farmer who rented his small holding from one of Mr. Scott's clients.[28] Walter not only resented hearing his folly censured but in youthful snobbery felt that it was presumptuous in anyone of Archibald's birth to intrude his advice. He rejected it with sulky civility. "I felt some twinges of conscience," he regretfully said later, "but they were unable to prevail over my pride and self-conceit."[29]

When Professor Dalzell at the end of the session required essays on the authors studied in the class, Walter had the audacity to turn in a composition arguing that Homer was inferior to Ariosto, supporting this "heresy," Scott records, "by a profusion of bad reading and flimsy argument." Dalzell could not contain his wrath, but at the same time— like the Oxford dons to whom Samuel Johnson quoted Macrobius— voiced honest surprise at the quantity of Walter's out-of-the-way knowledge. But, nonetheless, a dunce he was, said the Professor, and a dunce he would remain.[30]

During the middle of his second year with Dalzell, Walter fell ill and was sent again to Kelso. This second rustication dissolved even the faintest tincture of his Greek; he came to forget the very letters of its alphabet.[31] Though he now read only for entertainment, and had forsworn the Latin classics for no better reason than that they were akin to Greek, his interest in history induced him to tackle Buchanan, Mathew Paris, and some of the monkish chroniclers, and he had a strong relish for Lucian and Claudian, so that he retained some familiarity with their tongue.[32]

When he returned to Edinburgh his father decided that he should move on from his earlier study of arithmetic to a knowledge of mathematics. His tutor was Dr. MacFait, in his prime a distinguished teacher of this science. But age and domestic troubles had diminished his authority, and although Walter began ardently, and later believed that under more favorable circumstances he might have done well, he never acquired more than a smattering of the subject.[33] In the study of logic at the College he was more fortunate: Professor John Bruce approved his progress sufficiently to select him as one of his students to read an essay before Principal Robertson.[34]

Among his fellow students Walter continued popular. One of them was William Rae (known, for some orchard exploit, as Jackie Peartree), who was to become Lord Advocate. Another was Archibald Campbell, later a judge of the Court of Session under the title of Lord Succoth; still another George Ramsay, son of the eighth Earl of Dalhousie, a generous, high-spirited boy who in their high school days had been known and loved by everyone as "the *Lordie Ramsay* of the Yards." He rose to distinction as one of Wellington's generals and ultimately became commander in chief of the forces in India. Walter's closest friend, however, remained John Irving, with whom he read and walked as much as ever.[35]

Gradually they extended their ramblings until they had visited all the old castles within eight or ten miles of Edinburgh. On the road to Dalkeith was Craigmillar, with its rubble curtain wall and corner round-towers. And to the northwest was the village of Cramond, where the little River Almond slides into the Forth, passing nearby Lauriston Castle on the way.[36]

But Walter's favorite walk was to Roslin. Having started early in the morning, the two boys reached their destination in time to eat breakfast with the hearty appetite of youth.[37] Among its elms and chestnuts stood Rosslyn Chapel, bright in honey-colored stone, with its intricate buttresses and, within, its dark carved columns, the rich floral frothing of its vaulted ceiling, and the ornate garland-swagging of its famous "apprentice pillar."[38] Then they would explore the Castle, towering high above the pines and oaks clustered on the steep banks of the North Esk that looped around its foundations far below. From the foot of the Castle the two friends made their way along the deep gorge of the river, under granite crags, in the shade of gigantic oaks and silver hazels, amid daffodils, hawthorn, eglantine, and harebells, to where Hawthornden overhung the cliff, its roof green and violet with lichens. Thence they strolled on down the winding stream to the village of Lasswade, and started homeward early enough to arrive in George Square, ravenous, just in time for supper.[39]

Such long excursions on foot, sometimes almost twenty miles, argue vigorous strength in a lame boy of thirteen or fourteen, but Walter's parents had not yet given up hope of curing his infirmity. Among the remedies they now tried was another electrical apparatus devised by a Dr. Graham, "an empiric," Scott later said, "of some genius and great assurance," "with a dash of madness in his composition." When the magistrates refused Graham permission to give a course of lectures in Edinburgh, he extravagantly proclaimed that he "looked down upon them as the sun in his meridian glory looks down on the poor, feeble, stinking glimmer of an expiring farthing candle, or as God himself, in the plenitude of his omnipotence, may regard the insolent bouncings of a few refractory maggots in a rotten cheese."[40]

In their concern about his lameness, Walter's parents were ready to try even this quack. John Irving remembered helping him into Graham's contraption, the patient "seated in a large arm-chair, and hung round with a collar and a belt of magnets, like an Indian chief," confined within the glass and crystal intricacies of the machine. But the electrical treatment did no good, and neither did the "earth-bath," another of Graham's remedies.*[41]

* Graham used to come to Greyfriars' Church in a suit of white and silver, with a *chapeau bras*, his hair fantastically dressed in a double toupee, divided upon his head like the two tops of Parnassus. The Temple of Health, as he called his establishment, degenerated into a gambling hell, at which a beauty later notorious as Nelson's Lady Hamilton, then a *fille de joie*, appeared as the "Goddess of Health." When a young man, in a drunken quarrel there, was fatally stabbed through the bowels with a red-hot poker, the magistrates shut up the place.[42]

Walter had long understood that he was to follow the legal profession. All his father's hopes were concentrated upon having him attain fame as a lawyer. Neither of the two oldest boys had shown any inclination that way; Robert was now at sea and John had begun a military career. But Mr. Scott had no desire to see his third son acquire "the renown of a hero," and would have "laughed with scorn at the equally barren laurels of literature; it was by the path of law alone that he was desirous to see him rise to eminence, and the probabilities of success or disappointment were the thoughts of his father by day, and his dream by night."[43]

It had not, however, been determined whether Walter should be an Advocate or a Writer to the Signet. But now, feeling the technical knowledge of a Writer to be useful even if not essential to an Advocate, Mr. Scott decided that his son should serve the usual apprenticeship of five years to his own profession. Accordingly, on March 31, 1786, when he was fourteen, Walter entered into indentures with his father and began exploring what he calls "the dry and barren wilderness of forms and conveyances."[44]

He intensely disliked the drudgery of a law office and detested even more its close confinement. But he loved his father and was glad to be useful to him; he was also ambitious and knew that to get ahead he must work hard.[45] Therefore he labored diligently enough, on occasion covering more than a hundred and twenty pages in a swift legal hand without stopping for food or rest. Indeed, he retained to the end of his life some of the handwriting tricks of a law clerk, such as the flourish at the bottom of a page, a device originally adopted in engrossing to prevent the insertion of forged matter between the text and the signature. In later days his family often heard him mutter, after the habitual flourish, "There goes the old shop again!"[46]

His father gave him an example of faithful attention to business. "Punctual as the clock of St. Giles tolled nine, the neat dapper form of the little bald old gentleman was seen at the threshold of the Court hall, or at farthest, at the head of the Back Stairs"—the most direct way to the Parliament House from George Square—"trimly dressed in a complete suit of snuff-coloured brown, with stockings of silk or woollen, as suited the weather: a bobwig and a small cocked hat; shoes as black as Warren would have blacked them; silver shoe-buckles and a gold stock-buckle"; and adorned with "a nosegay in summer and a sprig of holly in winter."[47]

Although Walter was not an idle apprentice, sometimes he and one of his office companions played chess when they were supposed to be working and had to conceal the board hastily at the sound of his father's footstep on the staircase.[48] Presently Mr. Scott's visage would be thrust, in a peering way, through the half-opened door; and withdrawn, on seeing their absorption in legal papers, with a half-articulated "Humph!" which conveyed his doubts.[49] But Walter suspected that sometimes in his secret nook, in the afternoon, the old gentleman himself was poring happily over Wodrow's *Sufferings of the Church of Scotland* or Spottiswoode's ecclesiastical history when his apprentices imagined him to be deep in Dirleton's *Doubts* or Stair's *Decisions*.[50]

The boy's studies were lightened for him because he was allowed to choose his own law books and in his own peculiar way start them in the middle or near the end if he wanted to. A fellow apprentice was surprised by Walter's learning as much in this "hop-step-and-jump" method as he himself did in reading them straight through.[51] In addition, Walter's desk was always cluttered with miscellaneous volumes, mostly novels, which he was able to rent in larger numbers from the lending library now that he earned threepence a page copy-money by his clerical labors.[52]

One hundred and twenty pages put thirty shillings in his pocket, but they did not remain there long. He began seeing plays at the theater in the Old Playhouse Close.[53] He borrowed and purchased books from James Sibbald's circulating library in Parliament Square, ransacking its dusty shelves for old French and Italian books and flinging himself like a tiger on collections of old songs and romances. In this shop he now and then caught distant glimpses of writers, among them Andrew Mac-Donald, the author of *Vimonda*, and the great Robert Burns.[54] Walter also devoted a part of his earnings to attending an Italian class twice a week with Irving. Ambitious to read Ariosto and Tasso in their original tongue, he went on from them to Dante, Boiardo, Pulci, and *The Decameron*.[55] Deepening his knowledge of French, he devoured Tressan's romances, the *Bibliothèque Bleue* and the *Bibliothèque des Romans*, the innumerable volumes of La Calprenède's *Cassandre*, Scudery's *Artamène*, and Lesage's *Gil Blas*, as well as such chroniclers as Joinville, Froissart, Brantôme, and François de la Noue.[56] In his insatiable appetite, prodigiously, he even taught himself enough Spanish to read *Lazarillo de Tormes*, Hita's *Guerras Civiles de Granada*, and *Don Quixote*.[57]

Upon Hita's famous historical romance, which purported to be based on an Arabic manuscript by one Aben-Hamin, and which narrated the downfall of the Moorish kingdom, Walter probably based an ambitious poem, *The Conquest of Granada*, in four books, each of about four hundred lines, in a style imitative of Mickle's translation of the *Lusiads* of Camoens into heroic couplets. This effort he showed one of his fellow apprentices, but shortly afterward threw it into the fire.[58] Another early poem that has also disappeared, entitled "Guiscard and Matilda," he inscribed to Miss Keith of Ravelston.[59]

William Mickle and John Langhorne were among the poets Walter admired, and the former's *Cumnor Hall* had a peculiar enchantment for his ear which endured even to later years. "After the labours of the day were over," Irving remembered, "we often walked in the Meadows,"

among its formal alleys of old trees, "especially in the moonlight nights";
and Walter "seemed never weary of repeating the first stanza:

> "The dews of summer night did fall—
> The Moon, sweet regent of the sky,
> Silvered the walls of Cumnor Hall,
> And many an oak that grew thereby."[60]

In the faded lyricism of Mickle's poem there is also something faintly
akin to a ballad feeling that partly explains Walter's fondness for it.
From the age of ten he had bought the chapbooks and the penny and
halfpenny broadsheets of ballads that were still hawked about the streets
of Edinburgh, and he had a set of notebooks in which he copied those
he heard.[61] "My mother could repeat a great many," said Irving, and
Walter "used to come and learn those that she could recite to him."[62]

So close-knit a community as Edinburgh in the 1780s readily offered
a boy of a literary turn the opportunity of meeting men of letters. Under
the roof of his uncle Dr. Rutherford, in Hyndford's Close, he met Dr.
Cartwright, who then had some fame as a poet. The aged dramatist
John Home, who dwelt in a villa not far outside of town, had not forgotten the child he had met at Bath, and Walter was often a guest in
his house. One of his fellow students in the College, Adam Ferguson,
was the son of the famous Professor Adam Ferguson, in whose home
Walter met the venerable blind poet Thomas Blacklock. Through Dr.
Blacklock, who benevolently allowed the boy the run of his library, he
made a happy acquaintance with Ossian and intensified his enthusiasm
for Spenser.[63] He soon tired, to be sure, of "the tawdry repetitions of the
Ossianic phraseology," but he could have read forever the music and
brightly colored imagery of Spenser. Still too young to trouble himself
with the allegory, he found the knights and ladies and dragons and giants
enchanting. "God only knows," he exclaimed, "how delighted I was to
find myself in such society." With the facility of his memory in retain-
ing whatever pleased him, he could soon repeat endless stanzas.[64]

Professor Ferguson, an oddity in a hard-drinking, heavy-eating age,
was a teetotaler and a vegetarian and therefore never dined out except
with his relative Dr. Joseph Black, the great physicist, who was a kindred
spirit: it was delightful, Ferguson's son Adam used to say, to see the two
philosophers rioting over a boiled turnip! The Professor was also fussy
about the temperature of his room, which he regulated by Fahrenheit, and
was capable of throwing his wife and daughters into a commotion if,
looking at the thermometer, he discovered that it was one degree too hot
or too cold.[65] But he was hospitable in entertainment, taking pleasure
in throwing open his doors to the distinguished guests who were drawn
to Edinburgh to meet him. It was at his residence of Sciennes Hill House
in the winter of 1786–87 that Walter had the excitement of meeting
Robert Burns.[66]

He and his friend Adam, of course, "sate silent, looked and listened." But the youths were all eyes for the twenty-seven-year-old poet. Walter thought his manners, though rustic, had a dignified plainness, like a sagacious country farmer of the old school, with a strong expression of sense and shrewdness. The ploughman-poet was independent without presumption, firm but not forward. Among the learned company he conversed with modesty but complete self-confidence, not hesitating to differ from them in opinion. What impressed Walter most was his eyes, "large, and of a dark cast," that "glowed (I say literally *glowed*) when he spoke."[67]

In his youthful erudition Walter found Burns's acquaintance with English poetry rather limited. He also felt that though Burns had "twenty times the abilities of Allan Ramsay" and other less gifted poets, "he talked of them with too much humility as his models."[68] Years later, Scott subtly compared this exaggerated praise to "the caresses which a celebrated Beauty is often seen to bestow upon girls far inferior in beauty to herself, and 'whom she loves the better therefor.' "[69]

Only once at this meeting did Walter attract the poet's attention. Burns had noticed on the wall a print by one Bunsbury, portraying a soldier dead in the snow, his dog in misery by his side, on the other his widow with a child in her arms. Burns was moved to tears. Beneath the picture were some lines from a half-forgotten poem, "The Justice of the Peace." Burns asked who had written them: neither he nor anyone else in the company noticed the author's name in very fine print below. But Walter remembered that it was by Langhorne and whispered the information to a friend. He passed it on to the poet, who gave the boy a look and a word of thanks that filled him with pleasure.[70]

Working for his father sometimes took Walter out of town. Once when the two were driving from Selkirk to Melrose, Mr. Scott stopped the carriage at the foot of a hill and said good-naturedly, "We must get out here, Walter, and see a thing quite in your line."[71] He then led his son to a rude stone at the edge of a slope half a mile above the Tweed, which marked the place where

> gallant Cessford's life-blood dear
> Reeked on dark Elliott's border spear.

It was at this spot, called "Turn-again," that the battle of Melrose was fought in 1526 between the Earls of Angus and Home over the possession of the young King James V, and here a retainer of the Buccleuchs had mortally wounded Kerr of Cessford.[72] The field lay within the boundaries of a property later known as Abbotsford.

Through his father's Highland clients Walter became acquainted with their untamed region of lakes and mountain glens. In the first autumn of his apprenticeship old Alexander Stewart of Invernahyle, whose tales of the '15 and the '45 had enchanted his childhood, invited him for a visit.[73] The youth's excitement was sharpened by the heady glow of independence; this was to be his first excursion on a pony by himself.[74] When on the long ride from Kinross through the waste regions rising to the Wicks of Baiglie he at last looked down from the ridgy height, his heart swelled within him. There below lay the valley of the Tay with its lordly stream; "the town of Perth, with its two large meadows, or Inches, its steeples, and its towers; the hills of Moncrieff and Kinnoul faintly rising into picturesque rocks, partly clothed with woods; the rich margin of the river, studded with elegant mansions; and the distant view of the huge Grampians, the northern screen of this exquisite landscape." "I recollect pulling up the reins, without meaning to do so, and gazing on the scene before me as if I had been afraid it would shift, like those in a theatre, before I could . . . convince myself that what I saw was real."[75]

There followed wilder scenes of mountain desolation, leaping waterfall, scaur, and lake.[76] The way was rough, the inns along the road primitive. Often Walter and his brown palfrey "messed together on the same straw, fed on the same oat cakes, and drank small ale out of the same bicker." But at the end of his journey he was greeted with a hearty welcome.[77]

Walter heard from old Invernahyle how he had fought a broadsword duel with the famous Rob Roy at the Clachan of Balquidder and more reminiscences of his campaigns with Mar and Prince Charles Edward.[78] Nearby was the rocky cave in which he had hidden from searching English soldiers after the battle of Culloden in 1746.[79] And here still survived Invernahyle's miller, that "grim-looking old Highlander," who at Prestonpans was cutting down with his Lochaber ax an English officer, Colonel Whitefoord, when his master arrested the blow. It was to this intercession that Invernahyle owed his own life, for the Colonel later extorted his pardon from the Duke of Cumberland.[80]

Another business errand took Walter to some of his own relations of the Clan Campbell. At the end of his journey he found himself on a bleak rock overhanging their primitive tower, looking down on a tiny patch of cultivated ground. Stretched half-asleep in their tartans on the heath were Campbell, his three sons, and half a dozen gillies, amid guns, dogs, and heaps of game. In the courtyard below, a group of women were loading a cart with manure. Walter was astonished to discover that among these were the Laird's own lady and her three daughters, all quite untroubled at being found pitching dung. Retiring to their "bowers," they then reappeared dressed for dinner with no traces of their morning's toil except for faces glowing with health. The first course, a gigantic haggis, was borne into the hall in a wicker basket by two half-naked Celts, followed by a strutting piper blowing a tempest of dissonance.

For all this semisavage scene, Walter found the young ladies well informed and very agreeable, and the evening wound up with songs and dancing.[81]

To one of these professional journeys Walter owed his first sight of Loch Katrine. He was charged with serving a summons of removal against some Maclarens, refractory tenants of Invernahyle's brother-in-law. The Maclarens had intended to emigrate to America and agreed to sell their lease, and then, repenting their bargain, announced that nothing would make them move. Such was the terror they excited in the countryside that no King's messenger dared approach them without a military force.

Walter got an escort of a sergeant and six men from a regiment at Stirling and boldly rode up the Teith into the Trossachs, along the birch-and-pine-fringed shores of Loch Vennachar, and on to Loch Katrine. "The sergeant," he said, "was absolutely a Highland Sergeant Kite, full of stories of Rob Roy and himself, and a very good companion." When they came to the Maclarens' farm at Invernenty, they found the house deserted. They stayed overnight, helping themselves to some food, and returned unmolested. "The Maclarens," Scott concluded, had "probably never thought of any serious opposition, received their money, and went to America, where, having had some slight share in removing them from their *paupera regna*, I sincerely hope they prospered."[82]

In the second year of his apprenticeship, when he was sixteen, Walter broke a blood vessel in his lower bowels. He was so dangerously ill that his uncle Dr. Rutherford doubted his recovery. In the confinement of his bed, he was bled and blistered, not allowed to speak above a whisper, nor to eat more than a spoonful or two of boiled rice. His slow improvement his uncle considered little less than miraculous. Even so, his diet was still limited to a scanty allowance of vegetables. As the ravenous appetite normal to a growing boy returned, he felt starved. His talkativeness was rigorously suppressed; he could not open his lips "without one or two old ladies who watched my couch being ready at once to souse upon me, 'imposing silence with a stilly sound.'" It was a raw, cold spring, but the treatment prescribed allowed him no more covering than a single thin counterpane. He had several relapses, and on each one he was bled and blistered till he had barely a pulse.[83]

His gradual convalescence left him extremely weak. A nervousness afflicted him that he had never felt before, a tendency to start at slight alarms, indecisiveness in feeling and acting, touchiness about trifling irritations, nebulous fears of misfortune. These he blamed on the distasteful vegetable regimen, although he later admitted that they might have resulted from the disorder, not the cure. But he submitted with no outward murmur to the severe discipline and bore himself with a patience and courage that won the admiration of his family.[84]

During the weary hours of his convalescence, propped upon pillows, he passed hours looking out of his window at the Meadow Walk.[85] Day after day, too, John Irving relieved Walter's mother or his sister at his bedside, and the two boys played chess, the windows wide open, despite the bitter weather. Walter flung himself with enthusiasm into the game that had been a favorite of so many of the knights and paladins who were his heroes, but his interest did not survive into manhood. He came to think it a shame to throw away upon a mere game, however ingenious, the time in which he might be acquiring a new language. "Surely," he said, "chess-playing is a sad waste of brains."[86]

Meanwhile his counterpane was piled high with books—Shakespeare, Spenser, Drayton, Vertot's *Knights of Malta*, which delighted him by its fusion of reality and romance, and Orme's *History of Indostan*, whose maps and plans made the military campaigns as clear as they were fascinating. His mathematical studies with Dr. MacFait had taught him the meanings of the words used in fortification, and he had a fair knowledge of geography; he amused his hours of solitude by arranging seeds, shells, and pebbles to stand for battling armies. He made small crossbows to mimic artillery and, helped by a friendly carpenter, modeled a fortress which, like that of Tristram Shandy's Uncle Toby, was any beseiged place he wanted it to be.[87]

When he was strong enough for the journey he went again to Kelso, where he completed his recovery. His uncle Captain Robert Scott had now retired from the naval service of the East India Company and had bought the villa of Rosebank, whose grounds sloped down to the river Tweed. Walter happily took up his quarters with Uncle Robert and soon felt it a second home in some ways more agreeable than his own. Captain Scott had none of his brother's indifference to literature but warmly sympathized with Walter's enthusiasm for border lore and ballads. Uncle and nephew were soon closer friends than when, a man and a little boy, they had strolled the streets of Bath and the child had excitedly clapped his hands at *As You Like It*.[88]

# 2

## *Themis Ascendant over Aphrodite*

## *( 1 7 8 8 – 1 7 9 2 )*

R OSEBANK WAS AN ELEGANT two-and-a-half-story villa with half-dormers projecting above the edge of its hip roof. A curved bow window rose the full height of the gray stone walls, which were clothed in clambering vines; there were tall chimneys crowned with chimney pots, and a greenhouse jutting out from a lower wing. Before the house extended a lawn, and beyond flowed the Tweed, with stately chestnuts dipping their branches almost in the water.[1]

Walter read, idled in the garden, and slowly regained his strength. In the course of his ramblings he met a pretty tradesman's daughter of the village.[2] Like Edward Waverley, the hero of his first novel, he was now at that age when "Female forms of exquisite grace and beauty began to mingle in his mental adventures."[3] Although he had shown his schoolmates that they could not dismiss him as a cripple, his lameness still made him diffident of his attraction for girls. But the humble, blue-eyed Kelso beauty did not frighten him, and she did not look away from him because he limped.

Her father, however, was a straitlaced Presbyterian who would have distrusted deeply the intentions of a young lawyer toward the daughter of a small tradesman, and Walter may have suspected that his Uncle Robert would also disapprove. The boy and girl managed to meet unseen, and exchanged secret letters.[4] "Your goodness, your gentleness, your kindness," Walter exclaimed, "have filled me with the sweetest feelings I have ever known."[5] If only he could believe she was not indifferent to him, not offended by his boldness! His emotion overflowed into verse:

> Lassie can ye love me weel?
>> Ask your heart, and answer true,
> Doth that gentle bosom feel
>> Love for one who loveth you?

> . . .

> Lassie gin ye'll love me weel,
>> Weel I'll love ye in return,
> While the salmon fills the creel,
>> While the flower grows by the burn.[6]

The hours not spent with his Jessie lagged wearily; daylight dragged like a tortoise to the time when he might again be with her. He found no sport now in fishing the Teviot till twilight, no enjoyment in beating the woods with dog and gun. How dismal to wander over the crumbling walls of Roxburgh Castle or brood in the ruined Abbey, now powerless to throw over him the spell they had once cast, since she was not there![7] When he clasped her to his breast, he felt,

> I held all Heaven within my arms,
> Its bliss in thy caress.[8]

All her letters he unwillingly burned when he had read them, fearing "they might be discovered by some curious person and the course of our true love made to run less smooth even than it does."[9] His letters he urged her to destroy also, but she found some artful hiding place in which to conceal them and the poems Walter wrote to her. It is from these, and from the story as she confided it years later to an anonymous biographer, that we learn the few facts known about this early love. Though the details in the unpublished manuscript are scanty, they are directly from the lips of the girl who had stirred Walter's emotions.[10]

Soon the lovers were separated. On his recovery from his illness, he was called back to Edinburgh. Walter was plunged in despair.[11] The danger of discovery made Jessie forbid him to write her from there; he did not know how he could endure the miserable hours until he could "speed on the wings of love to Kelso." "I have no doubt," he wrote her before leaving, "an end would quickly be put to our meetings were they known by your friends or by mine, but if I can help it they shall never know it. . . . I do not see why young people should not be allowed to be as happy as old ones, and dislike nothing so much as seeing the latter hunt after the former like so many staunch terriers if they are but suspected of following their own honest inclinations."[12]

He was aware, he continued, that her home was not a very agreeable one, and could easily sympathize, "having had no little experience of a similar wretchedness"—a reference, doubtless, to the grim austerity imposed by his father's Calvinism. But if their parents refused to seize the joys of life, "we at least may help ourselves to them when they should chance to come within our reach." "You have honored me," he ended, "with the flattering avowal I most wished for, and relying on the duration of your love, which I prize above all the riches and honours of the world, I now for a time—Heaven grant it be brief—bid you adieu."[13]

Within a few months Walter found some subterfuge for a return visit to Kelso. There were trysts by sunrise and twilight, along the verdant late summer banks of the Tweed, among the golden yellow corn rigs, with dew sparkling on the daisies and red poppies at their feet.[14]

> With thee each look a pleasure darted,
> In those delightful days
> Our hearts and hands were never parted:
> Brightly each gaze met gaze,
> And ev'ry speech was praise . . .[15]

In the times of waiting to see her again he wrote his sweetheart long letters, which he gave her when they met, letters telling her of his poetic enthusiasms, quoting fragments of medieval love lyrics, copying ballads he had memorized, among them two that he remembered from the lips of his Irish nurse-girl when he was a child of five at Bath.[16]

He himself, he confessed to Jessie, had "been spoiling a vast quantity of good paper" with his poetic efforts. "I have addressed the moon—that most berhimed of planets—so often I am ashamed to look her in the face. I have made odes to nightingales so numerous they might suffice for all that ever were hatched, and as for elegies, ballads, and sonnets and other small ware, truly I can assert their name is legion . . ." Still more daring, he had attempted "an epic poem of hundreds upon hundreds of lines—a chronicle in verse of the wondrous doings of some of those famous Knights whose names, even, I doubt much you have ever heard."[17]

Their growing intimacy, Walter and Jessie knew, would be viewed with more than disfavor by their families. But he urged in verse the consummation of their desires and no doubt pleaded even more warmly when they were together. "At last," the biography says, "the one became as thoughtless as the other. They regarded nothing except the pleasure they were receiving and bestowing."[18] "The Minstrels of old were well rewarded," Walter begs in one letter. "I trust your poor 'Rymour' will taste of your sweet bounty without stint as a fitting reward for his labours in your service."[19]

Walter's legal duties for his father prevented his hurrying away to Kelso as often as he desired, and even when he was there he could not sally forth from Rosebank whenever he wished. One letter to Jessie breaks off, "I hear my uncle coming to take me with him to pay a visit to my aunt at the Garden so hastily conclude."[20] After a separation more than ordinarily prolonged, he had barely seen his love before she was called away from Kelso to nurse a sick relative. Her departure was so sudden that she had no time to send him word. His cautious inquiries failed to discover where she had gone. He returned to his desk in Edinburgh gnawed by uneasiness.[21]

He realized that in town he had no means of learning where Jessie was; he must wait until he obtained leave from his father to visit Rosebank again. His anxiety generated a restlessness that distracted him from his studies sufficiently to excite remark. When at last he was able to return to Kelso he still caught no glimpse of Jessie. But this time his guarded questions produced a startling answer. During the whole time he had been in Edinburgh, she too had been there taking care of an invalid aunt and was still in the town now. He did not dare ask the aunt's name and address. However, in a place he knew so well, he felt sure he could search Jessie out.[22]

He explored all parts of Edinburgh, high and low, rich and poor, stumping in every direction, peering up at windows, peeping under the brims of bonnets. But neither at an open casement nor tripping along the cobbles did he glimpse the form of his vanished love. He retraced his steps again, through every street and muddy alley, into every close, up and down every steep and narrow wynd. She had disappeared. With a heavy heart he at last gave up the search.[23]

Suddenly chance revealed what all his roving through the streets had been unable to discover. Descending the staircase from a visit to an acquaintance, he came face to face with his sweetheart and learned that her sick aunt lived in that same house in the flat above. With what glowing excitement they fell into each other's arms! From that moment Walter paid more frequent visits to his friend than ever before, seizing every opportunity to slip upstairs unobserved. The only drawback was that Walter often had to hide in a closet until the invalid was asleep or Jessie could find an excuse to leave her alone. Surrounded by crockery, dry haddocks, barley meal, marmalade, and jam on the shelves, with a ham suspended from a hook above his head, he stood in cramped and silent rigidity within the closet.[24]

Jessie gave him paper and pencil to help pass the time of his stuffy imprisonment.[25] For all the ardor of the lover, he could not help feeling the comedy of his plight:

> Instead of loving words from you,
>     No sort of sound I hear
> Save an old woman's sighs and groans
>     That make my stomach queer.
>
> Though tired of standing all this time
>     I darena stir a leg,
> Though wishing sair to stretch my arms
>     I canna move a peg.

. . .

> Untouched the tempting honey pots
>     Upon their shelves remain,
> For that I taste upon your lips
>     Makes me all else disdain.

> Come hither! You my closet are
>     Where all my sweets are stored,
> Oh save me from your aunt's good things
>     And some of yours afford.[26]

Although Walter found her lips and the pressure of her breast no less sweet than they had been among the meadows of the Tweed, the absurdity of their embarrassments made his concealment seem almost a game. Sometimes he risked discovery by a noise or whispered jest, at which Jessie, losing her own self-control, was unable to repress a giggle. Luckily her aunt was hard of hearing, or often dozing, and his recklessness went unpenalized.[27] Despite her excited laughter, Jessie could not help worrying about their behavior and voicing the immemorial fear that her lover might blame her for the very favors she granted him. His reassurances have more the tone of eighteenth-century gallantry than of romantic love:

> Heed not what the world may say
>     Should they spy our goings on;
> Put off till the evil day
>     What till then must be unknown.
> They may blame ye—who would doubt it?
>     Dinna fash your thumb about it.

. . .

> For what were our young arms designed
>     If not to twine in fond embrace?
> And long as "like loves like" we find,
>     Lips on lips have proper place.
> Though prudes such law condemn and knout it,
>     Dinna fash your thumb about it.

. . .

> Then to my heart once more be pressed,
>     And as such natural bliss we prove,
> Convince ourselves that we are blessed
>     As well and truly as we love.
> Though some may whisper, blame, and shout it,
>     Dinna fash your thumb about it.[28]

Indeed, all the verse Walter addresses to his sweetheart after they have refound each other in Edinburgh breathes a less devotional and exalted passion than he had voiced before their separation. Perhaps the undignified stratagems to which they were reduced came to seem not merely ridiculous but tiresome. Perhaps a rusticity not merely unobtrusive but charming in Kelso seemed less appealing in the capital. He had never imagined, even in the early days of their love, that she shared his devotion to books; he had doubted whether she knew so much as the names of the famous knights inspiring his poetic dreams. Possibly, now, his future dignity as an advocate made him aware, as he had not been before, of the gulf between their stations. And possibly the conversation of the young men with whom he had been mingling lately made him realize how little except youth and ardor he and the shopkeeper's daughter had in common.

Slowly, the secret romance was losing its power. Walter's visits began to come at longer intervals and be of shorter duration. Nor did Jessie rekindle his devotion by the reproaches with which she greeted his neglect. But although she could make her slackening lover feel discomfort and guilt, the vehemence of her language did not make him more tender.[29] Like *Marmion*, Walter "tired to hear the desperate maid threaten by turns, beseech, upbraid";[30] as her indignation grew strong, quarrels succeeded tears. She was angrily convinced that she had been superseded by a rival, and she did not intend to surrender her swain without a struggle.[31] Indeed her suspicions might have had some foundation; for only a little later we learn that a certain pair of blue eyes shaded beneath a green mantle have made their fateful entrance on the scene.[32]

Jessie's tirades only hastened their final separation. How they parted and under what circumstances is unknown, but it was in resentment, with Walter determined never to see her again. Although Jessie presently married a young medical student who established himself as a doctor in London, where she became the mother of a thriving family, she regarded Walter's desertion with lasting bitterness.[33]

During this period his father had taken counsel with him about his future profession. He generously offered, if Walter wanted to be a Writer to the Signet, to take him immediately into partnership. Mr. Scott was in his sixtieth year and might retire before long. Though his business was considerably diminished, it could be reanimated by a vigorous younger man and even now offered the immediate prospect of a handsome independence. But he admitted that he would prefer Walter to enter the more ambitious profession of the bar and let his younger brother Tom take the partnership.[34]

Walter was touched by his father's kindness. Although he chafed at the old man's austerity, he respected his rectitude, gratefully recognized his care, and repaid his devotion with love. He would gladly have relieved his father of his professional burdens, but he knew that in such a relationship they would often disagree. Tom was old enough to work into the business—he had completed his studies at the High School in 1787—and his easygoing nature was more yielding, Walter knew, than his own.

He saw, too, that his father would be disappointed if he did not turn to the bar. As for himself, it would be no sacrifice; he did not like the element of subservience in the relationship of a Writer to his clients. He had observed that the utmost exertions and the greatest services had not always protected his father from losses and ungracious treatment at the hands of his employers. Walter did not think much of his own abilities as a speaker, but the career of an advocate was the line of ambition and liberty. Finally, it was the profession for which most of his friends were destined. He therefore willingly agreed to his father's desire. In 1789–90 he had taken Dugald Stewart's course in moral philosophy and Alexander Fraser Tytler's universal history; now in 1790–91 he enrolled in the class in Scots Law, and the following year took Civil Law. He was given a small rear room in the basement at George Square to use as his study.[35]

The lectures on the Roman or Civil Law at the University were part of the preparation for both Advocates and Writers to the Signet; those on Scots Law were required for the Advocates.[36] The Civil Law chair, Scott remarks sharply, "might at that time be considered as in *abeyance*, since the person by whom it was occupied had never been fit for the situation, and was then in a state of dotage."[37] The Scots Law lectures, however, were given by David Hume, the nephew of the philosopher, the penetration and clarity of whose legal analysis Walter admired without measure. These lectures brought him into daily contact again with old High School friends, like Adam Ferguson and John Irving, of whom he had seen little during the past year, as well as bringing him new friends.[38]

These future advocates, he found, had none of his father's narrow distrust of literature as a distraction from their professional studies. On the contrary, they shared Walter's literary enthusiasms and felt that for the higher branch of legal practice an acquaintance with almost every realm of science and literature was a necessity. As he himself was to put it later, "A lawyer without history or literature is a mechanic, a mere working mason; if he possess some knowledge of these, he may venture to call himself an architect."[39]

Walter consequently applied himself now with profound seriousness to all his studies. He had completely recovered from the illness that had brought him to Rosebank. Indeed, he bade farewell to sickness and medicine for the next twenty years, enjoying a vigor so robust as to know only an occasional bout of indigestion or a headache after a night's drinking. His frame hardened; he had grown tall and muscular; his arms were enormously strong.

So restored to health, he worked hard. In the Scots Law class, he felt a mounting admiration for Hume's powers of analysis and synthesis. The intricate fabric of the Scots Law, formed originally under the influence of feudal principles, then "innovated, altered, broken in upon by the changes of times, of habits, and of manners, until it resembles some ancient castle, partly entire, partly ruinous, partly dilapidated, patched and altered during the succession of ages by a thousand additions and combinations," Hume both explained and methodized. "Neither wandering into fanciful and abstruse disquisitions . . . nor satisfied with presenting to his pupils a dry and undigested detail of the laws in their present state," making his survey a luminous presentation of their origins and principles, Hume was, Scott later wrote enthusiastically, an architect to the law of Scotland.[40]

Fascinated, the young law student impressed Hume's lectures on his mind by copying them out *twice* from the notes he had taken in class. Rereading them only made him feel more deeply the powerful grasp of Hume's legal understanding. One copy, in a neat hand, he had bound and presented as a gift to his father. Old Mr. Scott was delighted. They were proof of his son's industry and attention to his professor; in addition, he remarked, they would give him "very pleasant reading for leisure hours."[41]

A fellow student in Walter's law classes was William Clerk, the younger son of the famous naval theorist John Clerk of Eldin. The Clerks were a cadet branch of the Clerks of Penicuik.[42] Walter had one childhood memory of Will's distinguished father. As a small boy he had been on the edge of a group of men to whom Clerk was illustrating by means of cork models his celebrated maneuver of dividing the line in naval battle. The child had picked up one of the little models and been jokingly scolded when the tactician missed a line-of-battle ship whose absence crippled the demonstration.[43]

Will Clerk was brilliant, lazy, high-spirited, a relentless after-dinner debater who never rose from the table until he had borne down his opponents. Flashing in wit, ribald in humor, blunt in speech, he loved argument more than action. The first day he saw Walter in the classroom Clerk was struck by something odd in his look when he was in a pensive mood, a strange play of the upper lip with the underlip sucked in as if he were a hautboy player. Walter laughed at this as a good joke; he, who had never touched a musical instrument and couldn't even sing a note! Clerk also observed that Walter was untidy in dress, with a pair of old corduroy breeches much glazed by the rubbing of his staff. On an evening walk early in their friendship Clerk rallied him on his garments. Walter waved his stick, saying, "They be good enough for drinking in—let us go and have some oysters in the Covenant Close."[44]

Clerk and Walter became daily companions. The clerks and apprentices in Mr. Scott's office displayed considerable jealousy of this new alliance. At an annual supper their coolness became marked, and Walter demanded an explanation. "Well," replied one of them, "since you will have it out, you are *cutting* your old friends for the sake of Clerk and some more of these dons that look down on the like of us." "Gentlemen," Walter replied, "I will never *cut* any man unless I detect him in scoundrelism; but I know not what right any of you have to interfere in my choice of company. . . . As it is, I fairly own that though I like many of you very much, and have long done so, I think William Clerk well worth you all put together." The presiding officer of the banquet had sense enough to pass this off with a laugh, and the evening ended without disturbance.[45]

One morning, calling on Clerk at his home in Princes Street, Walter showed him his stick all hacked and battered. He had been attacked in the street the night before by three ruffians, he said, and defended himself for an hour.[46] "By Shrewsbury clock?" his friend jestingly echoed Falstaff's boast. "No," said Walter, smiling, "by the Tron." But from then on he called his walking stick his "Shrewsbury."[47] Clerk's brother James, who was in the navy and at the time stationed at Leith, was in command of a lugger on which the two young men sometimes took little trips to sea with him. Meeting in a Leith tavern once before going on board, James introduced Walter to his sailor friends. "You may take him for a poor lamiter," James told them with some salty naval oaths, "but he is the first to begin a row, and the last to end it."[48]

But Walter and Will Clerk worked together as well as frolicked. They agreed to prepare for their examinations by catechizing each other during vacation on various points of law every morning in the week except Sunday, coming alternately to each other's houses. All Will's resolution, however, could not drag him out of bed early enough to reach George Square in time. Daily, therefore, Walter trudged the two miles to Princes Street, climbing from the Cowgate to Parliament Square, and then going down the Mound, that huge fill of earth that crossed the hollow between the Old Town and the New where the Nor' Loch had been. Before seven o'clock he was beating Will from his slumbers and bombarding him with Heineccius's *Analysis of the Institutes and Pandects* and Erskine's *Institutes of the Laws of Scotland*. With question and answer they hammered away at each other, not slackening throughout the two whole summers before their examinations.[49]

In Walter's studies at the University, he was deeply impressed by Tytler's skepticism about rash generalizations and the construction of grandiose historical systems. Tytler was an empiricist in the tradition of Hume, who insisted upon careful examination of evidence and the complexity of fact, and warned his students against the dangers of a premature endeavor to reduce everything to general principles. At the same time, with the Scottish sociological disciples of Montesquieu, Tytler stressed the shaping power of institutions, of heredity, and of environment with an emphasis that was uncompromisingly deterministic.[50]

Walter's conception of history was decisively influenced by his teacher. And his boyhood reading, chaotically though it had jumbled fiction, favorite poets, playhouse ditties, Border-raid ballads, legendry, and obscure chroniclers, had unconsciously assembled for him, he came to realize, "a powerful host of examples in illustration" of "the deduction of general principles."[51] This, he later thought, was as it should be: from the dramatic and exciting in history a boy could be led to observe parallels, compare events, and uncover the trends beneath surface conflicts. The value of history, in fact, was both practical and philosophic, or rather the practical was the philosophic; progress was achieved only by avoiding the errors of our ancestors and improving on their improvements.[52] In all these respects, Scott's ideas on the scope and aim of history were essentially those of the eighteenth-century rationalist historians.

His course in philosophy with Dugald Stewart strengthened these convictions. Stewart was not an original thinker; the entire stress of his teaching was upon the advancement of human welfare in the light of a common sense inspired by noble ideals of truth and virtue. Like the French *philosophes* he had no interest in the "mists of metaphysics" and was primarily concerned with life in society, the study of social man; but unlike them he was no iconoclast and had none of their passion for building radical abstract systems.[53]

Stewart was a brilliant lecturer of an impressive presence. Standing before a class, with his large bald brow, his bushy eyebrows, his gray eyes luminous with emotion, he spoke in a musical voice with a slight *burr*, rising into a glorious rhetoric that for many of his listeners was like the opening of the heavens.[54] In after-years Scott felt that Stewart's analysis of the human mind was fine-drawn and metaphysical, adding, "There is much of water-painting in all metaphysics, which consists rather of words than in ideas."[55] But in Stewart's eloquent panegyric of a moral philosophy based on a commonsense analysis of man and society he found the germ of his own practical ethics as truly as James Mill, another of Stewart's pupils, found the inspiration of his own system of utilitarianism.

Mill thought of society as a building or a machine. He drew the conclusion that many customs and institutions were inefficient or irrationally obstructive and should be scrapped by a bold course of logical innovation; he had no doubt that reason was quite adequate to order human behavior for the best. Scott, more cautiously, would not depend upon reason alone. Institutions, he felt, were not lifeless structures but organic growths, rooted to some degree in habits and emotional loyalties from which they derived a vital part of their strength. Drastic changes, he concluded, could be risked only if we were quite certain that they would not tear up some great root on which the health of the social organism depended.

Not that Scott feared change or action. These were both parts of a full life, of doing and observation, which he early embraced with zest. "I saw," he said, ". . . that to gain a place in men's esteem I must mingle and bustle with them."[56] In this his judgment was reinforced by the influence of Professor Adam Ferguson, his friend Adam's father. Though he had retired from teaching in 1785, before Walter resumed his studies at the University, the intimacy between the two boys created a close tie with the Professor that lasted until his death, when Scott paid tribute to him as "my learned and venerable friend . . . whom I have known and looked up to for thirty years and upwards."[57]

"The most animating occasions of human life," Ferguson taught, "are calls to danger and hardship, not invitations to safety and ease."[58] Existence, he said, is a perilous game, in which happiness "arises more from the pursuit than from the attainment of any end."[59] Like Hume and Tytler, he never tired of emphasizing the "variety of mankind," "the multiplicity of forms which different societies offer to our view," hiding within a kaleidoscopic complexity the essential uniformity that was a cardinal tenet of his rationalist generation. Piercing beneath that outward confusion, however, to underlying principles, Ferguson insisted that character, not wealth or population, was a nation's strength, and demonstrated the hazards of an advanced state of civilization, which he saw as above all the submergence of patriotism and civic virtue in selfishness and political quietism.[60]

All these ideas excited by their professors, and a thousand more, were bubbling and fizzing in the brains of the young men with whom Walter mingled in the University.[61] Besides Irving, Will Clerk, and Adam Ferguson, there was Colin Mackenzie, who had been his poetic rival in High School, John James Edmonstone of Newton, George Abercromby, Thomas Douglas, later Earl of Selkirk, the calmly fastidious George Cranstoun, David Boyle, who ultimately became Lord Justice-Clerk, Patrick Murray of Ochtertyre,[62] and the fantastic and rattle-pated Charles Kerr of Abbotrule.[63]

With Colin Mackenzie, Charles Kerr, and another young man named Colin MacLaurin, Walter formed a Poetry Society, having only themselves as members.[64] With a number of the others he joined the Literary Society, in which they read and then discussed papers on all sorts of topics, literary, historical, philosophic.[65] He did not think himself a good speaker, except when he was animated by enthusiasm, and he did not find it easy to organize his ideas. "I was like the Lord of Castle

Rackrent, who was obliged to cut down a tree to get a few faggots to boil the kettle." Yet the odd and ponderous lumber in his brain and his recondite historical knowledge often did him yeoman service. His memory, he said, was "like one of the large, old-fashioned stone-cannons of the Turks"—hard to load and fire but exploding with powerful effect when an object came within its range.[66]

All told, he maintained a fairly good standing among these companions. Fired to emulation, he read industriously to fill the gaps in his knowledge in which they outshone him.[67] Two of the papers he read before the Literary Society he also submitted as essays to Dugald Stewart. In the first, "On the Origins of the Feudal System," which he delivered in the winter of 1789, he argued against the common view that it was invented by the Lombards and depended upon the king's being regarded as the sole lord of all lands, which were distributed on military tenure. In place of this view, he endeavored to prove that the feudal organization of society appeared in all nations under certain common circumstances.[68] The other paper, in the following year, "On the Manners and Customs of the Northern Nations," drew upon an acquaintance with Anglo-Saxon, Danish, Norwegian, and Icelandic lore that had led him even this early to dabble in reading Old Norse and Anglo-Saxon. It greatly impressed Stewart, who said, "The author of this paper shows much knowledge of his subject, and a great taste for such researches."[69] Walter also read a paper "On the Authenticity of Ossian's Poems"—against—and one "On the Origin of the Scandinavian Mythology."[70]

On January 4, 1791, he was honored with admission into the Speculative Society, mainly a debating club of young advocates, where they trained themselves in forensic skill. Among the topics argued at their weekly meetings were: "Ought there to be an established religion?" "Ought any permanent support to be provided for the poor?" "Should the slave trade be abolished?" "Has the belief in a future state been of advantage to mankind?" "Ought any crime to be punished with death?" "Is it for the interest of Great Britain to maintain what is called the balance of Europe?" and "Was the putting of Charles I to death justified?" the last of which was proposed by Scott. Among the debates in which he participated, he argued against divorce by mutual consent and against the proposition that justice was compatible with mercy, but for the idea that a national debt can promote the prosperity of a country.[71]

In this Society Walter's medieval learning won him the jocularly admiring nickname of "Duns Scotus." He was soon elected librarian and, the winter after his admission, secretary and treasurer. A new member named Francis Jeffrey, who was two years his junior, remembered being struck, his first night at the Speculative, by the secretary sitting gravely at the bottom of the table in a huge woolen nightcap. When the president took the chair, the odd figure pleaded a bad toothache as his apology for appearing in such a "portentous machine" before that worshipful company. But the strange apparition read aloud such a fascinating essay on ballads that the youthful Jeffrey at once asked to be introduced to him.[72]

Next evening he called on the secretary and was ushered into "a small den, on the sunk floor of his father's house . . . surrounded with dingy books." The chamber was crowded with Walter's curios.[73] There were more books than shelves; there were his six manuscript volumes of old ballads;[74] there was a small painted cabinet with Scotch and Roman coins. On the wall hung a claymore and a Lochaber ax, gifts of old Invernahyle, mounting guard over a little print of Prince Charlie, and hooked up below them a domestic curio called "Broughton's saucer," which was the subject of a family story.[75]

Like the elder Fairford, in *Redgauntlet*, old Mr. Scott, though a zealous subject of King George, had clients and business connections who were devoted to the Stuart cause. He therefore found it expedient, as many others did, to employ the polite phrases that had been devised to avoid a verbal clash of conflicting loyalties. "Thus he spoke sometimes of the Chevalier, but never either of the Prince, which would have been sacrificing his own principles, or of the Pretender, which would have been offensive to those of others." The Rebellion he called the *affair* of 1745, and those who had fought in it as *out* at a certain period.[76]

One autumn Mrs. Scott had noticed that every evening at the same hour a stranger muffled in a mantle came in a sedan chair and was ushered into her husband's private room, where he remained until long after the family bedtime. Mr. Scott answered her repeated questions with studied vagueness. At last her inquisitiveness could bear it no more; one night, when the bell rang for the visitor's chair, she braved the forbidden parlor with a salver, remarking that since they had sat so long they might like a dish of tea. The unknown, richly dressed and distinguished in demeanor, bowed and accepted a cup. His host knit his brows and coldly refused. The guest had barely withdrawn—his sedan chair was probably just moving away from the door—when Mr. Scott raised the window sash, took the empty cup, and threw it crashing to the pavement. "I can forgive your little curiosity, madam," he said, "but you must pay the penalty. I may admit into my house, on a piece of business, persons wholly unworthy to be treated as guests by my wife. Neither lip of me nor of mine come after Mr. Murray of Broughton's."[77]

John Murray of Broughton was the unhappy secretary to Prince Charles Edward who, following the defeat of Culloden, saved his own life and fortune by bearing evidence against his master's followers. When one of these, Sir John Douglas, a prisoner before the Privy Council in St. James's, was asked "Do you know this witness?" "Not I," he replied. "I once knew a person who bore the designation of Murray of Broughton—but that was a gentleman and a man of honour, and one that could hold up his head!"[78]

Not all Walter's University friends were drawn from among the ambitious young men who attended the lively meetings of the Speculative Society. At Dugald Stewart's lectures he often sat beside a poor divinity student with whom he occasionally took country walks. One day they ran into an aged "blue gown," one of those licensed beggars like Edie Ochiltree in *The Antiquary*, to whom he had sometimes given a trifle. Walter observed that his friend seemed embarrassed. "Do you know anything to the old man's discredit?" he asked. "Oh no, sir, God forbid!" the other cried, "but I am a poor wretch to be ashamed to speak to him— he is my own father. He has enough laid by to serve for his own old days, but he stands bleaching his head in the wind, that he may get the means of paying for my education."[79]

Some months later, running into the old man alone, Walter learned that his son had been ill. "I find, sir," the beggar told him, "that you have been very kind to my Willie . . . Will you pardon such a liberty, and give me the honour and pleasure of seeing you under my poor roof?" It would do Willie "meikle good to see your face." Next day Walter came to their neat little cottage near St. Leonard's, the beggar took off his blue gown, and they sat down to a leg of mutton that had been roasting on the fire, served with potatoes and excellent whiskey. "Please God," the old man said as they talked, "I may live to see my bairn wag his head in a pulpit yet."[80]

Telling his mother about it that night, Walter added that he would like to see his friend get a tutor's place in a gentleman's family. "Dinna speak to your father about it," she warned him; "if it had been a *shoulder* he might have thought less, but he will say the *gigot* was a sin. I'll see what I can do." Asking among the professors, she soon found the young man a place in the north of Scotland. "Thenceforth," said Scott, "I lost sight of my friend—but let us hope he made out his *curriculum* at Aberdeen, and is now wagging his head where the fine old carle wished to see him."[81]

The time was now fast drawing near when Walter would become an advocate. All the hours of lectures, the days and nights of drudging study, and the early mornings of drill with Will Clerk were to bear fruit. In May, 1791, the two friends petitioned to be tried in their skill in Roman Law, the Dean remitted them to examination, and they both passed on June 30, 1791. In accordance with the regulations of the Faculty of Advocates, the examination in Scots Law could not be taken until a full year later. But in due course, on July 6, 1792, they underwent this ordeal, triumphantly passed, and on July 11 "assumed the gown with all its duties and honours."[82]

After the ceremonies were over, Will and Walter mingled with the crowd of advocates in the Outer Court of Parliament House. When they had been there awhile, Walter said to his comrade, mimicking the voice of a Highland lass waiting at the Cross of Edinburgh to be hired for harvest work, "We've stood here an hour by the Tron, hinny [honey], and de'l a ane has speered our price." But a good-natured solicitor gave him a guinea fee before the Court rose. Walking down the High Street, Walter stopped in front of a hosier's shop. "This is a sort of a wedding-day, Willie," he said; "I think I must go in and buy me a nightcap." With his first fee of any size, however, he bought a silver taper-stand for his mother, which she proudly displayed on her chimney piece to the end of her life.[83]

It was a sort of wedding day for his father too. The Writer to the Signet was overjoyed at his son's achievement. His pride almost reached bursting over Walter's thesis—like Alan Fairford's, no doubt, "a very pretty piece of Latinity"—on the Title of the Pandects, "Concerning the disposal of the dead bodies of Criminals."[84] It was dedicated, probably on Mr. Scott's prudent advice, to Lord Braxfield, their neighbor in George Square, and, what was more important, the Lord Justice-Clerk of the Supreme Criminal Court of Scotland.[85] The young "callant" had realized his father's dearest hope.

That night, as was the custom, Mr. Scott celebrated by "a bit chack of dinner to his friends." The creamy paneling of the dining room gleamed in the bright light of clustered candles. The proud father's sable coat and knee-breeches, and his black silk stockings, were as funereal as ever, but above his snowy ruffles his pale anxious face became a pleased pink. More than an ordinary number of bottles were brought up from the cellar. Glass after glass was raised, glowing topaz and ruby, and the old gentleman grew very merry.[86]

# 3

---

# Bubbles in Champagne

## ( 1789–1792 )

O LD MR. SCOTT did not feel so merry, however, about Walter's habit of wandering all over the countryside. Since his recovery from the illness that had sent him to Kelso five years before, he had grown so strong that he could lift an anvil by the horn. He became a vigorous horseback rider, a tireless walker. On his first long walks with Clerk and George Abercromby, to be sure, he found their pace of four miles an hour too fast for him. They agreed on three, but at that rate he could limp along thirty miles a day, from five in the morning till eight at night, halting for midday refreshment at some village alehouse.[1]

During vacations he would ramble off on even longer trips, but throughout his apprentice days, even as a student at the University, he was repeatedly away for weekends. On one occasion he and a fellow apprentice at his father's, James Ramsay, and two other friends set out early for Prestonpans, ate their breakfast there, spent the morning exploring the ruins of Seton Castle and the battlefield on which Charles Edward's Highlanders had defeated the troops of Sir John Cope in September, 1745, dined sumptuously on dried haddocks and half a bottle of port each, and hiked the ten miles back to Edinburgh in the evening.[2]

Woods, water, wilderness, so led him on that sometimes he dreamily wandered farther than he had intended and alarmed his parents by not returning until long after he was anxiously expected. Once he and some friends set out on a fishing trip to the lake above Howgate. The next morning, Will Clerk persuaded Walter and John Irving to turn off the road and visit his family at Penicuik House. Here Clerk's cousin, Sir John Clerk, so entertained them with pictures and antiquarian conversation that the three forgot all about home for several days. Meanwhile their companions, who had not observed their failure to follow, walked on to Edinburgh, where in George Square, Walter's disappearance from the group caused no small consternation.[3] It would better become him to be studying law, his father said bitterly, "than to be scouring the country like a landlouper."[4]

A story about Sir John Clerk that amused Walter told how he had taken some English virtuosos to see a supposed Roman camp. Stamping on a particular spot, Sir John exclaimed, "This I take to have been the Praetorium!" "Praetorium here Praetorium there," a nearby herdsman said disgustedly, "I made it wi' a flaughter-spade" (turf spade). Some of Sir John's traits Scott later embroidered on the eccentricities of his childhood friend George Constable in creating the character of Jonathan Oldbuck of Monkbarns in *The Antiquary*.[5]

At one muirland cottage Walter took a fancy to a set of "lammer beads" that an old dame wore around her wrinkled neck. Though they were her pride, a sure charm against witchcraft and sore eyes, she was not unwilling to sell. "But I fear ye are not rich aneuch to buy them." "What do you ask for them, guid wife?" "I'll no gie them under sax pennies the piece." "But, guid wife, I'll gie ye twal pennies for them." They were off in an instant, lest the bold bidder should take back his offer. "Fair fa' yer sonsie face! ye're the honestest merchant I ever met wi'." Years afterwards, when Scott was married, he had them restrung and gave them to his wife.[6]

Mr. Scott did not readily get used to Walter's prolonged absences. On another walking trip he and his friends found themselves thirty miles from Edinburgh without a sixpence left among them. But they asked at cottage doors for a drink of water, and farmers' wives, seeing how worn out they looked, gave them milk instead of water, "so, with that, and hips and haws, we came in little the worse." His father, who knew pretty well how little money he had, met him with some impatient questions about what he had been living on. "Pretty much like the young ravens," Walter answered. "I only wish I had been as good a player on the flute as poor George Primrose in *The Vicar of Wakefield*. If I had his art, I should like nothing better than to tramp like him from cottage to cottage over the world." "I doubt," said his father acidly, "I greatly doubt, sir, you were born for nae better than a *gangrel scrape gut*" (a vagrant fiddler).[7]

Gradually, however, the old man realized that his son had a knack for getting along without mishap. One night Mrs. Scott was voicing some anxiety about the protracted absence of Walter and his brother Tom. "My dear Annie," said her husband, "Tom is with Walter this time; and have you not perceived that wherever Walter goes he is pretty sure to find his bread buttered on both sides?"[8]

On these walking trips Walter was willing to go anywhere, but if his suggestions were sought and then rejected he grew obstinate. "I have

broken off from a whole party rather than yield to any one."[9] This was
no hardship to him; from early youth the love of solitude had been a
passion, and in his teens he often fled from company "to indulge visions
and airy castles of my own."[10] "From the earliest time I can remember,
I preferred the pleasure of being alone to waiting for visitors, and have
often taken a bannock and a bit of cheese to the wood or hill to avoid
dining with company."[11]

As he grew to manhood, however, he saw this would not do. "Love
and ambition awaking with other passions" threw him into society.[12]
"Pride and an excitation of spirits," together with a real liking for
others and an enjoyment in observing character, made companionship
a pleasure as well as a rational necessity if one was to get ahead in the
world. Though association with others was no requirement of his
nature, people hardly ever bored him; he could find something interesting
or amusing in almost anyone.[13] But he still found it no less enjoyable to
lose himself in a glen or be alone upon a hilltop.

Although Walter loved landscape he responded most deeply to
scenes that had historic associations. He preferred wandering over the
field of Bannockburn to gazing over the entire famed panorama from
the battlements of Stirling Castle.[14] Crossing Magus Moor, near St.
Andrews, with some other travelers, he was inspired less by the bleak
grandeur of the country than by memories of the assassination of Archbishop Sharp in 1679. He gave his companions so horrifying an account of this murder that one of them, even though he knew the story
well, was frightened out of his night's sleep.[15]

He tried to sketch some of the places that interested him but discovered that he had no skill as an artist and was totally deficient in both
perspective and shading."[16] In his eagerness he even for a time took
lessons in oil painting, but found that he could neither draw nor paint.[17]
As keepsakes of places he wished to remember, he cut pieces from trees.
These he called his log-book, intending to have a set of chessmen carved
from them: the kings from Falkland and Holyrood, the queens from
Queen Mary's yew tree at Crookston, bishops from abbeys or episcopal
palaces, knights from baronial residences, rooks from royal fortresses,
and pawns from other places of historical note. But this whimsical design he never carried out.[18]

During term times, when the Court was in session, long jaunts were
not possible. But Edinburgh had diversions enough. All Walter's close
friends were members of a convivial group called simply The Club,
which met Friday evenings in a room in Carruber's Close and then ad-
journeyed to sup at a neighboring oyster tavern.[19] These eating places,
located in cellars or basements and therefore called "laigh shops,"
were dark but snug retreats where the young men regaled themselves
on raw oysters and porter, served in huge receptacles on a rough table,
in a dingy room lighted by tallow candles.[20] After the oysters had been

devoured, brandy and rum-punch circulated, voices grew louder, jokes broader, songs more ribald. No one joined the madcap laughter and high spirits more heartily than Walter. "The silly smart fancies," he wrote, "rose in my brain like the bubbles in a glass of champagne—as brilliant to my thinking, as intoxicating as evanescent."[21]

The suppers of The Club were masculine affairs, but to many of the laigh shops ladies and gentlemen resorted together, the ladies wearing masks after dark. When the board was cleared, fair lips did not hesitate to taste the punch.[22] Gay sallies mingled with witticisms not always of the most delicate, and there were country dances to the sound of fiddle, harp, or bagpipe. When the ladies retired, making their way home in sedan chairs or walking under the escort of a caddy with a paper lantern, the serious drinking of the night began.[23]

The eighteenth century was a drinking century, Edinburgh was a drinking town, and lawyers were a drinking lot. Lord Newton, one of the judges of the Court of Session, felt himself all the better fitted for business after six bottles of claret, judges often mounted the bench straight from the last night's debauch, and some of them drank from a bottle by their side while they tried a case. Bankers and merchants were no less bibulous. Looking one night into a side room at Johnny Dowie's tavern, a gentleman saw a heap of young men snoring on the floor. "Wha may thae be?" he asked. "Oh," said Johnnie, "just twa–three o' Sir Willie's drucken clerks!"—employees in Sir William Forbes's bank.[24]

Nor were women free from these bacchanalian indulgences. Once, after a late and hilarious night at a tavern near the Cross, three of them wandered along the High Street with only a dim idea where they were. At the Tron Church, the moon, high in the south, threw the shadow of the steeple clear across the road. Mistaking this for a broad and rushing river, they sat down on its imaginary brink, took off their shoes and stockings, and kilting their petticoats high above their waists, waded across the stream, and then, resuming their shoes and hose, reeled happily on their way.[25]

Clubs like that formed by Scott's young friends made a jovial part of Edinburgh life. The Pious Club derived its name, not from any devoutness in its members, but from the pie house where they met.[26] The rules of the Dirty Club forbade its members to attend in clean linen.[27] The Hell-Fire Club, a gang of dissipated young men, held wild orgies in cellars, and the Sweating Club, somewhat milder than the London Mohocks earlier in the century, after getting drunk, sallied outdoors and merely jostled, pinched, and pulled wayfarers about instead of gouging out their eyes.[28] But not all the clubs numbered ruffians such as these. Although Walter's fellow members drank enough, and sometimes too much, it was all out of sociability and youthful bravado, to show that their heads could take it.

How well Walter himself managed is perhaps insinuated by one of his nicknames, Colonel Grogg.[29] In a party of four that included William Forbes, the son of the banker, he once downed three bottles. Drink made him drowsy rather than belligerent, although one evening there were high words between him and Will Clerk.[30] The next day Walter wrote a note of apology: "I am sorry to find that our friend Colonel Grogg has behaved with a very undue degree of vehemence in a dispute with you last night . . . As the Colonel, though a military man, is not too haughty to acknowledge an error, he has commissioned me to make his apology as a mutual friend, which I am convinced you will accept from yours ever, Duns Scotus."[31]

Ribald songs were not confined to the carousing young. Scott recalled more than one befuddled banquet at which a drunken old Tory, a devotee of the banished Stuarts, sang a ballad about the Scottish Regalia, composed in 1707, the time of the Union with England under Queen Anne. In this song the sceptre and all the other symbols were destined to the basest uses; the crown, for example,

> To make a can
> For brandie Nan
> To piss in when she's tipsey.[32]

Once Walter, who had never turned a tune in his life, was duped into believing that under the influence of liquor *he* had sung a song. In a prolonged drinking bout with Clerk, Edmonstone, Abercromby, and Patrick Murray he fell asleep, and when he awoke these wags persuaded him that he had done triumphantly well.[33]

The young men from Teviotdale had formed an Edinburgh club whose meetings Walter seldom missed, and here he ran into his old Kelso schoolfellow James Ballantyne. The two had lost touch when James had been bound apprentice to a solicitor, but he had been sent to Edinburgh for a winter to complete his professional education by attending the class in Scots Law. At the monthly supper meetings of this club, too, there was a good deal of drinking and a good deal of quarreling, at which, Ballantyne says, Scott never failed to be an effective peacemaker.[34]

Ballantyne's testimony differs from Scott's own, and from James Clerk's, who found him ever the first to begin a row and the last to end it. "In what scenes," Scott exclaimed, had not he and William Forbes "borne share together—desperate, and almost bloody affrays, rivalries, deep drinking-matches."[35] But as they cracked bottle after bottle at Dowie's or the Star and Garter, or cheerfully cracked skulls, perhaps, with their cudgels in Liberton's Wynd, neither young man anticipated their far more serious rivalry a few years hence.

According to another friend, Davie Douglas, Scott "loved the stimulus of a Broil."[36] Thirty years later, running into David Erskine of Cardroes, a companion of these days, Scott warmly welcomed him as "my old friend and boon companion, with whom I shared the wars of Bacchus, Venus, and sometimes of Mars."[37] How far he and his friends pursued the wars of Venus we do not know, but there were plenty of wenches to be boarded in the purlieus of Blackfriars' Wynd. As for the wars of Bacchus and Mars, if Scott's drinking abilities earned him the nickname of Colonel Grogg, the swashbuckling enjoyment of a fight that he inherited from his moss-trooper ancestors led to his being called Earl Walter. But Scott's belligerence was also derived from his rebellion against circumstance, which had shown itself as far back as his school-days when he fought in the Yards lashed to a board. He would not use his lame leg as an excuse for skulking out of a fight. It was the spirit, as he was to say, "that, in spite of manifold infirmities, made me a roaring boy in my youth, a desperate climber, a bold rider, a deep drinker, and a stout player at single-stick."[38]

By the time these brawls and revels at last broke up, staid citizens had long been in bed. All shops closed at eight. At ten the drums of the City Guard beat an unofficial curfew, which was also a signal that slops might now be emptied out of upper windows into the streets. The cry of "Gardyloo!" (Gardez l'eau), supposed to caution anyone below, was often followed so swiftly by a deluge of filth that many a wayfarer found himself besmeared.[39] The shout was therefore, Scott remarks, "like the shriek of the water-kelpie, rather the elegy than the warning of the over-whelmed passenger."[40] But gradually the lights went out, the sashes came down, and the last belated wanderer from Bayle's or Fortune's tavern staggered through the perils of some precipitous wynd.[41]

Not all the social pleasures of Edinburgh, however, centered around nocturnal drinking. There was bowling on the greens opposite Grey-friars' Church, south of Heriot's Hospital, and behind Holyrood Palace.[42] Golfers swung their clubs on the Leith and Bruntsfield links.[43] Ladies drank afternoon tea with one another. In the evenings, the after-dinner port or claret was followed by a rubber at the card tables or by rolling aside the drawing-room carpet for a dance to the tinkle of the harpsi-chord.[44] At Mrs. Alison Cockburn's tiny flat, just around the corner from George Square in Crichton Street, during one card party, Walter saw Soph Johnstone, an eccentric old harridan who wore a jockey coat and swore masculine oaths, kick his sister Anne in the shins under the table. The nervous girl had exasperated her by sliding her foot back and forth, and Soph demanded in loud indignation, "What's the lassie wabster-wabster-wabstering that gate for?"[45]

Lady Balcarres, once Dr. Rutherford's neighbor in Hyndford's Close, now shared a flat and sunk story in George Square with her cousin Anne Murray Keith. The two old ladies both loved cards, company, and gossip; Lady Balcarres was passionately devoted to the drama; and Mrs. Keith was not only deeply versed in belles-lettres but was full of fascinating stories "of the *Vieille Cour* and of ancient Scottish manners." Walter became a protégé of these two ladies, delighting to hear Mrs. Keith's reminiscences and privileged to escort Lady Balcarres in public places and attend her in her box at the theater.[46]

Although he was no musician—"songs and simple melodies" he enjoyed, but "complicated harmonies," he said, "seem to me a babble of confused though pleasing sound"[47]—he must occasionally, even if only under feminine persuasion, have made one of the audiences who flocked to St. Cecilia's Hall, in the Cowgate at the foot of Niddry Street. Here, in an oval auditorium with a concave ceiling, built on the model of the famed opera house at Parma, assemblages of the beauty and fashion of the city, facing each other in two curving tiers that sloped down to the center, listened to concerts of Corelli, Bach, and Haydn, with songs by Gluck and Paisiello, and, every year, one of the great oratorios of Handel.[48]

His widening social life led Walter to amend that carelessness in dress on which Will Clerk had rallied him in his student days. He could not appear in corduroys beside Lady Balcarres in a stage box, and now there were younger and brighter eyes than hers to rain influence. Clerk observed an improvement setting in around 1790 and jested about his beginning "to set up for a squire of dames."[49] When a dazzling beauty named Mary Ponsonby came to Edinburgh on a visit from Cumberland, Walter is reported to have been attracted by her charms and to have written several poems to her.[50] There were also those blue eyes, beneath the green mantle, whose light may have slain poor Jessie's hopes. One Sunday in the doorway of Greyfriars' Church, while the congregation were dispersing, rain began to fall; Walter offered the shelter of his umbrella, and escorted those bewitching eyes home. Her name was Williamina Belsches, her family lived not far from George Square, and the two young people soon fell into the custom of strolling back from church together. Though Walter was already nineteen at the time of their first meeting, Williamina was only in her fifteenth year; nothing, therefore, came of their companionship immediately, but in the course of the next two years his feelings for her were to deepen.[51]

The limp that did not prevent Walter from walking thirty miles a day did not keep him from attending the balls whose music and movement were among the entertainments of the winter and spring. Fashion was now forsaking the Old Assembly Rooms in Bell's Close and moving on to the George Square Rooms in Buccleuch Place or, over in the New Town, to the gorgeous new Assembly Rooms with their Tuscan portico projecting on rusticated arches into George Street.[52] The elder generation sighed for the vanished splendors of belles with hoopskirts and powdered hair alighting from sedan chairs and gentlemen in laced coats moving through the stately geometry of the minuet with ladies in ribboned stomachers. But the young men in their silver buckles, and their rose-cheeked charmers in tiny slippers and clinging satins, did not believe themselves one bit less glamorous than their grandparents, and rejoiced in the magnificence of the spacious Buccleuch Place rooms and the crimson walls, hangings, and canopies, the lofty ceilings, and the innumerable glittering chandeliers of the New Town.[53]

"When I was of the age at which lads like to shine in the eyes of the girls," Scott remembered, "I have felt some envy in a ballroom of the young fellows who had the use of their legs." Tucked away in a pocket he might have the orange that etiquette decreed each beau should give his partner at the end of the dance, but what else did he have to offer? He soon found that he had the advantage of his tongue. "It was a proud night for me," he recorded exultantly, "when I first found that a pretty young woman could think it worth her while to sit and talk with me, hour after hour, in a corner . . . while all the world were capering in our view."[54] The lad who loved solitude had indeed turned into a captivating talker, and the lame boy into a well-formed young man.

"The young Walter Scott," declared the Duchess-Countess of Sutherland, "was a comely creature." His halting leg was not deformed, he towered more than six feet in height, his chest was powerful, his head superbly set upon its column of throat, his hands large and strong. His brow was high, although curious observers noted that above it the lofty dome of skull, thatched with sandy hair, rose to a strange conical peak. He had a fleshy nose, clear pink complexion, flashing gray-blue eyes beneath thick-eaved brows, and very regular white teeth. In repose his face looked rather dull and heavy, but when he spoke or listened it changed constantly from playful to grave to tender, and his smile was full of "innocent hilarity and humour."[55]

With the coming of summer, when the balls and other festivities were over for the season, Walter usually spent some time with Captain Robert Scott at Rosebank. Uncle and nephew had retained their common tastes in sport, reading, and historical antiquities.[56] When Walter was in town he hunted out books that his uncle wanted to acquire—*Dodsley's Annual Register* and *Byron's Narrative* of his adventures on the coast of Patagonia—and dispatched copies of the essays he would deliver at the Literary Society for the Captain's suggestions on their style.[57] In the country, they fished, shot wild ducks and herons, coursed hares with greyhounds, and ranged far and wide on horseback.[58] Betweenwhiles Walter read in the garden and ate gooseberries and grapes from his uncle's vines. Once they rode over for a day to Smailholm, and dined on bread and cheese, cold beef, and rum beside the Orderlaw well.[59]

Another time Captain Scott suggested that they ride across the Cheviots into Northumberland. Here they visited Ford Castle, Chillingham Castle, and Copland Castle, and explored the battlefields of Chevy Chase, Otterburn, and Flodden, all of which Walter had been reading about in Pitscottie and other chroniclers. They shot muirfowl and pulled trout half a yard long out of the brooks, and feasted on heath-fed mutton, barn-door fowls, pies, and milk cheese. Before rising in the morning Captain Scott drank whey, and Walter did too when he learned that it would be brought to his bedside every morning by a very pretty dairymaid.[60]

Writing to Will Clerk one afternoon, Walter tells him that the weather is "most bitchiferous; the Tweed, within twenty yards of the window . . . swelled from bank to brae, and roaring like thunder." The day before, Walter and his uncle had been fishing on the Teviot and returned through St. James's Fair. "There was a great show of black cattle—I mean of ministers . . ." and the procession of the magistrates of Jedburgh, riding three abreast, but wearing boots only on the outer leg of the outermost men. The Kelso populace had jeered this economy, and inflamed by whiskey, onlookers and paraders were soon involved in a battle royal.[61]

Toward the end of the summer David Erskine, the Earl of Buchan—who had heard Walter declaim from the *Aeneid* in his High School days—invited him to dinner and bored him with a too prolonged history of the entire Erskine pedigree. From this Walter went on to a happy week with his old apprentice-friend James Ramsay in the commodious, elm-shaded house his family occupied at Kippilaw, where the two young men wandered about all day and in the evening played round games at cards with Ramsay's three sisters. Some of Walter's family were now in Kelso, and, like many another young man he was in agonies lest he should be obliged to escort them back to town. His fears were realized, but the journey, in lovely September weather, proved a pleasant one after all.[62]

Walter's admission to the bar in July, 1792, made no difference in his wandering habits. The court session closed the very day after old Mr. Scott's jubilant dinner of celebration, and almost before the lees were dry in the bottles Walter escaped to Rosebank. Here his father sent him two fair copies of his thesis, noting indignantly, at the same time, that Walter's last letter to him had been undated: "This is a monstrous blunder."

The politic move of dedicating the thesis to Lord Braxfield had not been unsuccessful. The Lord Justice-Clerk had called at George Square, Mr. Scott wrote, and particularly inquired about its author. He had pleasantly remarked that some case might turn up on circuit at Jedburgh which he could throw the young advocate's way and had added that he intended to give him a share of the criminal business of that Court. After this news the careful father dropped a hint: "I think it is probable he will breakfast with Sir H. H. MacDougall on the 21st [of September] on his way to Jedburgh"—meaning that Walter should present himself at the table of his Makerstoun kinsman and travel with his Lordship into that county town.[63]

Meanwhile, Rosebank was pleasant during the long August days. Early September brought rains that swelled the Tweed with red mud.

Walter built himself a seat in a large tree overhanging the stream, from which, looking down on the turbid waves while the west wind rocked the branches, he could fire out upon the gulls and cormorants as they screamed past his nest. With two scarlet-uniformed young soldiers who dwelt on the opposite bank he went duck shooting, wading through the bogs in an unkempt jacket and mosquito trousers, he wrote, like one of his own moss-trooper ancestors, "Walter Fire-the-Braes, or rather Willie wi' the Bolt-foot."[64] Evenings, he pored over Bartholine's book on Danish antiquities, and felt a little envious of Clerk, Ferguson, and Edmonstone, who were enjoying a trip through the mountains of Perthshire.[65]

But in mid-September he himself started out on an expedition to Hexham and the hills of Northumberland. On every hand old towers and castles rose jagged among wild lakes and mountains, and built into barns and gateposts there were inscriptions taken from the great Roman wall marching from sea to sea, grandiosely unimpeded by all barriers of rock, river, morass, and mountain peak. The inhabitants, he was surprised to learn, could neither read nor write, and spoke an odd Saxon dialect "approaching nearly that of Chaucer."[66]

Michaelmas term saw him at the head court in Jedburgh in the last week of September. The redoubtable Braxfield was a brutal judge, a dark, rough giant with savage eyebrows, threatening lips, and a growing voice, like a dangerous blacksmith. But he was kind to fledgling advocates unless they were what he called "Bar flunkies"—brainless fops[67] —and when Walter came to the Jedburgh assizes to make his bow he welcomed the young man cordially. But for reasons he left unexplained, Walter undertook no case; "I . . . might have had employment," Walter adds, "but durst not venture."[68] Braxfield savagely condemned nine convicted rioters to deportation.

At Jedburgh he ran into his friend Charles Kerr, whose estate of Abbotrule was not far south in the valley of Rule Water.[69] High-spirited but irresponsible, Kerr in their Edinburgh College days had been kept short of pocket money by severe parents, fallen into debt, and fled from his creditors to the Isle of Man. Here he had fallen in love with a pretty cottage girl and married her. When Kerr's father thereupon disowned him, Walter had begged his own father to intercede with the angry old man.

Considerably against his better judgment, Mr. Scott did. He thought the young man a fool and disliked Walter's intimacy with him. He had managed, however, to obtain from Kerr's parents a small sum that enabled Charles and his young wife to emigrate to Jamaica, where for some years he had earned a poor living drudging in an attorney's office. Suddenly, the estranged father died intestate, and Mr. Scott, again prompted by Walter, was now able to put the young man in possession of his considerable inheritance.[70] But he still regarded Charles as addle-brained; his present scheme of selling the reversion to his estate, Mr.

Scott was convinced, would lead to his ultimate ruin. This very summer he had therefore refused to remain Charles Kerr's legal representative.[71]

Nevertheless, the two young men met warmly. At the County Court dinner, Charles introduced Walter to his cousin Robert Shortreed, a man nine years their senior, who later became the Sheriff-Substitute—a Scottish legal office partly administrative, partly judicial—of Roxburghshire. Kerr knew Walter's passion for castles and ballads, and knew that he had long desired to visit the remote wilds of Liddesdale to examine the ruins of Hermitage Castle. The shepherds and farmers of this grim region were descended from the moss-troopers who had followed the banners of the Douglas, and they still recited some of the ancient riding ballads of their ancestors. If Scott wanted ballads, who better to guide him than Bob Shortreed, who knew the whole country like the palm of his hand and "maist feck o' the fouk in't"?[72]

Liddesdale is the southern corner of Roxburghshire, the dale watered by the River Liddel. Its great bleak rolling moorlands heaving themselves up into barren hills fifteen hundred feet high are just north of the Border and were the scenes of innumerable forays in the sixteenth century. Fifty peel towers had once dotted its savage slopes, but all had been totally destroyed, except for Hermitage at the head of the dale, where in 1566 Queen Mary had visited Bothwell, her Warden of the Middle Marches.[73] In the eighteenth century it was still a lonely region remote from stagecoach routes, with bad roads, often none. There were no inns; travelers had to depend on the hospitality of shepherd's hut, minister's manse, and farmstead.[74]

A day or two after their meeting, Shortreed and Walter set out from Abbotrule, the former on a pony of Charles Kerr's, Scott on a hack "belonging to auld Bob Leck," a horsecouper in Jedburgh. The first day they dined at the farmhouse of Willie Elliott at Millburnham, to whom Shortreed had written that he and Mr. Scott the advocate would take potluck.[75] Advocates were then "not so plenty—at least not in Liddesdale"— and were looked on as great men.[76] Willie Elliott welcomed Scott with some alarm and insisted on stabling his horse himself, "a' the fouk aboot the toun [farmhouse] being engaged wi' the Bog-hay."[77] From the stable, Shortreed relates the episode, Willie took a peep at Walter "outby the edge of the door-cheek." " 'Lord Bob,' " he whispered, " 'is *that* Mr. Scott the advocate!'—'Aye, Willie lad, that's just Mr. Scott the advocate.'— 'Odd' quo' Willie, gien his arm a rub, and his shouther a shrug like ane relieved from some embarrassment, 'the Deil ha' me if I'se a bit feared for *that* fallow, he's just sich anither chield as oursels I think.' "[78]

At dinner they lingered over Willie's punch bowl. Their host, Shortreed continues, "had a Vast o' bits o' stories and tales o' the traditions and manners o' the Country that he telled, and really verra weel. . . . Willie wasna ony way particularly gien to drink at *that* time. He took his glass freely aneuch nae doubt," and Scott "did sae too, as I did mysell.

Oh aye! [He] could hae sitten till he was half glowerin' just like other
fouk."[79] From Millburnham, they rode their steeds to Dr. Elliott's at
Cleugh-head, where they slept the night, both in the same bed, "for,"
adds Shortreed, "folk were na very nice in those days."[80]

Dr. Elliott had a great manuscript store of the ballads Scott was
seeking. The two men were quickly friends, and for several years thereafter the Doctor exerted himself to ferret out in the darkest recesses of
the mountains people who knew such poems. "The Doctor would hae
gane through fire and water" for his guest "when he ance kenned him."
Dr. Elliott gave Scott a Border war-horn found in the ruins of Hermitage
Castle, which a servant had been using as a grease horn for his scythe
until they discovered its history. "Cleaned out, it was never a hair the
worse—the original chain, hoop, and mouth-piece of steel were all
entire . . ." Scott exulted in the gift: "How *great* he was when he was
made master of *that!*"[81]

From the laird of Whithaugh, near Cleugh-head, Scott obtained the
music of "Jock o' the Cow" and "Dick o' the Side," but Whithaugh
"wasna verra sure" he had "the richt *lilt* for Dick o' the Cow."[82] So next
morning, after "a devilled duck or twae," "just to lay the stomach," the
ballad hunters started out from Millburnham at six o'clock for breakfast at Whithaugh, and then rode six or seven miles to Penton Linns,
where "auld Thomas o' Twizelhope," famous for his skill on the Border
pipe, was known to have mastered that tune.[83] Shortreed was astonished
to see that Scott's lameness did not prevent his getting over the roughest
ground. "He was the youldest [most active] young chield I ever saw, and
could beat us a' at walking or louping across moss-hags, and especially
at coming down a hillside. He took sich *spangs* as ye can hardly
imagine."[84]

Auld Thomas delighted his visitors with a hideous and unearthly
specimen of "riding music," and regaled them during the rest of the
morning on "a gude snaiker o' whisky punch . . . out of a bit stroupit
mug that he ca'd *Wisdom*"—a wooden vessel like a milk pail, which he
had possessed for more than fifty years. Having done due honor to
"Wisdom," they mounted and rode on over moor and moss to another
hospitable master of the pipe.[85] Before they returned to Whithaugh's
roof that night, Walter saw that with these repeated libations their host
"was electrified to such a degree as to be absolutely spherical on his
horse's back."[86]

At some farmhouse one evening they were surprised to have only a
bottle of elderberry wine at supper. Afterward, a young divinity student
was called upon to take the "big ha' Bible" and conduct a service, during
which the goodman of the farm nodded drowsily. Suddenly they heard a
clatter of horses' hoofs outside, their host leaped from his knees, rubbing
his eyes, and shouted, "By God, here's the keg at last!" and in tumbled
two sturdy herdsmen with the smuggled brandy he had been awaiting

from the Solway Firth. The "service" was forgotten; with a thousand apologies for the shabby entertainment he had given them so far, the jolly farmer mounted the keg on the table; and the entire party, including the dominie, caroused until daylight stream in.[87]

Everywhere Scott made "finds"—from wrinkled dames crooning to their grandbairns in solitary shielings far up some glenhead, from "plaided herds and buirdly hinds," from farmers and dominies, from villagers and pedlars, from parish ministers and the impoverished lairds of small holdings. For the most part these old ballads existed only as the lilts and rhymes of this oral tradition. Walter was filled with enthusiasm. His Liddesdale "raid," as he called it, was a great success.[88]

It was quickly arranged that he should come again. Over the course of the next seven years, Walter made, in fact, "seven raids a' thegither," mostly in the autumn but one in the spring, "roving amang the fouk haill days at a time."[89] "Eh me," Shortreed recalled, "sic an endless fund o' humour and drollery as he then had wi' him! Never ten yards but we were either laughing or roaring and singing. Wherever we stopped, how brawlie he suited himsel' to everybody! He aye did as the lave did; never made himsel' the great man or took ony airs in the company. I've seen him in a' moods in these jaunts, grave and gay, daft and serious, sober and drunk—" which, Shortreed adds, was rare, even in their wildest rambles "—but drunk or sober, he was aye the gentleman. He looked unco heavy and stupid when he was *fou*, but he was never out o' gude-humour."[90]

From this first raid Walter rode back to Jedburgh in the wildest of spirits, gay fancies seething up in champagne bubbles. The great war-horn from Hermitage Castle he "slung about his neck like Johnny Gilpin's bottle," while Shortreed "was entrusted with an ancient bridle-bit which we had likewise picked up.

> The feint o' pride—na pride had he . . .
> A lang kail-gully hung down by his side,
> And a great meikle nowt-horn to rout on had he,

and meikle and sair we routed on't, and 'hotched and blew, wi' micht and main.' O what pleasant days! And then a' the nonsense we had cost us naething. We never put hand in pocket for a week on end, Tollbar were there none—and indeed I think our haill charges were a feed o' corn to our horses in the gangin' and comin' at Riccartoun mill."[91]

Neither Scott nor his jovial guide had any reason to see these jaunts as prophetic of the future. No anticipation of the *Border Minstrelsy* or the *Lay* had entered Scott's mind, no glimmer of the marvelous line of his invention extending from Dandie Dinmont to the Death of the Laird's Jock. It burst upon Shortreed years later. "He was makin' himsell a' the time, but he didna ken maybe what he was about till years had passed: At first he thought o' little, I daresay, but the queerness and the fun."[92]

# 4

## Acolyte in the Outer House

## ( 1 7 9 2 – 1 7 9 5 )

IN NOVEMBER, 1792, the Outer House of the Court of Session saw two new advocates among the crowd of young lawyers gathered around the three great iron stoves, all waiting hopefully for a fee. Besides Scott and Clerk, this group included the calmly correct George Cranstoun, with his fastidious lips and contemplative blue eyes; Thomas Thomson, the struggling son of a poor clergyman; the brown-eyed William Erskine, another poor son of the manse from Perthshire; and, a little later, the witty Francis Jeffrey, with his vehement play of sarcasm and fancy.[1] Known as "The Mountain," in jesting analogy to the extreme Revolutionary group across the Channel in France, they all had more time than business on their hands.[2]

Nothing, however, seemed to worry them less. Hour after hour they passed in lighthearted merriment, telling stories and impudently mimicking both the bigwigs who swept importantly by and the Lords of Session in their purple cloth and crimson satin.[3] Scott swiftly became famous among them for his comic imitations and helped himself liberally to the abundant game provided by the bench. There was the ancient Lord Monboddo, notorious for his belief that babies were born with tails which the midwives, he argued, secretly pinched off—an argument that gained hilarious force because in his judge's robes he looked like an old stuffed monkey himself.[4] Even more fantastic was Sir David Rae, with his odd mumbling voice, his face between a scurfy red and a scurfy blue, his enormous nose, his "clumsy chin which moved like the jaw of a Dutch toy," and his strange stealthy tread, something between a walk and a "hirple." To a veiled beauty who appeared as a witness he said, "Young woman! you will now consider yourself as in the presence of Almighty

God and of this High Court. Lift up your veil; throw off all modesty, and look me in the face."[5]

It was not long before Walter had a reputation as a storyteller. One morning, finding the group around the stove convulsed with mirth, Clerk complained that Duns Scotus had stolen from him the tale at which they were laughing, and concealed the theft by disguising the details. "Why," answered Scott, adroitly dodging the main charge, "this is always the way with the *Baronet*. He is continually saying that I change his stories, whereas in fact I only put a cocked hat on their heads, and stick a cane in their hands—to make them fit for going into company."[6]

Clerk's soubriquet, Baronet, had been acquired by comparing his own caustic manner to that of Sir John Brute in Van Brugh's *The Provoked Wife*. His was not the only nickname. John James Edmonstone, for obvious reasons, was called Jean Jacques.[7] Adam Ferguson had gained his on a boating trip from Leith to Inchcolm, when in the fog his tall standing figure had been mistaken by a Newhaven fisherman for that of a comrade, and the mariner had bawled out, "Linton, ye lang bitch, is that you?" Delightedly his friends at once christened the lang bitch "Linton."[8] "Bitch" was not then applied only to females: Lord Kames, on retiring from the Court of Session, had looked back from the doorway at his former colleagues and cried heartily, "Fare ye a' weel, ye bitches!"[9]

So the young men gossiped, quizzed one another, and joked in their black bombazine gowns while they waited for clients, or paced up and down the stone floor among anxious litigants beneath the rafters gray with age-old dust and dim in the winter haze. But Walter did not linger in complete idleness for long. Before the end of November he received a guinea fee from Alexander Keith of Ravelston, a solicitor who was married to Walter's great-aunt and perhaps not uninfluenced by that fact in engaging him. But his presentation of the case before Lord Monboddo must have been satisfactory; Keith engaged him on two further cases, which he argued before the same judge. The three guineas that he thus pocketed were his total receipts during his first winter session of the Court. But such scanty earnings were not unusual for a fledgling advocate. Meanwhile the Outer House served as combined office, forum, and social club.[10]

The smallness of his income, to be sure, might well have been a source of some impatience to him, for Walter's heart was gradually falling captive to the blue-eyed lass he had first noticed at Greyfriars' Church. She was the only child of Sir John Wishart Belsches, a wealthy advocate with an estate at Fettercairn in Kincardineshire. But Williamina's family ranked high above Walter's own; she was barely sixteen; and he himself was just past twenty-one and at the opening of his legal career. The surviving records from the earliest two years of their acquaintance give no more than an occasional glimpse of her green mantle and blue eyes; even now, during his first year at the bar, when she was beginning to haunt his dreams, she makes only brief and tan-talizing appearances. The young lawyer knew how many obstacles there were to their union. Though his heart beat more rapidly at the thought of seeing her again this winter, he would have to wait and hope.[11]

A little before Christmas, 1792, Scott and some half-dozen friends set themselves to studying German. A constellation of brilliant poets and dramatists, Lessing, Goethe, Schiller, was beginning to draw European attention to German literature.[12] Almost everyone had read *The Sorrows of Werther*, many weeping with sympathetic melancholy, although there were those who responded with some hilarity to its succession of lachry-mose incidents. The ballad supernaturalism of Bürger and the melo-drama of Klopstock also aroused fervent enthusiasm, and there were students eager to plunge into the depths of Kant.[13] The well-known novelist Henry Mackenzie had fired Edinburgh to excitement four years before when, on April 21, 1788, he had read before the Royal Society an essay on the German theater.[14] Here was a thrilling new literature, casting off the pedantic shackles of classicism, colorful, romantic, often extravagant, but full of vitality.

The remarkable similarities between the German tongue and the Lowland Scottish dialect stimulated the interest of Scott and his friends.[15] They obtained as teacher a German physician, Dr. Willich, under whom they proposed immediately to explore Goethe and Schiller.[16] The good doctor thought they should begin on something simpler and suggested Gesner's *Death of Abel*. To his distress, however, they were unanimous in deriding the mawkish pieties of that work, jeering the overstrained sentimentality of Adam, voting Abel a bore, and vastly preferring the manliness of Cain and even Lucifer.[17]

Walter, disdaining the toil of grammar, tried to fight his way to a knowledge of the language by relying upon his acquaintance with Scot-tish and Anglo-Saxon, and made his companions howl at his blunders.[18] Nevertheless, with much laughter and a little study, most of them man-aged to acquire some reading skill, one of them even tackling Kant, while Clerk, Scott, Erskine, and Thomson found refreshment "in the more animated works of the German dramatists."[19]

Otherwise Scott's life followed its recent courses. At the Speculative Society, in March, 1793, he defended the Inviolability of the Person of the Monarch, a topic given sharp edge by the blade that had guillotined Louis XVI less than two months before.[20] He had hardly been aware of the summoning of the States General, the storming of the Bastille, and the march on Versailles that had brought Louis back to Paris a captive King. But as French aggression and the Reign of Terror swept on in a river of blood, they gradually deepened his repudiation of violence and distrust of revolutionary theories as panaceas for suffering and injustice.

Two notebooks of this year reveal his varied interests and studies.

Amid favorite bits of verse, scraps of conversation, and remarks on curious judiciary cases, there are notations on "Vegtam's Kvitha, or The Descent of Odin, with the Latin of Thomas Bartoline," Gray's English Version, and "the death of Balder," both from the Edda, and the northern historians. There is a page entry about the financial distresses of Charles I, "the death-song of Regner Lodbrog," translated by a gentleman in Devonshire, an Italian canzonet praising blue eyes, etymologies from Ducange, notes on the *Morte D'Arthur*, extracts about witches and fairies. There are couplets from Hall's *Satires*, notes on second sight with extracts from Aubrey and Glanville, a table of the Maeso-Gothic, Anglo-Saxon, and Runic alphabets. And, among many further entries, biographical notes on the Lady of Branxome, who appears in *The Lay of the Last Minstrel*, and a "List of ballads to be discovered or recovered."[21]

When the Court rose in March, Walter set out for Galloway, a part of Scotland he had not seen before, to get up the case of the Reverend Mr. McNaught, the minister of Girthon, whom he was to defend during the next session before the General Assembly of the Kirk. His client was accused of habitual drunkenness, singing lewd songs, ratifying irregular marriages while acting as a justice of the peace, and "toying at a penny-wedding with a 'sweetie wife' "—a wandering vendor of gingerbread. To prepare his case Scott wanted to acquaint himself with the neighborhood and the people involved.[22]

After he had finished in Galloway, he went with Adam Ferguson on a trip through Stirlingshire and Perthshire, staying at the homes of some of his colleagues of "The Mountain." At Tullibody, east of Perth in the tiny county of Clackmannanshire, they visited George Abercromby, and heard his grandfather tell how he had journeyed into the wild country of Rob Roy. The venerable laird described his courteous reception by a cateran in a cave where he dined on some collops sliced from his own cattle (whose carcasses he recognized hanging from the rocky vault) and afterward agreed to pay Rob Roy annual blackmail in return for the future safety of his herds against all freebooters whatever.[23] At Newton, "Jean Jacques" Edmonstone's home near the ruins of Doune Castle, Scott heard another old gentleman's vivid memories of the time John Home and some other Hanoverian prisoners escaped from a Highland garrison in 1745. Scott and Ferguson, on their way up the Teith to its sources in Loch Vennachar and Loch Katrine, stayed with Alexander Buchanan of Cambusmore and delighted in that landscape of oak-clad mountains, dark pines, and silvery birches. They also visited Blair-drummond, the home of Lord Kames; Ochtertyre, the home of John Ramsay, the scholar and antiquary; and "the lofty brow of ancient Keir," the seat of the Stirling family, directly facing the field of Bannockburn and looking toward the gray rock of Snowdon and the towers of Stirling town. When Scott came to write *The Lady of the Lake*, he was to make all this country, from Loch Vennachar to Stirling, the course of Fitz-James's fiery gallop on Grey Bayard after his duel with Roderick Dhu.[24]

On May 12 the Court reconvened. Defending McNaught before the General Assembly, Scott argued that although there was an act of 1584 that excluded clergymen from acting as justices, this law had fallen into disuse and had been virtually repealed by an act of 1708. As for the irregular marriages, many of the girls had been pregnant, McNaught had persuaded their seducers to do them justice, and it was surely better that their children should not be born out of wedlock. Against the charge of habitual drunkenness, Scott distinguished between *ebrius* and *ebriosus*, being drunk and being drunken. The evidence brought against McNaught showed only three convictions for drunkenness in fourteen years. This was not habitual drunkenness, any more than a man was a common swearer if he cursed while intoxicated or an idiot if while drunk he talked nonsense.[25]

To combat the charges of lewd singing and indecent behavior gave Scott more trouble. In repeating some coarse expressions used by his client, his voice grew so loud that he was rebuked by a member of the venerable Court. Consequently, when he had to deal with one of McNaught's lewd ditties, he recited it in such a faint voice that the members of The Club, mustered strong in the gallery to encourage him, scandalized the Assembly by shouts of "Hear! hear!—encore!" They were promptly thrown out. It was the indecency of the songs themselves, however, not the interruption, that wrecked his client's cause. McNaught was deposed from the ministry, and Walter dismally felt that he had made a failure of the most important case that had so far been entrusted to him.[26]

The brethren ejected from the Court were waiting for him in a nearby tavern, whither Linton conducted him. "Come, *Duns*," cried the Baronet, "cheer up, man, and fill another tumbler!"—here was one of the party going to sing "The Tailor." "Ah!" groaned Colonel Grogg, "the tailor was a better man than me, sirs; for he didna venture *ben* until he *kenned* the way." But soon the ditty was being sung and chorused:

> The tailor he came here to sew,
> And weel he kenned the way o't,

and the evening ended in jollity and high jinks.[27]

Walter's fee as advocate in this unhappy case was five guineas; it was with this that he bought his mother the silver candle-stand. His luck throughout the remainder of the session was better: he had eight cases, out of which he made seventeen guineas, a total for his first year's practice of eleven cases and twenty-three guineas earned. Three of his clients came to him through connections of his father's, but the remainder were from six other solicitors. He had appeared before the Lord President, Sir

Ilay Campbell, the formidable Braxfield, and several other members of the high tribunal.[28]

In July, with the rising of the Court, Scott and Clerk headed for Craighall Rattray, the seat of the Rattrays, relations of Clerk, near Blairgowrie in the Highlands of Perthshire.[29] The manor was approached through a little village where huge hemlocks and thistles overshadowed the kale patches, half-naked children tumbled in the dirt, and bare-legged girls in thin petticoats carried pails upon their heads. A bowshot beyond, beneath a double row of sycamores and ancient horse-chestnuts, a deeply shaded grassy avenue led to the portals of the old house.[30]

Years later, reading an anonymous novel entitled *Waverley*, as Clerk came on its hero's arrival at Tully-Veolan, he exclaimed, "This is Scott's!" The detail that flashed conviction on his mind echoed an experience they had had at the end of a long ride in which they had become much heated. Seeing the smoke of a clachan, or hamlet, Clerk ejaculated, "How agreeable if we should here fall in with one of those sign-posts where a red lion predominates over a punchbowl!" Almost these same words Clerk found in the novel: when Waverley gazes on the courtyard of the Baron of Bradwardine he beholds "a fountain, where a huge bear, carved in stone, predominated over a large stone-basin."[31]

From Craighall the two young advocates rode east into Forfarshire, the home of Patrick Murray of Simprin at Meigle. Here they were joined by Adam Ferguson, with whom they paid an overnight visit to Glamis Castle, which was only nine miles away.[32] Belonging to the Earl of Strathmore, this splendid structure was mostly the work of Inigo Jones, although there was a huge square tower centuries older. Scott found the approach magnificent, "courtyard, ornamented enclosure, fosse, avenue, barbican, and every external muniment of battled wall and flanking tower," surrounding the lordly head of the ancient keep with "seven circles of defensive boundaries." Indoors a winding stair in a cylindrical corner tower led to a low, vaulted hall hung with armor and the buff coat of Claverhouse; the drawing room had a cradle-vaulted ceiling and a noble fireplace; and somewhere there was a secret chamber the entrance to which was known only by the Earl, his heir, and one other person in whom they confided.[33]

The seneschal allowed Scott to drink from the famous "lion-cup" and to take his night's rest in Glamis's haunted chamber. The cup was a massive beaker of silver, double gilt, molded into the form of a lion, from which he drained a pint of wine. The haunted chamber was in a distant part of the building. As Scott heard the receding footsteps of his guide, and door after door closing behind him, he began to feel himself "too far from the living, and somewhat too near the dead." They had passed through the King's Room, the vaulted apartment where Malcolm II was said to have been murdered. Scott knew that there was no historical foundation for Shakespeare's play, but despite strong effort, "the whole night scene in Macbeth's Castle rushed at once upon me, and struck my mind more forcibly than even when I have seen its terrors represented by John Kemble and his inimitable sister." He was neither superstitious nor frightened, but he did feel those sensations, half-horror, half-pleasure, "which my countrymen expressively call being *eerie*."³⁴

A much longer trip from Meigle took Clerk and Scott to Dunnotar Castle, on the rocky coast of Kincardineshire. Approaching this ruined fortress by the deep chasm that cuts it off from the mainland, Scott and his friend saw its battered walls crowning the enormous cliff whose grim crags are lashed by the North Sea. Here, during the wars of the Commonwealth, the Scottish Regalia had been safeguarded, and from here they had been smuggled out before the castle surrendered. Exploring the neighborhood with the parish minister, Scott met in the nearby churchyard a wandering eccentric named Robert Paterson, known as "Old Mortality," who devoted his days to keeping legible the epitaphs on the tombstones of the Cameronians martyred under the religious persecutions of James II.³⁵

Back in Rosebank from these summer excursions, Walter began looking forward impatiently to his coming Liddesdale raid with Shortreed, after the autumn assizes in Jedburgh.³⁶ During the spring Charles Kerr had obtained permission to copy and send him a good many ballads from the pages of the *Hawick Museum*, including one called "The Frey of Stoupar," dealing with an English invasion from Northumberland. Walter's excitement mounted.³⁷ Who could tell what treasures he himself might next turn up!

At Jedburgh, Scott made his first appearance as counsel in a criminal court, where he helped an inveterate poacher and sheep stealer escape through the meshes of the law. "You're a lucky scoundrel," he whispered. "I'm just o' your mind," the thief answered, "and I'll send ye a maukin [a hare] the morn, man." Either at these assizes or the next, he had less luck in behalf of a notorious house-burglar. The man knew he had no chance but was grateful for Scott's efforts. He was penniless, so by way of fee he offered some advice. "Never keep a large watchdog out of doors —we can always silence them cheaply . . . but tie a little tight yelping terrier within; and secondly, put no trust in nice, clever, gimcrack locks —the only thing that bothers us is a huge heavy old one . . . and the ruder and rustier the key, so much the better for the housekeeper." Years later, at a judges' dinner, Scott recited,

> Yelping terrier, rusty key,
> Was Walter Scott's best Jeddart fee.³⁸

At these same assizes Scott was counsel for a client accused of having misrepresented as sound a cow that was afflicted with "the cleirs," a disease like glanders in a horse. Before Sir David Rae, Scott stoutly maintained the animal's healthiness; it merely had, he said, a cough. "Stop!

stop! sir," interrupted the Judge, "a cough has she! A Coughin' Coo, man! and wha ever heard o' a Coughin' Coo? I hae a great deal of kye mysel and healthy kye too, but I never heard ane o' them *cough* i' my days. If she coughs, Sir, she *maun* be diseased."[39]

Scott felt vexed at losing this case. Two or three days later, on his way into Liddesdale with Shortreed, they "saw a herd o' Singdon's kye feedin' by the roadside" and a fine young bullock in the midst of them coughing lustily. "Ha! Walter," said Shortreed, had old Rae "but seen and heard that a week ago, ye wadna hae lost your Case the other day."

> "A Daniel come to judgment," Scott replied, "yea a Daniel;
> O wise young judge, how I do honour thee!"[40]

During this trip he was hot on the traces of a ballad about Jemmy Telfer, a favorite of his, and also arranged with Shortreed and their friend Dr. Elliott to begin some digging operations at Hermitage Castle, where he had obtained permission from the young Earl of Dalkeith to let them look for the grave of the Cout of Keeldar and excavate the dungeon into which the Douglas had cast Ramsay, the Sheriff of Teviotdale.[41]

Once Shortreed came to Edinburgh and spent a hilarious afternoon at George Square with Walter and his brother Tom. A wild madcap, his solemn indentures to his father's business could not hold Tom back from carrying foolery to fantastic heights. "I never laughed sae muckle at any period o' my life as I hae dune wi' his brother Tam and him at their father's house in Edinburgh. It was just fun upon fun, and who to be the daftest the haill afternoon. Tam was out o' sicht the best laugher I ever met wi'." Even Mr. Scott's sedateness broke down at the younger son's infectious drollery. "Their father," Shortread said, "was exceedingly fond and indulgent . . . and seemed to enjoy our mirth mightily and sat and hotched on his chair."[42]

During the winter of 1793–94 Scott again "swept the boards of the Parliament House with the skirts of his gown; laughed, and made others laugh; drank claret at Bayle's, Fortune's, and Walker's, and ate oysters in the Covenant Close."[43] The German class resumed their studies; in February at a meeting of the Speculative Society, Scott took part in a debate on Parliamentary reform.[44] On his desk new novels "lay snugly intrenched beneath Stair's Institute, or an open volume of Decisions"; and his dressing table was littered with "old play-bills, letters respecting a meeting of the Faculty . . . all the miscellaneous contents of a young advocate's pocket, which contains everything but briefs and bank-notes."[45] Nevertheless, though slowly, his carer was steadily advancing. At the end of the year he had made thirty-seven entries in his fee book, and more than doubled the earnings of his first year with a total of fifty-five guineas.[46]

Part of the spring recess he spent in Liddesdale. He obtained orally only one additional ballad, "The Fray o' Support." This he heard, Shortreed said, "frae auld Jonathan Graham, the lang Quaker," a man over eighty, tall and thin like a walking skeleton, who came fifteen miles to "*skraugh*" it "in a loud stentorian voice." He drank brandy so heartily that he fainted and had to be revived by throwing water on his face, whereupon he "set to roaring the outlandish lilt again"—"the awfu'est and uncoest howling sound I ever heard," recorded Shortreed, "a' sort o' horrible and eldritch cries."[47]

The snow was still too deep for digging at Hermitage, but in spite of his inability to draw, Scott attempted a sketch of the Castle from the side of Arnton Fell, standing up to his knees in the white drifts. He achieved a sort of diagram having no artistic skill but sufficiently accurate so that, when he returned to Edinburgh in April, Clerk was able with a few oral instructions from Walter to make a spirited drawing of the Castle's huge mass, with the strange pointed arch in the middle of one broad tower and slits of windows peering distrustfully from its brown walls.[48]

The war France had forced upon Britain, which had been so disastrous for the troops of the Republic in the earlier part of 1793, had now swung the other way. The allies had been thrust back across the Rhine, and a young artillery officer named Napoleon Bonaparte, exactly two years older than Walter Scott, had driven the British out of Toulon. But patriotic feeling among solid citizens was high and Walter was full of martial spirit. He only regretted that his infirmity prevented his enlisting in the regiment of volunteers in which his young brother Tom was now a grenadier. But he had hopes of joining a volunteer corps of light horse that had been proposed and asked his uncle at Rosebank to be on the lookout for a "strong gelding, such as would suit a stalwart dragoon." He would even part with his collection of Scottish coins to be properly mounted.[49]

Irish medical students at the University, who looked on every British setback as a blow for Ireland, and Republican enthusiasts, who hailed every French victory as a triumph for freedom, were by no means of Scott's mind. One night in the Edinburgh Theatre they insulted loyalists in the boxes, called for revolutionary tunes, cheered seditious speeches, and hooted the national anthem. A few nights later, Saturday, April 12, 1794, Scott and a number of other young advocates assembled in the pit with cudgels, determined to see that "God Save the King" was sung without interruption. At the first note the Irish clapped on their hats and brandished their shillelaghs, and a battle broke out. After many heads had been cracked, the loyalists won the field, Scott himself scoring three broken heads. Though he and his friends "were bound over to the peace, and obliged to give Bail for their good behaviour," they exulted in their achievement.[50]

The Magistrates, however, were worried lest there be more serious outbreaks of violence on June 8, the King's birthday, always a danger time for rioting among the disaffected. They therefore accepted the offer of nearly a thousand gentlemen, among them the irrepressible Walter, to act as special constables. During the day the volunteers assembled in the New Church, heard speeches, and were armed with brown batons and treated with claret and sweetmeats. But aside from the smashing of the Lord Justice-Clerk's windows by a few boys there were no disorders. That night, in front of St. Giles, the constables were assigned to districts so that if a flag were hoisted on the steeple and the bells rung they could be on duty in five minutes, but once more the town remained entirely peaceful.[51]

Scott spent the summer again in Roxburghshire with Shortreed. One entire day they were at Hermitage, Walter "dandering about the braes and lying down on the banks o' the water" while half a dozen "chields wi' pickaxes and shovels" tried to find the grave of the Cout of Keeldar. According to legend, this gigantic warrior, fleeing the wicked Lord Soulis, had stumbled crossing the river and fallen into the stream in full armor, where the lances of his foes held him till he drowned. Lord Soulis, a monster of cruelty, the tale went, had later been done to death by his own followers in a huge boiling cauldron on the Nine-Stane Rig, a Druid Circle east of the Castle. Although the men dug in six or seven places, however, they had no luck in finding the grave of Keeldar. But when they were clearing rubbish out of the dungeon and knocked through the last bit of wall, Scott in his eagerness jumped into the pit, where he began throwing out chaff and then some bones, which moldered as soon as they got in the air.[52] In the course of the digging, a ring was found, a broad silver band which Walter thought must have belonged of yore to one of the "Dark Knights of Liddesdale," and which he thenceforth wore on his finger.[53]

His archeological enthusiasms did not prevent his having an eye for the pretty girls of Liddesdale. He was much taken with a blooming lass in a riding habit of black polka dots on a gray ground, Miss Jessie Scott of Skelfhill, whom he and Shortreed met at dinner one day at Millburn. "He talked o' naething else amaist the haill way hame but Jessie Scott, and ca'd her aye his *nut-brown maid*. We had gotten off the subject for a little though—now that I mind, for it was that same nicht (we war a wee hauf-cock, or maybe mair) after we had gotten up the nine-stane rig and were *jerryin on* to a place they ca' Fawdoninch" that Scott's horse "played plop doun wi' her nose in a moss-hag, when we were i' the very middle o' Blythe Blythe and Merry was she."[54]

After a visit to his uncle at Rosebank, Scott returned in September to an Edinburgh feverish with uneasy excitement.[55] The war with France and a bad harvest were inflaming unrest and disorder. The price of corn had been rising steadily; both in England and in Scotland many people were going hungry. In Edinburgh alone by the following February eleven thousand were being fed by charity. Sullen laborers rioted for bread and in village taverns cottagers damned King George and "Billy Pitt." In Dundee, always a turbulent town, angry weavers erected a Tree of Liberty. To an alarmed administration grappling with armed Jacobinism these outbreaks seemed treasonous. During the previous year alone Tom Paine, whom respectable people regarded as a dangerous rabble-rouser, had sold two hundred thousand copies of his *Rights of Man*. Its defense of the use of force to overthrow an oppressive government assumed the coloring of rebellion when it merged with denunciations of a war for national survival.[56]

The agitation for parliamentary reform, carried on by the London Corresponding Society, which had appeared innocent in peacetime, now became alarming, and its Secretary, a shoemaker named Hardy, was arrested by Bow Street runners. The fashionable lecturer John Thelwall was charged with high treason, together with the genial ex-parson Horne Tooke, who was overheard declaring in a tavern that Parliament was a nest of scoundrels. What were called treasonable conspiracies were discovered in Sheffield and Ireland.[57] In Scotland, a man named Watt, a government spy, was accused of plotting with James Downie, a mechanic, to seize the Castle, the Bank of Scotland, and the persons of the Judges, and to proclaim a republican government.[58]

It was to witness the trial of these last two that Walter hastened back to town from Rosebank.[59] Lord Braxfield was savagely determined that they and all other ringleaders of the "pro-Jacobin" faction should be convicted.[60] "Come awa', Mr. Horner," he whispered to an advocate in another case, "come awa', and help to hang ane o' thae damned scoondrels."[61] But in this case "the violent and intemperate gentleman who sits in the Judiciary" did not preside; it was tried by a Commission of Oyer and Terminer.[62] Walter tensely sat in Court from seven in the morning of September 3 till two the next morning, sustaining himself on cold meat and a bottle of wine. "The very desperate and improbable nature" of the plot, he thought, might have given it "no small chance of succeeding," and he even believed testimony linking the scheme with the theater riots of the preceding April.[63] At the London trials, Hardy, Thelwall, and Tooke were acquitted of treason, though convicted on some lesser counts, but Watt and Downie were both convicted and sentenced to death.[64]

From the trial Walter rode back to Kelso, accompanied by his brother John, now a captain in the army, who had been with his regiment at Gibraltar. Since 1783 no attempt had been made to recapture that great fortress from the British. But "if Jack has not returned covered with laurels, a crop which the *Rock* no longer produces," Walter wrote, "he has brought back all his own goodnature," and was "very agreeable company" over a bottle.[65] Walter's other engagements, however, allowed him to remain with John only a short time at Rosebank. He spent a single day in Edinburgh to see Watt beheaded—"the pusillanimity," he remarked, "of the unfortunate victim was astonishing"— and was then off again to Perthshire, where he "hunted and pranced" until just before the beginning of the winter session of the Court.[66]

At the home of his friend Stirling of Keir, he had been presented to Mr. and Mrs. Belsches of Invermay, members of a younger branch of Williamina's family, who had politely invited him to visit them. But, though he knew that she and her parents were now back from Kincardineshire, Williamina herself he had not seen, even five days after his own return to Edinburgh. How he felt anyone who has ever been a lover knows, but the actual record is still sparse. Eagerly though he longed for a meeting, he put a tactical constraint upon his desires: "This being Sermon week," he told his young aunt, Miss Chritty, "I did not chuse to intrude." "For the same reason," he added, "we are looking very religious and very sour at home. However it is with *some folks* selon les regles that in proportion as they are pure themselves they are entitled to render uncomfortable those whom they consider less perfect."[67]

In fact, Walter was finding his father's harsh and carping austerity more and more trying. For his son's literary enthusiasms Mr. Scott had little sympathy, and castigated his rural wanderings with the sneer that he "was born to be a wandering pedlar."[68] On some of his friends, such as Charles Kerr, Mr. Scott sternly frowned.[69] He looked with disapprobation on Walter's convivial social life, and his own puritanical rigor made George Square a house of gloom. He "absolutely loved a funeral," preserved "the list of a whole bead-roll of cousins, merely for the pleasure of being at their funerals," and, his son suspected, often paid for them as well. "He carried me with him as often as he could to these mortuary ceremonies," but whenever Walter found it possible he escaped.[70]

That entire winter of 1794–95 was one of the severest ever known. A snowstorm that began at Christmas rendered roads inpassable for more than six weeks. Even in March Scott wrote that Scotland "much resembled Siberia" and was "fit only for the habitation of Russian Bears." In the midst of this freezing weather the French were conquering Holland, and Scott's brother John, who had obtained a company in a Highland corps raised by MacKenzie of Seaforth, sailed from Portsmouth with his regiment for a secret destination.[71] Volunteers were drilling throughout the country, in fear that Britain itself might be invaded.[72]

Meanwhile Scott's legal practice modestly grew, his earnings for this third year reaching £84 4s. More than half this sum, however, came through his father's connections.[73] His last case in the spring was the defense of a young sailor named James Niven against a charge of murder. He had served with excellent character on a ship of war and been discharged because of a wound that disabled one hand. Firing a small iron cannon in Liberton's Wynd for the amusement of some young

friends, he had accidentally killed David Knox, the doorkeeper of the
Faculty of Advocates, with a fragment of iron bolt that had broken off
and remained in the weapon when he was ramming the powder home.
There was no suspicion of malicious intent, but the public prosecutor
argued that the young man's carelessness justified either a verdict of
murder or at least of culpable homicide.[74]

Scott opened so well for the prisoner that before impaneling a jury
Lord Braxfield and his colleagues deferred further action and ordered
both parties to present a written statement or "information" of their
arguments. Scott's "information" pointed out that his client had acted
without malice, the cannon was pointed horizontally on a street with a
sharp downgrade, and was a mere toy such as boys of all ages amused
themselves firing in the evenings. A poor ignorant lad could hardly
imagine that he was wrong in doing what he saw the sons of gentlemen
doing unchecked by either their parents or the magistrates. No doubt
he deserved some blame; no accident ever took place that might not have
been avoided had the chief actor been gifted with the power of prophecy
or an almost superhuman degree of prudence. But the fragment of iron
left in the gun had remained there without his knowledge, and he was
as innocent as if the accident had been caused by the bursting of the
gun. On this argument, which was presented just before the Court rose
in July, the case was put over to the winter, then to be proved to the
satisfaction of a jury. Their verdict, handed down on December 21 following, was "Not guilty."[75]

During the intervening summer vacation Adam Ferguson and John
Irving, Scott's friends since school days, were on a tour of Ireland.
Walter amused himself by imagining them in the mountains of Tip-
perary, "John with a beard of three inches . . . shaggy elf-locks, an ell-
wand-looking cane with a gilt head in his hand, and a bundle in a
handkerchief over his shoulder, exciting the cupidity of every Irish
raparee who passes him," and Ferguson, "exalted in state upon an Irish
garron, without stirrups, and a halter on its head, tempting every one
to ask—

> "Who is that upon the pony,
> So long, so lean, so raw, so bony?"

He could almost see Adam "grinning a ghastly smile," he wrote, and
almost hear his companion's hollow voice observing, "God! Adam, if
ye gang on at this rate the eight shillings and sevenpence halfpenny
will never carry us forward to my uncle's at Lisburn."[76]

But although he could joke cheerfully about his two friends, his
heart was already full of yearning for the coming of November, still a
long six weeks away. For then he expected Williamina to return to
Edinburgh from Fettercairn with her parents. During the summer he
had at last found courage to declare his love; he even found the

optimism to believe that she loved him; early in August she had sent him a letter that filled him with wild joy. It was true that she had not yet pledged herself to him and was counseling circumspection as "the most prudent line of conduct for us both, at least till better days." But she was not forbidding him to hope. His relief was so great that he shed tears; he felt on fire with longing. How could he bear to wait for their meeting? "O for November!"[77]

# 5

## *Weep When They Melt*

### *( 1790–1796 )*

Now, in the autumn of 1795, Williamina was nineteen, a pensive blue-eyed beauty whose dark brown hair, with its serene Madonna-parting in the middle, clustered in ringlets around a white expanse of brow. Her almost translucent pallor was illumined by the faintest rose-flush. Her lips were thoughtfully firm above a firm chin. Though her eyes could dance, beneath their dark brows and lashes they were more often calm and expressed a mild composure.[1]

Her father, Sir John Wishart Belsches, laid claim to be the heir, through his mother, of the baronetcy of his great-great-grandfather, Sir George Wishart.[2] Her mother, Lady Jane, was the daughter of the Earl of Leven and Melville. One of Williamina's great-grandmothers had been a Swinton, so that she and Walter were distantly related through their Swinton blood.[3] There was, nevertheless, a marked distinction in their social position, even though, in so tightly knit a community as Edinburgh, their families knew each other and might count kin a few generations back. The daughter of a baronet and granddaughter of an earl enjoyed a far loftier rank than the son of a cadet branch of a numerous clan, whose father was a mere Writer to the Signet.

Nobody, however, had raised any objection to the boy-and-girl friendship that had begun so casually five years earlier.[4] As the youth of nineteen had limped beside the fourteen-year-old girl on the stroll home from Greyfriars', Walter's mother usually walked behind them, sometimes perhaps alongside Williamina's mother, although there was no intimacy between the two ladies, and Mrs. Scott was twenty years older than Lady Jane.[5] Walter talked animatedly, no doubt about Ariosto and

Launcelot and Baldur the Beautiful and Border ballads, and Williamina's cheek glowed and her lips curved in laughter.

Little by little, in the course of 1791 and 1792, he found his feelings warming and deepening. Poor rural Jessie, from whom he was already falling away when he and Williamina first met, was now entirely forgotten; Rosaline vanishes without a trace when the true Juliet appears. As Walter reached twenty-one and took his place at the bar, the girl to whom he had offered the shelter of his umbrella had blossomed into sixteen, and he knew that he was in love. In the summer she and her parents were always at Fettercairn, their seat in Kincardineshire, from which they did not return to Edinburgh till winter. It was a weary wait; in Rosebank, even with the excitement of his first term as an advocate looming ahead, Walter wrote, "I have no prospect of seeing my *chère adorable* till winter, if then."[6]

But when she was once more in town, reality did not prove as serene as he had hoped. Late in that November, Charles Kerr, replying to a letter Walter had written "under considerable pain," hoped that "your writing to me at such a time did not increase your sufferings." "If your quill could relieve that agony in any degree, I congratulate myself upon holding so sincere a place in your heart."[7] It may be that in responding Walter tried to give his sentiments a turn of gallantry rather than of heartfelt fervor, for his friend next commented, "Your Quixotism, dear Walter, was highly characteristic. From the description of the blooming fair, as she appeared when she dropped her *manteau vert*, I am hopeful you have not dropped the acquaintance. At least I am certain some of our more rakish friends would have been glad enough of such an introduction."[8]

The green mantle was Williamina's walking cloak of silk, fancifully embroidered, and with a deep hood shadowing her rose-tinted pallor,[9] and Walter's emotions were in fact very far from rakish. But he was too shy, too unsure, too awkwardly timid, to woo her outright. However bold he might be with a village Jessie, however gaily he had voiced admiration for the nut-brown maid of Liddesdale, the deeper devotion for one whom he felt far above him now left him abashed and unable, save by some rare and difficult effort, to do more than hint his emotion. Possibly an attempt to be overt had met with a girlish repulse which elicited his pained outcry to Charles Kerr and made him afraid to express himself except by quoting medieval love lyrics and Renaissance poets or composing youthful imitations of them.

One such poem he wrote on St. Valentine's Day, 1793:

> Ah! why wilt thou not be my Love
>  Among these wild and pleasant mountains
> From whence the eye untired may rove
>  O'er mossy Banks and sparkling fountains

> Thy fleeting form I oft have chaced
>    O'er craggy rocks thy steps pursuing
> By fancy lured thro' Woods to haste
>    While Hope deluded to my ruin[10]

The poem went on to threaten the "obdurate maid," "Thou Savage in an Angels form," that he would turn friar and in the monastic shade of some lonely shrine send all his orisons to Heaven:

> No more I'll wear this Cypress wreath
>    No more petition or reprove thee—
> Silent I go to meet my death
>    Or learn the Art no more to love thee.

The arrival of another spring and Williamina's approaching departure for Kincardineshire created an emptiness to be filled with memories and longing. During Walter's excursions of the summer, to Glamis Castle and north to Dunnotar, he must have cast longing glances west to Fettercairn. And sometime during the course of that summer, on his first visit to St. Andrews, he carved her name in Runic characters in the turf beside the castle-gate.[11]

Many were the times during the following winter that from his window in George Square he looked out into the Meadow Walk for a glimpse of a bonnet with a certain blue feather matching the blue eyes beneath.[12] But there were also evenings in the Assembly Rooms when, orange in pocket, he learned that despite the intoxication of music and eager admirers tempting her to the gleaming floor, those blue eyes had light only for him, that clear face would mantle into rose and enrapture him with those dangerous smiles.[13] Once, in what season, or even in what year is not recorded, Walter and Williamina visited the abbey church of Arbroath together, and for Scott even years later its red sandstone arcades evoked that day like an enchanted dream.[14]

Walter had taken his youthful aunt, Dr. Rutherford's sister Miss Chritty, into his confidence. When in the summer of 1794 she was staying with friends at Pitcullen in Perth, he excitedly wondered whether she might also have been nearby at Invermay, the home of another branch of the Belsches family, "and all the &cs &cs which the question involves."[15] But when he himself met Mr. and Mrs. Belsches that autumn and received a polite invitation to Invermay, "want of time," he said, prevented his accepting it.[16] His real reason may have been that he knew or believed Williamina already on her way to Edinburgh; he would feel no desire to remain behind her among scenes where there was no possibility of their meeting. Some verses he wrote in Roxburghshire express his longing for the winter that would bring them together once more:

> Unpu'd on Yarrow's braes, the birk,
>> Untouched may Teviot's roses fa',
> While thy pale flowers shall cheer my way—
>> Laid by the maid that's far awa'—
>
> And while I wander, lorn and drear,
>> By many a time worn tottering ha',
> Thy spriggs shall make remembrance dear
>> Of pleasures past and far awa'.
>
> Droop sune, ye birks in Yarrow's shade,
>> While the keen north winds rudely blaw,
> Sune may thy roses, Teviot, fade,
>> Born on his whirwhins far awa'.
>
> Come, Winter, with thy ruthless train,
>> And clad again our hills wi' snaw,
> For lovely in thy stormy van
>> Thou bringst the maid that's far awa'.[17]

During the few weeks Walter was in Perthshire before the opening of the autumn term of 1794 his thoughts often turned northward, but he did not dare an expedition to Fettercairn, where he said, "I should have little title to go, as the knight and I are hardly acquainted."[18] Walter's intimacy with Williamina, in fact, did not extend to the rest of her family, and Sir John seems to have been unaware for some time longer of the young advocate's feelings for his daughter. The severe winter which that year made Scotland "fit only for the inhabitation of Russian bears" drew on into a frigid March. Williamina was in town the whole season, "and going a good deal into publick, which has not in the least altered," her lover said fondly, "the sweetness of her manners."[19] Though the records are scanty, it is clear that he saw her neither more nor less than before. "Matters remain," he confided to a cousin, "just as they did."

Walter had not yet formally declared himself to Williamina, but he felt sure that she must know he loved her. His emotions wavered between hope and fear. That she liked him was plain; did she love him? She was always gentle, generous in praise of his verse, sometimes warm, then again reserved; and just at the moment when he felt that he could not bear it, there would come another mantling smile. Was her reserve only maiden modesty, or was it a warning of friendly indifference?[20] When Williamina went back to Kincardineshire that spring of 1795 he still had not spoken out. In his incertitude he took counsel with Will Clerk, who had managed to impress him as deeply versed in the ways of the feminine sex.

Clerk himself had surmised Walter's emotions on discovering that his friend "wore a sort of medallion in the style of Tassie's heads about his neck"[21]—a trinket perhaps given him by Williamina. Subsequently Walter confided in Clerk. There were several others among their close intimates who either knew of the attachment from his lips or had been astute enough to read it in his demeanor: the gentle William Erskine and his sister Mary Anne, both of whom felt affectionate sympathy for his plight, the witty but compassionate Jane Anne Cranstoun and her brother George, and of course his mother and his dear Aunt Christy.[22]

Clerk counseled boldness. Instead of timidly hoping that Williamina would reveal her feelings, he should force matters into the open by a frank confession of his own. With infinite trepidation Walter drafted a letter following Clerk's advice. What he wrote remains unknown but may be imagined—a reminder of their long friendship, an avowal of his love, a trembling hope that the disparity in their positions and the meagerness of his earnings might not be obstacles to their ultimate union?[23] The letter once dispatched, he waited anxiously for her reply.

When it arrived, early in August, with what agitation he broke the seal! Then came a flood of relief. He read the dear epistle over "ten times a day," he wrote Clerk, "and always with new admiration for her generosity and candour—and as often take shame to myself for the mean suspicions which, after knowing her so long, I could listen to, while endeavouring to guess how she would conduct herself." To forestall disappointment, he had "struggled to suppress every rising gleam of hope"; now, in his exaltation, he felt overwhelmed by a sense of his own unworthiness. His contending emotions ended in a flood of tears.[24]

Despite his ecstasy over her letter, what Williamina said is far from clear. The letter itself has disappeared; its contents can only be inferred, partly from Scott's letters to Clerk, partly from the events that followed. No doubt she had a genuine regard for her companion and friend of these three years and did not want to hurt him. Her tender heart would not like him to think she would despise him because of his circumstances or his infirmity—the "mean suspicions" to which, in fact, he *had* listened. But though he was all joyous excitement at her "generosity and candour," her desire not to wound him might have made her somewhat less than candid. She did not forbid him to hope, but she emphasized the need of being circumspect. Meanwhile their relationship must remain unchanged.

Walter believed her to mean that when his progress at the bar enabled him seriously to consider an engagement they might return to the subject. "What she has pointed out is the most prudent line of conduct for us both, at least till better days, which, I now think myself entitled to suppose, she, as well as myself, will look forward to with pleasure."[25] All his apprehensions had been obsessed by the fear that his poverty and her father's rank were unconquerable barriers to his hopes. He thought all her cautions merely prudential. When this cloud was lifted he soared up into a radiant empyrean.

Nevertheless, beneath his elation hovered a shadowy trace of uncertainty. He sent her letter enclosed in one he wrote to Clerk, hoping his friend would melt his lingering doubts, confirm his sanguine hopes. That expert on love agreed that Williamina's reply was highly encouraging and recommended that he pursue the course she had indicated. Walter joyfully concurred. His misty misgivings evaporated in a glow of assurance. He failed to observe that she had not said he had won her heart. He overflowed with gratitude to his adviser, whose encouragement and counsel had directed an attack "which has succeeded in bringing the enemy to terms." Now for November! "Dicite Io paean, et Io bis dicite paean!" he quoted Ovid rapturously at the end of his letter; "Jubeo te bene valere, Gualterus Scott."[26]

Meanwhile, his literary interests had mounted on the wings of a new enthusiasm that mingled with his excitement as a lover. During the autumn of 1794, when he had been ballad raiding in Liddesdale, a well-known literary lady, Anne Letitia Barbauld, had paid a visit to Edinburgh. At a party given in her honor by Professor Dugald Stewart, Mrs. Barbauld read a manuscript translation of Gottfried Bürger's romantic ballad "Lenore," recently made by her friend William Taylor of Norwich, a philosopher whose name they all knew. Her listeners were thrilled by its macabre story of a specter bridegroom galloping away with his sweetheart to the tomb, and their delight in the onomatopoeic

> Tramp, tramp across the land they speed,
> Splash, splash along the sea

was unmarred by the fact that there are no such lines in Bürger's poem.[27]

Scott had returned to find Edinburgh still buzzing with this literary sensation. His close friend George Cranstoun, who was Mrs. Stewart's brother, repeated to him from memory the exciting "Tramp, tramp across the land they speed," and he too fell into ecstasy.[28] He must obtain the volume containing the original poem. No Edinburgh bookseller stocked German books; even in London they were seldom found for sale. But in the summer of 1795 Scott's kinsman Scott of Harden married a distinguished German lady, Harriet, a daughter of Count Bruhl, the Saxon ambassador to the Court of St. James, a famous chess-player and a patrician whose escutcheon boasted sixteeen quarterings.[29] She kindly sent to Hamburg for a copy of Bürger's works. Scott awaited its arrival with impatience.[30]

How much he saw of Williamina that winter is not known, but stimulated by his dream of marriage he labored assiduously. He was appointed one of the curators of the Advocates' Library.[31] At the end of that year, his third as an advocate, the number of entries in his fee book had increased from the twenty-six of the preceding year to forty-one, but some of them had been only modestly remunerative and his total earnings increased only to £92 11s.[32] His last case, in March, resulted in a verdict of "Not proven" for a client named William Brown, who had been accused of stealing some bars of iron from a merchant in Leith.[33] By that time Walter was eagerly looking forward to a trip north at the end of the month. He planned to make some archeological investigations of Fenella's Castle at Glencairn, but this was only two miles from Fettercairn: surely he could use his visit to the neighborhood as a pretext for getting himself invited to Williamina's home.[34]

Mr. Scott had heard him talking of this excursion and had no doubt that the real attraction was not the bones of the murdered Kenneth III. Williamina's fortune, he knew, would be far greater than any to which his son had prospect. He felt in duty bound to warn her parents of an intimacy of which he feared they were unaware and which without their approval might bring pain to all. Before Sir John Belsches set out for Kincardineshire, Mr. Scott therefore waited upon him. He wished no such affair to proceed, he said, without the express sanction of those most concerned in the happiness of the two young people. Sir John was surprised; he had not heard of Walter's intended journey. He thanked Mr. Scott for his punctiliousness but treated the matter lightly, plainly believing that the old lawyer was making too much of it. It was not until long afterward that Walter learned of his father's interference.[35]

In the midst of his preparations for departure Walter was working at red heat on a poem. When the volume of Bürger had come that spring he had gulped down "Lenore" in a fever of excitement. The book had not been than a few hours in his hands before he enthusiastically promised George Cranstoun's lively sister Jane that he would translate it into English for her. Scribbling frantically all night long, from just after supper, seething in a tumultuous fury, he threw down his pen at daybreak. He had finished it—sixty-six stanzas in a single night![36]

A sheaf of disorderly papers in his hand, he rushed off, heedless of the hour, to Jane Anne Cranstoun. At half past six her maid woke her, said Mr. Scott was in the dining room, wished to speak with her at once. Miss Cranstoun dressed hastily, thinking there must be some crisis. Walter met her at the door, begging her to hear his version of "Lenore," which he called "William and Helen." She listened with astonishment; its speed and drama took her breath away. Jane praised him warmly, asking if she might retain the manuscript for a few days to read it over more carefully. He told her to keep it until he returned from his visit to the country and dashed off proud and elated. "Upon my word," Jane exclaimed to a friend, "Walter Scott is going to turn out a poet."[37]

Jane Cranstoun knew the magnet that was drawing Scott north. The kindness of her heart inspired the idea that his poetic achievement might help plead his cause with Williamina. With the aid of William

Erskine she had a number of copies of the poem elegantly printed. One of these, richly bound and blazoned, she forwarded for Walter to give his sweetheart.[38] He had started out on March 28, on a pony named Earwig, with a servant on another pony, and accompanied by John James Edmonstone "on a most splendid Bucephalus." The next day saw them on the field of Bannockburn, where Patrick Murray of Simprim joined them and descanted enthusiastically upon the positions of the English and Scottish armies, "wheeling and caracolling as he became warmed with his subject."[39]

Next Scott and Edmonstone were at Ramsay's, in Ochtertyre, and after that at Cambusmore, from where they went on for three or four days among the winding lakes of the Trossachs. Returning to Callander the two friends separated, and Scott set out up Loch Lubnaig. This was unfamiliar country to him, so he dismounted and went most of the way to Lochearnhead on foot. Turning east, he made his way down Strathearn to Comrie, where he saw a fine waterfall and the remains of a large Roman camp, and from there went on to Perth. Here he saw "what gave me more pleasure than all the camps and cascades in my tour," Mary Anne Erskine. Recovered from an illness, and looking delightful, she was, unknown to him, listening with favor to the courtship of Archibald Campbell of Clathick.[40]

From Perth he wrote Jane Cranstoun an account of his wanderings, giving the post office at Montrose as his next address. "When I consider the Wilds, the Forests and the Lakes," she answered, "the misshapen rocks that were piled around you and the spirits with which you would whisper to them startling echoes, it amazeth me how you escaped from the spot—" to which she added, teasingly, "had you but dismissed the little Squire and Earwig and spent a few days as Orlando wd. have done all posterity might have profited by it, but to Trot quietly away without so much as one Stanza to despair—never talk to me of Love again, never, never, never—"[41]

After leaving Perth, Scott proceeded with more speed. "Like a Cloud upon a whirlwind," he wrote Erskine, "did I pass thro the fat Carse of Gowrie, thro Dundee, thro Arbroath, thro Montrose"—where at the post office he left Aberdeen as a forwarding address—and on to Benholm, where he was entertained by George Robertson Scott. Close to the modern house there was an ancient tower looking down a steep woody glen to the sea and commanding a wide prospect westward. "You will guess," his letter continued, "I was often to be found upon the Battlements straining my eyes towards the Distant Grampians"—distant to a lover's heart, though Williamina's home was only ten miles away.[42]

But the Circuit Court at Aberdeen was to open on April 15, and he had as yet received no invitation to Fettercairn.[43] If he advanced his antiquarian interest in Fenella's Castle as an excuse for going there now, he might, to be sure, obtain the desired invitation, but it would be more serviceable later, when he could remain longer. "For a thousand reasons," he told his friend, "I deferred any stay in the neighborhood till my return Southwards so I tore myself from that quarter of the country and sad and slowly trotted on to Aberdeen with many an anxious thought upon the shadows clouds and darkness that involve my future prospects of happiness."[44]

At Aberdeen, as a compliment to his father, who had been for many years the Edinburgh law agent of that town, Walter was made an Honorary Burgess and given the freedom of the city. He was hospitably entertained by his father's friends and spent several days with one of them, the elderly Alexander Leith of Freefield, at his home thirty miles northwest of the Burgh.[45] But his thoughts were at Fettercairn. "I am, you may believe, anxious enough," he told Erskine, "on one score and another and may well adopt the burden of the old song—'If it were na my heart's light, I wad die.' "[46] On April 25 he was at last able to start south for Dunnotar, hoping now to be invited to Fettercairn.

Jane Cranstoun had written him a letter, forwarded from Montrose, telling him what an impression his translation of Bürger was making in Edinburgh and gossiping about their circle of friends. Taylor's translation, she told him, was now published and was far inferior. "Dugald Stewart read yours to Greenfield," who was deeply moved, "big tears rolling down his innocent nose." "This here place," Jane went on, "is damned dull. Clerk is in the country getting strong, Erskine in London . . . Macfarlan hatching Kant and George Fountainhall, Monroe is making hot love to J. Dalrymple and—upon my sincerity I have nothing else to tell you—but that I am most affectionately Yours—Many an anxious thought I have about you." "Heav'n speed you," she exclaimed. "Be sober *and hope* to the end."[47]

At Dunnotar he was the guest of Mr. Walker in the manse. He had seen to it that Sir John Belsches knew he would be riding over to Glencairn, only two miles from Fettercairn, to explore the ruins of Fenella's Castle.[48] Sir John seems to have responded that he would be welcome as their guest during the several days he would be engaged in his antiquarian researches there, and to have mentioned, perhaps not altogether undesignedly, that Williamina was ill and would be unable to see company. Nevertheless, hoping for the best, Walter prepared to accept the Baronet's hospitality.[49]

He started two laborers excavating the clogged-up well of Dunnotar Castle. He obtained Mr. Walker's promise to let him know any finds they made and to send on whatever ballads he discovered, and eagerly mounted his steed.[50] Sir John and Lady Jane received him pleasantly, and at Glencairn also he put some workmen to digging the ring or vallum just outside the main rampart. He was soon fascinated to come upon vitrified stones that afforded unmistakable evidence that the Castle had been destroyed by fire.[51]

But this triumph was entirely outshone by one still greater that filled him with a delirium of delight: Sir John and Lady Jane invited him to prolong his visit.[52] Perhaps they merely wanted to study more carefully this young man who was in love with their daughter; perhaps they were not, as Mr. Scott had surmised, so much concerned for a wealthy marriage as for her happiness; perhaps they thought that if she loved him the match might not be impossible. And soon Williamina recovered from her indisposition. She was as dear and delightful as ever; and, sometime during the visit, no doubt, Walter read his translation of Bürger aloud in a voice charged with emotion. He remained at Fettercairn for seven beatific days.[53]

On May 5, two days later than he had originally expected to be back in Edinburgh, he rode off in a blissful haze, the rue of parting radiantly dissolved in joy.[54] On his way to Montrose he blithely visited Eagle, or Edzell, Castle, and climbed the hill of Caterthun to gaze longingly back on Fettercairn, some eight miles away, golden in the light of the setting sun and his heart's ecstasy.[55]

> Loth to resume my vagrant lot
>     While brightening in the distance far
> Thy beams yet gild one sacred spot
>     And fondly seem to linger there
>
> And linger still thou setting sun
>     And gild her walks and cheer her flowers
> And chase each care, and chase each pain
>     That cloud my gentle Favourites hours
>
> Mine be the blast on mountain brow
>     If evening sunbeams round her play
> And mine the storm and mine the snow
>     If hers the sheltered vale of May[56]

At the fishing town of Montrose, Walter spent a cheerful night with his old tutor James Mitchell, who was now married and the minister of the Established Church. It was "an electric shock" to that solemn man to learn that his former pupil had made this northern journey not exclusively to attend the Court at Aberdeen, but also to collect "ancient ballads and traditional stories about fairies, witches, and ghosts." Walter did not tell him that the source of his spirited gaiety was a bewitchment not at all ghostly. But when his host tried to pledge his support for the rigid evangelical party in the Church of Scotland, he said good-humoredly, "Nay, nay, Mr. Mitchell, I'll not do that; for if that were to be done, I and the like of me would have no life with such as you."[57]

Scott arrived home in a state of high elation. If Williamina's parents had not formally received him as her suitor, they had been far from discouraging. He was happy, too, in the praises his friends were giving

"William and Helen." Soon after reading it to Jane Cranstoun he had also read it to Alexander Wood, son of a well-known surgeon, who had been no less impressed with its wild unearthly imagery. Following its impassioned delivery Walter had stared into the fire and then burst out, "I wish to Heaven I could get a skull and two cross-bones!" Nothing easier, said Wood; let Walter only come with him to John Bell, the celebrated surgeon. From a closet in his library Bell allowed Scott to select a handsome skull and pair of bones, which he joyfully carried home in a handkerchief and mounted on top of a bookcase.[58] The next summer, at Cambusmore, he gave an inscribed copy of "William and Helen" to Lady Charlotte Home.[59] "Every day," Jane Cranstoun had told him, "adds to your renown."[60] Buoyantly he began a translation of Bürger's "Wild Huntsman" ("Der Wilde Jäger"), which he entitled "The Chase," and arranged with Manners and Miller, the Edinburgh booksellers, to publish the two poems in a little volume.[61]

But a blow was in store. When Williamina had written him her gentle though cautious letter, the previous summer, she had been heart-free. However, during that winter, in Edinburgh, unknown to Walter, she had seen much of the banker's son, William Forbes, Scott's companion in many a youthful brawl and drinking bout. Her mother perceived from Williamina's confidences when they talked about the parties she attended and the young men she met that she liked him from their first meeting. Polite and agreeably attentive as he had been, though, William Forbes had not yet spoken any word of love. That summer he was a guest at Fettercairn, and Williamina found herself enjoying his companionship more and more. Still, however, he made no move toward courtship. Only after he had left did he at last declare himself. Unlike Scott, who pleaded his love to Williamina herself, William Forbes formally wrote Lady Jane requesting parental approval of his suit.[62]

Lady Jane could offer no real objection. Both young people were well provided for; Williamina was an heiress, Forbes the son of a wealthy banker. His social position was unimpeachable. Lady Jane already knew well that Williamina's heart inclined toward him. And she had a will as well as a heart of her own. "Nothing could induce her," Lady Jane wrote this new suitor, "to say more than she thinks to please any one. . . . You may implicitly rely on every word she says as being the sincere sentiment of her heart."[63] But Lady Jane was sorry for the poor young man who had spent a week with them that spring. She felt some quality, some promise, in him that impressed her, and she had been touched by his evident devotion. "Not the mother who bore you," she told him thirty years later, "followed you more anxiously (tho' secretly) with her blessing than I."[64] But she could hardly wish her daughter to sacrifice her own happiness or believe that for her to do so would secure Walter's.

It was not long before Walter heard rumors that he had a favored rival. The thought that Williamina might marry someone else became an agony in which the most harmless things assumed the power to wring his heart. One evening in late August or early September, as he chatted confidentially with Mary Anne Erskine, her innocent talk of the desirability of her brother's getting married gave a sudden twist to the knife of his apprehension.

Mary Anne's thoughts had turned to marriage for her brother because of her own approaching marriage, which William Erskine announced to Walter a few days later. Memories of seeing her at Perth with Campbell of Clathick made the news not altogether a surprise. Despite his own heartache he replied with generous elation. "I must have a bottle extraordinary somewhere upon the score . . . I have been whistling, hallooing and I verily believe almost crying this whole morning to the utter astonishment of my Uncle . . ." he wrote from Rosebank. "There are not upon this earth two of her sex besides in whose happiness I feel myself equally interested."[65] In acknowledging his good wishes, Mary Anne said, "I have ever considered you as a brother . . . Well do I remember the dark conference we lately held together. The intention of unfolding my future fate was often at my lips, when the gloom of the chamber would have prevented your seeing them . . ."[66]

His own "uncertainties and dilemmas," however, looked darker and darker. Sir William Forbes, he was sure, was on his way to Kincardineshire to discuss marriage settlements in his son's behalf, or, as Walter bitterly exclaimed, " '*Dot & carry one*' is certainly gone to F[ettercair]n."[67] A fortnight later he was still desperately trying to hope that nothing had "occurred from the campaign of the formal Chevalier and his son Don Guglielmo." Perhaps now that Mary Anne was married and living in the North, she would have "opportunities of getting acquainted with the Lady in question." Walter was certain Mary Anne would like Williamina "for her own sake and I need not say how much I should be delighted to see a union take place between such kindred minds in each of whom I take such interest."[68]

But deep in his heart he knew that hope was a mere dream, and he could not bear the humiliation of having the world in general know of his distress. He begged Erskine, who had been skeptical about the outcome of his suit, to treat his attachment, if it were referred to in gossip, as no more than a casual gallantry. "I am not sure but what your judgement may be more correct than mine in what regards W——— and therefore your sailing orders are—If the subject is introduced to treat it lightly. No body can be surprised that such a Don Quixote as your friend should have a Dulcinea—you understand—I am satisfied Joan Keir regarded it in that light otherwise she would hardly have mentioned it—*verbum sapienti*—"[69]

His misery tore at him constantly. "Down busy devil down—But I still run about the country and gallop over stock and stile after the 'gude graie dogs' so that if Horace's *Atra Cura* insist upon riding the pillion *sedere post equitem* as honest Flaccus has it, I must een do my best to drop her jadeship into a Teviotdale bog." Only, Erskine must write to him—write—"the more frequently you write the better you enable me to banish the Blue Devils and white black Devils and grey which insist upon being the companions of my Solitude."[70]

On October 12 Williamina's engagement to William Forbes was announced. "This is not good news," wrote one of his brothers of The Mountain. "I always dreaded there was some self-deception on the part of our romantic friend, and I now shudder at the violence of his most irritable and ungovernable mind."[71] Scott is reported, indeed, to have rushed to Fettercairn to insist upon seeing Williamina, and, on receiving his dismissal from her own lips, to have left her, vowing angrily "that he would be married before her."[72] Though this vehemence of feeling is not out of character, there is no authenticated record of his having left Edinburgh till October 16, when he was with the Fergusons at Halyards, and three days later he attended his friend Edmonstone's wedding. He is then supposed to have returned to Rosebank and to have come back to Edinburgh at the beginning of November.[73]

But whether or not any such last interview with Williamina ever took place, his bitterness and grief were indeed intense. There can be no question that they were echoed in that passage of *Rob Roy* where Frank believes that he has parted with Diana Vernon for ever: "At length, tears rushed to my eyes, glazed as they were by the exertion of straining after what was no longer to be seen. I wiped them mechanically, and almost without being aware that they were flowing, but they came thicker and thicker. I felt the tightening of the throat and breast, the *hysterica passio* of poor Lear; and, sitting down by the wayside, I shed a flood of . . . the most bitter tears which had flowed from my eyes since childhood."[74]

Hardly less bitter was Walter's obstinate belief that Williamina had encouraged him, led him on, and then betrayed him. Various possibilities tormented him. Was she a heartless jill-flirt, a Criseyde easily persuaded to surrender Troilus for the victorious Diomede? Was she tempted, she who was an heiress already, by a mercenary marriage? Had her parents only pretended cordiality when he was their guest, and was she weakly yielding to their tyranny, as Edgar of Ravenswood in *The Bride of Lammermoor*, years hence, would bitterly believe to be true of Lucy Ashton? The gentleness of Williamina's demeanor had always misled him into thinking of her as meek; he did not know her as her mother did, and did not understand that she had really fallen in love with William Forbes and was not acting under the pressure of either of her parents.

Indeed, the truth was the precise opposite of his suspicions. Williamina had made up her own mind, Lady Jane had not forced but merely agreed in her daughter's decision, and Sir John—for what reasons are unknown—had even felt doubtful about it. It may even have been that Sir John preferred Walter. As late as the middle of December, Williamina did not know whether her parents would in fact consent to the marriage. "They may retreat," she wrote her fiancé, "but I never can—at the same time I am perfectly conscious of what is due from me to my father—and to his will I must submit my conduct tho my affections are no longer in my power." Of her love, she earnestly told Forbes, "believe that it can end but with the life of your W. B."[75] Whatever Sir John's objections, they were, however, overcome, and the couple were married on January 19, 1797.

Knowing none of these undercurrents, Walter was torn between seeing Williamina as a coquette, as greedy for rank and wealth, or as dominated by paternal rule. Wearily his imagination rotated through the round of all these explanations of her treachery, returning to each a thousand times. The anguish that tore his heart repeatedly sought relief in verse.

> By a thousand fond dreams my weak Bosom betrayd
> Believed thee for Love & for Constancy made,
> Believed that Indifference never could be
> Where gentle compassion had pleaded for me.
>
> .　.　.
>
> For grandeur, for wealth your poor friend you resign,
> If Bliss they can give, *O may it be thine*
> Farewell to the raptures of lowly degree
> You might have enjoyed with Love & with me.
>
> Unfriended by fortune, untutor'd by Art,
> I gave You my all—when I gave You my heart
> But many a gallant of higher degree
> Has none, W[illiamina], for Love or for thee.[76]

In "The Triumph of Constancy," an adaptation of Bürger's "Das Lied von Treue," which Scott made in the autumn following his rejection, the two rivals for the Lady's hand are called "The Baron" and "Earl Marshal." (William Forbes was the son of a Baronet, and one of Scott's nicknames was "Earl Walter.") After a desperate battle the Baron suggests that instead of going on with their duel, they leave their Lady to choose which shall be her lover. Earl Marshal immediately agrees.

> "Ah!" tenderly thought he, "too deeply with me
>         The goblet of Love has she tasted"—
> Alas! simple knight, thou couldst not foresee
> Tho' the flower of Affection at morn sprung for thee
>         Ere noon might its fragrance be wasted.

The Maid on her palfrey approach'd from afar
    And thus to the warriors said she:
"Sir Knights, since 'tis mine to determine the jar,
Sheath, Sheath your keen blades and desist from the war.
    I go forward, Lord Baron, with thee."

No blush of contrition her features besprente
    As lightly she rein'd round her steed,
No glance of compassion Earl Marshal she sent,
Who blasted and breathless remain'd on the bent
    Like a Corpse by blue lightning struck dead.[77]

Still another of these poems again underlines the lady's falsehood:

The violet in her greenwood bower,
    Where birchen boughs with hazels mingle
May boast itself the fairest flower
    In glen or copse or forest dingle.

Though fair her gems of azure hue
    Beneath the dewdrop's weight reclining,
I've seen an eye of lovelier blue
    More sweet through watery lustre shining.

The summer sun that dew shall dry,
    Ere yet the sun be past its morrow,
Nor longer in my false love's eye
    Remained the tear of parting sorrow![78]

Scott proudly concealed his wound from the world and slowly conquered his agony. But he long continued to feel bitterly that Williamina had jilted him. A full dozen years later, when a young lady broke her engagement to his friend James Ballantyne, Scott exclaimed indignantly that her conduct had been "most singularly and abominably profligate." He knew, he told James, "by never to be forgotten experience" the nature of his friend's feelings, "scarcely susceptible of comfort but from generous disdain of the wanton cruelty from which you suffer." And Ballantyne must have been Scott's confidant on some other occasion, when his indignation had been so powerful as to burst out in physical violence, for Scott reminded him: "Remember my breaking the wineglass upon a similar recollection."[79]

"Nothing is perhaps more dangerous," he wrote in later years, "to the future happiness of men of deep thought . . . than the entertaining an early, long, and unfortunate attachment. It frequently sinks so deep into the mind, that it becomes their dream by night and their vision by day—mixes itself with every source of interest and enjoyment; and, when blighted and withered by final disappointment, it seems as if the springs of the spirit had dried up along with it."[80]

Gradually, however, he came to think of Williamina's behavior more gently. Partly, he realized, her ambiguous encouragement had represented a genuine liking, partly a tender if mistaken endeavor to avoid giving him pain. And, partly, too, his unhappiness had been caused by obstacles neither her fault nor his, but the results of the conflict between the emotions and the restraints imposed by the world. "The period," he wrote, "at which love is formed for the first time, and felt most strongly, is seldom that at which there is much prospect of its being brought to a happy issue. The state of artificial society opposes many complicated obstructions to early marriages: and the chance is very great that such obstacles prove insurmountable. In fine, there are few men who do not look back in secret to some period of their youth at which a sincere and early affection was repulsed or betrayed, or became abortive from opposing circumstances."[81]

"Experience makes me alike an enemy to premature marriage and to distant engagements," he wrote in 1817 to a young friend who confided to him a troubled love affair.[82] And two years later, to the same: "What you say of your private feelings . . . is indeed distressing, but assure yourself that *scarce one person out of twenty marries his first love* and scarce one out of twenty of the remainder has cause to rejoice having done so. What we love in these early days is generally rather a fanciful creation of our own than a reality. We build statues of snow and weep when they melt."[83]

Nevertheless, his passion for Williamina Belsches had been deep, and his grief, though buried, remained profound. In no surviving letter does he ever mention Williamina's name again. Even when she had been long dead and he was recalling in the privacy of his *Journal* his first youthful visit to St. Andrews so many years before, his words read: "I remembered the name I then carved in Runic characters on the turf beside the castle-gate, and I asked myself why it should still agitate my heart."[84] After Williamina's marriage to William Forbes, he and Scott served together in the same cavalry regiment and gradually resumed their old companionship, but even then—and though Forbes was to prove a faithful friend during days of crisis—there is no record that Scott ever visited him and his wife in their home. The small world of early nineteenth-century Edinburgh must surely on occasion have brought Scott and Williamina face to face—on the street, in the theater or assembly, in the houses of friends. But in no remaining letter, in no written word, does he anywhere make mention of her or of any meeting.

To his dying day his suffering left its mark upon his entire being. It made his later behavior in love and courtship seem that of a different man. It shaped and colored his rendering of passion both as poet and as novelist; sometimes those who have been burned are able only with restrained and painful effort to portray fire. His young people seldom undergo the dreadful hunger and anguished heartache he himself had so painfully known. And though he is able to delineate an emotion both moving and controlled—as in Frank Osbaldistone's grief when he believes he will never see Diana Vernon again, and in the trancelike and despairing tragedy of Lucy Ashton and Edgar of Ravenswood—his lovers rarely breathe in a world of unbearable pain.

The lonely pride in which Scott recovered from his loss deepened that solitude within which his spirit had always dwelt. Earl Walter, Duns Scotus, Colonel Grogg—all those manifestations of his personality that made him a "roaring boy"—were in their own way real enough; but in the profoundest level of his being he lived alone. Still more important, these years of fruitless devotion made him distrustful of violent emotion, unreined passion, excess. The delicate child from Sandyknowe had hardened himself to the rough competition of the High School Yards. Now the romantic youth hammered himself into the man of reason, emphatic upon the need of subjecting both heart and will to the criticism of the head.

Though in later years Scott would often achieve what other men regarded as impossible, he never again lost sight of reality in pursuing the sirens of the imagination. He learned to comprehend the nature of the attainable and the ways of attaining it. He confronted obstacles with a determination to analyze, understand, and overcome. He became stoical in the great onslaughts of adversity. Monarch of his own mind, "God to aid," he said firmly, "I will not be dethroned by any rebellious passion that may rear its standard against me." "Come, firm Resolve," he quoted Burns—

> Come, firm Resolve, take thou the van,
> Thou stalk of *Carle-Hemp* in man.

His love for Williamina had found him a boy, lyrical, desperate, confused, flashing from blurred ecstasy to misery, from hope to despair. When he had disciplined his pain, it left him a man.

But it also left a wound whose scar never disappeared. "Brokenhearted for two years," he wrote in his *Journal* thirty years later, "—my heart handsomely pieced—but the crack will remain to my dying day."[85] And again, two years later still, "What a romance to tell," he exclaims, "and told I fear it will one day be. And then my three years of dreaming and my two years of wakening will be chronicled doubtless. But the dead will feel no pain."[86]

# PART THREE

*Minstrel of His Clan*

1796 – 1803

# 1

## The Busy Hum of Mankind

### ( 1 7 9 6 – 1 7 9 7 )

DESPITE THE FEARS of his friends, Walter's wretchedness did not
goad him to desperation or violence. He banked down the fires
of his inward heartburning and faced the world with an appearance
of tranquillity. Repelling a brooding self-pity, he forced himself to
carry on his ordinary pursuits and vigorously sought the distraction of
new activities. An observation in one of his novels more than a quarter
of a century later reflects this hard-fought conquest over despair: "Melancholy, even love-melancholy, is not so deeply seated, at least in minds
of a manly and elastic character, as the soft enthusiasts who suffer under
it are fond of believing. It yields to unexpected and striking impressions
. . . to such scenes as create new trains of association, and to the influence of the busy hum of mankind."[1] .

The initial negotiations for publishing Scott's two adaptations from
Bürger had been handled by William Erskine, who told the booksellers
emphatically that a mere indemnity against loss would not do: they
must make an offer.[2] Scott himself was no less independent; the publishers might determine the date of release and perhaps decide on the
title page, but there their dominion ended. "As to expressing in a
preface feelings which I do not feel, apprehensions which I do not apprehend, and motives by which I am no whit moved," that was "all
Blarney" and he would stoop to no such "common place apologies."[3]

Of the advance copies which he received early in that October of
1796 he sent one to Shortreed with another to be presented to Dr.
Elliott, explaining that his presence at Edmonstone's wedding would
make it impossible for him to visit his Liddesdale friends that season.[4]
Four copies he also gave to his old teacher Dugald Stewart,[5] and when

he reached Edinburgh distributed so many to other friends that the booksellers complained of a serious interference with sales.[6] Another copy he sent to William Taylor of Norwich, apologizing for having borrowed from the latter's translation the two lines—the only ones he had heard from that version—which had inspired his own.[7]

His Edinburgh friends greeted his verses enthusiastically. Erskine wrote, "The poems are gorgeous."[8] Stewart sent a laudatory letter; Ramsay of Ochtertyre praised the sound effects and the nature imagery and linked the use of the supernatural with "the magic of Shakespeare."[9] William Taylor found a few passages in "The Chase" too stately or abstractly metaphorical, and queried the accuracy of translation at one point, but commended its spirited rapidity of movement. Of "William and Helen" he said little; "praise might seem hypocrisy—criticism, envy." The entrance of the ghost, however, he thought unsurpassed, and admired the recurrence of

> The scourge is red, the spur drops blood,
> The flashing pebbles flee.[10]

Neither poem is in truth very good. In "William and Helen" the line "And fleet as wind the hazel bush" loses the weird alliteration of "Wie Wirbelwind am Haselbusch," and Scott's

> Let the wind howl through hawthorn bush!
> This night we must away

fails to attain the eerie quality of Bürger's vowels:

> Lass saussen, durch den Hagedorn,
> Lass saussen, Kind, lass saussen.[11]

Another defect of "The Chase," as Taylor noted, is its lingering trace of conventional poetic diction. But "William and Helen" achieves a dawning pre-Wordsworthian simplicity in

> And through the glimmering lattice shone
> The twinkling of the star

which is refreshingly different from stately rhetoric about Hesperus alone in the blue vault of evening and all that elaboration of marmoreal epithet and lifeless personification with which neoclassicism gradually brought about its own glacial death. And the beat of horse hoofs in both poems anticipates the clattering tread that was to ring through *The Lay of the Last Minstrel, Marmion,* and *The Lady of the Lake.*[12]

Financially, the two poems proved a dead loss. In London, at almost the same time, Taylor's translation appeared in the *Monthly Magazine,* and there were others by William Robert Spenser and by the poet laureate, Henry James Pye. England paid little attention, when so many argosies launched by better-known names were crowding the sea, to this tiny cockboat of an unknown Scotsman. A large part of the edition remained in unbound sheets which were later used when John Murray reissued the volume in 1807.[13] But Scott was not upset. He had enhanced his reputation among his own friends; instead of being affronted by the world's indifference he would show it presently that it had neglected something worth notice.[14]

George Constable, his old friend from the days when he had played on the sands at Prestonpans, had made him a gift of *Adelung's Dictionary*, and through Mrs. Scott of Harden he obtained the works of Goethe, Schiller, and many other German authors.[15] Scott's ardor was fanned by the fact that his old teacher Alexander Fraser Tytler had produced a spirited translation of Schiller's *The Robbers*.[16] Walter himself now tackled Maier's *Fust von Stromberg*, Iffland's *The Wards* (*Die Mündel*), and, in October, Schiller's *Conspiracy of Fiesco*. In the course of the next few years he translated all three, as well as Steinsberg's adaptation of Von Babo's *Otto von Wittelsbach* and Goethe's *Goetz von Berlichingen*.[17] These he declaimed to long-suffering friends: "I used to read *Fiesco*," he said years later, "to sobbing and weeping audiences, and no wonder, for whatever may be thought of the translation, the original is sublime." The most thrilling to him, though, was *Goetz*, whose hero is a robber Baron of the Rhine, not unlike a Border chieftain, and who, if not lame, has lost one hand.[18]

Scott achieved a rough and ready success in conveying the spirit of the original, but his cavalier attitude toward grammar resulted in many inaccuracies. And he often guessed at the meanings of words. "Bienenkorb," meaning beehive, he rendered as "where they raised beans," "Arbeit," or work, as "fatigue," "gefangen," caught, as "conquered."[19] "I remember among other comical blunders, I gallantly translated *Glatze* (bald head) into 'glasses,' and made a landlord's drunken customers threaten his crockery instead of his noddle!"[20] His style was often turgid and melodramatic. "They have had time to deliberate, let us take the trouble upon ourselves!" "If we durst but once serve the princes in the same manner who drag our skins over our ears." "The haughty vindictive man! I hate him!"[21] But in these plays Scott found not only an exciting novelty but a hint of how history might be made alive to a modern audience.

Of no little aid in his struggles with the German language was his young kinswoman, Scott of Harden's bride. When they first met, Walter was twenty-four or -five, but looked, she said, much younger. Having known the Courts of Saxony and St. James, Harriet Scott found him provincially awkward and a little bashful but with gleams of sense and spirit that revealed budding genius. She thought of herself as polishing his manners and even correcting his idiom; "The little two dogs," she told him, was not the right word order, and he laughingly accepted her criticism. She was "the first *woman of real fashion*," Scott said, "that *took him up*." When he came from Rosebank to visit her and her husband at Mertoun, he also often met Harden's mother, Lady Diana Scott, the daughter of the last Earl of Marchmont. In her youth she had known the brightest celebrities of the reign of Queen Anne, and delighted in telling anecdotes of those days and giving him reminiscences of Alexander Pope. Scott had the knack of drawing out other people so unobtrusively that they enjoyed feeling how much they knew and how helpful they were being to this modest young man.[22]

Returning near the beginning of November from a visit to Rosebank, in the coach at Kelso he found his old friend James Ballantyne. The dark-haired schoolboy was now a short young man of twenty-seven, with a bull neck and a black beard, a little plump and a little pompous, with one eyebrow drooping and one cocked to heaven. But he was a merry companion and affectionately delighted to run into his former schoolfellow. Having earned but little as a solicitor, Ballantyne admitted, he had allowed himself to be persuaded by some of the local nobility and gentry to establish in the conservative interest a weekly newspaper, the *Kelso Mail*. He was now on his way to Glasgow to buy types.[23]

Ballantyne was soon telling Scott how, on a trip to London to engage correspondents there, he had met the popular dramatist Thomas Holcroft and the famous William Godwin, author of *Political Justice* and that almost feverishly compelling novel *Caleb Williams*. Ballantyne found Scott "what is called *the old man*," full of anecdotes, legendary lore, and ballads. The two went at it torrentially, much to the entertainment of an elderly Quaker who was a fellow passenger. Only after the coach had stopped for midday dinner and they were digesting their meal did their conversation flag. But the Quaker then primed the pump: "I wish, my young friends," he said, "that you would cheer up, and go on with your pleasant songs and tales as before"—and so they resumed, capping story with joke till evening, when the coach rumbled into Edinburgh.[24]

That winter, as before, Scott attended the Outer House, joked around the stoves, and worked conscientiously on those cases that came his way. He and Clerk witnessed the trial of James Mackean, a shoemaker who had murdered the money carrier of a Glasgow bank, almost severing his victim's head from his body by the slash of a razor tied to the end of an iron bolt.[25] Continuing his translations, Scott labored on his rendering of *Otto von Wittelsbach* and began *Fust von Stromberg*.[26] His German studies were warmly aided by a new friend, James Skene, an Aberdeenshire laird four years his junior, just returned from two years in Saxony and now about to be called to the bar. Skene knew German well and possessed a good library of German books. Enthusiastic about literature and art, he also shared Scott's love of horseback exercise.[27]

Of this the two young men were soon to have more than enough. During the previous year, although the French had been defeated in South Germany and forced to retreat through the Black Forest to the upper Rhine, they had triumphed throughout the rest of Europe. In Italy the twenty-seven-year-old Napoleon Bonaparte had defeated the Austrians at Lodi, forced Victor Amadeus to cede Savoy and Nice to France, conquered all Lombardy as far as Mantua, set up the Lombard Republic as a puppet state, and compelled the Pope and the King of Naples to purchase truces by paying enormous blackmail in money and art treasures. France now dominated all the Continent and threatened an invasion of England. Ireland, in fiery rebellion under Wolfe Tone, impatiently awaited the help of an invading force.[28] On December 16, 1796, in fact, a French armada of seventeen ships of the line and twenty-six battleships and transports, carrying an invading force of fifteen thousand troops, set sail from Brest, intending to land them at Cork. This flotilla reached Bantry Bay before being driven back by a gale so violent that no boat could have survived an attempt to land through those lashing waters. Other invasion forces were building up in Holland and Flanders, now called the Batavian Republic, and might strike any time at England, Scotland, or Wales.[29]

The country strained every nerve to meet the danger. Chaotically improvised military forces—Regulars, Militia, Fencibles, Yeomanry, Foreign Auxiliaries, every kind of Volunteer—sprang into being, and began drilling, drumming, and trumpeting.[30] In Edinburgh the idea of a volunteer force of light horse broached almost three years earlier was revived again. Scott's lameness made it impossible for him to serve on foot, but mounted!—all the belligerence of his moss-trooper forebears flamed up in him at the thought. On horseback he could cut and slash with any man. Soon he had fired Skene and a group of other friends with his own glow.[31]

On February 14, 1797, they met in the Royal Exchange Coffee House and proposed forming a body of cavalry. A few days later the newspapers announced that more than sixty gentlemen had volunteered, that regular drills were starting, and that applications to join should be made to Walter Scott, Secretary to the Committee of Management. Their service was to be confined to Mid-Lothian but in the event of actual invasion might extend to all Scotland. This proposal was transmitted to the government through the Duke of Buccleuch, Lord-Lieutenant of Mid-Lothian. In April a letter from His Majesty accepted the offer, authorizing the volunteers to form two troops wearing the royal blue and red, to be called the Royal Edinburgh Volunteer Light Dragoons.[32]

Meanwhile the French sent out an expedition with instructions to burn Bristol and then cross to Wales, march across the mountains, and threaten Chester and Liverpool. This force actually did burn a farmhouse at Ilfracombe, and then, cruising along the coast of Pembrokeshire, landed troops on the beach at the lonely village of Fishguard. They were captured by Lord Cawdor, commanding the Castle Martin Yeomanry, the Cardigan Militia, and the Fishguard Volunteers, but the attempt underscored the importance of being prepared for attack at any point.[33]

On March 15, at a meeting of sixty-six of the eighty members of the Edinburgh Light Dragoons, Scott was unanimously elected quarter-master, secretary, and paymaster, and nine days later he wrote the Duke of Buccleuch that the Corps had almost reached its proposed complement of two troops of fifty men each.[34] They selected as their captain Charles Maitland of Rankeillor, who had been in the army for twenty years and seen service in Gibraltar, Ireland, and the West Indies. There were a first and a second lieutenant, and two cornets or color bearers, one of whom was William Rae and the other William Forbes, who only a few months earlier had been Scott's successful rival for the hand of Williamina. The commission of major was not filled at once, Scott told the Duke of Buccleuch, "as Lieutenant Adams of the Cinque Ports Cavalry does the Corps the honor of acting as their temporary Commandant." Later Captain Maitland became major, William Rae was advanced to captain, and James Skene replaced him as cornet. One of Scott's fellow troopers, with whom he speedily became friendly, was the Duke of Buccleuch's son, the young Earl of Dalkeith.[35]

Like many such volunteer regiments, especially when even those in the rank and file were gentlemen, the Corps was run jointly by the commanding officer and a Committee of Management. The Committee framed regulations, maintained discipline by remonstrance, and imposed or remitted fines. Problem cases were laid before a General Meeting, usually held on parade. Orders of the commanding officer were approved by the Committee and submitted to the entire corps before being issued. It was more like a well-conducted club than a military organization. The members received no compensation, except for £3 a year to make up for deficiencies in their equipment and an allowance of 31s 4d daily for the twenty days spent in quarters at Musselburgh each year. The government did issue their arms and agreed to pay them as regular cavalry whenever they were on active service.[36]

Scott flung himself into all his military duties with enormous zest. He had been made quartermaster purposely to spare him the rough duty of the ranks, but he would accept no special privileges. Long before dawn he roused himself to attend the five o'clock drills made necessary by the fact that most of the members of the Corps had other occupations.[37] At the Botanic Gardens in Leith Walk, or on the sands of Leith when the tide was out, spurring a tall, powerful charger named Lenore —bought for this very purpose—he would gallop furiously at the turnip stuck on top of a staff to represent a Frenchman, and make a violent swipe at it with his saber, shouting, "Cut them down, the villains, cut them down!" or muttering curses at the enemy.[38]

Soon he was one of the most popular men in the Corps. Nobody toiled harder at the severe daily drills, and the order "Sit at ease" was always the signal for a joke from Earl Walter.[39] At parade no one was prouder in full-dress uniform obtained from a regimental tailor at a cost of £22 and of more than peacock splendor—scarlet coat with blue collar and cuffs and silver epaulettes trimmed with silver lace, white-leather breeches, black boots fiercely spurred, and a helmet crested with leopard skin and a red and white hackle.[40]

Some of his friends found his martial ardor a bit ridiculous. "Scott is become the merest trooper that ever was begotten by a drunken dragoon on his trull in a hay-loft," wrote one of them in April. "Not an idea crosses his mind, or a word his lips, that has not an allusion to some damned instrument or evolution of the Cavalry—'Draw your swords—by single files to the right of front—to the left wheel—charge!' After all, he knows little more about wheels and charges than I do about the wheels of Ozokiel, or the Kings of Pelew about charges of horning on six days' date."[41] And back in George Square, as Walter hobbled wearily home from drill, an impish boy named Charles Kirkpatrick Sharpe snickered from a neighboring window at his limping gait in a gorgeous but dusty uniform.[42]

After a fortnight of drilling two or three hours a day, most of the volunteers could perform nearly all the ordinary maneuvers at hard trot and gallop. They had made such progress by May that those passed by Lieutenant Adams were obliged to drill only twice a week.[43] Scott throve on the exercise and gloried in their common devotion to duty. "In case of an invasion," he wrote, "one and all will be the word, unless with some very *black hearted* or *lily livered* rascals indeed."[44]

The danger of invasion was no mere hobgoblin of nervous minds. For on April 16, rebelling against a pay scale on which their families starved and uneatable shipboard rations with weevily biscuits and cheese crawling with long red worms, the sailors of the Channel Fleet at Spithead mutinied. They were joined by the crews of the squadron at Plymouth and by the North Sea Fleet at Yarmouth. England was left almost without naval defenses, while on the Dutch coast at the Texel a force of thirty thousand men were waiting to swoop across the Channel and fall upon its shores. The peril was so ominous that the Admiralty took unprecedented action: they offered the men a royal pardon and a redress of their grievances. Hardly was this mutiny settled when in May there was a renewed outbreak at St. Helens and the crews of all the battleships at the Nore seized their vessels. This was a more incendiary uprising; among the demands of the men was the right to dismiss their own officers.[45]

At the same time rumors were flying through London that the

Household troops had revolted.[46] "There does not seem anything," wrote an alarmed liberal politician in his diary, "to prevent their being masters of the Tower, the Mint, the Palace, and the Cabinet."[47] On the Continent everything was going no less badly. Spain was preparing to invade Portugal—now England's one remaining ally. Napoleon annihilated the ancient Venetian Republic, overran the Papal States, and overwhelmed Genoa. Out of these he created a cluster of satellite "Republics" uneasily administered by collaborators.[48] Despite these blows at home and abroad, the British Government held firm. It refused to yield to the outrageous demands of the mutineers at the Nore, the bulk of the country indignantly rallied to its support, and slowly in the course of June the mutiny collapsed.[49]

But the invasion threat was by no means ended, and among the poor, wartime prices created bitter suffering and unrest. The "militia lists" of those liable for service aroused violent resentment; the rich could buy substitutes and most of the burden fell upon workingmen, who protested in riotous crowds armed with clubs. In Berwickshire that summer, while Scott and his friends were drilling, a mob of several hundred tore the lists out of the hands of two deputy lieutenants. On the evening of August 28 in the little village of Tranent, between Musselburgh and Haddington, a dragoon, trying to force his way through a crowd of colliers, farm laborers, and carters, drew his saber and was pelted with stones. He escaped to Edinburgh, galloping like a madman.

The next day militia were sent to Tranent. To a mild plea from the leaders of the protesting parish the officers returned only an order to disperse. Some county volunteers spurred into the crowd, jeering and brandishing their sabers, and were met with an angry shower of rocks. The troopers charged, slashing right and left; the people resisted, seizing the troopers' bridles and opposing ash saplings to cold steel. Nervous officers gave the order to fire. The peasantry were driven out of the village into the neighboring moors and fields of ripened corn, and unarmed men, women, and boys cut down without mercy.[50]

Four men who escaped the massacre were brought up for trial that October. One of them, Neil Reidpath, a farm laborer, having no counsel, the presiding judge assigned Scott to defend him. He had represented one such client the preceding May. Scott argued that Reidpath had come to Tranent merely to get his name stricken from the militia list because he was above the age; he had been an innocent bystander and had taken no part in the riot. Producing five supporting witnesses, Scott managed to get Reidpath off with a verdict of "not proven."[51]

Throughout the disorders and distractions of the year—both the wound to his own heart and the gigantic events on the international stage—Scott had been energetically advancing his career at the bar.

The drills on Leith sands had far from exhausted him.[52] During the court session extending from October, 1796, to July, 1797, he had represented forty-eight clients and his earnings had leaped to £144 10s—the greatest jump of the five years he had so far been in practice. He could now rate himself as making reasonable if not spectacular progress.[53]

As his own professional activities grew, his father's dwindled and were more and more assumed by Walter's brother Tom. Mr. Scott, now sixty-eight, had suffered a paralytic stroke and was in enfeebled health. Often he could not leave his bedchamber and, a querulous invalid in nightcap and dressing gown, berated his daughter Anne, who served as his nurse, scolding her because he had dropped a glass that she was not by his side to take from his hand, or complaining angrily that the cushions were not comfortably arranged in the easy chair into which she lowered him when he left his bed. His handsome face was drawn and shrunken, his once-bright eyes dimmed, his characteristic censoriousness now an infirm petulance. Sometimes there would be a flashing return to his old decisive energy only to flicker down again like a guttering candle.[54]

The burden of his invalidism fell, of course, mostly upon his wife and upon Anne. Though Walter visited him in his chamber with pity, affection, and respect, and saw him at other times when he was well enough to be up and about, most of the young advocate's day was taken up in attendance at the Court of Session or in drilling with the volunteer dragoons, and his evenings at home were often devoted to reading or translating in his ground-floor den. During the summer and autumn he translated three poems of Goethe's: "The Erl-King,"[55] the fragment "from the Morlachian language" beginning "What yonder glimmers so white on the mountain,"[56] and "Frederick and Alice," a free adaptation of Rugantino's song "Es war ein Buhle frisch genug" from *Claudine von Villa Bella*.[57] Besides these, he plugged away at his translations of German drama. Before the end of the year he completed *The Wards*, *Otto von Wittelsbach*, and *Fust von Stromberg*.[58]

Notebook entries that spring and summer reveal his wide-ranging interests. He jots down reflections on a seventeenth-century murder trial; notes that Delrius explains fairy rings as traces of Witches' Sabbaths; refers to passages in Apuleius and the antiquary Anthony à Wood; records his progress in reading Marlowe's *Dr. Faustus*, Lessing's *Nathan der Weise*, and Gerstenberg's *Die Braut* (a German version of Beaumont and Fletcher's *Maid's Tragedy*); writes a long memorandum on the proper packing of military clothing and supplies needed when he is in quarters at Musselburgh; copies out curious quotations; identifies Andrew Morton, the author of *Everybody's Business is Nobody's Business*, as another *alias* for Daniel Defoe; reads an Elizabethan treatise on political economy; studies an account of military discipline in the armies of the Low Countries.[59] It is a record of insatiable curiosity.

His old friend Charles Kerr, who had been living for some time in Cumberland and grown so enraptured with the lake scenery that he had taken a house at Keswick, wrote Scott letters in which he repeatedly sang its praise. He wondered that his friend devoted so much of his vacations to the Highlands of Scotland; surely he must now be familiar "with every crag and precipice," nay, even all the goats.[60] The Court of Session rose in July, and in August Scott set out with his brother John and Adam Ferguson for a tour of the English lakes.[61]

On the way they stayed a day or two at Hallyards with Adam's father, the philosopher and historian, and while there visited the misshapen dwarf David Ritchie in the little hut he had built himself in the Manor Valley. The ugly little man hated people, but perhaps Scott's lameness conciliated him. He made them stoop through a doorway only three and a half feet high into a low dark room that became eerie when he drew the rusty bolt. Seizing Scott by the wrist, he demanded in grisly tones, "Man, hae ye ony poo'er?"—magical power. As Scott shook his head, a huge black cat leaped into the deep window-bole and stood with arched back silhouetted against the light. "*He* has poo'er," the dwarf said in a grim whisper, and gloatingly repeated it with a horrible grin. Half-bewitched, they sat in dead silence for some minutes. Then Ferguson plucked up courage to ask the dwarf to open the door. Slowly he did so, and as they stumbled out into the daylight Ferguson noted that Scott looked pale and shaken.[62]

A merrier adventure was a call on a neighboring laird whom Scott entertained with antiquarian lore, while among the gooseberry bushes Adam devoured fruit and flirted with one of their host's six pretty daughters. Suddenly, despite Scott's endeavor to keep the father distracted, he awoke to what was going on. With a roar his wrath descended on the swain—not for making love to his daughter, but for plucking and eating his own special gooseberries.[63]

Moving southward, they rode through the Cheviots to Carlisle and its eleventh-century Castle, from which the "bold Buccleuch" had rescued Kinmont Willie in 1596. From there they went on to Penrith, with its view of the Lakeland fells from Penrith Beacon, and Brougham Castle, the seat of the Musgrave family for five hundred years. Then came the winding reaches of Ullswater amid wild overhanging mountains and Hellvellyn towering at the southern end, and after that the wooded banks of Windermere. This was the southernmost point of their excursion, from which, wandering north again, they came to a halt, around the end of August, at the peaceful and sequestered watering place of Gilsland, some eighteen miles northeast of Carlisle.[64]

Here there were several resort hotels for the accommodation of those who desired to take advantage of the sulphur and chalybeate springs or visit Hadrian's Wall and the other Roman remains in the neighborhood. In the evenings Scott was amused by the fashionable and would-be-fashionable guests, the Lady Penelope Penfeathers and the Sir Bingo Binkses of the place; in the daytime he and Adam and John explored the countryside. At their hotel, he soon struck up an acquaintance with a pretty girl and took her to see the Roman wall. They strolled along the fifteen-foot-high structure, explored its turrets and milecastles, and lingered on the grassy slopes of the vallum running south of the massive stonework, flirting with each other while Walter picked her a bouquet of wild flowers and handed her a poem he had composed the night before:

> Take these flowers, which, purple waving,
>     On the ruin'd rampart grew,
> Where, the sons of freedom braving,
>     Rome's imperial standards flew.
>
> Warriors from the breach of danger
>     Pluck no longer laurels there:
> They but yield the passing stranger
>     Wild-flower wreaths for beauty's hair.[65]

But however strong the attraction, it soon yielded to one still more alluring. A week or so later Scott was riding with Adam Ferguson when they saw on horseback a graceful brunette with large dark eyes, pale olive complexion, and silken hair "black as the raven's wing." Fascinated, the two young men followed at a distance, keeping her unobtrusively in sight—or so they flattered themselves—until they were sure that she was one of the guests at their own hotel.

That evening there was a ball next door at the Shaws Hotel. Captain John Scott appeared in all the glory of his scarlet regimentals, and Adam too chose to wear the uniform of the Edinburgh Volunteers. How Walter wished that he also had brought with him those glittering black boots, the white-leather breeches, and that brilliant red coat with its blue trimmings and silver lace! Who would look at a limping young man in civilian dress when there were two soldiers in scarlet? There was some rivalry among the three companions about who should first be presented to the dark beauty of their morning's ride. John and Adam had the pleasure of sweeping her onto the dance floor, where Walter could only watch her supple grace and vivacity. But it was Walter who enjoyed the triumph of taking her into supper after the dance and seeing that he could bring a warmer flush to her cheeks, a brighter glow to her eyes.[66]

# 2

## A Hot Heady Young Man

### (1797)

WALTER WAS SOON SEEING the brown-eyed beauty daily. Of French origin, she still spoke with a marked accent.[1] Her willowy form, her clear olive cheek, her dancing dark eyes, her waving hair, so deep and rich a brown that in candlelight it looked as black as a raven's wing, her arch and teasing vivacity, all captivated him.[2]

Just as there were occasional gaps in the story of Scott's love for Williamina Belsches, there are details here for which the evidence, if there ever was any, has disappeared; but it is possible to put together most of the important facts about the young woman who had so aroused his ardor. Her name was Charlotte Carpenter, anglicized from Charpentier. Both her parents were dead, and she was, or rather she had been, for she was now almost twenty-seven, under the guardianship of the Marquis of Downshire.[3] Here at Gilsland Spa she was one of a party consisting of John Bird, Perpetual Curate of St. Mary's Church in Carlisle, his wife, and Miss Jane Nicolson, a middle-aged lady whom Lord Downshire had chosen as his ward's companion.[4] Miss Nicolson, Walter was told, was a daughter of the Dean of Exeter and granddaughter of Bishop Nicolson of Carlisle, and he gathered that Mr. Bird was her cousin.[5]

Mrs. Bird speedily discovered that young Mr. Scott was acquainted with her friend Major Riddell, who was in command of the regiment that had suppressed the Tranent riots that very August.[6] Walter's uncle, Dr. Rutherford, and his wife were also at Gilsland and soon met the Birds and Miss Nicolson. His new friends were consequently assured of the respectability of his connections and felt no concern about allowing him to pass the time with their pretty young charge.[7]

Miss Carpenter's charm was less that of ideal beauty than of a vivid bloom, a radiant gaiety, a vitality reflected in the changing curves of her face, her moving lips, her dark laughing eyes, the rapid changes of feeling imaged in her expression. Her movements were exquisitely light and buoyant, whether she was circling and sinking on the dance floor or poised proudly on horseback. Walter was enchanted; he could not keep his eyes from her.[8]

Favorite junketings at Gilsland were to drive in a wagonette or four-in-hand to the Roman fortifications at Birdoswald Crags and to Triermain Castle, only two miles from the Spa. There were also nearby walks; the Shaws Hotel stood on the summit of a leafy gorge through which tumbled the little River Irthing, with graded paths by which visitors could descend to the river level and go downstream to the medicinal well or upstream to the rocky and secluded glen. High above the gorge stretched the Roman wall, with a well-trodden path leading up to its breezy heights and a wide view of the country south. Around the hotels flowers glowed in bright beds and graveled walks wriggled through a leafy maze.[9]

Walter had strategy enough to attach himself to Charlotte and her friends on these excursions and was sufficiently adroit to get Charlotte to himself at the curve of a turret along the wall or around the corner of a battlement at the Castle. He escorted her across the gorge, delightedly watching her slippered feet tread the stepping stones between which glided runnels of water, half-hoping she would falter so that he might clasp that light and slender burden in his arms and bear it across the stream. On the other side nestled a glade secluded by cliffs and copsewood, with green turf and gray mossy boulders in the waving shade of a poplar bower. This became their own private retreat, where they were safe from the eyes and ears of others.[10]

Though her admirer could persuade her to these leafy *têtes-à-têtes,* Charlotte was by no means disinclined to the glitter and music of the dance floor.[11] The Shaws Hotel boasted a luxurious ballroom with an adjoining room for whist and cassino and was full of gaiety.[12] In the evenings waxen lights shone against the walls, silver salvers tinkled as the *chasse-café* glided around, and between sets Hessian-booted gallants in elegant pantaloons strolled beside rustling gowns in the blue night air between beds of pallid flowers.[13] Here Charlotte loved to appear in a pink satin décolletée, her slightly powdered hair piled high on her head with ringlets curling at her neck.[14] In this gleaming scene she laughed at Walter's efforts to pay her compliments in stumbling French, and he was apprehensively jealous of his possible rivals: "lordlings and witlings," he called them, "with limbs of lath and kerchief'd chin," boisterous sportsmen following spaniels wiser than themselves, fops trailing their sabers along the ground, "a walking haberdashery of feathers, lace, and furs."[15]

But his dandified rivals did not worry him long; he soon felt that he was making an impression on her heart. Eagerly he intensified his courtship. Although Charlotte had believed at first that she could not bring herself to marry a lame man and told him that he must "forget her," she found herself yielding to her lover's devotion.[16] But still, they had known each other less than three weeks: how could she be sure?— how could she trust in so sudden a passion?[17] For himself, he replied, "I can only protest to you most solemnly that a truer never warmed a mortal's breast." And she herself must allow that from the nature of their acquaintance they were entitled "to judge more absolutely of each other than from a much longer one trammel'd with the usual forms of Life." He had not concealed from her that he had known one previous attachment, but except for that "the feelings I entertain for you have ever been strangers to my bosom."[18]

Walter's plea that three weeks at a resort hotel had given them ample opportunity to know each other was, for all the persuasive smoothness with which he advanced it, of course nonsense. But no more so than many another argument of a young man violently in love; it speaks eloquently of the determination with which he was bent upon his purpose. Williamina had set his mind as well as his heart on thoughts of marriage, and since the blow of her refusal less than a year earlier, these thoughts had never entirely left him. He was now twenty-six; he was anxious to escape from the straitlaced atmosphere of George Square and the petulant domination of his father. This vivacious and radiant girl was like sunlight after darkness; she was warming to his ardor; and she was not beyond his star.

The whirlwind of his desire swept away Charlotte's resistance. Only, she insisted, he must obtain the approval of his parents; nor would she marry without that of Lord Downshire. He must not follow her and Miss Nicolson back to Carlisle, and they must not see each other until they had both had time to reflect. Reluctantly he removed himself to the little village of Cockermouth, in Cumberland.[19] There he struggled with the task of breaking the news to his father and mother. The paralytic stroke Mr. Scott had suffered had left him bedridden and querulous, and Walter guessed that he would disapprove of a foreigner and a stranger, even though she was now a British subject.[20] Nevertheless his son determined to put the best face on it and to make it respectfully clear that he intended to have his own way. He wrote his mother first.[21]

He would ill deserve their care and affection, he said, if he omitted consulting them and availing himself of their advice and instructions about his matrimonial plans. His brother John would describe the lady to them; "without flying into raptures," he would say only "that her temper is sweet and cheerful, her understanding good, and, what I know will give you pleasure, her principles of religion very serious." "Her fortune, though partly dependent upon her Brother, who is high in office at Madras, is very considerable—at present £500 a year." The admission that she was an orphan without relations he followed up with the impressive fact that her guardian was Lord Downshire. She was forsaking for him "prospects much more splendid than what I can offer" and coming to Scotland without a single friend. He would therefore expect her to receive every kindness. "I could write a great deal more upon this subject, but as it is late and I must write to my father I shall restrain myself. . . . Write to me," he concluded, ". . . send me your opinion, your advice, and above all, your *Blessing*."[22]

That same night, September 21, he also wrote to Charlotte. Although his father was in easy circumstances, he told her, since he himself was only the second son in a large family his success in life must depend upon his own exertions. Living at home, he had hitherto given himself little trouble about his private income as long as it took care of his personal expenses. Nevertheless, none of his contemporaries at the bar had far outstripped him, and he was expecting to be appointed a County Sheriff, which would pay him £250 a year and not interfere with but increase his practice. "O how dear these prospects will become to me would my beloved friend but permit me to think she would share them." She must not allow herself to be terrified by the idea of living in Edinburgh or by fears of losing her liberty. They would share its amusements together; "When Care comes we will laugh it away"; and domestic pleasures would repay the loss of freedom.[23]

As his pen raced over the paper that night his desires took fire; no matter what she said he was determined to see her again—in three or four days at the latest—before he had to return to Edinburgh and she left Gilsland for Carlisle. "All Westmoreland and Cumberland shall not detain me a minute longer." "Do not think of bidding me *forget you* when we meet again . . . Adieu—adieu. Souvenez vous de moi—"[24]

On Saturday, September 30, after having spent several rapturous days again in Gilsland, Scott arrived in Jedburgh on his way back to Edinburgh. He put up at the Black Bull Inn that evening in a state of glorious exhilaration. Shortreed must make a night of it with him, "ane o' the daftest nichts we ever had thegither," said that worthy. "She made him sair beside himsel that night. O ye *never* saw a man sae gay and enthusiastic as he was about her. We pledged her health a score o' times I daresay."[25]

But in George Square Walter found no such enthusiasm, only dour distrust. His elders came down upon his head, Mr. Scott, Mrs. Scott, even Uncle Robert. Who *was* this young female? A foreigner! And, what was worse, French! And no family, no information about her family, except an unidentified brother in distant India. Who had her father been? What had been his profession and station in life? What was her brother's name and what was his "high office" at Madras?

What was her connection with Lord Downshire, and how did he come to be her guardian? And serious principles of religion were well and good, but for all they could tell she might even, being French, be a Catholic. In his dazzled ecstasy none of these queries had occurred to Walter, but he was able to reassure them that she had been baptized a member of the Church of England. Though not Presbyterian, this was not so bad as being Catholic.[26]

Rather embarrassed, Walter wrote Charlotte. These details had seemed of so little importance to him, he told her, that he had never even thought about them, "till I felt awkward at not being able to answer my Uncle's questions." She must not think they originated in that pride of family she believed a Scottish characteristic; it was simply that they wanted to know all they could about a young lady "with whose alliance they have a prospect of being honored." But all his assurances still left the point clear: "You must have the goodness to furnish me with some answer to these questions."[27]

While he waited Charlotte's reply Walter escaped his family by going to Rosebank, where he moodily practiced the sword exercise to the astonishment of the local yeoman cavalry and bored himself by fagging at partridge shooting, "breaking fences and wading through stubble."[28] One day he went over to Mertoun with the purpose of enlisting the Scotts of Harden in his cause, but they had guests whose presence made it impossible for him to broach the subject. Was *she*, he wondered, at Allonby, the Birds' country place on the Solway Firth, or was she enjoying the Carlisle Hunt and its attendant balls and assemblies?[29] In his own uneasy solicitude he avoided the Kelso races and balls and was glad that the trial of the Tranent rioters brought him back to Edinburgh on October 9.[30]

A letter from Charlotte crossed that in which he had made his inquiries. She had written Lord Downshire and received his reply that he would be happy to hear from Mr. Scott. Her guardian told her to consult her own heart—"do you believe I had not done it," Charlotte assured her lover, "when I gave you my consent . . . it is very awful to think it is for life, how can I ever laugh after such tremendous thoughts." She was hurt to find that one of his friends thought the match imprudent, and if the word imprudence reigned among his family he must forget her; she had too much pride to think of connecting herself with those who thought her unequal to them.[31]

A fortnight later, Scott had still had no reply to his questions. Anxiously he wrote again. Perhaps she had left Carlisle—perhaps she was not well—perhaps she had forgotten him in the gaieties of the Carlisle Hunt? One after another the worried "perhapses" poured out of him, followed by a more uneasy doubt. Was she angry about his inquiries, or was it painful to answer them? If so, she should hear no more of them. Were her birth the most splendid in Britain it would not raise her in his esteem nor sink her were it otherwise. He "would soothe national or family fancies" if he could, but knew how to despise both. She must not believe "that either *Pride* or *Prudence*" dominated the thoughts of all Scotsmen.[32]

He was already looking, he continued, for a house to take ready-furnished for the first half-year; accommodations would be cheaper in the spring and she would then be able to consult her own taste in furniture. Surely a letter from her must come soon; couldn't he tease her out of her "shall I call it *Laziness*—you write with the same ease and spirit with which you converse and therefore you have no apology." She should have pity upon his anxiety. He hoped they could be together in Edinburgh before the twelfth of next month. "Do not fear but you shall have laughing enough in our ancient Metropolis."[33]

This letter was barely dispatched when he heard from Lord Downshire. Only one further thing need be stated, the Marquis said, to make Walter's proposal perfectly satisfactory: what was his present income and what provision could he make for Miss Carpenter in case of his death? Her good sense and her education were her chief fortune, said his Lordship, to whom her £500 a year seemed no more than a moderate income. In a worldly way, therefore, he continued, she could not expect much, but it was his duty as her friend and guardian to see that she was not left destitute. Her brother, to be sure, who had obtained his post in India through Lord Downshire, and who was doing well there, was very fond of her and would undoubtedly be generous. His Lordship also wished to know Walter's thought about providing for any children that might result from the union.[34]

Hard upon Lord Downshire's letter came a reply from Charlotte. "A very fine chain of *perhaps*" and of "pretty conjectures" he had written her; he excelled "in the art of tormenting" himself. Upon Miss Nicolson's advice, she had been awaiting her guardian's response before answering his "very proper inquiries" about her family. He should remember that when Miss Nicolson offered to give him information he had refused it. She couldn't reply about the house until Lord Downshire had approved the match, "and I believe you are a little out of your senses to imagine I can be in Edinburgh before the 12th of next month." "I am very much flattered by your Mother's rememberance, present my respectful compliments to her. You don't mention your Father in your last *anxious* letter, I hope he is better." She herself had devoted so much time to nursing Miss Nicolson through a violent cold that "I believe *only once* and that quite by accident I thought of you." "I am expecting every day to hear from my Brother, you may tell your Uncle that he is Commercial Resident at Salem, he will find the name in the India list."[35]

The morsel of information about her brother that Charlotte doled out in her very last sentence and her statement that she was waiting for Lord Downshire's reply before supplying more did not reassure Scott's family. This mingling of vagueness and paucity seemed to them to imply that she had something to conceal, and Walter must have insinuated their feeling, for her next letter three days later begins with an outburst of exasperation. "Indeed Mr. Scott I am not at all *pleased* with all this writing, I have told you how much I dislike it, and yet you still persist in asking me to write, and that by return of the Post, O you really are quite out of your senses."[36]

She would not have indulged him had he not hinted "that my silence gives an air of Mystery." There is nothing that can detain her, she continues haughtily, in telling him that her parents were French, of the name of Charpentier, that her father had a place under the Government at Lyons, "where you would find on inquiries that they lived in good repute and on *very good style.*" She had lost her father when very young, "before I could know the value of such a parent," and had been left in the care of Lord Downshire, "who had been his very great friend." Her mother, who died not long afterward, had always desired that she and her brother "should be Educated, and even christen[ed] to the Church of England," and consequently they had been sent to their guardian and come entirely under his care. They had taken the name of Carpenter when her brother went to India "to prevent any little difficulties that might have arrisened" from his having a French name.[37]

"I hope now you are *pleased*, Lord Downshire could have given you every information, he has been acquainted with all my family. You say you almost love him, but until your *almost* comes to a *quite* I cannot love you, O if you knew the hundredth part of his kindness to me . . ."[38] But at the end Charlotte allowed a little burst of pique to escape her again: "Before I conclude this famous Epistle I will give you a little hint that is not to put quite so many *Must*[s] in your letter, it is beginning *rather too soon.*" Then, having slapped his imperatives, she roguishly relented: "But I expect you to mind me, you *must* take care of yourself, you *must* think of me."[39]

Mysteries, however, in Charlotte's family background there were, for all her air of offended frankness. The biographical details she gave Scott were sparse and somewhat disingenuous. Indeed, some of the veils shrouding her origins are still unresolved; how much Charlotte herself knew remains a matter of doubt. Her father, Jean François Charpentier, had in fact held the respectable post of Écuyer du Roi de l'Académie de Lyons, an appointment in which he was Master of the Military Academy. Before that he had been for more than twenty years the controller of the household to the French Embassy at Constantinople.[40] Some time after his return to France, probably around 1769, he had married a young lady much his junior, Élie Charlotte Volère or Vollaire,[41] who is described as beautiful, lively, and accomplished. Charlotte, their first child, was born on December 16, 1770, and baptized Marguerite Charlotte the following day. Her brother, Jean David, who took the name of Charles Carpenter when he entered the service of the East India Company, was born June 15, 1772. Another child, Noël Felicien Marthe, born three years later, seems to have died young.[42]

The long-accepted story, which originated with Scott's son-in-law John Gibson Lockhart, asserts that M. Charpentier, a staunch royalist, foreseeing the Revolution, hedged against it by investing some £4,000 in English securities, including a mortgage on one of the Downshire estates, and died at the beginning of the national turmoil. Thereupon, says Lockhart, "Madame Charpentier made her escape with her children, first to Paris, and then to England, where they found a warm friend and protector in the late Marquis of Downshire, who had, in the course of his travels, formed an intimate acquaintance with the family, and, indeed, spent some time under their roof."[43]

There are details in this account, however, that are certainly erroneous and others that are dubious. No documentary evidence has ever been produced to show that M. Charpentier had any English investments whatever. Mme. Charpentier and her children did not make a last-minute escape from the Revolution; well before it began, in 1785, she was a resident in the parish of St. George's, Hanover Square, London, and Charlotte and her brother were in England perhaps as early as 1784 and certainly in 1787. Their mother, in fact, returned in 1786 to France where she died in 1788, still a year before the Revolution began.[44] And their father, far from having died, as Charlotte implied in her letter to Walter, before she "could know the value of such a parent," is registered as still in charge of his academy in 1785, though at the time of Mme. Charpentier's death she was described as a widow. The story of the mother and her orphaned children fleeing the Terror is thus a melodramatic fiction of Lockhart's.[45]

What led to the Marquis of Downshire becoming the guardian of M. Charpentier's children remains completely unexplained. Scandal has not hesitated, of course, to suggest that he seduced Mme. Charpentier in France and that Charlotte and her brother were his illegitimate children.[46] But there is as little evidence for this tale as for the story of a romantic flight. Lyons, to be sure, in the later decades of the eighteenth century, was aping the polished corruption of Parisian society. Richard Lovell Edgeworth, who came to Lyons in the closing months of 1771 and who boarded with M. Charpentier, portrays the town as "approaching fast to the dissipation and relaxation of morals which prevailed" in the French capital.[47]

But at the same time Edgeworth speaks in the highest terms of M. Charpentier and his wife. Their little daughter Charlotte was a year old; in the course of the almost two years that Edgeworth lived in their household their second child was on the way, and was born while he was still at Lyons. Edgeworth evidently liked and respected both his host and his hostess. They lived "in excellent and cheerful apartments upon the ramparts." M. Charpentier "had seen much of the world, and communicated agreeably what he had seen. . . . Madame Charpentier was young, beautiful, lively, and accomplished, of an excellent disposition, and," Edgeworth adds, "less fond of public amusement than most French women. During nearly two years that I was at Lyons I never had occasion to repent having established myself in her family . . ."[48]

Edgeworth makes no mention of Lord Downshire, nor has any record been discovered of his having been in France prior to 1773. He was born in 1753; at the time Charlotte was conceived he was a youth of sixteen. In 1766 he was at Eton and from there went to Magdalen College, Oxford, where he bore the courtesy title of Lord Fairford, not yet having inherited his father's title. He took his M.A. at Oxford in 1773.[49] Neither his youth, to be sure, nor his not being known to have been in France either in 1770 or in 1771, makes it impossible for him to have been the father of Mme. Charpentier's two children. But neither do they make it more probable.

A further possibility is that at some later time he became Mme. Charpentier's lover. But Charlotte's surviving letters to her guardian, purely respectful in tone, never convey the slightest suggestion that she thought of him as any other than a deeply revered protector. And she possessed a miniature of M. Charpentier, portraying him as a handsome man in a blue coat and powdered hair—with no resemblance to Lord Downshire—which she kept by her bedside to her dying day.[50] It may be, of course, that Lord Downshire concealed her true paternity from her and fostered her innocent belief in her own legitimacy. Painful elements, however, in Charlotte's family history there certainly had been, even though to Richard Lovell Edgeworth all had seemed harmonious. In later years Scott came to realize their existence but refrained from pressing Charlotte for confidences about them: "I never enquired," he told his son-in-law in 1827, but he suspected "domestic distress and disagreement between Made. Charpentier and her husband."[51]

It may easily be, though, that Lord Downshire was quite innocent of their discord. For there was yet another person, whose role is even more shadowy and ambiguous, and who now enters the story. In 1778 Wyrriot Owen, a spendthrift young Welsh landowner on the edge of bankruptcy, granted a mortgage on his property at Great Nash, Pembrokeshire, to a lawyer named George Morgan. And the latter endorsed the deed with a declaration that the money was not his but was held in trust for Madame Élie Charpentier, "wife of the Sieur Charpentier Écuyer du Roi de l'Académie de Lyons." That July, in addition, Owen endorsed to her a bill of exchange on Paris for £250 in English money. The same month he granted a trust conveyance of his estate to his creditors and a year later died unmarried, leaving debts of almost

£26,000. It should be noted, however, that even in 1780, a year after Owen's death, M. and Mme. Charpentier were still living together in Lyons.[52]

Was Owen the seducer of M. Charpentier's young wife, and was he trying to make financial provision for her before he lost his estates? The evidence does not tell, but in 1785 the case went before the Master of Chancery, and in due course he allowed the mortgage but ranked it after the other debts. Mme. Charpentier's children were unaware of all this —there is indeed no evidence that she ever received any money or knew anything of these transactions—and when in 1788 she died at Paris her claim dropped into oblivion.[53]

Nevertheless, Wyrriot Owen's endeavors to provide for Mme. Charpentier make it not beyond all likelihood that it was he, rather than Lord Downshire, who was responsible for breaking up M. Charpentier's family. Whether the injured husband presently became suspicious of the paternity of their children and disowned them as well as his frail wife; whether she fled with the children; whether she had ever lived with Owen; whether, if so, he deserted her or she severed her connection with a man she gradually realized to be a rake and squanderer—all these are conjectures to which we have no answers.

Nor do we know precisely when either she or her children first came to England, nor why Lord Downshire took them under his protection. Charlotte herself said that he had been her father's "very great friend," but when that friendship could have been contracted remains unknown. He was almost thirty years younger than M. Charpentier; close friendships between men past middle age with those much their junior are unusual, and so is the choice of so young a guardian. Be that as it may, having now become Earl of Hillsborough, and having in 1786 married a granddaughter of the first Baron Sandys of Ombersley, he appears as the guardian of Mme. Charpentier's children. And on May 13, 1787, Margaret Charlotte Charpentier and her brother John David, as they were now called, were baptized into the Church of England at St. George's, Hanover Square.[54]

Baptized in the same ceremony with the younger Carpenters, as they were now called, was Antoinette Adelaide Dumergue, daughter of Charles François Dumergue, a surgeon and dentist who had come to England in 1776.[55] His first wife had been a Mlle. Charpentier and was perhaps related to M. Charpentier. Dumergue anglicized his Christian names, became dentist to King George III, and made a great success in London.[56] It may have been Dumergue who brought Mme. Charpentier and her children to England. Certainly he was their warm friend; Charlotte may have lived with the Dumergues in 1784–85, and in 1789–92 she was assuredly a member of the comfortable Dumergue household in New Bond Street. It may be that during the intervening period Charlotte was in France; she is said to have received part of her education at a French convent, and her French accent and imperfect English would not contradict this possibility.

There is a final glimpse of Mme. Charpentier in Paris just before her death in 1788, dwelling in the neighborhood of the Théatre des Italiens on an allowance from Lord Hillsborough. Though still only in her forties she was often ill, and a sympathetic French abbé dropped in every few days to look out for her welfare. She was not managing very well financially; she sent tradesmen to this Abbé de Chazelle, asking him to pay their bills until she received her next remittance from London. She owed the linen draper, the wine merchant, and the upholsterer. The last time she had gone to England she had left owing Chazelle almost 700 francs; she wheedled a watch-chain from him, saying, "I beg you to let me have it for 150 francs," and immediately put it on a watch for her son. She died owing the pitying abbé 332 francs 10 sous.[57]

On March 17, 1789, through the influence of Lord Hillsborough, Mme. Charpentier's son was appointed to a good place in the service of the East India Company, subject to a payment of £200 a year to his sister. He changed his name to Charles and sailed for the Orient. In 1793, on the death of his father, Lord Hillsborough became the second Marquis of Downshire.[58]

There is now another gap in our knowledge of Charlotte's story until 1797, when she reappears with Miss Jane Nicolson as her companion. How this connection came about is not certain. She may have been recommended to Lord Downshire by M. Dumergue, for whom her elder sister, Miss Sarah Nicolson, acted as housekeeper.

In the spring of that year, however, Miss Carpenter had attracted a suitor of whom Miss Nicolson disapproved. She told Lord Downshire; he decided at once that Charlotte should be packed off to see the Lake country. She and Miss Nicolson were accordingly dispatched to Miss Nicolson's cousin Mr. Bird, at Carlisle, with the request that he help them find proper accommodations. Mr. Bird and his family, just leaving for a holiday at Gilsland, invited the two ladies to come with them.[59] There she had caught the eyes of three young Border Scotsmen as she swept dashingly by on horseback. Soon one of them, a blue-eyed, flaxen-polled young lawyer, fell desperately in love with her brown eyes and dark hair.

When they met, Charlotte, like Walter, had thus, although even more recently, undergone the experience of a broken courtship. The only suggestion of how seriously she may have been involved is that Lord Downshire deemed it expedient to remove her from London. As she quizzed and teased her Scottish lover she certainly conveyed no impression of an aching heart. She may well, however, have been eager for emancipation from the control of her vigilant duenna: in one letter she displays a flash of resentment that Miss Nicolson "took so much upon herself."[60] With no very culpable deceit she allowed Scott to believe her several years his junior, though she was in fact eight months older than he. She protested ostentatiously that her pride would not allow her to marry into a family that did not regard her as their equal, but the evasions, omissions, and ambiguities in her account of her own family show that she very much wanted to marry Scott.

If he really believed what he wrote his mother, that for his sake Charlotte was forsaking "prospects much more splendid" than he could offer, he was probably quite mistaken. Her allowance was comfortable, even generous, but it was entirely dependent on her brother, and would not entitle her to expect a dazzling match even were there no doubts about her birth and background. On the other hand, neither was a struggling young advocate any spectacular prize. Scott had not yet made £150 a year and would inherit no more than a fifth share of a moderate fortune. To do Charlotte justice, she was marrying neither money nor genealogical grandeur. But this was a view of the matter that did not commend itself to George Square, a fact that accounts for an occasional slight exasperation in Charlotte's tone. Through her irritations at his family's queries, however, and her assumptions of coyness, it is possible to see a true if not very romantic affection for her lover, and a responsible awareness of how serious was the tie they were contemplating.

Scott did not intend to allow what he regarded as the absurd whims of his family to balk his happiness. "My resolution," he wrote Charlotte, "is *fixed and unalterable*"; if they did not give way he would "leave both them and this country to seek my fortune abroad." He sent her a miniature of himself in his blue and scarlet uniform—"a stranger" whom she will perhaps welcome for his sake—and she sent him a lock of her hair to be braided into a ring.[61] There was also another ringlet she had sent to London to be made into something mysterious, "I believe a Tooth-pick-case," wrote Charlotte mischievously. "I have had almost all my hair cut off."[62] He envied the little packet containing his portrait because it would soon be with her, while he was chained like a galley slave a hundred miles from the love he ardently wished to join. "Soon, *soon* may it be."[63]

In another letter, written before she could have had time to reply, he begged her to forgive him for having importuned her with prayers to join him in November and for having used the unwarrantable word "must." It was only because of his yearning to call her his own "as soon as *prudence propriety* and all these extremely wise matters" would permit; he would try to avoid making her think again that he was " '*really out of my senses*.' "[64] While he waited and longed for her his only pastimes were galloping on Leith Sands and at night making translations from the German—one of which was Goethe's "Erl-King." "Adieu ma belle Amie. Je vous aime toujours."[65]

Writing again, four days later, he apologized for having insisted, at the demand of his parents, on those inquiries she had satisfied "with so much ease and credit to yourself."[66] He had been unable so far to come to any final discussion with his father, whose infirm state made any agitation bad for him. He was very old, affectionate but hot-tempered, and full of those clannish prejudices almost universal in his youth. But Walter was resolute that his father's obstinacy must yield, he said, repeating his words of a few days before. If not, "I am firmly determined to resign my prospects here and seek my fate in the West Indies and my friends well know that if my resolution is taken heaven and earth cannot divert me."[67]

Thanking him for "The *Stranger*," Charlotte could not restrain a troubled outcry. Why had he so many fears? "Have your friends *changed*, pray let me know the truth, they perhaps don't like me *being french*."[68] And in her next letter, "All your apprehensions about your friends makes me very uneasy, at your Father's age prejudices are not easily over-comed, old people you know have so much more *wisdom* and *experience* than we have, that we must be guided by them, if he has an objection on my being french I excuse him with all my heart." And she tried to rally her lover out of his melodramatics about going to the New World: "You talk of going to the West Indies, I am sure your Father, and *Uncle*, says you are a *hot heady* young man." "I must believe that when you have such an Idea you have then determined to think *no more* of me—I begin to repent of having accepted your picture, and . . . will certainly send it to you *back again* if you ever *mention* or even *think* about the West Indies, your family would then *love me* very much, to forsake them for a *Stranger* . . . I think I hear your Uncle calling you a *hot heady* young man, *pray* is it not so."[69]

But Walter did not have to threaten long. No further attempt to persuade his father was needed. The sad old paralytic, straining his poor lips to form his words, withdrew his opposition to the marriage.[70] The victorious lover wrote: "I cannot deny that some of my friends are pleased to think me a little of the *hot-headed* character you describe." His brother the Captain "makes most regular enquiries after you." His sister will be happy to know her. He will convey her "*baisemains a Made. ma Mere.*"[71] It remained only to received word from her guardian: "I am actually *crazy* with impatience to hear from Lord Downshire, surely if he had meant to discountenance my addresses, he would have written instantly."[72]

And, indeed, Lord Downshire proved all complaisance. On November 5 an exultant Walter was on his way to Carlisle.[73] As soon as he had spruced up at the Crown and Mitre he dashed from English Street to the Market Place and hurried up Castle Street to Miss Carpenter's lodgings above Mrs. Palmer's china shop.[74] Charlotte resisted his urgings that they marry at once but agreed to a wedding during the Christmas holidays.[75] For a delirious two days he told her how she would "dance and laugh wi' our bra' Scotch Lassies and Lads."[76] Then he was obliged reluctantly to tear himself away and leave Carlisle for the opening of the Court. "How often," he wrote her, "did I look back upon the towers of its Castle and Abbey till they mixed with the blue sky."[77]

Charlotte had denied his desire for an immediate marriage because her annual allowance from her brother had not yet arrived and her little stock of money was almost exhausted. She had to appeal, in fact, to Lord Downshire for a small advance, so that she might purchase a few things, promising him that she would be very economical.[78] But then her remittance came, an order from Charles Carpenter dated March 16, 1797, making over to her "the whole of my half-commission payable in England on account to the investments for 1796 amounting to Pagodas 2438," as well as any commission he was entitled to as assistant at the Madras depot and as commercial resident at Salem from November 1794 to December 31, 1795.[79] A pagoda had the value of 7s 8d, so that the sum named amounted to more than £860.

Joyfully Walter now announced the forthcoming event to his young aunt, Miss Christian Rutherford. All the difficulties his father had made were melted away. The "main article" of "the uncertainty of her provision" was removed by the assurance that her remittances would be "regular and even larger in the future." The objection of her birth— " 'Can any good thing come out of Nazareth' "—since "it was *birth merely and solely*," had been abandoned. He and Charlotte intended to live in the New Town, he concluded happily, where they would be Miss Chritty's neighbors.[80]

The entire Scott family thawed. Mrs. Scott wrote Charlotte her blessing and sent her husband's love.[81] John and Anne, who had been spending some time at Ashestiel with Colonel Russell and their aunt, and Walter's two other brothers, Tom and Dan, all begged that she keep a corner of her friendship for them. Dr. and Mrs. Rutherford said they would be most happy to render Edinburgh agreeable to their new niece.[82] And presently it was discovered that when Charlotte's brother had first gone out to India he had been intimately acquainted with and in some degree under the charge of Mr. Scott's old friend and relation, Simon Haliburton of Muirhouselaw, who spoke most warmly about Charles.[83] This did a good deal to reconcile Mr. and Mrs. Scott to the match. Charlotte was pleased; "as they are not in *love*, and Scotch," she slyly wrote Lord Downshire, "they hold a great deal to family."[84]

Walter rented from a Mrs. Macleod a small house at 50 George Street for six months at ten guineas a month.[85] His mother found a maidservant who understood marketing and could set down a decent dinner or supper.[86] He hired an odd-job boy named Robert, whom he began drilling in waiting on the table.[87] Mrs. Scott was busy buying linens and cutting tablecloths,[88] and Walter purchased a few spoons, teaspoons, and other articles of plate.[89] Their little establishment, he wrote Charlotte, had a pleasant drawing room communicating by a glass door with a small parlor that would be his office and study. The glass they could cover with green baize, so that his conferences with his clerk would not disturb her. The two bedrooms were small, and the main one rather inconveniently opened off the dining room. "The servants' accommodations are very bad a bed [room] off the kitchen for the maid and a kind of Cockloft for the Man Servant to which he ascends by a ladder—if the House was on fire little Robert would be roasted like a Tod in a Hole."[90]

On November 21, Scott moved into the house and excitedly wrote from there. "Look at the *date* my dear Charlotte, pray look at the date and tell me where I am got to now."[91] The drawing room was in a state of glorious confusion: a venerable law book lying in one corner with an old Scotch song stuck between its dusty pages, a volume of German plays in another with a brief for a bookmark, the fireplace blocked off by a bed and bedding, over which were flung a lawyer's gown and coif, a light dragoon's helmet, and a saber, two young lawyer friends playing piquet and impatient to attack the bread and cheese, porter, biscuits, and wine that Walter had gotten in as provisions.[92]

For economy's sake he had sold his servant's horse but hoped Charlotte wouldn't think it extravagant for him to keep Lenore and remain in the cavalry. It involved some expense, he told Charlotte, but gave him access to the Duke of Buccleuch and others who might be useful, and the service was a little *Stylish*.[93] "How very *angry* I should be with you," she wrote back, "if you was to part with Lenore." Did he really believe anything involving his health and pleasure an unnecessary expense? And "I am very glad you don't give up the Cavalry, as I love any thing that is *stylish*."[94] She is pleased that his friends already come to see him in their new house: "I hope I shall not frighten them away, I love those *sans ceremonie* visits"; but she hopes he "will not be so vulgar as to eat, that is if you are in Love."[95]

The marriage contract, settling upon Charlotte and her children whatever she had from her brother, had now been drawn up and sent to Lord Downshire for his approval.[96] Although Scott's father had at first been unwilling even to discuss giving them any financial aid, he was now very impatient to meet Charlotte, and his son thought he would probably give them enough to buy a comfortable house, which would save more than five per cent in rent.[97] His paralytic disorder, however, made it impossible to press him for a specific commitment. If they bought a house, Walter intended that the title should be to his wife and himself and the survivor in liferent and then to their children in fee.[98]

Charlotte felt happy to hear that his father was better pleased about money matters but added generously that Walter must not let that trifle disturb him.[99] He said stoutly that they would do very well; they had enough to live on "and I really do not think I was born to stick in the world."[100] Charlotte was gayly confident that he was right: "I have no doubt but that you will rise very high and be a *great rich man*."[101]

Almost every day now saw their domestic preparations more complete. He should not buy any more silver, Charlotte wrote him; "I find I am very likely to get mine over, which will be quite sufficient for our use and ornament."[102] She was also sending by wagon a box containing a tea set of French china and "two or three boxes as *avant couriers*."[103] Her friends the Dumergues gave them a handsome teapot, Lord Downshire sent her a beautiful shawl, and Walter's Uncle Robert took it into his head to dispatch them a cargo of pickled pork.[104] And, finally, James Skene had been able to provide stabling for Lenore in his mother's coach house around the corner in South Castle Street, where there would even be room to accommodate a chaise or phaeton for Charlotte.[105]

More congratulations poured in. In the Outer House, Scott's legal brethren of The Mountain greeted him with jokes and compliments, which he bore with the unblushing "indifference of an iron-browed Lawyer."[106] The Scotts of Harden sent their good wishes.[107] Mr. Haliburton paid a call. In the south of Scotland, Walter told Charlotte, he would show her the Haliburtons' burial place, at Dryburgh, "now all that remains to my father of a very handsome property" and "one of the most beautiful and romantic scenes you ever saw, among the ruins of an old Abbey. When I die, Charlotte, you must carry my bones to be laid there—but we shall have many happy days before that I hope."[108]

"What an idea of yours, was that," Charlotte flashed back, "to mention ware you wish to have your *bones laid*, if you was married I should think you was tired of me, a very pretty compliment *before Marriage* . . . if you have always those *cheerful* thoughts, how very *pleasant* and *gay* you must be.—Adieu my dearest friend if you love me take care of yourself as I have *no wish* that you should visit that romantic and beautiful scene the burying place, that will not be any temptation to me I can assure you."[109]

Walter dutifully responded with gaiety. He would teach her to dance reels and strathspeys and make her a little Scottish woman in everything but obliging her to eat haggis and sheepsheads. "I will give you a lesson from a Scotch song which has become a great favorite of mine . . .

> O she has left her costly gown
>> Made of the silk and satin
> And she has put on the Tartan Plaid
>> To dance among the Bracken
> She would not have an English Lord
>> Nor be a Lowland Lady
> But she is away wi' Duncan Graeme
>> And he had wrapped her in his plaidie.

In about three weeks I think I shall wrap you in *my Tartan plaid* and call myself the happiest of human beings—O I will be so good to my little stranger and love her *so dearly*."[110]

In another letter he says, "I admire of all things your laughing Philosophy and shall certainly be your pupil in learning to take a gay view of human life."[111] Together they will banish *tristesse* and live by her *gaieté de coeur*. "I shall endeavor to brush up my French in order to do honour to my lovely Mistress. I must remember it is your mother tongue and that will give it double charms to me." He will teach her Italian, in which he knows he will have a charming scholar, although it is so long since he has studied it himself that he fears he will be ill qualified as a teacher. "Addio! addio! Carissima Carlotta mia—being your first Italian lesson . . ."[112] "Etudiez votre francais," Charlotte writes, "I have a french grammar for you, remember you are to teach me Italian in return and call forth for all your patience I shall be but a stupid scholar."[113]

The wedding day was now rapidly approaching. Mr. Scott was too unwell to travel to Carlisle; he had become, Scott told Charlotte, no more than "the shadow of what he was a year ago."[114] His wife and Anne would be obliged to remain in George Square to take care of him.[115] John, however, would be happy to come and see his brother married. When the bridal party reached Edinburgh Charlotte could go directly to her own house in George Street, where Mrs. Scott would either receive her or wait upon her immediately after her arrival.[116]

But Charlotte begged Scott "to contrive matters so as we may not see any one, not even any of your family, the evening we get home, we shall be so tired, and such figures that I should not appear to *advantage*." And she insisted that she would prefer the ceremony to be entirely private. "I do not see the necessity of your Brother's coming, it would give him a great deal of trouble, and would really distress me."[117] Scott agreed not to bring John if she did not wish it but suggested that she consult Mr. Bird or Miss Nicolson to make sure that all legal requirements were being complied with. There must be some gentleman present "to give you away," and there had to be two witnesses at even "the most private ceremony."[118]

Lord Downshire also proved unable to attend the wedding. He was Lord Lieutenant of County Down, and inflammatory troubles there made it impossible for him to leave.[119] Charlotte was anxious about him; "I am always unhappy," she wrote, "while he is in Ireland."[120] But he sent his warmest good wishes and a gold watch as a wedding present to Scott.[121]

As the day drew near Scott's impatience grew almost ungovernable. The weather had turned bitterly cold and he worried lest his *pauvre petite* feel chilled among his bleak northern hills. He offered to bring her muffs and tippets,[122] but she replied that she was well provided with these comfortable things.[123] "Have you any furred shoes? if not you must allow me to take care of your poor little feet," Scott wrote anxiously. ". . . All our Scottish Nymphs use them in travelling. Indeed I wish you to be as much dressed in fur as possible, quite *à la Russe*."[124] He hoped, too, that they would have a sunshiny day for their homeward journey. "*My own* Scotland will not appear quite so savage as perhaps Charlotte expects. To say the truth It does look a good deal the better of sunshine for we have some tolerably Bleak country to pass thro'. Were it Summer I could take you a more pleasant route but in Winter the shortest road is the pleasantest."[125]

Charlotte was in state of nervous tension. "I would give a good deal if it was all over," she confessed, "I really dread the time don't think it is from want of *Love* that I say it, but a thousand fears—"[126] "O my dear Scott, on that day, I shall be yours *forever*, does not that sound very awful—"[127] "Dear Dear Charlotte," he returned tenderly, "how I adore you. Did you ever know a Man go mad with joy. O how slow I shall think my motions."[128]

He set out by the coach that left Edinburgh at midnight Tuesday, December 19. It was a fast day, and the George Square folks would have though him driving posthaste to the Devil if he had started on a journey before the clock tolled twelve.[129] He would get to Carlisle the next night; the return journey they would make in a more leisurely two days, stopping to sleep at Selkirk.[130]

The wedding took place on Sunday, December 24, 1797, in St. Mary's Church in Carlisle. The ceremony was performed by Mr. Brown, a minor canon of the Cathedral, and witnessed by John Bird and Jane Nicolson.[131] Through clouds the winter sun shone coldly on the Cathedral and on the bride's lodgings in nearby Castle Street. A snow storm was threatening, and the newly married couple hastily took their places in the stagecoach that was to carry them north to their future home.[132]

## 3

---

# Two Ballads to Begin the
# World Upon

## (1797–1800)

T HE DRIVING INTENSITY of the letters Scott tore off to his bride-to-
be during their headlong three months' courtship leaves no doubt
of the strength of his passion. They reveal, it is true, none of the
lyrical mysticism of Dante's ethereal devotion to Beatrice and none of
the sorcery that leaves the pale victims of La Belle Dame Sans Merci
wandering on the cold hillside—perhaps the very qualities in his tremulous and timid worship of Williamina Belsches that helped foredoom
his yearning. In their stead he looses the banner of a warm-blooded
impetuosity determined not to die for love but to conquer.

He had known that his family would oppose the match on which
he had fixed his will and that their prejudice would find reasons—of
prudence, of propriety—that he would have to batter down. When his
youthful walking companions had asked him where they should walk
and then decided to go somewhere else, he had broken away from them
all rather than yield. Now, if his family did not surrender, he would
break away from them—if need be, even from Scotland. In childhood
he had rebelled against circumstance and refused to be made a helpless
cripple by his lame foot. Now, rebelling against circumstance once more,
he set his heart upon romantic love, not with the romanticism that
wanders into despair, but with a romanticism indomitably bent to achieve
its aim. He had no doubts of Charlotte's love, and deep down he may
have felt that the affection beneath his father's crustiness and the tenderness that made his mother still call him "Wattie, my lamb" could not
hold out against him. Nevertheless he had been forced to fight for his
heart's choice, and he had gloriously won. Radiant with joy, he returned
to Edinburgh with his bride.

He was right about Charlotte. For all her light coquetry and teasing raillery she did love him and she had not married him merely to achieve a settlement in life. Realistic, perhaps even a little prosaic, she had no lofty sentiments, but she was not shallow, and she brought to her husband both a true devotion and a sense of duty. She loved Mr. and Mrs. Bird, she told him, because he was such a great favorite of theirs. She was gay, good-humored, agreeable, with a liveliness sometimes attaining wit. She had had no training in running a household: "It is very unlucky," she warned Scott, "that you are such a bad Housekeeper as I am *no better*, I shall try and I hope I shall improve."[1] She did both; although not very economical, she learned to set a good table and with French neatness kept an immaculate and comfortable home. She herself carefully cut her husband's hair; she made copies of his poems for him in her delicate handwriting; she saw that the fire in his study was cheerfully burning. When he was working, she often looked in with affectionate inquiries about his comfort and his progress.[2] She did not always understand him when he spoke of literature or his legal activities, but she listened warmly, responding with sympathy for any setback and with joy for his triumphs.[3]

With what anxiety, the day after their arrival in Edinburgh, she arranged her dark hair, put on her most attractive bonnet, and arrayed her trim figure in her most soberly appealing gown for the ordeal of meeting the family in George Square. But the invalid father welcomed her with his old-fashioned courtesy, Walter's mother was her kind and gentle self, his brothers were charmed by her brown eyes and gay grace, and Anne soon took her into her warm affection.[4] Mr. and Mrs. Scott were perhaps not so rapidly enchanted as their children by Charlotte's piquant face and her desire to please, but they too came to feel that, however hasty, their son's choice was not so unwise as they had feared. One of Charlotte's ways, however, did not go uncriticized. Her George Street landlady felt scandalized that her *Southron* lodger sat in her drawing room daily instead of reserving it exclusively for solemn holidays; and when Charlotte laughingly reported this to Mrs. Scott she had the surprise of perceiving that her mother-in-law agreed with the thrifty old dame.[5]

Among Scott's friends his attractive bride was welcomed with delight. The young advocates of The Mountain enjoyed coming to her little suppers and spending the evening, as they had done with Erskine and his sister before her marriage took her away from Edinburgh.[6] Charlotte's arrival, too, partly made up for the departure of Jane Cranstoun, who had been married the previous June to an Austrian nobleman, Godfrey Wenceslaus, Count of Purgstall, and had gone off with him to his Styrian estates.[7] Lawyers' jokes and lighthearted mimicry of the eccentricities of the Lords of Session were soon familiar entertainment to Charlotte. But what she enjoyed even more were the weekly suppers of the officers in the Light Dragoons, who had inaugurated an informal dining club and met once a week in rotation at one another's houses. She loved the bright scarlet and blue-trimmed uniforms with their silver lace and epaulettes, as she did anything *stylish*, and loved being toasted in gleaming wineglasses by gallant young men.[8]

From her ancient castle at Hainfeld the enthusiastic new Countess of Purgstall sent affectionate congratulations on Earl Walter's marriage. "You will imagine," Jane exclaimed, "how my heart burst within me, my dear, dear friend, while I read your thrice welcome letter. Had all the gods and goddesses, from Saturn to La Liberté, laid their heads together, they could not have presented me with anything that so accorded with my fondest wishes." She rejoiced that he was happy and that she was not forgotten—how she wished Schloss Reggersburg opened on Parliament Square or that she could steal Jack the Giant-Queller's shoes and kidnap them all snug in her old hall! "And is it then true, my God, that Earl Walter is a Benedick and that I am in Styria? Well, bless us all, prays the separated from her brethren, J. A. P."[9]

Scott and Erskine enjoyed the theater, and Charlotte too was so passionately devoted to its glitter that three or four times every month saw them at the playhouse.[10] Charlotte set off her figure smartly in elegant gowns and wore hats in the latest style which she had her friend Miss Dumergue send her from London. "If feathers are also worn in London," she wrote, "I shall be very glad to have one of the most fashionable."[11] She also proved one of the best lady whips in Edinburgh and could both sit a horse well and drive with dash.[12] Scott felt proud of her taste and rejoiced in her success.

On February 16, Edinburgh celebrated the great naval victory of Camperdown, which had smashed the French fleet the previous October and ended the menace of an invasion from the North Sea. All the windows of the heroic Admiral Duncan, who resided in George Square, were illumined with transparencies of battleships with colors flying. The volunteer regiments, including the Light Dragoons, with Scott among them, marched around the Square, drums beating and pipes squealing, filing out through Windmill Street. Thence, still tumultuous, they paraded along South Bridge, spanning the Cowgate, and North Bridge, and, turning into Princes Street, wound through the streets of New Town, returning to draw up finally before the Castle. The festal climax was an entertainment at Fortune's Tavern, attended by the Duke of Buccleuch and his two sons, the young Earl of Dalkeith and Lord Montagu.[13]

In London during the spring William Erskine met Matthew Gregory Lewis, author of *Ambrosio, or The Monk*, a horrendous Gothic romance of diabolic possession and damnation that readers devoured with appalled fascination. "Monk" Lewis had become an indulged darling in the most glittering circles of Mayfair and blossomed into an ornately dressed little dandy elated by his intimacy with dukes and duchesses. He was now beating up in all quarters for contributions to a poetic miscellany of the horrible and marvelous, to be entitled *Tales of Terror* and filled with the most blood-curdling evocations of vampires, succubi, and demons. Erskine showed him Scott's versions of "Lenore" and "The Wild Huntsman," and told him that Scott had translated other examples of German *diablerie*.[14] Lewis eagerly requested that Scott contribute to his "hobgoblin repast."[15]

Even though all the contents would appear anonymously, Scott was happy to oblige, offering in addition his version of the "Lied von Treue," his ghostly ballad from "Claudine," and some ancient Scots ballads, including one "of a young Knight carried off by the Elfin Queene."[16] Gratefully acknowledging the young author's compliance, Lewis explained his plan. Ancient ballads as well as modern were to be included —"Sir Gawaine's Foul Ladye and the Ghost that came to Margaret's door and tirled at the pin"—whatever involved witches, ghosts, and spectral shivers. He could not use the "Lied von Treue" or the Goethe, but he would welcome the other "*marvellous* traditionary ballads." He expected, he wrote Scott, to visit Edinburgh soon and should then request the opportunity to thank him in person.[17] Early that summer Scott proudly received an invitation to dine with Lewis at his hotel. To his fame as a novelist Lewis added no little reputation as the author of macabre ballads, such as "Durandarte" and "Alonzo the Brave and the Fair Imogen." He was the first writer of any widely acknowledged standing Scott had met since as a boy of sixteen he had gazed across the room at Robert Burns.[18]

The person whom he now saw, though perfectly well shaped, was the tiniest man he had ever beheld, a boyish figure with diminutive hands and feet. His small body was richly clad in garments of an extravagant foppery, he had queer protruding bug-eyes, he constantly dropped the titles of the noblemen and women among whom he moved as if they tasted sweet on his tongue. Scott was astounded. "You would have sworn he had been a *parvenu* of yesterday," he exclaimed, "yet he had lived all his life in good society."[19]

But Lewis's faults were only ridiculous ones, Scott found; he was good-natured and generous. He asked about his guest's literary projects, and Scott mentioned his translations of German drama. He had turned out completed versions of no fewer than five plays, including the recently finished *Goetz*, and was now engaged on Lessing's *Emilia Galotti*. He had suggested to the booksellers Cadell and Davies that these works form the first two volumes of a twelve-volume collection of the German theater that he was ready to undertake, but they had turned down the proposal.[20] Lewis immediately volunteered to find a London publisher for *Goetz of Berlichingen*.[21]

Edinburgh lionized the unreluctant celebrity in a swirl of receptions. Lady Charlotte Campbell, the lovely daughter of the even lovelier Elizabeth Gunning, gave parties for him.[22] "The angels might come down," Lewis wrote Tom Moore, "and beg Lady Charlotte Campbell to take them to sup with us."[23] There was a coruscation of dinners, entertainments, musicales, balls. One evening at Dalkeith, Scott saw a portrait of Lewis passed around among the guests. The artist had picturesquely flung about the figure a shadowy mantle, the folds half-hiding a dagger from the light of a dark lantern. Everyone affirmed it a good likeness except the Duke of Buccleuch, who said loudly. "Like Mat Lewis? Why that picture's like a MAN!" He looked around, and saw Lewis's head at his elbow.[24]

While the little novelist was in Scotland the Light Dragoons went into summer quarters in the fishing village of Musselburgh for their annual fortnight of training. Scott invited Lewis to visit him there for a couple of days. As quartermaster, he had planned all the billeting and provided for the forage. Members of the troop were required to mess together for breakfast, dinner, and supper, but were billeted either in lodgings or in the homes of friends. Scott's amusement at his ancient landlady's colloquies with the local fishwomen and his delight in their dialect much astonished his dandyish guest.[25] Lewis, however, was as excited as Scott when, one day before dinner, James Skene gave them a spirited recitation of Schubart's "Kap'lied":

> Auf, auf! ihr Brüder, und seid Stark,
> Der Abschiedstag ist da!

Next morning Scott showed them his own War-Song, scribbled by candlelight the night before:

> To horse! to horse! the standard flies,
> The bugles sound the call;
> The Gallic navy stems the seas,
> The voice of battle's on the breeze,
> Arouse ye, one and all![26]

There were nine more tirelessly patriotic stanzas. The dragoons, loyal to their quartermaster, praised it and adopted it as their official song, but in their hearts it never took the place of "Hey! Johnny Cope."[27]

Scott enjoyed, as much as ever, swashbuckling in uniform and galloping black Lenore on the sands of Musselburgh. At the end of the fortnight's training, there was a full-dress review at which the corps presented an elegant silver cup to their commanding officer. The magistrates of Musselburgh gave a public dinner to the dragoons. Scott was praised for the efficiency of his arrangements. The entire corps had probably enjoyed the fortnight too; the wine consumption of the eighty odd men came to fourteen hundred bottles. Mid-July brought an annual inspection, and there was a grand field day at Drylaw Mains in October to look forward to.[28]

For the summer of 1798 Scott had rented a small thatched cottage at Lasswade, on the winding banks of the River Esk. Though no more than six miles from Edinburgh, the place was entirely rural. The little dwelling was comfortable and inexpensive—thirty pounds a year—with paddocks for Scott's mare Lenore and a cow, and with vegetable and flower gardens commanding a beautiful view. Downstairs there were a spacious dining room and a small room Scott called his oratory; upstairs, under the thatch, their bedroom.[29] Charlotte was waiting the birth of their first child—expected in October—and Scott kept busy writing and amused himself planting honeysuckle and roses.[30] Never was he prouder of his handiwork than when he had linked two crooked trees to form an ivy-twined archway at the entrance from the road. That evening, accompanied by his dog Camp, half black-and-tan terrier, half bulldog, he and Charlotte strolled arm in arm between the pink hawthorns on the path that led to Hawthornden.[31]

All up and down the Esk were sprinkled the country places of friends. Farthest away, at Penicuik, was the seat of Sir John Clerk, whose property included the Lasswade cottage. In the same neighborhood, Auchendinny, the villa of the novelist Henry Mackenzie, nestled in its hazel shade. Nearer Lasswade, on the south bank of the stream, just across from Roslin Castle, lay "haunted Woodhouselee," once the property of Hamilton of Bothwellhaugh, the assassin of the Regent Morton, now the home of Scott's old history teacher Alexander Fraser Tytler. Little more than half a mile from Scott's cottage, in a grove of beeches, rose Melville Castle, the estate of Henry Dundas, whose son had been one of Walter's schoolmates, and who as the great colleague of William Pitt, the Prime Minister, virtually ruled Scotland. And no great distance down the Esk, in its magnificent park, stood the impressive if heavy pile of Dalkeith Palace, the residence of Scott's fellow dragoon the Earl of Dalkeith.[32] "We have a great many neighbors," Charlotte wrote Lord Downshire, "by whom we are much visited." When they returned here next spring she added, Scott expected to have a second horse and she could take to riding again, after the birth of the baby.[33]

At Dalkeith, Scott struck up a happy friendship with the Duke of Buccleuch's sister, the witty Lady Frances, wife of Archibald, Baron Douglas.[34] Now just turned fifty, in childhood she had been the pet of her blazingly brilliant stepfather Charles Townshend and had grown from a wise, merry little girl to a clever and charming though by no means pretty woman. She laughed at her own diminutive figure and in youth had replied to an admirer:

> Your eyesight!—but no more of that!
> For what though I be short and fat
>      If you believe me tall?
> If love can change grey eyes to blue
> I need not rail, where thanks are due,
>      Nor Cupid blear-eyed call.[35]

"Quite the ugly old woman of a fairy tale," Scott said, she "had still the air d'une grande dame—there was no mistaking her for the hen-wife even in a check apron but you might have supposed her a Banshee in disguise. . . ." He soon admired her as an "accomplished lady, one of the wittiest best humoured and most sensible women."

Another guest at Dalkeith was Lady Douglas's favorite cousin, Lady Louisa Stuart.[36] The daughter of the Earl of Bute and granddaughter of Lady Mary Wortley Montagu, Lady Louisa had learned literary taste from her father's great library at Luton Hoo, loved Clarendon and Plutarch, read French, Spanish, and Portuguese, knew all the intimate history of the past hundred years, and scribbled verses and witty prose in secret. Though she shared the romantic enthusiasm for wild and beautiful landscape, her ironic mind derided the romantic cult of sentimentality.[37] "Madame de Staël," she wrote, "defied any one to express 'le sentiment' in English. We may have no word corresponding, but we have a phrase '*All my eye and Betty Martin.*' "[38] But Scott soon found that Lady Louisa, despite her sharp wit, was swift and warm in friendship, and formed with her a tie of lifelong affection.

While the corn yellowed in the fields and apples reddened on the bough, Scott began his first original ballads.[39] "The Fire-king" he turned out as another ballad for Lewis's miscellany. "Glenfinlas"—the Glen of the Green Women—was based on a Highland legend of two hunters benighted in a solitary hut, or *bothy*. Merry over their venison and whiskey, one young man wished that the party might include some pretty lasses. Instantly two beautiful damsels clad in green glided in, singing and dancing. One hunter was seduced into leaving the hut; the other distrustfully resisted his siren. Day came; the enchantress in the *bothy* vanished. Searching in the forest for his friend, all that the hunter could find were his gnawed and scattered bones.[40]

Scott's versification is melodious, and there are a few stanzas of fair landscape description—

> The moon, half-hid in silvery flakes,
>      Afar her dubious radiance shed,
> Quivering on Katrine's distant lakes,
>      And resting on Benledi's head—

but the story is spun too thin and moves too slowly. And at the end the shower of blood, the mangled arm, and torn-off head fail to achieve their intended horror. The straightforward prose introduction to the poem, in which Scott told of the young hunter's wish for a couple of pretty girls, is superior to the elaboration of the poem and Lord Ronald's overluscious imagery:

> What lack we here to crown our bliss,
>> While thus the pulse of joy beats high?
> What, but fair woman's yielding kiss,
>> Her panting breath and melting eye?[41]

"The Eve of St. John" has Smailholm for its central scene.[42] Since Scott's childhood at Sandyknowe the old peel tower had grown even more ruinous. Vandals had torn away its iron-grated door, thrown it on the rocks below, and damaged the interior. On a visit to Mertoun that autumn he asked its owner, Scott of Harden, to arrest these depredations, and his kinsman jestingly demanded a ballad in return.[43] The story, once more, is supernatural: a lover slain by a jealous husband, returning from his bloody grave to a midnight tryst with the adulterous wife, brands her wrist with the red-hot grasp of his hand.[44] Scott tells it with more speed and power than he had brought to "Glenfinlas," and his language is nervous and concrete:

> The bittern clamour'd from the moss,
>> The wind blew loud and shrill.[45]

The irregular accents, however, are sometimes handled so clumsily that the reader is thrown out of the saddle and has to pick himself up and mount again; there are lines of which *no* reading satisfies the ear. The emotional impact, too, is partly spoiled, near the close, by the spectral lover's moralizing on murder and lawless passion.

An unfinished ballad "The Gray Brother" starts out well but quickly goes astray.[46] Its pace is more rapid than that of "Glenfinlas," its rhythms more skillful than those of "The Eve of St. John." But there is something ludicrous about a pilgrim reaching Rome after forty days of penitential travel only to turn right around the very morning of his arrival and journey back to Scotland again. And from the first publication of the poem it has been remarked that the lyrical descriptions of the valley of the Esk are irrelevant and out of tone with the gloomy theme. They are, in fact, hardly more than a poetic postal directory of the neighbors whose hospitality Scott had been enjoying that summer.[47]

Scott had sent one of his German translations and a copy of his War Song to Jane Purgstall and told her at the same time that he and Charlotte were expecting a child. "I cannot tell you," she replied, "how happy your little translation and eke your March made us. . . . Write! Write! It is a duty you owe your talents."[48] And, of the child: "What sort of a genius he will be, is a very anxious speculation indeed; whether the philosopher, the lawyer, the antiquary, the poet, or the hero will prevail—the spirit whispers unto me a happy *mélange* of the two last—

he will lisp in numbers and Kick at la *Nourrice*."[49] "Present my fondest wishes to his Honour; and don't, we pray, give him a name out of the List of Round Table Knights, but some simple Xian appellation from the House of Harden."[50]

In October, Scott and Charlotte were back in Edinburgh, no longer in George Street, but in a house he had rented at 10 South Castle Street.[51] Here, on the fourteenth, Charlotte gave birth to a boy, and a letter was sent off to the Marquis of Downshire asking him to be the child's godfather.[52] But the following day the baby died. Charlotte was still very ill when Lord Downshire's congratulations and acceptance of the office were followed by letters of sympathy to both parents for their loss.[53] "I have been most kindly taken care of by all Scott's family," Charlotte replied; "his Mother could not have had more tenderness for her own daughter than she had for me and I was also attended by Dr. Rutherford with the utmost attention and kindness. I cannot say enough of their goodness." Within two or three days she was to be allowed to go out for an airing and hoped soon to be restored to health.[54]

During the autumn Scott showed his new poems to all his friends. He now felt himself "set up for a poet," he said humorously, "like a pedler who has got two ballads to begin the world upon"; and he showed his precious wares "requesting criticism—a boon which no author asks in vain."[55] He also sent copies to Matthew Gregory Lewis in London.[56] His friends' responses surprised him. One reader disliked precisely the lines another admired. In vain he "cut and carved, tinkered and coopered"; in vain "he placed, displaced, replaced, and misplaced." Everybody was displeased by the concessions made to others, and Scott found himself blamed "for having made two holes in attempting to patch up one."[57] Lewis's criticisms were the most stringent of all.[58] A martinet about accuracy of rhyme and rhythm, he took sharp exception to bumpy lines and complained about such pairings as "choir" and "lore," "arose" and "pursues," "bone" and "skeleton." "A *bad* rhyme," he grumbled, "is, in fact, no rhyme at all."[59]

Marking all the proposed corrections on a copy of "Glenfinlas," Scott found that they canceled one another out. The only two stanzas left were mediocre necessities, neither good nor bad. He then and there decided that when a friend whose judgment he respected told him a poem had no merit whatsoever he would cast it aside but that he would ignore minute criticisms.[60] This proved difficult with the pertinacious Lewis, whom Scott granted "the finest ear for rhythm I have ever known,"[61] and who returned insistently to the attack. Lewis argued, Scott defended, but ultimately he accepted all five of the emendations his mentor demanded in "The Chase," a few in "The Eve of St. John," and an unknown number in "Glenfinlas." About "William and Helen," however, he was more obdurate. Lewis suggested thirty-four changes; Scott rejected thirty-one, accepted one, and may have taken two more.[62]

Meanwhile, Lewis had found a London bookseller named Bell who agreed to bring out *Goetz of Berlichingen* and pay the translator twenty-five guineas, with an additional twenty-five if a second edition was called for.[63] "I have made him distinctly understand," wrote Lewis, "that, if you accept so small a sum, it will be only because this is your first publication." (Lewis either did not know or had forgotten about the little edition of "William and Helen" and "The Chase" in 1796.) Lewis advised Scott's putting his name to the published drama. "*I* see no reason to the contrary, and Bell is very anxious to have it. He is to send your five and twenty Guineas to Edinburgh immediately, so that *Goetz* will at least furnish Mrs. Scott with the price of a Pad-Nag, and his iron hand may be turned into Horse-shoes."[64]

Despite Bell's eagerness to bring it out, he was so dilatory about the printing that Lewis had to give him "a dressing" for not getting on faster. Then, while the typesetter was at work, a gust of wind blew some of the manuscript out of the window, and one page was lost. But Lewis was equal to the emergency. He at once obtained a German copy and retranslated the missing passages himself.[65] The little volume appeared in March, 1799, with Scott's name on the title page.[66] Critics made some mildly favorable comments, and enough copies were sold to justify a second printing, so that presumably Scott received his additional twenty-five guineas. There was, however, no rush of purchasers beating a path to the booksellers' doors.[67] Nor was there any injustice in this neglect. The significance of Scott's labor on the play is not what he did for Goethe but what Goethe did for him. These rapacious but courtly robber barons, with their feuds and forays, their castle sieges, stolen cattle, and captive knights, were Teutonic compeers of Auld Wat of Harden and all those Border clansmen whose raids rang in his own imagination.[68] Why should *he* not become the minstrel of their wild deeds, transmuting them into art?

The publication of the play, however, gave Scott some literary standing when, in March, he took Charlotte on a trip to London.[69] Their stagecoach struggled through bad weather and heavy snows on the road. At Stilton they bought two cheeses to send home by wagon, one for George Square and one for Castle Street, and dined with Scott's youngest brother Daniel, who was in some mercantile occupation there.[70] At the capital they lodged in New Bond Street opposite the Dumergues, who entertained them and Lord Downshire at dinner. Lewis introduced Scott to literary lions and titled friends. Scott was more eager, however, to examine the antiquities of the Tower and Westminster Abbey, which he had not seen since his Aunt Jenny had brought him to London as a child of four. He was more eager still to make researches among the manuscripts of the British Museum.[71]

During their courtship Scott had mentioned to Charlotte his hope of being made a County Sheriff. He undoubtedly took advantage of this

London visit to press his case in influential quarters. In his Liddesdale ballad-collecting he had received some help from Mr. Andrew Plummer, an elderly scholar and antiquary who was the Sheriff-Depute of Selkirkshire.[72] Mr. Plummer was getting too infirm for his work; he was often ill and seldom left his home of Sunderland Hall, where he lived with three spinster sisters "as old and musty," Scott said, "as any Caxton or Wynkyn de Worde in his library."[73] Most of the time Mr. Plummer spent among his books, walking out of the parlor once a day to his garden. Only a fool or a fox hunter, he said, would do more.[74] His age and ill health made it plain that he would not live much longer.

Although Mr. Plummer could not precisely nominate his successor, his favor carried weight and he liked Scott. The young advocate also had the powerful support of the Duke of Buccleuch. Most important of all, however, was Mr. Henry Dundas, Pitt's Secretary of War, who controlled all the Crown patronage in Scotland. Although Dundas had been pleased with Scott's manners and conversation at Melville Castle, it was essential to secure his active patronage. Fortunately, Scott was not only on friendly terms with his son Robert who was now a fellow cavalryman, but also had the support of his nephew, Robert Dundas of Arniston, the Lord-Advocate, and of William Dundas, Secretary to the Scottish Board of Control.[75]

While Scott was still involved in all these London activities, he received word on April 19, of his father's death.[76] During the past year the old man had endured a series of paralytic attacks. Lying helpless in his bed with dimmed eye and fallen lip, his memory impaired, he sometimes appeared unaware of which member of his family was bending over his pillow, and could only stammer unintelligibly in response.[77] Though occasionally the old fire flashed in his eyes and lucidity returned for a moment, the light of life was trembling in the socket. There had been no way of telling, however, that he might not linger on for many months.

News of the danger had reached Scott too late for him to be in Edinburgh at the deathbed. He wound up his business in London as quickly as possible.[78] His father's hopeless state, he wrote in consolation to his mother, made his death not only a release for him but "the happiest change, if the firmest integrity and the best spent life can enable us to judge." The affection and attention of her children, he hoped, would help alleviate her grief.[79]

Mrs. Scott and Anne were both exhausted by their attendance on the sickbed. When the summer came, Walter and Charlotte consequently asked them to stay at Lasswade until autumn.[80] Scott was working away on a Gothic melodrama which he called *The House of Aspen*, derived from a tale by Veit Weber, *Der Heilige Vehme*.[81] Charlotte was carrying a second child, and Scott therefore reluctantly declined an invitation from Patrick Murray to go off on a little tour with him.[82] He was, however, in Edinburgh for a time in August, where he met Richard Heber, a young man who was an ardent collector of rare books.[83]

Heber now represented Oxford in Parliament, but since his undergraduate days he had been far more interested in gilt bindings than in government. He was extremely rich: "No gentleman," he remarked, "can be without three copies of a book, one for show, one for use, and one for borrowers."[84] He bought whole libraries; ultimately his collections overran eight houses in England and on the Continent. Beginning with the classics, his enthusiasms expanded to early English drama and medieval literature. Illuminated vellums, volumes in calf and morocco, were the Melusinas of his imagination. Almost instantly he and Scott were deep in friendship. Leaving an all-night party just before dawn, they decided to climb to Arthur's Seat, and returned with ravenous appetites for breakfast. They talked ballads and romances endlessly, Heber offered the rich stores of his library to Scott's investigations, and on the shelves of every dusty bookshop Heber rummaged he began poking for materials that might interest his new friend.[85]

In his bibliomaniac prowlings about Edinburgh, he had observed on the High Street by the Cross a small shop with the sign "Rare Old Books." Heber plunged within and discovered not only some of "the small old volumes, dark with tarnished gold," of which he was in search, but found in the bookseller—a handsome young fellow named Archibald Constable—a man who was a warm and able bibliophile. Whenever he came in to chat with this knowledgeable person, Heber saw in the shop another visitor, a wild-looking scarecrow-figure with unshorn sandy hair and staring eyes, perched for hours on top of a ladder poring over some folio, his gangling legs drawn up under his chin. The shabby reader was a student named John Leyden. He proved to be a fellow bibliophile and in his high screech voice was soon pouring out a torrent of erudition about ballads and traditional lore.[86]

Leyden had entered Edinburgh University in 1790. Extremely poor, he subsisted largely on bread and water, but his appetite for learning was unbounded. Although a candidate for the ministry, he frequented every classroom, learning everything from languages to medicine and the natural sciences. Fellow students laughed at this uncouth fellow from Roxburghshire, even the professors smiled, but Leyden knocked down his deriders, disarmed his victims by the geniality that followed his belligerence, and confounded his teachers with "the portentous mass of his acquisitions in almost every department of learning."[87] "Dash it all, man," he would say in his grating voice, "if you have the scaffolding ready you can run up the masonry when you please."[88] Foreign languages were but so many hedges surrounding the fruits and flowers of literature; the single one he refused to attempt was English. "Learn English!" he exclaimed. "Never! It was trying to learn that language that spoiled my Scots."[89]

This odd acquaintance, half-Orson, half-Pico della Mirandola, Heber introduced to Scott. The raucous scholar, it turned out, was the same man whose initials Scott had seen over the past two or three years signed to verses in the *Edinburgh Magazine*—chiefly translations, from Greek, Norse, Arabic, Icelandic, Persian. They had excited his curiosity because he had felt in them something that suggested the unknown "J. L." to be a fellow Borderer.[90] Leyden flung himself heartily into furthering Scott's ballad-collecting, and Scott persuaded him to send Lewis a ballad he had written, called "The Elf-King," which the latter accepted for his *Tales of Terror*.[91] When Heber departed for London, he left Scott and Leyden in the Advocates' Library, keenly excited over an old version of *Sir Tristrem* that they had discovered in the Auchenleck Manuscript.[92]

It was not long before Leyden was a frequent visitor at Lasswade. Charlotte enchanted him with her pretty face, and he astonished her by downing dozens of cups of tea and bellowing old Scots songs in the tones of a revolving saw.[93] Once Scott obtained a fragment of an old historical ballad but was disappointed not to be able to recover the rest. Two days later, sitting with some guests after dinner, he heard a distant sound like "the whistling of a tempest through the torn rigging of a vessel which scuds before it." The noise grew louder; suddenly Leyden burst into the room, with violent and enthusiastic gestures, stridently chanting the desired ballad in his saw tones. He had learned of "an old person who possessed this precious remnant of antiquity" and had walked between forty and fifty miles, and back again, solely to get it.[94]

The summer brought Scott a budget of affectionate chitchat from Jane Purgstall. "Such is the electric charm of your penmanship," she confided, "that I declare to God I am such an idiot I cannot look at your letter yet without crying." She had been unable to find any new ghost stories for him, although the Count's own great-grandmother had been taken away by the Devil while she was supping in a large company one night. "Another of the family, with all her Diaments on, was handed by said Gentleman as if to her Carriage; but the street open'd and swallow'd them up: and no power can hide the opening which is before the house in Gratz even to this day." In Paris, Jane had seen a comedy that was the rage there: "The first scene was a King and all his Court perfectly happy, and all their happiness consisted in Eating." She was looking forward to *Tales of Terror*, but she scolded the notion of Scott's appearing anonymously: "If you do not give your name to your part of the Collection I must really say it is very ridiculous and what you know must make me angry, and so doubly wrong. A very pretty thing indeed when a man has real genius to let another get the credit for it, and poor me lose the love of such a friend."[95]

That autumn Scott was invited for several days to Bothwell Castle, the seat of Lord Douglas on the Clyde. His host and hostess and her cousin Lady Louisa Stuart showed him the red donjon tower, circular without and octagonal within, the banqueting hall, the round dungeon known as "Wallace's Beef Barrel," and the lofty red curtain-wall facing the river.[96] On an excursion to the ruins of Craignethan Castle, Scott was so delighted with the scenery that Lord and Lady Douglas pressed upon him the lifetime use of a small house belonging to them which was enclosed within the ancient walls. Grateful as he felt for their generous suggestion, he could not give them an immediate answer; his appointment as Sheriff of Selkirk might soon take place, and if he obtained it he could not have his summer home so far away as Lanarkshire.[97]

His little excursion inspired Scott to begin a ballad on Bothwell and Blantyre, but after less than a dozen quatrains he broke off and left it unfinished.[98] He also wrote a fragment describing the scene from the crest of Cheviot, looking down past Bowmont Water into the valley of the Till and the disastrous field of Flodden where James IV was slain.[99] A longer but likewise uncompleted ballad, "The Shepherd's Tale," tried to fuse a legend about Claverhouse with another about Thomas of Ercildoune. In the latter, a horse jockey who has sold a black stallion to a strange antique personage daringly comes at midnight to the top of the Eildon Hills to be paid. He is taken into a cavern where enchanted chargers and armed warriors stand ranged in stalls. The wizard points out a sword and a horn that will dissolve the spell. When the dealer blows the horn it rings out in a blast that shakes the earth, the horses stamp, the warriors clash their armor.

> "Woe, woe," they cried, "thou caitiff coward,
> That ever thou wert born!
> Why drew ye not the knightly sword
> Before ye blew the horn?"

The unfortunate wretch is cut to pieces and hurled from the cave.[100]

At about this time, Scott thought of making this same tale the core of a prose tale of chivalry in the style of *The Castle of Otranto*. The mysterious stranger was to turn out to be none other than Thomas of Ercildoune. He wrote some seven pages of this romance, entitled *Thomas the Rhymer*, and then abandoned the idea. Another fragment, equally brief, he called *The Lord of Ennerdale*. Both lay forgotten for many a year thereafter, gathering dust in an old cabinet.[101]

From this traffic with old legends Scott was called to attend the autumn assizes at Jedburgh. Then, after a week in Liddesdale with Shortreed, he went for a few lays to Rosebank, where he probably discussed his mother's future plans with his Uncle Robert.[102] She was giving up the house in George Square and buying a smaller one in George Street; the following spring the Captain gave her £200 to aid this purpose, in return for which Scott bound himself during his uncle's life to pay ten pounds every Whitsuntide.[103] One morning, while he was still at Rosebank, James Ballantyne called to ask the contribution of a few paragraphs about some legal question to his weekly newspaper. When Scott brought his article to the printing office in Kelso he also showed Ballantyne a few of the pieces he had written for Lewis's collection and enthusiastically recited some of Lewis's stanzas.[104]

Ballantyne expressed regret that the book was so long in appearing; it was now about a year and a half that it had been hanging fire. Scott's own poems, he told the author, especially the Morlachian fragment from Goethe, were far better than anything Lewis could do. Scott did not agree but was pleased. Just as he was on the point of leaving, he casually asked Ballantyne why he didn't try to get some book printing "to keep his types in play during the week." The idea had not struck Ballantyne before; he knew nobody in the Edinburgh trade, he said, but his types were good and he thought he could work cheaper than the town printers. "You have been praising my little ballads," Scott replied with a good-natured smile; "suppose you print off a dozen copies or so of as many as will make a pamphlet, sufficient to let my Edinburgh acquaintances judge of your skill for themselves." Ballantyne agreed, and Scott took his departure.[105]

Soon after the winter session opened, Mr. Plummer, the aged Sheriff-Depute of Selkirkshire, died. Scott's efforts in London and Edinburgh now bore fruit. The Duke of Buccleuch immediately pressed his influence with Mr. Dundas. The Earl of Dalkeith and Lord Montagu, Scott's fellow volunteers in the Dragoons, added their voices. Scott also had the favor of Lord Napier of Ettrick, the Lord-Lieutenant of the County. As Scott had expected, Dundas's son and his nephews warmly supported his candidacy.[106] Country gentlemen like Pringle of Whytbank spoke in his behalf, and Scott wrote requesting the interest of Riddle of Camieston and his relation Sir John Riddell.[107] On December 16, 1799, Scott received the appointment. It added £300 to his annual income and, since it required only his occasional presence in Selkirkshire, did not interfere with his living in Edinburgh for most of the year and continuing to practice as an advocate.[108]

Scott's cousin Jane Russell communicated this happy event to her brother James in India, together with other news of the past few months, including the birth of the child Walter and Charlotte had been expecting.[109] It was a girl, born on October 24. This time all went well. On November 15 the infant was baptized Charlotte Sophia by the Reverend Dr. Daniel Sandford of the Episcopal Church of Scotland. Although Lord Downshire was unable to be present, his name appears as one of the child's sponsors, with Miss Sophia Dumergue and Scott's mother.[110]

Miss Russell's letter included one other bit of family news. A few days before Christmas, Scott's younger brother Tom married a Miss Elizabeth Macculloch. "I believe his friends were a good deal astonished and not very much delighted." But he had been determined, his sister Anne said, and there had been no help for it. The lady was twenty-four or -five and no beauty, "one of those common looking people you would never think of looking twice at," but "very good humored . . . and in short," Miss Russell wound up, with a flash of her rapier, "a very proper wife for Tom . . . who . . . is but a light horseman."[111]

Hearing from Lewis that *Tales of Terror* was at last in the hands of the printer, Scott decided to put aside the sample pamphlet of his own ballads that he had suggested to Ballantyne.[112] Some months before, however, he had put together a small eighty-page quarto volume, which, in addition to his own "Erl-King," "William and Helen," and "The Chase," contained three poems by Lewis, two by Robert Southey, and one by a Dr. J. Aiken.[113] Ballantyne set this little volume up in type before the end of the year; it bears the date 1799 on the title page, and its title, *An Apology for Tales of Terror*, is an obvious allusion to Lewis's delayed anthology. Until late in the following spring, however, Scott took no further steps. But when Lewis wrote him in May that "only 17 Ballads are yet printed out of 60" he lost patience; shortly thereafter he allowed Ballantyne to run off a dozen copies of his own little volume for private distribution. It was the first production of the Ballantyne Press—a press that would become famous as *The Lay of the Last Minstrel*, *Marmion*, and *The Lady of the Lake* were followed in the years to come by the long series of the *Waverley Novels*. Scott was much pleased by the well-designed pages and the handsome typography of Ballantyne's work.[114]

"I have been for years collecting old Border ballads," he told Ballantyne, "and I think I could, with little trouble, put together such a selection from them as might make a neat little volume, to sell for four or five shillings. I will talk to some of the booksellers about it when I get to Edinburgh, and if the thing goes on, you shall be the printer."[115] Ballantyne was delighted, but the effervescent Leyden protested. "Dash it, does Mr. Scott mean another thin thing like *Goetz of Berlichingen*? I have more than that in my head myself: we shall turn out three or four such volumes at least."[116]

The exclamation was a flash of fire to Scott's enthusiasm. The long time of "makin' himsel" had come to fruition. The days of dreaming and Sandyknowe and hearing the tales of old Robert and Barbara Scott and Sandy Ormiston, Hardiknute, Satchells, and Blind Harry, the accumulating of penny broadsheets, the country tramps and explorations of Roslin, Craigmillar, Dunnotar, Fenella's Castle, Hermitage, and Bothwell, reading Pittscottie and Fordun, the Border raids in Liddesdale and drinking in from the lips of withered crones and wrinkled shepherds the old songs kept alive by tradition—all now fell into place in one glorious design. This would be no mere selection of a few ballads but nothing less than a monument of his country's song. *The Minstrelsy of the Scottish Border* was born.

# 4

---

# *The Birth of the* Minstrelsy

## *(1800–1802)*

SELKIRKSHIRE was a small rural county through whose shouldering hills wound the river Ettrick and the Yarrow and for a few miles in the north the Tweed.[1] Some two-thirds of its entire acreage were included within the vast estates of the Duke of Buccleuch.[2] In ancient times the higher land between the valley of the Tweed and the valley of the Ettrick and Yarrow, which is still called the Ettrick Forest, had been densely wooded with oak, birch, and hazel, and until the sixteenth century it had been a royal hunting ground roamed by red deer. But James V had turned thousands of sheep into the royal domain to graze, and the trees had been destroyed for pasture.[3]

There still remained, however, on the heights rising above the Ettrick at Bowhill oaks clustered thick among beeches, elms, firs, and scarlet-berried rowans, while birches waved around Newark Tower, and Harewood glen by the riverside was a tangle of laburnum and wild roses.[4] In the south the mountainous region above Moffat swelled in huge hills shaggy with heath around the blue waters and silver sands of St. Mary's Loch and bleak with crags and bogs about the dark tarn of Loch Skene.[5]

Mostly the countryside was one of lonely sheep farms and tiny hamlets. The only two towns of any size, Galashiels and Selkirk, boasted no more than a few thousand inhabitants. Galashiels, on the banks of Gala Water, some distance above its confluence with the Tweed, tanned hides and wove woollens. Farther south, climbing the steep slopes above the Ettrick almost like an Italian hill town, was Selkirk, the county seat and a royal burgh.[6] From an early time the craft of shoemaking had flourished there; in the rebellions of 1715 and 1745 its dwellers had been forced to supply the Jacobites with thousands of pairs of shoes. Though shoemaking was now dying out its inhabitants were still nicknamed "the souters of Selkirk."[7]

Scott threw himself energetically into his duties as Sheriff. An honor guard welcomed him into office. "The trumpets call me," he gaily wrote Heber, "to swagger in a cocked skyscraper and sword, preceded by a Band of halbardiers the antiquity of whose persons and weapons might entitle them to be bodyguards to the Cout of Keeldar—moreover a company of Volunteers whose legs move in such uniformity as would be most aptly represented by the treddles of a weaving loom—such are the attendants of the Man whom the King delighteth to honour."[8] On a superb new horse—named Brown Adam after a ballad hero—Scott executed a series of highhearted leaps that brought a murmur of admiration from the troops.[9] Watching him from the rear rank was a young sheep-farmer named William Laidlaw, to whom a companion growled in a deep voice, "Will, what a damned strong chield that would have been had his left leg been like his right ane!"[10]

Primarily the office of Sheriff was that of a county judge. Scott's predecessor, Andrew Plummer, had lived to an advanced age and during his later years had seldom stirred from his home, delegating the bulk of his work, including that of handing down decisions, to the Sheriff-Substitute whom a Sheriff was empowered to appoint. Scott had determined, however, that he would preside over the Sheriff Court in person whenever his legal duties in Edinburgh did not make this impossible. When he was unable to hear a case himself, instead of leaving the decision to his Sheriff-Substitute, he rendered it in writing on the basis of written reports of the arguments and evidence.[11]

His first official act, the choice of his Sheriff-Substitute, presented a ticklish problem. There were two rival candidates, each a good choice but each backed by different gentlemen among those who had supported Scott's appointment as Sheriff. He diplomatically proposed leaving the decision to two referees acceptable to both sides. One of the referees, however, refused to serve. But this proof of friendly impartiality was clear enough evidence that Scott had no cavalier disposition to ignore the recommendations of his supporters. He thereupon felt free to pass over both gentlemen in favor of a third candidate objectionable to neither faction. His choice was Charles Erskine, a solicitor—in the Scots phrase a Writer—at Melrose, an efficient and hard-working man, who became his friend and trusted agent.[12]

Letters from one to the other were soon flying back and forth between Edinburgh and Selkirk. A strict examination, Scott wrote his Sheriff-Substitute, must be made of the weights and measures in Galashiels and Selkirk, and any tradesmen giving short weights, especially butchers and bakers, must be handsomely fined.[13] Erskine must send him the Old Charter from James V, which would be found in a little odd-looking box on top of the Selkirk charter chest.[14] What was this folly and absurdity of Mr. Riddle's bringing suit in the Sheriff Court to demand that Mr. Henderson recant calling him "Damned Liar, Damned Villian, and Scounderal and Blackguard"?—"Who ever heard of a Sheriff judging in a case of Scandal?" (In point of law, a Sheriff *could* try an action for scandal but had no power to order a public recantation.)[15] The political brawling in Selkirk over the coming elections, Scott directed, must be curbed by imposing bail for all breaches of the peace. "If any more of these violent proceedings take place, my hand will fall heavy on the perpetrators, be they of what party they may."[16]

Once Scott had settled into his work as Sheriff his professional life fell into a regular routine. During the winter and summer terms of the Court of Session he was in Edinburgh pursuing his career as an advocate; during the spring recess and again from the middle of July to the middle of November he was in the country, riding from Lasswade to perform his duties as Sheriff in Selkirk and to attend the autumn assizes in Jedburgh. In the midst of all these activities, both in town and country, he industriously kept on gathering, arranging, and writing illustrative notes upon the ballads of the *Minstrelsy*.

He was now comfortably prosperous. His father had trained him to keep accounts carefully. (Old Mr. Scott himself, however, had not been altogether businesslike; large sums due him from his clients had to be traced through masses of old papers, so that it was almost two decades before his estate was finally settled.)[17] Scott's own surviving financial records are not complete, but among them his cash book for 1799 shows receipts of £1,445, and for 1800 the figures rose to £1,518.[18] To be sure, no large part of these totals came from his professional efforts as an advocate. The year of his marriage, 1797, his fifth as an advocate, his earnings shrank to less than £81, but the following year they jumped to 129 guineas and from that time on rose steadily.[19] The bulk of his income, however, was derived from three main sources: the £300 a year he was now beginning to draw as Sheriff, Charlotte's allowance from her brother, and his own share of his father's estate. In 1801, when he acquired 39 North Castle Street, his receipts shrank to £1,037; he must have been obliged to break into his capital to make the purchase.[20]

It is not clear whether Charlotte's income from her brother was paid on any regular schedule, but during the four-year period beginning with her marriage there are documents showing that she received about £2,324, and there might have been further sums of which the records have vanished.[21] In 1799, furthermore, £1,512 were invested in 3 per cent consols for her benefit.[22] Assuredly, then, she began her married life with rather more than the £500 a year of which Scott had told his parents, although in later years he estimated her income as £300. What is certain is that at no time after their first twelve months as a married couple did they have less than £1,000 a year.

Scott's account book for 1799 shows total expenditures of about £966. Household expenses came to £192; rent and servants' wages, £94; rent for Lasswade, country expenses, and books, £198; taxes, £29; traveling, £66; incidentals, £10. Personal expenses for Charlotte and the baby—£91—were exceeded by the upkeep of Scott's horse—£104—and were doubled by the £192 spent on wines and liquors.[23] The late eighteenth century was not only a drinking age; it was one to which the horse was as important as the automobile is to the twentieth.

When Scott cantered over the hills and valleys to Ettrick Forest, he usually lodged at Whitebanklee, a little inn at Clovenfords, a coaching station on the south road from Edinburgh, within easy riding distance of Selkirk.[24] Clovenfords was also only a few miles from the vales of Ettrick and Yarrow, where he hoped to find more ballads for James Ballantyne to print in the *Minstrelsy*. The number already in his possession was growing, and his plans for the collection were advancing steadily.[25]

Meanwhile he proposed that Ballantyne take the daring step of transferring his business from Kelso to Edinburgh. The town needed a good newspaper; Ballantyne could be its editor at the same time that he continued to publish the *Kelso Mail*. In addition there were fair openings for both " a monthly magazine, and [a] Caledonian annual Register." Ballantyne might also obtain a share in the well-paid work of printing Session papers. Finally, in book publication "an Edinburgh press might have superior advantages even to those of the Metropolis." If the printer needed financial assistance to make the move, no doubt it could be obtained.[26]

At the moment, nothing came of these suggestions. Meanwhile, however, Scott pressed ahead rapidly on the Border ballads. Another collecting trip to Liddesdale, he wrote Heber, would be necessary but could "only be undertaken in the summer on account of the Bogs."[27] Through Dr. Robert Anderson, the editor and biographer, he met Robert Jamieson, who was also planning to bring out a collection of Scottish ballads. Scott invited the two men to spend a day with him at Lasswade to talk about these projects. He himself was interested mainly in historical ballads based on incidents in the old Border raids; Jamieson, it turned out, in romantic ballads with no necessary foundation in fact.[28] Jamieson found Scott "beforehand with him in the greater part of the provincial poetry he had collected" but was able to supply his host with a number of ballads from the manuscripts of Mrs. Brown of Falkland. In return Scott gave Jamieson several poems, including some he had intended to publish himself, although he could not persuade himself to surrender either "Brown Adam" or "The Gay Goss Hawk."[29]

Introduced by a letter from Anderson, Scott sent Bishop Percy copies of "Glenfinlas" and "The Eve of St. John" in testimony of his grateful respect for "The Editor of 'The Reliques,' *upon which he formed his taste for ballad thinking and expression*."[30] The venerable scholar voiced so warm an interest in which ballads he intended to print that Scott outlined his plans and listed the poems he had gathered or still hoped to obtain. It was not long before the Bishop was answering Scott's queries about the old metrical romance of *Eger and Grime* and promising to send him a ballad on the escape of the Earl of Westmoreland, and Scott was telling his clerical correspondent the delight with which he had read the *Reliques* in boyhood.[31]

Dr. Currie, the editor and biographer of Robert Burns, likewise agreed to look through the poet's manuscripts for the old ballads he had collected. Of "Glenfinlas" Currie wrote, "I have read your 'green ladies.' It is a very noble poem."[32] Richard Heber offered generous assistance, and through Heber, Scott was presently involved in scholarly correspondence with George Ellis, a retired diplomat living near Windsor who was one of the founders of that wittily satiric weekly *The Anti-Jacobin*. Ellis had become fascinated by medieval romance, edited in 1790 a collection entitled *Specimens of the Early English Poets*, and was now engaged in editing *Specimens of Early English Metrical Romances*. Gradually Scott's researches also brought him into correspondence with Robert Surtees, an antiquarian at Durham, the scholarly Francis Douce, and the fiery and eccentric Joseph Ritson.

But most vigorous of all in aiding Scott's labors was the faithful John Leyden. Following his introduction to Edinburgh society by Heber and Scott, the gawky young scholar had become a riotous drawing-room sensation. In fashionable gatherings his strident voice rose in dispute or in top flood of spirits poured out loud monologues devoted to his own exploits, while his arms sawed the air in abrupt and violent gestures. The hoydenish Duchess of Gordon, not fastidious about polish, found him a delicious oddity; Lady Charlotte Campbell, too, was charmed and insisted on his dancing with her. Not at all abashed by his own clumsiness, Leyden wrote next morning a lively verse-squib in the character of her ladyship's dancing bear. At an evening party where everyone had grown silent in anticipation of a song, he astounded the company by bursting out with a Border ditty in a yell like an Indian war-whoop. "Dash it all, man," he answered a friend's remonstrance, "they would have thought I was *afraid* to sing before them."[33]

Despite these distractions Leyden was a tireless coadjutor. No lope across the countryside was too long for him to undertake if at the end there might be a dozen verses of a ballad to be taken down from the lips of some quavering gaffer. Although he had agreed to edit a sixteenth-century work, *The Complaynt of Scotland*, for the young bookseller Archibald Constable,[34] in the early summer Leyden set out to comb Liddesdale and from there went on to Carlisle to examine the Glenriddell MS and see if he could not turn up some trace of the old ballad "The Duel of Graeme and Bewick."[35] Meanwhile, Scott had obtained for him the commission of preparing for publication a catalogue of the manuscripts in the Advocates' Library, which might lead to his being entrusted with making a catalogue raisonée of that library's entire great collection.[36] In mid-July Leyden set out to conduct two German boys on a tour of the North and West of Scotland, from which he returned early in October turbulently contending that Ossian was "far from being a forgery of Macpherson's": even now there were current in the Highlands a prodigious number of Ossianic songs of transcendent merit.[37]

At Lasswade cottage Scott and Leyden toiled during the day on ballads and skirmished with each other in the evenings about "the old disputes between the Cameronians and their opponents. You know," Scott explained to Heber, "I am a bit of a Cavalier not to say a Jacobite, so I give his Presbyterian feelings a little occasional exercise."[38] Although much work still had to be done on the historical or "raiding" ballads, and not even all the romantic ballads had been obtained, they made such progress that by November the greater part of the first volume was sent to Kelso for printing.[39] Excited by the old ballads, Leyden wrote two imitations, one on the Cout of Keeldar, one on the violent death of Lord Soulis, the Liddesdale tyrant, from which Scott quoted enthustiastically:

> On a circle of stones they placed the pot
> A circle of stones but barely nine
> They heated it red and fiery hot
> Till the burnished brass did glimmer and shine

> They wrapped him in a sheet of lead
> A sheet of lead for a funeral pall
> They plunged him in the caldron red
> And they melted him lead and bones and all.[40]

Scott also tried his hand at further ballad imitations, writing one called "Helen's Cave," which has disappeared, beginning another called "The Reiver's Wedding," and turning out a third about Thomas the Rhymer.[41] Besides these, he had still other literary irons in the fire. There were, of course, his contributions to *Tales of Terror*, or, as Lewis had now decided to call his miscellany, *Tales of Wonder*. And Scott's Gothic tragedy *The House of Aspen*, Heber was urging on John Kemble for production at Drury Lane. "Pray let the theatrical potentate take his full time to consider whether he is to extend his golden (I mean *gilded*) sceptre to the Scottish stranger or no."[42]

Charles Kerr was glowingly convinced that Scott would achieve fame both in literature and in law. "Go on," he exhorted; "and with your strong sense and hourly ripening knowledge, that you must rise to the top of the tree in Parliament House in due season, I hold as certain as that Murray died Lord Mansfield. But don't let many an Ovid, or rather many a Burns (which is better) be lost in you." Why should not Lord President Scott "be a famous poet . . . when we have seen a President

Montesquieu step so nobly beyond the trammels in the *Esprit des Lois*"?[43]

Busy as Scott was at Lasswade, he found his literary work a relaxation from the demands of the spring. The war had been going badly; Napoleon Bonaparte had made himself the dictator of France under the title of First Consul; and disastrously scanty harvests at home had driven the price of wheat to four times its prewar figure and the 6d loaf to 1s 5d.[44] "The people," Scott explained, "are starving, actually starving and very tumultuously disposed." The Volunteers had consequently been called back to military duty in April and May. Scott's corps was on patrol duty day and night to prevent the poor from plundering. The Dragoons were jeered and pelted by rioters; one fellow seized the reins of Brown Adam and Scott had to slash at him with his saber, almost cutting off his fingers.[45]

In the course of the spring Charlotte had had a severe attack of influenza and even by May remained far from well. Her recovery, Scott thought, might be speeded if she went driving in the country that summer. He therefore wrote to ask if Heber could not pick up for him in London a low four-wheeled phaeton that was both neat and cheap. In a postscript he added a comment and command from Charlotte: "first that she is very impatient and secondly that you must put your glass quite close to your eye when you inspect the state of the wheels— Is she not a saucy Dame?"[46]

When the little carriage at last arrived in June, Scott and Charlotte were delighted by its elegance and by its bargain price—only a trifle over £34, although Scott's brother had been assured that nothing suitable could be obtained for less than forty guineas.[47] Heber's long silence before reporting success had made them imagine, Scott wrote, that "the gallant knight had fallen into the snares of some fair Armida," but the outcome put their suspicions to the blush. In gratitude Scott sent a copy of one of those scarce little books he knew their friend prized, a grammar of the Biscayan language printed at Salamanca.[48] All at Lasswade remembered Heber with great kindness, he concluded, especially the bull-terrier Camp, who "loves a pair of wide trousers for your sake" and was always chasing someone so clad, only to be "disappointed when it does not turn out to be his old friend."[49]

Late in July he wrote to thank Heber for Way's verse translations of D'Aussy's *Fabliaux*, edited and annotated by Heber's friend George Ellis, whose researches on the metrical romances Scott had offered to aid in any way within his power. Way's translation might do honor to Dryden, he remarked, but Ellis' notes and illustrations were the most valuable part of the publication. He and Charlotte were just setting out in the phaeton for an excursion through Selkirkshire, where she drove "every where with her own fair hands."[50] They had been offered a beautiful site "for a cottage upon the Braes of Yarrow," but on looking it over Scott concluded that it did not quite meet their desires. Consequently, as he wrote Heber after their return, he decided to retain their little place on the banks of the Esk.[51]

In October Heber reported unhappily that Kemble had turned down *The House of Aspen.*[52] Scott took the news calmly. Managers, he said, were the best judges of how they should spend their money and likely to know pretty well what was likely to please the public—"these things grieve not Cecil." He would not submit the play to any other manager. "Pray consider the *H. of Aspen* therefore as your own property—I wish to God it were worth the trouble it has cost you." The "dishonored Ms" might at least serve to amuse Heber and his friends. Scott's reply ended with one bit of personal news: "Erskine *married* to a daughter of Professor Robison the Illuminé—a lovely girl who will make our peerless blade very happy."[53]

During this summer one of the guests at Lasswade had been a young doctor named John Stoddart who was making a tour through England and Scotland. He was full of enthusiasm for two unknown poets named William Wordsworth and Samuel Taylor Coleridge who in 1798 had published a strange little volume entitled *Lyrical Ballads.* When he crossed the Border again he stopped off in Cumberland to visit Coleridge at Keswick and Wordsworth at Grasmere and sang Scott's praises to them. That December he sang their praises once more to Scott. They had completed the second volume of *Lyrical Ballads,* with some exquisite poems of natural feeling; Coleridge was writing a wonderful poetic romance called *Christabel.* Both Wordsworth and Coleridge, he added, "assured me that they should be happy in your personal acquaintance, and I promise you no small mental treat in theirs."[54]

Matthew Gregory Lewis's *Tales of Wonder* appeared at long last in January, 1801, and was coldly received.[55] Lewis had outwearied anticipation by delaying too long; the *nouveau frisson* was now old. His chamber of horrors evoked only a shrug instead of a shudder. Prepared to be carping, readers complained that the portly and high-priced volumes included too many well-known pieces from the past, too little that was either strange or startling. Reviewers called the collection "Tales of Plunder." In the holocaust of denunciation Scott was happy that his contributions not only escaped censure but even received some praise. Like Lord Home at the battle of Flodden, he said, he did so far well as to survive.[56]

With the new year Scott's editorial labors on the *Minstrelsy* immersed him in a torrent of scholarly correspondence. To Bishop Percy he expressed his doubts that John of Agurstane, mentioned in the ballads about the Battle of Otterburne, belonged to the Northumbrian family of Hagerstoune; it seemed more likely that the warrior was a Rutherford of Edgerstone, anciently spelled Adgurstane.[57] And with

George Ellis he embarked on a series of letters that began with a discussion of the medieval romance of *Sir Tristrem* and grew to take in an enormous range of Arthurian romance.

*Sir Tristrem*, one of the many variants of the story of Tristram and Iseult which had spread all over Europe, existed in an incomplete metrical version running to 204 eleven-line stanzas that formed part of the Auchinleck MS in the Advocates' Library. Scott had at first intended to include the poem in his *Minstrelsy*, but as those ballads swelled into two volumes he decided to publish it separately. Throughout March he and Leyden went over the Auchinleck MS, listing all the romances and the number of folios in each.[58] In addition to *Sir Tristrem*, Scott told Ellis, the manuscript had "an excellent Romance of Arthur and Merlin—I believe unique—Another termed Sir Otuel—the beginning of which is very spirited; it is a Romance of the Douze Pairs and Charlemagne. Also Orfeo and Herodeis (a Gothicized edition of Orpheus and Euridice) where Herodeis is carried off by the fairies."[59]

For the next three years Scott was intermittently occupied with *Sir Tristrem*. Ellis transcribed for him the ending of a French metrical version whose plot corresponded closely with that of the incomplete Auchinleck version. This, together with a suggestion sent by the antiquary Joseph Ritson, led Scott to toy with the idea of composing a conclusion in the same style as the rest of the poem. Sending Ellis a sample in "the villainous cramp stanza of our Thomas," he asked his friend's opinion.[60] Ellis applauded warmly: "If you seriously ask what the world would say to such verses as those you send me, I answer that such of the world as deserve to see Sir Tristram would be extremely pleased with them, and that *I*, after seeing them, shall be *perfectly ashamed of your acquaintance*, if, after having thus proved the facility with which you can execute the task, you should, through mere idleness, neglect to complete it."[61]

From *Sir Tristrem* their letters soared joyfully over broad fields of romance erudition. Gawain's Foul Ladie, Scott told Ellis, could be found in the history of Hrolfe Kraka edited by Torfaeus.[62] The tale of Ferembras was an altogether different one from that of the Ferragu who appeared in the *Orlando Furioso*.[63] Scott was having Leyden's younger brother transcribe for Ellis the whole of *Sir Otuel*.[64] He felt thunderstruck at Ellis's doubts that Adam Davie was the author of *King Alisaundre*.[65] Did the Picts, as Pinkerton claimed, speak a dialect of Teutonic, or were they Celts?[66] A letter from Bishop Percy helped confirm Scott's opinion that the romance of Sir Eger and Sir Grime was identical with that called Sir Graysteil.[67] "You perfectly astonish me," replied Ellis. "Pray tell me what Bishop Percy says, for I am upon Tenterhooks."[68]

Scott was exceedingly eager that Ellis should publish among his *Metrical Romances* one called *Roswal and Lillian*, "the last metrical

Romance of Chivalry which retained popularity in Scotland" and which had been "sung in Edinburgh within these twenty years by a sort of reciter in the streets."[69] Ellis was thinking of including also Archbishop Turpin's history, containing "the battle between Roland and Ferragus . . . I have some doubt whether *your* Ferragus can be much more entertaining than that of Turpin. . . . Do you approve? Yea or Nay?"[70] "How can you be so *superfluous* as to ask?" Scott replied. Ariosto and Boiardo had known Turpin only through the medium of the Romancers. "You will be guilty of a heinous offense if you suppress the Archbishop's legend."[71]

Throughout these lively exchanges Scott was as busy as ever. In April, and once more in August, he was again wandering through Liddesdale and Ettrick Forest looking for ballads, although without much success.[72] On one of these trips Charlotte came with him in the phaeton. It was a queer sight, said Shortreed, to see it "cogglin' first up on ae side and on the other as we gaed alang the burn or the braesides," for there were few "or rather nae roads, and often our best course *was the bed o' a burn.*"[73] During May the Volunteers were in quarters at Musselburgh. They were now amalgamated with the Mid-Lothian Yeomanry, of which they formed two out of the six troops.[74] His duties as quartermaster, Scott remarked gaily, were "altogether inconsistent with romance; for where do you read that Sir Tristrem weighed out hay and corn; that Sir Launcelot du Lac distributed billets; or that any Knight of the Round Table condescended to higgle about a truss of straw?"[75]

His next letter to Ellis was in a different tone, announcing "a heavy family misfortune, the loss of an only sister in the prime of life." Poor Anne had not attained her thirtieth birthday. Her health had always been delicate, and she had been much weakened by nursing her father through his prolonged last illness. On May 25 she was buried in Greyfriars' Churchyard. Of the twelve children born to Walter and Anne Scott only four now remained; the oldest brother John, Walter, and the two younger brothers, Tom and Daniel.[76]

July and August saw Scott engaged in writing the essay "On the Fairies of Popular Superstition," which he used as an introduction to the ballad of "The Young Tamlane."[77] Much of its wealth of illustration, the quotations from Heywood on "The Blessed Hierarchie of Angels," from Gervase of Tilbury, and from other recondite authorities, as well as many odd plums of information in the notes to the *Minstrelsy,* he generously acknowledged, he owed to Leyden's curious reading. He himself had digested and worked the essay into shape, but its materials had been originally compiled by Leyden.[78]

That restless scholar, although he had qualified himself for the ministry, had come to feel that he could not confine his energies to the duties of a clergyman. He was eager to travel; his mind glowed with images of Africa, of America, the palaces of Gondar, the enchanted halls of the Caliph Vathek.[79] "The discoveries of Mungo Park," he told his friends, "haunted his very slumbers"; and when they tried to discourage his wild ideas of penetrating beyond the Niger, "Dark Cuchullin," Leyden replied, "will be renowned or dead."[80] "To divert his mind from this desperate project," appeals were made to William Dundas to get him an appointment in India, where his talents would be useful in studying native languages and culture. Scott also enlisted in Leyden's behalf Ellis's influence among government circles in London.[81]

The only available commission, it turned out, was that of a surgeon's assistant, who must have a medical and surgical degree and pass a medical examination at India House. Undismayed, Leyden undertook to qualify himself within six months.[82] He had run up his "scaffolding" by casually auditing medical classes at Edinburgh University; nothing could be easier than getting the degree. For five months, aided by the distinguished surgeon John Bell, he toiled incredibly.[83] His labors did not prevent his attending evening parties, at one of which he was with difficulty restrained from settling an argument about muscular action by taking out of his pocket a human hand he had been dissecting that morning.[84] He qualified for the degree but annoyed the faculty by boasting so imprudently of his speedy achievement that he was obliged to seek his M.D. from the more complaisant University of St. Andrews.[85]

That September brought an odd visitor to Lasswade, the learned and waspish Joseph Ritson. Like Samuel Johnson, the antiquary paraded a hatred of Scotsmen. With a fiery Jacobinism that cursed all kings he inconsistently united a sentimental devotion to the dethroned Stuarts. He was also a ferocious vegetarian, a dogmatic atheist, a snarling controversialist. About ballads he was a precisian who had savagely mauled the aged Percy for sophisticating the purity of his texts with editorial improvements. Ritson's conscience recoiled with horror from the slightest conjectural emendation as inexcusable tampering, and his dyspeptic stomach steeped his verbal onslaughts in spleen. He despised most of his fellow scholars with venomous acrimony. He so terrorized Warton that he abstained from publishing for the last seven years of his life; he faced the intemperate Pinkerton with a fury as shrill as his own; only of Herd did he speak respectfully.[86]

Introduced by Ellis, Ritson arrived, however, predisposed to be pleased. "There are no men in the world," he had written Scott, "I am so desirous of seeing as Leyden and yourself." And Scott's welcome warmed even this "most rigid of our British Antiquaries" to an amiable glow.[87] Ritson was no less delighted by the "multifarious and many-tongued lore" of Leyden's conversation. Scott himself disarmed Ritson, he said playfully, by having "a tincture of Jacobitism," in addition to which there was the splendid fact that old Beardie, his "great grandfather (every Scotsman has a great grandfather), was *out* at Killicrankey and Sheriffmuir—fought a duel with a *whiggish* father in law—narrowly escaped the gallows—and finally died with a beard which would have done honor to any hermit because he had sworn never to shave till 'the king came home.' [All this was cal]culated to delight Ritson . . ." "Not to mention," Scott added, "that I can repeat ballads like any *seannachie*."[88]

Under these happy circumstances Ritson's asperities melted into a universal complaisance. Most of the two volumes of the *Minstrelsy* had now been printed;[89] Scott showed him the proofs "and was gratified to find that the plan met his approbation." More important still, he convinced Ritson of the authenticity of the ballads: "I believe I succeeded perfectly in removing every doubt from his mind." After studying the Auchinleck MS, Ritson even agreed with Scott in dating it within the reign of Edward III and strongly supported Ellis's recommendation that in printing *Sir Tristrem* Scott should substitute "th" for the old "þ" and "y" and "gh" for the ambiguities of the medieval "ȝ".[90] But Scott wondered how long this love feast would last. "Alas! I fear when he comes to peruse some particular parts of the poems he will resume the scalping knife."[91]

Leyden, always fond of horseplay, could not resist the temptation to tease their guest's horror of animal food by pretending to believe it manly to devour any food that came to hand, vegetable or animal, cooked or raw. While the poor vegetarian shuddered with horror, Leyden galloped "his Border hobby-horse full tilt against the Pythagorean palfrey of the English antiquary."[92] On one afternoon of Ritson's two-day visit, returning for dinner from a stroll with some other guests, Scott asked what had happened to "the learned cabbage-eater." "Mr. Leyden, I believe," replied Charlotte, "frightened him away." It turned out that, forgetting Ritson's creed, she had offered him a slice of cold beef. He had voiced such horror that Leyden, regarding this as rude to their hostess, had first tried to ridicule him, and then, growing angry, threatened to "thraw his neck." Scott shook his head, Leyden vehemently justified his own violence, Scott took a large feather-duster and tickled his ears until he broke down into laughter.[93]

For all this flurry, Ritson left Lasswade cordially disposed toward both Scott and Leyden. "I have two prodigious geniuses," he told a correspondent, "who are ready to give me every satisfaction."[94] Ellis sent congratulations that the visit "had such a friendly termination." "After having softened the Arch-enemy of your nation you have nothing to apprehend from other Sceptics; and, as Pinkerton cannot be so ungracious as to pick a quarrel with Ritson on such a point, the Antiquity of our MS. (I call it *ours* from having participated so largely in its contents) is forever established."[95] And Leyden triumphantly wrote to Heber: "You sent down to Scotland your old Lion—Walter Scott and I pared his claws and drew his teeth and returned him upon your hands a perfectly tame and domestic animal."[96]

Lasswade cottage saw a succession of other guests during the autumn. Clad in a shooting jacket, with a colored handkerchief round his neck, Scott would receive them with a look of boyish gaiety. "Hah!" he exclaimed to one group, "welcome, thrice welcome! for we are just proposing to have lunch, and then a long, long walk through wood and wold . . ." Only those could appreciate such a life, he went on, who knew what it was to "*daidle* out half the day in the Parliament House, where we must all *compear* within another fortnight; then to spend the rest of one's time in applying proofs to condescendences, and hauling out papers to bamboozle judges, most of whom are *daized* enough already. What say you, Counsellor Erskine? Come—*alla guerra*—rouse, and say whether you are for a walk today."[97]

Erskine cheerfully agreed, adding, "I'll tell you what I have thought of this half-hour: it is a plan of mine to rent a cottage and a cabbage-garden—not here, but somewhere farther out of town, and never again, after this one session, to enter the Parliament House." "And you'll ask Ritson, perhaps," Scott laughed, "to stay with you, and help to consume the cabbages. Rest assured we shall both sit on the bench one day; but heigho! we shall both have become very old and philosophical by that time."[98]

"I see you are admiring that broken sword," he addressed another guest. "In order to grasp that mouldering weapon, I was obliged to drain the well at the Castle of Dunnotar. But it is time to set out; and here is one *friend*"—a large dog—"who is very impatient to be in the field. He tells me he knows where to find a hare in the woods of Mavisbank. And here is another," caressing the bull-terrier Camp, "who longs to have a battle with the weazels and water-rats, and the foumart that *wons* near the caves of Gorthy: so let us be off."[99]

On their walk to Roslin, Scott's foot slipped as he scrambled toward a cave on the edge of the steep bank. Down he crashed toward the river's brink, but halfway his fall was broken by a large hazel root, which slowed his descent so that instead of smashing on the stones below his body slid through the tangled thickets and came to rest on the bank of the stream. Instantly he clambered erect, heartily laughing, "Now, let me see who else will do the like." Vigorously he climbed the cliff again, hauling himself up by laying hold of the branches and trunks of trees, and they entered the cave.[100]

One of the friends Scott had made through Leyden was the prickly and struggling poet Thomas Campbell, who had come from Glasgow to attend law lectures and in 1799 published *The Pleasures of Hope*. The poem had been a success but had earned no large sums; and with Campbell, born of a proud but reduced Highland family, poverty rankled. Now he was proposing to bring out an edition of his works by subscription, a project that Scott urged his friends to support. He was a real poet, Scott warmly told Ellis; "If a small sum could be realized for him he might get into some line of active exertion, for though poetry is a very pretty amusement yet I am afraid we must class it with fire and water, which according to our Scotch proverb are good Servants, but bad Masters."[101]

In the same letter Scott congratulated Ellis upon his engagement to be married. Ellis's bride-to-be, a sister of Admiral Sir Peter Parker, was already entering with enthusiasm into her future husband's literary interests and had transcribed for Scott a copy of *Sir Grime, Sir Eger, and Sir Graysteel*, which he gratefully said would "hold the most distinguished place in my little Book-room."[102] In return he sent Ellis a complete transcript of *Guy of Warwick*, the dullest romance, he remarked, except for *Bevis of Hampton*, that he had ever attempted to peruse. Now, in extending his felicitations to Ellis, he added a piece of news: "*The Minstrelsy of the Scottish Border* will, I think, soon salute—not *your* hands—but those of the fair Transcriber."[103]

Ellis also congratulated Scott upon the expected birth of another child. The baby, a boy, was born on October 28, shortly after his parents had returned to Edinburgh for the winter, and was barely six weeks old when the family moved from South Castle Street to the newly built, more spacious home in North Castle Street.[104] "It will be some time before I can get my few books into order, or clear the premises of painters and workmen," Scott wrote; "not to mention that these worthies do not nowadays proceed upon the plan of Solomon's architects, whose saws and hammers were not heard, but rather upon the more ancient system of the builders of Babel." Augmenting the confusion were the squalls of the baby, Walter, "a fine chopping boy, whose pipe, being of the shrillest, is heard amid the storm, like a boatswain's whistle in a gale of wind."[105]

For the next twenty-five years 39 North Castle Street remained Scott's Edinburgh home. Just one door north of George Street, it was a comfortable three-story gray-stone dwelling with a deeply sunk basement. To the right of the entrance a curving bay of three windows rose to a shallow cornice. Left of the door each story had another room with a wide window flanked by fluted Corinthian pilasters, but these were surmounted by the pediment of the adjacent dwelling and looked as if they belonged to that building. The topmost floor of Scott's house, oddly enough, really did belong to this neighbor and was completely sealed off from the lower floors.[106]

Within a few days the sawing and the hammering died down, and perhaps the pipe of the new baby diminished. Scott settled himself to his literary labors and his correspondence in a "den" behind the dining parlor, with a Venetian window looking out on a garden patch of green hardly larger than the room itself.[107] In his mail he found a pretty compliment. On his honeymoon, Ellis informed him, he had read all of *The House of Aspen* aloud to his wife, and they were both "extremely delighted with it."[108] Scott felt pleased that they had derived pleasure from the play, but his own opinion of it had changed; he now saw its faults clearly.

"At one time I certainly thought, with my friends, that it might have ranked well enough by the side of the Castle Spectre, Bluebeard, and the other drum and trumpet exhibitions of the day; but the *Plays of the Passions*"—the dramas by Joanna Baillie—"have put me entirely out of conceit with my Germanized brat; and should I ever again attempt dramatic composition I would endeavor after the genuine old English model."[109] In fact by this time Scott was recovering from the German measles that had mottled English literature with a rash of Gothic melodrama. He was to move steadily away from the monstrous absurdities of its horrors and in the direction of good sense. A decade later he dismissed the play as "a sort of half-mad German tragedy which I wrote many years ago, when my taste was very green."[110]

Scott spent Christmas, 1801, at Hamilton Palace in Lanarkshire. Through Lady Charlotte Campbell he had made the acquaintance of Lady Anne Hamilton, whose father, the Duke of Hamilton, shared her admiration for "Glenfinlas" and "The Eve of St. John." Scott quickly found himself on cordial terms with the entire family, including Lady Anne's brother Lord Archibald and her sister Lady Susan.[111] Deep in the woods of the estate were the ruins of Cadyow Castle, the ancient baronial residence of the Hamiltons, darkened by ivy and creeping shrubs, and overhanging the brawling torrent of the river Evan. The surrounding oaks, many of them over twenty-five feet in girth, had been part of the ancient Caledonian forest that once stretched from the German Ocean to the Atlantic, and some of these very trees might have witnessed the rites of the Druids. Among them, too, had formerly roamed herds of ferocious wild-cattle, milk-white, with white manes and black muzzles, horns, and hoofs.[112]

A morning's ramble suggested to Scott the idea for a ballad interweaving these scenes with the daring assassination of the Regent Murray by Hamilton of Bothwellhaugh. He gallantly promised Lady Anne that when the poem was finished it should be addressed to her,[113] but the combined labors of seeing the last pages of the *Minstrelsy* through the press, preparing for publication a supplementary volume of modern imitations of the ancient ballads, and toiling on over *Sir Tristrem*, as it turned out, prevented his completing the ballad for Lady Anne until well into the following summer.[114]

On his return from Hamilton, he enclosed in his letter of thanks for the hospitality with which he had been entertained his own translation of *Fiesco*, which Lady Anne had expressed a desire to read, together with a copy of Horace Walpole's fable "The Entail" for her father. "I hope his Grace will do me the honor to accept it with my respectful Compliments and that it will recall to his recollection the beautiful French translation of which he repeated so many lines."[115] Her brother Lord Archibald, Scott told her, should not allow his interest in reforming the laws of the country to be dampened by the fact that he had no legal education: "valuable alterations in the Law of a Country are most likely to be accomplished by those who have *not* received a professional education," because the mind of the law student, "bent to the existing system," becomes unable to distinguish between beauties and defects where he has been taught to regard everything as sacred.[116]

In a stagecoach, possibly on his return journey from Lanarkshire, Scott had found that his only fellow passenger was Thomas Campbell, and the two had beguiled the time repeating poetry to each other. Scott asked for something of Campbell's own. He replied that he had one thing he had never printed, "full of drums and trumpets and blunderbusses and thunder"; he didn't know "if there was any good in it." He then recited "Hohenlinden." Excited, Scott exclaimed, "But do you know that's devilish fine. Why! it's the finest thing you ever wrote." One hearing had given it to Scott by heart. He repeated it to Leyden, who, rambunctious as ever, had quarreled with Campbell but couldn't resist the poem. "Dash it, man, tell the fellow that I hate him; but, dash him, he has written the finest verses that have been published these fifty years."[117]

*Minstrelsy of the Scottish Border* appeared in February, embellished with a frontispiece engraving and magnificently printed by James Ballantyne at his Kelso press. The two volumes were dedicated to Henry, Third Duke of Buccleuch. There were eight hundred copies, of which fifty were on large paper. Writing to Cadell and Davies, the London booksellers who were publishing the work, Scott had suggested a price of eighteen shillings. On the back of his letter, however, the Edinburgh booksellers Manners and Miller, noted their agreement with young Mr. Archibald Constable that one guinea would not be too high a price; one hundred copies had been sold in ten days, though the price, not yet announced, was assumed to be at least a guinea.[118]

Scott sent complimentary copies, among others, to the Duke of Buccleuch, to Bishop Percy at Dromore, and to Anna Seward, who had delightedly praised "The Eve of St. John" and "Glenfinlas."[119] He sent a copy, together with Leyden's edition of *The Complaynt of Scotland*, which had been published late in 1801, to George Ellis, and eagerly awaited his judgment. He hoped, he said, that "the threatened third volume will be more interesting to Mrs. Ellis than I can *hope* the dry antiquarian detail of the first two should prove."[120] "You will be pleased," he wrote Lady Anne, "to hear that the sale here is rapid—how they will suit the London *market* (as the Booksellers say) I cannot even guess."[121] But they did well in England too, and sold out in six months,[122] although on the small first edition Scott's half-share of the profits amounted to only £78 10s.[123] Enlarged by the third volume of modern ballads on which Scott was already engaged, there were successive re-editions in 1803, 1806, 1810, 1812, and 1821.[124]

Still more gratifying was the critical reception of the volumes. "I have been devouring them," wrote George Ellis, "not as a pig does a parcel of grains (by which simile you will judge that I must be brewing, as indeed I am), putting in its snout, shutting its eyes, and swallowing as fast as it can without consideration—but as a schoolboy does a piece of gingerbread; nibbling a little bit here, and a little bit there, smacking his lips, surveying the number of square inches which still remain for his gratification, endeavouring to look it into larger dimensions, and making at every mouthful a tacit vow to protract his enjoyment by restraining his appetite."[125]

Letters of enthusiastic delight poured in from every side. Anna Seward, "The Swan of Lichfield," lamented that her "bright luminary," Dr. Erasmus Darwin, was no longer alive to share her raptures.[126] She did not care very much, to be sure, for folk poetry; her taste was predominantly neoclassical. The ballads Scott had taken such pains to recover she thought "uncouth rhymes totally destitute of all that gives metre a right to the name of poetry." But her eulogy of his original contributions to the publication outshone her blindness to the old ballads. His critical essays and historical notes she described ecstatically as "elegant prose raiment" to the poems.[127]

Most commentators, however, applauded with no reservations whatever both the editor and the poems he had gathered. That noble and learned book-lover, John Duke of Roxburghe, wrote warm congratulations and conveyed a complimentary message from Earl Spencer; the antiquarian Chalmers overflowed with hearty praise; Joseph Ritson welcomed his presentation copy as "the most valuable literary treasure in his possession"; even the atrabilious Pinkerton issued *ex cathedra* "his decree of approbation." Among all the ranks of the bibliophiles and scholars there was no voice of dissent in the chorus of praise for Scott's achievement. *Minstrelsy of the Scottish Border* was a ringing success.[128]

## 5

---

# *The Threatened Third Volume*

# *(1802–1803)*

THE CHORUS OF PRAISE for the *Minstrelsy* left Scott in no doubt that he should go ahead with what he had called "the threatened third volume." Ballad imitations were fast becoming a literary mania. A collection of them ought not only to go brilliantly but to push the sales of the two volumes already in print.

Within less than two months James Ballantyne was already beginning to set some of the new volume in type. He had also almost completed printing the text of *Sir Tristrem* and was asking Scott for the glossary and introduction, which, he urged, should be copious, "to give a Royal octavo *thickness*, corresponding to its other dimensions and to make it worth the one pound one shilling sterling, which I believe is to be the price." The printer was delighted by his connection with the publication of Scott's work. He had not merely gained financially; it had opened up prospects that might advantageously influence his entire destiny. "I shall ever think the printing the *Scottish Minstrelsy* one of the most fortunate circumstances of my life."[1]

He was still hesitating about the move to Edinburgh that Scott had proposed. "To say truth, the expences which I have incurred, with a a resolution to acquire a character for elegant printing, whatever might be the result, cramp considerably my present exertion, and throw obscurity over my future views. A short time, I trust, will make me easier, and I shall then contemplate the road before me with a steady eye. One thing alone is clear: that *Kelso* cannot be my abiding plan for aye; and that, sooner or later, migrate I must and will. But at all events I must wait till my plumes are grown."[2]

In this same letter Ballantyne passed on a communication from an attorney named John Davidson, who owned the land on which the battle of Otterburn had been fought. In his notes to the *Minstrelsy* Scott had quoted Godscroft's statement that the battlefield was twelve miles from Newcastle; the actual distance, Davidson pointed out, was at least thirty-two miles. Scott recorded the corrections for the next edition, but in thanking his informant suggested that Godscroft might have been thinking of Scots miles, which would have been nearer the mark.[3] This was the first in a flood of such correspondence. Pinkerton wanted to know if there were any portraits of "the Flower of Yarrow."[4] From Yorkshire another correspondent sent a ballad called "Jock of the Milk," which Scott had already seen in the Glenriddel MS and refrained from publishing because he suspected it to be a modern fabrication.[5] Ritson sent a copy of "Ye Litel Wee Mon," which had gotten entangled with the version of "The Young Tamlane" that Scott had published, and convinced him that it was really part of another ballad, so that Scott dropped the interpolated lines from later editions.[6]

These later editions were also enlarged by the inclusion of further ballads that Scott found in his explorations of Ettrick Forest or that were given him by fellow antiquaries and enthusiasts. Toward the end of April he and Leyden spent a joyful week or two in Selkirkshire, "where in defiance of mountains, rivers, and peat-bogs, damp and dry," they turned up "a compleat and perfect copy of "Maitland with his auld berde graie.'" Copied down from the recitation of an old shepherd, this ballad retained numerous archaic words "which neither the reciter nor copier understood—such are the military engines *Sowies*, *Spring-walls* (Springalds) and many others." "I do not suppose," Scott enthusiastically told Ellis, "that the poem was composed later than the days of Blind Harry."[7]

During this excursion Scott met William Laidlaw, the young volunteer who had seen him caracoling on Brown Adam when he assumed office as Sheriff of Selkirkshire. A nephew of Charles Erskine, Scott's Sheriff-Substitute, Laidlaw had a farm at Blackhouse on the Douglas Burn beyond St. Mary's Loch. The copy of "Auld Maitland" had been made by James Hogg, a sheep-farmer and self-taught poet. Scott read it aloud, his *burr* becoming pronounced in his excitement, while Leyden paced the room "like a roused lion" and clapped his hands.[8]

From the farm they rode to Whitehope for dinner, going down a narrow glen and over by Dryhope to see St. Mary's Loch and the peel tower. After dinner Scott admired Laidlaw's noble greyhound; the animal was so handsome, he said enthusiastically, that he wished he could have two of her puppies. Before saying a cordial farewell he interestedly took the address of the shepherd-poet, James Hogg. On his return to Edinburgh he sent Laidlaw the two volumes of the *Minstrelsy* and was delighted presently to receive from Laidlaw two greyhound puppies, which he named Douglas and Percy.[9]

With the summer Scott was back in the Forest again. Around the middle of July the Earl of Dalkeith held an encampment at the Loch of the Lowes, which Scott attended, taking Camp with him.[10] From there he visited Laidlaw at Blackhouse. The next morning the two men rode to the vale of Ettrick by Dryhope. Beyond Chapelhope, at the west end of the Loch of the Lowes, green mountains close in on the marshy ground where the infant Yarrow finds its way to the Loch, and although there were hills separating the Yarrow from her sister stream they were so moist and boggy as to be dangerous to horsemen. Throughout their ride Scott told anecdotes; Laidlaw listened in such fascination that he often forgot the treacherous ground and only awoke at the last moment to their peril with a shout of "Stop! for God's sake, sir! We must try another place."[11]

On the way Scott missed the gold watch given him by Lord Down-shire, but Laidlaw was sure he must merely have left it under his pillow. They stayed overnight at Ramsey-cleuch, a farm tenanted by Laidlaw's cousins Walter and George Bryden. From here Laidlaw sent back to inquire about the watch and dispatched a farmhand to fetch James Hogg.[12] Posting over the water, the man found Hogg in the field by Ettrick-house and "told me," Hogg said, "that I boud to gang away down to the Ramsey-cleuch as fast as my feet could carry me." "Wha can be at the Ramsey-cleuch that want to see me, Wat?" "I couldna say, for it wasna me they spake to i' the bygangin', but I'm thinkin' it's the Shirra an' some o' his gang."[13]

Hogg was rejoiced; since Scott's visit in the spring he had seen the *Minstrelsy* and copied down from his mother's chanting a number of ballads that he had sent for the next edition. He flung down his hoe and dashed home to put on his Sunday clothes, but before getting there met Scott and Laidlaw coming to see him.[14]

"Jamie the Poet," as his neighbors called him, was some nine months older than Scott, strong and athletic, with brown face and hands, stringy hair, and a large mouth with irregular teeth. His schooling had been confined to two periods of three months each before he was eight years of age, but in adolescence he had taught himself to read and write and had begun composing dreamy poems when he was in his twenties. Only the previous year, 1801, he had published a volume entitled *Scottish Pastorals*.[15] He took his guests into his thatched cottage, brought out a bottle of wine for their entertainment, and to Scott's delight Hogg's mother chanted "Auld Maitland" for them.

Had it ever been in print, Scott asked her. "O na, na, sir, it never was printed i' the world, for my brothers an' me learned it an' many mae frae auld Andrew Moor, an' he learned it frae auld Baubie Mettlin, wha was housekeeper to the first laird of Tushielaw. She was said to hae been another nor a gude ane, an' there are many queer stories about hersel', but O, she had been a grand singer o' auld songs an' ballads."

"The first laird of Tushielaw, Margaret?" asked Scott, "then that must be a very old story indeed?"

"Ay, it is that, sir! It is an auld story! But mair nor that, exceptin' George Warton an' James Stewart, there war never ane o' my songs prentit till ye prentit them yoursel', an' ye hae spoilt them awthegither. They were made for singin' an' no for readin'; but ye hae broke the charm noo, an' they'll never be sung mair. An' the worst thing of a', they're nouther richt spell'd nor richt setten down."

"Take ye that, Mr. Scott," exclaimed Laidlaw. Scott answered with a hearty laugh, while the old dame, giving him a smart rap on the knee, retorted, "Ye'll find, however, that it is a' true that I'm tellin' ye."[16]

Hogg brought a huge bundle of ballads and poetic fragments to dinner at the Brydens'. During the meal their hosts talked rather long-windedly about the relative profits from the black-faced forest breed called "short sheep" and the Cheviot breed called "long sheep." With quizzical solemnity Scott asked, "How long must a sheep actually measure to come under the denomination of a long sheep?" Walter Bryden innocently replied, "It's the woo', sir; the lang sheep hae the short woo' an' the short sheep hae the lang thing, an' these are just kind o' names we gie them, ye see." Laidlaw could not restrain a great guffaw, Scott's assumed seriousness gave way, and the whole company joined in the laughter. The evening grew steadily jollier. Both Scott and Hogg were such good mimics and storytellers—although Hogg's songs, said Laidlaw, were "sometimes a little low"—that tears of mirth ran down George Bryden's face.[17]

Next morning, before Scott rose from his bed, his watch was brought into his room. All five men then started out up the wilds of Rankleburn to see if there was anything left of the farm of Buccleuch, according to Satchells the ancient domain of the Scotts. They crossed the haughs at a gallop, Camp scampering about them and Scott leading an imagined charge shouting, "Schlachten, meine kinder, schlachten!" while Hogg cantered laughing at his side. Scott's mount spiritedly leaped every drain, rivulet, and ditch, rearing and plunging so that it was a wonder to Hogg that he kept his seat. "Mr. Scott," he exclaimed, "that's the maddest dei'l of a beast I ever saw. Can you no gar him tak' a wae mair time? He's just out o' ae lair intil another wi' ye."[18]

At Buccleuch they found no remains of tower or fortalice, but there were the foundations of an old chapel and beside the dam the ruins of the mill, of which Satchells had written:

> Had heather bells been corn o' the best,
> The Buccleuch mill would have had a noble grist.

In the chapel Scott searched in vain for the font of blue marble out of which, according to tradition, the heirs of the Buccleuch had been baptized. Among the loose stones all they could find was half an old pot, thickly encrusted with rust. This Scott tried to believe an ancient helmet, but Laidlaw, finding it smeared with pitch, said, "The truth is, Mr. Scott, it's nouther mair nor less than an auld tar-pot, that some of the farmers hae been buisting their sheep out o' i' the kirk lang syne."[19]

After visiting the peel tower of Tushielaw and the old castle of Thirlstane, they dined that evening with Laidlaw's aunt, Mrs. Bryden of Crosslee. The following day, taking his departure for Clovenfords, Scott warmly shook hands with Hogg and asked him to come sometime to Lasswade. "I will there introduce you to my wife," he said. "She is a foreigner, as dark as a blackberry"—a description that produced on the shepherd-poet the impression that she must be some kind of blackamoor —"and does not speak the broad Scots so well as you and me . . ."[20] Laidlaw came with Scott as far as Yarrow Church, describing so vividly the grand scenery at the head of Moffat Water, the famous waterfall of the Grey Mare's Tail, and the dark tarn of Loch Skene that Scott determined to return soon and find his way to the southern borders of that county.[21]

Late in August he made one of a gay party at Minto House in Roxburghshire. During the previous winter the Earl and Lady Minto had done a good deal of entertaining in Edinburgh, and Scott had probably made their acquaintance at that time. Lady Minto's sister was married to Lord Malmesbury, to whom George Ellis had been diplomatic secretary when that peer was the British ambassador at the Hague. Now at Minto in the waning summer evenings a lively circle gathered in the shadowy drawing room without candles and told hobgoblin stories till suppertime, sometimes laughing, sometimes shrieking, and "so vociferous," wrote Lord Minto, "that they have merited the title of Pandemonium."[22] Scott was "a most capital addition to the Hobgob-linites," said his Lordship; "besides an inexhaustible fund of spectres" he had "a rich store of horrid murders, robberies, and other bloody exploits committed by and on our own forefathers, the Elliotts. Mr. Scott is a particularly pleasing and entertaining man."[23]

Sometimes the fun grew a little too violent for Lord Minto and Lady Malmesbury, who retreated upstairs to the library and formed "a comfortable fogram party"—a party of old fogies—"pitying the noise and fatigues of youth, which we hear like the distant roar of the sea."[24] It was also too much for one of the guests, Tom Campbell, who felt uncomfortable among the "fashionable, proud folks" and found their slang as unintelligible "as the cant of the gipsies." Only Lady Malmesbury, he said, spoke "a sentence of either good sense or amusing nonsense." But Scott had no such discomforts: his shaggy brows came down, and his eyes assumed a mournful aspect when he narrated some dismal and mysterious story or dilated and glowed while his whole face grew radiant as he told a comic tale that made the entire company helpless with laughter.[25]

Before coming to Minto, he had finished "Cadzow Castle," the poem he had promised Lady Anne Hamilton the Christmas before. "Inclosed," he wrote her, "the long promised Ballad kisses your Ladyship's hands." He was happy to learn that Lady Anne and her sister Lady Susan liked it and that Lady Douglas admired it so greatly as to ask for a copy.[26] Acknowledging their praise, he made a number of improvements and additions, including a stanza describing that Lord Lindesay who in forcing Queen Mary to abdicate the throne had savagely "pinched with his iron glove the arm of his weeping sovereign."[27]

Tom Campbell also admired "Cadzow Castle." Its verses, he told Scott, were perpetually ringing in his imagination—

> "Where mightiest of the beasts of chase
> That roam in woody Caledon,
> Crashing the forest in his race,
> The mountain bull comes thundering on—

"and the arrival of Hamilton, when

> "Reeking from the recent deed,
> He dashed his carbine on the ground.

"I have repeated these lines so often on the North Bridge that the whole fraternity of coachmen know me by tongue as I pass. To be sure, to a mind in sober, serious street-walking humour, it must bear an appearance of lunacy when one stamps with a hurried pace and fervent shake of the head, which strong, pithy poetry excites."[28]

Despite house parties and wanderings in Ettrick Forest, from the spring through the autumn Scott continued working hard on the *Minstrelsy*. Longman and Rees had taken over the publication from Cadell and Davies; Longman himself came down from London and offered Scott £500 for the copyright.[29] The first two volumes were to be published in a new edition of a thousand copies, with fifteen hundred copies of volume three.[30] There were more explanatory historical notes to write; Scott polished those ballads of his own composition that he intended to include among the modern imitations; he corresponded with friends and strangers showering him with contributions.

Ballads old and new swam in upon him like goldfish bent on displaying themselves in a bowl. Mat Lewis sent a melancholy confection in fifty-four stanzas, called "Sir Agilthorn," in which a knight bids his lady a lachrymose farewell before spurring off to his death on Flodden Field:

> Flow, flow, my tears, unbounded gush!
> Rise, rise, my sobs, I set ye free;
> Bleed, bleed, my heart! I need not blush
> To own that life is dear to me.[31]

The Reverend Dr. John Jamieson, who was compiling a dictionary of the Scottish tongue, weighed in with "The Water Kelpie," whose hundred and ninety-two lines were so loaded with dialect words as to require almost that number of etymological notes.[32] A sharp-witted young man aptly named Charles Kirkpatrick Sharpe—the same who as a boy had grinned at Scott limping home from military drill in his rumpled uniform—offered him five old ballads, "The Twa Corbies," "The Douglas Tragedy," The Queen's Marie," "Lady Dismal," and one beginning "Lady Anne sat in her bower," as well as two imitations he had written himself, "The Lord Herries, his Complaint" and "The Murder of Caerlaverock."[33]

Scott was enchanted with "The Twa Corbies," which he had never seen before, although he noted its resemblance to the English ballad of "The Three Ravens." "The Douglas Tragedy" he had possessed only in "a very corrupted and inferior copy," and no more than fragments of "The Queen's Marie."[34] To "Lady Anne," he said, he was a perfect stranger—not a surprising confession, since she was a fraud, arrayed in medieval trappings by Sharpe himself.[35] Of the fifth ballad he agreed with Sharpe's own evaluation: "poor 'Lady Dysmal' hath not beauty enough to save *her* from oblivion. I am sensible that her age—a thing at present much admired among ladies—is her only merit."[36] But Sharpe's own two avowed ballads Scott warmly admired. "Lord Herries" was "one of the most happy imitations of ancient strains of minstrelsy which I had ever the good fortune to peruse"[37] and "The Murder of Caerlaverock" "might readily pass for a first-rate minstrel composition." He begged Sharpe's permission to include both in his third volume.[38]

Even Anna Seward, swept from her neoclassical moorings, sat down, glossary in hand, and turned out a ballad entitled "Rich Auld Willie's Farewell," in which sheep sprattle, floods swoom, and spunkie lads "geck and play, The flowrie haughs amang."[39] Politely asking permission to print this composition, Scott told her it was hard to realize that she came from the wrong side of the Border.[40] He himself was thinking, he went on, of writing a comic ballad, and he outlined the story of "The Reiver's Wedding," which he had begun at Lasswade some eighteen months before. It combined Auld Wat of Harden's foray after the bassened bull with that drum-head marriage to Meikle-mouthed Meg by which the young Knight of Harden had slipped from the hangman's noose.[41] After two dozen quatrains, however, Scott again laid the poem aside and left it unfinished.[42]

Delighted at having her own poem included in Scott's collection, Miss Seward in her next letter begged to have her name placed among the subscribers to the volume.[43] The ballads, Scott responded, were not being published by subscription; he had a small patrimony, which, with his professional income and his appointment as Sheriff of Ettrick Forest, made his "literary pursuits more a matter of amusement than object of emolument." He hoped she would honor him by accepting the third volume when it was published.[44]

Miss Seward apologized for her error. "I *knew* your profession, but professional Gentlemen, even of easy fortune, and much respectability, have published by subscription."[45] Scott replied good-humoredly that he did not think there was anything degrading about publishing by subscription, which was sometimes necessary in high-priced publications. "Still, however, it is asking the public to pay for what they have not seen, and carries with it if not the reality at least the appearance of personal solicitation and personal obligation." But neither would be like Miss Seward to believe he had "the vile vanity of wishing to hold myself forth as despising to reap any profit" from literary pursuits, which would "be ineffable conceit and folly in a man much richer than myself."[46]

Before the opening of the autumn session Scott took a final run into Ettrick. There was his usual work as Sheriff to be done: among other cases, a woman had been "ridden down by the Minister." If this had occurred in Selkirkshire, he wrote Erskine, a precognition must be taken with a view to a trial, and if the story seemed bad the minister must be taken into custody until he found bail. Scott himself was in Selkirk on October 4, and a little later was questing after ballads again with Will Laidlaw.[47]

This time he got to see Moffat Water and the Grey Mare's Tail. "Besides the risque of swamping in bogs and breaking my neck over *scaurs*," he wrote, "I encountered the formidable hardships of sleeping upon peat-stacks and eating mutton slain by no common butcher but deprived of life by the Judgement of God."[48] The going was so rough that at Birkhill they put up their horses in a shepherd's byre and proceeded on foot. Their path ran down the east side of a small rivulet toward a pass into Annandale. Between the Giant's Grave and the heathy brae of Mirkside the stream cut its way through opposing rocks of graywacke. The Grey Mare's Tail thundered from the grim heights above, boiling among huge crags with a white smoke of mist on its three hundred feet of roaring fall. The footing grew so difficult that Laidlaw and his cousin George Bryden worried about Scott's lameness, but he derided their fears. At the steepest descents Camp leaped down ahead, waited while Scott lowered himself by hands and arms, and then jumped up to lick his face.[49]

Next morning Laidlaw accompanied Scott on his return to Selkirk, going down the bare glens of Yarrow where once oaks had towered and red-berried rowans clung to the rocks. A small brook ran from the green hills of Whitehope into the Douglas Burn, and here a huge and solitary old hawthorn waved its boughs in the breeze. Laidlaw wondered if it must not be four or five hundred years old, and if red deer must not often have lain in its shade; and the two men pictured the landscape when the region was a royal forest, with alders reflected in the brook, birches and aspens clustering in the dell, and tall pines upon the heights.[50]

On this excursion Scott was pleased by recovering "three Covenanting Ballads—The defeat of Montrose at Philiphaugh—The Battle of Bothwell Brigg and the preceding Skirmish at Drumclog or Loudon hill," poor enough as poetry, but affording "room for some curious notes."[51] Later in the year Laidlaw sent a copy of another version of "Sir Patrick Spens," which his father's herd had obtained from a crazy old woman, and a copy of the ballad of "Coldiknows" taken down from the recitation of Jane Scott. This ballad, she told Laidlaw, the ewe milkers used to sing "coming home from the Bought at night." "Graeme and Bewick," for which Scott had long been searching, was known, Laidlaw had discovered, to a tinker named John Kennedy, who also had another quite different ballad called "The Gallant Graeme."[52]

In Edinburgh that fall, through Scott's influence, the *Scots Magazine* published a series of letters by James Hogg describing a trip through the Highlands.[53] All the poetry of *Sir Tristrem* was now printed, but the publication of that "preux Chevalier," Scott decided, would have to wait until the second edition of the *Minstrelsy* was completed.[54] For the third volume, he informed Miss Seward at the end of November, he was beginning a "Romance of Border Chivalry and Enchantment which will extend to some length."[55] About a fortnight later he conveyed the same information to Ellis, casually adding that it would be "in a Light Horseman sort of stanza." Thus appear the earliest hints of *The Lay of the Last Minstrel*.[56]

Scott began the poem at Lasswade during the summer or autumn of 1802.[57] The galloping rhythms of his irregular four-beat lines he derived from the memory of hearing Dr. John Stoddart recite a part of Coleridge's *Christabel*.[58] He repeated his own opening stanzas to Will Erskine and George Cranstoun, but they were so startled by his metrical novelties that they found little to say. Assuming that they thought more poorly of the effort than their good nature wanted to admit, Scott threw the manuscript in the fire. But they found their memories haunted by what they had heard and talked about the poem throughout the whole of their tramp back to Edinburgh. Sometime later one of them asked him with great interest how the romance progressed. Much surprised to learn its fate, he urged Scott to go on.[59]

So encouraged, Scott resumed the poem while he was in quarters with the Light Horse at Musselburgh. In a charge on Portobello sands he was kicked by a horse, and during the three days he was confined to his lodgings James Skene found him, pen in hand, dashing off the first canto.[60] In the course of December, however, he received through the young Countess of Dalkeith a communication that led him to lengthen and complicate his poem.

An aged gentleman named Thomas Beattie, who had an estate at Mickledale near Langholm, had sent her a tale of a man named Will Moffat coming upon a misshapen goblin with distorted features, who wandered over the moor crying, "Tint, tint, tint." He took the creature home with him, where it ate and drank, proving especially fond of cream. Any of the man's children it was able to master, it beat and scratched. Enraged, Moffat struck the creature a violent blow. "Ah, ah, Will Moffat!" it cried, "you strike sair!" One sultry evening, while the goblin was playing with the children, a shrill voice called, "Gilpin Horner! Gilpin Horner! Gilpin Horner!" "That is me, I must away," the creature exclaimed; it disappeared and was never heard of more.[61]

The Countess playfully demanded that Scott composed a ballad on this story,[62] and he began weaving it in with the wild ride of William of Deloraine, Michael Scott's enchanted volume in the tomb at Melrose Abbey, and the ordeal of battle before Branksome Tower. As the tale elaborated itself, it grew too long for inclusion among the modern ballads of the *Minstrelsy*. Like *Sir Tristrem*, it would have to be published, Scott realized, as a separate volume.[63] Thus the Border ballads had gradually led to three successive enterprises—the modern imitations, the independent appearance of *Sir Tristrem*, with Scott's completion of that poem, and, finally, what was growing into his first long poem, *The Lay of the Last Minstrel*.

Meanwhile John Leyden had been granted his degree as surgeon and doctor by St. Andrews and had received an appointment that would take him to India.[64] December brought the time when he would be obliged to sail. After taking a last farewell of his Edinburgh friends, he had gone to Roxburghshire to say good-bye to his parents. But at the hour of midnight, just as his cronies were drinking a solemn bumper to his health, a figure burst into the room muffled in a seaman's cloak, traveling cap thick with snow. "Dash it, boys," came the well-known sawtones, "here I am again!"[65]

Toward the middle of December, however, he finally did set out for London, bearing with him for George Ellis the running copy of *Sir Tristrem*.[66] Ellis would speedily discern, Scott warned him, that although Leyden was learned he was unpolished. "But he dances his bear with a good confidence and the Bear itself is a very goodnatured and well-conditioned animal." Ritson, Scott added, would be delighted by "the arrival of Leyden, whom he loves with a love surpassing the love of women."[67]

Scott's faith in Ellis's understanding was not misplaced. "Leyden would not have been your Leyden," Ellis wrote genially, "if he had arrived, like a careful citizen, with all his packages carefully docketed in his portmanteau." Instead, all his ideas were "perfectly bewildered, he was tired to death, and sick," and he had mislaid Scott's poem. But he assured his host and hostess that "he remembered to have left [it] somewhere or other and consequently felt very confident of recovering [it]. In short, his whole air and countenance told us 'I am come to be one of your friends'; and we immediately took him at his word so that now we are *old* friends."[68]

Ellis's friendship proved immediately useful. On Leyden's arrival in London he had been seized with a violent fit of stomach cramps. The clerks at India House coldly refused to permit any delay; he must proceed to the Downs, they told him, and board the *Hindostan* at once or surrender his appointment. But Ellis was able to arrange for Leyden to go out later on the *Hugh Inglis* with Lord William Bentinck, who had just been appointed Governor of Madras.[69] On January 12, the night after Leyden was to have gone on board, the *Hindostan* was wrecked going down the river and some fifty of those on board were drowned. "I write you now from the Lobby of the East India House," Leyden told Scott, "to inform you that G. Ellis has saved my life, for without his interference I should certainly this precious day have been snug in Davy's locker."[70]

Leyden's reunion with Ritson did not prove so happy as his meeting with Ellis. To his boisterously beefy high spirits the eccentric little antiquary's hatred of animal food was an absurdity he could never sufficiently deride. At dinner Leyden complained that the joint he had ordered was overdone. "Indeed, for that matter," he cried, "meat can never be too little done, and raw is best of all." He sent the waiter rushing to the kitchen for a raw beefsteak, which he devoured before the horrified vegetarian. Ritson could never afterwards "be prevailed upon to regard him, except as a kind of learned Ogre."[71]

The second edition of the *Minstrelsy* was now pressing on rapidly to completion. Laidlaw had sent the promised copy of "Graeme and Bewick," as well as "The Laird of Logie." "Mrs. Scott is much obliged to George Bryden for the game," Scott wrote, "and so are my books for the Tod's tail, which I have bane'd and mounted on a stick to give them a weekly switching. I am afraid there are too many of them which have the dust seldom removed in a more legitimate and honourable way. I had, however, a struggle with my wife before I could rescue it from her, for being packed with the game she claimed it as being part and pertinent thereof . . ."[72]

Scott's family was growing rapidly. "My little Sophia"—almost three and a half years old—"is a thriving lively Scotch girl," he wrote his brother-in-law Charles Carpenter, and her brother, about a year younger, "uncommonly stout, healthy, and robust; in short quite a model for a little Hercules."[73] And on the second of February, Charlotte had presented him with another daughter, whom they named Anne, after Scott's mother.[74] His worldly affairs, too, were going well. The Government proposed to increase the salary of Sheriffs to £400 a year. The Border ballads were at last returning a handsome profit for his exertions, and although it could not be hoped that *Sir Tristrem* would bring him much, he might confidently expect that his growing reputation would command a good price for *The Lay of the Last Minstrel.*[75]

During the spring of 1803 Scott drove on steadily with this poem. "Mr. Scott sends for Lady Dalkeith's perusal," he wrote in March, "three cantos of an unfinished poem in which her Ladyship will recognize her friend Gilpin Horner . . . The poem has drawn itself out to such a length that it cannot be received into the 3rd vol. of the *Minstrelsy* when finished it will consist of four or five cantos. Mr. Scott has thoughts of publishing it separately and inscribing it to Lord Dalkeith if his Lordship will permit it to be honored with his name."[76]

As soon as Charlotte had made a recovery from the birth of the new baby, Scott took her on a jaunt to London during the spring vacation of the Court of Session. Here they stayed with the Dumergues, who now lived at 15 Piccadilly, the corner of Whitehorse Street. They reached town just in time for Scott to see Leyden in a hurried last farewell before he had to dash off to the Isle of Wight, from which he was sailing for Madras.[77] "When I got to Portsmouth," Leyden wrote him on April 9, "neither ship nor purser had arrived and I then regretted most sincerely that I had left you with so much precipitation." He had now been two days on board and the vessel had not yet weighed anchor.[78]

The gentle bear was full of tenderness in parting. "Money may be paid," he continued, "but kindness never. Assure your excellent Charlotte, whom I shall ever recollect with affection and esteem, how much I regret that I did not see her before my departure, and say a thousand pretty things, for which my mind is too much agitated, being in the situation of Coleridge's devil and his grannam, 'expecting and hoping the trumpet to blow.' And now, my dear Scott, adieu. Think of me with indulgence, and be certain, that wherever, and in whatever situation, John Leyden is, his heart is unchanged by place, and his soul by time."[79]

London was a bustle of friends eager to welcome Scott.[80] At the Dumergues' hospitable board he met Matthew Boulton, the famous Birmingham manufacturer and silversmith, who flirted with Charlotte. "He was a wise man," Scott playfully told the gallant Boulton, "who said, 'Trust not thy wife with a Man of fair tongue.' "[81] Probably through Richard Heber, Scott met the antiquary Francis Douce, who had much admired the first two volumes of the *Minstrelsy*, and who generously placed his great literary resources at Scott's disposal. He renewed his acquaintance with James Mackintosh, whom he had often met at Professor Dugald Stewart's and who had now made a brilliant name for himself at the English bar by his Lincoln's Inn lectures on the law of nature and nations.[82]

Another new friend made during this London visit was the humorous and eccentric William Stewart Rose, whose father had been Pitt's Chancellor of the Exchequer and who was himself the reading clerk of the House of Lords and the author of a translation of *Amadis of Gaul.*[83]

Scott also made the acquaintance of the wealthy banker Samuel Rogers, the author of that bloodlessly elegant poem *The Pleasures of Memory*.[84] Just touching forty, Rogers in his youth had knocked on Samuel Johnson's door in Bolt Court and conversed with Boswell, and now knew Fox, Sheridan, the Holland House circle, everyone of importance in London. Pale, with cold blue eyes, and lips tight above a sardonic shelf of chin, Rogers was famous for a biting wit; he had such a small voice, he remarked, that nobody listened if he said pleasant things.

Rogers had just moved into a small classic mansion at 22 St. James's Place, looking out on the Green Park, where he initiated the famous literary breakfasts he was to give for the next fifty years. Here, amid Titians and a Raphael Madonna hanging gold-framed against crimson damask walls, with mantelpieces by Flaxman and luxuriously bound volumes and rare editions shelved in bookcases painted by Stothard with scenes from Boccaccio, Chaucer, and Shakespeare, his illustrious guests were expected to be brilliant upon topics chosen by their host.

Through Mat Lewis, Scott caught a glimpse of a circle that had achieved a different kind of fame. The author of *The Monk*, no ascetic, gave a gay supper party in Argyle Street, "where the company"—Scott quotes the Duke in *Twelfth Night*—was " 'fairer than honest.' " Among these ladies of pleasure was the notorious courtesan Harriette Wilson, "a smart saucy girl with good eyes and dark hair, and the manners of a wild schoolboy." "Whore from the earliest opportunity, I suppose," Scott commented, Harriette "lived with half the gay world at hack and manger" and later included the Duke of Wellington among her lovers. Her sister, Lady Berwick, "had whitewashed herself and cut Harriette. This was not to be forgiven, and as both had boxes at the opera, and Harriette's was uppermost," she entertained herself "now and then by spitting on her sister's head."[85]

In the intervals of his London social life, Scott made extracts from Douce's collection and from the manuscripts in the library of the Duke of Roxburghe, all of which were to be used in *Sir Tristrem*.[86] These labors completed, he and Charlotte went with Heber and Douce to visit George Ellis and his wife in their home at Sunninghill just outside Windsor Park. Although Scott had been in friendly correspondence with Ellis for two years, they now met for the first time. Ellis was a man of fifty, with sharp gray eyes, a brown face as thin and keen as a battle-ax, and a quizzical nose at the tip of which clung a small drop of moisture. Witty, well bred, and warmhearted, Ellis was both a brilliant conversationalist and a splendid listener. Mrs. Ellis, small and graceful, with a quaint wit of her own, Ellis called "Ladyfair." Scott felt at once as if they were all old friends. Before the end of a happy week, he was reading them the first three cantos of *The Lay of the Last Minstrel*, beneath a huge oak in Windsor Forest.[87]

From Sunninghill Scott and Charlotte went on with Heber to Oxford, where they met Heber's brother Reginald. At breakfast in Brasenose College, Reginald Heber read aloud his poem "Palestine," which had just won that year's poetry prize. The verses on Solomon's Temple, Scott observed, failed to note one striking fact, that no tools had been used in its erection. Reginald retired to a corner of the room, and returned in a few minutes with the added lines:

> No hammer fell, no ponderous axes rung,
> Like some tall palm the mystic fabric sprung.
> Majestic silence . . .[88]

Escorted by the Hebers the Scotts made a trip to nearby Blenheim, the nation's gift to the Duke of Marlborough. And of course they explored all the wonders of Oxford. They paced the great quadrangle of Christ Church beneath the bell spire of Tom Tower and ascended the noble stairway rising under its magnificent fan tracery to Wolsey's dining hall with its elaborately carved roof. On the gently curving High they beheld St. Mary's Church and its porch of twisted baroque columns. They saw the splendid dome of the Radcliffe Camera towering above its octagonal base, the Bodleian Library, the arched and stone-vaulted Divinity School, Wren's masterly Sheldonian Theatre, the lovely reredos of New College Chapel, the classical façade of Queen's College. They strolled through the Colonnades of St. John's and into its beautiful gardens. They walked in the cloisters of Magdalen, where its bowers soar beside the quietly flowing Cherwell. Too much richness crowded into too brief a time to be all clearly retained, the visit left in Scott's memory as he returned to London "a grand but indistinct picture of towers and chapels and oriels and vaulted halls and libraries and paintings."[89]

Before he had left Scotland, the third volume of the *Minstrelsy* had been very nearly printed, and he was now eagerly expecting copies to give his southern friends.[90] He had written to James Ballantyne, who had at last made the move to Edinburgh and whose printing works were located at Abbeyhill near Holyrood, directing that copies be sent his mother, his brother Tom, and his uncles Dr. Rutherford and Captain Robert Scott. Others went to James Hogg and Colin Mackenzie, one set on fine paper to the Duchess of Buccleuch at Dalkeith House, and another to Lady Charlotte Campbell. The remaining ten on fine paper Scott asked Ballantyne to send to him in London. "I think they will give you some *éclat* here, where fine printing is so much valued."[91]

"I have settled," he went on, "about printing an edition of the *Lay*, 8vo. with vignettes, provided I can get a draftsman I think well of. We may throw off a few superb in quarto. To the *Minstrelsy* I mean this note to be added, by way of advertisement:—'In the press, and will speedily be published, *The Lay of the Last Minstrel*, by Walter Scott, Esq., Editor of the *Minstrelsy of the Scottish Border*. Also, *Sir Tristrem, a Metrical Romance*, by Thomas of Ercildoune, called the Rhymer, edited from an ancient MS., with an Introduction and Notes, by Walter Scott, Esq.' "[92]

Unfortunately, Ballantyne ran into some labor trouble among the printers' devils and the papermakers, which delayed publication, so that it is uncertain whether Scott received his fine-paper copies of the *Minstrelsy* before he was obliged to leave London. "I never heard," he commented, "of authors *striking* work as the mechanicks call it until their Masters the Booksellers should increase their pay, but if such a combination could take place the revolt would now be general in all branches of literary labour."[93]

The middle of May saw Scott back in Edinburgh with glowing memories of his southern holiday. "How often do Charlotte and I think of the little paradise at Sunninghill and its kind inhabitants," he wrote Ellis. "I don't know why the human and vegetable departments should differ so excessively. Oaks and beeches, and ashes and elms, not to mention cabbages and turnips, are usually arrayed *en masse*; but where do we meet a town of antiquaries, a village of poets, or a hamlet of philosophers?" Ellis and his wife, Scott urged, must unroot themselves from their forest and see how the hardy blasts of the northern mountains would suit them for a change of climate.[94]

The second edition of the *Minstrelsy* was published in Edinburgh before the end of the month and a little later in London. Sales were a bit slower than those of the first edition; Scott and Ballantyne had been optimistic in believing that the third volume of modern imitations would prove a dazzling attraction.[95] And indeed these concoctions on the whole may well be left in oblivion. Leyden's "Lord Soulis" and "The Cout of Keeldar" have a lurid vigor, and Sharpe's two poems, which Scott praised, "Lord Herries His Complaint" and "The Murder of Caerlaveroc," rise above mediocrity.[96] Aside from these, however, only Scott's own contributions are of any importance: "Glenfinlas," "The Eve of St. John," "Cadzow Castle," "The Gray Brother," and parts of "Christie's Will" and "Thomas the Rhymer."[97] Even these would command little attention save for Scott's later achievement. The true value of the *Minstrelsy* lies rather in the ancient ballads Scott discovered and in his introductions and notes.

Swelled by a considerable number in the second edition and further augmented by a trickle of inclusions in later editions, the number of these ballads Scott printed came to seventy-two. The magnitude of his accomplishment may be appreciated from the fact that this represents almost one-quarter of the authentic old ballads known today, which total little more than three hundred.[98] Thirty-eight of the poems Scott was the first ever to put in print. Two more had appeared in broadside versions that did not come to light until later; one, "Willie's Ladye," had been published, very much modernized, in Lewis's *Tales of Wonder*; and one, "Sir Hugh le Blond," Scott erroneously believed to be the original form of "Sir Aldingar," in Percy's *Reliques*.[99]

Among Scott's outstanding harvests were the colorful "Sang of the Outlaw Murray," "Jamie Telfer," "Kinmont Willie," with its exciting rescue and rough humor, the beautiful though fragmentary "Douglas Tragedie," "The Twa Corbies," with its sinister insinuated betrayal, "Clerk Saunders," the supernatural fantasy of "The Demon Lover," "Kempion" (Kemp Owyne), "The Wife of Usher's Well," and the haunting pathos of "The Cruel Sister." Among those of which he printed important variations are "Sir Patrick Spens"—(although his added stanzas diminish rather than intensify the power of the standard version)—"The Battle of Otterbourne," a Scottish version of "The Hunting of the Cheviot," "Tamlane," and that stark melodrama of murder by poisoning, "Lord Randal."

Scott's editorial principles, like those of Bishop Percy and most other scholars of his time, were not quite those of present-day scholars. "It is no doubt highly desirable," he granted, "that the text of ancient poetry should be given untouched and uncorrupted."[100] But the great difficulty of the early editors, as he noted in defending Percy against the diatribes of Ritson, "was not how to secure the very words of old ballads, but how to arrest attention upon the subject at all."[101] They had to create the sensibilities by which their discoveries were to be judged, and make readers whose tastes were formed on Pope and Johnson realize that these folk poems were not crude and shapeless barbarities.

This was not always easy. Many corruptions were liable to creep into poems transmitted by oral tradition, "impertinent interpolations from the conceit of one rehearser, unintelligible blunders from the stupidity of another, and omissions equally to be regretted from the want of memory of a third."[102] What more reasonable than for an editor to use his learning and insight to restore the primitive vigor of diction and boldness of coloring? So felt Percy, and so felt Scott and almost all their fellow antiquaries; Ritson's frantic insistence that not a comma must be added nor the most obvious corruption rectified was highly unrepresentative. Scott loved poetry more than he loved a meticulous historical accuracy, and he wanted his ballads to appear at their best.

He therefore freely admitted that for his own versions he combined the most vivid and poetic lines from the various copies in his possession. No more than some of the editors of Shakespeare did he hesitate to make conjectural emendations where he felt sure he could discern the original meanings through the corruptions. More, for narrative clarity or dramatic structure, he did not scruple to transpose lines and even stanzas from one part of a ballad to another. Finally, there are no few places where, without warning, Scott substituted epithets or lines of his own for those of the original, even inserted entire quatrains of his own invention.

More scrupulous than Percy or Pinkerton but still pretty high-handed even for his own time, Scott's liberties would be regarded as scandalous in a scholar today. But, as Dame Una Pope-Hennessy remarks, "He felt that people who read ballads for enjoyment do not want to be confronted with the oldest or most accurate, but merely with the most satisfactory version."[103] And deep in his heart he identified himself with the old ballad singers, felt himself a *makar* like them with some of their creative privileges, a last minstrel for whom these lays were eroded torsos that he might recarve to bolder beauty. "*Doch Homeride zu seyn, auch nur als letzter, ist schon.*"[104]

In "The Dowie Dens of Yarrow," Scott altered twenty-eight out of sixty-eight lines, turning, for example,

> A better rose will never spring
> Than him I've lost on Yarrow

to

> A fairer rose did never bloom
> Than now lies cropp'd on Yarrow.[105]

In "Fause Foodrage," Professor Child notes, there are almost forty minor alterations.[106] "Jamie Telfer of the Fair Dodhead" has numerous variations and transpositions, and several inserted quatrains, including

> My hounds may a' rin masterless,
>     My hawks may fly frae tree to tree,
> My lord may grip my vassal lands,
>     For there again maun I never be.[107]

Furthermore, in this poem Scott changes the heroes from the Elliotts to the Scotts and invents stanzas bringing the Scotts of Harden and Buccleuch and others of his clan into the story:

> Warn Wat o' Harden and his sons,
>     Wi' them will Borthwick Water ride;
> Warn Gaudilands and Allanhaugh,
>     And Gilmanscleugh and Commonside.

> \* \* \*

> The Scotts they rade, the Scotts they ran,
>     Sae starkly and sae steadily!
> And aye the ower-word o' the thrang,
>     Was—"Rise for Branksome readilie!"[108]

Scott could not resist the same temptation in "The Sang of the Outlaw Murray," where he humorously has the marauding Scott of Buccleuch tell King James that it is below the royal dignity to treat with an outlaw:

> Then out and spak the nobil King,
>     And round him cast a wilie ee—
> "Now, had thy tongue, Sir Walter Scott,
>     Nor speak of reif nor felonie:
> For, had every honest man his awin kye,
>     A right puir clan *thy* name wad be!"[109]

Lockhart is therefore quite mistaken when he claims that Scott had "interpolated hardly a line or even an epithet of his own."[110] He is on firmer ground, however, when he continues in eloquent panegyric: "To the task of selecting a standard text among such a diversity of materials, he brought a knowledge of old manners and phraseology, and a manly simplicity of taste, such as had never been united in the person of a poetic antiquary. From among a hundred corruptions he seized, with instinctive tact, the primitive diction and imagery; and produced strains in which the unbroken energy of half-civilized ages, their stern and deep passions, their daring adventures and cruel tragedies, and even their wild humor, are reflected with almost the brightness of a Homeric mirror . . ."[111]

But even here Lockhart's praise falls partly aslant of the reality. Sometimes, far from restoring "the primitive diction" of a corrupted stanza, Scott is breathing his own life into a dead quatrain; and the "wild humor" is occasionally an urbane joke superimposed by the nineteenth-century poet upon the fifteenth-century folk-rhymer. Nevertheless, it is true that Scott's artistic tact fuses his own work so harmoniously with the original that even a sensitive reader may easily find it impossible to tell one from the other.

Scott believed his own skill at such literary detective work to be infallible; he prided himself on having a nose for sniffing out the spurious from the genuine. "I scarce know anything so easily discovered as the piecing and darning of an old ballad; the darns in a silk stockings are not more manifest."[112] He observed that most ballad forgeries give themselves away by excess. They "abound," he shrewdly noted, "with an extravagant use of old words and are in fact usually composed from the glossary of some old author without the ingenious imitator being capable of discovering the proportions which the words requiring explanation in old compositions bear to those which are still in common use."[113]

His judgments, however, were not quite so conclusive as he imagined. Laidlaw inserted stanzas in "The Demon Lover" of which Scott felt no suspicion. And the ingenious antiquarian Robert Surtees palmed off on him three ballads of his own composition, "Lord Ewrie," "The Death of Featherstonhaugh," and "Barthram's Dirge." Scott included these in the *Minstrelsy*, and Surtees never had the courage to admit the deception.

Scott's errors, nevertheless, are few; his insight and scholarship commanding, his introductions and notes fascinating. As Lockhart said, they "teemed with curious knowledge, not hastily grasped for the occasion, but gradually gleaned and sifted by the patient labour of years";[114] they were rich in striking quotations and out-of-the-way information, not only from the chroniclers and historians—Holinshed, Godscroft, Pittscottie, Satchells, Robertson, Spottiswoode, Pinkerton, Camden's *Britannia*, Stowe's *Chronicles*, Sadler's *State Papers*[115]—but from hosts of other recondite sources, both in print and in manuscript. They were crammed with dramatic anecdote, ranging over all Scottish history, from struggles to control the throne to the wildest Border feuds.

All this, which might have been pedantic in many another writer, was handled with ease, simplicity, and grace, skillfully arranged, vigorously worded. The past that had stretched out stiff like some petrified giant of legend began breathing with passion; wild deeds long buried in dust suddenly leaped into bloody life. When, a decade later, an anonymous novelist made his dazzling appearance, and all the world were puzzling themselves with the mystery of his identity, Christopher North exclaimed impatiently, "I wonder what all these people are perplexing themselves with: have they forgotten the *prose* of the *Minstrelsy*?"[116]

# PART FOUR

## Ascent of Helicon

### 1803–1810

# 1

---

# *That Wretched Beast Is Alive*

## *(1803–1805)*

Some quarter of a century after the publication of the *Minstrelsy*, Scott remembered it as having been coolly received south of the Border. "The curiosity of the English," he wrote, "was not much awakened by poems in the rude garb of antiquity, accompanied with notes referring to the obscure feuds of barbarous clans, of whose very name civilized history was ignorant."[1] But by 1830 he had long been used to enormous sales; in 1803 he was well pleased with his success, and the fact was that cultivated readers both south and north of the Tweed were hearty in their approval. The volumes became widely known abroad as well. Publishers on the Continent brought out successive editions; they were translated into German, Danish, and Swedish; and across the Atlantic editions in the United States spread Scott's name through the New World.[2]

At Lasswade that summer, with the *Minstrelsy* now off his hands, Scott pressed forward happily on the *Lay* and on his Introduction and Notes to *Sir Tristrem*. When in July his duties as Sheriff took him to Selkirkshire, he met at the little inn at Clovenfords a young man named Clement Carlyon, who was there for the fishing. Scott's sudden arrival strained the landlady's resources, but young Carlyon agreed to share a bed with a friend, Scott slept in a smaller bed, and the three shared the parlor. Scott was immediately fascinated by Carlyon's name. "You are a Cornishman, of course, and can tell me whether there is any seaport at present in Cornwall of your name, for such there certainly was in former days . . ." Carlyon did not know, but referred him to an antiquary named Polwhele, who was investigating the *Morte d'Arthur* for a history of Cornwall.[3]

There was "but one family of the name in Cornwall," Carlyon told Scott, "or as far as he ever heard, anywhere else," and "they were of great antiquity. Does not this circumstance seem to prove," Scott asked Ellis excitedly, "that there existed in Cornwall a place called Caerlion, giving name to that family? Caerlion would probably be *Castrum Leonense*, the chief town of Liones, which in every romance is stated to have been Tristrem's country, and from which he derived his surname of Tristrem *de Liones* [Lyonnesse]. This district, as you notice in the notes on the *Fabliaux*, was swallowed up by the sea." All these details fitted in with Scott's theory that "the Caerlion mentioned by Tomas" was "a very different place from Caerlion on Uske—which is no seaport."[4]

Together with his duties as Sheriff and his scholarly investigations, Scott's activities in the militia made strenuous demands on his labors. The Peace of Amiens had completely broken down. Bonaparte had bullied the delegates of the Cisalpine Republic into making him the president of their puppet state, now renamed the Republic of Italy. He had seized Piedmont, pounced on Switzerland. He was threatening the Ottoman Empire and Sardinia, stirring up trouble in Persia and Afghanistan, boasting that he would chase the British out of Bengal, demanding that they evacuate Malta. On May 18 Britain had again declared war.

The renewal of hostilities led to furious preparations against invasion. Napoleon was speeding the construction of battleships and bombarding dockyard officials from the Scheldt to the shores of Biscay with imperious secret orders. He had arrested ten thousand British travelers in France. Rumor had him building a bridge from Calais to Dover, digging a tunnel beneath the Channel, planning to transport his armies in balloons. Feverish endeavors were made to meet the danger. Stores were to be removed, bakers were told to have reserves of flour and oatmeal, families were provided with ten days' supplies of flour, meal, and potatoes.[5]

During the summer Scott's company was in quarters at Musselburgh. "Three regiments of militia, with a formidable park of artillery," he wrote Miss Seward, "are encamped just by us. . . . There are four other troops in the regiment, consisting of yeomanry, whose iron faces and muscular forms announce the hardness of the climate against which they wrestle, and the powers which nature has given them to contend with and subdue it."[6] Drums and bugles sounded above the rumble of drays in the streets; the evening quiet was broken by the pop of muskets and the thunder of the volley.[7]

Scott took as heartily to soldiering as ever. "I must own that to one who has like myself, la tête un peu exaltée, the 'pomp and circumstance of war' gives, for a time, a very poignant and pleasing sensation. The imposing appearance of cavalry, in particular, and the rush which marks their onset, appear to me to partake highly of the sublime."[8] As he galloped along the surge on Portobello Sands, his heart rose in fierce exultation. Once, at Lasswade, he was aroused from his desk by a volley of small shot fired through a window. Only five minutes earlier, Charlotte had been arranging flowers there; he leaped up with heavens knows what bloody visions. But through Camp's aid they ran down the culprit, who turned out to be only an unlucky sportsman firing wild.[9]

September brought a lull in these warlike doings, and a surprise visit from William and Dorothy Wordsworth, who were making a tour of Scotland. The two poets had looked forward to meeting since John Stoddart, three years before, had enthusiastically praised each to the other. Leaving their carriage at Roslin, the bony long-nosed poet and his brown-faced sister walked down the valley of the Esk to Lasswade, arriving before Scott and Charlotte had even risen that morning. Scott greeted them in the highest of spirits. The first four cantos of *The Lay of the Last Minstrel* were now completed, and he was soon reciting it to his fellow poet in an enthusiastic chant. "The novelty of the manners," said Wordsworth, "the clear picturesque descriptions, and the easy glowing energy of so much of the verse, greatly delighted me."[10]

Walking the tourists back to Roslin, Scott promised to meet them at Melrose two days later, on his way to the Circuit Court at Jedburgh. On September 18, the Wordsworths slept at the little inn at Clovenfords. On their mentioning Scott's name the landlady overwhelmed them with attentions. "Wherever we named him," said Wordsworth, "we found the word acted as an *open sesamum*; and I believe, that in the character of the *Sheriff's* friends, we might have counted on a hearty welcome under any roof in the Border country."[11] At Melrose the landlady refused to show them the beds, "or to make any sort of promise," Dorothy noted, "till she was assured from the Sheriff himself that he had no objection to sleep in the same room with William."[12]

In Melrose Abbey, Scott poured out a store of historical tradition and popular tales and drew their attention to the rich ornamentation of flowers and leaves sculptured in the pale red stone. It was unfortunate, Dorothy thought, that the insignificant houses of the town so encircled the ruins as to cut them off from the rural landscape and the river, but later Scott took them into the gardens and orchard of Mr. Riddell, from which they had a view of the Abbey through a wreathing of trees that concealed the surrounding buildings. They dined and spent the evening together at the inn.[13]

Next day, at Jedburgh, Scott begged them not to enter the Court: "I really would not like you," he explained, "to see the sort of figure I cut there." But they did see him, in his cocked hat and sword, marching in the Judge's procession to the sound of one cracked trumpet. After his official duties were over he introduced them to Will Laidlaw, who was serving as a juryman, and the four strolled up the woody banks of the Jed to the old ruined halls of Ferniehurst.[14]

Wind was tossing the branches of the elms, sunshine dancing among their leaves. Dorothy exclaimed, "What a life there is in trees!" How different, said Scott, was the feeling of a young lady who had been born and bred in the Orkney Islands and who came to spend a summer at Kelso. Nothing in the mainland scenery "had disappointed her so much as trees and woods; she complained that they were lifeless, silent, and, compared with the grandeur of the ever-changing ocean, even insipid." "And so back she has gone, and I believe nothing will ever tempt her from *the wind-swept Orcades again.*"[15]

With their dinner the Wordsworths had "*a bottle of wine*, that we might not disgrace the Sheriff, who supped with us in the evening, stayed late, and repeated some of his poem." The assizes being over the following day, Scott accompanied them up the Teviot to Hawick, entertaining them with legends and ballads about every rock and tower they passed, and pointing out Ruberslaw, Minto Crags, the Carter Bar, and the Cheviots. Before breakfast the following morning, from the top of the hill above Hawick, he showed them the wild glens of Liddesdale, regretting that his engagements would not allow him to be their guide among its lonely dales. Here on September 23 they parted.[16]

Dorothy Wordsworth was impressed by the strength of Scott's local attachments. "His whole heart and soul," she wrote, "seem to be devoted to the Scottish streams . . . and I am sure that there is not a story ever told by the fire-sides in that neighborhood that he cannot repeat . . . He is a man of very sweet manners, mild, cordial and cheerful."[17]

The Wordsworths pursued their journey homeward by Eskdale, passing Branxholm—the Branksome of the *Lay*—four miles south of Hawick. "We did not omit noticing Johnnie Armstrong's Keep," Wordsworth wrote Scott from his home in Westmorland; "but his hanging place, to our great regret, we missed." With his letter Wordsworth enclosed a copy of his sonnet on Neidpath Castle, which Scott had admiringly requested. "My sister and I often talk of the happy days we spent in your company. Such things do not occur often in life. If we live we shall meet again . . . Your sincere friend, for such I will call myself, though slow to use a word of such solemn meaning to any one, W. Wordsworth."[18]

But in one respect Wordsworth was puzzled by Scott. He seemed to have little hope or concern for rising to distinction at the bar and yet to think less of his powers as a writer than of his sports and social amusements. At the same time, when Wordsworth spoke of the profits of the legal profession, Scott remarked casually that "he was sure he could, if he chose, get more money than he should ever wish from the booksellers." To Wordsworth, still poor and struggling at the age of thirty-three, but solemnly convinced of his own poetical greatness, Scott's mingling of assurance and modesty was strange.[19]

Nevertheless it was genuine. Scott had no blown-up literary self-esteem, but the praise given the *Minstrelsy* had convinced him he could be a successful journeyman of letters. And the favorable response that *The Lay of the Last Minstrel* had already evoked from Erskine, Cranstoun, Ellis, and even Wordsworth made him quietly certain he could score a success with that poem. He therefore went ahead serenely with its composition. At the same time, for the newly founded *Edinburgh Review* he was making a first flight as a book reviewer.[20]

This quarterly had been established the previous year, with the rising young bookseller Archibald Constable as its publisher. Born in the brain of the witty and high-spirited English clergyman Sydney Smith, the project met with an enthusiastic response from three brilliant young advocates, Francis Jeffrey, Henry Brougham, and Francis Horner. Smith was now thirty-two and a bare two months older than Scott, Jeffrey two years younger, Brougham and Horner only twenty-five. All four were bursting with ideas, critical of society, interested in literature. Smith rose to prominence in the Church and but for his wit might have been made a bishop. Jeffrey became a critic of almost dictatorial power, Horner a distinguished economist, Brougham the stormy petrel of radical politics.[21]

Most of the critical journals of the time were either what amounted to publishers' organs, written by hacks who sneered or rhapsodized at their employers' bidding, or unscrupulous instruments of party politics, buttering or slashing up a book in accordance with its author's political affiliations. Smith proposed that the articles in the *Edinburgh Review* be written by contributors well informed in the fields they were dealing with and independent of the publisher's control. Although its position was to be one of a broadly progressive Whig liberalism, the *Review* would not damn a poem for its writer's politics. Nor would it be limited to literary criticism, but range over the whole world of thought and knowledge. Instead of the miserable two guineas that represented the usual reviewer's fee, its experts were to get sixteen guineas—many of them considerably more—for a sheet of sixteen printed pages. Each number of the new quarterly would consist of fifteen to twenty long articles devoted to the most important books of the day.

In Jeffrey's third-floor flat in Buccleuch Place the little group worked out their plans. The first number, under the editorship of Sydney Smith, created a sensation when it appeared on October 10, 1802. The members met as a sort of editorial board in a dingy room off Willison's printing office in Craig's Close, making a gay conspiracy out of preserving their incognito, stealing there singly, on Smith's insistence, by various lanes and back alleys. When Smith departed for London the following year, the editorial work was at first carried on by committee, but this proving impractical, the editorship was pressed upon Jeffrey. Within a year the *Edinburgh Review* had established itself as the leading quarterly in the kingdom.[22]

Jeffrey had of course known Scott since that night at the Speculative

Society, twelve years before, when he had seen him sitting at the foot of the table in a huge woollen night cap, heard him read an essay on ballads, and been led to visit his basement den in George Square. As fellow advocates they had paced the floor of the Outer House and mingled in conversational groups around its red-hot stoves. Short, aggressive, with a small, swarthy face, fiercely flashing dark eyes, and a huge circle of brow crowned by bristling black hair, Jeffrey poured out at these gatherings a rapid flow of fancy, sarcasm, persiflage, his lips vibrating with the vehement and never-ceasing play of his mind.[23]

It was Jeffrey, doubtless, who invited Scott to become a contributor to the *Review*. He was soon happily engaged on a long article dealing with two recent translations of *Amadis of Gaul*—one by Robert Southey from the Spanish prose of Vasco de Lobeira, and his friend William Stewart Rose's rhymed version of Herberay's French translation of Lobeira. Scott's review emphasized the importance of the romances of chivalry as a source of understanding the ages in which they were created. "The novels of Fielding and Richardson are even already become valuable, as a record of the English manners of the last generation. How much, then, should we prize the volumes which describe those of the era of the victors of Cressy and Poitiers!"[24]

Several years later, in a review of Ellis's *Specimens of Early English Romance*, Scott elaborated the same point. To form a just idea of the past, "These works of fancy should be read along with the labours of the professed historian. The one teaches what our ancestors thought: how they lived, upon what motives they acted, and what language they spoke; and having attained this intimate knowledge of their sentiments, manners, and habits, we are certainly better prepared to learn from the other the actual particulars of their annals." History, Scott summarized, told what they did, romance what they were.[25]

Both the review of *Amadis of Gaul* and another review by Scott, of Sibbald's *Chronicle of Scottish Poetry*, appeared in the *Edinburgh Review* for October, 1803.[26] But throughout that month Scott had to put aside further literary work; the Volunteers were again demanding his liveliest efforts. "A beacon light, communicating with that of Edinburgh Castle," he wrote, "is just erecting in front of our quiet cottage. My field equipage is ready, and I want nothing but a pipe and a *schnurbartchen* to convert me into a complete hussar. Charlotte, with the infantry (of the household troops, I mean), is to beat her retreat into Ettrick Forest, where, if the Tweed is in his usual wintry state of flood, she may weather out a descent from Ostend."[27] Late in October the militia were once more in quarters at Musselburgh, Dalkeith, and Lasswade for nine days. At the end, there was a great review, ten thousand strong on Portobello Sands, before their new Commander in Chief, the Earl of Moira, with boats, crowds of spectators, and waving flags and streamers.[28]

All this drilling and reviewing, complained Ellis, was delaying

Scott's literary projects. "You appear," he wrote in November, "to have been for some time so military, that I am afraid the most difficult and important part of your original plan"—for the Introduction to *Sir Tristrem*—"viz. your History of Scottish poetry, will be again postponed, and must be kept for some future publication." But these military alarms ought not to hold up the composition of the *Lay*. "That, I think, may go on as well in your tent, amidst the clang of trumpets and the dust of the field, as in your quiet cottage—perhaps indeed still better—nay, I am not sure whether a *real* invasion would not be, as far as your poetry is concerned, a thing to be wished."[28a]

Meanwhile, James Hogg, excited by the ballad imitations in the third volume of the *Minstrelsy*, had decided that he could do much better. He dashed some off and sent them to Scott, who warmly praised the beauties scattered among the crudities. The next time Hogg was in Edinburgh he called on Scott, who invited him and Laidlaw to dinner in Castle Street. In the drawing room Mrs. Scott, who had recently been in delicate health, was reclining on a sofa. Hogg made his best bow and promptly flung himself full length in his stained shepherd's clothing on a chintz sofa opposite her; "I thought that I could never do wrong," he explained, "to copy the Lady of the house." The shepherd dined heartily, drank freely, sang songs, and told stories. As the bottle circulated he progressed from calling his host "Mr. Scott" to "Sherra," and then on to "Scott," "Walter," and "Wattie"; by the time supper was served he was calling Mrs. Scott "Charlotte."[29]

"I am afraid," he wrote apologetically, "that I was at least half-seas over the night I was with you, for I cannot, for my life, recollect what passed when it was late . . . I have the consolation, however, of remembering that Mrs. Scott kept in company all or most of the time, which she certainly could not have done, had I been very rude." He would like Scott's advice, Hogg went on, about publishing his songs, which, although "certainly the *worst* of my productions," enjoyed "extraordinary repute in Ettrick and its neighborhood." What would Scott think about an engraving of the author as a frontispiece and about an introductory account of Hogg's life and education, which Hogg would write for Scott to transcribe, merely "putting He for I"? And, if Scott would allow it, "I will address you in a dedication singular enough. . . . You will not be in the least jealous, if, alongst with my services to you, I present my kindest compliments to the sweet little lady whom you call Charlotte. . . . Believe me, Dear Walter, your most devoted servant, James Hogg."[30]

Scott was not a man to miss the comedy in this quaint and clumsy effusion, with its innocent overfamiliarity and the glorious impudence of its proposal that he pretend to be the author of the Shepherd's own autobiographical preface. But if he laughed he also helped. Ultimately, through his good offices, *The Mountain Bard* was published by Constable, although without any such introduction as Hogg had suggested.[31]

Another kind of literary insolence, however, Scott subjected to a witty drubbing in reviewing Godwin's *Life of Geoffrey Chaucer* for the January number of the *Edinburgh Review*.[32] The swollen text of Godwin's two enormous quartos contained, Scott pointed out, "hardly the vestige of an authenticated fact concerning Chaucer, which is not to be found in the eight pages of Messrs. Thomas Tyrwhytt and George Ellis," and yet Godwin had repeatedly sneered at the researches of these scholars to which he himself had added almost nothing. Upon their biographical materials he had merely superimposed a voluminous embroidery of irrelevance and supposition.[33]

"Chaucer was born in London.—This is the subject," Scott continued, "of the first chapter. The commentary is a sketch of the history of London from the year of Christ 50, down to the reign of Edward III., with notices respecting the principal citizens and Lords Mayor . . . not forgetting Whittington and his cat. . . . But Chaucer must have gone sometimes to church,—and therefore Mr. Godwin feels himself obliged to give an account of the peculiar tenets of the Church of Rome . . . The author proceeds, with the most unfeeling prolixity, to give a minute detail of the civil and common law, of the feudal institutions, of the architecture of churches and castles, of sculpture and painting, of minstrels, of players, of parish clerks, &c. &c.; while poor Chaucer, like Tristram Shandy, can hardly be said to be fairly born, although his life has attained the size of half a volume."[34]

His work might have extended to still greater length, Godwin had solemnly explained, but for the assurance of his bookseller that two volumes were all the public would stand. "Upon perusing this sentence," Scott wrote, "the cold drops stood upon our brow at contemplating the peril we had escaped . . ."[35] It was an occasion for happy surprise that Godwin failed to record the tradition "that Chaucer, while in the Temple, was fined two shillings 'for beating a Franciscan friar in Fleet-Street.' " This might have introduced the history of Fleet Street, the Fleet Ditch, the Fleet Prison, and the fleet or Royal Navy, the penalty have justified a history of the silver coinage, and the Franciscan a history of the mendicant orders.

"But, above all, the cause of the scuffle, and the drubbing itself, would have led to many a learned dissertation. It is probable that one or both parties were in liquor. If so, when, how, or with what liquor did they become intoxicated? Was it with wine of Ape, or of Chepe; with Malverie, or with Hippocras? And can any light be thrown upon the combat, from the similar affray between Justice Shallow when an Inn's of Court man, and Samson Stockfish the fruiterer? Again, it is probable that the quarrel originated in some theological dispute,—and the vast and thorny field of controversy might have been accurately surveyed . . . Perhaps Chaucer offended the friar by the freedom of his conversation,—and why not insert all the jocose and satirical passages of the

Canterbury Tales? . . . All of which knowledge is unfortunately lost to the world, perhaps through the ill-considered interference of Mr. Phillips the publisher."[36]

The lighthearted burlesque of this article was contrary to Scott's usual principles as a reviewer. "In general," he wrote Ellis, "I think it ungentlemanly to wound any person's feelings through an anonymous publication unless where conceit or false doctrine strongly calls for reprobation." He did not approve the ostentatious superiority of tone habitually assumed by the *Edinburgh* reviewers, "nor have I either inclination or talents to use the critical scalping knife unless as in the case of Godwin where flesh and blood succumbed under the temptation." Godwin's dignified contempt of the men on whose labors he had depended was made still more ludicrous, however, by his own ponderous fatuity. "I was at a loss," Scott joked, "to know how a whole edition" of Godwin had been disposed of, "till I conjectured that, as the heaviest materials to be come at, they have been sent on the secret expedition . . . for blocking up the mouth of our enemies harbours."[37]

The French invasion-threats hinted in this allusion had by no means vanished. Alarm beacons stretched inland all along the coast. Throughout England and Scotland excited volunteers exercised in muddy fields and dashed in fierce assaults on thorny hedges. Edinburgh had become an armed camp; besides the regular garrison there were almost ten thousand volunteers. Lawyers wore uniforms under their gowns, "professors wheeled in the college area," shopkeepers measured out their wares in scarlet. On the last day of 1803 it became known that a severe gale had driven the Channel Fleet from its station. No defense lay between Britain and Napoleon's assembled barges.[38]

One night late in January the guard at Hume Castle saw a red glare in Northumberland and lit his own beacon. Down through the Border the fierce lights blazed from peak to peak; in Kelso, Hawick, Galashiels, and Selkirk the Volunteers flocked to arms.[39] At Jedburgh in the chill night drums beat through streets crowded with troops and bright as day from lighted windows.[40] Throughout Liddesdale, Scott said, men requisitioned every horse in the countryside and rode without drawing bridle to their rendezvous at Kelso, sweeping in to the tune of

> O wha dare meddle wi' me,
> And wha dare meddle wi' me'
> My name is little Jock Elliot,
> And wha dare meddle wi' me!

The men of Selkirkshire spurred without stopping the forty or fifty miles to their posts at Dalkeith and arrived at one o'clock on the following day.[41]

The signal, however, turned out to be a false alarm, and the troops dispersed. But drilling went on without cessation. Throughout the spring, sham battles and sham sieges rattled at Craigmillar, Gilmerton, and Braidhills.[42] In March a mock attack and defense on Leith Links turned into a riot because a regiment of kilted Highlanders refused to understand that the plan of battle made it their duty to be beaten. In May, Scott's regiment went into quarters again for three days.[43] During that same month its Adjutant, a fat, jolly drinker named Jock Adams, died and was buried with military honors in Greyfriars'. The band played the Dead March from *Saul*, and after they had fired a salute over the grave, Scott slyly remarked that the tune of "I hae laid a herrin' in the saut" would be appropriate for their withdrawal. The facetious suggestion took; out of the churchyard they marched in quick time to this rousing air.[44]

Scott's military zeal rather troubled the Lord Lieutenant of Selkirkshire, to whom he seemed more like a swaggering cavalryman than a Crown official. Lord Napier was a finicking old gentleman who fussed about the fashion of his neckcloth and whose orderly soul worried about the fact that Scott still had no dwelling in the Forest, where he was bound by Statute to reside for four months of the year. The law of residence, Scott knew, was not enforced, and he laid the old gentleman's insistence to nervous fidget. But as Lord Napier politely continued to urge how much pleasure he and the other gentlemen of the county would feel in having more of their Sheriff's society, Scott realized that it would be undiplomatic to remain at Lasswade. He therefore began looking around for a country house in Selkirkshire.[45]

His kinsman Scott of Harden suggested that Auld Wat's tower on Borthwick water might be put in repair for him. At first Scott was delighted by the idea of living in this ancestral fortress, but the southern extreme of Selkirkshire was hardly more convenient to his county business than Lasswade, and it was far more remote from Edinburgh.[46] Just as he was hesitating, the property of Ashestiel, on the south bank of the Tweed only six miles from Selkirk, became available for rental.

Its former owner, Colonel William Russell, Scott's uncle through marriage to his mother's sister Jean, had died; and his son and heir, James Russell, was in India. Scott had no use for the sheep farm, which was the larger part of the estate, but he could take the old farmhouse and its grounds and sublet the rest. He arranged to pay £325 a year and offered the sheep farm for £260 to "Laird Nippy," a distant cousin of Will Laidlaw, who occupied the neighboring Peel farm as a tenant of the Duke of Buccleuch.[47] But Nippy, who had not received his nickname for no reason, held out for paying no more than £240, and ultimately Scott accepted that figure.[48]

All that spring "little fidgetty pieces of business" kept him traveling backward and forward in Selkirkshire. But he found time to write two more critical articles which appeared in the *Edinburgh Review* for April: one on Ellis's *Specimens of the Early English Poets* and one on *The Life* and *Works of Chatterton.*[49] And on May 2 *Sir Tristrem* at last appeared.[50] Scott had reluctantly agreed to one "castration" in the text, "against my own opinion, and in compliance with that of some respectable friends: for I can by no means think that the coarseness of an ancient romance is so dangerous to the public as the mongrel and inflammatory sentimentality of a modern novelist."[51] But he had insisted on printing twelve unexpurgated copies, and sent one each to the Advocates' Library, and to Ellis, Heber, and Douce.[52]

Scott felt convinced that this text of *Sir Tristrem* was the earliest of all the English versions of the tale. The Auchinleck MS unquestionably dated from the time of Edward III, who had ascended the throne in 1327: it contained references to events in the preceding reign of Edward II, but none to any later occurrences.[53] And *Sir Tristrem* in turn seemed to be older than the rest of the manuscript; there were even signs, Scott argued, that the scribe had not fully understood certain more obscure parts of what he had copied. From these facts Scott found no difficulty in inferring that the date of its original composition must have been some still earlier time, in the thirteenth century.[54]

A poem on this subject was traditionally credited to Thomas Learmont, or Thomas the Rhymer, of Ercildoune, and Thomas could be proved to have been still alive in 1286. The opening lines of *Sir Tristrem*, indeed, gave him as its source:

> I was at Erceldoune:
> > With Tomas spak Y thare;
> Ther herd Y rede in roune,
> > Who Tristrem gat and bare . . .[55]

Scott thought this claim might be quite literally true. He did not, therefore, believe the Auchinleck MS version the very poem attributed to Thomas the Rhymer, but did feel sure that it contained "the essence of Tomas's work." Thomas's poem probably dated from the earlier half of the thirteenth century and this poem was "one of the spurious copies in queint Inglis" disparaged by Robert de Brunne in the following century.[56]

Scott was aware that the tale of Sir Tristrem was known to the French troubadours of the twelfth century. It was mentioned by the King of Navarre, and Chrétien de Troyes was even said to have composed a romance on the subject. But these allusions, Scott argued, were merely to the theme, not to any specific metrical romance.[57] No doubt there had been some real though remote Sir Tristrem who actually "swallowed a dose of cantharides, intended to stimulate his uncle, a petty monarch of Cornwall, and involved himself . . . in an intrigue with his aunt."[58] Thomas, however, had lived "on the borders of the ancient British kingdom of Strathclyde" among "a people, who perhaps had hardly ceased to speak the language of the hero." Even if the story "had already penetrated to France" and been sung by French poets a century before his time, he had possessed "immediate access to the Celtic traditions concerning *Sir Tristrem* with which the Anglo-Norman romancers were unacquainted" and had "brought back to its original simplicity, a story, which had been altered and perverted into a thousand forms, by the *diseurs* of Normandy."[59]

Parts of Scott's argument have been overthrown by the more detailed·knowledge available to modern scholarship and its more scientific methodology. The poem's mere assertion that its story came directly from the lips of Thomas of Erceldoune has, of course, no more weight as evidence than the unproduced Ossianic manuscripts to which Macpherson appealed. And Scott's assumption that the author of *Sir Tristrem* had close access to Celtic tradition is a mere flight of fancy; the poem is now known to be based upon a French original. Nevertheless, Scott's knowledge and imaginative insight cleared up a good many obscurities, and there can be no doubt of *Sir Tristrem's* antiquity and its importance as a romance document. Scott stands high among the pioneers who called this entire body of romance material to the attention of the world.

At the time he published the poem, none of his arguments were seriously challenged. George Ellis accepted them almost in their entirety. Reviewing the volume in the October *Edinburgh Review*, he could find no fault with it except its inflated price of two guineas and its tiny edition of only 150 copies.[60] Constable, in fact, had expected little popularity for so esoteric a work; the two guineas would at least cover the cost of paper and printing.[61] But Ellis found it "quite scandalous in him to make the book scarce at the moment of publication . . . to save himself the trouble of distributing. . . . Your name," he told Scott indignantly, "must have sold 500 copies just as easily as 150. . . ."[62] Robert Jamieson agreed: "I am persuaded, had the impression been 4 times as numerous, and sold for half a guinea a copy, it would have answered full as well to the Bookseller, and served the other end of its publication much better."[63] "I kiss the rod of my critic," Scott replied to Ellis, but pleaded that the price was not his fault: "I declined taking any copy-money, or share in the profits; and *nothing*, surely, was as reasonable a charge as I could make."[64]

A little extra money at this time, indeed, might well have come in handy. For Scott's youngest brother, Daniel, had got himself into a scrape. Long employed at the Custom-house, where he was in line for promotion, he had fathered an illegitimate child on some female whom Scott called "an artful woman." She was trying to force him to marry her, to avoid which Daniel had been obliged to flee Scotland. Now in Liverpool, he was about to embark for North America and thence for Jamaica, where Scott hoped he might find a clerical position.[65]

Perhaps Ellis, Scott thought, through his West Indian connections, might be able "to procure him such recommendations as may put it in his power to gain his bread." But even in trying to help as much as he could, Scott felt Daniel's fall too keenly to mention that the scapegrace was his brother; he described him merely as "a young man, a very near relation of mine." Daniel was good-natured, he told Ellis, wrote and figured decently, but was "a little *soft*, and can only be engaged in some subaltern employment." Ellis responded with a letter of introduction to a Mr. Blackburn, who had large estates in Jamaica.[66]

The unfortunate Daniel presently set sail from Liverpool for "the southern parts of the United States," probably for Charleston, where the Scott family had friends or connections. Thence he made his way to Jamaica and a post Mr. Blackburn found for him on a plantation at Manchioneal on the northeast coast of the island.[67] "Ten thousand thanks to you," Scott wrote Ellis, "for your kind attention to Daniel Scott's Interests—the climate he must encounter, it is a melancholy risque but I hope he will endeavor to guard himself against its effects by temperance and prudence. I sincerely hope and trust he will exert himself so as to give Mr. Blackburn satisfaction . . ."[68]

Despite the expense of sending Daniel abroad, Scott and Charlotte were not really pressed financially. News came from India that her brother Charles was planning to marry, and with it another £5,000 to be invested for Charlotte in the Funds, as well as enough Pagodas to pay her a lump sum of £211.[69] And on June 10 Captain Robert Scott died, leaving Rosebank to Scott in addition to some £600 from the rest of his estate.[70] For a while Scott was tempted to give up Ashestiel and retain his uncle's beautiful little villa and its twenty acres of land. But though he remembered happy times there, it would neither meet his own needs nor satisfy Lord Napier's demands that he have a residence in Selkirkshire. It was too near Kelso to be truly a country place; "besides, it is hemmed in by hedges and ditches, not to mention Dukes and Lady Dowagers, all which are bad things for little people."[71]

In the course of the year, consequently, Scott sold Rosebank for £5,000.[72] "I shall buy a mountain farm with the purchase money, and be quite the Laird of the Cairn and the Scaur."[73] Meanwhile he concluded his arrangements for renting the Ashestiel farmhouse[74]

Preparations for the move went forward steadily among all Scott's usual crowding activities. He vigorously argued to Ellis that the Castle Orgeillous of romance was located at Bamborough and that Sir Lancelot's Joyeuse Garde was at Berwick.[75] He arranged for the Town of Selkirk to lodge its prisoners in the Jedburgh jail and pay the expenses of their confinement there. He heard the trial of a man named Brown, who "stoutly and impudently denied stealing the cow" he was accused of having taken.[76] As executor to Captain Scott's estate, he conferred with solicitors and arranged for the public sale of Rosebank to the highest bidder. He fitted out Ashestiel "from sales, from brokers' shops, and from all manner of hospitals for incurable furniture."[77] At last, in mid-August, he and Charlotte and the children said farewell to

Lasswade. "I had to superintend," he remarked cheerfully, "the removal, or what we call a *flitting*, which, of all bores under the cope of Heaven is bore the most tremendous."[78]

Notwithstanding all these calls upon his time Scott worked steadily on his poem. "I proceed *doucement* with *The Lay of the Last Minstrel*," he wrote in June.[79] By August 21 he had completed the last two cantos, the fifth, which brought the narrative to a close, and the valedictory sixth, which was written in three forenoons while he was in quarters with the yeomanry.[80] "I wish very much," he told Ellis, "I could have sent you the *Lay* while in MS., to have had the advantage of your opinion and corrections. But Ballantyne galled my kibes so severely during an unusual fit of activity, that I gave him the whole story in a sort of pet both with him and with it."[81]

Ellis had suggested that the poem appear with illustrations by Flaxman. But Scott feared that Flaxman's genius was "too classical to stoop to body forth my Gothic Borderers"; they would risk "resembling the antique of Homer's heroes, rather than the iron race of Salvator."[82] He had already, in fact, been arranging to have the volume illustrated by engravings from a series of paintings by John James Masquerier. It was important, he told the artist, that the Minstrel should be depicted as wearing, not the Highland tartan, but the "Maud or Low Country plaid," "of the natural colour of the wool with a very small black check."[83] Ultimately, however, Scott decided to do without illustrations and suggested to Longman and Rees that the first edition be a handsome quarto in Ballantyne's best style. Seven hundred and fifty copies would cost at most £200 and might yield a reasonable profit at a guinea apiece.[84]

Once the last pages of the *Lay* had left his hands, Scott settled down to enjoying himself at Ashestiel. Among his neighbors was Mungo Park, the African explorer, who was now living at Foulshiels, the cottage where he was born, almost opposite Newark Castle on the Yarrow. Calling one day and not finding Park at home, Scott strolled along the banks of the stream looking for him. In a hollow he came on Park throwing stones into a deep pool and watching the rising bubbles. An idle amusement, Scott commented, for one who had seen such wild adventures. "Not so idle, perhaps, as you suppose," Park answered. "This was the manner in which I used to ascertain the depth of a river in Africa before I ventured to cross it—judging whether the attempt would be safe, by the time the bubbles of air took to ascend."[85]

Instantly Scott divined that Park was thinking of another expedition. And, in fact, Park told him, his thoughts were haunted by Africa; whenever he woke suddenly at night he fancied himself still a prisoner in the tents of Ali. Why, then, Scott suggested, run those risks again? He had rather, Park replied, brave Africa and all its horrors than wear out his life at home.[86] In September he paid Scott a farewell overnight visit. Next morning Scott rode partway home with him through the autumn fogs floating slow and heavy over the wild hills between the Tweed and the Yarrow. At the Williamhope ridge, leaping on a small ditch that divided the moor from the road, Park's horse stumbled and almost fell. "I am afraid, Mungo," said Scott, "that is a bad omen." Park smiled. "Freits [omens]," he said, "follow those who look to them." Spurring his steed, he disappeared in the mist. Scott never saw him again; he died attempting to reach the source of the Niger.[87]

All that autumn Scott spent in field sports. "I have not taken so good a swing," he wrote, "in many a day." Early in October he invited all the neighbors to Ashestiel for "a rousing *kirn*," or harvest home, which proved so convivial that next morning many a heavy celebrator still lay about drowned in slumber, and at last, "the dead like those in Chevy Chace were carried off in *carts and wains* by their weeping spouses."[88] In November, while Ballantyne's presses were groaning with the *Lay* and its notes, he was hunting hares with greyhounds.[89]

With December he was back in Edinburgh again, and by the end of the month the volumes were on their way to Longman and Rees while Scott and his family set out in a blinding snowstorm to spend their hogmanay at Ashestiel. "Our march has been ordered with great military talent—a detachment of minced pies and brandy having preceded us. In case we are not buried in a snow-wreath, our stay will be but short."[90]

*The Lay of the Last Minstrel* was published in the first week in January, 1805. Its success was instantaneous; within a few months Scott found himself famous.[91] The first edition melted from the booksellers' shelves. An octavo impression of fifteen hundred was presently exhausted. In the next year there followed two more, totaling almost forty-five hundred; the year after that, fifth and sixth editions coming to five thousand; and from then on the editions followed in bewildering succession. Within five years the sales reached almost fifteen thousand; within less than a decade they were touching twenty-seven thousand. In a period when the total population of England and Scotland was fewer than twelve million, and when the bare ability to read was far from being a general accomplishment, such sales were a spectacular triumph. And throughout Scott's lifetime—to trace it only that far—the demand continued unabated. In the entire history of British poetry there had never been anything like the popularity of *The Lay of the Last Minstrel*.[92]

Scott's half-share of the profits on the first edition was £169 6s. As soon as it was clear that a second edition would be called for, Longman and Rees offered £500 for the copyright. This Scott accepted.[93] No Scotsman ever made a worse bargain. The lucky publishers must have cleared thousands from the poem. The following October, however, when they were visiting Scott at Ashestiel, the junior partner, Owen Rees, insisted on presenting him with an additional £100. The two men had been riding together, Scott mounted on a fine horse named Captain, the successor to Lenore. In a desperate leap on the coursing field the animal fell and had to be destroyed; Rees demanded the pleasure of replacing the loss.[94] Scott named Captain's successor Lieutenant.[95]

The success of the *Lay*, however, was not merely popular and financial. Critical applause was almost universal. Thomas Campbell found in it inspired passages of the most exalted stamp and lauded the entire poem as a monument of Scott's genius that would be judged by future ages.[96] Anna Seward ranked the ride of William of Deloraine with the work of Burns: "Yours and Burns's poetic journeys transcend those of every other Poet."[97] Even Wordsworth commended the poem, although with the moderation that marked his praise of any living poet: "We think you have completely attained your object; the Book is throughout interesting and entertaining, and the picture of manners as lively as possible."[98]

The *Lay* made its victorious progress even into the loftiest circles. Those two great opponents in the political world, Charles James Fox and William Pitt, united in their admiration for it. Pitt praised it to his niece, Lady Hester Stanhope; she repeated his words to William Stewart Rose, who communicated them to Scott. At his dinner table the great Minister recited to his guests the picture of the old Minstrel's trembling hesitance when he began to play his harp. "This is the sort of thing," Pitt said emphatically, "which I might have expected in painting, but could never have fancied capable of being given in poetry." He questioned Scott's boyhood friend, the Right Honorable William Dundas, about Scott's situation in life, saying "that it would give him pleasure to advance the fortunes of such a writer." "He can't remain as he is," Pitt observed, and asked Dundas to "look to it."[99]

The critics were hardly less enthusiastic. The *Annual Review* found it an "elegant, spirited, and striking poem," abounding in poetical description, its versification managed with great judgment, a happy return from the stiffness of classical poetic diction "to the more varied measures and familiar style of our earlier poets."[100] The *Critical Review* hailed the "masterly hand" with which from the "rich but unpolished ore" of ballad poetry "Mr. Scott has wrought much of his most exquisite imagery and description."[101] Even the magisterial Francis Jeffrey, in the *Edinburgh Review*, struck repeated chords of admiration: "The whole night journey of Deloraine—the opening of the Wizard's tomb—the march of the English battle—and the parley before the walls of the castle, are all executed with the same spirit and poetical energy . . ."[102] There were, he continued, many other passages "in every part of the poem, which are still more striking and meritorious," some of them "in the very first rank of poetical excellence."[103]

Jeffrey, to be sure, together with numbers of other readers, took exception to Gilpin Horner as a tiresome irrelevance to the story. "The Goblin Page is, in our opinion, the capital deformity of the poem." The whole machinery was useless, "a perpetual burden to the poet, and to the reader," "an undignified and improbable fiction, which excites neither terror, admiration, nor astonishment, but needlessly debases the strain of the whole work, and excites at once our incredulity and contempt." "We entreat Mr. Scott . . . to take advantage of any decent pretext he can lay hold of for purging the 'Lay' of this ungraceful intruder."[104]

Scott good-humoredly granted the justice of these strictures. "The Dwarf Page," he confessed to Miss Seward, was "an excrescence," and he pleaded "guilty to all the censures concerning him." But his devotion to the Countess of Dalkeith left him unable to banish the page from the poem. "I don't know if you ever saw my lovely chieftainess—if you have, you must be aware that it is *impossible* for any one to refuse her request, as she has more of the angel in face and temper than any one alive; so that if she had asked me to write a ballad on a broomstick, I must have attempted it. . . . In the process of the romance, the page, intended to be a principal person in the work, contrived (from the baseness of his natural propensities, I suppose) to slink downstairs into the kitchen, and now he must e'en abide there." Scott admitted, also, that the sixth canto was redundant, "for the poem should certainly have closed with the union of the lovers, when the interest, if any, was at an end. But what could I do? I had my book and my page still on my hands, and must get rid of them at all events."[105]

But most readers were as little troubled by the existence of the Goblin Page in the poem as Scott was by the enormity of having inserted him. Nor were they any more perturbed by the occasional careless lines that some hypercritics puffed themselves up by disparaging. A later friend of Scott's, Morritt of Rokeby, remembered a dinner at which a fellow guest annihilated one of these carpers. All these cavilings, he said, reminded him of a lecture on sculpture given in Rome by the renowned Falconet, the creator of the equestrian statue of Czar Peter at St. Petersburg. The vain little artist had been criticizing the anatomical inaccuracies of the famous horse of Marcus Aurelius in the Campidoglio, finding as many faults as a horse dealer might in an animal he wanted to buy. But suddenly something came over him. He took a long pinch of snuff, eyed his own faultless model with a sigh, and exclaimed, "Just the same, gentlemen, I must admit that wretched beast is alive, and mine is dead."*[106]

---

* "Cependant, Messieurs, il faut avouer que cette vilaine bête est vivante, et que la mienne est morte."

# 2

---

# *The Pounding of Presses*

## *(1804–1805)*

A SHESTIEL stretched bright stone walls and gabled roofs along the
crown of a high bank thick with green ash trees descending steeply
to the Tweed.[1] From these the place derived its name; "stiel" or "steel"
means a steep, and the clustering ashes stood out in contrast to the oaks
and birches of the rest of the countryside.[2]

The valley here was hardly more than a mountain glen, now shallow runs bickering over stones and again deep pools whose smooth waters
reflected the overhanging foliage. Down a dark ravine east of the house,
hidden in tangled greenwood, a little brook dashed its brown and foaming cascades over sharp rocks.[3] Behind, to the south, rose a slow purple
slope of heathery mountain, still clad in those years with the remaining
wildwood of the old Ettrick Forest. Before the dwelling, bright on sunny
days, lay an old-fashioned flower and fruit garden, from which the
ground fell away to a wide haugh or meadow, and then, leafy with
trees, plunged still more abruptly to the banks of the stream.[4]

This was one of the legend-haunted regions of the Border. Upstream
stood the tower of Elibank, the home of Muckle-Mou'd Meg. Further,
in Peeblesshire, were Manor and Holms, which had been known to
Merlin Sylvestris. Minchmoor, across which Montrose had fled after
the battle of Philiphaugh, hung like a cloud in the west. Tale and ballad
linked every field and burn. Ashestiel itself had two ghosts—a heavy
tread called Jack Boots that could be heard hollow in a corridor, and in
a small pasture named the Piperdale park a murdered piper who blew
a spectral bagpipe on summer nights.[5]

Half farm, half manor, and very ancient in parts, the building was
considerably larger than Lasswade; on the face opposite the river

projected a good-sized ell.[6] To the east extended a green lawn from which a bank planted with strawberry beds slanted down toward the brook brawling through its shady linn. The front garden, sheltered from a road leading to the stables by high hedges of glittering crimson-berried holly, had two enormous heavy-branched apple trees and, in its center, a sundial dated 1660. There was also a smaller garden bordered with boxwood.[7]

The nearest main road was that from Edinburgh to Selkirk, which passed through Yair-bridge-end three miles away. Here parcels for Ashestiel were left by the coach between Edinburgh and Carlisle, and brought along to the ford, but if the Tweed was in flood the ford at Ashestiel became dangerous and wagons had to use the rough cart track on the right bank. Only when the top of a "riding stone" showed above the water could its rapid flow be crossed in safety.[8] Struggling through this ford during the days when the family were settling in, a wagon bringing a new kitchen range overturned. "The horse and cart were with difficulty got out, but the grate remained for some time in the middle of the stream to do duty as a horse-trap, and furnish subject for many a good joke when Mrs. Scott happened to complain of the imperfection of her kitchen appointments."[9]

"We are seven miles from kirk and market," wrote Scott. "We rectify the last inconvenience by killing our own mutton and poultry; and as to the former, finding there was some chance of my family turning pagans, I have adopted the goodly practice of reading prayers every Sunday, to the great edification of my household."[10] The church the family attended when they undertook the journey was at Traquair, which was in fact eight or nine miles away. For many supplies they depended on the Edinburgh coach. Once, when they had invited the Pringles of Whytbank to meet Lord Melville's nephew Robert Dundas and his wife, the carrier failed to arrive. Charlotte sent a hasty appeal to her neighbors for whatever they could donate in the emergency, and served a dinner dominated by four legs of mutton.[11]

For all the remoteness of the region there were more than a dozen gentlemen's families within less than a dozen miles. Nearby was the seat of Lord Elibank and the new house of the Pringles at Yair, some distance from their ancient tower of Whytbank. Not much further resided the Earl of Traquair and, across the Tweed, the Pringles of Torwoodlee. On the river at Elwyn, some ten miles below Ashestiel, there was Lord Somerville, a good friend who shared Scott's enthusiasm for coursing and salmon fishing.[12] At Sunderland Hall, surrounded by their brother's library, still dwelt the surviving elderly sisters of Scott's predecessor Sheriff Plummer, guarding his Caxtons and Wynken de Wordes, Scott said, like three ancient dragons in the Garden of Hesperides. "I suppose they trouble the volumes," he wrote, "as little as *the* dragon did the golden pippins"; but he contrived to coax them into giving him the run of the collection.[13] And a little farther south, at Bowhill, his friend the Earl of Dalkeith had what was then no more than a small shooting-lodge on the Yarrow.[14]

When Scott had first looked Ashestiel over, he had thought of taking James Hogg to run the sheep farm and watch the house in winter.[15] By this time, however, the Ettrick shepherd had loftier hopes than being Scott's *grieve* or bailiff. "I have no intention of waiting," he wrote, "for so distant a prospect as being manager of your farm, though I have no doubt of our joint efforts proving successful, nor yet of your willingness to employ me in that capacity." Instead he had set his heart on taking rank as a farmer himself. He had heard that the Duke of Buccleuch had a farm vacant at Eskdale. Scott, he suggested, might write the Duke "stating that such and such a character was about leaving his native country for want of a residence in the farming line. . . . I have nothing to bestow save my hearty thanks; and as Hamlet says, sure my thanks are too dear at a halfpenny."[16] Nothing came of Hogg's application at the time, but considerably later, after Lord Dalkeith had succeeded to his father's titles, he gave Hogg the life rent of the farm of Altrive.

The proposal, however, that Hogg manage Scott's farm was not renewed. Shortly after Scott took possession of Ashestiel, in the summer of 1804, he found a man for the post.[17] He had retained Peter Matheson, the coachman who had formerly served the Russells, to drive the carriage he had bought for Charlotte, and Peter had a brother-in-law named Tom Purdie, who desperately needed a job. Scott took him on, first as a shepherd, but soon promoted him to general charge of the farm. In Peter Matheson and Tom Purdie he acquired two retainers who gave him a lifetime of devoted service.[18]

There is a more picturesque version of how Tom came into Scott's employ, according to which Scott first saw him in the dock at the Selkirk Sheriff Court as a poacher. Tom did not deny his guilt, and he had been convicted before. But he had been unable to find work, his wife and children were hungry, and there was grouse in plenty on the moor. Nevertheless, poaching must be stopped; Scott imposed a heavy fine, with jail as the alternative. Purdie had no money, but he did not go to jail. When the Court rose, "Shirra," they told him, had paid the fine. Tom ran out to thank the Sheriff for his freedom. He was already gone. Without hesitation Tom started walking the seven miles to Ashestiel. Reaching the house by evening, he had a talk with the Sheriff. From it he went home to tell his wife that he had a job.[19] There is no mention, however, of Tom in the Sheriff Court records, and the story must be regarded as unsubstantiated.

The Scotts were soon settled down at Ashestiel. The children were all thriving: Sophia now five, Walter a stocky youngster of three, Anne almost two. In the August days they played about the garden, picking the pink-tipped daisies and watching the birds lighting on the sprays of hawthorn, the lambs frisking on the lea.[20] Charlotte was kept busy with household affairs and with the fowl pens, though she needed Scott's protection for the chickens against the wild cats that were always breaking in from the woods.[21] Scott directed the work of Tom Purdie and conferred with a Highland gardener named Mackay about the fruit and vegetable gardens down in the east end of the haugh.[22] There was also another gardener, who complained that ladies always wanted "peers, plooms, and apricocks, in season and out of season" and who explained his failure to grow early cabbages by saying, "There will be fine early cabbages in the how i' the summer."[23]

Scott did his writing in the dining room. Here two windows faced southeast on the garden and a "jargomelle pear-tree" on the wall, and a third window looked southwest over the lawn.[24] By this time he had adopted the working habits that he would maintain for the rest of his life. Formerly, when business or enjoyment had taken up the middle of the day, after he was supposed to have gone to bed he had devoted several hours to writing and study. But his doctor told him this course was likely to aggravate the nervous headaches that were the only illnesses he now knew. Consequently he began rising at five in the morning. He lighted his own fire if it was cold; he shaved and arrayed himself carefully in a shooting jacket or whatever garment he meant to wear till dinner time. He had radically amended the slovenliness of dress that had characterized his adolescence; although still not a dandy he was now a martinet about neatness and hated what he called the "bedgown and slipper tricks" in which some literary men indulged themselves.[25]

Before settling down to work he paid a quick visit to the stables to feed his favorite horse, Captain, or his successor, Lieutenant, or Brown Adam, none of whom would be fed by anyone but him. Six o'clock saw Scott at his desk, papers and reference books neatly arranged about him, Camp lying faithfully at his feet, and the two greyhounds Douglas and Percy, as fancy moved them, leaping in and out of a window always left open for them.[26] As he wrote, he joked with the dogs, whom he represented as understanding every word he spoke. These one-sided conversations he followed up with James Skene, who was a frequent guest, by imagining their replies if they could have spoken and giving sketches of their characters. Camp perfectly understood, he said, "that his master considered him as a sensible and steady friend, the greyhounds as volatile young creatures whose freaks must be borne with." When the rest of the household assembled for breakfast around nine, he had already, as he put it, done enough "to break the back of the day's work."[27]

In his rusty black jacket, with the early morning light streaming in through the eastern windows, Scott drove his pen steadily across his paper. During that first summer at Ashestiel in 1804 he wrote for the January number of the *Edinburgh* a review of Thomas Johnes's trans-

lation of Froissart and an amusing review of Thornton's *Sporting Tour*
of northern England and the Highlands. The great value of Froissart,
he notes, is the brilliance with which he makes the fourteenth century
live before our eyes, a superiority to the mere chronicler which "must ever
be the case, while we prefer a knowledge of mankind to a mere acquaintance with their actions."[28] The review of Thornton pokes good-natured
fun at this English sporting squire "poaching in the fields of literature"
and writing elaborate descriptions of all the horses, hawks, dogs, guns,
rods, baggage wagons, and troops of servants with which he invaded the
north, every pickled salmon, jugged hare, deer ham, and magnum of
claret he devoured at dinner, and every brace of snipe he shot or great
pike he caught from Loch Lomond and Inverary to Inverness and
Strathspey.[29]

After breakfast Scott labored for another couple of hours. Part of
this time he devoted to answering letters, though he seldom replied on
the day a letter was received. Important ones he deliberated about for
several days before answering, and with others he was still more dilatory,
often allowing them to remain unanswered for weeks, though he ultimately got around to most of them. By noon, saying, "Out, damned
spot," he could close his writing box and be "his own man" for the rest
of the day. In bad weather he worked in the afternoon as well, but otherwise he was out and riding by one o'clock.[30]

His horse bridled and saddled, the stable door was opened as a
sign that Scott was ready for him. Brown Adam, who would allow himself to be backed by no one else and who had broken one groom's arm
and another's leg when they made the rash attempt, was altogether
gentle with his master. He would immediately trot to the "leaping-on
stone" that Scott's lameness made it convenient for him to use, and there
stand silent and motionless as a rock. But when Scott was once mounted,
the animal displayed his joy by neighing triumphantly and rearing
through a brilliant series of curvettings.[31]

Since the publication of *The Lay of the Last Minstrel*, James Ballantyne's printing business had been growing steadily. When he had made
the move to Edinburgh toward the end of 1802, he had raised additional
capital to the amount of £1,000, half in a loan from Scott and half in an
overdraft from the Royal Bank of Scotland.[32] Presently he had moved
from Abbeyhill to a larger establishment nearby in Foulis Close, Canongate.[33] Now, as orders poured in upon him, he found himself unable to
handle them without increased financial backing. Therefore, "maugre all
delicacy," Ballantyne said, he applied to Scott, early in 1805, for a
further loan.[34]

Scott had on hand five thousand guineas from the sale of Rosebank.
He had thought of using all or most of this sum in the purchase of a
country property. But there was no estate on the market that he liked;
and meanwhile he had taken on the lease of Ashestiel. He was fond of

his old schoolfellow and knew that despite the absurdly majestic manner with which Ballantyne bore his swelling stoutness he was an industrious worker and an excellent printer. His business, too, was clearly prospering. Nevertheless Scott did not think it prudent to increase his loan. Instead, after advising with William Erskine on the matter, he suggested that he might become a partner in the printing establishment.[35] Ballantyne willingly acquiesced, and on March 14, 1805, they signed a partnership agreement.[36]

Ballantyne's capital, including his presses and stock, and the building in Foulis Close, was valued at £2,090. Scott canceled his promissory note for £500 and unpaid interest of £8, and advanced £1,500 in cash, making a total of £2,008, falling a little short of Ballantyne's contribution.[37] The books were to be balanced twice a year, at Whitsuntide and Martinmas, when Ballantyne was to receive one-third of the profits "in consideration of his taking the whole trouble of management," and the remaining two-thirds were to be divided between the two partners in proportion to their stock—that is, in almost equal shares.[38] Although Scott was to give advice and literary assistance in the conduct of the business, essentially he was a sleeping partner.

The partnership thus began with plant, stock, and other assets of an agreed value of £2,090 and £1,500 additional cash in the bank. If Scott had insisted upon Ballantyne's repaying his £500 loan and had then put this sum in the business, his own investment would have been the same, but they could not then have sustained the generous fiction that the printer was an equal partner. This he could have made a reality only if he had somewhere obtained another £500 and added it to their bank account. The method of adjustment actually followed seems tantamount to a gift of £250 from Scott to his new partner.[39] It is possible, of course, that he meant this as a recognition of Ballantyne's successful efforts in establishing the business as a going concern. There can be no question, however, that Scott was behaving with intentional liberality.

Much nonsense has been written about the fact that Scott did not blazon this business venture to the world. Some critics have found it undignified that an advocate should set up as a printer, incompatible with his position as a judge, even discreditable and dishonest. A court official, they have urged, should not be a partner in what they have represented as a secret commercial enterprise. John Buchan has sufficiently answered these arguments. "Before the modern development of joint-stock companies," he notes," "one of the commonest ways of investing spare capital was by lending money to some enterprise and receiving in lieu of interest a certain share in the profits."[40] Between this and being a legal partner the ethical distinction is tenuous. There was little more reason, however, even according to early nineteenth-century standards, for Scott to advertise the connection than there would be for a lawyer today to publish his stock holdings.

Scott made no special point of secrecy, although Erskine was the only friend whom he consulted. Nor can it be doubted that if Erskine, with his delicate sense of honor, had seen anything legally or morally wrong in the arrangement, he would have spoken out against it. The notion that Scott's connection with the firm remained unknown in commercial circles will not bear examination. The banks with which James Ballantyne and Company discounted bills could scarcely have failed to notice that Scott's name appeared on its bills and credits and they would have been slow-witted beyond all financial norms if they had never suspected that he had an interest in the business. Nor would the typecasters, the ink makers, the manufacturers of presses, the cloth and paper merchants, and others from whom they purchased supplies long remain ignorant. And, some dozen years later, when James Ballantyne and Company bought the *Edinburgh Weekly Journal*, there were even occasional newspaper references to Scott as one of the proprietors. Gradually, if not to every friend or fellow advocate, certainly to the business world, Scott's association with Ballantyne became well known. And, assuredly, therefore, known to publishers as well.

It has been suggested that what was wrong was not that Scott was a lawyer investing money in business but that he used his influence as a writer to throw orders to the printing establishment in which he was a secret partner. This argument is even more absurd. It was simply impossible that publishers should be unaware of what all the business world knew. But, even were this not so, Archibald Constable and Thomas Longman were not babes in the woods. When Scott made their publication of one of his poems conditional upon Ballantyne's printing it, would they have no idea why? When he would undertake editorial work for them only if Ballantyne were the printer? When he proposed far-ranging publishing schemes, again with Ballantyne as printer? When bank credits and discounted bills bearing his name and Ballantyne's were used interchangeably? Of course Constable and Longman knew, and what they knew other publishers soon knew too. If they gave their printing to Ballantyne, or undertook an enterprise that Scott suggested, it was not because they were deceived. It was because they thought it good business. Their correspondence, and that of Murray and Blackwood as well, shows that they were perfectly well aware of Scott's connection with Ballantyne.

Not long after the formation of the partnership, the printing plant moved to Paul's Work, at the North Back of the Canongate. This was near the foot of Leith Wynd, in the very shadow of Calton Hill.[41] Before the building an iron gateway opened into a small court with a narrow door below an outside, iron-railed staircase ascending to the counting room. Indoors, a maze of devious winding stairs connected rooms noisy with the hammering of wooden mallets and the pounding of presses, odorous with machine oil, moldy paste, and printer's ink daubed on the rollers. Adjoining the long case-room filled with toiling compositors the readers corrected proofs in a set of cubicles like sentry boxes; above was the stereo foundry; below, the damping room and the thumping presses and the drying room, where the moist printed sheets hung on horizontal bars.[42]

James Ballantyne lived nearby in a house at 10 St. John Street, a short private street entered by an archway from the Canongate, where an ancient seneschal in a faded uniform barred entry to all carriages and carts except those in the service of its residents.[43] Here, early in the partnership, Scott dined, and found as a fellow guest James's younger brother John Ballantyne, a rail-thin, lively little fellow with a hopping gait, a squeaky voice, and a hilarious gift of drollery and mimicry. He had spent some time in the London banking house of Messrs. Currie and was now engaged in carrying on, not very successfully, his father's business in Kelso, selling everything from children's toys to fine broadcloth.[44]

Old Mrs. Ballantyne, who acted as her son's hostess, was away from home on this occasion, and in her absence John's wife, Hermione, was asked to take the head of the table. From her seat she examined Scott while his rather heavy face brightened with amusement at her husband's chatter. Though he had no color in his cheeks, he was healthy-looking and handsome, with light brown hair straight on his brow and lighter eyebrows thick above sharp gray eyes. His upper lip, she noticed, was very long, and when he laughed she observed that his teeth, though small and regular, were somewhat discolored. On the little finger of his left hand he wore a ring of antique gold. She could not help being struck by his halting gait, although he walked rapidly in gigantic strides, setting his staff close to the lame foot. He seemed to her like a crippled Hercules.[45]

Scott set vigorously to work devising schemes to keep his partner's presses busy. He himself would edit the works of John Dryden with an introductory biography and critical notes. Then there might also be an edition of the works of James Thomson, the author of *The Seasons*. On top of these he projected an even more grandiose plan. "I have imagined," he wrote Ballantyne, "a very superb work. What think you of a complete edition of British Poets, ancient and modern? Johnson's is imperfect and out of print; so is Bell's, which is a Lilliputian thing; and Anderson's, the most complete in point of number, is most contemptible in execution both of the editor and printer. There is a scheme for you! At least a hundred volumes, to be published at the rate of ten a year."[46]

Learning that a London clergyman, the Reverend Mr. Edward Forster, who was a friend of Lord Somerville, was already contemplating an edition of Dryden, Scott suggested that they join forces.[47] He would be quite ready, he said, to act anonymously as Forster's assistant.[48] But Forster was delighted at the chance of obtaining Scott's name on the title page as a collaborator.

Soon they were discussing the division of the work. Would Forster like to undertake the political poems and translations, Scott asked, while he himself did the plays? "The reason I am anxious to take the Drama, at least the one half of it, is that I can be ready to go to press immediately, having a copy lying by me corrected and almost ready for printing, whereas the waiting for yours would lose us at least three or four months."[49] Ballantyne, who must of course have the priniting, would thus be able to begin almost at once. "Besides this is my own period of leisure, so that I could dedicate much more time to setting the old Bard in motion than when our courts sit down."[50]

Forster wanted his half of the work to be printed in London, but this Scott obdurately opposed. One of them would have to overlook the entire work "to prevent our repeating explanations which may have been already given." If the edition was to carry Scott's name—and "you think," he reminded Forster, "a good name is better than great riches"—it must be done where he could take charge of its execution. Therefore, if Forster insisted on his proposal he must carry on alone; if they were to be joint editors the printing must be done in Edinburgh.[51]

There was of course no reason why proofs could not have been sent to Scott from London for his correction; it would have caused no more delay than the plan they did adopt, of sending proofs to Forster in London for *his* suggestions. But Forster knew that Scott's name was more valuable on a title page than his own and had no desire to lose it. He was dismayed, though, at Ballantyne's estimate of costs and again protested. "His argument," Scott wrote confidentially, "is that you print too fine, *alias* too dear. I intend to stick to my answer, that I know nothing of the matter; but that settle it how you and he will, it must be printed by you, or can be no concern of mine. This gives you an advantage in driving the bargain."[52] Forster in fact gave way; subsequently he suggested a plan for their further collaboration with which Scott expressed himself "very pleased."[53]

Scott's conduct here cannot be defended as readily as in his dealings with publishers, banks, and other business enterprises. Quite possibly he knew nothing about the financial calculations on which Ballantyne based his charges. But the disclaimer, even if technically true, was misleading. Although Scott was entitled, of course, to insist that Ballantyne should do the printing, it would not have been amiss to reveal that he himself had a financial interest in that choice; it seems highly unlikely that Forster, not a businessman or publisher but a clergyman in distant London, could have known of the partnership. On the other hand, there is no reason to believe that Ballantyne's estimate was excessive. William Miller, the Albermarle Street bookseller, who was already Forster's publisher and the one to whom he had proposed the present work, would hardly have endangered his own venture by submitting to extortionate printing bills. Nor was Forster forced to yield; if Scott withdrew he would have been no differently situated than he had been before. Nevertheless, Scott's behavior toward Forster sounds more than a little disingenuous.

Forster's surrender made Scott dominant in their enterprise. And, indeed, before many months had passed—though by no maneuvers of his own—Scott became the sole editor. For William Miller now felt that Forster's name would not help its sales. He preferred that Scott's name should appear alone on the title page and that if Forster worked on the book at all it should be only as an anonymous helper.[54] This precisely reversed the subordinate capacity in which Scott himself had originally suggested that he work with Forster. "I was from the beginning," he told Miller, "not only ready but anxious to have my own name concealed and to act merely as his assistant."[55]

It is impossible not to suspect that Miller played Forster to obtain Scott, and discarded the clergyman when that object was attained. James Ballantyne voiced the hardheaded business judgment of Miller's decision. "No doubt," he said, the publisher's action must have given Forster pain; "and, very likely, he will think himself ill-treated. But what could you do? If, as you have reason to think, his name would hurt the work, it would be absurd to pay for it; if it would ruin the work, it would be madness to retain it. You can only feel the pulse of the London trade; and, be their estimate of Mr. Forster's literary talents just or unjust, it is by that estimate alone that your conduct must be regulated."[56]

Scott's sentiments were more sympathetic. He wrote Forster, "in the gentlest terms," expressing his "extreme unwillingness to hurt his feelings."[57] "I could have wished it otherwise," he told Miller, "and made every concession I possibly could to alleviate the pain he must necessarily have felt upon the alteration of the title-page."[58] But the publisher's refusal to have Forster as coeditor seemed to Scott no reason for giving up a project he had conceived long before they had known each other. "I have no idea," he wrote Ballantyne, "of being dragged through all the shops"—publishing houses—"in London because F's own bookseller holds him disqualified for the undertaking."[59]

Though the unfortunate clergyman felt aggrieved, he conveyed his dissatisfaction with "less acrimony," Ballantyne confided to Miller, "than I had anticipated—for I do sincerely lament the compulsory wound he has received."[60] But the indignity of being degraded to the status of an unnamed assistant his pride could not swallow; he withdrew altogether. Subsequently, indeed, he expressed a wish to continue receiving proofs, so that he might "see the work in its progress." In this wistful desire Ballantyne urged Miller that he be indulged.[61] Still later, in the Advertisement to the completed work, Scott emphasized his regret for the "unlucky circumstances" that had deprived him "of friendly assistance, which might have rendered his toil more easy, and the result more accurate."[62]

In this episode there can be no question that Miller's treatment of Forster was inconsiderate, even unscrupulous. What of Scott's? "Mr. Scott," Ballantyne wrote Miller, "though the most honourable and delicate, is one of the most resolute men in the world."[63] But we may justly feel that he showed more drive than nicety. Though he was not obliged to forego a design he had formed before he and Forster were acquainted, it would at least have been more fastidious to find another publisher than the one who had behaved so shabbily to his associate. Scott had not himself cuckooed Forster out of the nest, but he had allowed Miller to do so. That such sharp practice was not unusual among booksellers does not leave Scott absolutely blameless.

His vast scheme for a hundred-volume edition of the British Poets he had broached to Archibald Constable.[64] Already portly though barely twenty-nine, pink-faced and almost oppressively handsome, at once astute and daring, Constable was making the publishing world hum with his energies. He had launched the enormously successful *Edinburgh Review*, was negotiating for the copyright of the *Encyclopaedia Britannica*, and had recently purchased the copyright of the supplement to its third edition. He had taken a quarter share of both the *Minstrelsy of the Scottish Border* and *The Lay of the Last Minstrel*, and was the publisher of *Sir Tristrem*. A man of large ambitions, he responded with enthusiasm to Scott's grandiose conception.[65]

The previous year, however, Constable had already entered into an agreement with Thomas Campbell for a collection of *Specimens of the British Poets* not quite so inclusive in scope. This scheme Campbell at once offered to relinquish in favor of Scott's. "What is it," he asked Scott, "that Aeneas says of perishing by the hand of Achilles? I rejoice that the plan is taken from me by a hand so powerful, I really do my dear Scott. It would have gone to my heart to see any of the Hodman hods of literature proposing for this gigantic plan; but to see it in your hands, I am happy for the sake of taste and my native country. You will do it gloriously, deeply and strongly with research to inform us, with fire to warm us, and with taste to enlighten us."[66]

Though Scott had known of Campbell's plan, he had thought of it as more of an anthology, and had not realized the degree to which their intentions would overlap. However unconcerned he may have felt about replacing poor Mr. Forster on the Dryden, he would not hear of supplanting a brother poet whom he honored as highly as he did Tom Campbell. He therefore proposed that they share the editorial task. Campbell modestly doubted his ability to equal Scott's erudition, but warmly assented to the invitation.[67]

But poverty, and bitter experience with publishers, had made Campbell deeply suspicious of their good faith. They were "ravens, croakers, suckers of innocent blood and living men's brains." Even Cadell and Davies, "liberal enough as booksellers go," had told him "fifteen or sixteen lies" about how cheaply others could be had for this very job. He had demanded a thousand pounds for writing thirty lives; they said another man had "offered to stake his whole reputation on the work [at] £150—this was told me as a damper is thrown over muslin that is going to be singed." As for that "butteracious Bookseller," Archibald Constable, he was "a piece of the most fallacious fat meat that was ever packed into a human skin." Not two months before he had made Campbell "believe he was not made for a bookseller; but the cold grease" had subsequently appeared.[68]

Nevertheless, the spleenful poet admitted, Constable was "not the worst of the bunch" and he had "no objections to him."[69] But Constable soon showed the streak of grease. There were disputes about delivery dates, Constable's firm refusing to accept Campbell's declaration that he could not be bound to complete his part of the work in less than eighteen months. On more cautious reflection, too, Constable doubted that there was really room for so huge a collection. Worse, the publishers refused to admit poetical works Scott and Campbell agreed on as essential. On the rocks of these contentions the whole project foundered.[70] "As for the British Poets," Scott told Ellis, "my plan was greatly too liberal to stand the least chance of being adopted by the trade at large, as I wished them to begin with Chaucer."[71]

A year later, under different auspices, the scheme was revived. "A very excellent and gentlemanlike man, albeit a bookseller," wrote Campbell, "Murray of Fleet-street is willing to give for our joint lives of the Poets on the plan we proposed to the Trade a twelvemonth ago—A Thousand Pounds . . . I have seldom seen a pleasanter man to deal with." Excitedly Campbell's hopes burst into flame. "Now my dear Scott as to the laborious part of it I will traverse the island to get information and books and promise to devote myself to make ample amends by *my* industry for the superior stock of knowledge which you must be confessed to be able to contribute."[71a] But, alas, the gentlemanly Murray also proved hard to deal with. Murray consulted Constable; Constable threw cold water on the project. Scott decided not to undertake it, and although Campbell was willing to do it unaided Murray was unwilling to confide it to him alone.[72]

Throughout all these fruitless negotiations Scott's literary industry continued unflagging. In the April, 1805, *Edinburgh Review* appeared his amusing dissection of the melodramatic plot absurdities and emotional hysteria of Godwin's *Fleetwood: or The New Man of Feeling*,[73] of whose hero Scott observes that "a man who is transported with rage, with despair, with anger, and all the furious impulses of passion, upon the most common occurrences of life, is not a man of sentiment, but a madman; and far from sympathizing with his feelings, we are only surprised at his having the liberty of indulging them beyond the precincts of Bedlam."[74] "In short, the new Man of Feeling, in his calm moments a determined egotist, is, in his state of irritation a frantic madman, who plays on a barrel-organ at a puppet-show, till he and the wooden dramatis personae are all possessed by the foul fiend Flibbertigibbet, who presides over *mopping* and *mowing.*"[75]

During the spring recess of the Court Scott worked at Ashestiel on Dryden. The *Essay on Dramatic Poetry*, he thought, should "be thrown to the end of the first volume the rest of which will be occupied by the life, general critique, and other prolegomena"; and he would soon be ready to put into Ballantyne's hands the second volume, consisting of *The Wild Gallant*, *The Rival Ladies*, and *The Indian Queen*. Congreve's edition must be corrected from the original quartos and the two folios. "Malone's dates are very accurate and should be followed in arranging the plays—they differ considerably from those of Dr. Johnson and Congreve." Next he would tackle *The Conquest of Granada*, *The Spanish Friar*, *The Duke of Guise*, *Don Sebastian*, *King Arthur*. "I suppose you will think three plays enough in each volume." Surely, too, many of Dryden's letters might be recovered, and Mr. Bindley of Somerset House had a large collection of the controversial tracts of the period.[76]

Rising from these labors at noon, Scott would join James Skene, who was his house guest that April, in an afternoon of sport or rambling.[77] "Every day," says Skene, "we had some hours of coursing with the greyhounds, or riding at random over the hills, or of spearing salmon in the Tweed by sunlight . . ." Often this last sport was "renewed at night by the help of torches," with Lord Somerville coming up from the Pavilion at Alwyn to join them, or James Hogg making one of the company.[78]

"Burning the water," as it was called, was rough sport. The large salmon usually lay in deep pools, and it was hard to judge their position by torchlight, so that when the fisher made a violent thrust he was apt to miss, tumble souse into the water, and find spear and salmon gone, his torch extinguished, and the boat bobbing some distance down the stream. Once Scott went right over the gunwale and Skene just managed to grab the edge of his jacket as he plunged overboard. The pleasures of burning the water, Skene remarks, "consist in being penetrated with cold and wet, having your shins broken against the stones in the dark, and perhaps mastering one fish out of every twenty you take aim at."[79]

On one midnight expedition "leistering kippers," says Hogg, when they had reached the Rough Haugh of Elibank, they found their peat gone out and were unable to kindle their torches. Sending a messenger back the two miles for another fiery peat, they sat down on the greensward by the riverbank to wait his return. The night was mild, calm, and pitch dark. Scott asked the shepherd to sing his ballad of "Gilmanscleuch," which he had heard only once before, when Hogg had composed it some three years earlier. But the poet's memory broke down when he had given some eight or nine stanzas. Thereupon, to his astonishment, Scott took it up and recited all eighty-eight stanzas.[80]

At last the messenger returned, and with him old "Nippy" Laidlaw of the Peel farm carrying a lantern. Into the river they plunged in a frail leaking bark. The torches blazed, salmon began to appear in plenty, but the boat started to sink. When they reached Gleddie's Weal, the deepest pool in that part of the Tweed, Nippy was in terror and Scott laughed till the tears blinded his eyes. "For God's sake, push her to the side!" roared Peel. "Oh, she goes fine," replied Scott—

> "An' gin the boat war bottomless,
> An' seven miles to row."

While he was reciting these lines, down went the boat, plunging them all over head and ears in the water.[81] "I was three hours on the water last night and killed some salmon," wrote Scott; "the boat sunk with us however and concluded our sport with a sound ducking."[82] "That was a glorious night for Scott," remarked Hogg, "and the next day [he] was no worse."[83]

From mid-May to mid-July, as usual, Scott was in attendance on the Court of Session, but the summer saw the family again at Ashestiel. The very night before they left Edinburgh the copy of Ellis's *Specimens of Early English Metrical Romances* Scott had long been eagerly awaiting was at last delivered to him. Next day, after packing Charlotte, a fat maid, and "three childer" inside the chaise, Scott perched himself outside on the "dickie" with the driver, and devoured the first volume on the road, roaring, he told Ellis, "at the ludicrous turn you have given to the dullest of the old Romances." "Charlotte, to whom of course the narrative as well as the manner is altogether new, can scarcely persuade herself that the lively and delightful tales with which she is so much charmed have sprung out of the old *Rums* which she heard occasionally discussed at Sunninghill."[84]

During the summer Scott plugged away at Dryden. In his hours of relaxation, he said, "I ride, walk, fish, course, eat and drink, with might and main, from morning to night."[85] He turned out for the *Edinburgh Review* an article on Todd's edition of Spenser and an enthusiastic review of Ellis's work and Ritson's *Ancient English Metrical Romances*. From Sunninghill, Ellis, who had heard from Thomas Longman about the proposed edition of the British Poets—which was not abandoned till autumn—but did not know about the Dryden, urged upon him still another monumental project:

". . . Much as I wish for a *corpus poetarum*, edited as you would edit it, I should like still better another *Minstrel Lay* by the last and best Minstrel. . . . If, however, you don't feel disposed to take a second ride on Pegasus, why not undertake something far less *infra dig.* than a mere edition of our poets? Why not undertake what Gibbon once undertook—an edition of our historians? I have never been able to look at a volume of the Benedictine editions of the early French historians without envy."[86]

Ellis also broached this idea to Owen Rees, exciting that diminutive bookseller's brain, Scott said, with glittering visions of an immense *corpus historiarum.* "You have set little Rees's head agog about the Chronicles, which would be an admirable work, but should, I think, be edited by an Englishman who can have access to the MSS. of Oxford and Cambridge, as one cannot trust much to the correctness of printed copies. I will, however, consider the matter so far as a decent edition of Holinshed is concerned, in case my time is not otherwise taken up. . . . My present employment is an edition of John Dryden's *Works,* which is already gone to press." (He referred, not to the complete works, which ultimately came to eighteen volumes, but the earlier volumes of the dramas.) "As for riding on Pegasus, depend upon it, I will never again cross him in a serious way, unless I should by some strange accident reside so long in the Highlands, and make myself master of their ancient manners, as to paint them with some degree of accuracy in a kind of *companion* to the *Minstrel Lay.*"[87]

Thus we hear the first faint vibration in Scott's mind of *The Lady of the Lake,* though as yet voiceless and imageless, the emotion and the theme that was to sweep the strings in his opening invocation to the Harp of the North and evoke the sylvan scene of Loch Katrine. But so far these were but disembodied glimmerings; in August he filed his papers neatly away, put his books back on their shelves, and started out with Charlotte on a vacation among the Lakes of Cumberland and Westmorland and a visit to Southey at Keswick and to Wordsworth in his little cottage at Grasmere.[88]

Charlotte rode in the carriage—she was expecting another child in November or December—and Scott trotted on horseback at her side. Once again he saw the wild mountains rising above the twisting shores of Ullswater and the thick foliage fringing Windermere. Southey took him boating among the green islets of Derwentwater. With Wordsworth and the well-known chemist Humphry Davy, a fellow guest at Dove Cottage, he clambered up the steep ascent of Helvellyn, and from its summit the three men gazed over the vast encircling panorama, from Windermere, Esthwaite Water, and Coniston Water to the south, with the Irish Sea in the distance, around to the rolling ridges of the Pennine Chain to the east, and thence from Ullswater to the Solway Firth and the far-off Dumfriesshire Hills in the northwest.[89] The preceding spring a young man losing his way on the mountain had died in a fall from a precipice and not been found till three months later. Wordsworth and Scott were each inspired to write a poem on this subject, Scott's lines beginning:

> I climb'd the dark brow of the mighty Helvellyn,
>> Lakes and mountains beneath gleam'd misty and wide;
> All was still, save by fits, when the eagle was yelling,
>> And starting around me the echoes replied.[90]

From Grasmere, Scott and Charlotte went on to Gilsland, where they had first met. Here they revisited the scenes of their courtship, the green gorge of the Irthing, the poplar glade across its rushing stream, the breezy top of the Roman wall, the battlements of Triermain Castle, the ballroom of the Shaw Hotel, where she had been enchanting in a pink satin décolletée and he had been so bitterly jealous of those dandy "lordlings and witlings" whose rivalry he had feared.[91]

How his life had changed in a bare nine years! How different was he from the awkward but obstinate young lover of 1797, the struggling advocate, the fledgling author of a few poems! Now a happily married man, father of a growing family, an Edinburgh householder with a country home, Sheriff of Selkirkshire, he had won prestige for himself as a scholar and antiquary and laurels as the author of the most brilliantly and immediately successful poem in English literary history. Limping along the graveled paths between the bright flower beds, he had ample reasons to feel joy. But how his heart might have been shaken with wonder had he been able to foresee the unimaginable changes of the next nine years!

Suddenly, in the midst of their visit, came an alarm. Once again the beacon fires flamed north, south, inland. The French were rumored to be landing in Scotland. Volunteers, horse and foot, Scott knew, would be assembling at Dalkeith and Musselburgh. Leaving Charlotte at Gilsland, he leaped to saddle and galloped off. Through the night, to the pounding of his steed's hoofs, lines of a new poem formed themselves in his mind, his *Bard's Incantation*, beginning

> The forest of Glenmore is drear
> It is all of black pine and the dark oak tree;

and going on to the exhortation:

> O yet awake the strain to tell,
>> By every deed in song enroll'd,
> By every chief who fought or fell
>> For Albion's weal in battle bold.[92]

The hundred miles' fiery ride from Gilsland to Musselburgh he covered within twenty-four hours. The alarm had blown over, but the places of rendezvous were swarming with the Edinburgh troops and with the yeomen of Ettrick Forest who had poured down from their glens under the leadership of Pringle of Torwoodlee. Before the needless muster broke up there were a few sham battles and some evenings of high jollity. Then Scott turned his horse south again and rejoined Charlotte at Carlisle. From there the two returned to Ashestiel.[93]

Here, in October, Robert Southey repaid their visit. The two poets had become warm friends, and Southey regaled Scott with the sight of a fifteenth-century manuscript he had with him, containing among other items a Breton lay resembling the history of Robert the Devil, a romance called *Sir Isambras*, a long dull poem about heaven and hell, and a burlesque sermon with an anecdote in which Adam is asked "*a full great doubtful question*, saying, 'Adam, Adam, why didst thou eat the apple unpared?' "[94] Southey wrote a correspondent, "We were three days at Scott's, a much superior man, whom it is impossible not to like. He was delighted with the MS., and has commissioned me to offer fifteen guineas for it, for the Advocates' Library."[95]

During that summer and early autumn of 1805 Scott began one further piece of writing. The same impulse that made him dream of a Highland companion poem to *The Lay of the Last Minstrel* led him to start writing a prose narrative using his early recollections of Highland scenery and customs.[96] The tales of old Invernahyle in his childhood, his youthful ramblings through Stirlingshire and Perthshire, the stories of Rob Roy and the '45 he had gathered from the lips of many an old warrior—all these were glowing in his mind. "The ancient traditions and high spirit of a people who, living in a civilized age and country, retained so strong a tincture of manners belonging to an early period of society," he thought, "must afford a subject favorable for romance, if it should not prove a curious tale marred in the telling."[97]

With this idea he dashed off some seven chapters of a novel. These he showed to William Erskine for his opinion. It was unfavorable, a judgment that Scott accepted with unwavering good-nature. He had never attempted prose fiction since the abortive fragments on *Thomas the Rhymer* and *The Lord of Ennerdale*, and he harbored no notion that he possessed any particular talent for it. Having now some poetical reputation, "I was unwilling," he said, "to risk the loss of it by attempting a new style of composition." Therefore he unhesitatingly threw it aside. The unfinished manuscript he crammed into the drawers of an old writing desk, where it lay forgotten.

The title he had written on its first page was *Waverley: or, 'Tis Fifty Years Since*.[98]

# 3

# "My Staff But Not My Crutch"

## (1805–1807)

AFTER AGAIN SPENDING some jolly days and nights in quarters at Musselburgh, Scott returned early in November to Edinburgh and the glorious news of Trafalgar.[1] On the heavy swell of waters rolling in from the Atlantic toward the Cape and the Gut of Gibraltar, Nelson had smashed the combined French and Spanish fleets and, dying victorious in the cockpit of the *Victory*, became "one with England and the sea." Past midnight, in the early hours of November 6, through heavy fog, blazing flambeaux, and shouting coachmen, the tidings traveled to London; thence it rolled its way north. Though almost all the Continent lay prostrate under Napoleon's power, the invasion of England was now a danger that had passed.

Nelson's death in the hour of his triumph inspired Warren Hastings, an enthusiastic admirer of the *Lay* and the *Minstrelsy*, to suggest that Scott compose a naval epic with "our gallant Nelson" as its hero.[2] "I would be utterly devoid of the feelings of an author," Scott replied, "if I were not highly flattered by the approbation of Mr. Hastings, to whose genius and talents we owe the preservation of the British Empire in the East. The Compliment he pays me in supposing me capable of executing the colossal design which he has sketched out is in every point of view as high as unmerited."[3]

He would not dwell, Scott continued, "on my general incapacity to perform such a mighty task, for that might look like an affectation of modesty to hook in more praise." He simply did not know enough, however, about seafaring to write such a poem successfully; every honest tar would deride his efforts as "the effusions of a mere landlubber." With his "ancient *preux chevaliers* and border Moss-troopers" he ran no such risks; even if he misrepresented "their customs or manners there is no chance of their rising to call me to debate the point *en champ clos*, or to carry off my milk cows from Ashestiel." "After all, the fate of the hero of the Nile, of Copenhagen, and alas! of Trafalgar is almost too grand in its native simplicity to be heightened by poetical imagery."[4]

The glory of Nelson, therefore, did not suspend Scott's labors on "glorious John Dryden." Ellis had greeted with some alarm his announcement of this project. The mass of Dryden's writings, especially his comedies, contained so many obscenities; would it not be more judicious to make a selection of the tragedies, poems, fables, and prose writings rather than print the complete works?[5] "I will not castrate John Dryden," declared Scott. "I would as soon castrate my own father, as I believe Jupiter did of yore. What would you say to any man who would castrate Shakespeare, or Massinger, or Beaumont and Fletcher?" It might be very proper to make virginal selections of such authors for girls' boarding schools, but for libraries and collections the writings of a man of genius must be presented with no page torn out, even to get rid of the blots.[6]

"In fact, it is not passages of ludicrous indelicacy that corrupt the manners of a people—it is the sonnets which a prurient genius like Mr. Moore sings *virginibus puerisque*—it is the sentimental slang, half lewd, half methodistic, that debauches the understanding, inflames the sleeping passions, and prepares the reader to give way as soon as a tempter appears. At the same time, I am not at all happy when I peruse some of Dryden's comedies: they are very stupid, as well as indelicate; —sometimes, however, there is a considerable vein of liveliness and humour, and all of them present extraordinary pictures of the age in which he lived."[7]

Late in November came an invitation from Lord Minto's daughter to spend the Christmas holidays at Minto House and again make the teeth of the Hobgoblinites chatter at hair-raising stories by its flickering fireside. Signing herself "Demonia," she proclaimed

> A solemn council, forthwith to be held
> At Pandemonium, the high capital
> Of Satan and his peers,

and implored his presence; "each member amongst us," she wrote,

> this Motto has got
> That for Tales of Hobgoblins of Ghosts and *what not*
> No Mortal in Britain is like Walter Scott. . . .[8]

He replied in an epistle from "Gilpin Horner to Demonia":

> Infernal Maid, I greet ye well.
> Your favours came to hand from hell,
> So witty and so courteous too,
> That, give the Queen of Devils her due,

> I should have sworn each sable line
> Flow'd from the quill of Proserpine,
> But that the fair sign manual shew'd
> A blooming Princess of her blood,
> Whom in the Forest I had seen
> Reigning, herself, a Fairy Queen.[9]

He and Charlotte could not accept the invitation, for she was still waiting the birth of their child, already a little past the time when it had been expected. Even if it were born well before Christmas, she would hardly be in a condition to travel into Roxburghshire.[10] He therefore made his response a substitute for his presence:

> I'll take my passage on a blast
> Till Eildon's triple top is past;
> Then glancing down, a shooting star,
> Without a drag, shall be my car;
> Or lumps of ice shall be my sledge,
> To rattle down cold Lylliard's edge;
>
> . . .
>
> Astride one besom we may speed,
> At Melrose cloister till it halts,
> And sets us down in charnel vaults,
> Where Monks' unrotted bodies dwell
> And unlaid spirits haunt the cell,
> Oft seen to flit on leathern wing,
> And squeaking requiems heard to sing.
>
> . . .
>
> Then as the bloody cross's glow
> Stains the cold shadowy tomb below,
> We'll heave dread Michael's massy stone,
> And shudder at the frowning bone.[11]

Not until almost the end of December, on Christmas Eve, was the baby born. Despite the protracted delay, Charlotte made an excellent recovery. The infant, a fine sturdy boy, was named Charles, after her brother. The whole family, Scott told her old companion Miss Nicolson, were "healthy and strong; your little favourite Sophia turns out a very clever girl of her age and gives great content to her instructors." Walter, almost exactly two years younger, was a hardy four-year-old now nick-named Gilnockie, and Anne would soon be three.[12]

With this growing family to provide for, Scott was devoting serious thought to his future. He felt confident that he might continue to gain considerable sums as a writer, and yet, as the poverty of Wordsworth and the struggles of such men as Southey and Campbell showed, literature was a cruelly precarious means of earning a livelihood. At the same time he felt that his literary activities had hampered his success at the bar. Writers to the Signet, clients, judges, his fellow advocates, he knew, all felt dubious of the professional dedication of a man who flirted with the Muses.

"The goddess Themis," he observed, "is at Edinburgh, and I suppose everywhere else, of a peculiarly jealous disposition. She will not readily consent to share her authority, and sternly demands from her votaries, not only that real duty be carefully attended to, but that a certain air of business shall be observed even in the midst of total idleness." An advocate, however destitute of clients, ought nevertheless to "appear completely engrossed by his profession." "He should, therefore, seem perpetually engaged among his law-papers, dusting them, as it were; and, as Ovid advises the fair,

> " 'Si nullus erit pulvis, tamen excute nullum.' "[13]
> —If dust be none, yet brush that none away.

How could anyone believe in the legal industry of a man who found time to pour torrents of printed matter from the press?

In addition, although Scott was fascinated by the law as a study and would have found pleasure in the loftier judicial function, he did not enjoy practicing as an advocate contending for victories. But the Bar was the only way to the Bench, and that seemed a remote and phantom hope. "My profession and I, therefore," Scott summarized it, "came to stand nearly upon the footing which honest Shallow consoled himself on having established with Mistress Anne Page: 'There was no great love between us at the beginning, and it pleased Heaven to decrease it on farther acquaintance.' I became sensible that the time was come when I must either buckle myself resolutely to the 'toil by day, the lamp by night,' renouncing all the Delilahs of my imagination, or bid adieu to the profession of the law, and hold another course."[14]

Scott had not, in fact, been the failure he represents himself. His practice had become comprehensive and had included cases before the House of Lords, the Court of Session, the High Court of Judiciary, both in Edinburgh and on Circuit, the Sheriff Court, and the General Assembly. His legal earnings and the number of his clients had risen slowly but steadily from the beginning of his career. There is no record for 1804–5, but in the preceding year, his eleventh in practice, he had earned £228 18s. So slow a start was neither unusual nor incompatible with future eminence: after nine years at the bar Francis Jeffrey, who became Dean of the Faculty of Advocates and a Lord of the Court of Session, was earning only £240.[15] Furthermore, Jeffrey's long career as a critic and as editor of the *Edinburgh Review* would ultimately prove that the prejudice against lawyers being men of letters could be broken down.

But Scott's way was neither Jeffrey's truculent defiance nor timorous surrender. Though he would take no wild risk, he would still take his own course. Independence could be combined with common sense, resistance with realism. He would not give up literature, but neither would he make himself subservient to the bounty of booksellers. "I determined that literature should be my staff, but not my crutch, and that the profits of my literary labours should not, if I could help it, become necessary to my ordinary expenses."[16] He would not give up the law, but neither would he scrabble any longer for cases bringing in only a few uncertain hundreds a year. His responsibilities to his family demanded that he have an assured income; if he was to be a writer he must have a financial anchor to windward.

With the cool judgment he had learned to bring to bear upon accomplishing his will, he saw that he must obtain a post as one of the salaried officials of the law. Surely his powerful friends—the Duke of Buccleuch, Lord Dalkeith, Lord Melville—could get such an appointment for him. Had not the Prime Minister himself, the great Mr. Pitt, told his boyhood friend William Dundas that he would be happy to promote the interests of the author of the *Lay*? Scott's aim was to be made one of the Principal Clerks of the Court of Session. This would not oblige him to surrender his Selkirk sheriffdom, its duties would consume only between four and six hours a day during the six months the Court was in session, and its salary was £800 a year.[17]

Scott had been making efforts in this direction for a full year. Even before his poem had achieved its triumphant success, Lord Dalkeith was writing him, on February 2, 1805: "My father desires me to tell you that he has had a communication with Lord Melville within these few days, and that he thinks *your business is in good train, though not certain*."[18] What this probably meant was that he would be favorably considered for the first vacancy. But there was no retirement system; the usual procedure was that a Clerk resigned in favor of a successor or formally designated a coadjutor who then did all his work. This person either paid the retiring Clerk an agreed sum or made him an annual allowance out of the salary. One of the Clerks of Session, George Home of Wedderburn, in Berwickshire, had held his office for more than thirty years and was growing so deaf as to have difficulty in performing its duties. Home was an aged man; Scott now clinched matters by proposing to assume his labors and allow him the entire salary for his lifetime. Home not unnaturally leaped at this offer.[19]

The influence of the Duke of Buccleuch was brought to bear; the Government agreed to a new commission naming both men jointly.[20] Unfortunately, through a clerical error, it was made out to Scott alone. The mistake would make no difference as long as Scott was alive, but if he were to die Home would have no claim on the salary. It was a risk Scott could not allow the retiring Clerk to take. The document would have to be drawn afresh.[21]

Under ordinary circumstances this would merely have meant a short delay. But on January 23, 1806, the death of William Pitt dissolved the

Ministry, and the succeeding administration was bound to be a Whig coalition of Fox and Grenville. The northern Whigs rejoiced; at last they would have a chance at public places.[22] Although Scott had not been a rancorous politician and lived on friendly terms with many of them, he could expect no aid at their hands: "they must provide," he remarked, "for the Whiggish children before they throw their bread to the Tory dogs; and I shall not fawn on them because they have in their turn the superintendence of the larder."[23]

Worse still, Scott's old patron Lord Melville had been forced to retire from the Admiralty under charges of corruption during his incumbency as Treasurer of the Navy ten years before, and the Opposition was clamoring for his impeachment. There were accusations of misappropriations of funds, hints of worse.[24] Pitt had tried to protect him, but Pitt's death made it certain that he would be brought to trial. With all his enemies howling for his blood, Melville could be of no help, nor were the triumphant Whigs apt to look with much favor on one of his supporters. Although the inaccurate wording of the patent was plainly an official blunder, there was no small danger that it might be made the excuse for throwing out the appointment.

While Pitt's life still hung in the balance Scott had written asking Ellis to state his case to Lord Grenville. It was no favor, he insisted, but a matter of fair play, that a transaction completed between two private parties and approved by an existing administration be permitted to take effect. With the news of Pitt's death Scott hurried up to London. In this crisis anything might happen; even if his claim were not denied, the patent might lie on a table in Whitehall, under a growing pile of correspondence about it, gathering dust for months on end. He must strike quickly.[25]

Lord Somerville introduced him to Lord Spencer, who was installed as Secretary of State in the Home Office. That nobleman unhesitatingly granted Scott's request. "In the handsomest manner" he ordered "that the commission should issue as originally intended; adding that, the matter having received the royal assent, he regarded only as a claim of justice what he would willingly have done as an act of favour."[26] Lord Grenville concurred; Fox, now Foreign Secretary, Scott did not approach, feeling that to do so might appear an expression of "political opinions different from those which I had always professed. In his private capacity," Scott added, "there is no man to whom I would have been more proud to owe an obligation."[27]

"You are now to snap your finger at the Bar," Lord Dalkeith told him, "—But you are not to be idle—We shall expect much from your leisure—" Above all, he must steer clear of political faction: "Talk not, think not of Politics. Go to the Hills and converse with the Spirit of the Fell; or any spirit" but that foul fiend "the spirit of Party."[28]

To ministers in London, no doubt, the Clerkship at Edinburgh seemed a trifling affair. But Scott's speed unquestionably forestalled rival demands they might have found embarrassing to refuse. When his nomination as Clerk of Session appeared in the same *Gazette* (March 8, 1806) that announced the installation of Henry Erskine as Lord Advocate and John Clerk of Eldin as Solicitor-General for Scotland, the inclusion among these promotions of a prominent Tory excited the wonder of Parliament House, and resentful Whigs buzzed with spleen at the conduct of their party leaders in Westminster.[29] Had their voices been heard before Scott's the justice of his cause might not have been enough to gain a victory.

London, in fact, with this political upheaval, had become a violent arena of jealous ambitions—"people who have stood in the rain without doors for so many years, [now] quarrelling for the nearest place to the fire, as soon as they have set their feet on the floor."[30] Scott had managed to get his own affairs attended to before the real battles began. "There is much loose gunpowder amongst them and one spark would make a fine explosion."[31] "I have indeed," he wrote, "been rather fortunate, for the gale which has shattered so many goodly argosies, has blown my little bark into the creek for which she was bound . . ."[32]

Upon one reason for his success he put a humorous finger. "After all," he said in a letter conveying his thanks to Lord Dalkeith, "a literary reputation is of some use here. I suppose Solomon when he compared a good name to a pot of ointment meant that it oiled the hinges of the hall doors into which the possessors of that inestimable treasure wished to penetrate. What a *good* name was in Jerusalem a *known* name seems to be in London. If you are celebrated for writing verses or for slicing cucumbers, for being two feet taller or two feet less than any other biped . . . your notoriety becomes a talisman, an 'Open Sesamum' before which everything gives way till you are voted a bore and discarded for a new plaything."[33]

For Scott was now a London Lion, tasting to the full its cup of blandishment.[34] George Ellis was away at Bath, but old friends like Richard Heber, of course, Scott happily saw again, and stole off as often as he could to pore over the literary collections of Mr. Bindley in the liberties of Westminister.[35] The great world of fashionable society also insistently drew him into its glittering whirl. The Marquis and Marchioness of Abercorn (for whom Scott's father had been factor and who were now clients of his brother Tom) had him as their guest in Bentley Priory, at Stanmore, Middlesex.[36] Sallying out from his hotel at 79 Jermyn Street, almost around the corner from Samuel Rogers, he went nightly to receptions and dinners. He met the witty George Canning and John Hookham Frere; he was even invited to that great Whig stronghold, Holland House, in its ancient park.[37]

Here he dined for the first time on February 11, well after his business with the Government had been carried to its successful conclusion.

"I refused to go before," he explained, "lest it should be thought I was soliciting interest in that quarter, as I abhor even the shadow of changing or turning with the tide."[38] But now that he could not be accused of trying to curry favor, he willingly attended a great crush in the old Elizabethan mansion, being shown by liveried footmen from its noble entrance hall up the grand staircase to the long library rich with serried volumes and the lofty dining room with its gilded wainscoting.

Through William Sotheby, the translator of Wieland's *Oberon*, Scott also met the famous Joanna Baillie, whose *Plays of the Passions* he had long admired.[39] A niece of the famous anatomist Dr. John Hunter, and a sister of Dr. Matthew Baillie, physician-extraordinary to George III, Miss Baillie composed blank-verse tragedies that fascinated a distinguished audience. That fastidious connoisseur of all the arts, Sir George Beaumont, had sent them to Charles James Fox, who had responded with five pages of rapturous eulogy. Their scenes of witchcraft and the terrors of the supernatural, together with the elemental passions that were their themes, overpowered their readers. To be sure, Miss Baillie's tragedies had not been very successful on the stage, but that only proved, her enthusiasts said, the tastelessness of the average theatergoer. Although their magic has faded today, they were then compared with Shakespeare and Dryden.[40]

The famous authoress proved to be a plain little spinster of forty-four, living in rural Hampstead with her maiden elder sister. Scott took to her at once. Perhaps her eager attenuated face, sensitive mouth, and strong straight brows hinted to him the strange fire that led this small creature to deal in the emotions of fear, anger, envy, hatred, and love.[41] And Miss Baillie had sharpness and force as well. When Miss Mary Berry—the fashionable Miss Berry, Horace Walpole's Mary Berry—tried to patronize her, neglected a promise to visit her, and then wrote a careless note of insincere excuse, Joanna replied with flashing resentment: "If anything in the simplicity of my appearance has led you to suppose me of an easier and gentler temper than I am, I am sorry for the involuntary deceit."[42]

Miss Baillie, however, did not take so quickly to Scott. "I was at first," she said, "a little disappointed, for I was fresh from the *Lay*, and had pictured to myself an ideal elegance and refinement of feature; but I said to myself, If I had been in a crowd, and at a loss what to do, I should have fixed upon that face among a thousand, as a sure index of the benevolence and the shrewdness that would and could help me in my strait. We had not talked long, however, before I saw in the expressive play of his countenance far more even of elegance and refinement than I had missed in its mere lines."[43] In her demure Hampstead parlor that day the plain little poetess and the limping Scottish poet laid the foundations of a lasting friendship.

Another of Scott's conquests was Caroline, Princess of Wales. Separated from her husband since 1796, she was pursued by his relentless hatred. Like his grandfather Prince Frederick William and his great-grandfather George II before him, the Prince had also quarreled with his father and therefore befriended the Whigs, whom the King distrusted. They in turn lauded the obese and dissolute Prince as a model of royal virtue and professed to regard his Princess as the most abandoned of her sex. The Tories consequently—despite an undignified levity of demeanor in Caroline that gave some grounds for uneasiness—defended her as a much injured lady persecuted by a vindictive libertine. She now resided south of Greenwich Park, in Montague House, at Blackheath, where Scott was invited to dine.[44]

"She is an enchanting princess, who dwells in an enchanted palace," Scott told Ellis, "and I cannot help thinking that her prince must labour under some malignant spell when he denies himself her society. The very Prince of the Black Isles, whose bottom was marble, would have made an effort to transport himself to Montague House."[45] The Princess asked him to recite some of his own verses. He replied that he had none unpublished that he thought worth her Royal Highness' attention, but repeated one of the ballads from Hogg's *Mountain Bard* and told her about the Ettrick Shepherd. The Princess, pleased with the story and the poem, requested that her name be placed on Hogg's subscription list.[46]

Scott found himself a little embarrassed, however, by the familiarity of the Princess' manner. Taking him from the drawing room and the rest of the company to admire some flowers in the conservatory, she led him down some rather dimly lighted steps, descending them in a rapid skip. But his lameness made him hesitate in the dark. The Princess turned round. "Ah! false and faint-hearted troubadour!" she exclaimed in mock indignation, "you will not trust yourself with me for fear of your neck!"[47] Could it be, the startled suspicion flashed through his mind, that her Royal Highness was flirting with him?

Early on the morning of March 4, Scott started for home, his appointment as a Principal Clerk of Session triumphantly confirmed and the ultimate prospect of an assured £800 a year added to his income.[48] He had intended, indeed, to have left a bit sooner, but James Ballantyne, who had been with him in London, "was afflicted," Scott recorded, "with a severe diarrhea." This would "have contributed little to his accomplishments as an agreeable companion in a post-chaise, which are otherwise very respectable."[49] At Edinburgh, Scott was joyfully welcomed by Charlotte, Sophia, now growing into a big girl, Gilnockie, and little Anne, as well as by the faithful Camp and the two greyhounds, Douglas and Percy, eagerly bounding about. From Edinburgh the coachman Peter Matheson drove them to Ashestiel on April 5, where they were greeted by grinning Tom Purdie, the Highland gardener Mackay, "two cottages full of peasants and their children, and all my other stock, human and animal, in great good health."[50]

Plugging away at John Dryden again, he found himself somewhat regretting his brave boast that he would expurgate nothing. Some of the translations from Lucretius and Juvenal, another from Ovid's "Instructions to his Mistress," would bring "the Bishop of London and the whole corps of Methodists about my ears"; they were "not only double-entendres, but good plain single-entendres." "I fear," he told Ellis, "that, without absolutely gelding the bard, it will be indispensable to circumcize him a little."[51]

But Ellis now sternly held him to his word. No doubt it would have been better had Dryden not selected from the classical poets "such passages as were calculated to please the frequenters of a brothel," but Scott had pledged himself "to give, in a uniform edition, *all* that Dryden wrote." Though his purchasers might not wish to possess it for the sake of its prurient poems, they would be justified in expecting "to find every passage to which they may chuse to refer." Consequently he was "not at liberty to leave out the obnoxious passages."[52]

When the Court of Session resumed its sittings after the spring recess Scott took his new place at the Clerks' Table, just in front of the Bench. The Court sat from May 12 to July 12, and again from November 12, with a short Christmas holiday, to March 12. It did not sit, however, on Mondays, which were reserved for criminal cases under the High Court of Judiciary, nor on alternate Wednesdays, called *Teind Wednesdays*, when the Judges heard tithe questions.[53] At ten in the morning the Judges swept in and took their places, their red-satin-lined hoods on their heads and their purple robes billowing.[54] Depending on the amount of business before them, they remained in Court between four and six hours.

Part of the work of the Clerks was purely formal, but it was also their duty to reduce to technical written form decisions orally pronounced from the Bench. In new or complicated cases this could not be done without close attention to the proceedings and a complete grasp of all the documents involved, as well as an understanding of the legal principles and precedents invoked and a command of the whole vocabulary of legal forms. Outside of Court the Clerks had also a good many tasks, such as authenticating registered deeds by signatures and looking up law papers and authorities. More than one of the Clerks enjoyed a reputation for legal erudition that would have done honor to a Judge.[55]

Scott's colleagues at the Clerks' Table included John Pringle, the oldest of their number, Scott's old friend and schoolfellow Colin Mackenzie, James Ferrier, the father of the novelist Susan Ferrier, James Walker, and Hector Macdonald Buchanan of Drumalkiln, in whose veins flowed the Highland blood of Clanranald. It was not long before Scott was an almost annual visitor at Ross Priory, Buchanan's home on the shores of Loch Lomond. All the Clerks soon became an affectionate brotherhood. They and their families were constantly in one anothers' houses, and their children all called one anothers' fathers and mothers "Uncle" and "Aunt."[56]

Once when some of the uncles and aunts were coming to dinner at Castle Street, the kitchen chimney caught fire. Flames darted out into the room, thick smoke darkened the windows, the spit was coated thick with ashes. The servants broke into a pandemonium of excitement, knocking over pots and pans. A fine turbot lay on the floor an inch thick in soot. In the confusion Camp happily gnawed some cindery mutton chops. The fire was put out, but the meal was ruined. Scott laughed, and ordered dinner at the nearest hotel. Mrs. Macdonald Buchanan, arriving late, was amazed to be hurried out of the doorway in a crowd of other guests, and, still trying to get an explanation, hustled away toward Princes Street.[57]

It was not long before Scott and his fellow Clerks settled down into a routine. Every morning during term times a great coach lumbered from door to door, picking them up, and then drove across the North Bridge and turned into the High Street to deposit them at the Parliament House; many a morning Scott would hastily take a final huge gulp of tea and dash out of the door at Castle Street clutching a half-consumed scone in his hand.[58]

Since the death of Pitt, Lord Melville's enemies had been pressing forward with his impeachment. "I suppose," Scott wrote, "they are determined to hunt him down. Indeed, the result of his trial must be ruin from the expense, even supposing him to be honourably acquitted."[59] Under the strain the fallen statesman's health broke. "My heart bleeds," Scott exclaimed, "when I think on his situation—

> Even when the rage of battle ceased,
> The victor's soul was not appeased."[60]

The trial before the House of Lords in Westminster Hall lasted from April 29 to June 12. When the news came that it had ended in an acquittal, Scott flamed into exultation. The Magistrates of Edinburgh cravenly turned down an application that the town be illuminated in celebration.[61] But Melville's rejoicing supporters gave a great public dinner in his honor on June 27. Five hundred and forty-one met in the Assembly Rooms, and there were seven or eight parties of from fifty to two hundred scattered around the town.[62] Two songs Scott wrote for the occasion were sung by the black-bearded and corpulent James Ballantyne in "the voice of a Stentor" and received by the numerous company with clamorous applause:

> Since here we are set in array round the table,
> Five hundred good fellows well met in a hall,
> Come listen, brave boys, and I'll sing as I'm able
> How innocence triumphed and pride got a fall.

But push round the claret—
Come, stewards, don't spare it—
With rapture you'll drink to the toast that I give.
Here, boys,
Off with it merrily—
MELVILLE for ever, and long may he live!

Stanza after stanza was followed with cheers, right to the culmination:

And since we must now set Auld Reekie in glory,
    And make her brown visage as light as her heart;
Till each man illumine his own upper story,
    Nor law-book nor lawyer shall force us to part.
    In GRENVILLE and SPENCER,
    And some few good men, sir,
High talents we honour, slight difference forgive;
    But the Brewer we'll hoax,
    Tallyho to the Fox,
And drink MELVILLE for ever, as long as we live![63]

The derisive allusion to "the Brewer" was a slap at one of Melville's most violent assailants, Samuel Whitbread, the owner of Whitbread's Brewery, and "the Fox" was understood to mean Charles James Fox. In the other ditty, which Ballantyne also gave out in his bass bellow, Scott mentioned both again:

Once Whitbread had *hops* of conviction we hear,
But now he's got wormwood to bitter his beer,
For when to the Peers the fair Question was put
The Brewer of mischief has turned out a Butt.

The party now find themselves in the wrong box:
Though they thanked the Committee and voted with Fox,
They've found out the odds betwixt merit and Jaw
And the damnable difference 'twixt Justice and Law.[64]

No objections were voiced to the attack on Whitbread, but the reference to Fox, who was gravely ill, gave deep offense to his devotees. The Countess of Rosslyn, indeed, never forgave Scott to her dying day. Though she regretted that anything should "make a coolness" between them, the song was "an uncalled for mark of personal disrespect to Mr. Fox," whose example of the forgiveness of injuries, she said, she admired but could not put into practice where he was concerned.[65] "Poor Lady Roslin is gone," Scott said in 1810, "with all the various talent and vivacity that rendered her society so delightful. I regret her loss the more as she died without ever making up some unkindness she had towards me for these foolish politics."[66]

But if Scott's loyalty to Lord Melville—"the architect of my little fortune"[67]—angered people like Lady Rosslyn and Dugald Stewart, it brought him the warm friendship of many others. Acknowledging a copy of one of the songs which Scott sent him through William Stewart Rose, Canning depreciated the "loud and petulant" expressions of annoyance, and voiced approval and gratitude for his praise of his old patron.[68]

In the midst of these political agitations Scott was again involved in the affairs of his brother Daniel. Old Mrs. Scott was anxious to provide for the education of his illegitimate child and tried to bring about an arrangement.[69] She would agree, Scott wrote, "to the terms last proposed by" the mother's family, "which though high are I think little enough for getting rid of such a scrape."[70] Nor had this weakling brother been doing well in Jamaica. "Your Daniel (who I am afraid is no prophet)," Ellis commented, "did not perhaps foresee the advantages in point of intoxicating power which a vertical sun gives to rum over whisky imbibed in Scotland."[71]

Poor Daniel was too soft and his drink too hard for the West Indies; when he was ordered to subdue a revolt among a band of rebellious Negroes he showed the white feather and was dismissed in disgrace.[72] He returned to Scotland a dishonored man, "with ruined health and blasted prospects."[73] His mother compassionately took him in, but Scott, to whom cowardice was almost the one unforgivable weakness, would not even see him. Overwhelmed by shame and shattered by dissipation, Daniel's constitution gave way altogether. On July 20, 1806, he died. Scott remained unyielding. He refused to attend his brother's funeral and wore no mourning.[74]

An exile who had done far otherwise was John Leyden. He had been appointed physician and naturalist to the Mysore survey at a salary of £1,000 a year, was studying oriental languages and literature, lived magnificently with a retinue of fifty servants,[75] traveled with "a guard of spearsmen on foot" like "Johnny Armstrong and his merry men," and was saluted by "the astonished Natives" as "Bahader" or "great warrior."[76] For fifteen months, however, he had been ill with an inflamed spleen and fever. "I conjure you by all things dead and alive," he told Scott, "to write me . . . If I die of this I have ordered myself to be scalped and hung up in your cottage as proof positive that you have brought down my grizzled head with sorrow to the grave."[77]

"I am ashamed to have written so far," Leyden continued, "without enquiring for the good, the kind, the sweet, the dear Mrs. Scott. I am ready to cry when I think of her. Good God what would I give—I would swim the Annan though I don't swim any more than a stone—to have the pleasure of drinking tea with her again and astonishing her tea-pot. . . . Pray, my Dear Mrs. Scott, lay aside that pretty unbelieving face of yours."[78]

Scott responded with a budget of news—about Ballantyne's new quarters, the success of the *Lay*, editing Dryden, his new position as

Clerk of Session, Constable's growing bulk and business, and the move from Lasswade to Ashestiel. "Here we live all summer like little kings and only wish that you could take a scamper with me over the hills in the morning and return to a clean tablecloth with a leg of forest mutton and a blazing hearth in the afternoon. Walter has acquired the surname of Gilnockie being large of limb and bone and dauntless in disposition like that noted chieftain. Your little friend Sophia is grown a tall girl and promises to be very clever. . . . We have moreover a little round-about girl with large dark eyes as brown, as good humoured, and as lively as the Mother that bore her and of whom she is the most striking picture. Over and above all this there is in rerum natura a certain little Charles . . . but of this gentleman I can say but little as he is only five months old and consequently not at the time of life when I can often enjoy the honour of his company."[79]

Before he left town for the summer Scott saw Lord and Lady Melville and dined with them at Melville Castle. He was happy to find that his old patron had completely recovered from his ordeal. "I never saw the veteran statesman looking better or in more high spirits." Lord Melville was full of a pleasant visit he had made to Lord and Lady Abercorn at Bentley Priory just before returning to Edinburgh and flattered by his reception in almost every town he had passed through on his homeward journey— "nothing but huzzaing and cheering" all the way.[80]

Throughout the summer Scott kept himself busy in the solitude of Ashestiel. "Our whole habitation," he told Lady Abercorn, "could dance very easily in your great Salon without displacing a single moveable or endangering a mirror. We have no green pastures nor stately trees, but to make amends we have one of the most beautiful streams in the world winding through steep mountains which are now purple with the heath blossom." His portable desk having been delayed in some slow conveyance, he had been obliged "to sally forth and shoot a crow to procure a quill" with which to write his letters.[81]

He wrote for the October number of the *Edinburgh* a humorous review of Beresford's *Miseries of Human Life* and a review of the *Miscellaneous Poetry* of the Honorable William Herbert.[82] He began work for Constable on a two-volume selection from the curious Elizabethan papers of Sir Ralph Sadler, which contained many fascinating details about the imprisonment of Mary Queen of Scots in Tutbury Castle.[83] He edited and wrote a biographical introduction for a volume of Civil War memoirs, consisting of *The Life of Sir Henry Slingsby and Memoirs of Captain Hodgson*, which was printed by Ballantyne and published in October by Constable.[84] His own ballads and lyrical pieces, previously scattered, were collected into a single volume published by Longman, who paid him £100.[85] And checking details in Dryden continued, of course, to keep him abundantly busy. "Will you slip into my book-room"—in Castle Street—he asked Skene, "and on the ground shelves next the window" locate the volume of the *Biographia Britannica* containing the article on Gilbert Burnet, and give it to the old house-keeper to send out to Ashestiel by the carrier.[86]

If in the next two months Skene could find a moment to spend at Ashestiel, "you know the way," Scott told him, "and the ford is where it was; which by the way is more than I expected, after Saturday last, which was the most dreadful storm of thunder and lightning I ever witnessed. The lightning broke repeatedly . . . betwixt us and the Peel Wood"[87] "within a hundred yards of our farm house but fortunately did no damage except that the concussion threw down the bricks etc. from the top of the chimneys" and "the thunder was so tremendous as actually to affect my hearing for some time."[88] "Charlotte resolved to die in bed like a Christian, the servants thought it was the end of the world, and I was the only person that maintained my character for stoicism, which I assure you was some merit, as I had no doubt that we were in real danger."[89]

"Our rivers and brooks, always sufficiently rapid, became the most furious torrents . . . Ricks of hay, whole acres of young and old trees, even cattle and horses, came swimming past us without the possibility of our giving any assistance." One gentleman "has totally lost a large and valuable garden which a small rivulet, that in general winded very peaceably through it, chose to carry off entirely. Minto House was in great danger, the inhabitants driven to the upper floors as the lower part of the mansion was quite filled with water. A heroic cook-maid secured a sirloin of beef in her retreat, otherwise the plague of famine would have been added to the distress of the sufferers."[90]

From these tempestuous doings Scott turned to the more peaceful exertions of shooting some grouse to send Lady Abercorn.[91] Trying to tempt her to a visit, "we have the best mutton in the world," he wrote her, for which "the air of our hills makes an excellent sauce. Then we have pigs and poultry, and a whole apparatus of guns, fishing-rods, salmon spears and nets," not to mention the possibility of "hare soup, for am I not Sheriff of the County and may I not break the laws when I please and course out of season?"[92]

While Scott was riding with Adam Ferguson, Skene, and Hogg to pay a visit to the Laidlaws at Blackhouse Tower, the greyhounds caught the scent of what their masters took to be a fox or a roe deer. Hounds and horses were soon in hot pursuit through the fog veiling the lonely hill-tops. At the end of the chase they found that the victim was a stately old he-goat, who had "fought a stout battle for his life, but now lay mangled in the midst of his panting enemies."[93] Another time, Scott and Skene explored the region of Borthwick water together, on their way to pass a week at Langholm with Lord and Lady Dalkeith. On this occasion there was an otter hunt, with yeomen dashing recklessly from crag to crag, a scene that Scott later transmuted into the fox hunt in *Guy*

*Mannering*, together with the character of Tod Gibbie, who was suggested by a half-witted, stuttering creature called "Tod Willie."[94]

On such expeditions the two men covered on horseback all the vales
of Ettrick and Yarrow and their tributary glens, St. Mary's Loch and
the Loch of the Lowes, the Teviot and the Ale, and all the lonely countryside of Buccleuch and Harden, Minto, Roxburgh, and Gilnockie. Everywhere they found a hearty welcome from the farmers at whose houses
they stopped for dinner. The brisk mountain air and the day's riding gave
them a keen appetite for the homely fare, and the popularity of "the
Sheriff" was unbounded. Sometimes Skene, who was a gifted amateur
draftsman, brought out his sketching pad and pencil to render the wild
scene, while Scott sat beside him on the brae, reciting an old ballad or
telling the tradition of the glen.[95]

One of their earliest rides was to the bleak mountainous tract above
Moffat, with the cascade of the Grey Mare's Tail and the dark tarn of
Loch Skene. Ascending to the lake they were bewildered in the thick
fog, and, says Skene, "as we were groping through the maze of bogs,
the ground gave way, and down went horse and horsemen pell-mell into
a slough of peaty mud and black water," entangled in plaids and
floundering nags. "We rose like the spirits of the bog, covered *cap-à-pie*
with slime, to free themselves from which, our wily ponies took to rolling
about on the heather, and we had nothing for it but following their
example." As they approached the gloomy loch, the "thick folds of fog
rolling incessantly over the face of the inky waters" now and then were
rent asunder to reveal "a glimpse of some projecting rock or naked
point of land, or island bearing a few scraggy stumps of pine," and
out of the cheerless waste "a huge eagle heaved himself from the margin
and rose right over us, screaming his scorn at the intruders."[96]

The Tweed, of course, they ranged from its source to Berwick,
splashing through every ford in its course. No matter what its state of
flood, though there was a bridge, Scott "scorned to go ten yards about,"
said Skene, and even crossed fords on foot, though his lameness made
him unsteady on the slippery stones. Once the two men were both on
the same tottering stone in the middle of the Ettrick when Scott remembered a story about a kelpie and began telling it. In the midst of
his laughter, his foot slipped or the stone wobbled, and down he went
into the pool, pulling Skene in with him. Their clothes were drenched
and Scott's stick floated away down the stream, but "he was as ready
as ever for a similar exploit before his clothes were half dried upon his
back."[97]

Scott's mornings, as usual, were industriously devoted to Dryden.
The extracts he had made in London from Mr. Bindley's volumes and
Heber's first edition were doing him yeoman's service. He had now got
over the difficult ground of *Absalom and Achitophel* and *The Medal*, on
both of which he had very full historical notes. Could Heber, he appealed,

help him get hold of a rare pamphlet attack on Dryden, "The Whip and the Key," as well as Shadwell's *The Medal of John Bayes,* and Shadwell's translation of the Tenth Satire of Juvenal?[98] To his old schoolteacher Dr. Adam he also addressed an appeal: Was there any justice in Samuel Johnson's criticism of the Latin of Dryden's title *Threnodia Augustalis* "as not being classical"?[99]

Dryden, however, was not the only subject of Scott's summer correspondence: Miss Seward had asked him his opinion of the Ossian controversy and must be answered. He had no doubt, he told her, that most of the poem "must be ascribed to Macpherson himself and that his whole introductions notes &c &c is an absolute tissue of forgeries." The original Gaelic poems were not "much better than those of the Scandinavian Scalds"—often "vigorous and pointed, often drivelling and crawling in the very extremity of tenuity." Macpherson cunningly adopted the beginnings, names, and leading incidents of an old tale; the Highlanders, recognizing these, were seduced into imagining his sentimental elaborations the same poems they had heard in infancy. "There is something in the severe judgment passed on my countrymen 'that if they do not prefer Scotland to truth they will aways prefer it to enquiry.' When once the Highlanders had adopted the poems of Ossian as an article of national faith you would far sooner have got them to disavow the Scripture than to abandon a line of the contested tales."[100]

His own plan of writing a Highland poem as a companion piece to the *Lay,* Scott was still turning over in his mind. But more and more he realized his "comparative deficiency in knowledge of Celtic manners."[101] Such an undertaking would necessitate a journey into the country to refresh his "faded or inaccurate recollection of the scenery" and enhance his store of "the traditions still floating in the memory of the inhabitants."[102] In the course of the autumn, therefore, while the heather blossoms deepened to imperial purple on the hills, he put the project aside.[103]

In its place he found himself revolving the idea of another poem inspired by the fatal battle of Flodden. "I have disbanded on this occasion all my border riders although I may come to want their assistance as much as the King is said to have done that of Johnie Armstrong after he was hanged."[104] This poem Scott thought he would call *Flodden Field,* but within a few months he changed its title to *Marmion.* He began the poem in November.[105] In January the energetic Constable got wind of it. Resolved to shut out all rivals, he determined on a magnificent stroke. Without having seen a single line of it, he offered Scott immediate payment of a thousand guineas for the poem. Scott, "without hesitation," accepted.[106]

# 4

# *Red Flodden's Dismal Tale*

## *(1807–1808)*

CONSTABLE'S MUNIFICENCE startled the literary world. One thousand guineas for an unseen, unfinished poem! "It was a price," said Scott, "that made men's hair stand on end."[1] Even at this hair-raising sum Longman and Rees, to be sure, would have been happy to share in its publication, but they had broken off relations with Constable. That burly bookseller had taken into partnership three years before a hard-drinking, rough-spoken young Angus laird, Alexander Gibson Hunter of Blackness, who brought him £3,000–£4,000 of additional capital, but who managed to embroil him not only with Longman but in other bitter disagreements.[2] Although Scott did not take sides in the present quarrel, he considered himself bound in honor not to withdraw the poem from a fellow townsman whose firm had been so useful to Scottish literature.[3]

It would not be wise, Constable realized, to forego the active co-operation of London publishers. He therefore offered a quarter share each in the copyright to William Miller and young John Murray. These booksellers were delighted. Murray, not yet a power in the publishing world, but coming on fast, sent thanks for them both. "You have rendered Mr. Miller no less happy by your admission of him; and we both view it as honourable, profitable, and glorious to be concerned in the publication of a new poem by Walter Scott."[4]

Scott and Ballantyne were now rolling along on a high tide of prosperity. Ballantyne's lively younger brother John had become a salaried employee of the printing firm at £200 a year, two-thirds debited to his brother, one-third to Scott.[5] The presses in the Canongate were thundering out profits. In 1806 they were £786 10s 2d; when the books were balanced at Whitsuntide 1807 they had risen to £960 11s 7d and the capital had increased to some £7,250.[6]

During the winter Ballantyne was in negotiation with Murray over a new flood of ideas born in Scott's brain for the purpose of keeping the presses busy. He proposed an edition of the novelists with biographies by Scott, Defoe's Works, Swift's Works. (As a commercial proposition, noted Murray, "Swift more uncertain than Dryden.") Then there were the plays of Beaumont and Fletcher ("Respectable and valuable work," said Murray, "but not extensive"), minor poets ("Barker is now printing such things—Wyatt, Surrey, &c"), Daemonology, Le Sage (but Murray would consider only *Le Diable Boiteux*), Nash's pamphlets, Memoirs of the House of Somerville, Popular Tales ("They never sold, and do not sell"), Boyd's Works—presumably Hugh Boyd, believed by some to be the author of the *Letters of Junius*.[7] Although none of these projects were undertaken at the moment, Scott did do several in later years.

Two more on Ballantyne's list demand attention. The first is "An anonymous work." Murray commented, "perfectly approved." What this referred to is not clear; it may have been that novel called *Waverley*, which Scott had begun and tossed aside the year before. The second is "New Poem," about which Murray observed, "Only one opinion upon the subject. *Most certainly.*"[8] This was unquestionably the poem that became *Marmion*. It had been proposed to Murray, he had liked the idea, but before he had made a firm offer Constable's lordly gesture had swept it out of his grasp. No wonder he appreciated Constable's generosity in sharing it.

While the poem was shaping itself in Scott's mind, he heard from the Durham antiquary Robert Surtees of Mainsforth. With the spurious ballad of "The Death of Featherstonhaugh"—which fooled Scott—Surtees enclosed another concoction of his own, which he represented as a manuscript note in a copy of Burthogge "On the Nature of Spirits."[9] Scott introduced part of the ballad into the first canto of *Marmion* and derived from the note the episode of Marmion's combat with the supposed Elfin Knight.[10] "The extract of the ghostly combat, between Bulmer and his aerial adversary," he told Surtees enthusiastically, "is like the chapter of a romance . . ."[11]

Writing the poem did not prevent his maintaining a heavy and far-flung correspondence, sometimes carried on from the black table of the Clerks in the Court of Session. Adam Ferguson had become Secretary to the Governor of the Channel Islands and was now stationed at St. Helier. He envied Adam his situation in Jersey, Scott wrote him: "Claret in plenty" and "Blithe French lasses with their black eyes and national vivacity scratching each other for the honour of dancing and flirting with Mr. Secretary." With what contempt Adam "must recollect a nipperkin of whiskey punch and the lang-trained frost-bitten Dearies" of Scotland![12]

Robert Jamieson, Scott's fellow ballad-collector, was now in Russia, at Riga, whence he wrote home "the most horrible details of the French excesses in Prussia and of the unutterable blindness and execrable treachery of the Court of Berlin."[13] His volume of ballads had just been published by Constable and, Scott told him, "been very well received by the public." Another friend, Thomas Thomson, had recently been made Depute-Clerk-Register at Edinburgh and needed an assistant who was well acquainted with old handwriting and Scottish antiquities; Scott was sure Jamieson could obtain the appointment.[14]

There had been no letter from Leyden since the one Scott had received last July, but in December, through a son of the novelist Henry Mackenzie, there came word of him. Young Mackenzie had "found our eccentric friend an earnest spectator of a combat between a tiger and a buffalo exhibited for the amusement of the Nabob. Upon recognizing his Scottish friends Leyden's yells of joy are said fairly to have drowned those of the tiger." Enlivened by that news, Scott prepared with his family to spend the Christmas holidays at Mertoun again under the hospitable roof of the Scotts of Harden.[15]

The year ended in weather of extreme violence. Early in January Scott returned to Edinburgh and resumed work on *Marmion*.[16] In place of the Introduction describing the old minstrel and the recurrent inter-polations about him which had framed the narrative of the *Lay*, Scott planned to introduce each canto with a pastoral epistle to one of his friends, although he had originally thought of publishing these separately as *Six Epistles from Ettrick Forest*.[17] The first epistle, addressed to William Stewart Rose, he now sent to Lady Abercorn, promising that she should see more when he came up to London in March.[18] A little later he also confided some of the opening of the poem to Anna Seward.[19]

Miss Seward had questioned whether the historical background of *Marmion* might not be wounding to Scottish patriotism. Should he give "poetic immortality . . . to the most disastrous event in their military annals"?[20] Scott, however, had no fears. "It is very true that my friend Leyden has said

    'Alas that Scottish Maid should sing
      The Combat where her lover fell,
    That Scottish Bard should wake the string
      The triumph of our foes to tell.'

But we may [say] with Francis I that at Flodden 'all was lost *but our honour*' an exception that includes everything that is desirable for a poet."[21]

The Princess of Wales was among those who early saw a part of the manuscript.[22] In the Introduction to Canto III there was a passage lauding her father, the Duke of Brunswick, who had been slain in the battle of Jena:

Hast thou no elegiac tone
To join that universal moan
Which mingled with the battle's yell
Where venerable Brunswick fell?—

. . .

On thee relenting Heaven bestows
For honour'd life an honour'd close—
The boon which falling heroes crave,
A soldier's death, a warrior's grave.[23]

"Of course the Introduction to the 3rd Canto was impatiently turned to," her Royal Highness had one of her ladies-in-waiting write, "and I am commanded to say that nothing so gratifying to the Princess' feelings could have been done . . ."[24] The following month the Princess herself sent Scott a silver vase in token of her gratitude.[25]

In a letter to Surtees, outlining his plan, Scott quoted the part of Canto I in which Marmion is entertained at Norham Castle by Lord Heron and hears the harper chanting a barbaric lay—the very poem that Surtees had sent to Scott in December. "In the notes I will give your copy of the ballad and your learned illustrations. Holy Island is one of my scenes: also Whitby. I have occasion for an abbess of Whitby, and also for a Nunnery at Lindisfarne."[26]

*Marmion*, however, was not Scott's only preoccupation during the early part of 1807. He was violently excited by the proposals of the victorious Whig government to make radical changes in Scotland's courts of law and administration of justice. The old structure was to be torn down and rebuilt into close conformity with the institutions of England. This was a violation, Scott believed, of the Act of Union of 1707, a deadly blow at Scotland's independence; he reacted with painful intensity.[27] "The Clerks &c all go"—who could tell, perhaps the Court of Session itself would be destroyed, or changed past all recognition— "adieu a long adieu to all their greatness!" It was more than he could bear.[28]

When the proposed changes were debated by the Faculty of Advocates, Scott spoke against them. His forcefulness and eloquence surprised even those who knew him well. After the meeting broke up, he walked down the Mound on his way to Castle Street between Jeffrey and another reforming Whig. These two, by no means as disturbed as Scott, complimented him on his rhetorical powers but were playful about the theme that had so aroused his feelings. They had altogether underestimated his passionate agitation. "No, no," he exclaimed, "—'tis no laughing matter; little by little, whatever your wishes may be, you will destroy and undermine, until nothing of what makes Scotland Scotland shall remain." Seldom, even among friends, had he so allowed his emotions to overmaster him. He turned away to conceal his distress, resting his head against the wall of the Mound until he recovered his self-control, but Jeffrey saw tears rolling down his cheek.[29]

The Clerks of Session had entrusted to Colin Mackenzie their pleas for compensation if their office was abolished, but while he was in London he became seriously ill and Scott was chosen to replace him. Promptly at the end of the winter term, therefore, he hurried south.[30] The need for haste made it impossible for him to stop off, as he had intended, and visit Surtees at Durham and also prevented his looking in on Wordsworth, who had been lent the farmhouse on Sir George Beaumont's estate at Coleorton and was staying there with Coleridge.[31] The weather was freezing cold all the way; at Morpeth a blinding snowstorm almost halted Scott in his journey. But on the morning of March 20 he arrived in London, where William Miller the bookseller found him comfortable lodgings in Bury Street.[32]

To his surprise and relief, the Ministry, he learned, were in the act of going out. They had introduced a bill, which George III opposed, to open commissions in the Army to Catholics; the bill had been withdrawn, but the King tried to secure their pledge that they would never again press for concessions to Catholics, and the ministers resigned.[33] "Castlereagh, Rose, Hawkesbury &c come in," Scott wrote his wife jubilantly, "and Lord Melville is to be at the head either of the Admiralty or of the Treasury. There's a turn for you—match it in your novels if you can. When I think what I witnessed last year in this very place it almost turns me dizzy."[34]

No longer need the Clerks of Session worry; Scott knew that he would be "an acceptable Solicitor in their behalf."[35] "Contrary to many who held the same political opinions in sunshine," as he wrote his brother-in-law, Charles Carpenter, in India, he had held fast his integrity "during the Foxites's interval of power" and now found himself "very well with the present administration."[36] Lord Melville did not return to office, as Scott had expected, but he was right in appraising his own position. "The present President of the Board of Controul in particular is my early and intimate friend since we carried our satchels together to the High School of Edinburgh."[37] Best of all, "the Law of Scotland will remain as it was or at least be touched with a respectful and lenient hand."[38]

The change of Ministry even held out hopes that Scott himself might begin to be paid for his clerical labors. Though he jestingly referred to them as "an Irish sinecure," "all work and no pay," he felt that he ought to be relieved of his "Old Man of the Sea," George Home.[39] Canning, Frere, Robert Dundas, "a party of the *new men*," with whom he dined shortly after his arrival in London, all agreed. They were "highly delighted," he reported, "with my firm adherence to them in adversity and I hope to reap some good fruits from it."[40] "I think since the sun shines on our side of the hedge I have as good a claim to share in its warmth as any body else. I am sure I did not fear the bad weather."[41]

An act of Parliament made it impossible to pension off Home, but a new Judicature Bill might create an additional Clerk.[42] If this were done, "I shall get the salary," Scott wrote Charlotte, "and the new brother succeed to George Home."[43] Or, perhaps, "I shall ride the new Clerk as G. Home rides me so that while [Home] draws my salary I shall draw the salary of the new comer. What turn the Bill will take is yet uncertain but we shall know in the beginning of this week. It is probable I may be one of the Commissioners appointed to draw up a report to parliament on the Subject, as two are to be taken from the Clerks."[44] In the end, Parliament was again dissolved on April 27, and the whole matter blew over till after the election of the new Parliament.[45]

Directly upon his arrival in London, Scott had seen Colin Mackenzie. Very gaunt, and enfeebled in voice, he had braved "the most bitter easterly winds I ever felt," Scott said, by remaining in the metropolis until Scott could replace him, but at last consented to go down to the milder climate of Devonshire.[46] George Ellis, who had also been ill, looked "weak and emaciated to an incredible degree considering how thin he always was." He now felt better, however, and received Scott "with his usual affection."[47] The Dumergues were all well. At their house on the day he came to town Scott met Mrs. Fitzherbert, the mistress of the Prince of Wales, but did not realize at the time who she was.[48] The next day, Saturday, he had breakfast with Lord Dalkeith, and spent all of Sunday with him and the Countess.[49]

Socially, Scott was more lionized than ever; his days were a succession of dinners, balls, and routs, and he found droll the degree to which his card rack was "covered with invitations from Secretaries of State and Cabinet Ministers."[50] For the Easter holidays the Marquis and Marchioness of Abercorn invited him to Bentley Priory, where the gay and brilliant party included Lady Charlotte Lindsay, the Earl and Countess of Aberdeen, William Sotheby, the great Shakespearean actor John Philip Kemble and his wife, and the beautiful madcap Duchess of Gordon.[51]

Lord Abercorn was a man of towering vanity; he wore all his orders and decorations even when he hunted and traveled, and insisted that the servant who made his bed wear white kid gloves.[52] But he also had some pretensions to literary taste and enjoyed the image of himself as Scott's patron. Though he was not at all well satisfied with Thomas Scott's services as his man of business, it was pleasant to have an almost feudal relationship with the rising poetic star of the day.[53]

Scott smiled to himself at his Lordship's grandiosities and privately nicknamed him the Marquis of Carabas but mingled liking and respect with his amusement. There were even elements of good judgment in this pompous nobleman; Scott willingly showed him the parts of

*Marmion* that he had so far written and adopted a suggestion he made about the Introduction to Canto I. Immediately after a panegyric on Pitt, Scott had written a tribute to the memory of his great rival Fox, who now lay buried by Pitt's side in Westminster Abbey. Though Lord Abercorn himself had been a follower of Pitt, he felt that this passage might well be heightened to still loftier eulogy.[54] He even composed one couplet—

> For talents mourn untimely lost
> When best employed and wanted most—[55]

which Scott used as the opening of a dozen revised and inserted lines. Thus modified, the introduction was sent to Ballantyne under Lord Abercorn's frank to be set up in type.[56]

On his return from Stanmore to London, Scott almost immediately went down into Hampshire with William Stewart Rose to Gundimore, Rose's villa on the sandhills looking across the Solent to the Isle of Wight.[57] Between the one-storied house and a balustraded terrace lay a formal garden with ancient pilasters, Roman cinerary urns, and a mask of Seneca gushing water into a basin. This was sheltered from the winds by a screen of tamarisk and ilex, but through an iron-grilled gate came a glimpse of the far horizon and the blue sea. Indoors there was a long gallery crowded with books, a room with Greek works of art, and another with Persian decorations.[58]

From Gundimore, under Rose's frank, Scott sent Ballantyne several manuscript sheets of *Marmion* and corrected proofs of Canto III. The printer had criticized the first draft of Fitz-Eustace's song, "Where shall the Lover rest," and sketched out what he thought would be a better rhyme-scheme for the stanza. "I am much obliged to you for the rhymes," Scott amicably replied. "I presume it can make no difference as to the air if the first three lines rhyme . . . For example," he added mischievously, "would this do?

> Should my heart from thee falter,
> To another love alter
> (For the rhyme we'll say Walter)
> Deserting my lover."[59]

Together Scott and Rose rode the neighboring New Forest, under whose trees William Rufus had been slain by Tyrrel's arrow. Among its wide expanses of heath they came on browsing cattle and donkies and the descendants of its original wild ponies; under its ancient oaks and beeches they startled occasional red deer and fallow deer. Here and there they explored the remains of Celtic camps and barrows.[60] Through the influence, probably, of Rose's father, who was soon to be Treasurer of the Navy in the new administration, they embarked on the royal yacht, which took them across to the Isle of Wight.[61]

They landed at Cowes and spent a morning clambering among the gloomy Gothic ruins of Carisbrooke Castle, where Charles I had been imprisoned during the Civil War. A fresh breeze then brought them to Portsmouth and a dinner of fowl pie and madeira before going ashore to see the wonders of the Dockyard. Scott was fascinated by the forging of the anchors: "the gloomy light of twenty furnaces," "the red glare of the heated iron," the gang of smiths like "ghastly spectres," and "the clang of . . . hammers dinning" as if they were a crew of Vulcans "forging the thunderbolts." But he was troubled by the brutal faces and what seemed to him the degrading punishment of the convicts chained in irons.[62]

Following a call upon the Port Admiral and an inspection of some of the ships of the line at Spithead, they reembarked for Christchurch. The weather had turned squally; the little frigate rolled and pitched, the sea dashed over the deck, and Rose became very sick. Scott, to his surprise, was not, but since it was too wet on deck retired to his cabin, where he lay eating sea biscuits and cold fowl. Giving up the idea of getting back to Gundimore by sea, they landed at the little village of Lymington and made the rest of the journey by post chaise.[63] Before Scott returned to London, he and Rose mounted on horseback again and went on a visit of a few days to Rose's father at Cuffnells, from which, after an all-night stagecoach ride, Scott reached London on April 15.[64]

The capital was once more a whirl of gaieties. Scott dined with Robert Dundas and the Chief Baron, with Lord Somerville, with Lady Douglas,[65] and dined again with Lord Abercorn in the large house he had taken in St. James's Square.[66] I have breakfasted twice with the Marchioness, who admits me to her boudoir," he wrote Charlotte teasingly, "—there's for you." "The said Marquis has taken prodigiously to my poetry and we are upon a footing of intimacy which his Lady says is very unusual with this great man." A week later Scott was to dine with the Abercorns yet again; "Tom will be there and I fancy the Marquis designs to give him a lecture."[67]

Wordsworth had arrived in London shortly after Scott, and the two poets breakfasted together on April 21. Later that day, at a dinner at Acton, Scott met the new bride of his friend Wolfe Murray, a lively little brunette who talked vivaciously. Unhappily the other feminine guests were "a pack of the ugliest old hags I ever beheld in my life," "the rooms were floored with marble and deadly cold"—in short, there was "nothing pleasant except Mrs. Murray and the wine, which was superb." There were also dinners with the Dumergues, a great rout at the Abercorns to which eight hundred guests were invited,[68] and after the opera on Saturday night a glittering ball at Lady Castlereagh's.[69]

That same afternoon Scott had again visited the Princess of Wales at Blackheath. She welcomed him with open arms. "As soon as she saw me," he wrote Charlotte, "she cried out, 'Come my dear Walter Scott and see all my improvements,' and accordingly she whisked me through her grotto and pavilion and conservatory and so forth, asking me slily at the same time if I was not afraid to be alone with her." "The Princess will emerge from all her distresses," Scott predicted: "she is to be at the Court on the Birthday and I think may soon look forward to a time when she will be enabled to gratify her friends and make her enemies her foot-stool."[70]

Through all these festivities Scott's thoughts were often with his family at Ashestiel. Charlotte, "the Laird and his sisters and brother, not forgetting the Black Child"—Camp, who was now growing elderly— what were they all doing?[71] To Charlotte he wrote constantly. "Kiss my little girls and boys and pray tell me how the schooling goes on." Walter, he knew, was learning to dance: "The Laird I suppose is capering suc-cessfully."[72] "I expect to see Charles running races with the rest when I return, which must now be very soon. I rejoice to hear that the old black gentleman is in handsome enjoyment of his health."[73] "And now, my dearest Lotty, I am impatient to know what you are doing at home. I have always a little vision of you sitting with all the monkies teasing you and poor old Kiki sleeping upon the hearth rug."[74] "Believe me dear Mimi Ever your own W. S."[75] "Once more adieu! my sweet Mimi."[76]

It was not to be thought of that Scott's London visit should draw to a close without his again spending a weekend with George Ellis and his wife at Sunninghill. The morning after Lady Castlereagh's ball, there-fore, he set off on the top of the Windsor coach, sitting between "a mon-ster of blubber who must have weighed at least twenty stone" and a voluble old girl resembling the Wife of Bath, "who gave us the history of her three husbands and her five apprentices and of her own success in the tallow chandling line," while the fat man assured them "that the peas in his own garden were at least two inches taller than any we saw on the road." As the two talked, Scott thought how strangely varied his society was within a few hours, from dining with the Princess of Wales and supping with the Prime Minister's lady to riding outside a stage with a female tallow chandler.[77]

At Windsor he saw George III in the fifteenth-century Chapel and then took a chaise through the Park. "Sunninghill," he reported to Char-lotte, "is looking beautiful." The grass was frothed white with daisies and blue with violets: "I send you a sample" of the violets "because I know you love them so much."[78] Ellis was now much recovered in health and in very good spirits; Mrs. Ellis was disappointed that Scott had not brought Charlotte south with him. His host and hostess made him recite from *Marmion*, and he wrote several more parts of the first two cantos while he was there. These were duly forwarded to Ballantyne under Lord Abercorn's frank.[79]

With the first week in May, Scott's southern sojourn was drawing to an end.[80] He saw the Matthew Boultons in Soho, said good-bye to the

Dumergues, and had a quiet farewell dinner with William Miller. Most of his baggage he sent by sea with his manservant; he intended himself to travel as inexpensively as possible by stagecoach.[81] He and Wordsworth had seen each other several times at breakfast;[82] now they arranged to leave London together, taking the coach by the west road. This would bring Wordsworth to Loughborough, only eleven miles from Coleorton, and allow Scott to pay his long-promised visit to Anna Seward at Lichfield and perhaps to spend a day at Mainsforth with Surtees. They started out at half-past four in the morning of Wednesday, May 5.[83]

Miss Seward's father had been Residentiary Canon of Lichfield, living in the Episcopal Palace, a beautiful Charles II building in the Cathedral Close, where she still dwelt. When she was a little girl her poetic efforts had been encouraged by the famous Dr. Erasmus Darwin, author of *The Botanic Garden*, and in the course of time a profuse outpouring of ornate sonnets and florid elegies had given her fame as the "Swan of Lichfield." On Samuel Johnson's visits to his native town she had met and disliked that old but still violent literary lion, whose lofty arrogance she found intolerable from one of low birth. She was a bluestocking of the most ultramarine dye, equally ready to admire fashionable mediocrity and reject unfamiliar merit. Her taste had been shaped by the classicism of Pope and Collins; she rejected with equal distaste the imitative talent of William Hayley and the genius of Wordsworth and Coleridge.[84]

Like many highbrows, however, she was not stupid, and unlike many more, she loved to admire and praise. She welcomed Southey's poetry with enthusiasm; her ecstasy about his own Scott found almost embarrassing. She had considerable independence of character: she and one of the vicars-choral of the Cathedral, a married man named John Saville, had fallen in love with each other, and although there had been no liaison Anna admitted candidly "she did not know what might have happened if Saville had not been more afraid of the devil than she was!"[85] She was a voluble conversationalist, often polysyllabic and pedantic, sometimes brilliant, full of entertaining anecdote, always warmhearted, irresistibly alive. Now in her sixtieth year, she had the remains of some beauty, with auburn eyes the same hue as her auburn hair,[86] but with advancing age what Scott chivalrously called her "majestic presence" had swollen into a stout amplitude of flesh.[87]

Their meeting was an immediate success. Like nearly everybody who came to know her, Scott liked her immensely. And although he had warned her that he was less a man of letters than "a rattle-sculled half-lawyer, half-sportsman, through whose head a regiment of horse has been exercising since he was five years old; half-educated—half-crazy, as his friends sometimes tell him,"[88] she too at once fell captive to her guest. "On Friday last," she wrote a friend, "the poetically great Walter

Scott came 'like a sunbeam to my dwelling,' " and with characteristic flamboyance she went on to describe him as "this proudest boast of the Caledonian muse."[89]

His features were not elegant, she thought, but his expression was "open, ingenuous, and benevolent." Fair complexion, brown hair, flaxen eyebrows, all these she found rather commonplace; but then, of his light gray eyes, added romantically, "deep thought is on their lids; he contracts his brow, and the rays of genius gleam aslant from the orbs beneath them." His upper lip was too long, but his mouth played in "the sweetest emanations of temper and heart." "His conversation an overflowing fountain of brilliant wit, apposite allusion, and playful archness . . . the accent decidedly Scotch, yet by no means broad." His memory, like Johnson's, astonished her; his recitation, also like Johnson's, she felt "too monotonous and violent." She showed him the passage in Cary's translation of Dante dealing with his own ancestor Michael Scott, but he confessed that he did not like the *Inferno*: "The plan appeared to him unhappy; the personal malignity and strange mode of revenge presumptuous and uninteresting."[90]

Scott stayed two nights at the Palace. After leaving Lichfield he headed north, rejoining the Great North Road again at York, but found that he would not have time to visit Surtees at Mainsforth. Disputed elections were raging in every town he passed through; post horses were unobtainable, and the public coaches were crowded inside and out with drunken voters swilling brandy every furlong for the good of their country. After three nights during which he had not been to bed once, he arrived in Edinburgh on May 13. There he found Lord Melville working hard on election business.[91] The Tories, Scott predicted happily, would win a smashing victory; the Foxites were "weaker than water"; he himself was believed to stand high in favor with the ministers. "I look wise say nothing and gain the credit of being in the secret and knowing how to keep it."[92]

In Castle Street he delighted Charlotte with a smart new cap Lady Abercorn had selected for her, which he was sure would "be the envy of the Edinburgh Belles." The children were all in great health and spirits and beginning to talk a little French under Charlotte's instruction, but we do not hear how poor old aging Camp was feeling or what progress Walter was making in his dancing lessons.[93]

Soon after Scott's return he was again busily at work on *Marmion*. After dinner one night at Castle Street, he read the first two cantos to a small group that included James Hogg and an artist and civil engineer named John Morrison. The Ettrick Shepherd praised the accuracy with which Scott described St. Mary's lake, but Morrison objected that the shore had no "trace of silver sand" and that instead of being treeless, as the poem said, there were some good trees, including a fine old ash. Led away by the beauty of the poem, exclaimed Hogg, he had forgotten the trees. "A few facts, or a little sound criticism," commented Scott, "is infinitely more welcome to me than any praise whatever. I am sorry that I had not observed those trees, as the part is now printed off."[94]

Scott had expected to have *Marmion* ready for publication by Christmas. But a number of obstacles conspired to delay his intentions. Until the middle of June he was occupied in doing for Constable what he called the "by-job" of preparing for the press the state papers of Sir Ralph Sadler,[95] a diplomat who made "a figure in history in the reigns of Henry VIII, Edward VI, and Queen Elizabeth," and whose talents almost brought about a marriage in 1543 between the infant Queen of Scots and the young Prince of Wales.[96] Sadler, again, was in charge of the same unhappy Queen in 1585 when she was a prisoner in Tutbury Castle.[97] Scott was not doing the editorial work, merely the historical notes and an introductory memoir of Sadler's life, but even this commission necessitated his going through all the papers and "a little interfered," he told Surtees, "with the progress of my new poem."[98]

Worse than this literary delay, however, his brother Tom was suddenly in serious trouble. Since his marriage in 1799 Tom had been working manfully at swelling the size of his family and losing the clients he had inherited from his father.[99] He now had five children, including a baby son born only that June. The law agency of the city of Aberdeen, which his father had held for so many years, slipped out of Tom's grasp.[100] The management of the Marquis of Abercorn's Duddingston property was now his main source of income, and for the past three years the Marquis had been increasingly dissatisfied with him. Without permission he had started a brickworks on the estate, he was incorrigibly sloppy about keeping financial records, and could not be prevailed upon to submit his half-yearly accounts.[101]

The exasperated nobleman had already concluded that Tom was unworthy of his confidence and only Scott's intercession had prevented his dismissal. Now, "finding himself pressed," said Scott, "to make up the money belonging to another client," Tom had not hesitated "to apply the term's rents of the Duddingstone estate to make up his deficiency." When this was discovered, Tom went into hiding, "leaving me," Scott told Lady Abercorn, "to settle his account with the Marquis as best I can." Since his Lordship had retained Tom on Scott's plea, he felt responsible: "I would rather become a hack author for my own and my family's daily bread than the Marquis should lose a penny on my account . . ." "I am not afraid of being unable to make up this loss to the Marquis [ultimately] for I have never exceeded my income and am worth about six thousand pounds independent of my House, furniture, Books, and farm stocking, which are worth at least £4,000 more."[102]

Although Tom had thus tried him, he had always been Scott's favorite brother. The weakling Daniel was now dead. The military brother, John, was a dull dog who was interested only in playing whist with his fellow officers; he and Scott were not unfriendly, but saw little of each other. Despite Tom's irresponsibility, he was affectionate, gay, lively in mind, and handsome, with "an excellent heart and humor that used to put the table in a roar."[103] Scott never ceased to cherish the generous illusion that he was enormously gifted. He unhesitatingly set himself the task of straightening out Tom's affairs.

But the shock of Tom's misconduct made Scott almost sick with anxiety and grief. His own fortunes might be ruined, his wife and his own four children subjected to suffering, through this folly.[104] It was too hard to see his own savings dissipated by having to pay for Tom's criminal negligence.[105] For three days Scott was in a fever, and even in the ensuing weeks violent nervous headaches sometimes left him almost unable to write.[106] "Who could have thought," he exclaimed bitterly, "this miserable young man would have behaved so cruelly ill . . ."[107]

It was plain that Tom's business would have to be wound up. Other creditors speedily presented themselves; they must be persuaded to accept a composition.[108] When they saw that Scott would make himself responsible they left Tom undisturbed, and he returned to Edinburgh, to live with his family at Gorgie Park.[109] The leases of the two farms he held on the Abercorn estate, Midfield and Brunstane, however, had to be sold for what they could bring. The Marquis, who owned a tenth of the brickworks, offered to buy Tom's two shares for £3,000.[110] Two of the creditors, named Gillon and Riddell, proved especially rapacious, possibly because Gillon was himself going bankrupt.[111]

Tom took a violent dislike to Guthrie Wright, a Writer to the Signet who was called in to help clarify his tangled records and who acquired Midfield. But although Wright charged heavy fees he was not unsympathetic and concluded that Tom's troubles were more the consequence of carelessness than of dishonesty. "I really don't know," he wrote Scott, "whether the mistakes for Tom may not balance those *against* him . . . in settling the debt due by the Marquis to Arch. Macdonald he accidentally discovered a payment of £50 for which he had not taken credit and I understand he made several similar discoveries . . ."[112]

Influenced, perhaps, by these revelations, and even more by friendship for Scott, Lord Abercorn behaved with generous liberality. Most of the other creditors also, including even those who had no ties of blood or family friendship, proved not unkind.[113] Scott oscillated between hope and fear. At one time he thought Lord Abercorn would sustain no loss whatever; then, as more debts swelled the total to £3,400, he desponded.[114] Ultimately some preferred creditors were paid in full and the rest accepted ten shillings in the pound, which Scott hoped might be increased to twelve.[115]

"I have put things into such a train," he was able to report, "as to avoid a personal loss which would not only have deprived me of the power of assisting my Brother's family but very much cramped me in maintaining my own . . ."[116] In the end his own loss came to only the few hundred pounds he had lent Tom and always "regarded rather as a gift than a loan."[117] There might even be enough left from the wreck of Tom's fortunes so that his wife and children would not go out "naked and helpless into the wide world."[118] "Thank God," Scott exclaimed, "everything has turned out better than I ventured to hope."[119]

The financial worry, however, had made him chafe even more at the fact that old Mr. George Home, healthier than ever, still drew the entire salary for the clerical labors Scott performed in the Court of Session. Home was "as deaf as a post and as capable of discharging his duty as I am of dancing a hornpipe"[120]—surely he might be retired on a pension or under one of the provisions of the new Judicature Bill? But he continued to be as immovably fixed on Scott's back as the Old Man of the Sea on the shoulders of Sinbad the Sailor. Could not Lady Abercorn, Scott asked, intercede with Lord Melville to hasten "the progress of any good office he may intend me"?[121]

Disentangling Tom from his troubles had badly delayed the writing of *Marmion*. Scott had intended to devote more pains to its composition than he had given his previous work "and to be in no hurry again to announce myself as a candidate for fame." Much of the first three or four cantos, therefore, "were laboured with a good deal of care, by one by whom much care was seldom bestowed." Now, however, while negotiations were still in progress and he did not know how much money he would actually lose through Tom, he felt it necessary to recoup his fortunes by hastening publication.[122] On a business trip to Dumfries, where he and Guthrie Wright were meeting Lord Abercorn to settle some of the details about the Duddingston estate, he took the manuscript of the poem along to work on in his spare time.[123]

The Marquis did not arrive until some two or three days after they did. While they were waiting, the two men visited Sweetheart Abbey and Caerlaverock Castle, Scott delighting his companion by reciting old legends and poetry from morning till night, and enchanting him even more by reading aloud his own poem. Invited to comment on it, Wright said that Scott had brought his hero into Scotland by a very strange route. "Did ever mortal coming from England to Edinburgh go by Gifford, Crichton Castle, Borthwick Castle, and over the top of Blackford Hill? Not only is it a circuitous *detour*, but there never was a road that way since the world was created!"[124]

A most irrelevant objection, replied Scott stubbornly; "it was my good pleasure to bring Marmion by that route, for the purpose of describing the places you have mentioned, and the view from Blackford Hill—it was his business to find his road and pick his steps the best way he could." How would Wright have him come, by the post road, "as if he had been travelling in a mail-coach?" No, said Wright, but he might have come the natural way by Dunbar and the sea coast, and had the chance to stay with the famous Earl of Angus, Archibald Bell-the-Cat, at Tantallon Castle, and seen the Bass Rock. "By Jove you are right!" exclaimed Scott. "Before he and I part, depend upon it he shall visit Tantallon." Of this conversation were born parts of Cantos V and VI. "When the poem was published," said Wright, "I remember he laughed, and asked me how I liked Tantallon."[125]

The latter part of August found Scott once more at Ashestiel, creeping ahead slowly on Dryden and taking his harp down from the willows, he told Miss Seward, to sing again of Marmion.[126] She was indignant at Francis Jeffrey's slashing review of Southey's epic poem *Madoc*. "I despair of reconciling you to my little friend Jefferies," wrote Scott, "although I think I could trust to his making some impression on your prepossession were you to converse with him. I think Southey does himself injustice in supposing that the *Edinburgh Review* or any other could have sunk *Madoc* even for a time." Such a poem could not be an immediate success. "We know the similar fate of Milton's immortal work in the witty age of Charles II."[127]

As for the rapacious share of the profits swallowed by the booksellers, this was not so strange when you considered the "singular nature of their mystery. A Butcher generally understands something of black cattle" and a jockey of horseflesh; but booksellers were "the only tradesmen in the world who . . . deal in what is called 'a pig in the poke.' " They had to make up their losses on the trash they published by fleecing the able writers. "A Bookseller publishes 20 books in hopes of hitting upon one good speculation as a person buys a parcel of shares in a lottery in hopes of gaining a prize." This was iniquitous for Southey, but not bad for literature; it gave everyone a chance.[128]

The warm August days passed as Scott meditated and composed *Marmion*. A knoll with some tall old ashes on the neighboring Peel farm, where he loved to sit alone, came to be known as the Sheriff's Knowe.[129] Another favorite seat was beneath a huge old oak at the very edge of the haugh of Ashestiel, where he would idly toss a reed into the water and watch it floating along the Tweed or listen to the singing of a milkmaid as she carried her pail down the dale.[130] Sometimes, on horseback, accompanied by one of the dogs, he wandered as far as the still lake of St. Mary and the sources of the Yarrow, returning late through the quiet twilight.[131] Again, he would race Lieutenant full speed over brake and fell across the hills from Ashestiel to Newark: "Oh, man, I had many a grand gallop among these braes when I was thinking of Marmion."[132]

At the beginning of September he had to spend a few days in Edinburgh. From there he and Charlotte went to Bothwell Castle to see the Falls of Clyde and visit Lady Douglas. On their return journey through the wild glens of Lanark and Peebles, the weather, which had been very rainy, "became a perfect hurricane." Bridges were broken down, others left standing as if in the middle of a lake, with water flowing round both ends; often the road was entirely under water; terrified peasants had deserted their cottages; the town of Peebles was half drowned. They walked, waded, and rode before the carriage in places where the perilous way was quite invisible. "Next day, all the roads being impassable for a carriage, we had to walk home"—about eight miles of sopping country intersected by brooks—and arrived at Ashestiel on September 7 to discover that a good part of Scott's crop had been carried off by the Tweed.[133]

*Marmion* was now progressing rapidly. Two more cantos, he told Miss Seward, "will compleat the adventures of this doughty warrior."[134] At the same time he was pressing forward on his other projects. For the Sadler papers he asked Henry Ellis, the Librarian of the British Museum, to send him transcripts of some of the diplomatic records preserved there.[135] The edition of Dryden was entirely printed, except for his life of the poet, of which he now had the proof sheets for almost half, and he was pushing the index maker to complete that job. He was urging William Miller to reprint the black letter *Morte Arthur*: "I have referred to this curious work so frequently in *Marmion* that I am sure if that poem sells a small edition of the Romance (say 500 or 750 at most) will go off." Ballantyne could do it handsomely and not extravagantly! a small quarto would look more antique.[136]

Toward the end of October, Scott's regiment went into quarters again at Musselburgh.[137] Here he wrote the dramatic stanzas describing the battle of Flodden. In the intervals of drilling he delighted in walking his powerful black steed along Portobello sands within the beating of the surge; "now and again," said James Skene, "you would see him plunge in his spurs, and go off as at the charge, with the spray dashing about him." As they rode back to Musselburgh he often repeated to Skene the stanzas he had been composing during pauses in their exercise.[138]

"I am just now," he told Lady Louisa Stuart, "very busy dressing your cousin James IV in his court suit"—the scenes of Marmion's reception by that monarch at Holyrood—"his clothes are all cut, sew'd, and ready to put on, so I must bid your Ladyship farewell to attend his royal levee."[139] He wrote the introduction to Canto V in Edinburgh and that to Canto VI during the Christmas festivities at Mertoun. In January, "Marmion is, at this instant," he wrote Lady Louisa, "dying on the field, and there I have been obliged to leave him for these few days in the death pangs. I hope I shall find time enough this morning to knock him on the head with two or three thumping stanzas."[140] Three days later, January 22, "I have finished *Marmion*," he triumphantly wrote Lady Abercorn.[141] The last canto was done in four days "and sent piece-meal to the press as the ink dried on the paper."[142]

He had decided that it would help the sale of the *Dryden* if *Marmion* was published first.[143] He was expecting the last two proof sheets from James Ballantyne, with the concluding Envoy to the Reader, around the end of the month. "God grant the thing may go."[144] At the very end he happened to be at a dinner Ballantyne gave in St. John's Street. When the ladies retired he sat silent for some time, then said, "James, it's a strange thing to ask, but I should be glad if you would go with me to the library for a quarter of an hour." To the other guests he explained, "To tell you the truth, gentlemen, our worthy landlord and I are just about finishing a new poem, and a few lines have just struck me, which I should be glad to send to the printing house before the sheet is printed off."

In the library, at the close of the twenty-fourth stanza, after the lines

> Tweed's echoes heard the ceaseless plash,
>   While many a broken band,
> Disorder'd, through her currents dash,
>   To gain the Scottish land;

he added:

> To town and tower, to down and dale,
> To tell red Flodden's dismal tale,
> And raise the universal wail.
> Tradition, legend, tune, and song,
>   Shall many an age that wail prolong:
> Still from the sire the son shall hear
> Of the stern strife, and carnage drear,
>   Of Flodden's fatal field,
> Where shiver'd was fair Scotland's spear,
>   And broken was her shield![145]

The poem was published on February 23.[146] Advance copies in a splendid quarto went out—one to the Princess of Wales, with drawings by James Skene illustrating the scenery of the poem; others to Lord Minto, the Governor General in India, to Lady Abercorn, to the Earl and Countess of Dalkeith, to Ellis, Surtees, Douce, Heber, and Southey; and some, less splendid, to Charles Carpenter in India, Will Laidlaw, and a circle of other friends.[147]

"The long-promised *Marmion*," he wrote Lady Abercorn, "at length has the honour to kiss your ladyship's hand."[148] "I have to request your acceptance," he told Surtees, "of a thumping quarto entitled *Marmion*."[149] It was "a goodly volume in point of size," he explained to Southey, "but I had not time to write the poem shorter."[150] "When you have run over *Marmion*," he said to Ellis, "I hope you will remember how impatient I shall be to hear your opinion *sans phrase*. I am sensible I run some risk of being thought to fall below my former level, but those that will play for the gammon must take their chance of this."[151]

# 5

## The Greatest Elephant

## Except Himself

### (1808)

M ARMION WAS STILL more dazzlingly successful than *The Lay of the Last Minstrel*. Even at the staggering price of one and a half guineas the entire first edition of two thousand copies was sold out in less than two months.[1] A second of three thousand was hurried through the press and melted away so rapidly that before the end of May a third was thundering out, making a total of eight thousand published in little over three months. Before the end of the year these were almost exhausted; two editions of three thousand each followed in 1809; two more amounting to five thousand in 1810. In 1811, the poem's fourth year, nine thousand were issued and its cumulative total of twenty-eight thousand surpassed the number the *Lay* had sold in seven years. Long past the remainder of Scott's life, the sales of the two poems rose to ever more dizzy heights.[2]

Constable's daring had been amply justified. The floridly handsome publisher and his rough-spoken partner Hunter were both overjoyed. Neither the two booksellers nor the author had any vision of future discord. The elated Constable asked Scott to sit for a portrait which he commissioned from the celebrated Henry Raeburn, and in the course of the year the artist painted a canvas representing Scott seated by a ruined wall with Camp at his feet and Hermitage Castle and the mountains of Liddesdale in the background.[3] As a further token of his delight Constable sent Scott the gift of a hogshead of claret.[4] Its contents came to be known simply as "Marmion," and for many a month thereafter on festive occasions did the Sheriff call for "a bottle of Marmion."[5]

Most of Scott's friends were as enthusiastic as the public. Words-

worth, to be sure, expressed only moderate rapture. "I think your end
has been attained. That it is not the end which I should wish you to propose to yourself, you will be well aware, from what you know of my
notions of composition, both as to matter and manner. In the circle of
my acquaintance it seems as well liked as the *Lay* . . ."⁶ But Ellis's praise
was uncompromising: "Everybody has already read *Marmion* more than
once"; "it delights all ages and all tastes."⁷ "All the world are agreed
that you are like the elephant mentioned in the *Spectator*, who was the
greatest elephant in the world except himself."⁸

There was universal agreement, however, that the introductory
epistles were mere interruptions having no such dramatic involvement in
the story as the passages portraying the Last Minstrel. "I did not wish
[them] away," wrote Southey, "because, as poems, they gave me great
pleasure; but I wished them at the end of the volume, or at the beginning
—anywhere except where they were." They were like intermissions at a
play: "You are alive to know what follows, and lo—down comes the
curtain, and the fiddlers begin with their abominations." "The story as
a whole" Southey thought "made of better materials than the *Lay*"; "in
parts it has pleased me more. There is nothing so finely conceived in
your former poem as the death of Marmion; there is nothing finer in its
conception anywhere."⁹

"The popularity of *Marmion*," Scott confessed, "gave him such a
*heeze* he had for a moment almost lost his footing." Wherever he went he
found himself surrounded by a buzz and glare of ecstasy. One witty observer, however, Mrs. Grant of Laggan, leaving a brilliant assembly
where Scott had been bathed in adulation, denied that he ever lost his
balance: "Mr. Scott always seems to me like a glass, through which the
rays of admiration pass without sensibly affecting it; but the bit of paper
that lies beside it will presently be in a blaze—and no wonder."¹⁰

Francis Jeffrey's judgment of the poem dissented from the general
laudation. The belligerent little critic was a radical in politics, not literature. He disliked poetic innovation, and in the *Edinburgh Review* had
already ferociously assailed Southey as a poor poet and Wordsworth
as rather worse—which, as Fowler Wright remarks, "was making three
errors about two men."¹¹ Both of his victims were rancorously indignant.
Southey described him as "up to my elbow in stature, and in intellectual
stature . . . up to my ankle."¹² Wordsworth thought he displayed "a gross
want of the common feelings of a British Gentleman," and added, "let
him take care to arm his breech well, for assuredly he runs desperate
risque of having it soundly kicked."¹³ Jeffrey's review of *Marmion* was
not discourteous, and it contained ample praise, but it was written in a
strain of lofty condescension, and almost every phrase of approbation
was balanced by one of niggling qualification.

Though the "intrinsic merits" of *Marmion* "are nearly, if not altogether equal" to those of the *Last Minstrel*, Jeffrey thinks its success "will

be less brilliant." "It is a good deal longer, indeed, and somewhat more ambitious; and it is rather clearer, that it has greater faults than that it has greater beauties . . . It has more flat and tedious passages, and more ostentation of historical and antiquarian lore: but it has also greater richness and variety . . . ; and if it has less sweetness and pathos . . . it has certainly more vehemence and force of colouring . . ."[14] "From the moment the author gets in sight of Flodden field . . . he never stoops his wing, nor wavers in his course; but carries the reader forward with a more rapid, sustained, and lofty movement than any epic bard we can at present remember."[15]

On the other hand, though Scott had made chivalry temporarily fashionable, Jeffrey disapproved of the entire design.[16] "Fine ladies and gentlemen now talk indeed of donjons, keeps, tabards, scutcheons, tressures, caps of maintenance, portcullises, wimples, and we know not what besides; just as they did in the days of Dr. Darwin's popularity, of gnomes, sylphs, oxygen, gossamer, polygnia, and palyandria." But "To write a modern romance of chivalry, seems to be as much a phantasy as to build a modern abbey or an English pagoda."[17]

All this Scott could have read with smiling composure, but it must have staggered him to find himself accused of having "throughout neglected Scottish feelings and Scottish characters!"—"He who had just poured out all the patriotic enthusiasm of his soul," exclaims Lockhart, "in so many passages of *Marmion* which every Scotchman to the end of time will have by heart; painted the capital, the court, the camp, the heroic old chieftains of Scotland, in colours instinct with a fervour that will never die; and dignified the most fatal of her national misfortunes by a celebration as loftily pathetic as ever blended pride with sorrow,—a battle-piece which even his critic had pronounced to be the noblest save in Homer!"[18]

What led to Jeffrey's fantastic accusation is beyond imagining, but what he found distasteful in *Marmion* is not hard to unearth. It is more than Scott's delight in the picturesque barbarism of glaives and hauberks; it nourishes the very lifeblood of the poem and breathes in its spirit. Jeffrey was one of those radical Whigs who were more bent on reform at home than on resistance to Bonaparte abroad. All Europe was prostrate beneath Napoleon's heel. England, they cried, must not bleed herself to death in a hopeless war. Far better to make peace while she could, and leave the unconquerable victor in possession of his spoils.

The very opening epistle of *Marmion* showed how Scott despised these counsels of defeatism. The surrender that the *Edinburgh Review* urged, he felt passionately, was not only ignoble, it was disastrous. How could there be peace with Napoleon?—had he not repeatedly violated his pledged word, and once England's defenses were gone how much liberty would he leave her even at home? Inspired by these convictions he had burst into praise of the buried Pitt:

> The mind that thought for Britain's weal,
> The hand that grasp'd the victor steel
>
> .  .  .
>
> Now is the stately column broke,
> The beacon-light is quench'd in smoke,
> The trumpet's silver sound is still,
> The warder silent on the hill!
>
> .  .  .
>
> While faith and civil peace are dear,
> Grace this cold marble with a tear,—
> He, who preserved them, PITT, lies here![19]

Even Scott's magnanimous praise of Pitt's great rival, Fox, was not of a kind to propitiate Jeffrey and the advocates of peace at any price:

> *Here*, where the end of earthly things
> Lays heroes, patriots, bards, and kings
>
> .  .  .
>
> If ever from an English heart,
> O, *here* let prejudice depart,
> And, partial feeling cast aside,
> Record that Fox a Briton died!
> When Europe crouch'd to France's yoke,
> And Austria bent, and Prussia broke,
> And the firm Russian's purpose brave,
> Was barter'd by a timorous slave,
> Even then dishonour's peace he spurn'd,
> The sullied olive-branch return'd,
> Stood for his country's glory fast,
> And nail'd her colours to the mast![20]

This threnody Jeffrey thought "a remarkable failure. . . . The manner in which he has chosen to praise the last of these great men, is more likely, we conceive, to give offence to his admirers, than the most direct censure. The only deed for which he is praised is for having broken off the negotiation for peace; and for this act of firmness, it is added, Heaven rewarded him with a share in the honoured grave of Pitt! It is then said that his errors should be forgotten, and that he *died* a Briton —a pretty plain insinuation that, in the Author's opinion, he did not live one; and just such an encomium as he himself pronounces over the grave of his villain hero, Marmion."[21]

When the proofs for the April number of the *Edinburgh Review*, containing this attack, were put in Jeffrey's hands, he felt a sudden qualm. That very evening, he remembered, he had been invited to dine with the Scotts. How would Scott take this castigation? He sent the copy around to Castle Street, with an apprehensive note saying that he scarcely dared put it in Scott's hands and earnestly hoped it would make no difference in their friendship. "Though I cannot reasonably suppose you will be pleased with everything I have said, it would mortify me very severely to believe I had given you pain. If you have any amity left for me, you will not delay very long to tell me so."[22]

Scott sent Jeffrey word that the article had not spoiled his appetite, though he hoped neither the publishers nor the public would agree. Of course Jeffrey was to come to dinner. Scott welcomed him heartily. "As I don't believe the world ever furnished a critic and an author who were more absolute *poco curantes* about their craft," Scott remarked, "we dined together, and had a hearty laugh at the revisal of the flagellation."[23] But Charlotte felt differently about it. Instead of chattering vivaciously in her foreign accent she maintained a cold and taciturn politeness. And as their guest was making his farewells in the hall her repressed feelings darted out for a moment. "Well, good-night, Mr. Jeffrey—dey tell me you have abused Scott in de *Review*"—and her black eyes stabbed at him. "I hope Mr. Constable has paid *you* very well for writing it."[24]

The words had a concealed Gallic sting in them. Constable had paid Scott a thousand guineas for the poem, and as publisher of the *Edinburgh Review* he paid Jeffrey's editorial salary. He was thus subsidizing an onslaught which might, for all that could be foreseen, reduce his own sales and injure one of his own authors. But for the time the poet, bookseller, and critic remained on terms of cordial friendship. Scott had even, in fact, been trying to persuade Southey to write for the *Edinburgh Review*.

Although that impecunious poet had a small government pension it was inadequate to his needs. He earned a precarious living by toiling at editorial hack-work, translating, and reviewing. He had been unlucky with his poems: *Thalaba the Destroyer* had been published by Longman on the most miserable terms, and *Madoc* had made only twenty-five pounds.[25] Despite the severity and flippancy with which Jeffrey had reviewed them, Scott told Southey, he knew the critic to have "the most sincere respect both for your person and talents." The *Edinburgh* paid ten guineas a sheet and was soon to increase this rate; Southey might "add £100 a-year, or double the sum" to his income "with almost no trouble." "Pray think of this, and if you are disposed to give your assistance, I am positively certain that I can transact the matter with the utmost delicacy towards both my friends."[26] But Southey would have nothing of this proposal. "I have scarcely one opinion," he replied, "in common with" the *Review*; when he wrote his "moral feelings must not be compromised."[27]

Scott replied that he perfectly understood Southey's scruples about the *Review*. "Indeed, I dislike most extremely the late strain of politics which they have adopted, as it seems, even on their own showing, to be cruelly imprudent. Who ever thought he did a service to a person engaged in an arduous conflict, by proving to him, or attempting to prove to him, that he must necessarily be beaten? and what effect can such language have but to accelerate the accomplishment of the prophecy which it contains?"[28]

On the other hand, about the publication of his poems Southey felt differently. "My friend Constable," Scott had told him, "I find anxious to be connected with you." Southey replied eagerly. He had on the stocks "a poem called *The Curse of Kehama*, of which Hindoo superstition is the basis, as the Mohammedan faith was the basis of *Thalaba*." What would Constable give for this poem? "If his offer tempted me to proceed, I would communicate it to Longman (to whom I should consider myself so far bound), and give him the refusal of it at that price. On his refusal it should be Constable's."[29]

Meanwhile Southey labored energetically at translations of *Palmerin of England* and *The Cid*. "My expectations from *Palmerin*," wrote Scott, "are very high."[30] A little later he was expressing his admiration: "I like it very much, although it is, I think, considerably inferior to the Amadis. . . . One discovery I have made is, that we understand little or nothing of *Don Quixote* except by the Spanish romances."[31] "I am most anxious to see the *Cid*."[32] "*The Chronicle of the Cid*," Southey replied, "is just gone to press—the most ancient and most curious piece of chivalrous history in existence—a book after your own heart."[33]

It turned out that Southey had forestalled one of Scott's own editorial plans.[34] "I am very glad the *Morte Arthur* is in your hands," Scott told him magnanimously; "it has long been a favourite of mine, and I intended to have made it a handsome book, in the shape of a small antique-looking quarto, with wooden vignettes of costume."[35] "I was I believe to have had the use of a very ancient copy . . . in the possession of Mr. Dent the member of Parliament commonly and alliteratively termed Dog-Dent. If you can get at him I presume he will not be so much of the Dog in the Manger as to refuse you the same favour."[36]

Scott resigned this enterprise to Southey the more willingly that his own hands would be fully occupied. He had completed, to be sure, the work on his edition of Dryden, which was on the verge of publication. But Constable, eager to bind Scott to him, now proposed a complete edition of Swift. For the Dryden he had paid 40 guineas a volume, a total of 720 guineas for its eighteen volumes.[37] For the Swift, Constable munificently offered more than double that sum, 1,500 guineas.[38] "It will occupy me occasionally for two years," Scott optimistically told Lady Abercorn, "but labour is to me really pleasure and the profit is not to be despised."[39]

In general his financial affairs were in a state of high prosperity. At Martinmas, 1807, the capital of James Ballantyne and Company had risen to around £7,200; by Whitsuntide 1808 it was a little over

£7,500.[40] The partners expected to divide profits of £1,200 and still have a sinking fund of £700–£800 for the payment of interest and the gradual extinction of company debts. "If all continues well," Scott exulted, "I have no doubt the next year's dividend may prudently be raised to £1,000 to James and £500 to me."[41]

In addition Scott had lent the firm £2,000, of which £800 was his own and the remaining £1,200 a loan from his brother, Major John Scott, and was proposing to advance a further large sum. The business was expanding so rapidly that it constantly needed more working capital, but if Scott had paid in these amounts as increases to his own share it would have destroyed the approximate equality he and James had so far maintained in the business.[42]

The arrangement Scott proposed was thus advantageous to both partners. "It is therefore my decided idea," wrote James Ballantyne's brother John, "that the Company should take from the partner willing to advance it £1,100 more at the Trade allowance of 15 p.c."[43] Although this, as Scott himself pointed out, was more than a bank would charge, a proportion of it would come out of his own pocket by cutting down "his interest in the free profit." A bank, on the other hand, would demand security that they might not find it convenient to give.[44]

Nevertheless, Scott said fairly, "while Bills belonging to the Company are discountable without such security, or if the Company on its own credit can procure a stationary loan at £5, per Cent it would be unjust that a partner should force a loan upon them. I mention this because I shall have a large sum of money to dispose of at Whitsunday and the state of my family requires I make the most of it I can. What Ballantyne and Company have no occasion for I will probably employ in some literary speculation."[45]

Despite this cheerful clink of gold, Scott remained hopeful that he might not be obliged to wait for the death of George Home to come into the receipt of his salary as Clerk of Session. His friend Colin Mackenzie was still in poor health. If he should have to retire it seemed only reasonable "that any new Clerk should come into my place and that I, who have served two years for nothing, which may be considered as equal to paying between £2,000 and £2,400, should be put in full possession of the emoluments of my office."[46]

In addition Scott had hopes that when the new Commission on the Administration of Justice in Scotland came into existence, he might be made its Secretary. He had the support, he wrote Lady Abercorn, of all his brethren at the Clerks' Table, Lord Melville was friendly to him, the Chief Baron warmly cordial, and the Lord Advocate, Archibald Campbell-Colquhoun—husband of his old friend Mary Erskine—promised to write the Chancellor, Lord Eldon, in his behalf.[47] Among the Lords of Session only Sir Ilay Campbell, its President, kept silent. "I may say with Falstaffe on a similar occasion, 'Good faith this cold-blooded Man loves me not'—yet I know he neither dare nor will be an active adversary, for it is not in his nature to be either a good friend or a bold enemy.—Every other person seemed happy to shew me kindness, the Justice Clerk sent me his answer in two lines

> "Tho' all mankind thy rivals be
> Thou Marmion art the Clerk for me."[48]

"If any channel occurs to your Ladyship in which the matter could be privately stated to the Chancellor it would probably greatly aid our claim. You see my dear friend how little I fear wearying your kindness in my behalf—"[49] "The place, though temporary, is highly respectable, and if I discharge the duty properly may or rather must pave the way to my getting forward in some shape or other."[50]

In March Joanna Baillie came on a visit which both she and the Scotts found thoroughly agreeable. With her demure reserve and good breeding, she proved an ideal guest.[51] In Scott's experience these were unusual qualities in women of literary pretensions. "Miss Baillie," he told Charles Kirkpatrick Sharpe, "is the only *writing* lady with whose manners in society I have been very much delighted. But she is simplicity itself, and most of them whom I have seen were the very cream of affectation." Even Miss Seward, whom he liked, was no exception, "for she was both affected and exigeante."[52]

Scott was delighted for Miss Baillie's sake that Mrs. Siddons was in the northern capital, "I believe to take her farewell of the Edinburgh audience."[53] But although as an actress he thought no one came "within a hundred degrees of what she was" at her best, as a woman he found her vain, foolish, and pretentious, spoilt by adulation, possessed of little sense and no taste.[54] Charles Mayne Young, however, an excellent actor "and an enthusiast in his profession," who was also in Edinburgh, was "a well-educated and gentlemanlike man" whom Scott was glad to entertain in Castle Street and introduce to Miss Baillie.[55]

Joanna, for her part, enjoyed her stay, and was pleased not only with her host but with Charlotte and the four children. "When I visited her," she said, "I saw a great deal to like. She seemed to admire and look up to her husband. Her children were well bred and the house was in excellent order. And she had some smart roses in her cap, and I did not like her the less for that."[56]

Meanwhile, "All the Whigs here are in arms against *Marmion*," Scott wrote Lady Abercorn, "—if I had satirized Fox they could have borne it, but a secondary place for the god of their idolatry" exasperated them. "I suppose the crossed critics of Holland House will take the same tone in your Metropolis."[57] His prophecy was quickly realized. Through a mistake in binding, some copies of the poem had gone out with the tribute to Fox in its briefer early form, lacking the additions suggested by the Marquis of Abercorn. The *Morning Chronicle* now raised the cry that this had been done on purpose, the more laudatory version going to Fox's followers and the original one to the Pittites.[58] Soon all the Whigs both in London and in Edinburgh were raging.[59] They would be surprised, laughed Scott, "to know that the couplet in question was written by so distinguished a friend of Mr. Pitt as Lord Abercorn."[60]

These outcries, however, proved as little injurious to the sales of the poem as Jeffrey's criticism in the *Edinburgh Review*. "Indeed Jeffrey's flagellation," Scott remarked cheerfully, "is of a kind not calculated to do much harm and has more the appearance than the essence of severity." The quotations were "carefully selected from the best passages of the poem," and "the criticism of the plan" applied with equal force to Ariosto and Tasso. "I suspect Jeffrey made an odd sort of compounding between his own character and mine . . . and was willing rather to amuse the public with cracking his whip than to annoy the culprit with laying on the lash."[61]

Scott's bargain to edit Swift met hearty disapproval from Lady Abercorn. She scolded him sharply for wasting his time on hack work when he ought to be engaged in original creation. But he defended himself vigorously. No popular writer, he agreed, should give malevolence the excuse for saying that he was publishing too often and writing too hastily. Furthermore, works of imagination, like the web of the spider, were spun from within their creators and left them feeling exhausted until they had assembled within themselves a sufficiency of poetic ideas to create another. As a small farmer he knew that after wheat he should plant turnips; "according to the best rules of agriculture I take it that an edition of Swift will do well after such a scourging crop of *Marmion*."[62]

A little later, following the publication of *The Works of John Dryden*, Scott made a similar defense of his editorial labors to Anna Seward. "Jeffrey, I hear, has reviewed my edition of Dryden and censures me for employing my time in editing the works of others. But what would he have? I have neither time nor inclination to be perpetually making butterflies that he may have the pleasure of pulling their legs and wings off . . . The critics tell me a poet ought to take care of his reputation and really I think, like honest Bob Acres, that the least thing Reputation can do in return is to take some care of the poet, and mine I am resolved shall do so. As to the unfading laurels which they are kind enough to Promise me if I will dedicate my time solely to the Muses, I care not for rewards which from their very nature are to be posthumous. Neither is it easy to gull me with these fair promises. The immortality of poetry is not so firm a point of my creed as the immortality of the soul—

"I've lived too long and seen the death of much immortal song

"Nay, those that have really attained this literary immortality have gained it under very hard conditions—to some it has not attached till after death, and I like not such grinning honour, as Falstaff says of my namesake Sir Walter Blunt."63

His present intention, Scott remarked, was to write no more poetry during the two years that he estimated it would take him to edit Swift. This work he did not expect to be "half as difficult as Dryden, all the sources of information lying within reach; and . . . while labouring at Dryden I found time not only to make two trips to England but to write *Marmion*."64 He would, in fact, positively need something to occupy his "idle time" and therefore directed James Ballantyne, who was going to London, to sound out William Miller on bringing out a collection of romances of wonder. There might be six volumes a year, including not only such English works as Paltock's *Peter Wilkins* but translations from the German and other languages and the best Eastern tales, Persian, Arabian, and so on.65 For these he himself would provide notes and short memoirs of the lives of the authors and the character of their works, though he decided that his contributions to the enterprise must remain anonymous.66

Although Miller exhibited no interest in this proposal, he did suggest the republication of the *Somers Tracts*, a great collection of historical pamphlets Scott had used in editing Dryden.67 They ranged from the reign of Elizabeth to George I and would probably fill a dozen quarto volumes. This proposal Scott enthusiastically accepted. Three weeks later Longman and Rees nibbled at the romances of wonder, asking Scott to state his terms and furnish "a rough list of Tales sufficient to make about twenty-five volumes."68 This project fell through,69 but meanwhile Scott bound himself to supply Constable with prefaces and notes to Captain Carleton's *Memoirs* and to the *Memoirs of Robert Carey, Earl of Monmouth*.70

Between these last two, both of which were done during that very summer and autumn and published before the end of the year, he also edited for John Murray a historical novel entitled *Queenhoo Hall*, which the antiquarian Joseph Strutt had left unfinished at his death, and supplied the fourth volume with a conclusion imitative of the author's own style.71 This last Scott undertook in a mood of gay self-confidence: "I wish you would see," he wrote Ballantyne, "how far the copy of *Queen-hoo-hall*, sent last night, extends, that I may not write more nonsense than enough."72

Nor were Scott's labors limited to these enterprises. Since the success of Robert Burns, Scotland had been deluged with peasant authors who were bursting into song. "Poets began to chirp in every corner," Scott noted in some amusement, "like grasshoppers in a sunshine day. The steep rocks poured down poetical goatherds, and the bowels of the earth vomited rhyming colliers."73 One of these was a shoemaker named John Struthers who had produced in 1803 a volume entitled *Anticipations* and in 1804 another called *The Poor Man's Sabbath*. Struthers had been befriended by Joanna Baillie, and now Scott persuaded Constable to reissue the shoemaker bard.[74] "The Great Biblipolist," as Scott called Constable, gave the poet thirty pounds and had Ballantyne print the volume as "a small lady-looking book . . . in the best stile."[75]

At the same time Scott was trying to help a young German scholar named Henry Weber find backing for a monumental edition of the ancient metrical romances. Weber had first come to his attention in 1804 as a refugee medical student from Jena, and Scott had taken him under his wing.[76] He was a violent Jacobin, a fact he believed he was disguising from Scott, who amused himself by teasing the poor fellow but cared not a fig about his politics.[77] He was also affectionate, highly emotional, and teutonically addicted to strong beverages. But he turned out to be deeply versed in German versions of *Sir Tristrem* both in verse and prose, as well as in continental antiquities, and to be well read in the literature of modern Europe. He was an accurate bibliographer, a scholar who pursued knowledge for its own sake, an enthusiastic lover of letters.

"You will be interested in a plan which I have greatly at heart," Scott wrote Surtees, "to have these venerable poems"—the metrical romances—"carefully published." Such a work, Scott knew, would be "caviare to the multitude," but surely he could get a hundred subscribers at five guineas each for "three quarto volumes of romantic poetry. Will you be one of my round table?"[78] Weber had already transcribed many thousand lines, and in May he journeyed south to carry on his labors in London and Oxford.

Scott gave him letters of introduction to Heber, Douce, and Ellis. "He will explain his views in turn himself," Scott wrote Heber, "which I believe chiefly regard the [British] Museum."[79] Weber had also made, Scott told Douce, "a transcript of the *Paradise of Dainty Devices* from a Copy in the Advocates' Library, which he is very desirous of collating with yours if you will have the goodness to permit him."[80] "But how is this?" enquired Ellis, "—Weber tells me he is afraid Mr. Scott will not be able to do anything for the recommendation of his *Romances* because he is himself engaged in no less than five different literary enterprises, some of them of immense extent. Five? Why, no combination of flesh and blood can possibly stand this; and Sir John Sinclair, however successful in pointing out the modes of feeding common gladiators, has not discovered the means of training minds to such endless fatigue."[81]

Scott confirmed his inability to supply Weber with extensive help but laughed at the idea that he would collapse. "My giving my name to Weber's *Romances* is out of the question, as assuredly I have no time to do anything that can entitle it to stand in his title-page; but I will do all I can for him in the business. . . . Swift is my *grande opus* at present, though I am under engagements, of old standing, to write a

*Life of Thomson* from some original materials. . . . My health is strong, and my mind active; I will therefore do as much as I can with justice to the tasks I have undertaken, and rest when advanced age and more independent circumstances entitle me to repose."[82]

Though Scott denied that he was undertaking too much, the strain was indeed enormous. "Ay," he told his son-in-law Lockhart in later years, "it was enough to tear me to pieces, but there was a wonderful exhilaration about it all: my blood was kept at fever-pitch—I felt as if I could have grappled with anything and everything; then, there was hardly one of all my schemes that did not afford me the means of serving some poor devil of a brother author. There were always huge piles of materials to be arranged, sifted, and indexed—volumes of extracts to be transcribed —journeys to be made hither and thither, for ascertaining little facts and dates,—in short, I could commonly keep half-a-dozen of the ragged regiment in tolerable case." Lockhart remarked that he must have felt like a locomotive engine getting up steam to drag a score of coal wagons. "Yes," replied Scott, laughing, and making a crashing cut at the larches they were felling, "but there was a cursed lot of dung-carts too."[83]

April had been a wintry month. Even during its last week Scott was up to his knees in snow at Ashestiel, the roads were impassable, and the coal almost entirely consumed in temperatures like those of "Siberia or Nova Zembla."[84] Then came a change, and while the hills were still white the rivers ran red with rain. "The groom says he cannot get forage for the horses," Scott reported, "and the dairy maid protests that there is no food for the cows and the lambs are dying by scores as fast as they are yeaned,—and the pigs—and the poultry—and the dogs—and lastly the children are all in some danger of being actually starved. Seriously, I believe that if the weather does not mend speedily we shall have a terrible year in our South Highlands and still worse in the North."[85] Then suddenly, with May, spring came in a rush, and the farm was in glory, "all the twigs bursting into leaf and all the lambs skipping on the hills."[86]

But the change came too late to bring comfort to the heart of poor James Hogg. His whole flock of sheep had been destroyed by the frost,[87] although Scott thought he had been careless as well: "I heard he neglected his sheep and forgot his sheephook."[88] He was now pleading for a post as surveyor of taxes for the Ettrick Forest or gloomily fearing that he must enlist in the militia,[89] "for which his habit, manners, speech, and *tout ensemble*," said Scott, "render him utterly and ludicrously unfit."[90] *The Mountain Bard* had not sold well, and Hogg despaired of getting any more money from Constable. Waiting for the bookseller in his shop, he read *Marmion*, standing there in his plaid and counting off 240 copies of that poem sold in a single forenoon.[91] Scott sought the aid of Lord Dalkeith to see if, like Burns, Hogg might not receive an appointment in the Excise. This seemed "to be the *domus ultima* of

Scottish genius" and therefore "the most natural refuge for poor Hogg, who has certainly driven his pigs to a bad market."[92]

Unlike the Ettrick Shepherd, Scott appeared to have the golden touch. He corrected the last sheet of his edition of Dryden on April 25, and it was published early in May.[93] A few days before it was issued James Ballantyne reported from London that Miller had "sold *in one day* £2,000 worth . . . besides £1,500 in country orders."[94] Its literary and scholarly success was no less striking. The critique in the *Edinburgh Review*—not by Jeffrey, as Scott believed, but by the historian Henry Hallam—took exception to some of his views of seventeenth-century politics but paid high tribute to the accuracy of his researches, his mastery of the materials, and the soundness of his judgments, and agreed in essence with his evaluation of Dryden's achievement as a man of letters.[95]

Scott's work, indeed, is still recognized as a monument of its kind, "one of the best-edited books on a great scale in English."[96] Of Dryden, in fact, it might almost be maintained that even to this day there is no other; although Saintsbury's edition of 1882–93 was able to achieve a more accurate text, it left unchanged as "thoroughly trustworthy" Scott's elaborate apparatus of historical notes. To the richness and fullness of his illustrative material Scott had devoted enormous industry. He pored over the innumerable tracts and pamphlets "of that pamphlet-writing age" to throw light on *Absalom and Achitophel, The Hind and the Panther*, and the other political poems. The eight volumes of drama have less commentary than the rest, but for Dryden's heroic plays Scott read tremendously in the seventeenth-century theater and for his comedies delved deeply into the satiric squibs, backbiting gossip, and literary feuds of the time. His entire work is a mine of information about the age.[97]

Scott filled his first volume with a detailed critical life of Dryden. Written in a clear and impersonal eighteenth-century style, it is neither so intimate nor so vividly colorful as later biographies have often sought to be, but it is a model of judicious narrative and sane comment. Though Scott adds little to Malone's painstaking investigations of the facts,[98] he presents them with a skill unattained by that clumsy scholar. And if he does not equal the brilliance of Johnson's critical essay, his discriminations are always shrewd and reasonable. Scott surpasses both—and this is his characteristic achievement—in relating Dryden's work to his character and showing how his writings both molded and were molded by the climate of the age.[99] This was the approach to history which in his University days he had derived from Dugald Stewart and Alexander Fraser Tytler, and he now applied it with striking effectiveness to literary history.

His literary analysis is often penetrating. Butler's satiric *Hudibras*, for example, he notes, makes a burlesque use of "the same extravagant ingenuity in combining the most remote images" that is displayed in the metaphysical poetry of Cowley: "although Butler pursued the ludicrous, and Cowley aimed at the surprising," their work differed only as "the same face convulsed with laughter, or arrested in astonishment."[100] Scott's psychological insights are also sharp. Of Dryden's unhappy marriage to Lady Elizabeth Howard, he remarks that "it is difficult for a woman of violent temper and weak intellects . . . to endure the apparently causeless fluctuation of spirits" of a man laboring, like Dryden, "in the feverish exercise of the imagination." Therefore she easily construed unintentional neglect as intentional offense. One consequence can be observed in Dryden's work: "on no one occasion when a sarcasm against matrimony could be introduced, has our author failed to season it with such bitterness, as spoke an inward consciousness of domestic misery."[101]

Perhaps Scott's own memories of his unhappy infatuation for Williamina Belsches, and his reaction against its miseries, color his comments on romantic love as portrayed in the heroic plays. "The love introduced was not of that ordinary sort, which exists between persons of common mould; it was the love of Amadis and Oriana, of Oroondates and Statira; that love which required the sacrifice of every wish, hope, and feeling . . . and which was expressed in the language of prayer and adoration. It was that love which was neither to be chilled by absence, nor wasted by time, nor quenched by infidelity. No caprice of the object beloved entitled her slave to emancipate himself from her fetters; no command, however unreasonable, was to be disobeyed; if required by the fair mistress of his affections, the hero was not only to sacrifice his interest, but his friend, his honour, his word, his country, even the gratification of his love itself, to maintain the character of a submissive and faithful adorer."[102]

It was a madness of which Scott might perhaps have been capable at twenty-five. At thirty-six he dismissed it with amused contempt. The man of rational principle and conduct had superseded the romantic youth.

With the notes to his *Minstrelsy of the Scottish Border* Scott had already won a reputation for scholarship that ranged curiously from the Middle Ages to the sixteenth century, and the notes to his two narrative poems had enhanced that reputation. Now his edition of Dryden established him as deeply versed in the seventeenth century as well. As a six-year-old child he had declared Mrs. Cockburn "a virtuoso like myself." "Dear Walter," his Aunt Jenny had asked, leaning tenderly over his pillow, "what is a virtuoso?" "Don't ye know? Why, it's one who wishes and will know everything." What, his fellow countrymen were now beginning to wonder, did Walter Scott not know? His erudition seemed as solid as his imagination was brilliant. "Glorious John Dryden," as Claude Halcro dubs him in *The Pirate*, had for Scott proved glorious indeed.

6

---

# *The Ladder and the Oak*

## *( 1 8 0 8 – 1 8 0 9 )*

CONSTABLE'S ROUGH-SPOKEN PARTNER, Alexander Gibson Hunter, thought Scott had too many irons in too many fires—especially when the fires were those of booksellers other than Archibald Constable. Scott's commitments to William Miller and John Murray exasperated him. The agreement on Swift implied, he irritably felt, that Scott should undertake no other tasks until his labors for Constable were concluded. Whenever Scott stepped into the bookshop Hunter made his sentiments bluntly clear. But Scott, for the time, at least, courteously ignored Hunter's rudeness. He felt serenely confident of his ability to carry out all his engagements. He was already calling on his correspondents to send him all the information they could collect about Swift and planning to go to Ireland to see what could be found there.[1]

In June, however, he knocked off work for a little vacation in the Highlands. He and Charlotte spent several days with Lord Melville at Dunira and his country house near Crieff.[2] They visited the battlefield of Bannockburn and went as far as Loch Katrine with an oddity of a Welsh lady, Miss Lydia White, whom they had met at Edinburgh during the winter and who had been their guest at Ashestiel that spring.[3] "What Oxonians call a lioness of the first order, with stockings nineteen-times-nine dyed blue, very lively, very good-humoured, and extremely absurd," full "of eccentric affectation," Miss White was also, Scott conceded, a woman "of some talent."[4] "I stood a respectable siege; but she caressed my wife, coaxed my children, and made, by dint of cake and pudding, some impression even upon the affections of my favourite dog: —so, when all the outworks were carried the main fortress had no choice but to surrender on honourable terms."[5]

Miss White inspired Charlotte with her passion for sketching, and the two ladies exercised their pencils on "every object that fell in their way, from a castle to a pigeon-house. Did your ladyship," Scott asked Lady Louisa Stuart, "ever travel with a *drawing* companion? Mine drew like cart-horses, as well in laborious zeal as in effect; . . . I could not help hinting that the cataracts delineated bore a singular resemblance to haycocks, and the rocks much correspondence to large old-fashioned cabinets with their folding doors open. . . . All this nonsense is *entre nous*, for Miss White has been actively zealous in getting me some Irish correspondence about Swift, and otherwise very obliging."[6]

"I always rejoice from an *esprit de corps*," Lady Louisa responded, "when a woman gets the better of a man. But I do not like you editing this and that for booksellers. However, Swift is such a favourite of mine (don't be shocked, I know it is like speaking of one of the wicked) that I shall be glad to have his stile recommended and brought back into fashion and I hope to see Cadenus and Vanessa made into sense."[7]

Scott began on Swift, surrounded by Faulkener's Dublin edition of the Dean's works, Cibber's *Lives*, and Granger's *Biographical History of England*, the first obtained for him by William Miller and the other two by Constable. That bear, Hunter, had at least proved useful in getting him books that he needed.[8] As Scott settled down to work, a means of putting a hundred guineas or so in his brother Tom's pocket occurred to him. Why should not Tom try his hand at editing the plays of Thomas Shadwell? Despite the devastating satire of Dryden's *Mac-Flecknoe*, Shadwell's comedies by no means merited, Scott thought, the utter neglect into which they had fallen; and "your habitual acquaintance with the old Drama," he wrote persuasively, "would enable you to make very entertaining notes and illustrations." He himself would see that the press was properly corrected and revise Tom's manuscript.[9] "My collection of Shadwell is almost complete and I will send you when I get to town both the original editions and a modern one." "You are not aware," he cajoled his brother, "what is in you."[10]

Although Tom's affairs were gradually getting settled, he was not yet out of the woods. The preceding August there had been a "roup," or public auction, of his effects, but his Edinburgh house in Albany Street had not yet been disposed of.[11] Early in 1808 he had taken refuge on the Isle of Man, where he had obtained a commission in a regiment of Fencibles being raised by the Duke of Atholl.[12] Meanwhile, in order to pay a needed £500 into Tom's account at Sir William Forbes's bank, Scott would anticipate £750 still due from the brickworks.[13] Anything Tom could earn would come in very handy, and "I am perfectly sure," Scott added, "you will find great pleasure in this work . . ."[14] Before he left Ashestiel at the end of the summer he was able to write a further assurance: "Miller of Albemarle Street was here the other day and seems willing to give £120 for Shadwell's plays; if I cannot get £150 from

Constable I will promise him the refusal. This will be pretty picking, being all autant gagné."[15]

William Miller was only one of a number of guests at Scott's Tweedside farm during the summer and autumn. Among these was a new acquaintance who became a lifelong friend. Handsome, sweet-tempered, witty, well educated, and wealthy, the owner of enormous estates with a splendid Palladian mansion at Rokeby in Yorkshire, John Bacon Sawney Morritt was then thirty-five, just a year Scott's junior. He had traveled in Greece, tried to buy a portion of the Parthenon frieze, written an illustrated quarto defending the geographical accuracy of Homer's description of Troy, and brought out an elegant little volume of translations from Musaeus.[16]

He was a close friend of Lady Douglas and Lady Louisa Stuart, whom he had met in 1800 at an inn at Lake Windermere. He and some University friends had written on a shutter of the inn parlor a poem to Lady Douglas's dog, Mr. Tippits; Lady Louisa, upstairs, wrote a reply, which Lady Douglas tied around Mr. Tippits's neck. Off trotted the little animal, an innocent go-between; shouts of laughter sounded from the young men downstairs; above, Lady Douglas's daughters were in ecstasies at "Mama's impudence." The ice once broken, the two middle-aged ladies had found the young man and his friends delightful.[17]

Heralded by a letter from Lady Louisa, Morritt and his wife had reached Edinburgh late in June. Scott showed them all the sights of the town and took them rambling along the Esk to Roslin and Hawthornden, his old cottage at Lasswade and Dalkeith Palace.[18] Morritt attended one select dinner at which Scott and Jeffrey were the two lions. Morritt was dazzled by Jeffrey's acuteness, wit, and informational scope but thought Scott himself displayed "even a larger range of anecdote and illustration." One striking difference beween the two men Morritt noticed: Jeffrey entertained them "with the detection of faults, blunders, absurdities, or plagiarisms"; Scott "recalled some compensating beauty or excellence for which no credit had been allowed" and "set the poor victim on his legs again."[19]

Only once did the two reverse their roles. While the claret was circulating, Jeffrey lauded his fellow founders of the *Edinburgh Review*, Sydney Smith, Henry Brougham, and Francis Horner. Scott heartily agreed to the brilliance of Smith and Brougham, but Horner's humorless economic solemnities were too much for him. "I will not admire your Horner: he always puts me in mind of Obadiah's bull, who, although, as Father Shandy observed, he never produced a calf, went through his business with such a grave demeanour, that he always maintained his credit in the parish!"[20]

From Edinburgh the Morritts had gone north to Ross-shire and on their return in September came to Ashestiel. The house, Scott told them heartily, "had pigeon-holes enough for such of his friends as could live, like him, on Tweed salmon and Forest mutton."[21] Here they spent a glorious week, one day going to Melrose Abbey, another to Newark Castle, a third coursing with the greyhounds, Douglas and Percy, by Yarrow braes and St. Mary's Loch, Scott joyfully repeating legends and ballads.[22] One night, crossing the ravine and brook that separated Ashestiel from the Peel farm, children and all, they went to a *kirn* or harvest home at old Laird Nippy Laidlaw's, where Morritt and Scott drank whiskey punch and danced, Morritt said, "with Border lasses on a barn floor."[23]

Morritt was greatly struck by the happy faces of Scott's children. Sophia, close to her ninth birthday, was a demure child beginning to sing in a sweet wavering voice and was soon to start practicing on the piano.[24] Walter, "the Laird of Gilnockie," a sturdy seven, within another year would be following his father's footsteps by entering the Edinburgh High School.[25] Anne, now between four and five, delighted Scott's heart by memorizing readily the verses of old ballads like the "Wife in the Wilds of Kent."[26] Little Charles, the youngest, was "a stout cherry cheeked animal" in his third year, who tumbled about everywhere, from the orchard to the haugh, and frightened his parents that summer by falling into a deep part of the Tweed and almost drowning in its strong current.[27]

The children ate at the family dining table, and to be allowed "to sit up to supper" was the reward for being "good bairns." During the day they wandered in and out of the room where Scott was writing as freely as Camp and the greyhounds; he did not seem to be disturbed by their chatter and was always ready to answer their questions. When they asked him to tell them a story, he laid aside his pen, took one of them on his knee, and repeated a ballad or a legend. Then, with a kiss, he sent them back to their marbles or ninepins and resumed writing "as if refreshed by the interruption." He was often with them in their games, and for them the rainiest day was never dull when "papa" was at home.[28]

In the children's education Scott was much more concerned to stimulate their imaginations than to load them with learning. He detested the kind of children's books then becoming popular that tried to thrust scientific minutiae into the infant mind. History, he believed, could be taught best by telling its deeds of daring and excitement; the meanings behind the drama would sink into the mind later. The tales he told them, therefore, were often Lindsay of Pitscottie's quaint old stories of the Scottish past, or the romantic rhymes of Barbour's *Bruce* and Blind Harry's *Wallace*.[29]

On Sundays he told stories from the Bible, mainly from the Old Testament, and the excitement of Samson among the Philistines, of David and Goliath, Judith and Holofernes, Jael and Sisera, and Moses smiting the Egyptians, did not suffer beside the exploits of the Bruce and

Wight Wallace. When the family did not go to church he read from the Church of England prayer book, but he would subject his children to nothing like the wearisome redundance of sermons and prayers that had darkened his own childhood in George Square.[30] After a time, old Laird Nippy, though a dry and taciturn Presbyterian prejudiced against "English prentit prayers," came to be a fairly regular attendant at the Sunday service in Scott's parlor.[31]

Scott would not hear of sending Sophia or Anne away to boarding school, but obtained for them a governess, Miss Millar, a good-tempered, brown-eyed young woman, who lived henceforth with the family. Both Ashestiel and Castle Street were full of books, among which the children might browse freely, although Scott would not tolerate anybody dog-earing or breaking the back of one of his precious volumes. But more important to him than any degree of scholarly knowledge was the formation of character, and, like the ancient Persians of Xenophon's *Cyropaedia*, he ranked love of truth the highest of all virtues, and courage next.[32]

Like them, therefore, he regarded horsemanship as a prime feature of education. As soon as Sophia could sit a horse she became a companion of his mountain rides. And after her the other children were taught to think nothing of tumbles and to share his own "reckless delight in perilous fords and flooded streams" and his passion for horses. No child of his must be a coward. "Without courage," he said, "there cannot be truth; and without truth there can be no other virtue."[33]

On Sundays, Scott did not ride; the animals, he thought, were entitled, like human beings, to their day of rest. After the church service they walked—Scott, Charlotte, the children, and the dogs—all except poor Camp, who was growing old and feeble—to some favorite spot. One of these was the ruined tower of Elibank, some three miles from Ashestiel, where they would dine in the open air on a basket of cold provisions and Scott would mix his wine with icy water from the rushing brook.[34]

While Scott was thus rusticating with his family, his partner, the corpulent and black-bearded James Ballantyne, was thinking of becoming a family man. He had fallen in love with a Miss Stewart, a young woman of a prosperous Glasgow family. Her parents were disposed to favor his suit, but while admitting an affection for him, she herself hesitated about marrying a man markedly her senior. Scott was warmly interested in his old friend's behalf. Though it was long, he told James, since he had been a confidant in a love affair, eleven years of matrimony had not dulled his sympathies for the emotions James was feeling:

"The power of beauty I remember yet"[35]

Scott thought the young lady's request for time to make up her mind sensible and honorable. James must take care, however, during his year of probation, not to injure himself by undue humility or the anxiety of his own temper, and he must not let himself "be cast down by jealousy about trifles." "I have know several Falklands in real life but I never saw a Julia." If Ballantyne really thought it would be helpful for Scott to meet the girl and her parents, "I will be at your service." They could go to Glasgow together, spend a few days there, and return by the Falls of Clyde. Perhaps James might "prevail on the fair Lady and her *pa* and *ma* to go so far as Hamilton or even Lanark— It is a fine country to make love in."[36]

Toward the end of September, consequently, Scott and Ballantyne went to Glasgow together. There were assembled to meet Scott a company of friends who were eager to admire the distinguished guest. Ballantyne had forebodings of a heavy evening looming ahead. Their host had no shining powers of entertainment, and Scott usually behaved with quiet reserve, allowing Francis Jeffrey, or anyone else who loved displaying his eloquence, to monopolize the conversation. But Jeffrey was not here today, and these sober merchants were all waiting for the literary celebrity to glitter. Scott gave a spectacular exhibition of intellectual fireworks. Ballantyne was amazed; he had never heard anyone "so glowingly brilliant."[37]

Walking to their bedchambers that night he voiced his astonishment. "What," asked Scott, "did you never see me rear before?" "Rear?" asked Ballantyne. "No, I fancy not. But what do you mean by rearing?" "Why," Scott replied, "you have seen a lion in a menagerie stirred up by a long pole. Now I really felt myself called upon to rear today, even though the pole was not applied to me"; their host obviously had nothing to say, "the honest merchants were all dumb, and you are in love—what could I do?"[38]

The two men returned to Edinburgh, Ballantyne lost in dulcet dreams of marital bliss. Back in Ashestiel, Scott began to pore over the pages of Swift's *Examiner* and its attacks on Lord Wharton.[39] He had had several further interviews with Constable's partner, but had not yielded to Hunter's feeling that he should be engaged on no other tasks than the *Swift*. They parted without cordiality, although Scott's courtesy misled Hunter about the nature of the man he was dealing with.[40] He would find that Scott was not to be driven. Unknown to him, Scott's association with Constable and Company was already being threatened by young John Murray.

That London publisher remembered Jeffrey's extraordinary attack on *Marmion* and had read in the same number of the *Edinburgh Review* articles clamoring for peace with France, exalting Napoleon's armies as invincible, and predicting revolution in England if the war went on. "Walter Scott," he said to himself astutely, "has feelings both as a gentleman and a Tory, which these people must now have wounded:—the alliance between him and the whole clique of the *Edinburgh Review*, its proprietor included, is shaken."[41] Could not be himself snatch this great prize away from Constable?

He opened his campaign skillfully. Ballantyne would rise to the bait of printing orders, and through Ballantyne he could get to Scott. Murray wrote Ballantyne, broaching a Novelists' Library in numerous volumes. Ballantyne responded eagerly. He would have been quite willing to come to London to discuss the project, but that would not have suited Murray's plans at all. He wanted to meet Scott; he did not want to appear to be seeking a meeting. He had business to transact in the north of England, he said, and easily induced Ballantyne to suggest that they confer with each other in Yorkshire, midway between London and Edinburgh. Just before the middle of October the two men met at Ferrybridge, where the coach road crossed the Aire.[42]

Murray outlined his own plans. Ballantyne made no endeavor to conceal his belief that Hunter was making a breach between Scott and Constable imminent. Scott had already chalked out a design for an *Edinburgh Annual Register*, in opposition to the politics and criticism of the *Edinburgh Review*. Little persuasion would be needed to make him start a rival publishing house. And the author of *Marmion*, Ballantyne confided enticingly, had "both another Scotch poem and a *Scotch novel on the stocks*." These might head the list of the new house. Murray instantly offered his own active cooperation in the metropolis. The upshot was that he accompanied Ballantyne back to Edinburgh.[43]

The young London publisher had a scheme in his own mind. At Ashestiel he outlined it to Scott: a quarterly of Tory sympathies, opposing the *Edinburgh Review*. He had privately discussed this project with Mr. Canning, the Foreign Secretary, who had promised unofficial government support and confidential access to authoritative sources of information.[44] Scott was deeply interested. The position of the *Edinburgh Review* had been growing ever more violently partisan; on foreign policy Scott felt its persistent arguments for appeasement to be hardly short of treasonous.

It was true that the Napoleonic menace was now appallingly swollen. The Emperor had seized Portugal and forced its royal family to flee to Brazil. With an army of 100,000 men he had invaded Spain, bullied Charles IV and his son Ferdinand into abdicating, and put his brother Joseph on the throne. A revolt of the Spanish people had given the French troops under Murat a temporary setback, but they had speedily defeated this rabble and swept back to Madrid. Then in Portugal a rising British general named Sir Arthur Wellesley had defeated Junot at Vimeira. England went mad with joy; Napoleon's chain of victories was broken. When army politics deprived Wellesley of his command and his successors signed away his gains in the Convention of Cintra it was a terrible shock to the country. Wrote Wordsworth, "Britannia sickens, Cintra, at thy name."[45]

Scott agreed; he joined in the heady cry that England should give the Spanish rebels strong support. For Jeffrey and his cohorts, though, the Spaniards were a mob of peasants masquerading as regiments and their hidalgo leaders were deluded romantics brandishing the rusty arms of the Middle Ages; their resistance was a ridiculous affair of Don Quixote in the saddle and Sancho Panza in the ranks while Napoleon's military machine rolled unopposed along the highways. In the October number of the *Review* Jeffrey's article, "Don Cevallos on the Usurpation in Spain," voiced this view and urged that England should not bleed herself white in supporting a hopeless cause. If the French landed an army in Ireland how was England to be saved?[46]

Scott and twenty-four other prominent readers had immediately canceled their subscriptions. Lord Buchan laid his copy on the lobby floor of his house in George Street, opened the front door, and solemnly kicked the magazine out into the street.[47] "The *Edinburgh Review*," Scott wrote Constable, "*had* become such as to render it impossible for me to continue a contributor to it.—*Now*, it is such as I can no longer continue to receive or read it."[48] In an indignant dash Constable's pen scored through Scott's name on the subscription list the word— "STOPT! ! !"[49]

Scott therefore energetically supported Murray's plans. Nevertheless he declined the editorship; his hands were already too full for such an undertaking, and the editor, he pointed out, ought to reside in London. But he would do everything else in his power.[50] As editor he suggested William Gifford, the witty author of two brilliant satirical poems, *The Baviad* and *The Maeviad*, and, in 1800, one of the founders with Canning of the *Anti-Jacobin*. This post Gifford accepted. Soon Scott was in council about the new quarterly with Archibald Campbell-Colquhoun, the Lord-Advocate, and letters were flying back and forth between Edinburgh and Canning in London.[51]

At their request, Scott wrote Gifford a letter of advice.[52] The eight or nine thousand copies of the *Edinburgh Review* that were regularly sold, he pointed out, did not owe their popularity to its political opinions, with which not one out of twenty readers agreed,[53] but to the fact that it was ably conducted and independent of the influence of booksellers. Its contributors were handsomely paid. "The Editor to my knowledge acts on the principle that even Czar Peter working in the trenches must accept the pay of a common soldier." And he never allowed it to sink into a vehicle for puffing Constable's publications or running down those of his rivals.[54] In addition, Jeffrey had the art of giving life even to rather sober materials. Sometimes men of deep knowledge in specialized areas wrote with stupefying dullness; Jeffrey rendered their learning lively by colorful illustration or by drawing brilliant generalizations from their details. In these two ways the new periodical would do well to emulate its predecessor.[55]

One great advantage the new review would have would be its closeness to government channels of knowledge about public affairs. But it should not assume an exclusively political character; its articles on science and literature should challenge comparison with the best. And it should not degrade itself to a slavish support of administration policy but carefully maintain its independence. It would thus reap a decided ascendance over all competition through its early and accurate information upon political subjects without losing the respect of its readers.[56]

He himself, Scott promised, would be happy to serve "as a sort of Jackal or Lion's provider."[57] "My own studies have been rather limited, but I understand in some sort literary antiquities and history, and have been reckoned a respectable tirailleur in the quizzing department of the *Edinburgh Review*." Others who were "fit to be put into the van of the battle" were the Ellises, the Roses, and Malthus for political economy. William Erskine would also help in obtaining "some scientific articles and some Scotch metaphysics." "You can never want scholars while Oxford stands where it did. Richard Heber was with me during Murray's visit, and knowing his zeal for the good cause I availed myself of his advice." "In the mean while I am for gliding into a state of hostility without a formal declaration of war . . ."[58] "The first Number of our proposed Review if it can be compiled without the plan taking wind . . . will burst among the Whigs . . . like a bomb."[59]

Hard upon this letter Scott wrote to Ellis as an old colleague of Gifford's on the *Anti-Jacobin*, demanding his support. "You must hang your birding-piece on its hook, take down your old Anti-Jacobin armour, and 'remember your swashing blow.' " This new quarterly conducted from London must "offer to those who love their country," he argued, "and to those whom we wish to love it, a periodical work conducted with equal talent" to that displayed in the *Edinburgh Review* "but upon sounder principles. Is this not possible? In point of learning, you Englishmen have ten times our scholarship; and, as for talent and genius, 'Are not Abana and Pharpar, rivers of Damascus, better than any of the rivers in Israel?' Have we not yourself and your cousin, the Roses, Malthus, Mathias, Gifford, Heber, and his brother? Can I not procure you a score of blue-caps who would rather write for us than for the *Edinburgh Review* if they got as much pay for it? 'A good plot, good friends, and full of expectation—an excellent plot, very good friends!' "[60]

Scott's only fear was lest the new quarterly ape the rancorousness of its rival. Gifford, the Editor, was himself "a little warm and pepperish," but heat and acerbity should not be the leading characteristics of a publication. The acid vituperations of the *Edinburgh Review*, once a novelty, now affected "the tympanum of the public ear" no more than a parrot screeching "rogue" or "rascal." "Decent, lively, and reflecting criticism, teaching men not to abuse books only, but to read and judge them," would have a striking originality to "a public wearied with universal efforts at blackguard and undiscriminating satire."[61]

Although his brother Tom had not even commenced the editing of Shadwell's plays (and, in fact, if he ever did begin, certainly made no headway on them), Scott hopefully invited him to do clever reviews for the new quarterly. "I know no one who possesses more powers of humour or perception of the ridiculous"; they would send him "novels, light poetry, and quizzical books . . . by the packet" and he could "glide back" reviews in the same way. He might thus make himself powerful friends: "You must understand, as Gadshill tells the Chamberlain, that you are to be leagued with 'Trojans that thou dreamest not of, the which for sport sake are content to do the profession some grace.' . . . Constable, or rather that brute his partner, has behaved to me of late not very civilly, and I owe Jeffrey a flap with a fox-tail on account of his review of *Marmion*, and thus doth 'the whirligig of time bring about my revenges.' "[62]

For despite Scott's resolution to arm himself in Horace's triple brass and ignore literary attacks upon himself,[63] Jeffrey's arrogance had left behind it some rankling. "I have no fault to find with his expressing his sentiments frankly and freely upon the poem, yet I think he might without derogation to his impartiality have couched them in language rather more civil to a personal friend, and I believe he would have thought twice before he had given himself that air of superiority in a case where I had any chance of defending myself."[64]

Nevertheless, there can be no doubt that Scott's exertions for the rival review were dictated predominantly by principle. The London *Quarterly Review*, as it was to be called, must counter the pacifist influence of the *Edinburgh Review*; the very first number must carry an article tearing to shreds the shameful suggestion that England abandon the Spanish rebels. Ellis was the man to write this article on Spanish affairs—"God grant," Scott exclaimed, "it may be an exulting one."[65] The subject was one for which Southey would not do; though "my friend, an excellent man," and "a valuable contributor," he was bound to go wrong on politics, and "once wrong Gifford will find him absolutely intractable."[66]

They should even beg an article from Canning himself. "Though unquestionably our Atlas," he "might for a day find a Hercules on whom to devolve the burthen of the globe . . . I know what an audacious request this is; but suppose he should, as great statesmen sometimes do, take a political fit of the gout, and absent himself from a large ministerial dinner, which might give it him in good earnest,—dine at three on a chicken and pint of wine,—and lay the foundation of at least one good article?"[67]

With the aid of Scott's untiring efforts, the first number of the

*Quarterly* was whipped into shape. He asked William Erskine to review Curran's Speeches—"a rich subject"—and obtained and sent in an article on Fox's fragment of a *History of the Early Reign of James II.*[68] He himself wrote reviews of a book on Burns, of Southey's translation of *The Cid*, and of a biographical essay on Swift, as well as what he called "a whisky-frisky article" on the ludicrous *Caledonian Sketches* of Sir John Carr, who was "an incomparable goose," but an "innocent good-natured" creature who should not be mauled.[69]

Through Scott's solicitation Gifford also obtained the services of William Stewart Rose, Southey, and the Hebers.[70] Weber would be useful, Scott suggested to Ellis, on antiquarian subjects, but wrote badly: "you or I must re-write his lucubrations." "Constable, the great Edinburgh editor, has offended me by tyrannizing over this poor Teutcher, and being rather rude when I interfered. It is a chance but I may teach him he should not kick down the scaffolding before his house is quite built."[71] Among a growing list of contributors were Frere, "Rogers, Moore (Anacreon), and others whose reputations Jeffrey has murdered, and who are now crying wo upon him, like the ghosts in King Richard."[72]

That little critic was by this time worried about Scott's disaffection. He "offered terms of pacification," Scott reported, "engaging that no party politics should again appear in his review. I told him I thought it was now too late, and reminded him that I had often pointed out to him the consequences of letting his work become a party tool. He said 'he did not care for the consequence—there were but four men he feared as opponents.' —'Who were these?' —'Yourself for one.' —'Certainly you pay me a great compliment; depend upon it I will endeavor to deserve it.' —'Why, you would not join against me?' —'Yes, I would, if I saw a proper opportunity: not against you personally, but against your politics.' —'You are privileged to be violent.' —'I don't ask any privilege for undue violence. But who are your other foemen?' —'George Ellis and Southey.' The fourth he did not name."[73]

Scott thought Jeffrey had no suspicion of the bomb they were preparing for him, but he was mistaken. Several days before this conversation Jeffrey had written to Horner that the veteran playwright and novelist Richard Cumberland was starting a rival review, "and what is worse, I have reason to believe Scott, Ellis, Frere, Southey, and some others are plotting another."[74] Within another three weeks, in fact, the *Quarterly* was publicly talked about. Constable tried to find out if Scott was involved in it by asking him "if it was to be an Edinburgh publication," but Scott refused to be pumped: "I told him report said no."[75]

Scott's relations with Constable's house were now almost entirely severed. He heartily wished that he had never undertaken to do the *Swift*;[76] the circumstances accompanying its commencement and progress, he told them angrily, had been very unpleasant. "I have only to add that if it is likely to prove so dubious a speculation as it seems Mr. Hunter apprehends I am very willing, so far as I am concerned, to renounce the bargain."[77] Constable and Hunter put their heads together. They realized uneasily the causes of Scott's annoyance and made a conciliatory reply. They were anxious to assure him, they said, that they felt no dissatisfaction about any part of their agreement and would be very sorry to have him relinquish it. They hoped their relations with him might be restored to the old cordial footing.[78]

"We regret," their letter continued, "that you have not been more willing to overlook the unguarded expression of our Mr. Hunter about which you complain."[79] Scott pounced upon this. "I must remind you," he replied, "of what I told Mr. Constable personally, that no *single unguarded expression* . . . would have influenced me to quarrel with any of my friends. But if Mr. Hunter will take the trouble to recollect the general opinion he had expressed of my undertakings, and of my ability to execute them, upon many occasions during the last five months, and his whole conduct in the bargain about Swift, I think he ought to be the last to wish his interest compromised on my account."[80]

He would complete the *Swift*, since they did not wish to abandon it, but it would terminate their long and friendly intercourse.[81] Though he did not tell them so, he was already planning to establish the rival publishing house that had been hinted to Murray. "I have some reason," he told Ellis, "to believe that Ballantyne, whose stock is now immensely increased, and who is likely to enlarge it by marriage, will commence publisher. Constable threatened him with withdrawing his business from him as a printer on account of his being a Constitutionalist." His haughty despotism was likely to raise up a formidable opponent.[82]

Even as Scott and the troubled booksellers were exchanging these last letters he was announcing the new project to his friends. "I have had a high quarrel with Constable and Company," he told Southey. "The *Edinburgh Review* has driven them quite crazy, and its success led them to undervalue those who have been of most use to them— but they shall dearly abye it."[83] And to Morritt: "I have prepared to start against them at Whitsunday 1st the celebrated printer Ballantyne (who had the honour of meeting you at Ashestiel) in the shape of an Edinburgh publisher with a long purse and a sound political creed, not to mention an alliance offensive and defensive with young John Murray of Fleet Street, the most enlightened and active of the London trade."[84] Bitterly should "those misproud stationers Constable and Hunter" regret their insolence![85]

"I have only a parting request," he wrote them, "to make of your house, which is that the portrait for which I sat to Raeburn shall be considered as done at my debit and for myself."[86] Constable himself replied, in handsomely courteous terms, declining to give up the picture.

It was his private property, and however painful his feelings made it to refuse any request of Scott's, "I cannot think of parting with it, on any account whatever." He considered it "a strong pledge of the friendship with which you honored me, and I shall have a pride in preserving the Picture as a memorial of those days . . . this, with the repeated assurances when we last met of the good opinion you are still pleased to entertain of me personally, will in some degree operate to lessen the regret I feel . . ."[87]

But beneath their civilities both men were angry. Forgetting that Constable had already been the leading publisher of Edinburgh and the owner of the immensely profitable *Edinburgh Review* long before the success of *Marmion*, Scott chose to believe that he had created Constable's prosperity. And Constable, dropping into oblivion the fact that he had been given only a small share in the *Last Minstrel* and that the *Minstrelsy* had made Scott's name before that, imagined himself the architect of Scott's fame.

Later they were to make up their quarrel—and bitterly might Scott have reason to regret the renewal of their friendship. Their reconciliation, and their catastrophe, however, were still hidden in the future. At the moment they were hot against each other.

"Constable, like many other folks who learn to undervalue the means by which they have risen, has behaved, or rather has suffered his partner to behave, very uncivilly to me. But they may both live to know," Scott said grimly, "that they should not have kicked down their ladder till they were sure of their footing."[88] Constable's wrath expressed itself still more violently. "Aye," he said, with a savage smile, stamping on the ground, "there is such a thing as rearing the oak until it can support itself."[89]

# 7

## For Lucre and for Fame

## ( 1 8 0 9 )

Sᴄᴏᴛᴛ ꜱᴡɪꜰᴛʟʏ ʟᴀᴜɴᴄʜᴇᴅ into hostilities against the house of Constable. The new publishing firm that was to shake the great bookseller's supremacy was set up quickly. It would possess the enormous
advantage of bringing out all Scott's future poems, including the new
"Scotch poem" James Ballantyne had dangled before Murray. Originally
Scott had not intended to begin the poem before another year, but now
he started turning it over again in his mind.[1] No doubt he could be a
powerful force in enlisting other authors under the Ballantyne banner.
He proposed also to devise splendid schemes for reissuing wonderful
old books that had fallen into oblivion. The prospects seemed glorious.

With this heady optimism the publishing house of John Ballantyne
and Company was born. Its cash capital was £2,000, of which Scott
supplied a half-share, the other half-share being divided equally between
James and John Ballantyne. In later years, Scott's son-in-law, John
Gibson Lockhart, believed that Scott lent James £500 for his quarter-
share, but gave no better reason than that James, "not having any funds
to spare, must have become indebted to some one."[2] The Ballantynes,
however, were not, as Lockhart tries to make them appear, a family of
impecunious adventurers. Another brother, Alexander Ballantyne, had
already lent James £600 for investment in the printing establishment.
And James's credit was good enough so that he was able, if need be,
to borrow outside his family as well. The records simply do not show
where he or his younger brother John found the money for their quarter-
shares.[3]

It is true that when John Ballantyne came to Edinburgh three years
previously and entered the employ of James Ballantyne and Company

as a clerk at £200 a year, he had been in financial distress.[4] Through a mingling of negligence and ill-health he had made a failure of his father's general-merchandise shop in Kelso, been victimized by some unidentified person whom he bitterly designated—in a partly erased memorandum— as "the scoundrel," and found himself forced to go out of business. His furniture and goods were sold: "My effects at Kelso," he recorded in his diary, "with labour, paid my debts, and left me penniless."[5] Later, though, he must have recovered some of his losses, for not long after he entered on his duties in the Canongate he was able to lend James £300.[6] Now he was to act as manager for the publishing house that bore his name and receive a salary of £300 a year as well as one-fourth of the profits.[7]

John was thirty-four years of age, small in build, all skin and bones, but bursting with mercurial vitality and bounce. He rode well and loved all field sports from fox hunting to badger baiting; he was convivial at the wine bottle and the punch bowl; full of droll merriment, a brilliant comic mimic. His gay fancy exploded into recklessly imaginative manipulations of reality. He loved inventing tall tales, piling one fantastic impossibility on another. He skated between mendacity and romance, his fabrications so outrageous that they hardly seemed intended to deceive. When a gasping listener at last protested, "Is that true, John?" he would unblushingly reply, "Not a word of it. Any blockhead may stick to truth, but 'tis a sad hamperer of genius." He sang humorous songs in a sharp treble; told funny stories, in a voice half-croak, half-squeak, ludicrously twisting his mobile features. He overflowed with energy and zeal, was always good-humored, always elastically buoyant.[8]

At this time Scott knew him less well than he did his elder brother James.[9] It was only by degrees that he came to feel as fond of little "jocund Johnny" as he did of his old Kelso school-friend. Scott intended to control the publishing house himself, but Johnny knew all about accounts and credits, would be a good hand at keeping the books, and, with his liveliness and charm, make a wonderful figurehead through whom Scott could act when he did not wish to appear himself. Early in January, 1809, Scott sent him off to London to introduce himself to the leading publishers there, to talk over publishing plans with John Murray, and to take Murray's instructions about the Scottish management of the *Quarterly Review*, which the new firm would represent in Edinburgh.[10]

A number of reprint projects Scott acted upon speedily. Within the year John Ballantyne and Company issued a new edition of the autobiography of Lord Herbert of Cherbury, with a short prefatory memoir that Scott may have written himself.[11] Another project was a *Secret History of the Court of James I*, consisting of four curious seventeenth-century memoirs; still another, which Scott persuasively suggested that Murray join in publishing, a splendid annotated edition of the Old English *Froissart*, to be edited by Henry Weber.[12] Scott also threw together two volumes of fugitive poems entitled *English Minstrelsy*.[13] "The selection," he told Samuel Rogers, "is chiefly from the smaller pieces of dead authors, but it would be very imperfect without a few specimens from the present masters of the Lyre." The author of *The Pleasures of Memory* ranked high "in that honour'd class," and therefore Scott held out his "begging box." Rogers responded with a lyric, as did others among Scott's circle of friends. The volumes came out the following year with poems by Heber, Joanna Baillie, Southey, Canning, Tom Moore, three of Scott's own early lyrics, Coleridge's *Genevieve*, and Wordsworth's *Tintern Abbey*.[14]

Besides the *English Minstrelsy* and his antiquarian publications, Scott cast around for new works by living authors. Possibly, he suggested to Southey, John Ballantyne and Company might be interested in publishing the new periodical, *The Friend*, which he had heard that Coleridge was meditating.[15] And while John was in England he would talk over Southey's idea of a periodical *British Librarian*.[16] If Southey was determined to bring out his *Curse of Kehama* himself, Scott had no doubt the firm would be delighted to print it for him and "take payment . . . in copies of the work."[17] Beyond these suggestions, in the course of the next year Scott accepted for publication an erudite but ponderous work on a Scottish monastic order dating from the seventh century, Dr. John Jamieson's *Historical Account of the Ancient Culdees of Iona*.[18]

All these, of course, Scott expected to have printed by James Ballantyne. The Canongate presses were to be kept thundering as well with work already undertaken for William Miller. There was a collection of *The Ancient British Drama*, which Miller at first decided to hold within two volumes but which Scott persuaded him should run to three. There would even be ample materials, Scott noted, for a fourth and a fifth volume.[19] These in turn were followed by *The Modern British Drama*, which ultimately extended to five volumes.[20] When Miller abandoned his intended edition of Thomson, and Scott no longer had to write the introductory biography, he heaved a breath of relief: "Thomson will be a load off my mind and my hands."[21]

A further publishing scheme, which Murray had proposed in October, was a uniform edition of novels and tales, beginning with Defoe, for which Scott was to supply biographical memoirs and illustrative notes.[22] "I have little doubt," Scott wrote Murray confidently, "that 20 volumes of 700 pages will hold all the Novels, &c, that are worth reprinting . . ."[23] They should start out at once with the novels of Richardson, follow with Fielding and Smollett, and go on to later writers such as Fanny Burney, Mrs. Radcliffe, and Charlotte Smith.[24] The entire collection could be called *The Cabinet of Novels* or *The Cabinet of Tales and Romances*.[25]

But Scott's vaulting ambition soon magnified this plan into one of grandiose size. His imagination saw long shelves including some thirty-six British and eighteen foreign authors.[26] Certainly they must have Baron Trenck, perhaps Marmontel, and "Pray look out for 'Chaou Kiou Chouau; or, The Pleasing Chinese History'; it is a work of equal rarity and curiosity."[27] Volume was added to volume; the stunned Murray, who had thought of a modest twenty volumes at an outlay of £15 each, protested that it could not be completed in fewer than two hundred volumes involving an expenditure of at least £20,000.[28]

James Ballantyne put Scott's argument to the reluctant bookseller: "You might publish a part of the work during its progress" and thereby forestall all possible competition. "Mr. Scott thinks also that the publication of the first six volumes should be accompanied with a full detail of your plan, and an assurance to the public that it was in speedy progress, and would certainly be completed." There was no question of success: "Mr. Scott is so sanguine about this plan, that I believe he means to propose to you to embark £500 or £1,000 in it. I wish to God I had any money to embark." The cautious Murray, however, drew back, and the enormous enterprise never materialized.[29]

Since 1800, when he had first urged Ballantyne to come to Edinburgh, Scott's mind had been fascinated by the idea of a *Caledonian Annual Register*, modeled upon the English *Annual Register* and devoted to a summary of the leading historical events and most important intellectual developments of each year.[30] This vision he now started resolutely hammering into reality. Renaming it the *Edinburgh Annual Register*, he drafted a prospectus, obtained the promise of cooperation from Will Erskine and the two Mackenzies, father and son, on literature, from Lord Meadowbank on legal affairs, and from Professor Leslie on science. Though Leslie was "as abominable an animal as I ever saw," Scott said, he wrote with great eloquence and enthusiasm on mathematics, chemistry, and mineralogy.[31]

He asked Charles Kirkpatrick Sharpe to do history: "A lively luminous picture of the events of the last momentous year, is a task for the pen of a man of genius," and the *Register* would pay "£300 a-year—no deaf nuts."[32] But Sharpe declined to contribute as historian; "my ignorance," he explained, "of recent politicks is profound." He would, however, be glad to help in other ways.[33] "You grieve my praecordia," Scott replied, "by declining to give me the heavy lift I had promised myself but I still claim the subordinate assistance you are so good as to offer me and which I shall deem invaluable."[34]

Southey delighted Scott by taking on the historical section dealing with the war in Spain.[35] And Scott amused himself by turning out an anonymous article on "The Living Poets of Great Britain," in which he reviewed the comparative merits of Southey, Campbell, Wordsworth, and himself,[36] awarding his own poems both "a sugar plum and a buffet."[37]

"I read the history of the *Register*," he told Southey, "with great pleasure. Some points we differ on but they are daily becoming less important. The tone of candour and impartiality struck every one. . . . I know not," he added mischievously, "where they have picked up their poetical critic who is a dashing fellow but lets, I think, his tongue run a little before his wits; a common fault in his trade."[38]

As Scott's representative, James Ballantyne offered Murray and several other London booksellers a twelfth share each in the *Register*. "I look forward," wrote the sanguine James, "to this work as to an inheritance; for the assistance I have received is of the most splendid kind. Mr. Scott's words were, 'Ballantyne, tell Murray not to be hasty in rejecting these shares. If the other parties hesitate and refuse, tell him by all means to take them himself.'" But Murray and his fellow publishers felt skeptical and rejected the offer.[39]

Constable did not share their doubts. Earlier in the year Ballantyne had discussed the project with him, and he had now convinced himself that he had originated the idea. Furious at Scott's desertion, he told James that they could not honorably appropriate it without his consent. James knew that Constable was deluded but worried over how to disprove the claim. Scott sent for James to come to Castle Street and discuss the position. As James was leaving, he saw Constable at the door and slipped into the dining room to avoid a meeting in the hall. What took place in the study between Scott and the publisher is unknown, but it certainly led to no reconciliation.[40]

Murray and his London colleagues turned out to be well justified in their judgment. When the *Edinburgh Annual Register* for 1808 finally appeared in 1810 it lost money. And despite Scott's conviction that it could be built up into a success the volumes that followed continued to lose.

The incredible labors Scott poured into all these activities—organizing his new publishing firm, launching the *Edinburgh Annual Register*, writing articles for the *Quarterly Review*, sending Gifford pages of detailed advice and comment on it, corresponding with friends and possible contributors to all three enterprises—are all the more amazing because his days were more than usually occupied in official duties.[41] Through the influence of Lady Abercorn he had been successful in gaining the post of Secretary to the Commission on the Administration of Justice in Scotland, and this body, or its various committees, sat with few intermissions from St. Andrew's Day (November 30) all through December, January, and February.[42] The long hours of these meetings left Scott hardly any time for writing until after supper.[43]

None of these employments, however, deflected him from the fierce excitement with which he followed the war in Spain. He thrilled to the Declaration of Claremont that England would not desert any peoples who resisted the aggressions of Bonaparte. "Tell Mr. Canning," he wrote impetuously, "that the old women of Scotland will defend the country with their distaffs, rather than that troops enough be not sent to make good so noble a pledge."[44] He admired the firmness of the Spanish leaders in declaring "the Frenchified Spaniards traitors even when approaching Madrid with a victorious army. But they may have Roman pride," he added, "and want Roman talent to support it."[45]

All the advantages of skill and unscrupulous villainy appeared to lie with their crafty adversary. "We can only fight like mastiffs, boldly, blindly, and faithfully."[46] And Sir John Moore, who now commanded the British armies in the Peninsula, he feared, had too much caution to be a daring leader. "A general who is always looking over his shoulder, and more intent on saving his own army than on doing the service on which he is sent" would win no great victories.[47] What England needed was a general who had "*le Diable au corps*, and who, instead of standing staring" to see what the French intended to do, would "teach them to dread" *his* moves.[48] Scott was unfair to Moore—he did not know his problems—but the retreat to Corunna and the British evacuation of Spain seemed to him to confirm his judgment. "I would to God Wellesley were now at the head of the English in Spain."[49] "Had Wellesley been there, the battle of Corunna would have been fought and won at Somosierra, and the ranks of the victors would have been reinforced by the population of Madrid."[50]

The first number of the *Quarterly Review* appeared in March, 1809,[51] leading off with an article written or inspired by Canning. Surveying Napoleon's entire career, it appealed to the British nation not to lose heart. "To confine ourselves to a partial and gloomy view can never be wise. A nation may be ruined by despair; it cannot be much injured by hope."[52] This voiced the spirit in which the review was founded. It was Scott who had suggested seeking Canning's aid, and Scott's endeavors, Gifford gratefully acknowledged, had been of crucial importance: "You have, indeed, acquitted your promise nobly: yet nothing less was requisite to enable us to complete the first Number. Without your uncommon exertions we must have failed."[53]

The general tone of the *Quarterly*, however, Robert Southey found unnecessarily ferocious: "too much in the temper of the *Edinburgh*," he said, "to please me. No man dips his pen deeper in the very gall of bitterness than I can do . . . but I do not like to see scorn and indignation wasted on trivial objects—they should be reserved like the arrows of Hercules for occasions worthy of such weapons."[54] Scott agreed, but other readers relished its savagery. It gradually built up a London following and in Edinburgh was a success from the start. Within less than three weeks, "Ballantyne has only about 30 left of the last 200 received by sea," Scott reported to Murray, "and thinks he could easily have sold double the number forwarded—many announce themselves as steady customers and I have no doubt you may sell 1000 in Scotland quarterly."[55]

In the midst of two reviews for the next number, Scott was saddened by the loss of a faithful companion.[56] Old Camp had long been drooping. At Ashestiel the preceding summer he had no longer been able to go with Scott on his rides, but lay on his mat by the dining-room fire. While the servant was laying the cloth for dinner, he would say, "Camp, my good fellow, the Sheriff's coming home by the ford"—or "by the hill"—but the enfeebled animal could only falter a few steps out the back door toward the Tweed, or out the front door toward the little bridge over the Glenkinnon burn beyond Laird Nippy's gate.[57]

On the evening of March 3, in Castle Street, Scott's "old four-footed friend . . . stretched himself out in his basket and died."[58] The whole family were in great tribulation. Scott had been engaged to dine with the Hector Macdonald Buchanans, but excused himself on account of "the death of a dear old friend." In the little back garden beneath the study window where Scott usually sat writing, Camp was buried by moonlight that night. Nine-year-old Sophia and the rest of the family stood in tears while their father smoothed the turf over the grave.[59]

All winter Scott had been expecting to be called to London in connection with the work of the Commission to which he was Secretary. The summons depended upon the Chancellor, Lord Eldon, "and what depends," Scott commented, "upon his Lordship's doubts and hesitations is not likely soon to be decided."[60] Meanwhile, well into March, the Commission was busy "clouting" and "cobbling our old Scottish system of jurisprudence." Their chief disagreement was about introducing trial by jury into civil cases—they had always had it in criminal trials—and Scott himself confessed to grave reservations about the wisdom of the change.[62] "We have been tearing each other's throats out like our own highland terriers," he told Lady Abercorn, "about the Scottish Judicature Bill . . ."[63]

As the month drew to a close, however, Scott was in momentary expectations of setting out for the capital. He announced his departure on March 19,[64] but was obliged by urgent business to postpone it till April 2 or 3.[65] Then he was detained again. Finally he and Charlotte did get away at noon on April 5.[66] He bore with him various legal memoranda, including opinions on the subject of jury trial by the Lord Advocate, the Chief Baron, and Sir Ilay Campbell, the former Lord President of the Court of Session.[67]

Scott had planned to stop off on the road for a day at Mainsforth and at last meet Robert Surtees. He did pay this visit, but another one he did not make.[68] Only a few days before leaving Edinburgh he learned that Anna Seward was dead and had made him her literary executor with directions for the publication of her works. He had promised himself to see her in Lichfield, "had hoped to find her well, had wished she should have learned to know Mrs. Scott, in short had built a little scheme of two days happiness." The news was a shock: "her sudden death . . . comes over me like a dream."[69]

Scott and Charlotte arrived in London on April 10 and stayed again in Half Moon Street with her old friends the Dumergues.[70] Hosts of old friends and claimants for acquaintance contended for Scott's time. Lord and Lady Abercorn were not in town, but Scott and Charlotte were entertained by Morritt in his home in Portland Place, by the Marchioness of Stafford—a close friend of Charles Kirkpatrick Sharpe—at Cleveland House, and by the Princess of Wales, who "was in the highest possible spirits."[71]

Through Miss Hayman, a lady-in-waiting to the Princess, Scott had become acquainted with Mrs. Thomas Hughes, the wife of a canon of St. Paul's Cathedral, and spent a musical evening with her and her husband at their home in Amen Corner.[72] He had tea in Clarges Street with Mrs. Maclean Clephane, a Highland widow who was heiress of the Macleans of Torloisk, and showed her the manuscript of Miss Baillie's new play, *The Family Legend,* a tragedy based on the feuds of the Macleans and the Campbells.[73] At Tunbridge Wells the Scotts spent a few days with Sir Samuel Hood, the commander of the *Centaur* at the bombardment of Copenhagen and capture of the Danish Fleet. On their return they visited the famous and splendid baronial mansion of Knole, the home of the Sackvilles at Sevenoaks, and admired the Vandyke and Holbein portraits in the Great Hall and Brown Gallery.[74]

Scott's prestige in London was now of towering height; "the homage paid him," said Morritt, "would have turned the head of any less-gifted man of eminence." Scott smiled at it but enjoyed it: "All this is very flattering and civil; and if people are amused with hearing me tell a parcel of old stories, or recite a pack of ballads to lovely young girls and gaping matrons, they are easily pleased, and a man would be very ill-natured who would not give pleasure so cheaply conferred." "Well, do you want me to play lion today?" he would ask when he dined with the Morritts— "I will roar if you like it to your heart's content." But when the party shrank, and he and Charlotte were left alone with their host and hostess, he laughed at his own performance: "Yet know that I one Snug the joiner am—no lion fierce."[75]

His literary fame aroused no little jealousy. At a brilliant dinner party where Scott and Coleridge were among the men of letters encircling the table, there were signs of a desire to humble Scott by extravagantly eulogizing poets of smaller renown. Several of those present recited poems they had not yet published and were enthusiastically praised; Coleridge repeated more than one and was lauded to the skies. Scott heartily joined in the applause. When he was asked to give them something of his own, he replied that he had nothing worth their hearing but that he had seen some verses in a provincial newspaper that he thought very fine. He then repeated a poem entitled *Fire, Famine, and Slaughter*. It was received with only faint approbation. Criticisms followed; Scott defended the unknown author. Finally, a more bitter antagonist, fastening upon one line, cried, "This at least is absolute nonsense!" Scott denied it—the carper maintained his criticism—until Coleridge, who had been growing more and more uncomfortable, called out, "For God's sake let Mr. Scott alone—*I* wrote the poem."[76]

After a stay in the south of a little more than two months, Scott started homeward on June 15. On the way he and Charlotte enjoyed a two-day visit with the Morritts in their Yorkshire home at Rokeby.[77] Scott almost envied his friend this magnificent and picturesque estate: the river Greta and the Tees joined their rapid currents within its extensive domain. Nearby was Barnard Castle; the wooded landscape united the luxuriance of English foliage with the variety of glen, torrent, and copse seen in the north; the Tees flowed between wild cliffs in a deep trench of solid limestone and marble. From the height of the rocks, Scott said, its banks resembled the glen of Roslin.[78]

Scott and Charlotte found the children all well. Soon they were on their way to Ashestiel for the summer, taking with them in the place of Camp "a terrier puppy of the shaggy old Celtic breed" whom Scott christened Wallace.[79] All the living creatures on the farm seemed, Scott thought, to be bursting with happiness, and the place had "never looked so enchanting—the ground is quite enameled with wild flowers."[80] Here he settled down to work on Swift and think how he might help relieve the poverty of Southey.

Canning, he knew, had desired to offer Southey an official position in his own department, but the only vacancy paid a mere £300 and required constant attendance. There were professorial chairs, however, in both England and Scotland, "and there is hardly one," he told Southey, "unless such as are absolutely professional, for which you are not either fitted already, or capable of making yourself so, on short notice. . . ." There were also diplomatic posts, "should you prefer them to the groves of Academe. . . . What would I not give to secure you a chair in our Northern Metropolis."[81]

Southey replied that what he would like would be for the government to "create for me the Title of Royal Historiographer for England (there is one for Scotland) with a salary of 400£." There was also the Stewardship for the Derwentwater Estates, which was expected soon to be vacant and which would be a very desirable post.[82] Scott saw difficulties about "erecting a new office merely literary" for Southey's accommodation, but thought the Stewardship "a more probable opening." He promptly wrote off to Ellis urging Southey's claims;[83] to Southey himself Scott suggested obtaining the support of Sir George Beaumont and the Marquis of Bute. The choice of the Steward was in the hands of the Earl of Lonsdale, and although he and Lord Bute differed in politics they were personal friends.[84]

Lord Lonsdale proved to be favorable to Southey's application. For a few days the poet's hopes rose high. But he turned out to lack the necessary qualifications for the Stewardship. Nor could he be made Historiographer; though neither he nor Scott had known it, there already was one—"old Dutens at £406 a year."[85] Scott thereupon began pulling strings to obtain an increase in Southey's small pension upon the understanding that he surrender it if he became Historiographer when Dutens died.[86]

Through all these efforts for Southey, Scott toiled day in and day out on Swift. He immersed himself in "the dirty stream of scurrility by which Swift and his friend Pope were assailed during their lives,"[87] delved into the claim that Swift had carried on a treasonable correspondence with Ormond, sought to plumb the dark mystery of Swift's ambiguous relationship to Stella.[88] Through Lydia White he learned that an obscure Irish clergyman named Edward Berwick, whom the Earl of Moira had presented with a living in County Dublin, was deeply learned in Swift.[89] Everyone testified to Berwick's erudition: "'Go to Berwick,'" Scott said, "has not been more frequently called for in a ballroom than it was returned in answer to all my enquiries."[90] Soon the two men were exchanging lengthy letters, and Scott was "surprised and delighted" to learn through Berwick that Swift's correspondence with the fascinating Esther Vanhomrigh, the famous Cadenus and Vanessa letters, was still in existence.[91]

While he thus fagged at Swift, Scott was ruefully amused and a little annoyed to come upon Lord Byron's satiric attack on him in *English Bards and Scotch Reviewers*, published just the preceding March. Byron sneeringly dismissed Scott as a mercenary poet who wrote for "half-a-crown per line":[92]

> No! when the sons of song descend to trade,
> Their bays are sear, their former laurels fade.
> Let such forego the poet's sacred name,
> Who rack their brains for lucre, not for fame:
> Still for stern Mammon may they toil in vain!
> And sadly gaze on gold they cannot gain!
> Such be their meed, such still the just reward
> Of prostituted muse and hireling bard!
> For this we spurn Apollo's venal son,
> And bid a long "good night to Marmion."[93]

Scott had in fact accepted Constable's offer for the poem without bargaining, and, unless the hogshead of claret be counted, had made not an extra penny from its enormous popularity. "It is funny enough," he wrote Southey, "to see a whelp of a young Lord Byron abusing me, of whose circumstances he knows nothing for endeavoring to scratch out a living with my pen. God help the bear, if, having little else to eat, he must not even suck his own paws. I can assure the noble imp of fame it is not my fault that I was not born to a park and £5000 a-year, as it is not his lordship's merit, although it may be his great good fortune, that he was not born to live by his literary talents or success."[94]

The Highland poem that was to follow *Marmion* was now forming itself in Scott's mind. He may already have begun writing it when at the end of August he took Charlotte and Sophia with him for a little holiday among the wild lakes and mountains that were to be its background.[95] Once again, as in his youth, he stayed at Cambusmore with his old friends the Buchanans. With them he rode to Ross Priory and explored the islands of Loch Lomond, Arrochar, and Loch Sloy, the scenes of a hundred fierce fights between the Macfarlanes, the Colquhouns, and Clan Alpine. Amid the very landscape of his first canto he dashed off the rapid opening narrative of the stag hunt.[96] In a swift ride Scott himself tested out the possibility that Fitz-James, the hero of his poem, might make his desperate gallop from Coilantogle Ford, at the eastern end of Loch Vennachar, to the rock of Stirling.[97] At nearby Buchanan House, where Lady Douglas and Lady Louisa Stuart were guests of the Duke of Montrose, Scott joined them for a two-day visit.[98] Ten Highland rowers, "all plaided and plumed in their tartan array," took them boating among the islands of Loch Lomond, and Scott read the two ladies the stag chase as it had poured alive from his imagination.[99]

During September his best-loved aunt, Miss Christian Rutherford, was at Ashestiel with the family. Scott resumed "threading verses together, with what success," he told Lady Abercorn, "I am uncertain. But if I am not able to please myself at all it is but a step to the fireside and the poem will go into the smoke like half the projects of this world."[100] Miss Chritty warned him against daring to stake his reputation on still another long poem. "You stand high," she pleaded, "—do not rashly attempt to climb higher, and incur the risk of a fall; for, depend upon it, a favourite will not be permitted even to stumble with impunity."

Scott quoted the Marquis of Montrose in reply:

> "He either fears his fate too much
> Or his deserts are small,
> Who dares not put it to the touch
> To gain or lose it all.

"If I fail it is a sign that I ought never to have succeeded, and I will write prose for life; you shall see no change in my temper, nor will I eat a single meal the worse. But if I succeed,

> "Up with the bonnie blue bonnet,
> The dirk, and the feather, and a'!"[101]

It was a brave boast. If I fail, *I will write prose for life, nor will I eat a single meal the worse*. But when the time came, Scott made it good.

Miss Chritty's fears for the poem were dissipated by hearing the first canto. Scott also read it to Mungo Park's brother Archie, a passionate lover of the chase, who happened to be dining at Ashestiel. He listened with sharp attention, his hand on his brow, through the whole of the hunt, till the dogs threw themselves into the lake to follow the skiff in which their master had embarked with Ellen Douglas. At this he started up, struck the table with his fist, and wrathfully exclaimed that the dogs must have been ruined by being allowed to plunge into the water after so violent a chase. Scott felt much pleased at this evidence that his listener had lost all memory that the tale was a work of fiction.

He was not so pleased, however, to have his guest pierce through to the identity of Fitz-James as soon as he wound his bugle to summon his attendants. What enabled him to detect it, Scott thought, was that the lines of the poem here echoed "the lively but somewhat licentious old ballad in which the dénouement of a royal intrigue takes place as follows:

> "He took a bugle from his side,
>     He blew both loud and shrill,
> And four-and-twenty belted knights
>     Came skipping owre the hill.

> "Then he took out a little knife,
>     Let a' his duddies fa',
> And he was the bravest gentleman
>     That was amang them a'.

"This discovery, as Mr. Pepys says of the rent in his camlet cloak, 'was but a trifle, yet it troubled me' "; and Scott went to a good deal of trouble to efface the telltale signs by which the secret might be revealed before the end.[102]

Through September the weather was dreary, with continual heavy rain, obliging Scott "like Hamlet to forego a custom of my exercise" and amuse himself indoors. "In the course of which seclusion," he said, "I have of course blotted much paper."[103] With "no sun on the brae, and no fire in the chimney," he readily found himself caught up "by the inveterate habit of coupling the lines together by jingling rhymes, as I used to couple spaniels in sporting days."[104] He had made a good start by the time the family returned to Edinburgh.

One morning that autumn brought a change to the daily program in Castle Street. Young Walter had now reached the age of eight: "My little boy," the father wrote, "is just gone to the High School and it is with inexpressible feeling that I hear him trying to babble the first

words of Latin; the signal of commencing serious study for his acquirements hitherto have been under the mild dominion of a governess. I felt
very like Leontes

> "Looking on the lines
> Of my boy's face, methought I did recoil
> Thirty good years—"[105]

It brought back to him with a strange melancholy those days "when I
first crept swinging my satchel through George's Square with Robert
Dundas to learn tasks to which I could annex neither idea nor utility."[106]

In the course of the winter, father and son established a study
routine. "I condescend," Scott reported, "to hear him his lesson every
day."[107] But to this news he sadly made an addition about the Rector:
"Poor old Dr. Adam died last week after a very short illness, which first
affected him in school. He was lightheaded, and continued to speak as
in class until the very last, when, having been silent for many hours, he
said, 'That Horace was very well said; *you* did not do well,' then added
faintly, 'But it grows dark, very dark, the *boys may dismiss*,' and with
these striking words he expired."[108]

The High School, Scott quickly learned, had not changed. Walter
was soon battering his way through both the forms and the yard. "He
is flourishing in arts and arms,"[109] his proud father boasted, "*tam Marte
tam Mercurio* having gained forty places during the last fortnight"[110]
and "won two pitched battles. I was of course obliged to look grave on
these military successes but I am not sorry that he can *make his hand
keep his head* as we border folk say."[111]

Despite Scott's determination to have his new poem ready with all
speed for publication by his new firm, the winter saw no slackening of
his editorial work. William Miller published several volumes of those
*Somers Tracts*[112] that Lady Abercorn had upbraided Scott for doing
and that he had defended as little more than an amusement for which he
was paid £400 a year.[113] Scott did not complete this huge diversion,
however, until three years later, by which time it had extended to
thirteen volumes and earned him thirteen hundred guineas.[114] Miller had
found no difficulty in persuading Scott to begin as well an edition of
Grammont's *Memoirs of the Court of Charles II*. "I will make some
additions to notes," Scott promised him, "and endeavour to translate the
beautiful introductory *Epistle to the Count de Grammont* (though I am
uncertain how I shall succeed in imitating the exquisite facility of the
poetic fragments interspersed with the prose)."[115]

The biographical memoir and notes for the *Sadler Papers* had been
completed, and Constable brought out the entire work, in two volumes,
in the course of the autumn.[116] The bookseller's wrath with Scott had
subsided into a desire to end their estrangement. Anna Seward's will
had arranged for her letters to be published by Constable; he generously

allowed Scott to go through the twelve manuscript volumes, striking out passages in which the authoress had too gushingly praised him or too enthusiastically quoted his opinions, although their inclusion would clearly have helped the sales.[117] He also magnanimously volunteered his advice to the new firm on how to publish Scott's poem. He intended, he added quickly, no interference in their arrangements, merely "to shew you how gratefully I remember and how much I value your former friendship."[118]

Scott's replies were courteous but cool. All are in the frigid third person,[119] except one that acknowledges having heard from John Ballantyne "the handsome manner" in which Constable had behaved. "I have no doubt," Scott continues, "Mr Jo: Ballantyne will avail himself with gratitude of any hint your professional knowledge and experience may afford him. I assure you that I think with more regret than resentment (though certainly with cause for both) on the mode in which our connection was necessarily ended."[120] The door still remained firmly though politely closed.

John Ballantyne and Company now had quarters on South Hanover Street, between George Street and Princes Street.[121] On Scott's way home from Parliament House, instead of dropping into Constable's "shop" in the High Street to gossip, tell stories, and look through the books on the shelves, as he had formerly been in the habit of doing, he stumped down the Mound and stopped off at Jocund Johnny's "drawing room" to pore over black-letter volumes and stuff some of them into coat pockets made especially roomy for that very purpose.[122] The tiny, hopping figure of the manager was always there, always ready for stories and jokes. Bubbling, buoyant, bright-eyed, he was after the drone of some advocate under the dark rafters of the Court of Session, like a beam of sunlight on a winter day.

Little Johnny was by this time high in Scott's favor. To both the Ballantyne brothers he gave affectionately comic nicknames from Henry Carey's farce *Chronon hotonthologos*: stout and mock-majestic James was the pompous Alliborontiphoscophornio, and his flute-thin brother the zany Rigdumfunnidos.[123] James at first received his appellation with indignant incredulity passing into tragic horror, but Rigdumfunnidos was at once delighted with his cap and bells. Gradually, however, James grew mollified, and later, when over a convivial glass the comedian Charles Mathews imitated them both in their comic roles, as Scott passed the decanter, James would even chuckle faintly while Johnny screamed with laughter.[124]

Scott ended the year in a glow of satisfaction. The Highland poem was going rapidly and would undoubtedly be ready for publication by spring.[125] To various correspondents he gave scraps of information about it. "The scene Loch Katrine *tempore Jacobi quinti*," he told Morritt.[126] And to Mrs. Clephane, somewhat earlier: "The Douglases enter a good deal into my present sketches . . ."[127] On the very last day of the year he confided to Lady Abercorn that he had "made considerable progress."[128] She had been pleased to hear a rumor, she replied, that he was being paid "£2000, which I hope is true." Although, she added, "I am sure you never can get as much as it is worth."[129] "It is true my new ditty is sold," Scott answered, "but the price is two thousand guineas not pounds. When I was fond of horses I learned from the jockey to sell by guineas and buy by pounds."[130]

For some time the "new ditty" had had a name. It was "to be called *The Lady of the Lake*."[131] Scott felt calmly assured that it would make his fortune as a publisher.

# 8

## *A Nail in Fortune's Wheel*

## *( 1 8 1 0 )*

SCOTT HAD MADE one striking change in his first cloudy conception of *The Lady of the Lake*. Some five months before he began writing, he had thought of presenting it as a tale told for the amusement of the Young Pretender during his wanderings after the fatal battle of Culloden. He had planned to include among the characters in this supporting framework the heroic Flora Macdonald, through whose aid the Prince had escaped capture.[1] But as Scott turned the poem over in his mind he must have seen that this device merely echoed the machinery of *The Lay of the Last Minstrel* without sharing the pathos of the old bard's deep feeling for his own story. Perhaps, too, the universal feeling that the introductory epistles of *Marmion* were irrelevant intrusions led him to realize that his tale would gain nothing from bringing in either a real or an imagined teller. He therefore rejected this part of his original plan.

The root conception of the poem, however, he did not reject. He intended it to depend less on violent action and colorful scenery and more on a deeper rendering of character than he had previously attempted. He desired to paint vivid pictures of the faithful old James of Douglas and his daughter Ellen, and sharply contrasting portraits of the savage yet honorable Highland chieftain Roderick Dhu and the sagacious but noble-minded ruler James V, struggling to bring law to a tumultuous land. Scott's aim, in fact, was to shift his emphasis to the psychological, "the power of distinguishing and marking the *dramatis personae*."[2]

As he strove to make headway on the poem, his hours were more than ever taken up by his duties on the Judicature Commission. Its members, "like every other body that I know," he said, "left all their work to be done just at the time they were to make their report."[3] Every day during the Christmas holidays they met from eleven to five, and the Secretary toiled from nine in the morning till nine at night,[4] so "that I have never had a moment to put on my cap and bells."[5]

The Commission was giving the Clerks of Session indignant night-mares. They were willing enough to be paid a salary instead of fees, but the salary proposed by the Commission would disagreeably curtail their incomes.[6] The Lord Advocate, Archibald Campbell-Colquhoun, on whose support the Clerks had imagined they could count—"my *soi-disant* friend," Scott said—turned hostile and backed the recommenda-tions of the Commission.[7] All through the spring the conflict raged. Colin Mackenzie, now in restored health, was again sent to London to represent his brethren.[8] Through Scott's *Quarterly Review* connections he assured them the powerful championship of Canning and gained the interest of John Wilson Croker, the Secretary to the Admiralty and a member of Parliament for Ulster, who brought a host of Irish members to their aid.[9]

The struggle ended only in June. "The Compensation business was settled," Scott wrote Ellis, "upon the terms of a drawn battle though not till Canning went down to the House on a night particularly incon-venient to him to bid defiance to the Lord Advocate."[10] The salary was fixed at £1,100 a year, "with a chance of getting a hundred or two more by application to the Exchequer."[11] For Scott himself it would amount to £1,200, "which will make a very comfortable addition to my income when it pleases heaven to remember my Senior in office."[12]

Scott did a little good-natured grumbling because the Commission had still set its face against giving retirement pensions. "I think while they were making so many alterations in the court here they might have invalided my Senior and cash-drawer . . . by granting a man of seventy-five a pension for having discharged an important trust for forty years they would have been guilty of no public robbery. . . ."[13]

The preceding September the patent of Edinburgh Theatre, the first licensed theater in the town, had expired. When the new patent was issued Scott had joined the proprietors by purchasing a share and had become one of its trustees. These included the Lord Provost of the Town, the Dean of the Faculty, Henry Mackenzie, and William Er-skine.[14] The new trustees were eager to provide entertainment superior to what Scott called "the garbage of melo-drama and pantomime" pre-sented by the previous lessees.[15] The management of the theater was therefore transferred to the actor Henry Siddons, nephew of the great John Kemble and son of the renowned Sarah Siddons.[16] Even before young Siddons was officially installed Scott showed him the manuscript of Joanna Baillie's play *The Family Legend*, and was exhilarated to report him "determined to bring it out with all the force he can muster."[17]

Scott was soon enthusiastically corresponding with Miss Baillie about the production. Assuming the piece to run about nine nights, he assured her, she might expect it to earn her not less than £300 or £400.[18] The new theater, in Corri's Rooms in Leith Walk, was "quite *a bijou*,"[19] "the most complete little thing I ever saw of the kind elegantly fitted up and sufficiently large for every purpose."[20] Miss Baillie quite agreed about the desirability of an intimate theater: "Large theaters are a bane and pest to the Drama . . ."[21]

The staging of the play would be rendered most colorful, Scott told her, by the contrast between the dark green tartan of the Campbells and the glaring red of the Macleans.[22] But there was a great danger that "Highland prejudices . . . still glowing though in ember" might lead the Macleans, "a numerous and hot-headed clan," to take in dudgeon the portrayal of their chief as a coward. Finding that Mackenzie and Erskine agreed with him on this point, Scott recommended that Maclean "be called Duart (actually the name of his property) and the Clan either *Clan Gillian* or isles-men or Mull-men."[23] The handling of his character might also be strengthened, Scott thought, and "a touch or two might be thrown in to exasperate his jealousy of Argyle."[24] One scene in a cavern was too long; in another "the shrieks of the seer and the piper at Argyle's chamber door," though splendid in the reading, would sound ludicrous on the stage.[25]

Miss Baillie mildly agreed to all Scott's suggestions.[26] She even meekly accepted more drastic cuts demanded by Siddons to bring the play within normal performing time. Some of these, Scott felt, resembled less the work of a pruning knife than of a tomahawk,[27] but when he saw the drama acted he admitted that the curtailment "had the effect of tearing ornaments from a balloon. The piece was less elegant . . . but it rose more lightly."[28] Scott checked the Highland costumes; he wrote a prologue and Henry Mackenzie an epilogue; both men attended the rehearsals.[29]

Excited anticipation in Edinburgh mounted high. Scott wrote letters to all the chiefs of Highland clans inviting them to come to the opening night and make it a great Scottish occasion.[30] Even the Lord Provost—by profession a stocking weaver—was "filled with a new-born zeal for the drama" and spoke of Siddons with enthusiasm, "of Miss Baillie's powers almost with tears of rapture." This theatric rage, however, which had seized the worthy Magistrate, Scott learned, "was owing to a large order for hose, pantaloons, and plaids."[31]

On the night of January 29 the curtain rose to a packed and eager audience.[32] "The crowd was insufferable," the pit "an aggregate mass of humanity," Scott wrote the authoress, and the boxes crammed with the representatives of rank and literature.[33] Charlotte had deliriously brought "a party of thirty friends" to a small box, "which she was obliged to watch like a clucking hen till she had gathered her whole flock."[34] Scott was tense with fear lest a scene shifter or a carpenter or some minor actor make a blunder and shatter the enchantment that soon gripped the entire assemblage.[35]

The play scored a tremendous success. "The banquet-scene," Scott wrote its author, was impressive, "and so was the combat." The scenes "between Lorn and Helen in the castle of Maclean, that between Helen and her Lover and the examination of Maclean himself in Argyle's castle, were applauded to the very echo." "The scene on the rock struck the utmost possible effect in the audience and you heard nothing but sobs on all sides."[36] David Hume enthusiastically told Scott that Helen was "the finest model of female virtue firmness and feeling" ever exhibited on the stage. Robert Blair, the Lord President of the Court of Session, expressed "his delight at having witnessed and aided the triumph of a tragedy which may rival the best in our language." Jeffrey applauded with violent animation.[37] At the end, when Siddons announced that the play would be given *"for the rest of the week,"* he was greeted with thunders of enthusiasm, cheers, and hats and handkerchiefs tossed into the air.[38]

Throughout the week the tragedy played to great houses; "Your laurels flourish," Scott told Miss Baillie, "in all their original verdure." He had promised Sophia, Walter, and Anne that they should see a performance, and on the first night of the following week "I went with all my little folks who were delighted, and cried like little pigs over Helen's distresses."[39] "Little Charles did not cry . . . not because he was such a pebble-hearted cur as Lancelot's dog Crab which did not shed a tear when the whole house was drowned in sorrow, but simply because he was not there. We thought him rather too young to see [a] theatrical exhibition—it is like eating peas in the bloom to hurry our enjoyments before we can fully relish them."[40]

*The Family Legend* won the extraordinary triumph of playing for still a third week.[41] It was followed immediately by a revival of one of Miss Baillie's earlier plays, *De Montfort*.[42] This had been coldly received by London playgoers a decade before, but now upon the keyed-up Edinburgh citizens it had a "deep and powerful effect."[43] "What do you think," Scott asked, "of De Montfort presented to a tossing audience filled with dread horror and consternation? Siddons acted ten thousand times better than I ever saw him . . ."[44] "Even the critical Aristarch Jeffrey was melted into tears."[45]

Later in the spring the play was put on again, with Mrs. Siddons joining her son's company in the role of Jane de Montfort. It was "the very finest performance ever seen in Edinburgh," Scott wrote Miss Baillie. "Every body agrees that she was never more herself . . . She fairly cried herself sick at her own part," and in the front of the house innumerable handkerchiefs were soaked with tears. "Never was there such a night for laundresses."[46]

Scott's enjoyment of the theater brought him a growing circle of friends among the acting profession. Young Siddons's uncle, John Philip Kemble, the great Macbeth of the day and a student of dramatic antiquities, became a welcome and frequent guest at Castle Street and Ashestiel. The actor jovially addressed Scott's butler, a fat dignitary named John Macbeth, as "Cousin Macbeth," and horrified the man's soul by the late hours and the deep drinking into which he allured the usually abstemious master of the house.[47]

Kemble's own bulk rivaled that of the butler. On horseback he became a grotesque rotundity that made Scott chuckle during their afternoon gallops at Ashestiel. Once, near the Ettrick, they were chased by a bull. "Come, King John," said Scott, "we must even take the water," and he and Sophia plunged into the turbulent stream. Kemble, who often talked in blank verse, halted on the bank, and solemnly exclaimed:

> "The flood is angry, Sheriff;
> Methinks I'll get me up into a tree."

But there were no trees with limbs strong enough to bear him, nor could he speedily have heaved his stately poundage aloft. He was therefore forced, "with the rueful dignity of Don Quixote," to follow them ponderously into the river.[48]

His sister, Mrs. Siddons, shared Kemble's trick of forming the commonest utterance in iambics. When the Lord Provost of Edinburgh, with whom she was dining, apologized for the roast's being too heavily salted, she responded with grandeur: "Beef cannot be too salt for me, my Lord!" And Scott loved to recall a time at the Ashestiel dining table when she terrified a page by exclaiming in a tragic contralto: "You've brought me water, boy,—I asked for beer."[49]

One of the actors in *The Family Legend*, a young man named Daniel Terry, had been trained as an architect under the distinguished James Wyatt but abandoned that profession for the stage. A student of literature, he was also a connoisseur whose knowledge ranged from old china to antique furniture and from medieval armor to Renaissance paintings. His admiration for Scott became so extravagant that he even imitated his penmanship and his way of speaking. Scott used to say that if he were called on to swear whether a document was in his handwriting, the best he could do would be to say that it was either his or Terry's; and although the actor had been brought up in Bath, no stranger would have doubted that his *burr* was that of a native Scot.[50]

A small, lively man with mobile features, he strove to look like Scott and taught his tiny eyebrows to lower in Scott's meditative frown. When he and the comedian Charles Mathews were thrown out of a gig, Terry escaped unhurt but Mathews received an injury that made him limp for life. "Dooms, *Dauniel*," Mathews exclaimed when they next met, "what a pity it wasna your luck to get the game leg, mon! Your

*Shirra* wad hae been the very thing, ye ken, an' ye wad hae been croose [cocky] till ye war coffined!"[51]

After the excitement of seeing Miss Baillie's plays, Scott settled down to hardly more than his usual expenditures of energy. He had urged her to allow *The Family Legend* to be published,[52] and presently told her that "my booksellers" would give her fifty guineas for a first edition of a thousand copies and twenty guineas more when a second thousand went to press.[53] John Ballantyne and Company consequently brought it out later that spring. "The booksellers shall be content," Scott promised the authoress, "with as little profit as can in reason be expected."[54] In fact, the publication of plays was seldom profitable; he did not tell her that any loss would be partly his own. At the end of March, "The play," he wrote her, "is now groaning through the press." In the course of the year, however, it did reach a second edition.[55]

Scott was also busy discharging his responsibilities as Anna Seward's literary executor. "The crossest thing I ever did in my life," he confessed to Miss Baillie, "was to poor Miss Seward. She wrote me in an evil hour (I had never seen her, mark that!) a long and most passionate epistle upon the death of a dear friend whom I had never seen neither, concluding with a charge not to attempt to answer the said letter for she was dead to the world &c &c &c. Never were commands more literally obeyed. I remained as silent as the grave till the Lady made so many inquiries after me that I was afraid of my death being prematurely announced by a sonnet or elegy. When I did see her however she interested me very much and I am now doing penance for my illbreeding by submitting to edit her posthumous poetry most of which is absolutely execrable."[56]

Scott's other labors were progressing briskly. The third volume of the *Somers Tracts* had issued from the press. So had the *Ancient British Drama*, "which looks very well," he wrote William Miller, "and I hope will do equally." And on March 15 "The Grammont"—the *Memoirs of the Court of Charles II*—"is today entirely out of my hands."[57] A review of the *Sadler Papers* about to appear in the next number of the *Quarterly* was sent by Gifford for Scott's approval and correction. A touch or two by the author of the memoir and notes of the work under review, the Editor thought, would be just what the article needed. "Make what alterations you think fit; all is at your mercy."[58] And in the course of the winter or early spring, Scott had even found time to review Maturin's *The Fatal Revenge* and Evans's *Old Ballads* for the May *Quarterly*.[59]

But none of these tasks were permitted to slacken Scott's work on Swift. He was now looking into the historical background of some of the political tracts ridiculing "the intended establishment of a Dublin Bank."[60] He had learned, too, that Lady Castlereagh had a numerous collection of letters that Swift had written her ancestress Mrs. Howard, the favorite of Queen Caroline. Could Lady Abercorn, he asked, use her friendship with Lady Castlereagh to gain him copies of these letters? There had been a clash leading to a duel and a political break between Canning and Lord Castlereagh, which made it awkward for Scott, as a known friend of Canning, to request the favor himself—though, he explained, "I am sure I am a sincere well-wisher to Lord Castlereagh whose conduct since that unfortunate quarrel has been so manly generous and patriotic."[61]

These wranglings of the cabinet vexed Scott; they were, he said, a disgrace to the country.[62] He and Laird Nippy had celebrated the victory over the French at Talavera with the joyful belief that the British Army would soon be in Madrid.[63] But instead of seizing the opportunity thus presented to them, the heirs of Pitt were yielding to personal animosities and internal feuds.[64] And this at the very time when strange seethings in France portended danger to Napoleon's power! The war in Spain ought to be kept up by exertions proportioned to the magnificence of the object, and there should be squadrons of frigates with ten thousand men each on the northern coast and in the Mediterranean.[65]

Despite these political turmoils Scott pushed forward happily both on *Swift* and on *The Lady of the Lake*. With polite diffidence he had requested the honor of being allowed to dedicate the edition of Swift to the Marquis of Abercorn, not feeling sure that he would regard it as any great compliment.[66] But Lady Abercorn replied for her magnificent lord that he would accept it with pleasure; even more, he would welcome having Scott's next poem dedicated to him as well.[67] To this unblushing solicitation Scott responded with graceful courtesy: ". . . the next tale of Chivalry shall certainly be Lord Abercorn's, that is it shall be *yours* my dear friend and you shall dispose of it as you please."[68]

As Scott progressed into the poem Lady Abercorn became almost frenzied in her eagerness to hear about it. Why did he not tell her its story? "I am sure Mrs. Scott, who is always so good to me, would have written it for me."[69] And a few days later: "Now shall I give the last Minstrel a good *scolding* and mingle the notes of discord with the songs of other times. If you did not mean to fulfil your promise why did you make it? And why do you tantalize me with promises of *extracts* and all sorts of fine things . . . I am sure you will be for throwing all the blame upon poor *Charlotte;* but I am too well acquainted with her to believe she is to blame."[70]

He would soon send her a specimen, Scott replied soothingly, if not a whole canto. "The tale cannot be very well sent without the verses, being no great matter in itself. . . . I have tried, according to promise, to make 'a knight of love who never broke a vow.' "[71] The middle of March found Scott able to write that he was sending printed proofs of the first two cantos.[72] A month later he sent the third and fourth cantos. "The fifth is going through the press and so soon as the sixth is achieved you shall have it all."[73] Lord Abercorn was pleased. "As to the Dedication," he himself wrote grandly, "I should be a good deal more vain than I am, were I not aware, that I am receiving not conferring a compliment."[74]

In one feature of the poem Scott felt that he had not succeeded. The love story was shouldered aside by the more warlike conflicts, and Ellen's lover, young Malcolm Graeme, never became more than a pallid figure beside the princely James and the fiery Roderick Dhu. Just why this should be, Scott didn't know, but "the Border blood seems to rise in my veins whenever I begin to try couplets," and although "I am in my own person as Hamlet says *indifferent honest* . . . a robber or Captain of Banditti never comes across me but he becomes my hero."[75] With Ellen he thought he had done "tolerably well"; but Malcolm, "spite of my best exertions," remained a lifeless manikin, "what the players call a *walking gentleman*,"[76] "a perfect automaton."[77] "It is incredible the pains it has cost me to give him a little dignity."[78]

His comment gave Lady Abercorn the courage to ask if he had ever been in love, veiling her impertinence by adding that if she "could judge by his way of talking about Mrs. Scott," she would conclude that he had.[79] The inquiry brought all the old ecstasy and torment throbbing back with painful intensity. Once again he remembered a green mantle whose folds robed all love and mystery, recalled how his heart had yearned toward Fettercairn, saw once more those blue eyes brimming with tears and felt the bitterness of betrayal, lived over again the dull ache of the days and the long agony of the nights.

None of this tumult did he allow to agitate his reply, though the reader may feel it as a vibration behind the tempered words. "I have had in my time," he told Lady Abercorn, "melancholy cause to paint from experience for I gained no advantage from three years constancy except the said experience and some advantage to my conversation and manners."[80] Only thus far would he go in hinting his "three years of dreaming and two years of wakening";[81] only thus far in drawing open the heavy curtains of reserve that swathed his deepest personal feelings.

"Mrs. Scott's match and mine," he continued, "was of our own making and proceeded from the most sincere affection on both sides which has rather increased than diminished during twelve years' marriage. But it was something short of love in all its forms which I suspect people only feel *once* in their lives."[82] Possibly the years of domestic serenity had made him forget the fiery four weeks' courtship with which he had swept away Charlotte's hesitancies, but hours crowned by happiness blur more easily in memory than those seared deep by a desperate wound. Perhaps the love he had lost led Scott to believe his emotions had been more cautious when he risked his heart again. "Folk who have been nearly drowned in bathing rarely venture a second time out of their depth."[83]

In April three of the children fell ill with "a dangerous and in-flammatory fever." For a fortnight their eldest son struggled for life; only bleeding, blistering, and drastic medicines brought about his re-covery. Little Anne and Charles were not so severely affected, but they too were very ill. Sophia alone among them escaped, although she helped her mother in nursing her two brothers and her sister. Even after Walter was no longer in danger he was left "the merest skeleton," so emaciated that he "would disgrace any decent mummy."[84] When this danger was past, all three fell prey to whooping cough. Not until the second week in May were they out of bed and on their feet again.[85]

Worry and watching over the children delayed Scott's work on his poem, but during their convalescence he dismissed its valedictory lines from his pen:

> Receding now, the dying numbers ring
>  Fainter and fainter down the rugged dell,
> And now the mountain breezes scarcely bring
>  A wandering witch-note of the distant spell—
> And now, 'tis silent all!—Enchantress, fare thee well![86]

"Dear James," he wrote Ballantyne, "—I send the grand *finale*, and so exit *The Lady of the Lake* from the head she has tormented for six months."[87] Splendid royal quartos were soon on their way to close friends and noble patrons. With those he gave to George Canning and John Wilson Croker, Scott expressed his relief at being able to rid himself of this encumbrance; "never was man more tired of his wife (and that's a bold word) than I am tired of the said Lady."[88]

Handsome copies also went to Lady Dalkeith, Lady Alvanley, Joanna Baillie, Lady Stafford, Richard Heber, Southey, and other friends.[89] George Ellis, Scott knew, would be reviewing the poem for the *Quarterly*. With a copy for Mrs. Clephane, Scott sent a note of thanks to her daughter: "When you have time to read over *The Lady of the Lake* notes you will see how much I have been obliged to your Gaelic erudition." He added that he had been thinking of visiting the Hebrides that summer, but might put it off, since he knew her family would not then be at Mull.[90] Still other copies Scott sent to his brother the Major and to Tom.[91]

The younger brother now seemed to have weathered his troubles. Professor Playfair had bought his house in Albany Street for £2,000.[92] The debts were almost all paid off. The reversion on Tom's share of their father's estate would come to about £2,000, a sum almost equal to his and Scott's original inheritance. The interest on this and on his wife's little fortune, his salary, and a few other resources, should add up, Scott calculated, to a comfortable income.[93] Over the course of long months Scott had often been obliged to beg his brother "to keep his patience and his temper" and assure him that everything possible was being done to extricate him from his embarrassments[94] and enable him to show his face in Scotland again.

One small source of income Scott himself had managed to bestow on his brother. The Clerks of Session had at their command the appointment of a number of subordinate positions in the General Register House of Scotland. At the beginning of Tom's troubles, in 1807, one of these had fallen vacant. Tom would willingly have accepted it and its income of £400 a year. But Scott scrupulously promoted to it an experienced clerk who had grown gray in the department, moved another into the post he vacated, and put Tom only in the lowermost of these positions, called an Extractorship and paying about £200–£250. Before ever assuming the duties of his new office, however, Tom had gone in 1808 to the Isle of Man, leaving his duties to be performed by a substitute who received a portion of the fees.[95]

The arrangement was not unusual; Scott was doing all George Home's work and receiving none of the income. Sooner or later Tom's affairs would be settled, and he would be able to step into a small but secure position. It was a severe blow when, after meetings that had been protracted over an entire year, the Judicature Commission, among other reforms, recommended in December, 1809, the abolition of all the Extractorships, but there was some compensation in the fact that their holders would all be pensioned off and that thus Tom would receive £130 a year for life to console him for the loss of a job on which he had never done a day's work. It was the way the political system worked; Scott did not question it, though he would have preferred Tom to have the appointment and the original £250.[96]

There is no evidence that Tom followed up Scott's suggestions about editing Shadwell and he certainly contributed no reviews to the *Quarterly*. He had, however, been collecting and sending Scott information about Manx customs and antiquities that might turn into a history of the Isle of Man.[97] Scott's pleasure in his brother's peaceful industry was rudely shattered when, near the end of June, there was an attack on Tom's pension in the House of Lords. The Earl of Lauderdale, pointing out that he had never performed any of his duties as Extractor, denounced the whole affair as a piece of gross political jobbery. Lord Holland concurred. He had a great esteem, he said, for Walter Scott and thought it a duty to reward literary merit regardless of party, but Thomas Scott was another matter. He had been appointed to an office he and his brother knew would be abolished, Lord Holland charged, and was therefore claiming indemnity for what could not be pronounced a loss.[98]

Scott was infuriated. It was not true, he retorted, that he had known the post would be swept away; he had made the appointment months before the Judicature Commission had been created, and it was not

Tom's fault that he had been unable to perform the duties of his office. This was simply a Whig attempt to plunder poor Tom of a pittance that was now important to him, "to rend the bread from an unfortunate man." To Colin Mackenzie and Robert Dundas he wrote indignantly: "I think Lord Melville will rouse a little in such a cause."[99] Far from preferring the pension, Tom was losing a considerable salary "which no power short of an Act of Parliament could have taken from him."[100]

Lord Lauderdale's accusations were vigorously answered by Lord Melville, the Duke of Montrose attended the session in the House of Lords on purpose to support him, and the pension bill, including the provision for Tom, was safely passed.[101] "Everybody here execrates Lord Lauderdale's unworthy conduct," Scott wrote Tom, "even those of his own party in politics. The bill then went directly back to the Commons and I learn this morning that it has been read three times in the House in the same evening and now lies for the Royal Assent."[102] So Tom had "fairly doubled Cape Lauderdale" and "may bid Lord L. kiss your cujo."[103]

That August, Lord Holland dined in Edinburgh with the Friday Club. Scott, who had come home only a few days before from a fortnight in the Hebrides, turned up at the dinner. When he suddenly found himself face to face with Holland, he looked straight through him.[104] At dinner he spoke to nobody but his neighbors. He attacked his mutton with such black looks that one of them felt surprise at his using his knife only on the roast. The other had his knee battered under the table by Scott's knee shaking with rage. Lord Holland, mildly ready to behave as if Scott had ignored him in a fit of poetic absent-mindedness, made a friendly gesture. Would Mr. Scott honor him by taking wine with him? But Scott growled a refusal. After two furious hours at the table he flung down his napkin and stamped out of the room.[105]

Francis Jeffrey felt amazed. It was the only time he had ever seen Scott discourteous.[106] Holland was gently puzzled. "The bard seems very angry at me," he remarked, "but really I don't know what it is for. It can't be about his brother's business—at least, if it be, he has been misinformed; for what I said was that if the arrangement was about an office, it was a job; but if it was meant as an indirect reward of Walter Scott, my only objection to it was that it was too little."[107]

In later years Scott made up this quarrel with Lord Holland, and the two men came to enjoy each other's company.[108] But at the time he gloried in his display of umbrage. "We met accidentally at a public party," he wrote Tom. "He made up to me but I remembered his part in your affair and *cut* him with as little remorse as an old pen."[109] But still worse was the thought that his honor had been impugned; even months later it made his blood boil. "The feeling was born with me," he proudly declared, "not to brook a disparaging look from an emperour."[110]

On the trip to the Hebrides from which he had just returned he
had been the guest of Ranald Macdonald, the Laird of Staffa, brother
of his friend Hector Macdonald Buchanan.[111] Though he felt sorry that
Mrs. Maclean Clephane would not be on Mull, it was perhaps, he had
decided, for the best. Between the Macdonalds and the Macleans there
remained "aching scars of the old wounds" from the times when they
had been rival tribes, and, for all their polish, the Laird of Staffa and
Mrs. Clephane were still such violent Highlanders as to have some of
the lingering antagonisms of the Capulets and the Montagues. He might
have found it embarrassing to be the guest of the one while the other
was in residence on the island.[112]

Scott had looked forward to this holiday with wild enthusiasm.[113]
Charlotte and Sophia went with him;[114] the younger children, now
recovered from the whooping cough, were at Ashestiel, playing with a
black greyhound puppy named Lady Juliana Berners, a gift from Ellis
early in July.[115] With the rising of the Court in the middle of the month
Scott and his party set out on their journey. Staffa's other guests included Henry Mackenzie's daughter Hannah and Mrs. Apreece, a young
widow distantly related to Scott, who had made herself a brilliant
Edinburgh hostess. They traveled slowly by horseback through
Argyllshire to Oban, Scott's Highland terrier Wallace frisking about the
cavalcade.[116]

Staffa had promised them a barge with eight rowers, a piper, and
his own company for pilot. From Oban, on a racing tide, they were
soon passing close to the Lady's Rock in the Sound of Mull, the very
rock of Joanna Baillie's *Family Legend*. Two miles farther, on a wild
and barren crag, the huge square tower and castellated ruins of Duart,
the seat of the Macleans, frowned down on the narrow channel, grimly
confronting on the opposing shores the castles of Dunstaffnage, Dunally,
and Ardtornish, the fortresses of feudal chiefs who had warred incessantly with one another.[117]

Late that night, wet, cold, and without their baggage, which was in
a wherry that could not keep pace with their rowers, the party landed
on Mull. Charlotte lost her shoes, Sophia a collection of bright pebbles,
and none of the men had their razors, so that they looked, Scott said,
like a Sanhedrin.[118] Next day they rode across the island on Highland
ponies, escorted by gillies and a piper with broadsword, dirk, and
pistol. They were met by Staffa's boats, with pipes playing and colors
snapping in the breeze. These brought them in state to Ulva House,
Macdonald's residence, where they were greeted by a salute of
musketry.[119]

Next day, July 18, they visited Staffa and Iona. In spite of his
lameness Scott scrambled over the broken columns of Fingal's Cave to
the very depths of the enormous cavern, where the black basalt pillars
towered as high as the roof of a cathedral over the sea rolling in "with

a voice like ten thousand giants."[120] In Scott's honor their boatmen solemnly christened a great stone at its mouth the "Clachan an Bairdh Sassenach more," the stone of the great Saxon poet.[121] The pibroch awakened tremendous echoes in the vaulting while they downed libations of whiskey and a bard made a long Gaelic oration. Unable to understand a word, Scott "could only receive it," he said, "as a silly beauty does a fine-spun compliment—bow and say nothing."[122] But he did gather that he was being praised for "burnishing the armour of the mighty dead" and for being the friend of the chieftain Staffa.[123]

From Staffa they were rowed across six miles of open sea to Iona, that remote island where St. Columba had founded a monastery in the sixth century and from which "the light of Christianity shone forth on Scotland and Ireland."[124] On the beach a crowd of almost naked boys and girls clamored for charity and offered for sale green pebbles each of which was believed to have the virtue of granting a single wish.[125] Charlotte bought some for a necklace and Scott several to have set into a brooch for Joanna Baillie.[126] From the shore the party made their way to the remains of the thirteenth-century church, not beautiful, Scott thought, "but curious to the Antiquary."[127]

A gale was now threatening, and they had twenty miles to row back to Ulva against an Atlantic tide. The rough water and the keen blast made all the ladies seasick, and excited, Scott said, "a combustion in the stomachs" of all the men except himself and Staffa.[128] "Mine . . . was no otherwise troublesome than by demanding frequent supplies of cold beef and biscuits."[129] Tugging at their oars for five hours, and singing in wild chorus old ditties of clan battles, the boatmen got the party to Ulva at ten that night, wet to the skin and ready for bed.[130]

From this visit to the western islands Scott brought back impressions of bleak grandeur and misty visions of a poem set in its wild scenes. The bareness of that treeless landscape, "huge barren hills wrapped in endless mist torn by unceasing cataracts," made him reflect that those waters bore "no more proportion to the excavations and ravines" they gouged "out of the bosom of the hills than human passions do to the consequences of their indulgence." Someday he would have to compose a tale of stark and violent emotion enacted amid these stark island rocks.[131]

Long before his return to Edinburgh all England and Scotland were ringing with the praises of *The Lady of the Lake*. Throughout the entire spring anticipation had reached feverish heights. In May the English bibliophile Thomas Frognall Dibdin had written Scott that everyone in London was frantic for it: "We are all here panting 'like the hart after the water brooks' for your *Lady of the Lake*."[132]

When the volume at last appeared the enthusiasm of its readers burst all bounds.[133] Scott had accomplished, Heber exclaimed, what no writer had ever done before: ". . . produced in succession and that with trifling intervals three great works of genius without the least sensible exhaustion or deterioration of your powers." "The Harp of the North," he said ecstatically, "was never before so struck or so apostrophized."[134] Southey had found the book lying on his table when he returned home in the evening and had been unable to go to bed until he had finished it.[135]

Even Francis Jeffrey joined the applause. There were, of course, details in the poem to which he took exception, but his tone of magisterial superiority had completely vanished. He even sent the proof sheets of his review to Scott with a letter apologizing for past offenses. "I am now sensible that there were needless asperities in my review of *Marmion*. . . . But I think you have generosity enough to construe me rightly in stating all these things, and to believe me when I say that I am sincerely proud both of your genius and of your glory, and that I value your friendship more highly than most either of my literary or my political opinions."[136]

Remembering, no doubt, the time of the *Marmion* review and the dinner refrigerated by Charlotte's glacial courtesy, Jeffrey wound up his letter by inviting Scott to *two* dinners: one on Tuesday, August 14, with Archibald Alison, Professor Playfair, "and two American ladies who are very much your admirers"; the other on Thursday, with some friends of Sydney Smith, who were just returned from the Highlands. Presuming, Jeffrey inserted parenthetically, "that this review will break no squares between us."[137]

There was praise enough to justify his hope. The reflective Spenserian stanzas beginning each canto, Jeffrey thought, were written "with great tenderness and beauty."[138] The brilliant picture of the barges of Roderick Dhu breasting the waves of the Lake to the skirl of the pipes, the spears and axes of his clansmen glittering in the sunlight, their banners streaming—all he found splendid: "The effect of the sounds—and the wild character and strong peculiar nationality of the whole procession, are given with inimitable spirit and power of expression."[139] The sending of the Fiery Cross on its wild journey to summon the chieftain's followers, though not without some exaggeration, he said, "shows great power."[140]

His summary was, for Jeffrey, almost pure panegyric. The poem displayed "a medley of bright images and glowing, set carelessly and loosely together—a diction tinged successively with the careless richness of Shakespeare, the harshness and antique simplicity of the old romances . . . alternately minute and energetic—sometimes artificial, and frequently negligent, but always full of spirit and vivacity—abounding in images . . ." Its richness, profusion of incident, and shifting brilliance of color reminded Jeffrey of the witchery of Ariosto. *The Lady of the Lake*, he concluded, was superior to both its predecessors, "more polished in its diction, and more regular in its versification; the story is constructed with infinitely more skill and address; there is a greater proportion of pleasing and tender passages, with much less antiquarian detail: and, upon the whole, a larger variety of characters, more artfully and judiciously contrasted."[141]

Eulogies poured in from distant places. Adam Ferguson, now a captain in Wellington's army in Portugal, wrote from Lisbon that he received nightly invitations to evening parties to read aloud from it. His rendering of the stag hunt was "always followed with bursts of applause"; and "to the good offices of the *Lady*," he said, "I owed many a nice slice of ham and rummer of hot punch . . . during the long rainy nights . . ."[142] In the lines at Torres Vedras he read the battle scene from Canto VI to his crouching troops, "and the listening soldiers only interrupted him by a joyous huzza, whenever the French shot struck the bank close above them."[143]

The general public were delirious about the poem. The quarto edition of 2,050, selling at two guineas, lasted less than a fortnight. Four successive octavo editions followed, rising in numbers from 3,000 for the first of these to 6,000 each for the third and fourth.[144] Within three months, Scott wrote Tom, the sales had been "in number 14,000 copies and in value £9,000."[145] In another month sales had risen to 17,000; in eight days more to 20,000.[146] Editions were swallowed up faster than the printers could turn them out. On October 15, "the edition now gone to press will make up 23,000 and Ballantyne says it won't answer his orders."[147] And eight months after publication "no less than 25,000 copies have disappeared," he happily wrote John Leyden in India, "and the demand is so far from being exhausted that another edition of 3,000 is now at press."[148]

*The Lady of the Lake* had shattered all records for the sale of poetry, and the house of John Ballantyne and Company had scored a resounding triumph. Scott's earnings can only be conjectured. As author he had received two thousand guineas for the poem. But as publisher he must have made much more. Only a quarter-share of the poem had been sold, to William Miller of London. The other three-quarters the Company retained, and on this Scott was entitled to half of all the earnings.[149]

His glittering success did not inflate his self-esteem. Though he might well have believed, he said, that "I had at last fixed a nail in the proverbially inconstant wheel of Fortune," he rated his own poetic talent modestly enough. "It must not be supposed that I was either so ungrateful, or so superabundantly candid, as to despise or scorn the value of those whose voice had elevated me so much higher than my own opinion told me I deserved. I felt, on the contrary, the more grateful to the public, as receiving that from partiality which I could not have claimed from merit."[150]

At the height of the furore James Ballantyne addressed a solemn question to Scott. "Will you excuse me, Mr. Scott, but I should like to ask you what you think of your own genius as a poet, in comparison with that of Burns?" "There is no comparison whatever," Scott replied decisively, "—we ought not to be named in the same day."[151] Around the same time, stepping into Scott's library, James found ten-year-old Sophia alone there. "Well, Miss Sophia," he asked, "how do you like *The Lady of the Lake?*" "Oh," she responded, "I have not read it; papa says there is nothing so bad for young people as reading bad poetry."[152]

Her eight-year-old brother had not even heard of the poem. One afternoon he came home from the High School, his face smeared with blood and tears. "Well, Wat," said his father, "what have you been fighting about today?" "He had been called a *lassie*," the boy said. "Indeed!" exclaimed his mother, "this was a terrible mischief to be sure." "You may say what you please, mamma," Wat answered, "but I dinna think there's a *waufer* [shabbier] thing in the world than to be a lassie, to sit boring at a clout." One of the boys, it turned out, had called him "The Lady of the Lake"; Wat thought he had been called a girl, an insult that demanded a blow.[153]

Scott told this story at the Clerks' Table; a few days later one of his colleagues was at Castle Street. "Gilnockie, my man," he said, "you cannot surely help seeing that great people make more work about your father than they do about me or any other of your uncles"—why did the boy think that was? Wat pondered a moment, then replied gravely, "It's commonly *him* that sees the hare sitting." His father's quickness of eye when they were coursing after hares was the only distinction the child knew.[154]

The popularity of the poem had fantastic reverberations. Crowds set out to overrun the once lonely scenery of Loch Katrine. It was just before the season when people went on excursions, and in consequence every house and inn for miles around was jammed with a constant succession of visitors and did a booming business.[155] The lake had formerly been visited by fifty or sixty carriages a year; within the first six months after the publication of *The Lady of the Lake* the number rose to 297![156] One canny inn-keeper built a new hotel at Callander to take care of the hosts who were eager to see Ellen's Isle. A peasant named James Stewart made a small fortune showing the scenes of the poem to excited tourists.[157] Traffic so increased that "the post-horse duty in Scotland rose to an extraordinary degree."[158] It became more fashionable to see the Trossachs than to make the Grand Tour of Europe. The hordes of sightseers who then began pouring into those mountain glens has never ceased.

# The War-Horn Braying

## (Criticism: *The Lay of the Last Minstrel, Marmion, The Lady of the Lake*)

THE THREE COLORFUL LONG POEMS Scott had brought out in the course of six years had raised him to a peak above all rivals. The great poetic voices of the preceding half-century—Gray, Goldsmith, Johnson—had fallen silent in death; no other commanding voices had taken their place. Though Scott himself was among the earliest admirers of Wordsworth and Coleridge, those two poets had still slowly to create the understanding that would respond to their strange new mingling of the natural and the visionary. And none of Byron's dark and fiery heroes had yet appeared to startle and enthrall the world. Scott stood alone.

Child prodigy though he had been, his growth as a poet had not been rapid. But for the Scott of the long narrative poems and the still later novels, few would read his earliest ballads and lyrics, and if they did, might well feel amazed at the young Jane Cranstoun's thrilled enthusiasm when she heard him recite "William and Helen." Scott really first emerged as a poet in some of the daring emendations, fusions, and invented lines in the *Minstrelsy*, but all this work must be regarded as no more than preparatory for *The Lay of the Last Minstrel*, in which he finally reached full stride. It was late for a poet; Scott was then thirty-five, an age at which all the marvelous fruition of Shelley and Keats had long been cut short by death.

In Scott's first three narrative poems there is thus none of the amazing development that takes place from *Queen Mab* and *Alastor* to *Prometheus Unbound*, or from *Endymion* to Keats's great odes. But if *The Lay of the Last Minstrel* does not attain the greatness of the later work of these two poets, it has passed beyond their youthful wandering richness; it is the work of an assured maturity. *Marmion* and *The Lady of the Lake* were to be more closely knit in structure, but neither was a leap from incoherence to control. Scott's apprentice days were in the past. From the time of the *Lay* onward, he might sometimes be careless; he was never uncertain.

The metrical debt of the *Lay* to Coleridge, Scott himself exaggerated with characteristic generosity. Certainly he was struck with the magic of *Christabel* when he heard parts of it from the lips of John Stoddart, and no doubt Coleridge made him see more vividly than ever the possibilities of the irregular beat, the tetrameter couplets interwoven with other variant rhymes, now and then broken by a trimeter.[1] But almost if not absolutely all of this was in the ballad forms that thronged to Scott's memory, and his handling of the beat evokes a tension emotionally very different from Coleridge's atmosphere of slow and haunted terror. Scott's rhythm is not that of brooding enchantment but of speed, boldness, movement, unfaltering as the flight of an arrow.

The very opening of the *Lay* is in contrast to *Christabel's* still and midnight darkness. "The feast was over in Branksome tower," it sets out briskly, with rapid pictures of the lofty hall, the glowing fire, the steel-clad warriors, the saddled horses, a sense of imminent action:

> Nine and twenty knights of fame
> Hung their shields in Branksome-Hall;
> Nine and twenty squires of name
> Brought them their steeds to bower from stall.[2]

Then come the nervous questions and answers:

> Why do these steeds stand ready dight,
> Why watch these warriors, arm'd, by night?—
> They watch, to hear the blood-hound baying:
> They watch, to hear the war-horn braying;
> To see St. George's red cross streaming,
> To see the midnight beacon gleaming:
> They watch, against Southern force and guile.[3]

Soon William of Deloraine is clattering through the darkness of that nocturnal journey to Melrose Abbey and the tomb of Michael Scott; until the end of the tale the great gallop of swift verses never slackens.

Scott makes brilliant use of the old minstrel who tells the story to the assembled ladies of Newark Castle. Like the medieval framework in *The Rime of the Ancient Mariner*, like the mariner imposing his spell on the wedding guest, the minstrel mediates between past and present, establishes an emotional environment, and gives the poem esthetic distance. Both Coleridge and Scott summon up out of remote times narrators to whom the wild and sometimes eerie narrative poses no problems of credence. For them the Spectre Bark, Life-in-Death, the enchantress Lady of Branksome, the wizard Michael Scott, the Goblin Page, are all realities, and the reader accepts their belief.

It is true that Scott's minstrel, outliving all his fellow bards by almost a hundred years, is seen as still surviving into the latter part of the seventeenth century, but Scott gives the old man such truth and pathos that the anachronism does not touch our minds. The feeble wanderer, fallen on days of neglect, but still loving his harp and his art, is a breathing figure; as his fingers make an uncertain warbling amid the strings and then sweep with more assurance over the chords, while he smiles and catches fire with his theme, we cannot but believe. His survival into a more skeptical age is even made the means of giving him a deeper solidity; he knows that men now begin to doubt some of the wonders he still believes:

> "I cannot tell how the truth may be;
> I say the tale as 'twas told to me."[4]

The return to the ancient harper at the close and beginning of each canto, his tremulous pleasure in the praise of the listening ladies, the growing confidence of his wild notes, all make the story *his* story and give it the authority of his faith.

He does not doubt the widowed Lady of Branksome's command of sorcery nor her bitter determination to use her powers, if need be, to ensure that her daughter shall never marry the family's hereditary enemy Lord Cranstoun:

> "Your mountains shall bend,
> And your streams ascend
>     Ere Margaret be our foeman's bride."[5]

On her behest, Deloraine spurs breathlessly over hill and stream to the pillared arches of the Abbey, there under the dim lights to heave aside the massy stone from the wizard's tomb and take his Book of Might.

Some of the lines picturing the chancel foreshadow, though they do not attain the full magic of Keats's rendering of, Madeline's moonlit chamber in *The Eve of Saint Agnes*:

> Full many a scutcheon and banner riven,
> Shook to the cold night-wind of heaven . . .
> The moon on the east oriel shone
> Through slender shafts of shapely stone,
>     By foliaged tracery combined;
> Thou would'st have thought some fairy's hand
> 'Twixt poplars straight the ozier wand,
>     In many a freakish knot, had twined; . . .
> The silver light, so pale and faint,
> Shew'd many a prophet, and many a saint,
>     Whose image on the glass was dyed . . .
> The moon-beams kiss'd the holy pane,
> And threw on the pavement a bloody stain.[6]

The morning scene in which Margaret steals out to a meeting with her lover echoes one from *Christabel* and anticipates Keats's description of Madeline and Porphyro creeping forth from the castle at dawn:

> Why does she stop, and look often around,
>     As she glides down the secret stair,
> And why does she pat the shaggy blood-hound,
>     As he rouses him up from his lair;
> And, though she passes the postern alone,
>     Why is not the watchman's bugle blown?
>
> The ladye steps in doubt and dread,
> Lest her watchful mother hear her tread;
> The ladye caresses the rough blood-hound,
> Lest his voice should waken the castle round;
> The watchman's bugle is not blown,
> For he was her foster-father's son.[7]

There is a fine stroke of realism when Cranstoun, returning from this rendezvous, encounters Deloraine and unhorses him; Deloraine is a tried warrior, but he is worn out with a night's hard riding, and is stretched senseless on the plain. Though there is magic in the story, there are no impossible feats of arms. At Lord Cranstoun's order the Goblin Page conveys Deloraine's body to the Lady of Branksome's door, and then embarks on his own course of malicious mischief. Invisibly he leads the boy-heir of the Buccleuchs into the forest to be lost, and himself magically takes the child's place within the castle walls.

The child falls into the hands of an English host, come to demand that Deloraine be surrendered to them for having broken truce in a border raid. Bale fires blaze out warning of their approach; there ensues a tumult of Border clansmen riding in to the castle's defense. The gathering is no distant echo of Homer's catalog of the ships. When Thomas Hardy said he had been reading the *Iliad* and it was very good, almost as good as Scott, he was making a daring joke but not invoking a fantastic parallel.

> Mount, mount for Branksome, every man!
> Thou, Todrig, warn the Johnstone clan,
>     That ever are true and stout—
> Ye need not send to Liddesdale;
> For when they see the blazing bale,
> Elliotts and Armstrongs never fail—[8]

Watt Tinlinn leaps down from a shaggy nag, cursing the invaders:

> "They crossed the Liddel at curfew hour,
> And burn'd my little lonely tower:

> The fiend receive their souls therefor!
> It had not been burnt this year and more."[9]

It is characteristic of Scott that even in a scene of such high excitement he can make a joke. Scores of other clansmen follow, from Teviot, Aill, and Ettrick: Thirlestane with his motto, "Ready, aye ready"; the aged Knight of Harden; Scotts of Eskdale; warriors from Yarrow-cleuch, Hind-haugh-swair, Woodhouselee, Chester-glen—all shouting their gathering-cry of "Bellenden."

The English army draws up before the castle, crimson banners waving, helms and shields glistening, kettledrums sounding. On the battlements ax and spear gleam, sable smoke eddies from towers where cauldrons of pitch and molten lead seethe and bubble. The English demand that Deloraine be turned over to them and that two hundred of their force be garrisoned in the castle as a guarantee against future raids. The child they will take to London to be bred as King Edward's page.

The Lady of the castle proudly defies them. Deloraine will fight in single combat to cleanse him of the charge against him.

> "For the young heir of Branksome's line,
> God be his aid, and God be mine;
> Through me no friend shall meet his doom;
> Here, while I live, no foe finds room."[10]

The English are about to attack when a rider brings them warning that a Scottish host under Douglas, Maxwell, and Home are marching to the castle's relief. Lord Dacre fiercely cries, "And let them come!," but Lord Howard counsels accepting the terms. The approaching force, as yet unknown to the castle's defenders, will soon be there; ten thousand Scots are too many against whom to risk a kingdom's power.

> "Let Musgrave meet fierce Deloraine,
> In single fight, and, if he gain,
> He gains for us; but if he's cross'd,
> 'Tis but a single warrior lost;
> The rest, retreating as they came,
> Avoid defeat, and death, and shame."[11]

Dacre sullenly yields, and it is agreed that if Deloraine vanquishes Musgrave the child shall be returned and the English army retreat to Cumberland. When the Scottish army arrives, consequently, instead of joining in battle, the two hosts mingle in truce and the leaders of both sides feast together within the castle. Though its Lady has been treating Deloraine with magic potions, she fears that he will not be sufficiently recovered to do battle. If so, Harden or Thirlestane may have to fight in Deloraine's place. But the following morning brings a surprise:

> Himself, the Knight of Deloraine,
> Strong, as it seem'd, and free from pain,
>     In armour sheath'd from top to toe,
> Appear'd, and craved the combat due.
> The Dame her charm successful knew,
> And the fierce chiefs their claims withdrew.[12]

In the combat Musgrave is slain. Suddenly, from within the castle, half-naked and ghastly, Deloraine appears. It has been Lord Cranstoun disguised in his armor who has fought the match. Now Cranstoun leads the child to his mother. "For this fair prize," he says, kneeling at her feet, "I've fought and won." The Lady yields and pledges her daughter's hand to her family's noble foe:

> "Not you, but Fate has vanquish'd me;
> Their influence kindly stars may shower
> On Teviot's tide and Branksome's tower,
>     For pride is quell'd, and love is free."[13]

The marriage takes place in the last canto. Much of the narrative detail is anticlimactic. Though the successive ballads sung at the festivity —Albert Graeme's "For love will still be lord of all," Fitztraver's song of the Lady Geraldine, Harold's of the lovely Rosabelle—are appropriate enough in theme, they seem mainly designed to fill it out to the length of the other cantos. Scott still had to dispose of the Goblin Page, who had been one of the original sources of the poem but who, as he jokingly said, had "contrived, from the baseness of his natural propensities . . . to slink down into the kitchen."[14] With a flash of lightning and a dread-voiced summons "Gylbin, Come!" he disappears, and Deloraine believes he sees in the gloom the awesome figure of Michael Scott. In the terrified confusion no mention is made of what happens to the wizard's Book.

Though the Goblin Page is disposed of clumsily, Jeffrey and the critics who have echoed him have been merely conventional in deploring the Page as a blot on the story. His malicious tricks are as much a part of the poem's design as the Lady of Branksome's dabbling in enchantment. They are woven essentially into the plot; without the Page's agency the child heir of Buccleuch would not have been taken by the English, the combat to redeem him would have been unnecessary, and the reconciliation between the Scott clan and the Cranstouns given no cause. Objections to the Page are but a lingering of the neoclassical feeling that the grotesque should not be mingled with the heroic, and are of no more weight than the protest that in a serious poem Scott does not fear occasionally to be comic.

Despite its flawed ending, the poem is a great achievement. It is full of dash, brilliance, and glowing color. Its pace is almost breathless. Above all, it is steeped in the very atmosphere of the wild and disorderly sixteenth century it portrays and the Border conflicts between Scotland and England that Scott knew so well. It powerfully re-creates the colors of the time, vigorously reflecting the confusion of bravery, fierceness, and credulity with flashes of gentleness and nobility which jostled in that tumultuous world. Though its people are not subtly conceived, they are people, neither pallid shadows nor ideal images but full-blooded and passionate. They dwell in a real world, not the fairy land of Ariosto or of French courtly romance. For all the romantic elements in *The Lay of the Last Minstrel*, it glows with the steel light of human truth. Scott has conjured up a vision of the past the essential elements of which are revealingly true.

The scene of *Marmion* broadens from the Border clash of the *Lay* to the conflict between the entire might of England and Scotland, and comes to its climax in the slaughterous battle of Flodden Field. More tightly constructed than the earlier poem, it has no declining aftermath; when Marmion's eyes glaze on the battlefield the ending swiftly follows his death. Sardonically, a peasant's body is mistaken for his and buried in his ornate Gothic tomb, and De Wilton and Clare are peacefully united.

The introductory epistles were an ill-judged intrusion on the narrative, as many of Scott's friends noted at the time of publication. Though their passages of meditation, landscape painting, and reminiscence often have their own pensive interest, no reader welcomes these interpolations to an exciting story, any more than between some of the fiery scenes of *The French Revolution* we should exult in finding sections of Carlyle's *Reminiscences*. The epistles might better have been published separately, as had been originally intended.

Scott liked to believe that "the force in the *Lay*" was "thrown on style,—in *Marmion*, on description."[15] This is the kind of pleasant fancy in which authors sometimes indulge after the event. The descriptions in *Marmion* are neither more numerous nor more brilliant than those in the *Lay*, and if a sensitive reader were presented with passages from each that did not betray their origin by local references it is doubtful that he would be able to assign them on stylistic grounds alone to their proper poems. The versification, like that of the *Lay*, is rushing, hasty, a bit careless, but vibrant and rich in imagery.

Only Milton, among poets in English, excels Scott in the emotional reverberations of his place names. Milton ranges, of course, over vaster reaches: the globe, the heavens, and the remotest regions of the past are not too grandiose for his great theme. Scott remains within the more limited geographical and historical setting he has chosen, but the concrete names give the poems extraordinary color and solidity. Although local names stud the *Lay*—Penchryst Pen, Woodkerrick, Eskdale, Murdieston, Rangleburn—*Marmion* displays even deeper hues of historical association, from the somber majesty of Holyrood to the solemnity of Holy Island, the trumpet clangor of Tantallon, and the dark resonances of Flodden itself.

The opening scene glows with splendor. Marmion—warrior, statesman, royal favorite, envoy from Henry VIII to James IV—is received at Norham Castle in Northumberland. St. George's banner streams from the ramparts, Marmion's entourage paces over the drawbridge into the Castle yard, Marmion on his red-roan charger, his cheeks browned and furrowed, his helmet burnished gold, his armor plate of Milan steel. Pursuivants in tabards and silver scutcheons welcome him at the donjon-gate:

> They hail'd him Lord of Fontenaye,
> Of Lutterword and Scrivelbaye,
>     Of Tamworth tower and town.[16]

Beneath the glitter, though, certain elements in Marmion's character are swiftly established. The harper chants a wild Border-ballad:

> Scantly Lord Marmion's ear could brook
> The Harper's barbarous lay;
> Yet much he praised the pains he took,
>     And well those pairs did pay.[17]

When Heron's nephew voices fears that the Palmer who will serve as Marmion's guide holds converse with demons, Marmion brusquely scorns his anxiety:

> —"Let pass," quoth Marmion, "by my fay,
> This man shall guide me on my way,
> Although the great arch-fiend and he
> Had sworn themselves of company."[18]

The Palmer, he sneers, will do well enough to charm the way with "some lying legend." The following morning at dawn Marmion crosses the Tweed into Scotland. With him goes the Palmer, his dark, gaunt visage almost hidden by his cowl.

While Marmion is making his way from the Border up to Edinburgh, on Holy Island at Lindisfarne a nun is being sentenced to death. Constance de Beverley had broken her vows and is condemned to be walled up alive within the convent's secret underground vaults. Seduced by Marmion, she had fled and lived with him disguised as his page, then later been abandoned when, to add to his estates, he sought the hand of the Lady Clare. He had gotten rid of De Wilton, the Lady's betrothed by an accusation of treason, supporting the falsehood with forged documents. Though De Wilton claimed the right to defend his honor in combat, Heaven had not sustained the innocent; he had been defeated by Marmion and forced to flee abroad. Now the betrayed Constance, just before her death, gives the Abbess evidence of Marmion's villainy.

The earliest readers of *Marmion*, who had no Lara or Manfred to compare him with, were startled by his mingling of evil and magnificence, and tended, as Scott had foreseen, to be shocked not so much by the seduction of Constance as by his committing the mean crime of forgery. But Scott's note is correct in pointing out that from the Middle Ages on, forgery had been common; there is an entire chapter on the subject in Coulton's *Five Centuries of Religion*, and indeed forgery had no more frequent reason than the desire, like Marmion's to add to one's own possessions. The names of two of his lordships may even remotely insinuate this strain in his machinations, "Lutterword" and "Scrivelbaye," with their echoes of the manipulation of uttered words and the arts of the scrivener or scribbler.

Skeptic though Marmion is about the teachings of the Church, his conscience troubles him, and in his mind he hears again

> the desperate maid
> Threaten by turns, beseech, upbraid.[19]

The belief in the supernatural which he shares with many other unbelievers leads to his midnight encounter on the moors of Gifford with the Elfin Knight, who tumbles him in the mire. His opponent is in reality the Palmer in disguise—in fact doubly disguised, for the Palmer is in turn none other than De Wilton, secretly come home from the Holy Land to regain his good name.

Then come the scenes of the Scottish camp and Court, the prancing steeds, the heralds, Bute, Islay, Marchmount, Rothsay, the Lord Lion King-at-arms, the sable turrets of Edinburgh and the Castle on its height, the innumerable tents of the armed host, the gorgeous pageantry of Holyrood. King James rejects all peace overtures and warns Marmion:

> "Perchance our meeting next may fall
> At Tamworth, in his castle-hall."[20]

Marmion replies with equal haughtiness;

> "Nottingham has archers good,
> And Yorkshire men are stern of mood;
> Northumbrian prickers wild and rude.
> . . . Many a banner will be torn,
> And many a knight to earth be borne,
> And many a sheaf of arrows spent,
> Ere Scotland's King shall cross the Trent:
> Yet pause, brave Prince, while yet you may!"[21]

But James, blindly infatuated, is unmoved:

> "Southward I march by break of day."[22]

In Edinburgh the Abbess finds De Wilton and gives him the proofs of Marmion's guilt. These he shows at Tantallon to Marmion's host, the old Earl of Angus.

> "A letter forged! Saint Jude to speed!
> Did ever Knight so foul a deed! . . .
> Thanks to Saint Bothan, son of mine,
> Save Gawain, ne'er could pen a line."[23]

The Earl provides De Wilton with armor and readmits him to the order of knighthood. When Marmion is ready to depart for England, Angus sternly refuses to take his hand:

> "The hand of Douglas is his own;
> And never shall in friendly grasp
> The hand of such as Marmion clasp."[24]

Marmion is infuriated:

> "An 'twere not for thy hoary beard,
> Such hand as Marmion's had not spared
> To cleave the Douglas' head!"[25]

Douglas orders his men to raise the drawbridge and drop the portcullis; Marmion dashes the rowels into his charger:

> Like arrow through the archway sprung,
> The ponderous gate behind him rung;
> To pass there was such scanty room,
> The bars descending, razed his plume.
>
> The steed along the drawbridge flies,
> Just as it trembled on the rise.[26]

On the march south Marmion learns that at dawn, clad in armor and mounted on the Earl's own steed, the Palmer has ridden off, and in a sudden light divines his identity.

From here the poem moves swiftly to the carnage of Flodden. The battle scenes are a superb tumult.

> They close, in clouds of smoke and dust,
> With sword-sway, and with lance's thrust; . . .
>
> And, first, the ridge of mingled spears
> Above the brightening cloud appears;
> And in the smoke the pennons flew,
> As in the storm the white sea-mew.[27]

Marmion is mortally wounded:

> His hand still strain'd the broken brand:
> His arms were smear'd with blood and sand:
> Dragg'd from among the horses' feet,
> With dinted shield and helmet beat,
> The falcon-crest and plumage gone,
> Can that be haughty Marmion![28]

The poem does not fall into the errors that weakened the last canto of the *Lay*. There are no irrelevant interpolations and no prolonged gatherings of loose ends. As Marmion lies dying the battle rages on; a single last stanza tells how De Wilton fights valiantly, regains his heritage and his good name, and is united with Clare; and the end still pulsates with the high excitement of Marmion's death.

It is not true, as some critics have argued, that the great national catastrophe of Scottish arms and the death of James IV make it impossible for us to care about the fate of Marmion. Such a generalization would mean that all concern for Sidney Carton must be drowned in the blood of the Reign of Terror, and the grief of Troilus forgotten amid the fall of Troy. And has anyone ever felt in reading *War and Peace* that the tremendous drama of the retreat from Moscow left us indifferent about what happens to Prince André, Pierre, and Natasha? From the beginning of *Marmion* to the end the dark villain-hero holds our interest and is the center of attraction, and the crashing scenes around him only enhance his dramatic fascination.

Nor can I feel, with Lockhart, that "The combination of mean felony with so many noble qualities" is a "blot in the poem"[29] or that we cannot sympathize with so ambiguous a protagonist. The second of these statements is indeed demonstrably untrue, as Byron's glamorous hero-villains were soon to prove. Marmion is far more subtly and powerfully conceived than any of the characters in the *Lay*, and far more complex, in his mingling of courage, pride, brilliance, and pollution, all tinged with guilty superstition and shot through with pangs of remorse. And Marmion is perhaps no inappropriate representative of the unscrupulous, powerful, wily, glittering, and monstrous Henry VIII, who is his Sovereign.

The real weakness in the poem is that Marmion has no antagonist of like stature and is brought to death and defeat at the hands, not of De Wilton, whom he has injured, but of some unknown soldier on the battlefield. De Wilton and Clare are but pallid figures, and Constance is little more substantial, no more deeply conceived than Lord Cranstoun and Margaret in the *Lay*. But there the lightness of the character drawing did not matter, for Cranstoun has no enemy of greater solidity to overthrow and is at least an active agent in the outcome. De Wilton is not; even his recovery of the forged letter is achieved by luck rather than a clearly planned course of action. Had Scott realized him more vividly and brought him into a more violent and effective clash with Marmion the poem might have risen to still more dramatic heights.

So reflection suggests, but it is doubtful if many have had such thoughts in the heat of reading. The glow and color, the rapidity of movement, the splendor of description, the rising excitement, the rush from Marmion's dash across the drawbridge at Tantallon to the tumult, bloodshed, and tension of Flodden, and always Marmion himself, double-hearted, dazzling, and unworthy, sweep all before them. On a broader canvas than the *Lay*, holding in imagination all sixteenth-century Scotland as she faced her powerful southern foe, *Marmion* paints a picture of almost epic scope and impressiveness. This time it is not merely a Border fray that is the background but the deadly clash of two great kingdoms.

*Marmion*, unlike the *Lay*, sustains its dramatic intensity to the end. In turn, *The Lady of the Lake* surmounts *Marmion*'s crucial flaw. Roderick Dhu and James V, predestined antagonists, give the poem two almost evenly matched and powerful opponents. The fiery and vindictive clan chieftain, inflamed by his people's wrongs, though half a barbarian, is still capable of a noble chivalry; the daring King, striving for his country's welfare, though susceptible to angry resentments, is both astute and magnanimous. They are two lions locked in mortal combat. For all that they do not meet before the last third of the action, the struggle between clan and crown, not the tenuous love-story of Ellen Douglas and Malcolm Graeme, is the real theme of the poem. It is foreshadowed in Roderick's first angry speech about the King's ruthless suppression of the Border clans, and in his proud determination that Clan Alpine shall not submit.

Almost always a better critic of his own work than the Jeffreys and Giffords, Scott knew well that in spite of his efforts he had not managed to endow Malcolm with much vitality and had totally failed to give him a significant role in the plot. Somehow his outlaws, he noted humorously, always seized the center of the stage and brushed into the wings the young lover whom other poets would have made into the romantic hero. He could find nothing really vital for Malcolm to do.

With his other principle figures, however, he was entirely success-ful. James, in his resentment at the domination over the country form-erly maintained by the powerful Douglases, has banished the entire family, even Ellen's father, the Earl of Bothwell, who had been the protector of his youth. The aged Bothwell, drawn back irresistibly to his native land, refuses to rebel against the king he still loves. When, to save Roderick from retribution for having sheltered him, he journeys to Stirling to surrender himself to imprisonment, perhaps death, his daughter Ellen shares his proud integrity. Suppressing her anguished fear for him, in one of those noble utterances to which the human heart can rise, she says:

> "He goes to do what I had done
> Had Douglas's daughter been his son."[30]

In their brave simplicity the words are both splendid and utterly convincing.

We are early given hints that Fitz-James, who calls himself simply "the Knight of Snowdon," is other than he seems:

> His ready speech flow'd fair and free,
> In phrase of gentlest courtesy;
> Yet seem'd that tone, and gesture bland
> Less used to sue than to command.[31]

And when in the island cave he sees Douglas's sword,

> "I never knew but one," he said,
> "Whose stalward arm might brook to wield
> A blade like that in battlefield."[32]

Again, as he dreams of Ellen that night, his vision changes into a phantom warrior that still strangely resembles her, and he exclaims:

> "Can I not mountain-maiden spy,
> But she must bear the Douglas eye?
> Can I not view a Highland brand,
> But it must match the Douglas hand?"[33]

Scott believed with justice that the main strength of *The Lady of the Lake* lay in its wealth of exciting incident, but the lovely landscape-painting of its wild Highland scenery that later drew hosts of visitors to the Trossachs is also justly famous. There is a series of ever changing pictures—the huge peaks bathed at sunset in living fire, the glens and ravines dark below, the tumbled crags and tangled trees—

> Grey birch and aspen wept beneath;
> Aloft, the ash and warrior oak
> Cast anchor in the rifted rock;
> And, higher yet, the pine-tree hung
> His shatter'd trunk—[34]

the lake hollowed out among its encircling heights:

> One burnish'd sheet of living gold,
> Loch Katrine lay beneath him roll'd,
> In all her length far winding lay,
> With promontory, creek, and bay,

> And islands that, empurpled bright,
> Floated amid the livelier light,
> And mountains, that like giants stand,
> To sentinel enchanted land.[35]

No less striking is the splendid flotilla of Roderick's barges sweeping down the mirrored lake, banners glancing, water sparkling, and pibrochs echoing from the hills:

> Spears, pikes, and axes flash in air.
> Now might you see the tartans brave,
> And plaids and plumage dance and wave:
> Now see the bonnets sink and rise,
> As his tough oar the rower plies;
> See, flashing at each sturdy stroke,
> The wave ascending into smoke . . .[36]

One of Scott's greatest skills, indeed, is his ability to mingle picture and action, so that instead of making a static set-piece he fuses painting and movement. This is true of the superb stag-hunt with which the poem opens, in which Fitz-James's horse draws his last laboring breath and leaves his master to struggle on foot through rocks and snarled undergrowth to sound his horn on the shore of the lake; it is true of the running of the Fiery Cross with which Roderick Dhu summons Clan Alpine to war; and is true again of Fitz-James's great gallop from Loch Vennachar to Stirling, which in its thunderous beat of hoofs rivals and perhaps surpasses Deloraine's nocturnal ride to Melrose.

In the sending of the Cross, many a reader has shared the gasp and shudder that Edmund Gosse felt quiver down his backbone when the summons and its curse reverberate through the cavern:

> A sharp and shrieking echo gave,
> Coir-Uriskin, thy goblin cave
> And the grey pass where birches wave,
> On Beala-nam-bo.[37]

The messenger dashes off:

> Speed, Malise, speed! such cause of haste
> Thine active sinews never braced.
> Bend 'gainst the steepy hill thy breast,
> Burst down like torrent from its crest;
> With short and springing footsteps pass
> The trembling bog and false morass;
> Across the brook like roebuck bound,
> And thread the brake like questioning hound;
> The crag is high, the scaur is deep,
> Yet shrink not from the desperate leap . . .[38]

Fitz-James's ride has the same marvelous rush:

> Bounded the fiery steed in air,
> The rider sate erect and fair,
> Then like a bolt from steel crossbow
> Forth launch'd, along the plain they go
>
> .   .   .
>
> Blair-Drummond sees the hoofs strike fire,
> They sweep like breeze through Ochtertyre
>
> .   .   .
>
> They bathe their courser's sweltering sides,
> Dark Forth! amid thy sluggish tides,
> And on the opposing shore take ground,
> With plash, with scramble, and with bound.
> Right-hand, they leave thy cliffs, Craig-Forth!
> And soon the bulwark of the North,
> Grey Stirling, with her towers and town,
> Upon their fleet career look'd down.[39]

The poem is full of suspense and dramatic confrontations. In a glen on the verge of a precipice the madwoman Blanche* warns Fitz-James in a symbolic song that his guide is false and that Roderick's henchmen wait to ambush him:

> "It was a stag, a stag of ten,
>     Bearing its branches sturdily;
> He came stately down the glen,
>     Ever sing hardily, hardily.
>
> "It was there he met a wounded doe,
>     She was bleeding deathfully;
> She warn'd him of the toils below,
>     O, so faithfully, faithfully!
>
> "He had an eye, and he could heed,
>     Ever sing warily, warily;
> He had a foot, and he could speed—
>     Hunters watch so narrowly."[40]

Then the arrow of Murdoch of Alpine pierces her heart and Fitz-James's blade cleaves Murdoch's breast, shedding that first blood which a seer had warned would portend final victory.

Hard on this follows Fitz-James's encounter with the unknown clansman and the sudden appearance of Roderick's men from behind every crag and copse on the hill:

---

* Blanche is a poetic forerunner of the pathetic and deranged Madge Wildfire in *The Heart of Mid-Lothian*, with her haunting snatches of song.

"These are Clan-Alpine's warriors true;
And, Saxon, I am Roderick Dhu!"[41]

But Roderick had given his word to conduct Fitz-James safe as far as Coilantogle Ford. The clansmen vanish among the heather, the two stride on. But at the Ford, his pledge fulfilled, Roderick demands that they fight to the death. Fitz-James, fired with admiration for a noble foe, pleads with him to submit to the King, promising that James will inflict no injury on him or his clan. Roderick scornfully rejects the offer. They fight; Roderick is wounded, and sinks unconscious from loss of blood. Fitz-James's squires arriving at this moment, are ordered to bear the wounded chief to Stirling.

There Ellen comes to plead both for her imprisoned father and for Roderick. Through Fitz-James she attains an audience with James V. To her surprise though not ours, he turns out to be none other than Fitz-James himself:

"And Snowdoun's Knight is Scotland's King!"[42]

He has already taken Douglas back into his favor with all the warmth of old affection:

". . . Bothwell's Lord henceforth we own
The friend and bulwark of our Throne."[43]

He has given orders that the fighting with Roderick's followers is to cease, but it is too late to do anything for that noble and savage opponent. Roderick is dead. James regrets his death and mourns his loss, not as one who might have been transformed into a powerful supporter, but as a valuable human being:

"My fairest earldom would I give
To bid Clan-Alpine's Chieftain live!"[44]

There remains only Malcolm Graeme to be punished for having sheltered the outlawed Douglas:

"Fetters and warder for the Graeme!"
His chain of gold the King unstrung,
The links o'er Malcolm's neck he flung,
Then gently drew the glittering band,
And laid the clasp in Ellen's hand.[45]

As in both *The Lay of the Last Minstrel* and *Marmion*, the personal stories of the characters in *The Lady of the Lake* are woven into a larger conflict. In the *Lay*, the Scots north of the Border and the English south of it; in *Marmion* the two kingdoms; in *The Lady of the Lake* the wild and unsubdued Highlands and the Lowlands moving toward the reign of civil law—all mirror the hostility of great opposed forces. Scott's sympathies, in all three, are divided. Save for pure national feeling there is little to choose between Dacres and Deloraine; both are valiant, lawless, and turbulent. And if sixteenth-century England is threatening in its might, it is the Scottish James IV, not the English King, who ill-advisedly decides on war when he might have had peace.

But in *The Lady of the Lake*, although the issues are more complex, and Scott does justice to them, his ultimate judgment is clear. Pointing down at the waving fields and green pastures sloping gently south and east, Roderick expresses the grievance of the Highlanders:

> "These fertile plains, that soften'd vale,
> Were once the birthright of the Gael;
> The stranger came with iron hand,
> And from our fathers reft the land.
> Where dwell we now! See rudely swell
> Crag over crag, and fell o'er fell.
> Ask we this savage hill we tread
> For fatten'd steer or household bread;
> Ask we for flocks these shingles dry,
> And well the mountains might reply,—
> 'To you, as to your sires of yore,
> Belong the target and claymore!
> I give you shelter in my breast,
> Your own good blades must win the rest.'
> Pent in this fortress of the North,
> Think'st thou we will not sally forth,
> To spoil the spoiler as we may,
> And from the robber rend the prey?
> Ay, by my soul!—While on yon plain
> The Saxon rears one shock of grain;
> While, of ten thousand herds, there strays
> But one along yon river's maze,—
> The Gael, of plain and river heir,
> Shall, with strong hand, redeem his share."[46]

Roderick voices the bitterness of a proud and valiant people despoiled of their heritage by hordes of alien invaders. Though his mountain glens are wildly beautiful they can give only a rude livelihood to a few hunters. What else is there to do but despoil the descendants of the despoilers? No set treatise, as Walter Bagehot observed a generation after Scott's death, could more accurately convey the historical relationship between Highlander and Lowlander. And quoting Bagehot almost a century later still in 1946, the historian G. M. Young goes on to note how brilliantly Scott renders this antagonism, not in abstractions, but dramatically in words that "come naturally to the lips of a man who thinks in terms of flocks and herds."[47]

But if Roderick speaks for the past, James V embodies the future. Ancient days and ways cannot be restored without breeding new wrongs. The Lowland Scots have become relatively peaceful farmers and craftsmen slowly evolving an ordered society. The raids and reprisals must cease, the old barbarities and bloodshed die like the vanished Picts—but through peace, not annihilation. James urges the cessation of past hatreds, though if need be he will put down violence by force of arms. He offers the Highlanders an opportunity for a share in a gradually emerging prosperity. He stands for the establishment of law and order in a unified realm.

The defeat of the barbaric and heroic Roderick is a symbolic resolution of the conflict. Even on the verge of their desperate struggle James has pleaded against it:

> "I ne'er delay'd
> When foeman bade me draw my blade;
> Nay, more, brave Chief, I vow'd thy death;
> Yet sure thy fair and generous faith,
> And my deep debt for life preserv'd,
> A better meed have well deserv'd;
> Can nought but blood our feud atone?
> Are there no means?"—"No, Stranger, none!"[48]

But Roderick's fierce pride and giant force are emblematically outmatched by James's technical skill in wielding his sword—another symbolic rendering of the confrontation of past and future. Bleeding from three wounds, his claymore forced from his hand, Roderick is brought to his knees. Still he refuses to yield:

> Like adder darting from his coil,
> Like wolf that dashes through the toil,
> Like mountain-cat who guards her young,
> Full at Fitz-James's throat he sprung;
> Receiv'd, but reck'd not of a wound,
> And lock'd his arms his foeman round.[49]

They fall, "The Gael above, Fitz-James below." Roderick's knee on James's breast, his grip on his opponent's throat, he raises a dagger snatched from his side. But his loss of blood has been too great. His sight already misting, he strikes down and the dagger buries itself in the heath as he collapses on the body of his foe.

Though Roderick is brave and chivalrous, his virtues are not enough; James's victory is the victory of civilization over barbarism. "No villain need be. Passions spin the plot." And, though there were to be villains in Scott's future work, both in verse and prose, from the freebooter Bertram of *Rokeby* to the half-tragic Ramorny of *The Fair Maid of Perth*, they would seldom be figures of pure evil and seldom be the dominant forces in the narrative. The most meaningful human contentions, for Scott, are enflamed not by the dark forces of depravity but by the conflict of loyalties rooted in warring values.

Even in the bright morning of his literary career he has found his essential theme. For a great artist there is an underlying absorption that runs through his most significant work and that he finds himself overwhelmingly impelled to penetrate in all its depths. What that interest was for Scott first emerges unmistakably in *The Lady of the Lake*. It is the clash of loyalties locked in combat on the stage of time, of men struggling in the torrent of history. More profoundly still, it is the collisions of history itself, the contention between different degrees of civilization and different states of society, between a predatory tribalism and the establishment of an ordered society, between the endeavor to hold back—sometimes even to turn back—the clock of history and the forward movement of its hand, between the desire to hold on to ways of life rooted in the past and the forces making for progress, between the powers of stability and change.

It was to be a lifelong exploration. As Scott's insights deepened they grew ever more complex. Neither a bland historical optimist nor a stubborn pessimist, he did not see all change as either advancement or decline. Often, the strands of good and evil were intricately entwined in both contending systems of values. The great struggle was to extend through all his future work—Highlander and Lowlander, pastoral Scotland and commercial England, Catholicism and Protestantism, established church and Covenanter, freedom of conscience and authority, law and rebellion, tyranny and constitutional government, feudalism and nationalism, barbarism and culture, Europe and Byzantium, Christianity and Islam. These fell encounters of mighty opposites dominate Scott's greatest work and provide his most exciting theme.

# PART FIVE

## *Monarch of Parnassus*

### 1 8 1 0 - 1 8 1 6

# 1

---

# *A Bower in Good Green-Wood*

## *( 1 8 1 0 – 1 8 1 1 )*

THE TIME was now fast approaching when Scott's seven-year lease on Ashestiel would expire. Though he might remain as a tenant at will,[1] sooner or later Colonel Russell would be returning from India to reside in his ancestral home. Scott had taken pleasure in pruning and planting trees under which he could see his cousin strolling in future years, but it would be even more enjoyable to create his own groves on his own land.[2] Russell's agent demanded a rise in the rent from £85 to £105, which seemed to Scott a heavy sum to be paying for a place he must someday leave. He agreed to the increase, stipulating that the fishing rights must remain entirely at his disposal, but instead of entering into a new lease he arranged to stay on from year to year.[3] Meanwhile reviving his old dream of a mountain farm that would make him a "laird of the Cairn and the Scaur,"[4] he began looking around again for a domain of his own on the Tweed.

This would probably require a much larger outlay of cash than for the moment Scott had at his disposal. The great sums *The Lady of the Lake* was bringing in were being absorbed by the initial expenditures of John Ballantyne and Company. Before books can be sold they must be printed; the printing was done, of course, by James Ballantyne, but whatever the credit arrangements between the two firms, paper, printing, binding, and distribution had ultimately to be paid for. In addition, John Ballantyne, like all publishers of the day, carried on a retail bookshop in which he sold both old books and those of other publishers. He valued his stock at £7,000 to £10,000, of which only a small part was represented by his own publications.[5]

The expansion of James Ballantyne's printing establishment also involved an outlay of capital. He now had eleven presses in operation, and Scott wanted to bring their number up to twelve and if possible fourteen. If these were to be kept busy there must be corresponding increases in their fonts of type. In the long run, all this would be good business and Scott might hope to profit both as a partner in the publishing house and as a partner in the printing plant. Great prospects, therefore, he was confident he had; but ready money he had not.[6]

Constable, to be sure, was warm to restore their old friendly footing, an object he might have had in mind when he generously advised John Ballantyne on the publication of *The Lady of the Lake*. He would have liked to join forces with the new firm. "With all the insinuating appearance of candour he assumes when it serves," John reported to Scott, Constable urged a coalition in which each would take a share in the other's publications, and argued "the superior advantage of possessing a number of small divided good risques to that of having one or two large ones."[7]

So strongly did the astute Constable desire a share in one of Ballantyne's tentative projects that he offered the most extraordinary inducements. He vigorously emphasized how valuable it would be to both firms for him to have a half or even a quarter share of a literary work that Ballantyne, even in writing to Scott, with mysterious discreetness calls "an object you wot of. 'It would make no change of publishers— would bring all the things into one focus' "— "(his focus I fancy)," John interpolated—and Constable " 'in return would impart a proportionate share of *Marmion*,' " which Scott had sold him outright.[8] That he was willing to convey back a part of this valuable property reveals how ardent he was for a share in the new production.

What was this secret enterprise? Ballantyne does not say, and neither does Scott. But in John Ballantyne and Company's printed announcement of "New Works and Publications for 1809–10" there had been a title that might have caught Constable's eye.[9] This was an anonymous novel called *Waverley: or 'tis Sixty Years Since*. The story had not appeared; in the intervening months Constable might have nosed out its authorship. It was even possible that Scott himself had made some forgotten reference to it before laying it aside five years previously. Possibly, too, Constable had learned of the "Scotch novel" discussed with Murray, or John Ballantyne had dropped some artful hint in his ear the preceding spring. And now, only a few weeks before, Scott had hauled out the unfinished manuscript and given it to James Ballantyne for his opinion.[10]

James's judgment had been encouraging but not enthusiastic. "What you have sent of *Waverley* has amused me much; and certainly if I had read it as part of a new novel, the remainder of which was open to my perusal, I should have proceeded with avidity. . . . The language is spirited, but perhaps rather careless. The humour is admirable." On the other hand, James was not so much impressed as he had been by the opening of *The Lady of the Lake*; he thought the account of Waverley's reading unnecessarily minute and saw no connection between these studies and his character. Waverley himself, James said, "I think excellent and interesting, and I was equally astonished and delighted to find in the last-written chapter that you can paint to the eye in prose as well as in verse. . . . Should you go on? My opinion is, clearly—certainly. I have no doubt of success, though it is impossible to guess how much."[11]

This moderate approval Scott found insufficient; the pages were once again tossed back into the drawer of the old cabinet. Whether or not this unfinished work was the one that John Ballantyne now dangled before his great rival, he played the eager bookseller adroitly. Constable was anxious to know if he had given the London trade any share. No, said John, but reminded him "of the conversation on the same subject we held in the spring." "*If* we parted with any share of this it would only be to those from whom we . . . expected to derive the greatest reciprocal advantage" in the form of "employment as printers, and large purchases of our publications!" But since the enormous success of *The Lady of the Lake* "we could not *now* accept of either as a bribe to give any assurance of a share in this work which, *if we could*, we would keep to ourselves."[12]

"I thought it better to leave the matter thus open," the wily John explained to Scott. "I conceived it would have done no good to have told this plump,"[13] resolved though they were to retain the whole. That would have removed Constable's only motive for secrecy and risk having their determination conveyed to London, where it was to their interest to foster precisely those hopes of profit that allured the great Edinburgh bookseller. Thus the two competitors parted after their fencing match, with assurances of reciprocal friendship.

Scott's own feelings toward Constable, indeed, were no longer hostile. There had been a friendy interchange of letters between them during the spring, in which Scott had agreed as a personal favor to let the publishers bring out a third edition of *Sir Tristrem* and Constable had conveyed his partner's regrets for his obnoxious conduct. Scott would not harbor a grudge. "I am sure," he responded, "if Mr. Hunter is really sorry for the occasion of my long absence from your shop I will be happy to forget all disagreeable circumstances and visit it often as a customer and amateur."[14]

It was no longer in his power, though, he explained, to return to Constable's firm as an author. In the months since the breach, the Ballantynes had diverted "a large capital . . . from another object and invested it in their present Bookselling concern" under Scott's promise that they would have the publication of his future books, "a pledge not to be withdrawn without grounds which I cannot anticipate. But this is not a consideration which need prevent our being friends and well-wishers."[15]

Constable might well rue the connection he had lost. His own temper and his partner's insolence, as Scott noted the following year, had already cost him a full £5,000.[16] But neither had James Ballantyne and Company gone unscathed. Printing orders that might have come to them Constable had bestowed elsewhere; and after four volumes of *Swift* had been printed by their presses, Constable, claiming they were too slow, had given all the remaining fourteen volumes to a rival printer. Now one of James's presses was idle, and the plant was in danger of losing the *Somers Tracts* as well.[17]

The annual profits of £900 and £450 respectively upon which he and Scott had agreed would leave only £400 for the sinking fund. This, Scott pointed out, was not nearly enough when they needed to buy additional types, discount bills, liquidate debts, and build up their capital. "It would be a pity to make our Milk Cow yield blood"; unless they could "put the establishment on a more productive footing the necessary though unpleasant consequence must be an abatement of the dividends to the partners from next Martinmas."[18]

Nor had the publishing house done so well as Scott had hoped. Grahame's *British Georgics* had been a dead loss, Dr. John Jamieson's *History of the Culdees* had done so badly that much of it had ultimately to be sold as waste paper, and the three volumes of Anna Seward's *Poetical Works* were lingering unbought in rows. *Defoe's Works* had moved slowly but had at last sold out. Large numbers, finally, of *Edinburg Annual Registers* for 1808 still weighed down their shelves. Scott, nevertheless, had the most unbounded confidence that ultimately this work would prove a good investment. "The *Register*," he exclaimed, "I will pawn my life upon."[19]

He was investing heavily, too, in his German protégé, Henry Weber, whom he had commissioned to produce a great edition of the works of Beaumont and Fletcher. In addition to this, Weber was doing a collection of *Tales of the East*,[20] and Scott felt sure that he could successfully edit an elegant but inexpensive Shakespeare with original commentaries and a selection of the best notes from former editions. For this purpose he would "willingly advance a few hundreds"; it would drive out all rivals from the field, bring in a good profit, and be a credit to the firm.[21] He had also accepted for publication the *Northern Antiquities* on which Weber had collaborated with Robert Jamieson,[22] and had insisted on taking Arthur Clifford's bulky collection of *Tixall Poetry*. About this last project both the Ballantynes had the gloomiest forebodings: it ought, James said, "to be got rid of at almost any sacrifice. We would not now even ask a London bookseller to take a share, and a net outlay of near £2,500, upon a worse than doubtful speculation, is surely 'most tolerable and not to be endured.' "[23] It proved indeed as bad a loss as he and his brother had predicted.

The only triumphant exception was *The Lady of the Lake*, the sixth edition of which was now roaring through the presses.[24] This was cause enough for exultation, and although Scott warned James that they might have to retrench their dividends he contemplated the future cheerfully. He had made good headway on Swift; by the end of August he had dispatched Volume XIII of that work to the printer.[25] It was a relaxation to turn during the golden hours of vacation to coursing hares by day and spearing salmon by night. "I should be delighted," he told a correspondent, "to furnish you with an unpublished tale for your own exclusive adaptation, but—as the Neapolitan beggar said to the stranger who exhorted him to industry—'Did you but know how lazy I am.' "[26]

He had not been too lazy, however, to be of service to James Hogg, who that summer had published a collection of songs to Scottish airs, which he had called *The Forest Minstrel* and dedicated to the Countess of Dalkeith as "the Stay of Genius and the Shield of Merit." Hogg sent him two copies, begging him to transmit one to the Countess. Scott put the volume in her hands with a sympathetic word about the Ettrick shepherd's lot and was later able to give him one hundred guineas from her ladyship.[27]

Later that summer Scott welcomed to Ashestiel his Highland friends, Mrs. Clephane and two of her three pretty daughters, whom he had failed to see when he was at Mull. "Our Hebridean syrens and their Lady Mother," as he called them, were all three full of Highland lore and story, and Margaret, the eldest daughter, behaved like one of her own heroines when she dislocated her arm in a bad fall at Melrose Abbey, enduring a painful setting of the joint without a single wince or groan.[28] After their departure, inspired by one of their stories, *Minnie's Benison*, five-year-old Charles distinguished himself by clapping a spoonful of hot porridge on the head of his seven-year-old sister Anne.[29]

In September came John Richardson, a friend of Scott's since 1800, who had studied law at the University of Edinburgh, but who had removed to London in 1806 and become the head of a firm of parliamentary solicitors. One day they went fishing, Richardson trolling the stream and Scott quoting Izaak Walton and reciting Border ballads. With them was Tom Purdie, who mistook Richardson for a Southron and plainly gave him no credit for any skill as an angler, boasting grandly of the size of the fish he himself had taken there.

After catching several fine trout, Richardson hooked something more powerful than he had yet pulled in, running out his reel. "Hold up your rod!" cried Scott excitedly; "give him line!" Richardson's rod broke, but he still managed to play his reel and finally pulled in a large trout. Scott jumped in the water, seized the fish, and threw it on the grass. Pressed to admit that it was as heavy as the biggest of those he had been so vainglorious about, Tom gave a smile of bitter incredulity; but just then up came Lord Somerville's fisherman with a scale in his basket, and the trout proved to weigh seven pounds. "Weel," said Tom, discontentedly letting it fall on the turf, "weel, ye are a meikle fish, mon—and a meikle *fule* too," he sank his voice to a lower key, "to let yourself be kilt by an Englander." Surreptitiously he gave the trout a kick on the head. "To be ta'en by the like o' him, frae Lunnon!"[30]

For all his boasted laziness Scott was not idle during the autumn. In his before-breakfast labors he plugged away at Swift, polished and emended for the November *Quarterly Review* an article on Crabbe that Murray asked him to look over, and made English versions of some Gaelic poems garnered from Margaret Clephane.[31] In Edinburgh, during a fortnight's official duty at the Register House, he reworked an ancient "March of the Monks of Bangor," telling of their massacre by a heathen King of Northumberland in the year 610.[32] Then, back at Ashestiel again in late October, when a cold prevented him from riding out, he spent the time "brushing the jackets of some old Swiss ditties upon the battles of Sempach, Morat, and other encounters with the Knights of Austria and Burgundy," which were "not good as poetry," he said, "but curious."[33]

As a *jeu d'esprit* for the 1809 *Edinburgh Annual Register*, he dashed off some anonymous poetic imitations—one of George Crabbe, entitled "The Poacher," others of Moore and himself.[34] He amused himself by planning still others, of Wordsworth, Southey, and perhaps Campbell, with a ghost story in the manner of Mat Lewis, but left these unfinished. By way of introduction he wrote a prose extravaganza called "The Inferno of Altesidora," in the style of Cervantes, in which literary criticism was humorously pictured as a tennis match, with Jeffrey, Gifford, and other leading reviewers of the day striking books back and forth in public favor.[35]

With the end of October the weather broke. The wind came roaring down the vale of the Tweed and howled around Ashestiel so tempestuously that Scott was glad to get back to his snug study in Castle Street.[36] Here he settled down to driving ahead on Swift. Matthew Weld Hartstonge, one of his Dublin correspondents, was putting him in touch with a surviving representative of the Dean's family, Mr. Theophilus Swift, and had sent him much valuable manuscript information. But what a strange, absurd tale, Scott exclaimed, was that "of Swift having been obliged to give up living at Kilroot on account of his having attempted a rape on a farmer's daughter": "Rapes were not at all in the Dean's way at any time of his life . . ."[37]

Scott also went on giving the *Quarterly Review* the assistance of his pen. That periodical was now selling four to five thousand copies of each number and had made itself into a formidable opponent to the *Edinburgh Review*. One book that Murray had sent him Scott refused to review; Cromek's *Remains of Nithsdale and Galloway Song*. The collection was mere "sweepings" and its editor "a perfect Brain-sucker living upon the labours of others."[38] Southey's *Curse of Kehama* presented Scott with some difficulties; he must do justice to the *Review* by noticing the blemishes and to the author by pointing out its brilliances.[39] Ultimately he solved the problem by slurring over the absurdities and throwing as much weight as possible on the beauties. It was "infinite pity," he remarked to Ellis, that Southey, "with the true obstinacy of a foolish papa . . . *will* be most attached to the defects of his poetical offspring."[40]

During the winter, dramatic versions of *The Lady of the Lake* were presented in Edinburgh, in Dublin, and in London.[41] "Messrs Morton and Reynolds play-carpenters in ordinary to Covent Garden," Scott reported, "are employed in scrubbing careening and cutting her down into one of those new sloops called a Melo drama . . ." He expressed polite approbation, "but entre nous I wished them at the bottom of Loch Katrine with all my heart."[42] The Siddons production at Edinburgh, written by Edmund John Eyre, had scenery painted from sketches made of the actual landscapes of the poem. Though Scott lounged in the green room of the theater, chatting with Henry Siddons, he carefully avoided seeing a line of the script: "I would not willingly have the public of this place suppose I was in any degree responsible for the success of the piece."[43]

The play did well at the box office, but Scott thought it only fairly good. His words had been rearranged into blank verse, which made them seem to him like "an old friend with a new face." He felt silently disappointed in Mrs. Henry Siddons as Ellen: "She had somehow got a little too *Columbinish*, and fell short in the dignity which should mingle even with the playful simplicity of a high-born maiden." Young Daniel Terry, on the other hand, did superbly as Roderick Dhu: "I am certain," said Scott, "he will one day make a figure."[44]

As usual the Scotts spent Christmas at Mertoun with their Harden relatives, having set out in the midst of a snowstorm on December 23.[45] Besides the mince pies Charlotte had made and brought in the big carriage their host's copious board, in the days that followed, groaned with fat geese and applesauce, ducks, chickens, turkeys, and Westphalian hams, codlins in cream, strawberries and raspberries in Bordeaux, cheese cakes and tarts, syllabub, and white and red wine.[46]

With them as a fellow guest was Dr. Robert Douglas, the minister of Galashiels. The old Doctor still preserved, as he may have told Scott, a letter written him over thirty years before by Mrs. Alison Cockburn, describing a child genius of six who had dazzled her one evening when she visited her distant relatives in George Square.[47] The snow lay piled up outdoors, but the fires were blazing within. Dr. Douglas grew warm with the contents of a black teapot, the elders talked, the children of both families mingled in joyful hubbub, and the holiday passed happily. Despite the snowdrifts the return journey was made without mishap, and the Castle Street household were home in time for Twelfth Night.[48]

Early in 1811 Scott's hopes of being paid as a Clerk of Session were suddenly revived. Mr. Pringle, the oldest of the Clerks except for George Home, died on February 14, and Lord Melville proposed that Scott be appointed to the vacancy and someone else be associated with Home.[49] Scott thought there might be difficulties about making a new arrangement of this kind. It would be easier to let his venerable colleague retire on a two-thirds pension; he himself would willingly make up the difference out of his own pocket.[50] But Home objected to formal retirement. He countered by suggesting that Scott be given Mr. Pringle's place and that he himself, despite his total deafness, return to his own duties, his fellow clerks all lending a hand to make them as light as possible for him.[51]

There turned out, however, to be a rival candidate for the vacancy, David Hume, the Professor of Scottish Law at the University.[52] Hume, who was hoping to be made a Baron of Exchequer, swore that he would not take the post, then reversed his decision and said he would, and then reversed himself once again, offering to resign his pretensions in Scott's favor.[53] While Hume vacillated, and Home obstructed, Scott tried vigorously to pull strings in his own behalf. Although he had the highest respect and liking for his old law professor, he felt that his own satisfactory performance of his duties gave him superior claims.[54] But political forces stronger than he could command were brought to bear, and for a third time the irresolute Hume changed his mind. "Upon my honour," Scott exploded, "I think it a little hard that any man should have an office *forced* upon him after repeated refusals formally communicated to his friends and competitors."[55]

But Hume took the place and Scott was passed over. To make it up to him retirement was pressed on Home.[56] He stubbornly refused, however, to apply for a pension; it might be said, he argued, "that this is a job by which the Parties have secured to themselves a Joint Interest in the office and are now endeavouring to burden the Publick with a double sallary."[57] Scott felt exasperated at the old man. "He pretends scruples at being a pensioner on the public yet never considers he has been this five years the pensioner of an individual."[58] If the hard-hearted conduct of "this Scotch Shylock" forced Scott to resign, where would Home stand? Perform the duties of the office he could not; he would then be forced to take the very step he now balked at.[59]

Lord Melville argued with Home in vain; so did the Lord President,

Robert Blair. "Call it folly or obstinacy or what my friends or his friends chose," Scott reported Hume's words, "no argument should prevail on him to resign unless I resigned first."[60] At last, however, after a full month of resistance, he weakened and consented to apply for the super-annuation. Surprisingly, he then even declined to accept Scott's offer to make up the difference between two-thirds and full pay.[61] At last the way was opened for Scott to begin drawing a salary for the work he had been doing over the past five years.

There were further legal complications that had to be surmounted. As a formal proof of disinterestedness Scott put his resignation in the hands of Robert Dundas, to "make use of as your prudence suggests." It would then be for the wisdom of the Lords of the Treasury to decide whether there was any difference to the country between accepting Home's resignation and leaving Scott in the Clerkship and doing the same thing circuitously by accepting both resignations and making out a new commission. Had Pringle's place been given him, Scott could not resist pointing out, none of the conflict need have occurred: "Mr. Geo. Home must then have had his pension and Mr. D. Hume would have got my office instead of Mr. Pringle's."[62]

It had been pleasant in the midst of these contentions to hear from John Leyden and learn that he was doing well. He had become an Indian judge, far outstripped Sir William Jones in his knowledge of oriental languages, and composed a book on the literature and language of Indo-Chinese nations.[63] "It is impossible," he wrote, "not to beg to be remembered to my dear Mrs. Scott": the Lasswade cottage and its blazing ingle were "the happiest scenes of my youth. God bless you and your family My dearest Scott."[64] The dancing bear of a decade before had become a state dignitary and was "flourishing like a green bay tree."[65]

Leyden sent Scott a creese with a brilliant hilt and a blade "em-brued . . . in poison as fatal as that of the Upas."[66] The glittering, evil-looking thing was "worthy of the bowels of Bonaparte," Scott exclaimed, "I should have said his guts for bowels he hath none."[67] In the death struggle against the continental Dictator it had sometimes seemed to Scott as if Napoleon were served by a devil and as if there were an evil fate on everything his foes attempted.[68] The Spaniards were ruining their own cause and defeating their own valor and patriotism by a false pride that would not allow them to acknowledge their own weaknesses. If only they would profit by the example of the Portuguese and put themselves under British command and British discipline![69]

When Masséna began his retreat from Torres Vedras, Scott burst into exultation. He had followed the whole Peninsular campaign with furious absorption, poring over huge maps of Portugal and Spain, tracing the marches and countermarches of the French and English troops, and marking their positions with black and white pins. He carried these maps with him even between Edinburgh and Ashestiel, and Charlotte often complained of their being spread out in her carriage.[70]

The French débacle now filled him with fierce joy. Hundreds of horses and mules lying hamstrung on the line of march; artillery, baggage, sick, wounded, all abandoned; their rear constantly harassed by pursuers; their flanks turned whenever they attempted a stand![71] "And all owing," Scott exclaimed, "to the coolness and generalship of Wellington"; "I rejoice with the heart of a Scotsman in the success of Lord Wellington and with the soul of a Seer to boot. I have for three years been proclaiming him as the only man we had to trust to."[72] "Not fettered by prejudices, not immured within the pedantries of his profession," the great commander was "a man of genius and talent" who would smash the French military machine. That would destroy the evil domination: "The downfall of Bonaparte's military fame will be the signal of his ruin."[73]

The turn of the tide in Spain inspired Scott with the idea for some wild stanzas of celebration on the theme; the earnings he would donate to the Portuguese war sufferers. "Silver and gold have I none but that which I have I will give unto them."[74] The organizing scheme of the poem he borrowed from Hita's *Guerras Civiles*, one of the favorite books of his boyhood, that had inspired the destroyed poem of his youth, *The Conquest of Granada*.[75] "You remember," he told Morritt, "the story of the last Gothic King of Spain descending into an enchanted cavern to know the fate of the Moorish invasion—that is my machinery."[76] Written in Spenserian stanzas, to please Will Erskine, the poem was called *The Vision of Don Roderick*.[77] "My friends and booksellers the Ballantynes of Edinburgh have very liberally promised me a hundred guineas for this trifle."[78]

Scott began the writing in Edinburgh during the spring vacation. A literary acquaintance named Robert Pierce Gillies found him in his library writing busily, with his little wire-haired terrier Wallace by his side. Scott recited the stanzas he had been composing and invited Gillies to return to supper. "I have just begun to copy out the rhymes that you heard today." The following morning he hoped to have eight or ten more stanzas written: "Wallace will not suffer me to rest after six in the morning. Come, good dog, and help the poet." The little dog at once leaped into a chair beside his master. Scott offered him a newspaper, which the animal seized and held in his mouth, sitting up alertly and looking very wise and contented. "Very well," Scott said with satisfaction, "*now* we shall get on."[79]

His first draft was completed at Ashestiel in dispiriting weather. "Nothing but everlasting rain hail and easterly blights and no walking without being wet to the skin and gaining a good headache for the day from the severity of the damp and cold."[80] Nevertheless he had been able to do a good deal more in the country than would have been possible in the endless interruptions of Edinburgh. As he prepared to return to town he was able to tell James Ballantyne that a great deal of the poem was done, "at least in *dead* colours as the painters say."[81]

But he found all of *Don Roderick* hard going, and dismissed as "a Rhodomontade piece of goods."[82] "This patriotic puppet,"[83] "this damned Spaniard, whose national sloth is infectious," Scott complained with humorous impatience, moved only with "characteristic Spanish gravity and tardiness" and refused to leave his hands.[84] But at last the task was completed. While he copied it out as fast as he could for the press, Charlotte made another copy for Lady Abercorn, "that your Ladyship may be possessed of it as soon as it is finished."[85]

Barely had Scott settled down in Castle Street again when he and all Edinburgh were shocked to hear of the death of Robert Blair, the President of the Court of Session.[86] "Party made no division about Blair"; his integrity and legal erudition were universally respected.[87] "Eh, man!" John Clerk exclaimed once after Blair had just demolished his argument before the Court, "God almighty spared nae pains when he made your brains."[88] Scott had been on the warmest terms with his superior and parted from him just "the day before in great health and spirits after much laughing at some nonsense or other."[89]

On the very day of the Lord President's burial, May 29, came the further news that Lord Melville had died in his sleep the night before. The two men, early and attached friends, and for long years neighbors on the northeast side of George Square, had thus been lying, "suddenly dead, with but a wall between them."[90] Even more than by the death of Blair, Scott was grieved by the loss of Lord Melville. The patriot who had served his country so nobly; the early patron of Scott's own fortunes; their architect, as Scott had often called him, to whom he owed both his Sheriffdom and his position in the Court of Session; the good kind old man, who had dined in Castle Street that very winter, and who entered so simple-heartedly into the ways of the family that the children had always been allowed to sit up for supper whenever Lord Melville was there![91] Only that spring Lord Melville had been instrumental in getting George Home to retire.

Lord Melville's last service had, in fact, made into a practical possibility Scott's dream of buying some land and building a little cottage where he could gather his family around his own fireside under the shelter of his own rooftree. Sometimes in the discouragements of the previous winter he had almost lost heart and felt half-inclined to pull up stakes and try his fortune in another clime. If Robert Dundas went to India as Governor-General and were "willing to take me with him in a good situation," he had moodily confided to Tom, "I would not hesitate to pitch the Court of Session and the booksellers to the Devil."[92] Even in February he had been obliged to turn down one property he could not afford. "Langfaugh is beyond my mark," he said regretfully. "I have not at present above £10,000," and to buy so large an estate would be beyond his means.[93]

Now, however, with the prospect of an added £1,300 a year, he began looking about in good earnest. Andrew Lang's land would not do, he told his Sheriff-Substitute, Charles Erskine: it was too near Selkirk. "I must be on Tweedside if possible."[94] In the course of May he narrowed down his search to two adjacent holdings. Either would suit him, but together they "would make a very desirable property indeed." About halfway between Selkirk and Melrose, they extended a mile along "the beautiful turn of the Tweed above Gala-foot." They might be had "for between £7000 and £8000 or either of them separately for about half the sum." Scott was eager to buy them both.[95]

Sober reflection convinced him that at the moment he would be wiser to confine himself to one. The actual payment of his salary was hanging fire; it might still be months before he began receiving it. Robert Dundas, it seemed to him, had not been pressing this matter as vigorously as he might, and Scott also felt hurt at the negligence of his friends in the government. "I think they use me coldly and unworthily which I feel more than any pecuniary disappointment for 'bread we shall eat or white or brown.' "[96] In the meanwhile, though, if need be, he could borrow a thousand or two from his brother the Major, and for the rest "I must have recourse to my pen."[97] John Ballantyne, to be sure, might find it hard to advance "so large a sum as the copyright of a new poem supposing it to be made payable in the course of a year at farthest from the work going to press," but this was a difficulty that would have to be surmounted.[98]

In spite of some poor speculations, the publishing house—thanks, no doubt, largely to *The Lady of the Lake*—seemed to be prospering. They were still short of cash, but this was partly because there was £4,718 due them that had not yet been paid, and partly because, unlike other publishers, they had paid for their printing in advance. But this would not last: "As the Printing Office gets easier they will be able to give credit." In a financial statement dated May 23, 1811, John Ballantyne valued their book stock at £10,000 and gave their realized capital as now £3,500. Over the two-year period that the firm had been in existence, John wrote Scott, "you will observe that your £1000 capital has now grown 2064 being a clear profit of 50 p[er] Cent p[er] an[num]."[99]

Scott therefore decided to go ahead with his land purchase. Of the two holdings he preferred the one to the northeast, which consisted of 110 acres called Newarthaugh, belonging to Dr. Douglas, the Galashiels minister. Scott employed Charles Erskine and Nippy Laidlaw to negotiate for him.[100] The minister proved a tough man to bargain with. "Mr. Laidlaw and I have this forenoon had a hard prigg with the Doctor," wrote Erskine. Nippy did his best, but to no avail. Dr. Douglas demanded 4,000 guineas, "I told him I would give £4,000, he said he would take no less."[101] After some further haggling, "I asked him 14 days to advise on it." This the Doctor granted. He was willing also to take £1,500 down and the rest, if Scott desired, in a five-year mortgage on the property, but he would not lower his price a penny.[102] "We could not break the Doctor down," reported Erskine.[103]

Scott agreed to these terms. Considering the £140 rent paid for the land by the present tenant-farmer, and the fact that thirteen acres were planted, Erskine thought that "altho' dear your purchase is not extravagant."[104] Dr. Douglas agreed to give Scott possession on Whitsunday, 1812, and wrote him a letter outlining the conditions of the sale, specifying that the tenant would "flitt and remove" by that date, and wishing the new landowner "health long to enjoy the fruits of my labours and outlay."[105] On June 20, Scott wrote his acceptance.[106]

The farm he had thus acquired ran along the Tweed for about half a mile of rich meadow, with an unplanted dirt bank going up steeply to the rolling ground behind.[107] Dr. Douglas had never resided there, and what he called his "labours and outlay" was, except for the erection of a new barn, a long course of neglect. The land lay undrained and poorly enclosed, much of it covered only with heath. The huge staring barn overshadowed the farmhouse, a cottage of four rooms and a kitchen, with a kail yard on one side, a squashy enclosure where pigs squelched and snorted. The whole miry hollow was named Cartley Hole, sometimes humorously modified into Clarty—"Dirty"—Hole. The few trees were thin and scraggly; Dr. Douglas had done little planting except for a straight length of dark firs. This looked so tall and narrow that Scott, thinking it resembled a black hair-comb stuck in the ground, called it "the Doctor's redding-kame." Only at some distance from the house were there plantations which though young were thriving.

Most observers would have found the place bare and unattractive.[108] But three things about it enchanted Scott. One was that the contours were noble; when they were planted with oaks intermingled with chestnuts, red beeches, and elms the bleak and bony hills would become majestic. Though Scott cared little for agriculture he loved trees and exulted in the prospect now opening before him of being able to compose a landscape of living trunks and leaves clothing the swelling curves and hollows of the earth itself.[109]

"I cannot enter into the spirit of common vulgar farming," he exclaimed to Joanna Baillie, "though I am doomed in a small way to carry on that losing trade. It never occurred to me to be a bit more happy because my turnips were better than my neighbors . . . But planting and pruning trees I could work at from morning till night . . ." And what an enjoyment to reflect that while you were thus pleasing yourself you were "contributing to the welfare of the country and that your very acorn may send its ribs of oak to future victories like Trafalgar."[110]

The river, too, was beautiful—a bold and rapid stream flowing broad and bright over a bed of milk-white pebbles, darkening here and there into a deep pool overhung by birches and alders.[111] Across the glinting water the opposite banks rose in a long slope feathery with foliage beyond which the undulations rolled away to the heathered and lonely heights of Minchmoor. With the cloud shadows racing blue over yellow fields and mists swirling up gray and silvery and broad washes of golden sunlight, the hills surrounding his own domain were an unceasing drama.

But, above all, this valley was steeped for him in the glamor of tradition and history. There was the Tweed itself flowing like time before his door with all its memories of the past. Directly across the stream, in a hollow of the hills, were the traces of that ancient British barrier the Catrail. In a glen to the east, he felt sure, Thomas of Ercildoune had walked, and beyond its hollow the land rose again to the triple peaks of the Eildon Hills violet in the dawn and green in the sunset.[112] The very rise just before his farmhouse was that historic spot called "Turn-again," the place his father had shown him when he was a youth a quarter of a century before—

> Where gallant Cessford's life-blood dear
> Reeked on dark Elliott's border spear.

Nearby were Skirmish-field and Charge-Law, over which had raged the bitterly fought battle of Melrose and where his own ancestors had followed the banners of Buccleuch. The land that would now be his had seen the last of the great clan battles of the Border.[113]

No wonder he wrote his friends "a poet has bought himself a farm"[114] and felt his heart swell at the thought of building a bower "in good green-wood" of the trees he would plant with his own hands rising around his walls.[115] He would keep the haugh by the river for pasture and twenty-four acres above the road for arable, making the rest into coppice and woodland.[116] Close to the house would be his garden and, directly adjoining, the household offices, "for you must know I like to spend time in

> "Twisting of collar my dogs to hold,
> And combing the mane of my palfrey bold."[117]

Only a little downstream, just above the slight bend where the Gala mingled its waters with the Tweed, an ancient Roman road descending from the Eildon Hills crossed the river in a shallow ford. These lands had been ruled of old by the Abbots of Melrose. All melted to a bright glow in Scott's imagination. Before he had even taken possession of his new domain he had named it Abbotsford.[118]

# 2

---

# *The Shirra's Flitting*

## *( 1 8 1 1 – 1 8 1 2 )*

"SO YOU HAVE BECOME the Laird of Abbotsford," wrote Joanna
Baillie hard upon the news of the purchase. "A respectable-
sounding name this; and would become a large estate fully as well as
a little farm; and I hope it will be the name of a good estate with a
good house upon it too, in which your prosperous descendants—ages
after this—will proudly point out the picture of the first Laird. . . . Many
happy days may you and Mrs. Scott and the children have in your new
habitation! But don't let all the idle Travellers, who come to visit the
country and the ruins which you have made famous, make an Inn of
your house for their own convenience and that they may boast in their
stupid Tours afterwards of the great attention they received from their
*friend* Mr. Scott."[1]

The words were ominously prophetic. And within little more than a
month Scott was busy making part of them a reality by striving to swell
his holdings of land.[2] A larger farm adjoining Abbotsford on the south
came up for auction, and he bid as high as £6,000—"far beyond the
value," he admitted, before finally giving up. "Another much more to my
purpose," he added, "will be in the market in a year or two."[3] In his
heart revived the ancestral craving to be the lord of broad acres, looking
out over his own realm of waving fields and wooded hills. It would prove
a fatal hunger.

The dwelling he planned to build was modest enough, just a
pleasant cottage close to a "little garden (having no pretension to fruit
walls) . . . like some of your beautiful old rectories," with the stables,
dairy, and poultry yard clustered beside the house.[4] William Hayley
recommended placing these structures at a little distance, with a covered

arcade between.[5] As for visitors, though Scott loved to fill his home with guests, he thought it would be ample to have "two spare-bedrooms, with dressingrooms each of which will on pinch have a couch bed." Ten people were enough to fill Ashestiel, but there had been times when it had lodged thirty-two without complaints. "I cannot relinquish my border principle of accommodating all the cousins and *dunawastles* who will rather sleep on chairs and on the floor than be absent when folks are gathered together."[6]

The bedrooms, however, Scott thought, might all be small, provided they were airy and comfortable, and the drawing room and dining room need be no larger than would pleasantly suit a company of twelve or so. One little dream upon which he insisted was that the drawing room open into a small conservatory with a marble fountain, and glass doors leading out to the garden. Gradually his imagination gleamed with further glorious inspirations—"a large boudoir or recess" on one side of the drawing room, with bookshelves and cabinets for guns and curios; outside this room, commanding the vales of Tweed and Gala, a wooden balcony having pillars wreathed with creepers and broad steps descending to the river meadow; below the balcony a trellis-screened walk by which the servants could get from the kitchen door to the dairy and other outbuilding.[7]

All these modest elaborations of his simple cottage Scott poured out to William Stark, a brilliant Glasgow architect suggested by Daniel Terry. There must also be a master bedroom with two dressing closets, a schoolroom and two bedrooms for the children, two water closets, a kitchen, scullery, servants' hall, pantry, and servants' bedrooms. The slate roof should not slant too sharply; steep roofs were ugly, and there would always be people to clear the snow. The local stone, unfortunately, was either a dirty dark-red freestone or a dull blue, which Scott disliked; he would therefore, although it would cost a little more, send to Sprouston, in Roxburghshire, for the beautiful grayish-white freestone of that county. The whole design—which he still called a cottage—Scott buoyantly believed might be made a reality for about £1,500.[8]

"I have got permission," he exulted to Stark, "to make all preparations for setting early to work in spring. The present farmhouse and offices are new and substantial, and may, with judicious additions, be converted into excellent offices. Clearing away the modern work from the interior of Melrose Abbey has afforded an excellent pile of building stone (a rare commodity in this country) to the purchase of which I hope to be preferred. I wish to build a wall and simple cottage, a laborer's (not a lodge) at the bend of the approach."[9] "Pray, as you are a ruling elder, solve me a case of conscience," Scott wrote James Ferrier, one of his fellow Clerks. "They are clearing out the modern additions from Melrose Abbey—will it be absolute sacrilege to build my cottage with the stones these operations afford, providing I can get them for next to nothing?"[10]

Stark came to Ashestiel with Terry, looked over the proposed site of the house at Abbotsford, and sketched "a most beautiful fanciful and at the same time convenient plan," with which Scott was delighted.[11] Lady Abercorn sent him a drawing of a cottage made by a Mrs. Long, "a person of great taste," for which he also expressed admiration.[12] But there were practical difficulties, he explained, about making a highly irregular roof watertight in the harsh Scottish climate. However, he tactfully added, he had gladly borrowed several hints from the design.[13] When Stark had turned out more detailed drawings, Scott's praise was enthusiastic—"a beautiful plan for a cottage indeed I think the prettiest I have ever seen" and "the interior the best laid out, and most commodious house I ever saw."[14] He does not give Stark's estimate of the cost. "*But* (for these horrid three letters always meet one in the teeth)" the amount made him wince.[15]

The design would demand "a great pouch full of money," far more than he could spare out of his ordinary income. Nevertheless, to spoil the plan by mean little economies was more than his heart could bear. "I am terribly afraid I must call in the aid of Amphion and his harp, not indeed to found a city, but if it can rear a cottage it will be very fair for a modern lyre."[16] At first Scott thought of a poem about the Bruce, and even made some headway on the project, but laid it aside when he reflected "that an English story might have more novelty."[17] Soon he was announcing a "grand project" to Morritt: "Nothing less than a fourth romance in verse, the theme during the English civil wars of Charles I and the scene your own domain of Rokeby."[18]

He therefore determined—"like a *canny Scot*," he said—that when he had to leave Ashestiel he would rough it temporarily in the little Cartley Hole farmhouse. The tenant, a man named Redford, would have moved out by that time and the place could be made to do "untill a years savings shall make up a purse to finish my intended mansion."[19] The farmhouse had "five tolerable rooms in it kitchen included and if all come to all," he told Joanna Baillie, "we can adopt your suggestion and make a bed in the barn. So you see I keep the lee-side of prudence in my proceedings."[20]

Meanwhile, July had seen the publication of *The Vision of Don Roderick*, the poem whose profits Scott dedicated to the Portuguese war sufferers. He showered small privately printed copies among his personal friends and correspondents and sent one of these as well as a large-paper copy to Lady Abercorn.[21] "I don't know if you are so great an admirer of Spenser as I am," he told Heber, "or whether you will allow of an imitation of his style without the rust of his *y-clads misers* and other peculiarities of phrase and orthography. I have studiously resisted all temptation to use complicated and involved construction and I hope the *sense* such as it is will be so evident that he who runs may read."[22]

The clarity at which he aimed he achieved, and even some passages of elaborate and ornate brilliance. But the design, a mere sequence of historical tableaux, is essentially undramatic. Don Roderick descends into a palatial subterranean hall where two bronze giants show him visions of the future fate of Spain. First, following his own defeat and death at the hands of the Moors in 714, there are the gardened harems of Alhambra; then the restored Christian era, with its blood-bedabbled conquests of Montezuma and the Incas, its golden ingots, and its tortured victims of superstition; next the slow decline of the Spanish monarchy under two centuries of corrupt and incompetent court intrigue; and last, Napoleon's cynical invasion of the tottering realm, the resistance of the Spanish patriots, and the great battles of Vimeiro, Talavera, and Fuentes de Onoro, in which Wellington was now smashing the Emperor's armed might.

All these scenes, however, though often picturesque, are no more than a series of colorful pageants; and the old Gothic kings, the Moors, the rule of Philip II, and the sleepy decline of the Escorial had in fact very little to do with the true theme of Scott's enthusiasm, the splendor of Wellington's exploits and the valor of British arms. Fully half the poem was but a prelude to the great hammer-blows echoing in Scott's heart. Despite his utmost pains bestowed upon them, the scenes, as he too truly said of the draft he had sent James Ballantyne in May, remained painted "in *dead* colors,"[23] and attained to none of the glow he achieved when his emotions caught fire. There was no climax because there was no connection; the martial thunders of the conclusion rang clamorous and noisy rather than glorious, oratorical rather than eloquent. Even the final passages of panegyric to Britain's heroic sons are no more than a magnificent rhetoric. Scott's sincerity of intention proved no substitute for an inspiration that failed his call. The poem remains, at best, a competent exercise in craftsmanship—as he himself called it, a "Drum and Trumpet performance."[24]

The public, however, received it well. "*Don Roderick*," said Scott, "has greatly exceeded my calculation as to popularity."[25] The reviewers, too, were predominantly laudatory. They all praised the vividness of the descriptions; most of them thought the successive visions handled with harmony and ease, although some doubts were felt about the propriety of mingling historical and allegorical figures. The effect, said one critic, was as strange as that of the paintings in the Luxembourg, where the "naked limbs and tridents, thunderbolts and caducei" of the Immortals contrasted so oddly "with the ruffs and whiskers, the queens, archbishops, and cardinals of France and Navarre."[26] Jeffrey complained of the irrelevance of the romantic earlier scenes and remarked that the poem had "scarcely any story, and scarcely any characters," but commended as brilliant in themselves the enchanted vault, the Gothic kings and Moorish invaders, with their harnessed knights, ravished damsels, and magic statues.[27] The *Quarterly Review* noted that the poem had none of "the interest derived from suspense" but ranked it above Gray's poem *The Bard* and all other poetic apparitions of the future, except for "Adam's Vision from the Mount of Paradise and the matchless beauties of the sixth book of Virgil."[28]

The summer following the publication of *Don Roderick* passed uneventfully. Richard Lovell Edgeworth, who had heard that Scott might visit Ireland for his researches on Swift, invited him to Edgeworthstown whenever he should come, and Scott replied that he would feel pride and pleasure in doing so. He had greatly enjoyed both Edgeworth's own writings and the novels of his gifted daughter Maria Edgeworth. He hoped they had not believed the idle rumor that he was guilty of the "very silly and impertinent review" of her *Tales of Fashionable Life* that had appeared in the *Quarterly Review*. The hilarious "Irish journey in the inimitable tale of *Ennui*" from those brilliant volumes had left his sides sore with laughter.[29]

In the middle of July, Scott was delighted to escape to the birches and alders, the long days, and the "somewhat clear" skies of Ashestiel.[30] It was the last summer the family would be spending there before their migration to Abbotsford in the following spring. As they basked "among gooseberries and currants," Scott looked forward to the move with a mingling of eagerness and nostalgia.[31] But change, he realized, was an inevitable part of human existence. Was not his feudal chief Scott of Harden even now enthusiastically supporting the construction of a railway into Berwickshire and converting all the Roxburghshire and Merse lairds to the project?[32] No doubt his relation's "Hobby horse," on which he wanted to make "every one canter along with him," would some day become a serious reality, and there would be railways running through the valley of the Tweed and even into Liddesdale.[33]

Scott did not want young Walter to fall behind in his Latin during these summer holidays. Consequently they read Caesar and Virgil together for two hours every morning, shifting to Buchanan's psalms on Sunday—"a great exertion," confessed Scott, "for my impatient temper."[34] "It is hard to say whether the preceptor or the scholar finds the task more wearisome,"[35] "because my knowledge of the language is more familiar than grammatical and because little Walter has a disconsolate yawn at intervals that is quite irresistible and has nearly cost me a dislocation of my jaws."[36] "However between yawning and scratching our head we get on pretty well."[37]

Although the new cottage at Abbotsford would not be started for another year, there were changes in the outbuildings that he wanted to begin next spring. He asked the permission of Mr. Redford, the departing tenant, to bring in building materials during the autumn and to put up a laborers' hut on the bank just west of the road. That October he also wanted to plant the western end of the haugh with acorns and seedlings and to repair the dike against winter floods. The bank below the road Scott intended to replant in turnips again as soon as Redford got off his own crop in the spring. All Redford's "away-going crop corn as well as fallow and dung" he was willing to buy at a fair valuation.[38]

The seedlings and acorns on the haugh were the beginnings of Scott's dream to surround Abbotsford with noble English oaks. He told his friends his plans; they responded with acorns by the cartload.[39] The Earl of Clarendon was eager to send all Scott desired: "If I had any magic at once to make them into a Grove, I need not say that it should be such a one as I thought the Muses would be most likely to haunt."[40] Morritt sent acorns from Rokeby by coach, Hartstonge from Ireland by ship.[41] "I assure you," Scott told Morritt, "I will plant them in your name with my own hands and those of my little people and we will promise ourselves a *Morritt grove* when the fit time shall come around."[42]

Lord Glenbervie sent acorns; either George Ellis or Joanna Baillie sent a bag of them from Windsor Forest; the Marchioness of Stafford sent some to Leith. Scott gloried in the thought of his "future oaks."[43] Bare though the place was now, "Wood rises very fast with us every-where," he said; and he foresaw the time when he would "be embosom'd in a little wood."[44] "I am torturing my brains for the best means of con-quering the prim regularity of artificial plantations which I think may be done by putting in plants of different ages and even sowing some part of the ground."[45]

Acorns, however, were not the only arrivals Scott welcomed to his little estate; at the end of August came his Irish correspondent Harts-tonge. "The mail will set you down within a mile of my dwelling," Scott directed him, "at a small hamlet called Clovenfords. You have but to name the day and I will have a servant waiting for you with a chaise; if you cannot do that let the hostler shoulder your portmanteau and shew you the way to Ashestiel shout lustily for the boat over the Tweed and you will be with us in an instant."[46]

Scott took his guest to see "all that is memorable in our wilds," including the bare slopes that were to be the future forests of Abbots-ford.[47] One mild September morning they strolled to the pond at Faldon-side and from there up to Cauldshiels Loch, little Walter scampering along with a toy boat which he launched onto the water and which Scott had to wade after when it was blown out by an untoward breeze.[48] On his return to Dublin, in his letter of thanks Hartstonge enclosed copies of various rare compositions by Swift, including a letter "to Mrs Pratt," "exceedingly witty," a bottle of lavender water for Charlotte, and a poem commemorating his visit, which he had written at Clovenfords: "On leaving Ashestiel, Ettrick Forest: the seat of Walter Scott, Esq."[49]

Almost upon the heels of his departure appeared the Kembles, the stout tragedian gasping with asthma but gallantly bouncing over the hills with Scott on an excursion to the Braes of Yarrow.[50] October saw Daniel Terry and William Stark at Ashestiel, "hammering with 'cauk and keel'" at the plans for the Abbotsford cottage.[51] At the same time came James Ferrier, bringing his gifted daughter Susan, who during the previous year, unknown to anyone, had written a novel entitled *Marriage*, which she was to publish anonymously in 1818. The weather had turned broken and stormy, but in spite of wind and rain Charlotte took Susan out on short afternoon carriage drives, the men cantering by their side and ten-year-old Walter jogging on a pony. In the evenings Scott recited ballads and Terry dramatically read plays aloud.[52]

The night before their departure there was a perfect hurricane; the next morning, while the horses were being harnessed to their carriage, Scott wrote an impromptu in Susan's album:

> The mountain winds are up, and proud
> O'er heath and hill careening loud;
> The groaning forest to its power
> Yields all that formed our summer bower.
>
> . . .
>
> How much we forest-dwellers grieve
> Our valued friends our cot should leave
> Unseen each beauty that we boast,
> The little wonders of our coast,
> That still the pile of Melrose grey
> For you must rise in Minstrel's lay,
> And Yarrow's birks, immortal long,
> For you but bloom in rural song
> Yet hope who still in present sorrow
> Whispers the promise of tomorrow
>
> . . .
>
> When the wild whirlwind shall be still
> And summer sleep on glen and hill
> And Tweed unvexd by storms shall glide
> In silvery maze his stately tide
> Doubling in mirror every rank
> Of oak and alder on his bank
> And our kind guests such welcome prove
> As most we wish to those we love.[53]

From the Isle of Man now came word from Scott's brother Tom that at last he had an opportunity to settle himself. The Manx Fencibles had been disbanded that spring, but his wife's cousin Colonel Ross, formerly Governor of Demarara, had returned to England with a large fortune, and was using his influence in Tom's behalf. At first there had been talk of a post in the Demarara Customs, paying £1,200 a year and offering opportunities to "make a large fortune in a few years." This had fallen through; the Colonel's own brother decided to take it himself.[54] Tom had disappointedly thought of taking orders, a step that Scott discouraged on the ground that the clergy were miserably paid,[55] but that he privately regarded as "a sneaking line" unless its adoption was "dictated by a strong feeling of principle."[56]

Colonel Ross had presently offered Tom appointment as the Paymaster of his own Regiment, the 70th.[57] Two sureties of £1,000 each were required. "If General Stuart will be security for him for £1,000," Scott wrote his mother, "I would propose that Tom should give me an assignation in security to the extent of £500 over the funds in the Trustees . . ." In justice to his own dependents Scott thought he should be protected against the risk of losing the entire £1,000, but for Tom's sake he was ready to chance half of it rather "than refuse my assistance at this moment."[58] General Stuart, however, said it was not at all the line for Tom, and declined to assume any financial responsibility; so did their cousin Alexander Keith of Ravelston, to whom Tom appealed in a vain hope that "matrimony may have enlarg'd his heart, and he may be disposed to stand my friend."[59] Ultimately, Tom's brother-in-law Robert McCulloch became surety for the other £1,000.

Old Mrs. Scott offered to give Walter security upon £500 she intended to leave Tom, "the money to lye for your relief as long as He is in that situation, so that if it is lost it is Lost to Himself, but I hope in God what he has suffered will make him more cautious for the future. I would have wished it had been a situation where he had nothing to do with money but I am happy to get him in Active Life again."[60] Scott accepted their mother's offer, dropping his suggestion that Tom give him any security. "This will leave his share of my father's funds altogether unburthened."[61] Whether he would ever claim the financial protection she was giving him, he wrote his mother, "might depend much upon my circumstances at the time, but I cannot but think Tom will be as cautious in his conduct or fully more so if he thinks it may involve his own family as if it only concerned mine."[62]

Whether Tom's predecessor could retire at once depended upon Lord Palmerston, the Secretary at War. In the hope of accelerating Palmerston's decision, Tom went to London. Scott always believed that "a little personal influence" was helpful; he therefore wrote Heber and Ellis, requesting their good offices.[63] "If you can assist poor Tom in this matter," he told the former, "you will do me a most essential kindness and at the same time do a very good and benevolent action." He himself, he added, was "busy planting [and] ornamenting" at Abbotsford, "where I hope we may one day crack a social bottle of Claret."[64]

The end of October saw Tom's affairs successfully concluded, and not long afterward he was gazetted as Paymaster of the 70th. Scott sent his brother's wife £100 to help discharge any debts he might have on the Isle of Man,[65] and settled back happily to building his dike against the winter floods of the Tweed.[66] When there was a violent storm, early in November, he observed with satisfaction that although the water came up "within nine inches of the top of my barrier," "the flood-dyke . . . held out bravely."[67] He begged his neighbor Alexander Pringle "for a large double-stemmed birch which, among other damage, the late tempest has blown down in Yair Craig Wood . . . It would suit me particularly to make rustic pillars for a little porch before a cottage at Abbotsford."[68] By October 19 the children had already returned to Edinburgh, where Scott and Charlotte expected to follow them in another three weeks.[69]

"Kiss the Oes [grandchildren] for us," he wrote his mother. "Do not plague yourself with more than one at a time."[70] Indeed, four lively youngsters might well be a strain on an old lady now in her eightieth year. Scott himself, as he sometimes realized with surprise, had passed his own fortieth birthday. "Our little folks," he wrote Leyden, "whom you left infants are now shooting fast forward into youth . . . Charlotte and I are wearing on as easily as this fasheous world will permit; the outside of my head is waxing grizzled but I cannot find that the snow has cooled my brain or my heart. Adieu dear Leyden pray brighten the chain of friendship by a letter when occasion serves . . ."[71]

But Leyden never replied. On the very day Scott's letter was written he had thrown himself into the surf to be the first member of the British expedition to set foot on Java. The surprise attack had given them instant possession of Batavia.[72] Leyden dashed, still perspiring from battle, into a damp and long-closed library of rare Indian manuscripts; by nightfall he shivered with fever. Three days later he was dead.[73]

Before closing Ashestiel for the winter, Scott and Charlotte were busy packing their household goods for moving. "I leave to my better half the care of furniture and china, yet there are such things as books and papers, not to mention broad-swords and targets, battle-axes and helmets, guns, pistols, and dirks . . . besides the bustle of ten thousand directions, to be given in one breath of time, concerning ten thousand queries, carefully reserved for that parting moment, by those who might as well have made them six months before."[74] Scott himself would be back during the holidays "to see how things go on at Abbotsford," but the Hardens were not to be at Mertoun, so the rest of his family would remain in Edinburgh. "In the Christmas vacation," he wrote Charles Erskine, "I shall claim a goose from you."[75]

Scott soon made two glorious additions to the collection of targes and claymores that were to embellish the future curio room at Abbotsford. "I have a very important matter to settle," he excitedly broke off a letter to Joanna Baillie, "—no less than to close a treaty for the gun and arms of old Rob Roy."[76] Part of "a small lot of ancient armour and other curiosities . . . the stock in trade of a Virtuoso who is leaving off collecting,"[77] the weapon was a long-barreled Spanish piece engraved with Rob Roy's initials.[78] "I defy any one to say that there is a single article among the two hundred which can be of use to a human being excepting indeed a snuff Box, and that is useless to me as I never take snuff."[79]

"I have moreover a relique of a more heroic character—it is a sword which was given to the great Marquis of Montrose by Charles I and appears to have belonged to his father our gentle King Jamie."[80] This was a gift from John Ballantyne, who had bought the library of Montrose' descendant, Graham of Gartmore. Graham had at first resisted selling it: "No, by God, I am bad enough; but not quite so low as that yet." But Ballantyne declined to strike a bargain unless the owner flung the sword into the scale; if he did, John wheedled, "I will, in twenty-four hours, make the whole a ready-money transaction." "Take it, and be damned to you. My poverty, but not my will consents."[81]

The prize now hung over the chimney piece of Scott's library in Castle Street, and on a nearby wall a contemporary portrait of the brilliant soldier who had worn it.[82] "And here it is," he later crowed delightedly to John Morrison. "This is the very sword sent by King Charles to the gallant Montrose, the general of his armies in Scotland." But Morrison refused to handle the weapon: "It was drawn against the cause in which my fathers bled, and I should account it pollution to touch it." "Morrison, if you had lived in those times you would either have been killed or hanged." "And why not? . . . Might not this lucky hand have saved the hangman's trouble, as a predestined arm achieved in the case of his descendant and successor, bloody Clavers? But we will let the old fellows sleep." "So be it," said Scott.[83]

Shortly before Christmas little Walter had the measles, "with a tremendous quantity of spots and swelling."[84] But they went off quickly, and as soon as it was clear that he was recovering Scott made his way to Ashestiel, from which he could ride over to see how his workmen were getting on at Abbotsford.[85] In the midst of the snow he spent three days planting Hartstonge's acorns on a knoll with his own hands. Then he was called back to Edinburgh by the news that all the other children had caught the measles from Gilnockie.[86]

Scott felt desperately alarmed. The disease, he knew, had been fatal to several of his brothers and sisters and had ravaged the families of his friends.[87] Little Charles was in graver danger than the others, and even after seeming to get better had a frightening relapse. Scott trembled with terror. Slowly, however, they all recovered, although in the middle of January Charles was still very weak.[88] From the moment the children began mending, Scott deluged them with asses' milk. "Really it operates," he remarked in jesting relief, "as if they had been like Dogberry written down asses' colts, for they have overcome under its genial influence all the peaking, pining and consumptive coughing" that usually followed the illness.[89]

On January 17, Scott attended the funeral of his old patron, the Duke of Buccleuch.[90] "I thought the last time I saw him (about a month before his death)," Scott said, "that the hand of fate was upon him." He had died quietly in the arms of his son and was buried in the family vault at Dalkeith.[91] "Few men have been followed to the grave," Scott wrote, "with so many tears of friendship and gratitude."[92] "My friend Lord Dalkeith succeeds to the power and fortune of his father with some points which these evil times require, for with all his father's good-nature he has something in him that will not allow it to be trampled upon and I think that in our homely ballad rhyme he is likely to prove

> "—a *hedge* about his friends
> A *heckle* to his foes—"[93]

The illness of the children had interrupted Scott's progress on Swift, but he had now completed almost all the editorial work and was ready to begin writing the life. He was relying, he wrote Berwick, on him "for light upon the melancholy chapter of Vanessa."[94] Berwick did not disappoint him. He had seen "the original rough drafts of all Vanessa's letters to Swift in her own hand," and had made copies of them; he also had revelatory knowledge about Swift's conduct to Stella. "I think his unaccountable behaviour hastened the death of the one and broke the heart of the other."[95] Lady Louisa Stuart added a strange story that had come to her directly from the lips of Swift's friend Dr. Patrick Delaney. As he was going into Archbishop King's library, "Swift rushed out with a countenance of distraction, and passed him without speaking." The Doctor found the Archbishop in tears. "You have just met the most unhappy man upon earth," King said solemnly, "but on the subject of his wretchedness you must never ask a question."[96]

Scott was now drawing his full court salary. Old Mr. Home, however, had thought better of refusing Scott's offer to make up the difference between his pension and his former salary and magnanimously agreed to accept £960 a year instead of the £800 to which he was entitled.[97] In view of the Treasury's long delay before deciding that Home's retirement and Scott's succession were both legal, he had hoped he might be granted what he called "a *back-spang*" of a quarter or two— particularly as it was costing him around £300 to outfit Tom for his post as Paymaster.[98] A windfall of £325 or £650, as he remarked to his mother, would be "no deaf nuts" under the circumstances.[99] The Treasury seems to have felt no such impulse of generosity, but even so Scott's income had taken a leap of over £1,000.[100]

The cost of his Tweedside cottage, on the other hand, would come to much more, and, as he had already told Morritt, he had decided to write another poem. "If I build," he wrote Surtees, "I must have money, and I know none will give me any but the booksellers; so I must get up into my wheel, like a turnspit, or lose the pleasant prospect of one day placing roast mutton before you at Abbotsford. I think of laying my scene near Barnard Castle, where there is some beautiful scenery, with which I am pretty well acquainted."[101] He would rekindle his memories by revisiting Rokeby that summer. He had sketched out a story that pleased him but was keeping it dark, lest it be "piddled upon by some of your Ready to Catch literati as John Bunyan calls them."[102]

But he began bombarding Morritt with questions. "What the deuce is the name of that wild glen where we had such a clamber on horseback up a stone staircase?—Cats-cradle or Cats castle I think it was." What was that traditional tragedy of Morritt's old house at Mortham and its ghost? Was there some book on the scenic beauties of Teesdale?[103] Morritt responded delightedly with pages of antiquarian lore about Barnard Castle and Rokeby since the time of William the Conqueror. Scott must certainly see the neighborhood again under his guidance: " 'I know each dale and every alley green,' between Rokeby and the Lakes and Caves . . ." And when the inevitable influx of cockney romancers and sentimental tourists followed the publication of Scott's poem, "I shall raise the rent of my inn at Greta Bridge . . . as I hear the people at Callander have made a fortune by you."[104]

Early in February Scott sent Tom Purdie instructions about the planting at Abbotsford. Tom must take pains not to put the shrubs in regular rows but mingle them as if they had been sown by chance. On the bank above the house, and in the hedge between the haugh and the garden, there should be privet, holly, sweetbriar, honeysuckle, wild rose, and a white convolvulus, which would thrive beautifully with blackthorn. Near the edges of the plantation he should take care to scatter red oaks and red beeches. He must avoid all formality of arrangement, sometimes placing a score or two of oaks with a sprinkling of other trees, sometimes chestnuts or elms. He should not forget to leave room for shrubs.[105]

At the end of the month, Scott himself was at Abbotsford for a few days, "planting, ditching, and fencing" and dirtying himself to the knees laying out walks.[106] He had decided, he told the builders, Messrs. Sanderson and Paterson, of Galashiels, to move the farmhouse "a little more to the westward and incline it somewhat to the South" and had made a few "trifling alterations in the plan the piggery being turned into a coal house &c." Their estimate for digging the foundation seemed reasonable; he would come out again on March 19 or 20 and mark the exact location for them.[107]

If they could erect the lodge in sufficient time, he went on, it would provide accommodation for the family of his coachman, Peter Matheson, until Scott's own family arrived for the summer, when it would be needed as a temporary kitchen and servants' hall. The stone from Hailes and Sprouston was so dear that he had decided to use local stone from Dryburgh, much as he disliked its color. Large slates would enable him to keep the roof at a somewhat lower pitch. Wood for the house must be bought immediately so that it could be laid down for an entire year's seasoning.[108]

Late in March winter returned violently.[109] "We are here in a most extraordinary pickle," Scott wrote after a fortnight of freezing weather, "considering that we have just entered upon April when according to the poet 'primroses paint the gay plain' instead of which both hill and valley are doing penance in a sheet of snow . . . Mail coaches have been stopped, shepherds I grieve to say lost . . . all the hardships of a January storm at this late period of spring."[110] At the beginning of May, while masons laid the foundations of the cottage and built a garden wall, the snow was not only heavy on the summits of the hills but thick on the lower ground.[111] Seven days later it was swirling down furiously through a howling northeast wind.[112]

Through all this, while the children remained in Edinburgh, Scott and Charlotte had been camping out in the partly dismantled rooms of Ashestiel with Macbeth, the butler, and a lame dairy maid, "keeping house by ourselves" and all clubbing "their skill to make up the dinner."[113] During the day, at Abbotsford, they had been "planting trees and shrubs amongst the snow of this dreadful season arguing the faith of a saint," Scott said, on their part, "and the patience of a martyr on the part of the things committed to the earth."[114] The first parcel of acorns from Hartstonge, which they had planted with so much care, proved to have been almost entirely devoured "by those foes to Forest ground the Mice. I have replanted the same spot with the assistance of Mrs. Scott with my own fair hands."[115]

Suddenly, overnight, it was "absolute summer, greatly to the refreshment of the young lambs and grass and corn." The sun glowed down upon the sapling trees and infant shrubs, and the parents prepared to fetch the children from Castle Street.[116] Since they were going to live so near Melrose Abbey, Scott wrote Sophia, she must learn all about it. He hoped Walter had "plied his lesson hard" and that Anne and Charles had been good children. "You must kiss them all for me and pat up little Wallace. . . . I think we shall be home on Thursday or Friday so the Cook can have something ready for a beefsteak or mutton chop in case we are past your dinner hour."[117]

The poem that was to pay for their new home had not been forgotten. "My work *Rokeby* does and must go forward," Scott told Morritt, "or my trees and inclosures might perchance stand still. But I destroyed the first canto after I had written it fair out because it did not quite please me."[118] "I am hammering my brains upon an odd subject," he wrote Miss Clephane. "I will not tell it to you because I may possibly fling it all in the fire but it is . . . nearer that of *Marmion* than any of the other attempts I have made. But my cottage is rising and the fates will have it so that like Vanburghs house it must rise to the clinking of noise. All our children are thank God now quite strong again and Walter begins once more to look like the laird of Gilnockie after the rude shaking which the measles gave him."[119]

The clinking trowels of the masons and his own hammer blows at *Rokeby* did not take up all Scott's attention. Even in the midst of planting, path making, writing, building, and preparations for moving, he still found time for a host of interchanges with his friends. Pringle of Whytbank had recently suffered an attack of the gout; perhaps "among the enclosed volumes" of Weber's *Tales of the East*, just published by John Ballantyne, he might find "some talisman to charm away the time at least, if not the pain."[120] Charles Kirkpatrick Sharpe had composed a risqué ballad about a lady who blissfully submitted to being raped; the verses reminded him, said Scott's note, of another "witty ballad on a similar subject in which a fair lady is assailed by a naked Spectre:

"And in his hand withal
A thing which we for modesty
A pistol chose to call."[121]

Almost on the tail of this indelicate exchange Scott was called upon for his congratulations on a wedding. His fair widowed cousin, the witty lion-huntress Mrs. Apreece, had caught as her second husband a great lion indeed, none other than the famous Humphry Davy.[122] "I am not going to claim an Epithalamium," she wrote saucily.[123] Scott's acknowledgment recalled that he and Davy had met some half-dozen years earlier, when they had climbed Helvellyn with Wordsworth.[124]

Despite his momentary irritation over the sneers of *English Bards and Scotch Reviewers*, Scott had cherished no grudge against the "whelp of a young Lord Byron"[125] who was their author. Barely a month after the publication of *Childe Harold's Pilgrimage* he was praising the poem to Joanna Baillie. It was a very clever poem, he told Joanna, though one hardly speaking well for "the writers heart or morals." There was an "impudence at least equal to the noble lord's other powers" in gravely claiming "sympathy for the ennui arising from his being tired of his wassailers and his paramours. . . . Yet with all this conceit and assurance there is much poetical merit in the book and I wish you would read it."[126]

He sang its praises to Morritt even more enthusiastically. Byron's misanthropy gave "an odd poignancy to his descriptions and reflections"; it was "a poem of most extraordinary power and may rank its author with our first poets."[127] Morritt agreed; he had found the descriptions "so spirited, and the sentiments, however gloomy and mischievous . . . so powerful and drest in such brilliant poetry" that he had "hardly laid the book down without longing to take it up again."[128]

Morritt's letter also told a lively bit of gossip about Lady Holland, who rejoiced in the possession of a chamber pot made of silver. "This little appendage of domestic luxury," to which she applied herself assiduously, had "become so essential to her ladyship's comfort" that, "disdaining the China substitute" in ordinary use, she even carried it with her when she visited her friends. At one country house the chambermaid brought this chalice to the underbutler; "it was *his* business," she said, "to clean *plate*." "The underbutler appealed to the Major domo, alleging that a *pot-de-chambre*, though of silver, did not fall within his jurisdiction." From these "ladies and gentlemen of the second and third tables" the dispute raged through the housekeeper and butler up to Lady Holland's host and hostess, who had ever since been angry at her fastidiousness.[129]

Scott capped Morritt's stercoraceous story with another he had often heard from Robert Dundas of Arniston. There was a tremendous silver vessel at Arniston Castle, not reserved for any one person, but brought into the dining room after dinner, when the ladies had left the table and the serious drinking had gotten under way, for the general comfort of all the men. One unlucky day the ladies sat longer at table than usual, but when the bell rang the ancient butler had "no doubt it was the well-known signal." Into the room he stalked, "a man of a most reverend and dignified appearance . . . bearing in both hands this brilliant Heirloom," which for all its antique design was of unmistakable purpose. Absorbed in bearing his enormous burden, he had reached the top of the room and placed it "on its usual throne before he perceived his blunder," exclaimed "God forgie me," and beat a hasty retreat, shrouding the embarrassing object in a huge napkin. "This story," Scott concluded, "the Chief Baron tells with great humour."[130]

The time of the removal to Abbotsford was fast approaching.[131] "Are you not sorry," asked the Ettrick Shepherd, "at leaving *auld Ashestiel* for *gude an' a'* . . .?"[132] And Joanna Baillie wrote, "If I should ever be happy enough to be at Abbotsford, you must take me to see Ashestiel too. I have a kind of tenderness for it, as one has for a man's first wife, when you hear he has married a second."[133] Their neighbors, too, felt mournful to see the family go. "I am apt to think you will be a Tweedside Laird," old Nippy Laidlaw told Scott, "but Mrs. L. and me will be sorry to part with Mrs. Scott; you! and your dear Children. . . ."[134] Years later Scott was touched to learn that Nippy had carefullly kept in good repair the turf seat on what was still called "the Shirra's knowe."[135] There were sad hearts, as well, among the poor cottagers whom Charlotte had relieved from her larder when they were hungry and dosed from her medicine chest when they were ill.[136]

But the day of departure came. On May 21 they started out for their new home. Twenty people were clamoring around Scott, with twenty different demands, all stunning his ears.[137] "Our flitting and removal from Ashestiel," he wrote Daniel Terry, "baffled all description; we had twenty-four cart-loads of the veriest trash in nature, besides dogs, pigs, poneys, poultry, cows, calves, bare-headed wenches, and bare-breeched boys."[138]

The flitting, in fact, turned into a parade. Charlotte rode in the carriage, with Miss Millar, the governess, chubby little Charles, and Anne, and Peter Matheson driving. Scott and the two other children were outriders, Sophia perched on horseback and Gilnockie digging his heels into the sides of a pony. Menservants and maidservants under the command of Tom Purdie stowed themselves on farm wagons creaking along under loads of household gear. Sheep, cows, and pigs plodded along, bleating, mooing, and grunting.

The neighbors stared delightedly at "the procession of my furniture," Scott said, with "old swords, bows, targets, and lances" glinting in the sun. "A family of turkies was accommodated within the helmet of some *preux* chevalier of ancient border fame and the very cows, for aught I know, were bearing banners and muskets."[139] So, attended by ragged, rosy peasant children carrying fishing rods and spears, and leading greyhounds and spaniels, the caravan splashed through the ford and wound its way down the Tweed. Scott was now, as Joanna Baillie had hailed him, the Laird of Abbotsford.

PLATE I: *Scott's mother, Anne Scott.* (THE SCOTTISH NATIONAL POR-
TRAIT GALLERY)

PLATE II: *The College Wynd, Scott's birthplace.* (THE NEW YORK PUBLIC LIBRARY)

PLATE III: *Walter Scott at the age of six: the "Bath miniature."* (THE SCOTTISH NATIONAL PORTRAIT GALLERY)

PLATE IV: *Scott's great-grandfather, "Beardie."* (ANTHONY HOWARTH, AMERICAN HERITAGE)

PLATE V: *Number 25 George Square, Scott's father's house and Scott's home until his marriage in 1797.* (THE SCOTTISH NATIONAL PORTRAIT GALLERY)

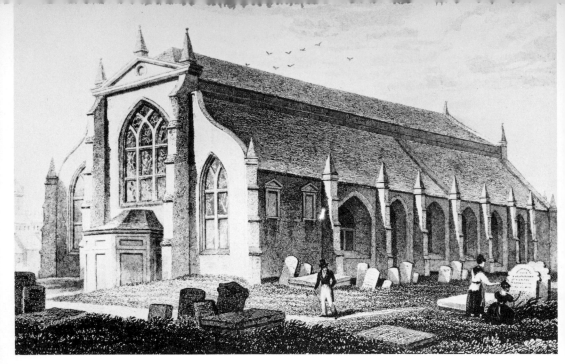

PLATE VI: *Greyfriars' Church.* (THE NEW YORK PUBLIC LIBRARY)

PLATE VII: *Holyrood Palace.* (THE NEW YORK PUBLIC LIBRARY)

PLATE VIII: *The Kirk of St. Giles.* (THE NEW YORK PUBLIC LIBRARY)

PLATE IX: *Professor Daniel Rutherford, Scott's uncle. Engraving by Holl after a portrait by Sir Henry Raeburn.* (THE SCOTTISH NATIONAL PORTRAIT GALLERY)

PLATE X: *The West Bow.* (THE NEW YORK PUBLIC LIBRARY)

PLATE XI: *Edinburgh Castle.* (THE NEW YORK PUBLIC LIBRARY)

PLATE XII: *Kelso Abbey*. (THE NEW YORK PUBLIC LIBRARY)

PLATE XIII: *Scott's meeting with Robert Burns at Sciennes House, the home of Professor Adam Ferguson.*

PLATE XIV: *Professor Dugald Stewart, under whom Scott studied philosophy at the University of Edinburgh, 1789–1790. Drawing by Sir David Wilkie, 1828.* (THE SCOTTISH NATIONAL PORTRAIT GALLERY)

PLATE XV: *Williamina Belsches, Scott's early love.* (THE SCOTTISH NATIONAL PORTRAIT GALLERY)

PLATE XVI: *William Erskine, later Lord Kinnedder, a lifelong friend of Scott's. Portrait by William Nicholson.* (THE SCOTTISH NATIONAL PORTRAIT GALLERY)

PLATE XVII: *Walter Scott. Portrait by William Nicholson.* (THE SCOTTISH NATIONAL PORTRAIT GALLERY)

PLATE XVIII: *William Laidlaw, Scott's companion on some of the Border "raids," and later his factor at Abbotsford.* (THE SCOTTISH NATIONAL PORTRAIT GALLERY)

PLATE XIX: *James Hogg, "the Ettrick Shepherd." Portrait by William Nicholson.* (THE SCOTTISH NATIONAL PORTRAIT GALLERY)

PLATE XX: *Scott's meeting with Hogg at Ettrick Cottage.*

PLATE XXI: *Charlotte, Scott's wife. Portrait by James Saxon.* (ABBOTSFORD)

PLATE XXII: *Lasswade Cottage, Scott's summer home 1798–1803.* (THE SCOTTISH NATIONAL PORTRAIT GALLERY)

PLATE XXIII: *Number 39 Castle Street, Scott's Edinburgh home 1801–1826. Watercolor and pencil sketch by J. M. W. Turner.* (THE PIERPONT MORGAN LIBRARY)

PLATE XXIV: *George Street, where Scott's mother lived 1800–1819.* (THE NEW YORK PUBLIC LIBRARY)

PLATE XXV: *Ashestiel, Scott's country home 1804–1812. Illustration by J. M. W. Turner for* Marmion. (THE NEW YORK PUBLIC LIBRARY)

PLATE XXVI: *James Ballantyne, Scott's friend from boyhood, and partner in the printing firm of James Ballantyne and Company.* (THE SCOTTISH NATIONAL PORTRAIT GALLERY)

PLATE XXVII: *John Ballantyne, Scott's literary agent,
and partner in the publishing house of John Ballantyne
and Company.* (THE SCOTTISH NATIONAL PORTRAIT
GALLERY)

PLATE XXVIII: *George Gordon Noel, Lord Byron.
Portrait by T. Phillips.* (THE NATIONAL PORTRAIT
GALLERY, LONDON)

# 3

## My Old Cossack Manner

### ( 1 8 1 2 − 1 8 1 3 )

THEIR ARRIVAL at Abbotsford was a wild hubbub. "Everything went wrong. The horses jibbed at entering the stables; the cows and sheep ran out of the pastures as soon as they were put in; the hens flew out of the chicken yard—the kitchen fire would not burn, the oven would not bake, the jack would not go, the pump would give no water, the men swore, the maids wept," Charlotte scolded. Everyone hurried to Scott "with complaints of each other." At last he could bear it no longer. He dashed out, "burst into a tremendous passion," shouted a lot, cursed a little, "and in half an hour everything and everybody were in their right places."[1]

In comparison with Ashestiel their quarters were uncomfortably cramped. The whole family had to be crammed into the four small rooms and kitchen of the little farmhouse formerly tenanted by the Redfords. "Our only sitting room," wrote Scott, "is about twelve feet square and all the others in proportion: so that upon the whole we live as if we were on board of ship."[2] Their tiny parlor served as drawing room, dining room, schoolroom, and study. Scott had no room to himself; his desk was pushed up against a window and an old bed curtain was nailed up close behind his chair. Here, when he was not busy with the spade, the dibble, or the chisel,[3] he retired to labor on the composition of *Rokeby*, "one poor noddle" hammering out verses[4] amid the clatter and clamor of carpenters and masons, the chatter of Charlotte's voice, and the babble of the children reciting their lessons to Miss Millar.[5]

Outdoors, Scott was walling in three-quarters of an acre for the garden and building the coachhouse, laundry, pantry, and storehouse. "An old coal-hole," he said, "makes our cellar." Upstairs, the room above their crowded sitting room was "subdivided for cribs to the children," and "a garret above the little kitchen with a sort of light closet make bedroom and dressing-room decorated—lumbered, my wife says—with all my guns pistols targets broadswords bugle-horns and old armour."[6] The whole of these "temporary barracks,"[7] he remarked cheerfully, was little more than "a sort of poultry house."[8]

Until the Court of Session rose on July 12, Scott divided his time between Edinburgh and Tweedside, hurrying down to Abbotsford each weekend for bouts of digging and building.[9] An early digging operation was a grave for one of the two greyhounds, Percy, whom Scott buried on the bank between the house and the road. He intended, he wrote Terry, to set up over the spot an old stone, inscribed " '*Ci gist le preux Percie*,' and I hope future antiquaries will debate which hero of the house of Northumberland has left his bones in Teviotdale."[10]

All the expenses of wresting Abbotsford into shape left Scott feeling a little pinched for money. "I am getting deep into nursery men's books," he told Heber, "not to mention a set of offices which are rising not like 'some tall palm' but rather like a burdock."[11] Consequently, although his mouth watered at the news that the great library of the Duke of Roxburghe was being auctioned off in London, he decided that he would have to look on its treasures like the fox on the grapes. What with planting, walling, building, and "a wife and four bairns crying as our old song has it, 'Crowdy ever mair,' " he could not afford rare editions.[12]

But ultimately his wistfulness overcame him. After all, had he not at last "flung mine ancient rider George Home not upon the ground but upon the broad shoulders of the public who have granted him a super-annuation allowance"? How could he resist the temptation of "sporting forty or by our lady some fifty pounds in St. James's Square"? He there-fore marked down a number of items on which he begged Heber to bid for him,[13] and was presently delighted to learn that, in spite of the high prices, his friend had succeeded in obtaining *L'Hystoire de Guerin de Montglave* and a copy of *Huon de Bordeaux*, "the most beautiful of the old Romances."[14]

He was also delighted to receive from Charles Kirkpatrick Sharpe a comical drawing portraying the espousal of Meikle-mouthed Meg to the young Knight of Harden. "I think it is quite perfect," he told the artist donor, "the rueful helpless resignation of the heroe, the exhorta-tions of the priest, who obviously feels the drollery of the dilemma, the sly looks of the mother, the glee of the poor damsel, and the determined obstinate attitude of the baronial papa . . ."[15]

The letter with which Sharpe had accompanied his gift scornfully quoted a newspaper obituary eulogizing the Duchess of Gordon, then recently dead, as "The fair Fidele"; "there are fairer things," Sharpe spat, "than Pole-cats, sure."[16] Although Scott disliked speaking ill of people, he felt obliged to agree: "The fair Fidele with a pize to her!—

'twas as rampant a brimstone as ever came out of Billingsgate, whose sole claim to wit rested upon her brazen impudence and disregard to the feelings of all who were near her."[17]

From the fair Fidele, Sharpe turned his pointed tongue to an earlier Duchess of Gordon, the wife of the second Duke; he had, he told Scott, "a packet of letters" which proved that this great lady "had the turn of Sappho, and of many ladies mentioned by Brantome."[18] "What you tell me of the D. of G.," Scott replied, "is very curious and might enlighten the intellects of some of our judges who in a *cause célèbre* of our own day protested . . . that there were no such propensities . . ."[19]

Sharpe's indubitable knowledge of antiquities suggested to Scott what he called a "hobby horsical proposal" to amuse their winter evenings. "What think you of a selection of the most striking and absurd stories of apparitions witchcraft demonology and so forth tacked together with ironical disquisitions and occasionally ornamented with historical and antiquarian anecdotes and instead of a broomstick to slap three or four humorous drawings to the tails of our witches . . . We would carefully conceal names and I am certain might have a great deal of fun and afford some to the public. We could divide the literary part of the task as was most agreeable to you. . . . Pray let me interest you in this matter

> "For if you deign not to assist
> You make all this an idle dream."[20]

The collaboration Scott proposed never took place, but the idea of a work on demonology and witchcraft did not vanish from his mind.

Despite the bustle of getting settled down in their new home, Scott and Charlotte found time for an enjoyable reading of Maria Edgeworth's tales, which she had sent them from Ireland. Charlotte particularly admired *The Emigrants*; the portrayal of "Madame la Marquise," she said, was "the finest picture of a French woman of fashion that was ever given to the public." Scott himself liked *The Absentee* best of all: "I have grown as fond of Sir Terry as of Falstaff." And just as he hoped that Henry V, in an "incognito sort of manner which could give no scandal or offense to the Lord Chief-Justice," occasionally smuggled the fat knight into the palace for a convivial evening, "so, I have little doubt that when Sir Terry had made the most of his jockey contract and whitewashed himself, he certainly returned to Ireland and now and then saw Lord Clonberry."[21]

This first summer at Abbotsford brought the beginning of a friendly correspondence between Scott and Lord Byron. That rising star of the poetic world had repented his sneering attack on the author of *Marmion* and seized upon an opportunity to extend him an olive branch. He had attended an evening party where for more than half an hour the Prince Regent had expressed his enraptured delight in the writings of Walter

Scott. This eulogy Byron immediately passed on, for Scott's ears, to John Murray, the publisher, "thinking that it might not be ungrateful for you to hear." Despite the Prince's scandalous life of luxurious libertinism, he was also a man of taste, deeply versed in literature and the arts. He preferred Scott, Byron said, "far beyond every other poet of his time"—no small tribute from a royal personage who had read, as it appeared to Byron, "more poetry than any prince in Europe."[22]

In reply Scott sent Byron "my best thanks for the flattering communication which you took the trouble to make Mr. Murray on my behalf" and told him of "the high pleasure I have received from the *Pilgrimage of Childe Harold* . . . This leads me to put your Lordship right in the circumstances respecting the sale of *Marmion*, which had reached you in a distorted and misrepresented form . . . The poem, my Lord, was *not* written upon contract for a sum of money—though it is too true that it was sold and published in a very unfinished state (which I have since regretted) to enable me to extricate myself from some engagements which fell suddenly upon me from the unexpected misfortunes of a very near relation."[23]

"I am sure your Lordship's good sense will easily put this unimportant egotism to the right account, for—though I do not know the motive would make me enter into controversy with a fair or an *unfair* literary critic—I may be well excused for a wish to clear my personal character from any tinge of mercenary or sordid feeling in the eyes of a contemporary of genius. Your Lordship will likewise permit me to add, that you should have escaped the trouble of this explanation, had I not understood that the satire alluded to had been suppressed, not to be reprinted. For in removing a prejudice on your Lordship's own mind, I had no intention of making any appeal by or through you to the public . . ."[24]

"I feel sorry," Byron answered, "that you should have thought it worth while to notice the 'evil works of my nonage' as the thing is suppressed *voluntarily* and your explanation is too kind not to give me pain. The satire was written when I was very young and very angry, and fully bent on displaying my wrath and my wit, and now I am haunted by the ghosts of my wholesale assertions."

Byron went on to give a more detailed account of his conversation with the Prince Regent. "He talked to me of you and your immortalities, he preferred you to every bard past and present, and asked which of your works pleased me most, it was a difficult question. I answered, I thought the *Lay*. He said his own opinion was nearly similar; in speaking of the others I told him I thought you more particularly the poet of *Princes*, as *they* never appeared more fascinating than in *Marmion* and *The Lady of the Lake*; he was pleased to coincide and to dwell on the description of your James's as no less royal than political."[25]

Scott was soon enthusiastically inviting Byron to Abbotsford. His mother, Scott knew, had been a Scottish heiress, Miss Gordon of Gight, and Byron himself had spent part of his childhood in Aberdeen; could he not be persuaded "to revisit Scotland," which had "a maternal claim" upon him? "I am labouring here to contradict an old proverb, and make a silk purse out of a sow's ear,—namely, to convert a bare *haugh* and *brae* . . . into a comfortable farm." Though he could offer no better accommodations than "a couch in a closet," and though the ruins of Melrose might not tempt one who had seen the ruins of Athens, it would be a pleasure to entertain him.[26]

"I would rather cross-question your Lordship about the outside of Parnassus, than learn the nature of the contents of all the other mountains in the world. Pray, when under 'its cloudy canopy' did you hear anything of the celebrated Pegasus? Some say he has been brought off with other curiosities to Britain, and now covers at Tattersal's. I would fain have a cross from him out of my little moss-trooper's Galloway, and I think your Lordship can tell me how to set about it, as I recognize his true paces in the high-mettled description of Ali Pacha's military court."[27]

Military affairs were ringing through Scott's mind all that summer. At the very moment that his little cavalcade of swords and lances had left Ashestiel for Abbotsford, the Emperor Napoleon had precipitated his Grande Armée from Dresden against Moscow. In June the French crossed the Niemen and occupied Vilna. From there, with Barclay de Tolly's army ever retreating before them, they disappeared into the interminable reaches of Russia.[28] Scott felt a gleam of hope. Given those vast spaces and the Fabian strategy of delay and attrition, the colossus of the North might ultimately prove too much even for the prowess of Napoleon.[29] But few Englishmen shared Scott's faith; and the capture and destruction of Smolensk confirmed their gloom. Wrote the Secretary of War, "I cannot have one particle of hope for Russia."[30]

In England, too, conditions were dark.[31] Angry at the blockade of the Continent, the United States had countered by cutting off all commercial intercourse between the two countries. At a stroke the mills of Lancashire were deprived of their raw cotton; British exports to North America fell from £11 million to under £2 million. To appease American ire Britain rescinded the offending Orders in Council, but it was too late. The young Republic had already declared war. The double blow was calamitous. All but six of Manchester's thirty-eight mills had to close; a fifth of urban Lancashire was driven on the rates; in Nottinghamshire alone 15,000 frame workers went on poor relief. In Glasgow the weekly wages of hand-loom weavers fell from 17s 6d to 7s 6d. Food prices were 87 per cent above prewar level; the cost of potatoes and oatmeal had trebled.

But to hungry laborers it seemed that the machines that did the work of ten men for the wages of one were the real cause of their

misery. Mobs of starving frame-work knitters rioted; in Nottinghamshire, Derbyshire, Leicestershire, Staffordshire, Lancashire, and Yorkshire, men with blackened faces smashed machines, gutted factories,
seized arms from military depots. The yeomanry were called out. Parliament, in panic, made frame-breaking a capital offense. (Byron's
maiden speech in the House of Lords opposed this measure. "Can you
commit a whole country to their own prisons?") More than forty rioters
were sentenced to death, still more deported. On May 11, 1812, the
Prime Minister, Spenser Perceval, was assassinated in the House of
Commons. The savage joy with which this news was greeted by the
unfed workers of the North terrified the rest of the country.

The disorders convulsing the Midlands spread into Scotland. Only
a few days after Scott had moved to Abbotsford he learned of agitations
among the weavers of Galashiels. Swooping down "and arresting the
ringleaders at peep of day" on the morning of May 25, he forestalled
the "cutting of looms and webs": "I have had the examination of the
rascals upon my hands the whole day."[32] Their chief got away, but Scott
discovered bundles of letters and printed manifestos proving that the
rioters had been corresponding through every manufacturing town in
England and Scotland.[33] The Manchester Weavers' Committee had
levied "a subsidy of 2s. 6d. per man—(an immense sum)—for the
ostensible purpose of petitioning Parliament for the redress of grievances,
but doubtless," Scott was sure, "to sustain them in their revolutionary
movements." "You are quite right," he told Southey, "in apprehending
a *Jacquerie*; the country is mined below our feet."[34]

Just in time, the opening of the ports of Russia and of her ally,
Sweden, brought about a revival of trade. Unemployment diminished;
with bread in their bellies once more, the weavers grew less violent and
industrial unrest died down.[35] Early August brought word of Wellington's great victory at Salamanca, where almost the entire army of
Marshal Marmont was destroyed and Napoleon's domination of Spain
shaken to its foundations.[36] Scott assembled forty or fifty masons and
other workmen around huge bonfires at Abbotsford to celebrate the
glorious news.[37] In their glaring light the men drank "an ocean of
whiskypunch," and to the sound of pipes and violins "the people—at
least my subjects danced almost the whole night."[38]

Through August, on into the autumn and winter, Scott followed the
events of the war with devouring excitement. After twenty years of almost unending bloodshed, the struggle was reaching a crisis. Unlike
his little friend Jeffrey, belligerent at home but timorous abroad, Scott
had always insisted that England must not yield an inch. From the first
he had been sure that Spain would prove the Achilles' heel of Napoleon's
empire. Now the Emperor was battling on two widely separated fronts;
defeat in either Russia or Spain might be fatal.

In glorious weather Wellington's army marched on Madrid. Bands played in every village; girls welcomed his victorious troops with streamers, laurel crowns, and kisses. They entered Madrid on August 12, bells pealing, palms waving, fountains flowing wine, ballet dancers pirouetting before the columns. All night the capital gave itself up to feasts and wine, and during the days that followed to a round of fêtes, bullfights, and balls.[39] From Madrid, Wellington marched north to besiege the fortress of Burgos.[40]

Meanwhile, in far-off Russia, the armies of Czar Alexander were still retreating.[41] Though they made a stand on September 7 at the bloody battle of Borodino, they were obliged to give ground;[42] a week later Napoleon entered the deserted city of Moscow.[43] But his conquest had been bought at enormous cost. His army of almost half a million men had dwindled to fewer than 200,000, of whom 20,000 were sick.[44] And the victory proved fruitless; the Czar did not even answer his offers of peace. In the already chilling air of the empty and flame-blackened capital, under the golden domes of the Kremlin, Napoleon waited in vain for a Russian surrender that never came.[45]

"What say you to our friends the Russians?" Scott exulted. "If Alexander is firm I think he has the ball at his foot."[46] At last, on October 18, when a few snowflakes were already in the air, Napoleon gave his forces the order to retreat. They had been unable to obtain food supplies in Moscow, and they were now returning through country that they themselves had wasted.[47] Past charred villages, over an immensity of stripped fields filled with the stench of unburied corpses, the starving men struggled on.[48] With November 5 winter set in, a penetrating fog rose from the ground, snow began to fall in the darkness, a terrible wind howled out of the north and whirled thick, blinding flakes around the famished invaders.[49] Since leaving Moscow they had lost 40,000 men; as they staggered through the snow the Russians harassed their flanks.[50]

The dying agonies of the Grande Armée lasted all through November. Crossing the river Beresina, 12,000 were drowned and another 18,000 left in Russian hands. On December 5, Napoleon abandoned the survivors and set out by sled for Warsaw and Paris.[51] On the tenth, Scott wrote: "Glorious news today from the North—pereat iste!"[52] He had been right and the fainthearted counsels of Jeffrey and the Edinburgh Reviewers had been wrong. France was bled white; "Boney's Devil" had failed him at last.[53] A few days later, 10,000 typhus-ridden cripples—all that remained of a host of half a million men—tottered across the bridge at Königsberg into Prussia.

Beside these tremendous events—"the pass and fell incensèd points of mighty opposites"[54]—in which the fate of nations, the fate of his own country, hung in the balance, Scott felt his own activities to be almost ridiculously insignificant. "I would, were it in my power, blow up the ruins of Melrose Abbey and burn all the nonsensical rhimes I ever wrote if I thought either the one or other could survive the honor or independence of my country. My only ambition is to be remembered, if remembered at all, as one who knew and valued national independence and would maintain it in the present struggle to the last man and the last guinea though the last guinea were my own property and the last man my own son."[55]

But he had obligations to fulfill, and whether his desk saw him or not, men would nonetheless be dying at Borodino. So he set himself resolutely enough to going on with the composition of *Rokeby*. Work on Abbotsford was also progressing speedily. "We have got up a good garden wall, complete stables in the haugh, according to Stark's plan, and the old farmyard being enclosed with a wall, with some little picturesque additions in front, has much relieved the stupendous height of the Doctor's barn. The new plantations have thriven amazingly well, the acorns are coming up fast, and Tom Purdie is the happiest and most consequential person in the world."[56]

Scott's seedling trees were indeed rising rapidly. On a lookout spot that the children called the Spy Law almost all the new acorns sent by Hartstonge, which he and Charlotte had planted in May, were now sending up shoots that were already six inches tall,[57] and he was busily setting out a bare bank jokingly called "the thicket." The acorns he had received from the Marchioness of Stafford, however, and put down the preceding autumn in "the Sutherland bower" on his eastern boundary, were rooted out and nibbled by fieldmice.[58] But all over the property, he told Joanna Baillie, little oaks were now standing "nearly as tall as your knitting needle. I wanted to sow birches with them but found it difficult or rather impossible to get good seed which is extraordinary as this is certainly the country of birches."[59]

He was sometimes puzzled to identify unfamiliar plants and trees that were not indigenous to Scotland. "I asked a lady the other day what shrub it was that had a leaf like a saddle and was much edified by learning that it was a tulip tree."[60] But his ignorance did not compare with that of an admirer in Seville who had offered him a gift of some Spanish chestnuts. Scott had set apart a space for them, only to discover on their arrival that they had all been carefully boiled before being dispatched to him.[61]

Up the hillside, across the road from the house there was a fine spring of clear water, which Scott enclosed in a Gothic well-front made of some of the stones he had acquired from Melrose Abbey.[62] With the lime carefully blackened and moss put between the joints, it looked, he boasted happily, at least three hundred years old.[63] "In honor of an old Melrose saint I have put an inscription in a gothic Latin verse, AVE, AVE, SANCTE. WALDAVE," "and I intend that willows and weeping birches shall droop over it with a background of ever-greens."[64]

All these activities had forced Scott to give up his yawning and head-scratching sessions with little Walter over his Latin. "I am relieved of the labour of hearing Walter's lessons," he wrote Terry, "by a gallant son of the church, who with one" leg of flesh "and another of oak, walks to and fro from Melrose every day for that purpose."[65] The tutor, named George Thomson, a son of the minister of Melrose, had lost one leg in a boyhood injury, but tall and athletic, he was an expert at singlestick and a dauntless horseman. "In the Dominie, like myself," Scott said, "accident has spoiled a capital lifeguardsman." A faithful and simple-minded oddity, "Dominie Thamson" soon became an established member of the household.[66]

Building and planting had already cost Scott £1,000 that summer.[67] In addition, John Ballantyne had written him in July that the publishing house badly needed more capital: the bankers were closing their account until the overdrafts were reduced.[68] Scott endorsed a note and told John that Murray and Longman must stop shilly-shallying about purchasing a share of *Rokeby*. "If they refuse their paltry money assistance I think you might express your peremptory wish that they would come to the point. Constables foot is in that business. He persuades them that he will make a better thing & give them a larger share &c. & they are asses enough to believe him—the old *Registers* are also against us in the eyes of these honest gentlemen."[69]

In August, Scott endorsed another note. John was so worried that it affected his health and spirits. "If you suffer the present inconveniences to depress you too much," Scott told him, "you are wrong—and if you conceal any part of them are very unjust to us all. I am always ready to make any sacrifices to do justice to engagements & would rather sell every thing or any thing than be less than true men to the world."[70] In their desperation the Ballantynes thought of selling a quarter of their three-eighths share in *Rokeby* to raise cash, but Scott thought this would prove unnecessary. "Therefore do not be rash—it is a last expedient to be resorted to when others fail." Scott patched up various other temporary accommodations to take care of their more pressing needs and staved off their difficulties.[71]

With these troubles, however, *Rokeby* advanced but slowly—just when it needed to be done with speed. "James and Erskine have alternately thrown cold water about my ears so that I have lost much of my confidence. But I will do my best & make a bolt or shaft of it."[72] With a sudden resolve, he destroyed what he had already written and made a fresh start. "I threw the whole into the fire about a month since," he wrote Lady Abercorn in September, "being satisfied that I had corrected the spirit out of it as a lively pupil is sometimes flogged into a dunce by a severe schoolmaster. Since I resumed the pen in my old Cossack manner I have succeeded rather more to my own mind. It is a tale of the civil war of 1643 but has no reference to history or politics . . ."[73]

As the poem began to go more briskly, Scott's own spirits rebounded.

James Ballantyne paid him a visit, urging that he finish it in time to go to press for publication by Christmas. When he left he absent-mindedly carried off his host's black coat, "I suppose," Scott remarked humorously, to persuade his mother that he had lost flesh "through the abstinence of Abbotsford."[74]

Through a series of interruptions from idle visitors, Scott kept on writing. One intruder remained overnight and hung on till twelve the following day. "When I had just taken my pen he was relieved like a sentry leaving guard by two other lounging visitors."[75] But Scott held on to his temper and worked steadily. Despite the unmet bills, James's clamoring for speed, and intrusive strangers, he had in fact entirely recovered his assurance.[76] Mercurially, he began thinking of adding to his landed property. There were "some acres of ground on a little lake about a mile from my cottage which is exactly the lake of the fisherman and Genii."[77]

He even entertained himself by playing with another narrative poem at the same time that he was writing *Rokeby*. This was an elaboration of those lines gaily imitating his own poetic style, which, with imitations of Crabbe and Moore, he had anonymously inserted in the *Register* the preceding year. There had been much curiosity about their authorship, and Scott had been amused when rumor attributed them to William Erskine. It would be fun to work them up into a light romance to be published in a small pocket volume at the same time as the longer poem.[78] Would the reviewers be fooled by this playful hoax? —above all, Jeffrey, whom Scott thought unable really to understand poetry and lacking in the taste for its enjoyment.[79]

Erskine cheerfully entered into this plot, agreeing to look wise and say nothing. Even more, "What think you," he asked, "of putting down your ideas of what the preface ought to contain, and allowing me to write it over?" The new opening of *Rokeby*, he told Scott, was now admirable; and as for the other poem, though it was hard "to form any opinion of a work, the general plan of which is unknown, transmitted merely in legs and wings as they are formed and feathered," "What I have seen is delightful."[80] Erskine deepened the mystification by throwing into the preface quotations in Greek from Herodotus and Diogenes Laertius, and Scott carefully wove into his poem allusions more characteristic of Erskine than of himself.[81]

For all James Ballantyne's worries and grumblings, therefore, *The Bridal of Triermain*, as the poem was to be called, progressed simultaneously with *Rokeby*. "I share in your anxiety to get forward with the grand work," Scott assured James. But it was exhilarating to do the two together: "I feel the more confidence from coquetting with the *guerilla* of which I send you Canto II all but for six stanzas. The Canto III will contain the disenchantment." If people did guess that the poem was his, "why our comfort will be that it will sell the better."[82]

Together with these two poems, Scott was working hard to complete his edition of Swift. In the middle of July the faithful Hartstonge had sent him from Ireland a box containing a large bundle of Swift's papers, including his account books and the receipts of his livings.[83] "I have not yet," Scott told Constable, "got the letters betwixt Swift and Stella which I understand throw a new light on their intimacy. But I shall be in a condition in a few days to complete the omitted Vol. after which I think nothing need stop the press."[84] Hartstonge was having an artist make a copy of a fine original portrait of Swift that could be used as the frontispiece. "I am anxious to have Swift out of hand," Scott concluded, "having between purchases and expenditures no little occasion to realize my literary funds."[85]

Scott had promised that he and Charlotte and the two older children would visit Rokeby that autumn, but with bills and the needs of the two Ballantyne enterprises breathing down his neck he wrote Morritt begging off and asking his friend instead to refresh his memory by supplying him with some written details about the scenery and traditions of the Valley of the Tees.[86] Morritt, however, pleaded with him to reconsider. The booksellers were ill advised in their urgings; he must not risk his fame through haste.

"If you want a few hundreds independent of these booksellers . . . I happen at this moment to have five or six for which I have no sort of demand—so rather than be obliged to spur your Pegasus beyond the power of pulling him up when he is going too fast, do consult your own judgment and set the midwives of the trade at defiance. Don't be scrupulous to the disadvantage of your muse, and above all do not be offended with me for a proposition which is meant in the true spirit of friendship."[87]

The appeal was irresistible—and there was the added enticement that Lady Louisa Stuart would also be a guest at Rokeby.[88] Scott did not accept the offered loan, but he did use Morritt's friendly offices to have some of the Ballantynes' bills discounted.[89] He could not pay more than a week's visit; the Duke of Buccleuch wanted him at Dalkeith to help bring in Mr. Alexander Don as candidate for Roxburghshire in the coming general elections. On September 24 the journey to Rokeby began, Scott on horseback, Sophia and Walter on their ponies, and Charlotte following in the carriage.[90]

Scott halted at Flodden to show the field of battle to the children. *Marmion* had so vastly increased the business of the local tavern that the host begged the poet's permission to have the "Scott's Head" as his signpost. Scott demurred; nothing could be more appropriate, he said, than the foaming tankard already above the doorway. "The painter-man has not made an ill job," agreed the landlord, "but I would fain have something more connected with the book that has brought me so much good custom." Wouldn't Scott, he asked, holding out a well-thumbed copy of the poem, at least suggest a motto from it? Opening the volume, Scott chanced on the line, "Drink, weary pilgrim, drink, and pray—" "Well, my friend," he said, "what more would you have? You need but strike out one letter . . . and make your painter-man, the next time he comes this way, print between the jolly tankard and your own name— "Drink, weary pilgrim, drink and PAY."[91]

From Edgerston, where they slept that night, Scott sent James Ballantyne corrections and additions to the first canto of *Rokeby*, with directions that the printed sheets were to be sent on to Rokeby Park.[92] The following day, they crossed the Border into Northumberland. While they were passing through a small country town, one of the servants suddenly felt ill and Scott sent for a local doctor. In the black-coated, black-hatted dignitary who turned up, solemn as a medico in Molière, Scott was astonished to recognize a former blacksmith and veterinary from Ashestiel.[93]

"John Lundie!" he exclaimed. "In troth is it, your honour—just *a' that's for him*." "You were a *horse*-doctor before; now, it seems, you are a *man*-doctor; how do you get on?" "Ou, just extraordinar weel; for your honour maun ken my practice is vera sure and orthodox. I depend entirely upon twa *simples*." "And what may their names be? Perhaps it is a secret?" The doctor lowered his voice to a whisper: "I'll tell your honour; my twa simples are just *laudamy* and *calamy*!" "But John, do you never happen to kill any of your patients?" "*Kill*? Ou ay, may be sae! Whiles they die, and whiles no; but it's the will of *Providence! Ony how, your honour, it will be lang before it makes up for Flodden!*"[94]

After this little halt, Scott's party pressed on to Hexham and Corbridge and from there to Bishop Auckland.[95] Here, as they were going through the public rooms of the Castle, Scott was recognized by the venerable Bishop of Durham, Shute Barrington, who insisted on showing them the picture gallery himself. Although already in his seventy-ninth year, the vigorous old man had a horse saddled and rode with them some ten miles on their journey to Greta Bridge: "I still like," he said, "to feel my horse under me."[96] They arrived at Rokeby in time for dinner on Sunday.[97]

Eager to make the scenes of his poem vivid and precise, Scott started out gathering local color the very next morning. "I want," he told his host, "a good robber's cave and an old church of the right sort." These they found in the ancient slate quarries of Brignal and the ruined Abbey of Eggleston. Morritt laughed at the scrupulousness with which Scott noted down the names of wild flowers and herbs growing round the bold crags. He would not be on oath, Morritt exclaimed; "daisies, violets, and primroses would be as poetical." Scott replied that "in nature herself no two scenes were exactly alike, and that whoever copied truly what was before his eyes, would possess the same variety in his descriptions." But "whoever trusted to imagination, would soon find his mind circumscribed, and contracted to a few favourite images," the repetition of which would sooner or later produce a barren monotony.[98]

High above the Greta, hastening between its marble walls, Scott found a shallow cave into which he settled as his study. Still higher behind him loomed the tower of Mortham Keep; the cliffs were fringed with ancient and enormous yews whose sable canopy was pierced by a few huge firs. Their mingled needles muffled the narrow path to a silence broken only by the rushing of the stream. Here, at a rustic table strewn with guide books, notes, and maps, Scott tossed off his descriptive passages.[99]

Both Morritt and Lady Louisa Stuart were delighted by the opening of the poem. Heartened by their praise, Scott wrote rapidly; within the week he had finished Canto II and sent it off to James. "As far as mortal man may promise on such a subject," he reassured the anxious printer, "I have no fear of publishing by Xmas—& *Triermain* as soon after as may be."[100] Half of the latter poem he had brought with him; he meant to bring it out, he told Morritt, within the same week as *Rokeby*, and was gleefully anticipating "laying a trap for Jeffrey."[101]

The coming elections, however, necessitated Scott's return home, and after a delightful though too brief stay with the Morritts he and his family started out by way of the west road and Carlisle.[102] Ascending the valley of the Greta, they visited Bowes Castle, crossed the desolate waste of Stainmore Forest, and on their journey visited the Castles of Brough, Appleby, and Brougham. Carlisle was choked with election mobs; Lady Louisa and Lady Douglas, who caught up with them there, would have had trouble finding quarters if Scott had not had the forethought to take a private house that could hold them all. Even so, some of the servants were reduced to crowded accommodations; Scott heard Lady Douglas's personal maid exclaim pathetically as she stepped out of the carriage, a three-volume novel in hand, "Am I to sleep with the greyhounds?"[103]

Dalkeith, too, was in the fury of the election tempest. But in the midst of the turmoil, Scott met General John Malcolm, "the Persian envoy," a poet and a fellow Borderer, who read "some very splendid extracts" from his own translation of Firdusi's *Shahnameh*. "A fine time we had of it talking of Troy town and Babel and Persepolis and Delhi and Langholm and Burnfoot with all manner of episodes about Iskendiar Rustan and Johnie Armstrong. Do you know that poem of Ferdusi's must be beautiful."[104]

In Roxburghshire the election was fought with violent bitterness and its results were contested.[105] Scott felt that Alexander Don's chances of success were small. "I have *entre nous*," he confided to William Erskine, "little hope of it," although Don's rival, "my friend Elliott," was "the right boy for beshitting his own seat."[106] Despite this talent, as Scott had feared, Elliott ultimately won: "I am returned from the election," Scott wrote his Aunt Chritty, "as sulky as a Bear with a headache, for we were most completely beaten—lost the day by seven." The only consolation was that his old boyhood aversion, his uncle, Scott of Raeburn, had tried to perjure himself by challenging Scott's right to vote and in the dishonorable endeavor lost his own.[107]

Even worse than this political defeat, business conditions were increasingly bad. The Ballantyne enterprises still contended with insufficient capital. On the plea that they did not want to be obliged to part with any of *Rokeby*, John had obtained a credit of £700 from Sir William Forbes's bank, but barely was this in hand when there came the failure of a London debtor who owed them £1,200. On Scott's guarantee, however, John managed to get bills for £2,000 from Longman & Company for a thousand quartos of the forthcoming poem. Through Morritt's assistance Scott was able to forward another bill for £500, so that he believed they would be able to meet all demands on the firm. These obligations, though, he warned James, must be strictly redeemed: "We must not on any account consider them as a part of Capital."[108]

James himself felt that they could surmount their difficulties only by accepting an offer from Constable for a share of *Rokeby* and by persuading him to take a part of the *Edinburgh Annual Register* as well.[109] But Scott opposed this course. Though Constable's proposal merited consideration, "like most of our other folks he promises mountains which his end being gained will shrink into molehills." Still worse was "a stroke so fatal to our reputation as striking sail to Constable in our own harbours." Worst of all was the effect upon their credit with Sir William Forbes. "Today you beg an accommodation of £700 which he grants upon your anxious statement of a wish to keep the entire poem & tomorrow you show that this was a mere pretext by selling the said poem to Constable? How could you apply to them in any future emergency with the chance of having your statement believed."[110]

Deep down, Scott did not want to be bailed out by Constable. The obnoxious Alexander Gibson Hunter had retired from the firm and was now dead, and Scott cherished no hard feelings against Constable himself, but he disliked having to confess himself beaten. Consequently, he invented reasons. "You may as well believe that he will sell all he has & bestow it on the poor as give you a guinea that he can keep you out of— so do not cheat yourself by looking forward to printing or any other advantages beyond what may be the immediate consequences of the transaction."[111] "Nothing ultimately good can be expected from any connection with that house unless for those who have a mind to be hewers of wood & drawers of water."[112] These statements simply were not true; Constable had never been illiberal. A second argument, however, may have had more force: "Longman & Co will *certainly* be displeased though they may not think fit to show it, untill they can make you feel it."[113]

All these objections, Scott granted, must give way "to absolute necessity or to very strong grounds of advantage. . . . I should have thought some share of *Marmion* a good thing in the balance. But we will talk the matter coolly over & in the mean while perhaps you could see Sir W. Forbes or W. Erskine & learn what impression this odd union is like to make among your friends." But, "short of necessity to which I always defer I can hardly think the purchase of the *Registers* equal to the loss of credit & character which your surrender will be conceived to infer."[114] In the end Scott had his way; they continued the struggle without Constable's aid, trusting to making a grand success out of *Rokeby*.

For this purpose, and to comply with James's anxious desire that it be out before Christmas, Scott suggested shortening the poem by a canto. "If you can allow me six weeks or two months I can yet *though* with some awkwardness & difficulty drive it out to the original length— but otherwise it is literally *impossible*. 'Have mercy mighty Duke on man of Mold.' . . . I cannot carry an ounce more weight & run my race too." From the completed poem they might expect £3,000, "and there is enough for your money."[115] Ultimately, however, the poem was fully as long as any of its predecessors and ran, like all of them, to six cantos.

By mid-October, Scott was dashing ahead at the rate of a hundred lines a day. He was annoyed to learn that Longman had a copy of the first sheet and had been showing it to his literary friends in London. "Both John and you," he sternly reprimanded James, "know my absolute and perempt objections to any one having any part of the proofs but myself and I own I wonder equally at his presuming to take such a liberty and at his being supplied *contrary to my express wish* with the means of doing so. . . . I desire that not a single sheet may go out of your hands to any one whatsoever except by my express direction & this extends as well to your American correspondents as to any one else. You will understand this to be a serious and standing order."[116]

The end of October saw the first two cantos set up in type. Scott expected to finish the third before he left Abbotsford for Edinburgh on November 11.[117] James bombarded him with detailed criticisms and worried about the reception of the poem. Scott was calm and patient. "I return the proof sheet in which you will find most of your corrections attended to as usual."[118] "Your verbal objection I cannot give weight to. People disturbed in mind write madness as well as speak it."[119] "People in a thicket often *hear* when they cant see. I might dwell on this at length but there is I think neither use nor time in doing so. I have made some change however to meet your objection."[120] "As for what is popular, and what people like, and so forth, it is all a joke. *Be interesting*; do the thing well, and the only difference will be, that people will like what they never liked before, and will like it so much the better for the novelty of their feelings towards it. Dullness and tameness are the only irreparable faults."[121]

The remainder of the autumn passed quietly. Scott was grieved by the death of his little terrier Wallace, who would no longer sit watching with quizzical alertness while his master wrote.[122] In late October the children returned to Edinburgh for school and Scott invited Erskine for a visit to Abbotsford. "We have their cabbin to spare and I have twenty things to talk about."[123] At the same time Scott invited his dear Aunt Chritty and her sister Jane. "You cannot guess how anxious I am to shew you what I have been doing in this little handkerchief of a place —not to mention the part of *Rokeby* which is finished . . . The weather seems looking up to be very fine so pray start gallantly to your feet put up your clothes in a trunk and betake yourself to Gala water with all speed—"[124]

Also in the course of October Scott received a courtly letter from the poet George Crabbe. Hatchard, Crabbe's publisher, had forwarded to him a letter in which Scott had spoken highly of his *Tales in Verse*. "It would be affected in me to deny," wrote Crabbe, "and I think unjust were I to conceal, the pleasure you give me. . . . Mr. Hatchard tells me that he hopes or expects that thousands will read my 'Tales,' and I am convinced that your publisher might, in like manner, speak of your tens of thousands; but this is no true comparison with the related prowess of David and Saul, because I have no evil spirit to arise and trouble me on the occasion . . ."[125]

The elder poet's letter, Scott replied, had gratified his own long-standing wish that they might be acquainted. More than twenty years before, as a boy of eighteen, during a snowy winter in an old country house, he had come upon some extracts from Crabbe's poems "The Village" and "The Library" in a volume or two of *Dodsley's Register* and faithfully committed them to memory. When Crabbe became famous, he was delighted. "It was a triumph to my own immature taste to find I had anticipated the applause of the learned and the critical. . . . With respect to the comparative view I have of my own labours and yours I can only assure you that none of my little folks about the formation of whose taste and principles I may be supposed naturally solicitous have ever read any of my poems while yours have been our regular evening's amusement. My eldest girl begins to read well and enters as well into the humour as into the sentiment of your admirable descriptions of human life—[126]

"As for rivalry," he continued, "I think it has seldom existed among those who know by experience that there are much better things in the world than literary reputation and that one of the best of these good things is the regard and friendship of those deservedly and generally esteemed for their work or their talents. I believe many dilettanti authors do cocker themselves up into a great jealousy about what they are pleased to call their fame but I should as soon think of nursing one of my own fingers into a whitlow . . ."[127]

Robert Southey, Scott learned, had recently paid a visit to Rokeby: "I hope you liked Morritt as well as he liked you. . . . Now let me thank you for the *Omniana*, which I need not say highly amused me. Some trifles I can add: you were right in your original idea that Lord Herbert of Cherbury conceived himself to be odoriferous in person, although Henry More had the same whim. It was probably, I think, some perversion of the nose rather than any peculiar fragrance of the pores. I daresay with a certain degree of early training a man's organ of smelling might distinguish flavours as well as a common cur if he did not reach the accuracy of a pointer. I knew an old lady who really could smell partridges in the stubble as well as you or I might smell them on the spit. It is a pity she did not take the field, for as she persevered in wearing a small hoop and long ruffles, she would have pointed with admirable effect."[128]

In Edinburgh once more, Scott swept on with the composition of *Rokeby*. He felt elated by the two songs in Canto III, "O Brignal banks are wild and fair," and "a little dashing banditti song called and entitled Allen a Dale." He would send the sheets of the first three cantos under frank, he told Morritt: "I think you will be able to judge for yourself in about a week—pray how shall I send you the *entire* goose which will be too heavy to travel the same way with its *giblets*."[129] Soon Canto IV was almost completed. "I shall have another sheet ready this morning," Scott wrote James Ballantyne. "Hourra! your most serene highness."[130]

For all his high spirits and energy, completing the poem was uphill work. "I *must* turn the three hundredth page," he humorously complained to Gillies, "and *heu me miserum* have only arrived at two hundred and ten! I assure you I am so sick tired of this *grewsome* tale that I can hardly persuade myself to drag it any further."[131] But a spectacular blaze at Bishopsland High Street, which Scott saw from Calton Hill, proved useful for the fire in the following canto, and he recovered his gaiety.[132]

"It is too late," he wrote Morritt on December 10, "to enquire if Rokeby is insured for I have burned it down in Canto V. But I suspect you will bear me no greater grudge than at the Noble Russian who burnd Moscow."[133] "You are wrong about the lattices," he answered one of James's criticisms; "the bursting of a fire through the roof is usually its last operation—besides a Barons hall rarely rose to the top of the building."[134]

Scott had hoped to finish the poem in time for Christmas publication. This he did not quite make. The last of the copy was dispatched on December 31. "There is something odd and melancholy," he wrote James, "in concluding a poem with the year, and I could be almost silly and sentimental about it. I hope you think I have done my best. I assure you of my wishes the work may succeed; and my exertions to get it out in time were more inspired by your interest and John's than my own. And so *vogue la galère*." "If you are not engaged at home, and like to call in, we will drink good luck to it; but do not derange a family party."[135]

The remainder of the Christmas holidays Scott divided between Mertoun and Abbotsford.[136] *Rokeby* was published on January 10, a few days before he returned to Edinburgh.[137] As he sent off copies of the handsome quarto to his friends, his heart beat high with the hope that it would solve his financial problems. Let him but have another success like *Marmion* or *The Lady of the Lake* and all his worries would melt like mist in the sunshine. There would be ample capital to put his business enterprises on an absolutely solid foundation, ample to lay the cornerstone of his little mansion at Abbotsford.

# 4

## These Damned Affairs

### ( 1813 )

THE POEM from which so much was expected got off to a tearing start. In Oxford excited students beleaguered the bookshops for the earliest copies, "all as eager to hear it read as ever horse-jockies were to see the conclusion of a race at Newmarket." "Send me *Rokeby*," Byron impatiently ordered John Murray in London, "—Who the devil is he? No matter—"[1] The day after publication John Ballantyne reported that of its first printing—3,250 volumes, selling at two guineas—all but some 80 copies had melted from his Hanover Street shelves.[2]

James Ballantyne celebrated the event that night by a splendid party in St. John Street. "I wish we could whistle you here today," Scott wrote Morritt. "Ballantyne always gives a christening dinner at which the Duke of Buccleuch and a great many of my friends are formally feasted . . ."[3] Who all the guests were is not recorded, but they must have included William Erskine, quietly enjoying his friend's triumph, Archibald Constable, floridly handsome, dignified, and corpulent, the Ettrick Shepherd, brandishing his knife and fork over the roast, his red cheeks "a' jappit wi' the jice,"[4] and Scott's protégé Henry Weber, drinking his way through Scotch libations with German thoroughness. And, of course, there was little John Ballantyne, hopping up gleefully to sing comic songs in his high shrill tenor, and James, their stout host, trolling out ballads in his thundering bass, and other songsters: "he has always," Scott said, "the best singing that can be heard in Edinburgh."[5]

Joyfully Scott showered gift copies far and wide. One of royal size on hot-pressed paper went to Morritt, to whom the poem was dedicated; another to the Duchess of Buccleuch.[6] He would apologize to anyone else,

Scott wrote her Grace, "for heaping quarto upon quarto," but her Gilpin Horner had launched him on his career and therefore he must insist upon his privilege of overwhelming her with these wild tales.[7] His uncertainty about the financial success of the poem had vanished; the demand for copies was "continuing faster than they can be boarded," he told Morritt, and "now I have nothing to fear but a bankruptcy in the gazette of Parnassus."[8]

Still other volumes were sped to Lady Abercorn, James Skene, Joanna Baillie, Lady Louisa Stuart, George Ellis, the Princess of Wales.[9] "I hope you will like Bertram to the end," Scott wrote Miss Baillie; "he is a Caravaggio sketch which I may acknowledge to you—but tell it not in Gath—I rather pique myself upon."[10] Of this same heroic ruffian, "I trust," he wrote Lady Louisa, "I have brought out your old acquaintance Bertram pretty well & brought him to a dashing conclusion—for the rest I cannot say very much: but as Corporal Nym wisely observes, *'Things must be as they may'* . . ."[11]

With Ellis he joked about the way in which he had "converted a lusty bucanier into a hero." "Somehow, despite the most obstinate determination to the contrary, the greatest rogue in my canvass always stands out as the most conspicuous and prominent figure." To be sure, his own grandfather had been a shrewd cattle dealer, his great-grandfather a Jacobite and a traitor, his Border ancestors feuding skull-splitters and sheep-stealers. But more recently the family had been law-abiding enough: "I am myself as Hamlet says, 'indifferent honest'; and my father, though an attorney (as you will call him), was one of the most honest men, as well as gentleman-like, that ever breathed. I am sure I can bear witness to that—for if he had at all *smacked*, or *grown to*, like the sire of Lancelot Gobbo, he might have left us all as rich as Croesus, besides having the pleasure of taking a fine primrose path himself, instead of squeezing himself through a tight gate and up a steep ascent, and leaving us the decent competence of honest men's children."[12]

Among Scott's friends *Rokeby* was received with hosannas of praise.[13] Morritt of Rokeby not unnaturally thought it the finest of all his poems. Joanna Baillie was ecstatic about "Your lumbering 4[to] as you call it—the Noble poem of *Rokeby* as I call it . . . I wish you could have seen me when it arrived. My sister was from home, so I stirred my fire, swept the hearth, chaced the cat out of the room, lighted my candles, and began upon it immediately." It was "written with wonderful power both as to natural objects & human character, and your magnificent Bandit, Bertram, is well entitled to your partiality; for it is a masterly picture . . ."[14]

The Princess of Wales received the poem *"with transport"* and anticipated having it read aloud to her that very night, "this golden Now."[15] The breeze of royal favor was blowing still more warmly from the opposing camp: the Prince Regent now made *"pattes de velours,"* as Scott said, and after all the verbal "sugar-plums" Byron had passed on during the preceding July,[16] extended through the Royal Librarian a graceful gesture of ingratiation: "His Royal Highness, the Prince Regent, has been pleased to signify to me that Mr. Scott is to have the access to his Library whenever he comes to town, and His Royal Highness wishes him to be introduced whenever he is able to come."[17]

Scott felt both flattered and embarrassed by these overtures. Though the loose chatter and undignified behavior of the Princess had laid her open to scandalous rumor, she had always been most kind and civil to him: "I could not as a gentleman decline obeying any commands she might give me to wait upon her especially in her present adversity." But visiting her at Blackheath might give great umbrage at Carlton House; he had best avoid the problem by staying away from London. "So, though I do not affect to say I should be sorry to take an opportunity of peeping at the splendours of royalty prudence and oeconomy will keep me quietly at home till another day."[18]

Not all the comments on *Rokeby* were as laudatory as those of Scott's intimates. Tom Moore included among the squibs of his *Intercepted Letters; or The Twopenny Postbag* a little good-natured badgering. Scott, he said playfully,

> Having quitted the Border to seek new renown
> Is coming, by long Quarto stages to Town
> And beginning with Rokeby (the job's sure to pay)
> Means to *do* all the Gentlemen's Seats by the way.
> Now the Scheme is (though none of our hackneys can beat him)
> To start a fresh Poet through Highgate to meet him;
> Who by means of quick profit—no revises—long coaches
> May do a few Villas before Scott approaches.[19]

A bookseller named Thomas Tegg brought out a parody of the poem; a decade later, on a sightseeing trip to Abbotsford, he presented himself to Scott somewhat apprehensively. "I am sorry to say, Sir," he apologized, "that I happen to be the publisher of *Jokeby*, a burlesque of *Rokeby*." "Glad to see you, Mr. Tegg," responded Scott, genially, "the more jokes the better!"[20]

Scott and Charlotte spent the last of the Christmas holidays of 1813 at Abbotsford, "where we weary ourselves all day," he said, "in looking at our projected improvements, and then slumber over the fire, I pretending to read, and she to work trout-nets, or cabbage-nets, or some such article."[21] Soon after they returned to town, he was able to send off another section of the *Swift* manuscript to the printer. "I am as anxious as you," he told Constable, "to get him out this season & as early as possible."[22] By the end of January the quarto edition of *Rokeby* was almost exhausted and the octavo about to go on sale.[23]

Although Scott had hoped to bring out *The Bridal of Triermain* simultaneously with *Rokeby*, it did not appear until almost two months later.[24] The small anonymous volume fooled almost everyone. "They talk here a good deal," Scott gleefully wrote Lady Louisa Stuart, "of a new poem in profess'd imitation of no less a person than your Ladyship's humble servant . . . & many people wish to make me very jealous of it. I heard from second hand Mr. Jeffrey pronounces it superior to me in my own line so I must be under the mortal apprehension of being out-heroded." "It has not he says my great artery but there is more attention to stile more elegance and ornament . . ."[25] As luck would have it, however, Jeffrey escaped falling publicly into Scott's trap: fascinated by a young American charmer, he pursued her across the Atlantic to New York, where, entangled in the witchery of courtship, he had no mind for writing reviews.[26]

Lady Louisa reported that at Bothwell Castle the poem "was all approved except one part the ridicule of Lucy's lovers" (at the close of Canto II). "Walter Scott *never* wrote anything in such bad taste as this," exclaimed Lord Douglas, "it is quite *unlike him*." The real author, Lord Newbattle told them, was Robert Pierce Gillies.[27] "I will endeavor to convey to Mr. Gillies (*puisque Gillies il est*)," Scott replied demurely, "your Ladyship's very just strictures . . . But if he takes the opinion of a hacked old author like myself, he will content himself with avoiding such bevues in the future without attempting to mend those which are already made. There is an ominous old proverb which says, *confess and be hanged*; and truly if an author acknowledges his own blunders, I do not know who he can expect to stand by him; whereas, let him confess nothing, and he will always find some injudicious admirers to vindicate even his faults."[28]

The critics were completely hoodwinked. Including George Ellis, who could not be let into the secret because he might review the poem in the *Quarterly*, and review it there he did. "If it be inferior in vigour to some of his [Scott's] productions," wrote Ellis, "it equals, or surpasses them, in elegance and beauty . . . The diction undoubtedly reminds us of a rhythm and cadences we have heard before; but the sentiments, descriptions, and characters have qualities that are native and unborrowed."[29]

During the spring vacation Scott was back and forth between Edinburgh and Abbotsford, where he was superintending the planting of wild birch seed from Loch Katrine and pinasters sent by Joanna Baillie. The gardener, John Winnos, thought "the pinaster seed ought to be raised at first on a hot-bed and thence transplanted to the nursery so to a hot-bed they have been carefully consigned." Winnos, Scott explained to Joanna, was "the Sub-Oracle of Abbotsford the principal being Tom Purdie"; but Tom's talents lay "in catching salmon or finding a hare sitting, on which occasions being a very complete Scrub, he solemnly exchanges his working jacket for an old green one of mine and takes the air of one of Robin Hood's followers."[30]

There were now about seventy acres planted in woodland, and Scott was stocking a garden. He had been poring over Price's *Essay on the Picturesque as compared with the Sublime and the Beautiful*, and was "not without hopes," he slyly told Lady Abercorn, "of converting an old gravel-pit into a bower and an exhausted quarry into a bathing-house." If she heard that he had "caught a rheumatic fever in the gravel-pit or . . . been drowned in the quarry I trust you will give me credit for dying a martyr to taste."[31]

April brought a return of winter. Along Princes Street there were such tempests of wind and snow that Scott could not get to his office in the Register House "but was fairly blown home again and glad to get in harbor."[32] Abbotsford was deep in snow, "mortifying me to the core," he said, "by retarding the growth of all my young trees and shrubs. . . . We are realizing the nursery tale of the man and his wife who lived in a venegar bottle . . . and my Eve alleges that I am too big for our paradise."[33] But for all the tightness of their cottage quarters their little parlor was snug enough. While the snow lay without and a fire blazed within, they amused their evenings by reading aloud from Washington Irving's comic *History of New York*, by "Diedrich Knicker-bocker," the gift of a recent American visitor. "Our sides," Scott reported appreciatively, "are absolutely sore with laughing."[34]

Until the opening of summer the children's lessons, of course, kept them in Edinburgh. "You say nothing of Walter's schooling," Scott wrote Sophia. "I hope that goes on well." Poor Cuddy, the small donkey on which the two younger children ambled around the countryside, had lost the use of his hind legs and had to be shot. This would grieve little Anne, but he would give her a beautiful peacock and a peahen, presents from Mertoun, which were so tame that they would "come to the porch and feed out of the children's hands."[35]

Scott himself had received from Joanna Baillie the gift of a lock of hair from the head of Charles I, "cut from the head when his coffin was discovered about a month ago in St. Georges Chapel at Windsor."[36] "I did not think Charles's hair had been quite so light—that of his father and I believe of all the Stuarts till Charles II was reddish. . . . Tory as I am my heart only goes with King Charles in his struggles and distresses, for the fore part of his reign was a series of misconduct. However if he sowd the wind God knows he reaped the whirlwind, and so did those who first drew the sword against him, few of whom had occasion to congratulate their country or themselves upon the issue of those disastrous wars. And sound therefore be the sleep and henceforward undisturbed the ashes of this unhappy prince—in his private capacity he was a man of unimpeached worth virtue and honour and bore his misfortunes with the spirit of a prince and the patience of a Christian."[37]

Although the quarto of *Rokeby* had been overprinted by between 500 and 1,000, John Ballantyne now had only about 30 copies left. The first edition of the octavo was a double one, of 6,000, but within two months it went to press again.[38] "It has been wonderfully popular," Scott told Lady Louisa, "about ten thousand copies having walked off already, in about three months, and the demand continuing faster than it can be supplied."[39] Such sales, indeed, would have made almost any other poet delirious with joy; but they fell short of the 14,000 *The Lady of the Lake* had marked up in the same period of time, and never mounted to more than half the dizzy heights that poem attained.

What Scott needed right now, however, was nothing less than an equally splendid success. For the financial affairs of both the publishing firm and the printing office were badly embarrassed. Under the war strain, business conditions grew steadily worse; booksellers were failing and banks refusing loans.[40] Clarke of St. Andrew Street, Walker of Hunter Square, and numbers of smaller houses had all gone under, leaving masses of dishonored bills. These disasters in the business world added to the struggles of John Ballantyne and Company. Sir William Forbes and Company had closed their open account.[41] Booksellers in Liverpool, Inverness, and Aberdeen all owed the firm money; they were buying no more books than they could help and were offering in payment only bills that could not be discounted.[42] John tried in vain to get their debtors to pay up; "our Dublin correspondent," he reported desperately in March, "yet retains a large bill for *Rokeby* on which I counted"; "Laing & Miller send word they *cannot* at present pay the books they bought at the sale and *will* not."[43]

The main trouble was, as it had been from the beginning, that the publishing enterprise lacked capital. Its initial capital of £2,000 had been lent to the printing office, and not long afterward £3,000 more of its credit had gone to the same purpose. These advances could be paid back only in work. But the books that poured from James Ballantyne's presses repaid the publishing house only to the extent that they were sold, and according to the business practice of the time they could be sold only on credit. In addition, as James lugubriously pointed out, though Scott's own poems had sold brilliantly, some of the other publications he had insisted on their undertaking had been disasters.[44] John agreed: the *Register* lost money regularly, the *Beaumont and Fletcher* had done badly, and they had locked up a large sum of their capital in the *Northern Antiquities* and *Tixall Poetry*.[45] "By these adventures," James concluded gloomily, "nearly £15,000 (perhaps more) of stock has been created, without any capital whatever."[46]

The only solution, John thought, was to gain time by collecting as many of their outstanding accounts as possible, trying to pay their own most pressing debts, and in the meanwhile "selling off part of our stock

& part of the copyrights & narrowing the concern" or perhaps "winding it up altogether." He had told their debtors that he would prosecute ruthlessly unless payment were made by the end of March. If the printing office could only pay back its debt and find enough money to meet its weekly expenses, he could go to London and dispose of his unsold stock by tying it in with the purchase of some of the copyrights.[47]

"I have read over this melancholy statement," James noted, "& have in truth nothing to add to it or remark upon it." Amid his troubled apprehensions he could only hope "that I may not wholly lose your countenance & regard which has for so many years been the prize of my life."[48] "I know for my part," John wrote, "that I have lived upon the £300 per annum allotted, and can live under other circumstances and in an inferior situation on much less. . . . In the meantime I beg to suggest to you the propriety for your consideration of selling the very good furniture of this house of mine, about £150 of which belongs to the business . . ." This would, "no doubt," realize £600, so that he could contribute £450; "and the counting house would do quite as well at Foulis' Close in the High Street as here."[49]

There were only three possible courses: somehow or other to find additional capital and struggle along; to wind up the shaky publishing business and continue with the printing establishment, which still had many profitable accounts; or to liquidate both. James argued strongly against the last. Instead of having to raise the relatively moderate sums that would be enough for carrying on, all their debts would come down on them at once.[50] Their book stock (which John had estimated at a nominal value of £12,746, but for which he hoped to get perhaps £9,500)[51] would go at deadly losses. The types would do better, but having been used for several years "could only be disposed of at 40 per cent below cost," and the presses and printing materials "in proportion."[52]

As for the publishing business, even if they resolved to give it up they should do so, James thought, gradually rather than by a sudden stoppage. Their old stock could then be sold off little by little instead of at panic prices. There would be time for new editions of *The Lady of the Lake* and *Rokeby*, which could still be expected to bring in profits. Perhaps the *Register* might be made a success if it were "narrowed to one volume, and conducted at half the expense"; and they could complete "various works in hand, which if not completed will sell as waste paper." Above all, "time would be given to wait for the improving aspect of public affairs, and its necessary favourable effect upon commerce . . . and very importantly upon bookselling and printing."[53]

"My opinion therefore," James concluded, "is (solemnly averring that I keep myself and my own feelings as far as I can out of view) that it would be infinitely better to raise money, at any sacrifice, to pay the impending bills, and thus to go on for a period more or less . . . than . . .

to let the business go to ruin, and not even by that means avoid sacrifices perhaps heavier. . . . Our Stock though of slow sale, is the greater part of it good. *Beaumont and Fletcher* for instance must sell one time or other; and the sale of your own works will probably all come, like *The Lady of the Lake* to a regular 3000 a year, though both the *Lady* and *Rokeby* have been as yet over printed. . . .

"Suffer me just to add this, that I am really disinterested in this opinion, for I have long seen such misery in John, that I have felt with the country mouse, a crust with content & independence is preferable to luxury & fear. Poverty I know I could bear and I do not think I have done anything to merit anything bitterer. Indeed should any shock take place, my sufferings would be less on my account than on yours. I may be pardoned for saying this for I say it with truth."[54]

With one desperate expedient after another John carried the staggering business on from day to day, borrowing £150 here, renewing a bill for £150 there, calling on Scott for additional drafts. Forbes's Bank discounted one bill for £503, giving John £420 in cash, and promptly presented a bill of £500 from Morritt, which he could settle only by giving them back the £420 plus £80 out of his own last £100, leaving him with a bare £20 in hand. But he was expecting a remittance from John Murray in another few days and trusted he could borrow to meet their needs in the meanwhile.[55]

In the course of April, conditions improved a little and John's volatile spirits rose high. *Rokeby* was selling again; the demand for the octavo "is now getting like what I remember of the famine at Kelso 15 years ago, as long as meal was to be had however dear, the natives damned the millers & supped as little porridge as possible; but having made no provision for the evil day when the time arrived that they were sent empty away then came the tug! and the curses both loud and deep, and the fist, stone and staff arguments." They had in May, he remarked optimistically, comparatively few bills coming due.[56]

But these few bills, as this very letter made clear, amounted to £1,350 due on May 1 and another £1,500 in the course of the month, over £2,800 before May 31.[57] Nor, for all John's hydrogenous bounce, would that be the last. Scott had already advanced £5,000, little of which he saw any prospect of getting back. In the course of the next three months, just to prevent the bookselling business from going under, it would be necessary to raise between £4,000 and £5,000 more and then keep that large sum floating by renewals for another nine to twelve months.[58]

Despite John's rosy visions, therefore, Scott could not disguise from himself that the publishing house was a sinking ship. To try to keep it above water was madness; it would only ruin the printing office too. "The stock of J[ohn] B[allantyne] & Co," he made up his mind, "must be sold for its marketable value & all loss submitted to in silence."[59]

"Meanwhile," he told James, "I will do all in my power to keep up the credit of the house untill these affairs are wound up."[60] The high hopes of outrivaling Constable with which it had been launched only four years ago must be abandoned.

When the stricken publishing house had been liquidated perhaps Constable could be persuaded to restore to the printing business some of the trade he had withdrawn from it, and gradually it could be brought back to its former prosperity. John was consequently instructed to sell in London sufficient quantities of their published books to realize £2,000, no matter how great a discount he had to give to get rid of them. Another £3,000 or £4,000 worth he must exchange for the books of English publishers, to be sold for whatever they would fetch at Edinburgh. "Between these two expedients we may raise £4000 or £5000 & obtain time finally to sell off everything in Decr. or January. The loss in discounts will be very great but certainly it is better [to] submit to it at once than labour on in constant anxiety & apprehension."[61] Even if all their stock brought only £6,000 or £7,000, less than 50 per cent of its estimated value, sold it must be.[62]

While John thus struggled to realize cash in London, Scott set himself to raise what he could in Scotland. The only Edinburgh bookseller with resources great enough to help was Constable. Pocketing his pride, Scott approached the great publisher. Constable, all compliant magnanimity, expressed a desire to relieve him in any way he could. He was not ill pleased to receive a pledge that what might have been a dangerous rival would wind up its affairs.[63] And it would be a great stroke to become again the publisher of Scott's own works. He agreed to consider taking over the copyright and publication of some of John Ballantyne's list and meanwhile to buy some of the printed stock.[64]

But Constable was shrewd as well as generous. It was not for nothing that he had weathered the storms in which so many other vessels had gone down. The *Edinburgh Annual Register*, which he had been so eager to inaugurate, and so angry at losing, turned out, on examination of the books, never to have lost less than £1,000 a year. He declined to assume now the loss he had so luckily escaped.[65] Some of John Ballantyne and Company's other publications he rejected even more emphatically. Brewster's edition of *Ferguson's Astronomy*, Singer's *General View of Agriculture in the County of Dumfries*, the unfortunate *Tixall Poetry* and *Northern Antiquities*: what profits could be made out of such stuff?[66] "I like well Scott's *ain bairns*," exclaimed Constable, "but heaven preserve me from those of his fathering!"[67]

Scott had been sure Constable would buy the 3,000 or so unsold copies of the current *Register* and even harbored the grandiose hope that he would take off their hands some of the more than 6,000 back *Registers* that still crowded their shelves. Constable refused both, although he did agree to take 295 current *Registers*. Various other publications of theirs—*Tales of the East, Popular Tales,* Defoe's *Novels,* 720 copies of Scott's *Don Roderick,* 50 sets of *Beaumont and Fletcher,* and some 200 volumes of historical memoirs—purchased at 40 per cent below their list price, brought a total of £1,300, little more than half the sum Scott had expected to realize.[68] He was forced to offer Constable one quarter of the copyright of *Rokeby* for £800; Constable made a counterproposal of £700. On this they closed, the bookseller settling the entire price of £2,000 by bills payable in six, twelve, and eighteen months.[69]

These terms, Scott told Constable, he considered very liberal. "It is with great pleasure," he wrote, "that I regard it as a renewal of our long friendly intercourse which as it was broken off by untoward circumstances is I trust now to be renewed upon a permanent footing of mutual interest and mutual kindness."[70] To John Ballantyne he expressed somewhat less enthusiasm: "After many *offs* and *ons* and as many *projets & contre-projets* as the treaty of Amiens I have at length concluded a treaty with Constable in which I am sensible he has gaind a great advantage but what could I do amidst the disorder & pressure of so many demands & scarce a farthing to pay either James household or my own."[71]

Both judgments, however, were true. In regaining Scott, Constable had scored a tremendous victory, but he had not driven a hard bargain. His new partner Robert Cadell later declared that the books purchased from John Ballantyne's stock were resold to the trade at between one-half and one-third of what Constable had paid for them.[72] Scott had retained all his copyrights except the quarter share of *Rokeby* and regained a powerful and zealous ally.[73] "I do think," he exulted, "that by our joint exertions we shall get well through the storm & save *Bea[u]m[on]t* from depreciation, get a partner in our heavy things reef our topsails & move on securely under an easy sail & if on the one hand I have sold my gold too cheap I have on the other turnd my lead into gold. . . ."[74]

"Adieu, my dear John, I have the most sincere regard for you & you may depend on my considering your interest with as much attention as my own. If I have expressed myself with irritation in speaking of this business, you must impute it to the sudden extensive & unexpected embarrassments in which I found myself involved all at once. If to your real goodness of heart and integrity, and above all to the quickness & acuteness of your talents, you added habits of more universal circumspection, and above all the courage necessary to tell disagreeable truths to those whom you hold in regard, I pronounce that the world never held such a man of business. These it must be your study to add to your other good qualities, meantime, as someone says to Swift, I love you with all your failings, pray make an effort to love me with all mine."[75]

Even with Constable's aid not all their problems were solved. But the worst seemed over. To meet the bills that would be due in August, Scott suggested a public sale of their miscellaneous stock and the more showy books John could collect by exchange in London. This would bring in twice as much money as a sale to the dealers, "who at present neither can nor will buy either here or in London . . . The booksellers would *rage* but we have all the ill effects of their enmity already & never had the least advantage from their favour & Constable & probably Blackwood, the only publishers, may be secured to the printing house."[76]

The future Scott contemplated with courage. "Ratcliff the physician said when he lost £2000 in the South Sea scheme it was only going up 2000 pairs of stairs. I say it is only writing 2000 couplets & the account is balanced."[77] For some months to come he might still find himself pinched, but "by Christmas I have every reason to hope that I shall find myself a free man of the forest with some thousand pounds in my pocket besides my house and farm of Abbotsford."[78] "For the first time this many weeks I shall lay my head on a quiet pillow."[79]

He was soon "working at Swift like a dragon,"[80] while the peacock and the peahen strutted outside in the garden and a new pet, a silky-eared little spaniel named Fenella, coaxed to be caressed. As spring moved into summer, the garden at Abbotsford was glowing with wild flowers Morritt had sent from Thorsgill, and around the well red-currant bushes were blooming.[81] Through Terry, Scott bought from a London auctioneer a "splendid lot of ancient armour,"[82] although he was at a loss to know where it should be placed when it reached Abbotsford. He was also turning longing eyes toward an additional piece of land, the hilly tract east of Abbotsford, stretching from the old Roman road near Turn-again south to Cauldshiels Loch.[83]

The bare hills rising above that mountain mere drew him. Seized by desire, he thrust aside the memory of the tortuous financial shifts that for weeks had troubled his wakeful nights. After all, it was only writing two thousand couplets more! Rummaging out the unfinished fragment of the poem on the Bruce which he had laid aside when he began *Rokeby*, he decided to resume work on this composition. He would call it, he thought, *The Nameless Glen*. No doubt some eager publisher would give him all the money he wanted for it.[84]

He sounded out Constable about an advance.[85] The great bookseller was troubled; though he had weathered the financial storm in which John Ballantyne had been forced to strike sail, it had not been without more effort than he would avow. Constable did not have sufficient cash for the large advance Scott wanted, and even his credit was strained.[86] Unknown to Scott, he had outstanding bills amounting to more than £75,000, of which more than £42,000 were payable during that current year. But having so recently paid heavily to regain Scott, he did not want to alienate him again.[87] Scott politely but plainly told him that in the event of a refusal he would apply to Longman and to Murray.[88] "I am not sure," Constable wrote his young partner, Robert Cadell, "but Walter Scott's letter may bring me home this week."[89]

Cadell felt scandalized at Scott's "even hinting at such an idea as our paying say six or twelve months in advance for a Poem not written perhaps scarcely thought of." Suppose he were "summoned to the other world, and not a sheet at Press, how would we look? what would the world say to it? You will say I am a very gloomy fellow, but Mr. Scott is not like his Poems immortal. . . . Mr. S. has cheated us in *Swift*, humbugged us in *Rokeby*, &c and will continue to do so the greater halo he gets to creep in at . . . I think that £5000 is too much for his proposed poem, he wishes to squeeze us as he has done the B[allantyne]s they thought *Rokeby* was to perform wonders in their finances but the cream has gone to Mr. S. and what is left to them is very thin."[90]

So Scott's near-disaster looked to an outsider. The cheerfully prosperous face he presented to the world had prevented even the astute Cadell from realizing how narrowly he had squeaked through. The proposals to Constable that so outraged Cadell, however, were quite above board, and the publisher was under no obligation to accept them if he thought them unprofitable. Of the two alternatives he offered, one was that Constable either share half the poem with Longman, paying £2,500 in bills immediately discountable, or buy a quarter share at £1,250, leaving Scott to deal with Longman. In this case the management was to be with John Ballantyne as the agent for Scott's half.[91]

The other alternative was that Constable purchase the whole poem for £5,000, with the understanding that Longman be offered the right to buy a half or a quarter. In this case £2,500 was to be paid at once "in bills at discountable dates," £1,500 when the manuscript went to press, and a final £1,000 when 10,000 copies had been sold. Furthermore, all the remaining *Edinburgh Annual Registers*—some 9,000 in number—were to be taken off Scott's hands at the same price as those Constable had already bought. "I will frankly own," Scott said, "that it is only the desire of being quit of these *Registers* that would induce me to part with the whole poem on any terms. For I know by experience how much better it is to keep copyrights than to sell them but I am not unwilling to give up some advantage to be rid of these books and the trouble attending them."[92]

Constable temporized. He declined the unprofitable *Registers* but nibbled at buying a share of the poem, though he balked at the large sum demanded. Scott's reply was courteous but firm. "I think from your very sensible observations we may lay aside any thought of selling the *Register* at present." His price for the poem, however, he insisted was moderate: "It is considerably less than I have made on the share of *Rokeby* sold to yourself & surely that is no unfair measurement. . . . I

have thought this matter over & over and cannot depart from the conclusion I have formd. But I shall be far from being displeased with you
for entertaining a different opinion."[93]

Meanwhile he pressed for a quick decision. Except for gratifying
his desire about the land, he said, "I don't care a farthing whether the
bargain goes on or off," but "I have a very capricious person to deal
with."[94] The unnamed landowner, in fact, turned out to be so capricious that within another four days Scott's negotiations with him proved
fruitless, and the need to come to an immediate agreement about *The
Nameless Glen* vanished. The bargaining with Constable accordingly
was allowed to lapse. "You are quite right in the present time," Scott
wrote him, "not to pledge yourself deeper than you find quite convenient.
So it is unnecessary to talk more about this business just now."[95]

For the 1811 *Annual Register,* soon to be published, Scott had
written a biographical memoir of John Leyden.[96] He was striving to
complete his *Life of Swift* and was finishing the tenth volume of the
*Somers Tracts.*[97] At Abbotsford all his planting was flourishing; his new
trees, he told Morritt, rivaled "an expanded umbrella in height and
extent of shade."[98] His court of offices, including a little house for Peter
Matheson, he nicknamed "Peterhouse," gaily coupling the name of his
coachman with that of the oldest college in Cambridge.[99] In the gable
above Peter's quarters, to eke out the scanty sleeping space of the farmhouse, Scott fitted up for his bachelor guests a small cockloft of a
bedroom, reached by the same primitive means that "leads many a bold
fellow to his last nap—a ladder."[100]

He and Charlotte were looking forward to spending a few days at
the end of July with the Duke and Duchess of Buccleuch at Drumlanrig
Castle in Nithsdale.[101] From there they would go on to Longtown, in
Cumberland, where Scott had to settle with the Marquis of Abercorn
some business left over from Tom's management of that nobleman's
Scottish affairs.[102] These excursions would be rounded off with a visit
to Morritt at Rokeby and to Southey at Keswick.[103]

In the midst of his happy anticipations, Scott still had to find ways
of meeting the liabilities involved in gradually winding up the publishing business. Morritt's banker, Hoare, advanced £650 on Morritt's
note of hand for six months.[104] Scott called on the aid of Murray's
credit for three bills of £300 each.[105] Even with these sums, on the very
eve of Scott's departure, John Ballantyne sent a sudden and belated
emergency appeal for another £350. Scott was obliged to wake a servant
boy at three o'clock in the morning and rush him to Edinburgh with
an order for the money and an angry dressing-down for John.[106]

"Surely you should have written three or four days before the
probable amount of the deficit . . . These expresses besides every other
inconvenience excite surprize in my family and in the neighborhood."[107]
John must, Scott insisted, be more businesslike. "You say you *could*

*not suppose* Sir W. F. wd. have refused the long-dated bills; but that you *had* such an apprehension is clear . . . because three days before, you wrote me an enigmatical expression of your apprehensions . . . Suppose that I had gone to Drumlanrig—suppose the poney had set up—suppose a thousand things—& we were ruined for want of your telling your apprehensions in time.[108]

"The large balance due in January from the trade & individuals which I cannot reckon at less than £4000, will put us finally to rights & it will be a shame to founder within sight of harbour. . . . Now do not affect to suppose that my displeasure arises from your not having done your utmost to realize funds & that utmost having faild. It is one mode of exculpation to suppose one's self accused of something they [sic] are not charged with & then to make a querulous or indignant defense & to complain of the injustice of the accuser."[109]

Early on July 26, Scott and Charlotte set out for Drumlanrig. When the late Duke of Queensberry died in 1810 the Castle with his other estates and titles had been inherited by Scott's old patron, whose son was therefore now both Duke of Buccleuch and Duke of Queensberry. The huge Gothic structure, a magnificent quadrangular pile designed by Inigo Jones, crowned a high hill overlooking the open valley where the river Nith ran through a channel of broken rocks.[110] Unhappily, the enormous building had been allowed to become ruinous and dilapidated, and the park and the mountain slopes were almost denuded of trees, "the late abominable old Q," as Scott remarked in scandalized horror, "having laid the axe to the root" with a ruthlessly greedy hand.[111]

But as the two visitors surmounted the long ascent to the house, they could see their host and hostess on a balcony waving white handkerchiefs from its battlements, and soon four merry people were exchanging greetings.[112] Scott was glad to see the restorations and improvements that Duke Charles was vigorously making on the neglected estate. The lightless and airless cells many feet underground—"as grim a dungeon as ever knave or honest man was confined in," Scott remarked—were "in some danger of being converted into a wine-cellar."[113] Other transformations, though necessary, no doubt, for the purposes of the inhabitants, seemed to him less happy. "Thus a noble gallery which ran the whole length of the front is converted into bedrooms very comfortable indeed but not quite so magnificent."[114]

Even at Drumlanrig, though, Scott was followed by John Ballantyne's hasty messages. "It is a cruel thing upon me," Scott replied, "that no state you furnish excludes the arising of such unexpected claims as those for the taxes on the printing office." Why did John persist in these "strange concealments of debts and difficulties" until they were placed in legal hands for collection?[115] Two days later there was another demand. "I return your Draft accepted."[116] There would be nothing really to fear in winding up these matters were it not for "your odd ways of keeping all difficulties out of view till the very instant moment of ruin."[117] "On Wednesday"—August 4—"I think of leaving this place where but for these damnd affairs I should have been very happy."[118]

At the village of Longtown, Scott found that the Marquis of Abercorn had not yet arrived, but his major-domo and cook had already taken possession of the little inn and were making grandiose preparations for dinner. On the Carlisle road Scott ran into his Lordship's majestic cortège of four or five carriages, with the Marquis, blue ribbon of the Garter gleaming across his chest, prancing on horseback. Dinner was served with pomp, ducks and geese from the village pond disguised in numberless entrées, a bill of fare at the Marquis' place, and the landlady's chipped crockery and dented pewter polished and ranged in solemn display on her crazy old buffet.[119]

From Longtown, Scott turned south toward Rokeby. At Penrith another cry of distress from John caught up with him. Even the printing office did not seem to be doing well: "it cannot be thought," Scott commented wearily, "that I have either means or inclination to support a losing concern at the rate of £200 per month." If James could find a monied partner, "it might be the best for all parties for I really am not adequate to the fatigue of mind which these affairs occasion me though I must do my best to struggle through them."[120]

Morritt had looked forward to welcoming Scott "as soon as you are disengaged from the train of the Great Abercorn comet that draws you along in its perihelion."[121] But at Brough a letter saying that Mrs. Morritt was ill regretfully postponed the visit.[122] After a day at Keswick, therefore—during which Southey read him a part of his new poem, *Don Roderick*—Scott turned his steps homeward and his mind to wrestling with the solution of his business problems.[123]

There was no question that the affairs of the publishing house must be wound up as speedily as could be done without incurring needless losses. John Ballantyne had decided to establish himself as an auctioneer of books and *objets d'art*. As for Scott himself, he would sell all his copyrights, clear off the debts, and retire from the printing firm as soon as his own financial safety and regard for James's welfare made it possible. "Whatever loss I may sustain will be preferable to the life I have lately led when I seem surrounded by a sort of magic circle which neither permits me to remain at home in peace nor to stir abroad with pleasure."[124]

John argued that the publishing enterprise could be wound up more favorably if Scott sustained its credit a while longer. No doubt he might raise the money, Scott replied, but he did not think it honorable to do so when he had no assurance of being able to repay it.[125] Instead, "I certainly can write a poem & I can sell my books . . . to discharge these claims."[126] Aside from their "unlucky business" he had no debts of any consequence: "My sufferings will be rather from the eclat of such an affair than any other circumstance—for no one," he said, ominously foreshadowing the fateful decision with which, years hence, he would face his life's great disaster—"no one shall lose a penny by me."[127]

Meanwhile their adversity grew steadily darker: ". . . you will see," Scott told John, "matters are just £1000 worse than when I wrote from Drumlanrig. I will manage however to send the funds for Monday . . ." As for September, he could provide the £750 then due, though not until past the middle of the month—his Irish friend Hartstonge had offered him a credit of £500, but this could not arrive from Dublin before the twelfth, and the remaining £250 must wait until the twenty-first.[128] Their other needs, Scott decided, must be met by a renewed appeal to Constable, and the Ballantynes were instructed to lay a statement of their affairs before him.[129]

James drew a picture of their troubles for Constable that Scott himself declared unnecessarily alarming. "I am not so low in purse as I suffer John Ballantyne to suppose, having always kept about £400 or £500 by me for a pinch, and my very considerable income is paid quarterly."[130] In addition, besides copyrights and book stock, he had property—house, farm, freehold, money lent, and library—which he valued at well over £10,000. With his own resources, "credit of from £2000 to £4000 would amply suffice to put these matters out of all danger."[131]

But Scott's desperation showed nakedly through another sentence in his letter. "If you could oblige us with procuring the temporary assistance wanted, you should fix the price of the next poem yourself."[132] This on a poem for which, only two months earlier, he had been asking £5,000 in advance! The plan of this poem, he said, was now matured in his mind; he would be prepared to go to press in November. "How far, however, your situation will enable you to embroil yourself in other people's matters is a very different question, and, be assured, I should be the last person to press you so to do, though I am fully conscious that the temporary inconvenience is the only evil that can befall you."[133]

Constable's mouth watered at the prize Scott held out to him, but his own resources were in fact strained almost to the breaking point. Though he would take pleasure, he replied, in coming to Scott's aid, he could not without "the most injurious consequences" to his own credit, and "I am sure you would not expect me to endanger my own safety."[134] Nor did Constable see any way in which Scott might secure further commercial loans. Could he not obtain "the support of one or two of your wealthy friends, in guaranteeing a London account"? If so, Constable felt almost certain of success in recommending this arrangement to his own bankers.[135]

The shock Scott felt at this reply reveals how anxiously he had counted on Constable's help. "I have no wealthy friend who would join in security with me to such an extent," he told James Ballantyne. What made his problems all the more distressing was that he needed only time to solve them. He had no debts other than those arising from the business; his income was over £2,000 a year; and that winter he would be receiving from his father's estate some large sums at last recovered, after prolonged legal delays, upon the discharge of a mortgage on the Shetland properties of Scott of Scottshall.[136] It was a bitter pill when relief was so near.[137]

Suddenly his hopes rebounded. It flashed through his mind that he did "*have one* friend of the most undoubted responsibility" to whom he might appeal, the Duke of Buccleuch.[138] Although the Duke had recently told him of "heavy demands which have left me very bare,"[139] his fortune ensured that there would be no need of actual cash: a mere letter guaranteeing Scott's integrity would be enough. This would enable him to meet his financial obligations and save the copyrights of *The Lady of the Lake* and *Rokeby* from being sacrificed for a fraction of their value. "I am not desiring any loan from your Grace, which I know would be inconvenient . . . but merely the honor of your sanction to my credit as a good man for £4000 & the motive of your Graces interference would be sufficiently obvious to the London Shylocks as your constant kindness and protection is no secret to the world."[140]

Scott felt so confident of the Duke's reply that he authorized Constable to propose the matter to his London bankers, Brooks, Son, and Dixon.[141] While they waited, there was a complicated juggling of bills and counterbills between Scott and John Ballantyne.[142] "I protest," Scott exploded, "I don't know at this moment if even £4000 will clear us out. After all you are vexd & so am I and it is needless to wrangle about who has a right to be angry—but pray try to be as luminous as you can . . ."[143] "As for me I really can no more & I blush to think of the straits I am reduced to. . . ." "You have drained me as dry as hay . . ."[144]

During this same time, Constable, at Scott's request, had been going over John's financial statement. His analysis was gloomy. More than £18,000 worth of stock would realize, in his judgment, only £8,600; of almost £4,000 owing to the firm it would probably be able to collect no more than £1,500. These losses would leave its assets some £3,000 short of its liabilities. The printing house was in better shape, but if it had to be sold much of its stock would go for less than it had cost. All told, the amount that had to be made good came to £15,271. With skill and management this sum could probably be realized, but not "in anything like time for the acceptances. . . ."[145]

Despite this dismal picture, Scott thanked Constable and put a brave face on matters. "I think," he said stoutly, "the copy rights and book debts may both turn out better than your state holds out. . . . I do not anticipate any great difficulty in clearing all quietly and creditably if the Duke comes forward, and your bankers are, as they say, agreeable. . . . The vexation to me in this business has been John's sanguine temper, who perpetually fixd some point when he hoped to get on well, and as regularly disappointed me—something like the spoild children in Princes Street, whose maids [have] to carry them twenty or [thirty] yards in hopes they will then be able to walk, when behold, whenever they are set down, the ricketty brats roar louder than ever and will not budge a step."[146]

Underneath, though, Scott felt disheartened enough. The prospect Constable held forth, he told John Ballantyne, seemed little less than ruinous. "But he may have his own reasons for depreciating the stock & copy-rights . . . I cannot understand how out of near £4000 of debts only £1500 are to be counted as good—a total bankruptcy of the trade could scarce produce a greater defalcation."[147] But all now depended on the Duke. Why did he not reply?

As the month of August drew to a close and Scott scanned his daily mail in vain, he oscillated between hope and despair. Surely the Duke would not fail to help?—but then, Scott reflected, "he does not know the extent of the emergency"; and yet again, more ominously, "put your faith not in princes."[148] On August 29 he spent a day at Mertoun—"in fine spirits for company," he wrote John, "as you may suppose."[149] The following day, to James: "No letter today so the same uncertainty prevails . . ." The demands of the business had stripped him so bare that he had hardly a penny for the immediate expenses of his family. But he refused to apply to the banks for any help: ". . . it would be little better than swindling unless I have the most decisive assurance of support.[150]

"As to myself my dear James, I must take my fate as I best can. Constable need not suppose that I will go mendicating from the booksellers a contract for a new poem. I would no more do so than you would sing ballads in the street for your relief."[151] In the nervous tension of waiting and receiving no reply, Scott's heart sank almost to the depths of despair.

His apprehension and his wounded pride are echoed, more than two years later, in the anguish with which Sir Arthur Wardour, in *The Antiquary*, contemplates the loss of his estate and the fear of a debtors' prison. "That I should have been such a miserable dolt," poor Sir Arthur exclaims, "such an infatuated idiot, such a beast, endowed with thrice a beast's stupidity . . . I am like a sheep which I have seen fall down a precipice, or drop down from sickness . . ."[152]

When all was over, Scott wrote mournfully, he would make his way abroad. "Scotland & I must part as old friends have done before, for I will not live where I must necessarily be lookd down upon by those who once lookd up to me. But Scotland is not all the world, though to me the dearest corner of it. I will see justice done to everyone to the last penny & will neither withdraw my person nor screen my property untill all are satisfied."[153]

He could no longer write poetry, he told James. "My facility in composition arose from buoyant spirits & a light heart which must now be exchanged for decent & firm composure under adversity." "I assure you I am as sorry for you as for myself & for John also, though I cannot but blame him for suffering my delusion to continue long after his own must have vanished. But his mind is a light and sanguine one and I trust [he] will soon get over his present distress and thrive in his new vocation."[154]

James must beg Sir William Forbes personally for a fortnight's delay in paying the acceptances that were due there. "It is no doubt most unpleasant to ask it, but am I on a bed of roses? You can state that you are winding up the bookselling concern with all dispatch . . . and when a man . . . is labouring, & effectually labouring, to pay his debts he is surely entitled to some indulgence from his creditors." Scott himself decided to wait one more day. "I will not," he added, a ray of hope creeping in, "send this letter till tomorrow when we will see what the post brings."[155]

His postscript, on August 31, rang out with jubilance. "The enclosed from my princely Chief arrived this morning having miscarried to Edinr."[156] The Duke had in fact answered his letter at once: "I shall with pleasure comply with your request of guaranteeing the £4000— You must, however, furnish me with *the form of a letter* to this effect, as I am perfectly ignorant of transactions of this nature."[157]

Overnight, all their problems were solved. Scott's confidence surged back on a tidal wave of courage. The melancholy thought of parting from Scotland vanished like mist before the dawn. A stroke of the pen from his princely Chief had rescued him as nobly as if by armored troops in battle. Now he would ride on victorious: "And the bright Star of Branksome to carry us through."[158]

# 5

## A Cast for Fortune

### ( 1 8 1 3 − 1 8 1 4 )

IN THE VERY DEPTHS of Scott's financial anxieties he had received an embarrassing honor. The poet laureate, Henry James Pye, had just died, and the Prince Regent offered Scott the post. The poet Pye and his recent predecessors had done little to gild the bays that once adorned the brows of Ben Jonson and John Dryden; tumid New Year hymns and blandiloquent birthday odes to the royal family had made the office ridiculous. ("Milk and water verses," Scott called them, "about the 'natal day' and the 'new born year.'") But he suspected that his visits to the Princess of Wales had annoyed the Prince, and he hesitated lest a "busy misrepresenter may whisper in the Regent's ear that some Kensington House partialities" led to his refusal.[1] Furthermore, "£300 or £400 a-year," in his present situation, as he remarked to James Ballantyne, was "not to be sneezed at upon a point of poetical honour."[2]

What was he to do? The same letter in which he asked the Duke of Buccleuch to guarantee his credit requested the Duke's advice. The royal favor so offered might be "an opportunity of smoothing the way to my youngsters through life." On the other hand, he would be laughed at for taking it, and people might feel him greedy if, having made so much money by poetry, he accepted yet another public office that could be no great addition to his own income, but "might do real service to some poorer brother of the Muses."[3] He also wished to be entirely free "of Kings and Courts."[4] But still there seemed "something churlish & perhaps conceited in rejecting a favour so handsomely offerd." Nevertheless, Scott jibbed at the idea: "I should make a bad courtier & an ode-maker is described by Pope as a poet out of his way or out of his senses."[5]

The Duke of Buccleuch entirely agreed that the post was an absurd one. "The Poet Laureate would stick to you & your productions like a Piece of Court Plaister. Your muse has hitherto been independent. Do not put her into Harness." "Only think of being chaunted & recitatived by a parcel of hoarse & squeaking coristers in the anteroom to the Drawing room on a birthday for the edification of the Bishops, Pages, Maids of Honors, & Gentlemen Pensioners—Oh horrible, thrice Horrible—" Scott should write "frankly & openly to H.R.H. but with respectful gratitude—*For* he *has* paid you a Compliment. . . . I cannot but conceive that H.R.H. who has much taste, will at once see the many objections which you *must* have to his proposal, but which you *cannot write.*"[6]

"Good advice is easily followd," Scott responded, "when it jumps with our own sentiments & inclinations." He had consequently written at once to the Marquis of Hertford, the Lord Chamberlain, "declining the laurel in the most civil way I could imagine."[7] "I shall always think it the highest honour of my life," he told Lord Hertford, "to have been the object of the good opinion implied in your Lordship's recommendation, and in the gracious acquiescence of his Royal Highness the Prince Regent. . . .

"Will your Lordship permit me to add, that though far from being wealthy, I already hold two official situations in the line of my profession, which afford a respectable income. It becomes me, therefore, to avoid the appearance of engrossing one of the few appointments which seem specially adapted for the provision of those whose lives have been dedicated exclusively to literature, and who too often derive from their labours more credit than emolument."[8]

Scott had, in fact, a "poorer brother of the Muses" in mind for the position, and promptly wrote John Wilson Croker to give his friendship a jog. "I am in no small hopes that . . . the ball may be thrown into the lap of our friend Southey . . . It is a thing he would not probably solicit," but he had neither of Scott's reasons "for declining it and the choice would reflect the highest honor on the Prince Regent." As Scott probably felt, Southey, without being too good for the position, might restore it to some degree of dignity. Scott himself, of course, could not gracefully suggest to the Prince where to bestow the office he had declined: "But *you*," he told Croker, "may strike in with great propriety for which reason I send my letter under your cover to be forwarded to Carlton House or the Pavilion . . ."[9]

Hardly was this letter dispatched than one arrived from Southey affectionately hoping Scott had accepted the Laureateship.[10] Scott's reply confessed his own endeavor to obtain the post for Southey. "I did not refuse it from any foolish prejudice against the situation," he said tactfully, "—otherwise how durst I mention it to you, my elder brother in the muse?—but from a sort of internal hope that they would give it to you, upon whom it would be so much more worthily conferred. For I am not such an ass as not to know that you are my better in poetry, though I have had, probably but for a time, the tide of popularity in my favour. . . . If I had not been, like Dogberry, a fellow with two gowns already, I should have jumped at it like a cock at a gooseberry."[11]

It is hard to say how much of this was truth and how much diplomacy, though Scott's modest view of his own poetic talent was quite sincere. Southey probably quite agreed with Scott's estimate of their relative poetic merits, but his response was full of generous feeling: "We shall both be remembered hereafter, and ill betide him who shall institute a comparison between us. There has been no race; we have both got to the top of the hill by different paths, and meet there not as rivals but as friends, each rejoicing in the success of the other."[12] As for the laureateship, Southey had informed Croker that he would not write odes to order but that if he were at liberty to write upon great public events or be silent, as the spirit moved, he would accept the office.[13]

Presently the post was offered Southey and he took it, though its income turned out to be far lower than Scott had imagined. Originally a hundred marks, "it was raised for Ben Johnson," Southey said, "to 100 pounds and a tierce of Spanish Canary Wine, now wickedly commuted for 26£, which said sum, unlike the Canary, is subject to income-tax, land-tax, and Heaven knows what taxes beside." But to Southey even this small stipend was a godsend; he invested it in a life-insurance policy of £3,000 for his family.[14]

"Long may you live, as Paddy says," Scott congratulated him, "to rule over us, and to redeem the crown of Spenser and of Dryden to its pristine dignity. I am only discontented with the extent of your royal revenue, which I thought had been £400, or £300 at the very least. Is there no getting rid of that iniquitous modus, and requiring the *butt* in kind? I know no man so well entitled to Xeres sack as yourself, though many bards would make a better figure at drinking it. . . . When you have carried your point of discarding the ode, and my point of getting the sack, you will be exactly in the position of Davy in the farce"— Garrick's *Bon Ton, or High Life Above Stairs*—"who stipulates for more wages, less work, and the key of the ale-cellar."[15]

With the laureateship thus neatly disposed of, Scott settled down to Swift again. All was now printed except the *Life*, which was going through the press as the pages came from his pen. Constable talked of delaying publication till January, "a great indulgence for me,"[16] said Scott, since it might enable him to get sight of the Bishop of Ossory's copy of *Gulliver's Travels*, containing many MS notes by Swift himself. This had previously been refused, but the Bishop was now dead and all his books were to be sold.[17] "I would give almost any money to be the purchaser," Scott wrote Edward Berwick, "though I should be quite as well pleased if it fell into the hands of any amateur who had the liberality to allow me the use of the variations." He would be grateful if Berwick would put in a bid for him: "I should not grudge five or six guineas in the least."[18]

So a waning summer of unusual sunshine and serenity—in strange contrast to the anxieties that had agitated Scott's sleepless nights until the end of August—glided away into a golden autumn. "The children's garden is in apple-pie order, our own completely cropped and stocked, and all the trees flourishing like the green bay of the Psalmist."[19] Early in September his mother was staying at Lessudden, and he insisted that, being so nearby, she must not cheat him of a visit; he would send Peter Matheson, his coachman, to bring her over any day she pleased.[20] The following week the old lady came to Abbotsford. Though she was now eighty-one, she was enjoying "better health," Scott reported happily, "than for many years."[21]

Later that autumn John Richardson, who had come on a visit from London, was also a guest at Abbotsford.[22] Scott had been so busy about the house that he had not had much time for sport,[23] and Richardson was as enthusiastic an angler as ever. Scott climbed up into the garret to rummage for fishing tackle in the drawers of an old writing desk that had been stored there. Among the lines and flies he came upon a dog-eared wad of manuscript. It was the unfinished novel called *Waverley*, which he had begun some eight years before, put aside, planned resuming in 1810, and then abandoned again.[24] Although he had thought more than once of completing it, he had forgotten where it had been stowed away, "and was too indolent," he remarked, "to attempt to write it anew from memory."[25]

Now he looked over the opening chapters, found them not bad, and made up his mind to finish the story.[26] Perhaps a prose romance would do better than another *Rokeby*. Talking a little later to James Ballantyne, he hinted that he was considering "a complete change in his future strain of composition"; what would James think of his hopes as a novelist? "It somehow or other did chance," James later recorded, although he couldn't remember the reason, "that they were not very high." "Well," said Scott argumentatively, "I don't see why I should not succeed as well as other people. At all events faint heart never won fair lady. It is only trying."[27] What he lacked in talent, he thought, might be made up by the picturesque clash of ancient traditions and civilized manners and by his detailed knowledge of Highland and Lowland Scotland and all the "ranks of my countrymen, from the Scottish peer to the Scottish ploughman."[28]

First, however, the *Life of Swift* must be driven to a conclusion. And, despite the Duke of Buccleuch's £4,000 guarantee, Scott still had many pressing financial demands to meet. In September he sent

John Ballantyne no less than £950. "For God's sake," he enjoined John, "look forward how your own funds & those provided in London will come in to extinguish debts & remember mine must be paid as well as yours."[29] Furthermore, it turned out that Constable's bankers, Messrs Brooks and Company, wished to regard the Duke's guarantee merely as collateral security on Scott's credit with them and to have, in addition, a deposit of accepted London bills.[30]

For this purpose Constable suggested to Longman that they advance the money in bills that would merely be on deposit in the bankers' hands, and as security Scott would convey to them his half-share of the copyright of *The Lady of the Lake* and *Rokeby* and the whole of that of the new poem he was to write. Since his needs were only temporary, Constable explained, these bills would be taken up at maturity without any cash having been put up at all.[31] Scott felt confident of their acquiescence. "All I can say of the matter is that if they do not come handsomely forward we must look else where for London publishers and such may I should think be found."[32]

But, considerably to Scott's irritation, Longman and Company proved reluctant to increase their financial engagements. Constable therefore suggested he might obtain money "on what is called a redeemable annuity, on a Bond." Five thousand pounds would cost only £500 – £600 a year, Constable explained, and the Bond could be redeemed by paying the principal and six months' annuity in advance at any time. "This would, I think, be a most snug way of getting hold of the Cash."[33] Scott did not think this "snug" at all: "The terms of the annuity are too hard (if I understand them) to be resorted to if I can do better . . . If Longman & Co. decline I shall then resort to Cadell & Davies . . ."[34]

Scott even thought of throwing into the balance his new poem and selling the first edition outright for four thousand guineas. Should Longman persist "in declining the arrangement proposed I should be very well pleased," Scott wrote James Ballantyne, "that Messrs C. & D. had one half of the Copy right with the management & that Messrs Constable and you retained each a 4th."[35] Of course, he told Constable, he would "greatly prefer an arrangement with Longman" and would even prophesy "that if they let the thing slip just now they will repent it hereafter."[36]

To exacerbate Scott's monetary tribulations, the Assessor of the Income Tax suddenly made a demand that he pay a property tax on the sale of his copyrights in addition to a tax on the earnings of his books, and directed him to make a return of such profits from publications since April, 1811.[37] Scott determined to resist this claim, not only as "totally new and unheard of," but on grounds of right. "I think it clear," he argued, "that a double taxation takes place." In addition, "a book is not the work of one year, but of a man's whole life, and as it has been found in a late case of the Duke of Gordon that a fall of timber was not subject to property tax because it comprehended the produce of thirty years it seems at least equally fair that mental exertions should not be subjected to a harder principle of measurement."[38]

What gave the contention an ironical turn was that he had at the moment no material interest in opposing the claim. "The distress which commercial circumstances have brought on the bookselling trade," he wrote the Assessor, "has been so great that after I had received bills for £3000, for the price of *Rokeby* . . . I have had to repay every farthing of it, and a great deal more the Acceptors being for the time unable to retire their bills." Ballantyne and Constable could thus "establish to your satisfaction that I have realized no profit whatever during the period alluded to." Nevertheless, he concluded, "I think it necessary to add that I shall lay a case before the Crown Council in England . . . in order to obtain the best guide for my future regulation."[39]

Meanwhile, Scott's endeavors to solve his problems through the aid of either Longman or Cadell and Davies proved unsuccessful. "In this crisis," he wrote Constable on Saturday, October 16, "I am of course coming to town & I would be very glad to converse with you in Castle Street as most convenient either on Sunday evening or Monday morning at ten o'clock."[40] John Ballantyne failed him in obtaining some accommodations on which he had counted, and he had to defer repaying £600 to John Murray until the beginning of November.[41] John continued to importune him for cash. "For God's sake," Scott exclaimed irritably, "treat me as a man, and not as a milch-cow!"[42]

In the end, he was obliged to resort to Constable's proposed annuity. "I can have no choice whatever," he said ruefully, "in the matter of the loan but am most anxious to have it settled as soon as possible . . ."[43] "I think I will make one cast for fortune," he wrote John, "and buy a lottery ticket. Will you send for one to Sievewrights office and as you are not very lucky I would rather Mrs. Ballantyne or your mother took the trouble of buying it than you; as the doctrine of chances will be more in their favour. Or perhaps if Mr. Constable is walking that way he will make the purchase. I should have some confidence in his good stars."[44]

Little by little, though, things again straightened out. On November 16 he wrote Constable, "I enclose the deed the terms of which are more unfavourable than we talkd of: for I understood that my life was to be insured & that on redeeming the annuity I would have the benefit of the policy. In the circumstances however I must submit."[45] The following day he wrote the Duke of Buccleuch: "I have the honour to enclose the deed respecting the annuity transaction. . . . I intend to lodge with your Grace a regular assignment in your favour to a policy of insurance on my own life for £4000 so that in case of my dying before redeeming the annuity (which I trust, God willing, to do in the course of two years) your Grace may not have the slightest trouble other than may be caused by the loss of your obliged friend."[46]

During the course of these transactions Scott had received a troubled letter from Morritt. At Newcastle he had been told that Ballantyne had failed for £20,000, and "with great grief that you were likely to be a sufferer to a very great extent from his failure . . . For God's sake then my dear friend let not the consideration of the money advanced by Hoare upon Ballantyne's bill & my security increase your embarrassment for a moment. I will settle with Hoare when the time of payment comes and I trust . . . that you will not on any account endeavor to repay me till it is perfectly convenient to you. Should it never be so I shall grieve on your account but believe me not on my own."[47]

"I have the pleasure to say," Scott was able to reply, "that there is no truth whatever in the Ballantynes reported bankruptcy. They have had severe difficulties for the last four months to make their resources balance the demands upon them and I having the price of *Rokeby* and other monies in their hands have had considerable reason for apprehension and no slight degree of plague and trouble. . . . Upon the whole I see no prospect of any loss whatever & although in the course of human events I may be disappointed there certainly *can* be none that can vex your kind & affectionate heart on my account. . . . Thank God all real danger was yesterday put over—"[48]

Throughout all these months of financial strain Scott had been obliged more than once to come to the aid of his brother Tom. For well over a year Tom's regiment had been first at Stirling and then at Perth, but in July was ordered to march to Portpatrick to embark for Ireland.[49] There were, of course, accounts that Tom wanted Scott to settle—£27 odd—[50] and Scott sent him another £20 for expenses.[51] At Dublin the Regiment's orders were changed; they were to proceed to Cork to embark for Halifax, Nova Scotia. "To add to my other distress," Tom lamented, "my wife is far gone in the family way" and would have to stay at Cork "and be confined amongst strangers when I am on the wide ocean for America—God knows this is a dreadful prospect . . ."[52]

Scott settled Tom's regimental accounts, promised to pay a "boot account," and sent another £50.[53] On September 1 Tom sailed.[54] "He took no books with him except *Rokeby*," his wife reported to Scott, "and that only for your sake, he said 'it is all I shall ever see of him' and when I proposed to pack up a few that we had he said 'No, since I am to go into banishment I will leave all behind me that helpt to lead me wrong' but I know he cannot *live* without reading—and he tires dreadfully of the officers and their trifling conversation—"[55]

Early in November, Tom's wife gave birth to a little girl, who was named Barbara.[56] Throughout December nothing was heard of Tom; his wife worried over rumors of mishaps to the ship—shortness of provisions, fever, a mutiny of the sailors, shipwreck on the coast of Newfoundland.[57] The war between Britain and the United States still dragged on, and there was a possible danger that the vessel would be intercepted by American privateers. But in January came word of the safe arrival of Tom's regiment and at the end of that month a letter from Tom himself.[58]

The war in Europe was going better. Napoleon struggled against rising difficulties. Sweden had joined the Allies with an army of 30,000 under Bernadotte, Prussia and Russia had signed an alliance, Austria declared war on France. "What an awakening of dry bones seems to be taking place on the Continent!" Scott exclaimed to Byron. "I could as soon have believed in the resurrection of the Romans as in that of the Prussians—"[59] In Spain, Wellington had defeated Jourdain at Vittoria, stormed San Sebastian, besieged Pampeluna, and forced the French to abandon most of the country. "The great victories of Lord Wellington in Spain & the determined . . . resistance exhibited by the Continental powers," exulted Scott, "seem to augur a favourable termination of the war. Yet I think while Bonaparte lives & reigns peace is hardly to be hoped for. Sebastiani one of his favourite generals who knew his character well told a friend of mine that if Europe Asia & Africa were at Bonapartes feet he would be miserable until he had conquered America . . ."[60]

Following the French defeat at the battle of Leipzig all the Netherlands revolted. "We are here almost mad with the redemption of Holland,"[61] wrote Scott. The Prince of Orange was restored; in Edinburgh orange ribbons fluttered everywhere—Scott's daughter Sophia covered herself with them[62]—"and orange Boven was the order of the day among all ranks."[63] But Scott did not believe that there would be peace until the French themselves rebelled and shook the tyrant out of the saddle. "Bonaparte is that desperate gambler who will not rise while he has a stake left and indeed to be King of France would be a poor and pettifogging compromise, after having been almost Emperor of the world."[64]

Elated by the glorious prospects on the Continent, the Town Council of Edinburgh, in December, asked Scott to draw up an address of congratulation to the Regent, which that Prince acknowledged on presentation as the most elegant "a sovereign ever received, or a subject offered."[65] In gratitude the Magistrates, at a brilliant entertainment, presented Scott with the freedom of the city and a handsome piece of silver plate.[66] "To poor Charlotte's great horror," he said, he chose "the vulgar shape of an old fashioned Ale tankard," "an utensil for which I have a particular respect especially when charged with good ale, cup, or any of these potables."[67]

As a New Year's gift Scott sent Miss Baillie a bottle of whisky, "and right good whisky it is," she told him. "I drank your health in as large a driblet as a respectable private gentlewoman may venture upon: it is very potent as well as very good."[68] In Edinburgh, the year 1814 began magnificently. On Twelfth Night the Duke of Buccleuch gave "a splendid Gala" at Dalkeith, throwing open the doors of Van Brugh's great structure to three hundred guests and illumining all its rooms of state.[69] Sophia and Walter were invited with their parents and were dazzled by the gorgeous spectacle. "I think they have dreamed of nothing since," Scott wrote Morritt, "but Aladdins lamp and the palace of Haroun Alraschid."[70]

With the changes on the Continent Scott's protégé Henry Weber had decided to return to Germany, where a cousin who had been named one of the Commissioners of the Saxony Regency held out hopes of finding him employment.[71] He had always, despite Scott's aid, been miserably poor, and neither his edition of the *Metrical Romances* nor his *Beaumont and Fletcher* had been a success. And his habits, as Scott well knew, "like those of most German students were always too convivial."[72]

Lately he had been behaving strangely and drinking more heavily, though Scott had tried to warn him against excess and endeavored to keep him busy transcribing extracts for the *Life of Swift*. But during December he had gone on a long walking trip through the Highlands and accepted from the Highlanders, Scott guessed, "potations pottle deep to support him through the fatigue."[73] Soon after his return from this journey Scott invited him to dinner in Castle Street.

The two men were sitting quietly in the book-lined library at opposite sides of the great desk made on the model of Morritt's huge desk at Rokeby. The winter light began to fail; Scott was just about to ring for candles when he observed the German looking at him with a fierce intensity. "Weber," he said, "what's the matter with you?" Weber stood up. "Mr. Scott," he said, "you have long insulted me, and I can bear it no longer. I have brought a pair of pistols with me, and must insist on your taking one of them instantly."[74]

"You are mistaken, I think," Scott replied coolly, "in your way of setting about this affair—but no matter. It can, however, be no part of your object to annoy Mrs. Scott and the children; therefore, if you please, we will put the pistols into the drawer till after dinner, and then arrange to go out together like gentlemen." Weber agreed, laying down his pistol beside the other on Scott's manuscript. Scott locked them both in the drawer. "Let me request further," he said, "that nothing may occur while we are at dinner to give my wife any suspicion of what has been passing."[75]

As soon as Scott reached his dressing room he sent a message to one of Weber's friends. At dinner the two men were perfectly calm until the whisky and hot water were put on the table. Then, instead of inviting Weber to help himself, Scott mixed two moderate tumblers of toddy and handed one to his guest. Weber started up in a fury, then sank back in his seat. Was he ill? Charlotte asked; he replied that he was subject to spasms but that the pain was now gone. He seized the glass, gulped it down, and pushed it back to be refilled. Just then the friend Scott had summoned entered the room. Weber leaped up, rushed past him, and hatless and coatless, dashed out of the house.[76]

His friend pursued him to the end of Castle Street, trying to calm him, but in vain. That night he had to be confined in a straitjacket. Next day, however, he seemed better and was persuaded to go to his mother in Yorkshire. She placed him under medical restraint, in the care of a Dr. Bent.[77] He recovered sufficiently to write to Scott pathetically in February, but the improvement was not lasting.

Scott was saddened for Weber. He was fond of him, had tried to help him, and thought highly of his acquirements, "for besides a very extensive general acquaintance with literature he was particularly deep in our old dramatick lore, a good modern linguist, a tolerable draftsman and antiquary, and a most excellent hydrographer." Perhaps, Scott hoped, if he submitted "to the proper regimen of abstinence," he might still recover; "if not, it is miserable to think what may happen . . ."[78] "It is a most melancholy business and I fear has been helped by distress."[79] All endeavors to aid Weber ultimately proved fruitless; he died a lunatic in June, 1818, having been supported, according to Lockhart, during those last four years "at Scott's expense in an asylum at York."[80]

The last of poor Weber's scholarly work appeared in the summer of 1813, as contributions to Robert Jamieson's massive quarto *Illustrations of Northern Antiquities*, accounts of the old German sagas of the *Heldensbuch* or Book of Heroes and the *Nibelungenlied*. Lockhart claims, however, that the rhymed passages from the latter which Weber embroidered into his prose narrative really came from Scott's pen and were a gift to Weber. Scott also wrote the abstract of the *Eyrbiggia-Saga* that appeared in the same collection.[81]

Scott's work on the edition of Swift was now rapidly nearing completion.[82] He had expected to be correcting the last proofs before the end of January; only the letters of Vanessa, promised him by Berwick but not yet arrived, remained to be inserted in an appendix.[83] But there were still unexplained further postponements; by April, Scott was apologetically telling Hartstonge that "Swift after all is not *quite* finished, but very *very* nearly so . . ."[84] On April 27, however, he wrote Constable that the index and table of contents were now almost printed.[85]

Though Constable said nothing about it to Scott, he felt bitterly dejected about the delays that had prolonged the enterprise over a period of six years. "Had the work been completed three years ago when [the] Trade were mad about everything where Mr. Scott's name appeared," he grumbled to his partner, Cadell, "how differently should we have stood in this business." "*Don Roderick* helped to damn him—& the failure of

*Rokeby* completed it. In the meantime Lord Byron carries the laurel & we are left in a considerable scrape . . ."[86] Constable, furthermore, did not think much of the introductory biography: "The first volume of Swift disfigures the whole if anything can add to the *disfigurement* of this most vexatious of all Books. It has been a job to somebody and a damnable one to us."[87]

But as he contemplated the future Constable felt more cheerful: ". . . never mind we shall make it all up I trust by & bye whether by W. S. is a different question & yet a new Poem equal to *The Lady of the Lake* would do both him & us much good."[88] But it was not to be a new poem that would make it up. Shortly after the new year William Erskine had reread the manuscript of the first volume of *Waverley* and reversed his previous judgment; he was now sure it would prove the most popular of all his friend's writings.[89] This verdict reinforced Scott's own hopes of success. He gave it to John Ballantyne to be copied in another hand: "I have certain particular reasons," he said, "for being secret over this . . ."[90]

As soon as it was printed John showed it to Constable. He did not have the slightest doubt who had written it but took a few days to reflect, and then offered £700 for the copyright. Considering that the most successful of Maria Edgeworth's popular Irish novels had not brought her much more than a tenth of this sum, the offer was a generous one. Scott, however, coolly replied that if the novel were a failure this was too much and if it succeeded not enough. "If our fat friend had said £1000, I should have been staggered." Ultimately they agreed that the publisher and author should share the profits equally.[91] Constable never had more occasion to regret his caution.

After supper one night Erskine read aloud from the proof sheets of the first volume to a small party of friends. Scott continued in his determination that the novel be published anonymously; Erskine, therefore, did not reveal the author's name, and they thought they were hearing the first effort of some unknown aspirant to fame. But they listened excitedly, till dawn, and praised it as a work of the highest merit.[92] Not so James Ballantyne, who still responded with only moderate enthusiasm. "I could by no means get myself to think much of the Waverley Honour Scenes," he recalled later, ". . . but to my utter shame be it spoken when I reached the exquisite descriptions of scenes and manners at Tully-veolan, what did I do, but pronounce them at once to be utterly vulgar."[93]

Meanwhile Scott's financial involvements were all being steadily cleared away. In January he had repaid John Murray's loans in full and retired the bills from Morritt's banker, Hoare.[94] The Ballantynes were prosperous. John Ballantyne had transformed his Hanover Street premises into an auction salesroom for books and works of art, and was selling happily and successfully at the rate of £50 to £100 a day. James had ten presses constantly busy.[95] Though there was still about £10,000 worth of unsold stock piled in John's cellar, Scott felt hopeful that he could make Constable and Longman take it.[96] All the great debts were liquidated; in March, Scott repaid both Hartstonge and Charles Erskine.[97] That same month, Richardson wrote him that Sir Samuel Romilly agreed with his views about the illegality of a property tax upon the sale of copyrights, and the Lords of the Treasury directed the Income-Tax Commissioners to abandon the claim against him.[98] By the end of April, Scott wrote John Ballantyne that he had arranged all his affairs. "I promise you," he added, "I shall like very ill to be driven out to sea again."[99]

Scott's triumphant settlement of his own troubles progressed almost simultaneously with the victories of the Allied arms on the Continent. Wellington had crossed the French frontier, invested Bayonne, captured Bordeaux in March, defeated Soult in the battle of Toulouse in April. Meanwhile, in the north, Napoleon had been defeated at Laon, and the Allies had marched on Paris, stormed Montmartre, and made a victorious entry into the capital of Napoleon's empire.

Scott illumined all his windows in Castle Street with candles.[100] "Mine own eyes," he exclaimed, "have seen that which I had scarcely hoped my Son's should see, the downfall of the most accursed and relentless military despotism that ever wasted the blood and curbed the faculties of a civilized people.—I should have as soon expected the blade of a sword to bear a crop of corn, on its polished and hardened side, as any good or liberal institution to flow from Bonaparte. If he survives the ruin he has created, and it is strange he should even wish to survive it—it will be no slight proof of the Civilization of our age, which does not follow with private revenge even the most atrocious criminal."[101]

Napoleon's abdication on April 11 was not known in Scotland until the end of the month. Scott's heart burst with exultation. "Joy—joy in London now," he wrote, "—and in Edinburgh moreover . . . never shall we see—according to all human prospects—a consummation so truly glorious as now bids fair to conclude this long and eventful war. . . . Thank God it is done at last and although I rather grudge him even the mouthful of air which he may draw in the isle of Elba yet I question whether the moral lesson would have been completed either by his perishing in battle or being torn to pieces . . . like the De Witts by an infuriated croud of conscripts and their parents."[102]

His good spirits flowed over into his relations with his publisher. No sooner had he finished his editorial work on Swift than Constable suggested another task. He had acquired the copyright of the *Encyclopaedia Britannica* in 1812 and was now planning to issue a supplement. He offered Scott £100 each for articles on Chivalry and on Romance. Scott accepted, "rather from the idea that I am complying with what will be agreeable to you than any other motive"—presumably they "need not be very long."[103]

They had resumed negotiations on *The Nameless Glen,* which Scott had now decided to call *The Lord of the Isles.* Ultimately Constable agreed to pay fifteen hundred guineas for the management and half the copyright of all editions that should be published during 1815 and 1816, and to offer half of his share to Longman and Company.[104] Scott would have demanded better terms, he said, "but you have been kind and freindly, and kindness and freindship will, I hope, never be thrown away upon me. I assure you I shall be delighted that you make a right good thing of it."[105]

For later that summer he planned a voyage around the coast of Scotland, visiting the Clephanes at Torloisk and seeing "everything curious, from Fife Ness to Greenock, including Hhetlant the Orkneys and Hebrides."[106] This would enable him to refresh his memories of the Isles and give him materials for colorful descriptive passages in the poem. "I really think," he said, "that, with the advantage of my proposed tour . . . I may boldly set considerable value on the fruit of my labours."[107]

At Abbotsford, meanwhile, he was making a few improvements, adding a dressing room to one of the bedrooms[108] and building a staircase to the little room above Peterhouse that would not remind his guests "of an ascent to the Gallows."[109] The tiny combined parlor and dining room in which he wrote was being enlarged by "a recess for books and arms," made by throwing into it the adjacent little bedroom,[110] the laundry at the other end of the house was being transformed into "an eating closet," and a new laundry was being built outdoors.[111]

All these tasks kept Scott so busy that until June he found no time to settle down to the completion of *Waverley.* Then, however, he went at it with a dash. Writing rapidly and unceasingly, within three weeks he finished both the second and third volumes, and on July 1 threw down his pen.[112] To conceal the authorship from the typesetters, John Ballantyne continued copying it out for the printing office as speedily as Scott produced it. Aside from the Ballantynes and William Erskine, the only other friend, at the moment, to whom Scott confided the secret was Morritt.[113]

The story was rushed through the press and published on July 7.[114] Two days later, "a small anonymous sort of a novel in 3 volumes" went by mail to Rokeby. "I had a great deal of fun in the accomplishment of this task," Scott wrote Morritt, "though I do not expect that it will be popular in the South as much of the humour if there is any is local and some of it even professional. You however who are an adopted Scotchman will find some amusement in it."[115]

And somewhat later in the month Constable at last published Scott's edition of *The Works of Jonathan Swift*, nineteen volumes, octavo, in an impression of 1,250 copies.[116] Scott sent full sets to Hartstonge and Berwick, who had given him so much valuable aid, and copies of the *Life* to various others who had obliged him with information.[117] "Meanwhile," he wrote Hartstonge on July 18, "I have packed a square deal box as well and neatly as I could with the various treasures I received from you . . ." At the top of the box he included "two or three new publications for your acceptance. The first is *Waverley* a Novel in 3 Volumes of which the Good Town of Edinr. give me credit as the author. They do me too much honor, and I heartily wish I had both the credit and the profit."[118]

The whole first edition of *Waverley*, indeed, of a thousand copies, although issued in what publishers called "the dead season," was selling rapidly.[119] "It has made a very strong impression here," Scott said, "and the good people of Edinburgh are busied in tracing the author and in finding out originals for the portraits it contains."[120] Constable at once projected a second edition of two thousand copies.[121] But before Scott could learn its fate he was tossing on the German Ocean, on his way to Orkney, Shetland, and the Hebrides.

# 6

## Ultima Thule and Return

### ( 1 8 1 4 )

"You must know," Scott enthusiastically wrote Hartstonge, "that a committee of the Commissioners for the Northern Lights, are going to make a tour of Scotland and the isles . . ."[1] And to Morritt: "We have a stout cutter well fitted up and mand for the service by government; and to make assurance double sure the Admiral has sent a sloop of war to cruise in the dangerous points of our tour and sweep the sea of the Yankee privateers . . ."[2]

Scott had been invited to join the party as a guest, but the real object of the voyage was to survey the lighthouses along Scotland and select sites for additional ones. For this purpose the Commissioners were accompanied by Robert Stevenson, lighthouse builder and engineer to the Scottish Lighthouse Board. The Commissioners consisted of William Erskine, who had become Sheriff of Orkney and Zetland, Adam Duff, the Sheriff of Forfarshire and Kincardineshire—who, however, did not come on board till they reached Arbroath—and the stout and genial Robert Hamilton, Sheriff of Lanarkshire. The yacht, a cutter carrying six guns and a crew of ten, was under the command of Captain Wilson.[3]

On the eve of their departure the Duke of Buccleuch sent Scott a note of farewell. He and the Duchess had no commissions "for the Ultima Thule, except that you do not break your neck or Drown yourself. . . . If indeed you happen to meet with a tolerably sized Craken we should like to have it preserved for us in spirits."[4] The Duchess, the Duke said, was well, although Scott had thought that lately she had been looking thin and poorly.[5] She had just begun to read *Waverley*.

"The World will have it that you wrote it, or *nearly* wrote it—at all events it is much admired."[6]

In London, Lord Byron jested about Scott's voyage. "Oh! I have had the most amusing letter from Hogg, the Ettrick Minstrel and Shepherd," he wrote Tom Moore. ". . . Scott, he says, is gone to the Orkneys in a gale of wind, during which wind, he affirms, the said Scott, he is sure, is not at his ease, to say the least of it. Lord! Lord! if these home-keeping minstrels had crossed your Atlantic or my Mediterranean, and tasted a little open boating in a white squall—or a gale in 'the Gut,'—or the Bay of Biscay with no gale at all—how it would enliven and introduce them to a few of the sensations!—to say nothing of an illicit amour or two upon shore, in the way of Essay upon the Passions, beginning with simple adultery, and compounding it as they went along."[7]

The yacht sailed from Leith on July 29 at one o'clock and ran down the Firth of Forth before a fine gale.[8] Passing Inchkeith, Scott regaled his companions with tales of Mary of Guise; Craigmillar to the starboard evoked memories of Queen Mary; farther out he gave them tales of the Bass Rock and the ancient glories of Tantallon. By evening they had landed at the Isle of May, where vast numbers of sea fowl soared about the rugged perpendicular rock and the seventeenth-century lighthouse tower.[9]

Rounding the point of Fife Ness, they came into rougher water and "had a touch of a deep rolling pitching kind of a heezie hozie as the children call it which forced the most reluctant and stout of the party to restore to Neptune our coffee & toast."[10] Later that night they were nearing the Bell Rock, fifteen miles offshore from Arbroath, and Scott remained on deck until eleven, watching its revolving light flash brilliant white, then gleaming red, and then dark crimson over the heaving water.[11]

Next morning Scott was up early. The solitary column rose directly out of the waves, a round of rock half again as high as the tower of Melrose Abbey, the first thirty of its hundred and twenty feet solid masonry.[12] Seeing "some of the party looking very *white-like*," Stevenson suggested breakfasting in the lighthouse, and the steward was sent off with baskets of provisions.[13] The door, thirty feet above the surge, was reached by a rope ladder with wooden rungs; Scott disdained the suggestion of being swung aloft in a chair, and clambered up with his hands and feet. Within, the entire ponderous structure trembled from the pounding of the billows. They ascended through a series of round chambers communicating by oak ladders with brass rails, and ate a hearty Scotch breakfast in the loftiest room, right under the light.[14]

Before their departure they were asked to write in the lighthouse album. Erskine laid his hand on the page and said, "Mr. Scott, you must give us something more than Walter Scott." At first Scott tried to decline, then rose, looked out of the window a few minutes, came back, and wrote:

### PHAROS LOQUITUR

Far in the bosom of the deep
O'er these wild shelves my watch I keep;
A ruddy gleam of changeful light,
Bound on the brow of dusky night,
The seaman bids my lustre hail,
And scorns to strike his timorous sail.[15]

The run from the Bell Rock to Arbroath was violent. The entire party were sick again, Hamilton remained in bed all day, and Scott's servant, John, was ill "to a degree of misery" that made him "liker to a half drowned baboon than anything else."[16] On shore, joined by Adam Duff, Scott went to visit the ruined abbey church and make recommendations for its repair and preservation.[17] In these very sandstone aisles almost twenty years ago, Scott recalled, he had strolled with Williamina. Now she was nearly four years in her grave, and although he had long been married his heart filled at the memory.[18]

All this coast was full of that old heartbreak; next morning at seven the yacht was gliding under the walls of the ancient castle of Dunnotar, where Scott had excavated the old well and lingered in the desperate hope that he would be invited to Fettercairn. But soon they had passed Stonehaven and were in the harbor of Aberdeen, with the tower of King's College and the steeples of St. Machar rising above clustered roofs. Scott did not go ashore, but Stevenson, Duff, and Erskine went to look at the rocky cape of Girdle Ness, on which a beacon was to be erected.[19]

At Dun Bay the crags stood out bright yellow with the dung of countless seagulls. Farther along among these cliffs were the famous Bullers of Buchan, a huge cauldron of black rocks into which the sea rushed through a lofty stone arch with a noise like the bellowing of innumerable bulls. Rowing in on the flood, they found themselves in an immense round pot hemmed in by insurmountable dark walls towering up two hundred feet, with the tiny figures of a few men at the top silhouetted like pigmies against the sky. In a storm, an old fisherman said, billows sometimes boiled to the very summit of the savage hollow.[20]

On August 1 the yacht was off Fraserburgh, the extreme point of the Moray Firth, and after saluting the castle with three guns, stood out in a merry gale for Shetland. But the breeze soon failed, and they found themselves becalmed, with nothing to pass the time but ballads, recitations, backgammon, chess, and piquet. The yacht was out of sight of land, the sun set in the open sea, the moon rose; until next afternoon there were only light baffling airs.[21] Then came a stiff breeze, growing fiercer, until there was nothing but booming, trampling, and whizzing of waves about their ears. The yacht tossed; huge combers poured over the deck. They were caught in the fierce current of the "Sumburgh-rost," a violent tide sweeping down from Sumburgh Head that buffeted the yacht unmercifully. Neither Captain Wilson nor the pilot knew exactly where they were and began to think they must have overshot Fair Isle, lying in the lonely waste of waters between Orkney and the Shetlands.[22]

Next day there was still no sight of land. Scott proposed that Erskine, as Sheriff of Zetland, "issue a *meditatione fugae* warrant against his territories, which seem to fly from us."[23] In the course of the day they hailed two whalers out from Lerwick, but when at two that afternoon a lookout on the topmast called "Land," Scott felt uncertain whether they had sighted Shetland, Norway, or the Faroe Isles.[24]

It turned out to be Bardhead, the southern tip of Bressay, and by nine o'clock, still in bright summer twilight, the yacht was sailing up the sound to the harbor of Lerwick.[25] Here the coast guard hailed them "in the humiliating phrase, 'Sloop a-hoy!' " Outraged, Captain Wilson exclaimed, "I will teach the Lubber better manners than to call this vessel a sloop." Nearer, however, the voice called, "Cutter a-hoy!"[26]

The harbor was crowded with whaling vessels from Greenland, and the streets of Lerwick were full of riotous drunken sailors. Erskine promptly arrested some of the rioters. Lerwick looked poor; there were no wheeled carts or carriages on Shetland, and the streets were flagged, not causewayed.[27] The surrounding low hills, entirely devoid of trees, intermingled huge stones with stunted heather and patches of yellow flowers; on the mossy and sterile muirs grazed "miserable-looking, hairy-legged" sheep, "of all colours," Scott said, "even to sky-blue." The farmhouses he found "most wretched; worse than the worst herd's house I ever saw."[28]

In the center of a fresh-water loch near the town, Scott visited a Picts' castle, an enormous circular structure built without mortar. The walls, of natural stone, some eighteen feet thick, were pierced by a winding gallery that spiraled its way to the summit. Only three feet high, and lit at intervals by narrow slits looking inward, this corkscrew passage justified, Scott thought, the tradition that the Picts were a dwarfish race. He was fascinated by this ancient structure built with such enormous labor by a people who seemed to have known "neither the art of cement, or arches, or of stairs."[29]

From the harbor Scott's party hired a six-oared whaler-built boat to circle the adjoining small island of Bressay and the tiny Isle of Noss. Here they saw, split off from the Isle, a lofty and precipitous rock called the Holm, the summit of which was reached by a chair swung giddily on iron rings from two cables stretched over the watery gulf.[30] On Bressay the farm laborers working with spade and hoe were so unused to the recent introduction of horses for plowing that they were frightened by the plowman when he called *ho, gee,* and *wo.* "He speaks to the horses," they said, "and they gang—and there's something no canny about the man."[31]

The Zetlanders, indeed, Scott found deeply superstitious. Witches and dwarfish fairies called "Trows" abounded. The trows stole children, and carried them off to the interiors of green hills; sometimes they stole an adult and left a moving phantom behind in his place. The Zetlanders also believed that anyone who rescued a drowning man would live to receive a deep injury at his hands. Scott was told one tale of a stranded vessel whose crew were warping their way ashore by means of a hawser. Offering no help, the Zetlanders watched them in silence, till an old man reminded them that if the sailors were allowed to land they would consume all the winter provisions, whereupon an islander cut the hawser and all twenty were swept away.[32]

At Lerwick, Scott began a rhymed letter to the Duke and Duchess of Buccleuch:

> Hail to the Chieftain from his clansman true
> From her true minstrel Health to fair Buccleuch
> Health from the isles where Dawn at morning weaves
> Her chaplet with the tints that twilight leaves
>
> . . .
>
> Here rise no groves & here no gardens blow
> Here even the hardy heath scarce deigns to grow
> But rocks on rocks in mist and storm arrayd
> Stretch far to sea their giant colonnade
> With many a cavern seam'd, the dreary haunt
> Of the dun seal and swarthy cormorant
> While round their rifted brows, with frequent cry
> As of lament, the gulls & gannets fly
> As from their sable base with sullen sound
> In sheets of whitening foam the waves rebound.
>
> . . .
>
> Why should I tell of Mousa's castled coast
> Why of the horrors of the Sumburgh-rost
> May not these bald disjointed lines suffice
> Penn'd while my comrades whirl the rattling dice
> While down the cabbin-skylight lessening shine
> The rays & eve is chaced with mirth and wine[33]

During this stay in Zetland more Greenland whalers arrived and let off their spirits in drunken riot. A gentleman of Lerwick was pleased to see a party of sailors eating a leg of mutton beneath his windows, only to learn that they were devouring his own dinner, which they had violently carried off, spit and all, from his kitchen. Two other sailors who had stolen a sheep were brought before a red-faced, black-wigged Justice of the Peace; one of them denied that he had taken it but said that he had seen it carried off by a fellow with a red nose and a black wig: "Don't you think he was like his honour, Tom?" he appealed. "By God, Jack," replied Tom, "I believe it was the very man!" Erskine was kept busy clapping these jokers in jail.[34]

For several days Stevenson was away in the yacht surveying some of the northern isles, and Scott visited the nearby towns of Tingwell and Scalloway. At dinnertime on August 8, Stevenson returned and called at the hotel to say they would put out to sea that night. Scott's servant had been almost constantly drunk. "My things are in disorder," Scott told Stevenson. "My man John Macbeth, poor fellow, is now neither for use nor ornament."[35] But he managed to get packed, and by eight that night the party were aboard.[36]

In the morning they found the yacht approaching the wild island of Mousa, where they clambered around the ancient castle, and then returned on shipboard to beat their way down to Sumburgh Head.[37] Here they ran again into the Sumburgh-rost, contending violently with the wind and flinging white foam high on the broken cliffs. The rocks were of sand flag, which after every storm slid down in immense masses like avalanches.[38] Climbing alone to the brow, Scott had no difficulty in dislodging a fragment as big as himself, which "thundered down in tremendous style," "splitting upon a projecting cliff," and crashing "like a shower of shrapnel shot" into the sea raging among thousands of other fragments fallen from the peaks.[39]

Across Quendale Bay towered the even loftier cliff of Fitful Head, its pearly bulk rising almost a thousand feet above the stormy Atlantic. On the landward side of Sumburgh Head the slopes were carpeted with short grass; when Scott had gazed enough and wished to rejoin his companions, "sitting gently down on the steep green slope which led to the beach, I e'en slid down a few hundred feet . . ." He found them in the Old House of Sumburgh enjoying gin and water. The wind was rising, so they all went on board, and the yacht was "made SNUG—a sure sign," added Scott, "the passengers will not be so."[40]

"The omen was but too true," he wrote the next day, "—a terrible combustion on board, among plates, dishes, glasses, writing-desks, etc., etc.; not a wink of sleep." The Sumburgh-rost was worse than ever. "All the landsmen sicker than sick, and our Viceroy, Stevenson, qualmish. This is the only time that I have felt more than temporary inconvenience, but this morning I have headache and nausea . . ."[41] Throughout the earlier part of the morning they were followed by two very sportive whales, "gambolling and spouting up sheets of water,"[42] but as the yacht neared the Fair Isle these dropped behind.[43]

It was here in 1588 that the flagship of the Duke of Sidonia Medina had been wrecked after the shattered fragments of the Invincible

Armada had fled northward amid tempestuous seas. The tiny island, only three miles long and a mile and a half wide, the sole dot of land in over a hundred miles of heaving water, now had a population of about thirty families. Some of the men, "with long elf-locks, striped worsted caps, and shoes of raw hide," rowed out in frail skiffs to meet the yacht.[44] The islanders were miserably poor, Scott found, living in huts "dirty without, and still dirtier within; pigs, fowls, cows, men, women, and children, all . . . in the same room—the brood sow making (among the more opulent) a distinguished inhabitant of the mansion."[45]

On the morning of August 11, after a night's run, the yacht was in the Orkneys, off the flat island of Sanday.[46] In Tress Ness Bay they saw the huge carcasses of a school of 265 whales that had been driven up on the sand.[47] During a tumultuous passage to Linghold Bay the sea got into the galley and spoiled their dinner: the soup "poisoned with salt water—our cod and haddocks . . . soused in their primitive element— the curry undone—and all gone to the devil." Hamilton, something of a gourmet, was in despair, but they comforted him with bad puns, and the cook managed to provide a good dinner after all.[48]

Next morning before breakfast they were in Kirkwall Bay and could see the red freestone tower of St. Magnus Cathedral rising huge and square above the roofs of the town.[49] Scott was disappointed to find no letters from Charlotte, although he had written her from Arbroath, Fraserburgh, and Lerwick.[50] He hoped now, he said, that she would write at once to his next address at Campbelltown: "Do not put this off as I am truly anxious to know that you are all well."[51]

"The most useful thing I brought to sea with me," he told her, "was the umbrella—the most useless poor John. He has been quite intolerable & last night was so drunk that I told him this morning I must look for another servant at Martinmas—he is much dejected but it is really impossible to put up with his drunkenness added to folly & I can safely say he has not been one day sober to an end since we set out . . . Kiss all [the] children. . . . I hope Fifi"—Charlotte's little spaniel, Finella—"& Puss are both well."[52]

"The magistrates of Kirkwall," Scott recorded in his *Diary*, "present us with the freedom of their ancient burgh . . ."[53] The antiquities of the place were not very numerous—the Cathedral, the ruins of the Bishop's castle, and the old palace built by Patrick, Earl of Orkney. This last had a great hall lit by Gothic-shafted windows and approached by a spacious staircase of three flights of steps. The Cathedral, with its round arches and heavy Saxon pillars, Scott thought "rather massive and gloomy than elegant," and much of the carved ornament had been injured by time. Earl Patrick's seat bore "the royal arms *without any mark of bastardy* (his father was a natural son of James V) quarterly, with a lymphad or galley."[54]

Scott was much excited by stories about John Gow the pirate, who had once been the plague of the Orkney islands, and asked many questions about his exploits. Erskine's Sheriff-Substitute, Mr. Peterkin, drew up an account of Gow for him, and Stevenson supplied some details he had learned from a friend one of whose ancestors had captured Gow.[55] Seven years after this lighthouse voyage, when the still anonymous author of the *Waverley Novels* published a romance entitled *The Pirate*, Stevenson recognized local details he himself had supplied Scott and had no doubt who had penned the tale.[56]

At Kirkwall, Scott concluded his verse letter to the Duke of Buccleuch with some galloping tetrameters and sent it off:

> In respect that your Grace has commissioned a Kraken
> You will please be informd that they seldom are taken
> It is January two years, the Zetland folks say
> Since they saw the last Kraken in Scalloway-bay[57]

Though the monstrous creature lay in the offing a fortnight, they said, nobody had dared draw near it, fearing that the suction would drag down their boats. Scott of Scalloway received differing accounts of its size:[58]

> . . . the modest and diffident swore
> That it loom'd like the keel of a ship and no more
> Those of eye-sight more clear or of fancy more high
> Said it rose like an island twixt ocean & sky
>
> . . .
>
> And I think my Lord Duke your Grace would not wish
> To cumber your house, such a kettle of fish.[59]

Before leaving the Orkneys, the party visited the Standing Stones of Stennis and the Dwarfie Stone of Hoy. The former was a circle of sandstone monoliths, like those of Stonehenge, some seventeen feet in height. The Dwarfie Stone was a rock hewn into two chambers, each containing a bed of stone, with a connecting passage.[60] On August 17 the cutter was ready to sail. From an old hag of Stromness, who made her living by selling winds, Captain Wilson, "between jest and earnest" bought a favorable gale.[61]

"On board at half-past three," Scott wrote in his *Diary*, "and find Bessie Millie a woman of her word, for the expected breeze has sprung up . . . "[62] Before evening the cutter had gotten out of Scapa Flow and the Pentland Firth and was in the open Atlantic. On their lee boom they sighted a King's ship of about eighteen guns shortening sail, "apparently to take us under her wing, which may not be altogether unnecessary in the latitude of Cape Wrath, where several vessels have been taken by Yankee-Doodle."[63]

After dark it turned rainy, Bessie Millie's charm failed, and they found themselves beating against contrary winds.[64] Early next morning the cabin-boy Tim dashed below to tell them he had sighted an island. "What island can this be?" Scott called. Stevenson didn't know; they must have been blown out of their course during the night. Without bothering to dress, Scott hurried on deck, but soon came back. Tim had indeed discovered an island—the island of Great Britain, for they were off Cape Wrath.[65]

They had weathered Whitten Head, but the wind was now so adverse and the ocean so squally that they tried in vain to make headway. Hamilton and Erskine kept their berths, Scott and Duff sat on deck, "like two great bears, wrapt in watch-cloaks, the sea flying over us." The gale became so violent that Captain Wilson renounced doubling Cape Wrath as impracticable, and the yacht ran for shelter into Loch Eribol. Here they anchored within a reef of sunken rocks. Salmon, haddock, and lobster were plentiful, they heard, so John Peters, the steward, was sent ashore to obtain some for dinner.[66]

Next day, after a Highland breakfast of herring, haddock, fresh butter and eggs, bannocks of barley, oatcakes, tea, coffee, and whiskey, they explored the Caves of Smoo. The outermost, encrusted with stalactites, was eighty feet high and extended two hundred feet in from the Loch. An arch fourteen feet high and eight feet wide opened into a further cavern with a black lake whose deep and sullen waters were in constant agitation. High above, in a rough dome, two chasms admitted a dubious twilight; down one, a violent cataract foamed into the convulsed waters below, through the other there was a remote glimpse of blue sky. They crossed this seething water in a skiff, and landed on a slippery shelf of rock, and with torches penetrated a tunnel running some hundred feet deeper into the rock, the stalactites branching out like coral and gleaming like diamonds in the glare of their lights. At the end, this passage sank into a horrible gulf filled with inky water.[67]

Half-past six the following morning saw the cutter off Cape Wrath. Here, five hundred feet above the rocky shore, Stevenson proposed to build a lighthouse. Over the cliff soared two large eagles; at its feet the billows tossed boulders of a ton's weight as a child might toss a ball. At eleven o'clock, with light winds and a great swell of tide, they set sail for the Hebrides, and Scott watched the pink cliff of the headland dwindle to stern. The breeze stiffened, the cutter bounded over the waves at eight knots an hour, the hills of Ross-shire sank behind. Long after it was dark the party remained on deck, watching the phosphorescence of the water and the foam streaming away from the bows.[68]

Overnight the weather turned stormy, and gave the cutter such concussions that she reeled with every wave and trembled from head to stern. But somehow she beat her way past Lewis, and about three in the morning ran for shelter within the little harbor of Scalpa on the coast of Harris.[69] Next day they tried in vain to cross to Skye; contrary winds would allow them only to creep along the desolate Harris shore.

Not until five that afternoon were they able with the ebb tide to stand out into the Sound and see the high mountains of Skye rising ahead of them and behind them the sun sinking in red and orange splendor below the conical top of Bernera.[70]

On the morning of August 23, Scott woke under the Castle of Dunvegan. Hanging on a steep mass of rock high above the Loch of Folliart, its embrasured gun-battery looked out to the sea, and the ancient entrance rose by a flight of steps cut in the living stone to a portal into the courtyard. Macleod of Macleod came out to welcome the party with his Highland piper skirling, and the yacht responded with a three-gun salute. The visitors were shown the treasured drinking-cup dating from A.D. 993 and the silver-tipped drinking horn of Rorie More, and Scott accepted from his hostess an invitation to sleep in the haunted chamber.[71]

Tapestries covered walls of immense thickness; the windows looked out on the white ghostly shapes of three tall pyramidal rocks called Macleod's Maidens; an autumnal blast drove clouds across the moon and mists over the troubled billows; an angry cascade raving down the crags mingled its voice with the moaning of the wind.[72] "But woe is me," said Scott,

> "The wild romance of life was done
> The real history was begun.

"I felt nothing but that I had had a busy day had eaten a good dinner had drunk a bottle of excellent claret and was much disposed to sleep."[73] Nothing even momentarily troubled his rest but that the feather bed was too soft.[74] "And so to my eternal shame without troubling myself about the ghost of Rorie More or anyone of his long line I went to bed and slept quietly till my servant calld me in the morning."[75]

From Dunvegan the yacht made its way down the coast of Skye, past Loch Bracadale, Loch Eynort, and Loch Brittle, to Loch Scavaig.[76] Here among the bleak Cuillin Hills the voyagers saw the dark and solitary lake of Coruisk, which they called Corriskin, a gash of black waves among treeless brown crags and swirling mists.[77] The scene overwhelmed Scott with its savage grandeur. Observing his emotion, the others "left him to roam and gaze about by himself," said Erskine, "until it was time to muster the party and be gone."[78] Hobbling with uneven pace along the bare summit, he waved his stick in gestures that seemed strange to his distant observers; a sailor sent to tell him it was time to go returned saying, "Strange, he did not seem to know me."[79]

In the neighboring Loch of Slapin they visited a cave belonging to Macallister of Strathaird. Unlike the caverns of Smoo, it was marble-white, frosted into fanciful shapes like statuary, and with a limpid pool that might have been, Scott said, "the bathing grotto of a Naiad." Emerging, "I slid down the polished sheet of marble which forms the rising ascent, and thereby injured my pantaloons in a way which my jacket is ill calculated to conceal." The party were escorted back to the yacht by Mr. Macallister's two grandsons, whose pockets Erskine filled with almonds and raisins.[80]

At seven the next morning the yacht was coasting between the islands of Rum and Egg. They put in at Egg to see the cave where the Laird of Macleod had inflicted a hideous death on two hundred of the Macdonalds by kindling a fire at the entrance and suffocating them all. The stony floor was still strewn with the black and chocolate-colored bones of the victims. Scott picked up and pocketed one of the skulls, to the horror of the sailors, who were convinced this would bring bad luck.[81]

Sure enough, the wind promptly turned tyrannical. Glasses and dishes smashed in the galley, portmanteaus and writing desks charged across the cabin, and the yacht kicked and bounced violently. Nevertheless they managed through a tremendous surf to land on the seal-haunted rocks of Skerry Vhor, where Stevenson proposed to erect a lighthouse. They avoided a square-rigged vessel believed to be an American and gained Iona before sundown.[82]

Haze and dullness delayed their sailing for Staffa until after dinner the following day, then cleared but returned heavily before nightfall,[83] so that not until the day after that were they able to visit Fingal's Cave.[84] Erskine, who had never seen it before, was overcome. "Would you believe it?" said Scott, "my poor Willie sat down and wept . . ."[85] The vast natural cathedral was indeed stupendous, its hexagonal pillars soaring to an enormous height, yellow, crimson, and cream-colored marble filling the spaces of the roof between the basalt columns, and the ocean roaring below over red and violet rocks.[86]

"We have now seen," Scott wrote in his *Diary*, "the three grandest caverns in Scotland . . ." Smoo, he thought, was so wild and savagely gloomy as to "convey an impression of terror"; "the dazzling whiteness" of Macallister's Cave "and the graceful dignity of its arch" gave it a "severe and chastened beauty"; but Staffa in its grandeur could only be called sublime.[87]

"We had scarcely left Staffa when the wind and rain returned." But Scott and Erskine were looking forward eagerly to seeing Mrs. Clephane and her daughters on Mull. In a heavy downpour they landed, struggled along a muddy cart-road to Torloisk, slipped in a swollen brook, and arrived soaked. Next morning the rest of the party joined them at breakfast.[88] Their hostess begged them to remain for several days, but time was running short, and Mrs. Clephane, Margaret, Anna Jane, and Williamina all waved their handkerchiefs from the windows as the party went down the hill to reembark.[89] Contrarily, the wind then fell away, and at six o'clock the yacht was still in sight of Torloisk, "which must have afforded amusement," Scott observed, "to the ladies whose hospitable entreaties we had resisted."[90]

It was now the last day of August. For the past two weeks Scott had sat almost daily in the forecastle chatting with the seamen or perched on an unsteady campstool jotting down notes while the wind dashed him with spray, although sometimes a member of the party stood over him with the umbrella that had proved so much more useful than John.[91] He was sunburned a dark brown; his hands, he said, were "the colour of Yorke tan."[92] Since leaving Skye his imagination had been full of *The Lord of the Isles*, much of which was to unfold in these scenes.

As the yacht crept past the shores of Ardnamurchan and the castle of Mingary and made its way into the sound of Mull his emotions took fire. Here was the Bloody Bay, where one ancient Lord of the Isles had overcome his own son in a desperate sea-battle.[93] On the shores of "woody Morven," just past Loch Alline, was the castle of Ardtornish, to which still other Lords of the Isles had summoned their own parliaments and from which one of them had "dated a treaty with the Crown of England as an independent Prince."[94] Standing out from Mull in the moonlight were the ruins of Duart Castle and across the water the magnificent summits of the chain of mountains bordering Loch Linnhe and, between Loch Awe and Loch Etive, the mighty bulk of Ben Cruachan. What scenes and what a history had his country![95]

On September 1 the party visited the castles of Dunstaffnage and Dunolly, Scott happily telling tales of the ancient glories of those fortresses.[96] At Oban, Stevenson learned that the Duchess of Buccleuch was dead but kept the news from Scott till he should learn it from his own letters.[97] In happy ignorance, therefore, Scott agreed with the Commissioners to run over to the coast of Ireland and see the Giants' Causeway before ending their voyage.[98]

He had still not heard from Charlotte: "I often ask myself," he wrote her, "what you are all doing & what can be the meaning of my having no letter either at Kirkwall or Torloisk but I suppose somebody would have written had any thing been otherwise than well and I know the posts are so awkward & so cross where seas & ferries are concerned that I think your letters might easily miscarry. . . . Kiss all the brats for me mostly kindly . . ."[99]

Suddenly it was Indian summer, and so warm that breakfast was served on deck beneath "a handsome awning to save our complexions, God wot," while a gentle breeze carried the yacht past the indelicately named Paps of Jura into the Sound. As they got out into the Runs of Islay and could feel the soft swell of the sea, the day was so clear that they could see Ulva in the blue distance and, still farther, the hills of Rum just distinguishable from the blue sky. In the course of the evening they lost sight of the Hebrides, and at dawn they were off the coast of Ireland.[100]

Yankee privateers had been seen off the Tiree Islands and were reported to have taken some vessels, so all that day they kept the yacht's guns loaded in case they had to fight for it.[101] Later, in fact, they learned that they had been repeatedly in the path of two American marauders, the *Peacock*, of twenty-two guns, and a schooner of eighteen guns, the *Prince of Neuchatel*, which had made many captures in the Irish Channel and at the back of Islay. But they themselves sighted no enemy vessel, and the evening passed with cards and backgammon in the cabin.[102]

At Portrush, unhappily, Scott heard the news that Stevenson had kept from him at Oban.[103] It grieved him deeply; "the shock of an earthquake," he wrote the Duke, could not have affected him more. "Of all whom I have ever seen, in whatever rank, she possessed most the power of rendering virtue lovely . . . Would to God I could say, be comforted . . ."[104]

Scott's letter crossed one the Duke wrote from Bowhill. "I am calm and resigned. The blow was so severe that it stunned me, and I did not feel that agony of mind which might have been expected. I now see the full extent of my misfortune; but that extended view of it has come gradually upon me. I am fully aware how imperative it is upon me to exert myself to the utmost on account of my children. I must not depress their spirits by a display of my own melancholy feelings. . . .[105] Whenever it suits your convenience I shall be happy to see you here."[106]

"Wake, or rather rise at six," Scott wrote in his *Diary* the day after he had learned of the Duchess's death, "for I have waked the whole night, or fallen into broken sleeps only to be hag-ridden by the nightmare."[107] He had no heart for the sights he had been anticipating so eagerly, and accompanied the others only that he might not spoil their pleasure. Dunluce he observed almost mechanically; at the Giants' Causeway he had a violent headache and did not even get out of the boat.[108]

The columns, he admitted, were remarkable; the horizontal strata of red and ocher against the black and dark gray checkered them to striking effect. Guides sold pieces of crystal, agate, or chalcedony from these rocks. Several of the party acquired specimens, "and, had I been quite as I am wont to be, I would have selected four to be capitals of a rustic porch at Abbotsford. But, alas! alas! I am much out of love with vanity . . ." He was relieved when the yacht stood out toward Scotland and came within sight of the beacon on the Mull of Kintyre.[109]

Early in the morning the ship's boat brought letters from shore, and Scott was relieved to find that at last he had a packet from home telling him that all the family were well.[110] "I have great need of some good news to raise my spirits a little," he wrote Charlotte, "after the deplorable intelligence of the death of our excellent friend. . . . My jaunt has compleatly answerd my purpose in every respect and has only been embitterd by this melancholy news at the conclusion. The Duke is more to be pitied than any human being living . . ."[111]

Capricious winds kept the yacht struggling around Arran for another day. When they had fought their way into the Firth of Clyde the wind then died away altogether, leaving them becalmed off the Renfrewshire coast until sunset.[112] "It is all," said Captain Wilson, "owing to the cave at the Isle of Egg," where Scott had picked up the charred skull. "Under this odium," Scott commented, "I may labour yet longer, for assuredly, the weather has been doggedly unfavourable." Aided by the tide, however, they finally reached Greenock on September 8.[113]

Here Stevenson brought on board a large packet of mail for everyone except Scott. It turned out that the postmaster, Mr. MacKechnie, had locked up Scott's letters so that he might have the honor of delivering them in person to "the man who had so often delighted his evening fireside." He handed them over with a small box of limes and the latest newspapers. On shore, with the news that Scott was aboard the yacht, flags were hoisted in fluttering welcome.[114]

At Glasgow the companions separated. With Erskine, Scott headed for Edinburgh in a glow of anticipation.[115] "I reckon this letter will reach you on Saturday morning"—September 10—he wrote Charlotte, "so that I may expect you in town (to my infinite joy) on Sunday or Monday at the very farthest. I will have a bit of dinner ready for you on Sunday and wait till five o'clock."[116]

# The Scent of Roast Meat

## ( 1 8 1 4 — 1 8 1 5 )

Scott returned from the Hebrides to find that the unknown author of *Waverley* was famous. The first edition of one thousand copies had been snapped up so fast that two days after publication Constable had rushed through a second two thousand.[1] No sooner was Scott back in Edinburgh than they agreed on a third of a thousand; in November this was exhausted and a fourth was called for. Before the end of 1814, five thousand copies had been sold; the profits were more than £2,100. Never had an anonymous novel had such a success.[2]

Even before Scott sailed from Leith, his friend Morritt had given him a foretaste of the book's reception. "How the story may continue I am not able to divine; but, as far as I have read, pray let us thank you for the Castle of Tully-Veolan, and the delightful drinking-bout at Lucky Mac-Leary's, for the characters of the Laird of Balmawhapple and the Baron of Bradwardine; and no less for Davie Gellatly . . ."[3] As soon as Morritt had finished the novel, "Were I to tell you all my admiration," he wrote, "you would accuse me of complimenting. You have quite attained the point which your postscript-preface mentions as your object—the discrimination of Scottish character, which had hitherto been slurred over with clumsy national daubing."[4]

Everywhere *Waverley* created a sensation. Edinburgh buzzed with it; London praised it to the skies. From England literary friends enthusiastically wrote about it to the Edgeworths in Ireland; in the wilds of County Longford the run on the three little volumes was so great that the desperate Edgeworths were unable to obtain them.[5] At last a neighbor lucky enough to have a set lent it to them on condition that each volume must be returned the moment it was read.[6] At evening readings the whole numerous family listened spellbound. "I wish," wrote Maria, "the author could have witnessed the impression it made— the strong hold it seized on the feelings of both old and young." With the last words of the story, "Aut Scotus aut Diabolus!" exclaimed Edgeworth; and Maria rushed to her desk to pour out pages of voluble thanks to the unknown author.[7]

Mrs. Edgeworth, however, had just turned a page; "There is a postscript," she observed. Their hearts filled with the wild Highland scenery, the death of Fergus MacIvor, and the devotion of Evan Dhu, no one felt much interested in a "Postscript, which should have been a Preface." But a sense of duty prevailed. "Well, let us hear it," said Edgeworth, resignedly. "Oh! my dear sir," burst out Maria, "how much pleasure would my father, my mother, my whole family, as well as myself have lost if we had not read to the last page! And the pleasure came upon us so unexpectedly—we had been so completely absorbed that every thought of ourselves, our own authorship, was far, far away."[8]

For what had the mysterious Author written? His object, he said, had been to describe his Scottish characters, not by caricature, "but by their habits, manners, and feelings; so as in some distant degree to emulate the admirable Irish portraits drawn by Miss Edgeworth."[9] Maria was overwhelmed by so high a compliment from so admired a source. "Thank you," she exclaimed rapturously, "for the honour you have done us, and for the pleasure you have given us . . . and believe me, every opinion I have in this letter expressed, was formed before any individual in this family had peeped to the end of the book, or knew how much we owed you."[10]

The reply to Miss Edgeworth's effusion was signed by James Ballantyne, but Scott certainly looked over his shoulder and perhaps even held the pen. "There are very few," this epistle said demurely, "who have had the opportunities that have been presented to me, of knowing how very elevated is the admiration entertained by the Author of *Waverley* for the genius of Miss Edgeworth. . . . 'If I could but hit Miss Edgeworth's wonderful power of vivifying all her persons, and making them live as *beings* in your mind, I should not be afraid': —Often has the Author of *Waverley* used such language to me. . . ."[11]

The reviewers, though more restrained than Morritt and Miss Edgeworth, were almost uniformly laudatory. The *Quarterly* hailed the novel as "a Scotch *Castle Rackrent*" but in "a much higher strain." Jeffrey, in the *Edinburgh*, broadly hinted his belief that Scott was the author and applauded "the extraordinary fidelity and felicity" of the character portrayal. The *Monthly Review* echoed this praise: ". . . all the subordinate characters are touched with the same discriminating force which so strongly marks their principals"; and it too hinted at the hand of Scott. So did the *British Review*, which recommended the book as no common novel but one of unusual originality and truth. The *Anti-*

*Jacobin* also guessed at the unknown author and had but one adverse comment to make—that no Chateau-Margaux sent from Bordeaux in 1713 could have been drinkable in 1745: "Claret two-and-thirty years old! It almost gives us the gripes to think of it."[12]

In Scotland fantastic rumors about the authorship circulated wildly. Some people named William Erskine, some the aging Henry Mackenzie, others Scott's brother Tom. Scott humorously suggested his old friend George Cranstoun.[13] "The Edinburgh faith now," he reported, "is, that *Waverley* is written by Jeffrey, having been composed to lighten the tedium of his late transatlantic voyage." But few people who knew Scott well had any doubt that he had written the book. His friend and fellow Clerk of Session, David Hume, pointed out to Scott that "the author must be of a Jacobite family and predilections, a yeoman-cavalry-man, and a Scottish lawyer," and slyly asked him "to guess in whom these happy attributes are united."[14]

Margaret Clephane, to whom Scott had so recently said farewell at Torloisk, wrote him: "I have found something here that speaks to me in the voice of a valued friend—*Waverley*. The question that rises it is perhaps improper to give utterance to. If so, let it pass as an exclamation.—Is it possible that Mr. Erskine can have written it? The poetry, I think, would prove a different descent in any court in Christendom. The turn of phrases in so many places is so peculiarly yours, that I fancy I hear your voice repeating them; and there wants but verse to make all *Waverley* an enchanting poem. . . ."[15]

Although Morritt had been in the secret almost from the start, he felt sure he would have known without being told. "The ballad of St. Swithin, and scraps of *old songs*, were measures of danger if you meant to continue your concealment; but, in truth, you wear your disguise something after the manner of Bottom the weaver; and in spite of you the truth will soon peep out." A week later he added: "After all, I need not much thank you for your confidence. How could you have hoped that I should not discover you? . . . no man who ever heard you tell a story over a table but must I think recognize you in a moment both in the fun & the sentiment."[16]

Nevertheless, Scott was determined not to remove the mask. "I shall not own *Waverley*," he replied, "my chief reason is that it would prevent me of the pleasure of writing again. . . . In truth I am not sure it would be considered quite decorous for me as a Clerk of Session to write novels. Judges being monks clerks are a sort of lay-brethren from whom some solemnity of walk & conduct may be expected. So whatever I may do of this kind I shall whistle it down the wind to prey on fortune. . . ."[17]

"I dont see," he added in a postscript, "how my silence can be considerd as imposing on the public—if I gave my name to a book without writing it, unquestionably that would be a trick. But unless in the case of his averring facts which he may be calld upon to defend or justify I think an author may use his own discretion in giving or withholding his name."[18] And, as for money, it was plain that Walter Scott might demand larger sums than would be conceded to an anonymous novelist.

Scott's original motive for secrecy was that the novel was a doubtful venture; he did not wish its possible failure to harm the reputation he had won as a poet. But he already had fame enough so that when *Waverley* too proved a success he felt no need to claim the added praise. His pleasure, he said, was like that of a man having a hidden treasure. "I did not the less feel gratitude for the public favour, although I did not proclaim it,—as the lover who wears his mistress's favour in his bosom is as proud, though not so vain, of possessing it, as another who displays the token of her grace upon his bonnet."[19]

He quickly realized, as well, that anonymity had practical advantages. The resounding triumph of this first novel made it certain that Scott would write further fiction. As a nameless author he "could appear or retreat from the stage at pleasure," write as often as he desired without being accused of "too frequent intrusions on the public patience." The very mystery, indeed, surrounding his identity would sharpen the curiosity about his books and stimulate the excitement of his readers.[20]

At the same time he himself would be able to avoid the tiresome importunities of admirers who wished to pursue him with praise or elongated discussions of his work. Scott never felt the least compunction about denying his authorship of the novels to anyone so ill-bred as to question him directly. Under such circumstances he believed himself justified in resorting to a lie; otherwise he would be at the mercy of the first impertinent intruder. With imperturbable courtesy he would usually add that if he *were* the author he would feel quite entitled to protect his secret by refusing his own evidence to disclose what he desired to conceal—thus leaving the question exactly where it had been before it was put.[21]

All these defenses for his secrecy Scott threw out at various times. But, as he well knew, "the ostensible reasons which we produce to ourselves as to others are very different from those which really influence our conduct."[22] His real reason he expressed by quoting Shylock: "It was my humour." It entertained him to enter slyly into discussions of the novels, tantalizing the curiosity of his companions by seeming slips and recoveries. It appealed to that mischievous trait in his makeup that sometimes peeped out in a sudden foxy expression. Now he would drop a hint from which people were sure they had caught him out, now withdraw again behind his smiling evasions. He enjoyed the fun and freedom of his flimsy disguise. He would remain suspected but unknown. It was his humour.[23]

He could hardly contain his glee when some readers attributed *Waverley* to his brother Tom. Opinion was divided, he wrote Tom:

"Keep this matter a dead secret and look knowing . . ." The joke would be still better if Tom were able to profit by it. "Send me a novel intermixing your excellent and natural humour with any incidents & descriptions of scenery which you may see particularly with characters and traits of manners. I will give it all the cobbling that is necessary and write it over again should that be required and if you do but *decently* exert yourself I have not the least doubt that it will be worth £500 & to encourage your labours you may when you send the manuscript draw on me for £100 at 30 days sight . . .[24]

"*In the meanwhile pray please to exert your energies*—you have more fun and descriptive talent than most people and all that you want in the mere practice of composition I can supply or the devil must be in it. . . . If you are not Sir John Falstaff you are as good a man as he . . ."[25]

Scott's generous partiality was mistaken, of course; Tom was not as good a man as Walter Scott and could not have imagined the weakest of the novels that were to pour from his pen. Whether he had the good sense to know this or whether, despite his assertion that he had begun one, he was too indolent to complete it, no manuscript of his ever arrived from Quebec.[26]

*The Works of Jonathan Swift*, published almost simultaneously with *Waverley*, was well if not ecstatically received. Little scholarly investigation had previously been done on Swift, and Scott's industry had achieved a valuable pioneer job. His diligent search had added about thirty poems to Swift's known work, about sixteen small pieces, and between sixty and seventy letters from Swift, including twenty-eight letters to Vanessa. His editorial notes showed a mastery "of the political intrigues of Queen Anne's reign" no less complete than his *Dryden* of the seventeenth century.[27]

His book-length *Memoir* of the Dean, Jeffrey said in the *Edinburgh Review*, with its good sense and "generous toleration for the 'Fears of the brave and follies of the wise,'" was not so much like the work "of a mere man of letters" as "of a man of the world." But, on the other hand, Jeffrey thought, Scott was "far too favourable to the personal character" of Swift, who was "extremely ambitious, arrogant, and selfish; of a morose, vindictive, and haughty temper." Nevertheless, the *Life* was drawn up "with great intelligence, liberality, and good feeling," and, Jeffrey admitted, perhaps somewhat to his surprise, was "quite fair and moderate in politics."[28]

Although later scholars have superseded much of Scott's work, his notes are still a valuable source of knowledge about the period.[29] He too generously included a number of dubious works among Swift's writings, not always so much out of belief in their authenticity as out of deference to the opinions of the helpers who had supplied them. Of several poems that one correspondent believed "juvenile attempts of Swift," he observed, "I own I cannot discover much internal evidence for the supposition";[30] and another uncertain piece he thought might "merit preservation as a literary curiosity."[31]

In the *Life*, his general portrayal of Swift is more sound than his command of particular biographical facts. Scores of investigators since Scott's day, digging through sources inaccessible to him, have uncovered many details of which he knew nothing and which came to light only through luck or long years of patient research. Some of these, indeed, have even deepened the mysteries surrounding the darker aspects of Swift's behavior and rendered that strange and tortured career still more enigmatic. Scott tended, moreover, to see Swift's character as something more consistent, less ambiguous and contradictory, than would be supported by modern psychology. In this, of course, his analysis reflects the rationalistic—but far from naïve—attitudes toward human nature that he had derived from his eighteenth-century teachers, though amplified and deepened by his own insight and experience. All told, the great contours of his portrayal of Swift are illuminating and true.

The undue leniency on which Jeffrey frowned is hardly discernible to a less censorious eye. Scott preferred, to be sure, to dwell upon Swift's virtues and genius rather than upon the failings that embittered and tormented his days. But he unequivocally condemned Swift's conduct toward both Stella and Vanessa, and even upon lesser weaknesses he did not hesitate to speak out sharply. The inverted snobbery, for example, of Swift's "whim of publicly sending the prime minister into the House of Commons to call out the first secretary of state, only to let him know that he would not dine with him if he dined late; the insisting that a duke should make him the first visit merely because he was a duke;—these, and other capricious exertions of despotic authority," Scott said roundly, were unworthy of Swift.[32]

The *Life* is written in a clear and unadorned style that never sinks below competence but seldom rises to eloquence. Sometimes the neoclassical balance of the sentences is managed with considerable skill: "In the pride of talent and of wisdom," Scott writes, "he endeavoured to frame a new path to happiness; and the consequences have rendered him a warning, where the various virtues with which he was endowed, ought to have made him a pattern."[33] Again, when he speaks of Stella's companion, Mrs. Dingley, as "a woman of narrow income and limited understanding, but of middle age and creditable character," the parallel adjectives achieve an effect close to wit.[34]

Like Scott's earlier exercise in biography, the *Life of Dryden*, his *Swift* is resolute in its avoidance of drama and color. It is strange to realize that only a few weeks after he finished writing it his pen was dashing off the picturesque and glowing pages of *Waverley*. Surely, a reader today may exclaim, Swift's story might have been made no less exciting? What of the bustle and brilliance of life among the wits of the London coffee houses, the glitter of great balls and dinners, the fever of political strife and foreign war, the royal mistresses and backstairs favorites, the dark underground correspondence with the exiled Stuarts, the dangers of the headman's ax, the flight of noble statesmen to France when their schemes crashed about their heads?

But to ask these questions is to misunderstand Scott's aim. In a way these qualities we miss *are* there, but they are subdued to cerebral statement. Our demands, both Scott and his contemporaries would have felt, were appropriate enough to the novel but unworthy of the dignity of literary history or biography, which should adhere to a tone of cool judicious narration. There was a distance that it was proper to maintain between the sobriety of fact and the exuberance of fiction. Though Boswell was admired, he was not imitated. Not until Carlyle would history take on the drama of the ballad and the novel and surge with fuliginous excitement.

That excitement Scott now proposed to capture in *The Lord of the Isles.* He had long meditated its scene, ever since he had first visited the western islands in 1810 and felt his imagination stirred by the idea of a poem steeped in their wild grandeur. Two years earlier he had even begun the poem, a fierce tale of Bruce's lonely seaborne wanderings ending in the great slaughterous victory of Bannockburn. Some portions of this he had then recited to Morritt, but had laid aside for *Rokeby.*[35] His mind now teeming with fresh memories of Ardtornish and the lonely heights of Skye, he was ready to resume writing.

He was not so clear, however, about Carrick and Turnberry Castle, where Bruce had landed, and he remembered that just before setting out on the lighthouse voyage he had received from an unknown admirer a volume of spirited poems dealing with the superstitions of Galloway.

> Why gallops the palfrey with Lady Dunore?
> Who takes away Turnberry's kine from the shore?
> Go tell it in Carrick, and tell it in Kyle,
> Although the proud Dons are now passing the Moil . . .[36]

Perhaps this Joseph Train could supply him with information about the present state of Turnberry—"whether any vestiges of it remain, what is the appearance of the ground, the names of the neighboring places," and any traditions there might be about Bruce's surprise descent.[37]

Train responded with a colorful account of the supernatural fire on the shore which Bruce was believed to have seen from the turrets of Brodick Castle the night before he swooped down.[38] Scott shot back a barrage of eager questions. According to Barbour, "the fire was kindled on Turnberry Neuk. Does this correspond with the situation of the Bogle Brae? or what is the exact position of the Bogle Brae with regard to the Castle, to the sea, and to the Isle of Arran?"[39] Soon Train was sending Scott long pages crammed with antiquarian lore and Scott was plunging forward furiously with his poem.

But, as usual, of course, *The Lord of the Isles* was far from being the only work Scott had in hand. He supplied a preface and an abundance of notes for the *Memorie of the Somervilles*, a curious family history of his old friend and neighbor at Alwyn;[40] he annotated a reprint of an antique treatise, Samuel Rowland's *The Letting of Humour's Blood in the Head Veine;*[41] and he was already turning over in his mind a novel that he was to call *Guy Mannering*. Early in October he sent John Ballantyne the last proofs of the *Somerville*, and later that month he reminded Constable that thirty copies were to be dispatched to Lord Somerville in London.[42]

Despite these labors, by November 10 three cantos of *The Lord of the Isles* were finished.[43] "Those Lords were famous for oppression in the days of yore," he humorously wrote Terry, "and if I can judge by the posthumous despotism exercised over me, they have not improved by their demise. The *peine forte et dure* is, you know, nothing in comparison to being obliged to grind verses; and so devilish repulsive is my disposition, that I can never put my wheel into constant and regular motion, till Ballantyne's devil claps in his proofs . . ."[44]

"To talk upon a blither subject, I wish you saw Abbotsford, which begins this season to look the whimsical, gay, odd cabin, that we had chalked out. I have been obliged to relinquish Stark's plan, which was greatly too expensive. So I have made the old farm-house my *corps de logis*, with some outlying places for kitchen, laundry, and two spare bed-rooms, which run along the east wall of the farm-court, not without some picturesque effect. A perforated cross, the spoils of the old kirk of Galashiels, decorates an advanced door, and looks very well. This little sly bit of sacrilege has given our spare rooms the name of *the chapel*. I earnestly invite you to a *pew* there . . ."[45]

Within another few days, however, Scott had returned to Edinburgh for the winter and was hoping to have *The Lord of the Isles* out by Christmas.[46] Though neither he nor Byron looked on each other with a jealous eye, he knew that many readers were beginning to regard them as rivals, and he felt sure that this poem would at least uphold his claims to be no unworthy brother in the Muse. But he had at the same time the highest admiration for Byron's brilliant genius; when *The Giaour* had been published the previous year he had written the younger poet a letter of the most cordial praise.[47] Byron, for his part, looked on Scott as the supreme poet of the day. "If they want to depose him, I only wish they would not set me up as a competitor. . . . I like the man—and admire his works to what Mr. Braham calls *Entusymusy*. All such stuff can only vex him, and do me no good."[48]

While Scott was in the Hebrides, Byron sent him an inscribed copy of *The Giaour*, which quietly remained among other unopened packages in Castle Street until the autumn, when Scott hastened to acknowledge it. "I must have seemed ungrateful," he remarked apologetically. "If I were, however, ten times more modest than twenty years' attendance at the Bar renders probable, your flattering inscription would cure me of so unfashionable a malady."[49] What Byron had emblazoned on the title-page was: "To the Monarch of Parnassus, from one of his subjects."[50]

Not many days later, after dinner one evening, while Scott was looking for a book in another part of the library, James Ballantyne picked up this volume. "Will you allow me to carry this book home for a single evening?" he asked. "I know its value, and, you may depend upon it, will immediately return it in safety." "O surely," replied Scott, "you are very welcome." Ballantyne reminded him of the autograph on the title-page. Scott had forgotten it: "What inscription? But inscription or no inscription, you are perfectly welcome." Ballantyne showed it to him. "James," said Scott, "Byron hits the mark where I don't even pretend to fledge my arrow."[51]

The printer knew that the following spring Scott intended to be in London and would probably meet Byron. He remarked that Scott must be looking forward to it. "Oh, of course," Scott answered. But after a few minutes, rising from his chair, he paced the room in a rapid hobble, a habit of his "in certain moods of mind," James had observed, and then halted, "bursting into an extravaganza of laughter." He had thought of a joke from Fielding's *Tom Thumb the Great*: "James," he cried, still laughing, "I'll tell you what Byron should say to me when we are about to accost each other—

"'Art thou the man whom men famed Grizzle call?'—

And then how germane would be my answer—

"'Art thou the still more famed Tom Thumb the small?'"

The fancy kept him in mirth for the rest of the evening.[52]

There were nevertheless many reasons why Scott was strongly desirous that *The Lord of the Isles* should be a success. Though the crisis of his financial troubles had been safely weathered, there were still hundreds of unsold volumes in John Ballantyne's basement to get rid of and many bills the settlement of which had merely been delayed. But Scott was confident now. "Time and I," he repeated the Spanish proverb, "against any two."[53] To meet present needs, however, Constable would have to pay him the balance of the profits on *Waverley*, allow him to anticipate £400 on the profits of the fourth edition, and grant him acceptances for the Somerville memoirs and the half profits on *The Lord of the Isles* when published.[54]

"I find," he wrote John on September 27, "that by the end of Jany. if the *Register* sells the debt will be reduced to between £2000 and £3000 & if money can be got on the P. O. [Printing Office] proportionally lower. As to the *Register* James is in despair, but his heart has been in his breeches about everything since I came home. . . . Debt reversions from Bankrupt estates, the resources of the P. O. & my own with such small sums as can be had from the stock will gradually melt down the remainder."[55] "I have little doubt that by Candlemas [February 2] we shall be clear within £2000. As for the stock

> "Twill be wearing awa, John
> Like snow wreaths in thaw, John

". . . If Constable is to get a new novel in spring he must take a good lug of stock with it, I promise him."[56]

But Constable was himself laboring under growing financial stress. The *Encyclopaedia Britannica* had proved a heavy burden, "but who would not have purchased the *Encyc. Brit.* under our then Circumstances?" he appealed to his partner. "Were it by any means in my power I would sell everything I possess, and retire to some quiet corner, if to live in little better than poverty, I hope in peace, and out of the world's eye."[57] In his desperate need Constable was forced to sell Longman a half-share of the *Edinburgh Review.* He was therefore in no position at the moment to take over any of John Ballantyne's stock, even for the sake of a successor to *Waverley.*

Meanwhile, in the middle of October, while James Ballantyne was on a visit in Kelso, a distraint for debt was served on him in Edinburgh. Scott exploded at "the astonishing news of James's utter disregard to his own credit"; ". . . he is even worse than you," Scott told John, "for you generally give a day or two's notice at least of the chance of dishonor & this pound[g] is little better."[58] Poor James had thought he had provided against this danger: "It is one of fifty things which happen to sour the temper," he commented dolefully, "and I by no means wonder that you see it under a different aspect from that in which I regard it . . ."[59]

Since Constable shrank from encumbering himself with any more of John's unsalable books, that cheerful little manipulator suggested to Scott that Longman, Murray, and Blackwood be invited to bid not only for the new novel but for the fifth edition of *Waverley.* Constable had not been promised all future editions; perhaps a slice of its fat profits would melt their resistance to absorbing a load of stock.[60] Scott at once vetoed this proposal. "Your expedients are all wretched," he told John. It was true that he was not technically committed to let Constable retain *Waverley,* but so long as Constable complied with the conditions of their agreement he considered himself bound in honor. "I never will give Constable or any one room to say I have broke[n] my word with him in the slightest degree—[61]

"I intend the new novel," he continued, "to operate as something more permanent than a mere accomodation . . . I will print it before it is sold to any one & then propose 1st to C[onstable] and Longman 2d to Murray & Blackwd. to take the whole at such a rate as will give them one half of the free profits—granting acceptances which upon an edtn of 3000, which we will be quite authorized to print, will amount to an immediate command of £1500; to this we may also couple the condition that they would take £500 or £600 of old stock. I own I am not solicitous to deal with Constable alone—nor am I at all bound to offer him the new novel on any terms—but he knowing of the intention may expect to be treated with at least—although it is possible we may not deal."62

Scott had come to realize, in fact, that Constable was in difficulties. "I am much surprised," he wrote John, "at their deep engagements to the P.O. in the way of accomodn. and it certainly takes much off the feeling of displeasure which I entertaind at some parts of their late conduct . . . James has plied them pretty well— . . . So they have actually given us a good lift & we cannot be surprized if they tire in these foul ways. . . . 'Coragio Bully monster.' October is over & I will make the best fight I can till you like the God Thor bring your hammer to my aid."63

This meant, though, that Longmans, "the Leviathans of Pater Noster row," must be offered the new tale. "My idea is that you or James write to them to the following purport—that a novel is offerd you by the author of *Waverley* with the desire that you print 2000 and publish yourself or arrange with publishers—the name is *Guy Mannering*—that you have proceeded accordingly & that the authors further desire is that the work may be out either before Mr. Scott's poem or as soon thereafter as may be—that having resolved as they are aware entirely to relinquish publishing you only wish to avail yourself of this offer to the extent of helping off some of your stock & therefore wish to know if it would be agreeable to them to take such a work at prime cost vizt. Print paper & authors half of profits & grant acceptances at six mos. along with a handsome order of your other stock at usual credit."64

One further proviso Scott demanded, in loyalty to his old publisher: Constable must be allowed to share in the novel "to the extent of the Scottish sale." It was necessary, however, that Longman be given the management, "for we must have *their* bills for the whole." He was sure that they would respond eagerly to this "scent of roast meat."65

John Ballantyne had been urging warmly that Scott avow the authorship of *Waverley* and allow its successor to appear under his own name. How much more might he extract from the publishers, how many more copies might be sold to the public, how eagerly people would buy and compare *The Lord of the Isles* and *Guy Mannering*, if it were suddenly revealed that Walter Scott and the mysterious author of *Waverley* were one and the same! But Scott continued to refuse:

"No, John, I will not own the book—
      I won't, you Piccaroon.
When next I try St Grubby's brook
The A. of *Wa*—shall bait the hook—
      And flat-fish bite as soon,
As if before them they had got
The worn-out wriggler,
                                    Walter Scott."[66]

Scott's prediction proved correct—"The A. of *Wa*—" *did* "bait the hook" sufficiently for Longman, who found the "scent of roast meat" irresistible. They undertook the publication of *Guy Mannering* on precisely the terms Scott dictated—"namely, granting bills for £1500, and relieving John Ballantyne and Company of stock to the extent of £500 more." Constable learned of the transaction only when Longman offered him the share in the edition on which Scott had insisted. But, whatever his feelings may then have been, of course he took it.[67]

During all these business proceedings Scott drove ahead on *The Lord of the Isles* with fiery speed. The fourth canto, with Bruce's voyage from Skye to Arran, flowed from his pen.[68] Soon he was deep in Canto V, using Train's story of the supernatural fire on the Bogle Brae;

             . . . never did a mortal hand
      Wake its broad glare on Carrick strand;
      Nay, and . . . on the self-same night
      When Bruce cross'd o'er, still gleams the light.
      Yearly it gleams o'er mount and moor,
      And glittering wave and crimson'd shore—[69]

From there he dashed on into the last canto, the shock of Bannockburn:

             Loud from the mass confused the cry
             Of dying warriors swells on high,
             And steeds that shriek in agony!
             They came like mountain-torrent red,
             That thunders o'er its rocky bed;
             They broke like that same torrent's wave
             When swallowed by a darksome cave[70]

On December 16 Scott sent the last stanza to James Ballantyne;[71] three days later he announced to Constable, "The whole is now set up except a sheet or two of notes which Mr. Ballantyne wishes me to add to bring the work to the size of *Lady of the Lake*. He will have them this day."[72]

Right after the holidays, he promised Constable, they would have "a gaudeamus over *The Lord of the Isles* in Castle Street." At the moment, after the strain of such furious composition, he intended to go to Abbotsford and "refresh the machine by a little exercise."[73] But the son of James Ferrier suddenly died, and Scott took over his colleague's

Parliament House duties.[74] On top of this, Walter, "despite of vaccination in infancy," "chose to make himself the town-talk, by taking what seemed to be the small-pox."[75]

"The medical gentleman who attended him is of the opinion that he *has* had the real small-pox, but it shall never be averred by me—for the catastrophe of Tom Thumb is enough to deter any thinking person from entering into a feud with the cows. Walter is quite well again, which was the principal matter I was interested in. We had very nearly been in a bad scrape, for I had fixed the Monday when he sickened to take him with me for the Christmas vacation . . . It is probable that he would not have pleaded headache when there was such a party in view, especially as we were to shoot wild-ducks one day together at Cauldshiels Loch; and what the consequences of such a journey might have been, God alone knows."[76]

Instead, Scott had consequently refreshed the machine by plunging into the composition of *Guy Mannering*. Joseph Train had sent him from Galloway "a local story of an astrologer" who predicted the future of a new-born child. This, mingled with memories of the same tale as he had heard it in childhood from his father's old servant John M'Kinlay, he wove into the opening chapters of the novel.[77] He progressed so rapidly that in less than a month he was able to tell Morritt two volumes were already in print. "I want to shake myself free of *Waverley*," he said, "and accordingly have made considerable exertion to finish an odd little tale within such time as will mystify the public, I trust—unless they suppose me to be Briareus."[78]

As he raced through page after page, imagination and memory almost effortlessly drew together the threads of his story. From his long-ago visit to Galloway in 1793, when he was defending the minister MacNaught, bits of forgotten experience flared into rekindled life; some of the names he gave his characters floated up from poor old drunken MacNaught's case. Caerlaverock Castle suggested some of the features of Ellengowan Old Place. Honest Dandie Dinmont and Ailie, his wife, were drawn in part from his old friends the Laidlaws, and Dandie's pack of Peppers and Mustards from that of a Liddesdale farmer who had only those two names to all his twenty dogs.[79] The oddities of Dominie Sampson—and his virtues too—were derived from Scott's children's faithful and eccentric tutor George Thomson. Some of the melodramatic details of identifying Van Beest Brown as the kidnaped Harry Bertram were based on the well-known lawsuit of the Dormont heir, which had come before the Court of Session as recently as 1811.[80]

Unlike his first novel, *Guy Mannering* was "a tale of private life," he told Morritt, "and only varied by the perilous exploits of smugglers and excisemen. The success of *Waverley* has given me a spare hundred or two which I have resolved to spend in London this spring bringing up Charlotte and Sophia with me."[81]

On January 8, 1815, *The Lord of the Isles* was published.[82] Scott impatiently waited to see what its reception would be. When it had been out seven days, "Well, James," he said to the printer, "I have given you a week—what are people saying about *The Lord of the Isles*?" James hesitated, embarrassed. "Come, speak out, my good fellow; what has put it into your head to be on so much ceremony *with me* all of a sudden?" James still remained silent. "I see how it is, the result is given in one word—Disappointment."[83]

Scott looked blank for a moment. He had fearlessly expected another triumph. But then his face cleared, and he remarked cheerfully that it was more wonderful that his popularity should have lasted so long, rather than that it should finally have given way. "Well, well, James, so be it—but you know we must not droop, for we can't afford to give over. Since one line has failed, we must just try something else . . ."[84]

The initial disappointment did not last. After a slow start, the first edition of eighteen hundred quarto copies sold rapidly;[85] within a month "people are tearing the printer to pieces," Scott wrote Lady Abercorn, "for the next edition."[86] Maria Edgeworth wrote ecstatically about the poem;[87] Richard Lovell Edgeworth told him it had held "the absorbed attention of our large circle . . . from nine o clock at night till two in the morning." The entire family thought it far more perfect than *The Lay of the Last Minstrel*. It proved that "the last production of a man of real abilities may be allowed to be superior to his former writings, and that the success of one performance need not necessarily dazzle the public eye so as to prevent it from seeing the beauties of his subsequent productions."[88]

By this time Scott had completed the last volume of *Guy Mannering*[89] and James Ballantyne was working the Printing Office overtime to get it set up in type. One night after twelve he came in with a letter in his hand. "I am going to make a small alteration, Sandy," he told one of the men; "just unlock the form, will you?" Looking at the letter, Ballantyne altered three lines on one page and one on another. "That will do now, I think, Sandy, but first pull a sheet till I see."[90]

After checking over the two pages, he said, "Bring me the printed sheets—they'll have to be destroyed," and went off, forgetting he had left the letter lying on the bank. Almost at once he remembered, and came back for it, but Sandy had had time to snatch a glimpse of it. Though he told no one at the time, "I kent the hand weel, and the signature," he often boasted in later years, "and it was 'Walter Scott.' I had a great lang ballant in [his] ain hand o' write at hame, so that I was nae stranger to it. It would hae likit to see what the difference was that was made in the sheets, but he made me carry them up to his room. So you see, gentlemen, I kent the grand secret, when it *was* a secret."[91]

During the course of the printing, James Ballantyne gave a taste of *Guy Mannering* to William Blackwood. Scott had suggested him as one of the booksellers who might be approached if neither Constable nor Longman accepted his terms; originally a dealer in rare books, Blackwood was now the Edinburgh agent for John Murray and was himself drifting into publishing. It would do no harm in the future to have still another flatfish to snap at the hook.

"He would not allow me to look at it," Blackwood reported to Murray, "but he read me a few pages. The painting is admirable and quite graphic—Scottish to the life. If Walter Scott be the author of the novel, he stands far higher in my opinion in this line than in his former walk. Ballantyne made great professions of his regret that we were not the publishers"—how sincerely Blackwood felt uncertain. "Keep all this most strictly to yourself . . . there would be the devil to pay if Constable knew that I had seen or heard a line of it."[92]

The novel appeared on February 24.[93] "The work of six weeks" at Christmastime, Scott said, it was greeted by the reading public with wild acclaim. The reviewers, to be sure, engaged in some grumbling. They sought, and were happy to find, evidence that the unknown author had written himself out in his second novel.[94] *Waverley*, said the *British Critic*, showed "the brilliancy of genius"; *Guy Mannering* the "irregular efforts of a powerful but exhausted mind." The *Critical Review* lamented that the book was "too often written in a language unintelligible to all except the Scotch"; the *Quarterly* solemnly adjudged that it would be "improved by being translated into English."[95] But none of the reviewers denied that they had read it with interest, and there were candid admissions that only "the Author of *Waverley*" and "one endowed with the sublimity of genius" could have written it.[96]

The mass of readers paid no attention to any qualifications; they were too busy devouring the book. If the publishers had been hooked by the mere scent of roast meat, the public swallowed the whole noble haunch in a great feast. The day after publication the entire first edition of two thousand copies was sold out. Within three months second and third impressions, coming to five thousand copies more, had also disappeared.[97] Lending libraries in Edinburgh had as many as thirty copies and had requests for thirty more: ". . . everybody wanted the first volume at the same moment."[98]

In country towns the excitement was no less high. One provincial bookseller hit on the expedient of binding the novel in portions of a hundred pages and lending them out at twopence a night. Private families joined purses to buy it, listened to it read aloud, and then sold it to the highest bidder.[99] Scott had mounted to a new peak of triumph. The unknown author of *Waverley* and *Guy Mannering* had sprung into a fame transcending that even of the poet.

# 8

## The Northern Eagle

### (Criticism: *Rokeby, The Bridal of Triermain, The Lord of the Isles*)

Scott's attainments as a narrative poet should not be lost in the dazzle of his emergence as a novelist. He is a novelist, indeed, both in verse and in prose, and nowhere more so than in his growing concern with the portrayal of character. Hardly an important figure in *Rokeby* but is rendered as robustly as Roderick Dhu and Fitz-James, and filled out more solidly than the vigorously outlined Ellen and Douglas; not even minor ones, like the treacherous minstrel Edmund, are as tenuous as Malcolm Graeme. Philip of Mortham, a man of violent passions and some nobility, torn by remorse, is, with Marmion, a Byronic hero-villain and precedes both *Lara* and *The Corsair* by a year.[1] The mean and double-dealing Oswald Wycliffe and his instrument, the bold former pirate Bertram Risingham, are drawn in strong contrast, as are the two rivals for the hand of Matilda of Rokeby, Oswald's sickly and retiring son, Wilfrid, and the virile young O'Neale.

Wilfrid's courtship of Matilda has echoes of Scott's unhappy passion for Williamina Belsches, and his character reflects the more pensive side of Scott's own, derived from that crippled childhood when the world of imagination was his main resource.[2]

> Hour after hour he loved to pore
> On Shakespeare's rich and varied lore,
> But turn'd from martial scene and light,
> From Falstaff's feast and Percy's fight,
> To ponder Jaques' moral strain,
> And muse with Hamlet, wise in vain;
> And weep himself to soft repose
> O'er gentle Desdemona's woes.[3]

But Wilfrid's is a weakness that Scott had tempered himself to overcome.

> Woe to the youth whom fancy gains,
> Winning from Reason's hands the reins,

—"Pity and woe" for those who fail

> The mind to strengthen and anneal
> While on the stithy glows the steel![4]

Though the portrait is sympathetic, Scott can barely repress his scorn for Wilfrid's soft resignation.

Not so had been his own response to Williamina's rejection, but bitterness and resentment, and the determination to plunge into the world of action. What he made of himself, when "he realized the truth about life and human nature" and decided that if he wished to win men's esteem he must mingle and bustle in the world, as Professor Grierson points out, is more nearly embodied "in the daring and active Redmond."[5] Redmond is the young Walter Scott who galloped his black charger along the surge on Portobello sands, cracked the skulls of Irish brawlers in the Edinburgh Theatre, and hacked with his sword at the Tranent rioters.

> He loves to wake the felon boar
> In his dark haunt on Greta's shore,
> And loves against the deer so dun,
> To draw the shaft, or lift the gun.[6]

> If brides were won by heart and blade,
> Redmond has both his cause to aid . . .
> And high was Redmond's youthful name
> Blazed in the roll of martial fame.[7]

Matilda was drawn in part from Williamina, who had died in 1810, but Scott now saw her in a kinder light than in the days of his angry return from Fettercairn.[8] She is really touched by her timorous suitor; though she cannot love him she shrinks from wounding him.

> All Matilda could, she gave
> In pity to her gentle slave;
>
> . . .
>
> Yet, loath to nurse the fatal flame
> Of hopeless love in friendship's name,
> In kind caprice she oft withdrew
> The favouring glance to friendship due,
> Then grieved to see her victim's pain,
> And gave the dangerous smile again.[9]

She is torn, too, by conflicting loyalties. Until the struggle between Charles I and Parliament sharpens into Civil War, her father supports Wilfrid's suit. When Oswald espouses the rebel cause, however, he swears that his daughter shall not marry the son of a traitor. But the royal forces have just been decisively beaten at Marston Moor; Rokeby is captured and consigned as a prisoner to Oswald, whose goodwill, Matilda realizes, he may well need if the Roundheads are ultimately triumphant. Futhermore, Matilda is moved by Wilfrid's devotion, though Redmond stirs her more deeply; and Redmond, confided to her father's care by a ruined Irish chieftain, is hardly her worldly equal. The claims of love, fidelity to the King, filial obedience, policy, and rank are all tortuously entangled.[10]

The action of *Rokeby* is thus dominated by the bitter hostilities of Roundheads and Cavaliers.[11] But Scott is not so successful in rendering these antagonisms as he was later in *Woodstock* with the old royalist Sir Henry Lee, the dissolute Cavalier Wildrake, Markham Everard, the moderate Roundhead, and Desborough and Harrison, the Puritan fanatics. The Lord of Rokeby barely appears on the scene and nowhere reveals what the royalist cause means to him; Oswald is a Parliamentarian out of calculation and greed for money and power; Mortham, though he has thrown in his lot with the rebellion, is more involved in personal guilts and agonies than in its triumph. Though history and individual fate are thus interwined, they are not fused as they were in *The Lady of the Lake* and were soon to be in *Waverley*.

Mortham's role in the convoluted plot is tinged with overtones of those Shakespearian tragedies in which Scott and Wilfrid had both steeped themselves. His relationship with the other characters is involved, and is rooted in past events almost two decades earlier than the opening of the poem. In that time, Mortham's marriage, like Othello's had been opposed by the father of his bride. And soon, again like Othello, Mortham had been deceived into believing his wife faithless, and mingled with the rage of Othello the jealousy of Leontes and Posthumus. Surprising her in the arms of a supposed lover, he had slain them both, only to learn that the man was really her brother, sent to bring about a reconciliation with her father. Not long after these events, Mortham's only child, an infant son, had been abducted by an armed band.

Mortham's deceiver has been his kinsman Oswald, a more cowardly fusion of Iago and Roderigo, who had failed in his endeavors to seduce the bride. Mortham wandered to the Spanish Main, where he made himself the leader of a band of buccaneers, striving to drown his grief and remorse in blood. Thence, with a horde of pirate gold. he has recently returned to England and has been caught up in the Civil War. Here the climactic drama of the poem begins.

Oswald too has returned to his own estates, working with the victorious Roundheads. But still fearing Mortham's vengeance, he has hired Bertram, a former member of his crew, to kill Mortham in the confusion of battle. Bertram may take the gold; Oswald himself will seize Mortham's estates. Bertram despises Oswald, but feels for Mortham a hatred that is half thwarted love. He had admired Mortham's daring leadership, and is now infuriated by the cold scorn with which he has cast off his former henchmen. Bertram's contemptuous agreement to further Oswald's schemes is motivated less by greed than by the resentment of rejected devotion.

The narrative technique with which all these complications are gradually unfolded is a Faulknerian intricacy of deliberately displaced revelations that must be fitted one by one into the elaborate mosaic of the plot. The same procedure is followed with Redmond, of whom we learn at first only that he had been brought up as Rokeby's page, then that he is the grandson of the Irish chieftain Turlough O'Neale, and only at the very end that he is Mortham's stolen son. But Scott has not attained command of his striking new method. Instead of achieving psychological complexity and depth, as it does in Browning, or dramatic intensity from the moment and circumstances of revelation, as in Faulkner, the many strands are confusing and sometimes merely melodramatic. The reader hunts through labyrinths to discover that Mortham's unnamed and faithless friend was Oswald and to learn that Mortham's wife was a daughter of the O'Neale; now and then he has to reread in order to clarify these interwoven relationships, and even so they occasionally blur in memory. The truth is that Scott is already moving toward being a novelist; in a narrative poem the effects at which he is aiming could be realized only through a subtler and more detailed portrayal of character than *Rokeby* manages to accomplish. Scott is attempting to transcend the long ballad poem and write a novel in verse; he solves some of its problems but falls short of success.

The landscape description on which he expended so much effort is but little more successful. Realizing that the neighborhood of the Greta and the Tees was not, like Scotland, a part of his very blood, he had revisited Morritt there and jotted down painstaking notes on the wild flowers, the herbs, and the rocks, to ensure that the scenery should be both accurate and vivid. But colorful as some of the details were, they were not a part of his heart and his imagination; peeping and botanizing for a few days will not do the work of a lifetime. And Scott carried the effort to laborious excess: the opening of the second canto has no fewer than nine successive stanzas carefully describing the course of the Tees from Oswald's castle at Brackenbury past Rokeby to its junction with the Greta—thereby giving some substance to Thomas Moore's joke that he was writing a poetic guidebook to English landed estates.

Not so had Scott proceeded when he was writing *The Lady of the Lake*. Though he had seen Loch Katrine and Loch Vennachar again just before he began the poem, his memory was steeped to its very depths in the Highland scene, and its loveliness and grandeur poured out of him in joyous flowing richness. Later, in comparing his novels with those of his imitators, he realized that this was the reason for his superiority over them. They had to pore laboriously over rows of ponderous tomes to get up all the historical facts. He might need to refresh his recollection of particular details, but the sense of the past and all its larger outlines he had absorbed into his imaginative life.

Despite the degree to which *Rokeby* fell short of Scott's conception, it has many splendid passages. The individual dramatic scenes, indeed, almost consistently surpass the whole. The opening is superb in the dramatic contrast between the cringing suspense with which Oswald waits to hear if Mortham has been slain, but dares not ask, and the surly disdain with which Bertram baits his anxiety. Arriving in the dead of night, at first he maintains a scornful silence, wolfing down food and drink ferociously.

> With deep impatience, tinged with fear,
> His host beheld him gorge his cheer . . .
> Now Oswald stood a pace aside,
> Now paced the room with hasty stride,
> In feverish agony to learn
> Tidings of deep and dread concern,
> Cursing each moment that his guest
> Protracted o'er his ruffian feast,
> Yet, viewing with alarm, at last,
> The end of that uncouth repast.[12]

Oswald finally presses him for his news. Pretending to believe that he is concerned over the outcome of the battle, Bertram begins, and gives an intentionally prolonged account of the engagement, still withholding the information that the murder has been done. Oswald at last can bear it no longer, and bursts out with the direct question:

> "Wretch! hast thou paid thy bloody debt?
> Philip of Mortham lives he yet?"[13]

Bertram laughs.

> —"Now, Oswald Wycliffe, speaks thy heart!
> Now play'st thou well thy genuine part! . . .
> What reck'st thou of the cause divine
> If Mortham's wealth and lands be thine?"[14]

But he still torments Oswald by spinning out his answer.

"Hearts are not flint, and flints are rent;
Hearts are not steel, and steel is bent;
When Mortham bade me, as of yore,
Be near him in the battle's roar,
I scarcely heard the trumpets blow. . . ."[15]

Only after further cat-and-mouse play does he at last give Oswald the
news he is fearfully awaiting:

"!Twas then I fired my petronel,
And Mortham, steed and rider, fell.
One dying look he upward cast
Of wrath and anguish—'twas his last. . . ."[16]

Mortham, however, is not dead, though when Bertram meets him
again, superstitious like Marmion, he half believes he is seeing Mortham's ghost and guiltily retreats before the stern figure of the leader
he has tried to kill. Mortham once more vanishes, not to return until
the end of the poem, when Redmond is revealed as his son. Meanwhile
Bertram leads a band to Rokeby, where Mortham's treasure is stored.
But Wilfrid has arranged that night to bear Matilda and the gold away
to safety. Though Bertram's spy, the minstrel Edmund, unbars the
castle gate and admits the robbers, in the confusion of combat the
structure is set aflame, and with Redmond's aid Matilda and Wilfrid
escape.

. . . From each loop-hole flashing light,
A spout of fire shines ruddy bright,
And, gathering in united glare,
Streams high into the midnight air. . . .[17]
Till bursting lattices gave proof
The flames have caught the rafter'd roof. . . .[18]
In gloomy arch above them spread,
The clouded heaven lower'd bloody red;
Beneath, in sombre light, the flood
Appear'd to roll in waves of blood.
Then, one by one, was heard to fall
The tower, the donjon-keep, the hall.[19]

The last canto ends in a tumult of violent action. Bertram escapes
from the flames and learns from the minstrel Edmund that Oswald
now knows the secret of Redmond's birth and that Mortham still lives.
But Redmond and the lord of Rokeby are both in Oswald's hands.
Bertram knows he will be ruthless; all his old devotion to Mortham
flares into hatred of the schemer. He sends Edmund to summon
Mortham and his royalist force. Oswald now believes he can blackmail
his way to triumph. Unless Matilda agrees to marry Wilfrid he will

have both Redmond and Rokeby beheaded as traitors. Her father smiles scornfully.

> "The maiden is my only child,
> Yet shall my blessing leave her head,
> If with a traitor's son she wed."[20]

Matilda nevertheless yields an anguished consent. Wilfrid intervenes:

> "Dear maid,
> Couldst thou so injure me," he said,
> "Of thy poor friend so basely deem
> As blend him with this barbarous scheme?"[21]

Dearly as he had hoped to wed her, he will not accept the sacrifice. Worn out with struggle, weakened with the wounds he had sustained in fighting their way through the robbers amid the flaming ruins of Rokeby, Wilfrid dies.

Aghast at this deathblow to his plots, Oswald gives the order:

> "Slave! to the block!—Or I, or they,
> Shall face the judgment-seat this day!"[22]

But a furious thunder of hoof beats is heard; through the Gothic arch a horseman gallops—Bertram—and with one shot Oswald lies dead. His soldiers tear Bertram to the ground, hacking with swords, stabbing with spears.

> He took a hundred mortal wounds,
> As mute as fox 'mongst mangling hounds;
> And when he died, his parting groan
> Had more of laughter than of moan.[23]

One of the soldiers speaks his epitaph:

> "Fell as he was in act and mind,
> He left no bolder heart behind:
> Then give him, for a soldier meet,
> A soldier's cloak for winding-sheet."[24]

Mortham's band of horses dashes up with banner and bugle. Father and son are united, the two houses of Mortham and Rokeby joined.

The poem is rich in interpolated lyrics that blend with their setting. "O, Brignal banks are wild and fair" voices the minstrel Edmund's guilty feeling that his criminal ways have estranged him from normal human ties. "A weary lot is thine, fair maid" reflects the troubled uncertainty of Matilda's future. Wilfrid's song "The Cypress Wreath"— "O, Lady, twine no wreath for me, Or twine it of the cypress tree"—

conveys his unhappy foreboding of his own fate.[25] The unity of tone between them and the surrounding narrative is effectively maintained.

But *Rokeby* in its whole ambitious design surpassed Scott's powers. If it was true, as he had told Ballantyne, that the world would not expect of him a narrative in which the interest turned primarily on character, it was also true that he was not ripe for it and did not become so till he had turned decisively to prose. He had no models from which he might have derived a hint. None of his poetic contemporaries or immediate predecessors, except possibly Crabbe, had any trace of what he was trying to do. Scott admired Crabbe's bleak modern realism but could not adapt it to his own purposes. Byron would attain a fiery emotional intensity in the portrayal of a single character who was contradictory rather than complex. Perhaps in Chaucer's *Troilus and Cryseyde* Scott might have found a medieval ancestor of his aim; but it is doubtful if he could have applied Chaucer's detached though sympathetic analysis to his own dashing and impetuous temperament. Toiling over his difficult and unwonted task, Scott did indeed, as he had feared, labor the spirit out of it. Only a richer and more delicately shaded rendering of character than *Rokeby* embodies could have made it the triumph Scott hoped for. Instead, he tried to crowd too much into too concentrated a compass. It remains a splendid conception only partly realized.

*The Bridal of Triermain* is a slighter effort. Scott first conceived it as a jest intended to seem an anonymous imitation of his own style. Like *The Lay of the Last Minstrel*, though more playfully, it weaves a medieval story into a more modern setting. There are, in fact, three stories, the eighteenth-century courtship of Arthur and Lucy, the Arthurian legend of "Lyulph's Tale," and the twelfth-century romance of Sir Roland de Vaux. None of them is serious, but the first is the lightest, even if some of its details are probably derived from Scott's courtship of Charlotte at Gilsland Spa, now seen in memory with a gentle, half-amused tenderness.

This part of the poem, of course, is not really autobiographic. Arthur's humility perhaps mirrors the desperate uncertainty of Charlotte's limping lover, but she had been no rich and high-born damsel wooed by a suitor of humbler birth. On the other hand, Arthur's jealousy of the gallants who whirl her in the "glittering ball," and of dandies in brilliant uniforms and skin-tight pantaloons, may well reflect some of the young advocate's feelings about the gorgeously dressed rivals contending to steal his sweetheart's smiles. The scene resembles that of *The Rape of the Lock*, but the satire in which it is tricked has none of Pope's exquisite froth of wit. Lord Douglas, with aristocratic touchiness, thought its mockery "in bad taste"; it is not, but it is heavy-footed and may have just a trace of envious pique. And the rendering of

Arthur's tenderness for Lucy is too archly sentimental, with too many repetitions of "my Lucy" in languishing possessiveness.

In the medieval core of the poem, the flaw is that Scott is not taking it with imaginative seriousness. It is handled neither with the deep emotional conviction of true romance nor with Ariosto's decorative vivacity nor with Spenser's allegorical richness. King Arthur's seduction by Guendolen, the enchantress of the mysterious castle, Malory would have seen as a foreshadowing of the evil that was to destroy the Round Table. Arthur's reception by the laughing damsels of the castle both Ariosto and Spenser would have made into a riot of sensuousness.

Scott's painting of the luscious scene is only a pale reminiscence of the Bower of Bliss. Lovely hands unbuckle Arthur's armor, anoint him with perfumes, wreath him with a myrtle crown.

> Then o'er him mimic chains they fling,
> Framed of the fairest flowers of spring.
> While some their gentle force unite,
> Onward to drag the wondering knight,
> Some, bolder, urge his pace with blows,
> Dealt with the lily or the rose. . . .
>
> One, while she aped a martial stride,
> Placed on her brows the helmet's pride;
> Then scream'd, twixt laughter and surprise,
> To feel its depth o'erwhelm her eyes.[26]

Charming though some of this is, there is none of the Renaissance carnality of pearly flesh, swelling breasts, wanton glances, and glowing warmth, and none of the wild tumult of the Venusberg. Arthur's seduction itself is dismissed in a few colorless lines far short of Archimago's lady of liquid air baiting her hook for the Red Cross Knight. Nor is the emotional temptation rendered with greater power, and since neither the spirit nor the senses are overwhelmed, the entire episode seems no more than a vision in colored mist.

Arthur's parting from Guendolen is handled with more power. Lifting a loving cup to her lips, Guendolen drinks.

> And strange unwonted lustres fly
> From her flush'd cheek and sparkling eye.[27]

Arthur bends from the saddlebow to take the vessel.

> A drop escaped the goblet's brink—
> Intense as liquid fire from hell,
> Upon the charger's neck it fell.
> Screaming with agony and fright,
> He bolted twenty feet upright—

> From Arthur's hand the goblet flew,
> Scattering a shower of fiery dew . . .[28]

When the King has regained control of his frantic steed the magic castle has disappeared, and nothing remains on its former site but a lonely stream brawling among fragments of rock.

Sixteen years later Gyneth, the fruit of their lust, appears at Camelot to claim Arthur's pledge that if there should be a daughter she shall wed the bravest of his knights. Hints of corruption are in the air; Mordred is there, and Lancelot, stealing glances at Guenevere. Gyneth blends in her human form a wild faery heritage; her mother's blood runs in her veins. Arthur decrees a tournament, with Gyneth as the prize of the victor, but warns her to halt the combat before lives are lost.

> A proud and discontented glow
> O'er shadow'd Gyneth's brow of snow . . .[29]

She is the child of her mother's wrath and the penalty of Arthur's transgression. All the knights of the Round Table save Lancelot, Tristrem, and Carodac contend for her; the battle grows fierce, swords strike flame, steel coats are riven, pennons stream gore, knights die even at her feet, staining her sandals red; and still Gyneth does not throw down Arthur's scepter and end the slaughter. Suddenly the skies grow dark, a whirlwind howls, and Merlin arises from a chasm in the earth.

His appearance ends the strife. Merlin pronounces Gyneth's doom:

> "Long shall close in stony sleep
> Eyes for ruth that would not weep;
> Iron lethargy shall seal
> Heart that pity scorn'd to feel."[30]

Yet her retribution will not be eternal. Her cruelty has not been altogether her own; her heart has been warped by her mother's vengefulness. She shall slumber in the enchanted castle until she is awakened by a knight as valorous as any of the Table Round.

The third and concluding canto becomes a highly embroidered version of the quest of the Sleeping Beauty. Five hundred years have passed. The twelfth-century Sir Roland de Vaux of Triermain has heard Gyneth's story and sets out to find the dark tower. In the Valley of Saint John he sees at last the shapeless rocks turn in the moonlight to buttressed walls as gray turrets rise in the mist. A solemn knell tolls midnight. A fiery meteor rolls through the sky. But as he makes his way through the vale the castle vanishes, then reappears, then vanishes once more amid a chaos of crags. Only when he angrily dashes his ax against a boulder at the foot of a huge cliff does it shatter and disclose a winding

stair that ascends to a platform where the portal of the castle is again
revealed.

Within he passes through a series of symbolic dangers and temptations. In a white marble gallery African maids with barbaric vests and
assegais lead Lybian tigers licking savage jaws. The tigers spring;
Sir Roland slays them with his sword and wins his way to an open
portal. He has passed through the Hall of Fear. Beneath a lofty dome,
in a chamber strewn with gold and silver, red Indian maidens offer him
baskets of jewels. Courteously he refuses them. He has overcome the
temptation of Avarice. In a courtyard where fountains toss rainbow jets
skyward, dark-eyed Oriental nymphs with bare breasts offer the blandishments of Sensuality. He kisses one of the sirens and presses the hand
of another but moves on. His way descends into a dark vault pitted with
lakes of black water where European damsels strive to give him the
royal robes and crown of Ambition. These too he rejects. He has surmounted all the tests triumphantly.

> "Quake to your foundations deep,
> Bastion huge, and Turret steep!
> Tremble, Keep! and totter, Tower!
> This is Gyneth's waking hour!"[31]

Within a bower draped with crimson curtains Roland approaches the
couch of King Arthur's child.

> Doubt, and anger, and dismay,
> From her brow had pass'd away,
> Forgot was that fell tourney-day,
> For, as she slept, she smiled.[32]

> Still her dark locks dishevell'd flow
> From net of pearl o'er breast of snow.[33]

The castle walls burst, and in the green valley, "Blushing like the rose's
flower,"[34] Gyneth is clasped in his arms.

So pretty a trifle should not be subjected to rigorous analysis. And
yet it must be admitted that Scott has not augmented in any way the
insights of romance.[35] Ariosto is more full-blooded and colorful, steeped
in the richness, vividness, and excitement of his bright-hued dream
world, half-laughing at it but half-entranced. Spenser's deeper vision
allegorizes romance into a strongly felt tension between the world and
the spirit. Though the inspiration of *The Bridal of Triermain* is romantic, it is a romance of surfaces. Scott could neither bring them Ariosto's
gay enthusiasm nor regard them as the veil for Spenser's profoundly
felt truths. He is charmed, not entranced; the story is too unreal. Nor
does he see in it any meanings that men have not seen before; it is

not for him a symbol of eternity. He brings to it, in Coleridge's sense, only fancy, not imagination. His fancy is graceful and alluring, but it is no more than fancy.

In *The Lord of the Isles*, however, Scott's imagination is again fully engaged. He has left the fairy regions of romance and is once more in the realm of history. And history that aroused his deepest emotions— King Robert Bruce's struggle against England with its culmination in the proud victory of Bannockburn. Scott's heart had keened in *Marmion* to the terrible disaster of Flodden; now it leaped to the triumph that had made Scotland free. The poem which he had dreamed for years, but put aside for *Rokeby*, had lain like a banked fire in his mind. With the lighthouse voyage to the western islands in the summer of 1814 the glowing coals had flared into flame.

How much he may have rewritten of the fragments he recited to Morritt is not known, but in three feverish months between his return from the Hebrides and the middle of December the poem poured out of him. Its story opens at Artornish in 1307 on the day of Edith of Lorn's wedding to Ronald, the Lord of the Isles. In the Sound of Mull, off the rocky coast above which the fortress towers, the Bruce's skiff labors against adverse winds while Ronald's fleet of galleys sweeps by:

> Streamer'd with silk, and trick'd with gold,
> Mann'd with the noble and the bold
>     Of Island chivalry.
> Around their prows the ocean roars
> And chafes beneath their thousand oars . . .
>
> And each proud galley, as she pass'd,
> To the wild cadence of the blast
>     Gave wilder minstrelsy.[36]

Bruce is still an outlawed fugitive, striving to forge effective resistance to England's domination. Toward nightfall, as the wind roars higher, he gives up the effort to beat against it and runs his skiff into the shelter of the castle, where he demands for himself and his little band the hospitality due even to nameless wanderers.

> "Warriors—for other title none
> For some brief space we list to own,
> Bound by a vow—warriors are we"—[37]
>
> "Though urg'd in tone that more express'd
> A monarch than a suppliant guest,"

the Warder replies,

> "Be what ye will, Artornish Hall
> On this glad eve is free to all."[38]

But within the castle there are hearts far from joyous. Edith of Lorn unhappily believes Ronald a reluctant suitor; their marriage has been put off by repeated "Excuse that shunn'd the spousal day."[39] Ronald in fact has fallen in love with King Robert's sister Isabel, whom he has seen at the Court of Edward I in England, and wishes there were some way in which he could withdraw from the marriage without kindling a feud. Edith's love and her pride are wounded by his indifference.

At the feast Ronald tries to drown his gloom in wassail. His brow now flushed, now faded, he falls into fits of apathy from which he rouses himself to loud bursts of forced gaiety. In the midst of these tensions, Bruce, his brother Edward, and Isabel, her face hidden by a veil, are shown into the hall. Edith's brother, the Lord of Lorn, fiercely suspects the identity of the strangers; to enrage Bruce into revealing himself he has a minstrel chant a song vaunting his own victory in a hand-to-hand battle with the King. Edward furiously grasps his sword, but Bruce bids him be still, and addresses the singer:

> "Well hast thou framed, Old Man, thy strains,
> To praise the hand that pays thy pains; . . .
>
> Enough of this—And, Minstrel, hold
> As minstrel-hire, this chain of gold,
> For future lays a fair excuse,
> To speak more nobly of the Bruce."[40]

Tumult breaks out. Ronald calls, "Forbear!"

> "Not in my sight, while brand I wear,
> O'ermatched by odds, shall warrior fall,
> Or blood of stranger stain my hall!"[41]

Lorn denounces Bruce as the murderer of his kinsman the Red Comyn before the very altar of Greyfriars Church in Dumfries; how should he expect sanctuary anywhere for himself? Voices rise, swords flash, Bruce's sister flings off her veil and appeals for peace.

Ronald flushes red as her eye seeks his.

> "Fear not," he said, "my Isabel!
> What said I—Edith—all is well—
> Nay, fear not—I will well provide
> The safety of my lovely bride—
> My bride?"—but here the accents clung
> In tremor to his faltering tongue.[42]

In the height of a brawling debate threatening to turn to bloodshed arrives the Abbot who is to perform the wedding rites, and it is agreed that he decide the conflict. The Abbot strives to denounce Bruce, but finds he cannot; his body is convulsed.

> "De Bruce, thy sacrilegious blow
> Hath at God's altar slain thy foe:
> O'ermaster'd yet by high behest,
> I bless thee, and thou shalt be bless'd! . . .
>
> "Avenger of thy country's shame,
> Restorer of her injured fame,
> Bless'd in thy sceptre and thy sword,
> De Bruce, fair Scotland's rightful Lord,
> Bless'd in thy deeds and in thy fame. . . ."[43]

Lorn ragingly calls his followers.

> "Call Edith—call the Maid of Lorn!
> My sister, slaves!—for further scorn,
> Be sure nor she nor I will stay."[44]

But in the turmoil Edith had marked Ronald's slip of the tongue. Sure that she is disdained and that he loves Isabel, she has fled heartbroken on the Abbot's bark. Her brother is incensed.

> "Man every galley!—fly—pursue!
> The priest his treachery shall rue!"[45]

Ronald, however, barely notices Lorn's fury. Shaken by the Abbot's words, carried away on a flood of emotion, he pledges fealty to Bruce. The King's situation is still full of peril. Lorn's power is near; English war vessels ride the Clyde. The King's own followers are dispersed; musters must be raised. Edward is to place Isabel in the safety of a convent while Ronald and his page Allan go secretly with Bruce to the safety of Skye.

Among its bleak cliffs and granite crags the fugitives presently meet a band of five men whom Ronald recognizes by their bonnets to be followers of Lorn. These claim to have been shipwrecked there; with them is a minstrel boy of delicate frame, who at the sound of Ronald's voice screams and turns his face to the wall, his neck reddening with a blush. He is a recent captive of war, they say, a mute from childhood. Any reader will at once realize that this must be Edith in male garb, but both King and her former fiancé are blind to her disguise.

The strangers offer a meal of a deer they have just slain.

> "Sit to your cheer—unbelt your swords."
> Sudden the captive turn'd his head,
> And one quick glance to Ronald sped."[46]

Ronald insists on a separate board and a separate fire, and says that he and his companions are on a pilgrimage in which they have sworn never to lay aside their swords. During the night they keep vigil, first Ronald, then the Bruce, last Allan. Toward morning the page's reveries melt into dream; the shriek of the minstrel arouses him too late. A dagger finds his heart. But in the struggle that follov ~s the King and Ronald slay all five of their opponents, the last of them hampered at a crucial moment by the minstrel's clinging to his raised arm.

Edward arrives with news that Scotland is in arms, Stuart and Douglas aroused, Bruce's storm-tossed fleet reassembled in Brodick-Bay, and Lennox waiting with a band in Arran to cross to Carrick. Edward I is dead on the Border, and the country is ready to shake off England's yoke. Off the coast of Arran, Ronald sues for Isabel's hand. Edith has fled, he knows, from Artornish; her brother has rejected the match.

The King agrees that it would be hard if Ronald were held by a tie she and her brother have broken, and promises to urge his suit, but will not force his sister's compliance. As they speak, the minstrel leans his head against the mast, tears trickling through the fingers that hide his eyes. At Arran, in the Convent of Saint Bride, the Bruce learns that Isabel desires to become a nun. But even if her thoughts were not on Heaven, she says in response to Ronald's hopes,

> "I'd spurn each proffer he could bring,
> Till at my feet he laid the ring,
> The ring and spousal contract both,
> And fair acquittal of his oath,
> By her who brooks his perjured scorn,
> The ill-requited Maid of Lorn!"[47]

Impulsively the minstrel leaps forward, clings to her neck, then stoops and kisses her hand. Later, Isabel finds on the pavement of her cell a ring bound with a scroll:

> " 'Twas with this ring his plight he swore,
> With this his promise I restore;
> To her who can the heart command,
> Well may I yield the plighted hand.
> And O! for better fortune born,
> Grudge not a passing sigh to mourn
> Her who was Edith once of Lorn!"[48]

The truth of the mute minstrel's identity flashes on Isabel. She sends word to her brother, praying him to leave the boy in her charge. But it is too late. The attempt on Carrick is already under way, and the youth has been sent with a message to one of Bruce's followers there.

The beacon signals are burning.

> The light, that seem'd a twinkling star,
> Now blazed portentous, fierce and far.
> Dark-red the heaven above it glow'd,
> Dark-red the sea beneath it flow'd,

> Red rose the rocks on ocean's brim,
> In blood-red light her islets swim . . .[49]

The minstrel falls into the hands of the English at Turnberry Castle and is condemned to death as a spy, though their commander offers to release him if Lorn claims him as liegeman. But Lorn carelessly glances at his tartan, not troubling to look at his face.

> "Wearer nor plaid claims care of mine.
> Give him, if my advice you crave,
> His own scathed oak, and let him wave
> In air, unless, by terror wrung,
> A frank confession find his tongue."
> "O brother! cruel to the last!"
> Through the poor captive's bosom pass'd[50]

Bruce and the Lord of the Isles, though, are lurking near in ambuscade. Ronald cries:

> "By Heaven they lead the page to die,
> And mock me in his agony!
> They shall abye it!" On his arm,
> Bruce laid strong grasp, "They shall not harm
> A ringlet of the stripling's hair;
> But, till I give the word, forbear."[51]

Turnberry is stormed.

> Unsparing was the vengeful sword,
> And limbs were lopp'd, and life-blood pour'd,
> The cry of death and conflict roar'd[52]

Ronald raises the minstrel where he has sunk half-fainting on the plain. The opposing forces are mown down, though Lorn escapes on his bark moored beneath the fortress. Bruce enters his ancestral halls.

> "Wide let the news through Scotland ring,
> The Northern Eagle claps his wing!"[53]

The last canto opens on the eve of Bannockburn. Bruce has regained almost all Scotland. Ronald has fought bravely at his side. Edith of Lorn has rejoined Isabel in Saint Bride's. The King has at last reluctantly consented to his sister's taking conventual vows. She has told him in secret who the poor minstrel really is, and he has seen the growth of Ronald's remorse at his faithlessness. Isabel pleads for him with Edith:

> "Now dwells he on thy juster claim
> And oft his breach of faith he blames—
> Forgive him for thine own!"

> "No! never to Lord Ronald's bower
> Will I again as paramour"—
> "Nay, hush thee, too impatient maid,
> Until my final tale be said!
> The good King Robert would engage
> Edith once more his elfin page,
> By her own heart, and her own eye,
> Her lover's penitence to try—"[54]

Edith reddens at the idea of again wearing man's attire and at the forwardness of seeking out her truant lover. But a dozen rationalizations besiege her heart. They had been plighted in youth, it is the King's command, she is his ward, she will remain only a single day, hidden in her disguise she will see Ronald once more, hear him name her name, then bear back to solitude the knowledge that he had rued his falsehood.

> . . . Love, howe'er the maiden strive,
> Must with reviving hope revive!
> A thousand soft excuses came,
> To plead his cause 'gainst virgin shame.[55]

She obeys the King's command. He stations her among a group of old men, priests, and serfs on a hill above the battlefield. The fight begins and rapidly swells into carnage.

> Rushing, ten thousand horsemen came,
> With spears in rest, and hearts on flame,
>     That panted for the shock!
> With blazing crests and banners spread,
> And trumpet-clang and clamour dread,
> The wide plain thunder'd to their tread,
>     As far as Stirling rock.
> Down! down! in headlong overthrow,
> Horseman and horse, the foremost go,
>     Wild floundering on the field!
> The first are in destruction's gorge,
> Their followers wildly o'er them urge;—
>     The knightly helm and shield,
> The mail, the action, and the spear,
> Strong hand, high heart, are useless here![56]

From the hill Edith sees the English forces rallying from the rout, hears the call of their trumpets, believes in her agitation that they are surrounding Ronald's islemen. Distracted, she forgets that she is supposed to be mute:

"O God! the combat they renew,
        And is no rescue found!
And ye that look thus tamely on,
And see your native land o'er thrown,
O! are your hearts of flesh or stone!"[57]

Those around her take it for a miracle, and seize axes, clubs, and spears. But the English host is already shattered. In the victorious field the Lord of the Isles drops on his knees before the Maid of Lorn.

The tableau is moving. But nearly all readers have felt that the love story is overwhelmed by the great national drama through which it weaves. At the time the poem was published reviewers thought the fault was that the battle of Bannockburn was a gigantic digression in the love tale of Ronald and Edith, but it may more reasonably be said that their story is a distraction from the liberation of Scotland. They are the weakest and least vividly realized aspect of the poem; they are subordinated both in length and vigor of development to the delineation of the character of Bruce and the celebration of his cause; all the most glowing parts of the narrative center brilliantly on him. If Scott had concentrated his story on the heroic figure of the King and his historic deeds he might have made it a poem of great power.

But the issue must be examined more closely. No one complains that the battle of Waterloo is a mere episode in the story of Fabrice del Dongo or that Chaucer makes the fall of Troy a background to the tragedy of Troilus and Criseyde. These three, however, are richly and fully conceived human beings, and Stendhal and Chaucer show the historical or the legendary background as it is seen through their eyes or as it molds their fates. Ronald and Edith are only a conventional hero and heroine, and although it would be untrue to say that Scott never realizes them with depth or feeling, he does not give them consistent and moving reality. His imagination is less profoundly engaged by them than by Bruce, and thus they have only occasional flickers of life.

This accounts for the awkward and even mawkish elements in those sections of the poem that center on them. Ronald's coldness to Edith is convincing, but not his change of heart, which is merely stated, never shown. We are left unregenerately wondering if, since Isabel is beyond his grasp, he has not merely returned to Edith as a consolation. The failure of both the Bruce and the Lord of the Isles ever to realize that the effeminate minstrel is a woman is fantastic, and that Ronald, who has known her so long, and the King, who has seen her so recently, should not recognize her is completely unbelievable. Edith's behavior, moreover, as the disguised minstrel, is sentimentally irritating; both her repeated blushes and her perpetual drip of tears are wearisome.

The few touching and noble parts of the love story do something to soften the adverse judgment on the purely romance elements in the poem. If Scott's heart was not wholly engaged and he could not rise on the wings of romantic love, he never fails to kindle, and to kindle us, to the moments of generosity and noble feeling.

No such apologies are needed for the presentation of Bruce and his trials and triumph. The great figure of the King towers a giant of strength and judgment. But he is far from being a lifeless colossus in marble. His sympathies, his moments of amusement, his self-blame for past errors of rage and ferocity—all humanize him. His calm dignity restrains even his fiery brother Edward and dominates the furious passions swirling through the feasting hall at Artornish. He can do justice to the greatness of Edward I, his most implacable foe, in the very moment of rejoicing at his death:

> ". . . Blot the story from his page,
> Of Scotland ruin'd in his rage,
> You read a monarch brave and sage,
> And to his people dear."[58]

Of the kingliness brilliantly sketched in the James V of *The Lady of the Lake* Robert the Bruce is a fully realized portrait. He is the first in Scott's great gallery of kings and queens.

The stormy scene of fourteenth-century Scotland is evoked with splendid force. There are the rocky coast of Morven, the lights of Artornish above the rough waves, the wild seas and desolation of Skye, the unearthly grandeur of Staffa. But, more, there are the fierce thanes and island lords, half-kings, half-barbarians, with their brutalities, their rivalries, their shifting allegiances, their treacheries, and the fragmentation of a world that is only beginning to feel itself as one. That forging into unity from which Scotland will emerge, no longer betrayed by the jealous struggle for power and dynastic rivalries, no longer a feudal or conquered dependency of England, but an independent kingdom, is the real and triumphant theme of the poem.

## 9

*Sceptred Kings and Laureled Conquerors*

*( 1 8 1 5 )*

H IS PURSE pleasantly swelled with his literary earnings, Scott set out by sea for London on March 31. He had had John Ballantyne take the after-cabin for Charlotte and Sophia;[1] after a six years' absence from London he looked forward eagerly, he told Morritt, to seeing Ellis, Heber, Gifford, and other old friends. "I dont include Mrs. Morritt and you because we are much nearer neighbours and within a whoop and a hollow in comparaison—"[2]

He knew he must expect to find changes:

> "For many a lad I loved is dead
> And many a lass grown old.

"To make some amends I am carrying up to see some of her English friends a Scotch girl of fifteen who shews that my wife & I are now old married folks. I wish her to see the lions and the tower and Westminster Abbey and the wild beasts and the rest of the Royal Family before she grows too wise or rather too conceited to enjoy vulgar pleasures . . ."[3]

The voyage was stormy. The wind, Scott said, blew "in constant and methodical opposition." A collier brig ran afoul of their smack in the dark and almost sank them to the bottom of the sea. Lastly, "we struck on a rock and lay hammering for two hours untill we floated with the rising tide."[4] Despite these mishaps, however, on April 8 they were breasting the waters of the Thames amid a clamor of barges and wherries.[5] Countless masts and spars crisscrossed above wharves and warehouses, but unbelievably higher still, soaring beyond all the jumble of roofs at their base, towered the walls of the enormous cathedral surmounted by its immense floating dome and the remote golden ball and cross.

Before nightfall the Scotts were settled in with Charlotte's faithful friends the Dumergues in their home at the corner of Piccadilly and Whitehorse Street. Scott at once sallied out to reknit old ties.[6] George Ellis, who had long been ailing, proved to be dangerously ill; two days later he died.[7] Scott was filled with sorrow for the kind heart who had helped so generously when he was working on *Sir Tristrem* and the *Minstrelsy*, who had filled page after page of long letters with encouragement, information, and enthusiasm, and who had so warmly praised all his work from the first cantos of the *Lay*, recited so long ago under the oaks of Sunninghill. "During my remaining space upon earth," he wrote Mrs. Ellis, "I can never hope to meet a friend with so many qualities which at once command esteem respect and affection."[8]

Among the friends waiting to greet him in London was Joanna Baillie, who had invited Sophia to be her guest in rural Hampstead during part of the family's visit. "I trust that you still consider her as too young to go into all the hurry of company that you must encounter," Joanna had written; "I almost tremble for you when I think how you will be beset by your innumerable admirers in this country"[9]—"Make up your mind to be stared at only a little less than the Czar of Muscovy, or old Blücher."[10] "Sophia will be delighted to be your honord guest," Scott replied, "and I will be charmd with the opportunity of making her acquainted with you."[11]

Scott was indeed a greater lion than ever. "Let me know when he comes," said the Prince Regent, "and I'll get up a snug little dinner that will suit him." "Let us have," the Regent went on expansively, "just a few friends of his own—and the more Scotch the better." The company at Carlton House accordingly included the Duke of Gordon, the Marquis of Huntly, the Earl of Fife, John Wilson Croker, Lord Chief Commissioner Adam, and Scott's early friend the second Lord Melville, in addition to the Duke of York, and the Vice-Chamberlain Lord Yarmouth, who was the son of the Regent's mistress, the Marchioness of Hertford.[12]

The portico of Carlton House opened on an overwheming marble hall with porphyry columns, cornices carved with Etruscan griffins, and a great circular double staircase sweeping past giant bronzes of Chronos and his clock and Atlas bearing the map of Europe. The throne room had a canopy of helmets and ostrich plumes and a fender supporting the eagle of Jupiter subduing prostrate dragons; the walls of the circular dining room were lined with silver and set with pierglasses reflecting forests of Ionic pillars; the crimson drawing room gleamed in the radiance of a lovely chandelier with three circles of lights surrounding a cascade of glasses hung above a blue velvet carpet adorned with the insignia of the Garter.[13]

There was a rose satin drawing room and a blue velvet room; there was a library, a golden drawing room, a Gothic dining room, another dining room, and a conservatory, forming with their open double doors a continuous chamber three hundred and fifty feet long, its walls paneled with golden moldings and emblazoned shields, its windows curtained in crimson, its ceilings spandreled and traceried. The conservatory was a miniature cathedral whose clusters of carved columns rose in a lofty nave and side aisles and whose stained glass windows poured multi-colored light on the gleaming marble pavement. At the western end of this enormous vista a wide Gothic door opened on the green of a quiet garden where nightingales sang among the weeping trees and peacocks fanned their iridescent tails in the setting sun.

Where in all this ornate magnificence the "snug little dinner" took place we are not told. But the Regent was enchanted with Scott and exerted all his powers to charm his guest.[14] Although now in his fifties, and bloated by dissipation and self-indulgence, enormously fat, with pendulous jowls raddled by potations of cherry brandy, and a huge backside tightly swaddled in white satin, he still had the remains of the handsomeness that had once made him an Adonis. His manners, when he so desired, were exquisite. He was the most cultivated Prince in Europe, a man of taste, a connoisseur of art and architecture, a lover of music and literature. He had an immense zest for life, and he was far from stupid. He could be gracious and caressing, witty and playful.

The Prince immediately called his guest of honor "Walter."[15] Scott told stories of the old Scottish judges and lawyers, among them one about Lord Kames, who when he went on circuit always played chess with a friend in one of the assize towns. One spring night they kept at it until the small hours; at dawn the battle was still not decided. "Weel, Donald," said Lord Kames, "I must e'en come back this gate in the harvest, and let the game lie ower for the present." In October he was back, but not in the home of his old friend, who had meanwhile been indicted on the capital charge of forgery. Lord Kames presiding, his former host was tried and found guilty. The Judge solemnly donned his cocked hat and sonorously pronounced the dread sentence: "To be hanged by the neck until you be dead!" Then, taking off his beaver, and giving a familiar nod, he concluded in a whispering chuckle, "And now, Donald, my man, I think I've checkmated you for ance."[16]

Around midnight the Regent, looking significantly at Scott, called for "a bumper, with all the honours, to the Author of *Waverley*." But Scott was already an adept at this game. Filling his glass to the brim, he said, "Your Royal Highness looks as if you thought I had some claim to the honours of this toast. I have no such pretensions, but shall take good care that the real Simon Pure hears of the high compliment that has now been paid him." The company all drank off their claret, but before they resumed their seats the Prince exclaimed, "Another of the same, if you please, to the Author of Marmion—and now, Walter, my man, I have checkmated you for *ance.*"[17]

Scott had been given the privilege of using the Regent's library and was not slow to take advantage of it. There was, he was fascinated to find, a collection of "most curious papers respecting 1715 and 1745," which had belonged to Prince Charles Edward's brother, Cardinal York.[18] In a long and gracious audience, the Regent talked about the Stuarts with Scott. "Ah, Walter, if you had lived in those days," he teased, "you would have been a keen Jacobite." "If I had lived in those times," returned Scott, "I should not have had the honour to be known to your Royal Highness."[19] But in the Regent's queer nature, too, there was a streak of romance which deeply sympathized with the unlucky dynasty that his own family had supplanted on the throne. "Baron Adam who was present says the impression upon his mind was a doubt whether the P. R. or I was the greater Jacobite."[20]

Later still there was an even more select dinner party, at which the Regent sang songs, told stories, and continued affectionately to call Scott by his first name.[21] "The Prince and Scott," said Croker, "were the two most brilliant story-tellers . . . I have ever happened to meet."[22] Not long after this dinner, the Regent sent Scott a gold snuffbox set in jewels with a medallion of the donor's head on the lid, as a token "of the high opinion his Royal Highness entertains of your genius and merit."[23]

Scott felt gratified to be so distinguished, and he was pleased by the Regent's good manners and good humor. But though he had seen that flamboyant being at his best, he was under no illusions about him. He refused to concede that the Prince had any exceptional abilities; how could one form a fair judgment, he asked, of a man whose position entitled him to introduce whatever subject he chose, discuss it as long as he chose, and dismiss it when he chose? He judged as severely as any radical all that there was of disgrace and folly in the Regent's life, but he could not feel bitterly about a Prince who loaded him with honors. In private letters Scott called him "our fat friend," and he always wished him well.[24]

About one point, however, he needed to make no allowance for the prestige of Royalty—the Prince's courtesy. James Ballantyne asked if the Regent had ever questioned him about his authorship of *Waverley* and what his answer had been. Scott glanced at Ballantyne with a look of mild surprise. "What answer I might have made to such a question, put to me by my Sovereign, perhaps I do not, or rather perhaps I do know; but I was never put to the test. He is far too well-bred a man ever to put so ill-bred a question."[25]

Even more memorable for Scott than being entertained by his Sovereign was at last meeting Lord Byron. Between them the two men divided the sovereignty of the literary world; each wholeheartedly admired the other. The previous October John Murray had brought Byron a gift from Scott, "a superb Turkish dagger" as a "mark of his love (a poet's love) for you."[26] No sooner had Scott arrived in London than Byron invited him to an evening party.

"We are at present guests with some old friends," Scott replied, "from whom I cannot easily disengage myself so soon as tomorrow evening. But I am much more desirous to see *you* than Kean or Garrick if he could be called to life again. Murray tells me you are to be in his shop by three o'clock when I hope to have the pleasure I have long wished of making your personal acquaintance."[27]

In John Murray's drawing room at 50 Albemarle Street the two accordingly met.[28] The younger man was a full sixteen years Scott's junior—he had barely turned twenty-seven—and, except for his club foot, was as beautiful as Apollo. "Byron's countenance," said Scott, "is *a thing to dream of*." No one had ever looked more perfectly an artist's idea of a poet. "The prints give one no impression of him—the lustre is there . . . but it is not lighted up." He could well understand Lady Caroline Lamb's saying to herself when she first saw Byron in a crowded room, before she even knew who he was, "*That pale face is my fate*."[29]

Far from being the bad-tempered monstrosity he was rumored, Byron proved touchingly sweet and courteous. He and Scott agreed on everything except politics and religion. When Scott remarked that he might change his views in a few years, Byron replied, rather sharply, "I suppose you are one of those who prophesy I shall turn Methodist." "No," Scott answered, "I would rather look to see you retreat upon the Catholic faith, and distinguish yourself by the austerity of your penances."[30] Byron smiled gravely and did not dissent; but, as Hesketh Pearson remarks, he ended in Greece, not in Rome.[31] Scott was unable to take Byron's radicalism seriously; it was all wit, fireworks, and dislike of some of the Ministers in office. Byron was really "as much an aristocrat as was consistent with good sense and good breeding." "At heart," Scott concluded, he was "a patrician on principle."[32]

"Like the old heroes in Homer we exchanged gifts." In return for Scott's dagger, a weapon beautifully mounted in gold, "which had been the property of the redoubted Elfi Bey," Byron sent him "a large sepulchral vase of silver" with "inscriptions on two sides of the base." "The bones contained in this urn," ran one, "were found in some ancient sepulchres within the long walls of Athens, in the month of February 1811." The other was a quotation from Juvenal: "*Expende—quot libras in duce summo invenies?—Mors sola fatetur quantula sint hominum corpuscula.*"[33] "Weigh it—How many pounds to the mightiest general? —Death alone tells what trifles are the puny bodies of men."

During the whole of this London visit Scott was also serving as the legal adviser of Margaret Maclean Clephane, who had become engaged to Lord Compton, the eldest son of the Marquis of Northampton.[34] The marriage settlement proposed by the Marquis Scott thought rather "narrow" and noted that the Northampton family solicitor had the in-auspicious name of Boodle.[35] Miss Clephane was heiress both of Torloisk and of her grandmother's estate at Kirkness;[36] she ought, Scott insisted, to have at least £4,000 a year as Dowager Marchioness.[37] As he fenced cautiously with the solicitor, Scott's feelings fluctuated. "I do not believe the family are very rich and I understand the estate is encumbered— But there is quite enough of money to support the dignity very hand-somely and much land which is always rising."[38]

These financial negotiations, however, Scott brought to a victorious conclusion; the ominously named Mr. Boodle, indeed, proved to be "a *fowl*"—"the most polite way," Scott explained, "of calling a man a goose."[39] Lord Northampton readily agreed that Miss Clephane's jointure be £3,000,[40] which, with the reversion of Torloisk and Kirkness, would assure her, if Lord Compton died, of somewhere between £5,000 and £6,000 a year.[41] And if Lord Compton succeeded to his father's title, Scott reported triumphantly, the income of the estate would be more than £18,000—"no bad prospect for our young lady."[42]

Early June saw all the deeds ready for signing. "As I have now happily brought so near to a close all I can do for you here," Scott told Miss Clephane, "I have resolved to set sail on Sunday . . ."[43] Margaret Clephane was affectionately grateful. To a friend she wrote, "Do you know, through it all, who has been father, brother, everything to me?— Mr. Scott."[44]

Meanwhile, Scott's social life was a delirious whirl. He escorted Charlotte and Sophia to glittering parties. Only after Sophia had been "noticed and caressed" for a month did her proud father send her out to Miss Baillie's cottage in the quiet lanes of Hampstead "to save her Tweedside complection."[45] At Covent Garden, Scott and Charlotte were enchanted by the sensational new actress Eliza O'Neill, whom he found "the sweetest Juliet I ever saw."[46]

London eagerly booked him—even for breakfast. He breakfasted with Daniel Terry,[47] and probably with Samuel Rogers;[48] he break-fasted in a company that included his old friend Wordsworth and the novelist Amelia Opie at the Mount Street residence of Sir George Phil-lips. Mrs. Opie he enchanted. Why, she asked him, with his powers, had he never tried the drama? Pride, he told her; he wouldn't dance attendance on managers and ignorant actors. Once, however, he had thought of writing a tragedy on the same theme as *The Family Legend*, but his drama would "have had no love in it." His hero, the uncle of the heroine, would have been a misanthrope, "with only one affection in his heart, love for his niece, like a solitary gleam of sunshine, gilding the dark tower of some ruined and lonely dwelling."[49] Mrs. Opie later rhapsodized about the beauty of Scott's face, "the fire of his blue grey eye"; she was mortified when Dr. John Brown contradicted bluntly, "The face is nothing but a roast-beef and plum-pudding face, say what you will!"[50]

Throughout every day Scott was kept on the go. There were, of course, his innumerable conferences with the Clephanes, with the Marquis of Northampton, and that goose, Mr. Boodle. But between these meetings, he was always hurrying to something else. He attended the Royal drawing room in dress coat, bag wig, and sword;[51] as many as three times in a single day he had to dress for "a grand déjeuner." At a Sunday evening musicale of Lady Salisbury's, with Charlotte, he heard a *"musicienne"* named Madame Simon—"the most preposterous animal"—recite, play, sing, and gesticulate like "twenty mad French." "London," he summarized, "gets more absurd than ever."[52] After his exhausting round of pleasures, he was glad to embark for home on June 11.[53]

But the stirring events on the Continent were too much for him. In barely more than a month he was again leaving Edinburgh. Throughout the nine weeks Scott had been in London, Napoleon had been approaching the crisis of his last effort to dominate Europe. All through the previous winter the vanquished Emperor's veterans had scowled in ferocious gloom. Sullenly in their native villages the old *moustaches* recalled their vanished glories and muttered fierce oaths against poor unwieldy Louis XVIII in the Tuileries. "Corporal Violet," they whispered hoarsely, would return in the spring with the violets. On the night of March 7, Vienna learned that Napoleon had escaped from Elba. His eagles, once more on the move, would soon, he proclaimed, alight on the spires of Notre Dame. Marshal Ney promised King Louis to drag him back to Paris in an iron cage, but no sooner did he see the little gray-coated figure than he was swept away by surging emotion. Six days later Napoleon was at Fontainebleau and Louis was groaning his bulk across the Flemish border.[54]

The Allied Powers denounced the escaped prisoner as an international outlaw. Britain, Russia, Prussia, Austria, each pledged 180,-000 men and put the Duke of Wellington in command of this host. Napoleon crossed the Belgian frontier, beat the Prussian advance guard at Charleroi, forced Blücher to fall back at Ligny, defeated the Prince of Orange at Quatre Bras. In the cold dawn of June 18, only twelve miles south of Brussels, Wellington faced the victorious French at a place called Waterloo. At dusk all was over. On that bloody field 15,000 of the Duke's army and more than 30,000 Frenchmen lay wounded, dead, or dying.[55] But Bonaparte's desperate gamble had failed. The vainglorious and demonic genius that had terrified Europe for almost twenty years was at the end of his career. Ahead there was only the surrender to the commander of the *Bellerophon*, the long voyage south in the Atlantic, and the weary years at St. Helena.[56]

Edinburgh was already wild with the news of Waterloo by the time Scott's little coastal vessel reached Leith from London. "So this strange eventful history of Politics has after all changed like the scene of *The Rehearsal*," he commented, "& Boney like his brothers of Brentford

> "Ere a pot of good ale you could swallow
> Is come with a whoop & is gone with a hollo."[57]

What an age was this to live in!—what scenes of terrible carnage there had been—what high congress of the triumphant Powers there was to be! How low had the pride of France been laid in the dust, and what an assemblage of armed might held her haughty capital in subjugation! Scott was on fire to get across the Channel at once, to Brussels, to Waterloo, to Paris.

But he could not leave immediately; he was pledged to attend Margaret Clephane's wedding to Lord Compton on July 24. A few days later, though, he could take off. Meanwhile, he wrote away to London for passports.[58] He determined to earn the cost of this excursion by throwing off a little volume describing his travel adventures, written in the form of a series of imaginary letters.[59] He would call it *Paul's Letters to His Kinsfolk*. Half profits on an edition of three thousand would bring him in a tidy £450. He empowered John Ballantyne to offer the other half in equal shares to Constable, Longman, and Murray. All three publishers quickly accepted.[60]

Scott gladly accepted as companions on his journey three country neighbors who were eager to join him—John Scott of Gala, Alexander Pringle of Whytbank, and a young advocate named Robert Bruce.[61] He only regretted that James Skene could not make one of their party: "Would to God you were joining with me my Dear Skene to hear the Tow row row of the British drums insulting the walls of that capital where so much mischief had been hatched against Britain and Europe."[62]

On July 28, at five o'clock in the morning, Scott and his fellow travelers were off, rolling merrily along in the Wellington coach. Highspiritedly, he told stories of his youthful rambles to Crichton Castle, Borthwick, and Lammermuir, of fishing parties and practical jokes with Clerk and Cranstoun. At Lauder they halted for breakfast, Scott jovially quoting:

> "Their breakfast so warm to be sure they did eat,
> A custom in travellers mighty discreet."[63]

Two nights later they were at York and next day attended Sunday morning services in the magnificent Minster under the grisaille windows; they reached Lincoln at nine that night and saw the great Tower, the Norman west front, and the Galilee Porch by brilliant moonlight. At Cambridge they visited the Gothic chapel of St. John's College, saw the statue of Pitt in the Senate House and the library of Trinity,[64] and crowned a hearty supper with such libations of Trinity's famous "bishop" that next day everyone suffered from "a general complaint of thirst."[65]

On the way to Newmarket and Bury St. Edmunds, Scott was so entertaining that a fellow passenger thanked him for his anecdotes: "You have a good memory, sir," said he; "mayhap, now, you sometimes write down what you hear or be a-reading about?" Scott gravely replied that he did now and then put down a *few* notes. In the afternoon Scott sat outside on the box, where he became lost in thought, murmuring to himself, smiling and sometimes waving his hand, while a neighbor, a solemn professor in a broad-brimmed beaver, "cast many a curious sidelong glance . . . evidently suspecting that all was not right with the upper story."[66]

At Harwich they learned that the packet had sailed the day before and that there would be no other for two days, but at their landlord's suggestion they hired a cutter for twenty guineas and sailed at two in the afternoon on August 3.[67] The weather was abominable; the wind blew so violently off the Dutch coast that they couldn't land that night; they were all seasick. Not till next morning did they get ashore at Helvoetsluys. First by boat up the Maas and then by carriage, they reached Bergen-op-Zoom at seven that night.[68]

Here they inspected the fortifications by twilight amid a few drops of rain and livid flashes of lightning. Everywhere the landscape was devastated, "houses dismantled chateaux of the noblesse deserted & gone into disrepair trees cut down." The French had ravaged the country. "The people always call them Les Voleurs & even the tea-spoons & linen of the beds & tables in the inns did not escape them. One fat dame with tears in her eyes described her set of damask napkins in a tone that would have grieved your very heart."[69]

"We travell," Scott wrote Charlotte, "in a long black queer looking hearse of a thing open on all sides but with curtains to draw if it rains . . ." It was pulled "by three horses with a driver who shrieks at them like a highland drover pushing on his bullocks." Everywhere they were grossly overcharged, "yet why should we complain when we can dine on a most capital french dinner with two courses & a desert of mulberries cherries of the finest sorts, capital greengage plumbs peaches nectarines &c and drink Burgundy as much as we please for not quite five shillings a piece."[70]

"On Sunday we were at Antwerp and saw the splendid churches of that city. The French have left little but their exterior architecture to boast of for all the fine paintings by Rubens & others were carried off to Paris & in this town the birthplace & habitation of the very first Flemish artists we hardly saw a single good picture."[71] But around the pulpit in the great cathedral there were statues and carved woodwork the despoilers had been unable to remove; and even stripped down to its bare bones the enormous structure, with its lofty tower and steeple, its three aisles on each side of the nave, and its clustered pillars and arches, was still magnificent.[72]

The great ship-basins in the Scheldt with which Napoleon had planned to make the city into a huge arsenal were still unfinished, and immense blocks of stone from the Namur quarries littered the quays. After a busy day's sightseeing, Scott and his friends returned exhausted to the Hotel du Grand Laboureur and a delicious French dinner with sauterne and burgundy.[73] Next morning they were up by seven and saw high mass celebrated at Mechlin Cathedral, the priest looking to Scott "as if engaged in some nice process of cooking, rather than in a devotional exercise." They reached the Hotel de Flandres in Brussels by two that afternoon.[74]

Here the Théâtre Français in the evening was brilliant with military uniforms, public places bristled with cannon taken at Waterloo, white Hermitage and claret flowed at the restaurateurs.[75] Scott called on the Duchess of Richmond and dined with General Sir Frederick Adam. "Tell Charles I see little boys like him riding in small cabrioles drawn by goats which trot along very knowingly. The dogs are also frequently harnessed to little brouettes but appear to suffer in this hot weather.[76] Scott could hardly contain his eagerness to see the field of Waterloo, however, and next morning was up by six.[77]

Mounted on a pony, and escorted by General Adam's aide-de-camp, Captain Campbell, and Major Pryse Gordon, he rode over the whole of that desperate ground, the battered chateau of Hougoumont, with its blackened orchard, the farm of La Belle Alliance, the ridge of St. Jean above La Haye Sainte.[78] All the earth was torn and pitted; casques, swords, carabins, bullets, cuirasses, old hats, torn shoes, littered the soil; brick walls were shattered and trees burned; the reek of dead bodies from the steaming carnage hung in a heavy and sickening stench.[79] Scott was given a little blood-stained notebook containing some popular French army songs and bought a grand cross of the Legion of Honor and two handsome cuirasses, "one for Bowhill, and one for Abbotsford."[80]

On the field, Scott ran into a Flemish peasant named John Da Costa, who was making a handsome living out of telling visitors Napoleon had seized upon him as a guide and kept him near at hand throughout the entire battle.[81] "As the cannon-balls flew over them, Da Costa ducked; at which the Emperor laughed, and told him they would hit him all the same." But at the crisis of the battle, according to the guide, when the Imperial Guard broke and fled, Napoleon hastily observed, "Je crois qu'ils sont mêlés," and turned pale as death. A General at his side said something; "Buonaparte answered, C'est trop tard—sauvons nous."[82] Months later, Da Costa was proved to have been hiding in a safe place ten miles from the scene of battle, but this did not prevent his gaining a prosperous livelihood from his fictitious reminiscences until he died in 1824.[83]

More veracious stories about the Duke of Wellington from officers who had been with him on the field enhanced Scott's admiration for the coolness and courage of that remarkable man. When one regiment of Belgians fled in disorder, "Lord Wellington rode up to them, and said— 'My lads, you must be a little blown; come, do take your breath for a moment, and then we'll go back, and try if we can do a little better'; and he actually carried them back to the charge. He was, indeed, upon that date, everywhere, and the soul of everything; nor could less than his personal endeavours have supported the spirits of the men through a contest so long, so desperate, and so unequal."[84]

In France the citizens of the *Grande Nation* still could not believe in their defeat. The men looked sullen and embittered; the women, weeping-ripe, were always ready to burst into sobs. They showed no remorse for the misery and devastation their armies had brought on the rest of Europe; all they could think of was their own humiliation and the ferocities that the Cossacks and the Prussians were now wreaking upon them.[85] "Coquins," "voleurs," "brigands," they called them to their faces —first making sure these barbarians understood no French and maintaining a tone and demeanor of perfect courtesy; and the Germans, mistaking these epithets for compliments, gravely removed their pipes from their mouths to respond, "Das ist gut," "Sehr wohl."[86] The Prussians, however, had the last laugh. After eating and drinking, at a hotel in Roye, "of the best the poor devils had left to give," Scott reported, they "called for their horses, and laughed in the face of the landlord when he offered his bill, telling him they would pay as they came back."[87]

But both the Germans and the Russians had bitter wrongs to avenge, and sometimes their outrages were hideous. "At Chateau Thierry the Prussians pillaged every house, violated the women and put the men to the sword." The Russians were like demons. "In one Seine valley town Cossack officers, after blowing up a woman on a pile of gunpowder, tried to roast the housekeeper of the château in which they were billeted for refusing to bring girls to amuse them."[88]

Scott and his companions entered Paris from the north, looking down on the capital from the heights of Montmartre.[89] Beyond a rough wooden palisade and an ominous gateway guarded by soldiers, knots of red-capped blackguards with enormous earrings glared from doorways; then came labyrinths of crazy medieval houses with tall fantastic gables, narrow roadways trickling with stinking water, ancient lanterns slung from ropes overhead.[90] In the center of the city, however, all changed. Here there were broad leafy boulevards, open-air cafés and restaurants, noble bridges arching over the Seine, the Louvre with the lilies of France again waving in the breeze, the formal gardens and gravel walks of the Tuileries, chestnut trees massing their foliage along the Champs Élysées, the Place de la Concorde, the victory column in the Place Vendôme, the bronze Venetian horses riding now triumphant above the Arc de Triomphe.[91]

For the great capital was a conquered city. Prussians in blue goose-stepped all the boulevards, Hungarian officers in dark green richly laced and furred paraded the Gardens of the Palais Royale, magnificent wasp-waisted Russian giants sauntered the Place de Carousel.[92] Near the Temple of Glory—now the Place de la Madeleine—the Band of the Emperor of Austria, in snowy uniforms, played military music. Scarlet-coated British troops guarded the Pont de Jena to prevent its destruction by revengeful Germans.[93] Filthy Cossack horsemen with uncouth beards and long lances dismounted from their ragged ponies to fraternize with the English, grinning "You Inglis, moi Russe, we brothers!" Only before the Louvre, pirouetting in blue and red decorated with silver, were there the French troops of Louis XVIII's Corps du Roi.[94]

Scott and his young friends engaged four bedrooms at the Hôtel de Bourbon in the Rue de la Paix, and at once hurried out to see the paintings and sculptures of the Louvre.[95] Never had there been such an assemblage of stolen masterpieces as Napoleon had plundered from all Europe. The Apollo Belvedere gleamed white in a spacious salon; in the Salle des Fleurs magnificent urns and vases were displayed against a background of columns and gray marble; paintings glowed close-crowded on every wall.[96] "I saw two Highlanders (common soldiers) & their wives," Scott wrote Charlotte, "busy admiring the famous Venus de Medicis & criticizing the works of Titian & Raphael."[97] He himself did not care very much for the sculpture but liked Salvator Rosa's *Witch of Endor*, a Wouvermans battle-piece of a cavalry attack on a bridge, and a handsome dog in a painting by Murillo.[98]

The visitors all dined that evening at Véry's in the Palais Royale, went to the Opéra Comique, and afterwards consumed ices in the Café des Mille Colonnes,[99] "where a magnificent, diamonded *Madame* in crimson velvet—reputed to have been a favourite of Bonaparte's—sat at a raised table among golden inkstands, flower vases, and bells for summoning waiters."[100] Next day began, for Scott, a crowded and glittering social life. The glowing orb of his fame was rising over all Europe. Sir John Malcolm escorted him to meet the Duke of Wellington in his splendid hôtel set in flowering gardens.[101]

Scott found the great commander, in his plain, unpretentious uniform, the most downright man he had ever met, utterly devoid of humbug.[102] Any other victorious leader would have been tempted to glorify himself by praising, and even overpraising, his opponent, but the notion never crossed the Duke's mind. There was nothing very rare about Napoleon as a General, he said; he was no better than his marshals. His own victory he owed entirely to the British regiments who had served under him in Spain, the best infantry in the world. When someone who intended to visit St. Helena asked if he had any message for Napoleon, he laughed. "Only tell Boney that I hope he finds my old lodgings at Longwood as comfortable as I find his in the Champs Élysées."[103]

Three nights later Scott was a guest at the grand ball with which the Duke celebrated Blücher's being given the Order of the Bath.[104] When their host greeted Blücher with a hearty welcome, Scott exclaimed, "A few weeks ago these two men delivered Europe!"[105] Wellington wore a plain Field Marshal's uniform, but it glittered with stars. Blücher, white-haired, bushy of eyebrow and mustache, wore blue with a splendid diamond cross and talked gleefully with the ladies who surrounded him. The rooms gleamed with candles; rainbow-hued gowns and gorgeous uniforms whirled in the waltz; a conjuror performed feats of magic, and a "grimacier" made comic faces and snorted. In the illuminated gardens, under gay tents and awnings, tables were loaded with refreshments. At supper Scott sat at the Duke's own table, where the band played near the open windows.[106]

Lord Cathcart, who had been the British Ambassador to Russia, invited Scott to a great dinner and presented him to Czar Alexander. Scott was wearing the red and blue uniform of the Edinburgh Light Horse; the Emperor, observing his limp, asked in French in what engagement he had been wounded. Scott, also speaking French, explained that it was a natural infirmity. "I thought Lord Cathcart mentioned that you had served," Alexander said. "Oh, yes; in a certain sense," Scott replied, "—in the yeomanry cavalry, a home force resembling the Landwehr, or Landsturm," "Under what commander?" the Emperor persisted. "Sous M. le Chevalier Rae." But Alexander was pertinacious. "Were you ever engaged?" Remembering the Edinburgh "bickers" of his boyhood, Scott could not resist saying, with a perfectly straight face, "In some slight actions . . . the battle of the Cross Causeway and the affair of Moredun-Mill."[107]

"The dinner," Scott told Charlotte, "was quite Russian in compliment to the Emperor whom our military jokers call the Imperial Dandie. We had first brandy—then cake—then oysters—then cheese—then brandy again—then a world of other things." On this occasion Scott met "Old Platoff," the famous Hetmann of the Cossacks, "and we said a world of pretty things to each other by signs."[108] The following morning, cantering along the Rue de la Paix with his Cossacks, Platoff spied Scott, leaped off his horse, and enfolded him in a great bear-embrace, kissing him moistly on both cheeks. Through an aide-de-camp he invited Scott to join his staff at the next great review, promising to mount him on their gentlest Ukrainian horse.[109]

Through all these convivialities Scott was vigorously seeing Paris. On the anniversary of the assumption of the Virgin he attended high mass at Notre Dame.[110] He visited the Gardens of the Luxembourg, where the Prussian troops were camped close to its magnificent flower-beds.[111] He saw the tombs of Voltaire and Rousseau in the Pantheon, and climbed to the top of the cupola—the loftiest height in the metropolis—to admire the panorama in the clear and smokeless air.[112] Escorted by the savant and archeologist, M. Chevalier, he went through the noble Library of St. Geneviève; another day, in the King's Library, he pored over rare manuscripts, including a batch of letters by Anne Boleyn and the letters of Henri IV to the Fair Gabrielle.[113] At the Jardin des Plantes he beheld enthusiastic Russians greeting the bears as "friends and fellow-countrymen."[114]

Sallying out in the morning under the August sun, when he passed the blind begger on the Boulevard des Italiens, he would bestow a pat on the man's dog and drop a coin in the wooden cup the animal held in his mouth.[115] He breakfasted at Tortoni's, where duelists could be seen devouring cold pâtés, game, fish, broiled kidneys, iced champagne, and liqueurs.[116] Along the avenues, in the intense heat, lemonade vendors sold their cool drink from castellated turrets borne on their backs.[117] He dined all over Paris—at the Quadron Bleu in the Boulevard du Temple, in a small restaurant in the Rue St. Honoré, at Beauvillier's, in a little cabaret on the quais by the Seine.[118] "I am quite a Frenchman in eating & drinking," he reported to Charlotte, "& turn up my nose at roast beef and port-wine—fricasses & champagne are much better—then you have the most delicious fruit huge bunches of grapes peaches & nectarines for nothing at all."[119] One night he gambled a few Napoleons at the Salon des Étrangers and won seven or eight.[120] Another night, at the Théâtre Français he saw Talma and Mlle. George in *Britannicus*; still another, at the Grand Opéra, he was one of an enormous crowd and had an ice on the boulevard on the way home.[121]

He saw the Duke of Wellington repeatedly, sitting next to him "by special invitation" at supper and hearing all "about his campaigns & particularly about the Battle of Waterloo." Viscount Castlereagh and Lady Castlereagh showered civilities and invitations upon him.[122] At the Académie Royale de Musique, where Wellington appeared in Lady Castlereagh's golden box and Austrian officers in gleaming white sat opposite, Scott watched Vestris in the ballet *L'Enfant Prodigue*, with blandishments of danseuses in gorgeous palaces followed by scenes of sandy desert, arid and oppressive.[123]

He went to Versailles with Lady Castlereagh, setting out in an azure-blue fiacre with scarlet wheels. They perambulated all the pomp and magnificence of that immense structure; the glitter, gold, and grandiose murals of the Galerie de Lebrun, the Salles de la Guerre et de la Paix, the Salle des Miroirs sparkling with reflections; the vistas of green park and stately architecture, the broad walks, glowing parterres, gleaming statues, marble-edged canals, sculptured fountains and basins. At five in the afternoon the "Grands Eaux" were turned on. An old gentleman in powdered earlocks, cocked hat, and buckles announced excitedly, "C'est le Jupiter qui commence!" The spectators shouted loudly as thousands of shimmering jets leaped skyward, arched in white streams, played gleaming over the shining limbs of bronze divinities and snorting steeds and dolphins in shrouds of crystal spray.[124]

An August 30, at the British Embassy—formerly the palace of the Princess Pauline Borghese—Lady Castlereagh gave a great ball for the emperors of Russia and Austria and the King of Prussia.[125] Here, in the course of the evening, Castlereagh told Scott a ghostly story of an adventure he had had in a desolate country house in Ireland. His bed was at one end of a long dilapidated room and at the other a great fire of wood and turf in a huge gaping chimney. Waking in the middle of the night, he watched the darkening embers on the hearth. Suddenly they blazed up, and a naked child stepped out. Advancing slowly toward Lord Castlereagh, it grew at every step until, three paces from his bed, it had become "a ghastly giant, pale as death, with a bleeding wound on the brow, and eyes glaring with rage and despair. Lord Castlereagh leaped from his bed, and confronted the figure in an attitude of defiance." It retreated, diminishing as it had previously grown; "he followed it pace by pace, until the original childlike form disappeared among the embers."[126]

The following day Scott attended the grand review of the Russian troops to which Platoff had invited him.[127] In the Place Louis Quinze, "the very spot where Louis XVI was beheaded," the Cossacks of the Guard kept the ground, giants in red jackets and wide blue trousers, with forests of pikes. The Emperors, the King of Prussia, the Duke, and all the "brilliant attendance of staff officers" were massed in a stand to the south. Behind stretched the long colonnade of the palace, to one side the Tuileries gleaming through the gardens and orange trees, and before the assembled monarchs "a superb row of buildings" beyond which rose "the bronze pillar erected by Napoleon to commemorate his victories" over these very princes whose victorious armies now dominated his fallen capital.[128] Russian bands played. The great square glowed like a furnace, "so fiercely were the sunbeams reflected from the arms of the host." Then came regiment after regiment, twenty thousand men, arms glancing, the pointed steel of fixed bayonets glittering, wave after wave, sparkling in the hot sun, thick as sheaves in a wheatfield.[129]

"It may give you some idea of the feelings of the French once so fond of spectacles," wrote Scott, that "there were not a hundred of their nation looking on."[130] The Parisians indeed were deeply crestfallen over their defeat. Though they prattled in public places with their usual vivacity, there was a sullen dislike of "Louis L'Inévitable" and a gloomy hatred of their conquerors. The few severities of the victors, like the execution of Labedoyère, they condemned as frightful atrocities. One lady told Scott it was "un horreur" unmatched in the annals of France. "Did Buonaparte never order such executions?" he asked. "Who? the Emperor?—Never!" "But the Duc d'Enghien, madame?" "Ah, parlez-moi d'Adam et d'Eve."[131]

The day of Scott's departure was now rapidly approaching. But he still rushed about with undiminished zeal. He visited the site of the Temple, in one of whose noisome cells Marie Antoinette and the little Dauphin had been imprisoned. He drove to the Place de la Bastille and saw a model of the colossal monument Napoleon had intended to erect there—an elephant in bronze, with a turnpike stair in one leg, discharging a jet of water from its trunk into a marble basin.[132] At a bookseller's in the Rue Serpente he priced a costly collection of French historians edited by the Benedictine monks and bought a description of Paris in several volumes.[133] Through the courtesy of M. Chevalier he was shown the famous collection of Baron Denon, the Egyptian and Phoenician papyri, the Watteaus and Rembrandt prints and a moonlight scene by Claude, a statue of Napoleon and Canova's bust of the King of Rome.[134] He went to Malmaison and with Lady Alvanley gazed on the sunset from St. Cloud.[135] Later one of Lady Alvanley's daughters sang in the warm summer evening. The scene moved Scott to compose the lyric beginning:

> Soft spread the southern summer night
> Her veil of darksome blue;
> Ten thousand stars combined to light
> The terrace of Saint Cloud.[136]

September 8 was Scott's last day in Paris.[137] He and Scott of Gala would be returning by themselves; Bruce and Pringle had set off for a trip to Switzerland.[138] After breakfast Scott and Gala separated to pay farewell visits to their friends. But Gala found himself irresistibly drawn back to the Palais Royale to buy more souvenirs. There he found Scott, who laughed heartily. "*Your* visits don't seem to have occupied much more time than my *own*, and here we are, in the midst of temptation, like a couple of moths, as we are." In a tobacconist's shop Scott found a snuffbox representing a cross section of a little tree, with the knots and veins carefully imitated. "We must not forget Tom Purdie, by-the-bye," he exclaimed, "—this is the very thing for him."[139]

In Lord Castlereagh's mail pouch, "with all the diplomatic secrets of Europe,"[140] Scott got off a last-minute letter to Charlotte: "I have bought some little trinkets for the party at Abb [otsford] necklaces & so forth . . . at the famous Palais Royale. If I find I can get anything of the lace kind easily brought over I will try to get a veil for you. Lady Alvanley has promised to smuggle it for me."[141] He also had a silk shawl for his mother and another for Miss Millar, and snuffboxes for some of the Abbotsford workmen.[142] "Kiss all the party for me and make much of poor fifi & puss. I saw a fine puss today of a sort of ash colour with long hair like silk a pretty creature."[143]

Early next day the two Scotts were off by way of Rouen and Dieppe. At Marli, Scott gaily added a quatrain to the old song:

> Who is't keeps guard
>     At Versailles and Marli?
> Who but the lads
>     That eat bannocks of barley.[144]

At Louviers the landlady of their inn grossly overcharged them for "pieds de cochon à la St. Menehauld," which they hadn't even ordered. Scott protested vehemently, but she won. "Eh bien, Madam," he concluded, "vous pouvez attendre une visite des alliés en peu de jours. Je vous assure que les *Prussiens* ne vous payeront ainsi." "C'est possible, Monsieur," she returned serenely.[145] That night there was a fierce banging on the door of the garret where the two men slept. Scott shouted in English—"forgetting where I was"—that he would shoot the first who tried to break down the door and the noise ceased. "Next morning we found the cause was the arrival of some benighted travellers English like ourselves who had mistaken their room & were no doubt surprized at the intimation they received from within."[146]

When they arrived at Rouen a service was going on in the Cathedral. The nave and lantern were handsome, Gala thought, but the Ionic colonnade in the screen and the Grecian transepts were incongruous. They saw the tombs of Richard I and the Duke of Bedford and hastily inspected the Palais de Justice and the statue of la Pucelle; Scott was eager for home and had no more patience for sights. At Dieppe they found a packet sailing for Brighton late that night.[147]

Slowly the lights of Dieppe receded in the darkness as the packet labored with adverse winds in the Channel.[148] Six astounding weeks these had been. The torn, blood-imbrued soil of Waterloo; the broad avenues of Paris, the bright air and the orange trees, the brilliant restaurants, glittering theaters, glowing salons and ballrooms; the military might parading to the rolling drums and shrilling fifes, even the skirling bagpipes of his native land; the hoary Cathedral with its gargoyles staring down over the historic walls of the Louvre and the Tuileries; the shimmering ballet of water before the enormous façade of Versailles—and among all these the powers of the earth, the kings and conquerors, the two emperors, Platoff, Blücher, and, towering in his lofty eminence, the great Duke. And in their midst had walked, caressed and courted, the descendant of cattle reivers, the little lame boy of Sandyknowe, a conqueror too, Monarch of Parnassus, laureled with Apollo's crown.

# 10

---

# Sweet Heathen of Monkbarns

## ( 1 8 1 5 – 1 8 1 6 )

AFTER BEING BATTERED in the Channel for forty hours, with noth-ing on board to eat but some oysters and a crust of bread washed down with vin ordinaire, the boat reached Brighton on the morning of September 12.[1] Scott and Gala were borne ashore to the pebbly shingle on the backs of a couple of sailors.[2] When the customs inspector heard Scott's name he would hardly look at the trunks: "I might have had them stuff'd with lace if I had known . . ."[3] That night they were off for London and next day at Long's Hotel in Bond Street.[4]

From here they called on Lord Byron, and Scott brought him back to the Hotel for a gay dinner with Terry and the comic actor Charles Mathews. The youthful Gala stared at "Byron's beautiful pale face, like a spirit's—good or evil," but thought him terribly "*bitter.*" When Scott told a story about a young officer with a ghastly head wound who had staggered on, dying, to deliver a message to the Duke, Byron said, "Ha! I daresay he could do as well as most people without his head—it was never much use to him."[5] Byron also expressed doubts of the veracity of imaginative people; they all, he said, "were addicted to mix fiction (or poetry) with their prose." Why, he exclaimed, "the celebrated courtesan of Venice about whom Rousseau makes so piquante a story," was prob-ably, "if one could see her a draggled-taild wench enough."[6] These same remarks that the sober-minded Gala found cynical, Scott thought only the sport of high-spirited gaiety. "A most brilliant day we had of it," he said. "I never saw Byron so full of fun, frolic, wit, and whim; he was as playful as a kitten."[7]

Next morning at six Scott and Gala took the coach for the North, accompanied by Mathews, who had a theatrical engagement at Leamington.[8] On the Wye, a few miles above Matlock, they visited Haddon Hall and saw on the gate the punning arms of the Vernons, "Ver non semper viret." Upon the great hall of this mansion, with its dais, long gallery, and massive table, and the adjoining bedroom with its strange cornice of boars' heads and peacocks and its velvet bed with peacocks and coronets, Scott later modeled Lady Peveril's rooms in *Peveril of the Peak*. Wild traveling through northern Derbyshire, Dovedale, and the Peak brought them to the Devil's Cavern, which they explored in a boat, and the Speedwell lead mine, whose limestone galleries they descended.[9] At Sheffield, Scott bought himself a planter's knife in Rogers's shop; at Ripon they visited the Minister and Fountains Abbey.[10]

When they reached Rokeby, Morritt's wife proved to be ill, so they did not linger, but passing on by way of Barnard Castle, Brough, Appleby, and Penrith, drew near Carlisle.[11] "I am always glad to visit Carlisle," Scott told Gala; "I was married here, and never spent happier days than when I used to take excursions in the neighborhood."[12] Again he visited the Cathedral, and, sauntering on the Castle esplanade before its Gothic gate, recited "Kinmont Willie." At their inn Scott was tickled to read, scratched on a pane of glass, a quatrain about Corby Castle, "the only rhimes" of which the philosopher Hume "was ever known to be guilty."

> Here chicks in eggs for breakfast sprawl
> Here Godless boys God's glory squall
> Here Scotchmen's heads do guard the wall
> But Corby's walks attone for all.[13]

It would be a good joke, Scott wrote Morritt, "to advertize the poetical Works of David Hume with notes critical historical and so forth." These might include an "inquiry into the use of eggs for breakfast a physical discussion of the causes of their being addled, a history of English church music and of the choir of Carlisle in particular, a full account of the affair of 1745, with the trials, last speeches, and so forth, of the poor *plaids* who were strap'd up at Carlisle and lastly a full . . . description of Corby, with the genealogy of every family who ever possessd it." "Even without the usual waste of margin the poems of David would make a decent twelve Shilling touch."[14]

On September 24, Scott and Gala had passed Johnny Armstrong's tower and were once more in Scotland. These bare hills were full of memories of his youthful jaunts. He was still wearing on his finger the ring he had found in the ruins of Hermitage, silver with hearts around the rim. "I should like well another raid into Liddesdale some day; I have not seen it for many a year." But there was no time now for pausing; it was drawing on toward sunset and Scott wished to reach home that night. Presently they were passing "Branxholm's lordly tower." Sometime after dark Scott gladly drew up at Abbotsford and was soon comfortably stretched out in his easy chair before the glowing fire of his snug little parlor.[15]

During his absence Charlotte and the girls had decked out the furniture in bright new chintz of the latest fashion. They waited eagerly for Scott to notice this sprucing-up, but alas he remained unaware of it. At last Charlotte burst out, no longer able to hold in her disappointment. Scott was full of remorse for his blindness; between then and bedtime he repeatedly tried to console "Mamma" by exclamations of praise.[16]

Next morning when he set out for a ride he had a surprise. His white charger Daisy was brought to the door, but instead of standing quietly to be mounted, as he had always done, "looked askant at me like a devil, and when I put my foot in the stirrup . . . reared bolt upright." Scott fell heavily to the ground. Twice he tried to mount; each time Daisy grew frantic. "He had certainly," Scott remarked, "taken some part of my conduct in high dudgeon and disgust." Later, laughing, "Troth," he added, "maybe some bird had whispered Daisy that I had been to see the grand reviews at Paris on a little scrag of a Cossack, while my own gallant trooper was left behind bearing Peter and the post-bag to Melrose."[17] Whatever Daisy's equine reasons, he remained unreconcilable, "and wars and rumours of wars being over," Scott sold him to John Ballantyne. Henceforth he would "stick to a good sober cob."[18]

Now that he was home from his Continental holiday, Scott was eager to get started on his third novel, which he had decided to call *The Antiquary*. Constable, who "had been admitted almost from the beginning into the *secret* of the Novels," undertook its publication.[19] But first various other commitments must be cleared out of the way. Even in the effervescence of sightseeing and mingling with kings and conquerors in Paris, Scott had written and sent James Ballantyne the first two of *Paul's Letters* and a poem entitled *The Field of Waterloo*.[20] Out of the poem also sprang an offshoot, "an odd wild sort of thing," Scott said, "which I intend to finish separately and call it *The Dance of Death*."[21] And although he had thought it probable that *The Lord of the Isles* would be his "last poetical adventure upon a large scale,"[22] he was amusing himself with a romantic poem called *Harold the Dauntless*.[23] The completion of *Paul* had to await the arrival of some of the books he had bought in France. Then, however, he would "proceed instantly with *The Antiq$^y$*."[24]

During October *The Field of Waterloo* went through the press, and James Ballantyne wrote down his usual painstaking comments. He didn't like its opening line, "Fair Brussels, thou art far behind"—"It is tame, and the phrase 'far behind' has, to my feeling, some associated vulgarity." "Stet," replied Scott. In the second stanza a repetition of the article "the," James said, was cacophonous. "Would not *its* do?" "Th. is a bad sound," Scott answered. "Ts a much worse. Read *their*." To another criticism he responded, " 'Cousin, thou wert not wont to be so dull!' " "I do not know such an English word as stance," James commented. "Then we'll make it one for the *nance*," Scott retorted. On one of the battle descriptions James remarked that it was "very spirited and very fine" but too much like a passage from *The Lord of the Isles*, "and really, to borrow from one's self is hardly much better than to borrow from one's neighbours." And only a few lines lower came a couplet that echoed one in *The Lady of the Lake*. These passages Scott went to some labor to change.[25]

The profits of the first edition of *The Field of Waterloo* were to be contributed to the relief of the widows and orphans of soldiers slain in the battle.[26] Constable proposed, and Scott agreed, that they should print six thousand copies, selling at five shillings.[27] The poem was published around October 21. Though it did well enough—within a month it went into a second edition of three thousand and before the end of the year into a third—[28] it was not one of Scott's inspired efforts, and reviewers delightedly but on the whole justly called it "a falling-off." One wit wrote:

> On Waterloo's ensanguined plain
> Full many a gallant man was slain,
> But none, by bullet or by shot,
> Fell half so flat as Walter Scott.[29]

Despite this joke there were vigorous and colorful sections in the poem, including a contrast between Napoleon and Cataline:

> That Chieftain, who, of yore,
> Ambition's dizzy paths essay'd,
> And with the gladiators' aid
>     For empire enterprised—
> He stood the cast his rashness play'd,
> Left not the victims he had made,
> Dug his red grave with his own blade,
> And on the field he lost was laid,
>     Abhorr'd—but not despised.[30]

Nevertheless Scott's lines nowhere rose to the brilliant and sulphurous heights of Byron's *Ode to Napoleon:*

> Is this the man of thousand thrones,
> Who, strew'd our earth with hostile bones,
>     And can he thus survive?
> Since he, miscall'd the Morning Star,
> Nor man nor fiend has fallen so far.[31]

Byron himself, however, greeted Scott's poem with generous enthusiasm. Reading aloud the lines

> For high and deathless is the name,
> Oh Hougomont, thy ruins claim!
> The sound of Cressy none shall own,
> And Agincourt shall be unknown,
> And Blenheim be a nameless spot
> Long ere thy glories are forgot

he struck the page, exclaiming, "I'll be damnd, if they will, Mr. Scott, be forgot!"[32]

All Scott's financial problems now seemed things of the past. John Ballantyne's spirits bubbled over. In Hanover Street he was banging down his auctioneer's hammer on many a plump sale. He had bought himself another horse named Little Waterloo, drove Daisy in a gig, wore a bright green coat with big buttons, and was thinking of buying a villa at Stockbridge. "Constable—pish!" he wrote in his *Diary*.[33] Scott's spirits were also rising high. Once more he was busy molding his slopes and planting them with foliage. The north side of the hill above Abbotsford he sowed thickly with pinasters recently received from Joanna Baillie. The old gravel-pit, which had been an eyesore, he covered over with rich soil and planted with laurels, holly, and cedars sheltering a rustic seat called Joanna's Bower.[34]

But his ideas were growing expansive. Mere landscaping was not enough; his land hunger was reviving. "Money has tumbled in upon me very fast," he wrote Morritt, "and I am enabled to make a very nice little purchase adjoining to Abbotsford . . . You who gave me so kind a shove when I was pinched with my long-dated bills will I know rejoice that your friendship has not been throwing water in a sieve."[35] The property was the farm of Kaeside, several hundred acres including "a large lump of wild land,"[36] "a fine stretch of bog and heather,"[37] undulating east from the Tweed; this addition, Scott rejoiced, "greatly more than doubles my domains."[38] What was more, it was very cheap —only £3,400, of which he paid down £400, and granted George Moss, the former owner, a mortgage on the estate for the remainder.[39] Less than a fortnight later Scott was offered £600 more than he had paid.[40]

His delight was enhanced by the fact that his own dominions would now include the little hillock of Turn-again, where the Scott clan had rallied after the battle of Melrose and the Knight of Cessford had bled his life into the ground.[41] Besides this, it extended to within quarter of a mile of Cauldshiels Loch, "a very sweet wild sheet of water," the border of which he was hoping to acquire.[42] Among the solitary shepherds who approached its banks there was a belief that in its waters lurked a monster they called a water-bull.[43] "A very cool-headed sensible man told me he had seen it in broad daylight—he scouted my idea of an otter and said the animal was more like a cow or a horse."[44] Soon Scott was trying to buy from Nicol Milne a hundred acres that half-circled the lake.[45]

While the bargain with Mr. Moss was going forward, Charlotte was in Edinburgh for the Music Festival, and was still there when he wrote to tell her "the great news." He himself had happily remained on Tweedside; he had no ear for sonatas and symphonies and found pleasure only in old native melodies. "For my part," as he put it, "I would not give one 'wheeble of a whaup' [cry of a curlew] from the moss at Keaside for all the fine music you have heard."[46] But he was glad Charlotte was enjoying Cherubini, Beethoven, Pergolesi, and Mozart, and Braham and Madame Marconi singing Händel's *Messiah*.[47] Meanwhile, he dined with the Duke of Buccleuch at Bowhill, had William Erskine and Robert Bruce to dinner at Abbotsford, and exchanged hospitality with Dr. Douglas, the minister at Galashiels.[48]

Although Scott and the old clergyman had long been friends, since the purchase of Abbotsford they had seen each other more often. One night, with the Doctor still snugly seated in the Abbotsford parlor, his daughter saw the hands of the clock nearing twelve. She tried to nudge her father to start for home. "Toot, toot, lassie! Dinna fash!" exclaimed Scott. "Bide a wee, lassie! Dinna break good talk! The Doctor is in excellent vein tonight. Let him finish his story, and then we won't go, but have one story more, and the stirrup-cup of toddy!" Not until the small hours did the Doctor walk home by clear moonlight.[49] When, toward the end of this year, Scott paid him the last of the purchase money,[50] he enclosed the check in a rhyming letter:

> "—So, Doctor and friend,
> We come to an end;
> The gowd's thine,
> And the land's mine."[51]

*Paul's Letters to His Kinsfolk* was proving a wearisome job, but Scott fagged at it steadily.[52] Constable had decided that it would be "safe & prudent" to print six thousand copies of this book too. Scott agreed: "It is a work of momentary interest—the more that can be made of it at first the better."[53] But the proofs were slow in arriving: "James *must* press on with it . . . and without humming and hawing. . . . *The Antiqy.* goes on instantly after or rather before *Paul* is done at press. . . . For GODS SAKE push it on, what signifies my slaving myself to death if we do not get forward."[54]

Some little time off from this drudgery Scott did allow himself, writing a kind of war song for the burghers of Selkirk, who in early December were going to fight "a terrible match at football" with the men of Yarrow and Ettrick. The game would be played at Carterhaugh under the auspices of the Duke of Buccleuch. Over the field would wave the banner of Buccleuch, "a very ancient and curious pennon with the armorial bearings embroidered on one side and on the other the war-cry of the name which was *Bellenden* from their usual place of rendezvous." James Hogg was composing a song for Yarrow, and of course their Sheriff must provide one for the Sutors of Selkirk. He begged Lady Compton's aid in making or finding some wild tune to go with his own "immortal verse."[55]

Earlier that year the Ettrick Shepherd had been in a violent sulk with Scott. He had conceived the idea of a volume to be entitled *The Poetic Mirror*, consisting of poems by his brother bards edited by Hogg and published for his own benefit. Nearly all had declined, but he especially resented Scott's refusal and had written him a letter beginning "Damned Sir" and ending "Believe me, Sir, yours with disgust." Scott had merely smiled, and when he learned that Hogg was ill in Edinburgh sought to pay his medical bill without the Shepherd's knowledge. Soon, however, the huffy poet repented his rage.[56]

"I think it is great nonsense," he wrote Scott, "for two men who are friends at heart" to "be professed enemies." He realized that he had been intemperate: "I desire not a renewal of our former intimacy, for haply, after what I have written, your family would not suffer it; but I wish . . . that when we meet *by chance*, we might shake hands, and speak to one another as old acquaintances . . . for I find there are many things which I yearn to communicate to you, and the tears rush to my eyes when I consider that I may not." Scott wrote Hogg "to think no more of the business, and come to breakfast the next morning."[57]

The great football match, or "wappenschaw," as Scott called it, was fought on December 4. Two thousand spectators had gathered on the meadowbank.[58] Scott's son, young Walter, now fourteen years of age, gallantly mounted and "dressed in forest green and buff," with an eagle's feather in his green bonnet and "a large gold chain with a medal," rode over the field with the Duke's standard while war pipes played.[59] Scott's song was chanted:

> Then up with the Banner! let forest winds fan her!
>   She has blazed over Ettrick eight ages and more;
> In sport we'll attend her, in battle defend her,
>   With heart and with hand, like our Fathers before.[60]

The Duke of Buccleuch tossed out the ball and the match began. In the first game the Selkirk players were joined by men from Hawick and weavers from Galashiels and battered down all opposition.[61] "In the second Torwoodlie meaning to restore equality caused the Galashiels men about fifty in number to change sides," and after a bitter struggle of four hours Selkirk lost.[62] Scott threw up his hat and suggested a deciding game with a hundred picked men on each side, but the sun of the brief December day was already declining, and the Sutors were angry at being deserted by Galashiels. After dark, drunken fistfights broke out among the heather, showers of stones flew, and men from both sides got ducked in the river.[63]

At Bowhill, however, there was a joyous party with a banquet and a ball that ended only with the dawn.[64] "Sophia danced till six in the morning as did the Banner bearer."[65] Anne, who was only twelve, is not mentioned as present, and even if she was there would almost certainly not have been allowed to remain up for the ball, but it may have been on this occasion, playing with the Duke's little daughters, that she was overheard saying to her namesake, Lady Anne Scott, "Well, I do wish I were Lady Anne too—it is so much prettier than Miss." Thenceforth, with cheerful mockery, her own family often called her Lady Anne.[66]

At dinner Hogg unobservantly started to seat himself at a side table for the young Earl of Dalkeith and the other children. Scott took his arm, and explaining that the table was for the "little lords and ladies," led him to a place "between himself and the Laird of Harden." Hogg didn't quite catch what Scott said; his touchy humor interpreted Scott's action as seizing him by the arm, telling him the table was reserved for the nobility, and seating him at an inferior board. "The fact is," Hogg explained, "I am convinced he was sore afraid of my getting to be too great a favourite among the young ladies of Buccleuch!"[67]

By the last third of December, Scott was impatient to begin *The Antiquary*. His mind was teeming with oddities for the portrayal of his title character, the eccentric and middle-aged Jonathan Oldbuck of Monkbarns. Nearly all his other literary tasks had been cleared from his desk. He had almost completed *Harold the Dauntless*, "a strange rude story founded partly on the ancient northern traditions" of the Berserkers, whose "fits of martial frenzy make such a figure in the Sagas of Scandinavian origin."[68] *Paul's Letters* were being rushed through the press. "The recess of our court which takes place tomorrow for three weeks will give me ample time to finish this job," Scott said confidently. "I shall then set myself seriously to *The Antiquary* of which I have only a very general sketch at present. But when I once get my pen to the paper it will walk fast enough."[69]

These last words he echoed to James Ballantyne on December 29. *Paul* had been a tiresome chore:

> "Dear James—I'm done, thank God, with the long yarns
> Of the most prosy of Apostles—Paul;
> And now advance, sweet Heathen of Monkbarns!
> Step out, old quizz, as fast as I can scrawl."[70]

*Paul's Letters* appeared early in January, 1816. For all Scott's boredom with the book, it was well received.[71] Within a short time

Constable sold fourteen hundred copies, and two further editions brought the total printing up to nine thousand.[72] The Edgeworths were lukewarm about the first two chapters, but when they reached the Battle of Waterloo they burst into fire. "Polybius never brought his reader so entirely into the field of battle," exclaimed Edgeworth, ". . . nor did Plutarch, or Homer, the greatest of all masters, inspire the reader with more interest for the individual heroes whom they describe." Scott's pen should be employed in history: "It narrates, instructs, and entertains . . . and opens every now and then glimpses of that patriotic flame which kindles the heart of a rising generation."[73]

Despite Edgeworth's praise, the truth is that *Paul's Letters* is a hack job, written, for the most part, in a pedestrian style that reveals Scott's lack of enthusiasm for his task. It is clear and intelligent journalism illumined by the reasonableness and good sense he brought to almost every undertaking. He sternly condemns the brutality of the Prussians, but he understands what bitter provocation they had suffered. He shows no hatred for the French. Unlike Byron, his eyes are not dazzled by the Emperor's glamor; unlike many other contemporaries, he does not fall into hysterical raving. He arraigns Napoleon's self-aggrandizement but grants his greatness. The Waterloo chapters are indeed the best parts of the book. But the blazing emotion brought to them by readers who had tensely waited for news from Belgium is faded; and the excitement was in the situation, not in the mere competence of the handling.

With the new year, "as fast as he could scrawl," Scott was racing ahead on *The Antiquary*. But, as usual, he was also busy in a dozen other ways. Mungo Park's brother had been ruined by a bank failure; Scott tried to find him a post as a bailiff. Archie Park was good-humored and steady, a fisher, shooter, and horseman; "his experience, knowledge and honesty would make him a real treasure . . . Lord Byron may among his friends hear of some one who would like an overseer, five parts Dandie Dinmont with one part of civilization."[74] Ultimately Scott got Park an appointment as Controller of the Customs at Tobermory.[75]

Still another unfortunate man was Scott's own cousin William, whose prosperous but tight-fisted father, old Raeburn, clutched every penny and refused the slightest aid while his middle-aged son worried over a large family and a thin purse on a small farm. William was seeking to obtain the Collectorship of Taxes for Roxburghshire. Scott did all he could to help; he canvassed the countryside for supporters; he wrote letters in his cousin's behalf; he urged William to campaign vigorously. "Now keep a good look out on *old* friends," he adjured, "& try to make *new* and I think you will prove the winning horse." "So ride Reaburn ride."[76]

Meanwhile Scott had struck his bargain with Nicol Milne for the part of Abbotslea that bordered on Cauldshiels Loch and brought his own estate up to around six hundred acres.[77] Adam Ferguson, his jollity undamped by the two years he had spent in a French military jail, was now quartered in Ireland but was thinking of retiring from the army on half pay.[78] Adam must not be reduced to seven shillings a day, Scott exclaimed, but "must get some snug thing to help out." On his own new farm there was "a mansion about the caliber of the *Lairds ain house*"; why should not Adam and his sisters live there during the summer? It would be near enough to be sociable and distant enough to be independent, and blackcocks for shooting were plentiful. Adam was welcome to it for the mere cost of the window tax, fifty shillings. Think of "laying our auld grey pows together as we used to do our young rattle-pates"![79]

His old music teacher, Alexander Campbell, Scott helped out by presenting him a song for publication in *Albyn's Anthology*. Campbell was "half musician half poet and in right of both capacities half mad" but a good man and very poor.[80] The poem, "Lullaby of an Infant Chief," was one Scott had composed to the old Gaelic air "Cadul gu lo," "Sleep on till day," to be sung in a dramatization of *Guy Mannering* that Daniel Terry had hacked out for production on the London boards.[81] Not until too late did Scott reflect that people might infer a connection between the author of the song and the author of the novel, but then he shrugged his shoulders: " I cannot see . . . how acknowledging the one is fathering the other."[82] Some aid, as well, he gave Terry in rearranging the dialogue of the novel and modifying its plot for stage purposes. At this excursion into what he called "the art of Terryfying" he felt much amused entertainment.[83] "For my share in it," he told Terry, "Dumple it out as you list so it pleases the public & serves you."[84] Terry's play was produced on March 12, with splendid success, at Covent Garden.[85]

Through Scott's influence, too, Maturin's tragedy *Bertram* was accepted for production at Drury Lane by Lord Byron, who was on the committee of management.[86] The play would "either succeed greatly," Scott predicted, "or be damned gloriously, for its merits are marked, deep, and striking, and its faults of a nature obnoxious to ridicule." Maturin's last act was bad: "He piddles (so to speak) through a cullender, and divides the whole horrors of the Catastrophe (though God wot there are enough of them) into a kind of drippity-droppity of four or five scenes, instead of inundating the audience with them at once in the finale, with a grand '*gardez l'eau.*' "[87] The poor author, Scott wrote Byron, was "almost mad with gratitude to your kindness."[88]

Byron himself was just upon the verge of his own catastrophe and all the scandal that attended his separation from his wife. On January 6 he had sent her a note asking her to leave home with her child as soon as possible. Joanna Baillie was violently indignant at his behavior:

". . . he has used her brutally; . . . no excuse can be pleaded in his behalf but *insanity*." She urged Scott to use his influence to see that Lady Byron received a generous separation allowance: "There is nobody whose good opinion he is more anxious to preserve than your own."[89]

But, as Joanna had feared, Scott said, "How can I meddle in such matters?" and declined to intervene. He did not believe that Byron would ultimately resist whatever should be fair and honorable to Lady Byron.[90] Scott proved to be right. "Wherever the wrong lies," Byron said, "it does not lie with her: she is perfect in thought, word, & deed."[91] He signed the separation agreement and left England, never to return. The brilliant September day Scott had spent with him in London proved to be the last on which they ever met.

"So Lord Byron's romance seems to be concluded," Scott said in valedictory. "But Lord Byron wt. high genius and many points of a noble and generous feeling has Child Harolded himself and Outlawd himself into too great a resemblance with the pictures of his imagination. . . . In the meanwhile I think my noble friend is something like my old peacock who chuses to bivouac apart from his lady and sit below my bedroom window to keep me awake with his screeching lamentation. Only I own he is not equal in melody to Lord B. for *Fare thee well and if for ever* is a very sweet dirge indeed—"[92]

As Scott steadily added page after page to *The Antiquary*, he did not cease to turn out other work. For the *Quarterly Review* he wrote a long article, almost 24,000 words, on the historic Culloden Papers, and for the same periodical a critique heartily praising Jane Austen's *Emma*.[93] For Alexander Campbell's further use in *Albyn's Anthology* he composed a number of lyrics, including the stanzas with which he completed the fragmentary old poem "Jock of Hazeldean."[94] In still another undertaking perhaps Edgeworth's declaration that he should write history bore fruit. Southey had given up the historical part of the *Edinburgh Annual Register*, and Scott had agreed to supply its History of 1814 and 1815.[95] He appealed to Terry for his aid in getting material, "especially foreign books & pamphlets. I am indifferently well stocked with those which were published before October as I brought many from Paris. But I want anxiously to know if there has yet appeared any narrative of Boneys doings from the time he left Waterloo till his leaving Paris & from that time until his embarkation."[96]

Early in 1816, on James Ballantyne's plea, Scott reorganized their business relationship. James, for long years a middle-aged bachelor, once again desired to marry and although still a somewhat timid lover, felt more confident of success than when he had wooed but failed to win Miss Stewart of Glasgow. His choice now was a young lady almost twenty years his junior, the daughter of Robert Hogarth, a prosperous farmer at Carfrae in Berwickshire. Although Hogarth was believed to have a fortune of almost £30,000, which he proposed to divide among his six children, he did not make his consent to the match dependent upon Ballantyne's being a man of means. Knowing, however, of the troubles from which the Ballantyne enterprises had so recently emerged, he desired to be assured that his prospective son-in-law should not again be so endangered. James therefore asked Scott to release him from their partnerships and allow him to become merely the salaried employee of the Printing Office.[97]

Nearly all the money that had saved the firm, James knew, had been poured into it by his partner, who still had a claim upon it, indeed, for the £3,000 he had advanced as a personal loan. No doubt Scott would be a lenient creditor; nevertheless the debt existed. "I am singularly and almost hopelessly ignorant in these matters," James confessed, "but I fancy the truth is, that owing to the bad success of the Bookselling speculation, and the injudicious drafts so long made on the business that throve, I am de jure et de facto wholly dependent upon you." He begged Scott for his advice: "I know no man so wise, and none more honourable. It will be hard, very hard, if from contingencies attaching no great portion of blame to me, I must resign this last hope, but I must never drag a kind and confiding woman into the pit after me."[98]

Hogarth's son George, who was a Writer to the Signet, desired a complete discharge of the partners of John Ballantyne and Company, leaving Scott to wind up its affairs and pay off all its remaining debts. Scott, who knew that James would never have gone into the business but for him, readily consented. The proposal, he said generously, "not only fully meets my concurrence, but is what I designed to request for my own sake . . ." He further agreed to take upon himself all the responsibilities of the Printing Office, including James's share of its debts, except for the £3,000, which would remain as a personal loan from him to James. This, however, he had no intention of pressing. James would become his manager at £400 a year. Finally, on Scott's suggestion, it was provided that James on his own volition might at any future time be readmitted as a partner.[99]

The Hogarths were cautious but not greedy. The old farmer liked his daughter's black-bearded middle-aged suitor, agreed with her that he was a man of talent, and wanted only to be certain that he had a comfortable income and no liability for crushing amounts of commercial debt. Early in January the discharges were signed and sealed.[100] James tried not to rhapsodize about his bride, but was clearly proud of her. She was "a lover of reading," he said, "particularly of poetry and belles lettres." "She is not beautiful certainly, and certainly she is not plain, of a pleasing exterior, good taste, a clear understanding, and a disposition eminently kind . . ."[101] Scott was pleased for his old friend. "James Ballantyne gives us his last Bachelor dinner tomorrow," he told

Terry, "& then moves off in all typographical state."[102] The wedding took place on February 1.[103]

James thus happily settled in life, Scott himself settled down to completing *The Antiquary*. The middle of March saw James's bride in St. John Street and James back among the clanking presses of the Canongate, setting the novel up in type. From Abbotsford, where he had installed himself as soon as the spring vacation released him from the Court, Scott sent in successive batches. James would have the end of the second volume, he wrote, within the week, and "if I have health I have no doubt all will be in his hands by the 12th April."[104]

During the proofreading Scott asked John Ballantyne, who chanced to be with him, to look up a passage in Beaumont and Fletcher that he wanted to use as a chapter motto. John searched in vain for the lines. "Hang it, Johnnie," cried Scott, "I believe I can make a motto sooner than you will find one." On the spot, in fact, he invented one; "and from that hour, whenever memory failed to suggest an appropriate epigraph, he had recourse to the inexhaustible mines of *'old play'* or *'old ballad.'* "[105]

Beside him as he wrote reclined a new dog, an enormous bloodhound a full "six feet from the tip of the nose to the tail."[106] The animal had just been given him by Alexander MacDonell of Glengarry, upon whose proud Gaelic chivalry Scott had modeled some of the characteristics of Fergus MacIvor in *Waverley*. Named Maida, after the battle in Spain, the creature was "between the deer greyhound and mastiff with a shaggy mane like a lion," "the noblest dog ever seen on the Border since Johnnie Armstrong's day," Scott exclaimed.[107] Soon Maida was sitting beside his master at every meal, "his head as high as the back of my chair."[108] "He is fully as large as a shetland pony and kills foxes most amiably."[109]

Yet, fantastically, this powerful killer was terrified by Hinze, the family's favorite cat. Puss kept him, Scott told Joanna Baillie, "in the greatest possible order, insists upon all right of precedence, and scratches with impunity the nose of an animal who would make no bones of a wolf and pulls down a red-deer without difficulty. I heard my friend set up some most pitiful howls and I assure you the noise was no joke—all occasioned by his fear of passing puss who had stationed himself on the stairs."[110]

Throughout March and in April the weather was atrocious, "snowing and hailing eternally,"[111] so that except for having Charlotte's company, Scott declared, he was like

> "The spirit who bideth by himself
> In the land of mist and snow—"[112]

But the snow wreaths were just as well, for as soon as a lull permitted he was playing truant from his task and out walking "over my bogs and clay fields till my legs ache."[113] Despite these temptations, however, he was able to announce late in April that *The Antiquary* would be published within another fortnight.

Suddenly, on the night of May 8, Scott received word that his brother, Major John Scott, was dying.[114] The Major had retired from the Army in 1810 with his digestion much impaired, and had suffered ever since from bilious complaints. A sedate bachelor of dull mind and frugal habits, he had lived with his mother and spent his evenings playing whist at Fortune's Tavern with other retired officers. Throughout all 1815 he had been a fretful invalid.[115] Scott had hardly expected him to survive the winter, but with the milder weather of early spring he had seemed to gather strength. Then came the return of frost and he took a turn for the worse.[116]

Scott hurried back to Edinburgh over the dark and icy roads. He arrived in the early hours of the morning, but he was too late. His brother had died at four o'clock the previous afternoon. Their mother, he wrote Tom, had "borne this severe shock with great firmness" and was "perfectly well in health, and as strong in her mind as you ever knew her. She feels her loss, but is also sensible that protracted existence, with a constitution so irretrievably broken up as our brother's could have been no blessing."[117]

"His death under all the circumstances," Scott told Morritt, "cannot be termd a subject of deep afliction and though we were always on fraternal terms of mutual kindness and goodwill yet our habits of life, our tastes for society, and circles of freinds were so totally different that there was less frequent intercourse between us than our connection and real liking to each other might have occasioned. Yet it is a heavy consideration to have lost the last but one who was interested in our early domestic life, our habits of boyhood, and our early friends and connections."[118]

John had left an estate of almost £6,000, which he divided between his two brothers. His gold watch he wished to be given to Scott's son Walter "as his male representative," but this, Scott told Tom, "I can accept only on condition *your* little Walter will accept a similar token of regard from his remaining uncle." In the course of nature now it could not be long before Tom would inherit another £3,000 from their mother. Surely he could give up his paymastership and bring his family back to Scotland? "I do not feel quite so *young* as I was when we last met, and I should like well to see my only brother return to his own country . . ."[119]

While Major Scott lay dying, *The Antiquary* made its entry into the world. It was published on May 4. Book dealers and readers seized on it with excitement. "We have had a most wonderful subscription among the Trade," Constable wrote Scott.[120] Even the critics surrendered and were obliged to admit that the Author's mind was not "exhausted," although the immortal idiot on the *Quarterly* still complained of the "dark dialect of Anglified Erse" in which some of the dialogue was written.[121] But readers throughout Britain, Erse linguists all, gulped down the tenebrous dialect undismayed. Within six days six thousand copies were sold and another printing was hurrying through the press. This was "very flattering to the unknown author," who was "a greater Mystery than ever."[122] But soon the masquerade was to grow still more complicated when a second unknown entered the lists.

# 11

## Time Looms Gigantic

### (Criticism: *Waverley, Guy Mannering, The Antiquary*)

"THE PRESENT WORK," Scott wrote in the introduction to *The Antiquary*, "completes a series of fictitious narratives, intended to illustrate the manners of Scotland at three different periods. *Waverley* embraced the age of our fathers, *Guy Mannering* that of our own youth, and *The Antiquary* refers to the last ten years of the eighteenth century."[1] But there is no evidence that Scott had any such plan in mind while he was writing *Guy Mannering*, and even to *The Antiquary* it was probably more or less an afterthought. Of the three novels only *Waverley* is built around important historical events—those of the Jacobite uprising of 1745. The other two center primarily on the private lives of the characters, although in *The Antiquary* the Napoleonic wars are in the background, the mysterious Lovel is at one point suspected of being a spy, and near the end there is a mistaken alarm of a French invasion.

Scott rightly claims, nevertheless, that all three reflect the manners and the social history of their successive times. *Waverley* shows the last confused and broken effort of the clan chiefs to dominate Scotland. Their defeat at Culloden ends the old feudal society forever. In *Guy Mannering* Godfrey Bertram's banishment of the gypsies and his campaign against the smugglers represent a premature and ill-thought-out endeavor to subdue old folkways to an order for which his world is not yet ready. *The Antiquary* portrays in the declining fortunes of Sir Arthur Wardour and the decay of the ancient house of Glenallan the further disintegration of traditional values—and reveals in the dominant role given to the plebeian Whig, Jonathan Oldbuck of Monkbarns, the growing significance of a middle class that mediates between old and new. Almost at spaced intervals—1745, the 1770s, 1795—the three novels mirror the social changes of the second half of the century.

In the very opening chapter of *Waverley* there is a passage that may well be taken as the program not merely for these three novels but for all the splendid series that was to follow them. He intends, Scott says, to throw "the force of my narrative upon the characters and passions of the actors—those passions common to men in all stages of society, and which have alike agitated the human heart whether it throbbed under the steel corselet of the fifteenth century, the brocaded coat of the eighteenth, or the blue frock and dimity waistcoat of the present day."[2] But at the same time that he thus insists on the essential constancy beneath all the varied patterns, he emphasizes the powerful ways in which men and women are shaped by the society of which they are a part, by the beliefs and attitudes of their milieu, in short, by the particular culture of their time. "The state of manners and laws,"[3] the social and historical forces that have created the community, he points out, are no less crucial for character than the deep-rooted essences of human nature itself.

This is Scott's revolutionary insight as an imaginative writer. For Chaucer, Troilus was a courtly medieval knight; for Shakespeare, the figures of Brutus and Octavius, of Hector and Achilles, differed in no significant ways from a sixteenth-century aristocrat, and a Roman mob was an Elizabethan mob. This is no less true of Scott's great eighteenth-century predecessors, Richardson and Fielding, splendid as were their achievements in the novel. Their characters live, as it were, in a clear present; though they are influenced, of course, by their personal antecedents and circumstances, they have no historical background. But the characters in Scott's novels are the products both of their own and of the collective past.

Scott is working, of course, as Georg Lukács says, in "direct continuation of the great realistic social novels of the eighteenth century."[4] But the perceptions that were left only implicit in Fielding and Smollett become with Scott "the driving spirit of literary portrayal."[5] What they render as the feelings and the material circumstances of men and women, Scott sees in relationship to the history of the time, and for him "the great transformations of history" are "transformations of popular life."[6] He thus becomes, Lukács concludes, the "great poet of history, because he has a deeper, and more genuine and differentiated sense of historical necessity than any writer before him."[7]

In all these ways Scott was himself both the product of his own eighteenth-century education and a creative builder upon it. If his teacher Dugald Stewart had convinced him that there is a core of human nature which for all its variety of forms is fundamentally unchanged, his wide reading from youth upward had been seminal in assembling a host of powerful examples of the richness and variety of human behavior. Another of his teachers, the elder Adam Ferguson, had stressed "the multiplicity of forms" of different societies, and Alexander Fraser Tytler had made him skeptical of the tendency to reduce everything to general principles, the excessive systematization of an insufficient foundation of fact.[8] And, above all, the writings of Edmund Burke had made him aware of the power of custom, of tradition, of deep social, cultural, even ancestral forces, in molding men's minds and hearts.

Scott was thus simultaneously both a rationalist who knew how much was irrational in human conduct, and an empiricist who never ceased steadily to contemplate the evidence. His view of human nature involved a radical emphasis on shaping forces that, if present at all in the minds of previous writers, had been no more than latent there. Instead of regarding men as either entirely the same in all ways at all times or as malleable without limit, he insisted that they were both the same and different. Steering a course between the extremes of innate and external determinism, and between fate and free will, he showed his characters as in a thousand ways the result of their heredity, their surroundings, their occupations, and at the same time portrayed the ineradicable essences, even the personal idiosyncrasies, irresistibly asserting themselves through all the impersonal forces. They fuse, as in the work of no novelist before him, the power of the historical past, of the social present, and of the human eternal.

This is the reason for those deliberately paced first five chapters of *Waverley* that have often been undervalued by impatient readers. For a part of their misunderstanding, indeed, Scott's own sense of humor must share the responsibility. In his odd freedom from literary vanity, it amused him to depreciate the talents of the unknown Author, both to those who did not know his identity and to those who did. With *Waverley* he began a long course of demure comment: its opening chapters, he remarked cheerfully, were "tedious and unnecessary," its structure as a whole "managed without much skill."[9] "The hero," he told his friend Morritt, "is a piece of sneaking imbecility and if he had married Flora she would have set him up upon the chimney-piece as Count Boralaski's wife used to do with him." (Joseph Borowlaski was a Polish dwarf who exhibited himself at fairs.)[10]

Readers who desired to be thought discerning but found it troublesome to think for themselves have borrowed Scott's belittlements, and criticism has continued to repeat them. There have been shining exceptions, notably John Erskine, John Buchan, David Daiches, Georg Lukács, Patrick Cruttwell, E. M. W. Tillyard, and most recently Francis Hart, and among the historians G. M. Young and George Macaulay Trevelyan—all of whom have made penetrating contributions to a realization of Scott's true achievement. But writers might conclude that a humor of modesty is on the whole more dangerous to their reputations even than a puffed-up conceit. It is hardly an exaggeration to say that half the uncritical clichés of Scott criticism are drawn from his own self-disparagements.

Unbiased readers may see for themselves how little foundation there is for these strictures. The opening of *Waverley* is indeed slow—intentionally so, for it was a fundamental element in Scott's design to begin quietly and gradually accelerate to that torrential rush of narrative which rises to the clangor of battle at Prestonpans and reaches a climax in the grim row of rebel heads impaled above the gates of Carlisle. But, more important still, these five chapters are establishing the influences that render inevitable the young Edward Waverley's responses to all his later experiences. His dual heritage, the Hanoverian connections of his father, the Whig politician with his positions under government, and the ancient loyalties of the baronetcy of Waverley Honour, the dormant sympathy of his Tory uncle Sir Everard Waverley for the dethroned Stuarts—all combine to insure that in a public crisis the young man will be torn between opposing forces.

Thus, far from being irrelevant or unnecessary, the details of Waverley's dreamy youth draw the lines of that imaginative character that will make him susceptible to the romantic appeal of the Highlands, the magnetism of Fergus MacIvor, the lofty nobility of Flora, and the devoted loyalties of the Stuart cause. His long hours in the Gothic library at Waverley Honour, the magic landscapes of Ariosto, Tasso, and Spenser's *Faerie Queene*, the "splendid pages of Froissart," the courtly glitter of Brantôme, and those "female forms of exquisite grace and delicacy" mingling "in his mental adventures"[11] are all destined to bear their fruit when Waverley finds himself in the banqueting hall at Glennaquoich, beside the waterfall listening to the notes of Flora's harp, and beset at Holyrood by the blandishments of the young Chevalier.

Justice has hardly been done, furthermore, to the balanced and realistic detachment with which Waverley's character is portrayed. Though much of it has roots in the youthful Scott, the mature novelist sees his hero quite clearly, even with a certain irony, in his weaknesses as well as in his virtues. Waverley's lack of self-discipline, his failure "in habits of firm and assiduous application,"[12] his proneness, not to the absolute delusion of Don Quixote, but to coloring reality with his own imagination, his pliability under the urgings of strong personalities who know their own purposes and seek to mold his conduct—these are to be the sources of all his vacillations and misadventures.

Scott shows Flora and Fergus MacIvor, too, understanding him better than he understands himself. Not all Flora's judgments, to be sure, reflect Scott's, but many of her perceptions do. She pays tribute to Waverley's bravery, delicacy of feeling, and sense of honor and therefore refuses to wed him without love, as for the Stuart cause she might not hesitate to do with a coarser man who would neither observe nor care. But Waverley, she feels, deserves better than a loveless marriage, and his is not her world of heroic and tragic dedication. "High and perilous enterprise," she tells Rose Bradwardine with a trace of scorn, "is not Waverley's forte." He belongs "in the quiet circle of domestic happiness" at Waverley Honour, refitting its library, rearing garden temples, and repeating verses "to his beautiful wife, who shall hang upon his arm"[13]—*shall*, because Flora has already determined that he must marry Rose, who will give him the love he merits.

Flora's brother Fergus, with less scrupulosity, has not hesitated to play on Waverley's pliancy and entrap him into offering his services to Prince Charles Edward. But he too responds to Waverley with esteem and friendship, and when he sees his own ambitious schemes crashing into ruin, refuses to involve him any further. Though the two men had previously quarreled over Rose Bradwardine, he now generously urges Waverley to ask her hand. "She loves you," he tells Waverley, "and I believe you love her, though perhaps you have not found it out, for you are not celebrated for knowing your own mind very pointedly." "He said this," the narrative adds, "with a sort of smile."[14] So remote from Scott's purpose is it to make us see his central character as a hero of romance.

*Waverley*, in fact, for all its epic sweep, wild scenes, and clashing drama, is not a romantic novel at all but an ironic novel of a young man's education. Its hero, as E. M. W. Tillyard notes, begins as an "innocent let loose upon the world" and ultimately becomes "the young man who grows up. He is the young romantic, slightly ridiculous as well as generous, who gradually sheds his illusions through the discipline of crude and genuine experience."[15] Far from being the romantic hero of a romantic tale, Waverley is the realistic protagonist of a realistic novel.

These facts Scott constantly emphasizes for us with touches of subdued comedy. How different from the sentimental novel is his treatment of Waverley's fledgling infatuation for the rather inelegantly named Miss Cecilia Stubbs, whose charms are so easily swept from his heart by the glitter of his own military gold-laced hat and his broadsword. But Cecilia is not a Rosaline to Flora MacIvor's Juliet; on the contrary, Flora deliberately makes herself the Rosaline to the gentle Juliet of Rose Bradwardine. Here, again, Scott gives us an almost Restoration mockery of the conventions of romantic love. In the scene where Waverley reads from Shakespeare, and the ladies exclaim against the speed and levity with which Romeo transfers his affections, Flora disagrees. "Affection can, now and then," she remarks—and note the qualification—"withstand very severe storms of rigour, but not a long polar frost of downright indifference. Don't, even with *your* attractions, try the experiment upon any lover whose faith you value." And her witty deflation of the enduringness of hopeless love Evan Dhu Maccombich collapses still further with a comic comparison. It is exactly, he says, like Duncan MacGirdie's mare, whose owner tried to reduce her to doing without food, but "just as he had put her on a straw a day, the poor thing died!"[16]

Repeatedly the novel strikes this note. On Waverley's first excited trip into the Highlands his imagination seethes with the romance of his situation: "Here he sate on the banks of an unknown lake, under the guidance of a wild native, whose language was unknown to him, on a visit to the den of some renowned outlaw, a second Robin Hood perhaps, or Adam o' Gordon, and that at deep midnight . . ." But Scott promptly reminds us of the prosaic occasion of the bizarre adventure and Waverley's endeavor to banish the crude facts from his memory: "The Baron's milch cows! This degrading incident he kept in the background."[17] And when Sir Everard and his sister rank Waverley's inconclusive military exploits "with those of Wilibert, Hildebrand, and Nigel, the vaunted heroes of their line," we remember the reality and Flora's less ecstatic insight that "he would never have been his celebrated ancestor Sir Nigel, but only Sir Nigel's eulogist and poet."[18] As the novel is drawing to a close, Waverley himself sees all his tumultuous adventures as a youthful fling: "the romance of his life was ended, and . . . its real history had now commenced."[19]

The detail with which Waverley is portrayed makes it clear that although he is indeed, as David Daiches has noted, a "symbolic observer"[20] of the historical events in which he participates, he is far from being that alone. He is not merely an average young Englishman; he is too sensitive and imaginative for that, and these deeper qualities give his responses a profounder value. Though he is swayed by the conflicting passions of the '45, and its violent struggles—to a degree that makes him wince at a newspaper aspersion on "the *Wavering-Honour* of W–v–rl–y H–n–r"[21]—he is neither a detached onlooker nor a mere piece of flotsam on the wild waves of events.

His divided feelings in essence are exploratory of the issues. He feels committed to the reign of law and justice and of stable government. He hesitates to desert a dynasty that has ruled Britain peacefully for forty years and take the sword for the descendants of a king who forfeited the throne by his lawless tyrannies. His temporary defection is brought about only by an overwhelming accumulation of pressures: his father's disgrace and dismissal from office, Sir Everard's Jacobite sympathies, the injustice of the loss of his own military commission (resulting from the trickery of Donald Bean Lean and Fergus MacIvor's machinations), the beauty of Flora, the glamor of Fergus's personality, and the adroit beguilements of that attractive Prince the young Chevalier.

For all these purposes the structure of *Waverley*, far from being "managed," as Scott said, "without much skill," is superbly contrived. Possibly, as Robert Louis Stevenson believed, the best plotted of all Scott's novels, it is certainly one of his outstanding triumphs in plot construction. The skillful building of the foundation has been already suggested, and the scenes at Tully-Veolan, Waverley's jaunt into the Highlands, first to the cateran's cave, then the meeting with Fergus, the visit to Glennaquoich, and the invitation to the "hunt," all follow by masterful interlinkings. From there on, the story moves with steadily increasing momentum: Waverley's arrest, his recapture by the Highlanders, his journey as a semiprisoner from Doune past Stirling and Linlithgow to Edinburgh, his meeting with Charles Edward and seduction into rebellion, the battle of Prestonpans.

Throughout the last third of the novel, the speed and dramatic intensity mount even higher. There are Waverley's angry conflicts with Fergus, in whose character he discovers more and more flaws, his disillusion with the rebellion and its wrangling leaders, the disintegration of the Highland forces. A significant touch, however, is Waverley's half-comic but nevertheless perilous embarrassment on his journey to London, with the prying Mrs. Nosebag, who almost pierces his incognito; so ludicrous a danger would never disconcert a hero of romance. The trial of Fergus and Evan Dhu rises to epic heights, with Evan's moving plea to the Court that he and five of Fergus's followers be hanged and his chieftain spared. The extraordinary proposal evokes startled laughter among the spectators. Evan Dhu looks around him sternly:

"If the Saxon gentlemen are laughing because a poor man, such as me, thinks my life, or the life of six of my degree, is worth that of Vich Ian Vohr, it's like enough they may be very right; but if they laugh because they think I would not keep my word, and come back to redeem him, I can tell them they ken neither the heart of a Hielandman, nor the honour of a gentleman."[22] When sentence is pronounced and the judge urges Evan to beg for grace, his response is defiant: "Grace me no grace; since you are to shed Vich Ian Vohr's blood, the only favour I would accept from you is to bid them loose my hands and gie me a claymore, and bide you just a minute sitting where you are!"[23]

Hard upon this follows Fergus's farewell to Waverley. "We part not *here!*" Waverley exclaims. "O yes, we do; you must come no further. Not that I fear what is to follow for myself: Nature has her tortures as well as art; and how happy we should think the man who escapes from the throes of a mortal and painful disorder, in the space of a short half hour? And this matter, spin it out as they will, cannot last longer. But what a dying man can suffer firmly, may kill a living friend to look upon."[24]

Then in turn, after Fergus's stoic heroism, comes the voice of everyday reality again, in Alick Polwarth's valedictory on the two Highlanders: "The heads are ower the Scotch yate, as they ca' it. It's a great pity of Evan Dhu, who was a very weel-meaning, good-natured man, to be a Hielandman; and indeed so was the Laird o' Glennaquoich too, for that matter, when he wasna in ane o' his tirrivies."[25]

Scott spends little time on the romantic details of Waverley's courtship. We have soon realized Rose's tenderness for him, and even as early as the beginning of his fancied passion for Flora there had been a hint of his feelings about Rose, when they were "jarred" by the jocular cynicism of Fergus's assumption that he himself might easily make her his bride and himself the master of her inheritance. During the "long polar frost" of Flora's cold indifference, though Waverley still asks, "What is it to me that Fergus MacIvor should wish to marry Rose Bradwardine?"[26] unconsciously those feelings grow. "Upon my word, I cannot understand how I thought Flora so much, that is so *very* much handsomer than Rose."[27] And he observes to himself, "Her manner, upon the whole, is most engaging";[28] "She has a more correct ear than Flora, though a less accomplished musician"; "She has more feeling too."[29]

It is hardly too much to say that although this is all psychologically sound, the narrative tone, far from being that of romance, is coolly realistic, detached—almost mildly amused. And the marriage arrangements Scott chooses to treat not primarily in terms of Waverley's moonlight declaration by the *jet d'eau* in the garden, which is dismissed in a few words, but of Bailie MacWheeble's enraptured exclamations: "Lady Wauverley! ten thousand a year! Lord be gude unto me!" and his legal preparations to make "a sma' minute, to prevent parties frae resiling."[30] This is capped by the Bailie's exultant glee at the technical maneuvers with which he has ousted the Baron's cousin from the lairdship of Tully-Veolan: "I circumvented them; I played at bogle about the bush wi' them; I cajoled them, and if I havena gien Inch-Grabbit and Jamie Howie a bonny begunk, they ken themselves."[31] Here is realistic comedy, not highflying romance.

The voice of reality has never been lost, indeed, throughout all the turbulent drama of the action. It permeates the richly diversified delineation of character, ranging from the rather frigid sanity of Major Melville and the warm sanity of Colonel Talbot—although Talbot is as bigotedly English as Fergus is Scottish—to the humorous oddity of the Baron of Bradwardine, the boldness and passion of Fergus, and the idealism of Flora. What a throng of living and breathing figures they are—the Baron, with his simple loyalty, his Latin tags and quotations from old Scots verse, his pedantic insistence on his feudal right to pull off his Prince's boots, his courage both in victory and in misfortune; MacWheeble and his legalisms; the rascally Callum Beg and the devoted Evan Dhu; daft Davie Gellatley, drooping and bedraggled after the sack of the Castle, but showing a flash of sense that enables him to save his fugitive master, and later dancing in his new finery, rejoicing, "Bra'

Davie, bra' Davie";[32] oafish, quarrelsome Balmawhapple, whose brave death with a cloven skull at least proved, Scott remarks characteristically, what many had doubted, "that the unfortunate gentleman actually had brains";[33] the polished and brilliant Prince Charles Edward exerting all his adroitness to hold his restive and jealous followers in a difficult accord.

The eccentrics, the heroic, and the spiritually elevated among Scott's characters are made authoritatively convincing by being portrayed against a broad background of the normal and average. Their success, as Walter Bagehot notes, depends upon establishing an identity between their extremes and "the ordinary principles of human nature . . . exhibited in the midst of, or as it were by means of, the superficial unlikeness. Such a skill, however, requires an easy, careless familiarity with normal human life and common human conduct."[34] That familiarity Scott demonstrates not only in the creation of "normal" people like Major Melville and Colonel Talbot, and Waverley himself, but also in his full and revealing picture of the entire social background of his story.

Nowhere does Scott show his own balance and sanity more clearly than in his rendering of Charles Edward's desperate attempt to regain the throne for his father. Despite Scott's supposed Stuart sympathies, he does not idealize either the Jacobite cause or its partisans. Donald Bean Lean is a wily trickster, disloyal to both sides, who disobeys the Prince's orders for his own ends and is caught ultimately in his own treacheries. Evan Dhu and Callum Beg are devoted only to Fergus, their feudal chief, and would follow any banner he dictated; Callum would shoot even the Prince if Fergus told him to. Fergus, though brave, chivalrous, free-minded, and sincerely loyal to the Stuart dynasty, is dangerous, dishonest, Machiavellian, callously disingenuous in his methods, ridden by personal ambition, and avid to be created Earl of Glennaquoich. Most of Charles Edward's other supporters are portrayed as contentious, jealous, rent by faction, the clans restrained only with difficulty from tearing each others' throats. The Highland chiefs are self-deceived with the belief that in the event of failure they can safely retreat into their trackless glens. Their Prince himself, despite his alluring qualities, is revealed as a dissembler in dealing with his brawling followers; he comments wearily on the guile entailed by his royal trade.

Only Cosmo Comyne Bradwardine, in fact, and Flora MacIvor are depicted as purely and selflessly devoted. The Baron, for all his simple virtues, is more than a little ridiculous, and Flora is a fanatic. After the retreat north, she bitterly blames herself for having encouraged her brother in a course that could end only in disaster—not that she regrets even then her loyalty to the Stuart claim but that she allowed it to blind her to the wild impracticality of the attempt and the desperate gulf between their hopes and the remote chances of success. It needs no deep study of the particular history of the period and the confused tumult of the '45 to know whether, in this panorama of motive and action, Scott is giving us romance or reality.

That same emphasis on reality marks the few scenes of war and battle in the book. Here, if anywhere, an ardent writer of romance might have allowed himself free rein—fluttering banners, clanging swords, thunderous volleys, rattle of musketry, screaming horses, streaming wounds. But Scott not merely restrains himself in length and melodrama, he restricts himself to what Waverley can see. In this respect it may be useful to note that Scott need not yield pride of place even to such justly admired achievements as the battle scenes in *The Red Badge of Courage* and *The Charterhouse of Parma*. Unlike Crane's hero, Waverley is, of course, no raw recruit, and unlike Stendhal's Fabrice del Dongo, no amateur confused by the meaningless chaos of what turns out to have been the Battle of Waterloo. Waverley has had some training in the art of war. When a party of English cavalry approaches to dislodge Fergus's band, Waverley can "plainly see the standard of the troop he had formerly commanded, and hear the trumpets and kettle-drums sound the advance, which he had so often obeyed." The contrast between "the well-known word given in the English dialect" and the Highland gibberish of the barbarous Gaels around him gives him the sensation of being in "a dream, wild, horrible, and unnatural."[35]

"Waverley felt his heart at the moment throb as it would have burst his bosom. It was not fear, it was not ardor—it was a combination of both, a new and deeply energetic impulse, that with its first emotion chilled and astounded, then fevered and maddened his mind. . . . The clans rushed forward, each in its own dark column. As they advanced they mended their pace, and the muttering sounds of the men began to swell into a wild cry." Then the rising sun dispels the morning mist and shows the two armies closing. "Forward, sons of Ivor," cries Fergus, "or the Camerons will draw the first blood."[36]

But after this brief thrilling moment, instead of going on, Tillyard points out,[37] Scott calmly observes, "The rest is well known" and brings the conflict to a conclusion with a rapid summary: "The battle was fought and won, and the whole baggage, artillery, and military stores of the regular army remained in possession of the victors."[38] Never were the possibilities of sensationalism and spectacle shouldered aside more speedily. It is not the historical battle as such that is the mainspring of Scott's creativity but its impact on Waverley—above all as Waverley is revealed in the feeling of humanity that leads to his rescue of the unknown English officer. The chapter ends on one of Scott's characteristic touches of humor: Evan Dhu's dry dismissal of the death of Balmawhapple—"There was mair *tint* [lost] at Sheriffmuir"—and Lieutenant Jinker's effort to prove that his disaster was not the fault of his mare.[39]

Nothing could therefore be more clear than that it is a mistake to think of Scott primarily as a historical romancer. He is no belated minstrel sentimentally eulogizing the past. Nor is he primarily a historian, though a gifted historian he certainly is, with a superb grasp of the feeling and atmosphere of the times he paints. But above all he is a *novelist*, outstanding in his talent for dramatic narrative and penetrating in the vivid and accurate rendering of human nature. Criticism falls far short of realizing his achievement when it repeats the conventional image of him as the romantic glorifier of a merely picturesque past. Although his materials are often those superficially thought of as "romantic," fundamentally he is an unfaltering and clear-sighted realist.

But his realism was deeply permeated with the sense of history; that is his revolutionary significance as a novelist. He saw history as more than causation, more than logic: it was the struggle between opposing schemes of values. "He was the first artist," Karl Kroeber notes, "to conceive of history as the evolution of competing styles of life."[40] In *Waverley* his analysis of the entanglement of Jacobitism in Scotland's feudal past explores the intricate motivations and total tensions that clarify its tragic failure. "And thus history," Francis Hart sums it up, "becomes . . . a process of individual ordeal caused by personal involvement in the collision. Part of the experience of collision is caused by the felt impingement of the past—any past—on the present—all presents."[41] Such a past is in fact a symbolic present: not only do the roots of the present reach down into that past, in essence its meanings reach up to live in us and its passions are ours.

*Guy Mannering* partakes of this depth. Its point of departure, however, is the effort not to reverse the course of history by reviving the past, but to speed its evolution. Godfrey Bertram's endeavor as a magistrate to enforce the letter of the law tears down established relationships that have entwined themselves in the needs and emotions of the community. His reprisals for the petty derelictions of the gypsies, whom he had long allowed to dwell on his wastelands, represent a thoughtless cruelty that violates a higher law of humanity. He and his family are to suffer for it.

The story opens a bit before Bertram starts on this course. Again, as in *Waverley*, although this time with no account of his previous background, we have an Englishman wandering into Scotland. Getting lost after nightfall in the black mosses of Drumfriesshire, the youthful Guy Mannering comes by moonlight to the ruins of Ellangowan Old Place and huddling beneath its turrets the humbler modern dwelling of its impoverished laird Godfrey Bertram. Mannering is hospitably taken in, and that night Bertram's child, a boy who is named Harry, is born.

As a hobby Mannering has cultivated the art of astrology, though with no real belief in its claims. Idly casting the infant's horoscope, he discovers that according to its rules there will be several precisely marked periods of peril in the youngster's life. Around this prediction—derived both from Joseph Train's anecdote and the story Scott had heard in childhood from his father's old servant John MacKinlay—he had originally intended to build the novel. But his own rationalism could not take astrology seriously; nor, he thought, did it "retain influence over the general mind sufficient even to constitute the mainspring of a romance,"[42] far less of a solid work of fiction. He therefore reduced this element in the design to a mere picturesque strand. The main focus of the story is not on fate but on justice—the downfall of Bertram's ancient house and its ultimate restoration.

While Bertram sees his patrimony dwindle away, he bolsters his self-esteem by obtaining appointment as a magistrate. Like many weak and previously easygoing men, he takes his new dignity solemnly and distinguishes himself by his severity. He heavily fines poachers and orchard breakers, sends beggars to the workhouse, prosecutes wandering pedlars. He helps the revenue officers harry the smugglers, drives the gypsies from his estate. Though the west coast of Scotland is more orderly than it had been a generation earlier, it is not ready for this rigor of law enforcement. His neighbors surprise him by their disapproval, a feeling that the narrative itself shares.

"Even an admitted nuisance, of ancient standing, should not be abated without some caution. . . . We are not made of wood or stone, and the things which connect themselves with our hearts cannot, like bark or lichen, be rent away without our missing them."[43] Housewives no longer have their gossip with the beggars and pedlars, the ribbons and toys they formerly bought, and the pleasure of giving poor mendicants a handful of oatmeal; their husbands are exasperated to be obliged to pay more for their brandy, tea, and tobacco. Everyone sympathizes with Bertram's victims. "Ellangowan, that had been a name among them . . . *him*, to be grinding the puir at that rate!"[44]

Bertram himself feels guilty as he runs into the banished gypsies sullenly hauling their carts from their demolished cabins. They were not worse than they had been when he had allowed them to feel themselves his dependents, and what had he done to make them better? "Some means of reformation ought at least to have been tried, before sending seven families at once upon the wide world. . . . There was also a natural yearning of the heart on parting with so many known and familiar faces. . . ."[45] Suddenly on a high bank above the road appears the wild figure of Meg Merrilies, the Queen of the tribe, her tangled hair streaming from a red headdress, a sapling bough in her extended hand.

"Ride your ways, Laird of Ellangowan," she exclaims, "ride your ways, Godfrey Bertram! This day ye have quenched seven smoking hearths—see if the fire in your ain parlour burn the blither for that. Ye have riven the thack off seven cottar-houses—look if your ain rooftree stand the faster. Ye may stable your stirks in the shealing at Derncleuch—see that the hare does not crouch on the hearthstane at Ellangowan. . . . There's thirty hearts that was hae wanted bread ere ye had wanted sunkets and spent their life-blood ere ye had scratched your finger. Yes, there's thirty yonder, from the auld wife of an hundred to the babe that was born last week, that ye have turned out from their bits o' bields, to sleep with the tod and the black-cock in the muirs! Ride your ways, Ellangowan. Our bairns are hinging at our weary backs: look that your braw cradle at hame be the fairer spread up. . . . And now, ride e'en your ways; for these are the last words ye'll ever hear Meg Merrilies speak, and this is the last reise I'll ever cut in the bonny woods of Ellangowan."[46]

Retribution follows soon. In a clash with the smugglers a revenue agent is murdered, and at the same time Bertram's five-year-old son disappears. The vessel of the smugglers burns at sea and neither their leader, a Dutch captain named Dirk Hatteraick, nor any of the crew reach shore. It cannot be learned whether the child has been murdered, kidnapped and lost in the flaming lugger, or stolen by the dislodged gypsies. Meg Merrilies, traced and questioned, denies indignantly that she would have revenged herself on the laird by doing any injury to the child, whom she has always loved. But the boy remains unfound. Agonized by the loss, his mother dies in premature child-birth, leaving her widowed husband with a baby girl. Bertram has paid bitterly for his clumsy inhumanity.

But he is punished further. In the course of years, more and more of his estate slips into the hands of his unscrupulous law-agent, Gilbert Glossin. It is not without meaning that most of the technicalities Glossin has wrested to his employer's disadvantage are, like Bertram's own harshness to the gypsies, within the law, and that at last, as Ellangowan is about to be sold, Bertram suffers the fate he has inflicted. Ill and broken, he is carried from his house, and dies on the green before his ruined towers.

But Glossin too has been unjust, and from motives not of wounded pride but of greed. The long pendulum of time has reached one extreme of its swing; its counterswing is now about to begin. Mannering returns from a career in India in which he has risen to the rank of Colonel. He is too late to help his old host, but he gives shelter and protection to Bertram's daughter, Lucy. Recently widowed, Mannering himself has a daughter, Julia, a young lady about Lucy's age. In the East, Julia and a young volunteer named Brown have fallen in love with each other, and unknown to Mannering the young man has followed them back to Europe. Though he knows nothing of his parentage except that he is an orphan of Scottish origin, Brown is of course Godfrey Bertram's abducted son.

This "stale romance of the missing heir,"[47] as Tillyard calls it, Scott had derived not from fiction but from the quite recent case of the Dormont heir, which had been before the Court of Session only a few years before. The plot is also, of course, deeply rooted in folklore, but in 1815 it had not become a stock theme of sensational novelists. And instead of trying to keep us in suspense about Brown's identity, Scott suggests it by every device short of outright statement. Remembering that Hatteraick, the smuggler leader, was Dutch, we know who Brown is as soon as we learn that he had been adopted by a Dutch merchant. As in Greek drama the only uncertainty is how the classical recognition is to be brought about.

First, however, Brown must be shown to deserve restoration to his heritage. This is the significance of the brilliant Charlies-hope episodes. Traveling by foot from Cumberland into Liddesdale, Brown saves from footpads a sheep farmer named Dandie Dinmont and accepts an invitation to spend a week at his farm. The warmth of their immediate friendship is a testimony to both. The rude hospitality of the farmhouse, with its hams and bannocks and home-brewed ale, the welcome of Dandie's wife, Ailie, their rosy-cheeked children, and their dogs, the fox hunt on the rugged scaurs, the nocturnal salmon-hunt, are a natural world in which acceptance is an index to character. Brown's stay at Charlies-hope is not a mere interlude and it is not an idyll; it is a touchstone. Brown is revealed to have those human qualities the absence of which cost Godfrey Bertram so dear.

The narrative interest in Brown is thus not that of moral development but of gradual self-recognition. How and when will he recover the memories that the five-year-old child had lost? In a lonely alehouse he meets Meg Merrilies, now an old woman. She stares at him and mutters to herself, "The laird's dead: aweel, death pays a' scores; he was a kind man ance." "Ye hae a face and a tongue," she tells Brown, "that puts me in mind of auld times";[48] and to him this wild-looking woman seems like something he has dreamed. Later, beneath the crumbling towers that he does not know are those of his own family, he plays on his flageolet a half-forgotten tune and is startled when a girl bleaching linen at a nearby spring takes up what he only then recalls as its words:

> . . . The bonnie woods of Warroch Head
> That I so fain would see.[49]

But not until in Mannering's house, where his former tutor Dominie Sampson sees his resemblance to his dead father, does the full flood of memory burst forth. "Harry Bertram, look at me!" "Yes, that was my name! And that is the voice and the figure of my kind old master!"[50] Under the questioning of the advocate Paulus Pleydell, he recalls the struggle in Warrock Wood, Meg Merrilies saving him from being slain by the smugglers, and his voyage to Holland as a half-starved child. Mannering's horoscope, which without knowing its significance Brown has always worn in a small velvet bag round his neck, supplies the final proof of his identity as Bertram.

Linked with the turn in Bertram's fortunes is another main theme, an inward development in Mannering. He had felt for the young man in India a dislike that was partly scorn of his low mercantile background, partly an objection to his dubious birth, partly jealousy of the interest displayed by his wife and daughter. But even there he had come to feel that he had been unjust. Though stern and overconscious of class differences, he is a man of integrity; he cannot at once overcome his prejudices, but rectitude compels him to work for the reinstatement of the man he now feels he has wronged. And to him, of course, unlike Dinmont, it makes a difference to discover that the obscure Brown is really the heir to an ancient name. As they are brought closer together he warms to the man he is striving to restore to his heritage.

Bertram's return also changes Mannering's relation with his daughter, Julia. He had severely condemned the surreptitious elements in their previous courtship, but now he realizes that his own forbidding austerity had not encouraged Julia's confidence. Though she has covered her tremors beneath an assumption of teasing impertinence, her love has been overlaid by fear. The scene in which he brings himself to an understanding with his child is full of grave tenderness. Julia is embarrassed; she hides it with false courage but breaks down under his gentleness and reproaches herself for her failure to understand him. "No more of that, Julia," he says, "we have both been to blame. He that is too proud to vindicate the affection and confidence which he conceives should be given without solicitation, must meet much, and perhaps deserved, disappointment. . . ."

"Oh, no danger, no fear!" Julia exclaims. Let her but have his approval, she continues, and he cannot prescribe any rule too severe. "Well, my love," he responds, kissing her forehead, with a mingling of affection and irony, "I trust we shall not call upon you for anything too heroic."[51]

The portrayal of the story's two heroines, Julia Mannering and Lucy Bertram—especially that of Lucy—leads to a complaint recurrently made of Scott: that, as Buchan puts it, he "was not often happy in his younger gentlewomen."[52] The impeachment is partly true. When the heroine exists merely to fulfill the reader's expectation of what Scott called "wedding cake," he himself was unable to work up much interest in her, and she remained a rather thinly realized figure. Such young women, however, are not untrue to nature. Most young girls, like most young men, have very little personality save to the fond gaze of their parents or their lovers; they are no more than a kind of amorphous human protoplasm with few qualities beyond that very modest degree of nubility that may suffice to get them a mate. "Let us own," remarks one commentator, "that Sir Walter opened his doors to a good number of bread-and-butter misses. Was it because he had observed that in fact the world holds a large number of pretty and well-behaved young women who are not distractingly interesting?"[53]

In so doing Scott draws from life itself, but he also saw and painted greater complexities. If some of his young women show only the everyday reality we perceive when the feelings are not deeply engaged, there are many more who both possess and are portrayed with vivid qualities and psychological depth. To an alert reader they have variety and personality that may be overlooked by the unobservant eye. Among Scott's three dozen or so young heroines there are of course failures, but they are by no means all alike and are often sharply differentiated, not merely in person but, what is more important, in character.

This is assuredly true, in *Waverley*, for example, of Flora MacIvor and Rose Bradwardine. Flora has none of that impassioned sexuality that writers of romance like to attribute to "dark" heroines. Though she may arouse desire she feels none, and it is even conceivable that she might frighten any other suitor than Waverley. Her fate is tragic, but her tragedy is that of her cause, not of passing her life unwed. Flora can be the bride only of her own idealism; she is one of history's vestal virgins. The timorous Rose violates still further the conventions of romance by falling in love with Waverley even before he is amorously aware of her, and, for all her shyness, is ultimately revealed to have gone far in taking active steps to help and protect him among his perils in the Highlands. That is not the behavior of what Alexander Welsh calls the "proper heroine."[54]

So much cannot be said of Lucy Bertram. She is indeed as dim as our neighbor's daughter and does justify Welsh's label. She does no more than the things expected of her—grieves for her father's death, accepts her fate with resignation, feels gratitude to Colonel Mannering for his protection, proves unwilling to lead on a rich suitor, and when Harry Bertram's identity is discovered responds with a warmth of love found mainly in novels to a brother she has never known. Lucy *is* the colorless figure mistakenly regarded as Scott's norm.

Not so Julia Mannering. Sometimes braving her father's anger, sometimes skirting the verge of insolence, sometimes moving even his gravity to a half-smile as she mocks the innocently unconscious Dominie Sampson to his face, Julia is always her glowing and vivacious self. She is in temperament both pert and romantic, what Scott's age called a "quizz," and even the dignified Colonel melts to her raillery. She irresistibly recalls the lively dark-haired girl Walter Scott married, rallying him on his desire to be buried in Dryburgh Abbey, driving gaily with him over all the roadless wilds of Liddesdale, and startling the solemn proprieties of Edinburgh by sitting in her drawing room even when she had no visitors.

There is no need to labor the extraordinary richness with which *Guy Mannering* paints Scottish life, from the genre pictures of Charlies-hope to the broad comedy of Pleydell frolicking in the Edinburgh tavern among his drinking companions and the mingled satire and drama of the reading of Miss Margaret Bertram's will. The scenes of danger and violence are powerful: Meg Merrilies hiding Bertram from the smugglers at the Kaim of Derncleuch, the escape from the burning jail at Portanferry, the capture of Hatteraick in the cave, and Meg rejoicing even as she dies that Bertram has been restored: "If my curse brought it down, my blessing has taen it off. . . . Stand out o' the light, and let me look upon him ance mair."[55]

Meg Merrilies is one of the great figures in Scott's fiction. Half-crazy, savage, and noble, "she is the fate," Buchan notes, "that presides over the action, an embodied destiny."[56] Her curse, perhaps, brings down Godfrey Bertram's fate upon his head; but she saves his helpless child from death, she knows him at once when she sees him again as a young man, she saves him in the jail and in the cave, and she helps restore him to his name and heritage. Her speech is that of a sibyl and a tragic heroine: "Do you see that blackit and broken end of a sheeling? There my kettle boiled for forty years—there I bore twelve buirdly sons and daughters. Where are they now?—where are the leaves that were on that auld ash-tree at Martinmas? . . . Do you see that saugh tree? It's but a blackened rotten stump now—I've sat upon it many a bonnie summer afternoon, when it hung its gay garlands over the poppling water. . . . It will ne'er be green again, and Meg Merrilies will never sing sangs mair, be they blithe or sad."[57]

*Guy Mannering* suffers as art from the fact that its thematic interest is divided between Harry Bertram's restoration and Colonel Mannering's humanization in understanding. Neither dominates the story—a fact that is reflected structurally as now the one and now the other disappears from the narrative for considerable stretches. This would not matter esthetically if there were a still broader theme that embraced them both; there is not. Godfrey Bertram's impiety, which precipitates the action, is lost and forgotten in a host of character portraits and a broad picture of Scottish life in the 1770s. The pace, though, is so brisk and the episodes so brilliant that in the excitement of reading we hardly notice the flaw. But it is there, and it makes the novel, delightful as it is, a less triumphant achievement than *Waverley*.

The period of *The Antiquary* is the very close of the eighteenth century, almost a generation later than that of *Guy Mannering*, but in it the present is even more dominated by the past. Sir Arthur Wardour, like Godfrey Bertram a gentleman of dwindled means, still looks on the world with all the haughty consequence of his ancient name. He regards with Tory condescension the prosperous Whig, Jonathan Oldbuck of

Monkbarns, a descendant of German artisans, borrows money from him, and resents the plebeian caution with which Monkbarns refuses to lend him more. The only other resource he can think of for repairing his shattered fortunes—just as all his judgments and values are sunk in the entombed past—is to dig in the ruins of St. Ruth's Priory for the family treasure that the charlatan Dousterswivel has gulled him into believing lies buried there. The Earl of Glenallan is still another victim of the past, haunted by sins committed a generation earlier. He leads a life of entombed misery which is nothing but a ritual of grief for crimes in that dead past.

Oldbuck, the titular antiquary of the story, is in part a comic foil both to the Earl of Glenallan's sorrowful immersion in former days and the deluded self-importance Sir Arthur founds on the lost grandeur of his family. Like his study, cluttered with old books and battered curiosa, some genuine, some spurious, Oldbuck's mind is filled with disordered erudition and muddled antiquarian theories, and he is as vain of his learning as Sir Arthur is of his lineage. But the past which for Wardour and Lord Glenallan governs their unhappy present is for him only a jumble of ragbag facts and pedantic crotchets.

Entertaining Wardour at dinner, Monkbarns can grow heated over whether the Picts were Goths or Celts. He writes hobby-horsical essays on castrametation, and standing proudly on the barren soil of the Kaim of Kinprunes, which he acquired in exchange for an equal expanse of fertile cornland, he can imagine he traces the praetorium of Agricola's encampment in an expedition against the Caledonians. "Praetorian here, Praetorian there," breaks in the bluegown beggar Edie Ochiltree, "I mind the biggin o't"[58] (recall building it). The earthwork on which Monkbarns is trying to confer such classical dignity was only a shelter thrown up by the cowherds some twenty years earlier.

For all the delight Edie takes, however, in pricking Oldbuck's delusions, he too is something of an antiquary. "That old rascal," Oldbuck says when he has recovered from his annoyance, "knows more ballads and traditions than any other man in this and the four next parishes."[59] But Edie is no less capable than Oldbuck of inventing antiquities and devising legends, not as a quirk of pride, but rather for the love of mischief or to aid the living.[60] And although he enjoys teasing Monkbarns, he also likes and respects him. "I hae aye said ahint your back," he tells him, "that, for a' the nonsense maggots that ye whiles tak into your head, ye are the most wise and discreet o' a' our country gentles."[61] Edie and Oldbuck are the comedy duo who between them are to solve the problems of the other main personages in the novel.

Around the two cluster a circle whose involvements in the past range from the farcical to the tragic. The Reverend Mr. Blattergowl, the local minister, is one of the only three people in the parish who still cling to wearing a wig; Caxon, the barber and hairdresser, laments the passing of powdered hair. Dousterswivel, the fraudulent German adept, pretends to be able by necromantic arts to locate the buried treasure of the past. Oldbuck's Highland nephew, Hector MacIntyre, is another fool of genealogy, fierily enslaved to the pride of his fifteen unblemished descents. Even Oldbuck himself, for all the mere whimsicality of his antiquarianism, is in a way also a sufferer from the past; the old-bachelor caustic cynicism he likes to assume is the consequence of an early disappointment in love. And at the tragic end of the scale stands old Elspeth Mucklebackit, once a servant of the Glenallans and darkly entangled in their sins, who regards her whole life as a punishment for her implication in their history of incest and death.

The entire novel is thus constructed around the recovery, the redemption, the true understanding and use of the past. The twisted attitudes must be straightened and the mistaken interpretations corrected if the present is to be healthy and free. Nothing, therefore, could be more mistaken than the superficial wit of E. M. Forster's analysis of it, in *Aspects of Fiction*, as a disconnected sequence of melodramatic episodes: the rescue of Sir Arthur and Isabella Wardour from the rising sea, the duel between Hector MacIntyre and the mysterious Lovel, the treasure hunt in the ruins of St. Ruth's Priory, the torchlight funeral of the Countess of Glenallan, the death by drowning of the fisherman Steenie Mucklebackit, the revelation that Lovel is the lost son of Lord Glenallan and neither the child of incest, as the old Countess had deceived her son into believing, nor illegitimate, but the legal heir. Both the melodrama of these events and the comedy of Monkbarns and Edie Ochiltree are in fact essentially fused into the significant action of the novel, which explores the way in which the present is rooted in the past and rectifies the errors of that present by putting it into a sound relationship with the past. Far from being a cluttered ragbag of a story, like Oldbuck's study and his historical lore, the novel when truly understood is seen to have the clearest thematic unity.

This is not to say that it is successful in all its aspects. Lovel, its young hero, has too little real vitality to make intelligible the warm interest that Edie Ochiltree and its elderly hero Jonathan Oldbuck both feel for him. He is, as Waverley and Harry Bertram are not, much more nearly the conventional pasteboard hero that conventional criticism has dismissed all Scott's heroes as being. He is consequently a rather unsatisfactory focus for so much concern among the other characters and his restoration to his proper name and rank a somewhat inadequate symbol of their redemption.

But even Lovel is not completely colorless. He is human enough to be bored by Oldbuck's relentless longueurs about Agricola's camp, though he politely conceals it, and amused by Edie's destruction of the antiquarian's fantasy; later he mildly banters Monkbarns on that comic embarrassment. During the picnic at St. Ruth's when Hector's attentions to Miss Isabella Wardour and Oldbuck's interminable archeological disquisitions prevent him from devoting himself to that young lady as he would like to do, his distraction is humanly real. He understandably resents Hector's snobbish questioning of his right to mingle in a society of ladies and gentlemen. He angrily accepts Hector's challenge to an exchange of pistol shots and will listen no more than his firebrand opponent to Edie Ochiltree's attempt at peacemaking between them. But his love for Isabella Wardour and hers for him are but pallidly realized, and for the most part we neither feel his reality strongly nor care deeply what happens to him.

Part of the trouble, to many readers, may seem to be how Lovel and Isabella talk. Nearly all the humbler characters in *The Antiquary*—Edie Ochiltree, the fisherman Saunders Mucklebackit, the housemaid Jennie Rintherout, Mrs. Heukbane and the other gossips in the Fairport post office—speak a racy and picturesque Scots that cunningly simulates the tone and rhythm of actual speech. Sir Arthur and Monkbarns use an English less tinged with Scottish words, but their utterance is strongly colored with their characters and personal idiosyncrasies. But Lovel and Miss Wardour, like many of Scott's young ladies and gentlemen, employ a formal Augustan very distant from the way in which people generally express themselves aloud.

Hear Isabella Wardour endeavoring to discourage Lovel's suit: "I am much embarrassed, Mr. Lovel, by your—I would not willingly use a strong word,—your romantic and hopeless pertinacity; it is for yourself I plead, that you would consider the calls which your country has upon your talents, that you will not waste, in an idle and fanciful indulgence of an ill-placed predilection, time, which well redeemed by active exertion, should lay the foundation of future distinction; let me entreat that you would form a manly resolution—"

"It is enough, Miss Wardour," Lovel replies;[62] and it assuredly is.

But let us compare her speech with that of the witty heroine in a novel universally and justly admired among its other triumphs for its psychological realism. Here too the lady is responding to an undesired declaration of love: "From the very beginning, from the very first moment, I may almost say, of my acquaintance with you, your manners, impressing me with the fullest belief of your arrogance, your conceit, and your selfish disdain of the feelings of others, were such as to form the groundwork of disapprobation on which succeeding events have built so immovable a dislike; and I had not known you a month before I felt that you were the last man in the world whom I could ever be prevailed on to marry."[63]

Thus, in *Pride and Prejudice*, Elizabeth Bennet rejecting Fitzwilliam Darcy. But although we may smile in passing, the complex structure of Elizabeth's speech does not in the slightest degree lessen our belief in her reality. She has been so firmly established in our minds, and we are so fascinated by her wit and charm, that she might, as she almost does, involve herself in all the convolutions and syntactical intricacies of Henry James, or dazzle us with the aphoristic glitter of George Meredith, and we should still believe in her, as we do in Lambert Strether and Sir Willoughby Patterne.

The truth is, of course, that in imaginative literature all dialogue is a matter of convention and of adjustment to an established atmosphere. Even dialogue that sounds almost stenographic—like that of Ernest Hemingway—does not actually repeat the slovenly, ungrammatical, and elliptic way in which most people actually speak. The gabble of Miss Bates, which so wearies Emma Woodhouse and so amuses us, is a miracle of concision and cogency in comparison with that of the bores who afflict us in actual life. "Realistic" speech is an illusion skillfully devised by an artist who has completely realized his characters and contrived for them an utterance that mirrors their inward natures. Provided this has been done, there is literally no kind of utterance so artificial that it cannot command our credence.

The dialogue at which Scott aims and attains in the highly formal style he gives his ladies and gentlemen is one that completely and precisely expresses the speaker's meaning. It is the way in which people *might* speak if they were clearly aware of every shade of their thought and feeling, knew just which aspects they desired to express and with what emphases, and were capable of articulating these intentions with the most exact precision. It is the way in which we have already found Flora MacIvor and Waverley, Julia and Colonel Mannering, all expressing themselves, but we may well have failed to notice it because they are indeed created characters. If we sometimes do not believe in Lovel and Isabella Wardour, the fault is not in their words, but in the fact that Scott has not imagined them in the deepest part of his artistic being. Our rebellion against their language is only a part of our failure to be engaged by them.

The novel has other faults. For some readers the horseplay of Edie's tricks on Dousterswivel is too farcically out of tone with the more serious parts of the story and Dousterswivel so ridiculously transparent a swindler as to make Sir Arthur exaggeratedly credulous. Even the humors of Monkbarns, entertaining though they may be, are a bit prolonged and overindulged. Edie is too conveniently on hand wherever he is needed, to overhear secrets, foil dishonesty, act as providential messenger, ultimately to serve as counselor, arbiter, and instrument of fate. The story of the Glenallan family, though an essential element in the thematic structure, is brought in so late that it appears contrived and melodramatic; and the long-delayed establishment of Lovel as the heir to the title, when it at last comes, reads like a mechanical *coup de théâtre*.

Nor, though we do not mind either Sir Arthur being saved from

financial ruin or Lord Glenallan being freed from his dark burden of
guilt, has either been so deeply realized that we care greatly about his
good fortune. Wardour has been weak, foolish, extravagant, gullible, and
ludicrously self-important. The humiliation of his exposure before
Monkbarns and the few days of agony in which he fears being jailed
for debt are more than balanced by his recovered prosperity and the
marriage of his daughter to the heir of an Earl. Lord Glenallan has taken
refuge from remorse and grief in gloomy self-flagellation and passive
withdrawal from life. We are told that they have learned from their
troubles, and both express regret for their errors, but in the speedy
conclusion they are given no action that convinces us they have changed.

But in every other respect *The Antiquary* is triumphant. It is rich
in its portrayals of Scottish life, the world of the manor, the burgh
town, the fishermen's huts. It is full of the most varied and vivid pictures
of human nature. Almost all its characters breathe with reality; as
Virginia Woolf remarks, every time we read the story we notice different
things about Oldbuck. "Thus, Scott's characters," she says, "like Shakespeare's and Jane Austen's, have the seeds of life in them." Especially
his peasants: "Images, anecdotes, illustrations, drawn from sea, sky,
and earth, race and bubble from their lips. They shoot every thought as
it flies, and bring it tumbling to the ground in metaphor."[64]

Again and again the language vibrates with colloquial poetry. In
the scene where Sir Arthur and his daughter huddle with Edie on the
ledge of the cliff while the rising waves dash at their feet, the Baronet
desperately offers the old man a fortune if he can find a means of escape:
" 'Our riches will soon be equal,' said the beggar, looking upon the
strife of the waters,—'they are sae already; for I hae nae land, and you
would give your fair bounds and barony for a square yard of rock that
would be dry for twal hours.' "[65]

Or take the words of Saunders Mucklebackit as in dry-eyed grief he
repairs the "auld bitch of a boat" from which his son has been drowned:
"And what would ye have me to do," he asks Oldbuck, "unless I
wanted to see four children starve, because ane is drowned? It's weel wi'
you gentles, that can sit in the house wi' handkerchers at your een when
ye lose a friend; but the like o' us maun to our wark again, if our
hearts were beating as hard as my hammer." In a passion he strikes the
boat's patched side: "Yet what needs ane be angry at her, that has
neither soul nor sense?—though I am no that muckle better mysell. She's
but a rickle o' auld rotten deals nailed thegither, and warped wi' the
wind and the sea; and I am a dour carle, battered by foul weather at sea
and land till I am maist as senseless as hersell."*[66]

*Beautiful and effective as the speeches of Edie Ochiltree and Saunders
Mucklebackit are—and those of Evan Dhu Maccombich in *Waverley* and Meg
Merrilies in *Guy Mannering*—one may wonder if they are much truer to "reality"
than the ordered clarity Scott gives to his ladies and gentlemen. We know ladies

To the surprise of readers who think of Scott as a hidebound Tory, he allows Monkbarns not merely to defend the French Revolution against what he dismisses as the "prejudiced horror" of Lord Glenallan but to reduce that aristocrat to silence: "If a set of furious madmen were now in possession of the Government," Oldbuck says, "it was what often happened in great revolutions, where extreme measures are adopted in the fury of the moment, and the State resembles an agitated pendulum, which swings from side to side for some time ere it can acquire its due and perpendicular station. Or it might be likened to a storm or hurricane, which, passing over a region, does great damage in its passage, yet sweeps away stagnant and unwholesome vapours, and repays, in future health and fertility, its immediate desolation and ravage."[67]

But with the mistaken alarm of a French invasion, the old Antiquary has no doubts where he stands; starting up from his bed in his two double nightcaps he seizes the sword his father used in the '45. Edie Ochiltree is no less martial, and when Oldbuck asks what stake the beggar has to defend, replies with stout patriotism: " 'Me no muckle to fight for, sir? Isna there the country to fight for, and the burnsides that I gang daundering beside, and the hearths o' the gudewives that gie me my bit bread, and the bits o' weans that come toddling to play wi' me when I come about a landward town? Deil!' he continued, grasping his pikestaff with great emphasis, 'an I had as gude pith as I hae gude-will and a good cause, I should gie some o' them a day's kemping.' "[68]

Above all, Scott shows his characters as responding both to the great events that shake a nation and to their personal crises in terms of their own and their country's past. They are molded by the forces that have shaped their native land, by the pressure of the past upon the present. That is Scott's great insight, and no writer before him had attained it with his passion and clarity.

He had made that knowledge the very flesh and bones of his first three novels. Time, and the historical pressure of time, even when their events are not predominantly historical, everywhere dominate them. In a way, indeed, all three are primarily concerned with time—not the private time of the individual, but the public time that makes the world he lives in different from the worlds of his father and his grandfathers. In *Waverley* the Jacobite leaders and the young Chevalier seek to turn time backward to the state existing before the Revolution of 1688; in *Guy Mannering*, Godfrey Bertram tries to move time forward; in *The Antiquary*, Sir Arthur Wardour and the Earl of Glenallan must cease

---

and gentlemen, or what passes for them, and we know that their words, alas, seldom attain these Augustan qualities. But most of us do not know peasants, and have allowed the poets, from Wordsworth to John Millington Synge, to convince us of their eloquence. The poetry of their utterance may be less a datum of fact than a creation of literary art.

living in the past and adapt themselves to present time. And time is thus to loom gigantically through all Scott's future work.

With *Waverley*, *Guy Mannering*, and *The Antiquary*, even more clearly than in his narrative poems, Scott has grasped the theme that henceforth he is to explore in a thousand ways. Hemmed in and propelled in opposing directions by the clash of vast impersonal forces, how is the individual to survive and achieve a meaningful and fruitful life? Among those forces, which are those that come to be a dead hand, which nurture and enrich, which mingle benefit and bane? The *Waverley Novels*, in their long sequence are a tremendous endeavor to grapple with these immemorial struggles of the human spirit.

# PART SIX

## The Great Unknown

## ( 1 8 1 6 - 1 8 2 1 )

# 1

## *Is Not the* Truth *the* Truth?

## *( 1 8 1 6 )*

**D**ESPITE CONSTABLE'S DESIRE to hold on to Scott, he had continued
to feel restive about the financial demands entailed by their association. He had not been very helpful to the printing house: the endless
stream of orders Scott hoped for had proved a dwindling trickle. During
the previous October his partner Cadell had failed to satisfy monetary
appeals from John Ballantyne. "I am afraid," Cadell wrote Constable,
"I have lost us an *Antiquary* or a *Guy*, but most unfortunately . . . I
could not do otherwise under present circumstances. . . . John, to back his
request, sent a note of Mr. S., who says in a *P.S.*, '*I have begun at odd
times the———.*' The words were entirely obliterated, so that I rather
suspect it is something newer even than *The Antiquary* . . . I do not
know if you approve, but I would, I think, do the same over again." So
great a sum as John had wanted "must gravel us more than all the
*Antiquaries* would do us good."[1]

To be sure, Constable had tried to smooth over these difficulties by
suggesting to Scott that he be allowed to bring out a new edition of
*The Lady of the Lake.* Scott agreed but left the arrangements to John
Ballantyne, suggesting that perhaps they might combine it with a
quarto edition of *The Vision of Don Roderick.* "But then Murray is to be
settled with," Scott warned John. "You will of course take care that no
preference is given in the matter which can give offence in Pater Noster
Row."[2] But Scott felt dubious of Constable's affable professions and
determined that he must be taught a lesson. "Dear John," he wrote, "I
have seen the great Swab who is supple as a glove & will

"Do ALL which some interpret NOTHING."[3]

Early in April, therefore, Scott instructed James Ballantyne to open confidential negotiations with William Blackwood.[4] James solemnly began by pledging the bookseller to breathe not a syllable of his proposal to anyone but John Murray. He was empowered to offer them the publication of a work of fiction, like *Waverley*, of which he was not at liberty to give either the title or the author's name.[5]

Except that it was to be in four volumes, James was nebulously vague about its contents. The work, however, Scott envisioned as "four tales illustrative of the manners of Scotland in her different provinces" and dedicated "To his loving countrymen, whether they are denominated *Men of the South, Gentlemen of the North, People of the West,* or *Folk of Fife.*"[6] "Was it by the author of *Waverley*?" Blackwood asked. The author chose to remain veiled, repeated James; people must form their own conjectures about his identity. He went on to outline some of the terms: the book to be printed by the following October, the author to have half-profits on all editions, the publishers to take £600 worth of John Ballantyne's stock.[7]

The author, Blackwood excitedly wrote Murray, *must* be Walter Scott, "for no one else would think of burdening us with such trash as John B.'s wretched stock." Blackwood tried to obtain other terms, but James insisted that he was instructed not to depart from a single particular. The other novels "had been taken on the same conditions, and he knew they would be greedily accepted again in the same quarter."[8] But James himself professed gratitude for the orders Blackwood had given the printing plant—nearly £1,400 in the past three years—and an eagerness "to accomplish that union of interests which I had so long been endeavouring to bring about."[9] Blackwood felt convinced that the new novel would equal if not surpass the others. He was on fire to close with the offer. But not a word, he reminded Murray, to anyone else!— Ballantyne assured him that they had received the first offer.[10]

Murray agreed with Blackwood that the unnamed author must be Scott. No untried novelist could propose such terms and be sane. He also agreed that they should be promptly accepted. Even though the title page was not to bear the magic words, "By the Author of *Waverley*," a loss that was likely to hamper the first success of the book, it was worth almost any concession to prevent Constable from acquiring a sort of prescriptive right to publish this unrivaled novelist.[11] But James, exceeding his instructions in his eagerness to conclude the bargain, had offered the booksellers more than the terms Scott had carefully determined. Scott promptly demurred.

"James has made one or two important mistakes in the bargain with Murray and Blackwood," he wrote John. "Having only authority from me to promise 6000 copies he proposes they shall have the copy-right *for ever*. I will see their noses cheese first."[12] James had also told Blackwood that the publishers might see the first two volumes in print and "that if on perusal we did not like the bargain," Blackwood told Murray, "we should be at liberty to give it up."[13] "No such thing," said Scott decisively, "—a bare perusal at St. John Street only." Furthermore, in payment he must have London bills as well as Blackwood's. Most important of all: "It is NOT stipulated that we supply the print & paper of successive editions. This must be naild & not left to understanding."[14]

If Murray and Blackwood agreed to these provisos, well and good; if not, Constable must be tried instantly, "but he must do more than others since he will not or cannot print with us. For every point but this one I would much rather deal with Constable than any one, for he has always shown himself both spirited, judicious, & liberal & gets off his books faster than anybody, our fathers in the Row not excepted." There was nothing wrong with the great Swab, evidently, that entire conformity to Scott's desires would not splendidly remedy. But he did not propose to accept a particle less than his demands, and they must be met at once; there was "no use in suffering the thing to be blown upon." Great things must be done, for this was to be "a new cast . . . of the net which has hitherto made such miraculous drafts."[15]

An approach to Constable proved unnecessary. Murray and Blackwood meekly agreed to all Scott's conditions.[16] But he did not intend to be sewed up in their pockets either; within less than a fortnight he empowered John Ballantyne to be his agent in making certain other proposals to Constable. These were for a three-volume *History of Scotland*, originally written for his children, which he believed he could revise and have ready for publication by the following Christmas. Constable was to have the publication of 10,000 copies, giving Scott half-profits and doing the printing with Ballantyne. But there were further conditions. Constable must in the course of the year employ the printing plant for work amounting to £600. He must take over the publication of the *Edinburgh Annual Register*, beginning "with that now at press for 1814," on terms to be arranged, he must retain Scott for its literary management. Finally, Constable must buy "of the above work, Copies or Setts to the amount of one Thousand pounds."[17]

Constable did not as yet know of the agreement Scott had concluded with Murray and Blackwood, but he may have feared Scott was slipping away from him. Although the *Register* had never been the glittering success that both he and Scott had once expected, it had during the last two years turned the corner.[18] It was no longer a white elephant; under skilled financial control—*his* control—it might still do all they had hoped. The *History of Scotland* would almost certainly do well. The small share of *Guy Mannering* to which he had been restricted showed the results of resistance; even some sacrifice was worth making to hold on to the greatest literary gold mine of the age.

Cadell agreed, but felt less hopeful about their purchases. "I enclose a copy of the agreement as to the *History of Scotland*," he wrote. "Do not let L. and Co. off one *bodle* of this bargain. They should as well as we take a share of the burdens attending Mr. Scott and his concerns."[19] He was hardly pleased upon learning that for all their efforts the new work of fiction had already been sold to a rival market at that very time. "This I *will* say, that there was a monstrous want of candour in the Author of these books going past us in the way he has done, when we undertook the *History* and *Register* he should have told us of the other, and his reason for going elsewhere."[20]

William Blackwood, however, was scandalized to hear that Constable had acquired the *History of Scotland*. He did not share Cadell's doubts of its success. And James Ballantyne, he protested, had proposed this identical work to him and promised that he should have it. "I confess," he wrote Murray, "I am sadly mortified at my own credulousness. John I always considered as no better than a swindler, but James I put some trust and confidence in. You judged more accurately, for you always said that 'he was a damned cunning fellow!' . . . If we live a little longer, we shall see what will be the end of all their cunning, never-ending labyrinths of plots and schemes. Constable is the proper person for them; set a thief to catch a thief: Jonathan Wild will be fully a match for any of the heroes of the 'Beggar's Opera.' My blood boils when I think of them . . ."[21]

Blackwood's remarks about Constable are a key to the justice of this outburst. For although Constable was certainly an astute businessman, known in the trade as "the Crafty," nowhere else is it suggested that he was dishonorable, far less that he was dishonest. Nor was Blackwood unable, for the purposes of his own game, to subdue the boiling of his blood. " 'He has need o' a lang spoon that sups wi' the Deil,' and since we are engaged let us try if we can partake of the broth without scalding ourselves. . . . I shall endeavor to the best of my power to repress my bile, and to turn their own tricks against themselves. One in business must submit to many things, and swallow many a bitter pill, when such a man as Walter Scott is the object in view."[22]

In the end, therefore, Blackwood decided that the broth more than balanced the taste of the pill. "I am not over fond of all these mysteries, but they are a mysterious set of personages, and we must manage them in the best way that we can."[23] Employing first James, then John, as his agents, Scott had managed to get Constable, Longman, Blackwood, and Murray all hotly bidding for the unknown novelist. He had now so adroitly balanced their claims that it was the author rather than the booksellers who commanded the situation. Blackwood and Cadell both looked with bitter envy on the plums their rivals had been able to snatch.

For Scott this system of agreements was of enormous utility. It linked his fortunes with no fewer than four of the leading publishers of the age and enabled him, if it seemed desirable, to call upon their good offices. This was no small advantage, for although his own affairs were easy at the moment, economic distress was rising throughout the country. The time might come when he would find it useful to be able to call upon their financial resources.

Ominous signs had first appeared in agriculture. During the long years of war the cost of food had mounted. Farmers bought or rented marginal land at high prices and still sold their grain at fat profits. "On they went bidding over each others' heads," Scott noted, until land values were monstrously inflated.[24] With the defeat of Napoleon, the opening of foreign grain supplies burst the bubble. The poorer lands went out of cultivation; farmers could no longer pay their rents and mortgages. It should teach "the landed interest," Scott observed, "that their connection with their farmers should be of a nature more intimate than that of mere payment and receipt of rent and that the largest offerer for a farm is often the person least fit to be preferd as a tenant."[25]

As the year wore on, conditions grew worse. Distressed farmers were unable to be buyers. Hardship spread into business. Trade stagnated, manufactured goods remained unsold on shelves, factories shut down. Banks all over the country called in their loans; some had already closed their doors and stopped payment. No one, not even the rich, appeared to have any money to spare. Tradesmen's books bulged with bad debts. The journals were filled with bankruptcy notices. One historian summarizes, possibly with slight exaggeration: "The only thing which seemed to sell in the universal ruin were Scott's novels."[26]

People with dwindling resources clamored for the repeal of the 10 per cent income tax, and the Government gave way before the pressure. Scott himself felt that they were wrong in allowing themselves to be bullied. Though he could as readily as anyone else "find some hundred uses for the two hundred which it claws annually out of my pocket," it seemed to him as fair as any tax and superior to most.[27] "With a certain relief upon the agricultural interest which might be compensated by severer regulations to prevent the evasions of the commercial it might, from its great amount and facility of collection, stand instead of the less productive & equally oppressive taxes which may be put in its place."[28] "I foresee the extreme shake which the rejection will give to public credit already staggered."[29]

These reflections were sharpened by the contrast between the dark present and the shining hours of 1814 when all Europe had been aglow with victory. He had just finished the military history of that year for the *Register* and was ransacking books and pamphlets in French, Spanish, German, and Italian on all its other aspects. He appealed to Constable to send him material on the disputes between the King of Spain and the

Cortes, the rise and progress of "our foolish war with America," the cession of Norway to Sweden, "the internal state of France under the Bourbons," "works on Indian affairs "[30]

In the midst of all these energetic preoccupations, he received a visit from Joseph Train, who had provided him with so much antiquarian information for *The Lord of the Isles* and *Guy Mannering*. Train was an exciseman whose duties usually kept him in the neighborhood of Newton Stewart; the previous June he had tried to pay a call on Scott in Castle Street and been disappointed to find he was in London.[31] Now he appeared, a tall, red-faced fellow laden with gifts: a Roman battle-ax, the head of a Roman spear, an antique purse that had once belonged to Rob Roy.[32]

At dinner Charlotte served a pair of ptarmigans; after dinner Sophia played Scottish airs on the harp. Before breakfast next morning, Train pored over the books in Scott's library and admired the paintings—a full-length portrait of his host, a fine view of the island of Staffa, a portrait of Viscount Dundee, the famous Grahame of Claverhouse. He appeared, remarked Train, looking at that beautiful and melancholy face, much milder and gentler than one would imagine from the stories of his cruelties. "No man," replied Scott, "has been more traduced by the Historians." Might he not, asked Train, be made the hero of a romance as interesting as Wallace or the Pretender? (He did not add that Prince Charles Edward had not long since appeared in a novel entitled *Waverley*.) "He might," said Scott, "but your western zealots" —the Covenanters—"would require to be faithfully pourtrayed to make the picture complete."[33]

Train saw he had found a theme that excited Scott. "And if the story was delivered as if from the mouth of Old Mortality in a manner somewhat similar to *The Lay of the Last Minstrel* . . . ?" he asked. "Old Mortality! Man! who was he?"[34] Momentarily, it seemed, Scott had forgotten his own meeting, some twenty years past, with the old man repairing the Covenanters' tombs in the Dunnotar churchyard. But as Train summoned up the details he himself recalled and promised to collect more in Galloway, Scott's own memories flowed back. With them a flame of imagination was lighted that soared into one of his greatest creative achievements, the novel Scott was to call *Old Mortality*.[35] It would be the second of the four tales to be issued by Murray and Blackwood.

No sooner had the Court of Session risen in July than Scott and Charlotte set out to show the glories of the Highlands to Miss Dumergue and Miss Sarah Nicolson, who had been their guests in Castle Street for several weeks. Scott had some misgivings about the expedition; their kind Piccadilly friends, accustomed only to London and Paris, might not take happily to bumpy roads and bad inns. He therefore limited the tour to ten days, going only to Loch Katrine and Loch Lomond, returning by Bothwell Banks and the Falls of Clyde.[36] His fears were only too well founded. Wind blew and rain fell in sheets. The weather was so infamous throughout the trip that he ruefully echoed the drunken landlord of the inn at Arrochar, "I declare I am perfectly ashamed of it."[37]

At Abbotsford the weather settled into an unceasing tempest for the next month. Their two metropolitan guests cared nothing for scenery or country amusements, which were all Scott had to offer, and "expected *fiacres* at the milestane cross and a pair of oars at the Deadmans heugh. . . . I walked them to death—I talked them to death—I showed them landscapes which the driving rain hardly permitted them to see and told them of feuds about which they cared as little as I do about their next-door news in Piccadilly. Yea I even played at cards and as I had Charlotte for a partner so ran no risque of being scolded I got on pretty well." On August 20 the two ladies departed, "deeply impressed with the conviction . . . that the sun never shone in Scotland." "That noble luminary" promptly came out in "the first fair day which we have seen this month."[38]

Scott had now almost completed the first volume of his four. Given the group title of *Tales of My Landlord*, they would impishly appear under a ludicrous pseudonym. A schoolmaster who sent Joseph Train some traditionary gleanings had facetiously signed his letter with a nickname derived from his use of the birch on his pupils. Scott seized on this as the name of an imaginary editor of the tales, "Jedediah Cleishbotham, Parish Clerk and Schoolmaster of Gandercleuch." ("Cleish" is Scots for flog.) It would be fun to see if readers identified Jedediah with the Author of *Waverley*.[39]

Scott called the opening tale *The Black Dwarf*. Its first 192 pages threw William Blackwood into such a fever of enthusiasm when he was allowed to read them that he was unable to sleep. Before going to bed, he wrote Murray nine quarto pages of rhapsodic comment. "There cannot be a doubt as to the splendid merit of the work. It would never have done to have hesitated and higgled about seeing more volumes. . . . The next relates to the period of the Covenanters. I have now neither doubts nor fears with regard to the whole being good . . ." Exuberantly, a week later, he embarked for London, simmering with excitement about "our book."[40]

There he received from James Ballantyne two printed copies of the completed tale, with assurances that the author was making "rapid progress on the 2d. vol."[41] But when he read the later chapters he was not quite so happy. The story that had begun so splendidly, he felt, limped to but a feeble ending. William Gifford, to whom Murray showed the book, agreed. When Blackwood returned to Edinburgh he learned that Ballantyne too had shared their disappointment. Never one to beat around the bush, he told the printer bluntly that he thought the conclusion should be changed and even ventured to outline what struck him as a better resolution of the plot. Worried for both his own investment and the author's fame, he would be willing himself, he stated, to pay for reprinting the canceled sheets.[42] James passed these proposals on to Scott. His temper shot up like a rocket.

"My respects to the Booksellers," he fired back, "& I belong to the Death-head Hussars of literature who neither *take* nor *give* criticism. I know no business they had to show my work to Gifford nor would I cancel a leaf to please all the critics of Edinburgh & London . . . I never heard of such impudence in my life. Do they think I dont know when I am writing ill as well as Gifford can tell me. . . . I beg there may be no more communications with critics. These *born idiots* do not know the mischief they do to me & themselves. I DO by God."[43]

James, trying to be diplomatic, toned down the language of this outburst and omitted several of its most explosive sentences, although he told Blackwood he was transcribing it verbatim. His version concluded: "I am extremely sorry they showed my work to Gifford . . . They are mistaken if they think I don't know when I am writing ill, as well as Gifford can tell me. I beg there may be no more communications with critics."[44]

But poor Blackwood was appalled at even this response to his well-meant suggestions. "I never had for one moment," he wrote humbly, "the vanity to think, that from any poor remark of mine, or indeed of any human being, he would be induced to blot one line or alter a single incident, unless the same idea occurred to his own powerful mind. . . . I trust the author will do me the justice to believe, that it is quite impossible for any one to have a higher admiration of his most extraordinary talents . . ." As for Murray's having shown the story to Gifford, "Mr. G. is the only friend whom he consults on all occasions, and to whom his most secret transactions are laid open. He gave him the work, not for the purpose of criticism, but that as a friend he might partake of the enjoyment he had in such an extraordinary performance."[45]

It was not long, however, before Scott had recovered his good humor and was able to laugh about his own annoyance. Blackwood ought to know, he joked, "that if he consults critics before books are printed, the authors must necessarily look on it as tormenting them before their time." And Gifford, Scott added, thought everybody had leisure "to sit hatching their eggs for ten years as he does over Ben Jonson."[46] *The Black Dwarf* was done with, critics or no critics; unlike Gifford, Scott worked rapidly, though he had subjected his current book to a change of plan. The memories lit by Joseph Train had caught fire—the pale haughty courage of Claverhouse, the cruel persecution of the Covenanters and their dour fanaticism, the lonely landscape of seventeenth-century Scotland, its bleak moors and hills rolling vast from isolated castle to tiny village and remote manor. His second tale, *Old Mortality*, was growing as his imagination glowed. It would fill a full three volumes. *Tales of My Landlord* would not, therefore, contain four tales but be limited to two. "I finished the half of Vol III," Scott reported, "in four rainy days."

After a summer that was the worst in memory, rain had in fact continued pelting down almost all autumn.[47] For all this, Scott had been glad to welcome Morritt ("though you dont vote for the income tax")[48] for a prolonged visit to Abbotsford in September. "I think (barring downright rain) I can promise you some sport of one kind or other."[49] Although the unhappy climate continued to weep, they did have rural exercise. "I hope," Scott wrote after Morritt had returned home, "this will find you well recovered of all the colds and wettings which you caught in the land of mist and snow, and not quite shivering when you think of the banks of the Tweed."[50]

During October there was a flurry of discord between Scott and James Ballantyne. Part of James's original capital in the printing business had been in the form of a £600 loan from his brother Alexander. James had tried to protect his brother by suggesting that he be given a mortgage on the plant in Foulis Close. When Scott refused his consent, James pointed out that *he* had raised no objection to *Scott's* stipulation that a loan of £1,200 from his brother the Major be covered by a mortgage if he so required. John Scott had not in fact demanded that security, and no such mortgage existed, but James Ballantyne had agreed to it. Why should his brother be denied what Scott had demanded for his own? The circumstances, Scott had replied, were not the same; the Major's loan had been made to the firm, Alexander Ballantyne's to his brother. It was his personal debt, not a responsibility of the business.[51]

Now James Ballantyne was no longer a partner, and suddenly Alexander had a pressing need for his money. James did not wish to bother Scott; he went to John, who undertook to raise the money for him on bills that James signed as the manager of the firm. The first of these, for £200, had fallen due; James was away from Edinburgh, but he had left the money in cash for John to pay. Unfortunately, John had been delayed two days in returning to town himself, the bill had been presented, and was dishonored. Scott was very angry. Here was a debt of James Ballantyne and Company about which he had known nothing. For it to be dishonored was gravely damaging to the credit of the business, to *his* credit. How had it come to exist?[52]

James explained, humbly apologetic. He had provided the money; it was just bad luck that it had not been paid. But that, of course, was not the point. As manager James was still empowered to sign bills for the Company; he was not entitled to use the Company's credit for his personal debts. This view of the matter had not occurred to James, who was aghast. "I protest I never knew I was doing wrong, but thought I was wonderfully clever in getting money without troubling you."[53] "I assure you, Sir, I should very nearly as soon FORGE your own signature as use one which implicated your credit and property for what belonged to me personally."[54]

John tried to take the blame on himself, and pointed out that as soon as he had reached Edinburgh he had sent his clerk to the bank and paid the protested bill. "I was as completely unaware of the impropriety of James's accepting in the firm as himself, or I should not have suggested it. In truth, his own name would have done as well . . . Of course the circumstance will never occur again. I am sure the Bank are satisfied that the money lay for payment from the Saturday preceding."[55] Scott had never imagined that James intended anything dishonorable. In the end, too, he accepted the explanation that he had not realized the seriousness of the irregularity, and his anger cooled.[56]

Early in October the *Edinburgh Annual Register* was published;[57] by the beginning of November, Scott had penned the last lines of *Old Mortality*.[58] The rising tide of his prosperity now revived his cherished but long-delayed plan of making Abbotsford into a small Scottish manor. In the thirty-four feet separating the old farmhouse from the "chapel" containing his guest rooms he projected an irregular connecting structure. There would be a handsome dining room, a little boudoir, and even, at last, a den in which Scott could write alone. "Above I will have two comfortable bedrooms with dressing closets."[59]

A gifted architect named Edward Blore, who had just made designs for his friend Surtee's *History of Durham*, turned out an ingenious plan for Abbotsford with two beautiful elevations, one of the entrance front and one facing the river.[60] In the spacious dining parlor all one wall would be a great bay window looking toward the Tweed and the opposite wall a Gothic window glowing with stained glass. Outside this window ran the greenhouse or conservatory Scott had so long desired.[61] The boudoir was to have windows with armed knights and armorial bearings in the glass, designed by Daniel Terry's wife,[62] and would accommodate on a superb cabinet serving as a pedestal a splendid bust of Shakespeare, the gift of the London cabinetmaker and dealer in antiques, George Bullock.[63] He promised his aid in decorating the interiors and made several casts of grotesques from Melrose Abbey that Scott thought would be delightful for cornices.[64]

Into his little mansion he joyfully intended to build some of the carved stones from the Edinburgh Tolbooth, the old "Heart of Mid-Lothian," long the meeting place of the Scottish Parliament but for the last hundred years the town jail.[65] Now, with the erection of a new jail on Calton Hill, the Magistrates were razing this venerable Bastille and had promised Scott the copestone of the doorway and several niches that had sheltered the statues of saints "till John Knox knocked them down."[66] "Better get a niche *from* the Tolbooth," Scott jested, "than a niche *in* it."[67] He liked to think of his own home being thus linked with the historic past, and "it were a pity the ancient ornaments should be destroyed or thrown away."[68]

The new rooms would double the size of the Abbotsford buildings. Better still, they formed no "cut-lugged bandbox with four rooms on a floor and two stories rising regularly above each other," but rambled picturesquely with all sorts of "*outs* and *inns*," angles and notched gables, "variety and depth of shade." "I have always," Scott confessed, "had a private dislike to a regular shape of a house although no doubt it would be wrong headed to set about building an irregular one from the beginning."[69] This home would have grown like a living thing, thrusting out wings and hollowing into the earth as one of the oaks he loved threw out branches and put down roots. It was almost lucky that he had lacked the money in 1812 to build a new house at once. But now the *Tales of My Landlord* would provide a great lift and "help out these mighty operations against they are set agoing."[70]

Before the end of November, in fact, *The Black Dwarf* and *Old Mortality* were in boards, and the exultant booksellers, headily sure of success, ordered a second edition even before the four volumes went on sale.[71] Murray thought the work as a whole superior to all three of Scott's previous novels. "You may go on printing as many as you can," he wrote Blackwood, "for we certainly need not stop until we come to the end of our unfortunately limited 6000."[72]

Scott shared this confidence.[73] *The Black Dwarf*, to be sure, although he had refused to alter it at Blackwood's behest, was, he agreed "wishy-washy enough."[74] He had begun it well, "but tired of the ground I had trode so often," he confessed to Lady Louisa Stuart. "So I quarrelled with my story & bungled up a conclusion as a boarding school Miss finishes a task which she had commenced with great glee & accuracy."[75] But *Old Mortality*, he thought, was "the best I have yet been able to execute."[76] "The subject," he told Daniel Terry, ". . . lies among the old Scottish Cameronians—nay, I'll tickle ye off a Covenanter as readily as old Jack could do a young Prince . . ."[77] His treatment, he well knew, was "full of the strongest light & shadow, all human passions stirr'd up & stimulated." "I am complete master of the whole history of these strange times both of persecutors & persecuted so I trust I have come decently off for as Falstaff very reasonably asks is not the *truth* the *truth*."[78]

Terry and Lady Louisa had now been added to the company of those who knew the secret. Terry disagreed with Scott's censure of *The Black Dwarf*; he thought Elshender "a very interesting person." But *Old Mortality* was Nature itself: ". . . from Balfour of Burley to Guse Gibbie I dwell upon them all . . . as upon people whom I have known and events that I have shared in."[79] Lady Louisa had devoured the two tales: "I got into sleep from a kind of fever of mind . . . It seemed as if I had been an eye & ear witness of all the passages, and I could not lull the agitation into calmness."[80]

Though the Marchioness of Abercorn and her magnificent lord fancied themselves Scott's patrons, they were not members of the inner circle, and she bombarded him with bewildered guesses about the new literary sensation. Could these novels, she asked him, have been written by Mr. Mackenzie? "I cannot even imagine whom you mean," Scott replied, "by Mr. Mackenzie as the author of the *Antiquary*. I should think my excellent old friend Mr. Harry Mackenzie . . .was too much advanced in years and plunged in business to amuse himself by writing novels and besides the stile in no degree resembles his."[81]

No, no, Lady Abercorn protested; she meant his son. About this surmise Scott expressed equal doubt. "I cannot think it at all likely that Young Harry Mackenzie wrote these books. I know him very well and have no idea that he has either time or disposition to bestow it on such compositions. He is high at the bar and has a great deal too much to do for writing novels. His brother James might be more likely to amuse himself in that way but I think this also is unlikely."[82]

In this same letter he announced that he was sending her Jedediah Cleishbotham's four volumes, "which I am strongly inclined to swear," he added solemnly, "are the production of the unknown author of *Guy Mannering*."[83] In her response the poor lady recurs to the hypothesis that the novels are being written by his brother Tom. Her frustrated voice rises almost to an epistolary squeak. "But who can it be who is capable of such productions and will not own them? I wish it was your Brother with all my heart."[84] Scott, however, continued to be a relentless tease. "If Tom wrote these volumes he has not put me in his secret. He has certainly powers both of pathos and humour . . . but I greatly doubt his possessing the steadiness of application necessary to write twelve or thirteen volumes in the space of two or three years."[85]

Scott did not, of course, seriously expect the Jedediah Cleishbotham disguise to deceive anybody. Only a goose could believe in this schoolmaster whose name meant Jedediah Thwackass of Gander's Hollow. But would his readers realize that Jedediah was another avatar of the ghostly author of *Waverley*? Anyone, to be sure, with a sense of style must see that the two were the same. But how many readers, nay how many critics, had a sense of style? Scott found his joke richly entertaining. There were critics who insisted that the volumes could not possibly be the work of that strange author; they lacked the "constant description of scenery that makes him so tiresome."[86] Other clever critics were convinced that they must, like the *Iliad*, have been produced "by three or four different hands" working together; they "could point out traces of the patch-work, which it was perverseness or want of taste not to distinguish."[87]

The dispute raged on, to Scott's enormous enjoyment. People were delighted to exalt the new unknown over the head of his admired predecessor. And, above all, "The murder is now out, and it does not signify disputing," Lady Louisa wrote Scott in high amusement. "Mrs. Thomas Scott," it was reported, "owns all the four books to be hers, with some help from her husband, and some licking over by her brother-in-law. *Verily I think the 'oman be a witch indeed I do spy a great peard under her muffler.*"[88]

In the midst of all this, the volumes sold merrily. Within six weeks, both editions of *Tales of My Landlord* were exhausted and a third was in the press.[89] John Murray was ecstatic. "Although I dare not address you as the author of certain *Tales*," he wrote Scott, "—which, however, must be written either by Walter Scott or the devil—yet nothing can restrain me from thinking that it is to your influence with the author of them that I am indebted for the essential honour of being one of their publishers. . . . I never experienced such great and unmixed pleasure in all my life as the reading of this exquisite work has afforded me; and if you witnessed the wet eyes and grinning cheeks with which, as the author's chamberlain, I receive the unanimous and vehement praise of them from every one who has read them, or heard the curses of those whose needs my scanty supply would not satisfy, you might judge of the sincerity with which I now entreat you to assure the author of the most complete success.[90]

"After this," Murray went on, "I could throw all the other books which I have in the press into the Thames, for no one will either read them or buy. Lord Holland said, when I asked his opinion: 'Opinion? we did not one of us go to bed all night, and nothing slept but my gout.' . . . Heber, who found it on his table on his arrival from a journey, had no rest until he had read it." Frere, Hallam, Boswell, William Lamb, all agreed that it surpassed all other novels. Gifford said he had never read anything like it; his admiration increased every time he thought of it. "Lord Glenbervie came to me with tears in his eyes. 'It is a cordial,' he said, 'which has saved Lady Glenbervie's life.' . . . Heber says there are only two men in the world, Walter Scott and Lord Byron. Between you, you have given existence to a third."[91]

# 2

---

# *The Grim Skeleton*

## *( 1 8 1 6 — 1 8 1 7 )*

SCOTT SEEMED TO MOVE from triumph to triumph. Whether as the anonymous author of the *Waverley Novels* or as the schoolmaster of Gandercleugh, whatever he wrote met with acclaim. But it had been accomplished at a cost of relentless and unflagging toil. In Edinburgh he spent endless hours seated at the Clerks' Table and his own desk in Castle Street; at Abbotsford he rose at five, wrote till noon, and crowded the rest of the long day with physical activity. He hobbled vigorously over the hills in all weather, splashed through streams, spent whole afternoons in soaked clothes. How long could his energies support such reckless demands? How long could he perform such prodigies of exertion?

During this winter, indeed, he began to be plagued by cramps in his stomach. These bouts of discomfort he silently submitted to, "endured as man of mould might," he said later, "and endeavoured to combat by drinking scalding water."[1] But he cast around in his mind for some way to cut down on his labors. There was no reason, as a number of his friends had suggested, why he should not aspire to some legal post of less toil and more prestige.[2] No doubt the notion of his youthful friend Kerr of Abbotrule that he might one day be Lord President Scott had long since become only a dream, but surely he was a sound enough lawyer to merit a seat on the Bench. He might even enjoy what Jeffrey called "the dignified ease of a Baron of Exchequer."[3]

The salary was no great object; it was only £400 a year more than he would relinquish as Clerk of Session and Sheriff of Selkirkshire. "But there is a great difference in rank and also in the leisure afforded by a Barons situation, and a man may without condemnation endeavour at my period of life to obtain as much honour and ease as he can handsomely come bye." He was acceptable, he felt sure, to the Chief Baron, his old patron Robert Dundas of Arniston. And there was no one else "making violent love to this situation."[4]

So he put it, in appealing for the support of the Duke of Buccleuch. His Grace entirely agreed that Scott's hopes were more than reasonable. His legal qualifications were respectable, the political party in power were his friends, and he was the most famous of living Scotsmen. But the Duke's own influence at the moment was of dubious strength. "To say the truth," he told Scott, "I am little inclined to apply to the present Government after the rebuff I got about the situation of Lord Register— a rebuff which I may forgive, but can never forget. What I should most dread in the present instance is some smothered promise to the Lord knows whom for the reversion of the office." Scott might depend, however, "upon my best endeavours."[5]

Scott knew, of course, that he must wait for a death or resignation to create a vacancy. And then his first and most natural channel of application would be the Chief Baron. But when the time came he believed his chances would be good; he stood well at Carlton House and he ought to have the support of the Scottish members of the Cabinet, "who naturally will desire to *give their own fish-guts to their own Seamaws*." His promotion, furthermore, would yield the Government two more posts to hand out. "In other respects I may plead that I served the public six of the best years of my life for nothing. . . . And so enough of this selfish scribbling . . ."[6]

Everything done on the matter that could be done, Scott turned his attention in other directions. He did not diminish by one bit the multitude of his undertakings. He had not allowed himself to be caught by Murray's fishing letter about the paternity of the *Tales of My Landlord*. "I have a mode of convincing you that I am perfectly serious in my denial—pretty similar to that by which Solomon distinguished the fictitious from the real mother—and that is, by reviewing the work, which I take to be an operation similar to that experiment of quartering the child. But this is only on condition I can have Mr. Erskine's assistance, who admires the work greatly more than I do . . ."[7]

Scott had a good deal of fun concocting this anonymous article with Erskine, and in the offices of the *Quarterly Review* it was regarded as a great joke.[8] Most of Scott's own part of it he devoted to illustrating the period of *Old Mortality* from contemporary sources, but he also defended the novel against the angry outcry of Dr. Thomas McCrie, the biographer of John Knox, that it gave a biased caricature of the Covenanters.[9] This accusation Scott considered a mere piece of Presbyterian touchiness. At first he had not intended even to read McCrie's attack. "I own I have my suspicions of that very susceptible devotion which so readily takes offense: such men should not read books of amusement; but do they suppose, because they are virtuous, and choose to be thought outrageously so, 'there shall be no cakes and ale?'—'Aye, by our lady, and ginger shall be hot in the mouth too.' "[10]

He also amused himself, however, by depreciating the slovenly construction of his own novels, and disparaging their heroes as uninteresting in character and inconsistent in behavior.[11] In *The Black Dwarf* the explanation of Elshender's conduct was "too long delayed from an obvious wish to protract the mystery" and "at length huddled up so hastily, that . . . we cannot say we are able to comprehend more of the motives of this principal personage than that he was a madman, and acted like one . . . We have dealt with this tale very much according to the clown's argument in favour of Master Froth—'Look upon his face, I will be sworn . . . his face is the worst part about him, and if his face be the worst part about him, how could Master Froth do the constable's wife any harm?' Even so we will take our oaths that the narrative is the worst part about the *Black Dwarf* . . ."[12]

This article appeared in the January, 1817, number of the *Quarterly*; in the previous number Scott had reviewed Canto III of *Childe Harold's Pilgrimage*.[13] The poem was so steeped in Byron's personal emotions that the review unavoidably touched upon them. "If you think it likely to hurt him either in his feelings or with the public," Scott wrote Murray, "in Gods name fling the sheets in the fire & let them be as *not written*. . . . No one can honor Lord Byrons poems more than I do and no one has so great a wish to love him personally . . ."[14] Scott even regretted that he had not responded to Joanna Baillie's appeal to intervene at the time of Byron's separation from his wife: "things appeard to me to have gone too far yet even after all I wish I had tried it for Lord Byron always seemd to give me credit for wishing him sincerely well & knew me to be superior to what Commodore Trunnion would call the pigs-kitchen brash of literary envy & petty rivalry."[15]

The *Childe Harold* review was both just and generous. Some of Lady Byron's friends resented it; Byron was deeply moved. "He must be a gallant as well as a good man," he exclaimed to Murray, "who has ventured in that place, and at this time, to write such an article, even anonymously. . . . It is not the mere praise, but there is a *tact* and a *delicacy* throughout, not only with regard to me but to *others*, which, as it has not been observed *elsewhere*, I had till now doubted whether it could be observed *anywhere*. Perhaps some day or other you will know or tell me the writer's name. Be assured, had the article been a harsh one, I should not have asked it."[16] "When I tell you," Byron wrote Moore a week later, "that Walter Scott is the author of the article in the *Quarterly*, you will agree with me that such an article is still more honourable to him than to me."[17]

Toward the end of January appeared *Harold the Dauntless*, published as another work by "the author of the *Bridal of Triermain*." Unlike that poem, with its fanciful Arthurian story, it was an experiment in the manner of the Norse skalds.[18] It had, Constable boasted, "considerable success," but Scott's great days as a narrative poet were past. Scott himself was dissatisfied with it. "I begin to get too old and stupid I think for poetry and will certainly never again adventure on a grand scale."[19] In many of the stanzas of the poem, the rollicking anapests suggested a sort of jollity about rape and rapine:

> Woe to the realms which he coasted! for there
> Was shedding of blood and rending of hair,
> Rape of maiden, and slaughter of priest,
> Gathering of ravens and wolves to the feast.
> When he hoisted his standard black,
> Before him was battle, behind him wrack . . .[20]

In later discussion of his poetical work, Scott dismissed the poem with scant attention, and his judgment may be allowed to stand.

But even in his novels Scott interpolated short poems and fragments of verse as chapter headings. In the course of the years, they came to almost the total length of *The Lay of the Last Minstrel*, *Marmion*, and *The Lady of the Lake*.

Only in the ballad or the lyric, though, was he ever to write moving verse again. His muse had always been hasty and impetuous, impatient of lingering to steep every line in riches. His way had rather been to seize and ride off swiftly with a carelessly heaped-up and glowing plunder of poetic loot like one of his own forebears bringing home the spoils of a Border castle. At his most splendid, his poems had been half-ballad, half-epic, though not without the deeper tones of both. But what he now most deeply desired to say could no longer submit to the dominion of verse. He needed the broader if more loosely woven fabric of the novel. Instinctively, from the moment he resumed *Waverley*, he knew that this was his grand medium. Henceforth his epics would be in prose.

Oddly enough, however, in a poetic trifle tossed off at the turn of the year Scott anticipates some of the mocking gaiety if not the glitter Byron would later bring to his *Don Juan*.[21] Entitled *The Search After Happiness*, Scott's poem is based on Casti's *La Camiscia Magica*, the widely known tale of the king who is told that his melancholy can be cured only by wearing the shirt of a happy man, and after long search finds that the only happy man he can discover owns no shirt. Scott slyly begins by reassuring his readers that he will not shock their modesty with any of the spiciness of the original novella:

> Yet fear not, ladies, the *naive* detail
> Given by the natives of that land canorous;
> Italian license loves to leap the pale,
> We Britons have the fear of shame before us,
> And, if not wise in mirth, at least must be decorous.[22]

His playful picture of all the medical sages peering and probing into the monarch was written amid his own bouts of stomach cramp and doses of hot water:

> Physicians soon arrive, sage, ware, and tried,
>     As e'er scrawl'd jargon in a darken'd room;
> With heedful glance the Sultan's tongue they eyed,
> Peep'd in his bath, and God knows where beside
>
> . . .
>
> More and yet more in deep array appear,
> And some the front assail, and some the rear;
>
> . . .
>
>     And then in solemn accents spoke their doom,
> "His majesty is very far from well."[23]

This "doggerel tale,"[24] as he called it, Scott gave John Ballantyne for a little weekly pamphlet named *The Sale-Room* which he began publishing at the beginning of the year, and the poem appeared as No. 5 on February 1.[25] John was now in high fettle. "Another year finds me the same man in the same mood, and wholly unchanged except in external circumstance," he wrote in his *Diary* on New Year's Day; "moving in my little library at Patriot Hall; Poll in firm health chattering on his table beside me." How glorious it was to be able to write, "Dined with James—told him as a matter of course to reckon on me next week for £400." But in March came an even more magnificent entry—"purchased myself a proprietary in the Bank of Scotland!"[26]

James Ballantyne too was prospering. Although he was no longer a partner in the printing plant, his salary was £400 a year, and Scott rewarded both him and John handsomely for their services as his literary agents. Toward the end of March, in partnership with his brother and Scott, James bought the *Edinburgh Weekly Journal* for £1,850, a bid of just £20 more than was offered by William Blackwood. James assumed the editorship of this newspaper, and John wrote its dramatic criticism. It brought its proprietors profits of around £600 a year.[27]

The passing months had brought no relief to Scott's health. His repeated cramps grew worse, and he did not help them by persisting in his established alternations of sedentary labor and violent exercise. At Abbotsford during the Christmas holidays he was outdoors during the stormiest weather. Walking on the steep bank above Cauldshiel Loch in a fury of wind and rain, he was nearly blown over the brink when the gale got under his plaid.[28] Before his return to Edinburgh he endured three nights of agonizing cramp, which "threatened to send me out of this excellent world."[29] During the course of January and February, cramps recurred with increasing violence.

On the night of February 28 he had a seizure so torturing that he fainted. He passed a sleepless night in such pain that it took all his self-control, he wrote Joanna Baillie, not to "groan, roul, and roar like a Bull calf." "Truly I thought the grim skeleton was about to take my harp out of the Minstrel's hands."[30] Nevertheless, he rose the next day and performed his duties in Court as usual. He did, however, write an appeal to Joanna's brother, Dr. Matthew Baillie, for his advice.[31]

Before any reply could reach him there was a crisis. On Tuesday, March 4, he had seemed enough recovered to dine at Dalkeith. But during the evening he again felt unwell and, declining to stay all night, as he usually did, returned home. At midnight came another attack that kept him in agony and Charlotte in terror for all the rest of the night. But Scott still refused to surrender. Next day, after lying in bed until two, an indulgence he had not allowed himself for thirty years, he resolutely dressed for dinner. Tom's wife was with them on a visit from Canada that was ending the following day, and they had planned a little farewell party; it would be a shame to spoil the evening's fun.[32]

Dinner was merry. The family and their guests, among them James Ballantyne, Hogg, and Mrs. Henry Siddons, still surrounded the candle-lit table at nine o'clock. Suddenly Scott was assailed by such excruciating torture that he was unable to suppress a scream that electrified them all.[33] He staggered upstairs and was put to bed, "roaring," he said, "like a bullcalf," and "having broken up the good company in most admired disorder." His great wolf-hound Maida "clamored wildly and fearfully . . . and could hardly be got out of the room." From his bed Scott sent down word begging that the party go on; it would do him good, he insisted feebly, to hear Mrs. Siddons sing. But the guests left, and doctors arrived and closeted themselves with the sufferer.[34]

Ballantyne turned from the door in trembling agitation. As he and Hogg walked down Castle Street, "I have often seen him look jaded of late," he observed mournfully, "and am now afriad it is serious." Hogg was all the more appalled because James had spoken his own fear. "Haud your tongue," he exclaimed wrathfully, "or I'll gar you measure your length on the pavement! you fause down-hearted loon that you are! Ye daur to speak as if Scott was on his death-bed! It cannot be! It *must* not be! I will not suffer you to speak that gate."[35]

But despite the Shepherd and despite the doctors Scott grew worse. During the night his diaphragm became dangerously inflamed. Every medicine he was given his stomach rejected. "All sorts of remedies were applied as in the case of Gil Blas's pretended colic but such was the pain of the real disorder that it out-devild the doctors hollow. Even heated salt which was applied in such a state that it burnd my shirt to rags I hardly felt when applied to my stomach."[36] Finally "the men of art had recourse to profuse bleeding and liberal blistering. This brought the disease to reason after about four and twenty hours much of which was spent in such acute agony that what intervals of rest intervened felt like the sleep of the poor Indian during the intermissions of his torture. The medical gentlemen used me as monarchs do a rebellious province, and levied such exactions of my blood and bones as I shall not forget in a hurry I promise you."[37]

The malady proved to be gallstones.[38] There was at that time no surgical treatment for the disorder, and the doctors were unable to deal with its roots. They could only keep on bleeding and blistering, while Scott gasped, he said, "in the Clown's universal exclamation of 'O Lord Sir!' "[39] These drastic and bloody countermeasures left him feeling "totterish" and weak as water. "My head is still as giddy as a top and I have been these five or six days endeavouring to get rid of the consequences of the remedies."[40] But somehow or other, though limp and enfeebled, he survived both his illness and its treatment and was willing to credit the doctors for the outcome. "They beat off the foul fiend and I am bound to praise the bridge which carried me over."[41]

He was then put on a diet, forbidden meat, restricted to porridge for breakfast, and limited in his allowance of wine. "They tell me . . . I must renounce every creature-comfort as my friend Jedediah calls it. As for dinner and so forth I care little about it—but toast and water and three glasses of wine sound like hard laws to me."[42] In reality, though, he did not mind very much: "I never drank wine to intemperance and am totally indifferent about the meat I eat so that I shall comply regularly being like Master Christopher Sly loath to fall into my *tantrums* again."[43] But he refused to swallow panada, a gruel of bread boiled to a pulp in water and flavored with currants or nutmeg; he spurned "all foreign slops," he insisted firmly, "and adhered to our ancient oatmeal manufacture."[44]

For a considerable time he "could neither stir for weakness and giddiness nor read for dazzling in my eyes nor listen for a whizzing sound in my ears nor even think for lack of power of arranging my ideas."[45] As March drew on, however, he began to mend. Slowly and cautiously he started to work again. "My head," he admitted, "is still Whiggiggish."[46] For John Kemble, who was making his farewell appearance on the Edinburgh stage, he wrote a poetic address, which the actor gave before a sobbing and cheering audience at the end of a superb performance of *Macbeth* on March 29.[47] For Daniel Terry, who had named an infant son after Scott, he sketched out a melodrama that he designed as a gift for his godson. The action would begin with the midnight arrival of a phantom cavalcade at a ruined Galloway castle and a ghostly banquet in its baronial hall. He felt sure, he told Terry, that when his health had been restored by outdoor air and exercise, he would be able to write it in a fortnight.[48]

He was eagerly looking forward to being at Abbotsford in April and getting started on the additions to the house. Through Terry he had been introduced to an architect named William Atkinson, who also became the Duke of Buccleuch's architect at Bowhill. Blore's plans for Abbotsford were thrown out, and Atkinson made an entire new design. The greenhouse, according to his plan, would be built out from a passage, so that one need not go through the dining room to reach the bedrooms in the Chapel. Scott's books were growing so numerous that he would install bookcases in the dining room as well as in the study. The best bedroom should have a large double dressing room. The southern bedroom would become Charlotte's, "and from the dressing room thereof will I myself sally to my morning walk on the leads."[49]

The country was still so gripped in an iron frost at the end of March[50] that Charlotte worried about Scott's going to Abbotsford. "I am sure that the *charms of his Bog* would tempt him to remain out in the cold and wet the worse thing for him but trust soon that he will be as well as ever."[51] And he continued to have "some recurrence of my vile spasm with an oppressive pain in my chest."[52] But he was longing to plant his foot once more upon the heather.[53] On April 13, though he still had bouts of great pain, he was once more on the banks of the Tweed.[54] With him came Maida, bounding over the whin and sniffing in the gorse, and a "leetle poopy dog" recently given Scott by Terry.[55] This was a greyhound pup at first named Marmion but later renamed Hamlet because of his inky black coat.[56]

For a neighbor and tenant Scott now had his old companion William Laidlaw, who had lost so heavily in the agricultural decline of the preceding year that he had been obliged to give up the lease on his Mid-Lothian farm.[57] Scott invited him, "till some good thing casts up," to make himself and his family comfortable at Kaeside. "Without affectation," he assured Laidlaw, "I consider myself the obliged party in this matter—or at any rate it is a mutual benefit, and you shall have grass for a cow and so forth—whatever you want. I am sure when you are so near I shall find some literary labour for you that will make ends meet."[58]

Nearby, soon, Scott hoped, would also be Adam Ferguson, his friend since schooldays. In 1810 Scott had bought from his neighbor John Usher a glen called Dick's Cleuch,[59] "a strange secluded ravine full of old thorns, hazels, guelder roses, willows, and so forth, with a dashing rivulet."[60] Now Usher also agreed to sell Scott his property of Toftfield, which in addition to the old house of that name had a good new house not far east of Abbotsford.[61] The glen bordered on Huntly Wood and was, Scott believed, that very Huntly Bank where Thomas the Rhymer, in the ballad, was supposed to have met the Queen of the Fairies. The little ravine he had renamed the Rhymer's Glen, and the new house, on the suggestion of the Fergusons, he named Huntly Burn.[62] Here Adam would dwell with his two sisters and be a jolly neighbor. "The garden seems to be very nicely arranged indeed,"

Scott wrote him, "& I trust is as well sown & stocked. The new fence is in great measure up and gives you a very pretty paddock . . ."[63]

As the ground thawed, Scott was ready to lay the foundations of his own addition.[64] His imagination seethed with his plans. The outside was to be "in the old fashioned Scotch stile" with "notch'd Gable ends & all manner of bartizans."[65] Perhaps at the center of the old farmhouse he would throw out three sides of an octagon which would become square, like an old border tower, as it rose over the roof of the building.[66] The niches of the Tolbooth would fit beautifully into this tower, two of its massive triangular stones carved in fleurs-de-lis, and thistles would crown the summit, and "the gate of the Parliament house with a carved lintel having the crown & cypher of Charles 1st" would form a splendid entrance porch.[67] He also had several scutcheons from the College and a chance of obtaining from "the west sides of St. Giles's church . . . a projecting octagon window which rests on the shoulder of a kneeling Apostle."[68]

Inside the octagon tower would twist the staircase, and the old stair-hall would be made into a handsome lobby between the parlor and the schoolroom.[69] The drawing room was to blossom out in a wide bay window.[70] Opening by folding doors into the new boudoir another square lobby would become an armory, with Scott's Waterloo cuirasses and helmet, his suit of Gothic mail, and the splendid suit of Indian armor that had once belonged to "the celebrated Jalabad Sing, Son of Nadir Shah."[71] The door from the study into the dining room should be disguised as a bookcase, and within his private apartment Scott intended to have his "whole set of curious Italian Novels," which were "not altogether fit to be left out to everybody's handling."[72] Perhaps, if he found that the new gas lighting had no smell, he would install it throughout the entire house.[73]

Even the domestic offices fascinated Scott's attention. The laundry and wash house he would transform into a servants' hall and kitchen, which would make them conveniently nearer for serving meals; the old kitchen and scullery would become the laundry and wash house.[74] Outdoors his invention ran riot. Possibly he would have a glassed-in grapery as well as the greenhouse for Charlotte's plants.[75] "I am much puzzled how to occupy the space called *Aviary*. Birds are out of the question for Mr. Hinse the brindled cat would clear the colony: besides they would be neglected in my absence—"[76] "I fear the fountain must be given up"; there was not a strong enough water pressure. Though a fountain "might play from the cistern that supplies the water closet," this would provide only a trickle "not worth the expense of keeping it piddling like an old woman."[77]

When the plans arrived from Mr. Atkinson, the masons had already begun "practicing on a piggery."[78] Scott had discovered that his new property of Kaeside had a fine quarry of dark blue whinstone, which he could use for the rubble work. Hammer-dressed and laid in courses, it would harmonize beautifully with the soft gray of the freestone from Sprouston and be far more substantial than stucco.[79] Indoors, the wainscoting and other woodwork must be of oak, "& I will go a fishing for oak trees as I may."[80] He had almost forgotten his illness and was in great spirits as the work got under way.

It pleased him that in these hard times he was able to give employment to so many laborers. Even during the winter, indeed, he had kept more than thirty men working on his land. "This I do not call charity because they executed some inclusive plantations and other works which I could never have got done so cheaply and which I always intended one day to do. But neither was it altogether selfish . . . because I was . . . incurring the expence of several years at once and certainly would not have done so but to serve mine honest neighbours who were likely to want work but for such exertion."[81]

He had made two important changes, however, from the schemes of public relief adopted in Edinburgh. All his laborers he paid by the job, on piecework. He would not let himself be cheated by idlers. "If you do not keep them to their bargain it is . . . forfeiting the very advantage you have in mind—that namely of inducing the labourer to bring his heart and spirit to his work."[82] But it was even more necessary to pay not a penny less than the going rate. Men must not be led to resent their employment as charity or as cheating them out of their just wage, nor should they feel, as some underpaid workers did, "that this sort of half pay" was "not given them for the purpose of working but to prevent their rising in rebellion."[83] Only by making a fair bargain and keeping them to it could you preserve men's self-respect and maintain "those habits which render them honorable and useful members of society."[84]

With his plantations flourishing and his foundation walls rising, Scott now turned his attention to his next novel. He intended to give Constable the first chance at it; since it would delay the *History of Scotland*, he could not fairly propose it to anyone else.[85] Besides, he was a little irritated with the obstreperous Blackwood, who had managed to bring about another jar over the *Tales of My Landlord*. Six thousand of these having been sold by January 31, Scott had given Murray and Blackwood permission to print 3,000 more—a total, he told Morritt, "which will be worth £2500 to the worthy pedagogue of Ganderscleugh."[86] But when the sales then slowed up, Blackwood first instructed James Ballantyne not to hurry with the printing, and a little later told him to suspend it.[87]

The edition, James replied, was already almost all run off and ready for delivery. He would forward Blackwood's letter to the author for his instructions.[88] What did the author have to do with it? demanded Blackwood pugnaciously; the publishers were the best judges of when a new edition was needed. "While we still have 600 or 700 on hand it is not to be thought of."[89] Naturally the author was interested, James responded; he had a large sum of money due him on the delivery of the edition. The author had agreed, however, on one concession: he would take bills at nine months instead of six "to give full time for the sale of the remaining books on hand."[90]

Evidently Blackwood argued the point, but Scott was adamantine. "I am sick of the encroachments of these gentlemen," he wrote James, "and will not give up an inch beyond what you proposed, that is nine months bills. . . . There is no end of this—Were they to refuse the offer you have made I have no doubt but the edition might be sold to Constable & Longman upon very advantageous terms . . . I am really tired of being supposed to receive favours when I am in fact conferring them . . . I wish you had written to Murray but it now seems [too] late."[91] This ungracious fellow Blackwood had to be put in his place.

Constable must consequently be sounded out at once on the new work. "I have a good subject for a work of fiction in petto," Scott wrote off to John Ballantyne. "What do you think Constable would give for a smell of it? . . . I do not mean a continuation of Jedediah because there might be some delicacy in putting that bye the original publishers."[92] This novel would therefore bring the author of *Waverley* back into competition with his supposed rival. The wiry and wily little auctioneer dangled the bait; the portly bookseller rose to it voraciously. Here was his chance to snatch Scott back once and for all from Murray and Blackwood. Scott had taught Constable his lesson.

It was arranged that John Ballantyne bring him out to Abbotsford on Monday, May 5. "You must attend," Scott instructed John, "that the usual quantity of stock is included in this arrangement that is £600 for 6000 copies."[93] As for the other terms, "My sum is £1700 payable in May: a round advance by'r lady but I think I am entitled to it considering what I have turnd off hitherto . . ." Of course they must both stay overnight. "I can give you good accomodation as I have access to the spare rooms so you need not fear the cold hospitality of the stable."[94]

Although Scott had undergone a return of his cramp only the day before, he greeted his guests in high spirits. He did not yet have a title, but his story was already clear in his mind. It was to be laid in Rob Roy's country, and Rob himself was one of the principal characters. "Might he make a suggestion? asked Constable. "What! Mr. Accoucheur," laughed Scott, "must you be setting up for Mr. Sponsor too—but let's hear it." *Rob Roy*, the name of the real hero, said Constable, was the best possible title for the book. "Nay, never let me have to write up to a name," responded Scott. "You well know I have generally adopted a title that told nothing." But during a cheerful dinner Constable genially pressed his suggestion, he was all compliance about terms, and at last won Scott's agreement: *Rob Roy* let it be.[95]

They rose from the table and strolled on the grass before the doorway. Jocund little John Ballantyne was almost bouncing with glee. "Is Rob's gun here, Mr. Scott?" he asked: "would you object to my trying the auld barrel with a *few de joy?* "Nay, Mr. Puff," replied Scott, "it would burst, and blow you to the devil before your time." Constable had a more tart humor. (He had once ruined a business deal by remarking that he had five geese named after Longman and his partners.) "Johnny, my man," he exclaimed, "what the mischief puts 'drawing at sight' into *your* head?"[96]

Scott laughed at this allusion to John's financial expedients, but he perceived that the little man was ruffled, and quickly changed the subject. " 'Tis a long time, Johnny," he said, "since we have had the Cobbler of Kelso." Jauntily, John at once perched himself on a boulder and sang one of Scott's favorite songs, imitating a shoemaker in dialogue with his pet blackbird. "Nothing could be richer than the contrast of the bird's wild sweet notes," which John rendered with wonderful skill, and "the Cobbler's hoarse cracked voice, uttering all manner of endearing epithets."[97]

In the cool May twilight Scott felt buoyantly assured of all his powers. They were surging back unimpaired by the illness that only two months before had made him believe he was on his deathbed. This evening he had allowed himself a few glasses of claret over the three permitted by his doctors and could feel their warmth coursing through him. He limped back and forth on the greensward, talking and laughing, inventing episodes for *Rob Roy*. Both the Highland outlaw and Bailie Nicol Jarvie were vividly before him. He was sure, he told his companions, that he would make a hit with the Glasgow merchant, "whom he would *ravel up with Rob*." Then and there he fairly outshone himself "in an extempore dialogue between the bailie and the cateran," Constable remembered, "not unlike what the book gives us as passing in the Glasgow tolbooth."[98]

Traveling back to Edinburgh next morning, John adroitly clinched Constable's agreement to take £600 more of John Ballantyne and Company's unsold wares. Scott had also made it a condition that Johnny, as his literary agent, should get one sixth of the book's profits—to be paid out of the publisher's share, not the author's.[99] "Dear James," John wrote excitedly, "I am at this moment returned from Abbotsford with entire and full success . . . Wish me joy: I shall gain above £600 Constable taking my share of stock also." At some later date he added to the bottom of the note: "I did gain above £1200."[100]

But although Scott seemed to have turned the corner of his illness, he was still far from being fully recovered. Porridge for breakfast, a sparsity of meat, and a stringent limitation of wine at dinner became his regimen. He was directed to have frequent hot baths and forced to take opium when he was wracked by cramp.[101] For exercise he tried horseback riding again, but could not mount without help. For some weeks he was unable to sit erect in his saddle without a servant on each side to hold him. "I was very proud," he told Robert Gillies, "when I was once more able to ride a little way by myself."[102]

On his return to Edinburgh for the Court Session, he frightened his friends by his drawn face and wan color. Many of them, with poor mournful James Ballantyne, feared he had not long to live. Gillies met him in Charlotte Square, mounted on a Highland pony. Though it was now summer, the day was cold and bleak, and the sun shone through a bank of cloud. He was "riding *for the wholesomes*," he said, "which I detest as much as any man can do." Worn almost to a skeleton, he sat "slanting on his horse, as if unable to hold himself upright; his dress was threadbare and disordered; and his countenance, instead of its usual healthy colour, was of an olive-brown—I might almost say, black tinge."[103]

"The physicians tell me," Scott went on, "that mere pain cannot *kill*; but I am very sure that no man would for *other* three months encounter the same pain that I have suffered, *and live*. However, I have resolved to take thankfully whatever drugs they prescribe, and follow their advice as long as I can. Set a stout heart to a *stey brae* is a grand rule in this world."[104]

But all that summer and autumn he struggled against languor and lassitude. For his sick eyes even the loved and familiar surroundings of Cauldshiels Loch had lost their beauty:

> The sun upon the Wardlaw Hill,
> In Ettrick's vale, is sinking sweet;
> The westland wind is hush and still,
> The lake lies sleeping at my feet.
> Yet not the landscape to mine eye
> Bears those bright hues that once it bore;
> Though evening, with her richest dye,
> Flames o'er the hills of Ettrick's shore.
>
> With listless look along the plain,
> I see Tweed's silver current glide,
> And coldly mark the holy fane
> Of Melrose rise in ruin'd pride.
> The quiet lake, the balmy air,
> The hill, the stream, the tower, the tree,—
> Are they still such as once they were,
> Or is the dreary change in me?[105]

This one cry of weariness was his only complaint. Among his friends he joked about his illness. And instead of slackening his labors he toiled harder than ever. With iron determination he was resolved to defy his weakness and his pain.

# 3

## A Great Laird

### (1817)

Aʟʟ ᴛᴏʟᴅ, Scott believed, the doctors had drained him of one-third of his blood.[1] They made him give up beer and ale, "pastry, fruit &c, and all that tends to acidity."[2] Merely consuming buttermilk on his oatmeal porridge brought on another severe attack—"a warning to meddle as little with acids as I possibly can."[3] "At the same time I am as strong as a horse in many respects, for within a few hours after the paroxysm is over I find no difficulty in taking exercise as usual"[4]—three or four hours in the forenoon and two after dinner. Again and again "the infernal spasms" returned, "as if all the imps that tend to plague poor Caliban were washing, wringing, and ironing" that "unshapely but useful bag . . . my stomach."[5] On July 11 he was assailed with dreadful violence; he was unable to keep down the laudanum given him to relieve his agonies, "and they were obliged finally to have recourse to Monsr. de Porceaugnac's treatment—a *lavement*."[6]

But only a day later, hard upon the rising of the Court of Session, he was off with undaunted vigor on an excursion to the Lennox and Drumlanrig, bringing with him Charlotte, Sophia, and Adam Ferguson.[7] He desired to refresh his memories of the scenes of Rob Roy's exploits and see the outlaw's cave at the head of Loch Lomond. On Sunday they were with Hector MacDonald Buchanan, at Ross Priory near Dumbarton, whence a boat took them up the lake to the wild scenes of Glen Falloch. In Glasgow they visited the ancient Cathedral and its Laigh Kirk, among whose pillars Rob Roy would whisper his cryptic warning to Francis Osbaldistone. At one of the weaving plants in the thriving city Scott was delighted to see the process of "singeing" muslin—removing all the knots and irregularities from a finished web by passing it with lightning speed over a bar of red-hot iron. "The man that imagined this," he exclaimed, "was *the Shakespeare of the Wabsters*—

"Things out of hope are compass'd oft with vent'ring."[8]

After leaving Glasgow, the travelers circled down the coast of Renfrew and Ayrshire before striking inland. They reached Drumlanrig on the evening of July 19. Scott sent on to the Duke of Buccleuch a high-spirited epistle heralding their arrival:

> From Ross where the clouds on Ben-Lomond are sleeping
> From Greenock where Clyde to the Ocean is sweeping
> From Largs where the Scotch gave the Northmen a drilling
> From Ardrossan whose harbour cost many a shilling
> From old Cumnock where beds are as hard as a plank Sir
> From a chop & green peace & a chicken at Sanquhar
> This eve please the fates at Drumlanrig we anchor.[9]

They spent almost a week at the magnificent old castle, laughing, exploring the enormous structure, going on picnics. It was so huge, Scott wrote Joanna Baillie, that "one would require a clew or a plan" to find one's way "from tower to tower and gallery to gallery." The Duke had already replanted five hundred acres of the woods cut down by the Duke of Queensberry and planned to increase them to more than a thousand. "At his various seats this hard winter he has employd daily upwards of nine hundred and forty labourers at the expense of £70 per day. This is something better than hoarding useless thousands or squandering them in profuse luxury or losing them at games of hazard. . . . I send you all this disjointed chat amidst a great clamour of preparation among the young and old of the castle for a sally to some remote place among the hills where we are to dine on the turf. What I would give that you were with us, only they are singing so many Jacobite songs that it is thought the full length pictures of King William and Queen Mary which hang in the ante-room will walk out of their frames like that in the Castle of Otranto and march off in their royal robes to some mansion where their canvas ears may avoid being shocked with such sounds."[10]

After a rainy trip home, over Hart Fell and past the defiles of the Grey Mare's Tail, Scott's party reached Abbotsford on the night of July 26.[11] Here Scott settled down resolutely to a summer's work. The oaks he had planted were rising; though he could not yet walk beneath their shade, he told Lord Montagu, he could "contrive to lie under them which is the more classical & pastoral posture. Read the veracious Gulliver's account of the Windsor forest of Liliput and you will have some idea of the solemn gloom of my Druid shades."[12] His masons were busy—"my addition rises with more noise though less splendour than the temple of Solomon"[13]—and Scott himself often had his hand in the mortar tub.[14]

The literary labors facing him were formidable. Turning over in his mind the article on Chivalry promised for the *Encyclopaedia Britannica*, he requested from Constable a copy of Sainte-Palaye's *Mémoires sur l'ancienne chevalerie*.[15] Within a week of his return from Drumlanrig he had finished the History of 1815 for the *Edinburgh Annual Register* and at once plunged into writing *Rob Roy*.[16] Probably as an aid to handling the chapters involving Squire Inglewood and the unscrupulous law-clerk Jobson, he asked Constable to lend him Richard Burn's *Justice of the Peace and Parish Officer*.[17] Shortly after the middle of August the *Register* was published.[18] During that same month he also supplied Longman and Company with a 40,000-word introduction for their richly illustrated quarto, *The Border Antiquities of England and Scotland*, which appeared in September.[19] Before the end of August, despite recurrent twinges of cramp, he completed the first volume of *Rob Roy*.[20]

Constable felt gloriously confident that its sales would far out-distance those of its predecessors. Orders were already pouring in; at this rate the first impression of 6,000 copies would not last three weeks. Daringly he urged increasing this printing to the unheard of number of 10,000.[21] In the United States today, with more than twelve times the population of Great Britain in 1817 and a far higher proportion of literacy, this would hardly be paralleled by 120,000 copies. But Constable was sure of himself—"the Author has done me the honour," he boasted, "to acknowledge that I can sell Books *when I fairly set to it*."[22] Scott at once agreed. Constable was "a dashing dog," he wrote James Ballantyne, "worth the whole bunch for spirit & adventure."[23]

In the midst of all these activities Scott found time during the summer to exchange antiquarian facetiae with Charles Kirkpatrick Sharpe and carry on a serious discussion of the evils of unemployment with Morritt. The title of Baron, he reminded Sharpe, was sometimes given to holders of very small estates—for example, "the Baron of Kincleven whose property consisted of a ferry over the Tay near Stobhall and a few acres bestowed on his ancestor for fathering (with reverence) a fart of Queen Mary's." Her Majesty had made this "little mistake in stepping into the boat whereupon the boatman steppd forward & cravd pardon of the company." Greatly pleased by the fellow's politeness, the Queen demanded, "Whose knave art thou?" Learning that he was a bondsman of the Earl of Mar, she at once "askd his freedom of her cousin Jock & moreover the Barony aforesaid which the Earl conferd on him accordingly."[24]

Morritt had been working in Parliament for reforms in the Poor Laws. These problems, "into which you have ventured for love of the country," Scott wrote him, "form a sad quagmire. They are like John Bunyan's Slough of Despond into which . . . millions of cart loads of good resolutions have been thrown without perceptibly mending the way."[25] Peasant farmers in ever larger numbers had been forced to sell their small holdings and descend into the ranks of hired farm laborers. One-fifth of the rural population was on parochial relief and the national contribution to the poor rates had risen since 1750 from £700,000 to almost £8 million.[26] In the hideously proliferating industrial towns unemployed factory workers overflowed filthy cellars and airless courts and sank into drunkenness and vice while their children toiled fifteen hours a day at labor that crippled their limbs, rotted their lungs, and stunted their minds.[27]

In Scotland conditions were not so bad, Scott told Morritt, because there were fewer towns, the agricultural classes were more knit together, and the peasantry had endured hard fare and lodging from their infancy. But in both countries the crying evils were those of the industrial districts. Why should financial adventurers be allowed to bring hordes of people into crowded slums, assume no responsibility for the conditions they had created, and then fling them into destitution by discharging them as soon as there was a stoppage of trade?[28]

Scott himself thought that factory owners should be taxed in proportion to the number of hands they employed and the money applied to relieving the industrial poor. "If it should be alleged that this would injure the manufacture[r]s I would boldly reply 'And why not injure or rather limit speculations the excessive stretch of which has been productive of so much damage to the principals of the country and to the population whom it has in so many respects degraded and demoralized' . . . I cannot but think that the necessity of making some fund before hand for the provision of those whom they debauch and render only fit for the almshouse . . . would be a measure just in itself and beneficial to the community. But it would never be listend to—the weavers beam and the sons of Zeruiah would be too many for the proposers."[29]

It was a relief to turn his attention to his masons at Abbotsford. The last story was now rising rapidly. Sophia thought the new addition looked beautiful. "We spend most of our time in airing ourselves upon the top, and I think it will be wonderful if it is finished without any of us breaking our necks."[30] The niche from over the gate of the old Edinburgh Tolbooth, with its fleurs-de-lis and thistle carving, Scott now planned to build into his north gable.[31] "Most of our scutcheons are now mounted & look very well as the house is something after the model of an old hall (not a Castle), where such things are well in character." He also had a place for one of the jail doors and its stone frame.[32] "They are now busy with the roof & chimneys and we shall have all winter for preparing the woodwork."[33]

Despite these building operations Scott progressed rapidly on *Rob Roy*. One morning, coming out of the house, he found a mason putting aside a tub. " 'What wad ye dae wi' that tub,' says the Shirra, 'if ye wanted to sit on it?' 'I wad whummle't up, of course,' says he. 'Man, that's the very word,' said the Shirra, 'I've been huntin' for a' mornin'.' "[34] ("Nae doubt, nae doubt," Bailie Nicol Jarvie says to the imprisoned and despairing Owen, "—ay, ay—it's an awfu' whummle—and for ane that held his head sae high—")[35] Scott gave the man half a crown. "He wad far rather hear us say shule than shovel," reported one of the laborers, "an' an auld-farrant oot o' the way word was often as guid as a day's wage."[36]

During the second half of August, Lady Byron came to Abbotsford for a day's visit, and the Scott family took her on an excursion to the banks of Yarrow.[37] It would have seemed, Scott thought, that "Lady Byron, young, beautiful, with rank and fortune and birth and taste and high accomplishment and admirable good sense," had every quality likely to bring happiness to Lord Byron, and that he, "whose talents were so high" and who had a marked tendency to like those who could admire and understand his genius, would have been happy with her. And yet how miserable their marriage had been! Remembering the painful story, his "heart ached for her all the time we were together."[38]

Still, Scott felt certain reservations that his sympathy for her would not allow him to do more than hint. "She has . . . a great deal of firmness and a certain decision of character which perhaps is more graceful in adversity than it might have been at all times in prosperity. So at least it seemed to me: and I sure I should not have felt such strong kindness towards her had she been at the height of her fortune and in full enjoyment of all the brilliant prospects to which she seemed destined."[39] Will Laidlaw, who met her at Scott's dinner table, put the same observation more bluntly. "Her ladyship is a beautiful little woman with fair hair, a fine complexion, and rather large blue eyes. She looked steadily grave, and seldom smiled. I thought her mouth indicated great firmness, or rather obstinacy."[40]

On the morning of August 30, while the family were at breakfast, the rattle of a chaise was heard on the road from Selkirk. Soon a card was handed to Scott at the table. It was signed by Washington Irving; he was on his way to the ruins of Melrose Abbey, and asked if Scott would find it agreeable to see him in the course of the morning. With the note was a letter of introduction from Tom Campbell.[41] Scott joyfully leaped to his feet. Since the cold spring of 1813, when he and Charlotte had laughed their sides sore over Diedrich Knickerbocker's *History of New York*, he had warmly admired Irving.[42] The unexpected visitor was more than welcome; he must be persuaded to stay several days.[43]

From the slope above the dwelling Irving looked down on the ever-green-draped walls of the old farmhouse and the "Chapel," with the masonry and scaffolding of the new building rising in between. Great masses of hewn stone lay tumbled all over the forecourt. Above the portal, making it look like a hunting lodge, a great pair of elk horns branched out of the foliage. From this doorway, with a rabble of small dogs all yelping loudly, dashed the great black greyhound Hamlet and, leaping on a block of stone, began barking furiously. Then came Scott, hobbling vigorously with a stout staff, the huge staghound Maida treading gravely by his side. He was clad in an old green shooting-coat, brown pantaloons, and a worn white hat.[44]

Calling out a hearty greeting, he grasped Irving by the hand. "Come, drive down to the house; ye're just in time for breakfast, and afterwards ye shall see all the wonders of Abbotsford." Irving pleaded that he had already had his breakfast. "Hoot, man," cried Scott, "a ride in the morning in the keen air of the Scotch hills is warrant enough for a second breakfast." Irving was whirled into the dining room and quickly seated at the table, surrounded by the excited family—Charlotte, Sophia, now a slight, blue-eyed girl of seventeen, Anne, dark-haired and black-eyed, with an expression of sly gravity, Walter, already over six feet in height though only sixteen, and Charles, a lively eleven-year-old.[45]

Scott was full of plans for entertaining their guest. After breakfast he himself had things to attend to—doubtless a chapter or so of *Rob Roy* —but Charles knew all about Melrose Abbey and could take Irving there for the morning. Consequently Irving went to Melrose with Charles.[46] The custodian of the ruin, Johnny Bower, a little old man in a blue coat and red waistcoat, overflowed with praise of Scott. "He'll stand and crack and lauff wi' me, just like an auld wife—and to think that of a man that has such an awfu' knowledge o' history!"[47] Johnny boasted that he himself had located the very tomb in which the wizard Michael Scott lay buried by noting how the moonbeams slanted through the stained glass of the oriel window to the red cross below. "I pointed out the whole to the shirra," he said happily, "and he could na' gainsay but it was varra clear."[48]

When Irving returned from Melrose, Scott was ready for a ramble. All the dogs gamboled ahead of them, Hamlet leaping gracefully, the silky-haired setter Finette padding at Scott's heels, the dignified staghound Maida pacing solemnly while the younger animals jumped on his neck, worried his ears, and tried to tease him into a frolic. Now and then he would seize one of them, tumble him in the dust, and then glance at the two men as if to say, "You see, gentlemen, I can't help giving way to this nonsense." "I have no doubt," remarked Scott, "that when Maida is alone with these young dogs, he throws gravity aside, and plays the boy as much as any of them; but he is ashamed to do so in our company, and seems to say, 'Ha' done with your nonsense, youngsters;

what will the laird and that other gentleman think of me if I give way to such foolery?' "[49]

At the quarry on the Kaeside property Scott stopped to joke with the men cutting stone for his new building, who all paused for a "crack wi' the laird." One of them, a rugged, silver-haired old fellow with sparkling blue eyes, Scott asked for a pinch of snuff. The old man drew out a horn snuff-box. "Hoot, man," said Scott, "not that old mull; where's the bonnie French one that I brought you from Paris?" "Troth, your honor," replied the other, "sic a mull as that is nae for week days."[50]

Their ramble had gradually taken them up into the hills. "Now," said Scott, "I have brought you, like the pilgrim in the Pilgrim's Progress, to the top of the Delectable Mountains, that I may show you all the goodly regions hereabout. Yonder is Lammermuir and Smailholm; and there you have Galashiels, and Torwoodlee, and Galawater; and in that direction you see Teviotdale, and the Braes of Yarrow; and Ettrick stream, winding along, like a silver thread, to throw itself into the Tweed."[51]

For all his response to the legendry of the names, Irving could not help confessing faint disappointment in the sight, "a mere succession of gray waving hills, line beyond line, as far as my eye could reach," with the far-famed Tweed "a naked stream, flowing between bare hills, without a tree or thicket on its banks." Scott hummed a moment and looked grave and then defended the stark beauty of his stern and solitary slopes. "When I have been for some time in the rich scenery about Edinburgh, which is like an ornamented garden, I begin to wish myself back again among my own honest gray hills; and if I did not see the heather at least once a year," he added, giving the ground a thump with his staff, "*I think I should die.*"[52]

Irving pleaded that his own native country made him think of romantic landscape in images of hills crowned with woods and streams breaking their way through a wilderness. "Ay," Scott agreed. "You love the forest as I do the heather—but I would not have you think I do not feel the glory of a great woodland prospect." The poetry of American scenery led to the mention of Campbell's *Gertrude of Wyoming.* Scott praised his fellow poet "in that liberal style," Irving said, "in which I always found him to speak of the writings of his contemporaries." With a faint Scottish burr but with magnificent expressiveness he recited a number of fine passages from his friend's poems. "Campbell is, in a manner, a bugbear to himself. The brightness of his early success is a detriment to all his further efforts. *He is afraid of the shadow that his own fame casts before him.*"[53]

Suddenly the crack of a gun sounded among the hills. "That's Walter," explained Scott; "he has finished his morning's studies and is out with his gun. I should not be surprised if he had met with a black-cock; if so, we shall have an addition to our larder . . ." Irving asked about Walter's education. "Faith," replied Scott, "I can't say much on that head. I am not over bent upon making prodigies of my children. As to Walter, I taught him, while a boy, to ride, and shoot, and speak the truth; as to the other parts of his education, I leave them to a very worthy young man, the son of one of our clergymen, who instructs all my children."[54]

At dinner Scott laid aside his rustic dress, appearing in black; and Sophia and Anne had twined purple heather blossoms in their hair. The dogs all crouched around the table, Maida at Scott's elbow, Fenella, Charlotte's pet spaniel, beside her chair. Nearby reposed the plump bulk of Hinse of Hinsfeld, the large gray cat, sometimes nibbling a tidbit given him from the board, sometimes reaching out a soft lazy paw to cuff the ear of a passing dog and remind him to be respectful.[55]

The evening was spent in the little drawing room, which was also Scott's study and library, snug with Charlotte's chintz chairs and book-cases stocked with rare and antiquated volumes. Scott read aloud from Malory's *Morte d'Arthur*, and Sophia sang ballads in a sweet Scottish voice. Against one wall stood Scott's long writing table, surmounted by a brass-studded cabinet of polished wood, and above hung a glittering steel corselet and helmet flanked by gauntlets and battle-axes. There were also Tippoo Sahib's scimitar, a pair of spurs from Bannockburn, a Highland broadsword from Flodden Field, and Rob Roy's gun, the last of peculiar interest to Irving because he had heard in Edinburgh that Scott was writing a novel about that famous outlaw.[56]

Sunday morning, when the sun's rays slanted over the Eildon Hills into Irving's latticed window, he looked out through the eglantine over-hanging the casement and saw Scott in the courtyard chatting with his workmen. Irving dressed hastily and joined his host.[57] After breakfast Scott was busy for a while correcting proof sheets, which had come by mail.[58] Later he took Irving for a walk through the Rhymer's Glen, with its little burn dashing in waterfalls beneath mountain ash and weeping birch. "Here," he said, "is Huntly Bank, on which Thomas the Rhymer lay musing and sleeping when he saw, or dreamed he saw, the queen of Elfland:

> "Her shirt was o' the grass-green silk,
>     Her mantle o' the velvet fine;
> At ilka tett of her horse's mane
>     Hung fifty siller bells and nine."[59]

Farther among the hills they came on the remains of a Roman camp, and Scott showed Irving the praetorium, revealing "a knowledge of castrametation that would not have disgraced the antiquarian Oldbuck himself." Irving grew convinced, indeed, that many of the humors of Monkbarns were taken from Scott's "own richly compounded character" and some of the scenes of *The Antiquary* from the neighborhood of Abbotsford. When Scott told him several anecdotes of the noted beggar Andrew Gemmells he so easily recognized the image of Edie Ochiltree that he had to check himself from remarking on the resemblance.[60]

On the following day they made an excursion to Dryburgh Abbey, driving in an open carriage drawn by two sleek black horses. Scott pointed out Sandyknowe crags in the distance and, on its naked hill, Smailholm tower, at the foot of which he had lain as a small child.[61] Nearer, he called Irving's attention to the baronial tower of the Haigs, reciting Thomas the Rhymer's prophecy:

> "Betide, betide, whate'er betide,
> Haig shall be Haig of Bemerside."

At Dryburgh, among the red sandstone ruins of its church, Irving saw the family vault and the tombs and monuments of Scott's ancestors.[62]

Of all Scott's family, Irving thought, Sophia and Charles seemed most to understand his humors and delight in his conversation. Charlotte did not always listen closely; one morning at breakfast Scott was gleefully telling some anecdote about the laird of Macnab, "who, poor fellow," he remarked, "is dead and gone." "Why, Mr. Scott," she interrupted, him "Macnab's not dead, is he?" "Faith, my dear," Scott responded gravely, "if he's not dead they've done him a great injustice— for they've buried him." This joke passed unnoticed by Charlotte but was too much for Dominie Thomson, the children's tutor, who was just raising a cup of tea to his lips and in a great snort of laughter sprayed it all over the table.[63]

On another after-breakfast walk Will Laidlaw came with them and, as the day was showery, Tom Purdie, carrying Scott's plaid. Sophia had told Irving how obstinate Tom was in his opinions; he and Scott would dispute about something to be done on the estate until, worn out, Scott would exclaim, "Well, well, Tom, have it your own way." Then, after a time, Tom might look in the parlor door and observe, "I ha' been thinking over the matter, and, upon the whole, I think I'll take your honor's advice." Scott laughed heartily over this story. "It was with him and Tom," he said, "as it was with an old laird and a pet servant, whom he had indulged until he was positive beyond all endurance. 'This won't do,' cried the old laird in a passion, 'we can't live together any longer—we must part.' 'An' where the deil does your honor mean to go?' replied the other."[64]

Two or three times in the course of their walk there were drizzling showers, but Scott limped along undaunted. Finally the rain became so steady that Irving asked if they should not seek shelter. "True," responded Scott, "I did not recollect that you were not accustomed to our Scottish mists. This is a lachrymose climate, ever showering. We, however, are children of the mist, and must not mind a little whimpering of the clouds, any more than a man must mind the weeping of a hysterical wife. As you are not accustomed to be wet through, as a matter of course, in a morning's walk, we will bide a bit under this bank until the shower is over." Taking a seat in the shelter of a thicket, Scott called for his plaid. "Come," he said to Irving, "come under my plaidy, as the old song goes."[65]

When the downpour ceased they resumed their walk until they came to the banks of Cauldshiels Loch, where they embarked in a small boat recently given Scott by his neighbor Lord Somerville. As Irving stepped on board he noticed the name, "Search No. 2," and paused, repeating it aloud, trying to clarify a nebulous memory connected with it. "Pshaw!" cried Scott, "it's only some of Lord Somerville's nonsense— get in!" In an instant the ludicrous episode of "Search No. 1," from *The Antiquary*, flashed into Irving's mind. "Ah! I remember now," he said, laughing as he took his seat, but tactfully made no further remark on the subject.[66]

Scott told him that from time immemorial the lake had been supposed to be haunted by a bogle in the shape of a water bull; one man even claimed he had seen it. "Our streams and lochs are like the rivers and pools in Germany," he remarked, "that all have their Wasser Nixies or water witches . . ." He went on to speak of the fabulous beings, the elves and sprites, with which the Scottish peasants people their lonely glens and mountains. "Our fairies, however," he said, "though they dress in green, and gambol by moonlight about the banks and shaws and burnsides, are not such pleasant little folks as the English fairies, but are apt to bear more of the warlock in their natures, and to play spiteful tricks."[67]

Laidlaw and his wife were guests at dinner, together with a middle-aged lady whom Scott treated with marked esteem. When they were gone he spoke of them all with cordial friendship. "I wished to show you," he told Irving, "some of our really excellent, plain Scotch people; not fine gentlemen and ladies, for such you can meet everywhere, and they are everywhere the same. The character of a nation is not to be learned from its fine folk." The other lady was the daughter of a poor clergyman, who had died, leaving her destitute. She had set up a children's school and not only supported herself but paid off all her father's debts. "She is a fine old Scotch girl," added Scott, "and I delight in her more than in many a fine lady . . . and I have known many of the finest."[68]

On Wednesday morning, September 3, Irving was obliged to leave for a trip through the Highlands. Coming with him to the gate, Scott bade him a cordial farewell,[69] and at once settled down to writing rapidly and energetically. "I will get to CHIVALRY next week," he told Constable. "I will not have time to make the article long but will try to make it lively."[70] "Never fear Rob making his appearance," he reassured

James Ballantyne. "My health is greatly mended. I rise a mornings and sleep a nights—"[71] His confidence turned out to be premature. Hard upon it came another attack of cramps, tormenting though not so violent as those of the previous spring.[72]

But Scott refused to be discouraged. He was determined now to pay off the bond for which the Duke of Buccleuch had given his name. "I have hungered and thirsted," he wrote John Ballantyne, "to see the end of these shabby borrowings among friends; they have all been wiped out except the good Duke's £4000—and I will not suffer either new offers of land or anything else to come in the way of that clearance."[73] He had consequently decided on a continuation of the *Tales of My Landlord*. This he would begin writing as soon as he had finished *Rob Roy*; he believed he could have it ready for publication by "the King's birthday"—June 4, 1818. "I expect that you will be able to arrange this resurrection of Jedediah, so that £5000 will be at my order."[74]

The new work, in four volumes, was to be offered to both Constable and Longman. "Constable pushes books so much better than our London friends that I shall wish him to take the management . . ."[75] But a heavy proviso was attached to the bargain: the purchasers must take all John Ballantyne's remaining unsold stock.[76] John, who was in London, was instructed to sound out Longman and Company. He reported that Rees was away and that nothing could be concluded in his absence. They were disposed, however, to accept Scott's conditions, though they suggested that the price of the stock be referred to arbitration. Scott refused to consider any such counterproposal.[77] John Murray, "through an indirect channel," had offered even better terms than Scott demanded —but after the wrangles with Blackwood about the previous *Tales* Scott had no desire for this connection. James Ballantyne was therefore directed to lose no time in ascertaining what Constable was ready to give for the right to publish 10,000 copies.[78]

But the seniors at Longman's had "oped their oracular jaws and profferd mighty things"; it would be treating them badly "to shut them out of a bargain" that had "been mentioned to them by an authorized agent." They must have a half-share if they wanted it. Constable must also understand that "the *whole* remaining stock of J. B. & Co." were to be taken "on the same terms of discount acceptance etc as formerly, and that in November he would grant such acceptances "as will take out of the way the £4000 bond." "If Mr. Constable agrees to these terms you may close with him directly . . ."[79]

Adamant though Constable had been in the past about not clearing off John Ballantyne's shelves, he had no stomach for further fight. When Murray and Blackwood bore away the first *Tales* of Jedediah he had been sorely wounded. If he refused now, Scott might in resentment turn to his hated foes. Constable was infuriated, too, by the swiftly rising sales of a periodical recently established by his Scottish rival, *Black-*

*wood's Magazine*, which had not only eclipsed his own old *Scots Magazine* but insolently challenged the authority of his *Edinburgh Review* and grotesquely satirized him in its pages. All these defeats were so many vials of gall and wormwood. To lose a second manuscript from Gandercleuch was more than he could bear. He had already yielded to the extent of taking £600 worth of John's stock when he acquired *Rob Roy*. He had the strongest faith that Scott's star, high as it had risen, was destined to still greater triumphs. The haughty but fearful bookseller therefore immediately surrendered.[80]

So the last remains of Scott's ill-fated venture into publishing were liquidated. Despite the days of desperate contrivance and the sleepless nights it had cost him, it had not turned out too badly. By carefully nursing along the unsold stock—as James and John Ballantyne had both urged—and tying in its disposal with the sales of his novels, Scott had managed to emerge not only without loss but, through this final bargain, with a profit he estimated at £1,000.[81] "At one stroke," as Lockhart put it, "the Augean stable in Hanover Street" was cleared "of unsalable rubbish to the amount of £5270!"[82]

But in fact Scott's list of publications was not so bad as the picturesque image implies. Large lots of the *Edinburgh Annual Register*, in sets, Cadell thought, might be sold for disposal in America. For the rest, he suggested printing a cheap catalogue of the whole, together with some of their own surplus stock, and offering it at 25 per cent reduction. "By these plans we may reduce this said stock and get our own money for a considerable portion of it, packing the balance off at what it will bring."[83]

The Longman firm felt enraged when they learned that Scott had settled with Constable. "I cannot allow Mr. Rees to suppose," Scott replied, "that any faith has been broken with him or his partners."[84] As a prudent man, he was entitled "to hear the breath of more than one house on a transaction" which involved "a most important sum of money."[85] John Ballantyne's memoranda had been for Scott's consideration as well as theirs; he had as much right as they had "to consider and reject them. This I did by return of post for I totally disapproved of their proposal of referring the price to arbitration & I cannot conceive how I should be bound by a proposal of John neither authorized nor approved of by me . . . & not even accepted by them.[86]

"If they are displeased with what has been done for them," Scott went on pepperily, "or rather if they do not accept it as an actual boon & favour they shall not have any part of the work. They managed G[uy] M[annering] worse than any of the other novels & I am at least £800 out of pocket by their doing so. They have ceased to do the only good deed they ever did & they must not think to trepan me into an engagement which I have no mind for. Blackwood did not find his interest in this & no more will they."[87]

The London publishers persisted, however, in feeling ill used. They wanted the half-share reserved for them "*without* any part" of the unsold stock and angrily refused the terms accepted by Constable.[88] So far as Scott was concerned, "the Chequer was closed": if they wanted to engage in any further negotiation it must be not with him but with Constable. "It is very unpleasant for me to think that amid all this procrastinated splutter betwixt Longman & Constable the payment of my bond may be postponed."[89]

To the Edinburgh bookseller Scott wrote, "So you have the staff in your hand and as you are on the spot can manage it in your own way. Depend on it that, barring unforeseen illness or death, these will be the best volumes which have appeared. I pique myself on the first tale which is called *The Heart of Mid-Lothian*."[90] Constable desired to remain on good terms with Longman and was still ready to admit them to the undertaking but agreed with his partner that there was "no occasion for *any sacrifice on our part* to attain what is not in danger." Ultimately Longmans declined Constable's offer. "They have themselves to blame . . . and may grumble as they choose," said Cadell; "we have *Taggy by the tail*, and if we have influence to keep the best author of the day, we ought to do it."[91]

Scott's fear that the payment of his bond might be delayed proved justified. Constable's credit was already strained; without Longman to pay half he was in difficulties. The four volumes of the *Tales of My Landlord* existed only in Scott's mind, even *Rob Roy* was not completed, and Scott was ill. If in November Constable granted bills for £4,000 on work not to be delivered for at least another six months, what would his financial position be if Scott died?[92] This was the nightmare that terrified Cadell: "I say *to you* & to no one else that W. S. is not long for this world . . ."[93]

After cudgeling his brains Cadell worked out a wily and somewhat disingenuous scheme. In the name of the firm, he wrote Scott, "we will take upon ourselves the obligation of making good this payment of £4000 sterling, at the next term of Whitsunday . . . It being understood that this bond of £4000, when so paid or delivered up, goes in part of the sums to be made good by us in the transaction" with Mr. John Ballantyne.[94] The purport of this last phrase was to imply that if Scott did not write the novels then Constable was *not* liable for the bond. To Cadell's relief Scott raised no objection to this qualification, though doubtless, being a trained lawyer, he understood it very well and felt confident that he would not fail to fulfill his part of the contract. Though the bond would not be retired at Martinmas, as he had hoped, it would be at the following Whitsuntide.

"Come what will," Cadell jubilantly told Constable, "we are covered from any claim that can be made upon us should Mr. Scott die, for to you I mention this, but I am diffident of doing so *in writing* to any one."

The two men had been partners since 1811, and were now still more closely related; little more than a month earlier Cadell had married Constable's daughter. To his new father-in-law Cadell explained the point of the interchange with sly triumph: "My letter to W. S. is *as good as his* in the eye of the law and as to the Bond, why, should he die we have nothing *to do with it*, the Duke pays the Piper, and *our letter* stands *against his*."[95] "It would take up too much time to explain how this was managed tho I have no hesitation in telling you candidly that you *could* not have done it for you *would* not have done it & when I shall explain all the circumstances you will be apt to say that I am something of a h[umbu]g—I did not think I had so much *face* left . . ."[96]

Meanwhile Scott had concluded the negotiations for the purchase of Toftfield, which had protracted themselves into the autumn. "The terms are £10,000, which my late arrangements enable me to make easy. It is dear land but I could not expect it cheap & it suits me exactly." He was now master of all the haunts of "True Thomas," and of the whole ground of the battle of Melrose, from Skirmish-field to Turn-again.[97] "Dear John," he wrote exultantly, "I have closed with Usher for his beautiful patrimony which makes me a great laird. I am afraid people will take me up for coining. Indeed these novels while their attractions last are something like it."[98]

He was also "in treaty for a field or two more; one of which contains the only specimen of a Peel-house, or defensive residence of a small proprietor, which remains in this neighborhood. It is [in] an orchard, in the hamlet of Darnick, to which it gives a most picturesque effect."[99] Beside this, "My neighbor Nicol Milne is *mighty* desirous I should buy, at a *mighty* high rate, some land between me and the lake which lies *mighty* convenient, but I am *mightily* determined to give nothing more than the value so that it is likely to end like the old proverb *Ex Nichilo Nichil fit*."[100]

Building operations at Abbotsford were progressing rapidly. "I agree with you," Scott wrote Terry on October 29, "that the tower will look rather rich for the rest of the building; yet you may be assured, that with diagonal chimneys and notched gables, it will have a very fine effect, and is in Scotch architecture by no means incompatible." Indoors, on Terry's advice, he had given up his idea of coving the ceiling of his study but insisted in spite of Terry that it must have a west window— his eyes needed the light and a single northern window would not be enough. In the paneling of the dining room he wanted "a press on each side of the sideboard. I don't mean a formal press with a high door, but some crypt, or, to speak vulgarly, *cupboard*, to put away bottles of wine, &c." "We begin roofing tomorrow."[101]

Throughout all this building and negotiating of contracts Abbotsford entertained an unending succession of visitors, among them David Wilkie, the artist, who painted a picture of Scott and his family garbed as a group of peasants.[102] When Wilkie arrived he found the house full of guests. "I did not presume," he later told Washington Irving, "to ask Mr. Scott to sit for his portrait, for I saw he had not a moment to spare; I waited for the guests to go away; but as fast as one went another arrived . . . At length all went off, and we were quiet. I thought, however, Mr. Scott will now shut himself up among his books and papers, for he has to make up for lost time; it won't do for me to ask him now to sit for his picture. Laidlaw, who managed his estate, came in, and Scott turned to him. . . . 'Laidlaw,' said he, 'tomorrow morning we'll go across the water and take the dogs with us—there's a place where I think we'll be able to find a hare.'

"In short," Wilkie concluded, "I found that instead of business he was thinking only of amusement, as if he had nothing in the world to occupy him; so I no longer feared to intrude upon him."[103]

Nevertheless, though Scott's courtesy would not allow him to let them suspect it, his visitors had interfered with his work. "I have been dreadfully broken in upon by company here," he wrote Constable, "otherwise *R. R.* would have been out. But not having even a closet to be private in, my course has necessarily been retarded. But time lost shall and indeed must be made up, and you know how I can move upon a pinch. I have had a bad touch of the cramp on the change of weather, but it gave way to bleeding without any bad consequences—save the fright."[104]

On his return to Edinburgh in November, however, Scott settled down, in spite of his renewed pain, to finish *Rob Roy* with no further interruptions. But his illness recurred every three or four weeks, and made his sufferings severe. "My spasms," he wrote Joanna Baillie, "have been frequent and violent especially since the weather set in moist and dank . . ."[105] He did not feel that all the negations of his diet had done him any good. The cramps came with unabated virulence: "I lie in agony for several hours swearing I will take no laudanum & roaring like King Corny of the Black Isles," only to be obliged at last to take sixty or eighty drops and feel relieved of the pain, indeed, but all the following day to endure the depression of spirits which that medicine brought him.[106]

Thus Scott struggled on with the novel, despite both the pains of cramp and the lassitude of opium. One day Ballantyne, calling at Castle Street to dun him for copy, found him sitting at his desk with a clean pen and a blank sheet of paper. James uttered a solemn exclamation of surprise. "Ay, ay, Jemmy," said Scott, " 'tis easy for you to bid me get on, but how the deuce can I make Rob Roy's wife speak, with such a *curmurring* in my guts?"[107]

But get on he did, though there were times when he was obliged to spend an entire day in bed, and felt as weak as water the next day.[108] He thought seriously of going to Bath for his health; he had "a long-ing," he said, "to see the place in which I spent my fifth & part of my sixth year." Better still, if he could get a leave of absence from the Court of Session, he would prefer going to Italy. He wanted to see Rome before he died. Among these melancholy thoughts he pressed forward.[109] With a determined burst of energy he managed to finish the book some ten days before the end of December. His spirits rose again as he concluded. "Dear James," he wrote,

> With Great Joy
> I sent you Roy.
> Twas a tough job
> But we're dune wi' Rob.[110]

Though these last twelve months had represented days and nights of agonizing physical pain, the year had also been one of unexampled prosperity. Barely five years ago his straits had been so desperate that he had meditated exiling himself from his beloved Scotland. Now his debts were paid and his novels were bringing him an income of £10,000 a year.[111] That October, during a visit to Abbotsford, Constable had offered and he had tentatively accepted another £10,000 for the copyrights to all his novels and poems except for the quarter-share of *Marmion* belonging to John Murray.[112] He was, as he said, coining gold.

Only that autumn the new Lord Advocate, his old friend Allan Macconochie, had insinuated that it might not be long before he attained the Barony of Exchequer toward which he had turned his eyes.[113] Abbotsford was rapidly becoming the Scottish mansion of his visions. His tower was rising to the sky, and he planned to place in the garden court the old fountain of the Edinburgh Mercat Cross, which he had just been given, with its Gothic masks and graceful basin.[114] Soon he would be dreaming of tearing down the old Redford farmhouse and erecting a magnificent new wing soaring to an even loftier tower.[115] His estate extended to twelve hundred acres of rolling meadow and woodland waving with young oaks.[116] He was indeed "a great laird." More than that, he was a great artist, a wizard with a magic pen. Would he soar still higher, or did the future have some crushing blow in store?

# 4

## Reivings and Revolutions

### (Criticism: *The Black Dwarf, Old Mortality, Rob Roy*)

*The Black Dwarf* did not soar so high as Blackwood in his first excited reading had hoped; its lame and melodramatically contrived ending justified his disappointment. But its longer companion, *Old Mortality*, is one of the summits of Scott's achievement as a literary artist. And *Rob Roy*, despite a few cavalier flaws in its last huddled and hasty pages, is again a triumph. All three, even the less than satisfactory *Dwarf*, surpassed what any of Scott's contemporaries were doing. Though both *Old Mortality* and *Rob Roy* had shortcomings, in their proud and impetuous radiance the blemishes were of no more moment than spots on the face of the sun.

The first of the three is set in those lonely Liddesdale hills that Scott knew so well from his youthful days when he had been "raiding" the Border for ballads. The comic conversation in the opening chapter, about the short sheep having long wool and the long sheep short wool, Scott borrowed from one he had listened to in a farmhouse with Laidlaw and Shortreed. But he moved the period back to the beginning of the eighteenth century, shortly after the Act of Union in 1707. Although James II had been dead more than six years, there were recurrent plots to set the Pretender on the throne; and the age was still one of lingering family feuds, cattle reiving, and the burning of barns and farmsteads.

Young Earnscliff is the heir to such a feud. When he runs into a neighboring farmer, Hobbie Elliott, on Mucklestane Moor, Hobbie voices the folk morality that expects him to avenge his father's slaying. The Laird of Ellieslaw, Hobbie concedes, did not strike the actual blow, but his "friend stickit your sire after the laird himself had mastered his sword." Ellieslaw was thus a party to the deed, "and I am sure if ye

were sae disposed as to take amends on him, naebody could say it was
wrang, for your father's blood is beneath his nails—"¹

Earnscliff, however, like many of Scott's heroes, is a voice of more
enlightened ways. Blood feuds, he feels, should be allowed to die with
the past. "Fie, fie, Hobbie," he objects, "it was a foolish brawl, occasioned
by wine and politics—many swords were drawn—it is impossible to say
who struck the first blow."² But Hobbie remains unrepentant. He
shrewdly suspects that "the twa grey een" of Ellieslaw's daughter
Isabel have something to do with keeping Earnscliff "sae sober."³ Should
her father Richard Vere, the Laird of Ellieslaw, swoop down with his
followers on Earnscliff's ancestral tower, the servants need but ring
its great bell and Hobbie and his two brothers will be there "in the snapping of a flint"—"it wad be but a wee bit neighbour war, and Heaven
and earth would mak allowances for it in this uncultivated place—"⁴

The violence never long dormant in these wild regions does not
break out between Ellieslaw and Earnscliff but strikes at Hobbie himself. He has enraged Willie Graeme, known as the Reiver of Westburn-
flat, by saying that the bandit feared him. Angrily the Reiver determines
"to gie him a lesson not to let his tongue gallop ower freely about his
betters."⁵ Returning from a deer hunt, Hobbie finds his farm in ruins
and learns that his bride-to-be, Grace Armstrong, has been abducted.
As he nears the top of the bank above his house, his old nurse Annaple
hobbles up to him lamenting.

"Ohon! that I should live to see the day!—The steading's a' in a
low, and the bonny stack-yard lying in the red ashes, and the gear a'
driven away. But gang na forward; it wad break your young yeart,
hinny, to see what my auld een hae seen this morning." The habitation
is indeed "a wasted and blackened ruin. From among the shattered and
sable walls the smoke continued to rise. The turf-stack, the barn-yard,
the offices stocked with cattle . . . had been laid waste or carried off in
a single night."⁶

It is the reality of those scenes of theft and rapine that had filled
ballad after ballad in the *Minstrelsy*—"The Outlaw Murray," "Kinmont
Willie," and "The Raid of Reidswire."⁷ To the Red Reiver it is "nae
great matter after a'—just to cut the comb of a young cock that has been
crawing a little ower crously."⁸ But to Hobbie and his family it is
utter disaster. "It was a cowardly cruel thing," exclaims one of his
sisters, "to harry a puir family to the bare wa's this gate." "And leave
us neither stirk nor stot," says his youngest brother. "Harry and I ha
been to gather what was on the outby land, and there's scarce a cloot
left. . . . We are ruined stoop and roop."⁹

In his desperation Hobbie appeals for help to Elshender, the Black
Dwarf, a grotesque and deformed monstrosity who lives in solitude in a
stone hut he had built himself on the Moor. There he finds in his loneli-
ness an unhappy refuge from the derision, ingratitude, and cruelty he

has known in his past life. Local superstition, which Hobbie more than half shares, credits "Cannie Elshie" with supernatural powers, and the furious hatred of mankind that the Dwarf repeatedly voices enhances the fear he inspires. But for all his terrifying appearance, Elshender has revealed streaks of crabbed helpfulness; the human sympathies he believes he has abandoned he is unable to tear from his heart.

The Dwarf gives Hobbie a gnomic hint where to look for Grace Armstrong's abductor, and flings him a bag of gold to rebuild and restock his farm. Hobbie is afraid the money may be the fraudulent wages of a satanic compact: "I dinna ken, Elshie; to be free wi' you, I dinna like to use siller unless I kend it was decently come by; and maybe it might turn into sclate-stones, and cheat some poor man." "Ignorant idiot!" retorts the Dwarf, "the trash is as genuine poison as ever was dug out of the bowels of the earth. Take it—use it, and may it thrive with you as it hath done with me!"[10]

Elshender, of course, is in fact an educated man who has abandoned the superior station he once held, and he still wields power in the world he has left behind. When Isabel Vere, the daughter both of his chief betrayer and of the woman he had once loved, straying from a hunting party, passes before his hut and speaks to him with kindness, he softens and gives her a rose. "Do not part with it," he tells her. "Come to me in your hour of adversity . . . and the heart and the doors that are shut against every other earthly being, shall open to thee and thy sorrows."[11]

Scott has devised for Elshender an acid and malevolent rhetoric that mingles the fever of the Gothic novel with the fury of Timon and the despair of Manfred. "Pass on your way," he tells Hobbie and Earnscliff when they first meet him, "the breath of your human bodies poisons the air around me—the sound of your human speech goes through my ears like sharp bodkins."[12] Later, to Earnscliff, he claims that when he has aided others it has been only to perpetuate the mass of human misery. "You are one on whom I look with the least loathing." "Were you on your sickbed, I might, in compassion, send you a cup of poison."[13]

And when Isabel Vere, recoiling from a forced marriage with the repulsive Sir Frederick Langley, does seek Elshender to implore his aid, he receives her at first with a sneer of bitterness: "Is mine the form of a redresser of wrongs?"[14] "Hast thou not heard it said in thy mortal world, that I have leagued myself with other powers as deformed to the eye and malevolent to the human race as myself?"[15] "I but mocked thee, girl, when I said I would relieve thee."[16] But he relents. "Be gone to thy dwelling. Fear nothing with which they threaten thee. Thou hast asked my protection—thou shalt find it effectual."[17]

The words are those of the stage, even of melodrama, but in the emotional aura with which Scott surrounds the Dwarf, they have power.

Elshender's sulphurous utterance is, as Hazlitt put it—although he thought that here Scott failed—"what the heart whispers to itself, what the imagination tells in thunder."[18] The portrayal of the heartache that may be engendered by physical deformity, and by the thoughtless cruelty it sometimes evokes in others, reveals that, like Byron, Scott knew the mood of rebellion, though he had conquered it. The distorted body of the poor Dwarf is a magnified projection of the crippled foot and limping gait that Scott and Byron shared. "All the bitter blasphemy of the spirit which, from infancy to the tomb, swelled up in Byron," Lockhart perceptively observes, "all this black and desolate train of reflections," Scott must have "encountered and deliberately subdued."[19]

The distress that brings Isabel to the Dwarf's hut has its sources in a Jacobite conspiracy in which Richard Vere is one of the leaders. The plotters assembled in Ellieslaw Castle are seen with an entirely disillusioned gaze. Though they are less quarrelsome than the Highland chiefs in *Waverley*, none of them except Vere's kinsman Mareschal-Wells has anything approaching the fiery courage of Fergus MacIvor. Almost to a man, they are venal, cynical, and self-centered. There is no Baron Bradwardine, no devoted Flora.

Vere's scheme needs the support of Sir Frederick Langley, and Langley will move no further unless he is given the hand and fortune of Isabel Vere. The Laird of Ellieslaw would like his daughter to believe him a loving father, would like to seem so even in his own eyes, but intrigue and power are more important to him than her happiness. His difficulties are compounded by the declaration of Mareschal-Wells that he will not "see any violence put on the will of my pretty kinswoman."[20] Isabel must be brought at least to seem to agree of her own free will to the hated marriage.

It is at this point that the whole story disintegrates into lurid theatricality. Scott has complicated his plot in a way that confronts Vere with an insoluble problem—to obtain his daughter's consent in what has become literally a matter of hours. Her surrender might have been made convincing under a slow pressure of months, but Vere must accomplish it in a single interview. Vere himself feels twinges at sacrificing his daughter to his ambition, but remembering that "if he failed, he himself was a lost man,"[21] he drowns his scruples.

Granted the situation, the main points of Vere's strategy are mustered skillfully. Scott always knows the emotional forces needed to move one of his characters to a required course of action, but sometimes, as here, he tries to rush the process. Vere tells Isabel that his life is in danger, but pretends to be unwilling even to name the sole course that can melt Langley's resentment. Only reluctantly does he allow her to learn that her marriage alone can save him. Feigning in turn to regard this sacrifice as altogether impossible, he then brings her to insist on it over his seeming protest.

It is not until after this colloquy that Isabel is reminded of the rose and Elshender's promise and appeals from the unnatural father who would have betrayed her to the Dwarf, who as "Father Elshie"— although, as Hobbie says, he is a "queer-looking father"[22]—has truly made himself a spiritual father to the countryside. "I come to you, father,"[23] she says, and Elshender, a Prospero clamped within the twisted body of Caliban, now becomes a father to Isabel too.

The ending is a glare of stage fire—the vaulted chapel of Ellieslaw Castle, the unhallowed wedding group assembling at midnight, the voice of the Dwarf from behind the tomb of Isabel's mother interrupting the first words of the marriage service with a harsh "Forbear!"[24] Ellieslaw's expenditures have brought his lands and fortune under the Dwarf's control, and by some mysterious proviso Elshender may dispose even of Isabel's inheritance from her mother; he himself is now revealed to be Sir Edward Mauley, who has long been supposed dead. Without his consent to her marriage she will be penniless: "Thank Heaven," he tells Langley, "that thou art prevented from wedding qualities with which thou hast no concern—portionless truth, virtue, and innocence." As for Vere, he may seek safety from the Government by flight abroad; Mauley contemptuously promises him a monetary allowance. "He will rejoice," says the Dwarf, "—for to breathe air and to handle gold is to him happiness."[25]

The Gothic melodrama of this dénouement appears all the more artificial in contrast to the solid realism with which Scott has drawn the Liddesdale moors and farmsteads and peopled them with a crowd of flesh-and-blood Borderers from Hobbie to the neighbors who rally round him in his troubles. Are they "to sit and see our friends' houses burnt ower their heads," asks one of them, "and no put out hand to revenge them? Our fathers did not do that, I trow?"[26] Even Elshender derives some of his reality from our seeing him as he appears to their eyes. "Ye mind ye said yoursell," Hobbie's grandmother reminds him, "he was mair like a bogle than a living thing." "Hout, mother," he replies, "Elshie's no that bad a chield; he's a grewsome spectacle . . . and a rough talker, but his bark is waur than his bite."[27]

But the scene in the chapel turns Elshender into a sensational figure out of Mat Lewis or Mrs. Radcliffe. Richard Vere, who might have been a complex study of a father torn between love for his child and his ambitions as a political manipulator, remains, for all his faint qualms, only a dissembling hypocrite. Though Earnscliff seemed at first destined for the crucial role of overcoming his heritage of vengeance against Ellieslaw and resolving the hostility between their two houses, he dwindles into a supernumerary employed only incidentally for that purpose. The love between him and Isabel, failing to weight the story with this deeper import, is given no more than a sentimental wedding-bells significance. What should have been Earnscliff's central function in the thematic structure, so far as it is worked out at all, is taken over entirely by the Dwarf and then marred in execution. When Scott had recovered from his exasperation with the overcandid Blackwood, he himself recognized that he had spoiled what might have been a splendid novel.

Of the four stories originally designed to make up the *Tales of My Landlord* and illustrate "the manners of Scotland in her different provinces," *The Black Dwarf* was that dealing with her southern border. Its period was earlier than any Scott had portrayed before, and in its successor, *Old Mortality*, taking place in the west of Scotland, he moved still further into the past, the later part of the seventeenth century. The conspiracy of Richard Vere had been imaginary, although, as the novel indicates, there actually was a French expedition to restore the Pretender in 1708, which reached the Firth of Forth before it was forced to turn back. But *Old Mortality* centers around a real historic event, the uprising of the Covenanters at Drumclog in 1679 and their decisive defeat three weeks later at Bothwell Bridge. The issues of religious freedom that inflamed their revolt were not to be resolved until almost a decade later. In many ways, though, their uprising was a forerunner of the Revolution of 1688, and *Old Mortality* is, as Welsh says, a study of revolution.

In the novel, Henry Morton is the central figure around which events swirl. His father, Silas Morton, had fought for the Covenanters at Marston Moor, but after the death of Charles I had defended the legitimate succession to the throne at the battle of Dunbar. In Henry Morton's heritage there is thus a tension between liberty of conscience and the claims of legal government. The times have sharpened this tension to fierce discord. The restored monarchy has reasserted the policy of controlling church polity and ritual. The Scottish Privy Council is bent with tyrannous rigor on enforcing conformity; the extremists among the Covenanters have responded with lawless violence. Henry Morton is caught directly between the clash of these opposing fanaticisms.

The explosive situation is foreshadowed on a comic level by the "wappenschaw" of the opening chapters. This traditional mingling of military games and rural sports the Government has revived with the aim of fostering accord among both Cavaliers and Puritans. At first it seems that gaiety and good feeling will carry the day. For the uncommitted, the gathering is an excuse for fun and drinking; for the royalist Lady Margaret Bellenden her small muster of retainers represents a display of loyalty and feudal duty; for Morton his presence on behalf of the estate of Milnwood is a reasonable obligation and a welcome chance to display his marksmanship by shooting at the popinjay before the eyes of Lady Margaret's niece Edith.

Not so for old Mause Headrigg, whose Puritan zealotry confusedly links the popinjay and prelatry with a worship of the Golden Calf. Yielding to her fantastic arguments, her son Cuddie, a ploughman of the Bellendens, fails to appear in Lady Margaret's train. The only available substitute, the doltish and undersized Goose Gibbie, blinded by a huge helmet that has slipped down before his eyes, is ludicrously somersaulted over the head of his wildly galloping horse, to the laughter of the onlookers and the humiliation of his mistress. Mause volubly defends her son's disobedience. "Thir ridings and wappenschawings, my leddy, I hae nae broo o' them ava."[28] Her son shall not "make murgeons or Jennyflections, as they ca' them, in the house of the prelates and curates, nor gird him wi' armour to fight in their cause."[29] "Ye're ower learned and ower godly for me to dispute wi'," Lady Margaret wrathfully retorts, and dismisses both mother and son from her service.[30]

Cuddie does not share his mother's religious enthusiasm, but he is used to doing her bidding, and tries in vain to silence her clamors when the Milnwood household in which they have found refuge is subjected to the visitation of a squad of redcoats. "Whisht, Mither, whisht!" he exclaims. "I will not whisht, Cuddie," she replies, "I will uplift my voice and spare not,—I will confound the man of sin, even the scarlet man." "She has her leg ower the harrows now," Cuddie says in despair, "stop her wha can."[31] And thus, after escaping from detention in the confusion of Drumclog, he has nowhere to go except to join the rebels.

But Mause's obstinacy is only a farcical variation on the resistance the Government's repressions have aroused among all the Covenanters. Presbyterian ministers have been driven from their churches, and the open-air conventicles that their followers then held in the fields declared illegal. The few "indulged" ministers allowed to return to their pulpits could do so only at the price of acknowledging the bishops and the supremacy of the crown. Landowners were held responsible for the conformity of their tenants and servants, and even association with religious offenders made a crime. Enforcement of the law was put into the hands of a brutal soldiery given the power of arbitrary fines and imprisonments.

Henry Morton has tried to steer a course of reasoned moderation between these partisan extremes. His reluctance both to defy the law and to injure its victims is rooted in humane feeling and in principle, but to the passionate contenders he seems merely prudential and self-serving; he is subjected to the distrust and antagonism of both sides. "I am weary," he exclaims to himself, "of seeing nothing but violence and fury around me,—now assuming the mask of lawful authority, now taking that of religious zeal."[32]

Significantly, while Morton is blamed for indifference, the real cynical opportunism exemplified by the innkeeper Niel Blane goes unrecognized and uncondemned. He directs his daughter to be "eident and civil" to all, both Whig and Tory: "When the malt begins to get aboon the meal, they'll begin to speak about government in Kirk and State, and then, Jenny, they are like to quarrel: let them be doing,—anger's a drouthy passion, and the mair they dispute, the mair ale they'll drink; but ye were best serve them wi' a pint o' the sma' broust, it will heat them less, and they'll never ken the difference."[33]

During the evening at Blane's inn after the shooting at the popinjay, Morton is revolted by the insolence of the soldiers under the bullying Bothwell. Leaving the tavern with a stranger, he learns that his companion is one of the rebels and in danger from the troopers who are combing the countryside for him. But the man turns out to have been an old comrade-in-arms of his father, John Balfour of Burley, and Morton remembers that Burley had once saved his father's life. Strongly as he dissents from Burley's use of force, he cannot surrender his father's preserver to probable death. Sheltering him for a night in a barn at Milnwood, Morton is thus drawn against his will into taking sides.

Morton does not then know how far Burley has already gone in lawless resistance. But the next morning he overhears some broken words that escape Balfour's lips in his sleep: "Thou are taken, Judas—thou art taken—Cling not to my knees . . . hew him down! —A priest? Ay, a priest of Baal, to be bound and slain, even at the brook Kishon. . . . Strike—thrust with the cold iron—put him out of pain . . . were it but for the sake of his grey hairs."[34] Burley is in fact one of those desperate men who on Magus Moor murdered Archbishop Sharpe, the Primate of Scotland.

Later, Burley defends the assassination. "You are of opinion," he demands of Morton, "that the justice of an execution consists, not in the sufferer's crimes, or in his having merited punishment," but "rests solely in the robe of the judge, the height of the bench, and the voice of the doomster?" Morton, however, refuses to accept this defense of revolutionary justice. "That the Almighty, in his mysterious providence, may bring a bloody man to an end deservedly bloody, does not vindicate those who, without authority of any kind, take upon themselves to be the instruments of execution, and presume to call themselves the executors of divine justice."[35] But he is forced to grant that sometimes a slayer, like Robert Bruce, who killed the Red Cuming, becomes the restorer of his country's freedom.

But the fanaticism and ferocity of Burley, from which Morton recoils in horror, is no less rife among the royalists. When Lady Margaret Bellenden asks the coldly relentless Claverhouse if there is no law to compel submission from recusants like old Mause Headrigg, he replies with ominous composure, "I think I could find one."[36] And hearing of the Covenanters now assembled in armed defiance on Loudonhill, "When the adder crawls into daylight," he remarks grimly, striking his boot-heel on the floor as if he were crushing a noxious reptile, "I can trample him to death; he is only safe when he remains lurking in his den or morass."[37]

Claverhouse and Burley are mirror-images of each other, alike in their fanaticism, their unscrupulousness, and their brutal contempt for human life and moral sympathy. Burley believes deception, treachery, and murder are justified by his religious aims. Claverhouse draws a distinction between what he calls "the fanaticism of honour and that of dark and sullen superstition . . . between the blood of learned and reverend prelates and scholars, of gallant soldiers and noble gentlemen, and the red puddle that stagnates in the veins of psalm-singing mechanics, crack-brained demagogues, and sullen boors." "God gives every spark of life," Morton replies, "—that of the peasant as well as of the prince."[38]

It is the reply of the book, and it is sometimes heard from other lips than Morton's. Among the royalists, Lady Margaret pleads for Morton's life, although his father had been one of those responsible for her own husband's death in the Civil War. "The shedding of this young man's blood will not call back the lives that were dear to me; and how can it comfort me to think that there has been maybe another widowed mother made childless, like mysell, by a deed done at my very door-stane!"[39] And on the opposing side Bessie Maclure saves Lord Evandale from her fellow Covenanters by hiding him in her hut, though her own two sons have been slain by Claverhouse's forces: "But, alas! betraying Lord Evandale's young blood to his enemies' sword," she says, "would ne'er hae brought my Ninian and Johnie alive again."[40]

In the rage engendered by civil strife such compassion is almost drowned and lost. Morton's appeal for moderation, law, and tolerance in behalf of the rebels repels even his old friend Major Bellenden: "I would not have believed this," he exclaims, ". . . if half mankind had sworn it! . . . Rebellious in cold blood, and without even the pretext of enthusiasm."[41] Lord Evandale, a royalist, and Morton's rival in love, does magnanimously contrive to obtain his life from Claverhouse as a personal favor. In his more crucial endeavors, though, to act as an intermediary between the Covenanters and the Government he fails. The flag of truce that under his urging is sent to the insurgents is ignored and Claverhouse's nephew is shot down; the reasoned plea for moderate concessions to the rebels which Morton draws up and which Evandale carries to the commander of the royal forces is summarily rejected.

The same fierce counsels prevail in the camp of the Covenanters, with whom Morton has felt compelled to associate himself. Here the temporizing Laird of Langcale and the moderate clergyman Poundtext are overborne by the wild enthusiasm of the fanatical preacher Macbriar, the frenzy of the maniac Habbakuk Mucklewrath, and the uncompromising ferocity of Burley. Even after the catastrophic defeat of their untrained forces at Bothwell Bridge, their vindictive bigotry unites in condemning Morton to death for having urged peaceful negotiation and for having released Lord Evandale on parole.

Morton's peril arises once more, as it has already done repeatedly, from that very moderation that had once made him seem fainthearted and indifferent, but which in every moment of crisis has led him to speak out clearly and heroically to both royalists and Covenanters. His scornful refusal to deny that he had sheltered Burley, his defiant assertion before Claverhouse of the liberties of Scotland, have twice endangered his life. Again and again he has risked death by clashing with Burley and the other rebel leaders. Now, for these gloomy and defeated men, his humanity itself condemns him.

The moment is tense. The clock is ticking away Morton's last moments. The insane Mucklewrath is about to put forward the hands of the timepiece, Morton's captors are already fingering their weapons, when they are stopped by one of them. "Hist!" he says, "I hear a distant noise." "It is the rushing of the brook over the pebbles," says another. "It is the soughing of the wind among the bracken," says a third. "It is the galloping of horse," says Morton to himself. "God grant they may come as my deliverers!"[42] Shots are fired; soldiers rush in. They are a part of Claverhouse's forces.

Morton and Macbriar are captured; the lunatic Mucklewrath dies drenched in blood. Macbriar, hailed before the Privy Council, is tortured and condemned to death. He meets his fate bravely. "You send me to a happy exchange,—to the company of angels and the spirits of the just, for that of frail dust and ashes; ye send me from darkness into day, from mortality to immortality, and, in a word, from earth to heaven!"[43]

But Morton now survives through those very qualities that have so often led him to the verge of destruction—his belief that human beings are more valuable than dogma, that human life is more important than abstractions. Though he has clearly committed himself to the side of the Covenanters, he has striven for a peaceful settlement, preserved Major Bellenden, Lady Margaret, and her niece from the fury of the rebels, saved the life of Lord Evandale. More than the mere champion of legality, though he has fought for law when he saw it wrested to cruelty, he has warmly defended a still higher law of humanity.

Claverhouse himself consequently makes a distinction between him and the other rebel leaders. "What a pity it is," Morton exclaims as Macbriar is taken away to die, "that with such self-devotion and heroism should have been mingled the fiercer features of his sect!" "You mean," Claverhouse responds, "his resolution to condemn you to death?"[44] And Claverhouse tells him, "There is that about you which I respect in an enemy as much as I like in a friend."[45] On the security of Claverhouse and Evandale, Morton's life is spared under condition that he go abroad so long as the King shall please. After the Revolution of 1688, when William and Mary ascend the throne, Morton is enabled to return to Scotland.

Since the time of Scott's contemporary Dr. Thomas McCrie, eminent scholars have disagreed on the accuracy with which Scott portrayed the Covenanters.[46] In our own day David Craig echoes McCrie's accusation that it is an unfair caricature, but R. S. Rait has insisted that it is literally accurate.[47] "Official statements of the Covenanters," Craig admits, "were couched in a strained jargon based on the Old Testament"; in contrast, both their daily speech and their field sermons, he claims, were direct and colloquial. He therefore finds Mause Headrigg's utterance implausible and Macbriar's sermon after Drumclog only "an elaborate concoction of Biblical rhetoric."[48] Here, again, Rait dissents: "There can be no doubt," he contends, "that the Covenanters did so speak."[49]

But this aspect of the debate overlooks the aims of Scott's art. Here, as in the language of Meg Merrilies, Saunders Mucklebackit, and Hobbie Elliott, he is not striving for a completely naturalistic speech, not for the language of everyday life, but one that will convey the spirit animating its speakers, vibrant with those solemn Bible overtones that inspired them. Little as Scott shares the enthusiasm of either Kettledrummle or Macbriar, he does not burlesque them. In the mouth of Macbriar "the language of Scripture" does indeed, as Scott says, have "a rich and solemn effect, like that which is produced by the beams of the sun streaming through the storied representation of saints and martyrs on the Gothic window of some ancient cathedral."[50]

Nor does Scott misrepresent his peasants; Craig himself can be charged with unfairness when he dismisses Mause as merely ludicrous and her son Cuddie as a blockhead.[51] To see no more than this is to overlook the mingling of sincere piety and maternal love in the one and the shrewd and earthy common sense of the other. "Oh, hinny,' hinny!" Mause exclaims when Cuddie is hailed before the Council, "glad and proud and sorry and humbled am I, a' in ane and the same instant, to see my bairn ganging to testify for the truth gloriously with his mouth." "Whisht, whisht, mither," he cries impatiently; "Odds, ye daft wife, is this a time to speak o' thae things? I tell ye I'll testify either ae gate or anither."[52] Not only here, but throughout the book, the two speakers are far more than a stupid clown and a crazily presumptuous old woman.

If Scott delineates the leaders among the Covenanters as almost maddened by their wrongs, he makes it amply clear that they were justified in their bitterness. Morton feels "revolted by the tyrannical and oppressive conduct of the Government, the misrule, license, and brutality of the soldiery, the executions on the scaffold, the slaughters in the open field, the free quarters and exactions imposed by military law, which placed the lives and fortunes of a free people on the level with Asiatic slaves."[53] On the other hand, it is not true that the Covenanters at Drumclog and Bothwell Bridge were fighting solely for the right to worship God in their own way; they were demanding, in the words of the Solemn League and Covenant, "the extirpation of Prelacy" and nothing less than the enforcement of their mode of worship on all of Scotland. But the actual tyranny of the Crown was no less ferocious than the tyranny of which they desired to be guilty.[54]

The fact Scott demonstrates is that rebellions are not led by philosophers or even by men exclusively rational and dedicated to reason. Within their ranks there will be men like Burley, driven by the lust for power, ruthless, implacable, and untrustworthy, but fearless, insidiously persuasive, and keen in judgment; there will also be madmen like Habbakuk Mucklewrath and enthusiasts like Macbriar, too possessed for compromise and too sincere for deceit; men of moderation like Poundtext; timorous followers like the Laird of Langcale, almost helplessly drawn on by the passions of those surrounding them; and many like Cuddie Headrigg, involved by the force of accident or circumstance. Further, men of all these kinds not only form inevitable parts of any movement of revolt, but play necessary roles in its course. Morton yields to these realities when he recognizes that though he does not desire to be their associate they are the rebellion. Scott has drawn a paradigm of a revolutionary movement.

It is the great achievement of *Old Mortality*. Scott, who had inveterately opposed the later stages of the French Revolution, and seen them lead to the dictatorship of Napoleon, has been impelled in the study of history to perceive that there are rebellions that are not only inevitable, but, with all their confused entanglement of right and wrong, essentially justified. The Covenanters were the early swell of that great flood that in 1688 was to overthrow a tyranny and sweep a dynasty from the throne. Luckier or wiser in its leaders, it achieved a settlement more stable and more nearly sound than emerged from the fury of 1789. The great issues, the great forces, and the human weaknesses and perils in such an upheaval are all given life and illumination in the tumultuous movement of *Old Mortality*. Breathing with the passions of men and women, it is at the same time a philosophic construction of a historical pattern.

Another kind of revolution, less violent, but no less crucial, forms the background of *Rob Roy*. It is the revolution from the older world of the feudal landowner and the clan to the new world of commerce. Since the times of the Tudors, of course, merchants and bankers had been growing in power. At the close of the seventeenth century their aid weighed decisively in enabling the landed aristocracy and the religious opponents of James II to bring in William and Mary. The Act of Union in 1707 further strengthened the mercantile prosperity of both England and Scotland. When Queen Anne died and George I was proclaimed King, the financial support of the merchants standing behind the Whigs established the Hanoverian dynasty and was powerful enough to crush the Jacobite uprising of 1715.

These historical facts determine the structure of *Rob Roy*. Its action moves between England and Scotland; the scenes in commercial London are balanced by those in commercial Glasgow, and those in wild Northumberland by those in the lonely Highland valleys of the upper Forth. The divisions in the scene and action reflect the careful balancing of the characters—William Osbaldistone, the daring London businessman and entrepreneur standing against the way of life symbolized by Sir Hildebrand Osbaldistone, the fox-hunting Jacobite country squire; Bailie Nicol Jarvie, the shrewd Glasgow merchant, against that of Rob Roy, the dislodged Highland drover turned cattle thief and Jacobite agent.[55] Scott sharpens the antitheses and parallels by making the two Osbaldistones brothers and the Bailie and Rob Roy cousins. The novel is a mirror of world forces.

Nor does Scott observe their working with any backward-looking regret.[56] Unlike Edmund Burke, who mourned the rise of the stock jobber as the decay of chivalry, Scott sees the businessman as a creative force and his life as no less adventurous and exciting and a good deal more fruitful than the life of the knight errant. He had before him the example of Constable, who was bringing out *Rob Roy* itself in a venturesome first edition of 10,000 copies, whose *Encyclopaedia Britannica* was spreading knowledge and enlightenment, and who paid magnificent sums to its learned contributors. Scott's own career, indeed, in his dealings with his publishers and his involvements in printing, shows him as an ardent man of affairs, keenly alert to both the challenges and the significant role of business.

William Osbaldistone is a man of Constable's boldness and Scott's mettle. *Rob Roy*, to be sure, gives us only glimpses of his business activities, but had Scott lived in an age ripe for a novel dealing with the world of business, he might, like Balzac, have given us a Nucingen, or anticipated Wells or Dreiser in presenting a Ponderevo or a Cowperwood. And he would have rendered the patent-medicine monarch or the streetcar king with quite as much understanding as he brought to princely gamblers like the young Chevalier and royal manipulators like Louis XI. Scott understands well that William Osbaldistone is a man animated less by greed than by the exercise of his financial talents:

"It seemed to be necessary to him, as to an ambitious conqueror, to push on from achievement to achievement, without stopping to secure, far less to enjoy, the acquisitions which he made. Accustomed to see his whole fortune trembling in the scales of chance, and dexterous at adopting expedients for casting the balance in his favour, his health and spirits and activity seemed ever to increase with the animating hazards on which he staked his wealth; and he resembled a sailor, accustomed to brave the billows and the foe, whose confidence rises on the eve of tempest or of battle."[57]

Nicol Jarvie, his Scottish analogue, is more cautious; he is careful of his cash but neither ungenerous nor lacking in financial courage. With some qualms he offers his Highland kinsman aid of "an hundred pund" and, uncertain that he will ever see his money again, falteringly adds, "or even twa hundred."[58] When Osbaldistone's business is struggling with sudden financial demands, and the rapacious MacVittie and MacFinn have treacherously thrown Osbaldistone's agent Owen in jail, Jarvie stakes much more than the bail he puts up to set him free, for he risks becoming responsible for a part of the liabilities of the London firm. But Jarvie does not share the towering financial adventurousness that characterized his Scottish contemporary John Law; it is the London speculator Osbaldistone who exemplifies that spirit.

Osbaldistone Hall and Sir Hildebrand are Old England but not that of Sir Roger de Coverley or even of Squire Western; they are fallen into a vegetative and fat-witted decay rendered with an almost savage satire.[59] Sir Hildebrand, though good-humored and kindly, and revealing traces of his youthful familiarity with the life of courts and camps, now allows his estate to sink into neglect and lives for little more than eating, drinking, and hunting. His six sons, except for the unprincipled Rashleigh, are boorish and illiterate; only Rashleigh and their kinswoman the lively and enchanting Diana Vernon ever open a book from the library their forebears have accumulated. Osbaldistone Hall is Horseback Hall in all its crassness, lost in lethargy, lacking even the impulses of aspiration and responsibility.

This Northumberland backwater is devoid of the virtues that mark Tully-Veolan in *Waverley*. For all the Baron of Bradwardine's absurdity and pedantry, he is a man of high and noble principle, his quotations from Virgil, Ovid, Barbour, and Lindsay are the marks of a true if somewhat antiquated culture, and his loyalty to the Stuart cause is a living flame, not the dead, hollow, and empty verbal jingle it has become in Osbaldistone Hall. Though *Waverley* has shown clearly enough the brainlessness of Balmawhapple, the wrangling of the Scottish clan chiefs, and the unscrupulousness and personal ambition that sullied Fergus MacIvor's fire, it had rounded out the picture with the Baron and Flora.

*Rob Roy* demonstrates, however, why Jacobitism never permeated northern England as it did the Highlands of Scotland. And even its Scottish scenes reveal why Jacobitism ultimately failed there both in 1715 and 1745. Rob Roy MacGregor is reduced to desperation by the enmity of powerful neighbors and is therefore drawn almost inevitably into plots for a change of government, but he would willingly be a peaceful cattle-breeder and dealer. Firebrands like Garschattachin are hardly more impressive than Balmawhapple as leaders of a rebellion. The material interests of Scotland are changing: already the Highland chiefs have been brought into commercial relations with the south by the sale of oak from their forests to businessmen like Osbaldistone; and thriving lowland merchants like Nicol Jarvie are not eager to endanger their prosperity by a violent change of government.

The wild life of the Highland glens no more glorifies the old Scotland than that of Northumberland does old England. Instead of glamor, Frank Osbaldistone finds dirt, violence, ignorance, and squalor. If Rob Roy's wife, Helen MacGregor, has a certain barbaric grandeur in her bitter sense of her sufferings, her response to them is one of savage and terrible ferocity. Her fierceness, transposed to another key, has already appeared in the scene at the clachan alehouse, with the Highlanders provoking a fight by their objection to sharing the accommodations of a public inn, "muttering to each other, drawing up their plaids, and snorting and snuffing the air after the manner of their countrymen when working themselves into a passion."[60] The words "snorting and snuffing" marvelously underline their preposterous sensitivity; and no less risible is the description of the naked slumberers around the wall of the tavern, who during the scuffle that follows only raise "their shirtless bodies to look at the fray," exclaim, "Oigh! oigh!" and fall "fast asleep again," before the swords are returned to their scabbards.[61]

This spectacle of men deliberately lashing themselves into a tantrum, ludicrous enough here, Scott can also modulate, in a later scene, to almost tragic power, when Rob Roy justifies his outlaw life by a wrathful enumeration of his wrongs, "his light grey eyes contracting alternately and dilating their pupils until they seemed actually to flash with flame, while he thrust forward and drew back his foot, grasped the hilt of his dirk, clenched his fist."[62] When Frank offers sympathy and aid for his sons, Rob's mood changes swiftly. "I thank ye—I thank ye—but let us say nae mair o' this. I did not think the eye of man would again have seen a tear on MacGregor's eyelash."[63]

So far, then, is Scott from idealizing the old England and the old Scotland and violently opposing the new. His loyalties were not rooted in an uncritical devotion to the past; in *Rob Roy* he shows the ancient and traditional ways of life as straitened and savage, and now dead or dying, and celebrates the new. If Rob Roy is heroic, Nicol Jarvie does not lack courage, not even physical courage, and emerges as the hero of commerce. His analysis of the economy of the Highlands is penetrating. His enthusiasm for the prosperity that has been brought about by the Act of Union is clearheaded and enlightened:

"There's naething sae gude on this side o' time but it might hae been better, and that may be said o' the Union. Nane were keener against it than the Glasgow folk, wi' their rabblings and their risings, and their mobs, as they ca' them nowadays. But it's an ill wind that blaws naebody gude—Let ilka ane roose the ford as they find it—I say, let Glasgow flourish! whilk is judiciously and elegantly putten round the town's arms, by way of byeword. —Now, since St. Mungo catched herrings in the Clyde, what was ever like to gar us flourish like the sugar and tobacco-trade? Will ony body tell me that, and grumble at the treaty that opened us a road west-awa' yonder?"[64]

But Bailie Jarvie is not idealized. He can urge a prosaic materialism to the point of arguing how many thousand acres of farmland might be created by draining Loch Lomond and leaving only a canal for transporting coal between Dumbarton to Glenfalloch. Contradictorily he has nevertheless a strain of sentiment: "The Hieland blude o' me warms at thae daft tales, and whiles I like better to hear them than a word o' profit, gude forgie me!"[65] And, if needs must, though he is a man of peace, he can fight too, seizing the red-hot coulter and setting fire to his wild opponent's plaid. Primarily, though, he is the practical businessman and, if *Rob Roy* has a hero, the hero of the book. He is the foil to both Frank Osbaldistone and Rob Roy: the middle-aged realist against the young romantic, the progressive Lowland merchant against the Highland champion of a dying feudal past.

Thematically, *Rob Roy* is thus far more significant than has been generally recognized. Any tyro, of course, can find defects in its technique and structure. The story is told as the first-person autobiographical narrative of Osbaldistone's son Frank, addressed in old age to his friend and business partner of many years, Will Tresham; and the reader finds it incredible that Frank should never before have confided it to an almost daily intimate. And although the narrative begins in the tone of the mature man looking back on his past, Scott endows it with none of the haunting overtones of foreshadowing and reflective insight gathered from later experience that Dickens, for example, so subtly uses in *David Copperfield* and *Great Expectations*. Frank Osbaldistone might be recording these recaptured experiences from day to day for all that the supposed perspective on the past colors its presentation.

More important, after the opening scenes, Frank's father, the elder Osbaldistone and head of the firm, who should have been made central to the thematic development of the novel, disappears until almost the end, is seldom even heard from, and plays no vital role in the action. His place is taken by Bailie Nicol Jarvie, who not only becomes a father-surrogate for Frank, but embodies all the significant thematic functions he should have shared with William Osbaldistone. After the middle of the book Sir Hildebrand also vanishes until the close and thus leaves its pattern to be worked out in Scotland alone. Though the relation between a financial crisis in the Highlands and the rebellion of their chiefs is made clear, Scott fails to convince us that the downfall of even the great firm of Osbaldistone and Tresham could so shake the entire northern half of the kingdom. Nor does he ever make quite plain how the firm could be ruined by the absence of the financial documents Rashleigh Osbaldistone has stolen, inasmuch as nearly all of them are non-negotiable instruments that can be realized by William Osbaldistone alone.

Finally, there can be no doubt that the dénouement of the story, as Scott himself recognized, is huddled with implausible rapidity to its "happy ending." It is cavalier beyond even Scott's wont to kill off all Sir Hildebrand's sons in a single paragraph to make Frank the heir of Osbaldistone Hall. And though the reader is willing enough to have Diana Vernon marry Frank instead of being consigned to a nunnery, he is startled to find this accomplished in two pages. The truth is that the logic of the story would have required another volume to be worked out in convincing and concrete detail. This Scott himself frankly confessed: "I had too much flax on my distaff," he wrote his friend Morritt, "and as it did not consist with my patience or my plan to make a fourth volume, I was obliged at last to draw a rough coarse and hasty thread."[66]

But after conceding these shortcomings—and they are not slight—all significant criticism rests. Unlike the slow opening of *Old Mortality*, with its thematically relevant but rather tiresome image of the old man among the graves, *Rob Roy* moves magnificently from the very beginning. One of Scott's great gifts is what Aristotle declared to be the essential characteristic of poetry, the representation of men in action; and in *Rob Roy* we find ourselves caught at once in the grip of a swift and yet poetic narrative fusing the colors of romance and reality. From the opening chapter, when young Frank Osbaldistone is summoned back from Bordeaux and his lackadaisical daydreaming of himself as a poet, the action hardly slackens. On his obstinate refusal to enter into his father's business, he is promptly disinherited and banished to his uncle's residence at Osbaldistone Hall.

There follow the comedy and adventure of the journey north; his encounter with the mysterious Campbell (whom we do not at the moment suspect to be Rob Roy); Frank's welcome from Sir Hildebrand; his meeting with his ugly, insinuating, silken, and sinister cousin Rashleigh and his half-scornful, half-jealous conflicts with those loutish Yahoos, his five other cousins; his conversations with the Scottish gardener, Andrew Fairservice; his intimacy with the frank, high-spirited, irresistible Diana Vernon, who renders both the reader and Frank her captivated admirers.

The gardener, Andrew Fairservice, who becomes Frank's knavish and saucy Sancho Panza, is among Scott's most superb character-creations. He is, as John Buchan truly observes, "one of the great serving-men of literature . . . a real but low type of Scot, cunning, avaricious, indifferently loyal, venturesome in his own interest but a craven in the face of bodily peril, an incorrigible liar and braggart, and never more impertinent than when his bluff is called."[67] But he is full of the mother wit of his class, with his hatred for episcopacy and the Church of Rome—"the muckle hure that sitteth on seven hills, as if ane wasna braid eneugh for her auld hinder end"[68]—his greedy rascality, his scorn for the "clinkum-clankum" of poetry,[69] and the incessant flood of bold, shrewd, and humorous observation that pours from his disgraceful mouth.

Andrew is more, however, than a bravura portrait; he is a parody of almost all the qualities that make Nicol Jarvie both a focal center of sanity and soundness in the book and the mediator who resolves all its major conflicts. Andrew's cunning parodies Jarvie's shrewdness, his avarice Jarvie's thrift, his conceit Jarvie's self-esteem, his contempt for poetry Jarvie's practicality, his pharisaical intolerance the Bailie's staunch Presbyterianism. Nearly every one of Nicol Jarvie's virtues Andrew's selfish rascality degrades into sneaking vices.

Soon after Frank's arrival in Osbaldistone Hall his father calls his nephew Rashleigh south to the post of business responsibility that his son had declined. Frank has already suspected his dissimulation, but from the moment of his cousin's departure we share Frank's gradually tightening sense of being entangled in a web of intrigue spun by Rashleigh. His subtlety and prepotence seem to envelop Frank in ambiguous dangers; even when he is far off in distant London, Frank suspects him of pulling secret strings, being accountable for unanswered letters, controlling fate itself. With the catastrophic announcement of his father's ruin, Frank in a blinding glare of illumination sees Rashleigh as an implacable, a Machiavellian, a diabolically powerful enemy.

From that moment Scott surrounds Frank's every step with an extraordinary atmosphere of peril. Even during his ride to Glasgow it is as if Rashleigh's vindictive spirit hangs about him, following with silent tread down the clattering precipices, across bogs and turf, pursuing with low breathings among nocturnal, solitary hills. Amid the gloomy shadows of the Laigh Kirk, in Glasgow, the ominous tension grows terrifying when the mysterious voice from behind the massive round pillars whispers, "You are in danger in this city," and Frank glimpses only a dim phantom figure disappearing among the dreary vaults of the dark church.[70]

The scenes in the Glasgow Tolbooth are a glowing chiaroscuro of light and shade—as Scott had anticipated—with Rob Roy's henchman Dougal and Bailie Nicol Jarvie wonderfully intermingling comedy and drama. From then, with the journey into the Lennox country, the pace even accelerates, and the excitement, never slackening, soars into epic narrative. The wild nocturnal episodes in the alehouse at the Clachan of Aberfoil are like a painting by Rembrandt pierced by the grotesque comedy of Cruikshank. The arrest of the travelers by the government troops, the defeat of the latter at the hands of the wild Highlanders, the news of Rob Roy's capture and the brutal murder of the cringing hostage, Rob Roy's escape from the forces of the Duke of Montrose, the recovery of the missing documents, all the later sequence of events culminating in the doomed Jacobite uprising of 1715, are one tremendous rush.

Frank Osbaldistone himself hardly perceives the full significance of the events in which he is involved and the forces that have buffeted him. He has some of Waverley's weaknesses and suggestibility but neither his sensitivity nor his depth. Though he is placed like Henry Morton in difficult situations, he falls far short of Morton's high sense of responsibility and his understanding. He finds his problems murkier and more mysterious than Morton does his, but they are personal rather than problems of principle—hostility to Rashleigh, loyalty to his father, love for Diana. He never sees them as related to great social issues. Thus he illustrates Scott's themes without himself understanding them.

This does not mean that he is not a real person, solidly presented. He is still another proof, indeed, of how lacking in foundation is the charge that Scott's young heroes have no personality. But Scott's way in portraying his characters is neither psychological analysis nor the direct endeavor to plumb their unconscious, but their presentation in action. Instead of being dissected or hunted through a labyrinth of clues, they are *there* before us, and their behavior declares their natures. It is not that they have no complexity or that Scott is limited to simple characters. His art is equal to the achievement of subtlety without a parade of subtlety.

In the beginning of *Rob Roy*, Frank Osbaldistone is a callow and conceited young spoony with a fancy picture of himself as a poet and the notion that there is something very fine in defying his father and refusing to go into his business. He entirely fails to comprehend his father's character, and imagines—even in the midst of certain doubtful tremors— that if he holds out long enough his father will give way. There is a high and truthful perception in Scott's rendering of that youthful obstinacy and those tremulous fears, and in the shocked surprise with which Frank finds himself disowned. Then come the thoughtless, silly-clever high spirits, during his journey north, of Frank's amusing himself with the cowardice of his fellow-traveler Morris, the immature bravado of his drinking and boasting among his cousins at Osbaldistone Hall, the alternate play of his hot resentment against Rashleigh and the ease with which that adroit trickster manipulates him even while Frank believes himself brilliantly clever, and the way in which Frank convinces himself that his sulky exhibition of jealousy to Diana is both dignified and manly.

But Frank is not entirely a fool; he is capable of dignity, courage, decision, and intelligence, and grows in all these in the course of the story. He is of real service to his father in regaining the documents Rashleigh has stolen. He recovers from the inflated notion that he has a soul too high and sensitive for the world's practical uses. He has the sense to respect the worth beneath the Bailie's bourgeois surface and to be guided by him. He has the grace to love Diana and the heart to be wrung when he believes that he has lost her.

Diana herself is one of Scott's proudest masterpieces. She takes us by storm with her gay and lively talk, her unconventional freedom of action, her moments of discouragement so bravely resisted, her intelligence, and her fineness of spirit. Modern readers, who are used to hoydens in fact as well as in fiction, may miss some of her surprising flavor and freshness, though they cannot miss her charm. Not that she is really a hoyden: unlike some of the equally uninhibited heroines of Restoration comedy, she remains a lady, neither coarse in conversation nor unchaste in conduct: but she refines all their dash into a noble wine of gallantry. Her true spiritual sisters, however, are neither the Miss Prues and Perts of seventeenth-century satire nor the Brett Ashleys and marijuana girls, but a more shining company: Shakespeare's Beatrice in *Much Ado About Nothing* and the lively Elizabeth Bennet of *Pride and Prejudice*. "Whatever she says or does," as Buchan puts it, "we are her devoted henchmen, believing fiercely in her beauty, her goodness, and her brains."[71]

And never has Scott handled the emotion of love between man and woman with more passion and intensity. "Those who have been taught that Scott could write but tamely of love"[72] may read the scene when Diana bends in the moonlight from her horse to say, as they both believe, good-bye to Frank forever. Its depth of feeling is all the more moving from the restraint the two impose upon themselves. Her father waits impatiently on his horse a few paces away. "Her face, not perhaps altogether unwillingly, touched mine—She pressed my hand, while the tear that trembled in her eye found its way to my cheek instead of her own. . . . It was *but* a moment."[73] Then the two riders move on and disappear, leaving Frank alone in the darkness:

"I remained motionless . . . gazing after them, as if endeavouring to count the sparkles which flew from the horses' hoofs. I continued to look after even these had ceased to be visible, and to listen for their footsteps long after the distant trampling had died in my ears. At length, tears rushed to my eyes, glazed as they were by the exertion of straining after what was no longer to be seen. I wiped them mechanically, and almost without being aware that they were flowing, but they came thicker and thicker. I felt the tightening of the throat and breast, the *hysterica passio* of poor Lear, and, sitting down by the wayside, I shed a flood of the first and most bitter tears which had flowed from my eyes since childhood."[74]

The love story and its resolution, though the latter is inartistically sudden, are woven into the resolution of the novel's main themes. The elder Osbaldistone has been an unbending and arbitrary father; Frank has been an indifferently understanding son. Nor have the relations of Sir Hildebrand and his heirs revealed any closer ties. Here too Bailie Jarvie's role is catalytic and serves as a resolving force. In a world where sons show small respect for their fathers and fathers ignore or disinherit their sons, pious remembrances of "My father, the Deacon" are ever rising to his lips. He makes himself a father to Frank, and brings him and his real father together in bonds of deeper understanding.[75]

Frank's entry into the partnership in Osbaldistone and Tresham, which he had formerly declined, his inheritance of Osbaldistone Hall, and his marriage to Diana draw into a unity the previously separate worlds of finance and of the landed gentry. Though Frank was not the poet he imagined himself to be, he and Diana share a genuine sensitivity to art and literature; they will restore the moldering library in the old Northumberland estate and revitalize its decayed cultural tradition. Frank is not, of course, a self-portrait of Walter Scott, but his story merges in significant ways with that of Scott himself, the scion of an old Scottish family, who enters the world of law and business, is a partner in a printing house, mingles an interest in money and literature, builds a country house in Roxburghshire, and is soon to be offered a baronetcy. But Frank does more than reflect his creator. He symbolically illustrates one of those fusions that repeatedly occur in history and which took place later that century in England, for example, when the heiress of the Coutts banking fortune mingled in the worlds of government and literature and when the Barings acquired rural estates, a title, and social prestige, and entertained men of achievement in science and the arts.

In four years Scott had written six novels, none flawless, but all save one enduring masterpieces. *Guy Mannering* and *The Antiquary* had stopped the mouths of those reviewers who feared that with *Waverley* he would have exhausted himself. They in turn proved to be only the first great peaks in an entire range. *The Black Dwarf* reached no such heights; what should have been its summit was broken off as if an accident had sliced away a mountaintop. But then had come *Old Mortality* and *Rob Roy*, two further towering heights in the chain. Beyond them, soon to rise into view, lay *The Heart of Mid-Lothian*. After that in the mists, nobody, not even Scott, could tell how many more there would be, of what shapes, or how high.

---

# *The Moving Hand*

## *( 1 8 1 8 )*

DURING THE LAST ten days of 1817 the final chapters of *Rob Roy* had been rushed through the press and the novel was published on December 31.[1] Some readers who suspected Scott's authorship and knew he had visited the outlaw's cave the previous summer were disappointed to find no mention of that wild hideaway. Other romantic souls were upset that Rob himself was portrayed neither as a Robin Hood despoiling the rich for the poor nor as a Red Cross Knight, but as the cattle reiver and blackmailer he had been in reality. Everyone, though, was fascinated by Bailie Nicol Jarvie, the Dougal creature, and the cowardly and insolent Andrew Fairservice; and the wild, gallant, witty, and incomparable Diana Vernon enchanted all hearts. Within two weeks Constable's huge printing of ten thousand was snapped up; three thousand more went to press at once; tens of thousands followed.[2]

Scott spent the Christmas holidays at Abbotsford, working on the melodrama he had promised Terry.[3] Snow was deep on the hills and the roads too slippery for much riding;[4] and "by remaining too long on the ice while the Darnick men were playing a great match at curling with the Melrose folks" Scott brought on himself another attack of cramp, though this time it was only a mild one.[5] In January the weather turned so stormy that he was obliged to postpone a hare hunt he had arranged for the amusement of the young Earl of Dalkeith. He promised that his own greyhound Hamlet would "be ready" at the next opportunity "to meet any Laertes" the youngster chose to match against him.[6]

No sooner was Scott back in Edinburgh than he cleared his desk for action. The conception for the heroine, Jeanie Deans, had been warming in his imagination for almost a year—from the time he had received from a Mrs. Thomas Goldie an account of the real Scottish heroine Helen Walker, who had saved the life of her condemned sister by journeying on foot all the way to London to plead for her pardon.[7]

Now he set to work with force. Cadell reported a visit from him on January 15, "in great glee" and "looking as healthy as possible. He is to begin the new *Tales* immediately. . . . He wants all the tracts, pamphlets, etc., that we can get him about Captain Porteous's mob, for the tale, *The Heart of Mid-Lothian*."[8] He worked with such speed that at the end of the month Cadell excitedly announced a considerable portion of "the *new Tales of My Landlord* . . . at the press!!!"[9]

Laboriously as he toiled on his book, Scott did not forget his Tweedside estate.[10] He and some of his Darnick neighbors were constructing roads to provide work for the poor of all the surrounding parishes.[11] He himself had built a sawmill on his property[12] and planned to convert one of his steadings "into a little hamlet for labourers, which we will name Abbotstown."[13] His tenants should be charged reasonable rents and be paid for their work "at the ordinary rate," but they must keep their cottages and gardens neat and not break his timber, destroy birds' nests, or trample down his planting. "The art of making people happy is to leave them much to their own guidance, but some little regulation is necessary. . . . I think we might settle a few families very happily here, which is an object I have much at heart, for I have no notion of the proprietor who is only ambitious to be lord of the 'beast and the brute,' and chases the human face from his vicinity."[14]

On January 16 there was a tremendous storm in Edinburgh. "All the gothic pinnacles on the new Episcopal Chapel are blown down, & have fallen on the roof & forced their way into the body of the building so that the horns of the Bishops Mitre have got into the guts of the church."[15] Scott trembled for the fate of his tower at Abbotsford. But a few days later he was relieved; a roof in the neighborhood had been blown clean off, Tom Purdie reported, and "was lying in the road like a saddle," but of the tower not a stone had been shaken. Nor had a slate been lifted from his roof, "though about two yards of slating were stripped from the stables in the haugh."[16]

He was anxious now to complete his building operations. The plastering, of course, could not be done while there was still frost and would have to wait until March, but meanwhile there was all the woodwork. He sent the builders, Sanderson and Paterson, plans of the oak cases for his bookroom and of the dining-room arch and told them he would be at Abbotsford on the weekend of February 14. "The cellars may be settled at the same time."[17] It did not matter, he remarked cheerfully to Laidlaw, that the garret bedrooms were dark: "they are intended for the accommodation of travelling geniuses, poets, painters, and so forth, and a little obscurity will refresh their shattered brains."[18] He had been "undisturbed by qualms or crambos in the stomach" since the beginning of January.[19]

During the last half-year Scott had gradually confided to Laidlaw more and more of the management of the estate. Tom Purdie, though "thoroughly honest and very clever in his way," Scott said, "has no kind of generalizing, and would often like to save sixpence in his own department at the expense of my paying five shillings in another." Under able direction the land could yield "£150 or £200 saved on what we must otherwise buy; and if we could arrange to have mutton and beef occasionally from the farm in winter, it would be a still greater saving."[20] Laidlaw ran the new sawmill, he superintended the planting, he kept an eye on the cattle.

"I am glad the saws are going," Scott wrote him. "We may begin by and by with wrights . . ." And "I like the idea of the birch-hedge much, and if intermixed with holly and thorns, I think it might make an impenetrable thicket . . ."[21] Black Italian poplars were also the "most beautiful of plants which love a wet soil."[22] How did the two oxen "Ogg and Bashan come on?" "Will you make Tom remember . . . not to plant his pleasure trees . . . in lines along the walks but take advantage of any little hollow or change of ground to place them in groupes of four or five together." Then there were the hagberries and Bullace plums to be planted, the sluice to be cleared, the haugh to be marled. At the entrance to the glen "George must stick in a few wild roses honeysuckles & sweet briars . . . to produce the luxuriance we see in the woods which Nature plants herself." "Our old & valued house-maid Bell"—"a good-tempered bustling affectionate girl"—"is going to be married to one of the Darnick Turnbulls. . . . We shall be in the hiring market therefore for a house-maid as well as a maid for Abbotsford."[23]

From the day Laidlaw settled into the Kaeside farmhouse Scott had also kept his promise to provide literary employment.[24] Laidlaw compiled the Chronicle section of the *Register*;[25] he did articles on volumes of African travels and on Mariner's *Account of the Natives of the Tonga Islands*.[26] Blackwood's new magazine, a Tory rival to the Whig *Edinburgh Review*, had got off to a rather feeble start in April, 1817, and the publisher slyly angled for Scott's support by suggesting that Laidlaw conduct its Chronicle department.[27] For his friend's sake Scott softened his distaste for that pugnacious bookseller. He would be, he assured Blackwood, completely neutral, "reserving the privilege of contributing any trifling assistance to either or both publications." As for payment, since he could supply only occasional small pieces, "I would be very unreasonable to exact any emolument for such trifles."[28]

"It is, however, in your power," he went on, "to interest me more deeply in the success of your attempt, in the event of your securing, as you propose, the assistance of my friend, Mr. William Laidlaw, on the footing of a regular contributor." He was "a man of a singularly original and powerful mind, acquainted with science, well skilled in literature," and "a good antiquary." He would have Scott's "best advice and frequent assistance." "But, my good sir, if I am to give this sort of pledge," Laidlaw must receive "at least £120 per annum."[29] He was now project- ing "a series of letters under the signature of Maugraby," which Scott would revise and correct. His own contributions, he warned, would probably be very few indeed.[30]

Blackwood shrewdly understood Scott's insinuation, and the angler himself was hooked by the great fish he was trying to catch. Laidlaw got the post and Scott adhered to his word. Presently he was writing Blackwood, "I return the Chronicle, and an article which we must see in proof, as, clubbing our information, we had but just time to have it copied over. . . . If I find I am essentially assisting my friend Mr. L., I have little doubt of occasionally assisting the *Magazine*, as much as any curious stray information, anecdotes, &c., may be gathered in this country."[31]

For six months the periodical was a failure. Its editors, two men named Pringle and Cleghorn, were making it a monument of dullness. Then Blackwood took drastic action. He fired the editors, seized the reins himself, renamed it *Blackwood's Magazine*, and threw open its pages to a brilliant group of contributors who filled it with startling controversial matter—brutally cutting book reviews, wild and fantastic satire, fero- cious attacks on the *Edinburgh Review* and all its gods of the Whig domination. Almost overnight, the leading article of the October number, the notorious "Chaldee MS," made *Blackwood's* into a scandalous suc- cess.[32]

It was elaborated during an after-dinner meeting, with bumpers of wine and shouts of laughter, by a triumvirate of authors who formed a sort of unofficial editorial board.[33] They consisted of James Hogg, the Ettrick Shepherd, "bustling in all flushed";[34] John Wilson, the son of a Paisley manufacturer, a Glasgow and Oxford graduate, now thirty-two years of age, a swaggering giant of a man, with bright yellow hair and icy blue eyes; and a dark, slender young man of twenty-three, also an Oxford graduate, named John Gibson Lockhart.[35] The article they hilariously concocted pretended to be a recently discovered oriental manuscript, but through its disguise of Biblical imagery it transparently derided the literati and booksellers of Edinburgh.

Blackwood himself appears as "a man in plain apparel" whose "name was as it had been the colour of ebony," and his rival Constable is in- troduced as "a man crafty in counsel and cunning in all manner of workmanship."[36] The manuscript then goes on to tell how Constable appeals to Scott for aid against Blackwood, saying to himself, "I will arise and go unto a magician which is of my friends: of a surety he will devise some remedy, and free me out of my distresses.

"So he arose and came unto that great magician which hath his dwelling in the old fastness, hard by the river Jordan, which is by the Border.

"And the magician opened his mouth and said, Lo! my heart wisheth thy good, and let the thing prosper which is in thy hands to do it.

"But thou seest that my hands are full of working and my labour is great. . . .

"Moreover, thine adversary also is of my familiars.

"The land is before thee: draw thou up thine hosts for the battle . . . and defy boldly thine enemy, which hath his camp in the place of Princes [Blackwood's shop at 17 Princes Street]; quit ye as men, and let favour be shown unto him which is most valiant.

"Yet be thou silent; peradventure I will help thee some little.

"But the man which is Crafty saw that the magician loved him not. For he knew him of old, and they had had many dealings; and he perceived that he would not assist him in the day of his adversity."[37]

Constable was enraged by this squib, deeply resenting its derision over his jealous fears of being supplanted. Other booksellers and authors also fumed over its stinging portraits; its outrageous personalities and profanities struck like a thunderbolt; and the devout were scandalized by its Biblical parody. All Edinburgh took sides, offended, tickled, furious, delighted.[38] Scott himself disapproved, though he could not help laughing. "Edinburgh is rather too narrow," he wrote Blackwood, "for satire so markedly personal . . . I am not greatly pleased with the mode in which one or two of my particular friends have been mentioned, as, for example, Playfair, Charles Sharpe, and Robert Jamieson. You will readily hold me acquitted of the childishness of resenting the good-humoured pleasantry exercised towards myself, with which I was really entertained . . ."[39]

Alarmed by Scott's strictures, Blackwood had hastened to pay a propitiatory call at Abbotsford. Scott was in bed with another attack of cramp but received him for half an hour. Unless these assaults on his friends ceased, he said frankly, it would be impossible for him to help the magazine any further. The publisher humbly gave "a solemn engagement that no personalities should disgrace the work in future. Now for all this fine fashion I should have bid Blackwood & his magazine go to the devil," but "having Laidlaw in tow with his helpless family (for what says the Bard)

> These piteous things ca'd wife and weans
> Wad melt the heart o' very stanes

inclined me to suspend my wrath & listen to the bibliopolist's promise of recantation & amendment."[40]

Nevertheless, though for Laidlow's sake he would not summarily withdraw his support, he followed up this conversation by writing Blackwood a note of reiterated warning. If the magazine persisted in being "a receptacle for articles, however able, composed in the same tone, I could not, consistently with my feelings of what is due to the literary society of Edinburgh, continue my permanent assistance. The field for fair pleasantry is wide enough without enlarging it at the expense of exciting, and not unjustly, feelings of personal and private resentment."[41]

"The parody of the two beasts," as Scott called it, had also attacked Blackwood's trade rivals, but this Scott looked on with a more tolerant eye. "Surely these gentlemen," he exclaimed to Laidlaw, "think themselves rather formed of porcelain clay than of common potter's ware. Dealing in satire against all others, their own dignity suffers so cruelly from an ill-imagined joke! If B. had good books to sell, he might set them all at defiance. His *Magazine* does well, and beats Constable's: but we will talk of this when we meet."[42]

Though *Blackwood's* pursued its merry career of travesty and violence, the publisher moderated its tone in dealing with Edinburgh, and Scott made regular small contributions. "The two papers you mention as having particularly pleased you," young Mr. Lockhart wrote a friend in February, "are the work of two very different persons, the first, 'Dandy Dinmont,' being mine, and the 'Depravity of Animals'— certainly one of the best pieces of grave burlesque since Swift—Walter Scott's. W. Scott is much interested in Blackwood and his *Magazine*, and has communicated something to each of the last five numbers."[43]

Early February brought an event that Scott had long eagerly awaited.[44] The Act of Union with England in 1707 had pledged that the ancient regalia of Scotland should never be removed from its soil, and they had been deposited in a locked oak chest bolted within the Crown Room of Edinburgh Castle. But through the years it was rumored that they had been illegally spirited away to England. Were they still in that locked chest, or had they been perfidiously removed?[45] In 1815, Scott had contrived to set the Regent's curiosity agog to solve this mystery, although even with the Prince's support it was not until January, 1817, that Scott finally received orders to prepare a scroll of warrant for the purpose.[46] But governmental red tape was interminable; it was still another year before John Wilson Croker wrote Scott from the Admiralty that he had paid the necessary fees and was sending the official instrument to the Lord Advocate.[47]

Scott was on fire with excitement. On February 4 the Commission assembled in the Crown Room.[48] Dim light filtered through the iron-grated windows and fell on the chest, "strewd with the dust of an hundred years about six inches thick."[49] Its keys had been sought in vain; it would have to be forced open. The blows of the hammer echoed with a deep and hollow sound.[50] When the ponderous lid groaned up, folds of old linen were seen—and, within, the regalia, just as they had been left in 1707: the fourteenth-century crown gleaming with rough jewels, the scepter of James V surmounted by a great beryl, the sword of state, a gift from Pope Julius II to James V, its scabbard all gilded silver filigree-work of oak leaves and acorns, and the silver mace of the Treasurer of Scotland.[51] The discovery was instantly announced by running up the royal standard above the Castle, to the shouts of the garrison and the multitude assembled on Castle Hill.[52]

Next day a number of the Commissioners brought the ladies of their families to see the precious find. Sophia, worked upon by her father's emotion, almost fainted when the lid was removed. One of the Commissioners playfully lifted the crown as if to place it on the head of a young lady. Scott was aghast; in a voice vibrating between anger and horror, he stopped the sacrilege with a passionate "No, by God!" Huskily whispering, "Pray, forgive me," he turned aside, and saw that Sophia was also deathly pale. Drawing her out of the room, he walked with her down the Mound. "He never spoke all the way home," she said later, "but every now and then I felt his arm tremble; and from that time I fancied he began to treat me more like a woman than a child."[53]

People were clamoring for a sight of the regalia. The government determined that they should be permanently displayed in the Crown Room. Scott began pulling strings to have Adam Ferguson made Custodian; Adam needed some income beyond his small army pension and could be given one or two rooms as living quarters in the Castle. Scott spoke to Lord Chief Commissioner Adam, he wrote Henry Dundas, he wrote Lord Melville. "If you happen to see Lord Melville," he pressed the Duke of Buccleuch, "pray give him a jogg in Adam Ferguson's matter. . . . I trust a good deal to Willie Adam, who is an old sneck-drawer."[54]

The Lord Chief Commissioner supported Ferguson as Custodian but urged upon the Prince Regent that Scott himself be given the title of Keeper of the Regalia and elevated to a Baronetcy.[55] Scott learned, however, that his kinsman Keith of Ravelston claimed the right to be made Keeper by virtue of his descent from the Earls Marischal of Scotland, in whom it had been hereditary. Scott would not mortify him by standing in his way, though if it were his Royal Highness' pleasure, he told Lord Melville, "while disposing of keeping the regalia to others," to make him a Baronet, he would proudly accept that honor.[56] Despite Scott's generosity Keith's pretensions were disallowed; late in the summer Ferguson was chosen Keeper, with an allowance of £300 a year,[57] and during the autumn the Lord Chief Commissioner privately told Scott that his own title might soon follow.[58]

Meanwhile, during January and February, Scott's health seemed to be restored. Cadell, who only a few months before had been convinced that Scott was not long for this world, now derided the dark rumors among London publishers. "*The Row* are all wrong about Mr. Scott," he wrote Constable on February 6. "I saw his doctor yesterday, who said he was amazingly well, and had not had the periodical return of cramp he has been accustomed to have for some months past. . . ." Scott was in high spirits, making rapid progress on *The Heart of Mid-Lothian*, and was already turning over in his mind the tale that was to follow.[59]

This had suddenly come to him during the weeks when he was waiting for the contents of the chest in the Crown Room to be brought to light. "As I maintain a correspondence with Mr. Jedediah Cleishbottom," he playfully wrote Lady Louisa Stuart, "I intend to recommend to him a tale founded upon an earlier adventure of these same Regalia."[60] During the Civil War they had been deposited in Dunnotar Castle; a clergyman's wife had smuggled them out when it was besieged by an English army; she and her husband had been tortured by Cromwell without revealing their hiding place and after the Restoration had returned them to Charles II. "I think this may be made a capital story & Jedediah without any sacrifice of his own opinions may make his peace honourably with his presbyterian friends if he can make a lively picture of a good divine of that persuasion & his good dame."[61]

As usual, though, his fictional labors were far from being the only literary work he had on hand. For *Blackwood's Magazine* he wrote a laudatory review of Mary Shelley's *Frankenstein* (which he imagined to be her husband's); for the *Quarterly* a review of Kirkton's *True and Secret History of the Church of Scotland*, recently edited by his friend Sharpe. He agreed to review Walpole's letters to George Montagu for the *Quarterly* if he could find time, and was unable to resist the request of an old school companion, Sir Howard Douglas, to review his *Essay on the Principles and Construction of Military Bridges*, though he said that he must get the help of some friend to deal with the technical parts. No sooner were these reviews completed than John Murray persuaded him to review the fourth canto of *Childe Harold's Pilgrimage*.[62] Notwithstanding all these tasks, he was able to assure Constable that *The Heart of Mid-Lothian* proceeded "in force."[63]

At Abbotsford the entire structure of his new building was now completed except for the doors and windows, which were being made in George Bullock's workshop in London. He was still waiting, however, for the plans of the archway in the armory, the niches and sideboard end of the dining room, and the chimney pieces and groins of the parlor. He sent Terry measurements for all the carpets[64] and Bullock a reminder that he was depending on him for a "French bed," "dining tables, sideboard, eating room chairs, & heaven knows what besides, not forgetting grates: a very necessary thing in Scotland."[65] "I shall be glad," he wrote Laidlaw, "when the plumbers finish their job, for I depend more on these private comforts in the present state of my health than I like by any means."[66]

Lately, indeed, he had endured another recurrence of his attacks of cramp. They had seemed to be returning less often, coming only at intervals of every five or six weeks,[67] but with the persistence of snow and frost throughout March there had been two within a single fortnight.[68] Though he knew that cold or fatigue of any kind brought them on with renewed virulence, this was hard to remember for "one whose pleasures lie chiefly in the open air."[69] "I have so much the habits of robust health that I am too apt to run after my workpeople in all weathers," he confessed, "but I suppose time and pain will make me wiser at last."[70]

During the earlier part of the spring vacation Sophia kept house for Scott at Abbotsford; the weather was still "too severe," he told Southey, "for Mrs. Scott to face the country till the sun comes earlier over the hill."[71] But Adam Ferguson was with them, getting ready to move into Huntly Burn, and there were country neighbors to talk with, not to mention the pleasure of conversing with the dogs and with the oxen, Ogg and Bashan, as they turned up the glebe. Nearby, visiting his father, was Captain Basil Hall, who told Scott stories of his voyage to the Loo-Choo Islands and of a visit to Napoleon at St. Helena. The former Emperor had been astounded by one detail in Hall's account of the islanders.[72]

" 'What arms have they?' said Bony. 'None' answered Hall. 'Ah! you mean no fire arms, but they have swords, bows, slings, spears'— 'No such thing nor any other weapon so far as we could discover'—B. in great surprise 'Diable! pas meme de poignards!' A ridiculous counterpart to this story was that when Capt. Hall told it to old Vansittart he laughed heartily and immediately gave a similar proof of technicality by admiring the simplicity of the savages who could exist without coind money . . ."[73]

Late in April, cold still gripped the countryside. "Everything is backward and disconsolate here," Scott wrote the Duke of Buccleuch, "—constant sleet and snow & the ewes lambing in the midst of it—all the distant hills white as January and the air feeling not very unlike it." When the Lord Chief Commissioner paid a visit to Abbotsford on his way to try a case at Jedburgh, Scott and young Walter rode to the trial with him over ground ringing like iron beneath their horses' hooves. "By the bye," Scott added, "the said Walter gets a commission this year as Cornet of the County yeomanry so becomes a standard bearer in good earnest."[74]

Despite the severe weather Charlotte had now come from Edinburgh.[75] During the night of April 28 they heard "a violent noise, like drawing heavy boards along the new part of the house." Writing Terry about it two days later, "I fancied something had fallen," Scott said, "and thought no more about it. This was about *two* in the morning. Last night, at the same witching hour, the very same noise occurred. Mrs. S.,

as you know, is rather *timbersome*, so up got I, with Beardie's broadsword under my arm,

> 'So bolt upright,
> And ready to fight.'

"But nothing was out of order, neither can I discover what occasioned
the disturbance."[76]

A few days later Scott was shocked to hear from Terry that on the
night of the twenty-ninth, at the very hour of the mysterious noises,
George Bullock had suddenly died. Scott felt all the more distressed[77]
because in his letter to Terry he had complained of the delay in receiving
his doors and windows from Bullock, whom he had facetiously called,
after the hero of one of the *Arabian Nights* tales, the Prince of the Black
Marble Islands, and written: "Surely our friend's heart is grown as
hard as his materials; or the spell of the enchantress, which confined
itself to the extremities of his predecessor, has extended to his whole
person."[78]

On May 11, Scott returned to Edinburgh for the spring session of
the Court.[79] Terry had scored a great success on the London stage with
a dramatization of *Rob Roy*, and Scott thought *The Heart of Mid-
Lothian* might also contain materials for a good play.[80] "There is in
Jedediah's present work," he confided, "a thing capable of being woven
out a Bourgeoise tragedy. I think of contriving that it shall be in your
hands sometime before the public see it, so that you may try to operate
upon it yourself. This would not be difficult, as vol. 4, and part of 3d,
contain a different story. *Avowedly*, I will never write for the stage; if
I do, 'call me *horse*.' "[81]

Once installed in his library at Castle Street, Scott devoted himself
with such determination to finishing *The Heart of Mid-Lothian* that,
breaking his usual habits, he wrote not only in the morning but after
dinner. The belated summer had at last arrived and was suddenly as
warm as August. One evening a group of young men in George Street
were having a party. Their open window looked north towards Scott's
little back garden and the window of his study. As the bottles went
round, their host grew silent and withdrawn; and one of his guests,
young John Gibson Lockhart, expressed a fear that he was unwell.

"No," said he, "I shall be well enough presently, if you will only
let me sit where you are, and take my chair; for here is a confounded
hand in sight of me here, which has often bothered me before, and
now it won't let me fill my glass with a good will."

Lockhart looked out of the window and "saw this hand which, like
the writing on Belshazzar's wall," troubled their hour of conviviality.

"Since we sat down," said their host, "I have been watching it—it
fascinates my eye—it never stops—page after page is finished and
thrown on that heap of MS., and it still goes on unwearied—and so it

will be till candles are brought in, and God knows how long after that."

"Some stupid, dogged, engrossing clerk, probably," exclaimed one of the guests. "No, boys," said their host's father, "I well know what hand that is—'tis Walter Scott's."[82]

Later that month Lockhart was presented to Scott, and dined with him at the table of Home Drummond, the grandson of Lord Kames. A few weeks earlier Scott had read the young man's translation of Schlegel's *Lectures on the History of Literature*, which Blackwood had just brought out and had praised it to the publisher as "the best translation from the German ever made"; no doubt he had read some of Lockhart's pleasant "Sketches of Foreign Scenes and Manners" that had been appearing in *Blackwood's Magazine* since the previous June. Strongly though Scott had censured the ferocious and acid personal satire of the "Chaldee MS," he saw clearly that here was a young man of high talent.[83]

Lockhart was the son of a Lanarkshire minister. At Glasgow University he had been a gold medalist in Greek, then had a brilliant career at Balliol College; in 1815 he had come to Edinburgh to read law. Now a briefless advocate, he had recently returned from a trip to Germany, and was reading studiously and trying his wings as an author while he waited for legal employment. Both his professional standing and his literary avocations strongly resembled what Scott remembered as his own a quarter of a century earlier.[84]

Slim, pale, and handsome, Lockhart was as elegant as a Velazquez grandee, but with a somber shadow of El Greco melancholy in his dark eyes, and the demeanor of a hidalgo. A demon of sarcasm lurked in the compressed smile of his thin lips. A slight deafness made him reserved, in reality shy, though he hid his diffidence in freezing hauteur or disguised it in biting and supercilious wit. "The Scorpion which delighteth to sting the faces of men,"[85] he had called himself in the "Chaldee MS." But his feeling of superiority was genuine too; he had a Calvinistic strain in his blood that did not induce humility. He could display a brutality only possible to those who are inwardly vulnerable. His secret heart, though, was like the heraldic emblem of his family, "a heart within a fetterlock," shrinking, affectionate, and tender. A man of deep and loyal devotion, among those he loved his chilly pride melted into a touching sweetness, his wit dissolved into warm gaiety.

After the ladies left the dinner table Lockhart found himself seated beside Scott, who drew him out about his recent tour of Germany. At his inn in Weimar, he told Scott, he had asked the waiter if Goethe was in town. The man stared as if he did not know the name. "Goethe der grosse Dichter," Lockhart added. The man still shook his head doubtfully; finally the landlady suggested that the traveler might mean "the Herr Geheimer-Rath Von Goethe." Scott laughed. "I hope you will come one of these days and see me at Abbotsford," he said, "and when you reach Selkirk or Melrose, be sure you ask even the landlady for nobody but *the Sheriff*."[86]

A few days later Lockhart received from James Ballantyne a note asking if he would like to write the History of 1816 for the *Edinburgh Annual Register*. Scott was overworked and had suggested him for the task. Lockhart agreed; when he called at Castle Street to thank Scott he found himself for the first time within the study through whose window not long since he had seen that moving hand.[87]

The room was small and square, dominated by an enormous double desk and by books on three walls—history and biography on one side, poetry and drama on the other, law books and dictionaries behind Scott's huge elbow-chair. Folios and quartos, bound in brown calf, with a few in blue morocco, gilded, ranged in ordered rows, save where a loaned volume was replaced by a wooden block bearing the name of the borrower. On the desk stood a handsomely carved box lined with crimson velvet and holding silver ink-bottles and a taper stand. Over the fireplace mantel hung a portrait of Claverhouse surrounded by a radiating star of broadswords and dirks. Green tin boxes, such as solicitors use for deeds, were piled on each side of the Venetian window, and on top of one pile the fox's tail mounted on an antique silver handle which Scott used to dust a book when he picked it up. In one corner rose a carpeted ladder with strong oaken rails, with the cat Hinse fat and sleek on its topmost step.[88]

As Scott talked he neatly folded letter covers or twisted paper into spills, while Maida laid his head across his master's knees. If the wars had gone on, Scott told Lockhart, he would have been willing enough to continue the historical summary. His imagination stirred to the plumed troops, the neighing steed, and the shrill trump, but he had no heart to record radical riots and the passing or rejection of Corn Laws and Poor Bills. His health was impaired; though he did not mean to give up writing—his smiling eye glanced to a pile of manuscript on the desk—he felt entitled now to write only what he enjoyed—"Juniores ad labores."[89]

On May 25, Scott joyfully sent the Duke of Buccleuch the discharged bond for his guarantee of £4,000. "My dear Lord," he wrote gratefully, "to wish that all your numerous & extensive acts of kindness may be attended with similar advantages to the persons whom you oblige is wishing you what to your mind will be the best recompense . . ."[90] Thus the last obligation connected with John Ballantyne and Company was now repaid, and Scott's future stretched before him in a glorious golden sunlight.

The present moment also had its pleasures. He now had at Abbotsford a Border piper who, when Scott left there in May, had been making his bagpipes skirl while Walter and a young cousin clanked broadswords on the lawn.[91] Only that spring Scott had been elected to "the Club," the famous Literary Club established by Dr. Johnson, Burke, and

Reynolds, and would be able to dine with his fellow members at the Thatched House in St. James's Street whenever he went to London.[92] Within another few days Adam Ferguson would be moving into Huntly Burn, and his boyish-hearted old friend would henceforth be a near neighbor.[93] The new bedrooms at Abbotsford were all finished, "snugger than snug," including his and Charlotte's; he would have a private sitting room to write in; and the rest of the work was being completed fast.[94]

He had not quite succeeded in having *The Heart of Mid-Lothian* ready for publication by the King's Birthday, but he did pen its last page by the beginning of July.[95] It had spun itself out to a greater length than he had foreseen and filled an entire four volumes. What had been intended as its companion tale would have to be published separately when it was written. But Scott was well pleased with his work. He had enjoyed doing it and felt sure it would be a success. He sent Terry the first three volumes on July 10 and proofs of the last volume on the following day.[96] On July 15, Constable wrote William Godwin, "We shall publish 4 new vols. of *Tales of My Landlord* in a few days." Two days later the smack *Caledonia* sailed from Leith with a cargo consisting of nothing else than copies of *The Heart of Mid-Lothian* consigned to the London trade.[97]

As always on these occasions, James Ballantyne gave a magnificent dinner in St. John Street to celebrate the great event. Young Mr. Lockhart, present for the first time, felt as convinced as most of the others that "THE GREAT UNKNOWN," as James mysteriously called him, was none other than that Walter Scott who sat so unpretentiously among the other guests. The banquet was, in one of James's favorite words, *gorgeous*, the board heaped with turtle and venison and overflowing with iced punch, ale, and Madeira.[98]

The toasts following the feast were a ritual. First their bulky host rose and sonorously intoned the words of Macbeth:

> "Fill full!
> I drink to the general joy of the whole table!"

Then came, "The King, God bless him!" Following this, James said, "Gentlemen, there is another toast which never has been nor shall be omitted in this house of mine—I give you the health of Mr. Walter Scott with three times three!" Afterwards Mrs. Ballantyne retired, and the bottles passed around two or three times. At last came the great moment.[99]

James rose again, "every vein on his brow distended, his eyes solemnly fixed on vacancy, to propose, not as before in his stentorian tone, but with 'bated breath,' in the sort of whisper by which a stage conspirator thrills the gallery—'*Gentlemen, a bumper to the immortal Author of Waverley!*' " Preserving his incognito, Scott joined the uproar of cheering. When silence was restored, James proceeded to lament the obscurity in which this illustrious man chose to conceal himself from the world's applause and "to thank the company for the manner in which the *nominis umbra* had been received." Lockhart, watching, was entertained by "the cool, demure fun of Scott's features during all this mummery" and even more by "Erskine's attempt at a gay *nonchalance*."[100]

Though James announced the title of the new novel, he did not allow it to be discussed. "Success to it crowned another cup; but after that no more of Jedediah." In his resounding bass James trolled out "The Maid of Lodi"; then came other songs and toasts—"The Bay of Biscay, oh!" and George Thomson, the friend of Burns, singing "Willie brew'd a peck o' malt."

When Scott, Erskine, and the more staid or elderly guests said good night the scene changed. Claret and olives gave way to broiled bones and a mighty bowl of hot punch. James, "*ore rotundo*," lauded the new novel. "One chapter—one chapter only." was the cry. After "Nay, by'r Lady, nay!" and a few other coy denials, he brought out proof sheets and began reading,[101] giving them with splendid dramatic power the interview between Jeanie Deans, the Duke of Argyll, and Queen Caroline in Richmond Park. His listeners were carried away, and responded heartily to his "One bumper more to Jedediah Cleishbotham!" As a valedictory James sang "The Last Words of Marmion," and the night's revelries ended.[102]

The enthusiasm of Ballantyne's guests was no more than a foretaste: the book created a tidal wave of delight that swept the entire United Kingdom. "I have not only read it myself," wrote Lady Louisa Stuart from a country mansion in England, "but am in a house where everybody is tearing it out of each other's hands, and talking of nothing else." Scott had drawn "to the very life" her great-uncle, John Duke of Argyll, of whom she had heard so much in girlhood that she felt as if she had seen and lived with him. Dumbiedikes and Rory Bean were "delightful"; the end of poor Madge Wildfire "most pathetic"; the meeting at Muschat's Cairn "tremendous"; Carlisle in *Waverley* not more moving than the trial of Effie Deans and her imprisonment in the Tolbooth.

Lady Louisa was not, to be sure, unqualified praise. The unnecessary opening chapter, with its Edinburgh lawyers, she found tiresome and the legal pedant Bartoline Saddletree a bore. The fourth volume flagged a little; the death of Sir George Staunton at the hands of his stolen son was "a lame, huddled conclusion. I know you so well in it, by the by! you grow tired yourself, want to get rid of the story, and hardly care how."

But how unsurpassed was all the rest! Scott had "effected what many have tried to do, and nobody yet succeeded in, making the perfectly good character the most interesting." How often "the wise good heroines" of other novelists tempted one to exclaim, " 'Upon my word she is enough to make anybody wicked.' . . . Had this very story been conducted by a common hand, Effie would have attracted all our concern and sympathy, Jeanie only cold approbation. Whereas Jeanie, without youth, beauty, genius, warm passions, or any other novel-perfection, is here our object from beginning to end."[103]

# 6

## Such Grinning Honours

### ( 1 8 1 8 – 1 8 1 9 )

EVEN WHILE SCOTT ground out the last volume of *The Heart of Mid-Lothian*, negotiations were already under way for a Third Series of *Tales of My Landlord*. As had been originally intended of the Second Series, this work was to consist of two novels filling four volumes. John Ballantyne as Scott's agent trickily pursued his usual policy of letting Constable worry lest the prize fall into the hands of Blackwood or Murray. "Both John and James Ballantyne," the burly publisher testily wrote Cadell, "have shown an evident desire to quarrel with us for several months past. John's mode of doing business with us is quite abominable . . ."[1]

Constable chafed, but held on to his temper. "I will do all that propriety and prudence dictate to avoid any open rupture . . ."[2] John adroitly inflamed his fears: "There is no bargain with any one *as yet* about the new *Tales*, but there have been *attempts* from Princes Street." Still worse, Murray was coming down to Scotland in August and would certainly visit Scott; Constable dreaded *his* tampering. If only some arrangement could be made before Murray arrived! Impishly the little strategist now relaxed and tightened the screws at the same time. "John says that the author does not want money just yet, but may soon, when bills will do, but that both he and 'James, poor fellow,' as he observed, must have *slices*."[3]

Cadell thought it might help if he himself had a frank conversation with Scott. "I would not be mealy-mouthed—we must be so no longer. Others drop this and get on with astonishing success: we must go and do likewise." Following a friendly visit to Abbotsford, he joyfully reported to Constable: "I do think we stand very well with him, and bid fair to retain the place we hold."[4] They did; when John outlined an agreement to them two months later, the booksellers were relieved, after all their fears, to find that it made no unreasonable demands. To be sure, Scott did demand "slices" for his two maddening henchmen, but at least this time there were no unsold books to be absorbed. The remaining clauses were even surprisingly generous— "the bare advance of a portion of the profits; in fact, for such a work, and from such an author," Cadell exulted, "the terms are most favourable . . ."[5]

John Ballantyne too was in high glee. He was prospering as an auctioneer, his services to Scott were profitable, and his puckish spirit delighted in the tricksiness he brought to literary bargaining. Several times a year he went to London, Brussels, and Paris to pick up rare books, *objets de vertu*, Venetian lamps, porcelains, Milanese cuirasses, old Dutch cabinets, works of art.[6] The previous autumn, it was true, he had burned his fingers in a business deal with a man named Ainslie, and Scott had felt obliged to warn James Ballantyne against backing his bills.[7] "I own that it surprizes me that knowing John as you do know him you should again plunge deep in his bill-transactions. . . . I will assist John myself & have done so in all feasible matters but *not* with credit . . ."[8] John's share of the profits of *Rob Roy*, however, more than balanced his losses, and in the end, somehow or other, he emerged not seriously hurt.[9] "John Ballantyne . . . like a cat," Scott commented, "can tumble out of a ten-pair of stairs window and light on his feet . . ."[10]

Just this last February he had bought Trinity Grove, a handsome little villa near the Newhaven Road on the Firth of Forth.[11] Its gardens, though small, were designed to seem extensive, with many trellised alleys, leafy paths, and mysterious bowers leading out of the bright flower-beds and plots of green. Opening on a perfumed conservatory, the sitting rooms glittered with mirrors and gleamed with portraits of beautiful actresses, Peg Woffington, George Anne Bellamy, Kitty Clive. In Jocund Johnny's own gay nature, with his love of burlesque and invention heightened to wild mendacity, there was a vivid strand of the theatrical, and he delighted to entertain actors and actresses, *danseuses* and singers, whenever they came to Edinburgh. Here Braham sang in his clear tenor, Liston jested, Mathews displayed his brilliant gifts of mimicry and parody; "here," as Lockhart put it, "Kean reveled and rioted —and here the Roman Kemble often played the Greek from sunset to dawn."[12]

Before Scott left town for Abbotsford that summer he brought Lockhart with him to one of John Ballantyne's parties. The dinner table, unlike James's sedate British board, abounded in continental delicacies, Périgord and Strasbourg pâtés, a boar's head from Coblentz, a turkey stuffed with truffles from the Palais Royal, and champagne foaming in shining glasses. Johnny disported himself in airy frolic around one of his guests, a floridly handsome man of impressive dignity. Lockhart asked Scott the identity of this gentleman, and was startled to learn that he was Archibald Constable.[13]

Scott expressed surprise that anyone could have lived two winters in Edinburgh without knowing the great bookseller by sight. Lockhart was amazed at Constable's polished manners and majestic presence. For him a publisher or any tradesman could not really be a gentleman; he had not, he confessed, imagined him "a man of such gentlemanlike and even distinguished bearing." "Ay, Constable is indeed a grand-looking chield," Scott said, smiling. The publisher put him in mind, he said, of Fielding's observation "that Joseph Andrews had an air which, to those who had not seen many noblemen, would give an idea of nobility." Lockhart reports the remark without seeming to realize the light flick at his own unconscious snobbery.[14]

He was still too much of a stranger to understand some of the pleasantries of the evening. When Scott said to Constable, "Will your Czarish Majesty do me the honour to take a glass of Champagne," Lockhart asked his lively little host what this meant. "Oh!" said Johnny, "are you so green as not to know that Constable long since dubbed himself *The Czar of Muscovy*, John Murray *The Emperor of the West*, and Longman and his string of partners *The Divan*?" "And what title," queried Lockhart, "has Mr. John Ballantyne himself found in this new *almanach imperial*?" "Let that flea stick to the wa'," responded John: "When I set up for a bookseller, the Crafty christened me *The Dey of Alljeers*—but he now considers me as next thing to dethroned."[15]

July 12 found Scott again on the Tweed.[16] The weather was delightfully warm and sunny, "Scotland has absolutely been Italy,"[17] and in Joanna's Bower and the Rhymer's Glen the laurels and evergreens were thriving.[18] Before the end of the summer Scott expected to see his greenhouse stocked with plants. The new dwelling looked splendid, with "antique corbeils" on the ceiling of the lobby—"you never saw such delightful grinners."[19] Scott was expecting a visit from the artist William Allan, who would advise him on grouping his armor, and urged Terry to come in August or September. "Wherefore wipe your mind's eye pull up the breeches of your resolution, & set forth manfully for the north that we may talk over many things you wot of."[20]

Promptly on arriving at Abbotsford, Scott set himself to complete his review of the last canto of *Childe Harold's Pilgrimage*.[21] Though Byron's "redwood [downright mad] Jacobinism" was a "crazy passion that makes a moderate man like me tremble at [the] idea of turning the world upside down," Scott felt more assured than ever that Byron was "a poet of great talent." And at least "his misanthropy" was now "less clamorous," "his fastidiousness towards the world . . . less intensive."[22] Joanna Baillie, fierily loyal to Lady Byron, was determined to find the poem "dull and obscure" and consigned its noble author to the Devil,[23] but Scott thought this canto the most brilliant of the four.

Early August brought a young American visitor named Edward Everett. Only twenty-four, he was at the beginning of his career, but he had already been appointed Professor of Greek at Harvard and was now spending several years traveling and studying in Europe before assuming his chair.[24] Except for Charlotte's little dog Ourisque, who growled at him furiously, all the family liked their American guest. He chatted with Sophia, and throughout his visit flirted playfully with fifteen-year-old Anne, audaciously snipping off an end of her sash and wearing it as a knight of romance wore his lady's favor.[25]

At dinner, Everett noted, they were regaled by the new piper, a hedger and ditcher during the day, who paraded up and down the lawn "dressed in his tartans, and playing national airs on the bagpipe." Everett was charmed by the warmth and familiarity of Scott's relation with his daughters: Sophia, who was always borrowing bits of finery from Mama or Anne, he playfully called "Miss Feuclothes," from the Scottish legal term *feu* for a tenure distinguished from ownership; and Anne, who was fonder of gay dress but who tore her garments jumping over hedges, he named "Miss Bonnierags."[26]

Throughout the meal Scott overflowed with stories. An Edinburgh lady of his acquaintance, he said, sent her Highland servant to tell a guest that dinner was served; the man found the visitor vigorously using a toothbrush, and returned to the dining room to say the gentleman would come at once—he was sharpening his teeth. Another servant, told to fetch his master's portmanteau on leaving the home of a friend, was asked if he was sure he had packed all his employer's belongings. Scott repeated Andrew's reply with a mischievous twinkle in his eye: "*At least*, your Honor."[27]

Barely had Everett made his farewells than the painter William Allan arrived and then Sir James Stuart, who sketched in pencil, together with a sister who wrote verse.[28] "I hope I shall have Mr. Allan here once more," Scott wrote Sir James, "before I quit this castle of Conundrums for Edinburgh. I wish you could ride up and meet him. . . . I think he is just the person whose mind and pencil are like to communicate fire to yours and encourage you to prosecute the noble talent with which you have been gifted."[29]

During the brilliant rainless days of August Scott took Charlotte and Sophia with him on a little excursion to Drumlanrig and Rokeby. The Duke of Buccleuch had been much distressed by a persistent cough, but "has now taken something recommended by Dr. Lincoln—poppy-juice & double distilled vinegar . . . which allays the irritation without the unpleasant effects of paregoric or any other opiate. . . . He is always at the family breakfast which I like much to see."[30]

When they had "kept the Castle in a gay uproar"[31] for a week, the travelers proceeded through the ripening farmlands to Rokeby. "This is heavenly weather," Scott wrote John Ballantyne, "and I am making the most of it, as I shall have a laborious autumn before me. I may say of my head and fingers as the farmer of his mare, when he indulged her with an extra feed—

> "Ye ken that Maggie winna sleep
> For that or Simmer.

We have taken our own horses with us, and I have my pony, and ride when I find it convenient."[32] After a pleasant week among Morritt's land of woods and streams, they were back at Abbotsford on August 30.[33]

Scott at once began work on his new novel. Instead of being about the Scottish regalia, as he had planned, it was a strange tragic tale of two lovers drawn toward doom, which he was to call *The Bride of Lammermoor*. "The story is a dismal one," he wrote James Ballantyne, "and I doubt sometimes whether it will bear working out to much length . . ."[34] By September 6 he had already made a start and was toiling hard. "I found the lion in his den, very busy," wrote Cadell;[35] but nevertheless Scott laid his pen aside and took his visitor for a stroll. How, besieged as he was by lion hunters and interrupted by his work people, Cadell asked, did he ever find time to compose? "I know that you contrive to get a few hours in your own room, and that may do for the mere pen-work, but when is it that you think?"[36]

"Oh," said Scott, "I lie *simmering* over things for an hour or so before I get up—and there's the time I am dressing to overhaul my half-sleeping half-waking *projet de chapitre*—and when I get the paper before me it commonly runs off pretty easily. Besides, I often take a doze in the plantations, and, while Tom marks out a dyke or a drain, as I have directed, one's fancy may be running its ain riggs in some other world."[37]

But in this world too his fancy was running its colorful course. There must be fanlights of stained glass, he wrote Terry, above the windows and door in his greenhouse lobby. The door handles would be ebony: "I never saw ebony handles but they sound as if they should be very handsome."[38] The designs Blore had made for the dining-room chairs and sideboard he decided he did not like; ". . . they are I think *knobbish* and out of character. . . . I do greatly affect the plain & massive & would prefer the sideboard to be made of very handsome wood with plain massive legs . . ."[39]

Early in October those two briefless advocates and rash satirists, John Gibson Lockhart and his friend John Wilson, were invited for their first visit to Abbotsford.[40] They found Scott walking in the grounds with Lord Melville, Adam Ferguson, and five or six young people. "I am glad you came today," Scott said, "for I thought it might be of use to you both, some time or other, to be known to my old schoolfellow here, who is . . . the great giver of good things in the Parliament House. I trust you have had enough of your pranks with your friend Ebony, and if so, Lord Melville will have too much sense to remember them."⁴¹

As Scott proudly showed them his new building and its fantastic battlements, Ferguson observed gravely that it had "much the air of some old fastness hard by the river Jordan." The young folks laughed at this allusion to the scandalous "Chaldee MS"; Scott chided, "Toots, Adam! toots, Adam!" But when he told how one of his dikes had been destroyed by a winter flood of the Tweed, Adam groaned another quotation: "Verily my fine gold hath perished!" Scott lifted his staff as if to belabor Ferguson's back but then could not help laughing himself.⁴²

At Peterhouse they found Peter Matheson, Scott's coachman, and his brother-in-law, Tom Purdie, directing the laying of turf for a bowling green. "Here," said Scott, "I mean to have a game at bowls after dinner every day in fine weather—for I take that to have been among the indispensables of our old *vie de chateau*." But later he told Lockhart why he had chosen that location: Peter was a devout Presbyterian and led family worship every night. "I wished to have a smooth walk and a canny seat for myself within ear-shot of Peter's evening psalm."⁴³

Dinner₁ began gaily with "Potage à la Meg Merrilees," a soup invented in Scott's honor by M. Florence, the Duke of Buccleuch's chef. Scott was in buoyant spirits, full of stories of the High School Yards, the Cross-causeway, the boyish exploits of Lang Linton and the Beau, and, as the champagne bubbled, toasts to the memory of Green Breeks. Outside the window John of Skye played pibrochs, then marched into the dining room on Scott's summons to down at a single gulp a large bicker brimful of Glenlivet, and resumed playing until the autumn moon streamed in so brightly that it dimmed the candles.⁴⁴

Later Scott proposed that they climb his western turret to see the valley in the moonbeams. The stairs were dark, steep, and narrow, but soon a party crowded the bartizans. The Tweed and Gala glimmered silver in the valley beneath the black mass of the Eildons. "If I live," Scott exclaimed, "I will build me a higher tower, with a more spacious platform, and a staircase better fitted for an old fellow's scrambling." Down below, in response to a word from Scott, John of Skye began playing "Lochaber no more," and they descended with its music trembling in the air.⁴⁵

Though the wainscoting of the new dining room was not yet finished, the chamber was ablaze with lights. Young and old danced reels, Scott beating time with his staff and Dominie Thomson with his wooden leg. Mulled wine and whiskey punch flowed, Lord Melville proposed a bumper to the rooftree, Adam Ferguson sang "Johnnie Cope" and called on the young ladies for "Kenmure's on and awa'," and as the merry evening closed Scott made the whole party join hands in a circle to the chorus of:

Weel may we a' be,
Ill may we never see,
God bless the King and the gude companie![46]

Next morning, rising between six and seven, Lockhart heard his host's voice outside on the green, talking with Tom Purdie about the draining of "the Blue Bank," a field of clay near Toftfield.[47] Scott had already put in a morning's labor at his desk, and though his stomach had again been giving him some uneasiness[48] he was hungry for breakfast. He cut thick slices of bread from a huge brown loaf on a wooden trencher at his elbow and helped himself generously from a plate of kippered salmon. He had borrowed an edition of Goethe from Lockhart and, between munches, dwelt enthusiastically on the lyrics in *Faust*, on the pathos of the scene before the Mater Dolorosa, and the subtlety of the character portrayals of Margaret and Mephistopheles. But, he remarked, blood would out: consummate artist as Goethe was, he was still a German; nobody but a German would have had the arrogance to pit his work against the *Book of Job*.[49]

Before breakfast was over the post bag brought Scott the huge shoal of mail that came almost every day. Though friends like Croker were generous in extending him their franking privilege, he had to pay for most of the letters he received. They seldom cost him less than £150 a year, "and as to coach-parcels," he added, "they are a perfect ruination." One morning last spring, he told his guests, he had carelessly opened a great lump of a dispatch, never doubting it had been franked. It turned out to be a play entitled *The Cherokee Lovers*, which a young lady in New York wanted him to revise, provide with a prologue and epilogue, and have produced at Drury Lane; on looking at the wrapper Scott found that he had been charged five pounds for postage. Then, only weeks later, he had absent-mindedly broken the seal of another bulky parcel: "Conceive my horror when out leaped the same identical tragedy of *The Cherokee Lovers!*" The fair authoress had feared the ship bearing the first copy might be lost at sea and "judged it prudent to forward a duplicate."[50]

At one o'clock Scott reappeared with a dozen letters sealed for the post and a packet addressed to James Ballantyne, which he dropped at the turnpike gate as he drove his guests to Melrose and Dryburgh.[51] On their return they found Charlotte on the porch with two strangers clad in the Macgregor tartan, who had turned out, however, to be a lawyer and a Unitarian preacher from New England. They had shown such vexation on learning Scott was not at home that she had never doubted they bore introductions, but since then they had aroused her suspicions by parading her about the house and grounds asking impertinent questions, including a demand to know not only Scott's age but her own.[52]

He had therefore barely had time to give them a cordial handshake when she broke in to remark that her husband would be glad to see their letters. They had none, of course, and Scott bowed the crestfallen tourists out the door, observing that the dinner hour approached and they were no doubt walking to Melrose. Charlotte was indignant, but Scott soon regretted his annoyance. "Hang the Yahoos, Charlotte—but we should have bid them stay dinner." "Devil a bit," said Adam's brother, Captain John Ferguson; the Americans were trying to sniff out the Author of *Waverley*. "The one asked Madame if she deigned to call her new house Tullyveolan or Tillietudlem—and the other, when Maida happened to lay his nose against the window, exclaimed, 'pro-di-gi-ous!' " "Well, well, Skipper," Scott replied, "for a' that, the loons would hae been nane the waur o' their kail."[53]

Neither Skipper John nor Adam had been officially let into the "secret" at this time, though both were told later.[54] Even Scott's children did not positively know, but they had their lively suspicions; they had not failed to notice that Mama seemed perfectly acquainted with the characters and events in the novels even though she left the pages of "her" copies uncut. One morning at the breakfast table Dominie Thomson thoughtlessly helped himself to an egg penciled with "a peculiar hieroglyphic." "That's a mysterious looking egg, Mr. Thomson," Anne remarked saucily, "what if it should have been meant for *the Great Unknown?*" What was this, Scott asked, coming in just then and laying his stick on the carpet beside his chair; didn't everyone know "that the keelavined egg must be a soft one for *the Sherra?*" Anne blushed, but slid out of her dilemma by alluding to Jocund Johnnie's pride in being the representative of Jedediah Cleishbotham. "Upon my word, papa," she teased, "I thought Mr. John Ballantyne might be expected."[55]

Throughout October Abbotsford was a whirl of visitors, John Richardson from London, Terry's wife and her father the well-known landscape painter Alexander Naesmyth, Lord and Lady Compton, whose marriage arrangements Scott had made in 1815, and who were now returned from a prolonged stay in Italy.[56] To celebrate Walter's seventeenth birthday Scott entertained all these guests at a grand jollification with the whole corps of the Selkirkshire Yeomanry Cavalry in which the young fellow was a Cornet. Eighty people crowded into the parlor, Walter bursting with pride in his uniform.[57] "I assure you the scene was gay and even grand," Scott told Morritt, "with glittering sabres, waving standards, and screaming bagpipes . . ."[58]

But neither guests nor gaieties slackened the relentless drive of Scott's pen. He had even taken on further literary tasks, agreeing to be one of eight shareholders in a publication entitled *Provincial Antiquities and Picturesque Scenery of Scotland*, with a group of illustrators including Edward Blore, John Thomson, and the great Joseph Mallard Turner.

The artists were to be paid individually for each picture they supplied; Scott would share in the profits, but contracted to furnish the accompanying descriptive text without remuneration on condition of being given all the drawings and paintings.[59] Before the end of October he was enthusiastically outlining for Blore a roll call of subjects—Borthwick, Crichton, Dalkeith, Edinburgh Castle, Holyrood, a long, excited list.[60]

Beyond this, he was negotiating with Constable for another three-volume work, *New Travels on the Continent*, similar in plan to *Paul's Letters*.[61] He had now been dreaming for some time of seeing Switzerland and Italy, and perhaps Spain. His doctors recommended a vacation as the best means of curtailing those long hours at his desk which they regarded as the true cause of his attacks of cramp; no doubt the Court of Session would grant him a twelvemonth's leave of absence. In addition to both these reasons, the Duke of Buccleuch had been in poor health, and his friends were trying to persuade him to escape Scotland's cold damp winters in a warmer clime. How glorious to spend sunny days together in the vineyards of southern France or the orange groves of Italy![62]

On November 7, agreements were signed for these *Continental Travels*, Scott to have half-profits with the publishers paying him £3,000 for the other half, on an edition of 10,000 copies.[63] "If health or the Court prevent his going," Cadell wrote his partner, "we must just get John to procure a novel or something in its place . . . What with the *Continental Letters*, the new *Tales*, and the *History of Scotland*, we have a prodigious stake in the great man"; but they had recently taken an insurance policy on Scott's life and this would "enable us to go further than any others dare to do . . . I have little doubt we will in due time get all matters made smooth; if he lives there is no fear."[64]

It was not for his own life but the Duke's that Scott felt afraid. In the few weeks since the visit to Drumlanrig his strength was much less, his spirits lower, and he was visibly unwell. The sad change "in voice, in person, in features, and in spirits" all argued "the decay of natural strength and the increase of some internal disorder which is gradually triumphing over the system."[65] His generous noble-hearted friend! Scott's own heart sank with pain and sorrow.

He endeavored himself, without voicing alarm, to hint the desirability of a trip abroad, but the Duke did not wish to go. He felt deeply attached to Scotland and had a strong sense of his duties there.[66] Scott consequently wrote the Duke's brother Lord Montagu suggesting that he might be able to be more persuasive. He himself, of course, would tell the Duke nothing of this letter; "I am as much afraid of [his] irritability as of any symptom I have observed & it would not fail to be affected by the idea that his health was the subject of our correspondence. He was half angry with me for recommending a migration to Dalkeith and yet . . . the extreme heat within doors at Bowhill & the damp without would try a stronger constitution than most unhappily he is at present possessd of."[67]

Meanwhile Scott tried to keep up the Duke's spirits by writing him a series of cheerful gossipy letters headed "Edinburgh Gazette Extraordinary." George Cranstoun had become the life-owner of a beautiful estate on the Clyde. It was reported that Lord Seaforth's daughter, the Honorable Frances Mackenzie, was going to marry the Danish sculptor Thorwaldsen in Rome.[68] Those two fiery young men, Lockhart and Wilson, "under the names of the Leopard and the Scorpion," had been assailed in a virulent pamphlet entitled "Hypocrisy Unveiled and Calumny Detected" and were in a rage at being slashed with their own weapons. They had both challenged the anonymous author to a duel, but the unveiler of hypocrisy chose to remain safely hidden behind his own veil.[69]

Wilson was in a hysterical frenzy, Lockhart angry but more controlled. Scott recommended to both a return to calm. "It would be vain to preach total insensibility," he wrote Lockhart, "but a man should have as much as possible the circum pectus aes triplex of Horace."[70] He had disapproved the severe attacks on Playfair and Sharpe; the young satirists had themselves provoked the hostility they now resented. "For yourself with your talents natural and acquired you have I trust a long and splendid career before you and you must expect that it will be occasionally interrupted or even obscured by the efforts of the envious and malevolent."[71]

In an "Edinburgh Gazette Extraordinary No II" Scott listed for the Duke's amusement "the miscellaneous trash" he had been dashing off during the summer and autumn. "For the love of Jeffrey the Editor— the first time this ten years—" he had contributed to the *Edinburgh* a laudatory review of Maturin's *Women: or, Pour et Contre*. Then, "for the sake of Mr. Constable the publisher" an article on "Drama" for the *Encyclopaedia Britannica*. "For love of the cause I espoused," an analysis of the errors and distortions in "General Gourgaud's Account of the Campaign of 1815" appearing in the November *Blackwood's*. Finally his *Quarterly Review* article praising *Childe Harold*, Canto IV, "for the love of myself I believe," Scott said facetiously, "or which is the same thing for the love of £100."[72] Scott made no mention at all, however, of the consignments of *The Bride of Lammermoor* that had been going to James Ballantyne since the beginning of September.

Either in London or when she visited Abbotsford, Lady Compton had learned of the baronetcy Commissioner Adam had told Scott the Prince Regent proposed to confer upon him. "I feel considerable regret," she wrote from Torloisk, "that this will probably be among my last letters to you addressed to the hands of Walter Scott a name to which no title can add dignity . . ."[73] He had in fact built higher towers than any he could erect on the Tweed or any title bestowed by any prince enhance. It was nevertheless not unpleasant to receive an official communication from the Home Secretary announcing the royal accolade. "I understand from Lord Sidmouth," Scott replied to Lady Compton, "that the honor you wot of may perhaps hang over my head untill I go up to London, which assuredly I will not do till Spring, as I should not like to have the appearance of running headlong to meet such a thing . . ."[74]

"Our fat friend being desirous to honour literature in my unworthy person," Scott wrote Morritt, "has intimated to me . . . that with consent ample and unanimous of all the potential voices of all the ministers, each more happy than another, of course, on so joyful an occasion, he proposes to dubb me baronet. It would be easy saying a parcel of fine things about my contempt of rank and so forth . . . yet coming, as it does, directly from the source of feudal honour, and as an honour, I am really gratified by it. Especially as it . . . is his Royal Highnesses pleasure to heat the oven to me expressly without waiting till he has some new *batch* of baronets ready in dough. . . . As things now stand, Advance Banners in the name of God and Saint Andrew. Remember I anticipate the jest 'I like not such *grinning* honours as Sir Walter hath.' After all, if one must speak for themselves, I have my quarters and emblazonments free of all stain but border theft and high treason, which I hope are gentlemanlike crimes . . ."[75]

Charlotte's pride in this honor conferred upon her husband was darkened a few days later by a letter from India.[76] Her brother Charles Carpenter had died at Salem on June 18 and only after a five months' journey round half the world had the news reached them. She was overwhelmed by grief. Not long before, they had heard that he was planning to return to England.[77] Though Charlotte and her brother had not seen each other for over twenty years, they had written regularly.[78] "She has not that we know of," Scott told Morritt, "a single blood relation left in the world, for her uncle Chevalier de la Volère, Colonel of a Russian regiment, is believed to have been killd in the Russian campaign 1813." Her last link with her far-off childhood in France was gone. Even her husband and her children did not prevent her feeling that she was a stranger in this cold northern clime. In her sorrow she retired to her room. Only after two days was she able to mingle again with her family.[79]

Scott, though stunned by the news, had never met Charles Carpenter and could not feel it as she did.[80] His brother-in-law's estate, they learned, was life-rented to his widow and was then to be divided equally among Scott's children. "There is upwards of £30,000 safe in the British funds and about £10,000 more or less still in India, which he was in the act of realizing in order to his return here when it pleased God to cut him short after a very few days illness. The eventual fortune thus secured to my young people leaves the fruits of my labour much at my own disposal & makes my mind very easy upon futurity."[81]

The first thought of all four children when they learned of this inheritance "was a unanimous wish to [give] up all to their mother. This I explain to them was out of the question, but that if they should be in possession at any time of this property they ought among themselves to settle an income of £400 or £500 on their mother for her life . . ." "She will not need it, but it is pleasant to see them grateful & affectionate." The bequest made Scott himself "neither richer nor poorer *directly*" but took away "a necessity of saving cheese parings and candle ends." A fortune of £10,000 would ensure his daughters "the choice of marrying suitably or of an honorable independence as single women," and he would be able to help "my poor brother Tom's family, besides pleasing myself in plantings and policies of biggings with a safe conscience."[82]

Through all these concerns Scott continued to worry about the Duke of Buccleuch. Though he had only jested when he talked about his own "grinning honours," behind his friend's shoulder might there not be a Death's head grinning those more ghastly honours? But the Duke refused to believe himself seriously ill and felt annoyed at his brother's concern. "He mentioned your Lordship's letter," Scott reported to Lord Montagu, "with small thanks to the anonymous informers who had been the cause of so much anxiety to you and whose information he treated with great scorn."[83] He had ceased to consult Dr. Lincoln and placed himself in the care of another doctor; Scott suspected that Lincoln "had recommended either a change of climate or something that the Duke was determined not to submit to."[84] Scott did persuade him, however, to consult Dr. Scott, a physician settled at Darnlee in Darwick.[85] Dr. Scott's examination led him to suspect that the Duke had water on the chest with "something of an unpronounced gout as the original cause of the malady. . . . He agrees with all the other medical men . . . in earnestly recommending a warmer climate."[86]

After prolonged resistance the Duke at last gave way. "I do not wish to set up my opinion against . . . the Doctors'," he wrote Scott, "and their plan *may* be the best." But the thought of passing the solitary winter months away from his family and friends had put an idea into his head. Would Adam Ferguson come with him as a companion on the same terms as the mentor of a young lord sent abroad, "or as a Spanish ambassador once said of poor Gartshore who travelled with me: 'Voilà apparement le Menteur de Lord Dalkeith.' "[87] "Depend on it," Scott replied joyfully, "Adam will go."[88]

Adam did agree; Scott was delighted. He was "exactly the companion of all hours"—

> "A merrier man
> Within the limits of becoming mirth
> You never spent a pleasant hour withal."[89]

In London, Dr. Matthew Baillie confirmed Dr. Scott's diagnosis of water on the chest and feared the Duke's lungs were partially affected.[90] Scott felt relieved to learn that his Grace would take with him Dr. Lincoln, "who is so steady in adhering to his point and will not care though the Duke should look at him as the Devil looks over the cathedral of the same name."[91] It was decided that the Duke should set sail for Lisbon, where the Duke of Wellington had courteously offered as a residence his own palace, Las Necessidades.[92] "Were I Lord Melville," wrote Scott, "I would send a press gang to way lay your Grace at Montagu House, seize the Capt., Florence, & Lincoln as able-bodied sea men, clap you all on board a frigate, & only liberate you in the chops of the channel."[93]

This matter so happily settled, Scott concentrated with renewed energy on *The Bride of Lammermoor*. He would finish it with all speed, and instead of going to Italy by way of Switzerland join the two travelers in Lisbon or Spain next summer.[94] Meanwhile, Edinburgh itself was having a burst of springlike weather. Here in December the thermometer stood at fifty-three at midnight, roses were blooming, and all the leaves remained green.[95] "Never was such a season," Scott exclaimed, "flowers springing, birds singing, grubs eating the wheat—as if it was the end of May. After all, nature had a grotesque and inconsistent appearance, and I could not help thinking she resembled a withered beauty who persists in looking youthy, and dressing conform thereto."[96]

On New Year's Eve at Abbotsford the air was still summery, and outdoors "the ladies," Scott wrote Adam Ferguson, were all, including his sisters at Huntly Burn, "alert as larks."[97] That night about a hundred children gathered in front of the house "to dance to the pipes and get a piece of cake and bannock and pence apiece (no very deadly largesse) — in honour of hogmanay." Their parents too made merry with them. "Like Fortunio in the fairy tale," said Scott, "I have my gifted men— the best wrestler and cudgel player—the best runner and leaper—the best shot in the little district—"[98]

During the first half of January, Scott set in motion the steps necessary for being granted his baronetcy, though he did not intend to go to London until spring to receive it. "At the Secretary of State's," John Richardson told him, "you must—before your Patent issues—produce a certificate from the Heralds' College, that your Arms are there registered. On the registration of your Arms you produce your pedigree to what extent you chuse. . . . Your fees at the Heralds' College . . . are not great things. The main charge is the deposit at the Secretary of State's office. They will there ask from you £380 of which you will receive back probably from £10 to £15. In all I should think £400 would clear you every where."[99]

One of Scott's reasons for being pleased with "le petit titre" had been that it might help his "views towards the Court of Exchequer should a favourable opening occur."[100] Now the Duke of Buccleuch heard in London that one of the Barons of Exchequer intended to resign. He sent word urging Scott to renew his application for a seat on that bench.[101] The circumstances, however, were all changed. He had learned that his old schoolfellow William Rae was also in the field. For Scott the small increase in salary made little difference; the principal gain was in legal prestige and longer vacations.[102] Pleasant though these would be, they were not pressing. "The Otium cum dignitate if it ever came will come as well years after this as now." But for Rae, who was only Sheriff of Mid-Lothian, the augmented income was important, and he had done a great deal to deserve such a promotion. "I would not, for the world," Scott exclaimed, "stand in Jackie Peartree's way."[103]

He therefore at once announced this resolution to Lord Melville. "It would be a strange point that I should wish to struggle . . . or interfere with the interest of so old & valued a friend & so meritorious a public character as Sir W. Rae." He himself must be taken to have withdrawn his card. "I wish to be laid entirely out of consideration where his interest is concernd." Perhaps at some future time there might be another vacancy on the bench, and then they might like to have his sheriffdom and Clerk of Session seat to bestow on someone.[104]

To Adam Ferguson, who was in London with the Duke, Scott minimized his generosity. "Immediate promotion would be inconvenient to me rather than otherwise because I have the desire like an old fool as I am *courir un peu le monde*." He was "determined to roll a little about, for I have lost much of my usual views of summer pleasure here." Where could he roll with more pleasure than to Lisbon, where he would be able to join Adam and the Duke in the Palacio las Necessidades, and then, if he could travel through Spain without getting his throat cut, move on to Madrid and Gibraltar?[105]

Happier still, the day would come when after these foreign jaunts they would all be together again in Scotland, the Duke's health completely restored by a southern clime. They would set out with the horses, "the Maid of Lorn (recovered of her lameness) and Charlie Stuart (reconciled to bogs) and Sybill Grey (no longer retrograde)" and all his Grace's "military and civil aids de camp with all the rout of younkers and dogs and a brown hill side introductory to a good dinner at Bowhill or Drumlanrick—Amen and God send it."[106]

# Death on the Pale Horse

## ( 1 8 1 9 )

" "A MEN AND GOD WROTE IT." There was reason for the words, for the Duke's health was gravely impaired and Scott's own still gave cause for uneasiness. The few months since autumn in which he had experienced no recurrence of cramps gave small assurance that he was cured, and he did not desist from his usual exertions. For the *Provincial Antiquities* he wrote out long accounts of Crichton and Borthwick castles.[1] He tried to obtain a promotion for Joseph Train, the antiquarian exciseman, who had gone on sending him pages of curious material, about penny weddings, Galloway traditions, the gypsies of Fife, the fishermen of Findhorn and Nairn.[2] He sent Laidlaw directions about planting lime seeds sent by Lord Montagu;[3] limes were noble trees and would make a magnificent avenue.[4] He advised his impoverished cousin William Scott, the son of the grasping old laird of Raeburn, about a lawsuit in which he had become entangled with a neighbor.[5]

The negotiations on the sale of Scott's copyrights to Constable, which had begun a full year before, had not yet been concluded. They were now to cover the two novels of the current series, *The Bride of Lammermoor* and a shorter companion tale called *A Legend of Montrose*, and Constable was hesitating about the additional £2,000 Scott asked. He had not "the least wish," Scott responded, "of pressing . . . a losing or even a doubtful bargain"; "I should not feel happy at taking a guinea more from you than you could fairly afford. . . ." He believed, however, that he could make even more if he retained the copyrights in his own hands, and only the certainty of a large sum could tempt him.[6] "I stand out for £12,000," he wrote Adam Ferguson, "Tell this to the

Duke; he knows how I managed to keep the hen till the rainy day was past."[7]

Ultimately Constable yielded, with the understanding that payment was to be made in six bills of £2,000 each, the first due in two years and the rest at yearly intervals thereafter. They signed the agreement on February 2, 1819; it covered Scott's shares in the copyrights of his poems and the entire copyright of *Paul's Letters* and of all the novels from *Waverley* through the unfinished third series of *Tales of My Landlord*. One provision bound Constable, under a penalty of £2,000, never to divulge the name of the Author of *Waverley* during his lifetime.[8] Just after the deed was signed, no man could guess, Scott told a friend gleefully, at how large a price Constable estimated his "eild kye" [old cows].[9]

Scott was now planning to go up to London in April and receive his baronetcy, taking Walter with him for his first sight of the great capital.[10] The young fellow had decided that he wished to enter the army; this would be a good opportunity to look out for a commission.[11] "Walter would have gone to the Bar had I liked," Scott wrote his brother Tom; "but I was sensible . . . that I should only spoil an excellent soldier to make a poor and undistinguished gownsman."[12] While in town Scott would also talk to people in behalf of poor luckless William Scott and see if he might not get some official appointment that would eke out his insignificant income—perhaps that of Lyon Clerk at Arms. On the spot he could accomplish more than could be done by letter. "An application of this kind is a single-barreled gun which can only be fired once and therefore I wish to be within gun-shot before letting off my carabine."[13]

February 15 saw a spectacular opening night at the Edinburgh Theatre Royal—a dramatized version of *Rob Roy*. Though nobody said so to Scott, it was common rumor that he had written the original novel; his appearance in the box Charlotte had taken for the occasion was the signal for a burst of enthusiasm in the crowded theater.[14] Among the friends filling the box was young Mr. Lockhart, whom Charlotte had invited just the day before.[15] The production scored a resounding success; repeatedly the actors were interrupted by thunders of applause; night after night all Edinburgh jammed the theater.

Scott felt enchanted beyond everything with the performance of Charles Mackay as Bailie Nicol Jarvie.[16] "It was the living Nicol Jarvie" in all his self-consequence, vulgarity, generosity, irritability, and good nature, said Scott. His fear of Rob Roy, his pride in being related to him, and his desire to intermeddle with and advise him, "I thought would have made me expire with laughing. His despairing exclamation of 'Ah Rab! Rab!' after the other had been provoked into a tirade of Highland wrath was quite irresistible."[17]

In the character of Jedediah Cleishbotham, Scott wrote the actor a letter of praise. "Friend Mackay—My lawful occasions having brought me from my residence at Gandercleuch to this great city, it was my lot to fall into company with certain friends, who impetrated from me a consent to behold the stage-play, which hath been framed forth of an history entitled Rob (*seu potius* Robert) Roy . . . Wherefore, having surmounted those arguments whilk were founded upon the unseemliness of a personage in my place and profession appearing in an open stage-play house, and having buttoned the terminations of my cravat into my bosom . . . I . . . beheld the show with great delectation, even from the rising of the curtain to the fall thereof.[18]

"Chiefly, my facetious friend, was I enamoured of the very lively representation of Bailie Nicol Jarvie, insofar that I became desirous to communicate to thee my great admiration thereof, nothing doubting that it will give thee satisfaction to be apprised of the same." As a further mark of approval, "I now send thee mine in the form of a five-ell web (*hoc jocose*, to express a note for £5), as a meet present for the Bailie, himself a weaver, and the son of a worthy deacon of that craft."[19]

This play, possibly, and some hints of the aid Scott had been lending Terry in adapting his novels to the stage, gave rise to a newspaper rumor that he was now himself composing a drama.[20] "I am greatly in hopes it may be true," wrote Southey, "for I am verily persuaded that in this course you might run as brilliant a career as you have already done in narrative—both in prose and rhyme;—for as for believing that you have a double in the field—not I! Those same powers would be equally certain of success in the drama, and were you to give them a dramatic direction, and reign for a third seven years upon the stage, you would stand alone in literary history."[21]

But Scott forcefully denied any such intent. "To write for low, ill-informed, and conceited actors, whom you must please, for your success is necessarily at their mercy, I cannot away with. How would you . . . relish being the object of such a letter as Kean wrote t'other day to a poor author, who, though a pedantic blockhead, had at least the right to be treated as a gentleman by a copper-laced, twopenny tearmouth, rendered mad by conceit and success?" And, besides, think of what London theater audiences were like. "One half come to prosecute their debaucheries, so openly that it would degrade a bagnio. Another set to snooze off their beef-steaks and port wine; a third are critics of the fourth column of the newspaper; fashion, wit, or literature, there is not; and, on the whole, I would far rather write verses for mine honest friend Punch and his audience."[22]

During that winter and spring John Gibson Lockhart was becoming a familiar guest in Castle Street. He was not a young man who yielded easily to admiration, but Scott conquered his prickly superciliousness. Never was there a lion with less roar. Let the lawyers of

Edinburgh cross swords and the wits glitter at their most dazzling, nobody was more delighted than Scott to sit by, with no jealous desire of rivalry. But his own conversation was full of vivid flashes and sound reflection, lit by quaint humor and homely wisdom, enriched by a marvelous stock of queer stories;[23] his talk, Lockhart said, was like "sunlight, which gilds the most indifferent objects and adds brilliancy to the brightest." "Whatever subject be mentioned, he at once steals a beam from his mirror and scatters such a flood of illustration upon it that you feel as if it had always been mantled in palpable night before."[24]

The great Whig lawyer Henry Cockburn thought Scott's conversation as brilliant as Jeffrey's and delighted in "the halting limb, the burr in the throat, the heavy cheeks, the high Goldsmith-forehead, the unkempt locks, and general plainness of appearance, with the Scotch accent and stories and sayings, all graced by gaiety, simplicity, and kindness."[25] The wise, brooding face and the rugged sagacity made mere cleverness trivial. Those who were taken in by more flashy talents, to be sure, sometimes even thought Scott commonplace, as a child might think a clear stream shallow though deep enough to drown in. To a young man who echoed these depreciations Cockburn replied: "I have the misfortune to think differently from you—in my humble opinion, Walter Scott's *sense* is a still more wonderful thing than his *genius*."[26]

Scott's health still did not allow him a steady round of dining out, and he seldom accompanied Charlotte and his daughters to evening assemblies. But he often went to the theater, and he enjoyed dining with close friends at his own board or theirs, though he went early to bed. Even more often, after a quiet family dinner, he drove in an open carriage to Ravelston or Portobello, coming home by Corstorphine or along the shore; or sometimes creeping around the esplanade of Holyrood, up past the tottering gables of the Canongate, and through the dark streets of the old town to the Grassmarket drowned in the darkest shadows of the Castle Rock, recalling all the way long-buried memories of past splendor and bloodshed.[27]

Breakfast, not dinner, Lockhart noted, was Scott's heartiest meal. He came to it from several hours of work and sat down to a table amply supplied—a round of beef, a pasty, a cold sheepshead, eggs, porridge, a huge brown loaf on a broad wooden trencher. He ate no other meal till dinner, when his favorite dishes were old-fashioned ones, like haggis and cockieleekie, but he ate and drank sparingly. His young observer was surprised to discover that neither his palate nor his sense of smell was refined. "I have seen him stare about, quite unconscious of the cause," says Lockhart, "when his whole company betrayed their uneasiness at the approach of an over-kept haunch of venison." He could not "distinguish corked wine from sound" or tell Madeira from Sherry. About port he was fond of quoting Home's epigram:

> Bold and erect the Caledonian stood,
> Old was his mutton, and his claret good;
> Let him drink port, the English statesman cried—
> He drank the poison, and his spirit died.

He really liked no wines except champagne and claret, and even to these he preferred "mountain dew"—Scotch whiskey—served in ancient Highland quaighs, little wooden cups inlaid with silver.[28]

In quiet evenings at home there was ballad singing and the harp— "Otterbourne," "The Bonnie House of Airlie," "Jenny dang the Weaver," —conversation, story-telling, and reading aloud. There was no music on Sundays, but Scott was fond of reading Shakespeare with his circle and having them join in. They also read Dryden, Johnson—Scott deeply admired both *London* and *The Vanity of Human Wishes*—and scenes from Beaumont and Fletcher. Among modern authors they read Joanna Baillie, Crabbe, Southey, Lord Byron, and Wordsworth—of whose poems Scott most liked the "Song for Brougham Castle," "Laodamia," and some of the sonnets. Whatever poem Byron had just published Scott was sure to read aloud, even on a Sunday, with a delighted emphasis that revealed his enthusiastic admiration.[29]

Early the previous January the Duke of Buccleuch had arranged to sail for Lisbon in the H.M.S. *Liffey*. But all through that month and well into February the vessel was held in Portsmouth by contrary winds.[30] On February 15 the Duke wrote to remind Scott of a promise to sit to Raeburn for his portrait. "My prodigious undertaking of a west wing at Bowhill is begun. A library of forty-one feet by twenty-one is to be added to the present drawingroom. A space for one picture is reserved over the fire-place and in this warm situation I intend to place the Guardian of Literature. I should be happy to have my friend Maida appear. . . . Raeburn should be warned that I am as well acquainted with my friend's hands and arms as his nose—and Vandyke was of my opinion. Many of R.'s works are shamefully finished—the face studied, but everything else neglected."[31]

"I write in great haste," responded Scott, "anxious to take the chance however remote that this letter may find you still wind-bound." He would arrange with Raeburn about the portrait. It could be placed in no house where he had been happier or for which he had "so long a train of kind and affectionate recollections."[32] The Duke believed that he had already taken a turn for the better in England, and the observation of others seemed to confirm it.[33] When the *Liffey* at last sailed around the end of February the son of Lord President Hope, who said farewell to him on the deck, "was pleasingly surprized to find his health and general appearance very much improved."[34]

Scott's own malady, however, had returned with piercing and dangerous intensity.[35] This time he had none of the fever and vomiting that had characterized his previous seizures, but the opiates the doctors found necessary to relieve the spasms so constricted his bowels that he was obliged to take strong laxatives as well.[36] During the course of six or seven hours he would be given six grains of opium, three of hyoscyamus, and as much as two hundred drops of laudanum.[37] Even in the agonizing "pull-devil—pull-baker contention" that resulted,[38] however, Scott joked about his desperate rushes from bed to water closet. They reminded him, he wrote, of a certain "American Sachem to whom an English Captain presented a lock and key," with which the savage chief "was so much delighted that neglecting all other duties he spent a whole week in locking and unlocking his back door."[39] But Scott's cramps did not desist; they came more often and with greater violence. The fits of sickness brought on with them a jaundice that left him looking like a yellow ghost. The Bank of England, he jested feebly, might coin him into deniers, "like Bardolph's nose,"[40] and he might sit for the very image of Plutus, the god of gold.[41]

When the Court rose on March 12, in the hope that "a mouthful of fresh air on Tweedside" "might renew health and appetite," Scott "crawled out" to Abbotsford.[41a] But in the next ten days he endured four more attacks so agonizing that the entire household was terrified.[42] "Within these four hours," he wrote on March 14, he had endured such pain "as to darken my eyes, so that I could not tell my daughters from each other."[43] On the night of March 22, the spasms lasted from six-thirty "till half-past four in the morning without a moment's intermission,"[44] and for eight hours he could not help screaming.[45] His left leg was so swollen with inflammation that he had to be carried about like a child; his right leg faired better because its lameness, he thought, made its muscles less irritable.[46] Pain never left him for twenty-four hours at a time;[47] four days he remained in bed, so weak with bleeding, blistering, and dosing[48] that he could not even bear being shaved, and his arms so mangled with lancets that he could not hold a pen.[49] He felt, he said, "as I suppose the town of Saragossa did when it had been so desperately attacked and defended."[50]

A crisis came when Charlotte was closing the house in Castle Street and Sophia and Anne were alone with their father and the servants in the country.[51] Despite her own terror Sophia managed the distracted servants,[52] sent for Dr. Clarkson and James Skene to come to the bedside. Together they bent over Scott's wan face on the pillow, and Skene felt for his pulse. Without opening his eyes, Scott murmured, "I am not *yet* gone."[53]

Presently he rallied and surprised Skene by a question. Did he remember a small round turret overhanging the street at Aberbrothwick? He had once, Scott went on, seen a mob tugging with a hawser to pull down its weather-beaten head. "Now that is exactly the condition of my poor stomach. There is a rope twisted around it, and the malicious devils are straining and tugging at it, and faith, I could almost think that I hear them shouting and cheering each other . . ."[54]

Not till the end of March did his illness relent somewhat, when it seemed to yield a little to immersion in warm baths,[55] into which he was lowered in the strong arms of Tom Purdie, to lie still in the water, Tom said, "like a haulded salmon" till the spasms ceased.[56] Scott thought that he could not have endured six more days of agony.[57] Following an afternoon in which he fell into a gentle doze he awoke feeling better. But he could eat only whey and oatmeal porridge, waving away "the vain imaginations of soups and jellies with which they tried to cram me";[58] for ten days he was able to swallow nothing "but toast & water & a tea spoonful of boiled rice."[59]

On March 31 he seemed so much recovered that he was taken outdoors for two airings; he believed that he had turned the corner. "But I am weaker than water," he wrote James Ballantyne, ". . . & *dare not* face any thing like continued thought or exertion. I am like the old carrier John talks of who at ninety making his usual march lost appetite for his supper & began to think for the first time in his life he was what folks calld weary."[60] At last, however, Scott found himself sleeping at night "instead of counting the hours" as they hollowly sounded on "a clock that never by any accident strikes right." He was "thin, exhausted, and ghastly to the last degree," but little by little he seemed gaining strength.[61]

In the pale mid-April sunlight he began crawling about on his white pony Sybil Grey, "the very image of Death on the pale horse, lanthorn-jawed, decayd in flesh, stooping as if I meant to eat the poney's ears & unable to go above a foot-pace."[62] Still, for weeks he wavered between relapse and recovery, seeming "to lose rather than gain ground, all food nauseating on my stomach, and my clothes hanging about me like a potato-bogle [a scarecrow] with from five or six to ten hours of mortal pain every third day."[63]

During one of Scott's recurrent crises of agony there were two American visitors at Abbotsford, Professor George Ticknor, of Harvard, and the bibliographer Joseph Cogswell.[64] Scott found them both agreeable and accomplished men, but in his anguish, he said regretfully, he had given them only "Tom Drum's entertainment"—"which is to hale a man in by the heade, and thrust him out by both the shoulders."[65] Bleeding, blistering, calomel, and ipecacuanha went on endlessly, and his spasms never ceased. "If I had not had the strength of a team of horses, I could never have fought through it . . . I did not lose my senses, because I resolved to keep them, but I thought once or twice they would have gone overboard, top and top-gallant."[66]

Only toward the end of April could Scott feel that he had beaten back his disorder and exclaim:

"The game is done—I've won, I've won,
Quoth she, and whistles thrice."

"I am like Sancho," he said, "after the doughty affair of the Yanguesian carriers . . ." "But no broken-down hunter had ever so many sprung sinews, whelks, and bruises."[67]

Throughout Scott's sufferings all his servants, farm laborers, and country neighbors had been in deep consternation. Tom Purdie had lowered him into his warm bath as gently as if he were an infant. Old Tom Hutson, the Bowhill gamekeeper, "crept down twice from Falshope to see how I was coming on and to ejaculate if any aild the Shirra it would be sair on the Duke."[68] From Jedburgh Robert Shortreed's wife sent loaves of her own home-baked bread.[69] Baby, the Misses Fergusons's housekeeper at Huntly Burn, came over to Abbotsford to offer her services as a sick nurse, and Adam's sisters abounded in attentions and homely gifts: "I have drunk scarce any thing," Scott wrote to Lisbon, "but delicious ginger-beer of Miss Bell's brewing since my troubles commenced."[70]

Everyone sent remedies for cramp and jaundice—"as many," Scott wrote the Duke, "as would set up a quack Doctor—three from Mrs. Plummer—each better than the other—one at least from every gardner in the neighborhood besides all sorts of recommendations to go to Cheltenham, to Harrowgate, to Jericho for aught I know." John Bruce, the Highland piper, "spent a whole Sunday in selecting twelve stones from twelve south running streams with the purpose that I should sleep upon them and be whole." Scott told him "the recipe was infallible, but that it was absolutely necessary to success that the stones should be wrapd up in the petticoat of a widow who had never wished to marry again," and poor John of Skye "renounced all hope of completing the charm."[71]

Save through those days, however, when Scott was absolutely unable to move from his bed, he had forced himself to go on with *The Bride of Lammermoor*, creeping downstairs to his study and stooping painfully over his desk. Page after page was written in a blurred trance of suffering in which he did not know what words he was putting down, images and dreamlike actions rising somehow out of unconscious depths of the imagination while he himself struggled through a drugged nightmare world. During some of his torments he resorted to dictation, using the pen of John Ballantyne or Will Laidlaw, lying on a sofa and groaning as he writhed on his pillow.[72] "I began to dictate yesterday," he wrote Constable on April 8, ". . . This is a great point. But I must work by little & little. Last night I had a slight return of the enemy but easily bafled him."[73] A few days later he wrote the publisher, "John Ballantyne is here and returns with copy which my increasing strength permits me to hope I may now furnish regularly."[74]

The novel had now, in fact, far advanced toward its ending, and as soon as it was concluded Scott turned all his attention to *A Legend of Montrose*. He found John a better amanuensis than Laidlaw, whose excited interest in the story burst out in exclamations of "Gude keep us a'!—the like o' that!—eh sirs! eh sirs!" John provided himself in advance with a dozen well-sharpened pens and never ceased writing, though his eyes twinkled archly at the doings of Dugald Dalgetty and he smacked his lips audibly over the richer episodes. When the dialogue grew dramatic, spirit triumphing over matter, Scott rose from his couch, limping up and down the room, raising and lowering his voice, almost acting out the roles. Often, though, Laidlaw begged him to stop dictating when his groans filled every pause. "Nay, Willie," he would reply, "only see that the doors are fast. I would fain keep all the cry as well as all the wool to ourselves; but as to giving over work, that can only be when I am in woollen."[75]

Even during the darkest hours of his illness Scott never lost his determination to recover or his zest for life. He was delighted with *Peter's Letters*, a series of sketches of Edinburgh and its leading figures which Lockhart was contributing to *Blackwood's Magazine*.[76] He looked forward eagerly to the concluding volume of Southey's *History of Brazil*, and to reading his *Life of Wesley* in the course of the summer. "When I was about twelve years old," he wrote Southey, "I heard him preach more than once, standing on a chair, in Kelso churchyard. He was a most venerable figure, but his sermons were vastly too colloquial for the taste of Saunders."[77]

He was still full of projects for Abbotsford. "We wish much," he wrote Terry, "to have a plan of the great bed, that we may hang up the tester." He had received "a beautiful scarlet paper, inlaid with gold (rather crimson than scarlet) in a present from India."[78] He still needed a carpet for the great parlor; James Ballantyne had obtained for him a "very handsome bright steel cuirassier of Queen Elizabeth's time"; and he wanted "a good set of *real tilting* armour. . . . Hangings, curtains, &c. I believe we shall get as well in Edinburgh as in London; it is in your joiner and cabinet work that your infinite superiority lies."[79]

He felt delighted to hear that Terry was becoming stage manager of the Haymarket Theatre. "You must beware," he cautioned, "of stumbling over a propensity which easily besets you . . . I mean what the women very expressively call *dawdling*. Your motto must be *Hoc age*. . . . I must love a man so well to whom I offer such a word of advice, that I will not apologize for it, but expect to hear that you are become as regular as a Dutch clock—"[80]

He rejoiced to learn from Lisbon that Adam Ferguson thought the Duke's health mending. "But I hope you will by & bye get away to Cintra or some other of those sequestered retreats where there are shades & cascades to cool the air. . . . As for the Senhoras I have little doubt that the difference of food betwixt your military *Buffa rossa* and

*Florence's* high sauces & jellies will make them think that time has rather improved an old friend than deprived him of any of his powers of pleasing."[81]

To the Duke himself Scott reiterated that he would be proud to sit for the desired portrait. "But neither my late golden hue, for I was coverd with jaundice, nor my present silver complection, looking much more like a spectre than a man, will present any idea of my quondam beef-eating physiognomy. . . . It is doomd this letter is not to conclude without a request."[82] The Kirk of Middlebie was vacant, and Scott put in a plea for George Thomson, "long the grinder of my boys & therefore deeply entitled to my gratitude & my good offices . . . He is nearer parson Abraham Adams than any living creature I ever saw, very learned, very religious, very simple, & extremely absent."[83]

On May 1 when Lockhart rode out to Abbotsford with John Ballantyne, he was shocked at the change in Scott's appearance. His face was meager and haggard, and the flaxen hair, which not many weeks before had been only flecked with gray, was now almost white. But his eyes were bright; as he ate his rice pudding and sipped his toast and water he pushed around the bottles to the others and talked cheerfully of the stout battle he now seemed to think he had won.[84]

One day of despair there had been, he told them, when he feared his illness was affecting his mind. Remembering his father's last dreadful days, he had been terrified lest he too decline into a state of peevish doddering. Original composition he found impossible, but he had just been reading an old Bohemian ballad; if he could translate it into decent rhymes, perhaps he might dismiss his worst apprehensions. "You shall see," he concluded, "what came of the experiment." He then sent Sophia for the MS of *The Noble Moringer*, which she and Laidlaw had taken down from his dictation, and read its forty-three quatrains aloud. Though the verses were no masterpiece, they were plainly not the work of a failing brain; his listeners praised them perhaps more than they deserved. Good, he said; after he had made them a little "tighter about the joints," Lockhart should take the poem back to town with him for the *Edinburgh Annual Register*.[85]

Reading the long ballad, however, had exhausted him. He retired to bed, and a few hours later felt a sharp return of his pangs. He was given a large dose of opium and was put in the hot bath, and Dr. Scott of Darnlee was sent for. Even out on the bowling green Lockhart could hear Scott's groans. Lockhart thought this was no time for the family to be troubled with guests and decided to leave early the next morning, but at seven Scott tapped on his door.

"Don't think of going," he said. "I feel hearty this morning, and if my devil does come back, it won't be for three days at any rate. For the present, I want nothing to set me up except a good trot in the open air, to drive away the accursed vapours of the laudanum I was obliged to swallow last night. You have never seen Yarrow, and when I have finished a little job I have with Jocund Johnny, we shall all take horse and make a day of it."[86]

Lockhart stared; after such a night, he asked, wasn't a twenty-mile ride a bold experiment? Scott laughed; following just such an attack the week before he had ridden forty. There was a Burgh election coming up, and sick or well, he would always guard the Duke's interests. At eleven o'clock he mounted Sybil Grey and they rode to Selkirk, where Scott halted to do business at the Sheriff-Clerk's. Catching up to them later at a lively canter, he was in high spirits over the results of his canvass. At Philiphaugh he vividly described Montrose's defeat and escape with his few cavaliers over the steep heights of Minchmoor. Rough as the ground was, Scott told them, his mother in her girlhood had bumped over it in a coach and six on her way to a ball at Peebles, with footmen marching on each side to hold the carriage on the hills and drag it through the bogs.[87]

Next morning, all the better for his ride, Scott said cheerfully, he was up at cockcrow. The election was touch-and-go. The opposing candidate, young Pringle of Clifton, "this pantalooned little Jack-a-Dandie with his whiskers," must not be allowed to whisk Selkirk from under the Duke's nose.[88] He had fifteen votes, the Duke's candidate fifteen. A drunken tailor and a drunken baker had promised their votes to both candidates, and the remaining voter, a respectable farmer named Simpson, was undecided. If they could nail down two of these three, the Buccleuch forces would triumph.[89]

But Simpson, a tenant of Lord Minto and Pringle, was terrified at losing his farm if he voted against his landlords and hardly dared be seen talking to a Buccleuch man. This morning, therefore, across Bowden Moor and up the valley of the Ale, over bleak wastes and mosses, Scott was riding to an out-of-the-way rendezvous with the frightened farmer at Langmoss, "a spot where the devil might meet the conjuror." A wreath of smoke wavering in the air told him where the wavering farmer was waiting.[90]

"But he is fixd," Scott triumphantly wrote Lord Montagu next day. The Duke's commissioner, Charles Riddell, had said that Simpson was an honest man and an excellent farmer; there would be nothing wrong in promising him the preference among several good farms on the Buccleuch estates if Lord Minto and Pringle proved vindictive. This Scott had done. "We have now to gain back only one of our blackguards or to keep him *neuter* which will suit as well . . . I rode forty miles yesterday before dinner and ten this morning before breakfast with as much ease as ever I made a journey in my life. Pretty well for a gentleman who could not a month since bear the motion of a carriage for two miles."[91]

The news from Lisbon, though, was less encouraging. The Duke's restored vitality had not lasted long. Though he kept up his spirits, Adam Ferguson reported, his health was not really mending. Scott tried to believe that the warm sunlight might still induce a renewal of strength, but he awaited the next letter with anxious foreboding.[92] When he had gone to Yarrow just this last time and his horse had turned by habit up the avenue to Bowhill, his heart had sunk at the thought that this was a road he might not travel for a long time to come. When would that lofty hall and the bright drawing room ring to their laughter once more? Would they ever meet again? May 5 brought the answer to his hopes and fears. The Duke had died on April 20. It was for Duke Charles, not himself, that the rider on the pale horse had come.[93]

Scott wrote Lord Montagu at once to voice his sympathy and sorrow. Such excellent sense, high principle, and perfect honor were an inestimable loss to the country and to all those who knew his dead friend's merits. It deepened the pain to think of him dying so far from home, though the voyage had been advised with the best intentions. Scott thought that he had never really recovered from the death of the Duchess. "He wrote me within two days of that cruel event a most affectionate and remarkable letter . . . but I could see a grief of that calm and concentrated kind which claimd the hours of solitude & of night for its empire & gradually wasted the springs of life."[94]

Back in Edinburgh for the opening of the Court, Scott gave himself the painful task of writing an obituary of the Duke for the *Edinburgh Weekly Journal*.[95] Selkirk, he was obliged to tell Lord Montagu, was "irretrievably lost—the fatal news destroyd every hope of recovering our turncoats."[96] Pringle, in fact, won the election by seventeen to sixteen.[97] Scott buried himself in the labors of his study. Before he left Abbotsford he had sent Ballantyne the last pages of *The Bride of Lammermoor;* now he determinedly put aside his personal emotions and directed himself to the remaining work that had to be done on *A Legend of Montrose*.[98]

On May 19 the London and Leith Old Shipping Company asked Scott's permission to have the honor of naming a new vessel after him. Their other six vessels were called the *King George*, *Queen Charlotte*, *Lord Wellington*, *Lord Melville*, *Queen*, and *Caledonia*. It was much above his merits, Scott replied politely, but how could he decline "the first compliment of the kind which has ever been paid to a living literary man in his own country." He would like "to furnish the Colours or Flag necessary for the Vessell." In turn came a letter from the Directors expressing their thanks for "so handsomely bestowing upon the *Walter Scott* her first Colours the *British Flag*."[99]

Before Scott's return to town he had felt a brief flash of anger at Constable, who was proposing, now that he had acquired the copyrights of all the novels, to reissue the First Series of *Tales of My Landlord— The Black Dwarf* and *Old Mortality*—in an ornamented edition. To

Scott's indignation Constable casually announced that he was giving the printing not to Ballantyne but to a rival firm. "I need not recall to Messrs. Constable and Cadell," Scott snapped back, "what passed betwixt us in their shop and that there was an engagement as solemn as a pledge of honour could make it that the works with which I then parted should be printed as usual in Saint John Street. I should otherwise have given my own knife to cut my own throat . . . I am always sorry to write cross letters but this is a very serious matter with me."[100]

Though Constable at once gave way,[101] this project led to another outburst of spleen from Blackwood. His business affairs were not going well; there had been a breach between him and Murray, who had withdrawn his name from the *Magazine*;[102] and now Blackwood angrily learned that henceforth Constable was to have the *Tales* he had so vaunted himself on snatching away from that hated rival. He still had twelve hundred copies of the fourth edition unsold, he protested to James Ballantyne; no new edition was needed; but even if one had been he was in courtesy entitled to the first offer. This scheme was an injury that must be instantly repaired.[103]

Ballantyne replied that he was no longer the author's agent, merely the printer. He pointed out, however, that Blackwood's agreement gave him no right to any editions beyond the fourth. But it appeared "common justice and common sense," he admitted, "that this last edition should not come into the market until the stock in hand shall be sold off or otherwise settled, so that you may be no loser." He would therefore consider it a duty to transmit Blackwood's claim to the author.[104]

Blackwood fumed at this letter as a transparent evasion. It might be true that as a mere printer it was Ballantyne's "business to execute the order without consulting B. or any other letter of the Alphabet." But whether the Author changed his agent or not, that gave him no right to nullify arrangements made with his authority. "This fifth edition," he insisted, "is in direct violation of our bargain. . . . I will not give up any claims or compensation I may think myself entitled to, nor will I allow myself or my rights, even by Him, to be trampled upon . . . I have no formal proposal to make: it is for the author to do so through you."[105]

In reply Scott coolly referred Blackwood to the terms of their bargain. He would not have changed publishers if the sales had been satisfactory, but this was optional to himself. "Concerning Mr. Constable's right of publishing a new edition of these tales before the old one is out I am neither a judge nor a party. But I suppose the utmost they can demand is to have what remains of the edition taken off their hands."[106] This opinion Scott repeated to Constable: "As for Mr. Blackwood I suppose all he can ask is that the copies on hand be taken from him at sale price—He cannot suppose he is to keep the book forever out of the market."[107]

Blackwood talked of bringing suit. This threat complicated the negotiations already under way for Scott's next literary enterprise. *A Legend of Montrose* was almost completed, and Constable was pressing him to get on with the Scottish history he had agreed to do. "I have as much desire as Mr. Constable can," Scott wrote John Ballantyne, "to get rid of the *History of Scotland.* But my health peremptorily requires that I should go to the country & without my town historical library and the Advocates' Library to refer to it is absolutely impossible for me to do justice to this work." He had already, however, outlined another novel in his mind; Constable need not expect this story unless he gave up his contention that not he but Scott must indemnify Blackwood.[108]

"If Messrs. Constable are determined to make a lawsuit of it," he said, "we may both have expence and trouble." They knew as well as or better than he did how many copies of the fourth edition had remained unsold, and he could see no clause in their bargain making him liable to relieve Blackwood of them. There had been a mistake that he was willing to do his best to make up, but he would not be bludgeoned into assuming the entire burden as a penalty for having gratified their desire "to be the proprietors of the first as well as subsequent series of these tales." "I should be sorry," he summarized, "to be at law with both my publishers at once."[109]

But both suits blew over. The new novel was to be called *Ivanhoe*; as soon as Constable heard about it he became more accommodating. An agreement for 10,000 copies gave Scott £1,500 and half profits, the other half going one-third to Constable, one-third to Longman, and one-sixth each to John and James Ballantyne. In consideration of this bargain the partners also agreed, if Scott lost the dispute with Blackwood, to take any of the First Series of *Tales of My Landlord* that were thrown upon his hands at the price he was found liable to pay.[110]

Blackwood, too, after snorting defiance, and vowing he would yield to no compromise, accepted an offer of £1,500 for his unsold volumes.[111] He had "the assurance to say," Scott indignantly reported to Constable, "that *his taking this full advantage was merely out of respect for the author.* I have taken care it shall not stand on that footing. But it is as well the business is closed, though at some loss which I dare say you will fall to pay one day with some butter to send it down."[112]

In the dubious state of Scott's health there was no longer any possibility, of course, of his spending the summer abroad, as he had hoped. He would never, alas, see Lisbon and the fountains of Cintra with the Duke, or travel with him and Adam Ferguson to Madrid and the fabled rock of Gibraltar. The *Continental Travels*, therefore, must be put over or, if Constable preferred, given up, and he would take the option open to him of redeeming the bills that had been given as an advance.[113] Nor until he felt in full vigor again could he go even to London; the honors in store for him there would have to wait.[114] Walter's ambitions of a military career no longer required attention; Chief Commissioner Adam had been exerting his efforts, and the Duke of York had promised an early commission.[115]

Scott consequently settled down to concluding *A Legend of Montrose* and getting started on *Ivanhoe*. He was still far from well. On the day he learned of the Duke's death, "under the necessity of devouring feelings which I could not express," he had not only been sick at heart, his stomach had knotted in turmoil; that night he had a return of his spasms and "felt as if a phantasmagoria was going on around me."[116] In Edinburgh, he found himself unable to attend his duties at the Clerks' Table for several weeks. Under these circumstances he completed and sent in the last pages of *A Legend of Montrose*.[117]

Weak and worn, he longed for the green peace of the approaching summer at Abbotsford. There, even when wracked with spasms, he could work at *Ivanhoe* in his study, breathing the sweet country air, seeing the light glinting on the rippling waters outside his windows, and having occasional rambles on horseback over the rolling hills. "Would we were met on Tweedside," he wrote Adam Ferguson, "I am as tired of looking at these dead walls as ever schoolboy was weary of his dog-ear'd Cordery."[118]

On May 23 he believed that he had surmounted his sufferings and was getting well, even stout again.[119] But within three days he was ill once more, and even worse than before, with extreme sickness and weakness.[120] "I think the pain of finding myself obliged to give way to my malady," he said, "is worse almost than the evil itself. 'There is not only dishonour in it, bully monster, but an infinite loss.' "[121] And if these crises returned often, "with the same violence," he feared, "I shall break up by degrees and follow my dear Chief."[122]

For eight days he lay hardly able to stir from his bed.[123] When *The Bride of Lammermoor* and *A Legend of Montrose* were published on June 10 almost all Edinburgh believed that he was dying and that these four volumes were the last that would ever come from the hand of the Great Unknown.[124] The preposterous and self-important old Earl of Buchan came to Castle Street to pay a farewell call. He found the knocker muffled but tottered his way into the basement and elbowed upstairs past Peter Matheson, who tried to tell him he had strict orders to admit no visitors. His fingers were on the handle of Scott's bedroom door when Sophia came out. She tried to dissuade him; he patted her head as if she were a child. She was obliged to bid Peter to show him out. Peter found that his persuasions were in vain, and at last he gave the meddlesome intruder a shove. Only upon this strong hint did the Earl make an indignant retreat.[125]

Scott heard the noise in his room, where James Ballantyne had been keeping melancholy vigil at his bedside. Fearing that Peter might have injured the feeble old body, Scott asked James to go and explain that the family were so alarmed that the ordinary rules of civility did not apply. James found the Earl strutting about his library in towering ire. He had desired, he said, to embrace Walter Scott before he died and to tell him how pleased he felt that they would both be interred in Dryburgh Abbey. The main thing, though, was to relieve Scott's mind about the funeral, and the Earl himself had drawn up a complete plan of the ceremony, of which he himself would take charge and pronounce a eulogy over the grave. Despite his illness, Scott laughed over this till the tears streamed from his eyes.[126]

Through all the first half of June Scott remained very ill.[127] His cousin William Scott offered to leave his family and go with him to Harrowgate for the waters. Scott was grateful but refused; he was no great believer in the virtues of those waters, he said, and if he grew strong enough to move at all he had rather be at Abbotsford surrounded by his family.[128] Meanwhile he seemed to be sinking lower and lower. "The timbers of the raft were hard strained," he thought, "and liable to part company after a little more tossing."[129] One night he believed that he was dying and called his children around his bed to say a last farewell.

"For myself, my dears," Lockhart reports his saying, "I am unconscious of ever having done any man an injury, or omitted any fair opportunity of doing any man a benefit. I well know that no human life can appear otherwise than weak and filthy in the eyes of God: but I rely on the merits and intercession of our Redeemer." After a pause, he laid his hand on their heads: "God bless you! Live so that you may all hope to meet each other in a better place hereafter. And now leave me, that I may turn my face to the wall."[130]

Shortly after, he sank into a deep sleep from which they feared that he would never wake. Was the rider on the pale horse ravening for him too? "Every new shake," he had written his old friend Sharpe, "tells me the tree will fall early—Amen! I have the applause and friendship of the best, the worthiest, and the most distinguished of my contemporaries; and that gain'd—we must die when our day comes."[131]

# 8

## Mutations of Fanaticism

(Criticism: *The Heart of Mid-Lothian, The Bride of Lammermoor, A Legend of Montrose*)

Rᴇᴀᴅᴇʀs who had felt *Old Mortality* unfair to the puritanical conscience could not make that complaint of *The Heart of Mid-Lothian*. Ephraim Macbriar shows the extremes to which faith may be driven by fanaticism and persecution; Jeanie Deans reveals the heights to which it can rise with love. Macbriar defies man-made law to assert the supremacy of what he is certain is God's law; Jeanie will violate neither the law of man nor the law of God, but within obedience to both appeals to the mercy of a higher justice. If Macbriar's is the heroic fervor that will die, hers is the noble devotion that will save.

But it should be noted that Jeanie belongs with Macbriar among those who will not compromise; she is not, like Henry Morton, a mediatorial figure pleading for moderation between clashing extremes. Jeanie's character has been formed by the rigor of her stern Cameronian father, David Deans, who in the past has stood beside the most unyielding Covenanters. He carries their zeal to its utmost limit. But he follows no religious leader; he is a solitary Deanite; his conscience bows only to God. Jeanie is the child of his unbending rectitude. Determined though she is to save the life of the sister she loves, she will do so by no unlawful means; she will not tell the lie she believes forbidden by God.

The illegitimate child born in secret to her sister Effie has disappeared and cannot now be found. In order to suppress the crime of child murder, the law decrees that unless an unwed mother has told someone she was pregnant the disappearance of the child is to be taken as proof that she has killed it. But Effie had denied her condition; her lover, a wild young man named George Robertson, himself sentenced to death for an act of robbery, dares not come forward; the old hag who helped deliver the child has also disappeared. If only Jeanie will declare that her sister gave the least hint of her pregnancy, Effie will be freed.

Jeanie's problem, as so often in the world of Scott's novels, is sharpened by the surrounding historical circumstances. At the hanging of one of Robertson's confederates, the Captain of the City Guard, John Porteous, has caused the deaths of six or seven innocent people by commanding his men to fire on the crowd. Though disorderly, it had constituted no danger to public safety; his action had gone far beyond need. Porteous has consequently been convicted of murder and sentenced to death. But subsequently he has been reprieved by the Government in London; there is every reason to believe that he will presently be pardoned.[1]

The exposition that puts us in possession of these facts is low-keyed and rather deliberate, but it clearly sets the background for one of the thematic contrasts of the book—the mercy shown to a convicted murderer as opposed to the extreme penalty threatened for a crime only assumed and without supporting evidence. The wife of one of the citizens, Mrs. Saddletree, voices the popular judgment: "If the law makes murders, the law should be hanged for them; or if they wad hang a lawyer instead, the country wad find nae faut."[2]

Sternly indignant, a mob gathers. The growth of this mass movement, swelling in the night, is masterly in its tension and rising power. The mob burns down the door of the Tolbooth, the town jail, seizes Porteous, and hangs him from the gibbet in the Grassmarket. But it is quite unlike the drunken, screaming, frenzied rabble who in *Barnaby Rudge* storm Newgate, smash shops, desecrate churches, and put dwellings to the flame. The members of this mob are orderly.[3] They refrain from all other outrage, even leave a guinea in a cordage shop to pay for the rope with which they hang their victim, and commandeer a clergyman (who chances to be Jeanie's fiancé Reuben Butler) to attend Porteous's last moments. In its very lawlessness the mob behaves with sober deliberation, convinced that it is enforcing a legal sentence that the administrators of the law cynically ignore.

Effie's lover is one of the mob leaders. In the tumult and darkness of the jail, "Flee, Effie, flee!" he whispers to her. But half-stupefied, she only looks on him in "mingled fear, affection, and upbraiding," and sinks back apathetically.[4] She might, she observes later, "have fled frae this tolbooth on that awfu' night wi' ane wad hae carried me through the warld, and friended me, and fended for me. But I said to them, let life gang when gude fame is gane before it."[5] As death draws near, though, she trembles and begs her sister to save her. Must Jeanie do by deception what Robertson had failed to accomplish by force? Is justice to be won by defying both truth and law? Jeanie's problem is a variant of that to which the mob has given its answer. But, whatever she is to do, Effie's life now lies in her hands.

She is beset on every side. Forcing her to meet him alone by night at Muschat's Cairn, Robertson swears that Effie is innocent and tries to bully Jeanie into promising that she will tell the needed lie. Almost all Edinburgh, neither knowing nor caring whether her testimony will be true or false, hopes that it will save her sister. Bartoline Saddletree and his wife, in whose shop Effie worked as a helper, are sympathetic both to her lapse and the crime of which she is accused. "If she's been guilty," says Mrs. Saddletree, "she's been sair tempted, and I wad amaist take my Bible-aith she hasna been hersell at the time."[6] The very officers of the law—the Procurator-Fiscal, the King's Advocate, and the Judges—are not inhumane, and are willing to let Jeanie's word go unchallenged.

In her prison cell Effie sobs that she has not murdered her baby and begs Jeanie to save her. "If it be a wrang word, ye'll hae time eneugh to repent o't." She bitterly reproaches Jeanie's scruples as cold self-righteousness: ". . . it's whiles the faut of very good folk like you." "I dinna deserve this frae ye, Effie," Jeanie sobs. The jailer, Ratcliffe, himself a reformed criminal, cannot bear it, and breaks in: "It's d – – d hard, when three words of your mouth would give the girl the chance." Effie has grown so deadly pale that Jeanie almost weakens. "O, Effie, look but up, and say what ye wad hae me do, and I could find in my heart amaist to say that I wad do't."[7]

Jeanie's ordeal is rendered still more unbearable by the agony of her father. Poor David Deans does not know that Effie had not confided in her sister; he imagines that Jeanie's problem is whether she may even testify in a court whose spiritual authority he does not recognize. "Jeanie, if ye can, wi' God and gude conscience, speak in favour of this poor unhappy," he falters "—but if ye arena free . . . let God's will be done." His broken words are so ambiguous that Jeanie misconstrues them. "Can this be?" she asks herself. "A sister's life, and a father pointing out how to save it!—O God deliver me!—this is a fearfu' temptation."[8] She makes her painful decision despite the belief that even her father has tacitly given her his permission to lie.

It is not true, as V. F. Pritchett contends, that Jeanie is even unconsciously motivated by the jealousy of a plain elder sister for a younger and prettier sister. "Scott ignores the evident jealousy," writes Pritchett;[9] but there is no jealousy to be ignored. Whatever truth there may be in D. H. Lawrence's declaration that the artist is always a liar and that we should trust not him but his book, in this case the book itself denies Pritchett's assertion. Jeanie is seen to her inmost heart, and neither in her behavior nor in any emotions of which she is herself unaware is there a trace of such feeling.

In reality, the root of her conduct is not jealousy, not self-righteous moral superiority, but a humble obedience to what she conceives to be God's command. Though she is her father's daughter, she is not concerned, as he partly is, with the shame Effie has inflicted on her in the world's eyes; she does not reject the fallen sinner. Even as she arrives at her awful resolution her love is unswerving, and she already knows deep within her that she must save Effie by some other means, though she does not yet know what those means are to be. Her moral environment and her moral character are the forces that determine her conduct; and Scott's understanding of those forces goes deeper than a criticism that invokes a facile Freudianism and fails to give due weight to the pressures of her creed upon her nature.

Another error in reading the novel is to see the crime for which Effie is being punished as sexual indulgence. It is not; the taint in Effie is a far deeper one of which her seduction is only a consequence.[10] David Deans, who in his first anguish denounces her as a "vile harlot . . . foul with her sins," stresses far more the crime of which she is actually accused, calling her "a bloody Zipporah—a mere murderess," and grieves most at the evil example and disgrace of her supposed destruction of her child and "the stumbling-block and scandal it will be to all tender and honest souls."[11] The Saddletrees barely mention her lapse from chastity, and only with pity; no one else in the book says a word to condemn her sexual transgression. If Robertson were able to emerge from hiding and marry her, though her father might bitterly remember, the rest of her world would readily forgive and forget.

Effie's essential weakness is not sexual passion; it is a rooted strain of self-will and deceit that David Deans himself has unwittingly fostered. Jeanie had been brought up in the full severity of his principles; Effie is the indulged child of his old age. Her vivacity, charm, and beauty have insensibly relaxed his rigor; though she still fears him, her conceit and willful obstinacy are enhanced by the ease with which she can evade his condemnation. The only result of the puritanic rigor of her home is to make her rebel behind her father's back. It turns her into a liar and hypocrite secretly yielding to the gaieties her father's creed opposes.[12]

Concealing the fact that she has been meeting Robertson at dances on the green, she petulantly resists Jeanie's endeavors to win her confidence and to guide her. She has moments of self-reproach, but they do not last. "If there were as many dances the morn's night," she tells Jeanie, "as there are merry dancers in the north firmament on a frosty e'en, I winna budge an inch to gang near ane o' them";[13] and to herself she says, "But I'll no gang back there again. I'm resolved I'll no gang back. I'll lay a leaf in my Bible, and that's very near as I had made an aith, that I winna gang back."[14]

She is unable, though, to adhere to her vow for more than a week, during which she is unusually cross and fretful; and later she willingly seizes the chance to work for the Saddletrees in Edinburgh, where she will escape her father's sermons and no longer be under her sister's eye. But Effie is no dark Iseult, no fated victim of passion; her lawless love is only one strand in her self-indulgence, disregard of duty, and deceit. Her course of evasive falsehood is set against the behavior of her sister Jeanie, the heroine of truth.[15]

As Jeanie is called to the bar to give her evidence, Effie, her fair hair streaming back and her eyes gleaming with tears, exclaims, "O Jeanie, Jeanie, save me, save me!"[16] What Jeanie will do has been foreshadowed in the narrative by three chapter captions from *Measure for Measure*, but, as Francis Hart notes, it is not of Isabella that she should remind us but of Cordelia.[17] The issue is not one of chastity and carnality but of truth and falsehood. When Jeanie is asked what Effie told her, she can only reply, like Cordelia, "Nothing," and, when pressed, "Alack! alack! she never breathed word to me."[18]

In a stage version of the novel that Bernard Shaw once witnessed, the trial was followed by a scene in the prison. "If it had been me," exclaimed Ratcliffe, the jailer, "I wad ha sworn a hole through an iron pot," and the pit and gallery roared with applause.[19] No doubt he would have, and so, possibly, would we; but Ratcliffe had passed his life in the stews of Edinburgh and among the smugglers and thieves of Cumberland and Fife, and few modern readers have endured the rigors of Jeanie's spiritual shaping. Not to understand her reply is to be lacking in moral imagination.

For Jeanie has been sustained by the faith "that while she walked worthy of the protection of Heaven, she would experience its protection." She has felt an intuition, almost a revelation, that the means to save her sister would reveal themselves to her. "It came, as she described it, on her mind, like a sun-blink on a stormy sea; and although it instantly vanished, yet she felt a degree of composure which she had not experienced for many days . . ."[20] Significantly, in this novel whose themes are so tightly interknit, the means are revealed by a reference to the reprieve of Porteous.

"But *can* the king gie her mercy?" Jeanie has asked. "Some folk tell me he canna gie mercy in cases of mur—in cases like hers." "*Can* he gie mercy?" replies Mrs. Saddletree, "I weel I wot he *can*, when he likes. . . . there was Jock Porteous the other day."[21] Instantly Jeanie sees what she must do. She will go to London, and beg Effie's life from the King and Queen. "It's but speaking to a mortal man and woman when a' is done. And their hearts maun be made o' flesh and blood like other folk's, and Effie's story wad melt them were they stane."[22]

And she must go in person. "We *must* try all means; but writing winna do it—a letter canna look, and pray, and beg, and beseech, as the human voice can do to the human heart. . . . It's word of mouth maun do it, or naething . . ."[23]

She has shown her ability to melt hearts in the scenes with the jailer Ratcliffe. The hard and wicked old "heart of Mid-Lothian," as the prison is symbolically called, abode of misery and cruelty, is revealed in the heart of its hardened custodian to be susceptible to the call of human sympathy. "It gangs against my conscience," he has said when he refused to win Effie's confidence to betray her: "She greets, the silly tawpie, and she's breaking her heart already."24 Now it is Ratcliffe who suggests that Jeanie win her way to the Queen through the Duke of Argyle, and who, as "Daddy Ratton," provides her with a scribbled bit of paper that will protect her from thieves and footpads on her dangerous way to London.25

We are not surprised, therefore, when Jeanie wins over both the Duke and the Queen. "Alas! it is not when we sleep soft and wake merrily ourselves," she says to the Queen, "that we think on other people's sufferings. Our hearts are waxed light within us then, and we are for righting our ain wrangs, and fighting our ain battles. But when the hour of trouble comes to the mind or to the body—and seldom may it visit your Leddyship—and when the hour of death comes, that comes to high and low—lang and late may it be yours—O, my Leddy, then it isna what we hae dune for oursells, but what we hae dune for others, that we think on maist pleasantly. And the thoughts that ye have intervened to spare the puir thing's life will be sweeter in that hour, come when it may, than if a word of your mouth could hang the haill Porteous mob at the tail of ae tow."26

"This is eloquence," says the Queen,27 and it is—the eloquence of the heart. Jeanie's loving and noble heart has triumphed over all obstacles. The heart that seemed as closed and hard to her sister's appeal as the closed hard heart of the jail, has opened the heart of the jail and even the hearts of the great. They have indeed justified her faith that they were flesh and blood like other folk's, and the very stones of the prison have melted.

The last quarter of *The Heart of Mid-Lothian* has been blamed, and with justice, for falling away from the height Scott had so long sustained.28 But not for the reason often suggested: the story is *not* really ended with Effie's pardon. Both structurally and thematically the ending Scott wrote is necessary; neither Jeanie's meaning nor Effie's would be complete without it.29 In a novel of which the deepest concerns are truth and justice, law and mercy, it is not enough to end on a touching and joyful tableau.

The trouble with the long conclusion is not that it is superfluous or anticlimactic, but rather that Scott's artistic imagination has slackened. Jeanie's later life is handled in too much and too low-pressured detail; Effie's, conversely, in summary so condensed as to seem thinly melodramatic. What Scott's judgment rightly saw to be needed, his artistry faltered and failed to create.

After Effie's pardon she elopes with Robertson. The novel had long hinted that he was not what he seemed, painting him as half-Byronic rebel, half-melodramatic Prince Hal sowing angry wild oats among thieves. But he is not one of Scott's successes; his characterization is thin and stagy, and he talks the turgidly Luciferean rhetoric of a Gothic novel. Now he is revealed to be the rebellious son of a Church of England clergyman and the heir to a baronetcy. Effie's manners are polished during some years in a convent school abroad; her husband returns to England, sobered and repentant, to take his place in society as Sir George Staunton, and she becomes a ruling belle as the fascinating Lady Staunton. She slides into fashionable life as easily as Becky Sharpe or Lady Dedlock into Regency London or the daughter of a modern coal-miner into café society. Her wit dazzles the aristocracy: ". . . raillery in the higher ranks," Scott remarks, exactly "resembles flippancy among their inferiors."[30]

For of course Effie's character is not really changed. She is still an egotist, still disregardful of the feelings of others, still primarily intent on pleasure, still gilding her selfishness with vivacity and charm, still acting a role, as in the days when she had deceived her father and her sister. But now she sees herself for what she is, and her self-knowledge leaves her neither proud nor happy in her social triumphs. When Jeanie wonders at her skill in playing her part, the novel strikes the keynote again: "I daresay you are surprised at it," she responds, "for you, my dear Jeanie, have been truth itself from your cradle upwards; but you must remember that I am a liar of fifteen years' standing, and therefore must by this time be used to my character."[31]

Jeanie's life is passed in humbler paths. David Deans greets her with joyful tears: "Jeanie—my ain Jeanie—my best—my most dutiful bairn —the Lord of Israel be thy father, for I am hardly worthy of thee!"[32] She marries her Reuben Butler, who through the influence of the Duke of Argyle is given a living in the west of Scotland. Effie's grandeur does momentarily strike from Jeanie a spark of that jealousy she has not felt when they were both young, but it is her social rank, not her sexual charm, that Jeanie momentarily envies. And Scott has her confront it honestly: "Surely I am no sic a fule as to be angry that Effie's a braw lady while I am only a minister's wife?—and yet I am as petted [piqued] as a bairn, when I should bless God, that has redeemed her from shame, and poverty, and guilt, as ower likely she might hae been plunged into."[33]

But to overcome her temporary spleen against her sister Jeanie has only to tear the veil from its motives. Sitting on a stool at the foot of her bed, she says to herself, "From this place will I not rise till I am in a better frame of mind."[34] The brief remainder of Jeanie's story, as Lukács points out, is both psychologically and historically sound. Having risen to her heroic moment, she "returns to everyday life" and never again experiences "a similar upsurge in her life."[35] Existence is not an unending heroic drama; with the passing of her struggle between love and truth and its solution Jeanie's supreme ordeal is over.

The decision that the novel forces upon her is one far harder and more terrible than those that had faced any of the preceding Waverley heroes—harder than Edward Waverley's choice between Jacobitism and Hanoverianism, than Colonel Mannering's against class prejudice, than any in *The Antiquary*, than young Earncliff's against blood vengeance, than Henry Morton's between the Covenanters and the Government, than Frank Osbaldistone's between romance and business. For she comes to her choice already committed to a degree none of them share, caught between the claims of law and Law, of truth and Truth. The resolution of her dilemma cannot be achieved either by compromise or by accepting a single alternative, but only by transcendence.

It makes *The Heart of Mid-Lothian* one of the most deeply exploratory of novels. It is profoundly searching in its probing of the problems of justice and compassion as they weigh on human beings conditioned by the historical forces that have shaped them. The grim old prison, long since destroyed, that gives the book both its title and its symbolic meaning, enables us, as the opening chapter truly claims, to penetrate "new pages of the human heart."[36] Even among Scott's other triumphs the novel is unsurpassed. "Wert thou to live a thousand years," exclaimed William Hazlitt, "and write a thousand romances, thou wouldst never, old True-penny, beat thy own *Heart of Mid-Lothian!*"[37]

In *The Bride of Lammermoor* Scott returns to the theme he had marred in *The Black Dwarf*, but this time with magnificent success. The providential father-figure Elshender is eliminated, and only the hesitant wire-pulling father remains. Richard Vere becomes the timorous and tricky lawyer-politician Sir William Ashton, dominated by his overbearing wife, Lady Ashton, whose relentless will knows no hesitations. Earnscliff becomes the proud but ill-fated Master of Ravenswood, and Isabel becomes the unhappy Lucy Ashton, too weak to resist the pressures loaded upon her.

Edgar of Ravenswood is a hero of rationalism. Though the heir to a feudal tradition and to a bitter family hatred for the Ashtons, he struggles desperately against this heritage.[38] He desires to listen to reason and to believe conciliation possible. He can control his passions; though the hot-tempered Bucklaw forces him into a duel he coolly disarms his opponent and spares his life. He reproaches Blind Alice when he thinks she is urging him to blood vengeance. He disbelieves in supernatural portents and tries to devise natural explanations even for what seems to him Alice's wraith at the Mermaiden's Fountain. Despite his family's old loyalties he has no intention of being drawn into dark intrigues to restore the Stuarts. Remembering their behavior when they were on the throne, "I see little reason," he says, "that, as a man or a patriot, I should draw my sword for their descendants."[39] All his strivings to be a man of reason nevertheless lead implacably to catastrophe. The novel is at once a tragedy of character and a tragedy of fate.

Thereby it demonstrates Scott's complex awareness that in the tangled strands of human antagonisms enmeshed in the web of history not even the most enlightened and humane courses are necessarily destined to win the day and that compromise is no certain formula for success. Jeanie Deans refused to compromise, and triumphed through the force of love. Scott's earlier heroes strove to mediate between clashing fanaticisms, and survived by virtue of their generous humanity. But the circumstances in *The Bride of Lammermoor* are such that the Master of Ravenswood and Lucy Ashton are destroyed by the very endeavor to make reason and love prevail over raging unreason.

The Ravenswoods have been ruined through a series of lawsuits pursued with rapacious trickery by Sir William Ashton. In the crumbling tower of Wolf's Crag, their last possession, perched high above the North Sea, Edgar's father dies, a broken man, cursing his foe. Edgar has thus inherited a far more embittered feud than that of young Earnscliff, in *The Black Dwarf*. (The resemblance of their names even suggests the parallel—Earnscliff—Eagle's Cliff; Raven's-wood.)[40] Unlike Earnscliff, however, Edgar, over his father's dead body, at first embraces the heritage. "Heaven do as much to me and more," he swears, "if I requite not to this man and his house the ruin and disgrace he has brought on me and mine!"[41]

His enemy, Sir William Ashton, during the earlier years of Queen Anne's reign, has risen in the Whig administration to the office of Lord Keeper. Subtle, scheming, and acquisitive, though with no personal animosity to his victim, and cautious to timidity, Sir William well knows that if the Tories come to power some of his machinations may be uncovered. And he knows too that one of their most astute leaders, the Marquis of A———, is Ravenswood's kinsman. He therefore hesitates whether to arouse Ravenswood to desperation by some final crushing blow or to soothe him with diplomatic concessions.

The political background is rendered with firm impartiality.[42] The contending Whigs and Tories are shown as predominantly motivated by greed for spoils and power. The administration of justice is honeycombed with influence and bribery. Sir William is "a skilful fisher" in these "troubled waters of a state divided by factions."[43] The Privy Council are time-serving and venal; one of them, Lord Turntippet, as he himself says, has "complied wi' a' compliances, tane all manner of tests, abjured all that was to be abjured, and sworn a' that was to be sworn, for these thirty years bypast."[44]

But the Tories are no better. The Marquis of A——— is skillfully engineering a cabal to oust the Lord Keeper's friends and is willing, if

Sir William proves important enough, to bribe or frighten him into abandoning them. Though the Marquis has no intention of endangering his neck for the Stuarts, he keeps up a correspondence with Saint Germains and smilingly allows the Pretender's followers to believe him their friend. He professes himself Ravenswood's well-wisher, striving to retain him on a string by ambiguous encouragements but offering no tangible aid. "In my opinion," Bucklaw shrewdly tells Ravenswood, "he has some scheme in view in which he supposes you can be useful, and he wishes to keep you at hand, to make use of you when it ripens, reserving the power of turning you adrift, should his plot fail in the concoction."[45]

These are the treacherous waters that Sir William Ashton is timorously navigating. His irresolution is sharpened by his fear of his wife, a scion of the great house of Douglas, who looks down on his inferior birth, despises his faintheartedness, and hates Ravenswood for his poverty, for having a name more ancient than her husband's, and for being the heir to the estates they have engorged. But while she is in Edinburgh, and later in London, trying to advance her husband's fortunes by state intrigue, he breathes a little more freely.

His course is determined by meeting Ravenswood. Edgar had decided to seek him out and demand an accounting; in a grove of trees near Ravenswood Castle he finds the Lord Keeper and his daughter Lucy threatened by an enraged black bull. Not knowing their identity, seeing only two helpless fellow beings, he kills the charging animal with one shot of his gun. Lucy Ashton swoons; her father leaves the stranger with her while he goes to call the assistance of servants. Reviving, she strives to express her gratitude for the rescue. Edgar, who now realizes who they are, endeavors to escape. "I leave you," he says in troubled accents, "to the protection of those to whom it is possible you may have this day been a guardian angel."[46] When her father asks his identity, "Request nothing of ME, my lord," Edgar replies sternly; "I am the Master of Ravenswood."[47]

But Sir William, who is not unperceptive, can see that even in this brief encounter his daughter and the Master have made an impression on each other. He begins to entertain the thought of ensuring his own safety in the event of a political overturn by bringing about a marriage between the two and giving Lucy in dowry some of the property he had wrested from Ravenswood's father. It would not be an unfitting match; Sir William's own wealth is ample to provide for them, and Ravenswood's birth is superior to his own. And Ashton is really devoted to his daughter, whose gentle and affectionate nature he knows may easily be brought to love her rescuer. Both his tenderness for Lucy and his prudential concern for himself urge dissolving these old dissensions in marriage.

The wily politician's scheme thus both resembles and differs from Sir Richard Vere's endeavor to force a loveless match upon his daughter

Isabel. Lucy's malleability will need no forcing; her father is thinking of her welfare, not only of his own; and Edgar of Ravenswood is no such venal and repulsive figure as Sir Frederick Langley. Sir William does not forget his bold and overbearing wife, but he persuades himself to believe that she will fall in with his plan for uniting Lucy's happiness and his own security, and in his tragic cunning he overlooks the possibility that Lucy's pliancy may be more a danger than an aid.[48]

Her character is revealed in the very first scene in which she appears, when her father hears her singing to her lute. Her song, one of the subtlest and most haunting of Scott's lyrics, itself hints the nature of the singer:

> "Look not thou on beauty's charming,—
> Sit thou still when kings are arming,—
> Taste not when the wine-cup glistens,—
> Speak not when the people listens,—
> Stop thine ear against the singer,—
> From the red gold keep thy finger,—
> Vacant heart, and hand, and eye,—
> Easy live and quiet die."[49]

All of her shrinking from the dangerous ardors of life vibrates in these tremulous negations, mingled still with the faint realization implied in the one word "vacant" that such a yearning for withdrawal is almost the desire to renounce life itself. Her timid passivity would rather gaze than venture; she is ill fitted to contend against others; emotional strain may break her.

Her father blinds himself to the peril of involving her in a struggle with her iron-willed mother. Instead, therefore, of pressing before the Privy Council dangerous charges against Ravenswood that he could have made, he softens them. He opens negotiations with Ravenswood's Tory kinsman that may enable him to remain in office even if the Whigs fall. He takes Lucy on a fox hunt near Wolf's Crag, manages to run into Ravenswood as if by chance, and extorts from his courtesy a reluctant invitation to take shelter from a storm.

Ashton's arrival at Wolf's Crag painfully displays the Master's poverty. Old Caleb Balderstone, his one remaining faithful servant, in vain tries to cajole or exact from the neighboring villagers of Wolf's-hope the butter, eggs, fowls, and ale that would once have been feudal dues. For all the former consequence of the Ravenswoods, they had induced little devotion in their dependents, and with their wealth and power that little is now gone. The seigniorial past has been as far from ideal as the Lord Keeper's eighteenth-century world of legal chicane. Denied on all hands, Caleb is ludicrously reduced to stealing a brace of wild ducks from the cooper's fireplace.

Caleb himself is a symbol, at once comic and tragic, of his master's difficulties.[50] He embarrasses Ravenswood before their guests by dis-simulations to which the Master's pride will not stoop, talking of tapes-tries now rotted away as if they still existed, of silver vessels long sold, of table linens, of wine and ale in the empty barrels of the cellar. To conceal the barrenness of his larder he pretends that a lightning bolt down the chimney had destroyed the roast; to explain the absence of fine china, in a simulated accident, he smashes even the chipped crockery in the kitchen.

His appeals to the "gude auld times"[51] and the duties of vassals have become tricks to cheat, rob, and despoil the villagers; he supports what he regards as the "honor" of the house by duplicity and fraud. Ravens-wood's merits extort our sympathy for his retainer, but Caleb's mono-maniacal and unscrupulous fidelity makes him a nuisance to his master, sometimes a bore to the reader, and a criticism of the tradition he ex-emplifies. He is both a ludicrous and a pathetic emblem of the decayed fortunes of the Ravenswoods. But still more, as Hart notes, he also parodies the other destructive forces in the story—the deceits of the Lord Keeper, the fierce pride of Lady Ashton, the cynical opportunism of the Marquis. As "comic relief" Caleb embodies absurdly but sympa-thetically all the problems of the situation and the essence of the tragedy.

If Caleb's trickeries among the villagers reflect little honor on the feudal virtues he invokes, their tightfisted resistance is no less un-scrupulous.[52] The needs of the Ravenswoods had forced them to sell off some of their lordly rights, but even those that remain their former de-pendents deny. When Caleb reminds them that the lord of the manor is entitled to the first stone of butter after every calving, the first egg each hen lays on a Monday, they scratch their heads: "They could not say." For traditional dues that had never been recorded in writing they demand evidence—" 'twas not in the bond." "Their hens had caickled mony a day for the Lords of Ravenswood, and it was time they suld caickle for those that gave them roosts and barley."[53] Against ancient custom they oppose a slippery legalism that parallels Sir William's manipulations.

Ashton courteously praises the entertainment Caleb has managed to set before them, and sets about wooing a relaxation of Edgar's bitter-ness. He reminds Ravenswood of what is indeed the fact, that he had often sought a meeting with his father, and represents these endeavors as prompted by a hope to end their legal contentions through a peaceful settlement. He professes his desire to do so now on principles dictated by justice rather than by strict law. He invites his host to ride back with him and be his guest at Ravenswood Castle, where he may go over all the legal records and be satisfied. And, watching keenly, he can observe that Edgar and Lucy are being drawn into a mutual attraction.

Not, however, on Ravenswood's part willingly or without resistance. His hospitality has been forced from him, but his breeding obliges him to entertain them as honored guests. The following morning the Lord Keeper places in his hands papers that prove his protection of the Master before the Privy Council. Ravenswood is first shaken and then won over by the evidence. He presses Ashton's hand and begs his pardon for the injustice he had done him. Tears flow from Lucy's blue eyes. "Why should you weep," Sir William asks unctuously, "because your father, though a lawyer, is discovered to be a fair and honourable man?" Then, addressing Ravenswood, "What have you to thank me for, my dear Master, that you would not have done in my case?" "My generous friend!" exclaims Edgar, and with that word "he gave his feudal enemy the full confidence of an haughty but honourable heart."[54]

Sir William himself is touched by the unreserved self-abandonment with which the Master renounces his former enmity. "His eyes glistened as he looked upon a couple who were obviously becoming attached, and who seemed made for each other. He thought how high the proud and chivalrous character of Ravenswood might rise . . . Then his daughter—his favourite child—his constant playmate—seemed formed to live happy in a union with such a commanding spirit as Ravenswood"; and her delicacy "to require the support of the Master's muscular strength and masculine character."[55]

The growing love between the two is rendered with sensitivity and power. Lucy's gentleness and beauty had made their impression on Ravenswood even at the time he had rescued her and her father from the charging bull, but between the two meetings they have grown in Edgar's memory. During the visit to Ravenswood he recoils indignantly from Blind Alice's suspicion that he is there to revenge himself on Sir William's daughter by dishonorable means. "Be silent, woman!" he exclaims. "Know that this young lady has not on earth a friend who would venture farther to save her from injury or from insult." "And is it even so?" the old woman rejoins—"Then God help you both!"[56]

Alice attempts to warn Ravenswood against the connection she forebodes. The chasm between them—of background, of point of view, of feeling—is too deep to be filled in either by reason or by love for Ashton's daughter. "When did a Ravenswood," she demands, "seek the house of his enemy, but with the purpose of revenge?—and hither are you come, Edgar of Ravenswood, either in fatal anger, or in still more fatal love." "Can you say as Sir William Ashton says—think as he thinks —vote as he votes, and call your father's murderer your worshipful father-in-law and revered patron? Master of Ravenswood, I am the eldest servant of your house, and I would rather see you shrouded and coffined!"[57]

Ravenswood's rationalism rejects her suspicions. Can she believe he would levy war against the Ashtons in the bloody ways of old, or suppose him so foolish that he cannot walk by a young lady's side without plunging headlong in love with her? But Alice is firm. "Lucy Ashton loves you, Lord of Ravenswood!" "It is impossible," says the Master. "A thousand circumstances have proved it to me," she replies. He must flee Lucy's presence; if he does, her love will die like a lamp with nothing on which to feed. "Depart, Master of Ravenswood. . . . If you remain an hour under Sir William Ashton's roof without the resolution to marry his daughter, you are a villain—if with the purpose of allying yourself with him, you are an infatuated and predestined fool."[58]

The Master realizes the truth of her arguments. He leaves her, determined to say farewell to Lucy and remain no longer in the Castle that formerly belonged to his own family. "I wish her well," he says to himself, "and for her sake I forgive the injuries her father has done to my house; but I will never—no, never see her more!"[59] Lucy is waiting, though, at the fatal Mermaiden's Fountain. Her tears and the knowledge that she loves him overcome his resolution. Before the end of their interview they have kissed and exchanged vows and shared the broken goldpiece so ominously emblematic of their troth. "Never shall this leave my bosom," Lucy promises, "until you, Edgar Ravenswood, ask me to resign it to you—and, while I wear it, never shall that heart acknowledge another love than yours."[60]

Neither she nor the Master is entirely able to banish misgivings. Lucy fears her mother's anger and feels a secret awe of Ravenswood's fierce pride. He realizes that her ductility renders her susceptible to molding by those with whom she lives and reluctantly knows that his temperament would be more fitly mated with "a more independent spirit, resolved as himself to dare indifferently the storm and the favouring breeze."[61] But her very softness endears her to him, and once they are in love the qualities in each that might if perceived earlier have made them pause only deepen their attachment.

Their love has nevertheless unfolded from the first in an atmosphere of foreboding that both Ravenswood's enlightened rationalism and Ashton's opportunism strive to ignore. Even as the Lord Keeper penned his memorandum defending Ravenswood to the Privy Council, a black bull's head like that of the bull that charged him and Lucy gazes down from the carved vaulting above him—the crest of the Ravenswoods, with the grim motto, "I bide my time."[62] Though Caleb thinks Lucy "a winsome sweet creature," when the Master prepares to visit Sir William the old man falters out an ancient prophecy of Thomas the Rhymer:

> "When the last Laird of Ravenswood to Ravenswood shall ride,
> And woo a dead maiden to be his bride,
> He shall stable his steed in the Kelpie's flow,
> And his name shall be lost forever moe!"[63]

As Ravenswood enters his ancestral halls Lucy's younger brother Henry is terrified by his resemblance to a portrait of Sir Malise Ravenswood, known as "the Avenger."[64] Blind Alice delivers the warnings that the

Master dismisses as hate-inspired superstition. The Mermaiden's Fountain is regarded as a place of evil omen to the Ravenswoods. As Edgar and Lucy leave its brink, an arrow from her brother's bow brings down a raven—traditionally sacred to the Ravenswoods—and her gown is stained with the bird's blood.

All this development is masterly in its emotional intensity and its logical inevitability, swift, vivid, bathed in reality and haunted by muted rumblings of disaster. The solid world of politics and the village greed of Wolf's-hope are shown in a clear daylight. The crudeness of the gambling and tippling Bucklaw, with his willingness to marry for money, highlights the exalted character of Ravenswood. Those who say that Scott cannot portray love should not only remember Diana Vernon and Frank Osbaldistone, but the Master of Ravenswood and Lucy, with their doubts and hesitancies swept away in the flood of passion. And in the background there are the mutterings of the old graveyard hags, like the witches in *Macbeth:* "He wad make a bonny corpse," says Annie Winnie, "—I wad like to hae the streaking and winding o' him." "It is written on his brow, Annie Winnie," responds Ailsie Gourlay, "that hand of woman, or of man either, will never straught him—dead-deal will never be laid on his back . . . I hae it frae a sure hand."[65]

The threatened dangers are not long delayed. Lady Ashton returns home; she has already formed her own plans for Lucy's marriage—to Bucklaw, who has inherited a fortune. She contemptuously overrides her weak husband. The triumph of the Tories,[66] Sir William's loss of the Lord Keepership, the legal efforts of the Marquis of A——— to regain Ravenswood's estates for him, all strengthen her animosity. Ravenswood has been sent abroad on a mission for the new government; Lady Ashton keeps Lucy virtually a prisoner and intercepts all their letters. Ravenswood's seeming silence she represents as a repudiation of his engagement. Lucy displays unexpected powers of passive resistance, but relentlessly pursued, she weakens and falls ill. The pressure is at last greater than she can bear; Ravenswood arrives too late to undo the tangled web of deception by which she has been betrayed.

The tragedy is implicit in the characters of all those involved—the temporizing father whose schemes have undesignedly destroyed his daughter's happiness; her fierce and formidable mother; the pride and even the enlightenment of the Master, who has endeavored to overcome prejudice and hatred; the gentle, weak, and affectionate heart of Lucy. Like Lady Macbeth, Lady Ashton has been willing to sacrifice the child of her womb to her pride and her passions, and at the wedding to Bucklaw the witches' chorus swells again: "Do ye see yon dandilly maiden," Ailsie Gourlay asks, "a' glittering wi' goud and jewels"? "But that's the bride!" exclaims her companion. "I tell ye," Ailsie returns, "her winding sheet is up as high as her throat already, believe it wha list."[67]

The end comes swiftly—the retirement of the bridal couple, the cry, shrill and piercing, that arrests the festal music, the bloody figure of the bridegroom on the chamber floor, the dagger all smeared, Lucy crouched in the chimney corner, "her night clothes torn and dabbled with blood,— her eyes glazed and her features convulsed," gibbering madly, "So, you have ta'en up your bonny bridegroom?"[68] She dies in convulsions a night later. Ravenswood, responding to a challenge from her elder brother Colonel Ashton, rides in blind haste over the quicksand of the Kelpie's Flow and is instantly sucked down. On the rising tide, fallen from his hat, floats only a sable plume, which old Caleb takes up and places in his bosom.

*The Bride of Lammermoor* is the most perfectly constructed of all Scott's novels.[69] Its few coincidences—the charging of the black bull, the return of Ravenswood on the eve of the marriage—are engulfed in and even reinforce the flood of its passionate fatality. The note of Caleb's maniacal devotion is, perhaps, hammered over-insistently, but it is not out of key. No element in the story, in fact, is superfluous, its atmosphere is superbly unified. Though Scott had written it in drugged near-somnambulism, and though he himself, on rereading, felt it to be monstrous and grotesque, the truth is that its brooding fatality is fused with the reality it envelopes; its Gothic warnings are dark mists swirling through a solid world. Released by Scott's illness, his imagination dredged up primitive tremors from primordial deeps.

These were the things in the novel, of course, that Scott's waking mind rejected. In the daylight world their dark portents went beyond what his reason was willing to believe. His own rationalism, like Ravenswood's, recoiled from taking seriously the nightmares at which the heart still shivers. But they are no more blemishes in the seventeenth-century world of *The Bride of Lammermoor* than are the blasted heath and the witches in the eleventh-century world of *Macbeth*. Scott had built his characters firmly in the realm of human reality, and as the story unfolds the swelling ground-tone of doom only enhances the emotional inevitability of their behavior. In the four main figures, and above all in Ravenswood and Lucy Ashton, the historical moment and inward character merge as fate.

The conventional judgment of *A Legend of Montrose* is that it is a relative failure and that its breakdown as a novel is even aggravated by its most brilliant character achievement, Rittmaster Dugald Dalgetty, whose vitality so takes over the story as to run away with the plot and run away from its theme. The immortal Rittmaster, critic after critic since Jeffrey has repeated, is an irrelevant though glorious intrusion grown "too big" for the book in which he appears.[70] This critical view is given some seeming support from one of Scott's own humorous remarks: when he lights on a character like Dalgetty, he says, his imagination brightens but leads him so many miles from his road that he has "to leap hedge and ditch to get back into the route again."[71]

It is a characteristic joke, but like Scott's depreciatory observation on the structure of *Waverley*, it has been misleading to those who would automatically discount a boast but are happy to swallow any self-dispraise. In fact, *Montrose* is far from a failure, and the great central section of the story, which Dalgetty dominates, is not essentially digressive. The other main stream of the narrative, too, abounds in dramatic movement, from the splendid scene when Allan M'Aulay displays the hall of Darnlinvarach Castle lit by blazing pine torches held aloft by gigantic Highlanders, to Allan's anguished and long-foreboded attempt, near the end, to murder his friend Menteith.

This murderous assault, suggested by the historical murder of the young Lord Kilpont by James Stewart of Ardvoirlich, was what had first fired Scott's imagination to his theme, what Henry James would have called his original *donnée*. But that theme itself is fundamentally a study and a criticism of the clan spirit and the nature of the clan chieftain and their impact on history. In *A Legend of Montrose* what had been one of the subordinate themes of *Waverley* thus moves into a central position. If the Young Chevalier failed in his attempt to restore James III to the throne because he could not reconcile the warring hostilities of his Highland followers into fidelity to a unified national purpose, Montrose fails, and for the same reasons, to preserve Scotland for Charles I.

Scott sets up his main cast of characters with just and representative symmetry. The Earl of Menteith, a moderate Cavalier, and Angus M'Aulay, a clan chief of towering pride, together with his fierce and violently unstable younger brother Allan, are all three devoted followers of Charles I. They are balanced by Sir Duncan Campbell of Ardenvohr, a moderate Presbyterian, and the wily and politic Marquis of Argyle, supreme feudal head of all the Campbells, and the most powerful leader of the Presbyterian cause.

Ranald MacEagh, whose savage tribe, the Children of the Mist, are feudal enemies of both the M'Aulays and the Campbells, has been driven with the remnants of his people into the remotest and most inaccessible glens; he represents the clan spirit inflamed by suffering to extremes of hatred and ferocity. In the past the Children of the Mist have stormed Ardenvohr and slain all Sir Duncan's male children; and in the M'Aulay's dining hall they have left the decapitated head of an uncle with a piece of bread between its lifeless jaws. Allan M'Aulay is now devoting himself ruthlessly to their annihilation. It is of such inflammable and hostile elements that the great royalist commander the Earl of Montrose is striving to forge a military force that can counter the might, wealth, and cunning of the Presbyterian leader Argyle.

To their clan spirit and clan loyalties Dugald Dalgetty stands out in sharp contrast. Formerly a divinity student at the Mareschal College in Aberdeen, he has become a mercenary soldier and has fought on the Continent under Gustavus Adolphus, under Wallenstein, for the Spanish, for the Dutch, for whoever would pay his wage. A military pedant, voluble and opinionated, his self-complacence has nevertheless a sound core of experience and knowledge. He is as indifferent to inducements of political principle as Falstaff is to the claims of honor, and when Lord Menteith tries to argue that he should not hesitate "to embrace the cause of King Charles, in preference to that of low-born, roundheaded, canting knaves, who are in rebellion against his authority,"[72] Dalgetty replies bluntly that "fine words butter no parsnips"[73] and that he feels free to take any part in the civil embroilment that suits his own advantage:

"Loyalty is your pass-word, my lord.—Liberty, roars another chield from the other side of the strath—the King, shouts one war-cry—the Parliament roars another—Montrose for ever, cries Donald, waving his bonnet—Argyle and Leven, cries a south-country Saunders, vapouring with his hat and feather. Fight for the bishops, says a priest, with his gown and rochet—Stand stout for the Kirk, cries a minister, in a Geneva cap and band.—Good watchwords all—excellent watchwords. Whilk cause is the best I cannot say. But sure am I, that I have fought knee-deep in blood many a day for one that was ten degrees worse than the worst of them all."[74]

Menteith's loyalist idealism is revolted by Dalgetty's political cynicism and sordid emphasis on soldiering as a business. Only with difficulty does he conceal his disgust and indignation. But Montrose judges differently. Though as an aristocrat and a devoted follower of the King he understands and even shares Menteith's feelings, his professional generalship recognizes Dalgetty's military value. "We cannot, unfortunately," he tell Menteith, "do our work without the assistance of those who act on baser motives than our own. We cannot spare the assistance of such fellows as our friend the soldado."[75] He wishes he had twenty more to supplement the enthusiastic but wild and undisciplined valor of his Highland followers.

And although Dalgetty is the antithesis of the fidelities and the fanatical devotions of clansmen and clan chieftains, he is not so purely anti-idealistic as he superficially appears. He demands military rank and a daily wage before enlisting under Montrose, but agrees to accept half at the conclusion of a successful campaign and is not unduly greedy in making his bargain. And once bought he remains bought; when in the dungeons of Inverary the Marquis of Argyle tries to bribe him into betraying Montrose's military secrets by offering him double pay, his response is to seize the tempter by the throat and choke him into submission.

Forcing his way to freedom with his fellow prisoner Ranald Mac-

Eagh, wounded by Argyle's pursuing troops, Dalgetty is saved, nursed back to health, and guided through the mountain passes by Ranald's few remaining followers. Though shocked by the ferocious hatreds of that wild tribesman, Dalgetty remains faithful to their bond of comradeship and endeavors when they are once more with Montrose's army to hide his identity and protect him from the vengeance of his clan enemies the M'Aulays. Dalgetty renders effective service at the triumphant victory over Argyle's forces; it is fitting that when his horse Gustavus is killed Montrose should give the doughty Major his own horse, which Dalgetty names "Loyalty's Reward,"[76] and that the General should bestow on him the honor of knighthood.

Dalgetty is not a normative character, but he is a corrective one. If his pedantry and his unimaginative materialism render him blind to ideal aims, his steadiness is far more dependable than the moody pride and erratic loyalty of the clan chieftains. Logically and chronologically Dalgetty's common sense anticipates the business practicality of Bailie Nicol Jarvie, but he lacks both the sympathetic understanding that makes Jarvie admire his cousin Rob Roy and the vein of poetry that responds to high deeds and noble feelings. Dalgetty's imbalance, however, is far less disastrous than that of the clan feeling that despises him.

Ranald MacEagh, in turn, anticipates Rob Roy, as Dalgetty does Nicol Jarvie. Rob Roy is what Ranald will become in a world where injustice is done by law, not by deeds of blood and violence. But Ranald, conversely, is also the anarchistic outcome of the clan spirit carried to its last extreme, defiant of law and of humanity, loyal only to itself. "Give us the huts ye have burned," he exclaims fiercely, "our children whom ye have murdered, our widows whom ye have starved; collect from the gibbet and the pole the mangled carcasses, and whitened skulls of our kinsmen; . . . till then, let death and blood and mutual wrong draw a dark veil of division between us."[77] When he is slain by Allan M'Aulay, his dying speech to his grandson echoes this glorification of absolute freedom: "Farewell, beloved! and mayst thou die like thy forefathers, ere infirmity, disease, or age shall break thy spirit. Begone! begone! live free, requite kindness, avenge the injuries of thy race!"[78]

Allan M'Aulay lives by the same code; and with only the smallest modifications it is also the code of his brother Angus and the other Highland chieftains. Its flaws and hidden dangers are symbolically foreshadowed in the great scene that greets Menteith and Montrose shortly after their arrival at Darnlinvarach. Angus M'Aulay has seen in the home of an English ally, Sir Miles Musgrave, some massive silver candelabra and been unable to resist the boast that he has more and better candlesticks in his own castle. Worse, he has supported the mad vaunt with a huge wager he has not the means to pay. To make good his honor his friends must lend him funds desperately needed by the royal cause. From this unhappy consequence of his crazed pride he is rescued by the fantastic artifice of his half-crazed brother Allan:

"Behold, gentlemen cavaliers," Allan exclaims, pointing to the Highlanders with their flaming torches, "the chandeliers of my brother's house, the ancient fashion of our ancient name; not one of these men knows any law but their Chief's command—Would you dare to compare to THEM in value the richest ore that ever was dug out of the mine?"[79] "It is very odd," Angus M'Aulay remarks later, "how Allan, who between ourselves is a little wowf [deranged], seems at times to have more sense than us all put together."[80] And it is equally significant that only a madman's strained trick of metaphor can undo the damage threatened by the insanity of family vainglory.

The same clan feelings limit the effectiveness of the army Montrose has managed to amass. He sees clearly that the tactics necessary for final victory require the defeat of the Presbyterian forces in the lowlands and the command of the capital and the eastern coastal cities. But he cannot make the clan mentality of his followers understand these facts. They persist in regarding the struggle as a feud against Argyle and their other clan foes; after each of Montrose's splendid victories they melt away into their glens with their spoils and can only by desperate struggle be reassembled again. And for all his towering military genius, even Montrose cannot help sharing some of their feelings, and is sometimes not altogether reluctant to see the struggle deflected into a clan feud against his great rival Argyle. These difficulties doom his cause, and the final catastrophe at Philiphaugh is inevitable.

Lukács well analyzes the situation: "Only a Scottish clan war can be fought with an army of clan members. Montrose's followers will go through fire and water for him; yet in their conviction that the real enemy is not Parliament, but the hostile group of clans led by Argyle, they will yield neither to persuasion nor authority, however unlimited Montrose's authority when he moves within the bounds of clan ideology. And one of the subtle and grand features in Scott's characterization is that he does not permit a merely external resolution of this opposition. Montrose is indeed an aristocrat, a convinced Royalist, an army commander of distinguished abilities, a man of great political ambition, yet at heart he is also a clan chieftain. The clansmen's way of thinking also affects him inwardly; necessity, outer and inner, makes him give up his great plans and squander his energies in a petty clan war against Argyle."[81]

In the novel the historical dénouement is prefigured when Angus and Allan M'Aulay prove the first of Montrose's clan followers to desert his banner. This too is a consequence of clan pride. Allan and Lord Menteith have both been in love with Annot Lyle, an orphan foundling brought up in the M'Aulay household, but neither feels able to marry a maiden of unknown origin. Annot secretly loves Menteith. When Ranald Mac-Eagh reveals that she is the daughter of Sir Duncan Campbell, stolen when the Children of the Mist stormed his castle, the blemish of uncertain birth vanishes. With Montrose's approval and Sir Duncan's consent, Menteith weds her, thereby prefiguring the ultimate union of moderate Cavalier and moderate Presbyterian.

Allan, for all his friendship with Menteith, has long been jealous of Annot's love for him and has been haunted by visions in which he saw an unknown Highlander stabbing him to death. Now in fury he plunges a dirk into Menteith's breast and, making his escape, loses himself in the forest glens, where he devotes himself to the destruction of the few remaining Children of the Mist. Menteith recovers, but his convalescence is too prolonged to allow him to join in Montrose's later campaigns. Angus M'Aulay, furious at Montrose for having supported Menteith's pretensions rather than his brother's, leaves the camp with his followers, never to rejoin the royalist army. Thus family pride and clan feeling have been prepotent over all other loyalties.

Despite noble qualities, to which Scott does ample justice, the clan system he portrays is incapable of growth and is therefore doomed, though its death may be delayed for another hundred years. Indeed, none of the characters in *A Legend of Montrose* proves capable of learning from experience. The two M'Aulays violently refuse to learn. Though Dalgetty's prosaic virtues are a touchstone for deflating the proud and lofty assumptions of those surrounding him, he too is severely limited; he has neither imagination nor any of that higher nobility of feeling on which the others pride themselves. The Earl of Menteith cannot surmount his own aristocratic prejudices. In the end, he merely withdraws from the civil strife and retires into private life from the challenge of history. But even the lofty and heroic Montrose cannot escape the limitations of his own class and character. He too fails not only to fire his followers with a larger vision but to let it steadily inspire his own heart.

From characters who themselves learn nothing, however, a reader may learn much. It is doubtful that poor Emma Bovary learned a great deal from her whole unhappy life, but Flaubert makes her illumine a searching analysis of nineteenth-century society and its values. Scott's vision too is as much social as it is personal. No more than Flaubert, of course, is he didactic; his novels are not sermons, but presentative of reality. If we reflect once more upon *The Heart of Mid-Lothian*, we may observe with surprise that it is not the heroic Jeanie who learns from the painful struggle of her love with her conscience; her vision is from the beginning as pure and noble as it is ever to be. It is her sister Effie who in the end gains painful insights into her own heart, little though they aid her happiness. This does not make Effie more meaningful and moving than Jeanie; Jeanie far transcends her worldly sister both in significance and in her power to move our hearts.

Even more, in a way, however, than these triumphs of individual character portrayal, is the range and depth of the emotions Scott renders and the total panorama of society he conveys. Honor, courage, devotion, love; high loyalty and rational principal; sense and absurdity; prejudice, envy, resentment, cruelty, hatred—all are there. In *A Legend of Montrose* there are the clan leaders and their followers and all the ways in which the clan spirit is shaped by the nature of their feudal structure; in *The Bride of Lammermoor* the Whig and Tory politicians, the old and new time-servers, the villagers of Wolf's-hope, the strength of Ravenswood and the weakness of Lucy Ashton, devotion and deception; in *The Heart of Mid-Lothian* the reformist conscience and the lawyers, criminals, and middle-class citizens of Edinburgh. If through some holocaust all other historical records of late seventeenth-century and eighteenth-century Scotland were swept away, from these three novels alone it would still be possible to reconstruct a clear and richly detailed picture of its world.

# *Thou Shalt Continue, Thou Knave*

# *( 1 8 1 9 )*

THOUGH SCOTT had seemed to be on his deathbed on that night of June, 1819, he did not die. When he woke after prolonged slumber it was clear that the crisis had passed. Through the advice of Dr. Dick, formerly physician to the East India Company, he was put on a new regimen. "Calomel," he was now told, "not used in doses—which I had already employed in vain but in such very small quantities and so constantly as to maintain the effect of the mineral on the constitution, but not to bring on salivation—is, Lord love its heart, an absolute specific. Ten days' rigid attention to his directions have restored me to action and to appetite and to healthy digestion. I am now under the doom which Elbow denounces to Pompey: 'Thou shalt continue, thou knave thou, thou shalt continue,' and continue I will till I get quite round again."[1]

He was still extremely weak, though, and unable to resume his duties in the Court of Session. Scott intended to set out at noon on June 14 for Abbotsford, "and Papa thinks," Sophia wrote, "that, if he feels quite stout, he will not return here, but send Mamma back in about a fortnight, or three weeks, to arrange this house, and transport us all out to Abbotsford to remain the summer."[2] At the last moment, however, finding himself "a little fagged," Scott put off their departure for another day. Even then the exertion proved too great for him, and on his arrival he was forced once more to take to his bed.[3]

"I have been very *very* ill this three weeks," he wrote Terry on June 27. "This relapse has been I think produced by the journey from town to this place. Certes I have been a most wretched wight till yesterday . . . nothing about me is constant: my eyes dazzy—my ears ring: my nose smells all odd savours. I have the staggers worse than an old horse & feel as if I was wading amongst uncarded cotton or something equally unfit to support one's steps instead of stepping on the firm earth." "Still the Calomel has conquered at last."[4]

So drew to an end the more than three years of illness that had begun with stomach cramps in the winter of 1816–17. During the coming autumn and winter Scott was still to have occasional bouts of discomfort, though far milder than those he had previously endured, and gradually, under the influence of the calomel, they desisted altogether. He still looked thin and drawn, and it was long before he regained the weight or the ruddy color he had lost. He grew hale and hardy again. But these three years had aged him more than all the preceding ten. "The fire of his eye was quenched," said James Skene, "his step was more uncertain," and "he had advanced twenty years in the downward course of life."[5] Although he would be only forty-eight in August, he looked and felt himself an elderly man.

There was one singular aftermath to those days of blurred pain in which, drugged with laudanum, he had nevertheless struggled on through the labors of composition. When the bound volumes of *The Bride of Lammermoor* were put in his hands, he found it entirely strange to him. The actual catastrophe on which it was founded and its circumstances, he recalled clearly enough; but of his own handling of the tale not a scene, incident, or character woke even an echo.[6] He had written it like a man fey, living in a remote world of phantoms, and like a dream it had vanished. From what drowned cavern deeper than ever plummet sounded, past the warderless gates of horn, did it well up into the light? The bitterness of the Master of Ravenswood as he rode from his last interview with Lucy Ashton, his violent feelings for her hated clan, all the emotional turmoil in which he galloped to his doom in the Kelpie's Flow, seem to mirror things Scott had long buried beyond any willing recall—the pain of his long ride, a quarter of a century ago, from Fettercairn, his indignant belief that Williamina had loved him but yielded to parental pressure, and the fires of what his friends feared as his ungovernable mind.

But for many years now he had subjected such emotions to control. Save when he was taken unaware he blotted out the very recollection in oblivion. As he read the unfamiliar words of this haunted tragedy the uneasiness he allowed himself was only lest he had written "something altogether glaring and fantastic." But then he remembered that James Ballantyne had been the printer and proofreader and would have halted the presses if the story had grown too extravagant. "Well," asked James, when Scott told him of this blank in his memory, "upon the whole, how did you like it?" "Why," he replied, "as a whole, I felt it monstrous, gross, and grotesque; but still the worst of it made me laugh, and I trusted the good-natured public would not be less indulgent."[7]

Readers were more than indulgent to both novels; they received them with acclaim. "The Master of Ravenswood," said Lady Louisa, "is perhaps the best *lover* the author ever yet drew";[8] and Sydney Smith thanked Constable for sending him "the last novel of Walter Scott. It would be profanation to call him Mr. Walter Scott. I should as soon say Mr. Shakespeare or Mr. Fielding. Sir William and Lady Ashton are excellent, and highly dramatic. Drumthwacket is very well done; parts of Caleb are excellent. Some of the dialogues between Bucklaw and Craigengelt are as good as can be . . . When I get hold of one of these novels, turnips, sermons, and justice-business are all forgotten."[9]

Not everyone liked Caleb Balderstone; he was a caricature, said some of the critics, a mere humor harping too much on one string, and Scott later agreed that "he might have sprinkled rather too much parsley over his chicken."[10] But everyone saluted the comic conception of Dugald Dalgetty, everyone wished there were more of Montrose, and everyone was thrilled by the exciting scene between Dalgetty and Argyll in the dungeon of Inveraray. "And why no more?" asked Lady Louisa. "Where are the good couple who concealed the Regalia from Cromwell's soldiers? I am sensible that the actor should always leave the stage before the spectator is tired, but I verily believe that nobody is tired. Meanwhile I believe that most people would say of the four & twenty volumes, what I have known the parents of large families do of their children— 'You may think them a great many, yet there is not one we could spare.' "[11]

"I heartily wish you joy of the success of Jedediah," Scott triumphantly wrote Constable on July 4. "I think I can promise you his successor will be as popular."[12] He had already, in fact, begun dictating *Ivanhoe* to John Ballantyne. "I can scarcely snatch a moment to give you this welcome information," John told Constable, "as I am writing to his dictation from morning to night . . . It is no pleasant job stooping over a breast with a sticking-plaster upon it (which is my case), to write all day; but all our interests are too deeply concerned to admit of my hesitating."[13] After a laborious weekend, John left for Edinburgh on Monday, bearing with him a large batch of the new novel.

"I must entreat you," Scott warned James, "that upon *no account & to no person whatsoever* you either read or show any part of *Ivanhoe.* I do not wish to have the point agitated in any literary coterie whatsoever who is the author of that work until it is before the public."[14] This injunction he repeated to Constable.[15] For he was again amusing himself with the idea of a playful hoax upon his readers. This new novel had its scene not in Scotland but in the England of Richard Coeur-de-Lion. Could he fool people into believing it fathered by neither the Author of *Waverley* nor Jedediah Cleishbotham, but by still another ghost named Laurence Templeton?[16]

The twelfth-century setting of the story involved problems Scott had not dealt with before. His knowledge of the seventeenth and eighteenth centuries was exhaustive, and his rendering of Scottish dialect speech brilliantly convincing. But how was he to suggest the diction of English peasants and franklins living more than half a millennium ago? "I must take care my *Saxon* characters speak proper language, not unintelligible but not modern."[17] For the vocabulary of Gurth and Wamba—and perhaps to a lesser degree of Cedric and Athelstane—he consulted Horne Tooke's philological treatise *The Diversions of Purley*.[18] As a model in portraying a remote age James Ballantyne recommended Strutt's *Queen-hoo Hall*, which Scott had edited with a concluding chapter in 1808. This, Scott said decisively, would not do at all; its excessive antiquarian detail made it unreadable, valuable though it was to "men more desirous of information than mere amusement." But it lacked "what I hope to give *Ivanhoe*."[19]

Scott made such rapid progress in the writing that by July 17 he had almost completed Volume I.[20] The name of the hero, he decided, must be changed from Harold to Wilfred. As a result of Byron's poem, "Harold is over-scutched in this our generation."[21] On August 2, Volume II was far advanced.[22] The printing, however, was unaccountably slow. "James has sent me but two proofs," Scott complained, "the reason of which *drumbling* I cannot conceive."[23] "Why in Gods name," he wrote the culprit, "have I no proofs from you?"[24] James explained that Cowan, the paper manufacturer, had been slow in making delivery of the fine-quality paper that, with more elegant presswork and a new format, was to help give the impression that this novel was the work of a different hand. He was "utterly dismayd with the delay," Scott responded; "pray let it be hurried."[25] When on August 19 he had finished the second volume and the paper still had not arrived, he turned aside temporarily to other projects.[26]

Of these he had his customary sufficiency on hand. There was more text for the *Provincial Antiquities*, of which he sent James revised copy. There was an introductory memoir for the *Trivial Poems and Triolets* of Patrick Carey, a Cavalier poet whom Scott thought almost as fine as Lovelace. There was running copy for the *Edinburgh Annual Register*.[27] Finding that these odd jobs did not exhaust his energies, he wrote a considerable part of a new novel "on the dissolution of the Monasteries,"[28] but then laid it aside when on August 25 he again began receiving proof sheets of *Ivanhoe*. "Your correctors," he wrote James, "might save me much trouble by observing how proper names &c are corrected on the return proofs." There were "the same blunders again and again—Always Brian-de-Blois Guilbert for Brian de Bois-Guilbert, Athelstone for Athelstane etc. I have corrected these about twenty or thirty times."[29]

Abbotsford had now lost one of its inhabitants. On July 4 Walter had received the army commission he had so eagerly awaited, and was gazetted as Cornet, or color-bearer, in the 18th Hussars. "The only thing that is to be feared," Sophia noted with affectionate mockery, "is his dying of pride and conceit before he joins, as it is among the most dashing regiments in the service."[30] He was to leave with all speed, sailing first for London to buy his military outfit and thence for Ireland, to his regiment in Cork.[31]

Scott had decided not to accompany him to London. Although his health seemed almost entirely mended, he was still taking calomel and felt it safer not to risk so long a journey or leave home for any length of time. He would therefore put off his own trip till after Christmas.[32] Possibly the following summer he would go to Carlsbad; "I like the idea of Bohemia and its seven castles;[33] and he might learn something new instead of being stalked by "the confounded lion-hunters who haunt English Spaws."[34] Charles could then be left "at the famous institution of Ferdenbergh near Berne" to learn French and German.[35]

On July 14, Walter set out for London. At last he was launched on his own, "to swim without bladders," as his father put it, "on the great tide of human life."[36] "The girls were very dull after you left us," Scott wrote him; "—indeed on the night you went away Anne had hysterics which lasted some time. Charles was also down in the mouth & papa and mama a little grave and dejected."[37] Abbotsford seemed very empty without its tall, handsome heir clattering in with his gun and half a dozen black cocks after a day's shooting on the hills. The only house guest at the moment was George Huntly Gordon—the son of Major Pryse Gordon, one of the officers Scott had met in Belgium—who was now serving him as an amanuensis, a worthy person but no sparkling companion for a family missing its son. Even five days later, "Mamma & the girls are very well," Scott wrote, "but very cross. Luckily there is no one to suffer but poor Mr. Gordon who is far too deaf to be annoyd even by Xantippe herself."[38]

In London, Walter was the guest of his parents' old friends the Dumergues, in Piccadilly.[39] Through John Ballantyne, who was in town on business, Scott sent him letters of introduction for presentation in Ireland. "You will see your old friend with a new face," said one to Hartstonge; "be-furred, be-feathered, and be-whiskered in the highest military *ton*."[40] And another to Maria Edgeworth: "When this shall fall into your hands, it will be accompanied by a second edition of Walter Scott, a *tall* copy, as collectors say, and bound in Turkey leather, garnished with all sort of fur and frippery—not quite so well *lettered*, however, as the old and vamped original edition."[41]

"I wish you would look out for Walter," Scott wrote John at the same time. "As he is a very young purchaser probably you can give him a hint about some of his purchases & payments."[42] But John's aid did not avail very much; the cost of Walter's military "rattle-traps & foppery"[43] proved "abominably extravagant." "They say it takes *nine* tailors to make a man—apparently *one* is sufficient to ruin him."[44] The resplendant uniforms and other equipment, "horses not included, cost about £360; and if you add a couple of blood horses," which Walter would obtain in Ireland, "it will be £200 more, beside the price of his commission"—a thumping £750. A good deal to pay, Scott noted drily, "for the privilege of getting the hardness of his skull tried by a brick-bat at the next meeting of Radical Reformers."[45]

Walter must consequently be economical, Scott wrote him—have only two chargers, as his Colonel stipulated, and not drive a gig. "I detest that mania of driving wheel barrows up & down when a man has a handsome horse & can ride him."[46] And he would be well advised not to buy his mounts from his brother officers but from dealers; no wise officer would sell a good horse save at an exorbitant price.[47] By the end of July, Walter was in Cork.[48] "I need not say," Scott wrote him, "how anxious I am that you keep up your languages, mathematics, and other studies. . . ."[49] "Everything goes on here in the old fashion and we are all as well as possible saving" that Charles rode "to Lammas fair at Melrose yesterday in a private excursion and made himself sick with eating gingerbread . . ."[50]

Counting Walter's two horses, the cost of starting him out in life as a cavalryman came to more than £1,300.[51] He would also need an allowance: "Colonel Murray informs me," Scott wrote him, "that from £200 to £250 in addition to the pay of a cornet ought to make a young man very comfortable."[52] James Ballantyne also reported himself unable to discount "£850 of Constable's Bills & £800 of mine (which last he had impetrated from me sore against my will)," so that Scott found himself temporarily a bit pinched. He therefore decided to proceed at once with negotiations for his new novel, *The Monastery*, although he had not planned to broach this to the booksellers until September.[53]

It was plain that Constable's credit, however sound at bottom, was momentarily strained. Times were still bad—foreign markets glutted, wages slashed, buying power falling—and Scott noted among the Scottish banks a "general distrust which strikes everywhere, or rather a resolution to withdraw their capital (I mean the Banks) from discount to job in the funds."[54] But they would not refuse the bills of the great London house of Longmans; the Pater Noster Row publishers, consequently, must have the management of the new book. "Understand," Scott instructed John Ballantyne, "it is by no means my intention to change Constable on future occasions. I only want to give his credit a little repose. I can never forget that he sells better than anyone."[55]

Against half-profits on 12,000 copies Scott desired an advance of between £2,400 and £3,000, "in Longman's bills at dates discountable in Scotland." Of the other half of the profits, one-third to be reserved for Constable.[56] "But it is not to be offerd him till I[vanhoe] is out, as it would, you are aware, only raise such a clamour as we had in May."[57]

Should Constable then refuse, Longman might have his share as well. "If the London lads like these terms you may close with them without farther delay. . . ." "I am pledging my time and leisure for *my own* convenience not *for theirs* & if they do not like the terms I do not desire to deal with them . . ."[58]

On August 16 wee Johnny gleefully reported striking a bargain that even bettered his instructions[59]—no less than "£5000," Scott wrote James, "in Longman's beautiful & dutiful bills."[59] What a brilliant little haggler he was! "I wrote yesterday under the impression that John had not been [able] to execute my commission—he has wrought it out however. To be sure he is a devil for what boxers call a *rally*. I enclose excellent paper for £1400. . . . Vogue la galère."[60]

Though John was in high spirits from his success he was not well. He had had a miserable voyage to London, then felt somewhat better there, and after striking his glittering bargain, restless as "a flea in a blanket," said Scott, had gone to Brighton for the races. But there he had been ill again and decided to forego the raid he had planned on the bookshops and antique dealers of Paris.[61] "I am sincerely glad," Scott told James; he would do himself more good remaining quietly at home.[62]

Now that Scott's own health was entirely restored, Abbotsford rang with gay hospitality. His aunt, Miss Chritty, who had been suffering from an asthmatic complaint, came out for a stay and seemed to grow better in the lovely August weather.[63] Mrs. Maclean Clephane came with her two younger daughters, Williamina and Anna Jane, and the two Miss Macallisters, friends of Sophia and Anne, these last "rather empty cannisters," Scott thought, "though I dare say very good girls. Anne tired of them most inhospitably."[64] All told, "The House," he wrote his mother, was "like a convent, only the young vestals are very noisy."[65]

Their youthful voices were cheerfully melodious, but Mrs. Clephane thought poorly of John of Skye's piping. "Is he not an elegant man?" Scott tried to wheedle her. "He is a pretty man; but he understands little of his pipe," Mrs. Clephane said firmly. "His drones are not in tune with his chanter. He wants the Highland style altogether." Scott's uncle, Thomas Scott, agreed with her. "His ear is false," he said, "and he will never play well. My nephew, however, is fond of a good-looking man, which Bruce is, and he can make a noise . . ."[66]

On September 21, Abbotsford received a more glittering guest, Prince Leopold of Saxe-Coburg—later King of the Belgians—who was passing through Selkirk on his way to Carlisle.[67] Only at eight in the morning of that very day did Scott learn of his approach, through a note from the Magistrates asking him as Sheriff to join in their welcome. It flashed into his mind that if the Prince wanted to see Melrose Abbey, they could hardly avoid entertaining him. Charlotte, who was still in bed, let out a scream at the news: "What have we to offer him?" "Cake and wine," said Scott carelessly. "Cake!!!" she exclaimed in a tone of despair. "Where am I to get cake?"[68]

But, filled with curiosity, she set out with Scott, "not to miss a peep of the great man." In Selkirk a search of the whole town produced only one shoulder of cold mutton. Prince Leopold was given the freedom of the Burgh, the Bailie made a speech, a band consisting of one drum and one fife played.[69] Melrose was too far out of his way, declared Leopold, but he could not leave Scotland without seeing Scott in his own home. And—miraculously—when they returned to Abbotsford, Charlotte produced, in addition to the leg of mutton, broiled salmon, black cock, and partridges; there was a saucer of "the sour plums of Galashiels," Scott said humorously, and another of "the iron pears of Abbotsford"; and he brought out some fine old hock and "added a dram of whiskey lest the plums & pears should come to wrangling before H.R.H. got to Hawick."[70]

That the "emphatic monosyllable *The Prince* is not heard amongst us more than ten times a day," Scott told Lord Montagu, "is on the whole to the credit of my family's understanding." John of Skye was the only member of the household whose brain seemed unsettled; the Prince had praised his piping as better than any he had heard in the Highlands ("which by the way shows H.R.H. knows nothing of the matter") and since then the delirious piper had been pruning trees "without remorse to the tune of *Phail Phranse* i.e. the Prince's wellcome." Such, Scott concluded, was "a very full true & particular account of our royal visit, unmatchd since that of King Charles to the Castle of Tillietudlem."[71]

Though his allusion to Tillietudlem was in jest, it had a core of relevance. For Abbotsford, originally to have been a modest dwelling like an old English rectory, had grown to something not unlike a small Border castle whose rambling additions with their southwestern tower and battlements and bartisan dwarfed the old farm cottage hidden in its creepers.[72] Indoors the large new parlor, Scott thought, was "one of the pleasantest I ever saw," and the armory, with its stained glass, its grotesques, and its gleaming trophies, filled his heart with joy.[73]

Only that summer Terry had bought him a large consignment of new prizes: two superbly polished blue-and-gold pouldrons of the time of Louis XIV, a breastplate richly embossed with the order of the Golden Fleece, three breastplates and helmets of the time of Henry VII, one engraved with a red Maltese cross, two Venetian morions, more than a dozen swords, one an Andrea Ferrara. Besides these, Terry had acquired a strange assortment of other curiosities—an Indian Hookah, a magnificently gilt Persian plate, an Esquimaux jacket made of the intestine of a whale, two ancient reading desks, a Lochaber ax, a large South Sea fishhook, an Elizabethan lady's headdress, Addison's velvet slippers.[74] If the slippers "will serve you in your professional dress," Scott replied, "pray accept them from me . . . Addison, I know not why, is personally no such favourite of mine as Sir Roger de Coverley should make him."[75]

Around his dwelling Scott's lands rolled from the banks of the Tweed to the base of the Eildon Hills and from Darnick to the shores of Cauldshiels Loch, farmland and field verdurously hedged, shady glen and burn tinkling over its falls of rock, young woods in which the trees were beginning gloriously to rise. Now he was bargaining with his neighbor Nicol Milne for all of Faldonside, just south of Abbotsford, extending another half-mile along the Tweed and including Faldonside Loch. It might be bought, he believed, for about £30,000, which was probably £2,000 more than its market value, but the two combined properties would be worth £2,000 a year, and with "a little judicious planting . . . the estate might be rendered one of the most beautiful in this part of Scotland."[76]

While Scott indulged these swelling dreams he pressed on with *Ivanhoe*. Though he felt better than he had in years, he was still unable to "write very long at a time without feeling a very disagreeable pain in my back" and was obliged to continue employing an amanuensis, "which is grievous work for one accustomed to independence."[77] In spite of these difficulties the novel was completed by the time he was ready to return to Edinburgh, and *The Monastery* was proceeding rapidly. "I am led to expect *I*[*vanhoe*] will please the public," he told John Ballantyne, "because it is uncommon."[78]

Both John and Constable, however, were disturbed by advertisements appearing during October in the London *Morning Chronicle* for a rival "4th Series of *Tales of My Landlord*" containing a novel called *Pontefract Castle* and purporting to be the work of Jedediah Cleishbotham. Cadell pooh-poohed the whole matter as an unimportant hoax, but Constable feared it might endanger the sales of *Ivanhoe*, and John angrily published a denunciation in all the London papers. The real Author, he assured the public, had "no connection with this *catchpenny* Publication" and Constable was "taking *Legal Measures* to interdict" its appearance and "to *Punish* those concerned."[79]

The publisher, a man named William Fearman, responded in an advertisement deriding John's threats. "Jedediah Cleishbotham," he said, was "notoriously a fictitious name and belongs to no one. . . . It is open to anybody to assume it, as it is to write a continuation of *Tales of My Landlord*." There was "one straightforward and manly way," he suggested, "of settling the question: let the author come forward, not as Jedediah Cleishbotham, not under the wing of John Ballantyne, I shall then be able to decide whether the MS. I hold is or is not by the same person."[80]

Scott laughed at this attempt to smoke him out. He doubted, he told Constable, that the public would "mistake a Chestnut Horse for a Horse Chestnut." But both Constable and John were worried. "In the face of this piratical pretender," they thought, "Scott should 'drop the mask.'" "The Author who lends himself to such a trick," he replied, "must be a blockhead—let them publish and that will serve our purpose better than anything we ourselves could do."[81]

Ultimately Cadell persuaded Constable to do nothing, repeating soothingly that he was "annoying himself without cause."[82] With this the teapot tempest died away, though John Ballantyne wrote a letter to *Blackwood's Magazine* voicing contemptuous pity for Fearman,[83] while Constable grumbled that the London bookseller was a low fellow and hoped the work would not succeed.[84] The only effect of the squabble on *Ivanhoe* was that Constable induced Scott to drop his scheme of presenting it as the work of still another author. There were already enough imitators in the field, he argued strenuously; the novel should have the advantage of being announced as by the Author of *Waverley*.[85] Scott made no very obstinate resistance, and it was so agreed, though he did provide the book with a "Dedicatory Epistle" to a suppositious "Dr. Jonas Dryasdust" signed by the imaginary "Laurence Templeton."[86]

On November 27, Scott entertained another royal visitor in Castle Street, Prince Gustavus Vasa of Sweden. He was but half a prince, Scott wrote Walter, "for this Northern Star is somewhat shorn of his beams. His father you know was dethrond by Bonaparte . . . and one of his generals Bernadotte made heir of the Swedish throne in his stead. But this youngster I suppose has his own dreams of royalty, for he is Nephew to the Emperor of Russia," and it was said that the Swedish nobles wished to get rid of Bernadotte.[87] The young prince "took a long look" at the portrait of King Charles XII over the dining-room mantel "and we were all struck with the resemblance betwixt old Ironhead as the Janissaries calld him and his descendant."[88]

When *Ivanhoe* appeared on December 18 it aroused an enthusiasm that more than justified Scott's serene assurance. Throughout England, indeed, it was received with even more clamorous delight than any of the "Scotch novels."[89] The *Quarterly* called it a "splendid masque" and poured fervent praise on the bold and brilliant characterization of Coeur-de-Lion and the rollicking scenes with the Clerk of Copmanhurst. It noted, however, that Ivanhoe and Rowena were pallid figures and complained that some of the other principal characters—Front de Boeuf, Bois-Guilbert, and Locksley—failed to blend the light and shade found in real human beings.[90] But Sydney Smith, with no qualification, said roundly, "There is *no doubt* of its success."[91]

Edinburgh swelled the chorus of praise. "The work before us," Jeffrey remarked, "shows at least as much genius as any of those with which it must now be numbered." Rebecca was a "lovely being," and next to her "the heartiest interest in the story is excited by the outlaws and their merry chief . . . It is a splendid Poem, and contains matter enough for six good tragedies."[92] *Blackwood's Magazine*, for all its proprietor's frictions with Scott, was almost rapturous: "Never were the long-gathered stores of most extensive erudition applied to the purposes of imaginative genius with so much easy, lavish, and luxurious power, never was the illusion of fancy so complete." The tournament at Ashby-de-la-Zouche splendidly evoked "all the truth and graphic precision of Froissart."[93]

Though Lady Louisa Stuart was no ordinary reader, she eloquently spoke for the reading public. The storming of Torquilstone and Rebecca's trial, she wrote from Ditton, were read with breathless interest. "Few characters were ever so forcibly painted as hers; the Jew too, the Templar, the courtly knight De Bracey, the wavering inconstant wickedness of John, are all worthy of Shakespeare. . . . Yet I shall own I dislike one thing, the sudden death of Bois-Guilbert; it is too much a *makeshift*. What really may (and does) happen to people of violent passions, breaking a blood-vessel, would have staggered the reader less and answered the purpose equally well . . . I must not omit paying my tribute to Cedric, that worthy forefather of a genuine English gentleman, he is admirable."[94]

Despite the hard times and despite the thirty-shilling price entailed by its handsome post-octavo format, *Ivanhoe* sold with the speed of a racing fire.[95] Within less than two weeks the entire first printing of 10,000 copies was exhausted "and more demanded with more speed than the printers can accomplish."[96] John Ballantyne estimated with perky self-congratulation that his own small share in the profits of Scott's novels (and he had no part of *Waverley*, *Guy Mannering*, or *The Antiquary*) had already come to £4,250.[97] When he dropped in at Castle Street on Christmas Day, Scott said to him, "John, are you not astonished at the success of these things? Egad, *I* am."[98]

But Scott's prosperity was in gleaming contrast to the state of the country. The summer had been bad and the autumn was still worse. Both in England and in Scotland the signs of a sick economy grew ever darker and the rumblings of social discontent more desperate.[99] "The wages of Glasgow handloom weavers, once twenty-five shillings a week, shrank that autumn" of 1819 "to five shillings, or half what they had been in 1816."[100] Discharged soldiers and sailors begged, half-naked, in the gutters; the streets of manufacturing towns were silent and deserted save when strikes brought thousands of sullen specters surging over the cobbles to smash machines and put out the fires of furnaces. In Birmingham, laborers marched with inflammatory banners and liberty caps to field meetings harangued by radical orators.[101]

Disorder seemed imminent. Throughout the industrial North, workmen with bludgeons and pikes drilled under Peninsular veterans; Glasgow weavers were organized into battalions by streets. The Government urged magistrates to stand firm and marched its scanty army into the manufacturing districts. On August 16 there had been a clash that shocked and terrified the country. After weeks of drilling on the moors, more than fifty thousand Manchester workmen—a force larger than Napoleon's army at Waterloo—had marched with bugles, drums, and revolutionary flags to St. Peter's Field to listen to the radical agitator Orator Hunt. They were unarmed, but their menacing looks sowed fear.[102]

The alarmed magistrates ordered a detachment of yeomanry to force their way to the hustings. Jostled by the crowd, the yeomanry started slashing with their sabers; there was a panic, and in the fleeing masses eleven people were slain and hundreds wounded. The Government congratulated the magistrates on the firmness with which a gallant handful had suppressed a dangerous demonstration. In the nation opinion was divided.[103] The Duke of Wellington thought that the purpose of the reformers was neither more nor less than the plunder of the rich. In general, Tories and manufacturers agreed;[104] and there were liberals who believed the ferment among the laboring classes a prelude to revolution. But most of the Whigs and even some Tories and employers felt outraged; the Government had spilt blood, and the country did not like blood to be spilt.[105]

Despite the violence, Scott did not think there was any real danger of revolution. He remembered 1793 and 1794, "when the same ideas possessed a much more formidable class of the people," including farmers, shopkeepers, and other men of substance. "A mere mob," he said calmly, "will always be a fire of loose straw."[106] And despite the lying newspapers, with their wild talk of a "Peterloo massacre," the Manchester troops, he said, had not acted with needless violence. The meeting itself had been an illegal attempt at intimidation.[107]

But James Ballantyne felt horrified by the bloodshed and published in the *Edinburgh Weekly Journal* a strong denunciation of the magistrates. Scott immediately took him to task. Even if he were right in believing the authorities had acted prematurely, was he called on "to give these banditti the encouragement they will derive from the countenance of any one decent & well disposed Editor? Especially were you calld on to do this before you were Master of the facts or before any evidence had been adduced?"[108] Fifty thousand men were obviously not a deliberative body and could have been assembled for no purpose but to carry their point by force. So dangerous a situation might easily lead to "an Irish rebellion with all its horrors."[109]

He had therefore decided, Scott wrote, that he must withdraw from the *Journal*. "I cannot continue a partner where such mistaken views are inculcated[110] . . . I do not think my ideas are those of a party man—in fact I care very little about parties . . . But this seems to involve the great question of whether we shall have peace in our time or a bloody and remorseless struggle . . ." Fortunately the paper was so prosperous that his retirement would do it no financial harm. "I am sorry for all this —But as our judges are wont to say 'there is no help for difference of opinion.' "[111]

James was distressed by Scott's decision, agreed that his own judgment had been hasty and ill-advised, and begged Scott to reconsider. "Since you wish it and promise to be cautious," he replied placably, "I shall certainly remain a partner."[112] He did not desire James to support any cause he did not believe in, only to investigate thoroughly before taking a stand. "It can never be right for an Editor to argue *against* his own conviction but it may be often highly advisable that he should suppress an opinion formd even upon good grounds because the publishing it may lead to evil consequences."[113]

What was needed in Edinburgh, a number of men like Scott believed, was a strong and independent newspaper of Tory principles to counter the malcontent influence of the *Scotsman*. Young Mr. Lockhart approached Scott on the subject; "I agree," he replied, "with every word you write." Only last year he had been asked to talk to Lockhart on this same topic.[114] How would James Ballantyne do as editor? Except for "his foolish rigg about Manchester which was a mere capriole," he was a "well principled honorable man," fully versed in all the details of the business, and wrote a good style.[115] Or if he would not do, possibly the editorship might be pressed upon Washington Irving, who had "much humour and power of writing."[116]

Scott personally sounded out Irving. Would he "superintend an Anti-Jacobin" weekly paper at a salary of £500 a year? This might involve Irving in a warfare he preferred not to meddle in, or perhaps his "view of politics" might "not suit the tone it is desired to adopt; yet I risque the question because I know no man so well qualified for this important task, and perhaps because it will necessarily bring you to Edinburgh."[117] But Irving gracefully declined. "I have no strong political prejudices, for though born and brought up under a republican government . . . I have a deep *poetical* feeling for the old institutions of this country and should feel as sorry to see them injured or subverted as to see Windsor Castle or Westminster Abbey demolished . . ." He was "peculiarly unfitted," however, for such a post or "for any periodically recurring task, or any stipulated labour of body or mind."[118]

Meanwhile, Croker had written from London asking support for precisely such a newspaper, which was to be established in the metropolis.[119] Scott at once agreed; this *Constitution* or *Guardian*, "whatever the paper is calld"—though he thought the *Beacon* would be a still better name—could strike with more power than any local paper. If it kept "a port-hole or two open" to articles from Scotland it would "run like wildfire in this country . . . I would call our corner 'The Northern Lights.' Lockhart, who is a treasure both for zeal and capacity, promises they shall be vivid enough."[120] Wilson too would give ardent help. In London it was essential to obtain Canning's powerful aid. "He must not wear the kerchief now."[121]

Scott himself wrote three articles entitled "The Visionary," which were published in the *Edinburgh Weekly Journal* under the penname of Somnambulus and which had a still wider circulation collected in pamphlet form. They attacked the radical scheme of an equal division of all wealth, if it were carried out, as "a thousand times more fatal to the poor than even to the rich," and assailed the demand for universal suffrage as a wildly dangerous experiment in view of the illiterate state of the uneducated masses.[122] It gave Scott warm satisfaction to see a mason reading this pamphlet aloud to his fellow laborers eating their dinner before a new building in Leith Walk.[123]

In the weeks since Peterloo, though, social tensions had deepened, and the anger of the workers seethed. Young men in Lancashire surreptitiously made pikes, ground scythes, and converted hatchets, old swords, and mop-nails into weapons. At Newcastle, keelmen assaulted the magistrates with brickbats and cries of "Blood for blood!" At Manchester a constable was stoned to death.[124] In Glasgow a plot was discovered "to seize on a thousand 'stand' of arms . . . which had been sent from Edinburgh Castle," and the entire town was put under military guard.[125] "The Devil seems to have come up amongst us," exclaimed Scott, "unchaind and bellowing for his prey."[126]

Volunteer regiments were recruited to preserve law and order. "The loyalists," Scott reported to Morritt, "are arming fast. The Edinr. regiment is getting strong . . . and they are raising Sharp shooters and cavalry. A fine troop of the latter, all handsome youths and well mounted, made me wish myself twenty years younger that I might join them again. The highland Chiefs have offered their clans . . ."[127]

With this danger of a social war, Scott and his neighbor the laird of Gala volunteered to raise and equip a troop of three hundred men from Melrose and Galashiels. Torwoodlee also, Scott wrote Lord Melville, was ready to raise a company. His own neighborhood, he said proudly, was "steadily & firmly loyal." "They are almost all marksmen & would be a most formidable and steady light infantry. Any number of shepherds could be added if the Buccleuch tenantry were turnd out, all picked hardy mountaineers . . ."[128] Aside from its military uses, "such a corps could operate forcibly on the *morale* of the people. It would confirm the loyalty of the lower orders by showing confidence in them and it would intimidate the disaffected by showing plainly that they cannot rely on even the neutrality of the Scottish peasantry."[129]

The Government introduced more stringent laws, muzzling the cheap Press and forbidding private drilling, the bearing of arms, and some kinds of outdoor meetings.[130] All over England and Scotland volunteer regiments flooded into the drab factory towns with their bright uniforms and handsome horses. To the workers they seemed heartless oppressors in their scarlet dress, "their empty or fume-charged heads" swollen with "pride and folly."[131] In their own eyes, however, as they sharpened their swords in the village smithy and said farewell to wives and sweethearts, they were heroic saviors of their country. With the deepening of the icy winter a day of wrath threatened.[132]

But, for all the general gloom, Scott's fortunes seemed unassailable. Within a single year of widespread adversity he had written and published one short novel, *A Legend of Montrose*, and two full-length novels, *The Bride of Lammermoor* and *Ivanhoe*, all three selling better than any of their seven predecessors. Within five years he had produced ten novels thronged with living characters painted against a wide and varied background of the richest reality, and at least six of these were undoubted masterpieces. "Pray make the author go on," pleaded Sydney Smith; "I am sure he has five or six more such novels in him, therefore five or six holidays for the whole kingdom."[133]

# 10

## The Wind Has Blown Away

### ( 1 8 1 9 – 1 8 2 0 )

Though 1819 had seen Scott restored to health and rising to new heights of fame and prosperity, it had not been unshadowed. There had been the death of the Duke of Buccleuch—"The poor Duke who loved me so well"[1]—over whom Scott's heart still grieved. Another early friend and patron, Robert Dundas of Arniston, the Chief Baron of Exchequer, who had long been ailing, had died on June 17. In September William Erskine lost his wife, and in October Scott's kind neighbor Lord Somerville died at Vevey on his way to Italy. But before the year ended Scott was to know heavier blows.

His aunt Miss Christy, after having seemed to grow stronger during the warm summer weeks at Abbotsford, was now again losing ground. His mother, despite her eighty-seven years, still seemed well, "better indeed," Scott wrote his brother Tom on December 9, "than last year."[2] She lived cheerfully and comfortably in her little George Street home, still calling him "Wattie my lamb" but refusing to take a penny from him, and devoting one-third of her income of £300 a year to charity.[3] On Sunday, December 12, the old lady appeared in unusually high spirits. Coming to drink tea with their grandmother, Sophia and Anne found her vivaciously telling the Scotts of Harden all the differences between the real story of the Bride of Lammermoor and her son's handling of that tragic tale. But the very next day she suffered a sudden stroke that paralyzed one side and left her unable to speak.[4]

Dr. Daniel Rutherford, her stepbrother, said that she could not linger more than a few days. On Wednesday, he himself, after eating breakfast and dressing to pay her a visit, suddenly collapsed while he was playing with his cat "and died in his daughter Anne's arms, almost without a groan and in the course of a single minute."[5] Though Miss Chritty had not been told of her brother's death, she too was despaired of; "there is very little hope," Scott wrote Walter, "of her living so long as to make it necessary she should know it. . . . I need not tell you how I loved and valued her and how much I feel the approaching separation, for I hold it for certain that I shall never see her more."[6]

Three mornings later Miss Chritty died, but Mrs. Scott still breathed on, though speechless and barely able to move.[7] At her bedside Charlotte observed the old lady looking at her wistfully for some time and then turning an anxious gaze toward the door. Realizing that this was a mute appeal for the presence of her son, Charlotte sent for Scott. When he appeared in the doorway his mother beamed her joy. Within his hand her fingers pressed his, then managed to falter up and pat his cheek. From there they moved to the crown of his own white head, as if in blessing, while she struggled for utterance. But in vain; there came only sighs and wordless murmurs, and at last she closed her eyes.[8] On the morning of December 24 she quietly died, without knowing that her half-brother and sister were already gone.[9]

All three were buried in the graveyard adjoining St. John's Chapel at the west end of Princes Street. The old family burial place in Greyfriars' Churchyard was being crowded by other graves; "When poor Jack was buried," Scott said, "where my father and Anne lie, I thought their graves more encroached upon than I liked to witness."[10] He therefore decided that the brother and two sisters whose fate had been so singularly entwined in death should not be divided in the grave.[11]

In his mother's room he was touched to find a little pile of New Year's gifts that she had assembled for her family: ". . . she was a great observer of the old fashions of her period." His heart beat more sadly "to think that the kind heart was cold which delighted in all these acts of kindly affection."[12] Only the preceding New Year's Day she had given him a Baskerville folio Bible. Under her trembling handwriting on the fly-leaf he added the words: "This Bible was the gift of my grandfather Dr. John Rutherford, to my mother, and presented by her to me; being, alas! the last gift which I was to receive from that excellent parent, and, as I verily believe, the thing which she most loved in the world,—not only in humble veneration of the sacred contents, but as the dearest pledge of her father's affection to her. As such she gave it to me; and as such I bequeath it to those who may represent me—charging them carefully to preserve the same, in memory of those to whom it has belonged."[13]

There could now, of course, be no thought of going to London after Christmas; he would have to defer that journey until March.[14] But although the dangers of revolt in the country seemed to be subsiding, Scott and Gala still thought it needful to press forward with their plan to muster a company of volunteers. Lord Elcho had already organized a corps of eighty cavalrymen, of which Lockhart was a member,[15] riding about on various marches and countermarches, the Raid of Airdrie, the Trot of Kilmarnock.[16] "I think Harden will also raise a troop of Ettricke men," Scott wrote, "& put his son, a very fine lad, at the head of it."[17] How odd it was, he thought, that he, a lame man, "began life by raising Light Dragoons & now in the autumn of my days am embodying sharp-shooters . . ."[18]

The loyal response on Tweedside was swift and enthusiastic. "I sent my piper through the neighboring hamlets to play *Scotts blue Bonnet* and he was immediately joined by upwards of 100 young fellows who have volunteered to go to Carlisle or Newcastle."[19] "My company was full in 24 hours and I could have doubled it with the greatest ease. It was rather of the latest for me to get on horse back & command sharp-shooters, but the knaves would hear of no other leader, declaring they had almost all of them eat my bread and would fight for me to the death. . . . They are all hardy young fellows & are to wear forest green with their own grey plaids."[20] "I have my eye on a clever horse that stands sword and fire well and I assure you I don't think my old namesake Walter the Devil had better men at his back."[21]

Many landowners feared putting weapons in the hands of the poor and wanted to arm only the upper classes. This Scott regarded as a disastrous error that might lead "to that most dreadful of evils a *servile* or Jack Cade sort of war."[22] If it were true that the lower orders were not to be trusted, then "we have only to compute how long the poor will be of discovering the recondite secret that 100 are stronger than one . . . But it is not true. The poor ARE to be trusted in almost every situation where they have not been disunited by circumstances from their natural superiors."[23] The normal relationships of landowner and tenant, of farmer and laborer, created ties of understanding and loyalty that were broken only by harshness and cruelty.

Scott granted that among the manufacturing districts conditions were more unstable. In the days before the steam engine, when factories had depended on water power, their owners had been obliged to locate them beside streams and had lodged their hands in neighboring villages. "In bad times the Master had to provide for these people's sustenance, else he could not have their service in good, & the little establishment naturally lookd up to him as their head. But this has ceased since manufacturers have been transferd to great towns where a Master calls together 100 workmen this week and pays them off the next with far less interest in their future fate than in that of as many worn-out shuttles."[24]

Even so, before the end of 1819 the peril that had seemed so imminent had visibly declined, and with the new year Scott believed that it was quite over.[25] "Radicalism is going down fast & the common people begin to hear reason," he wrote Croker, "—but not the less willingly that a thousand sabres have made it glitter in their eyes."[26] "Matters seem very different," he observed on January 23, "from the pass at which they stood a month ago."[27] "In these circumstances it would only be imposing on government and misusing their money to engage in such a matter . . . The Ministers will consider whether . . . they think the services of such a corps are desirable, attended as they must be with the degree of expence necessary to render it really useful."[28]

With the return of tranquility the Government showed no desire to pay a daily allowance to large numbers of unnecessary troops. Scott agreed and wrote a letter of thanks to the Melrose volunteers. "Confiding as I do, in the good sense and good principles of our countrymen, I hope and trust that such a call will not again disturb the course of our peaceful occupations. . . . For myself, I can only say, that the feelings of gratitude towards those individuals who have on this momentous crisis offered me their support, are in proportion to the confidence they have shewn themselves willing to repose in me. . . . From what I know of the gentlemen who so handsomely agreed to act as officers, as well as of your own spirit and zeal, I think I might have boasted that I would have been the *only* inefficient man in the proposed corps. May that happy state of society long subsist among us which binds its different classes together by good will, mutual attachment, and reciprocal kind offices!"[29]

Nevertheless, times were still hard. January was severe, with deep falls of snow.[30] "It makes me shiver in the midst of superfluous comforts," Scott wrote, "to think of the distress of others." He sent Laidlaw £10 "to distribute among our poorer neighbors, so as may best aid them. I mean not only the actually indigent, but those who are, in our phrase, *ill aff*. . . . I think part of the wood-money, too, should be given among the Abbotsford folks if the storm keeps them off work, as is like."[31] And, a few days later, "Do not let the poor bodies want for a £5, or even a £10, more or less: —

> "We'll get a blessing wi' the lave,
> And never miss't."[32]

Early in January, through the kindness of Lord Bathurst—whom Scott had never met—there came an offer of a writership in India for Charles.[33] Scott himself had thought of the diplomatic service for the boy, feeling "his talents more to lie towards the business of life than the study of the law."[34] But this offer opened a prospect of enticing prosperity. "Papa does not think it his duty to refuse," wrote Sophia, "more especially as Charles, though extremely clever, is also extremely idle" and would not be likely to "turn out a good lawyer in this town, with so many opportunities of seeing and being in company, and so little taste for studying."[35]

For all the grief that he would naturally feel at "parting from an amiable and promising boy," Scott did indeed at first conclude that he should not turn down such an opening. "Young hawks must leave the roost and we poor Scotsmen must send off our sons as well as our black cattle." Charles was only fourteen and would not have to leave for another three years, but then he might step at once into £500 a year and be able to return with a handsome fortune before he was thirty.[36]

It developed, however, that the only appointment available was not as a writer but a much less glittering one as a cadet. "I should be very unjust to Lord Bathurst's undeserved and unsolicited kindness," Scott replied, "if I made my feelings of gratitude depend either upon the nature of the appointment or his success in attaining it and I am as sensible of his goodness . . . as I could have been if the original appointment of a writership had taken place." Charles's older brother, though, had already "embraced a wandering and perilous profession"; only the possibility of wealth and an early return could persuade a father to send his remaining son to India. "But a cadetship would leave me little chance of seeing him again . . ." Scott therefore gratefully declined, deciding to wait until a writership offered.[37]

Charles was not the only one of his young people of whose future Scott was thinking that winter. John Gibson Lockhart had fallen in love with Sophia and asked for her hand. He was "a young man of uncommon talents," Scott thought, "highly accomplished, a beautiful poet & fine draughtsman, & what is better, of a most honourable & gentlemanly disposition. He is handsome besides & I like everything about him except that he is more grave & retired than I (who have been all my life something of an *Etourdi*) like particularly, but it is better than the opposite extreme. . . . He will probably rise high, as his family are rich and his talents excellent & I have some interest."[38]

Sophia too had been early impressed by Lockhart's talents. "I would advise you," she had written her old governess, Miss Millar, in the preceding July, "to read a new book which will be out soon called *Peter's Letters to His Kinsfolk*, being a description of the society of Glasgow and Edinburgh. It is one of the most clever and at the same time rather severe books that has been written for ages; this is Papa's opinion."[39] But she had taken some time to feel sure of her heart. "Believe me," she had responded to Lockhart's avowal of love, "we do not know each other sufficiently to have any reasonable prospect of happiness. Though my name is Sophia Scott I know well that I am not in the least clever, and fear, greatly fear, that you give me credit for talent and information beyond what I possess. When I told Papa of your letter to me at Abbotsford it went no further than himself, so neither Mamma, brothers or sister, know anything of it."[40]

Her father, she firmly believed, had no serious objection, but he too thought they should consider carefully whether their "different tempers and dispositions" would be harmonious throughout life. "And now, Mr. Lockhart, for God's sake if you love me do not be so unhappy; it makes me quite wretched to think that you are so, and to feel that I, who would do anything for your peace of mind, am the cause. Do not answer this, as I know that any further correspondence of this kind, unknown to Papa, would be very wrong . . ."[41]

Sophia was right in believing that Papa would not oppose their marriage, and neither did Mamma. After all, Mr. John Gibson Lockhart, Advocate and established author, was already somewhat further advanced in his career than Mr. Walter Scott, Advocate and fledgling poet, had been in 1797, although certainly the daughter of Sir Walter Scott and Lady Scott of Abbotsford, as they were soon to be, might have aspired higher than Charlotte Carpenter, the obscure French orphan who had been the Marquis of Downshire's ward. Perhaps Charlotte would have preferred a man of wealth or title, but she did not deny Lockhart's merits, and he was accepted as a suitor.

"I have at last made up my mind," Sophia wrote Miss Millar in January, 1820, "to marry Mr. Lockhart . . . Anything I may say to prepossess you in his favour, in the present state of my feelings towards him, might appear to you overdrawn, but Papa has the highest opinion of him, and his opinion is worth all the world to me. That I might have made a much higher marriage in point of rank and wealth I have little doubt, but I am not one who can be persuaded that happiness can depend upon these two alone."[42]

All Lockhart's anxiety melted away in joy. "When I look back a few months," he wrote Sophia, "and compare what I am now with what I was then, how is it possible that my heart should not overflow with tenderness. My dearest Sophia, you have put great trust in me. God grant I may never cost you a minute's pain in return for all your kindness. If I can put any faith in my knowledge of myself, you are sure of always possessing whatever happiness my love can give you. I wish I had other things to lay at your feet—but I have no fear for my part—all will be very well, and we shall be very happy."[43]

Scott announced the engagement to Walter on January 17. "Mr. Lockhart has made his formal visits to Mama and so forth. I think Mama would have liked a little more *stile* but she has no sort of objections to the affair."[44] Scott himself was warmly pleased. "To me," he wrote Morritt, "as it seems neither of my sons have a strong literary turn, the society of a son-in-law possessd of learning and talent must be a very great acquisition . . . All I have to fear on Lockhart's part is a certain rashness which I trust has been the effect of youth and high spirits joined to lack of good advice, as he seems perfectly good humoured and very docile. So I trust your little friend Sophia, who I know has an interest in your bosom, has a very fair chance for such happiness as this motley world can afford."[45]

None of these events, either private or public, had deterred Scott from the steady routine of writing *The Monastery*, though somehow or other sixteenth-century Scotland did not inspire him as the seventeenth and eighteenth centuries did. Nevertheless he worked steadily and now expected to have the book completed for early spring publication. Though Constable had not been pleased to learn that Longman was to have the management, he had accepted the share offered him, but he felt that Scott was making a mistake in bringing it out so soon after *Ivanhoe*. Instead, as soon as that novel was finished, Constable thought, Scott should have set to work on the *History of Scotland*. "Longman and Co. would be quieted by the appearance of the *History*, and I am certain their interest as well as ours would be greatly benefited thereby. The author has the *History* so much at his finger-ends, that he could write it, if once fairly at work, without any kind of difficulty, and there would be no delay in the copying of MS."[46]

Constable was mollified, however, by Scott's accepting his suggestion of a novel set in the time of Queen Elizabeth and introducing that great ruler among its characters. The novelist, to be sure, rejected Constable's desire that it be entitled *The Armada* and deal with those stirring days of 1588 when England's fate seemed trembling in the balance. He preferred to build his story around the legend of the murder of Amy Robsart, told in Meikle's old ballad, one of the favorite poems of his youth. He wished to call the novel, like the ballad, *Cumnor Hall*, but further agreed when Constable proposed *Kenilworth* instead, though John Ballantyne disgustedly jibed that the result would be "worthy of the kennel." Constable was elated at his victory. "His vanity boiled over so much," said his partner Cadell, ". . . that when in his high moods, he used to stalk up and down his room and exclaim, 'By God, I am all but the author of the *Waverley Novels*!' "[47]

Down at Windsor Castle, on the night of January 29, poor blind old George III, who had for years been hopelessly mad, drew himself up in his bedclothes, said, "Tom's a cold!" and died.[48] Four days later, from the windows above Constable's shop facing the High Street, Scott, Charlotte, and their daughters, accompanied by Prince Gustavus Vasa, witnessed the proclamation of the new reign of George IV at the Cross of Edinburgh. "The weather was fine, the sun shone bright," says Lockhart, "and the antique tabards of the heralds, the trumpet notes of *God save the King*, and the hearty cheerings of the assembled multitude . . . filled the noble old street. . . . The Royal Exile surveyed it with a flushed cheek and a watery eye, and Scott observing his emotion, withdrew with me to another window, whispering, 'Poor lad! poor lad! God help him.' "[49]

Early in February Scott took Lockhart down to Abbotsford with him for a weekend.[50] At noon Peter Matheson brought the carriage to the Parliament Close, Scott dashed out of Court tossing off his gown, and they were away. He had the first volume of *The Monastery* in his hand and talked freely of how he had drawn the setting of Kennaquhair from Melrose and the Rhymer's Glen. "It was a relief," he said, "to interlay the scenery most familiar to me with the strange world for which I had to draw so much on the imagination."[51]

Sunday morning John Ballantyne, who had a hunting box in the vale of the Leader, brought Constable to breakfast. Scott read the Church service and one of Jeremy Taylor's sermons, after which they sallied out into the crisp air of a sunny day with Tom Purdie. Little Johnny, pale and emaciated as a ghost, was nevertheless as gay as ever, prancing along and making "a harlequin and piebald figure" in his green coat trimmed with buttons of mother-of-pearl, gold, and silver snipped from a coat that had once belonged to the great Marquis of Montrose. Tom Purdie strode ahead vigorously in one of Scott's old green jackets with white hat and drab trousers. Surrounded by Maida and his yapping tail of Mustards and Peppers, Scott, too, despite his limp, maintained a pace that tried the portly Constable, who puffed and panted up one ravine and down another, mopping his brow and exclaiming "it was not every author who should lead him such a dance," while Tom grinned at the bookseller's exertions.[52]

"This will be a glorious spring for our trees, Tom!" Scott exulted. "You may say that, Shirra," replied Tom; and then added, scratching his head, "My certy, and I think it will be a grand season for *our buiks* too." At Huntly Burn the "Weird-Sisters," as Scott called the Misses Ferguson, refreshed the winded publisher and his companions with a drink, and they went on down the brook to a little tree-sheltered cottage that Scott intended to convert into a summer home for Lockhart and Sophia.

> "Mine be a cot beside the hill—
> A bee-hive's hum shall soothe my ear,"

he quoted Samuel Rogers, but instead of the lines

> "And Lucy at her wheel shall sing,
> In russet gown and apron blue"

he gaily improvised,

> 'But if Bluestockings here you bring
> The Great Unknown won't dine with you.'[53]

Johnny Ballantyne, who had ordered his hunter, Old Mortality, to be brought here so that he might ride back to Abbotsford, mounted and capered about, eager to mark out the line for a future avenue to the cottage. If the country people saw him so engaged on Sunday, Scott told him, they would take the whole party for heathens, but Johnny clapped spurs to his horse and trotted off. "The deil's in the body," said Tom, "he'll be ower every *yett* [gate] atween this and Turn-again, though it be the Lord's day. I wadna wonder if he were to be *ceeted* before the Session." "Be sure, Tam," cried Constable, "that ye egg on the Dominie to blaw up his father—I wouldna grudge a hundred miles o' gait to see the ne'er-do-weel on the stool, and neither, I'll be sworn, would the Sheriff." "Na, na," said Scott, "we'll let sleeping dogs be, Tam."[54]

As they walked home, Scott's hand on Tom's shoulder, an argument arose about which trees should be cut down in a hedgerow they were passing. Scott, displeased, removed his hand, and Tom fell a few paces to the rear. At Abbotsford, Scott and his guests dropped into some garden chairs on the green before the porch to admire the new tower gleaming in the sunlight. Tom lingered lounging for a minute, then asked the Shirra "to speak a word." Together they stepped into the garden. Scott returned, his face twisted in a comical expression. "Will ye guess what he has been saying, now?—Well, this is a great satisfaction! Tom assures me that he has thought the matter over, and *will take my advice* about the thinning of that clump behind Captain Ferguson's."[55]

On Monday the party returned to Edinburgh, where Scott found himself wearying with the transports of the two young lovers and looking forward to being with Walter next month in London. "Lovers are rather tiresome folks to everybody excepting each other," he wrote his son, "so that the family in general, including myself, heartily wish them married and settled, there being at present small mirth towards, as the man says in the farce. . . . I begin to think it long since I saw you." Walter must see that his leave from his regiment extended to the end of April, when Sophia's wedding must take place if it were not to be put off till June, "superstition having attached ill luck to marriages formed in May *Male nubis Maia* you remember."[56]

*The Monastery* was published at the beginning of March.[57] With his usual freedom from vanity, Scott thought the book rather dull and came to a characteristic decision. No use trying to tinker with it and see if by sheer sweat he might not rework it into something better; it would have to do as it was, and the public would probably buy. But neither would he let himself be vanquished by the sixteenth century. Instead of plunging immediately into the composition of *Kenilworth*, he therefore resolved to write a sequel to *The Monastery*, to be called *The Abbot*, using some of the same characters, and seeing if he could not so fire his imagination this time as to transmute his resistant material into gold.[58]

This determination he announced to Constable, "sweetening" it by agreeing at the same time to sell the publisher all the future profits of the *Tales of My Landlord*. "He was all alive to the last intimation," Scott wrote John Ballantyne, "and talked of producing the *ready* whenever called upon—with a fortnight's notice . . ."[59] Constable, to be sure, urged that the new novel be entitled *The Nunnery*, perhaps thinking that readers would anticipate wild enormities behind its virginal walls.[60] The only objection was, Scott responded, that neither nun nor nunnery was to be mentioned in the book from beginning to end. He remembered that Harry Siddons had written a novel that its publishers had rechristened *The Mysterious Bridal.* " 'Saar,' as poor Harry used to say, 'there was neither mystery nor bridal in my poor book. So egad, Saar, the consequence was I took my own book out of the circulating library . . . and never found it out till I was far in the first volume!' "[61]

Though *The Monastery*, as Scott had foreseen, sold well, neither reviewers nor general readers liked it very much. The Euphuist, Sir Piercie Shafton, failed to amuse, and the White Lady of Avenel fell incongruously between farce and terror.[62] "When this ethereal personage," said one critic, "who rides on the cloud which 'for Araby is bound' . . . whose existence is linked by an awful and mysterious destiny to the fortunes of a decaying family . . . descends to clownish pranks, and promotes a frivolous jest upon a tailor's bodkin, the course of our sympathies is rudely arrested, and we feel as if the author had put upon us the old-fashioned pleasantry of selling a bargain."[63]

Scott agreed with the public that the book was "not very interesting; but it was written with as much care as the others that is with no care at all and

> 'If it is na weel bobbit we'll bobb it again.'

On these points I am Atlas."[64]

The time was now rapidly nearing when Scott was to receive his Baronetcy. Lady Abercorn thought this an insufficient recognition of his talents; he and the Duke of Wellington, she said, stood alone on an eminence above all other men.[65] But Scott merely laughed, and joked about the dangers he might be risking in the capital—the Government had just discovered the Cato Street conspiracy to assassinate the entire Cabinet over their wine and walnuts at dinner. "On my word I shall think of Damocles if I have the honour of dining with a Minister and shall never see a red box but I shall expect a poniard or pistol to bounce out of it."[66]

On Sunday, March 12, Scott went to Abbotsford with Charlotte to attend to a few business matters before he took the stagecoach to England,[67] and Charles was left alone in Castle Street. "As Pappa & Mamma are to the country and I am very lonely by myself," the boy appealed to Constable, "I take the liberty to beg that you will favor me with the lend of a copy of *The Monastery*, if it is convenient. Be assured I will take the greatest care of it."[68] On the morning of March 17, Scott set out for London.[69]

He was delighted to find Walter "the very true cut of a soldier" and "not at all *dandified*."[70] No sooner were they unpacked at the Dumergues' than Scott found himself spinning in a whirl of engagements. Through a howling mob of "Middlesex blackguards" excited over the general election entailed by the new reign, he drove to Whitehall and met Lord

Sidmouth.[71] At the Admiralty he called on John Wilson Croker, whose *Diary* notes, "He looks older and not so well as I had hoped to find him, but his spirits are excellent."[72] Scott presented Walter to the Duke of York.[73] He met the gigantic Belzoni, who had excavated the second pyramid at Gizeh.[74] At the table of Charles Arbuthnot, one of the Secretaries of the Treasury, he and the young soldier dined with the Duke of Wellington and "heard the great Lord in all his glory talk of war and Waterloo."[75]

Writing Charlotte as "the Lady Scott of Abbotsford—to be," he told her "your honours will be in the gazette on Saturday"—"the King has I believe signed the warrant."[76] On March 30, letters patent were passed granting him and his lawfully begotten heirs male "the dignity of a Baronet," and the announcement appeared in the *London Gazette* of Saturday, April 1.[77] Next day Scott and Walter had a merry time at Lord Melville's. Lord and Lady Huntley and other friends were among the guests; Lady Huntley, who played "Scotch tunes like a highland angel," "ran a set of variations on Kenmure's On & Awa" with fire enough, Scott told her, "to raise a whole country side"; and everyone drank "a bumper to the new Baronet."[78]

When the news reached Abbotsford, Tom Purdie disappeared the whole day chasing all the sheep to re-mark them with reddle "S.W.S." for Sir Walter Scott, returning at nightfall so spattered with crimson himself that he looked like a red Indian. "Oh, but he's an awfu' great laird now," Tom exulted, "and stands next to the Duke of Wellington, and aiblins he'll be made commander-in-chief, gudeness only kens, and I," Tom concluded happily, "shall be his heddy-camp."[79]

From Lockhart, Scott learned that John Wilson was a candidate for the Professorship of Moral Philosophy at the University of Edinburgh. Hastening to the Admiralty to enlist the support of Lord Melville, he found his old schoolfellow "extremely well disposed to be friendly." But Wilson must realize, Scott warned, that his violent jests and literary asperities had created enemies who would use every weapon to defeat him. "Our pleasant follies are made whips to scourge us." Wilson must conduct his campaign with great good temper; "wrath will do no good."[80]

Promptly forgetting his own counsel, "I am very angry with Castle Street," Scott added. "Not a soul has written to me save yourself since I came to London."[81] But a few days later he was appeased by a "packet" from Mamma, which arrived just as he was penning a letter to Sophia. "There is a certain veil of Flanders lace floating in the wind for a certain occasion from a certain godmother," he told his daughter, "but that is more than a dead secret. I think you should write a few lines to Miss D. assuring her of your unaltered regard &c . . ."[82]

After a quiet Sunday in Hampstead with Joanna Baillie and John

Richardson,[83] Scott was plunged into a renewed round of entertainment. Every evening he was fêted; "if I had three heads like Cerberus," he said, "I could eat three dinners every day and am fairly in a way to be smothered with kindness."[84] The Dumergues invited to a breakfast party a large gathering of ladies and gentlemen including Sir Alexander Boswell, the eldest son of Johnson's biographer, and Washington Irving, who brought with him the artist Charles Leslie.[85] William Atkinson, the architect who was to design the new addition to Abbotsford, gave a dinner where Scott met Benjamin Robert Haydon, whose enormous canvas of *Christ Entering Jerusalem* was creating a sensation.[86]

Scott's dinner-table conversation alone convinced Haydon that he had written the *Waverley Novels*. One story seemed to him characteristic in its humor—a one-eyed smuggler named Dick defied the law by returning from transportation. With awful anger the magistrates demanded how he had dared. "Please your honours," he replied, "I did not like the climate!" "I could hardly help thinking," wrote Haydon, "that Scott took a pleasure in exciting your suspicions that he was the author, without confessing it, chuckling that good breeding prevented you from opening your lips. . . . You thought, 'Here is a mysterious being, with whom allusion to a certain topic is forbidden:' and there you sat, listening to stories which convinced you you were right, and yet you did not dare to say so."[87]

So eager was Scott to see Haydon's picture that the very next morning he sallied out early to the gallery. When he arrived the doors were still closed; the attendant who presently came to open up found Scott patiently sitting on the stairs, his lame leg stretched out in front of him. Scott praised the painting to Haydon, but the artist himself was dissatisfied with the head of Christ, which he thought insufficiently grand and not in harmony with the rest of the design. "I had painted it seven times and had overwrought my imagination and my feelings. In fact I over-did it; and like all overdoings it was weak." Haydon listened eagerly, however, to Scott's vigorous insistence that he could make a good deal of money by exhibiting the canvas at Edinburgh.[88]

An early caller in Piccadilly was Allan Cunningham, who brought a request from Francis Chantrey that Scott pose for a bust. The following morning sittings began in the sculptor's studio in Ecclestone Street.[89] Chantrey wanted to show Scott in a poetic mood and began modeling his head as looking gravely upward. But the next morning he invited Scott to breakfast first. Richard Heber was there with some other acquaintances, and the two old friends became so mirthful that Scott's eyes twinkled ever brighter with laughter. "This will never do," Chantrey said privately to Cunningham. "I must try his conversational look, take him when about to break into some sly funny old story." He altered the pose of the head and touched the eyes and mouth slightly; when Scott came for the third sitting he smiled at the changes the artist had made. "Ay, ye're mair like yoursel now!" he exclaimed. "Why, Mr. Chantrey, no witch of old ever performed such cantraips with clay as this."[90]

In the midst of these sittings the King returned from Brighton and Scott prepared to present himself at the Levee for the ceremony of kissing hands. Cunningham found him in court dress, stiff coat, gleaming buttons and buckles, lace ruffles, queue, sword, and cocked hat, and could not help smiling. Scott looked at himself in the glass, and burst into laughter. "O Allan," he said, "what creatures we make of ourselves in obedience to Madame Etiquette! See'st thou not, I say, what a deformed thief this fashion is?—how giddily she turns about all the hot-bloods between fourteen and five-and-thirty?"[91]

The King welcomed Scott graciously, would hardly permit him to kneel, and shook hands with him repeatedly. "I shall always reflect with pleasure," he observed, "on Sir Walter Scott's having been the first creation of my reign."[92] Scott felt entertained at the electric transformation these words made in the royal entourage. "The fun was," as he remarked later, "that the folks in waiting who, I suppose, had not augurd any mighty things of my exterior, seeing me so well received, made me about five hundred scrapes and congees as I retired in all this grandeur of a favoured courtier."[93] In general, however, he did not feel that the dignity "inflicted" on him made the least difference. "Servants bow two inches lower, a door opens three inches wider, and there it rests except that in Scotland my degree places me among the old ladies at the head of the table and obliges me to carve, at which office I am very awkward and regret the old days of chivalry when this labour devolved upon the Esquires."[94]

Meanwhile, in Scotland, Lockhart was on yeomanry duty and Sophia was playgoing with Lady Scott in Edinburgh. "Mr. Raymond and I," she wrote her lover demurely, "were the best of friends possible during the whole evening. (You had better return quickly.) He has persuaded Mamma to take a box for his play, and offers to delay bringing it out till her return from the country . . ." Lady Scott, in fact, took the box for two successive nights, Sophia resumed later, "and as her Ladyship purposes to remain till the curtain drops both nights, I think we shall both have enough of Liston."[95]

Lockhart himself was involved in a more vital drama. "On Wednesday evening," he wrote Sophia, "the greater part of the roads leading from Glasgow were in the hands of the Radicals, and various places of encampment in the neighborhood were resorted to by the weavers from the villages. The drum was beat, such was their audacity, within a mile of the Barracks. But on the whole, the arrival of so many broad-backed Yeomen, etc., had the effect of chilling the ardour of all but the very hottest . . . The numerous executions which must occur in a very few weeks" might be expected to freeze the blood of the insurgents further, "but meantime . . . there is no prospect of entire tranquillity."[96]

Presently, though, Lockhart returned to Edinburgh, only to find that Sophia was at Abbotsford. "I don't remember being so downcast for a while—however as Bailie Jarvie hath it there's a braw time coming— On Friday we meet, my dearest, I trust to part no more . . . I found lying on my table another long letter from the Baronet in which he communicates his approbation of our arrangements for going into Perthshire &c I have settled everything so that you shall be sure of good quarters & the country you know is beautiful in the highest degree. We shall stay if you please over 2 days at Perth & see Scone & the other Lions in that neighborhood—then go to Crieff for a day & look at Drummond Castle—then to Stirling . . ."[97]

Sir Walter's stay in London was now fast coming to an end. He spent a Sunday at Ditton with Lord Montague and on his way back to town saw his "young Chief," Duke Walter, at Eton.[98] He and his own young Walter went to Woolwich in the Admiralty Barge, shooting the swift tide between the stone piers of London Bridge, inspected the Works, and enjoyed a grand nocturnal display of Congreve rockets, not getting back to town till one o'clock.[99] Scott witnessed the last day of the trial "of that bloody dog Thistlewood," the leader of the Cato Street conspirators who had tried to assassinate the Cabinet. "Ings the butcher was to have the heads and plucks of lords Castlereagh and Sidmouth for his fee, and he had his bags ready to carry them off in, and a large knife to amputate them."[100] In Strafford Place, Scott dined with Lady Abercorn and the Bishop of London,[101] and on the Saturday before his departure had a tête-à-tête breakfast with Lord Melville.[102]

"I wrote wishing to know what I could bring Anne and you & Mamma down that would be acceptable," he had told Sophia. "To little Charles also I promised something and I wish to know what he would like." There was jewelry for the bride from various friends, including a beautiful necklace from Lady Compton. "I think you will be quite an Indian princess, so instead of adding to your trinkets I send you on the other side a cheque for £50 for pocket money &c, which you will find convenient in your new situation."[103]

On Monday, April 24, he and Walter set out for Scotland, bowling along in the stagecoach with such speed that they reached Edinburgh on Thursday night.[104] Next day he was up and out of the house early; he had learned in London that John Ballantyne was ill, and he was worried about the little man.[105] "This ought to be the proudest day of my life," John recorded in his *Diary*. "Sir Walter Scott returned from London last night, full of fame and dignity, & made his *first* call on me this morning at Trinity Grove. Plain, simple & unaffected as ever; his friendship 'like an elder brother's love' (and how much more effectual!) was balm to my heart. What ought I *not* to do for this man!"[106]

Castle Street was already in a turmoil of preparation for the wedding. The drawing room, with its beautiful gray-green Empire sofa, was to be the scene of the ceremony. It took place, *more Scotico*, on the evening of April 29.[107] Walter made a brilliant figure in his bright hussar uniform, though his dignity was somewhat affronted by his father's suggestion that his mustache might be rendered more impressive by a touch of burnt cork.[108] Sophia looked delicately appealing, her dark hair and blue eyes contrasting with her clear, fair complexion beneath the veil of Flanders lace. Lockhart was serious and handsome with his grave hidalgo face.[109]

The house seemed lonely when the two young people had left for their honeymoon. But Scott felt that he had "consulted her happiness in the match, as became the father of a most attached and dutiful daughter who never in her life gave me five minutes' vexation. In the meanwhile the words run strangely in my ear

> "Ah me! the flower and blossom of my house
> The wind has blown away to other towers.

. . . They make rather a pretty couple & as they marry for love & with very fair prospects their present lot seems to be enviable. . . . I suppose by-and-by some kind suitor will carry off my black-eyed maid and then the old folks will be lonely enough."[110]

# 11

## The Rome of Augustus

### ( 1 8 2 0 )

T HE SUMMER OF 1820, however, proved far from lonely. Mrs. Maclean Clephane and her daughter Williamina turned up in Edinburgh, and Sir Walter hastened to invite them to dinner with a Polish countess "said to be superbly skilled in her native music."[1] On May 12, Lockhart and Sophia returned from their honeymoon, joining the family for a weekend at Abbotsford[2] and settling down afterwards in their Great King Street lodgings, only a little north of the Queen Street Gardens and less than a half-mile from Castle Street. For three days near the end of the month Sir Walter and Lady Scott entertained Prince Gustavus Vasa of Sweden at Abbotsford, asking the Scotts of Gala and the James Skenes to be of the party.[3] When the Prince took his leave he presented as a gift a seal engraved with Scott's coat of arms, "all our new blazonries," Scott wrote Walter, "cut on a fine amethyst and . . . on one side of the setting my name on the other the prince's—Gustaf."[4]

Scott had added to his property by purchasing for £2,300 some land he called "Heiton's grounds," which adjourned the Burnfoot cottage that was to be the Lockharts' summer home.[5] This beautiful bit of woodland, with its growth of firs in which blackcocks roosted, rounded out his lands so that they now, he told his son, "march with the Duke of Buccleuch all the way round that corner."[6] He had a fine plan for making the cottage itself snug and comfortable; it would cost over £500, but even if Lockhart were called elsewhere it would "make a useful farmhouse on the estate" and could be rented with the land around it for £200–£300 a year.[7] Trying to get the work on the cottage done, Scott spent a good deal of June "scambling back and forth" between Edinburgh and Abbotsford.[8]

There were also his court labors, which could not be scamped, and *The Abbot* to be completed. Lord Archibald Hamilton was reported to have complained in Parliament that Walter Scott wrote more books than any other man could read.[9] "His Lordship is greatly mistaken," Scott wrote Lady Abercorn tartly, "if he supposes that I neglect any part of my official duties"; on the contrary, he had often discharged not merely his own but those of his colleagues when they were ill. And as to how he employed his leisure hours, that was none of Lord Archie's business.[10]

"I really believe," her Ladyship replied, "party will make people do or say anything."[11] She was by now one of the favored circle admitted to the "secret" and was eagerly awaiting the new novel, of which rumor said that he had already completed the first volume. This report, he responded, was "quite erroneous unless the Second Sight be as common among the literati in London as it used formerly to be in the Hebrides." The truth was that "not above one half is written, so much have family affairs interfered with my literary amusements."[12]

At Lady Abercorn's request, Scott was also sitting for his portrait to an artist named John Watson. "If I look a little sleepy," he told her, "your kindness must excuse it, as I had to make my attendance on the man of colours betwixt six and seven in the morning."[13] "The dog which I am represented as holding in my arms"—little Urisk—"is a Highland terrier from Kintail, of a breed very sensible, very faithful, and very ill-natured. It sometimes tires or pretends to do so when I am on horseback and whines to be taken up, when it sits before me like a child without any assistance." His large wolf-greyhound Maida, he added, was weary of being painted; he had "sate to so many artists that whenever he sees brushes & a pallet he gets up and leaves the room."[14]

In consequence of all these employments, when Oxford and Cambridge simultaneously offered Scott honorary degrees, he found it impossible to journey southward to receive them. His friend Heber wrote that he was constantly pressed by the Vice-Chancellor of Oxford and other members of the University to bring Scott there so that they might testify "their respect & good will, by conferring upon you the honorary degree of LL.D. in full convocation in the Theatre on the 14 of June"; and added cajolingly that if Scott came, "I will promise faithfully to join you then, & afterwards, if you wish it, to accompany you to Cambridge on the same errand on the 2d & 3d of July."[15] But Scott felt reluctantly obliged to refuse.[16]

Though too busy to leave Scotland, he made time to give comfort and counsel to his numerous tail of dependents and henchmen. George Huntly Gordon, who had been his amanuensis the previous year, was finding his deafness a serious obstacle to earning a livelihood. In addition he was ill and for some time had been forlornly in love. "I can give no better consolation," Scott wrote, "than in the worn-out and wearying word, patience." Hard as it might be, Gordon should force himself to realize that "scarce one person in twenty marries his first love, and scarce one out of twenty of the remainder has cause to rejoice for having done so. What we love in those early days is generally rather a fanciful creation of our own than a reality. We build statues of snow, and weep when they melt."[17]

The words are among those rare and almost secret allusions that Scott makes to the deep wound of his own love for Green Mantle, now ten years in her grave. Had he come to feel that she had been only an entrancing phantasm of his imagination? a statue of snow, that had melted in the heat of the long day's laborious reality? But though that may well have been the verdict of maturity and though his marriage to Charlotte had brought abundant happiness, the crack that he had riveted together in his heart, as he was later to record, would remain to his dying day. Even here, in the bright noonday of honor and felicity, it haunts the only unavailing consolation he can give to the despair of youthful love.

For John Ballantyne he had more practical but hardly more fruitful counsel—to take better care of his health. John had recovered sufficiently to set out for London but had worsened on the trip, and despite that, "like an egregious fool," as he himself recorded, had traveled outside on the coach from Lowestoft. He arrived in pain, with his "voice gone" and a "dreadful pulse." Nevertheless he went to Epsom for the Derby and exposed himself in a driving rain. A party and "6 or 8 glasses of wine" completed the damage: he was confined to bed, where he was "blistered on the back" and suffered agonies. On Scott's advice he consulted Dr. Baillie, who told him that though his throat was bad his heart and lungs were sound, and that "care and sobriety would alleviate and finally cure" his ailments.[18]

"The words . . . chiefly to be insisted on," Scott repeated, "are *with care*. For, my good friend, you do *not* take care—at least not when any immediate prospect of fun or frolic crosses you . . . Have a little patience and be ennuyé for a few weeks or months, as becomes an invalid who wishes to get well, and your constitution will lose the habit of the disease and you may return to any prudent enjoyment of your habits of exercise. . . . I know the practice is very difficult, for the fidgetty, irritable state of a convalescent is more difficult to manage than the depressed feeling & habits of an actual invalid . . . But health is the jewel sans prix and we must do all to recover it."[19]

Scott's own health now continued "quite firm," as he wrote his brother Tom, "at no greater sacrifice than bidding adieu to our old and faithful friend John Barleycorn, whose life-blood has become a little too heavy for my stomach." Then followed a budget of news: his own "*petit titre*," Sophia's marriage to Lockhart, the cottage he was preparing for them, how handsome Walter was in his military uniform.[20]

"After my own sons, my most earnest and anxious wish will be, of course, for yours . . . and whatever line of life you may design him for, it is scarce possible but that I can be of considerable use to him." If Tom's youngster Walter, who was now thirteen, proved studious, and good at figures, it might be well to make him an accountant, a highly respectable and well-paying profession. But not if he was active, high-spirited, and adventurous; ". . . you will never be able to convert such a sword into a pruning-hook." This was why Scott had not sent his own Walter to the Bar; he would only have spoiled "an excellent soldier to make a poor and undistinguished gownsman."[21]

Let Tom therefore decide, and meanwhile put the boy under his care in Edinburgh: "I will do all that is in my power to stand in the place of a father to him." Should he seem fitted for a military life, "I think I can promise to get him a cadetship in the East-India Company's service; as soon as he has had the necessary education, I will be at the expense of his equipment and passage-money . . ." Once in India, he would thus be assured a good income, and have a great chance of a fortune. "I am aware this would be a hard pull at Mrs. Scott's feelings and yours; but recollect, your fortune is small, and the demands upon it numerous, and pagodas and rupees are no bad things."[22]

Lockhart's friend Wilson also needed Scott's help. His candidacy for the Chair of Moral Philosophy, as Scott had predicted, was running into stormy weather. His principal opponent, Sir William Hamilton, though then little known, was a distinguished philosopher; Wilson's own claims to be a philosopher of any kind, his foes derisively hooted, were of the most tenuous.[23] Scandalous imputations were smeared; the Whigs said, quite falsely, that he was a blasphemer and a bad husband and father, and, perhaps more plausibly, that while drunk he had sung an indecent song in a public tavern.[24] Wilson grew hysterically anguished; his skin was as sensitive as his own vituperations were violent.[25]

But the Tories generally supported him, Scott's friend David Hume defeated an attempt to pass a resolution against him in the Academic Senate, and Scott defended his character and intellectual powers in a letter to the Lord Provost. "I should have conceived myself guilty of a very great crime," he wrote, "had I been capable of recommending to the Moral Philosophy Chair, a Scoffer at Religion or a libertine in morals."[26]

The struggle, however, in fact had little to do with either ability or morals; it was a fight of Tories and Whigs. "It is odd," Scott said belligerently, "the rage these gentlemen have for superintending education. They consider it as their own province and set their mark on it as Sancho did on the cow-heel—Then their geese are all swans and the tory swans are all geese and they puff the one and slander the other without mood or mercy. But we gave them a day's kemping for once and carried the election by 21 against eight. I was obliged to canvass personally and stoutly among the Bailies and Deacons, and if Wilson fulfills the high promise which his talents and eloquence have made . . . I shall think I have done both Edinburgh and literature some service."[27]

Scott seized the occasion to read Lockhart another emphatic lesson on the dangers of personal satire. Especially in view of "the mean objects on whom" it was wasted, it was "like a gentleman fighting with a chimney sweeper—he may lick him, but cannot avoid being smutted in the conflict."[28] Such behavior was perhaps excusable "as a frolic of young men" but if persisted in would "fritter away your talents, hurt your reputation both as a lawyer and a literary man, and waste away your time in what at best will be but a monthly wonder."[29] Let Lockhart withdraw from *Blackwood's* blackguard skirmishing and instead employ his "wit and wisdom on general national topics," bestowing "deserved correction on opinions rather than men," and he could not but do his country "yeoman's service."[30]

To these strictures his son-in-law replied with serious and grateful agreement. He was sure Wilson realized that the responsibilities of his new dignity dictated his dropping all connection with the warfare of party politics, and "I am not so great a fool as to covet a single-handed post of that sort."[31] Wilson also expressed "deep and everlasting gratitude." "With every thing you say in your letter, *respecting retaliation*, I do most deeply sympathize. Your will is Law. My kind Friend Lockhart requested me to tell you that he too intended to leave the Beasts in their own mire . . ."[32]

In the middle of August a letter came from Washington Irving saying he had taken the liberty of dedicating a second volume of *The Sketch Book* to Scott; "the last sheet was going to the press, and I could not resist the impulse to express simply but honestly the feelings of my heart. . . . In the last number of *Blackwood* I perceive a very flattering notice of my *Knickerbocker*, which I presume is from the pen of Mr. Lockhart. I feel very sensible of the warm and friendly feeling that shines through his writing, and which induces him to give me more praise than even my vanity as an author can admit."[33]

Through all these interchanges, Scott was pressing forward daily on *The Abbott*. "Mr. Erskine . . . has seen the sheets of Vol. I," Lockhart wrote him, "& agrees with me perfectly that it at least equals *Waverley*, *Ivanhoe*, & *The Antiquary*."[34] "I hope it will do," Scott replied, "and am greatly encouraged by your sentiments and Erskine's. James Ballantyne, a good specimen of a certain class of readers, likes the second volume better than the first—So *Vogue la galère*."[35] James evidently felt, however, that part of the narrative was too longwinded; "What you say of the Episode," Scott agreed, "is very true but I do not like to cut the train of Queen Mary's vestment."[36] On August 1, "This matter is now very nigh done," he reported to James; "you will receive a dozen more pages on your return, so you may crush on boldly" with the printing.[37]

On the tenth, "The Great A is so far as I am concernd finishd within a days work," he wrote Constable exultantly, "and the press labouring hard."[38] Finally, by August 20, "I intend to set toughly and instantly to work" on *Kenilworth* "so soon as September commences."[39]

In the course of the summer Scott had filled Abbotsford with guests. "Abbotsford is no more like the Abbotsford you knew," he wrote Morritt enticingly, "than the Rome of Augustus was like the Rome of Numa. We have plenty of little pigeon holes of bedrooms, plenty of mutton on the hill & beef in the park & salmon and hares and grouse & poultry and so forth. And a parlour to eat them in, the model of which I take to have [been] Mr. Slender's own great chamber, which he makes the subject of asseveration when confirming his complaint against Falstaff."[40]

Responding to this invitation, Morritt arrived on August 15.[41] Lockhart returned from the Western Circuit, bringing Sophia with him, and since their cottage was still far from ready, they were stowed away in one of the little pigeon holes.[42] William Stewart Rose was there, with his eccentric servant Hinves,[43] "his clown," as Scott called him, "my old acquaintance Caliban."[44] In the party too were the actor Charles Young, together with Sir Humphry Davy,[45] and the venerable Henry Mackenzie, "The Man of Feeling," now in his seventy-sixth year but still hale.[46] Scott was momently hoping for the appearance of his old friend Heber, though "his movements are cruelly uncertain." When anyone drew up at the door early in the morning, Scott exclaimed, "There comes Heber after having travelld all night in the Selkirk mail."[47]

Rose and Davy were both impassioned anglers and set out almost daily for Lord Somerville's preserve under the guidance of Tom Purdie's brother Charlie, the most celebrated fisherman of the neighborhood. Rose on his *shelty*, armed with salmon rod and landing net, Davy in jack boots like a Dutch smuggler, fustian jacket dabbled with the blood of salmon, and a brown hat stuck full of fly hooks, the two men waded and cast all day long.[48] When the fishing party was larger it might wind up for a picnic banquet, boiled, grilled, and roasted, beneath a grand old ash arching over Charlie's cottage at Boldside, lasting often till the harvest moon shone on the banks of the Tweed. Sometimes the evening closed with a "burning of the waters." Though the Sheriff was not so agile as in his Ashestiel days, he was sure to be in the boat, holding a torch or taking the helm, exulting in the ruddy blaze striking flakes of light from the dark water and shining from the fiery spears.[49]

One clear September morning the party mustered on the porch after breakfast for a coursing match on Newark Hill. Only Rose remained faithful to fishing; even Davy joined them on a sudden impulse. Adam Ferguson had ridden over from Huntly Burn, and Laidlaw from Kaeside, his long legs almost touching the ground as he sat astride Hoddin Grey, his wiry Highlander. Mackenzie, in long brown leather gaiters, green jacket, and gleaming green spectacles, his locks even whiter than his white hat, but eager as a boy, was with difficulty persuaded to resign his steed to his Negro servant and ride with Lady Scott in the sociable. Tom Purdie had already gone ahead with all the greyhounds, but Maida gamboled about Sir Walter as, mounted on Sybil Grey, he flourished his huge hunting-whip.[50]

The cavalcade was just about to set out when Anne, screaming with laughter, broke from the line, crying, "Papa, papa, I knew you could never think of going without your pet." It was a little black pig who had become sentimentally attached to her father and who constantly tried to join the greyhounds and terriers, frisking about his pony. Poor piggy was dragged back with a strap around his neck; Scott cracked his whip at the creature, half-embarrassed at this ludicrous devotion, and tried to look stern, but was obliged to burst into a laugh. Watching the animal's reluctant withdrawal, he recited with mock pathos:

> What will I do gin my hoggie die?
>     My joy, my pride, my hoggie!
> My only beast, I had nae mae,
>     And wow! but I was vogie![51]

At Newark Hill, Lady Scott and Sophia unpacked the picnic basket from the carriage on the mossy rocks overhanging the Yarrow. After lunch Mackenzie mounted his pony; Scott marshaled the hunt in a broad line ascending the heather toward Blackandro. Davy, with glowing eyes, exclaimed, "Good heavens! is it thus that I visit the scenery of *The Lay of the Last Minstrel?*" and muttered to himself—

> "But still,
> When summer smiled on sweet Bowhill,
> And July's eve, with balmy breath,
> Waved the blue-bells on Newark Heath"[52]

Mackenzie saw the first sitting hare, shouted to slip the dogs, and spurred after them. Puss doubled down the steep, nags stuck fast in the bogs, riders tumbled in the peat hags. Sir Humphry plunged neck-deep in a treacherous wellhead that had seemed solid green turf; when he clambered out, smeared with slime and mangled watercress, Sir Walter triumphantly shouted, "Encore!" But soon after, in a brisk gallop, Scott put Sybil Grey to a leap beyond her powers and tumbled in a ditch while Davy cleared him at a bound. He scrambled up, unhurt, however, and resumed the chase.[53]

Scott and Davy enormously enjoyed each other's company; "the modesty of their mutual admiration," Lockhart remarks, "was a memorable spectacle." Each strove to make the other talk, Davy delighting in Scott's picturesque stories and Scott in the clear imagery and eloquence of Davy's scientific knowledge. One night, when their "rapt talk" had kept a circle round the fire till long past bedtime, "Gude preserve us!" Laidlaw whispered to Lockhart, "this is a very superior occasion! Eh, sirs," he added innocently, cocking his eye like a bird, "I wonder if Shakespeare and Bacon ever met to screw each other up?"[54]

Despite guests and gallops after hares, Scott was now getting on with *Kenilworth*. John Nichols's *Progresses and Public Processions of Queen Elizabeth*, he wrote Constable, were doing him "yeoman's service, for I am in *progress* myself. . . . What was the name of Dudley Earl of Leicester's first wife, whom he was supposed to have murdered at Cumnor Hall? I know it occurs in the Sidney Papers, and probably in the common genealogies, but I have no book here which contains the information. In Lyson's *Magna Britannia*, or some such name, there is something about this same Cumnor Hall. I wish you would have it copied out for me, and should like indeed to know anything that occurs to you about this same village of Cumnor, its situation, etc. I like to be as minutely local as possible."[55]

He was also eager to have Brady's *Clavis Calendaria*, an account of the calendar and the customs on saints' days and other holidays,[56] and welcomed Constable's offer of Ashmole's *Antiquities of Berkshire*. "I am advancing fast," he reported, "and with some confidence. I have littel doubt we will be out by Xmas. *Ivanhoe*"—which Constable had proposed reprinting—"may go to press whenever you have a mind. I will write to Ballantyne about it."[57]

*The Abbot* had been published on September 2.[58] Scott himself thought he had retrieved the ground he had lost in *The Monastery* and was glad he had not allowed the sixteenth century to defeat him; in the copy he sent Lockhart he inserted a slip of paper with a couplet whimsically glancing at his obstinate refusal to abandon what had seemed a barren subject:

> Up he rose in a funk, lapped a toothful of brandy,
> And *to it* again!—any odds upon Sandy![59]

Readers agreed with him, liked his heroine, Catherine Seyton, found deep pathos in the story of Queen Mary's captivity and escape, and flocked to Lochleven almost as years before *Marmion* had brought sightseers to Flodden and *The Lady of the Lake* had drawn vacationers to Loch Katrine and Ellen's Isle.[60]

"Some wise mortals," wrote Lady Louisa Stuart in amusement, "will have it that you wrote *The Abbot* to defend" George IV's estranged Queen, Caroline, "and see her pictured in poor Mary . . . But I forget— *The Abbot*, &c., are not yours; that point is cleared up. A lady, who has taken real pains to get at the truth, assures me your sister in law is certainly the author, a cousin of hers (Mrs. S's) fairly acknowledged it to herself. I begged to know the cousin's precise words. 'Why; on being asked the question she smiled and supposed Time would show; was not this owning it?' You may believe I submitted."[61]

"Whoever wrote *The Abbot* may be satisfied with its success, which was so compleat that it sent its readers back to *The Monastery*, and forced them to see the merits they had denied before. A secret triumph for me. Not that I liked this latter as well as *Waverley* and some of the others; but I thought it had a full share of what is in my mind the principal charm of them all—masterly touches of character. Mr. Morritt whispers the name of Kenilworth Castle; and with Mr. Sneer in *The Critic*, 'hopes no scandal of Q. Elizabeth?' I hope so to . . . ."[62]

"I do not design any scandel about Queen Bess whom I much admire," replied Scott, "altho' like an old *true-blue* I have malice against her on Queen Mary's account—But I think I shall be very fair—the story is a tragedy of Leicester's first wife and I have made it as far as my faculties would permit 'a pleasant tragedy stuffed with most pitiful mirth'—The mournful termination is certainly an objection to the general reader and may hurt its popularity."[63]

For all his whispered knowledge of *Kenilworth*, on September 12 Morritt had not yet seen the current novel and was clamoring for a copy. "Pray desire the anonymous author of *The Abbot*," he pleaded, "to send me his cargo to Rokeby, as *The Monastery* was left at my house in London, & if *The Abbot* is sent to the same place he will fall into the hands of a dainty widow to whom I let my house till next January & who will not know what to make of him. . . . *The Abbot* I hear is extremely popular, & two or three of my correspondents are in raptures with it. I long for the book because till I get it I dare not talk about it, as I shd betray more knowledge than I chuse to account for. I would buy it directly, but having by that means found myself in the possession of not a few duplicates of the author's other works I think this time I will wait till I get my copy; as I am often twitted with questions of how I come by my duplicates. I thot Queen Mary would take, & I rejoice in my sagacity. You understand Queens well . . .

"I have been all morning pulling about my pictures & hanging them in new positions to make room for [my] fine picture of Venus's backside by Velasquez, which I have at length exalted over my chimneypiece in the library. It is an admirable light for the painting & shews it in perfection, whilst by raising the said backside to a considerable height the ladies may avert their downcast eyes without difficulty, & connoisseurs steal a glance with drawing in the said posteriors as a part of the company."[64]

Reviewers gave *The Abbot* a mixed reception. The *Edinburgh* was predominantly captious. The title, it said, was bad, the Abbot having little to do in the book; the Popish zealots were "very tiresome personages"; Catherine Seytoun, "a wilful deterioration of Diana Vernon," was "far too pert and confident"; and Roland Graeme "little better than a blackguard boy." On the other hand, Catherine had "grand passages of enthusiasm and devoted courage," the escape from Lochleven was handled "with great effect and spirit," and the muster and battle of Langside were "full of life and colouring."[65] The *Quarterly* glowed enthusiasm. "Queen Mary . . . has at last fallen into the hands of an author that deserves her." Catherine Seytoun was "bewitching" in her "arch buoyance." "And the loves of Catherine and Roland are most skilfully interwoven with the fate of their mistress. Never was a double plot better connected."[66] *Blackwood's* too was favorable. Queen Mary signing her abdication it found "the best scene, and next to that" George Douglas changing the keys of her prison.[67]

The boyish pertness that the *Edinburgh* reviewer scored in Catherine Seytoun may have been partly drawn from Scott's son Charles. Now almost fifteen, engaging and precocious, the youngster was also idle and more than a bit conceited. He was getting too much for poor George Thompson to handle, and the good Dominie was not enough either of a disciplinarian or of a classicist to direct his further education.[68] Scott had therefore been considering placing him under some more rigid tutor, perhaps at Glasgow, and consulted Lockhart for this purpose. Lockhart approached Professor Jardine, who held the Chair of Logic at the University of Glasgow, to see if he would take Charles into his home but confessed to Scott that he had doubts about the plan.[69]

"If Charles comes to Glasgow," he wrote, "the whole of his progress will depend, exactly as you seem to suspect, on his keeping quite out of the way of the gaieties of the place. If he is to *dance* he had better do so anywhere than in Glasgow—but temptations offered by the zealous hospitality of the Citizens and the unwearied vanities of their womankind are not such as many of the young strangers that once give way to them have resolution to resist afterwards . . . You would be surprised with the account I could give you of *Liaisons dangereuses* formed by young gentlemen attending Glasgow College within my own recollection."[70]

One of Lockhart's college friends at Balliol, John Williams, had become Vicar of Lampeter in Cardiganshire and the master of the Grammar School there. Now twenty-eight, he was an excellent scholar and of a strong and decisive character. Why not, Lockhart suggested, put Charles under the Reverend Mr. Williams?[71] This, in the course of the autumn, Scott arranged to do. "Do you think it would greatly inconvenience Mr. Cadell, " he asked, "to take Charles with him to London in a fortnight or three weeks hence . . . it would be the greatest possible favour to Lady Scott and myself to have him under Mr. Cadell's protection as far as London where he might be clapped into a coach for Wales."[72]

Cadell replied himself that he would cheerfully take Charles under his care and that Lady Scott might be assured of his watchful attention to his charge.[73] "Nothing can be kinder," Scott replied," than your offer, which Lady Scott and I accept most willingly although we are sensible that we put a great tax on your kindness . . . I believe you will find Charles a good humourd companion and as little restraint on your movements as his situation will admit of. We will be most happy if you will spend a day with us at Abbotsford before your departure."[74] On Sunday, October 15, accordingly, the youngster set out with Cadell, bearing letters to Richardson and Terry and one to Charles Dumergue asking him to provide the boy with quarters during the three or four days he would be staying in London.[75] "Charles was in high spirits," Scott wrote Walter. "Poor fellow! he will think of this house often before he sees it again."[76]

Charles arrived at Lampeter on November 3. "His Latin," wrote Mr. Williams, "is much superior to his Greek, but there are serious defects even in Latin. Like Garrick as described by Dr. Johnson, he guides his translation by his own preconceived idea rather than by the rules of grammar. He even told me with a grave face that he did not think an intimate acquaintance with grammar necessary for understanding an author. . . . He must be taught that knowledge and skill are not hereditary, whatever doubts there may be respecting talents. His imagination is very lively. . . . He lays down his principles with a most amusing dogmatism and his tone and manner bring back irresistibly to my mind the account which the Lausanne pastor gives of Gibbon about the same age."[77]

Doubtless, Scott had forgotten and Mr. Williams did not know that his pupil's father had acted upon the same notions when he was studying German in his own youth. But now, at forty-nine, he thought differently. "My dear boy Charles," he wrote affectionately, "Your letters made us all very happy and I trust you are now comfortably settled and plying your task hard. Mr. Williams will probably ground you more perfectly in the grammars of the classical languages than has hitherto been done and this you will at first find but dry work. But . . . a perfect knowledge of the classical languages has been fixd upon and not without good reason as the mark of a well educated young man and though people have scrambled into distinction without it, it is always with the greatest difficulty, just like climbing over a wall instead of giving your ticket at the door.[78]

"Perhaps you may think another proof of a youth's talents might have been adopted, but what good will arise from your thinking so if the general practice of society has fixd on this particular branch of knowledge as the criterion. Wheat or barley were as good grain I suppose as *sesamum* but it was only to *sesamum* that the talisman gave way and the rock opend . . . Besides the study of grammar, from its very asperities, is calculated to teach youth that patient labour which is necessary to the useful exertion of the understanding upon every other branch of knowledge, and your great deficiency is want of steadiness and of resolute application to the dry as well as the interesting parts of your learning."[79]

All that autumn the fun and flow of guests at Abbotsford was unceasing. Constable and his son David arrived on the very day of Charles's departure,[80] and, soon after, Mrs. Clephane with her two younger daughters Williamina and Anna Jane.[81] Then came Lord Morpeth's eldest son, "a promising young man," with Lord Ashley, later the seventh Earl of Shaftesbury, whom Scott found "an original."[82] Near the end of October he entertained Mrs. Clephane's older daughter Margaret and her husband Earl Compton.[83] Sir Walter was as fond of his former ward as he had always been, and he thought Lord Compton "an excellent & honourable man" but privately felt him a bit tedious. "Entre nous," he confessed to Morritt, "he sometimes tires me by a *petitesse* a sort of minuteness in his mode of reasoning and in his pursuits. He is born to be a splitter of hairs in argument and a gatherer of pebbles in science."[84]

At the same time Joanna Baillie was at Abbotsford with her sister. "I have long wished to see you together," Scott had written Lady Compton, "which is something of a compliment to both."[85] Seventeen-year-old Anne found Joanna a refreshing novelty; "No one," she said wickedly, "would ever guess by her behaviour that she was an authoress." Anne added a notation of the arrival of still other guests: "Sir Alexander Don and a great pack of people come here today; Mamma is quite tired of people, as we have never been alone all the summer."[86]

Through all these comings and goings Scott plugged steadily at *Kenilworth*. "I will be in town Monday sennight," he wrote James Ballantyne on November 5, "but I will send much copy before that. I am glad you like what is done but am most anxious you should give your opinion on Queen Bess."[87] Constable was also preparing to bring out a second edition of Scott's *Dryden*, and Scott was revising the *Life* for that purpose. "I cannot expect so curious a haul of new materials as I got for Swift," he wrote; "however, something may be done. I am very glad that this work, which cost me so much labour, is going to press again."[88]

Finally, John Ballantyne, who planned to retire from business as a bookseller and auctioneer within another two years, was reentering the publishing field with a series of inexpensive reprints to be called the *Novelists' Library*, for which Scott agreed to write introductory lives. The first of these, a life of Fielding, he completed in mid-November. "I see not why if Fielding succeed as it will," he wrote John, "you should not go on with the Novels. I will see you on Tuesday and expect to find you greatly mended, the recovery once begun is rapid but *beware* of cold—"[89]

On November 9 took place what had become a grand annual event, the Abbotsford Hunt,[90] attended by all the local farmers and gentry.

They coursed the whole of Huntly Wood and on to Halidon and Prieston. "Saw twelve hares and killed six," Scott wrote, "having very hard runs and tiring three brace of grews completely.[91] George Craig, the bank manager at Galashiels, was kicked by Adam Ferguson's horse and at first refused to let his boot be drawn off, "protesting that he would faint if he saw the bone of his leg sticking through the stocking." At length Gala and Sir Walter persuaded him and were relieved to find that the damage was not serious though the pain was severe. "Some thought," Scott said, that Craig's reluctance was "to exhibit his legs in their primitive and uncloathd simplicity" because they had "an unhappy resemblance to a pair of tongs."[92]

The whole company then, some twenty-five in number, dined at Abbotsford, with the Sheriff in the chair.[93] The feast was gargantuan— a baron of beef, roasted, at the foot of the table, a salted at the head, tureens of hare soup, hotchpotch, and cockieleekie, geese, turkeys, sucking pigs, a singed sheepshead, haggis, blackcocks and moorfowls, bushels of snipe, black puddings, white puddings, and pyramids of pancakes.[94]

The beverages were no less copious—ale throughout the meal, with port and sherry in no less profusion. Quaighs of Glenlivet were filled brimful and tossed off like water. Wine decanters made their rounds; then came clamorous cries for hot punch and toddy. Bowls appeared, and soon the Ettrick Shepherd, his face red and glowing, was stirring the steaming mixture. There followed stories and reminiscences, the Sheriff telling his richest tales of rural life, Adam Ferguson fighting his Peninsular campaigns over again. Sheriff-Substitute Shortreed sang "Dick o' the Cow," his son Thomas "The Twa Corbies," Hogg "The Kye comes hame." The Melrose doctor trolled some of Moore's ballads, a weatherbeaten, stiff-bearded veteran called Captain Ormistoun sang "Cowdenknowes," a couple of retired sailors joined in bellowing "Bould Admiral Duncan upon the high sea," and Ferguson crowned the last bowl with "Ale, good ale, thou art my darling."[95]

At last some farmer who had fifteen or twenty miles to ride home remembered that his wife would be getting sorely worried about the fords. Ears till then deaf to all but jolly shout and song heard Dumples and Hoddins neighing at the gate, and it was agreed that the hour had come for *deoch-an-dorris*—the stirrup cup, a bumper all round of *mountain dew*. Somehow, everyone got home safely, except for Hogg, who made a bet that he would jump over his wall-eyed pony and broke his nose in the leap. One comely goodwife amused Sir Walter the next time he passed her home, remote in the hills, by telling him her husband's words when he tumbled off his horse. "Ailie, my woman, I'm ready for my bed—and oh lass," he added gallantly, "I wish I could sleep for a towmont, for there's only ae thing in this warld worth living for, and that's the Abbotsford hunt!"[96]

# Less Sunshine

## ( 1 8 2 0 – 1 8 2 1 )

NOVEMBER 13 saw Scott's dwindled family back in Edinburgh for the winter. Charles, of course, was at Lampeter; Walter was with his regiment at Cork; and Sophia was settled into her new home in Great King Street, "as nicely and orderly . . . as if she had been a married woman these five years." Even the "canine establishment" in Castle Street was "reduced to little Ouri";[1] at the last minute Lady Scott's tiny spaniel, Finette, scandalized her mistress by refusing point-blank to follow the carriage, and remained at Abbotsford "to keep old *Mai* company."[2]

Near the end of the month Scott was elected President of the Royal Society of Edinburgh. Though at first he had modestly felt it somewhat incongruous for a man of letters to preside over such a body, when it was pointed out that the Society had a section for literature as well as one for science he willingly accepted the honor.[3] "You are mistaken," he told James Ballantyne," in supposing I disregard the sciences, but I am ignorant of them and have enough to do in my own department."[4]

It tickled Scott's feeling for the absurd, however, to pretend that he now spoke with the magisterial voice of the natural historian. "I would have you in future respect my opinion, in the matter of *chuckie-stanes*, caterpillars, fulminating powder, and all such wonderful works of nature," he jokingly wrote Laidlaw. "I feel the spirit coming on me, and never pass an old quarry without the desire to rake it like a cinder-sifter."[5] And, to Morritt, "Talking of science, hast any philosophy in thee, Morritt? If you have, now is the time to clear any doubts which may hang on your mind about geology, phrenology, or anything terminating in ology, for I am installd President of our northern Royal Society in place of Sir James Hall—

"And Log the second reigns like Log the first."[6]

At his inaugural meeting Scott rather startled the grave naturalists by speaking of the story of the Laidly Worm[7] and quoting some pompous nonsense of the charlatan Jenkinson, in *The Vicar of Wakefield*, on "the cosmogony of the world."[8] Following this, "mulld wine & punch were manufacturd and consumed according to the latest philosophical discoveries,"[9] and his presidency "took place with great eclat."[10]

The reign of George IV, which had begun the previous January, could hardly be described, even facetiously, as opening with éclat or in the least resembling that of King Log. Its first ten months had been, on the contrary, nothing but one prolonged and roaring scandal. George and his brothers, the Royal Dukes—except, perhaps, for the Duke of York—had long been unpopular in the entire nation. The King, above all, was despised as an unprincipled wastrel and libertine. His almost hysterical loathing for his wife, Caroline of Brunswick, provoked hoots of derision, which grew more rancorous with his endeavor to have her debarred from assuming the title of Queen, his insistence on a bill to dissolve the marriage, and the introduction in evidence of a green bag alleged to contain proofs that she had been guilty of carnal relations with her own courier Bergami.[11]

Hastening back from Italy to claim her place and deny these charges, the Queen was tumultuously cheered by crowds who thought her shamefully persecuted. The mob were sorry only that she had not brought her lover with her. In London they enthusiastically unhorsed her carriage and dragged it with yells and din past Carlton House. The Duke of Wellington, stopped by some road menders with pickaxes demanding that he remove his hat in her honor, replied, "Very well, gentlemen, since you will have it so, God save the Queen—and may all your wives be like her!"[12]

Scott's attitude toward these royal dissensions had changed since those early days when he had seen her as "an enchanting princess" and exclaimed that "her prince must labour under some malignant spell."[13] Even then, to be sure, he had been startled by the immodesty of her dress and the strange suggestiveness of her manner; now she was a rouged and shapeless figure with a scandalous reputation, appearing sometimes in a black wig with voluminous curls, sometimes in a leonine yellow mane, followed by a crew of raggle-taggle supporters.[14] Scott had no illusions about the character of the dissolute King, but little more doubt that the salacious details of the green bag were not much exaggerated.[15] What an inglorious spectacle it was that "the two first personages in the state" should "expose themselves in this extraordinary pas de deux"![16]

The Queen's hatred of her husband, Scott knew, was amply justified. Her fighting Brunswick blood had "courage enough to dare the worst, and a most decided desire to be revenged of him, which by the way, is scarce to be wondered at. If she had as many followers of high as of low degree (in proportion), and funds to equip them, I should not be surprised to see her fat bottom in a pair of buckskins, and at the head of an army—God mend all." The support of the Whigs was of course just part of the game of politics, the outs seizing any handy weapon against the ins. And as for the London mob, their shouts were like those that had greeted a certain lady of notorious frailty in the gallery of an Irish theater: "Huzza for Lady C—and long may she live to cuckold the Chancellor!"[17]

The Divorce Bill passed the Lords by only nine votes, a margin so narrow that, despite the King's anguished protests, the ministry withdrew it rather than face certain defeat in the Commons. The whole episode, as one cynical observer put it, amounted to declaring the Queen a whore and the King richly to deserve her.[18] But exultant throngs chose to take it as an exoneration of the Queen and roamed the streets wrecking the windows of householders who failed to display lighted candles in celebration of her victory. In Edinburgh as well as London there were riots; the painter Haydon, who had just arrived there, in accordance with Scott's suggestion, to display his *Christ's Entry into Jerusalem*, saw a roaring mob that, "after smashing all the glass right and left," surged away with beating drum into St. Andrew Square.[19]

In George Street the windows of Francis Jeffrey and the Marquis of Bute shone brilliantly. But Scott was one of those who refused to comply, though he had been threatened by letter. If anything worse than broken windows were attempted, he sent out warning, instead of taking it meekly he would "become as great a heathen as the Dey of Algiers." His house was passed over, though many others, he reported, "were terribl[y] *Cossaqués*, as was the phrase in Paris in 1814 and 1815." Damage of £1,000 was done; on the following night, wise after the event, the magistrates had a force on hand that put down every attempt at riot.[20]

News of these doings reached London in distorted newspaper reports of an attack on Abbotsford, with Sophia in trembling alarm and Lockhart heroically repelling the assailants. No such thing, Scott answered an inquiry from Morritt: "The Sutors of Selkirk never meditated the least injury to me or my dwelling nor was there the least disturbance or window-breaking . . . A much less acute genius than yours, my dear Morritt, will comprehend that Lockhart displayd no heroism because there was no room for it and that Sophia was not alarmd because he and I were in no danger, being residing quietly in Edinburgh when the alleged row at Abbotsford was affirmed to have taken place. She is, thank God, very well and I suppose will raise me to the venerable rank of a grand sire early in the spring.—I have only to add that if a set of madmen had . . . come four miles to attack my peaceful house I would have fired from window and battlement and kept my castle while my castle could keep me."[21]

Soon after Haydon's arrival in Edinburgh he called at Castle Street to pay his respects. Sir Walter stumped down the stairs, waving his stick from the first landing and crying, "Hurrah! welcome to Scotland, Haydon." Gripping the painter's hand in his own huge paw, he went on, "How d'ye like Edinburgh?" "It is the dream of a great artist," Haydon replied. "Well done," Sir Walter exclaimed. A few days later at dinner with Daniel Terry and William Allan, Haydon told Scott he had been climbing Salisbury Crags. "Ah," said Scott, "when I was a youth I have often sat there thinking of my prospects in life. It is a glorious place!" "Gad," Haydon thought to himself, "I remember that in one of the novels," and later relocated the passage in *The Heart of Mid-Lothian* where Reuben Butler, after escaping from the Porteous mob, looks out from the crag musing on his own future.[22]

The mob violence Haydon had witnessed was suppressed, but the partisan emotions aroused by the royal struggle continued to inflame the hostility of the Whigs and the Tories. The more radical Whigs had long been holding a small annual dinner to commemorate the birthday of their hero, Charles James Fox. Now they resolved to enlarge their 1821 celebration to a public banquet, though since some of them were members of Parliament and had to be at Westminster soon after the new year, they advanced the date from January 24, the actual day of the birthday, to January 12.[23] The Tories promptly countered by a gigantic feast in memory of *their* tutelary deity, William Pitt. These two rival festivities took place on the same evening. The Foxites managed to muster around five hundred; the Pittites, Scott proudly reported, more than eight hundred, "a tremendous multitude." It overflowed several banqueting rooms, Scott presiding in one holding two hundred and fifty, where he "gaind a headache of two days by roaring to them for five or six hours almost incessantly."[24]

In the midst of these political banquetings, *Kenilworth* made its appearance in the same luxurious format that had distinguished *Ivanhoe*. It was at once a spectacular success.[25] "The task of introducing Elizabeth," said the *Edinburgh Review*, "is not only fearlessly but admirably performed, and the character brought out, not only with the most unsparing fullness, but with the most brilliant and seducing effect. . . . The deep and disgusting guilt" of Varney's plottings against Amy Robsart and Leicester's temptation, unfolding in counterpoint with the glittering pageantry at Kenilworth Castle, "make a splendid passage of English history read like the Newgate Calendar."[26]

Though the *Quarterly* thought Elizabeth not as fine as *The Abbot*'s portrayal of Mary, still she was "vivid and magnificent"; Leicester was "the best picture extant of the old courtier of the Queen." The building up of the charges that burst upon Amy were superb. "We are unconscious of her danger, till Varney's rapid recapitulation lights the train."[27] The ending, however, as Scott had predicted, was felt to be too tragic. "The immediate circumstances of Amy's death, as she rushes to meet what she supposes to be her husband's signal, almost pass the limit that divides pity from horror."[28]

Scott's friends praised the story without qualification. "You know," wrote Morritt, "when I first heard that Queen Elizabeth was to be brought forward as the heroine of a novel how I trembled for her reputation. Well knowing your not over affectionate regard for that flower of maidenhood, I dreaded lest all her venerable admirers on this side of the Tweed would have been driven to despair . . . The author, however, has been so very fair and has allowed her so many of her real historical merits that I think he really has, like Squire Western, a fair right to demand that we should at least allow her to have been a bitch."[29]

Mrs. Hughes, the wife of a Canon of St. Paul's, told Scott that *Kenilworth* was creating a sensation in the neighborhood of Oxford. Hosts of pilgrims crowded to Cumnor Place, Lord Abingdon was reviled for having torn down the old mansion, the parish clerk was making a fortune by showing its site, and every child could point out the location of the staircase down which the unhappy Amy had fallen. The landlord of the Jolly Ringers had changed its name to the sign of "The Black Bear, by Giles Gosling," and village children, who devoutly believed in the legend of Wayland Smith, often visited his forge to hear the clink of his hammer.[30]

"Pray do not imagine," Mrs. Hughes wrote, "that I am making an attempt to raise the veil of mystery which covers the 'Great Unknown.' "[31] Nevertheless, "Who but Sir Walter Scott, who is so rich already in fame, could afford to let such a hoard of honour be unappropriated?—and could any mortal Man but one who is already so distinguished bear to see another person run away with so much distinction?—yet I can conceive the merry pleasure it must be thus to keep all the world in ignorance of a fact which they are so desirous to ascertain—it matters not, however, what *I* think: nothing but your producing the author in a bodily shape will convince the public."[32]

Scott was in exultant health and spirits and had already outlined in his mind a new book. On New Year's Day he had announced its title to John Ballantyne as *The Buccaneer*.[33] John, too, for all his persistent ill health, was feeling buoyant. He had advanced the date of his retirement and was giving up his auctioneering business just fifteen years from the day he had come to Edinburgh. "Through Sir Walter Scott, and Sir Walter Scott alone," he wrote, "I am now worth, at least, seven thousand pounds." Could anyone have told him, he asked, that he should have attained such prosperity, "*what* should I have thought?"[34]

Scott's warnings that Lockhart's satiric excesses would involve him in trouble were not long in being realized. The editor of *Baldwin's London Magazine*, a man named John Scott, penned a fierce attack on Lockhart, singling him out as the secret editor of *Blackwood's* and denouncing him as a virulent libeler. Lockhart demanded an apology; this John Scott refused to make unless Lockhart gave his word that he was not *Black-wood's* editor.[35]

The demand put Lockhart in an embarrassing position. Though he was not "the" editor of the magazine, he could not deny that he had assumed editorial functions, and some of his satire had the sting of a poisoned dagger. If he replied, at best he could only be evasive. Belligerence might be more effective; Lockhart hurried up to London determined to make John Scott either retract or exchange pistol shots. Lockhart's second, however, an old college friend named Christie, could not get John Scott even to accept Lockhart's challenge; for now he insisted that Lockhart must first disavow having derived money either directly or indirectly from the management of *Blackwood's*.[36]

In a way, however, the modified demand took some of the pressure off Lockhart. He drafted a careful public statement denying that he was the editor or manager of the magazine and affirming that he received no emolument from its management. But through some strange chance this crucial part of his declaration failed to be included in the printed copy sent to John Scott. The latter remained silent; after giving him some time to reply, Lockhart on the counsel of John Wilson Croker fired a last salvo taunting him as a liar, scoundrel, and coward, and returned triumphantly to Scotland.[37]

John Scott was discredited as a craven; what more was there to be said? Croker felt that Lockhart's "rascally antagonist" was "rolled in the mire,"[38] and Sir Walter tried to dismiss the whole affair as "a dish of skim'd milk," "a foolish scrape with a blackguard," who "blusterd when at a distance" and turned pusillanimous near at hand.[39] There were observers, though, Constable among them, who thought Lockhart rather than John Scott "in the mire." He had brazened matters out by a display of physical courage, but his only reply to Scott's charges had really been a quibble, for he had certainly shared in the editorial functions of *Blackwood's* and written some of its most offensive pieces. Had John Scott pressed these points, Constable thought, he would have had Lockhart "completely in the Corner."[40]

Still others believed Lockhart's hasty trip to London a feint based on the calculation that John Scott was a coward. This suspicion did Lockhart an injustice; he had gone to London prepared to fight. Even Lady Holland, a leading Whig hostess, and therefore "ill enough disposed" toward Lockhart, dismissed this rumor and said that little as he was a favorite of hers, there was no denying he "had done all a man of spirit could do."[41] But the affair was not over, and chance was to draw Sir Walter himself into its dénouement in London.

His fellow clerks in the Court of Session had asked him to go with Sir William Rae, who had been made Lord Advocate in 1819, to see through Parliament a bill partly designed to relieve them of the labor of signing in person the thousands of formal writs issued from their offices. There was no objection from any of their legal colleagues, but three of the Whig Commissioners, it was feared, might give some trouble, their plea being, Scott said, "The horse . . . has too little to do and so we will load him with stones to make him carry full weight of some kind or other."[42]

Besides this purpose, Scott desired to welcome and pay his respects to Mrs. Carpenter, the widow of Charlotte's brother Charles, who had at last arrived in England from Madras.[43] He left Edinburgh with some reluctance and uneasiness; for Sophia, now in the last two months of her pregnancy, had been suffering extreme pain from cramps. Laudanum gave her relief, but left her most of the day, she wrote Lockhart, "a useless half tipsy girl."[44] Though the doctors said she was in no danger, Scott felt a father's worries, and Charlotte decided that she must remain with Sophia. "I would otherwise," Scott explained to Mrs. Carpenter, "have brought her up as well as my youngest daughter."[45]

Just on the verge of Scott's departure, Robert Dundas, who had agreed to take his place at the Clerks' Table, came down with an attack of gout, "so that instead of leaving him to do my business I must remain to do his."[46] But after a few days' delay Scott was able to get off, and by February 11 he had reached London. Here he called on Mrs. Carpenter, whom he found in melancholy spirits and feeble health.[47] She was eager to meet her sister-in-law but could not stand the strain of a land journey; she would have to wait for mild weather and come to Scotland by sea. "You never saw a creature so exhausted."[48]

Her legal papers made it clear that the sum Scott's children would ultimately realize from Charles Carpenter's estate would not greatly exceed £20,000, little more than half what had been originally presumed but around what Scott had calculated in making Sophia's marriage settlement. "So she is about £5,000 poorer," he wrote Lockhart, "than she once had some reason to hope for, but I suppose it will make no great odds to her or you. You have not only independence but wealth in your power if you take the right road to it, but you must lay aside your frolics and gambades . . ."[49]

Scott had reason for this last remark, for the "gambade" involving John Scott was marching to a violent and bloody conclusion. The editor of the *London Magazine* had grown truculent again as soon as Lockhart had returned to Edinburgh. He found it very suspicious, he claimed, that Lockhart's published statement contained declarations not included in the copy sent him.[50] Lockhart's friend Christie, after consultation with Sir Walter, drafted a sharp reply to these insinuations. John Scott then fierily demanded from Christie a public statement that his remarks implied no disrespect to Lockhart's opponent. Christie interpreted this as a trick designed to enable John Scott to retreat without loss of face. When he refused, John Scott challenged him to a duel.[51]

The two men met by moonlight at Chalk Farm on the night of

February 16. In their first exchange Christie fired in the air, but his second, seeing that John Scott had taken careful aim, loudly protested this gesture. Next time, therefore, Christie also aimed his pistol; Scott was pierced through the stomach and fell to the ground. The surgeon he had brought with him gave one look at his wound and disappeared. Christie and his second carried the bleeding man to the inn and then escaped from the constables.[52] Both men went into hiding, making ready to cross over to Calais till John Scott's fate was known.[53]

For ten days the wounded man lay in a fever, wavering between life and death. Then his fever shot upward; on the night of February 27 he died.[54] Christie later returned from France and surrendered himself to trial. When it was established that John Scott had been the challenger and that Christie had fired his first shot in the air, the jury were glad of the excuse to bring in an acquittal.[55]

Sir Walter drew the appropriate moral to Lockhart. He and his son-in-law knew very well whose rash verbal excesses had lit the match to the fuse. If Lockhart were entangled in another such affair he would not again have the sympathy of either the public or his friends. "Do not *promise* but *act* and act at once and with positive determination. Blackwood has plenty of people to carry on his Magazine, but if it should drop I cannot think it fair to put the peace of a family and the life not only of yourself but of others in the balance . . ."[56]

Nor had Lockhart's name emerged unblemished. However unjustly, in the minds of the ill-disposed there lingered doubts of his courage and a stain of journalistic disingenuousness on his literary standing. In fighting with dirt, as Sir Walter had warned, he had been begrimed. The "Scorpion" had wounded himself with his own sting.

Despite Scott's own semi-involvement in this wretched business, he had not neglected the errand that had brought him and the Lord Advocate to London. He and Sir William had to be in almost daily consultation about the bill they were pressing through Parliament, and for the purpose, instead of staying with the Dumergues, Sir Walter was lodging with his boyhood friend at the Waterloo Hotel in Jermyn Street.[57]

Here, less than a week after their arrival, he received the news that on February 14 Sophia had given birth to a boy. Though the birth was an entire month premature, both she and the child were doing well. "I give you joy a hundred times . . ." Scott wrote Lockhart. "I am inexpressibly relieved on account of my dearest Sophia, who has had such a grievous time of it."[58] To Sophia herself he wrote tenderly, ". . . the best I can wish for you is that your little boy may prove the same dutiful and affectionate child which you have always been to me."

"Love to Lockhart," Scott's letter concluded, ". . . and give your bantling a kiss extraordinary for Grandpapa. I hope Mungo"—the Lockharts' dog—"approves of the child, for that is a serious point. There are no dogs in the Hotel where I lodge but a tolerably conversible cat who eats a mess of cream with me in the morning."[59] "I expect from your description," he wrote two weeks later, "quite a cherubim of a grand child though not I hope representing in voice those who we are told in the prayer book continually do cry."[60]

His early morning breakfasts with the cat were almost the only times Scott had to himself. The bust for which he had sat to Chantrey the previous year was now in marble, but the sculptor wished to chisel a few finishing touches and Scott had to give him a series of further sittings.[61] In addition came the fashionable portrait painter Sir Thomas Lawrence with the request that Scott sit to him. The King had charged him with painting the most distinguished men of the age to adorn the great gallery that was now in progress at Windsor Castle. His Majesty desired that of Sir Walter Scott to be the first among those who had attained the highest honors in literature and science. Scott was of course obliged to comply, but so crowded were his days that when Lawrence invited him to select an hour he chose seven in the morning.[62]

"The King has commanded me to sit to Sir Thomas Lawrence . . ." he wrote Laidlaw. "I want to have in Maida that there may be one handsome fellow in the party." Would Laidlaw therefore "take the picture in the little armoury (I mean the oil picture with Maida & Panick)," have John Swanston pack it in a box, and send it to London by the Carlisle mail. "With that and one or two sketches which are here the honest gentleman may be introduced."[63]

The artist was trying to portray what he regarded as his subject's "noblest look." Sir Walter, however, chatted away, telling comical stories, and could only with much difficulty be brought back to an expression of inspired solemnity. One morning a guest in the studio had so many amusing but blackguardly anecdotes about Richard Brinsley Sheridan that Scott felt ashamed of laughing so much; one might have said to Sheridan, he remarked, as Lord Braxfield once did to a culprit at the bar, "ye're a vera clever chiel', man, but ye wad be nane the waur o' a hanging." Lawrence soon found that the best strategy was to repeat a few lines from Campbell or Byron; Scott would take them up or cap them with something better, and then his face would fire, his eyes sparkle, and the painter would seize the inspired moment.[64]

Like Maida, however, Scott was finding it more and more tiresome to pose for artists. "My picture," he wrote Charlotte, "comes on and will be a grand thing but the sitting is a great bor[e]. Chantrey's bust is one of the finest things he ever did. It is quite the fashion to go to see it."[65]

Socially, Scott found himself so sought after that sometimes he lost track of his engagements. "Yesterday I forgot where I was to dine . . . fortunately an accident reminded me that my Amphitrion of the day was Lord Castlereagh. Were I to tell this in a stage coach or in company what a conceited puppy I would seem, yet the thing is literally true, as well as my receiving three blue ribbands and a marchioness in my hotel in the same day."[66] He dined with the Duke of Wellington, he spent two days at Ditton with Lord Montagu and the young Duke of Buccleuch, he was obliged to defer a breakfast with Heber and Sir George Beaumont and tell them he would come at ten o'clock instead, he was "coaxd by very pretty ladies" at late nocturnal parties.[67]

"My time," he wrote his cousin Lady Davy, "escapes like Water through an Egyptian Vase by a thousand pores and is lost . . ."[68] Nevertheless, he managed in odd minutes to amuse himself by writing a number of imaginary letters in a seventeenth-century manner imitated cleverly enough, he believed, to fool even the antiquarians. It would be fun, he thought, to publish such a series, presented as drawn from the archives of a noble family, and see how they would go. To get variety of style, he enlisted Morritt and Lady Louisa Stuart, both of whom were in town, to concoct further letters for the hoax.[69]

Throughout all his engagements he was assiduous in courteous attentions to Mrs. Carpenter, putting his carriage at her disposal, emerging himself from a sitting at Chantrey's to take her and Miss Hooke, her companion, "a little howdy dowdy ugly thing," to see the King's apartments at Carlton House, and warmly urging both of them to come with him when he returned to Scotland.[70] Mrs. Carpenter continues to know her own mind," he wrote Lockhart, "as little as your sucking baby and is very delicate without, I think, being in actual bad health. I am almost sure the exertion of the Northern journey would do her good, but of course I dare not press what she seems afraid of."[71]

On Scott's urging, Mrs. Carpenter was prevailed upon to consult Dr. Baillie, who agreed with her doctor that she "had no formd complaint" but suffered "from a weakness both of spirits and body" demanding great care. Only by slow stages might she "regain a state of feeble and invalid health."[72] The two doctors united in advising that she should not risk traveling north until May or June. Scott consequently decided that as soon as his Parliamentary business was concluded he would return to Scotland without her.[73]

As always when he had been in London for any considerable period of time, he was eager to be home among family and friends again. He was impatient, too, to see his first grandchild, and concerned about Sophia, who had not made as rapid a recovery from her confinement as had been hoped. There had been a return of the cramps from which she had suffered, though these were now yielding to treatment with the doses of calomel that he himself had found effective. Gradually the pains subsided, she was able to sleep without opiates, and began to regain strength and appetite.[74]

She must "get well as soon as possible," Scott charged, "and be in good looks when I come down, as I have been keeping company of late with the choice beauties of the age," he added playfully, "& do not like thin, yellow-looking people. Moreover I have been feasting with dukes &

cabinet ministers on turbot & champagne & do not know how I shall relish live oysters & gin & water."[75] Before the end of the month, "All in Edinr. are quite well," Scott was able to report to Walter, "& no fears saving those of little Catherine," Sophia's maid, "for the baby, lest the fairies take it away before the Christening."[76]

The cottage at Huntly Burn had now been christened Chiefswood and was almost ready to be moved into. The old gardener James Scott, known as Cock-a-pistol, was busy there transplanting shrubs from Abbotsford with Tom Purdie's help, and walls were being made ready to receive fruit trees.[77] William Atkinson had also provided Scott with "a delightful plan for the addition" which would replace the old Redford farmhouse when it was torn down, and give him "a handsome library" and Charlotte "a drawing room and better bedroom with a good bedroom for company."[78] Its only drawback was that the outside was "modern Gothic, a stile I hold to be equally false & foolish." Scott and Blore were consequently "at work to Scottify it by turning battlements into bartizans," and had struck out, he thought, a picturesque and appropriate design.[79]

The Court of Session bill finally cleared Parliament on March 26. Despite Scott's anxiety to be home, he stayed on in London a few days longer to consult the Duke of York about Walter's future.[80] The young man was eager to enhance his military knowledge and hoped that he might be admitted to the army training college at Sandhurst. Scott strongly approved of a plan that could make him an ornament to his profession and a useful servant to his country. There were so many applicants, however, that he might not be eligible to take the entrance examination till some time after he had been placed on the waiting list.[81]

The Duke responded with the most friendly encouragement. He would reflect, he said, on whether he could put Walter on the establishment "without any very violent infringement on the rules" and even hinted that in his case he might "make an exception to the rule of seniority of standing & priority of application . . . when an opportunity occurd."[82] Meanwhile, Scott pointed out, the young soldier would have time to work hard at mathematics, principles of fortification, drawing, and languages, so that he might pass the examinations with credit. Just as Scott was about to start north, on April 6, he was able to report to Walter that his name had been put on the list and that he should now make formal application for Sandhurst through Colonel Murray, his commanding officer.[83]

Instead of going by sea, as he had originally planned, Scott took the stagecoach, and after a cold, windy journey arrived at Edinburgh on the night of April 10. He found everyone well, though Sophia still looked peaked from her severe illness. He distributed to Charlotte, Sophia, and Anne a consignment of gifts Mrs. Carpenter had put in his hands, card cases, fans, and some magnificent Indian shawls that were greeted with cries of admiration,[84] and added some tokens of his own to show that he was a loving husband, "a loving papa," and a proud grandfather.[85]

His return plunged him into a turmoil of commitments almost as crowded as those he had left in London. His unfortunate cousin William Scott of Raeburn was seeking election as collector of taxes for Roxburghshire, the struggle was close, and Sir Walter loyally canvassed for him and wrote scores of letters in his support.[86] He attended the christening of his grandson, who was named John Hugh Lockhart. He was present at the marriage of Adam Ferguson, who after fifty years of bachelorhood had surprised everyone by suddenly proposing to a widow.[87]

Scott found the lady "a good humourd purpose-like body *of no particular age*" who seemed to be very fond of Adam. His old friend's behavior at the wedding, however, struck Scott as irresistibly ludicrous: "I assure you the like hath not been since the days of Lismahagow."[88] Adam, as comic in solemnity as in jest, advanced toward his bride "in a jaunty military step with a kind of leer on his face that seemd to quiz" the whole ceremony, mingling "a proper & becoming tenderness" with a "*dégagé* air of military gallantry . . . which was one of the greatest exhibitions I ever saw."[89] Sir Walter had all he could do to keep a straight face, but he loved the dear fellow, rejoiced in his happiness, and was pleased that when the hilarious Captain left his sisters and Huntly Burn he would be moving no farther than Gattonside.

Though Scott had been glad to get back to Edinburgh after the smoke and dirt of London, he was even happier, as soon as Adam was married, to remove himself to Abbotsford for the spring vacation. Here a letter reached him from Viscount Sidmouth, the Home Secretary, dealing with the proposed establishment of a Royal Society of Literature.[90] The project, of which Scott had heard the outline from the Honorable John Villiers, was partly modeled upon the Académie Française; its members were to be drawn from the ranks of the most distinguished men of letters, and it was to encourage neglected men of literary merit with stipends of £100 a year. Scott thought poorly of the entire scheme, but it was this last aspect that he criticized most sharply.[91]

"For such a work of genius as the plan proposes to remunerate with £100 any bookseller would give ten or twenty times that sum and for the work of an author of any eminence £3000 or £4000 is a very common recompense." The conventional image of genius starving despised in garrets Scott considered a sentimental phantasm; a man of any literary ability who wrote diligently could earn anywhere from £500 to £5,000 a year. Who, therefore, except talentless hacks would contend for a "petty prize where failure would be a sort of dishonor and where the honour acquired by success might be very doubtful"? It was true that sometimes through ill fortune or flaws of character men of genius failed to prosper. But these were few (though Coleridge was one), and such exceptions might better be aided by a gift from the royal bounty or a crown pension.[92]

The membership created other problems. Some men of talent would refuse to join; others, like Byron, Jeffrey, and Moore, Scott gathered, were to be excluded for reasons moral or political. The only eager contenders would be the plodders and "the obscure pedants of the universities," and few men of any literary reputation would choose to be associated with these. Not all the prestige of Louis XIV in the plenitude of his power had been able to lift the Académie Française above mediocrity. Nor would such a body, even assuming it could be assembled, function well in awarding prizes. The Lake School of poets had one set of artistic standards, the *Edinburgh* reviewers another, and so on for twenty more. In practice they would be united only in recognizing flaws, and the prizes would be given not to works of genius but to those respectable dullnesses that had the fewest defects, a class sufficiently numerous to need no encouragement from a literary society.[93]

With these objections Lord Sidmouth warmly concurred and earnestly asked Scott's permission to show them to the King. "It is very unfortunate, & provoking, that the liberal Disposition of the Sovereign should have been surprized, & most strange that no Communication should have been subsequently made to any of Those without whose Knowledge & Advice, I presume to say, no Decision should have been taken, or rather no Approval given."[94] "Whatever use can be made of my letter to stop the very ill-contrived project to which it relates," Scott replied, "will answer the purpose for which it was written. . . . At all events, his Majesty should get out of it; it is nonsense to say or suppose that any steps have been taken which, in such a matter, can or ought to be considered as irrevocable."[95]

The Royal Literary Society did come into existence but upon a scheme that was to a marked degree modified in accordance with Scott's criticisms. "I believe," Morritt wrote him, "you have succeeded completely in your object, by the masterly exposure of the vices inherent in such a Plan." Lord Sidmouth had also sounded out Morritt, "& I tried to do the State some service by expressing what I think must be the opinion of every man whose knowledge of the world is drawn from beyond the walls of a cloister or a garret, & who does not wish to see royal literature set up as a mark to be pelted with rotten eggs." The King was accordingly advised "to keep his name & patronage entirely out" of the matter, and "to let the Society (if it chuses) act by themselves as beneficent individuals working for the cultivation of middling poetry & dull prose."[96]

Morritt had been dilatory about supplying his contributions to the imaginary seventeenth-century letters. "Pray, my good Lord of Rokeby," Scott appealed, "be my very gracious good lord, and think of our private letters. . . . I hold you accountable for two or three academical epistles of the period, full of thumping quotations of Greek and Latin in order to explain what needs no explanation and fortify sentiments which are indisputable. . . . I must write to Lady Louisa for further contributions . . .[97]

London and the world of literature seemed far away as Scott jogged over to Chiefswood or observed with pleasure the growth of his plantations on Turnagain and the gray fowl and partridges nesting among their foliage.[98] His pleasure in his hills, however, was suddenly disrupted by the news that Walter's fellow officers had been behaving badly and that in punishment the 18th Hussars were being sent to India.[99] They had been at odds, Scott was told, with their commander; they had drunk seditious toasts and broken out into rebellious democratic sentiments destructive of army discipline.[100] There were still other grave irregularities, including the drunken introduction of a common prostitute into their regimental mess.

"I am desirous to learn from you," Scott sharply wrote his son, "a plain statement of this business without either palliation or suppression and also whether you had any accession to their proceedings." It was equally out of the question for Walter to go to India or remain in the 18th. If Scott found it impossible to effect an exchange to another regiment, Walter would have to go on half-pay for a time rather than continue "in a corps where the officers have so far forgot their character as gentlemen and soldiers."[101]

Walter himself—"the ass," Scott said—was excited at the prospect of going to India. He talked "of being absent for five or six years, when I will be bound not one of them will see British land again till their beards are grey."[102] Scott refused his consent. "You can get neither experience in your profession," he wrote Walter, "nor credit nor wealth nor anything but an obscure death in storming some hill fort of some Rajah with an unpronounceable name. . . . You are much mistaken if you suppose promotion goes on fast in the East . . . I will write to you whenever I learn what I can do in your affair, but in the mean time I hasten to acquaint you that it is not my intention you should remain in the 18th or proceed with them to India."[103]

Walter replied angrily that the charges against his companions were lies or exaggerations and bitterly accused Sir David Baird, their commander, of being a capricious and bad-tempered tyrant. But Walter's own account, Scott responded, showed that they had behaved like blackguards, and drunkenness was no excuse either in the young man guilty of such a brutality as bringing a whore into the mess or in those who did not turn them out of doors as the fittest companions for each other. "A man may be violent & outrageous in his liquor but wine seldom makes a gentleman a blackguard or instigates a loyal man to utter sedition." The tone of Walter's letter was "that of a conceited young person possessd with a wrong sort of *Esprit de corps* and who is very *angry* because he has been very *wrong*. . . . I wish you to be aware that if I hear (and my ears are long ones) that you have again participated in such disgraceful orgies . . . it will (coute que coute) be the immediate signal for your removal."104

Walter was not lacking in spirit; subdued, he responded with a sneer about the misrepresentations of "the lawyers and gossips of Edinburgh." "The *lawyers* and *gossips* of Edinburgh whom your military politeness handsomely classes together in writing to a lawyer," his father replied, "know & care as little about the 18th as they do about . . . any other regimental number which does not happen for the time to be at Piershill or in the Castle. . . . Lawyer & gossip as I may be, I suppose you will allow I have seen something of life in most of its varieties, as much at least as if I had been like you 18 months in a cavalry regt." Walter must understand that he was *not* going to India. "That this letter may not be unacceptable in all its parts I enclose your allowance . . ."105

Eleven days later Scott's tone was gentler but no less firm. "I see you are still of the mind of the irritable prophet Jonah who persisted in maintaining '*he did well to be angry*' even in disputing with Omnipotence. I am aware Sir David is considered as a severe and ill-tempered man and I remember a story" that when "Tippoo's prisoners . . . were chaind together two and two his mother said 'God pity the poor lad thats chaind to *our Davie*.'" But Cornet Scott would reap more advantage from reflecting on *his own* errors than from studying Baird's.106 Meanwhile, he must at once send his written application to Sandhurst with Colonel Murray's consent. "I beg you will not take it into your wise noddle that I will act either hastily or unadvisedly in your matters. I have been more successful in life than most people and know well how much success depends first on desert and then on knowledge of the Carte de pais."107 Walter did as he was told, and with this the dispute ended.

While Scott was thus asserting his parental authority with Walter he was also having a disagreement with John Ballantyne. He had gladly seen John's retirement from the auctioneering business and volunteered his aid in John's publishing venture of the *Novelists' Library*. But he strongly opposed John's desire to give up Trinity Grove and live in the country. John's position as his literary agent demanded that they be able to consult each other often. This would be impossible if John removed himself to his native village of Kelso, as he had been talking of doing, or to any place equally remote.

In the course of the winter, however, John had grown seriously concerned about his declining health.108 Though he was saddened by his patron's disapproval, he felt that he had no other course. "Hard, but I cannot help it. I *must* go."109 Near the end of 1820 he had let Trinity Grove and taken residence at Kirklands, three miles from Melrose. But his heart was set on Kelso. During the spring he was on the lookout for a house there, and on April 2 settled on Walton Hall,[110] a rambling place with notched gables and thatched roofs near the end of Kelso's High Street and the gateway of the Duke of Roxburghe's park. For all his illness he was full of hopeful plans, stables for his two horses, Old Mortality and Jeanie Deans, a drawing room embellished with emblems of the chase, a pleasance with ornamental steps, a fountain, and a broad terrace overhanging the river Tweed.[111]

But his high spirits did not last long. Scott voiced his objections more emphatically. They were not capricious, he pointed out, but inherent in the nature of their relationship. If John persisted in "this Kelso scheme," he would have to consider it "a virtual resignation of the agency."[112] Perhaps John dimly knew in his heart what he would not admit to himself, that he would never see his alterations at Walton Hall completed. The truth was, though not even Dr. Baillie had suspected it, that he was dying of a rapid consumption. His brother James was moving to Heriot Row; John gave up Walton Hall, and took a lease on James's old house in St. John Street. Here on June 1 he began spitting blood.[113]

The end came with startling speed. Wrung with pity, Sir Walter visited him on his deathbed. Proof sheets of a volume of the *Novelists' Library* lay on his pillow, and poor little Jocund Johnny pulsated between fear and flashes of irrepressible hope.[114] The sum of £2,000, which he had life-rented to his wife he had gratefully left in reversion to his great friend and patron to help the completion of the new library at Abbotsford. Eagerly he began outlining what he thought would be the best style and arrangement for the bookshelves, only to be halted by an agony of gasping. On June 16 he died.[115]

It was the close, Scott said, of "an innocent, industrious, & joyous career." No death had so grieved him since that of the Duke of Buccleuch. Strange as it might seem to join them in this way, he told the Duke's brother Lord Montagu, there was "a sort of connection, for had I gone first your brother would have probably given me the same sorrow I am now paying to my poor friend, or had Ballantyne been the survivor he would have mournd for me as I did for my dear friend and patron."[116]

Scott and Lockhart saw John's body lowered into the grave in the Canongate Churchyard. As the gravediggers smoothed the sod over his coffin, the sky, which had been dark and slaty, suddenly cleared and the grass glowed green in the bright sunlight. Scott cast his eyes toward Calton Hill and its gleaming walls and towers, and then turned again to the grave. Poor happy little Rigdumfunnidos, with his harmless gaiety, his madcap jests and songs and stories, his blue dog-cart and its prancing steeds, his green hunting-coat with its silver buttons! Farewell to Jocund Johnny and his tricksy strategems, his cunning bargains, his faithful service, and his loving heart. "I feel," Scott said in Lockhart's ear, "as if there would be less sunshine for me from this day forth."[117]

# 13

---

# Chivalry, Church, and Crown

(Criticism: *Ivanhoe, The Monastery, The Abbot,
Kenilworth*)

*Ivanhoe* plunges back in time to an age over four hundred years earlier
than Scott has previously dealt with, and shifts his scene from Scotland into the heart of England almost two hundred miles south of the
Border. Consciously his aim was novelty of time and setting; perhaps, Scott
thought, readers were getting tired of Scottish scenes and characters.
But his mind—whether or not of set purpose—was still dwelling upon
the themes of *A Legend of Montrose*. The Highland clan system exemplified a feudal organization of society lingering on in a moribund
state among Scotland's remote mountain glens. What of the feudal
world at its height? What were the realities of feudalism during its
flood in the England of the gallant and lion-hearted Richard I? Was
Chivalry nobly splendid in its triumphant flower? Had its virtues been
lost in the days of its dying struggles?

Scott's response is the central conception of *Ivanhoe*. It is not simple
but complex, for although he was capable of errors and misinterpretations and even, as he cheerfully confessed, of fusing the manners of two
or three centuries, he had far too balanced a knowledge both of the
medieval world and of life in general either to reject totally or to idealize.
Scott's historical knowledge saved him from the naïveté with which
Mark Twain runs together the imaginary realms of Arthurian romance
with medieval Austria and Tudor England as all one mixture of superstition, cruelty, and horror; and he had none of the gloomy disillusion
with the present that led even so erudite a historian as Henry Adams
to glorify the thirteenth century.

The world of *Ivanhoe* is not the ideal unity Adams's vision saw in
the following century, but it is not more cruel and chaotic than the

twelfth-century reality or than the world usually is. Scott portrays it neither with the bright-hued enthusiasm of Froissart nor with the rose-tinted gaze of nineteenth-century romanticism; his medieval world has no Bayards, *sans peur et sans reproche*, and no Galahad, no Gawains or Tristrems or Lancelots. If it glows with vivid color, that color reflects the keenness of the eye that saw and the skill of the hand that painted it.

Not least is the relish with which Scott renders the picturesque details of the temporal scene, and which more than any other writer of his time he taught us to see too—glittering armor, gloomy dungeons, moats, drawbridges, massive castle walls, ample-boughed oak forests, dining halls with great fires roaring up huge chimneys. Still more is an enjoyment of physical violence, which—without approving it any more than we do—he shares with most of mankind. *Ivanhoe* is full of the atmosphere and sound of violence—the clanging steel, shattered lances, and blood-soaked knights of Ashby-de-la-Zouche; the hissing arrows and ringing blades, the crashing walls, and the flaming towers of the siege of Torquilstone; the last thunderous shock of Ivanhoe and Bois-Guilbert at Templestowe.

These are among the things that have led later generations of critics to dismiss *Ivanhoe* as a boys' book, but it is doubtful if the story is violent enough to gratify that zest in either the present generation of boyhood or their elders. The gunsmoke of television, mass murders in the films, sadism in the novel; our political assassinations, shootings in the streets, clashes of police and university students from Berkeley to the Sorbonne and Madrid, and bombings of civilian cities—all these involve volumes of bloodshed that leave the violence in all of Scott's work tame by comparison. Though there are plenty of anonymous deaths in *Ivanhoe*, only two of the major and individualized characters are slain, Front-de-Boeuf and Brian de Bois-Guilbert.

Fundamentally, of course, in a work of literature, the central issue is not the existence of even large amounts of violence, but whether it takes place mainly for purposes of sensationalism or for esthetically profounder reasons. Nobody dismisses *Macbeth* and *Hamlet* as boys' plays because of their overflowing blood-baths, or reads *In Cold Blood* only for its brutal and ferocious murders, though no doubt the fierce deeds they deal with also give them a dreadful fascination. But both Shakespeare and Capote, different as their kinds and degrees of insight may be, are using violence not as mere melodrama but as one of the deep-rooted elements in human nature and the human condition.

So Scott invokes not the theory of feudalism—though he does not ignore its theory—but its practice to portray the violence of a violent age. In the course of each of the three main actions into which the novel is symmetrically divided he emphasizes that analysis. After all the brilliant color, pageantry, and excitement of the tournament, he concludes: "Thus ended the memorable field of Ashby-de-la-Zouche, one of the most gallantly contested tournaments of that age; for although only four knights, including one who was smothered by the heat of his armor, had died upon the field, yet upwards of thirty were desperately wounded, four or five of whom never recovered. Several more were disabled for life; and those who escaped carried the marks of the conflict to the grave with them. Hence it is always mentioned in the old records as the 'gentle and joyous passage at arms of Ashby.' "[1]

The tone of this comment is unmistakable, and so is that permeating the concluding third of the novel, the trial by combat which is to determine whether Rebecca is to be freed as innocent or burned to death as a witch. The cold-hearted fanaticism, superstition, and cruelty of Lucas de Beaumanoir, the Grand Master of the Temple; the fear to testify in her defense of even those Rebecca has aided with her healing art; the exaggeration, distortion, and invention of trifles and irrelevancies to condemn her; even the contemptuous scorn of the proceedings voiced by Malvoisin and Bois-Guilbert, who in this case, despite their libertine skepticism, speak for the book itself—all conjoin in condemnation of the appeal to physical violence as a means of settling a problem of justice.

In the face of this critical judgment Scott is nevertheless rigorously fair in seeing both the trial and Beaumanoir in terms of the shaping influences of the age and of social and personal environment. Of the Grand Master, he writes: "He was not originally a cruel or even a severe man; but with passions by nature cold, and with a high, though mistaken, sense of duty, his heart had been gradually hardened by the ascetic life which he had pursued, the supreme power which he enjoyed, and the supposed necessity of subduing infidelity and eradicating heresy, which he conceived peculiarly incumbent upon him."[2] The sentence epitomizes Scott's understanding of how history makes men and men make history.

The great central action of the novel, the siege of Torquilstone, makes all these points even more emphatically and is the very core of Scott's criticism. The situation is crucial. Cedric, Athelstane, Rowena, Ivanhoe, Isaac of York, and Rebecca have all been captured by Front-de-Boeuf and his companions. Outside the Castle, under the command of the Black Knight, Robin Hood and his followers are pressing an attack on its walls. The wounded Ivanhoe lies helpless on a couch in a tower; at the window Rebecca gives him agitated reports of the progress of the siege. But antiphonal with these war bulletins is a debate between the Jewish maiden and her knightly patient on the virtues of feudal chivalry.

"Where Ivanhoe 'champions a chivalry, which he ironically associates with Christianity' and 'which rates life far beneath the pitch of honor,' Rebecca insists on the idleness of a code that makes a virtue of bloodshed and glorifies violence."[3] "The love of battle," Ivanhoe exclaims, "is the food upon which we live—the dust of the *mêlée* is the breath of our nostrils! We live not—we wish not to live—longer than while we are victorious and renowned—Such, maiden, are the laws of chivalry to which we are sworn, and to which we offer all that we hold dear." "Alas!" replies Rebecca, "and what is it, valiant knight, save an offering of sacrifice to a demon of vain glory . . . ? What remains . . . of all the travail and pain you have endured, of all the tears which your deeds have caused . . . ?"[4]

"What remains?" Ivanhoe cries. "Glory, maiden, glory! which gilds our sepulchre and embalms our name." But Rebecca asks sorrowfully if the rusted mail and the defaced sculpture on a moldering tomb are really "sufficient rewards for the sacrifice of every kindly affection," for domestic love, for peace and happiness? "By the soul of Hereward!" Ivanhoe responds impatiently, "thou speakest, maiden, of thou knowest not what. . . . Chivalry!—why, maiden, she is the nurse of pure and high affection—the stay of the oppressed, the redresser of grievances, the curb of the power of the tyrant—Nobility were but an empty name without her, and liberty finds the best protection in her lance and her sword!"[5]

Ivanhoe has the last word, but Rebecca would have only to remind him of their present circumstances to refute his argument. The chaotic strife that the chivalrous code not merely endures but inspires, the tyrannies it cannot repress, the evils it makes no effort to destroy, the sufferings of Rebecca's own people in Christian Europe, are painful answers to its pretensions. The scene is indeed, as Edgar Rosenberg observes, the moral center of the novel, "and it is certain that in the critical agon of the book the Jewess carries the day."[6]

Nor does the behavior of the characters speak differently than the words of Rebecca and the author. The Norman conquerors display neither magnanimity nor chivalry to the defeated Saxons. At Prince John's banquet he gives his sycophants the lead in treating his two invited Saxon guests, Cedric and Athelstane, with sneering discourtesy. The Prince himself is endeavoring to seize the throne of his brother, Richard Coeur de Lion, whose love has loaded him with favors. John's followers, defiant of their vows of feudal loyalty to Richard, and animated by no grievance against their royal master but only by their desire for greater wealth and power, feel no qualms about murdering their King if he ever escapes from his Austrian prison and returns to the rule they have all sworn to support.

The very names of some of them insinuate their natures: Malvoisin, "bad neighbor"; Front-de-Boeuf, "bull-brow"; Prior Aymer, "aimer," the worldly, luxurious, and pleasure-loving priest, whose amorous adventures often fill the night, until he creeps at dawn into the postern gate of his priory of Jourvaux. Maurice de Bracy, the leader of a band of mercenaries, sells his lances to whoever has the most flowing purse. Though he has some flashes of chivalrous idealism and even of generous feeling, he is hardly superior to a hired soldier like Dalgetty; he peddles the services of his band wholesale, whereas the Scottish soldier of fortune offers only his own body and military skill.

The two Knights Templar, Albert Malvoisin and Bois-Guilbert, almost openly despise their own knightly and ecclesiastic vows; both are infidels who no longer believe in the religion they have sworn to defend, and Bois-Guilbert in the Holy Land has lived *par amours* with both Christian and Saracen women. When King Richard reappears in England, Prince John's chief adviser, Waldemar Fitzurse, conspires to have the King ambushed and slain.

In this crisis of Prince John's fortunes, his three other chief supporters, whose fortunes are indissolubly bound with his, are off on a lawless and self-interested expedition of their own, seizing Athelstane and Cedric and the others in their train and conveying them to Torquilstone. All three expect to gain large ransoms from the two Saxon thanes. Front-de-Boeuf intends in addition to extort from the Jew Isaac of York his entire fortune by roasting him, if necessary, over the coals of a red-hot brazier. Bracy desires the person and the fortune of the Saxon heiress Rowena and is ready to marry her by force. Bois-Guilbert lusts for Isaac's daughter Rebecca and cares not whether he gains her by seduction or rape. In pursuit of their reckless, divisive, and unscrupulous personal aims these leaders of Norman chivalry, disloyal even to their chosen prince, ruin his chances of ruling a kingdom. Like Froissart's knight two centuries later, they might all say, "It is a good life to rob and pill." They are only grandiose gangsters in chainmail.

Their fates are symbolic. Front-de-Boeuf dies amid the flames of his own castle, roasted as he had intended to roast Isaac, while the mad Saxon crone Ulrica, who had been first his father's and then his own captive and despised mistress, screams her hatred and perishes with him in the blaze. Bracy is disarmed by King Richard and scornfully pardoned by the monarch, who disdains to take revenge on so mean a foe. Bois-Guilbert dies in the lists at Templestowe, his features convulsed, his brow flushed red as blood, slain not by the still unrecovered Ivanhoe but by the violence of his own passions. Thus the red thread of violence ravels to its fitting end.

In contrast to these representatives of Norman chivalry the Saxons come off better, though even they hardly shine. Athelstane, called the Unready, a descendant of the Saxon kings and thus after a fashion a contender for the throne, does not lack bravery and even has a strain of sense and good feeling in his heavy bulk, but he is an oaf, a sluggard, and a glutton. Cedric the Saxon, almost the last enthusiast for a Saxon restoration, blinds himself to the bovine qualities of this human ox, strives to bring about a marriage between him and the Saxon princess Rowena, and disinherits his son Wilfred of Ivanhoe for daring to fall in love with her. In his unrealistic dedication to a lost cause, Cedric resembles more than anyone else that tragic and fanatical devotee of the Jacobite cause, Redgauntlet, in a novel Scott was to write five years later.

The best and most manly figures among the Saxons are not these members of its old nobility but the serf and swineherd Gurth, with his courage, loyalty, and good sense, and the half-crackbrained jester Wamba, whose touching devotion to his master throws a gentler light upon Cedric himself. And Cedric in turn gains in stature by his treatment of these two, by his affectionate gratitude to his poor clown and by freeing Gurth for his services. He is more fully redeemed by his ability at last to accept the rule of the Plantagenet Richard and to allow love for his son to prevail over his dynastic fantasies.

This development in the story is given a comic parallel in the resuscitation of Athelstane, still ravenous for food and drink, and his renunciation of his claims both on the hand of Rowena and on the throne. That resuscitation is not "a botch," as Scott later thought, but a ludicrous demonstration of the unreality of Cedric's dreams. It is more fitting that Athelstane should linger on, a foolish food-champer, than that he be given a grandiose burial at Coningsburgh as a symbol of the heroic death of the Saxon cause.

In all this gallery, who speaks for the nobler qualities of chivalry? Primarily, of course, Ivanhoe, the titular hero. He is one of Scott's mediatorial figures, bridging the gulf between Saxon and Norman, adopting the chivalric code in its highest form, aiding the oppressed, becoming the devoted follower of Richard, fighting for the Cross in Palestine, humbling the pride of the cynical and overbearing Bois-Guilbert, and in the end, by wedding Rowena, symbolically uniting Norman knighthood and the Saxon heritage.

During the first third of the book Ivanhoe has a decisive role, first in disguise as the palmer, when he saves Isaac of York from Bois-Guilbert's plan of seizure, then in the thinner disguise of the Disinherited Knight, when he defeats all the Norman champions in the tournament at Ashby. But throughout almost all the rest of the narrative his wounds condemn him to a passivity from which he does not emerge until near the end, with the vain endeavor to curb Coeur de Lion's rashness and the heroic gesture of presenting himself at Templestowe as Rebecca's defender.

The role of King Richard is more complex and even contradictory. In the mêlée at Ashby, he has fought under the banner of Ivanhoe but so inactively as to get himself nicknamed the Black Sluggard, *le Noir Fainéant;* he has bestirred himself only when Ivanhoe was in danger. He puts himself at the head of Robin Hood's band of Saxon outlaws in pressing the assault on Torquilstone in which the oppressively lawless Norman leaders are crushingly defeated. At the mere terror of his return to England his brother John's abortive conspiracy begins to crumple; with the announcement of his presence armed supporters spring up out of the soil everywhere. He banishes the corrupt and subversive Order of the Temple from the land. The King is a providential force before whom oppressive violence collapses.

But, further, even more than Ivanhoe he is a symbol of national unity. He has no Norman disdain for his Saxon subjects. If he addresses De Bracy and Fitzurse in a tone of high command, he drinks and exchanges buffets with the Clerk of Copmanhurst and mingles readily with Robin Hood's band, and he treats Cedric with a distinguished courtesy splendidly differentiated from Prince John's ill breeding. When Cedric invites him to Rotherwood, "not as a guest, but as a son or brother," the King responds, "Cedric has already made me rich,—he has taught me the value of Saxon virtue."[7] When he at last reveals his identity at Coningsburgh, "Richard of Anjou!" exclaims Cedric. "No, noble Cedric," is the reply, "—Richard of England! . . . whose deepest wish is to see her sons united."[8]

If Richard is presented as redeemer, however, it should be noted that many of the evils he promises to eradicate are the dark results of his own irresponsible knight-errantry. Through his melodramatic preference for dashing off to Palestine and winning glittering but fruitless victories there, instead of attending to the duty of governing his own country, he has subjected England to the misrule of Prince John, a fickle, cowardly, and depraved would-be tyrant. Even after escaping from his Austrian prison Richard pursues the same reckless and headstrong courses, and might well have been slain by Fitzurse and his assassins but for Wamba's seizing Robin Hood's horn and summoning the outlaw bowmen.

Though Ivanhoe is himself no model of prudential conduct, even he is shocked by Richard's recklessness. "Your kingdom," he upbraids, "is threatened with dissolution and civil war—your subjects menaced with every species of evil"—"why, oh why, noble Prince, will you thus vex the hearts of your faithful servants, and expose your life by lonely journeys and rash adventures, as if it were of no more value than that of a mere knight-errant, who has no interest on earth but what lance and sword may procure him?"[9]

Richard replies that he has been obliged to remain concealed to give his friends and faithful nobles time to assemble their forces, when the announcement of his return may make his enemies tremble and subdue treason without unsheathing a sword. But he well knows that he could have remained in hiding less hazardously than wandering through the forest attended only by a Saxon jester. The King's behavior in the course of the narrative thus qualifies his role both as mediator and as redeemer, and provides ample justification for the book's more disillusioned conclusion about him:

"In the lion-hearted King, the brilliant, but useless character of a knight of romance, was in a great measure realized and revived; and the personal glory which he acquired by his own deeds of arms, was far more dear to his excited imagination, than that which a course of policy and wisdom would have spread around his government. Accordingly, his reign was like the course of a brilliant and rapid meteor, which shoots along the face of Heaven, shedding around it an unnecessary and portentous light, which is instantly swallowed up by universal darkness; his feats of chivalry furnishing themes for bards and minstrels, but affording none of those solid benefits to his country on which history loves to pause, and hold up as an example to posterity."[10]

Richard thereby illustrates the failure of the most heroic secular ideal the age of chivalry could imagine—that ideal that Ivanhoe had so enthusiastically defended and Rebecca sadly reproached with its errors and omissions. Though Scott's own heart beats to its clarion peal, his honesty as a historian will not allow him to pretend that it is any less gravely flawed at its height in feudal Europe than in its lingering manifestations among the Highland clans of the seventeenth century. The code of chivalry is not the stay of the oppressed; it is often no more than the mask of violence, rapacity, and bloodshed, and leaves unredressed more wrongs than it rights. In the person of Coeur de Lion it carries war abroad and allows anarchy to rage at home. Its achievements are irregular and irresponsible.

Its deepest failures are defined by the existence of those who lie outside the pale of such organization as it lays claim to. Cedric and Athelstane, heirs of the old Saxon aristocracy, are jeered and baited by the Norman chivalry. Robin Hood's band, descendants of the Saxon yeomanry, are outlaws both to the Norman barons and the Saxon thanes. Isaac of York, his daughter Rebecca, all the Jews, once the Chosen People, are now despised and persecuted by Norman and Saxon alike. But the Jews and the Saxons who despise them are linked through an ironical equation: as Jews are to Saxons, so Saxons are to Normans. In an emblematic subtlety with which Scott is not usually credited, both are the disinherited of their world. Ivanhoe, literally disinherited by his father, bears upon his shield at Ashby the motto "Desdichado," and it is significant that his last important action is to champion a daughter of the most deeply disinherited of all, the Jews.

Isaac and Rebecca are in fact at the moral heart of *Ivanhoe*. Both are what they are in response to the pressures of their world. If Isaac is in part both comic and contemptible, Scott shows clearly that his most unlovely and ludicrous traits are to an overwhelming degree the consequences of the cruelty with which he and his people have been treated. Exiled, harried, and despoiled, denied an entry into almost all trades except the manipulation of money and then reviled as bloodsucking usurers, the Jews are revealed in historical perspective not as villains but as victims. If Isaac is still the legendary moneylender, it is because Christians will not let him be otherwise. The existence of the Jew as outcast and scapegoat indicts the society that rejects him.

Scott thus retains the stereotype but inverts its meaning. Isaac is avaricious because his ducats are his only weapon; he is in terror because Front-de-Boeuf's brazier always glares behind him. Even the relatively amiable characters in the book join as a matter of course in verbal Jew-baiting—Robin Hood distastefully calls Isaac "good earthworm"—while to the Norman group he is "dog Jew," "infidel dog," and "Hound of a Jew." Isaac is made the butt of crude japes, recoiling from a gammon of bacon suddenly flourished beneath his nose by Wamba, and rolling down a flight of steps while Prince John snatches his purse from him and flings two of its gold pieces to the jester. But we are not allowed to forget the true nature of the joke; the Prince receives "as much applause from the spectators," we are told, "as if he had done some honest and honourable action."[11]

So derided and so periled, Isaac has reason enough to fear for his moneybags and even for his life, but it is not true, as Edgar Rosenberg contends, that "he reacts as badly as possible under pressure."[12] For his rescue by the supposed Palmer he responds with immediate gratitude. "Something would I do," he says, ". . . something for thyself," and offers the free use of the horse and armor he has keenly guessed that Ivanhoe desires.[13] Nor does he recoil with the warning that both may be lost in the tourney. "I care not," he says. "If there is damage it will cost you nothing—" Instead, he worries about the danger to his benefactor: "Good youth," he begs, "thrust thyself not too forward in this vain hurly-burly—I speak not for endangering the steed, and coat of armour, but for the sake of thine own life and limbs."[14]

Here Isaac is being no Shylock but a grateful human being, and so he is again in Front-de-Boeuf's dungeon when he strives to include within his own ransom the freedom of Cedric and his followers. "Grant me," he begs, "at least with my own liberty, that of the companions with whom I travel. They scorned me as a Jew, yet they pitied my desolation, and because they tarried to aid me by the way, a share of my evil hath come upon them . . ." Even when that endeavor is repulsed, he still tries to ensure that Ivanhoe is with him: "I am then," he asks, "only to be set at liberty with mine wounded friend?"[15] But when he discovers that Rebecca has been given to Bois-Guilbert, his humility is exchanged for outraged fury: "Robber and villain! I will pay thee nothing—not one silver penny will I pay thee, unless my daughter is delivered to me in safety and honour! . . . My daughter is my flesh and blood, dearer to me a thousand times than those limbs which thy cruelty threatens. No silver will I give thee, unless I were to pour it molten down thy avaricious throat . . ."[16]

It is striking here to find the impeachment of avarice turned upon the Christian, and still more to see that in the agony of parental love

Isaac ceases to think of his own danger and rises to the dignity of defiance. But in the total structure of the book his major function is to reveal how a people may be broken by cruelty and injustice. It is his daughter Rebecca who symbolizes their unbending inward resistance. More courageous than her father, a stranger to his "constant state of timid apprehension," she displays "a proud humility" that submits only externally to her unhappy position "as the daughter of a despised race."[17] Her loyalty to her father, like his devotion to her, enhances the moral stature of both—in sharp contrast, again, to the Christians, of whom Cedric has disinherited his son, Prince John is conniving at the murder of his brother, and Front-de-Boeuf has killed his father. Throughout the book, in fact, the Jews reveal more of the Christian virtues than the Christians. And when at the end Rebecca and her father prepare to exile themselves abroad, the meaning of their departure is that England still cannot behave with Christianity to its Jews.

Among the more sentimental of Scott's readers there have always been some who felt that Rebecca should have married Ivanhoe. But this is totally to misunderstand the book. Scott has made clear from the beginning not only that Ivanhoe is deeply and unalterably devoted to the enchantingly beautiful Rowena but that the religious sentiments of the age render it impossible for him to feel for a Jewess anything greater than a detached gratitude. In a later introduction to the novel Scott also noted his own feeling that "a character of a highly virtuous and lofty stamp is degraded rather than exalted by an attempt to reward virtue with temporal prosperity." But the historical argument is all-sufficient: as Hart cogently remarks, a marriage between Ivanhoe and Rebecca could be significant in a Disraeli novel set in the nineteenth century; in the actuality of the twelfth century it is an impossibility.[18]

There have been, to be sure, complaints that Scott's rendering of the twelfth century is distorted by anachronisms. Historians have pointed out that Edward the Confessor had no lineal descendants, that Cedric, Rowena, and Ulrica are not genuine Saxon names, that Ulrica's crazy death-chant reverts to paganism a full four centuries after England had been completely Christianized and that one of the deities she invokes, Zernebock, was not even a Scandinavian god but a Slavonic idol. Scott well knew, of course, that Athelstane's ancestry was fictitious, but it may be questioned whether any of these slips seriously misrepresents the nature of the age. And though all the ballads of Robin Hood date from over two centuries later, can there be any doubt that there were such bands of forest outlaws long before the fifteenth century?

In his *History of the Norman Conquest of England* Professor E. A. Freeman has denied that the hatred between Normans and Saxons endured into the twelfth century,[19] but he overlooks Scott's specifically describing Cedric the Saxon as a belated holdout maintaining a hopeless cause. Cedric's fanaticism is no more false to human nature, and there-

fore to the twelfth century, than the Irish nationalism that after 400
years of submersion made Ireland at last a free nation, or than the
Scottish nationalism that more than 250 years after the Union with
England has today again emerged as a political movement. It would
be far stranger if there were no one like Cedric in the twelfth century—
whether or not recorded in any surviving document—than if there were.
In all other ways, furthermore, Cedric is entirely representative of his
race and time; Scott's historical imagination could be impugned only if
he also portrayed Cedric's ardent Saxon patriotism as characteristic of
the age.

Ivanhoe stands far higher than all save a few of its critics have rated
it. Though it lacks the psychological depth of Scott's greatest work,
for narrative excitement it is unsurpassed. If its people do not always
speak with the living voice that Scott gives his eighteenth-century
Scottish characters, their words and their actions nevertheless tellingly
reflect the hearts and the minds of human beings. The critical insight
into the virtues and the shortcomings of the feudal system and the code
of chivalry is acute and in the main just. Both as a work of literary
imagination and as a feat of historical reconstruction, the novel is an
impressive achievement.

As a portrayal of the Middle Ages Ivanhoe has been blamed, and
with some justice, for showing little of the importance and power of the
Church. It is true that Prior Aymer of Jourvaux and the Clerk of Copmanhurst are rather inadequate representatives of the mighty institution
which in that very period was rearing the Winchester retrochoir, the
great structure of Lincoln Cathedral, and the marvel of Fountains Abbey,
and which had produced such exalted ecclesiastical figures as Anselm,
Thomas à Beckett, and Saint Bernard. But Ivanhoe is concerned with
the worldly manifestations of feudalism, not its religious faith. The
wild lawlessness and the political conspiracy that dominate its turbulent
events, and the violent lay ambitions of men like Front-de-Boeuf, Fitzurse, and Prince John, could hardly serve to delineate the working of
spiritual forces. Such an aim would demand a different book with
different characters. That aim provided the initial concept of Scott's
next novel, The Monastery.

It was not, however, the days when the Church gloriously dominated
all Europe that Scott determined to deal with, but those of the sixteenth century when it was everywhere under attack, and when in
Scotland it was plundered by the greed of the aristocracy lusting for its
lands and wealth and destroyed by the hammer blows of John Knox.
Scott's design, as he later explained, was "to conjoin two characters . . .
who, thrown into situations which gave them different views on the
subject of the Reformation, should, with the same sincerity and purity
of intention, dedicate themselves, the one to the support of the sinking

fabric of the Catholic Church, the other to the establishment of the Reformed doctrines."[20]

It is not clear which of two pairs of characters are intended primarily to represent the opposing forces of the Catholic Church and of Protestant Reform, Halbert Glendinning and his younger brother Edward, or the itinerant preacher Henry Warden and Father Eustace, the Sub-Prior of St. Mary's Abbey at Kennaquhair. From the beginning we have small doubt that Halbert will ultimately join the Protestants and that Edward will enter the monastery as a monk. But the forces that precipitate Halbert's final choice are only superficially realized, and the emotions that determine Edward's are irrelevant to the spiritual issues. Halbert would never, it is true, have been more than a conventional son of the Church. His devotion to sport, his delight in weapons, his disinclination for study, his desire to marry Mary Avenel, his bellicose pride, all render it little likely that he would be drawn to a life of religious withdrawal. Nevertheless until early manhood he has been an undoubting Catholic, and the machinery of his swift and easy conversion is unconvincing. We cannot take seriously his descent into the bowels of the earth with the spectral White Lady and her gift of the "Black Book"—the Bible in English, which, for that matter, we are not told that he ever reads. His resentment of the snobbish superiority of Sir Piercie Shafton sharpens his craving for rank and power but entails no change of faith. His initial horror at the heresy of the Reformer Henry Warden crumbles far too readily, even granted that he might admire the preacher's bravery and integrity. His ambitions and his energies lead him to seize the opportune and almost accidental chance to enlist in the forces of the Earl of Murray, an aggressive power-seeker who can further Halbert's own desires. But this jumbling of the supernaturally implausible and the psychologically unexplored does not add up to a persuasive conversion.

His brother Edward is handled far more convincingly. No less courageous fundamentally than Halbert, he is more studious, reflective, and sensitive, and he has long been the favorite pupil of Father Eustace. But it is frustration and despair, not a deep sense of vocation, that lead him to take monastic vows. He too is in love with Mary Avenel and has come to realize that she returns his brother's love. Edward's clashing emotions of love and hatred for his brother are powerfully drawn, but they confuse his motives for entering the cloister. Though men so impelled have often proved devoted servants of their church, Edward's choice ultimately tells us as little about the deepest roots of the Catholic faith as Halbert's does about the call of Protestant reform.

For these purposes, which should have been fundamental to the theme Scott states, Father Eustace and Henry Warden, in turn, are only relatively more satisfactory. They have been friends and fellow students abroad in their university days, and when they meet again they still feel love and esteem in the midst of their disagreement. Each respects the other's sincerity; each is utterly convinced of the truth of his own faith; each is sure that in candid debate he could win over the other, and earnestly desires to do so. But the contest never really materializes. Warden does not even appear until halfway through the story; he and Father Eustace confront each other only in its last third. Then they are given a number of eloquent though general interchanges, but the prolonged conflict, of word or action, which should have developed if they were to be the central spokesmen for this clash of faiths gets sidetracked in a flurry of concluding melodrama.

Their one significant confrontation, however, is well realized. In defense of the Church, the Sub-Prior invokes the learning and authority of its Fathers and its Councils against "a rash, self-willed, and arbitrary interpretation of the Scriptures, wrested according to the private opinion of each speculating heretic." Warden warmly appeals to the text of the Bible itself, rather than "the devices and decisions of men not less subject to errors than ourselves, and who have defaced our holy religion with vain devices, reared up idols of stone and wood," and established "that profitable purgatory of which the Pope keeps the keys." Father Eustace responds that it is such men as Warden "that should defend the bulwarks of the Church," who are battering a breach "through which all that is greedy, and all that is base, and all that is mutable and hotheaded . . . hope to advance to destruction and to spoil."[21] But this promising beginning is interrupted by the arrival of Edward Glendinning and, soon after, by the news that Murray is marching that way with a body of troops, and the debate is never resumed.

The fact is that although Scott was sincerely assured of the truth of the Christian religion and was a convinced Protestant, his mind had no bent toward theology—which, like metaphysics, he might have been inclined secretly to dismiss as "water-painting." His mingling of conservative feeling and unphilosophic rationalism made him almost equally unreceptive to abstract speculation, to mysticism, and to enthusiasm. He loved the wonderful fabric of medieval churches and abbeys, and regretted that the fanatical zeal of the Reformers had mutilated and destroyed so many of them, but the complex architecture of the thought of the Roman Church had nothing to say to him. The artist in Scott could respond to the beauty of its rituals, and he was deeply moved by some of its Latin hymns—among them the Stabat Mater and the Miserere—but the intercession of the saints, the virtues of relics, the doctrine of purgatory, the confessional, the power of the priest to forgive sins, and the sale of indulgences, were all for him the superstitions and iniquities they were to the Reformers.

On the other hand, he felt equally little sympathy for the frames of mind and of heart exemplified in Luther, Calvin, and Knox. He had suffered in childhood the excruciating boredom of long intolerant sermons preached in the Tron Kirk and in Greyfriars, and rebelled against the rigid straitness of his father's home. He rejected the gloomy pre-destinarianism of the Calvinist creeds and the way their votaries almost deliberately saddened life. The persecuting bigotry of the Covenanters had been no less cruel than that of the Inquisition, and their doctrines had often been even harsher and more irrational. Though individual insight might sometimes pierce through the errors of generations, it was in general true, Scott thought, that the accumulated wisdom of learned and earnest men was more likely to be sound than the notions of self-appointed judges who were too frequently ignorant and intoxicated with opinionated conceit. Intellectually, Scott conceded that there was partial truth in the positions of both the Reformers and the defenders of the Church of Rome, but emotionally neither side really enlisted his sympa-thies. In *Waverley* he *could* sympathize with both sides; in *Old Mortality*, while condemning the fanaticism of the Covenanters, he could feel for their wrongs, their sincerity, and their sufferings; in *The Heart of Mid-Lothian* he could exalt Jeanie Deans because her faith was irradi-ated and redeemed by love. In *The Monastery* Scott respects Warden and Father Eustace, but he is unable to identify himself with them or their causes. That is the primary reason for its comparative failure.

Scott himself analyzed two other weaknesses in the book—the White Lady of Avenel and the character of Sir Piercie Shafton. The White Lady is a mingling of Ondine, a family banshee, and a mischievous fusion of Puck and Ariel. She appears to the Avenels and the Glendin-nings in exhortation, prophecy, and warning, and she also plays undig-nified tricks upon strangers. The White Lady has never pleased many readers, some of whom have imagined that the cause of their dissatis-faction was the incongruity of a lovely and poetic water-nymph sousing reverend clerics in rushing streams and making japes with a bodkin. But tricksy and even malicious sprites appear as often in literature as more solemn or terrible spirits, and there is no reason for their not being combined in a single figure.

Scott himself thought that the trouble lay in the execution not the conception. But though the White Lady is no such triumph of the supernatural as "Wandering Willie's Tale" in *Redgauntlet*, she is not handled unskillfully. The real flaw lies elsewhere. It is that she does not belong in this book at all; she has strayed from the realm of romance into a different world of the imagination. She is not like the Bodach Glas in *Waverley*, which is seen only by Fergus MacIvor, or like the Bahr-Geist who in *The Betrothed* terrifies the Lady Eveline Berenger in the Chamber of the Red Finger. She is not like the baleful ghosts of Peter Quint and Miss Jessel in James's *The Turn of the Screw*, who for all we certainly know is seen only by the governess. The White Lady appears not only to Mary Avenel and the two Glendinning brothers, whose minds are as it were ready for her, but to the Sacristan, who has never heard of her, to Christie of the Clinthill, and to the Sub-Prior, the last of whom is even skeptically resistant. She is thus not a hallucination but an objective reality.

Such supernatural manifestations present no problems in other literary contexts. Prince Prospero in *The Masque of the Red Death* and all his fellow masquers see the blood-bedabbled figure stalking through the seven apartments of his sealed castle. Not only does Sir Bedivere see the white arm rise from the mere and seize the brand Excalibur, but the wounded Arthur has expected him to do so; and in Keats's *Lamia* the serpentine lady is no solitary delusion of Lycius but is beheld by the sage Apollonius and all Corinth. But in the otherwise solid historical world of *The Monastery* the White Lady occasions all the disbelief with which reason responds to the Cock Lane Ghost in the eighteenth-century London of Samuel Johnson. For Scott's own mind the White Lady is merely a colorful fancy, to which, in a world of despoiled monasteries and greedy nobles, he could give no serious imaginative belief. It is these deeper difficulties, rather than a mere stumbling in technical skill, that account for her failure.

The failure of Sir Piercie Shafton *is* technical. It does not matter that the wild verbal exaggerations of Lyly's euphuism did not become a popular literary affection until almost half a century later than the period of the novel; there have always been fantastics who devised grotesque jargons for themselves. Nor is the error, as Andrew Lang thought, that "a fashion which is to be caricatured should be a contemporary fashion."[22] The artificialities Molière mocked in *Les Précieuses Ridicules* are four centuries out of date, but his comedy still sparkles, and Mrs. Malaprop mutilates the English language in a ludicrous derangement of epitaphs which it is dubious that anyone ever really displayed in any time or place. Molière's *précieuses* are amusing, Mrs. Malaprop is amusing; Sir Piercie Shafton is not, or is so but seldom.

The reason, I think, is that Scott can imitate the formal rhetorical structure of euphuism and even its figures of speech, but cannot, as the successful parodist must, feel his way into its spirit. Euphuism is a kind of insanity. Only a literary madman, though a gifted and sometimes witty one, could quite so obsessively impose upon language its relentless patterns of parallelism and alliteration, and so grandiosely pile up decorations of simile and metaphor. Even in its absurdity *Euphues and His England* itself has a recurrent glitter and grandeur rising out of this lunatic excess. Scott's own good sense is too fundamental for him to be able to throw himself fully into the euphuistic mood. Willynilly, Sir Piercie is haunted by glimmers of sanity, and even in his most pompous elaborations of syntax never achieves Lyly's picturesque and monumental absurdity.

Sir Piercie is thus aimed at a mode of humor the very reverse of that in Scott's most characteristic and successful comedy. His best comic characters, such as Edie Ochiltree or Nicol Jarvie, may masquerade as simple peasant or prosaic merchant, but are actually men of shrewd wit and insight. Even the slightly touched Wamba, in *Ivanhoe*, is best when sense flashes through his freakishness and he observes of the Templar that "If he is but half a monk, he should not be wholly unreasonable."[23] Scott's gloriously entertaining bores, from Jonathan Oldbuck to Dugald Dalgetty, are not fools but men of brains and even some learning with bees in their bonnets. Sir Piercie was meant to portray silliness puffing itself up into ostentatious nonsense, but only now and then soars to those poetic heights of foolishness that are genuinely comic. His best moments are those in which he is deploring the "molendinary" background of the miller's daughter, Mysie Happer, whose dazzled adoration kindles his own devotion.[24]

*The Monastery* is far, however, from being as tiresome in its entirety as it is in the pages where Sir Piercie holds the floor, or as unconvincing as when the White Lady rises mistily on the historic stage. Most of the action moves vigorously; much of it is dramatically exciting. Lady Louisa Stuart was right in saying that the success of its sequel, *The Abbot*, should send readers back to *The Monastery* and force them "to see merits they had denied before." Its failures are formal and technical; they lower its achievement as a work of art but still leave much that is vividly effective, including the portraits of Father Eustace, Henry Warden, several glimpses of the Earl of Murray, many although not all the scenes in which Halbert and Edward Glendinning are the principle actors, and almost all those involving Sir Piercie's "lovely Molinara,"[25] the fair and devoted Mysie Happer.

*The Abbot* avoids nearly all the mistakes of *The Monastery*. Some of the major characters of the earlier book recur, but Sir Piercie is fortunately gone and the White Lady has vanished forever. Father Eustace has long since become the Abbot of St. Mary's, now shorn by the Reformers of much of its wealth and power and perilously surviving only through the sufferance of the Earl of Murray. The aging Henry Warden has ceased to be a traveling preacher but exchanges with his old friend and enemy fiery theological tracts that the readers of the novel are happily spared. Warden dwells mostly at Avenel, now the castle of Halbert Glendinning, who has married Mary Avenel and been granted the lands that once belonged to her family. Halbert has been elevated to knighthood by Murray, in whose favor he has risen high as an able military follower.

But Halbert and Mary, now approaching middle age, are childless. The Knight of Avenel, as he is called, is often away in the service of his lord, and she is left lonely in their island castle. She has taken as her page, almost as an adopted son, an orphan child who has been rescued from drowning in the lake. His grandmother and only surviving relation, Magdalene Graeme, a fanatical devotee of the Roman Church, consents to his remaining in the Lady's care and wanders off but enjoins him to remain secretly loyal to the faith in which he was born. This boy, Roland Graeme, the Lady of Avenel in her starved maternal affection pets and spoils. He is the protagonist of the story.[26]

Roland Graeme is Scott's first experiment in the creation of an uningratiating hero. He is arrogant, conceited, and quick-tempered, convinced without evidence that he is really of noble origin, devoted to his mistress, but quarrelsome and disdainful in his treatment of all his fellow dependents in the castle. He learns quickly and easily, but resists all direction and authority. He insolently despises the spiritual ministry of Henry Warden. (Though with some excuse; Warden has come with age and the triumph of the Reformers to assume an authoritarianism far less attractive than the courage with which he formerly risked martyrdom.) Roland at last gives inexcusable offense: in a brawl with his fellow servants he inflicts a dagger wound on one of them and is sadly dismissed from her service by the Lady of Avenel.

Sir Halbert takes the broil less seriously. Though he has never much liked the youth, he has noted his mettle and quickness of wit. He receives Roland into his own service and recommends him to the Earl of Murray as a page to Queen Mary in her island imprisonment at Lochleven. The Queen is at the same time to be allowed as one of her two ladies Catherine Seyton, the daughter of a devoted follower; it will be useful, Murray thinks, if he also has a representative there. Unknown to Murray and Glendinning, Magdalene Graeme has reappeared and brought about a meeting between Catherine and her grandson, whom she intends to have join each other in Mary's service. The young page has thus imposed upon him two warring obligations—to serve as Murray's spy and to conspire for the freedom of the Queen.

Roland's dilemma is sharpened by the fact that inevitably of course he falls in love with the arch and saucy Catherine Seyton. Mary's escape and the fortunes of the lovers are fused; her desire for their happiness and their sympathy for her sufferings deepen and heighten each other, and the story becomes at once the story of Mary's fate and that of Roland's development, his struggle between clashing loyalties and spiritual freedom. With a striking formal symmetry the scenes move from the opening at the island castle of Avenel, through the brawling factions whose swords clang against each other in the Canongate of Edinburgh, and through the political intrigues coiling in the dark corridors and winding stairways of Holyrood, to their culminating action in the island prison of the Queen at Lochleven. As Hart finely puts it, "The lonely mother who rescued the mysterious child from her lake now has her lofty historic counterpart in the lonely maternal figure on another dangerous lake."[27]

Mary of Scotland is the most superb of all Scott's royal figures. Her charm, her imprudent wit, her nobility, and her pathos are all irresistibly conveyed in the scene in which she first appears. The envoys of the Council, the fierce Lindesay and the merciless Ruthven, have appeared to demand that she sign her abdication and designate Murray as Regent. What warrant has she, asks the Queen, that they will adhere to their assurance of "honour and safety" if she yields her throne? "Our honour and our word, madam," replies Ruthven. "They are too slight and unsolid pledges, my lord," answers the Queen, "add at least a handful of thistle-down to give them weight in the balance."[28]

In a secret letter Lord Seyton has urged that a surrender to force cannot be binding, but Mary still hesitates. "Beware, madam," says Lindesay, gripping her arm with his gauntleted hand, "—beware how you contend with those who are the stronger, and have the mastery of your fate!" His grasp leaves a purple bruise on her flesh. He might have spared her, she remarks, so severe a proof that he has the greater strength on his side. "But I thank you for it—it is the most decisive token of the terms on which this day's business is to rest.—I draw you to witness, both lords and ladies, that I subscribe these instruments in obedience to the sign manual of my Lord of Lindesay, which you may see imprinted on my arm."[29]

Even Lindesay is abashed, and after the signature has been given feels moved by something like remorse. Falling on one knee, he kisses her hand. "Lady," he says, "thou art a noble creature, even though thou hast abused God's choicest gifts. I pay that devotion to thy manliness of spirit, which I would not have paid to the power thou hast long undeservedly wielded.—I kneel to Mary Stewart, not to the Queen."[30] And when the envoys have withdrawn, his voice sounds from the vestibule: "Chide not with me, Ruthven, for I will not brook it!" "I would I had as deep cause to be this lady's friend as I have to be her enemy."[31]

Though Roland Graeme's respect for Sir Halbert Glendinning and the magnetism of the Earl of Murray have almost impelled him to side with them, the glamor and sorrow of the Queen and the allure of Catherine Seyton move his heart. But he is repelled by the sibylline enthusiasm of his grandmother and her demand that he subject himself blindly to her will. He wearies of her religious vehemence as much as he had of Henry Warden's sermons, for in reality his youthful and secret Catholicism has been only an aspect of his obstinacy and pride and has had no roots in conviction. Now, listening to Elias Henderson, the preacher at Lochleven, it seems to him that there is much truth in his teachings and "that the profligacy of the Catholic clergy has brought this judgment on their own heads."[32] "If thou art won by the song of these sirens to aid that unhappy lady's escape from this place of penitence and security," Henderson tells him, "it is over with the peace of Scotland's cottages, and with the prosperity of her palaces—and the babe unborn shall curse the name of the man who gave inlet to the disorder which will follow the war betwixt the mother and the son."[33]

Reproached by his grandmother for his wavering and accused of abandoning his faith, Roland responds in an impassioned outburst: "I have been treated amongst you—even by yourself . . . —as one who lacked the common attributes of free-will and human reason or was at least deemed unfit to exercise them. A land of enchantment have I been led into, and spells have been cast around me—every one has met me in disguise—every one has spoken to me in parable—I have been like one who walks in a weary and bewildering dream; and now you blame me that I have not the sense and judgment, and steadiness, of a waking, and a disenchanted, and a reasonable man, who knows what he is doing, and wherefore he does it!"[34]

Against these rebellions and doubts Catherine Seyton urges that if he will throw in his lot with the Queen he will have for guerdon the prayers of oppressed subjects, ejected priests, and insulted nobles, "immortal praise by future ages," "—and I, sworn with you so early to the accomplishment of Queen Mary's freedom, will—yes, I will love you better than—ever sister loved brother!" And as she speaks, in the air above Roland's brow she traces the sign of the cross, and stooping toward him kisses that space between them. Roland is overwhelmed: "If his thoughts were not of unmixed delight, they at least partook of that thrilling and intoxicating, though mingled sense of pain and pleasure, the most overpowering which life offers in its blended cup."[35]

The decision is still not easy, but it is made inevitable by the page's very nature: "I will serve this poor Queen as a subject should serve an imprisoned and wronged sovereign—they who placed me in her service have to blame themselves—they sent me hither, a gentleman trained in the paths of loyalty and honour, when they should have sought out some truckling, cogging, double-dealing knave, who would have been at once the observant page of the Queen, and the obsequious spy of her enemies. Since I must choose between aiding her and betraying her, I will decide as becomes her servant and her subject . . ."[36]

It is Roland who forges the dummy keys that deceive the eyes of their jailers and who manages to make the substitution beneath their very noses, and it is Roland who, when Mary and her two ladies are embarked at midnight on the boat floating in the dark shadow of the castle, baffles pursuit by darting back and locking the garrison within their own prison doors. The unhappy Queen's freedom, of course, is not destined to last long; after the disastrous battle of Langside she takes the fatal step of throwing herself upon the protection of her jealous rival, Queen Elizabeth. But she has followed with compassionate tenderness the emotions of the two youthful lovers, and during the brief period of her liberty commends her page to the protection of Lord Seyton. When it is learned that he is not of ignoble birth but is the true and legitimate nephew of the Lady of Avenel, the last obstacle to his union with Catherine disappears.

The ending is no mere bow to romance, for the feelings of Roland and Catherine have been drawn with a sure touch and their fortunes are shadowed by the fate of the Queen. But Mary herself is the real triumph of the novel. "She is a queen," as John Buchan observes, "in dignity and fortitude, and more than a queen in brains."[37] Her beauty and grace are rendered with compelling power, her courage is made all the more convincing by one flurry of terror when in a nightmare she cries out for the absent and traitorous Bothwell. The devotion she inspires in Catherine and Roland give them depth and dignity.

Having thus painted Mary almost at full length, it was perhaps inevitable that Scott should be drawn to portray her great and powerful adversary Elizabeth. This he does in *Kenilworth*, and although she is not the central personage of the story, her nature and her power are its dominant force, controlling the lives of all the others as a star sways the movements of its planets. From her commanding position in her world follows every significant action in the narrative. She is the embodiment of sixteenth-century England, and *Kenilworth* is a masterly evocation of the time.

The truth of Scott's historical reconstruction is a matter of spirit rather than of particular events, for in many factual details he is almost recklessly anachronistic. The Earl of Leicester's marriage to Amy Robsart had taken place in the reign of Edward VI and had not been secret; Kenilworth was not his until long after Amy's death; and it was Leicester's much later marriage to Lettice Knollys that Queen Elizabeth so bitterly resented. There is evidence that the real Richard Varney and Tony Foster were not such villains as Scott paints them. When the splendid pageantry of Kenilworth took place in 1575, far from being a known dramatist, Shakespeare was still a small boy in Stratford. Nor did Walter Raleigh rise in the Queen's favor and receive his knighthood until years later. But such caviling is picayune; what Scott magnificently does is to capture the flavor, the color, the *élan* of the age. This he drew not only from the formal historians, but from an enormous lore in chronicles, chapbooks, Elizabethan ballads, and plays.

Elizabeth herself lives with towering vitality. Fierce, feminine, accomplished, leonine, and dangerous, she can subdue her surface vanity and caprice to a sagacity of judgment, a steeliness of will, and an imperious pride of command that awes and terrifies not only her courtiers but the statesmen and warriors who are the instruments of her power. Even her favorite, Leicester, can be appalled by the violence of her resentment when he has dared to threaten one of the court dignitaries: "God's death! my lord! what means this? We have thought well of you and brought you near to our person; but it was not that you might hide the sun from our other faithful subjects. Who gave you license to contradict our orders, or control our officers? I will have in this court, ay, and in this realm, but one mistress, and no master."[38]

She is no less arrogant with Leicester's great rival, the Earl of Sussex. "Do you bandy looks and words with me, my lord? methinks you might learn of my Lord of Leicester the modesty to be silent, at least, under our censure."[39] Even the court usher whose appeal has led to these outbursts of temper feels the rough side of her tongue: "You think yourself a great man, because but now we chid a nobleman on your account—yet, after all, we hold you but as the lead-weight that keeps the door fast."[40] Such is the high-tempered ruler on whose favor Leicester's precarious fortunes depend.

Unlike Sussex he is no skilled military leader, and unlike Burleigh he is no statesman and administrator; his lofty position at court he has won entirely through an adroitness and a brilliance of charm that have led many to believe that in the end Elizabeth's affections may overpower her determination to live and rule and die a virgin Queen. Leicester himself, irresistibly carried away by love, has secretly married Amy Robsart, the daughter of an obscure Devonshire knight; he may later, he trusts, be able to avow the match without losing the Queen's partiality.

But he has not sufficiently allowed for the degree to which his power hangs on Elizabeth's emotions as a woman. Though she has no desire to take a lord and master, she wavers on the verge of being in love with her glamorous favorite. Dazzled by the great prospect of becoming King, Leicester defers the revelation that he is already married, cannot resist giving his ingratiations a deepening tone of gallantry, and while he glides on the thinnest of ice hopes vaguely for he hardly knows what turn of fate or artifice.

Leicester is thus entrapped in an insoluble dilemma. From mere concealment he is drawn on into overt falsehood. When the Queen unexpectedly learns of Amy's existence he is led to support a hasty strategem of his principal retainer, Richard Varney. "My Lord of Leicester," Elizabeth demands, "will you warrant with your honour— that is, to the best of your belief—that your servant speaks truth in saying he hath married this Amy Robsart?" Desperately Leicester responds with a deceptive equivoque. "To the best of my belief—indeed to my certain knowledge—she is a wedded wife."[41] The Queen accepts the explanation and sets a week hence for a long-promised visit to Leicester's magnificent estate in Warwickshire. But her last words open a pit at his feet: "Varney, thy wife must be at Kenilworth, and forthcoming at my order."[42] Amy's doom is sealed, and her tragic death becomes inevitable.

Varney is an Iago-like figure in the depth and blackness of his villainy. But he differs from Iago in being genuinely devoted to what he conceives as the welfare of the man he misleads, though less in loyalty to Leicester's person than to his power, with which he himself expects to rise. He schemes to weaken Amy's health with drugs and thereby prevent her appearance at Kenilworth. This plan fails; she escapes from virtual imprisonment at Cumnor Place and manages to reach the Queen and appeal for her protection. But Amy's tongue is tied by her promise to Leicester not to reveal their marriage without his consent and by her belief that it will ruin him with their sovereign. It is easy for Varney, aided by her evident sufferings, to represent her as disordered in her mind. She is forcibly returned to his custody; with Machiavellian chicanery he even manages to convince his lord that she had been seduced by a former suitor. "And yet, Varney," the duped Leicester cries, in an anguished echo of Othello, "so young, so fair, so fawning, and so false!"[43] He is undeceived too late; deluded by Varney's imitation of the whistle with which her husband had always announced his arrival, Amy falls through a loosened trapdoor on the staircase landing and hurtles to her death in a pit below.

Leicester himself is portrayed not so much as a man completely without integrity as one weakening in his struggles among the coils of an ambition that even his love for his bride does not enable him to resist. More than once he almost determines to follow the dictates of love and honor, to confess his marriage, and resign himself to his disgrace at court and fall from Elizabeth's favor. But each time some twist of circumstance or trick of Varney makes him waver in his purpose. Even near the end, though he still believes in Amy's guilt, his love for her wells up again: "Sir Richard Varney," he writes, "we have resolved to defer the matter entrusted to your care, and strictly command you to proceed no further in relation to our Countess . . ."[44] Leicester's psychology is rendered with fidelity and power; if he is far short of the heroic, even the melodrama in which he has entangled himself never leaves him less than absolutely convincing. When on learning of his deceptions Elizabeth's tumultuous passion stops just short of sending him to the Tower as a traitor, it is plain that the dangers he has risked were far from imaginary.

The tragic victim, though, is not Leicester but Amy Robsart. And she is no weak and almost passive sacrifice, like Lucy Ashton; she beats her bright plumage passionately against the bars of her gorgeous prison at Cumnor Place and resists with beak and claw. "I tell thee, Varney," she says, "if thou knowest it not, that not Elizabeth on the throne has more pride than the daughter of this obscure gentleman of Devon."[45] Though she loves and has some fear of her exalted husband, she never ceases importuning him to lift her publicly to his side as his Countess. She has early seen through Varney, whom she scorns and hates. "You have a courtly conscience, Master Varney," she tells him, "and your veracity will not, I think, interrupt your preferment in the world, such as it is."[46]

At every step she fierily rebels against Varney's tortuous schemes. She ragingly refuses to believe that her noble husband could stoop "to so dastardly and dishonourable a plan" as asking her to pretend to be Varney's wife—that "cloak-brushing, shoe-cleaning fellow—*him* there, my lord's lackey."[47] Not until she has been racked almost to the madness Varney imputes to her does she come to fear him, and even then she will not allow him near her. Though Leicester strains in the toils of his servant's deceptions with something of the anguish of Othello, Amy has none of the sad resignation of Desdemona. She resists to the last, but all her courage, her proud will, her desperate struggles, only sink her deeper and more irretrievably in disaster.

The Queen, her jealousy and her power, of course, are crucial. The real might of the Crown is as central to *Kenilworth* as the ideal concept of chivalry and its corruptions are to *Ivanhoe*; and as central as the conflict of the Church and the Reformers and the struggle between Mary and her unruly nobles are to *The Monastery* and *The Abbot*. At the lofty summit of the Tudor pyramid is Elizabeth; below and contending for rank, wealth, and power a descending hierarchy from the glittering but unstable Leicester and the blunt but trustworthy Sussex down through their followers, faithful and faithless.

It is significant of the moral organization of the novel that these two factions mirror, although in no overschematized way, various facets of the natures of their leaders. Although there are traitors and tricksters in the Sussex camp, as well as the adroit but not ignoble careerist Raleigh, his supporters include the straightforward soldier Blount, the honorable Cornish gentleman Tressilian, and Tressilian's servant Wayland Smith, this last striving to fight fire with fire. Leicester's dependents range through the dissolute returned buccaneer Michael Lambourne, the miserly Tony Foster, the cheating astrologer and alchemist Alasco, to the subtle and false-hearted Varney. They image in even more deeply fuliginous hues the slipperiness of their master.

All the gorgeous pomp of the entertainment at Kenilworth, in its superficial refulgence, reflects in turn the hollowness that gnaws at Leicester's manhood. Alasco is able to trick him with the fool's-gold promises of alchemy because Leicester is himself a tinseled counterfeit. His castle battlements—those tremendous red sandstone walls whose ruins still loom over the green Warwickshire countryside—bristle with splendidly clad men at arms. But only some of these "gigantic warders" who crowd its gates and towers are real men; all the rest are "mere pageants composed of pasteboard and buckram,"[48] as empty as the lord whose power and grandeur they seem to proclaim. "Ironically," as Hart puts it, "Scott makes a moral emblem of the pasteboard theatricality of which his severer critics accuse him."[49] The showy unreality of Kenilworth epitomizes the garish unreality of Leicester as man and statesman.

It would be hard to conceive a fusion of subject and setting that more superbly imaged the meaning it reveals. The events of those few days of pageantry are the core and climax of *Kenilworth*, and in the same measure their overwhelming and empty décor is the visible symbol of its theme. Just as Scott looks beneath the pretensions of the Age of Chivalry and sees in sixteenth-century Scotland the worldly passions beneath the masks of faith and patriotism, so he pierces through the Renaissance grandeur of Elizabeth's court. He does not cynically deny the existence of truth and nobility. But he sees how heavily they are alloyed with the venal and the false, both in the institutions of the age and in the people who embody them.

# NOTES

In abbreviating dates I have followed the American usage of giving month, day, and year: thus, 12/31/99 for December 31, 1799, and 1/1/09 for January 1, 1809. Dates later than the nineteenth century and other dates that might be confusing to the reader have the year in full. For the abbreviations used to identify quotations from or references to manuscript sources, the printed writings of Scott, and other printed books and articles, see the explanations in the four sections of the Bibliography. Special abbreviations used are: "n.d.," meaning "no date"; "n.y.," meaning "no year"; and "p.m.," meaning "postmark."

PART ONE

Chapter 1

1. Chambers, *Traditions*, 1, gives the population of Edinburgh in 1760 as 70,000, but this is an exaggeration. Anderson, *Hist. of Edin.*, 607, says that in 1755 Edinburgh had 48,000 and Leith 9,000; Mitchell, *Abstract of Brit. Hist. Stud.*, gives their combined population in 1801 as 83,000.
2. Edinburgh details in these two paragraphs are from Chambers, *Traditions;* Fyfe, *Edin. Under S.W.S.;* Lindsay, *Old Edin.;* and Skinner, *Royal Mile.* Chambers, *Traditions*, 242, says Mr. Scott's

house was east of Gateway; Dr. J. C. Corson, in a personal note to the author, says west.
3. Rogers, *Gen. Mem.*, Lockhart, I, 8–10, 63, 63 fn.; Grierson, *Scott*, 8, fn. 1; Glen MS, 56–71.
4. JGL, I, 6–7, 62; Dr. Corson note.
5. JGL, I, 6–7, 62, 87–8.
6. *Ibid.*, 88.
7. *Ibid.*, 8, 62; Rogers, *Gen. Mem.*, 146.
8. JGL, I, 62–3; Chambers, *Traditions*, 230–1.
9. The Nor Loch was not drained till 1816.
10. Downey Douglas: Chambers, *Traditions*, 162.
11. Grierson, *Scott*, 8, notes that the latest MS letters addressed to Anchor Close are dated 1767.
12. NLS, MS letter, quoted by Grierson, *Scott*, 8. The quotation is the opening of Pope's "Epistle to Dr. Arbuthnot."
13. NLS MS letter, 1/25/79, Jane Russell to Mrs. Walter Scott.
14. JGL, I, 11; Allan, *Life*, 37.
15. JGL, I, 11–2, 64.

Chapter 2

1. JGL, I, 12, 15; Rogers, *Gen. Mem.*, for Janet's age.
2. JGL, I, 13.
3. *Ibid.*, 66.
4. *Ibid.*, 12.

5. *Ibid.*, 66–7.
6. *Poetical Works*, VII, *Marmion*, III, Intro., 137.
7. *Old Kelso Days with Scott;* Crockett, *Scott Country*, 5.
8. Personal observation.
9. Crockett, *Scott Country*, 3; *Scotsman*, 3/9/1921; personal observation.
10. JGL, I, 64; Crockett, *Scott Country*, 9.
11. Crockett, *Scott Country*, 9–10.
12. Slightly modified from *Marmion*, Intro., III, 137.
13. JGL, I, 66–7; Allan (Weir) says, though, that this was in Edinburgh.
14. JGL, I, 67–8.
15. The actual title is "The Capacity and Extent of Human Understanding, Exemplified in the Extraordinary Case of Automathes, a young Nobleman . . . left on a Desert Island." Attributed to John Kirkby. First published, London, 1745; reprinted in Weber's *Popular Romances*, 583–638, Edinburgh, 1817.
16. JGL, I, 14–5, 67–8.
17. *Ibid.*, 14.
18. *Poetical Works*, VII, *Marmion*, III, *Intro.*, 139.
19. JGL, I, 14.
20. Rogers, *Gen. Mem.;* JGL, I, 5.
21. JGL, I, 5.
22. *Ibid.*, 3, 52–4; *Poetical Works*, I, *Minstrelsy*, I, 210, Intro., fn. 2.
23. *Letters*, VIII, 332, fn. 1.
24. JGL, I, 54, 305–6, 309–11; *Letters*, I, 144–6. "Meg's" real name was Agnes.
25. *Ibid.*, 54–5.
26. *Ibid.*, 3–4, 55–6.
27. *Ibid.*, 4–5, 56–7.
28. *Ibid.*, 57–8; *G. Man*, XXXIX, xii; *Letters*, XII, 37, Basil Hall, 10/27/36.
29. *G.Man.*, XXXIX, xiii; JGL, I, 58.
30. *Peveril*, Pref., XXIV.
31. JGL, I, 50–1, 67; *Journal*, quoted by JGL, I, 52.
32. *Scotsman*, 7/9/1921, Dr. Wilson's daughter's reminiscences.
33. JGL, I, 16.
34. JGL, I, 68.

Chapter 3

1. Lindsay, *Old Edin.* 7–8; Lindsay, *Georgian Edin.*, 11.

2. Tait and Gray, *George Square.*
3. Contract in NLS between Walter Scott, WS, and James Brown. Quoted in *Letters*, VIII, 190, fn. 1. It is reasonable, since the first payment was made 5/15/73, to think the move was made in course of a year or so.
4. Tait and Gray, *George Square;* MacDonald, *Our Square;* personal inspection, courtesy of the present owner, the Reverend Mr. Ian Simpson.
5. Ferguson, *The Honorable Henry Erskine*, 134–5; NLS MS, 3234, reminiscences.
6. JGL, I, 8–9.
7. Tait and Gray, *George Square.*
8. *Chronicles of Canongate*, "Aunt Margaret's Mirror," 252.
9. JGL, I, 16. That Dr. Wilson had something to do with the experiment is shown by letter quoted in *The Century Memorial* by C. D. M. Lockhart, from A. M. Robertson at Bath to Dr. Wilson of Kelso, 8/11/75, expressing hopes of a cure "from his great youth." This letter was given to this Lockhart in 1871 by Wilson's daughter, then a very old lady (Glen MS; NLS MS, 7533, ff. 3–28).
10. JGL, II, 18; *Letters*, III, 62, 62 fn.
11. JGL, I, 16–8.
12. Cook, *New Love Poems*, 11–5, 17–21 (partly quoted in *Letters*, I, 4, 4 fn. 1).
13. *Misc. Prose*, XX, 167–272; "Review of *Life of Kemble* (quoted by JGL, I, 68–9).
14. JGL, I, 17.
15. *Ibid.*, 17–8.
16. *Ibid.*, 17; *SWS Quarterly*, IV, 184, 184 fn. giving as ref. Home's *Works*, I, 181; D.N.B.; and *Life of Home*, II, 507.
17. JGL, II, 9, 17.
18. *Ibid.*, I, 13; *Journal*, 669.
19. JGL, I, 495.
20. *Ibid.* 13–4.
21. *Letters*, IV, 38, Lady L. Stuart, 1/31/17; quoted also in JGL, III, 92–3.
22. JGL, I, 14–15; NLS MS letter, Dr. Duncan to Scott's parents, 9/16/76.
23. JGL, I, 18; *Journal*, 682, 6/27/30.
24. JGL, I, 18–9, fn. 1, 73; *Journal*, 682; *Antiq.*, ix; JGL, III, 63.

25. JGL, I, 18.
26. *Ibid.*, 73; *Scotsman* 7/9/1921, quoting Dr. Wilson's daughter's reminiscences.
27. *Scotsman*, 7/9/1921.
28. JGL, I, 74.
29. *Ibid.*, 72–3.
30. *Ibid.*, 70–1.
31. *Ibid.*, 72.

### Chapter 4

1. JGL, I, 9.
2. *Ibid.*, 20.
3. *Ibid.*, 197.
4. *Ibid.*, 20.
5. *Ibid.*, 87.
6. *Letters*, VI, 118–9, Lady L. Stuart, after 1/16/20.
7. JGL, I, 20–1.
8. *Ibid.*, 21.
9. Allan, *Life*, 39.
10. JGL, I, 27–8.
11. *Ibid.*, 74.
12. *Ibid.*, 17.
13. NLS, MS, 1554–9, Harriett Scott to JGL.
14. Lindsay, *Georgian Edin.*, 11–2.
15. Chambers, *Traditions*, 336–7.
16. *Chambers's Edin. Journal*, 3/7/40.
17. Letter to Maria Edgeworth, 2/24/24, quoted by JGL, IV, 164.
18. *Waverley*, cvi–cvii.
19. Quoted by Pope-Hennessy, 23.
20. *Waverley*, cvii.
21. *Journal*, 733.
22. Allan, *Life*, 37.
23. JGL, I, 21, 74 (*cf.* Glen MS, 7).
24. For Nicol see JGL, I, 25.
25. Glen MS, 7.
26. JGL, I, 21–2.
27. *Ibid.*, 75 fn.
28. NLS MS letter, Jane Russell to Mrs. Scott from Madras, 11/29/81.
29. JGL, I, 76–7.
30. *Ibid.*, 79–80.
31. *Ibid.*, 23.
32. Details about Edinburgh in this paragraph and those that follow are from Chambers, *Traditions;* Fyfe, *Edin. Under SWS;* Lindsay, *Old Edin.;* and personal observations.
33. C. K. Sharpe, quoted by Stalker, *Intimate Life*, 20.
34. Morrison, "Random Reminiscences," 786.
35. Chambers, *Traditions*, 264.

36. *Chambers's Edin. Journal*, 3/9/40.
37. *Ibid.*
38. *Lives of Lindsays*, II, 327; letter to Lady Anne Barnard, somewhat later than *Letters*, VIII, 327, 7/14/23. *Cf.* also Lady Anne to WS, *ibid.*, 43–4, fn. 1, 7/19/23.
39. *H. Mid-Lothian.* I, 79, Ch. VI.
40. Lockhart, *Peter's Letters*, 194–8.
41. *Ibid.*, 202; Dr. Corson tells me JGL was wrong in saying "purple velvet with blue cloth and silk."
42. *Chambers's Edin. Journal*, 3/7/40, 52–4.
43. JGL, I, 81.
44. *Ibid.*, 80.
45. *Waverley*, Gen. Pref. No. III, lxxiii.
46. *Ibid.*, lxxiv; Tait and Gray, *George Square*.
47. *Waverly*, Gen. Pref. No. III, lxxiv–lxxv.
48. *Ibid.*, lxxvi.

### Chapter 5

1. Glen MS, 7.
2. MS letter, from Mrs. Russell, 1/25/79.
3. NLS MS letters from Robert, 6/1/79, 9/21/79, 9/29/79; Glen MS, 5, quoting Marine Records (S. O. Marine Misc., V, 654, p. 31).
4. JGL, I, 10; NLS MS letters from C. Forbes, 12/16/79; and Mrs. Keith to Mrs. Scott, 11/9/80.
5. JGL, I, 94.
6. Allan, *Life*, 39.
7. *Poetical Works*, VII, *Marmion*, 295–6, fn. 2.
8. JGL, I, 94, fn. 41.
9. *G.Man.*, *Intro.*, ixxvii–xxxv.
10. JGL, I, 86; Tait and Gray, *George Square;* "Aunt Margaret's Mirror," 250.
11. "Aunt Margaret's Mirror," 254; letter to Joanna Baillie, 2/10/1872. quoted by JGL, IV, 5–6.
12. "Aunt Margaret's Mirror," *Intro.*, 246.
13. Letter to Joanna Baillie, 2/10/22, quoted by JGL, IV, 4–6.
14. "Aunt Margaret's Mirror," *Intro.*, 246.
15. Letter to Joanna Baillie, as above; also JGL, I, 86; IV, 4–6; "Aunt Margaret's Mirror," *Intro.*, 246, for last quotation of paragraph. WS says he was ten at time but NLS

MS letter, Dr. Rutherford to Mrs. Scott, fixes the date as 1/4/81.

16. JGL, I, 24.
17. *Ibid.*, 25–26.
18. *Chambers's Edin. Jo.*, 3/7/40, 52–4.
19. JGL, I, 25.
20. *Ibid.*, 24–5.
21. *Ibid.*, 27.
22. *Ibid.*, 84–5.
23. *Ibid.*, 23, 86.
24. *Ibid.*, 23.
25. *Ibid.*, 90.
26. *Ibid.*, 23.
27. *Ibid.*, 24.
28. *Ibid.*, 90.
29. *Ibid.*, 87.
30. *Ibid.*, 92.
31. *Ibid.*, 91–2.
32. *Ibid.*, 24.
33. *Ibid.*, 75.
34. *Ibid.*, 75–6. Corrected from Claud Russell MS, Abbotsford, which gives the story in a much simpler form.
35. *Journal*, 629, 4/25/29.
36. JGL, I, 28. The Doctor dated these July, 1783–Edin. H–S. MS.
37. *Poetical Works*, IV, 54; also quoted by JGL, I, 78.
38. JGL, I, 25; 90–1.
39. *Ibid.*, 35.
40. *Ibid.*, 100–1; *Waverley*, Gen. Pref., xvi.
41. *Waverley*, Gen. Pref., xvii.
42. JGL, I, 101.
43. *Ibid.*, 92–3.
44. *Ibid.*, 117.
45. Quoted by Grierson, *Scott*, 12–3.
46. JGL, I, 29.

### PART TWO

#### Chapter 1

1. JGL, I, 26.
2. *Scotsman*, 1/9/1921, and Dr. Corson note to author.
3. JGL, I, 26.
4. *Ibid.*, 26–7, 97.
5. *Ibid.*, 96; description from a boyhood portrait, though JB later became fat.
6. Glen MS, 7566, 133; letter of 6/27/1933 to Grierson.
7. JGL, I, 96–7.
8. *Ibid.*, 97.
9. *Redg.*, I, 299, n. I by W.S.
10. JGL, I, 30.
11. Crockett, *Scott Country*, 34.

12. JGL, I, 29–30.
13. *Letters*, III, 468, Sotheby, 3/21/14.
14. JGL, I, 29.
15. *Ibid.*, 30.
16. *Misc. Prose*, XXI, "On Landscape Gardening," 88–9; *Journal*, 391, 8/29/27.
17. JGL, I, 30–1.
18. *Ibid.*, 9.
19. Glen transcript from Marine Records (S.O. Marine Misc., V., 654, p. 31).
20. JGL, I, 31.
21. *Ibid.*, 100.
22. Fyfe, *Edin. Under SWS*, 24.
23. JGL, I, 31.
24. Fyfe, *Edin. Under SWS*, 26.
25. *Ibid.*, 25.
26. JGL, I, 31–2.
27. *Ibid.*, 32.
28. *N & Q*, 4th Series, III, 215, 3/6/1869.
29. JGL, I, 32.
30. *Ibid.*
31. *Ibid.*, 32–3.
32. *Ibid.*, 108.
33. *Ibid.*, 33.
34. *Ibid.*, 108. WS says ethics, not logic; but JGL points out that Bruce taught logic and that it was with Dugald Stewart that he took ethics and moral philosophy.
35. JGL, I, 100.
36. *Ibid.*, 104; but the inclusion of Craigmillar and Cramond is hypothetical. Description of details from personal observation.
37. JGL, I, 104–5.
38. Details from personal observation and lines attributed to WS in *Rosslyn Guidebook*, p. 82. The pillar is now white—either painted or whitewashed.
39. JGL, I, 104–5.
40. *Ibid.*, 103–4.
41. *Ibid.*
42. *Ibid.*
43. *Redg.*, I, 214, and JGL, I, 34, and Pref.
44. JGL, I, 34; *Minute Books of Society of Writers to the Signet*, 5/15/86, quoted by JGL, I, 111.
45. JGL, I, 34.
46. *Ibid.*, 121–2.
47. *Redg.*, I, 212–3, quoted by JLG, I, 157, who adds on the authority of Will Clerk, "nothing could be more exact . . . than the resemblance of

the Mrs. Sanders Fairford of *Redgauntlet*" to Mr. Scott.

48. JGL, I, 121.
49. *Redg.*, I, 13, but there is no question that it applies to Mr. Scott.
50. JGL, I, 7.
51. *Ibid.*, 34.
52. *Ibid.*, 113.
53. *Ibid.*, 34.
54. *Ibid.*, 36.
55. *Ibid.*, 35–6, 110.
56. *Ibid.*, 35–6; *Waverley*, Pref. xvii; JGL, I, 110. It is uncertain whether WS read *De la None* in French or English. Abbotsford library has the book in English (London, 1587), tr. by E[dward] A[ggis]. WS never acquired conversational facility in French.
57. JGL, I, 109.
58. *Ibid.*, 114. JGL spells it Meikle, but it should be Wm. Julius Mickle.
59. *Ibid.*, 102.
60. *Ibid.*, 113 and *Kenilworth* Pref.
61. *Letters*, XI, 342, Strong 5/10/30; *cf.* also MacCunn, 105.
62. JGL, I, 101. Dr. Corson says there were about twenty volumes in Abbotsford library; JGL alludes to only six of them. These, according to Dr. Corson, contained 112 chapbooks printed between 1776 and 1786 and selling from ld to 3d.
63. JGL, I, 117.
64. *Ibid.*, 28.
65. Fyfe, *Edin. Under SWS*, 65–6.
66. JGL, I, 115; *cf. SWS Quarterly*, I, Apr., 1927, ff. 42–7, "The Meeting of Burns and Scott," by John Hughes.
67. JGL, I, 115.
68. *Ibid.*, 115–6.
69. Quoted by Pearson, *Life and Personality*, 20.
70. JGL, I, 115.
71. *Ibid.*, 174.
72. *Poetical Works*, VI, *Lay*, XXX, 68, and n. D, 231–3.
73. JGL, I, 112.
74. *Ibid.*, 118.
75. *Fair Maid*, I, 17–8.
76. JGL, I, 119.
77. *Letters*, VII, 123, Maria Edgeworth, 4/?/22.
78. *Waverley*, Intro., cvi.
79. *Ibid.*, cv–cvi.
80. JGL, I, 118; *Waverley*, Intro., ciii–cv.

81. JGL, I, 119–20.
82. *Ibid.*, 121; *R. Roy*, Intro. lxxx–lxxxii, fn. 1. On the Teith was also Doune Castle, home of WS's friend John James Edmondstone of Newton, to whom during these years, WS paid an annual visit (Allan, *Life*, 56).
83. JGL, I, 36, 107; *Waverley*, Pref., xvii.
84. *Ibid.*, 37–8.
85. *Ibid.*, 37.
86. *Ibid.*, 107.
87. *Ibid.*, 107, 110, 37.
88. *Ibid.*, 107–8. JGL says the cottage was bought from Scott's father; Leishman says from Dorothea Jackson, daughter of Dr. Charles Jackson, on 5/24/88 (see Dr. Corson, *Bibliography*, #2849).

## Chapter 2

1. *Old Kelso Days; Scotsman*, 7/9/1921.
2. Cook, *New Love Poems*, 1; *cf. Letters*, I, lvii–lviii.
3. *Waverley*, I, 33.
4. Cook, *New Love Poems*, 1–3.
5. *Letters*, I, 1, Jessie.
6. Cook, *New Love Poems*, 3–4.
7. *Ibid.*, 5–7.
8. *Ibid.*, 7. The correspondence does not reveal Jessie's last name. Dr. Corson tells me a lady has discovered but refuses to divulge it.
9. Cook, *New Love Poems*, 11–2.
10. V and A MS. Biog.
11. Cook, *New Love Poems*, 7.
12. *Letters*, I, 2–3.
13. *Ibid.*, 3.
14. *Ibid.*, 9–10.
15. *Ibid.*, 9.
16. *Ibid.*, 11–20, 22–7; *cf. Letters*, I, 4–6, fn. 1.
17. *Letters*, I, 3–4; Cook, *New Love Poems*, 11.
18. V and A MS, Biog.
19. *Letters*, I, 8; Cook, *New Love Poems*, 24.
20. *Letters*, I, 7; Cook, *New Love Poems*, 12.
21. Cook, *New Love Poems*, 27–9.
22. *Ibid.*, 29.
23. *Ibid.*, 29–30.
24. *Ibid.*, 30–1.
25. *Ibid.*, 30.

26. *Ibid.*, 31–2.
27. *Ibid.*, 34.
28. *Ibid.*, 35–6.
29. *Ibid.*, 39.
30. *Poetical Works*, VII; *Marmion*, III, xv, 5–6.
31. Cook, *New Love Poems*, 40.
32. JGL, I, 136, 138.
33. Cook, *New Love Poems*, 40.
34. JGL, I, 44.
35. *Ibid.* and Dr. Corson note to author.
36. JGL, I, 44–5, 122.
37. *Ibid.*, 45. The unfortunate victim of WS's strictures was Robert Dick.
38. *Ibid.*, 123.
39. *G.Man.*, II, 89.
40. JGL, I, 45.
41. *Ibid.*, 157.
42. *Ibid.*, 123–4.
43. *Misc. Prose*, XII, *Napoleon*, V, 101, fn. 1.
44. JGL, I, 124.
45. *Ibid.*, 133.
46. *Ibid.*, 126.
47. See *Henry IV*, Pt. 1, V, 4.
48. JGL, I, 125.
49. *Ibid.*, 46.
50. JGL, I, 33; Duncan Forbes: "Rationalism," *Cambridge Journal*, VII, I, 20–35. See also Tytler, *Elements of Gen. Hist.*, I, 43–4.
51. JGL, I, 28–9.
52. *Letters*, VII, 34, Charles Scott, 11/21/21; *Letters*, VIII, 104, Montagu, 10/5/23.
53. Forbes, "Rationalism."
54. Fyfe, *Edin. Under SWS*, 30–1.
55. *Journal*, 560, 6/14/28.
56. *Ibid.*, 58, 12/27/25.
57. *Letters*, IV, 181, see 2/?/16, and fn. 2.
58. Ferguson, *Essay on History of Civil Society*, 74.
59. *Ibid.*, 81 (both quoted by Forbes, "Rationalism").
60. *Ibid.*, 48–51.
61. JGL, I, 43.
62. *Ibid.*, 124.
63. *Ibid.*, 134–6, although not named.
64. *Journal*, 677.
65. JGL, I, 128.
66. *Ibid.*, 42.
67. *Ibid.*, 43.
68. *Ibid.*, 146, 148, *Letters*, I, 16, Capt. Robert Scott, 9/30/90, says he gave this paper the preceding year and outlines the argument.
69. JGL, I, 129, 148.

70. *Ibid.*, 150.
71. Partly from JGL, I, 50; partly from Allan, *Life*, 68.
72. JGL, I, 151. According to Fyfe, *Edin. Under SWS*, 85, F.J. was admitted 12/11/92.
73. JGL, I, 152.
74. *Minstrelsy*, I, 227 fn.
75. JGL, I, 152. Dr. Corson, in a letter to the author, voices doubts that the particular source would be identifiable, but it may quite possibly have been of an individual pattern.
76. *Redg.*, I, 213.
77. JGL, I, 153.
78. *Ibid.*, 154.
79. *Ibid.*, 148–9.
80. *Ibid.*
81. *Ibid.*, 150.
82. *Ibid.*, 46, 158, and Glen MS, 2533.
83. JGL, I, 159.
84. *Ibid.*, 158–9. The Latin title is *Dispututio Juridica de Cadaveribus Punitorum* (Just. Dig. Lib. XLVIII, Tit. XXIV).
85. Lord Braxfield was the original of the judge in Robert Louis Stevenson's *Weir of Hermiston*.
86. JGL, I, 158–9; cf. *Redg.*, I, 128–9.

### Chapter 3

1. JGL, I, 127–8.
2. *Ibid.*, 38.
3. *Ibid.*, 39.
4. *Redg.*, I, 17.
5. JGL, I, 126.
6. Allan, *Life*, 118–9.
7. JGL, I, 128.
8. *Ibid.*, 128, fn. 1.
9. *Journal*, 108–9, 2/17/26.
10. *Journal*, 143, 3/28/26.
11. *Ibid.*, 58.
12. *Ibid.*, 143.
13. *Ibid.*, 58.
14. JGL, I, 39.
15. *Ibid.*, 40.
16. *Ibid.*, 39–40.
17. *Journal*, 118, 3/1/26.
18. JGL, I, 40.
19. *Ibid.*, 129, fn. 1.
20. Chambers, *Traditions*, 145.
21. *Journal*, 330, 3/13/27.
22. Chambers, *Traditions*, 145.
23. Fyfe, *Edin. Under SWS*, 125.
24. Chambers, *Traditions*, 138–9, 139 fn.
25. *Ibid.*, 143–4.

26. *Ibid.*, 149.
27. *Ibid.*, 155.
28. *Ibid.*, 153–4.
29. JGL, I, 129. JGL says from his corduroy (grosgrain?), but I doubt this.
30. *Journal*, 498, 3/4/28.
31. *Letters*, I, 9, Clerk (1788–90?).
32. *Ibid.*, V, 51–2, Buccleuch, 1/14/18.
33. JGL, I, 127.
34. *Ibid.*, 131–2.
35. *Journal*, 82, 1/26/26.
36. JGL, I, 114.
37. *Journal*, 498, 3/4/28.
38. *Ibid.*, 333, 3/21/27.
39. Chambers, *Traditions*, 148.
40. *Ibid.*, 148, fn.
41. Fyfe, *Edin. Under SWS*, 124, gives these as favorite drinking places of the Bar, as does Chambers, *Traditions*, 297–8. They are also mentioned in *Redgauntlet*.
42. Fyfe, *Edin. Under SWS*, 52.
43. *Ibid.*, 321.
44. *Ibid.*, 40, *who quotes* WS.
45. *Letters*, VIII, 38–9, Lady Anne Barnard, 7/14/1823.
46. *Ibid.*, 38.
47. *Journal*, 5, 11/21/1825.
48. Chambers, *Traditions*, 249–53.
49. JGL, I, 137.
50. *N & Q*, Vol. 157, p. 24, 7/13/1929.
51. JGL, I, 138–9.
52. Chambers, *Traditions*, 265–8; Fyfe, *Edin. Under SWS*, 34–6.
53. Tait and Gray, *George Square*; Lockhart, *Peter's Letters*, 61.
54. JGL, I, 138.
55. JGL, I, 137–8.
56. *Ibid.*, 108.
57. *Letters*, I, 16–7, Robert Scott, 9/30/90.
58. *Ibid.*, 7–10, Mrs. Scott, 9/5/88.
59. *Ibid.*, 11, Will Clerk, 8/6/90; 14, Clerk, 9/3/90; 9, Mrs. Scott, 9/5/88.
60. *Ibid.*, I, 18–20, Clerk, 8/26/91.
61. *Ibid.*, 10–2, Clerk, 8/6/90.
62. *Ibid.*, 13–5, Clerk, 9/3/90.
63. *Ibid.*, 24–5, fn., Walter Scott, WS to his son, 8/15/92.
64. *Ibid.*, 22, Clerk, 9/10/92.
65. *Ibid.*, 23, Clerk, 9/30/92.
66. *Ibid.*, 24.
67. Fyfe, *Edin. Under SWS*, 94, quoting Cockburn's *Memoirs*.
68. *Letters* I, 4, Clerk, 9/30/92.
69. JGL, I, 166.

70. *Ibid.*, 134–5, outlining the story, though without giving Kerr's name; various MS letters in NLS.
71. WS to his son, 8/2/92, 8/15/92.
72. Shortreed MS, NLS Acc. 2559, John Elliott Shortreed's account of Robert Shortreed's oral reminiscences. Partly used in JGL, I, 167 *et seq.*, and somewhat more in *Cornhill Mag.*, 73, 266–83. My quotations are all from the MS, but where JGL has them I give page references for the reader's convenience, though I have corrected JGL from original.
73. Shortreed MS; not in JGL.
74. JGL, I, 167.
75. Shortreed MS; not in JGL.
76. JGL, I, 168.
77. Shortreed MS; not in JGL.
78. JGL, I, 168, though he has somewhat altered the text.
79. Shortreed MS; not in JGL.
80. JGL, I, 169.
81. *Ibid.*, 171. Dr. Corson thinks this later than 1793 (see my comment on n. 87, which applies to this note also).
82. Shortreed MS; not in JGL.
83. JGL, I, 169, but much garbled.
84. Shortreed MS; not in JGL.
85. JGL, I, 169.
86. Shortreed MS; not in JGL.
87. JGL, I, 170. Dr. Corson thinks this was not in 1793 but a later year; but I have found no documentary evidence and have grouped a number of such anecdotes to create the atmosphere of the "raids."
88. Crockett, *Scott Country*, 146.
89. JGL, I, 167.
90. *Ibid.*, 170.
91. *Ibid.*, 171.
92. *Ibid.*, 168.

Chapter 4

1. JGL, I, 173. Descriptive details about the people and the Outer House are taken from Lockhart's *Peter's Letters*, 201, and MacCunn, *Sir W's Friends*.
2. JGL, I, 173.
3. *Ibid.*, 174; *Peter's Letters*, 202; Fyfe, *Edin. Under SWS*, 97.
4. Chambers, *Traditions*, 133.
5. Fyfe, *Edin. Under SWS*, 97–9.
6. JGL, I, 174.

7. *Ibid.*, 133.
8. *Ibid.*, 162, fn. 4.
9. Chambers, *Traditions*, 130.
10. MacDonald, *Juridical Review.*
11. *Letters*, I, 25, Clerk, 9/30/92.
12. JGL, I, 174.
13. *Poetical Works*, IV, *Minstrelsy*, 36–7, 44.
14. *Ibid.*, 38–40.
15. *Ibid.*, 41.
16. *Ibid.*, 42.
17. *Ibid.*, 43.
18. *Ibid.*, 42.
19. *Ibid.*, 44; JGL, I, 175.
20. JGL, I, 191; Allan, *Life*, 68. But JGL mistakenly dates it winter 1793–4; it was 3/19/93.
21. JGL, I, 172–3.
22. *Ibid.*, 177.
23. *Ibid.*, 182, but JGL imagines these were in the summer; MS letter to C. Kerr 5/10/93 shows during spring vacation (incl. Perthshire trip).
24. JGL, I, 183.
25. *Ibid.*, 178–80.
26. *Ibid.*, 181.
27. *Ibid.*
28. MacDonald, *Juridical Review; cf.* JGL, I, 230.
29. JGL, I, 183, puts this trip in the spring, but, I think, is undoubtedly wrong. Clerk was on this trip, as he was on that to Meigle, etc., and they were *joined* at Meigle by Ferguson, who had been on all the spring trip. From Craghill Rattray to Meigle is a logical progression. The places already visited from 3/12–5/12 are enough to have filled that time.
30. Descriptive details are from *Waverley*, I, 59–60, 62–3. WS says these were based on Craghill Rattray, though the house and gardens were from Ravelston and Bruntsfield (*Waverley*, I, 68). Clerk recognized them, as JGL says, I, 184.
31. JGL, I, 184; *Waverley*, I, 65.
32. JGL, I, 184.
33. *Ibid.*, 185–6, quoting "Essay on Landscape Gardening"; *Misc. Prose*, XXI, 77.
34. *Letters on Demonology and Witchcraft* (*Misc. Prose*, XXX), quoted by JGL, I, 186–7.
35. JGL, I, 185.
36. *Letters*, I, 26, Murray, 9/13/93.

37. NLS MS, 871, ff. 81–2, Kerr to WC 4/19/93; Kerr says "The Fray of Stoupar," but probably this is really "The Fray of Support." The *Hawick Museum* is a publication, not a place; see *Minstrelsy*, II, 61.
38. JGL, I, 188.
39. NLS, Shortreed Papers, inaccurately quoted by JGL, I, 189.
40. *Ibid.*
41. *Letters*, I, 29, Shortreed, 12/18/93; also NLS, Shortreed Papers.
42. *Letters*, III, 429, fn. 1.
43. JGL, I, 191.
44. Allan, *Life*, 68.
45. JGL, I, 191.
46. MacDonald, *Juridical Review.*
47. NLS, Shortreed Papers. JGL does not mention a trip at this time, but it seems to fit in, because during the preceding winter, WS had been arranging to dig at Hermitage and the sketching episode seems to precede the excavating. It must be the following summer that the digging took place, as any later in the spring would probably be too late for snow.
48. *Ibid.* The episode was more likely at this time than later, during the course of publication of *Minstrelsy*, as JGL claims.
49. JGL, I, 191–2.
50. *Ibid.*, 192–3, says end of April, but *Letters*, I, 30, Murray, 4/16/94, sets the date of the theatre riot as 4/12/96 (later WS was counsel for Donald Maclean, sued by Joseph Mason for £600 for injuries received during this riot (NLS MS, 1567, fn. 1).
51. *Letters*, I, 30–1, C. Rutherford, 6/8/94.
52. JGL, I, 194; NLS, Shortreed Papers.
53. JGL, V, 356.
54. NLS, Shortreed Papers.
55. *Letters*, I, 34, C. Rutherford, 9/5/94, says he came from Kelso 9/1.
56. Bryant, *Endurance*, 134–7.
57. *Ibid.*, 137.
58. JGL, I, 194.
59. *Letters*, I, 34, C. Rutherford, 9/5/94.
60. Bryant, *Eudurance*, 136.
61. Fyfe, *Edin. Under SWS*, 95–6.
62. Grierson, *Scott*, 27, quoting letter

from Robert to Henry Dundas, 6/21/94.

63. *Letters*, I, 34–5.
64. Bryant, *Endurance*, 138.
65. *Letters*, I, 35–6.
66. *Ibid.*, 37, C. Rutherford, 11/8/94. They were Mr. and Mrs. John Hepburn Belsches.
67. *Ibid.*, 38.
68. JGL, I, 39.
69. NLS, unpubl. letters WS, WS to his son, 8/8/92, 8/15/92.
70. *Journal*, 151, 8/8/26; also quoted by JGL, IV, 497.
71. NLS MS letter, WS to Wm. Scott, 3/19/95.
72. Bryant, *Endurance*, 134.
73. MacDonald, *Juridical Review*.
74. JGL, I, 198–200; Allan, *Life*, 86–8.
75. *Ibid.*
76. *Letters*, I, 41–2, Clerk, 8/23/95.
77. *Ibid.*, 40–2, Clerk, 8/23/95.

Chapter 5

1. The descriptive details are based both on portraits of Williamina and on the word portrait of Matilda in *Poetical Works*, IX, *Rokeby*, Canto IV, St. V, 11, 1–20, which Scott himself said was based on Williamina. See also *Letters*, V, 165, Maria Edgeworth, 5/10/18; *Journal* (Doyles ed.), I, 404, fn. 1; JGL, II, 255–6.
2. Sands, *Sir W's Congé*, 6–10.
3. *Ibid.*, 184.
4. JGL, I, 138–9.
5. Sands, *Sir W's Congé*, 24.
6. *Letters*, I, 25, Clerk, 9/30/92.
7. NLS MS, Kerr to WS, 11/22/92.
8. *Ibid.*, 12/19/92. Quoted by JGL, I, 136, without giving name of writer.
9. *Redg.*, I, 115; *cf.* JGL, I, 136.
10. NLS MS, 3220, f. 35.
11. *Journal*, 359, 6/16/27, says merely "thirty years ago."
12. Hughes, *Letters and Recollections*, 134.
13. *Rokeby*, Canto I, st. XXVIII, 1, 18.
14. JGL, II, 340, quoting *Journal*, 7/30/14.
15. *Letters*, I, 32, C. Rutherford, 6/8/94.
16. *Ibid.*, 37, C. Rutherford, Oct., Nov. 1794.

17. MS commonplace Vol. *Adversaria*, in NLS. Also pub. in *Poetry Review*, XL, 1940, 266.
18. NLS MS, WS to Wm. Scott, 3/19/95.
19. Grierson, *Scott*, 29, renders this "the meekness of her manners," but my reading of the original MS is "sweetness."
20. *Poetical Works*, IX, Rokeby, Canto I, st. XXVII, 11, 1–18.
21. Quoted in Grierson, *Scott*, 29.
22. Sands, *Sir W's Congé*, 71, fn. 1.
23. Inferences drawn from *Letters*, I, 40–1, Clerk, 8/23/95.
24. *Letters*, I, 40–1.
25. *Ibid.*, 40.
26. *Ibid.*, 42.
27. JGL, I, 204; *Poetical Works*, IV, *Minstrelsy*, 56–8.
28. *Letters*, I, 60, Taylor, 11/25/96, says it was Geo. Cranstoun; JGL, I, 29, says Miss Cranstoun; *Poetical Works*, VI, 292, in Intro. to "William and Helen," says "a gentleman."
29. *Letters*, I, 42, Clerk, 8/23/95.
30. JGL, I, 203, 214.
31. *Ibid.*, 206.
32. MacDonald, *Juridical Review*.
33. Allan, *Life*, 88.
34. JGL, I, 208; *Letters*, I, 48, Walker, 5/6/96; Sands, *Sir W's Congé*, 71, 74.
35. JGL, I, 139.
36. *Ibid.*, 204–5; *Minstrelsy*, IV, 59; Hall, *Schloss Hainfeld*, 333.
37. JGL, I, 204–5.
38. *Ibid.*, 205.
39. *Letters*, I, 45, Erskine, 4/25/96. For the name of the pony, NLS MS, J. A. Cranstoun to WS, 4/18/96. Cf. Sands, *Sir W's Congé*, 57.
40. *Letters*, I, 45–6, Erskine, 4/24/91, and 46, fn. 2.
41. NLS MS, J. A. Cranstoun to WS, 4/18/96 (addressed to Montrose and forwarded from there to Aberdeen).
42. *Letters*, I, 46, Erskine, 4/24/96.
43. Sands, *Sir W's Congé*, 59–60.
44. *Letters*, I, 46.
45. Sands, *Sir W's Congé*, 60–1. Entry in Register of the Honorary Burgesses of the Borough of Aberdeen, 4/19/96.
46. *Letters*, I, 47, Erskine, 4/24/96.

47. NLS MS, J. A. Cranstoun to WS, 4/18/96. Inaccurately and incompletely quoted by JGL, I, 208–9.
48. JGL, I, 208, mistakenly puts the visit in autumn. See *Letters*, I, 48, Walker, 5/6/96, and 48, fn. 1.
49. Sands, *Sir W's Congé*, 71.
50. *Letters*, I, 50–1, Walker, 5/6/96.
51. *Ibid.*, 48–9.
52. Sands, *Sir W's Congé*, 73.
53. *Ibid.*, 125.
54. *Ibid.*, 72.
55. *Letters*, I, 51, Walker, 5/6/96, and fn. 1.
56. Quoted by Grierson, *Scott*, 37.
57. JGL, I, 93, 208.
58. *Ibid.*, 204–5.
59. Sands, *Sir W's* Congé, 126, gives date as 8/26/96.
60. NLS MS, 2553, f. 74 Jane Anne Cranstoun to WS, 11/18/96.
61. Wm. Erskine P.S. to Mary Anne Erskine letter to WS, 9/12/96; *Letters*, I, 54–5, Erskine, 9/20/96, replying to one from W.E., 9/18/96; *Letters*, I, 57–8, Miller, 10/2/96.
62. Letter from Lady Jane to Wm. Forbes, (pub. in *Century Mag.*, July, 1899, 368–74), quoted by Sands, *Sir W's Congé*, 85–6. Not dated, but obviously *before* the engagement was announced 10/12/96. Therefore the words "last week," in the letter, mean the winter of 1795–6. *Cf.* Sands, *Sir W's Congé*, 87.
63. Quoted by Sands, *Sir W's Congé*, 86.
64. See Partington, *Post-Bag*, 232, Lady J. Steward to SWS, 10/23/1827; also quoted by Douglas in his edition of *Journal*, II, 55, fn. 1. Partington gives the date as 10/29/27, but this is impossible: WS received it 10/25 on getting home from Mertoun. "3" sometimes looks like "9."
65. *Letters*, I, 53, Erskine, 9/9/96.
66. NLS MS, M. A. Erskine to WS, 12/12/96. Inaccurate and incomplete in JGL.
67. *Letters*, I, 54, Erskine, 9/9/96.
68. *Ibid.*, 56, Erskine, 9/26/96.
69. *Ibid.*, but Grierson prints it "regards M"; "W" is my suggestion.
70. *Ibid.*, 56–7; Grierson prints "graer dog"; Sands makes it "graca." Grierson explains that it *means*

"grew" or "grey," the Scottish greyhound. But in *Poetical Works*, III, *Minstrelsy*, 118, 120, "Johnee of Breadislee," I find "graie," and I suggest that *this* is the proper reading.
71. JGL, I, 210.
72. Russell, "Some Recent Statements," 8.
73. *Letters*, I, 58, Shortreed, 10/16/96, and 57, fn. 2.
74. *R. Roy*, III, Ch. XVI, 243–4.
75. Grierson, *Scott*, 42.
76. NLS MS; also quoted by Grierson, *Scott*, 40–1.
77. NLS MS, 2232, ff. 34–6; also quoted by Parsons, *JEGP*, XXXIII, No. 2, 240–9.
78. NLS MS; also quoted by JGL, I, 211.
79. *Letters*, I, 246, James Ballantyne, ?/?/08.
80. *Kenilworth*, II, 144.
81. Sands, *Sir W's Congé*, 162, quoting from *Peveril*, I, 181.
82. *Letters*, V, 202, G. H. Gordon, 10/14/18; quoted by Sands, *Sir W's Congé*, 164.
83. *Letters*, VI, 208, G. H. Gordon, 6/12/20.
84. *Journal*, 359, 6/16/27.
85. *Ibid.*, 50, 12/18/25.
86. *Ibid.*, 426, 11/7/27.

PART THREE

Chapter 1

1. *Quentin*, II, 23.
2. MS M. J. Erskine to WS 9/12/96, postscript.
3. *Letters*, I, 54–5, Erskine, 9/26/96.
4. *Ibid.*, 58, Shortreed, 10/16/96.
5. JGL, I, 219.
6. *Poetical Works*, IV, *Minstrelsy*, 61.
7. *Letters*, I, 59, Taylor, 11/25/96.
8. MS, P.S. to M.J.E., 9/12/96.
9. JGL, I, 219–20.
10. *Letters*, I, 59–60, fn. 1.
11. These comparisons are partly indebted to Pope-Hennessy, *Laird*, 44–5.
12. This last sentence parallels a suggestion by S. Gwyn, *Life*.
13. *Poetical Works*, IV, *Minstrelsy*, 61–2. WS overmodestly and inac-

curately says they were scrapped and "consigned to the trunkmakers."
14. *Ibid.*
15. *Ibid.*, 63–4.
16. *Ibid.*, 44.
17. JGL, I, 205, 227, has many errors, which have been corrected from Emerson, "Literary Life," 29–32; Mennier, in MLR; and Falconer, "Two MS."
18. Letter to Mrs. Hughes, 12/13/21; see also Hughes, *Letters and Recollections*, 9/20/27, and *cf.* Ochojski, *WS and Germany*, 29–30.
19. My comment is echoed from Pope-Hennessy, *Laird*, 29–30.
20. WS's comments on himself are, as usual, depreciatory.
21. See also Ochojski, *WS and Germany*, 40, 42, 44, 49, for other howlers.
22. JGL, I, 215–6.
23. *Ibid.*, 216–7. *Cf. Letters*, I, 57, fn. 2, where Grierson thinks this the October journey mentioned in letter to Miller, 10/2/96, but I think JGL for once right. One would hardly go to Peebles by going first to Edinburgh.
24. JGL, I, 218.
25. *Ibid.*, 273.
26. Emerson, "Literary Life," 29–31; *cf.* Ochojski, *WS and Germany*, 29.
27. JGL, I, 224; MacCunn, *Sir W's Friends*, 267.
28. Bryant, *Endurance*, 167–70.
29. *Ibid.*, 202.
30. *Ibid.*, 127.
31. JGL, I, 224–5.
32. "WS Quartermaster," *Blackwood's Mag.*, Apr. 1930, 511–32.
33. Bryant, *Endurance*, 173.
34. "WS Quartermaster."
35. JGL, I, 225, anticipates the later setup. NLS MS letter, Buccleuch, 3/24/97, gives the initial staffing.
36. "WS Quartermaster."
37. JGL, I, 226.
38. "WS Quartermaster"; Cockburn, *Memorials*, 181.
39. JGL, I, 225–6.
40. "WS Quartermaster." The description of the uniform here I have corrected on the authority of Dr. Corson.
41. JGL, I, 228–9, fn. 1.
42. MacCunn, *Sir Ws' Friends*, 135.

43. *Letters*, I, 64, Murray, 3/8/96; "WS Quartermaster."
44. *Letters*, I, 64, Murray, 3/8/96.
45. Bryant, *Endurance*, 187–94.
46. *Ibid.*, 193.
47. *Ibid.*, 200.
48. *Ibid.*, 201–2.
49. *Ibid.*, 195–9.
50. Allan, *Life*, 110–5.
51. *Ibid.*, 116–7; *Letters*, I, 72, fn. 2, gives dates as 5/12 and 10/7/97.
52. *Letters*, I, 64, Murray, 3/8/96.
53. MacDonald, *Juridical Review;* JGL, I, 230.
54. JGL, I, 232–3; *cf. Chronicles*, I, 9–10.
55. *Letters*, I, 76–7, Rutherford, Oct.–Nov., enclosing a copy of the poem.
56. JGL, I, 215, "Klagegesang von der edlin Farren des Asarr Aga."
57. Emerson, "Literary Life," 34; Ochojski, *WS and Germany*, 30. Possibly at the time he also translated, under the title of "The Mermaid," Goethe's poem on the same legend Heine was to endow with deathless sorcery in *Die Lorelei*. See MS in NLS.
58. Emerson, "Literary Life," 29, 32; JGL, I, 215, 227.
59. JGL, I, 227–30, quoting selections from 3/15–7/1/96.
60. *Ibid.*, 230.
61. Morgan MS, WS to Robert A. Davidson, 8/17/97.
62. JGL, I, 231, MacCunn, *Sir W's Friends*, 332. The location of Ritchie's hut corrected by Dr. Corson.
63. *Ibid.*
64. JGL, I, 231; *cf. St. Ronan's Well*. The poem is in *Poetical Works*, VIII, 373.
66. JGL, I, 231–2.

Chapter 2

1. *Letters*, I, 75, Miss Rutherford, 10 or 11/?/97. Actually received in late Nov.
2. JGL, I, 232.
3. *Letters*, I, 69, Mrs. Scott, ca. 9/21/97; JGL, I, 233.
4. *Letters*, I, 67, fn. 2; Grierson, *Scott*, 46.
5. Glen MS, 7566, f. 55, quoting WS letter to Lord Downshire, 10/26/97.

6. NLS MS, C. Kerr to WS, 1/3/96. Further note C.K. to WS, 4/12/96. Kerr had come in Wales the previous year to know Mrs. Piozzi (the former Hester Thrale) to whose daughter, Queenie, Miss Nicolson had formerly been companion.

7. *Letters*, XII, 67, to Charlotte Carpenter, 11/14/97; Miss Carpenter to Lord Downshire, 11/21/97.

8. *Ibid.*, I, 86, Murray, 12/21/97: "not very frappant—a smart looking little girl with dark brown hair"; JGL, I, 232; *cf.* Pope-Hennessy, *Laird*, 63, quoting Hogg. Also *Letters*, I, 76, Rutherford: ". . . her person and face are very engaging"; WS says here "not a beauty by any means."

9. Pope-Hennessy, *Laird*, 51–2.

10. *Poetical Works*, XI, *Bridal*, Intro., Sts. I–III. *Cf.* Pope-Hennessy, *Laird*, 56, with whose identification of these details as derived from WS's visit to Gilsland Spa I agree.

11. *Poetical Works*, XI, *Bridal*, Intro., V.

12. Pope-Hennessy, *Laird*, 51.

13. *Letters*, I, 72, Charlotte, 10/6 or 7/97; *Bridal*, postlude to Canto II, St. II.

14. See miniature of Charlotte Carpenter painted around that time (reprod. in Pope-Hennessy, *Laird*, 63).

15. *Poetical Works*, XI, *Bridal*, postlude to Canto II, Sts. I–III.

16. *Letters*, XII, 58, Charlotte, 10/29/97.

17. NLS MS, Charlotte to Lord Downshire, 9/29/97.

18. *Letters*, I, 67, Charlotte, ca. 9/21/97. The "previous attachment" is clearly Williamina; he ignores Jessie.

19. *Ibid.*, 69, Mrs. Scott, 9/21/97. The letter is postmarked "Cocker mouth."

20. *Ibid.*, 84–5, Downshire, 11/23/97.

21. *Ibid.*, 75, Rutherford, 10 or 11/?/97; 68–70, Mrs. Scott, ca. 9/21/97; JGL, I, 233, but notes that contra JGL's implication to the contrary WS *says* he is writing his father at same time.

22. *Letters*, I, 68–70, Mrs. Scott.

23. *Ibid.*, 65–8, Charlotte, ca. 9/21/97.

24. *Ibid.*

25. NLS, Shortreed Papers.

26. *Letters*, I, 75, Rutherford.

27. *Ibid.*, 71, Charlotte, 10/6 or 7/97.

28. *Ibid.*, 72.

29. *Ibid.*, 71.

30. *Ibid.*, 73 and fn. 2.

31. NLS MS, Charlotte to WS, 10/7/97; in JGL, I, 236, but erroneously dated 10/4/97, and with manipulated text. No identification of who the friend was.

32. *Letters*, XII, 53–4, Charlotte, 10/18/97.

33. *Ibid.*, 54–5.

34. JGL, I, 240–1, Downshire to WS, 10/15/97.

35. NLS MS, Charlotte to WS, 10/22/97, partly quoted in *Letters*, XII, 53–4, fn. 1, and JGL, I, 241–2, with minor omissions and alterations.

36. NLS MS, Charlotte to WS, 10/25/97, partly quoted in *Letters*, XII, 57, fn. 1, and a manipulated text in JGL, I, 242–3.

37. *Letters*, XII, 57, fn. 1. There is no known explanation of why Charlotte's French mother should have wanted her children to be Church of England.

38. *Ibid.* These passages are not quoted in *Letters*, XII, 57, fn.

39. *Ibid.* But these are.

40. Grierson, *Scott*, 47–58; Glen MS, 2533, in NLS, on Lyons' birth register; correspondence in *Scotsman*, Apr.–Nov. 1930, between Grierson, Crockett, and Carswell.

41. On some of the baptism documents her name is given as Elie Marguerite, in others as Marguerite Charlotte, but clearly the same person. The husband's name is the same in all of them.

42. Glen MS.

43. JGL, I, 232–3.

44. Grierson, *Scott*, 49–50; Glen résumé, NLS MS, 2533. Mme. Charpentier returned finally to France (Paris) at the time of Lord Downshire's marriage in 1786.

45. *Scotsman*, Crockett Letter, 4/18/1931; Carswell letter, 4/23/1931; also Pope-Hennessy, *Laird*, 67–9. In 1791 M. Charpentier was listed by the Revolutionary Government

as an émigré and stated to be living in Alsace with his daughter Charlotte. Note that Charlotte's words are ambiguous: she says only "lost," not dead—and how old does one have to be to know the value of a parent?

46. *E.g.*, Robert Chambers in *Chambers's Journal*, 1833, quoted by Grierson, *Scott*, 47.
47. Grierson, *Scott*, 53, quoting R. L. Edgeworth.
48. *Ibid.*
49. NLS, Glen MS, 3256, f. 117; Crockett, *Scotsman*, 12/5/1931.
50. Still at Abbotsford. The collar is faced with Chinese red.
51. *Letters*, X, 310; JGL 11/14/27.
52. Grierson, *Scott*, 49–50; NLS, 2533, Glen, ff. 106–69.
53. Grierson, *Scott*, 49–50.
54. *Ibid.*, 50; Crockett, *Scotsman*, 7/12/1930; NLS, Glen MS, 2533.
55. NLS, Glen MS; Elizabeth Dexter's researches give the year as 1776.
56. Glen MS, 2533; *Chambers's Journal*, Aug.–Sept. 1926, ff. 575–6, J. A. Lovat-Fraser.
57. Grierson, *Scott*, 51–3.
58. *Ibid.*, 47; Crockett, *Scotsman*, 12/5/1930.
59. Grierson, *Scott*, 53.
60. NLS MS, Charlotte to WS, 11/14/97, *not* in JGL's *much* manipulated version of this letter, I, 245.
61. *Letters*, XII, 56, Charlotte, 10/24/97.
62. NLS MS, Charlotte to WS, 11/14/97—much manipulated in JGL, I, 245.
63. *Letters*, XII, 56, Charlotte, 10/24/97.
64. *Ibid.*, 52. Grierson erroneously says *before* 10/7, but WS refers to her objections to his "must" in 10/6, 7/97 (I, 71) and quotes her "out of senses" from 10/25/97 (XII, 57, fn. 1), and "when you look upon your dumb friend" also makes it obviously after his sending the miniature, 10/24/97 (XII, 55–6).
65. *Ibid.*, 53. Cf. letter to C. Rutherford, I, 76–7 (which is erroneously dated late Oct.; it must be mid- or late Nov.).
66. *Letters*, XII, 57, Charlotte, 10/29/97.
67. *Ibid.*, 59.
68. *Ibid.*, 58, fn. 1, Charlotte to WS, 10/26/97, inaccurate in JGL, I, 243.
69. *Ibid.*, 60, fn. 1, Charlotte to WS, inaccurate and incomplete in JGL, I, 243–4.
70. *Ibid.*, 61, Charlotte, 11/3/97.
71. *Ibid.*, 62.
72. *Ibid.*, 61.
73. *Ibid.*, Downshire, 11/5/97; see also Downshire's letter to WS, 10/29/97, which, with minor changes, is in JGL, I, 244, and Charlotte's to WS of early Nov. (which, however, is *not* dated 11/4, as JGL has it in I, 244–5. He has also changed the text).
74. Crown and Mitre: See *Letters*, XII, 64, fn. 2; Mrs. Palmer's, 51, fn. 1.
75. NLS MS, 2525, f. 13, Charlotte to Downshire, 11/26/97.
76. *Letters*, XII, 59, Charlotte, 10/29/97.
77. *Ibid.*, 64, 11/12?/97.
78. NLS MS, Charles Carpenter to WS, 11/4/97.
79. Berg MS, WS to Wm. Scott, 3/16/95, endorsed rec'd 11/20/95, so that it took about 8 months to go. This would make Chas. Carpenter's remittance of 3/19/97 arrive about 11/16/97.
80. *Letters*, I, 74–6.
81. *Letters*, XII, 66, fn. 2, Mrs. Scott to Charlotte, 11/12/97.
82. *Ibid.*, 67, Charlotte, 11/14/97.
83. *Ibid.*, 73, Charlotte, 11/21/97.
84. NLS MS, Charlotte to Downshire, 11/26/97; also quoted in *Letters*, XII, 76, fn. 1.
85. *Letters*, XII, 64, Charlotte, 11/12?/97.
86. *Ibid.*, 67, Charlotte, 11/14/97.
87. *Ibid.*, I, 84, Charlotte, 11/17/97.
88. *Ibid.*, XII, 69, Charlotte, 11/18/97.
89. *Ibid.*, I, 80, Charlotte, 11/17/97, XII, 69, Charlotte, 11/18/97.
90. *Ibid.*, 79, Charlotte, 11/28/97.
91. *Ibid.*, 72, Charlotte, 11/21/97.
92. *Ibid.*, 68, Charlotte, 11/18/97.
93. *Ibid.*, I, 80, Charlotte, 11/17/97.
94. NLS MS, 1549, f. 203, Charlotte to WS, 11/27/97. Only a frag-

ment in *Letters*, XII, 77, fn. 1; but the letter is in JGL, I, 246.

95. NLS MS, 1549, f. 207, Charlotte to WS, 12/6/97; this quotation is not in the part printed in *Letters*, XII, 83, fn. 1. Also MS, Charlotte to WS, 11/22/97, and 83–4, Downshire, 11/21/97, partly quoted in *Letters*, XII, 71, fn. 1.

96. *Letters*, I, 81–2, Charlotte, 11/22/97, and 83–4, Downshire, 11/23/97.

97. *Ibid.*, XII, 61, Charlotte, 11/3/97. Perhaps Mr. Scott altered because he was also buying a commission for John (XII, 69, Charlotte, 11/18/97) and thought it unfair to do nothing for Walter.

98. *Letters*, I, 84–5, Downshire, 11/23/97.

99. NLS MS, 1549, f. 189, Charlotte to WS, 11/14/97, incomplete and inaccurate in JGL, I, 245.

100. *Letters*, XII, 90, Charlotte, 11/18/97.

101. NLS MS, 1549, f. 203, Charlotte, to WS, 11/27/97, partly quoted in *Letters*, XII, 77, fn. 1.

102. NLS MS, 1549, f. 209, Charlotte to WS, 11/23/97.

103. *Ibid.;* and NLS MS, 1549, f. 215, Charlotte to WS, 12/6/97, the latter partly quoted in *Letters*, XII, 83, fn. 1 (but not this part).

104. NLS MS, 2515, f. 15, Charlotte to Dumergue, 12/10/97; Charlotte to WS, 11/23/97; Charlotte to Downshire, 11/26/97; *Letters*, XII, 81, Charlotte, 11/28/97.

105. *Letters*, XII, 79, Charlotte, 11/28/17; 90, 12/10?/97.

106. *Ibid.*, 67, Charlotte, 11/14/97.

107. *Ibid.*, 77, Charlotte, 11/25/97.

108. *Ibid.*, I, 83, Charlotte, 11/22/97.

109. NLS MS, Charlotte to WS, 11/27/97, manipulated in JGL, I, 246.

110. *Letters*, XII, 78, Charlotte, 11/28/97.

111. *Ibid.*, I, 79, Charlotte, 11/17/97.

112. *Ibid.*, 66, *Charlotte*, 11/12?/97.

113. NLS MS, Charlotte to WS, 12/2/97. JGL, I, 247, misrepresents this as a postscript to her letter of 12/10/97. This letter is correctly dated and partly quoted in *Letters*, XII, 82, fn. 1.

114. *Letters*, XII, 69, Charlotte, 11/18/97.

115. Inference from next letter, below.

116. *Letters*, XII, 63, Charlotte, 11/12/97.

117. NLS MS, Charlotte to WS, 12/2/97, partly quoted in *Letters*, XII, 82, fn. 1.

118. *Letters*, XII, 83, Charlotte, 12/5/97.

119. *Ibid.*, 87, Charlotte, 12/8/97 and fn. 1.

120. NLS MS, Charlotte to WS, 12/10/97, partly quoted in *Letters*, XII, 88, fn. 1.

121. Shortreed Memoir.

122. *Letters*, XII, 70, Charlotte, 11/18/97.

123. NLS MS, Charlotte to WS, 12/2/97.

124. *Letters*, XII, 91, Charlotte, 12/10/97; NLS MS, Charlotte to WS, 12/14/97, only partly quoted in *Letters*, XII, 93, fn. 1.

125. *Letters*, XII, 81, Charlotte, 12/4/97.

126. NLS MS, Charlotte to WS, 12/6/97, partly quoted in *Letters*, XII, 83, fn. 1, but not this part.

127. NLS MS, 1549, f. 225, Charlotte to WS, 12/14/97, in *Letters*, XII, 93, fn. 1.

128. *Letters*, XII, 93, Charlotte, 12/16/97.

129. *Ibid.*, XII, 92, Charlotte, 12/16/97.

130. *Ibid.*, 88, Charlotte, 12/8/97.

131. Charlotte's letter of 12/14/97 gives Thursday, 12/21, as the intended date; there is no explanation of why it was postponed to 12/24.

132. Letters, I, 88, Downshire, 12/26/97.

### Chapter 3

1. NLS MS, Charlotte to WS, 12/16/97.

2. *Letters*, I, 93, fn. 2; *ibid.*, I, 152, Lady Anne Hamilton 8/10/02; *Journal*, 176, 5/26/26.

3. *Journal*, 182, 6/7/26.

4. JGL, I, 249.

5. *Ibid.*, 248.

6. *Ibid.*, 249.

7. MacCunn, *Sir W's Friends*, 59.

8. JGL, I, 249.

9. *Ibid.*, 250–1, but JGL has done

some hanky-panky with the letter, which is in the Walpole Collection.

10. *Ibid.*, 249.

11. NLS MS, 3234, f. 62, Charlotte to Miss Dumergue, 4/29/98.

12. *Letters*, IX, 43, Jane (Mrs. Walter Scott), 3/23/25.

13. Tait and Gray, *George Square.*

14. JGL, I, 253.

15. Lewis to WS, n.d., but before that of WS to him, 5/29/98, which is quoted in JGL, I, 254.

16. Scott's letter is in Morgan Library MS.

17. JGL, I, 253-4, quoting Lewis to WS, n.d.

18. *Ibid.*, 254.

19. *Ibid.*, 255.

20. U. of Rochester Lib. MS, WS to Cadell and Davies, 5/5/98.

21. JGL, I, 256, which says Jan. '99, but in Partington, *Post-Bag*, there is a letter to WS on the subject, 12/15/98.

22. JGL, I, 254.

23. Quoted by MacCunn, *Sir W's Friends*, 116.

24. JGL, I, 255.

25. *Ibid.*, 256; "WS Quartermaster."

26. *Ibid.*, 256; Emerson, "Literary Life," 38; Ochojski, *WS and Germany*, 33.

27. JGL, I, 256; Pope-Hennessy, *Laird*, 49.

28. "WS Quartermaster" says the dragoons were all admitted to the freedom of the Burgh at this time, but Dr. Corson points out that the placque on the Musselburgh Town Hall gives the date as 3/25/99. WS could not have been present in *person* at that time, since he was in London.

29. JGL, I, 251-2.

30. NLS MS, Charlotte to Downshire, 8/24/98.

31. JGL, II, 21.

32. *Ibid.*, I, 252; Pope-Hennessy, *Laird*, 94.

33. NLS MS, Charlotte to Downshire, 8/24/96.

34. JGL, I, 265.

35. MacCunn, *Sir W's Friends*, 189-90, 192.

36. JGL, I, 265.

37. MacCunn, *Sir W's Friends*, 205, 207-10, 215-8.

38. Quoted by MacCunn, *Sir W's Friends*, 218.

39. JGL, I, 263-4.

40. *Minstrelsy*, IV, 167-8, 83-4. Emerson, 37, "Literary Life," points out that JGL errs in dating "Glenfinlas" and "Eve of St. John" as composed in the course of 1799; there is a letter from Lewis, 1/6/99, that refers to both.

41. *Poetical Works*, IV, *Minstrelsy*, 172. The ballad was certainly finished by the end of 1798, for on 1/?/97 Colin MacKenzie sent a copy to Anna Seward, which she acknowledged 2/3/97, and Lewis received a copy in 1798.

42. JGL, I, 264-5.

43. *Poetical Works*, IV, *Minstrelsy*, 67-8.

44. *Ibid.*, 183-94.

45. *Ibid.*, 187.

46. JGL, I, 265, says 1799, but Emerson, "Literary Life," 39, says 1798; Dr. Corson agrees. All three therefore date from 1798.

47. *Poetical Works*, IV, *Minstrelsy*, 218-29. P. 229 quotes *Critical Review*, Nov. 1803, with this criticism.

48. Partington, *Post-Bag*, 3-4; Purgstall to WS, 7/20/98. This is the same letter JGL, I, 250-1, quotes differently below.

49. JGL, I, 250-1.

50. Partington, *Post-Bag*, 4.

51. The first letter so dated that I can find is NLS MS, WS to Wm. Scott, 2/13/99, but WS had taken the first house for only six months.

52. JGL, I, 251.

53. NLS MS, Downshire to WS, 10/16, 19/98, and to Charlotte, 10/21/98.

54. NLS MS, Charlotte to Downshire, n.d.

55. *Poetical Works*, IV, *Minstrelsy*, 68-9.

56. *Ibid.*, 72.

57. *Ibid.*, 70.

58. *Ibid.*, 73.

59. *Ibid.*, 80-3.

60. *Ibid.*, 70-1.

61. Quoted in Partington, *Post-Bag*, 6.

62. JGL, I, 263, says he accepted all, but Emerson, "Literary Life," 41, says he accepted very few, and my own count, though not identical with Emerson's, in "William and Helen," is almost 30.

63. JGL, I, 256, says still negotiating in January, but Partington, *Post-*

*Bag*, 6, shows that agreement had been reached before 12/15/98.

64. Partington, *Post-Bag*, 6, Lewis to WS, 12/15/98.
65. Walpole Collection, MS. Lewis to WS, 3/5/98, says "will be published in the course of next week."
66. JGL, I, 257, says Feb., but see above. Scott's name erroneously appears on title page as "William Scott."
67. JGL, I, 257.
68. *Ibid.*, 257–8, *Cf.* Ochojski, *WS and Germany*, 52–4.
69. *Ibid.*, 256.
70. *Letters*, I, 89–90, to mother, 3/8/99.
71. JGL, I, 256–7.
72. *Ibid.*, 276. *Cf.* also references to Plummer in *Poetical Works*, I, *Minstrelsy*, 372; and III, 328.
73. *Letters*, I, 227, Ellis, 8/21/04, quoted by JGL, I, 377.
74. *Ibid.*, 229, Ellis, 11/23/04, quoted by JGL, I, 379.
75. JGL, I, 276–7.
76. *Ibid.*, 260.
77. *Chronicles*, 10–2.
78. JGL, I, 260.
79. *Letters*, I, 90–1.
80. JGL, I, 262.
81. *Ibid.*, 259; Emerson, "Literary Life," 45.
82. *Letters*, I, 92, Murray, 6/30/99.
83. *Ibid.*, XII, 157, fn. 1; JGL, I, 281.
84. Quoted in *Encyc. Brit.*, article "Richard Heber."
85. JGL, I, 281.
86. *Ibid.*, 282. *Cf.* also Cockburn, *Memorials*, 157, and *Misc. Prose*, IV, 154–5, "John Leyden, M.D."
87. JGL, I, 281; *Letters*, I, 110, fn. 1; *Misc. Prose*, IV, 137, "John Leyden, M.D."; MacCunn, *Sir W's Friends*, 113.
88. *Misc. Prose*, IV, 146.
89. MacCunn, *Sir W's Friends*, 116.
90. JGL, I, 282; *Misc. Prose*, IV, 154.
91. *Misc. Prose*, IV, 164; JGL, I, 283.
92. MacCunn, *Sir W's Friends*, 251.
93. NLS MS, Leyden to WS, 11/20/05; *Misc. Prose*, IV, 161.
94. *Misc. Prose*, IV, 165.
95. Partington, *Post-Bag*, 7–8; Purgstall to WS, 7/26/99.
96. JGL, I, 265.
97. *Ibid.*, 267.
98. *Ibid.*, 265–6.
99. *Ibid.*, 273.

100. *Ibid.*, 267–73. JGL, II, 272–3, makes numerous alterations in the text of the ballad. See Parsons, "Correct Text of Shepherd's Tale", *N & Q*, 164, ff. 75–7, 2/21/1933.
101. *Waverly*, Gen. Pref., xix; App., I, xxxvii–liii.
102. JGL, I, 274–5.
103. NLS MS, WS to Captain Scott, 4/19/1800; Fales Collection MS., WS to Ferguson, 6/1/01.
104. JGL, I, 275.
105. *Ibid.*
106. *Ibid.*, 276–7.
107. *Letters*, I, 94–5, Riddell, 11/22/99.
108. JGL, I, 277; *Poetical Works*, VI, 13.
109. NLS MS, Jane Russell to Col. Russell, 2/3/1800.
110. JGL, II, 26. Despite the fact that Sophia was baptized in the Episcopal Church, WS had not severed his connection with the Presbyterian establishment. In 1815 his son Charles was christened by Thomson of Duddingston, and WS represented the Selkirk Church of Scotland in the General Assembly 1807 and was reelected 1808. He was an elder in the Duddingston Church and kept up his connection with the Presbyterian Church till death.
111. *Ibid.*
112. *Letters*, I, 96, James Ballantyne, 4/22/1800.
113. Emerson, "Literary Life," 48.
114. JGL, I, 275. Note that although this pamphlet was printed by Ballantyne, it was *not* officially a publication.
115. *Ibid.*, 275–6.
116. *Ibid.*, 283–4, somewhat differently worded in James Ballantyne's recollections, NLS MS, 921, ff. 67–8.

### Chapter 4

1. Crockett, *Scott Country*, 157.
2. JGL, I, 277; *Letters*, I, 415, Lady Abercorn, 12/25/07.
3. Crockett, *Scott Country*, 157.
4. *Ibid.*, 364.
5. *Ibid.*, 404, 408, 396.
6. *Ibid.*, 355.

7. *Ibid.*, 358.
8. *Letters*, XII, 159, Heber, 4/5/1800.
9. *Ibid.*, 158.
10. *Trans. Harwick Arch. Soc.*, 66.
11. *Letters*, I, 229, Ellis, 11/23/04.
12. Queen Mary's House (Jedburgh) Collection, WS to John Rutherford, 3/9/1800, quoted in *Scotsman*, 9/12/1932.
13. *Letters*, I, 102, Erskine, 10/8/1800.
14. *Ibid.*, 103, Erskine, 10/18/1800.
15. *Ibid.*, 107, Erskine, 12/4/1800 and fn.
16. *Ibid.*, 105, Erskine, 10/21/1800.
17. *Ibid.*, III, 321, James Ballantyne, 8/24/13; IV, 259, Donaldson, 7/7/16; and XII, 488 fn.
18. NLS MS, 1741, Account Books, 1798–1801.
19. MacDonald, *Juridical Review*.
20. NLS MS, 1741.
21. Berg MS, Charlotte Carpenter, to Handley, 3/16/97 (£86, 14s, 8d); Morgan MS, Charlotte Scott to Downshire, receipt 9/13/98, £620; NLS MS, 2525, fn. 29, T. Handley to WS, 11/10/01, £842, 19s, 8d.
22. *Letters*, I, 122, Handley, 11/15/01.
23. NLS MS, 1742, Case Book 1797–1802.
24. JGL, I, 286; *Letters*, I, 117, C. Erskine, 1/4/01, and 118, fn. 1.
25. *Letters*, I, 96, James Ballantyne, 4/22/1800.
26. *Ibid.*, corrected from original MS. Quale, *The Ruin of SWS*, 24, reads this letter as "first tentative attempt to buy a share in the printing enterprise" and "lure James to the city," but I know of no supporting evidence for such an interpretation.
27. *Ibid.*, XII, 158, Heber, 4/5/1800.
28. *Ibid.*, I, 100, Jamieson, 8/13/1800, and fn. 1.
29. *Ibid.*, XII, 172, Heber, 10/19/1800.
30. *Ibid.*, 167, Percy, 10/6/1800; 167, fn. 1.
31. *Ibid.*, I, 108, Percy, 1/11/01 (in MS Rm. N.Y.P.L.).
32. *Ibid.*, 103–4, Currie, 10/18/1800, and 103–4, fn. 1.
33. JGL, I, 283; *Misc. Prose*, IV, 157–9; MacCunn, *Sir W's Friends*, 116.
34. ACLC, I, 202; *cf. Letters* I, 133, fn. 1.
35. *Letters*, XII, 164/5, Heber, 6/12/1800 and fn. 1.

36. *Ibid.*, 162, Heber 6/10/1800.
37. *Ibid.*, 171, fn. 1.
38. *Ibid.*, 172, Heber, 10/19/1800.
39. NLS MS, Leyden to Heber, 11/4/1800.
40. *Letters*, XII, 172, Heber, 10/19/1800.
41. NLS MS, Leyden to Heber, 11/4/1800.
42. *Letters*, XII, 158, Heber, 4/5/1800. JGL says Lewis showed *The Honce of Aspen* to Mrs. Esten, who recommended it to Constable; *cf.* Ochojski, *WS and Germany*, 57.
43. JGL, I, 274, Kerr to WS, 10/?/99.
44. Bryant, *Endurance*, 309, 317.
45. *Letters*, XII, 160, Heber, 5/5/1800.
46. *Ibid.*, 158–61, Heber, 4/5/1800.
47. *Ibid.*, 161–2, Heber, 6/10/1800; *Ibid.*, 164, Heber, 6/12/1800.
48. *Ibid.*, 161–2, Heber, 6/10/1800.
49. *Ibid.*, 164, Heber, 6/12/1800.
50. *Ibid.*, 165–6, Heber, 7/28/1800.
51. *Ibid.*, 173, Heber, 10/19/1800.
52. *Ibid.*, 170, fn. 2.
53. *Ibid.*, 171–2, Heber, 10/19/1800.
54. JGL, I, 285; Partington, *Post-Bag*, 12, Stoddart to WS, 12/26/1800.
55. JGL, I, 299.
56. *Poetical Works*, IV, *Minstrelsy*, 75–6.
57. *Letters*, I, 109–10, Percy, 1/11/01 (MS Rm., N.Y.P.L.).
58. NLS MS, Leyden to Heber, 3/21/01.
59. Morgan MS; in *Letters*, XII, 178, Ellis, 3/27/01.
60. *Letters*, XII, 186, Ellis, 8/21/01, and fn. 1; *Minstrelsy*, IV, 20.
61. *Ibid.*, 186, fn. 2.
62. *Ibid.*, I, 114, Ellis, 5/11/01.
63. *Ibid.*, XII, 185, Ellis, 7/13/01.
64. *Ibid.*, 112, Ellis, 4/20/01; XII, 181, Ellis, 4/20/01.
65. *Ibid.*, XII, 189, Ellis, 8/21/01; XII, 186, fn. 1.
66. *Ibid.*, 188, Ellis, 8/21/01.
67. Morgan MS., WS to Ellis, 9/24/01; section omitted in *Letters*, XII, 194–6. Also *cf. Letters*, XII, 192, Ellis 8/25–9/8/01.
68. *Letters*, XII, 193–4, fn. 1.
69. *Ibid.*, 194, Ellis, 8/25–9/8/01.
70. *Ibid.*, 195–6, fn. 2.
71. *Ibid.*, 195–6, Ellis, 9/24/01.
72. *Letters*, I, 112, Ellis, 4/20/01; XII, 186, Ellis, 8/21/01.
73. NLS, Shortreed Papers.

74. "WS Quartermaster."
75. *Letters*, I, 114, Ellis, 5/4/01.
76. *Ibid.*, 115–6, Ellis, 6/10/01, and fn. 2.
77. *Ibid.*, XII, 187, Ellis, 8/21/01.
78. MacCunn, *Sir W's Friends*, 115, *Misc. Prose*, IV, 165.
79. *Misc. Prose*, IV, 168–70.
80. *Ibid.*, 169.
81. *Letters*, I, 117, Ellis, 7/13/01.
82. *Misc. Prose*, IV, 170; *Letters*, I, 125, Ellis, 1/8/02; *Letters*, I, 111, fn. 1.
83. *Misc. Prose*, IV, 171.
84. *Ibid.*, 172.
85. *Letters*, I, 111, fn. 1.
86. *Ibid.*, XII, 194, Ellis, 9/24/01; MacCunn, *Sir W's Friends*, 122–6.
87. MacCunn, *Sir W's Friends*, 122.
88. *Letters*, XII, 197, Ellis, 9/24/01. The bracketed "All this was cal" is conjecturally added to supply a gap created by a hole in the original letter.
89. *Ibid.*, 188, Ellis, 8/21/01.
90. *Ibid.*, 195, 9/24/01.
91. *Ibid.*, 197–8, Ellis, 10/9/01.
92. *Misc. Prose*, IV, 167; JGL, I, 313–4.
93. JGL, I, 316–7. Note, however, that JGL himself indicates that the Gillies recollections on which these anecdotes are based may not be entirely reliable—Gillies was only thirteen years old in 1801—and that *Misc. Prose*, IV, 167, places in London the anecdote JGL tells on p. 314.
94. MacCunn, *Sir W's Friends*, 122.
95. *Letters*, XII, 197, fn. 1.
96. *Ibid.*, Leyden to Heber, 2/14/03. Leyden was mistaken, however: Ritson was far from tamed. Returning to London he fell into a fit of touchiness that ended "his long and amiable intercourse with Douce." Imagining that he detected in "his tranquil and unsuspecting friend . . . symptoms of manifold disaffection to himself and all his pursuits," Ritson fell into a rage, "would never take another drop of tea in Douce's house; never commune with him in the museum reading room; never even exchange with him the common forms of civility! And they are now separated by an 'oceanus disassociabilis' as effectually as Menou from Cairo,

or Bonaparte from Sir Sidney Smith!," *Letters*, XII, 197, fn. 1.
97. JGL, I, 315. This is also quoted from Gillies and must have been a composite of the recollections of others, passed on to him, not personally observed.
98. *Ibid.*
99. *Ibid.*, 315–6.
100. *Ibid.*
101. *Letters*, XII, 198–9, Ellis, 10/9/01.
102. *Ibid.*, 196–7.
103. *Ibid.*, 198; *cf.* also XII, 216, fn. 2, and Morgan MS, WS to Ellis, 3/2/02, partly printed in *Letters*, I, 137–8.
104. *Letters*, I, 119, fn. 1; JGL, II, 26.
105. *Ibid.*, 123, Ellis, 12/7/01; *cf.* fn. 1.
106. Descriptive details from personal observations plus photographs, drawings, etc.
107. JGL, III, 183.
108. *Letters*, XII, 205, fn. 1.
109. *Ibid.*, I, 124, Ellis, 12/7/01.
110. *Ibid.*, II, 495, Lady Abercorn, 5/17/11.
111. JGL, I, 297–8.
112. *Poetical Works*, IV, *Minstrelsy*, 200–1.
113. JGL, I, 298.
114. *Letters*, I, 149, Lady Anne Hamilton, 7/29/02.
115. *Ibid.*, 126, Lady Anne Hamilton, 1/17/02, and 130, fn. 2.
116. *Ibid.*, 127–8.
117. MacCunn, *Sir W's Friends*, 367.
118. JGL, I, 299–300, says January, but the letter quoted below shows that it had been on sale only ten days on Feb. 23. NLS MS, WS to Cadell and Davies, 2/23/02.
119. *Ibid.*, plus fn., and the fact that I saw at Bowhill the complimentary copy inscribed to Buccleuch.
120. *Letters*, I, 132–3, Ellis, 2/14/02; *ibid.*, 137, Ellis, 3/2/02, corrected from Morgan MS original.
121. *Ibid.*, 136, Lady Anne Hamilton, 2/23/02.
122. *Ibid.*, 176, Charles Carpenter, 3/6/03; JGL, I, 300; *Ballantyne Press*, 16.
123. But WS himself in Carpenter letter, above, says £100.
124. *Trans. Edinb. Bib. Soc.*, 1935–6; 1937–8. JGL, I, 300, gives the number of copies in these editions as totaling 4,500 nd estimates

(1838) that in the later editions of WS's *Collected Poetry* in which the *Ministrelsy* came to be included, the sales must have reached 15,000 more.

125. JGL, I, 300.
126. *Ibid.*, 301.
127. MacCunn, *Sir W's Friends*, 286–7.
128. JGL, I, 302–3.

### Chapter 5

1. NLS MS, James Ballantyne to WS, 3/30/02, partly quoted in JGL, I, 305–6.
2. *Ibid.*
3. *Letters*, XII, 377–8, Davidson, 4/2/02.
4. *Ibid.*, I, 138, Pinkerton, 4/24/02.
5. *Ibid.*, 140, 142, Cleaton, 4/2/02, 6/6/02.
6. *Ibid.*, XII, 218, fn. 1, Ritson to WS, 4/10/02; 219, Ellis, 5/10/02.
7. *Ibid.*, 217–8.
8. Laidlaw, "Recollections."
9. *Ibid.*
10. NLS MS, Leyden to Heber, 6/11/02.
11. Laidlaw, "Recollections."
12. *Ibid. Laidlaw* says only given by "a person of rank, a connection of his wife's," but there was no other such person than Lord Downshire.
13. Hogg, *Domestic Manners*, 51–2.
14. *Ibid.*
15. Lockhart, *Peter's Letters*, 79.
16. There are minor differences here between Laidlaw's account and Hogg's. Laidlaw, "Recollections," says this investigation with Hogg's mother was after breakfast next day; Hogg, *Domestic Manners*, 52–3, says same day.
17. Laidlaw, "Recollections"; Hogg, *Domestic Manners*, 54–5.
18. Hogg, *Domestic Manners*, 57.
19. *Ibid.*, 56.
20. *Ibid.*, 57.
21. Laidlaw, "Recollections."
22. Parsons, "WS in Pandemonium," 244 (occurred ca. 8/27/02).
23. *Life and Letters of Sir Gilbert Elliot, 1st Earl of Minto* (London 1874), III, 254–5.
24. *Ibid.*, 255.
25. Parsons, "WS in Pandemonium," 244.

26. *Letters*, I, 149, Lady Anne Hamilton, 7/29/02.
27. *Ibid.*, 150–1, Lady Anne Hamilton, 8/10/02.
28. JGL, I, 298–9.
29. *Letters*, XII, 277, Ellis, 11/29/02; Scott's memorandum of the Agreement (NLS) is dated 10/29/02.
30. JGL, I, 330.
31. *Poetical Works*, IV, *Minstrelsy*, 327.
32. *Ibid.*, 338–47.
33. *Letters*, I, 152–4, Sharpe, 9/13/02; *ibid.*, 155–8, Sharpe, 9/8/02; *ibid.*, 160, Sharpe, 10/17/02.
34. *Ibid.*, 153.
35. Child, *Ballads*, I, 218, says "on the face of it a modern composition, with extensive variations."
36. *Letters*, I, 156, fn. 1.
37. *Ibid.*, 156, Sharpe, 9/8/02.
38. *Ibid.*, 161, Sharpe, 10/17/02.
39. *Poetical Works*, IV, *Minstrelsy*, 334–6.
40. *Letters*, I, 144–5, fn. 1; Pope-Hennessy, *Laird*, 81.
41. *Letters*, I, 144–5, Seward, 6/29/02, quoted by JGL, I, 305–6.
42. JGL, I, 308–11.
43. *Letters*, I, 154, fn. 1, Seward to WS, 7/20/02.
44. *Ibid.*, 154–5, Seward, 8/16/02.
45. Partington, *Post-Bag*, 14, Seward to WS, 8/26/02.
46. *Letters*, I, 163, Seward, 11/30/02.
47. NLS MS, WS to Erskine, 9/24/02.
48. *Letters*, XII, 220, Ellis, 10/17/02.
49. Laidlaw, "Recollections."
50. *Ibid.*
51. *Letters*, I, 161, Sharpe, 10/17/02.
52. NLS MS, Laidlaw to WS, n.d., but certainly *after* the publication of *Minstrelsy* and *before* 1/21/03 (*Letters*, I, 169, Laidlaw), in which WS acknowledges having received "Graeme & Bewick," which he mentions in the earlier letter.
53. *Letters*, I, 158–9, Editor of *Scots. Mag.*, 9/21/02, and fn. 1.
54. *Ibid.*, XII, 221, Ellis, 10/17/02.
55. *Ibid.*, I, 166, Seward, 11/30/02.
56. *Ibid.*, XII, 231, Ellis, 12/?/02, but answering Ellis, 12/11/02, partly quoted in 228, fn. 1.
57. JGL, I, 319.
58. *Poetical Works*, VI, *Lay*, Intro., 23, 26–7. WS says "more than a year after Mr. Stoddart's visit," but the

only recorded visit was in the summer of 1807, two years previously. Not till the following December did WS become acquainted with *Christabel*. Possibly there was a later, unrecorded visit.

59. *Poetical Works*, VI, 27–8. For the prologue that he urged, WS substituted the machinery of the minstrel, Intro., 28.

60. JGL, I, 319.

61. MS letter at Bowhill, Beattie to Countess of Dalkeith (n.d., but Dec. 1802). WS mentions receiving the poem "Tom Linn," which accompanied it, from her in *Letters*, I, 171, Laidlaw, 1/2/03, and it is a fair inference that in passing on the one the Countess gave him the other. What is certain is that he could not have been seen the story of Gilpin Horner before December; therefore, if he started the poem in summer, his original narrative could not have included it, and weaving it into the main plot must have been, despite what he says in *Lay*, Intro., 21–3, a later interpolation, *not* "the occasion of its being written." WS had probably forgotten; the Introduction was written in Apr. 1830, 28 years later.

62. *Poetical Works*, VI, *Lay*, Intro., 22.

63. *Letters*, I, 175, Ellis, 1/30/03; also an undated note to the Countess at Bowhill, ca. Mar. 1803.

64. *Misc. Prose*, IV, "Life of Leyden," 171; *Letters*, I, 111, fn. 1.

65. *Misc. Prose*, IV, 174.

66. *Letters*, XII, 229, Ellis (after 12/11/02).

67. *Ibid.*, 231, Ellis (after 12/11/02).

68. *Ibid.*, 229, fn. 1.

69. Partington, *Post-Bag*, 15–6, Leyden to WS, 1/13/03.

70. *Ibid.*, 17, Leyden to WS, 1/25/03.

71. *Misc. Prose*, IV, 167, "Leyden," specifically puts it in London before Leyden's departure for India; cf. JGL, I, 314, which gives the episode as if it had happened at Lasswade.

72. *Letters*, I, 167, Laidlaw, 1/20/03; 171, Laidlaw, "Wednesday."

73. *Ibid.*, 176, Charles Carpenter, 3/6/03.

74. JGL, II, 26.

75. *Letters*, I, 176, Charles Carpenter, 3/6/03.

76. Bowhill MS, undated, but obviously just before WS went to London, where he read these same three stanzas to Ellis.

77. JGL, I, 324–6. He says WS arrived too late to see Leyden, but see next note.

78. *Letters*, XII, 236, fn. 1, Leyden to WS, is dated 4/9/03, and NLS MS, Leyden to Heber, 4/6/03, from the Isle of Wight fits in with the statement that he has been on board two days.

79. *Letters*, XII, 236, fn. 1. JGL quotes this, I, 324, but erroneously gives the date as 4/1/03.

80. JGL, I, 326.

81. *Letters*, I, 183–4, Boulton, 5/13/03.

82. JGL, I, 326.

83. *Ibid.*, 326; MacCunn, *Sir W's Friends*, 228–9, 232.

84. *Ibid.*

85. *Journal*, 36–7, 12/9/25.

86. JGL, I, 326.

87. MacCunn, *Sir W's Friends*, 243–4, 252, 254; JGL, I, 322, 326.

88. JGL, I, 327.

89. *Letters*, I, 181, Seward, given as March but should be ca. 5/5/03.

90. *Ibid.*, Seward.

91. *Ibid.*, 182–3, Seward, 4/21/03.

92. *Ibid.*

93. *Ibid.*, 181, Seward, 4/21/03.

94. *Ibid.*, 186, Ellis, 5/25/03.

95. *Ibid.*, JGL, I, 331.

96. *Poetical Works*, IV, *Minstrelsy*, 235, 270, 317, 313.

97. *Ibid.*, 91–230.

98. Child *Ballads*, includes 305.

99. Checked with the discussion of each poem in Child, *Ballads*, passim.

100. Child, *Ballads*.

101. *Poetical Works*, I, *Minstrelsy*, Intro., 64.

102. *Ibid.*

103. *Ibid.*, 18–9.

104. Pope-Hennessy, *Laird*, 74.

105. Henderson's ed. of *Minstrelsy*, III, 173.

106. Child, *Ballads*, III, 273.

107. *Ibid.*, II, 10.

108. *Ibid.*

109. *Poetical Works*, I, *Minstrelsy*, 385–6.

110. JGL, I, 332.

111. *Ibid.*
112. *Letters*, X, 490, Sharpe, 8/22/28.
113. *Ibid.*, I, 160, Sharpe, 10/17/02.
114. JGL, I, 333.
115. All these, for example, are quoted in the Intro. above.
116. JGL, I, 323.

PART FOUR

Chapter 1

1. *Poetical Works*, VI, *Lay*, Intro., 6–7.
2. JGL, I, 331.
3. *Letters*, I, 207, fn. 1.
4. *Ibid.*, 198–9, Ellis, 8/27/03.
5. "WS Quartermaster."
6. *Letters*, I, 188, Seward, summer 1803.
7. Cockburn, *Memorials*, 164.
8. *Letters*, I, 189, Seward.
9. *Ibid.*, 197, Ellis, 8/27/03.
10. JGL, I, 352.
11. *Ibid.*, 353.
12. Wordsworth, *Journals*, 394–5.
13. *Ibid.*
14. JGL, I, 353.
15. Wordsworth, *Journals*, 402.
16. *Ibid.*, 403–4.
17. Wordsworth, *Early Letters*, 493, Dorothy to Lady Beaumont, 5/4/05.
18. *Ibid.*, 342, Wordsworth to WS, 10/16/03.
19. JGL, I, 354–5.
20. *Ibid.*, 395.
21. ACLC, 48–50; Cockburn, *Life of Jeffrey*, I, 125–6.
22. ACLC, 51.
23. Lockhart, *Peter's Letters*, 32, 40.
24. *Misc. Prose*, XVIII, 38.
25. *Ibid.*, XVII, 17–8.
26. *Ibid.*, 21, 24.
27. *Letters*, I, 204–5, Ellis, 10/14/03.
28. "WS Quartermaster."
28a. JGL, I, 351–2, Ellis to WS, 11/10/03.
29. *Ibid.*, 356–8.
30. *Ibid.*, 358–60.
31. *Ibid.*, 358.
32. *Ibid.*, 335; Ball, *SWS as a Critic*, 162.
33. *Misc. Prose*, XVII, 56–7.
34. *Ibid.*, 58–9.
35. *Ibid.*, 64.
36. *Ibid.*, 67–8.
37. *Letters*, XII, 243, Ellis, 3/19/1800?.

38. Bryant, *Endurance*, II, 70–1; Cockburn, *Memorials*, 164, JGL, I, 404, erroneously dates these events 1805.
39. *Antiquary*, II, 310–3.
40. Minto, *Life and Letters*, III, 417–8.
41. *Antiquary*, II, 310–7.
42. JGL, I, 404.
43. "WS Quartermaster."
44. JGL, I, 471, fn. 1; "WS Quartermaster."
45. *Ibid.*, 365–6.
46. *Ibid.*, 366.
47. *Letters*, I, 213, memorandum; 217, Erskine, 7/19/04.
48. *Ibid.*, 213, memo of agreement.
49. *Ibid.*, XII, 245, Ellis, 5/4/04, but possibly a few days later. In MS letter to Longman and Rees, 5/3/04, WS says "on the eve of publication."
50. JGL, I, 363.
51. *Letters*, I, 221, Douce, 5/7/04.
52. *Ibid.*, 220–1, Curators; 5/7/04; 245, Ellis, 5/4/07.
53. *Ibid.*, XII, 192–3, Ellis, between 8/25 and 9/8/01.
54. *Ibid.*, XII, 186, Ellis, 3/23/01 (Morgan MS); *Poetical Works*, V.
55. *Poetical Works*, V, 139, *Sir Tristrem*, (Fytte First, I, 1–4).
56. *Letters*, I, 192, Ellis, 7/?/03.
57. *Poetical Works*, V, Intro. to *Sir Tristrem*.
58. *Letters*, I, 191, Ellis, 7/?/03.
59. Morgan MS, WS to Ellis, 3/27/01.
60. *Letters*, I, 230–1, fn. 2.
61. JGL, I, 363.
62. *Letters*, I, 230–1, fn. 2, Ellis to WS, 7/4/04.
63. *Ibid.*, XII, 262, fn. 1, Jamieson to WS, 10/19/04.
64. *Ibid.*, I, 231, Ellis, 11/23/04, but dated from XII, 262, fn. 2.
65. *Ibid.*, XII, 246, Ellis, 5/4/04. The child had been born somewhere around 1800 and was therefore now 3–4 yrs. old. (See *Letters*, II, 234, to Mrs. Scott, 1809, saying he is nine.) The girl's name was Currie Lamb; she was the daughter of a seedsman at Selkirk and the housekeeper of the Marquis of Abercorn at Duddingston. The Marquis was one of the clients of Tom Scott. Daniel may have met the girl either in Selkirk or through Tom at Duddingston.
66. *Ibid.*, XII, 246.

67. *Ibid.*, 266, fn. 1, Ellis to WS, 12/3/04.
68. *Ibid.*, 265, Ellis, 11/23/04.
69. NLS MS, S. Dumergue to Charlotte, 11/20/04.
70. JGL, I, 368–9. (I have a note saying that this equals about £500 income and £100 as trustee.)
71. *Letters*, I, 229, Ellis, 6/18/04; XII, 258–9, the same.
72. JGL, I, 329.
73. *Letters*, XII, 263, Ellis, 8/21/04.
74. JGL, I, 386, says he was tempted by the small estate of Broadmeadow, near the ruins of Newark Castle on the banks of the Yarrow, but Dr. Corson says it *had* been sold in 1803 and did not in fact come on the market again until 1825.
75. *Letters*, I, 253, Ellis, 5/27/04.
76. *Ibid.*, 226, Erskine, 7/10/04.
77. *Ibid.*, 223, W. Smith, 7/11/04; Princeton MS, WS to W. Smith, 10/26/04.
78. *Ibid.*, 224, Ellis 8/21/04. Thus dated in Morgan MS, but erroneously printed as 8/1/04.
79. *Ibid.*, XII, 262, Ellis, 6/18/04.
80. *Ibid.*, I, 353, Seward, 2/20/07.
81. *Ibid.*, 227, Ellis, 8/21/04.
82. *Ibid.*, 226–7.
83. *Ibid.*, XII, 378–9, Masquerier, 9/12/03.
84. NLS MS, WS to Longman and Rees, 5/3/04.
85. JGL, I, 373–4.
86. *Ibid.*, 375.
87. *Letters*, IV, 53–4, Whishaw, 11/24/15.
88. *Ibid.*, I, 228–9, Thomson, 10/6/04.
89. *Ibid.*, 230, Ellis, 11/23/04.
90. *Ibid.*, 231–2, Ellis, 12/30/04.
91. JGL, I, 383.
92. *Ibid.*, 394–5.
93. *Ibid.*, 395.
94. Dated by *Letters*, I, 260, James Ballantyne, 10/2/05, and XII, 278 (I, 258–9), Ellis, 10/17/04, part of which JGL wrongly dates 9/5/05.
95. JGL, I, 395; NLS MS, 851.
96. Partington, *Letter Books*, 100 Campbell to WS 2/9/05.
97. *Letters*, I, 242, fn. 1, Seward to WS 3/9/05.
98. Wordsworth, *Early Letters*, 457, Wordsworth to WS 3/7/05.
99. JGL, I, 393–4.

100. Quoted in *Poetical Works*, Vol. VI, *Lay*, 219–20, fn. 3.
101. *Ibid.*, 125, fn. 3; 195, fn. 1.
102. *Ibid.*, 220, fn. 3.
103. *Ibid.*, 48, fn. 1.
104. *Ibid.*, 210–1, fn. 1.
105. *Letters*, I, 242–3, Seward, 3/21/05.
106. JGL, I, 392.

### Chapter 2

1. JGL, I, 370; NLS MS, 3234, ff. 17–23; photographs, etc.
2. *Poetical Works*, VII, *Marmion*, Intro., and Canto I, 23–4; personal observation.
3. *Marmion*, Intro., and Canto I, 23–4.
4. NLS MS, 3234, f. 27; JGL says the haugh was narrow, but 27–8 ff. contradict him.
5. NLS MS, 3234, f. 104.
6. *Ibid.*, ff. 17–23.
7. *Ibid.*, f. 27.
8. *Ibid.*, f. 17.
9. JGL, I, 417.
10. *Letters*, I, 225, Ellis, here dated 8/1/04, but should be 8/21/04; *cf.* *Letters*, XII, 263.
11. NLS MS, 3234, ff. 17–8.
12. *Ibid.*, 18–9.
13. *Letters*, I, 227, Ellis, 8/21/04.
14. JGL, I, 370–1.
15. *Ibid.*, 371.
16. *Ibid.*; *Post-Bag*, 18–9, Hogg to WS, 1/1/04.
17. JGL, I, 372.
18. Chisholm: "Sir WS as a Judge"; Dr. Corson.
19. JGL, I, 372–3.
20. *Poetical Works*, VII, *Marmion*, Intro., and Canto I, 24–5.
21. *Letters*, XII, 277, Ellis, 7/20/05.
22. NLS MS, 3234, f. 27.
23. Russell, "Some Recent Statements," 28.
24. NLS MS, 3234, f. 22.
25. JGL, I, 417–8.
26. *Ibid.*
27. NLS MS, 924, f. 35, Skene to JGL, 3/7/34; JGL, I, 419.
28. *Misc. Prose*, XIX, Criticism, III, 114.
29. *Ibid.*, 87, 99, *passim.*
30. JGL, I, 418. JGL says he made it a rule to answer every letter the day it came and delayed a day or two only on those requiring delib-

eration, but the letters themselves contradict this statement.

31. JGL, I, 419.
32. *Ibid.*, 326; Ballantyne, *Refutation; cf.* Wright, *Life*, 222.
33. Dobson, *Ballantyne Press*, 17.
34. JGL, I, 396.
35. *Ibid.*, 400. JGL says WS had been inclined to buy Broadmeadow, but it had just been sold 6/1/03, did not come on market again till 1825, and there is no evidence WS ever thought of it.
36. NLS MS, 862.
37. Note that *contra* JGL, I, 346, this sum was less the one-third the amount WS derived from the sale of Rosebank, Ballantyne, *Reply to Lockhart*, 11–2.
38. NLS MS, 862. Quale, *The Ruin of SWS*, 29, is in error in saying that the agreement made WS the owner of only one-third of the stock.
39. Here I agree in essence with Wright's analysis, *Life*, 224, though correcting his arithmetic.
40. Buchan, *SWS*, 76.
41. Dobson, *Ballantyne Press*, 17.
42. *Ibid.*, 143–9.
43. *Ibid.*, 17–8.
44. JGL, II, 33–5.
45. Ballantyne, "Rambling Reminiscences," *Chambers's Edin. J.*, 10/12/43, 324–5.
46. JGL, I, 400–2; *Letters*, I, 240, James Ballantyne, 4/12/05.
47. *Letters*, I, 244, fn. 1, 245, fn. 1.
48. Houghton MS, WS to W. Miller, 10/20/05.
49. NLS MS, 2521, f. 155, WS to Forster, 3/17/05.
50. *Ibid.*
51. *Letters*, I, 245–7, Forster 3/24/05.
52. *Ibid.*, 247–8, James Ballantyne, 4/12/05.
53. *Ibid.*, 249, WS to Forster, 4/21/05 (p.m. 4/26/05).
54. NLS MS, 786, f. 49, James Ballantyne to W. Miller, 9/21/05.
55. Houghton MS, WS to W. Miller, 10/20/05.
56. NLS MS, 786, f. 49.
57. *Ibid.*
58. Houghton MS, WS to Miller, 9/21/05.
59. NLS MS, 786, f. 49.
60. *Ibid.*

61. NLS MS, 786, f. 51, James Ballantyne to Miller, 12/1/05.
62. Quoted in *Letters*, I, 245, fn. 1.
63. NLS MS, 786, f. 49, James Ballantyne to W. Miller, 9/21/05. This sentence is quoted in *Letters*, I, 245, fn. 1.
64. JGL, I, 403.
65. ACLC, II, 314–5. In 1806 the *Edinburgh Review* was selling 4,500 copies a number. See *Letters*, XII, 279, Ellis, 10/17/06.
66. Partington, *Letter Books*, 112, Campbell to WS, 6/6/05.
67. JGL, I, 403.
68. Partington, *Letter Books*, 102–3, Campbell to WS, 6/6/05.
69. *Ibid.*
70. Partington, *Post-Bag*, 23, Campbell to WS, n.d.; JGL, I, 403.
71. *Letters*, I, 258, Ellis, ca. 9/5/05.
71a. Partington, *Post-Bag*, 23, Campbell to WS, 11/4/06.
72. NLS MS, 1758, f. 23, WS to Campbell, 12/14/06. See also ACLC, I, Constable to Murray, 12/9/06, Murray to Constable 12/19/06.
73. Ball, *SWS as a Critic*, 162. JGL, I, 409, says that these reviews as well as those mentioned in the next note were written in the summer of 1805, which is impossible.
74. *Misc. Prose*, XVIII, *Criticism*, II, 135–6. In the July number of the *Edinburgh Review*, WS reviewed two cookery books and had an article on the Highland Society's report on the Poems of Ossian (Ball, *SWS as a Critic*, 162).
75. *Misc. Prose*, XVIII, 137.
76. *Letters*, I, 249–50, Forster, 4/21/05.
77. *Ibid.*
78. JGL, I, 419–20.
79. *Ibid.*
80. Hogg, *Domestic Manners*, 58–60.
81. *Ibid.*
82. *Letters*, I, 251, Forster, 4/21/05.
83. Hogg, *Domestic Manners*, 60.
84. *Letters*, XII, 274–5, Ellis, 7/20/05.
85. *Ibid.*, I, 261, Ellis, 10/17/05.
86. JGL, I, 406–7, Ellis to WS, n.d.
87. *Letters*, I, 258–9, Ellis, not, as printed, 9/5/05 but 10/17/05; see *Letters*, XII, 277, fn. 3.
88. JGL, I, 425–6. Though he does not mention the visit to Southey, see *Letters*, I, 287, Seward, 4/10/06, which makes it clear that WS saw

both men at the time; also I, 292, Southey, 4/?/06.
89. JGL, I, 425–6.
90. *Ibid.*, *Letters*, I, 292, Southey, 4/?/06; Wordsworth, *Early Letters* (1785–1805), 514 n.
91. JGL, I, 426; *Poetical Works*, VI, 370.
92. *Ibid.*, 426–7; *Poetical Works*, VIII, 357.
93. JGL, I, 427.
94. *Letters*, I, 262–4, Ellis, 10/17/05. Scott used this sermon in the ending that he added to *Queenhoo-Hall* in 1808.
95. *Letters*, I, 263, fn. 1, Southey to Wynne, 10/3/05.
96. JGL, I, 409.
97. *Waverley*, I, Gen. Pref., xx–xxi.
98. *Ibid.*, WS says, xxi, that the novel was "advertised to be published by" John Ballantyne, but this is an error of his memory. In 1805 John B. was not yet a publisher.

### Chapter 3

1. *Letters*, I, 268, C. Erskine, 11/6/05.
2. *Ibid.*, XII, 382, fn. 1.
3. *Ibid.*, 382₃, Colin Mackenzie, 12/29/05.
4. *Ibid.*, 383.
5. JGL, I, 429–30, Ellis to WS, n.d.
6. *Letters*, I, 264–5, Ellis, 11/29/05; *cf.* XII, 279–80.
7. *Letters*, I, 205.
8. Parsons, *M.L.R.*, XXXVIII, no. 3, 246, July 1943.
9. *Ibid.*, 247.
10. *Letters*, I, 265, C. Erskine, 11/6/05.
11. Parsons, *M.L.R.*, as above, 248.
12. *Letters*, I, 270, Nicolson, 12/24/05.
13. *Poetical Works*, VI, *Lay*, Intro., 8.
14. *Ibid.*
15. MacDonald, *Juridical Review.*
16. *Poetical Works*, VI, *Lay*, Intro., 17.
17. JGL, I, 399, 436.
18. NLS MS, 3875, Dalkeith to WS, 2/2/05.
19. JGL, I, 437; *Letters*, I, 369, Lady Abercorn, 7/20/07, says "as deaf as a post and as capable of discharging his duty as I am of dancing a hornpipe."
20. *Letters*, I, 273, Ellis, 1/25/06.
21. NLS MS, 1750, f. 60, C. Erskine, 2/5 or 2/12 /06; MS, 1753, f. 139. Mundell, 2/5 or 2/14/06.

22. My interpretation differs from JGL, I, 438, but largely agrees with Wright, *Life*, 192–4.
23. *Letters*, I, 273, Ellis, 1/25/06.
24. Historians have taken the view that Lord Melville was careless but not criminal.
25. *Letters*, I, 274–5, Ellis, 1/25/06.
26. *Ibid.*, 276, Dalkeith, 2/11/06; JGL, I, 438.
27. *Poetical Works*, VII, *Marmion*, Intro., 8–9.
28. *Letters*, I, 278, Dalkeith to WS, 2/20/06.
29. JGL, I, 455–6.
30. *Letters*, I, 279, Ellis (MS. p.m. 2/10/06, though printed as 2/20/06).
31. *Letters*, I, 277, Dalkeith, 2/11/06.
32. *Ibid.*
33. *Ibid.*, 276, Dalkeith, 2/11/06.
34. JGL, I, 439.
35. *Letters*, I, 279–80, Ellis, 2/10/06.
36. *Letters*, I, 302, Lady Abercorn, 6/9/06. JGL says "Stanmore Priory," but see *Misc. Prose*, XX, 182–4, "Abercorn."
37. *Letters*, I, 285, Ellis, 4/7/06; 277, Dalkeith, 2/11/06.
38. *Letters*, I, 277, Dalkeith, 2/4/06.
39. JGL, I, 462.
40. MacCunn, *Sir W's Friends*, 294.
41. *Ibid.*, 291.
42. *Ibid.*, 299.
43. JGL, I, 462.
44. *Ibid.*, 451.
45. *Letters*, I, 285, Ellis, 4/7/06.
46. JGL, I, 451–2.
47. *Ibid.*, 451.
48. *Letters*, I, 280–1, Sharpe, 3/3/06.
49. Morgan MS, in which p.m. establishes the date as 3/3/06; printed in *Letters*, I, 281–2, Ellis; and *cf.* XII, 280–1.
50. *Letters*, I, 283, Ellis, 4/7/06.
51. *Ibid.*, 284.
52. Partington, *Post-Bag*, 25, Ellis to WS, 5/13/06.
53. JGL, I, 452–3.
54. Lockhart, *Peter's Letters*, 202, says blue robes; corrected by Dr. Corson.
55. JGL, I, 453–4.
56. *Ibid.*, 455.
57. NLS MS, 924, f. 35, Skene letter to JGL, 3/7/34. Also in Skene, *Memories*, 64–6, where the episode is dated 1819—but this is impossible since Camp died 1809.

58. JGL, I, 455.
59. *Letters*, I, 285, Ellis, 4/7/06.
60. *Ibid.*, 280, Ellis, 2/10/06.
61. JGL, I, 458 fn.
62. *Letters*, XII, 285, Heber, 6/30/06.
63. *Ibid.*, I, 305, R. Dundas, 6/28/06.
64. Morgan MS and NLS MS, 855, which vary slightly from each other.
65. *Letters*, XII, 113, fn. 1.
66. *Ibid.*, II, 371-2, Lady Dalkeith, 8/14/10.
67. *Ibid.*, I, 280, Ellis, 2/10/06.
68. JGL, I, 459.
69. *Ibid.*, II, 86.
70. *Letters*, I, 295, C. Erskine, 5/25/06.
71. *Ibid.*, 264, fn. 2, Ellis to WS, 12/11/05.
72. JGL, II, 86.
73. *Letters*, I, 311, Lady Abercorn, 8/8/06.
74. *Ibid.*, 319, fn. 2.
75. *Ibid.*, XII, 269, Ellis, 1/5/05; 269, Heber, 1/7/05.
76. *Ibid.*, 267, fn. 1.
77. *Ibid.*, 269, fn. 2, and NLS MS, 939, f. 64, Leyden to WS, 11/20/05.
78. *Ibid.*
79. *Letters*, I, 305-9, Leyden, 7/5/06.
80. *Ibid.*, 312, Lady Abercorn, 8/6/06.
81. *Ibid.*, 311.
82. JGL, I, 461; Ball, *SWS as a Critic*, 148.
83. ACLC, I, 420, Constable to Geo. Chalmers, 6/4/06.
84. JGL, I, 462; Ball, *SWS as a Critic*, 148; *Letters*, I, 325, Constable, 10/7/06.
85. JGL, I, 461.
86. *Letters*, I, 315, Skene, 8/11/06.
87. *Ibid.*
88. *Ibid.*, 316, Lady Abercorn, 9/20/06.
89. *Ibid.*, 314-5, Skene, 8/11/06.
90. *Ibid.*, 316, Lady Abercorn, 9/20/06.
91. *Ibid.*
92. *Ibid.*, 312, Lady Abercorn, 8/6/06.
93. JGL, I, 423-4, quoting Skene's reminiscences; Skene, *Memories*, 35-6. WS used this episode in *Black Dwarf*.
94. Skene, *Memories*, 34, erroneously remembered the *G. Mannering* episode as an otter hunt too. Dr. Corson disagrees: "Tod Willie bears no resemblance to 'Tod Gibbie.'"
95. JGL, I, 420-1, 429.
96. Skene, *Memories*, 33; JGL, I, 422-3.
97. JGL, I, 424-5.

98. *Letters*, XII, 288-9, Heber, 8/28/08.
99. *Ibid.*, I, 387-8, Dr. Adam, 8/18/06, original still in Edinburgh H.S. Library.
100. *Ibid.*, 321-2, Seward, bet. 7/20 and 9/23/06.
101. *Ibid.*, 324.
102. *Ibid.*, 347, Seward, 1/13/07.
103. *Ibid.*, XII, 290, Heber, 8/18/16.
104. *Ibid.*, I, Seward, 1/13/07.
105. JGL, I, 462-3.
106. *Letters*, I, 349, Constable & Co., 1/21/07; JGL, I, 463.

Chapter 4

1. JGL, I, 463; Smiles, *Murray*, I, 76.
2. ACLC, I, 47; *Letters*, I, 309, Leyden, 7/5/06. *Temple Bar*, Dec. 1892, says £2,500, but WS was writing at the time.
3. NLS MS, 1758, f. 28, WS to Rees, 1/16/07; *Letters*, I, 348, James Longman, 1/27/07.
4. JGL, I, 463.
5. Dobson, *Ballantyne Press*, 110.
6. *Tait's Edin.*, Oct. 1839, 660.
7. NLS MS, 910, f. 35, quoted by Grierson, *Scott*, 83-4.
8. *Ibid.*
9. *Letters*, I, 341-2, Surtees, 12/17/06.
10. *Poetical Works*, VII, *Marmion*, Canto I, XIII, 58 and fn. See also n. H, ff. 383-4, and *Poetical Works*, II, *Minstrelsy*, 86-9.
11. *Letters*, I, 343, Surtees, 12/17/06.
12. *Ibid.*, 338, Ferguson, 12/16/06, and fn. 1.
13. Morgan MS, WS to Mrs. Ellis, 12/16/06.
14. *Letters*, I, 346, Jamieson, 12/16/06.
15. Morgan MS, WS to Mrs. Ellis, 12/16/06.
16. NLS MS, 2889, f. 17, WS to Wm. Scott, 1/7/07.
17. JGL, I, 496.
18. *Letters*, I, 350, Lady Abercorn, 2/11/07.
19. *Ibid.*, 351, Seward, 2/20/07.
20. *Ibid.*, 352, fn. 2, Seward to WS, 1/29/07.
21. *Ibid.*, 353, Seward, 2/20/07.
22. JGL, I, 466.
23. *Poetical Works*, VII, *Marmion*, 131-2 fns. I have quoted from the MS version, which was probably that which the Princess saw, rather

than from the modified version ultimately presented.

24. Partington, *Letter Books*, 8, Mrs. Hayman to WS, 2/22/07.
25. JGL, I, 466.
26. *Letters*, I, 356–7, Surtees, 2/21/07.
27. JGL, I, 460.
28. *Letters*, XII, 95, Charlotte 3/20?/07.
29. JGL, I, 460. But he makes it sound as if it happened in 1806, whereas it was probably not till 1807.
30. *Letters*, I, 358–9, C. Erskine, 3/14/07; 360, Surtees, 3/15/07. JGL says to use the British Museum, but WS never mentions it in any letter, whereas the Clerks of Session business recurs again and again and was therefore obviously the chief reason. That Mackenzie *was* in London, see *Letters*, XII, 97, Charlotte, 3/24/07.
31. *Letters*, I, 360, Surtees, 3/15/07; *P.B.*, 27, Wordsworth to WS, 3/2/07.
32. *Ibid.*, XII, 94, Charlotte, 3/20/07.
33. *Ibid.*, 94, fn. 1.
34. *Ibid.*, 94–5, Charlotte, 3/20/07.
35. *Ibid.*, 95.
36. *Ibid.*, II, 14, Charles Carpenter, 2/8/08.
37. *Ibid.* The school friend was Robert Dundas (later the 2nd Lord Melville).
38. *Letters*, XII, 95, Charlotte, 3/20/07.
39. *Ibid.*, I, 348, Lady Charlotte Campbell, 10/12/06; XII, 98, Charlotte, 3/24/07.
40. *Ibid.*, XII, 96–7, Charlotte, 3/24/07.
41. *Ibid.*, 99, Charlotte, 3/30/07.
42. *Ibid.*, 106, Charlotte, 4/14/07.
43. *Ibid.*, 99, Charlotte, 3/30/07.
44. *Ibid.*, 108, Charlotte, 4/19/07.
45. *Ibid.*, 115, Charlotte, 4/27/07.
46. *Ibid.*, 97, Charlotte, 3/24/07.
47. *Ibid.*, 101, Charlotte, 3/30/07.
48. *Ibid.*, 97, Charlotte, 3/24/07.
49. *Ibid.*, 95, Charlotte, 3/20/07.
50. *Ibid.*, 97, Charlotte, 3/24/07.
51. *Ibid.*, 101, Charlotte, 3/30/07.
52. *Ibid.*, 99–100, Charlotte, 3/30/07.
53. *Ibid.*, I, 302, fn.
54. *Ibid.*, XII, 100, Charlotte, 4/22/07.
55. JGL, I, 499; *Letters*, I, 385, Lady Abercorn, 9/19/07.
56. *Letters*, II, 35, Lady Abercorn, 4/3/08; *Poetical Works*, VII, Intro.

to Canto I, *Marmion*, 29, and 29 fn. 2; JGL, I, 466–7.

57. *Letters*, XII, 97, Charlotte, 3/30/07.
58. MacCunn, *Sir W's Friends*, 229–30.
59. *Letters*, I, 363, James Ballantyne, ca. May, '07.
60. JGL, I, 467, fn. 1.
61. *Letters*, XII, 102, Charlotte, 4/10/07.
62. *Ibid.*, 103, 4/10/07.
63. *Ibid.*, 105–6, Charlotte, 4/14/07.
64. *Ibid.*, 108, Charlotte, 4/19/07.
65. *Ibid.*, 110, Charlotte, 4/22/07.
66. *Ibid.*, 108, Charlotte, 4/19/07.
67. *Ibid.*, 110, Charlotte, 4/22/07.
68. *Ibid.*, 109–10, Charlotte, 4/22/07.
69. *Ibid.*, 113, Charlotte, 4/27/07.
70. *Ibid.*, 111–2, Charlotte, 4/27/07.
71. *Ibid.*, 95, Charlotte, 3/20/07.
72. *Ibid.*, 102, Charlotte, 3/30/07.
73. *Ibid.*, 115, Charlotte, 4/27/07.
74. *Ibid.*, 100, Charlotte, 3/30/07.
75. *Ibid.*, 104, Charlotte, 4/10/07.
76. *Ibid.*, 116, Charlotte, 5/10/07.
77. *Ibid.*, 113–4, Charlotte, 4/27/07.
78. *Ibid.*, 113–4, Charlotte, 4/27/07.
79. *Poetical Works*, VII, *Marmion*, 236, fn. 1; JGL, I, 466–7. JGL errs, however, in saying that WS reserved every Sat.–Sun. for either the Abercorns or the Ellises.
80. *Letters*, XII, 111, Charlotte, 4/22/07.
81. *Ibid.*, 115, Charlotte, 5/4/07.
82. *Ibid.*, 111, Charlotte, 4/22/07.
83. *Ibid.*, 115–6, Charlotte, 5/4/07.
84. *Misc. Prose*, IV, 206–7.
85. *Letters*, III, 29, Sharpe, 12/4/11.
86. *Misc. Prose*, IV, 216.
87. Quoted in Ashmun, *Singing Swan*, 8.
88. *Letters*, I, 325, Seward, 9/?/06.
89. JGL, I, 468.
90. *Ibid.*, 469.
91. Ashmun, *Singing Swan*, 254; *Letters*, I, 361, Lady Abercorn, 5/15/07.
92. *Letters*, I, 362.
93. *Ibid.*
94. Morrison, "Random Rem.," in *Tait's Edin. Mag.*, Sept., 1843, 573.
95. *Letters*, I, 366, Surtees, 6/12/07; JGL, II, 110. But JGL is mistaken in saying the work was done for a London publisher.
96. *Letters*, I, 364.
97. *Ibid.*, 365.
98. *Ibid.*, 366.

99. NLS MS, 2533 (Glen MS), ff. 49–57.
100. *Letters*, VII, 394, fn.
101. NLS MS, 1750, f. 69, WS to Lord Abercorn, 11/17/07.
102. *Letters*, I, 367, Lady Abercorn, 7/20/07.
103. *Ibid.*, VII, 350, Charles Scott 3/6/23.
104. *Ibid.*, I, 370, Lady Abercorn, 7/20/07.
105. *Ibid.*, 368.
106. *Ibid.*, 372, Surtees, 7/28/07.
107. *Ibid.*, 370, Lady Abercorn, 7/20/07.
108. NLS MS, 2533 (Glen MS), ff. 49–57.
109. Princeton MS, WS to Guthrie Wright, 8/14/07.
110. NLS MS, 1750, f. 67, to C. Ferrier (copy).
111. NLS MS, 2533 (Glen MS), ff. 49–57.
112. *Ibid.*, but also quoted in *Letters*, VII, fn. 1, Wright to WS 9/22/07.
113. *Letters*, I, 374, Seward, 8/11/07.
114. *Ibid.*, 381, Lady Abercorn, 9/16/07; NLS MS, 1750, f. 69, WS to Lord Abercorn, 11/17/07.
115. *Letters*, VII, 398, fn. 2.
116. *Ibid.*, I, 374, Seward, 8/11/07.
117. *Ibid.*, II, 15, Charles Carpenter, 2/8/08; *Letters*, I, 384, Lady Abercorn, 9/19/07.
118. NLS MS 1750, f. 69, Lord Abercorn, 11/17/07.
119. *Letters*, I, 374, Seward, 8/11/07.
120. *Ibid.*, 369, Lady Abercorn, 7/20/07.
121. *Ibid.*
122. *Poetical Works*, VII, *Marmion*, Intro. 10.
123. JGL, I, 470–1.
124. *Ibid.*
125. *Ibid.*
126. *Letters*, I, 374, Seward, 8/11/07.
127. *Ibid.*, 379, Seward, 9/?/07.
128. *Ibid.*, 380.
129. JGL, I, 464.
130. *Poetical Works*, VII, *Marmion*, Intro. and Canto I, 34.
131. *Ibid.*, Canto II, 83, 85.
132. JGL, I, 465.
133. *Letters*, I, 382, Lady Abercorn, 9/10/07; *cf.* also *Letters*, I, 377, Miss Smith, 9/9/07, and *Letters*, II, 87, Surtees, erroneously dated 1818 but should be 9/10/07.

134. *Ibid.*, I, 399, Seward 11/23/07.
135. NLS MS, 1809, f. 233, WS to Ellis, 10/5/07.
136. Morgan MS, WS to W. Miller, 10/11/07.
137. *Ibid.*
138. JGL, I, 465–6, Skene's reminiscences.
139. *Letters*, I, 392, Lady Louisa Stuart, 11/?/07.
140. *Letters*, II, 3, Lady Louisa Stuart, 1/19/08.
141. *Ibid.*, 3, Lady Louisa Stuart, 1/19/08.
142. *Letters*, II, 7, Lady Abercorn, 1/22/07.
143. *Letters*, II, 50, Seward, 4/23/08.
144. Morgan MS, WS to W. Miller, 1/24/08; *Letters*, II, James Ballantyne, n.d.
145. NLS MS, 921, ff. 176–7, James Ballantyne's reminiscences.
146. JGL, I, 485.
147. *Letters*, II, 1, Lady Minto, n.d. except "Tuesday," but probably 2/16/08, when he wrote to others that he was sending them copies of the poem. *Ibid.*, 16, Lady Abercorn, 2/16/08; 21, Ellis, 2/23/08; 29, Surtees, 2/26/08; XII, 298, Douce, 2/20/08; II, 23, Southey, 2/26/08; 17, Charles Carpenter, 2/16/08; NLS MS, 860, f. 9, Laidlaw, 2/16/08.
148. *Letters*, II, 16, Lady Abercorn, 2/16/18.
149. *Ibid.*, 20, Surtees, 2/20/08.
150. *Ibid.*, 23, Southey, 2/26/08.
151. *Ibid.*, 21, Ellis, 2/23/08.

Chapter 5

1. JGL, I, 503, says "one month," but See *Letters*, II, 42, Lady Louisa Stuart, 4/7/08, which says the 2nd ed. was then on the eve of publication. There may, however, have been some additional delay in printing this edition; see *Letters*, II, 63, Constable, 5/3/08, which says, "I am glad the new *Marmion* is at length out."
2. JGL overlooks the 3rd ed., mentioned in NLS MS, 3653, WS to Seward, 5/27/08, which says the "3rd edition is at press, 3,000 strong, to replace 2nd of like number [of] which the first 2,000

quartos is almost gone." *Letters*, II, 74, Lady Louisa Stuart, 6/16/08: "The press is now groaning" with the 3rd, making "the number of copies published within the space of 34 months amounting to eight thousand." Most of the rest of the figures are from JGL, I, 503.

3. JGL, I, 457.
4. *Letters*, II, 70, Lady Abercorn, 7/9/08.
5. Gillies, "Recollections," *Fraser's Mag.*, XII, 694.
6. JGL, I, 489.
7. *Ibid.*, 491.
8. *Ibid.*, 490.
9. *Ibid.*, 488.
10. *Ibid.*, 495.
11. Wright, *Life*, 206.
12. Partington, *Post-Bag*, 30, quoted by Seward to WS., 8/26/07.
13. Partington, *Letter Books*, 65, Wordsworth to WS, 1/18/08.
14. JGL, I, 493.
15. *Poetical Works*, VII, *Marmion*, 354–5, fn. 1.
16. JGL, I, 494.
17. *Ibid.*, 493. Plainly Jeffrey would not have approved either of Beckford's Fonthill Abbey or of the Pavilion at Brighton as the Prince Regent was transforming it in 1817.
18. *Ibid.*, 492.
19. *Poetical Works*, VII, *Marmion*, Intro., and Canto I, 26–9.
20. *Ibid.*, Canto I, 30.
21. *Ibid.*, 31, fn. 1.
22. JGL, I, 492. This account makes it sound as if it were the actual magazine, but WS's letter to Surtees, quoted below, says "the revisal," which sounds more like proof sheets.
23. *Letters*, II, 56, Surtees, 4/18/08.
24. JGL, I, 494–5.
25. L.B., 73, Southey to WS, 10/4/07.
26. *Letters*, I, 389, Southey, 11/?/07.
27. *Ibid.*, 386, fn. 1, Southey to WS, 12/8/07.
28. *Ibid.*, 400, Southey, 12/15/07.
29. L.B., 74, Southey to WS, 10/4/07.
30. *Letters*, I, 386, Southey 10/1/07.
31. *Ibid.*, 389–90, Southey, 11/?/07.
32. *Ibid.*, 387, Southey, 10/1/07.
33. *Ibid.*, fn. 1, Southey to WS, n.d.
34. *Ibid.*, XII, 298, fn. 2, Southey to WS, 12/2/07.
35. *Ibid.*, I, 401, Southey, 12/15/07.

36. *Ibid.*, II, 23, Southey, 2/26/08.
37. JGL, II, 1.
38. *Ibid.*, 10.
39. *Letters*, II, 27, Lady Abercorn, 2/28/08.
40. *Tait's Edin.*, Oct. 1839, 660, from Ballantyne pamphlet.
41. *Letters*, I, 409, John Ballantyne, 11/31[sic]/07.
42. Ballantyne Reply to Lockhart, 25,
43. *Letters*, I, 410, fn. 1, John Ballantyne to WS, 12/1/07.
44. *Ibid.*, 411, John Ballantyne, 11/31/07.
45. *Ibid.*
46. *Ibid.*, 405, Lady Abercorn, 12/15/07.
47. *Ibid.*, II, 10–1, Lady Abercorn, 2/5/08.
48. *Ibid.*, 12, Lady Abercorn, 2/8/08.
49. *Ibid.*, 10–1, Lady Abercorn, 2/5/08.
50. *Ibid.*, 10.
51. *Ibid.*, 29, Smith, 3/3/08.
52. In 1811? quoted by Pearson, *Life and Personality*, 71.
53. *Letters*, II, 29, Smith, 3/3/18.
54. Pearson, *Life and Personality*, 74.
55. *Letters*, II, 30, Smith, 3/3/08.
56. Gilfillan, *Life*, 96, quoting from Crabb Robinson's *Diary*.
57. *Letters*, II, 31, Lady Abercorn, 3/13/08.
58. *Ibid.*, 35, Lady Abercorn, 4/3/08.
59. *Ibid.*, 59, Lady Abercorn, 4/26/08.
60. *Ibid.*, 35, Lady Abercorn, 4/3/08.
61. *Ibid.*, 66, Mrs. Scott of Harden, 5/25/08.
62. *Ibid.*, 31–2, Lady Abercorn, 3/13/08.
63. BM MS, WS to Seward. They are dated 4/5/08, but something is wrong in the date. JGL says the article, in the October *Edin. Rev.*, was by Hallam.
64. *Letters*, II, 42–3, James Ballantyne, 4/?/08.
65. *Ibid.*, 44.
66. *Ibid.*, 43; also Morgan MS, WS to Longman and Rees, 5/11/08.
67. *Letters*, II, 44, James Ballantyne, 4/11/08.
68. *Ibid.*, 43, fn. 1, Longman and Rees to James Ballantyne, 5/6/08; Morgan MS, WS to Longman and Rees, 5/11/08.
69. *Letters*, XII, 394, Rees, 6/9/08; 395, fn. 1, Longman to WS,

6/16/08; NLS MS, 3653, f. 149,
WS to Longman, 6/19/08.

70. JGL, II, 11.

71. *Ibid.*

72. *Letters*, II, 109, James Ballantyne,
autumn/08.

73. *Ibid.*, II, 56, fn. 2.

74. *Ibid.*, 57, fn. JGL, II, 15, gets them
wrong. James Grahame's *The Sabbath* was not published "a year or
two before" Struthers, but in the
same year, 1804, and the 1818 volume was one of collected poems,
not a first issue, as he implies. See
*Letters*, I, 230 fn. For Grahame, see
*Letters*, II, 333, fn. 1, and XII, 272,
fn. 2.

75. *Ibid.*, Joanna Baillie, 5/7/08; 57,
Joanna Baillie, 4/7/08.

76. *Ibid.*, I, 227, Ellis, 8/21/04; XII,
292–3, Ellis, 7/1/07; 290–2, fn. 2.
Weber is not to be confused, as
JGL confuses him, with the "half-
starved amanuensis," who was Rob-
ert Leyden, a younger brother of
John, "sent down by some of the
London booksellers," and who cop-
ied the *Lay le Frein* for WS,
*Letters*, I, 227, Ellis, 8/21/04.

77. *Journal*, 129–30, 3/9/26.

78. *Letters*, II, 38–9, Surtees, 4/4/08.

79. *Ibid.*, XII, 301, Heber, 5/12/08.

80. *Ibid.*, XII, 391, Douce, 5/12/08.

81. JGL, II, 8, Ellis to WS.

82. *Letters*, II, 13, Ellis, 10/8/08.

83. JGL, II, 13.

84. *Letters*, II, 48, James Ballantyne,
4/22/08; 49, Seward, 4/23/18.

85. *Ibid.*, 58, Lady Abercorn, 4/20/08.

86. *Ibid.*, 46, Joanna Baillie, 5/7/08.

87. NLS MS, 3653, f. 147, WS to Seward, 5/27/08.

88. *Letters*, II, 100, Dalkeith, 10/25/08.

89. Partington, *Letter Books*, 90, Hogg
to WS, 5/?/08.

90. NLS MS, 3653, f. 147, WS to Seward, 5/27/08.

91. Partington, *Letter Books*, 90, Hogg
to WS, 5/?/08.

92. *Letters*, II, 99, Dalkeith, 10/25/08.

93. Yale U. MS, WS to Miller, 4/25/08.

94. *Letters*, II, 45, fn. 2, James Ballantyne to WS, 4/30/08. JGL erroneously dates merely the last
week in April.

95. JGL, II, 2.

96. Ball, *SWS as a Critic*, 61.

97. *Ibid.*, 60.

98. WS himself says this in his Pref.,
vi.

99. Pref., vi.

100. *Misc. Prose*, I, *Life of Dryden*, 38.

101. *Ibid.*, 76–7.

102. *Ibid.*, 102.

## Chapter 6

1. *Letters*, II, 62, Constable, 5/3/18;
74, Stuart, 6/16/08; Thomas Sad-
lcir, 8/14/08, *Athenaeum*, Feb.,
1908, 257.

2. *Letters*, II, 71, Lady Abercorn,
6/9/08.

3. *Ibid.*, 73, Stuart, 6/16/18.

4. *Ibid.*, 5, Stuart, 1/19/08.

5. *Ibid.*, 72, Stuart, 6/16/08.

6: *Ibid.*, 73.

7. *Ibid.*, 72, fn. 1, Lady Louisa Stuart
to WS, 6/11/08.

8. NLS MS, 1809, f. 235, WS to Wm.
Miller, 9/10/09; ACLC, I, 136,
Hunter to Constable, 5/11/08;
*Letters*, II, 62, Constable, 5/3/08.

9. *Letters*, II, 75, Thos. Scott,
6/20/08, corrected from Huntington MS; JGL, II, 52, fn. 1.

10. *Letters*, VII, 421–2, Thos. Scott,
8/25/08.

11. *Ibid.*, 416, Mrs. Thos. Scott,
8/21/07; *Letters*, II, 417, Thos.
Scott, 7/26/08, and fn. 4.

12. *Letters*, VII, 397–8; II, 74–5, Thos.
Scott, 6/20/08.

13. *Ibid.*, 417, Thos. Scott, 7/20/08.

14. *Ibid.*, II, 75, Thos. Scott, 6/20/08.

15. *Ibid.*, VII, 423, Thos. Scott,
10/8/08.

16. MacCunn, *Sir W's Friends*, 309–12,
315; *Letters*, II, 92, Baillie, 9/18/08.

17. MacCunn, *Sir W's Friends*, 199–
200.

18. JGL, II, 20.

19. *Ibid.*, I 501.

20. *Ibid.*, 502.

21. *Ibid.*, II, 22–4.

22. *Ibid.*, 22–4; *Letters*, II, 89, Smith,
9/17/08; *Letters*, XII, 392, Heber,
9/8/08, says WS is expecting
"Morritt today or tomorrow"; II,
92, Baillie, 9/18/08, says they left
two days ago.

23. JGL, II, 22–4.

24. *Letters*, II, 162, Mrs. Clephane,
2/5/09.

25. *Ibid.*, 259, Joanna Baillie, 10/27/09.

26. *Ibid.*, 65, Sharpe (1808).

27. *Ibid.*, 15, Charles Carpenter, 7/9/08.
28. JGL, II, 26–7.
29. *Ibid.*, 27–9.
30. *Ibid.*, 27–8.
31. *Ibid.*, 24.
32. *Ibid.*, 28.
33. *Ibid.*
34. *Ibid.*, 27.
35. *Letters*, II, 82–5, James Ballantyne, 8/19/08; *cf.* NLS MS, 862, f. 29, James Ballantyne to WS, 10/15/16.
36. *Ibid.*
37. NLS MS, 921, James Ballantyne Recollections, 196–9.
38. *Ibid.*
39. *Letters*, II, 112, Constable, "Tuesday" (10/11 or 10/18/08).
40. Wright, *Life*, 244.
41. JGL, II, 37.
42. *Ibid.*, 38.
43. *Ibid.*
44. *Letters*, II, 103, Gifford, 10/25/08.
45. Wordsworth, *Poetical Works*.
46. JGL attributes this article to Brougham, but it was by Jeffrey.
47. Pope-Hennessy, *Laird*, 122.
48. JGL, II, 39, fn. 1; *cf. Letters*, II, 126, Murray, 11/15/08.
49. *Letters*, II, 101, fn. 1, W. Erskine to Campbell-Colquhoun, 10/23/08; *ibid.*, 130, Thos. Scott, 11/19/08.
50. *Ibid.*, 130, fn. 2, Gifford to WS, 11/9/08.
51. *Ibid.*, and 100, Gifford, 10/25/08.
52. *Ibid.*, 101.
53. *Ibid.*, 107.
54. *Ibid.*, 102–3.
55. *Ibid.*, 104.
56. *Ibid.*, 105.
57. *Ibid.*, 104.
58. *Ibid.*, 108.
59. *Ibid.*, 107.
60. *Ibid.*, 122, Ellis, 11/2/08.
61. Morgan MS, quoted in *Letters*, II, 128–9, Ellis, 11/18/08.
62. *Letters*, II, 130–1, Thos. Scott, 11/19/08.
63. *Poetical Works*, VI, *Lay*, Intro. 16.
64. *Letters*, II, 116, Baillie, 10/31/08.
65. Morgan MS, WS to Ellis, 11/18 (incomplete in *Letters*, II, 127–30, and XII, 315–7).
66. *Ibid.*, but *cf. Letters*, II, 126, Murray, 11/15/08, in which WS expresses no opposition to Southey's doing the piece.
67. *Letters*, II, 128.
68. *Ibid.*, XII, 308, Ellis, 12/13/08; II, 136, Murray, 12/14/08; II, 106, Gifford, 10/25/08.
69. *Ibid.*, II, 161, Murray, 2/2/09; 157, Murray, 1/28/09; 158, Murray, 1/30/09.
70. *Ibid.*, 142–3, Sharpe, 12/30/08.
71. *Ibid.*, 129, Ellis, 11/18/08.
72. *Ibid.*, 143, Sharpe, 12/30/08.
73. *Ibid.*, 138, Ellis, 12/15/08; XII, 310, same letter: checked with Morgan MS.
74. *Letters*, II, 138, fn. 1, Jeffrey to Horner, 12/6/08.
75. *Ibid.*, 146, Murray, 1/4/09.
76. *Ibid.*, 125, Murray, 11/15/08.
77. *Ibid.*, 145, Constable & Co., 1/2/09.
78. JGL, II, 55, Constable & Co. to WS, 1/11/09.
79. *Ibid.*
80. *Ibid.*, 56.
81. *Letters*, II, 145, Constable & Co., 1/2/09.
82. *Letters*, II, 135, Ellis, 12/13/08.
83. *Ibid.*, 151, Southey, 1/14/09.
84. *Ibid.*, 153, Morritt, 1/14/09.
85. *Ibid.*, 165, P. Murray, 1/15/09.
86. *Ibid.*, 155, Constable & Co., 1/22/09.
87. *Ibid.*, 155, fn. 1, Constable to WS, 1/25/09.
88. *Ibid.*, 181, Seward, 3/19/09.
89. JGL, II, 57.

### Chapter 7

1. *Letters*, II, 28, Lady Abercorn, 2/28/08; 103, Mrs. Clephane, 2/5/09, saying he has "a world of questions to ask about Highland song and poetry" because "one day or other" he hopes "to attempt a Highland poem."
2. JGL, II, 58. The deed of Copartnery, as JGL says, is dated 7/19/09 (*Letters*, II, 207), but the correspondence shows that the firm was created in January and opened its Hanover Street premises in March.
3. Wright, *Life*, 227; probably, however, mainly from Ballantyne Trustees' pamphlet.
4. JGL, II, 34.
5. *Ibid.*, III, 461, quoting John Ballantyne's Diary, now in Morgan Library.
6. Ballantyne Trustees *Reply*, 17.
7. JGL, III, 461; see n. 5 above.

8. Ballantyne Trustees *Reply*, 34–5.
9. *Letters*, II, 195, Southey, 5/4/09.
10. *Ibid.*, 146, Murray, 1/4/09. JGL, II, 76. says in February, but this letter says, "Ballantyne sets off to-day to meet you," and speaks of John as holding up "his character with any Edinburgh Publisher." This must be John, because Murray has already met James.
11. Ball, *SWS as a Critic*, 150.
12. *Letters*, II, 168, Murray, 2/25/09.
13. *Ibid.*, 167; VII, 427, Thos. Scott, 2/24/09; II, 170, fn. 2.
14. *Letters, II*, 230–1, Rogers, 8/18/09; 170, fn. 2.
15. *Ibid.*, 151, Southey, 1/14/09; 160, Southey, 1/30/09.
16. *Ibid.*, 195, Southey, 5/4/09.
17. *Ibid.*, 205–6, Southey, 6/16/09.
18. *Ibid.*, VII, Thos. Scott, 10/15/10.
19. *Ibid.*, II, 113, Wm. Miller, 10/30/08.
20. Ball, *SWS as a Critic*, 52 fn., 151–2.
21. *Letters*, II, 113, Wm. Miller, 10/30/08.
22. *Ibid.*, 119 fn., Murray to WS, 10/26/08; Smiles, *Murray*, I, 86.
23. *Letters*, II, 119, Murray, 11/2/08.
24. *Ibid.*, 114, Murray, 10/30/08.
25. *Ibid.*, 120, Murray, 11/2/08.
26. Smiles, *Murray*, I, 86.
27. *Letters*, II, 119, Murray, 11/2/08.
28. Smiles, *Murray*, I, 86.
29. *Ibid.*, 89.
30. *Letters*, I, 197, James Ballantyne, 4/22/1800.
31. *Ibid.*, II, 136, Murray, 12/14/08; 134–5, Ellis, 12/14/08.
32. *Ibid.*, 143–4, Sharpe, 12/30/08.
33. *Ibid.*, 156, fn. 1, Sharpe to WS, 1/19/09.
34. *Ibid.*, 156, Sharpe, 1/26/09.
35. *Ibid.*, 213, Southey, 8/7/09.
36. *Ibid.*, 283, fn. 1.
37. *Ibid.*, 392, Lady Abercorn, 10/15/10.
38. *Ibid.*, 282–3, Southey (1810).
39. Smiles, *Murray*, I, 89.
40. James Ballantyne's Diary, quoted by Wright, *Life*, 250.
41. *Letters*, II, 95, Lady Abercorn, 10/14/08; 133, 11/31[sic]/08; 153, Morritt, 1/14/09.
42. NLS MS, 1567, Minutes of the Commission.
43. *Letters*, II, 157, Murray, 1/28/09.

44. *Ibid.*, 137, Ellis, 12/15/08.
45. *Ibid.*, 140, Ellis, 12/23/08.
46. *Ibid.*, 151, Southey, 1/14/09.
47. *Ibid.*, 139, Ellis, 12/23/08.
48. *Ibid.*, 160, Southey, 1/31/09.
49. *Ibid.*, 139, Ellis, 12/23/09.
50. *Ibid.*, 159–60, Southey, 1/31/09.
51. *Ibid.*, 167, Murray, 1/25/09.
52. *Ibid.*, 210, fn. 1.
53. *Ibid.*, 107, fn. 1, Gifford to WS, 2/20/09.
54. *Ibid.*, 171, fn. 1, Southey to WS, 3/11/09.
55. *Ibid.*, 182, Murray, 3/19/09.
56. *Ibid.*, 176, Murray 3/7/09. The two articles were a review of Richard Cumberland's *John de Lancaster* and a review of Thomas Campbell's *Gertrude of Wyoming*.
57. JGL, II, 79–80.
58. *Letters*, II, 172, Sharpe, 3/3/09.
59. JGL, II, 80.
60. *Letters*, XII, 303, Ellis, 12/2/08. There is now a tombstone over Camp's grave. It was erected in 1952 by Percy R. Stevenson.
61. *Ibid.*, II, 151, Southey, 1/14/09.
62. *Ibid.*, 133, Lady Abercorn, 11/31 [sic]/08.
63. *Ibid.*, 179, Lady Abercorn, 3/13/09.
64. *Ibid.*
65. *Ibid.*, 185, Murray, 3/27/09.
66. *Ibid.*, 186, Murray, P.S. dated 4/4/09.
67. NLS MS, 1567, f. 41, memo from Sir Ilay Campbell; JGL, II, 76. JGL says Scott also took Sophia and that she stayed at Hampstead with Joanna Baillie, but I am certain this is a mistake. In a letter to Miss Baillie (*Letters*, II, 332, 5/7/10), a little over a year later, WS writes: "I have no prospect *now* of being in London soon but the next time I come I am much tempted by your kind offer of a harbour for Sophia to bring her with me. She is a clever and tract-able child very capable of improv-ing by which she sees and hears and I would think a week or two of your society a most important ad-vantage indeed." The tone of this implies that Joanna does not know what Sophia is like, which would be very strange if Sophia had stayed with her only the preceding year, and it would be almost unna-

tural for him not to say "again" if
Sophia had been there before. JGL
probably hastily read this letter,
which had no year date, and failing
to note that other details place it in
1810, thought it earlier. Sophia did
accompany WS and Charlotte to
London in 1815. See, clinching it,
*Letters*, IV, 74, Miss Baillie,
1/3/15, saying WS will be delighted at "making her acquainted
with you."

68. *Letters*, II, 175, Surtees, 3/4/09;
247, Surtees, 9/17/09.
69. *Ibid.*, 186–7, White, 3/31/09.
70. *Ibid.*, 188, Miss Millar, 4/15/09.
71. *Ibid.*, 215, Lady Abercorn, 8/18/09;
JGL, II, 76; *Letters*, II, 218, Lady
Stafford, 7/21/09; 240, Lady Abercorn, 9/14/09.
72. *Letters*, I, 402, fn. 1; II, 191, Mrs.
Hughes, 5/4/09.
73. *Ibid.*, II, 189, Mrs. Clephane, Apr.–
May 1809; 191–2, Mrs. Clephane,
Apr.–May 1809.
74. *Ibid.*, 216, Lady Abercorn, 8/18/09.
75. JGL, II, 76–7.
76. *Ibid.*, 77–8.
77. *Letters*, II, 197, Southey, 6/14/09,
says two days; JGL, II, 79, erroneously says two weeks.
78. *Letters*, II, 204, Ellis, 7/8/09,
which shows that WS reached
home about 6/24/09.
79. *Ibid.*, 205, Ellis, 7/8/09.
80. *Ibid.*, 211, Morritt, 7/22/09.
81. *Ibid.*, 198–9, Southey, 6/14/09.
82. *Ibid.*, 197, fn. 1, Southey to WS,
6/16/09.
83. Morgan MS, WS to Ellis, 7/8/09.
The part quoted is not printed in
*Letters*, II, 204–5.
84. *Letters*, II, 205, Southey, 7/06/09.
85. *Ibid.*, 212, fn. 1, Southey to WS,
8/3/09, 8/6/09, 8/16/09.
86. *Ibid.*, XII, Ellis, 9/14/09.
87. *Ibid.*, II, 200, Berwick, 7/24/09.
Maggs Brothers MS has p.m. date.
88. *Ibid.*, 201.
89. *Ibid.*, 200; *cf.* 199, fn. 1.
90. *Ibid.*, 232, Lady Charlotte Rawdon,
8/20/09.
91. *Ibid.*, 222, Berwick 8/17/09.
92. JGL, II, 82–3. But JGL has the
times wrong: it was *before* WS's
trip to the Highlands and *not* in
Buchanan's house that WS saw the
attack.

93. *English Bards and Scotch Reviewers*, 175–84.
94. *Letters*, II, 214, Southey, 8/7/09.
95. JGL, II, 81, mistakenly says the
trip was in July. There are letters
from Ashestiel all through August
up to 8/28/09 (*Letters*, VII, 429,
Mrs. Thos. Scott) and none of
these mention a trip to Highlands,
but WS has just returned when he
writes Southey, *Letters*, II, 235,
9/10/09.
96. JGL, II, 82.
97. *Poetical Works*, VIII, *Lady of the
Lake*, Pref. 9–10.
98. *Letters*, II, 241, Lady Abercorn,
9/14/09.
99. *Ibid.*, 270, Lady Louisa Stuart,
11/7/09.
100. *Ibid.*, 239, Lady Abercorn,
9/14/07.
101. *Poetical Works*, VIII, *Lady of
Lake*, Pref., 5–6.
102. *Ibid.*, 6–8.
103. *Letters*, II, 252, Rogers, 10/4/09.
104. *Ibid.*, 261, Mrs. Clephane,
10/27/09.
105. *Ibid.*, 259, Baillie, 10/27/09.
106. *Ibid.*, 261–2, Mrs. Clephane,
10/27/09.
107. *Ibid.*, 272, Mrs. Thos. Scott,
12/27/09.
108. *Ibid.*, 272–3, Mrs. Thos. Scott,
12/27/09.
109. *Ibid.*, 294, Joanna Baillie, 1/31/10.
110. *Ibid.*, XII, 318, Ellis, 2/1/10.
111. *Ibid.*, II, 294, Joanna Baillie,
1/31/10.
112. JGL, II, 87.
113. *Letters*, II, 94, Lady Abercorn,
10/14/08.
114. JGL, II, 87.
115. NLS MS, 1809, f. 235, WS to
Wm. Miller, 9/10/09.
116. JGL, II, 87. JGL says in 3 vols.,
but only some large-paper copies
were issued in 3.
117. *Letters*, II, 273, Constable, n.d.,
but around Nov.–Dec. See 273, fn.
1, noting that Constable made the
offer in letter of 11/14/09.
118. NLS MS, 742, f. 36, Constable to
WS, 10/30/09.
119. *Letters*, II, 266, Constable (late
Oct. 1809), 271, 11/15/09; 273,
n.d., but after Constable to WS,
11/11/09.

120. *Letters*, II, 265, Constable, 10/30/09.
121. *Ibid.*, 183, Murray, 3/19/09, says will get possession in a few days.
122. *Blackwood's Mag.*, Nov. 1930, 717–28, A. Woods, "Sir Walter Scott's Man Friday."
123. JGL, II, 35.
124. *Ibid.*, 103, and fn. 1.
125. *Letters*, VII, 432, Mrs. Thos. Scott.
126. *Ibid.*, II, 306, Morritt, 3/2/10.
127. *Ibid.*, 261, Mrs. Clephane, 10/27/09.
128. *Ibid.*, 274, Lady Abercorn, 12/31/09.
129. L.B., 138, Lady Abercorn to WS, 1/12/10.
130. *Letters*, II, 286, Lady Abercorn, 1/21/09.
131. *Ibid.*, 261, Mrs. Clephane, 10/27/09.

### Chapter 8

1. *Letters*, II, 37, Surtees, 4/4/08.
2. *Ibid.*
3. *Ibid.*, 274, Lady Abercorn, 12/31/09.
4. Morgan MS, WS to Wm. Miller, 1/8/10.
5. *Letters*, II, 285, Lady Abercorn, 1/21/10.
6. *Ibid.*, 329–30, Croker, 5/1/10.
7. *Ibid.*, 326, Lady Abercorn, 4/14/10.
8. *Ibid.*, 330, Croker, 5/1/60.
9. *Ibid.*, 329–30 and 329, fn. 1, Croker to WS, 5/10/10.
10. *Ibid.*, XII, 319, Ellis, 6/16/10.
11. *Ibid.*, II, 276, Lady Abercorn, 12/31/09.
12. *Ibid.*, XII, 320, Ellis, 6/16/10.
13. *Ibid.*, II, 325–6, Lady Abercorn, 4/14/10.
14. *Ibid.*, 46, James Ballantyne, 4/22/08, and fn. 1; 76, Dundas, 6/24/08; 81, Campbell-Colquhoun, 7/?/08; NLS MS, 1750, f. 108, WS to Campbell-Colquhoun, 10/27/08. *Cf.* also Young, *Memoirs*, I, 554–5; WS to Young, 5/15/08; and JGL, II, 96.
15. *Letters*, II, 254, Baillie, 10/13/09.
16. *Ibid.*, 206, Southey, 7/16/09.
17. *Ibid.*, 217, Baillie, 8/15/09.
18. *Ibid.*, 218.
19. *Ibid.*, 220.
20. *Ibid.*, 258, 10/27/09.
21. *Ibid.*, 254, fn. 1, Joanna Baillie to WS, 10/21/09.
22. *Ibid.*, 218–9.
23. *Ibid.*, 253, Baillie, 10/13/09, and 219, fn. 1, quoting Thompson, *Man of Feeling*, 175–7.
24. *Letters*, II, 194, Lady Louisa Stuart, 6/11/09.
25. *Ibid.*, 254, Baillie, 10/13/09.
26. *Ibid.*, fn. 1, James Ballantyne to WS, 10/21/09.
27. *Ibid.*, 257, Joanna Baillie, 10/27/09.
28. *Ibid.*, 293, Joanna Baillie, 1/31/10.
29. *Ibid.*, 219, fn. 1, quoting Thompson, *Man of Feeling*, 175; 285–6, Lady Abercorn, 1/21/10; 289, Mackenzie, 1/29/10.
30. *Letters*, II, 219, fn. 1; 287, Joanna Baillie, 1/22/10.
31. *Ibid.*, 258, Joanna Baillie, 10/27/09.
32. *Ibid.*, 292, Joanna Baillie, 1/30/10.
33. *Ibid.*, 290, Joanna Baillie, 1/30/10.
34. *Ibid.*, 292.
35. *Ibid.*, 290.
36. *Ibid.*
37. *Ibid.*, 293, Joanna Baillie, 1/31/10.
38. *Ibid.*, 290–1, Joanna Baillie, 1/30/10.
39. *Ibid.*, 295, Joanna Baillie, 2/6/10.
40. *Ibid.*, 303, Joanna Baillie, 2/20/10.
41. JGL, II, 101, says "a continuous run of fourteen nights," but *Letters*, II, 294, Joanna Baillie, 1/31/10, shows that there *were* a few breaks. On the other hand, *Letters*, II, 300, Joanna Baillie, 2/20/10, implies that *Family Legend* played right up to the time when it was succeeded by *De Montfort*, 2/19/10.
42. *Letters*, II, 298, fn. 1.
43. *Ibid.*, 297, Sophia Baillie, 2/20/10.
44. *Ibid.*, 300, Joanna Baillie, 2/20/10.
45. *Ibid.*, 298, Sophia Baillie, 2/20/10.
46. *Ibid.*, 319, Joanna Baillie, 3/30/10.
47. JGL, II, 95. The butler actually spelled his name "McBeith."
48. *Ibid.*, 95–6.
49. *Ibid.*, 96.
50. *Letters*, XII, 335, Heber, 6/11/12; JGL, II, 102.
51. JGL, II, 103.
52. *Letters*, II, 292, Joanna Baillie, 1/30/10.
53. *Ibid.*, 292, Joanna Baillie, 2/6/10; 302–3, 2/20/10.
54. *Ibid.*, 313, Joanna Baillie, 3/18/10.
55. *Ibid.*, 319, Joanna Baillie, 3/30/10, and 303, fn. 1.

56. *Ibid.*, 314–5, Joanna Baillie, 3/18/10.
57. *Ibid.*, XII, 400–1, Wm. Miller, 3/15/10.
58. Partington, *Post-Bag*, 60, Gifford to WS, 4/30/10.
59. Ball, *SWS as a Critic*, 103; *Misc. Prose*, XVII, 119–37; XVIII, 157–71.
60. *Letters*, II, 323, Berwick, 4/10/10 (Maggs original).
61. *Ibid.*, 326–7, Lady Abercorn, 4/14/10.
62. *Ibid.*, 275, Lady Abercorn, 12/31/09.
63. *Ibid.*, 225, Morritt, 8/17/09.
64. *Ibid.*, 312, Lady Abercorn, 3/14/10.
65. *Ibid.*, 283, Southey (1810).
66. *Ibid.*, 95, Lady Abercorn, 10/14/08.
67. Partington, *Letter Books*, 137, Lady Abercorn to WS, Oct., 1808.
68. *Letters*, II, 111, Lady Abercorn, 10/29/08.
69. Partington, *Letter Books*, 138, Lady Abercorn, to WS, 1/12/10.
70. Partington, *Post-Bag*, 56, Lady Abercorn to WS, 1/22/10.
71. *Letters*, II, 286, Lady Abercorn, 1/21/10.
72. *Ibid.*, 312, Lady Abercorn, 3/14/10.
73. *Ibid.*, 324, Lady Abercorn, 3/14/10.
74. *Ibid.*, 324, fn. 1, Lord Abercorn to WS, 5/6/10.
75. *Ibid.*, 312, Lady Abercorn, 3/14/10.
76. *Ibid.*, 286, Lady Abercorn, 1/21/10.
77. *Ibid.*, 312, Lady Abercorn, 3/14/10.
78. *Ibid.*, 286, Lady Abercorn, 1/21/10.
79. Partington, *Post-Bag*, 134, Lady Abercorn to WS, 1/12/10.
80. *Letters*, II, 286–7, Lady Abercorn, 1/21/10.
81. *Journal*, 476, 11/7/27.
82. *Letters*, II, 286–7.
83. *Ibid.*
84. *Ibid.*, 324–5, Lady Abercorn, 4/14/10.
85. *Ibid.*, 332, Baillie, 5/7/10.
86. *Poetical Works*, VIII, 28–9, *Lady of Lake*, 23–7.
87. *Letters*, II, 328, James Ballantyne, Apr.–May 1810.
88. Yale U. Lib. MS, WS to Croker, 5/3/10.
89. *Letters*, II, 330, Lady Dalkeith, 5/7/10; 331, Lady Alvanley, 5/7/10; 332, Baillie, 5/7/10; XII, 318, Heber, 5/8/10; II, 340, fn. 1, showing Southey acknowledged receipt 5/11/10.
90. *Ibid.*, 337, Miss Clephane, 5/19/10. Scott's salutation does not indicate which of Mrs. Clephane's three daughters he was addressing, although it was probably the eldest!
91. NLS MS, 1036, f. 51, WS to Major John Scott, n.d., but ca. early July 1810.
92. *Letters*, XII, 438, Thos. Scott, 5/13/10.
93. *Ibid.*, VII, 432, Mrs. Thos. Scott, 9/27/09.
94. *Ibid.*, 430, Mrs. Thos. Scott, 9/10/09.
95. JGL, II, 107–8; *Letters*, III, 51, Lady Abercorn, 1/1/12. *Cf.* also Glen MS, 5. *Cf.* Wm. Wordsworth to unknown correspondent: "If any office should be at your disposal the duties of which would not call so largely upon my exertions as to prevent me from giving a considerable proportion of my time to study, it might be in your Lordship's power to place me in a situation where, with better hopes of success, I might advance towards the main object of my life; I mean the completion of my literary undertakings." *Letters of Wm. and Dorothy Wordsworth: The Middle Years*, II, 486.
96. *Letters*, VII, 435, Mrs. Thos. Scott, 12/?/09; 438, Thos. Scott, 5/13/10.
97. JGL, II, 108; *cf. Letters*, VII, 444, Thos. Scott, 8/26/10; 446, 9/26/10; 447–51, 10/15/10.
98. JGL, II, 109; *Letters*, II, 345, Thos. Scott, 5/25/10, and fn. 2; 353, 6/21/10, and fn. 2.
99. NLS MS, 997, f. 12, WS to Robert Dundas, 5/20/10.
100. *Letters*, II, 357, Richardson, 7/3/10.
101. *Ibid.*, 352, and VII, 441, Thos. Scott, 6/12/10; II, 353, and VII, 443, Thos. Scott, 6/21/20.
102. *Letters*, VII, 443.
103. *Ibid.*, 442.
104. JGL, II, 113.
105. Pearson, *Life and Personality*, 76–7; *cf.* Cockburn, *Book of the Old Edinburgh Club*, Vol. 3, 1910.
106. JGL, II, 113.
107. Pearson, *Life and Personality*, 77.
108. JGL, II, 113.

109. *Letters*, VII, 445, Thos. Scott, 8/26/10.
110. *Ibid.*, III, 53, Lady Abercorn, 1/1/12.
111. JGL, II, 133. It was at this time that WS wrote his lines on Staffa, not, as JGL says, in 1814.
112. *Letters*, II, 367, Morritt, 8/9/10.
113. *Ibid.*, XII, 320, Ellis, 6/16/10.
114. *Ibid.*, II, 363, Ellis (p.m. 7/29/10); Baillie, 7/19/10; 351, Baillie, 6/10/10.
115. *Ibid.*, 362, Ellis, 7/29/10, and fn. 1; Ellis to WS, 6/30/10.
116. JGL, II, 134; *Letters*, II, 359, Baillie, 7/29/10.
117. *Letters*, II, 358–9.
118. *Ibid.*, 359.
119. *Ibid.*, 360; 364, Ellis, 7/29/10.
120. *Ibid.;* 376, Lady Abercorn, 9/30/10; 374, Southey, 9/19–20/10.
121. *Ibid.*, 378, Lady Abercorn, 9/30/10.
122. *Ibid.*, 360, Joanna Baillie, 7/29/10.
123. *Ibid.*, 336, Ellis, 2/29/10.
124. *Ibid.*, 360, Joanna Baillie.
125. *Ibid.*, 377, Lady Abercorn, 9/30/10.
126. *Ibid.*, 361–2, Joanna Baillie, 7/29/10; 401–2, 11/23/10.
127. *Ibid.*, 360, Joanna Baillie, 7/29/10.
128. *Ibid.*, 360–1.
129. *Ibid.*, 368, Morritt, 8/9/10.
130. *Ibid.*, 361, 365, Joanna Baillie, 7/29/10.
131. *Ibid.*, 384, Smith, 10/4/10.
132. Partington, *Post-Bag*, 61, Dibdin to WS, 5/9/10.
133. JGL, II, 118. JGL, II, 117, says, "early in May," and WS did indeed send out some copies 5/7/10. But it was not published till considerably later: 6/29/10 (*Letters*, II, 354). WS tells Lady Abercorn that the 1st ed. "has not lasted a fortnight," which would suggest a publication date in June.
134. *Letters*, XII, 318, fn. 2, Heber to WS 5/14/10.
135. *Ibid.*, II, 340, fn. 1, Southey to WS, 5/11/10.
136. Partington, *Letter Books*, 16–7, Jeffrey to WS, 8/11/10.
137. *Ibid.*, 17.
138. *Edinburgh Review*, quoted in *Poetical Works*, VIII, *Lady of Lake*, 115, fn. 1.
139. *Poetical Works*, VIII, *Lady of Lake*, 85, fn. 1.
140. *Ibid.*, 134, fn. 1.
141. *Ibid.*, 301, fn. 1.
142. JGL, II, 167, quoting Ferguson to WS, 8/31/11.
143. *Ibid.*, 169, quoting Ferguson to WS, 8/31/11.
144. JGL, II, 119.
145. *Letters*, VII, Thos. Scott, 8/26/10.
146. *Ibid.*, II, 378, Lady Abercorn, 9/30/10; 387, Berwick, 10/8/10.
147. *Ibid.*, VII, 451, Thos. Scott, 10/15/10.
148. *Ibid.*, II, 441, Leyden, 2/20/11.
149. JGL, II, 117.
150. *Poetical Works*, VIII, *Lady of Lake*, Pref., 10–1.
151. JGL, II, 131–2.
152. *Ibid.*, 130.
153. *Ibid.*, 131.
154. *Ibid.*
155. *Ibid.*, 118–9.
156. *Letters*, II, 419, fn. 1, Sir J. Sinclair to WS, 11/6/10.
157. Partington, *Letter Books*, 90, Maria Edgeworth to WS, 6/23/12.
158. JGL, II, 119.

### Chapter 9

1. *Poetical Works*, VI, *Lay*, Intro., 24–5, 27.
2. *Ibid.*, 49–51, Canto I, i–iii.
3. *Ibid.*, 52, Canto I, vi.
4. *Ibid.*, 87, Canto II, xxii.
5. *Ibid.*, 61, Canto I, xviii.
6. *Ibid.*, 78, Canto II, x–xi.
7. *Ibid.*, 81, Canto II, xxvi–xxvii.
8. *Ibid.*, 114, Canto III, xxvii.
9. *Ibid.*, 126–7, Canto IV, vi.
10. *Ibid.*, 144, Canto IV, xxvii.
11. *Ibid.*, 148, Canto IV, xxx.
12. *Ibid.*, 170, Canto V, xv.
13. *Ibid.*, 177, Canto V, xxvi.
14. *Letters*, I, 243, Seward, 3/4/05.
15. *Ibid.*, III, 184, James Ballantyne, 10/28/12.
16. *Poetical Works*, VII, 52, *Marmion*, Canto I, xi.
17. *Ibid.*, 55, Canto I, xiii.
18. *Ibid.*, 67 Canto I, xxv.
19. *Ibid.*, 155, Canto III, xv.
20. *Ibid.*, 265, Canto V, xvii.
21. *Ibid.*
22. *Ibid.*
23. *Ibid.*, 327, Canto VI, xv.

24. *Ibid.*, 324, Canto VI, xii.
25. *Ibid.*, 324, Canto VI, xiv.
26. *Ibid.*, 326–7, Canto VI, xiv–xv.
27. *Ibid.*, 341–2, Canto VI, xxv–xxvi.
28. *Ibid.*, 345, Canto VI, xxviii.
29. JGL, I, 495.
30. *Poetical Works*, VIII, 173, *Lady of Lake*, Canto IV, x.
31. *Ibid.*, 47, Canto I, xxi.
32. *Ibid.*, 54, Canto I, xxviii.
33. *Ibid.*, 63, Canto I, xxxv.
34. *Ibid.*, 37, Canto I, xii.
35. *Ibid.*, 39, Canto I, xiv.
36. *Ibid.*, 86, Canto II, xvi.
37. *Ibid.*, 130, Canto III, x.
38. *Ibid.*, 133, Canto III, xiii.
39. *Ibid.*, 233, Canto V, xviii.
40. *Ibid.*, 193, Canto IV, xxv.
41. *Ibid.*, 218, Canto V, ix.
42. *Ibid.*, 293, Canto VI, xxvi.
43. *Ibid.*, 294, Canto VI, xxvii.
44. *Ibid.*, 297, Canto VI, xxix.
45. *Ibid.*, 298, Canto VI, xxix.
46. *Ibid.*, 220, Canto V, vii.
    G. M. Young, *SWS Lectures*, 153.
48. *Poetical Works*, VIII, 224, *Lady of Lake*, Canto V, xiii.
49. *Ibid.*, 230, Canto V, xvi.

PART FIVE

Chapter 1

1. *Letters*, II, 492, James Ballantyne, 5/12/11.
2. JGL, II, 181.
3. *Letters*, II, 400, Pringle, 11/20/10; *cf.* Dr. Corson, *Bibliography of SWS*, 385, no. 2816.
4. *Ibid.*, XII, 263, Ellis, 8/21/04.
5. *Ibid.*, I, 412–4, James Ballantyne, 10/30/10.
6. *Ibid.*, I, 414–5.
7. NLS MS, 861, ff. 14–5, John Ballantyne to WS, 10/?/10.
8. *Ibid.*
9. Grierson, *Scott*, 84, fn.
10. JGL, II, 151.
11. James Ballantyne to WS, 9/15/10, quoted in JGL, II, 151–2.
12. NLS MS, 861, ff. 13–5, John Ballantyne to WS, 10/?/10.
13. *Ibid.*
14. *Letters*, II, 308–9, Constable, 3/12/10, 3/13/10.
15. *Ibid.*
16. *Ibid.*, 442, Leyden, 2/20/11.
17. *Ibid.*, I, 415, James Ballantyne, 10/23/10, and fn. 1; II, 372, Constable, 8/29/10.
18. *Ibid.*, I, 415.
19. *Ibid.*; JGL, II, 153–4.
20. NLS MS, 862, f. 16, John Ballantyne to WS, 5/23/11.
21. *Ibid.*
22. *Letters*, II, 389, Polwhele, 10/11/10, and fn. 1; *cf.* 423, 12/30/10. The *Northern Antiquities* contained an abstract of the *Niebelungenlied*, translations of medieval romances from Old German, Danish, and Icelandic, the *Heldenbuch*, a series of romances (done by Weber) dealing with Attila and Theodoric, popular heroic and romantic ballads from the northern languages (contributed by Jamieson) and an abstract of the *Eyrbiggia Saga* (contributed by WS). See *Misc. Prose*, V, 355–413.
23. JGL, II, 153. Ballantyne is quoting Dogberry, in *Much Ado*, III, 3, 36.
24. JGL, I, 153.
25. *Letters*, II, 372, Constable, 8/29/10.
26. *Ibid.*, 375, Whitfeld, 9/24/10.
27. *Ibid.*, 370–2, Lady Dalkeith, 9/14/10; JGL, II, 193.
28. *Ibid.*, 369, Morritt, 8/9/10, shows that WS was expecting them about 8/20/10; II, 367, Miss Clephane, 8/9/10, says about 8/23/10; 380, Morritt, 10/3/10, shows they had come and gone.
29. *Ibid.*, 379, Margaret Clephane, 10/?/10. This time the address does indicate which Miss Clephane WS was addressing.
30. JGL, III, 366, fn. 1, but corrected from Richardson's own reminiscences in *North British Review*, Nov., 1864, 239–59.
31. *Letters*, II, 397, Murray, 10/26/10; 398, Margaret Clephane, 10/27/10. In the preceding year WS had written several others; see *Letters*, II, 189–90, Margaret Clephane, 4 or 5/?/09.
32. *Letters*, VII, 447, Thos. Scott, 10/15/10; II, 395–6, Lady Abercorn, 10/24/10.
33. *Ibid.*, II, 398–9, Margaret Clephane, 10/27/10.
34. *Ibid.*, I, 415, James Ballantyne, 10/29/10.
35. *Ibid.*; JGL, II, 171.

36. *Letters*, II, 399, Miss Clephane, 10/27/10.
37. *Ibid.*, 406–8, Hartstonge, 12/1/10.
38. *Ibid.*, XII, 325, Ellis, 7/6/10.
39. *Ibid.*, II, 409, Murray, 12/3/10.
40. *Ibid.*, 346, Ellis, 12/23/10, misdated, but corrected in XII, 326.
41. *Ibid.*, 414, Lady Abercorn, 12/22/10; also 470, Joanna Baillie, 12/31/10.
42. *Ibid.*, 403–4, Joanna Baillie, 11/23/10.
43. *Ibid.*, 410, Miss Smith, 12/18/10.
44. *Ibid.*, 463–4, Miss Smith, 3/12/11.
45. *Ibid.*, 415, Lady Abercorn,, 12/22/10.
46. *Ibid.*, XII, 327, Ellis, 12/23/10; II, 429, Mrs. Scott of Harden, 1/5/11.
47. *Ibid.*, II, 430; VII, 454, Thos. Scott, 12/30/10.
48. *Ibid.*, 429–30, Mrs. Scott of Harden, 1/5/11.
49. *Ibid.*, 436–7, Lady Abercorn, 2/15/11.
50. *Ibid.*, 438, Lady Abercorn, 2/15/11.
51. *Ibid.*, 440, Melville, 2/20/11; 443, Lady Abercorn, 2/22/11.
52. *Ibid.*, 435, fn. 2.
53. *Ibid.*, 452, Lady Abercorn, 2/25/11; 442–3, Lady Abercorn, 2/22/11; 446, Arbuthnot, 2/23/11.
54. *Letters*, II, 444, Lady Abercorn, 2/22/11; 452, Lady Abercorn, 2/25/11.
55. *Ibid.*, 445–6, Arbuthnot, 2/23/11.
56. *Ibid.*, 447–9, Lord Melville (1st Viscount), n.d. (3 letters, all late Feb. or early Mar.).
57. *Ibid.*, 454, Home to Lord Melville (1st Viscount), 3/6/11.
58. *Ibid.*, 457, Lady Abercorn, 3/3/11.
59. *Ibid.*, 458–9, Lady Abercorn, 3/3/11; 459, Arbuthnot, 3/8/11.
60. *Ibid.*, 461, Lady Abercorn, 3/10/11.
61. *Ibid.*, 460, Lady Abercorn, 3/10/11. But see *Letters*, III, 71, Lady Abercorn, 1/23/12, showing that Home later accepted *part* of WS's offer.
62. *Ibid.*, II, 465–9, Robert Dundas (later 2nd Viscount Melville), 3/14/11.
63. *Ibid.*, XII, 309, Ellis, 12/12/08.
64. *Ibid.*, II, 441, Leyden, 2/20/11, and 441 fn., Leyden to WS, 1/10/10.
65. *Ibid.*, 473, Southey, 4/10/11.
66. *Ibid.*, 473–4.

67. *Ibid.*, XII, 309, Ellis, 12/13/08; II, 474, Southey, 4/10/11.
68. *Ibid.*, II, 248, Ellis, 9/26/09; XII, 313, Ellis, 9/14/09.
69. *Ibid.*, 474–5, Southey, 4/10/11.
70. JGL, II, 159–60.
71. *Letters*, II, 475, Morritt, 4/10/11.
72. *Ibid.*
73. *Ibid.*, 480, Morritt, 4/26/11.
74. *Ibid.*, 482.
75. *Ibid.*, 477–8, Lady Abercorn, 4/30/11. WS does not mention Hito's work by name, but the reference is obvious, and furthermore, he had not long since thanked Richardson for a new copy of the book (*Letters*, II, 357, 7/30/10). In the notes to the poem WS atributes the story to *Historia Verdadeyra del Rey Don Rodrigo*, 1654.
76. *Ibid.*, 482, Morritt, 4/26/11.
77. *Ibid.*, 491, Erskine, 5/8/11.
78. *Ibid.*, 478, Lady Abercorn, 4/30/11.
79. *Ibid.*, III, 186–7, fn. 1, quoting Gillies, "Recollections."
80. *Ibid.*, II, 491, Erskine, 5/12/11.
81. *Ibid.*, 492, James Ballantyne, 5/12/11.
82. *Ibid.*, 509, P. Murray, 7/?/11.
83. *Ibid.*, 507, Morritt, 7/1/11.
84. *Ibid.*, 506–7, G. Thomson, 7/?/11.
85. *Ibid.*, 495, Lady Abercorn, 5/17/11.
86. *Ibid.*, 496–7, Mrs. Scott of Harden, (p.m. 5/25/11).
87. Cockburn, *Memorials*, 220.
88. *Letters*, II, 497, fn. 1.
89. *Ibid.*, 499, Lady Abercorn, 5/25/11.
90. Cockburn, *Memorials*, 220.
91. JGL, II, 163.
92. *Letters*, VII, 452, Thos. Scott, 11/1/10.
93. NLS MS, 2899, f. 103, WS to Wm. Scott, 2/3/11.
94. *Letters*, II, 476, C. Erskine, 4/12/11.
95. *Ibid.*, 492–3, James Ballantyne, 5/12/11.
96. *Ibid.*, 490, Wm. Erskine, 5/8/11.
97. *Ibid.*; cf. JGL, II, 194, which says WS *did* borrow £2,000 from the Major, but see below.
98. *Letters*, II, 493, James Ballantyne, 5/12/11.
99. NLS MS, 862, f. 16, John Ballantyne to WS, 5/23/11.
100. *Letters*, II, 500–1, C. Erskine, 6/2/11, and fn. 1; *Letters*, VII,

407–8, Dr. Douglas, 6/20/11, and fn. 2.

101. *Letters*, XII, 407, fn. 2, C. Erskine to WS 6/1/11.
102. *Ibid.*, II, 500, fn. 1, Laidlaw to WS, 6/1/11.
103. *Ibid.*, XII, 407, fn. 1, C. Erskine to WS, 6/19/11.
104. *Ibid.*
105. *Ibid.*, fn. 2, Dr. Douglas to WS, 6/19/11.
106. *Ibid.*, Dr. Douglas, 6/20/11.
107. JGL, II, 177.
108. *Ibid.*, 174.
109. *Letters*, II, 402–3, Joanna Baillie, 11/23/10.
110. *Ibid.*
111. JGL, II, 177.
112. *Ibid.*, 178.
113. *Ibid.*, 174–5.
114. *Letters*, XII, 329, Heber, 7/1/11.
115. *Ibid.*, 521, Lady Abercorn, 7/25/11.
116. *Ibid.*, 516, Hayley, 7/2/11.
117. JGL, II, 177. But JGL says, "The first hour that he took possession he claimed for his farm the name of the adjoining 'ford' "—actually WS did so only a short time after the purchase and *before* possession. Joanna Baille writes, "So you have become the Lord of Abbotsford," and WS must have used the name before that in writing to her.

### Chapter 2

1. Partington, *Post-Bag*, 67, Joanna Baillie to WS, 7/9/11.
2. *Letters*, II, 522, Lady Abercorn, 7/25/11; 530, C. Erskine, 8/8/11.
3. *Ibid.*, 532, Mrs. Scott, 8/14/11.
4. *Ibid.*, 514, Hayley, 7/2/11.
5. L.B., 222, Hayley to WS, 7/16/11.
6. *Letters*, II, 527, Baillie, 8/4/11.
7. Morgan-Fales MS, WS memo about Tweedside cottage ca. 8/?/11.
8. *Ibid.*
9. Russell, "More Recollections," 231–4, quoting WS to Stark, 9/3/11.
10. JGL, IV, 424, fn. 1, quoting WS to Ferrier, 9/18/11; *cf.* also NLS MS, 1750, f. 110. In the end, though, WS did *not* use stone from the Abbey.

11. *Letters*, III, 10, W. Erskine, 10/5/11.
12. Partington, *Letter Books*, 21, Lady Abercorn to WS, 11/22/11.
13. *Letters*, III, 50, Lady Abercorn, 1/1/12.
14. NLS MS, Acc. 2376, WS to Hayley, 12/12/11; *Letters*, III, 65, P. Murray, 1/18/12.
15. NLS MS, Acc. 2376, WS to Hayley, 12/12/11.
16. *Letters*, III, 68–9, Mrs. Clephane, 1/18/12.
17. *Poetical Works*, IX, *Rokeby*, Intro., 11.
18. *Letters*, III, 40, Morritt, 12/20/11.
19. NLS MS, Acc. 2376, WS to Hayley, 12/12/11.
20. *Letters*, III, 34, Joanna Baillie, 12/12/11.
21. *Ibid.*, 504–15, to various correspondents, 6/30–7/5/11; XII, 329, Ellis, 7/1/11.
22. *Letters*, XII, 328, Heber, 7/11/11.
23. *Ibid.*, II, 492, James Ballantyne, 2/12/11.
24. *Ibid.*, 513, Hayley 7/2/11.
25. *Ibid.*, 525, Joanna Baillie, 8/4/11.
26. *Quarterly Review*, quoted in *Poetical Works*, IX, 389, fn. 1.
27. *Edinburgh Review*, Jeffrey, quoted in *Poetical Works*, IX, 424–5, fn. 2, and 408, fn. 1.
28. *Quarterly Review*, Oct., 1811, quoted in *Poetical Works*, IX, 425–6.
29. *Letters*, II, 510, Edgeworth, 7/2/11.
30. *Ibid.*, 512, Mrs. Scott of Harden (7/17 or 7/24/11).
31. *Ibid.*, 523, Joanna Baillie, 8/4/11.
32. *Ibid.*, 513, Mrs. Scott of Harden (7/17 or 7/24/11).
33. *Ibid.*, III, 65, Murray of Simprim, 1/18/12.
34. *Ibid.*, 533, Mrs. Scott, 8/14/11; III, 8, Mrs. Scott, 9/30/11.
35. *Ibid.*, 522, Lady Abercorn, 7/25/11.
36. *Ibid.*, 529, Baillie, 8/4/11.
37. *Ibid.*, 533, Mrs. Scott, 8/14/11.
38. NLS MS, 1750, f. 107, Memo, WS to Redford, 8/24/11.
39. L.B., 69–70.
40. *Ibid.*, Clarendon to WS, 9/5/11.
41. *Letters*, III, 44, Hartstonge, 12/22/11.
42. *Ibid.*, II, 542, Morritt, 9/?/11.
43. Partington, *Letter Books*, 70; NLS MS, Acc. 2437, WS to Mrs. Prin-

gle, 11/4/11; *Letters*, II, 540, Stafford, 9/11/11.
44. *Letters*, II, 522, Lady Abercorn, 7/25/11.
45. *Ibid.*, 521-2.
46. *Ibid.*, 538, Hartstonge, 8/25/11.
47. *Ibid.*
48. *Ibid.*, *IV*, 97, Hartstonage (ca. 11/2–12/15/11).
49. *Ibid.*, III, 11, fn. 1, Hartstonge to WS, 9/26/11, and 12, WS to Hartstonge, 10/24/11. H's poem is dated 9/6/11.
50. *Ibid.*, 2, Lady Abercorn, 9/18/11, and fn. 1, Lady Abercorn to WS, 9/6/11.
51. *Ibid.*, 10, Wm. Erskine, 10/5/11.
52. S. Ferrier, "Recollections," *Temple Bar*, XL, 329–35.
53. NLS MS, 1750, f. 111, Grierson copy from Miss Ferrier's Album, there dated 10/13/11; also quoted in *Temple Bar* above.
54. *Letters*, VII, 399, Thos. Scott to WS, 3/15/11, and fn. 2, Thos. Scott to his mother, 11/2/10.
55. *Letters*, VII, 452, Thos. Scott, 11/1/10.
56. *Ibid.*, X, 28, Lockhart, 5/10/26.
57. *Ibid.*, VII, 400.
58. *Ibid.*, III, 6, Mrs. Scott, 9/?/11.
59. *Ibid.*, VII, 400; III, 14, Mrs. Scott, 10/27/11.
60. *Ibid.*, III, 7, fn. 1, Mrs. Scott to WS, 9/?/11.
61. *Ibid.*, 8, Mrs. Scott, 9/20/11.
62. *Ibid.*, 13-4, Mrs. Scott, 10/24/11.
63. *Ibid.*, VII, 331, Ellis, 10/18/11; NLS MS, 1750, f. 113, WS to Heber, 10/17/11.
64. NLS MS, 1750, f. 113, WS to Heber, 10/17/11.
65. *Letters*, III, 15, Mrs. Scott, 10/27/11. Thos. Scott left London for the Isle of Man 11/18/11 (*Letters*, III, 18, Mrs. Scott, 11/30/11), and fn. 1, from Tom, 11/27/11); *Letters*, III, 15, and VII, 464, Mrs. Thos. Scott, 10/27/11.
66. *Ibid.*, 12, Hartstonge, 10/24/11.
67. *Ibid.*, 20, C. Erskine, 11/9/11; 30, Surtees, 12/10/11.
68. *Leisure Hour* (1871), 490, WS to A. Pringle, n.d., but around end of Nov.
69. *Letters*, III, 12, Hartstonge, 10/24/11.
70. *Ibid.*, 14, Mrs. Scott, 10/27/11.

71. *Ibid.*, II, 535, Leyden, 8/25/11.
72. *Misc. Prose*, IV, 194-5.
73. *Letters*, III, 69, Mrs. Clephane, 1/18/12.
74. *Ibid.*, 25, Polwhele, 12/1/11.
75. *Ibid.*, 20, C. Erskine, 11/9/11.
76. *Ibid.*, 39, Joanna Baillie, 12/7/11.
77. *Ibid.*, 45, Hartstonge, 12/22/11.
78. *Ibid.*, 99, Joanna Baillie, 4/4/12.
79. *Ibid.*, 45-6, Hartstonge, 12/22/11.
80. *Ibid.*, 100, Joanna Baillie, 4/4/12.
81. *Tait's Edin. Mag.*, X, 578.
82. *Letters*, III, 69, Mrs. Clephane, 1/18/12.
83. *Tait's Edinburgh Mag.*, X, 578.
84. *Letters*, III, 41, Morritt, 12/20/11.
85. *Ibid.*, 46, Hartstonge, 12/22/11; 43-4.
86. *Ibid.*, 51, Lady Abercorn, 1/1/12.
87. *Ibid.*, 75, Southey, 2/23/12.
88. *Ibid.*, 56-7, Berwick, 1/16/12.
89. *Ibid.*, 75-6, Southey, 2/23/12.
90. *Ibid.*, 63, Joanna Baillie, 1/17/12.
91. *Ibid.*, 72, Lady Abercorn, 1/23/12.
92. *Ibid.*, 69, Mrs. Clephane, 1/18/12.
93. *Ibid.*, 73, Lady Abercorn, 1/23/12.
94. *Ibid.*, 56-7, Berwick, 1/16/12. WS also at this time wrote a prologue to *Helga*, a tragedy of Sir George Stewart Mackenzie, produced at the Edinburgh Theatre 1/22/12.
95. *Ibid.*, 56, fn. 1, Berwick to WS, 7/30/09.
96. Partington, *Letter Books*, 79-80, Lady Louisa Stuart to WS, 1/?/12.
97. *Letters*, III, 71, Lady Abercorn, 1/23/12.
98. *Ibid.*, 15, Mrs. Scott, 10/27/11; *cf.* III, 20, Lord Melville (1st Viscount), 11/17/11.
99. *Ibid.*, 15.
100. *Ibid.*, 71, Lady Abercorn, 1/23/12.
101. *Ibid.*, 30, Surtees, 12/10/11.
102. *Ibid.*, 40, Morritt, 12/20/11.
103. *Ibid.*, 41. Morritt, 12/20/11.
104. JGL, II, 197-203, Morritt to WS, 12/28/11.
105. Morgan MS, WS to Thos. Scott, 2/7/11.
106. *Letters*, III, 83, Polwhele, 2/29/12; 88, Morritt, 3/2/12.
107. NLS MS, 997, f. 15, WS to Sanderson and Paterson, 3/13/12.
108. *Ibid.* But many of these plans were never carried out. The Lodge was never built; the stone from Dryburgh was not used; there was no cottage till 1817.

109. *Letters*, III, 95, Surtees (p.m. 4/1/12).
110. *Ibid.*, 100, Joanna Baillie (p.m. 4/4/12).
111. NLS MS, 3109, f. 86, WS to Heber, 5/3/12; 3653, f. 153, WS to Hayley, 5/3/12.
112. *Letters*, III, 118, Duchess of Buccleuch, 5/8/12.
113. *Ibid.*, 104, Hartstonge, 4/20/12.
114. NLS MS, 3653, f. 153, WS to Hayley, 5/3/12.
115. *Letters*, III, 105, Hartstonge, 4/20/12.
116. *Ibid.*, 118, Duchess of Buccleuch, 5/8/12.
117. *Ibid.*, 102, Sophia Scott, 4/19/12.
118. *Ibid.*, 88, Morritt, 3/2/12.
119. *Ibid.*, 116, Miss Clephane, 5/11/12.
120. *Leisure Hour* (1871), 411, WS to Mrs. Pringle, 3/5/12.
121. *Letters*, III, 196, Sharpe. Wrongly placed in Nov.; Sharpe sent the ballad to WS in Mar. (see 196, fn. 1), and Scott would not delay answering for 8 months.
122. *Ibid.*, 95, Mrs. Apreece, 4/3/12.
123. *Ibid.*, 96, fn. 1, Mrs. Apreece to WS, 4/1/12 (also Partington, *Post-Bag*, 86). They were cousins "Scottice"—very distantly related.
124. *Ibid.*, 96, Mrs. Apreece, 4/13/12.
125. *Ibid.*, II, 214, Southey, 8/7/09.
126. *Ibid.*, III, 98–9, Joanna Baillie, 4/4/12.
127. *Ibid.*, 114–5, Morritt, 5/9/12.
128. Partington, *Letter Books*, 182, Morritt to WS, 4/?/12.
129. *Ibid.*, 181.
130. *Letters*, III, 114, Morritt, 5/4/12.
131. *Ibid.*, 107, Margaret Clephane, 5/4/12.
132. JGL, II, 181.
133. *Ibid.*
134. *Letters*, II, 500, fn. 1, Laidlaw to WS, 6/1/11.
135. JGL, II, 24.
136. *Ibid.*, 220.
137. *Letters*, III, 120, Gillies, 5/12/12.
138. *Ibid.*, 128, Terry, 6/9/12. The actual day of departure was not Whitsunday but Thursday, May 21. See *Letters*, III, 121, Blackwood, 5/20/12, and fn. 1.
139. *Letters*, III, 122, Lady Alvanley, 5/25/12.

Chapter 3

1. Hughes, *Letters and Recollections*, 80.
2. *Letters*, III, 151, Carpenter, 8/4/12; see also 135, Murray, 7/2/12, and 156, Lady Abercorn, 9/2/12.
3. JGL, II, 224. JGL says the window looked toward the Tweed, but in fact it faced the road.
4. *Letters*, III, 115, Morritt, 5/4/12.
5. JGL, II, 224.
6. *Letters*, III, 156, Lady Abercorn, 9/2/12.
7. *Ibid.*, 134, Miss Clephane, 6/20/12.
8. *Ibid.*, 131, C. Rutherford, 10/22/12.
9. JGL, II, 223.
10. *Letters*, III, 128, Terry, 6/9/12.
11. *Ibid.*, XII, 333, Heber, 5/14/12.
12. *Athenaeum* (1832), printed letter to Heber, 5/3/12.
13. *Letters*, XII, 333, Heber, 5/14/12.
14. *Ibid.*, 336–7, Heber, 7/1/12, and 336, fn. 4.
15. *Ibid.*, III, 128, Sharpe, 6/18/12.
16. *Ibid.*, 129, fn. 1, Sharpe to WS, 6/10/12.
17. *Ibid.*, 129, Sharpe, 6/18/12.
18. *Ibid.*, 143, fn. 2, Sharpe to WS, 6/28/12.
19. *Ibid.*, 143, Sharpe, 7/6/12.
20. *Ibid.*, 144–5, Sharpe, 7/6/12.
21. NLS MS, 3109, f. 13, copy of original in possession of Mrs. Meecham Surrey.
22. *Letters*, III, 135, fn. 1, Murray to WS, 6/27/12.
23. *Ibid.*, 138, 137, Byron, 7/13/12.
24. *Ibid.*, 138.
25. *Ibid.*, 138, fn. 1, Byron to WS, 7/6/12.
26. *Ibid.*, 140–1, Byron, 7/16/12.
27. *Ibid.*
28. *Ibid.*, 125, Southey, 6/4/12; 152–3, Carpenter, 8/4/12; *cf. Misc. Prose*, XIV, *Napoleon*, VII, 33, 45.
29. *Letters*, III, 152, Carpenter.
30. Bryant, *Victory*, 49.
31. Details in these next two paragraphs from Bryant, *Victory*, 50–52.
32. NLS MS, 966, f. 306, Lady Abercorn, 5/25/12, not in the part of this letter quoted in III, 152.
33. *Letters*, III, 152, Carpenter, 8/4/12.
34. *Ibid.*, 125–6, Southey, 6/4/12.

35. Bryant, *Victory*, 53.
36. *Cambridge Modern History*, IX, 472–3. The battle was fought 7/22/12.
37. *Letters*, III, 153, Carpenter, 8/4/12.
38. *Ibid.*, 156, Lady Abercorn, 9/2/12.
39. Bryant, *Victory*, 38.
40. *Ibid.*, 40.
41. *Misc. Prose*, XIV, *Napoleon*, VII, 90–100.
42. *Ibid.*, 101–4.
43. *Ibid.*, 110–3.
44. Bryant, *Victory*, 46.
45. *Misc. Prose*, XIV, *Napoleon*, VII, 125–6, 134, 137.
46. NLS MS, 1753, f. 210, WS to Southey, 11/26/12; this part is not in *Letters*, III, 197–8.
47. Bryant, *Victory*, 46; *Misc. Prose*, XIV, *Napoleon*, VII, 136, 141.
48. Bryant, *Victory*, 47.
49. *Misc. Prose*, XIV, *Napoleon*, VII, 165.
50. Bryant, *Victory*, 47.
51. *Ibid.*, 48.
52. *Letters*, III, 205, Morritt (p.m. 12/10/12).
53. *Ibid.*, 202, Morritt (p.m. 12/10/12).
54. *Hamlet*, V, ii, 61–2.
55. *Letters*, III, 173, Joanna Baillie, 10/11/12.
56. *Ibid.*, 153–4, Terry, 9/?/12.
57. *Ibid.*, 186. Hartstonge, 10/29/12.
58. JGL, II, 224.
59. *Letters*, III, 174, Baillie, 10/11/12.
60. *Ibid.*, 156, Lady Abercorn, 9/2/12.
61. JGL, II, 224.
62. *Letters*, III, 154, Terry, 9/?/12 (corrected by Dr. Corson).
63. *Ibid.*, 174, Joanna Baillie, 10/11/12.
64. *Ibid.*, 185, Hartstonge, 10/29/12.
65. *Ibid.*, 155, Terry, 7/?/12.
66. JGL, II, 226.
67. *Letters*, I, 418, John Ballantyne, 8/14/12.
68. Partington, *Post-Bag*, 91, John Ballantyne to WS, 7/?/12.
69. *Letters*, I, 416, John Ballantyne, 7/19/12.
70. *Ibid.*, 417–8, John Ballantyne, (p.m. 8/11/12).
71. *Ibid.*, 418–9, John Ballantyne, 8/14/12.
72. *Ibid.*, 417.
73. *Ibid.*, III, 157, Lady Abercorn, 4/2/12.
74. *Ibid.*, I, 419, John Ballantyne, 9/1/12.
75. *Ibid.*, 420, John Ballantyne, 9/2/12.
76. JGL, II, 228.
77. *Letters*, III, 164, Lady Louisa Stuart, 9/20/12. *Cf.* III, 296, fn. 1, for purchase of Abbotrule.
78. JGL, II, 227.
79. *E.g.*, *Letters*, II, 116, Joanna Baillie, 10/31/08.
80. JGL, II, 227–8, Erskine to WS (mid-Sept. 1812).
81. *Poetical Works*, XI, 7, Pref. to *Bridal*.
82. Dexter photostat, WS to James Ballantyne, 9/10/12.
83. NLS MS, 3663, f. 155, Hartstonge to WS, 7/16/12.
84. *Letters*, III, 161, Constable, 9/20/12.
85. *Ibid.*, 162.
86. JGL, II, 228.
87. *Ibid.*, 229, Morritt to WS, 9/?/12.
88. *Letters*, III, 162, Lady Louisa Stuart, 9/20/12.
89. JGL, II, 229.
90. *Letters*, III, 162–3.
91. JGL, II, 230.
92. *Letters*, III, 157, James Ballantyne (should be dated 9/25/12; *cf. Letters*, III, 162, to Lady Louisa Stuart, which says WS expects to spend the night of 9/24 there, and III, 178, which should be dated 9/20/12, and which tells James the same thing).
93. JGL, II, 230–1.
94. *Ibid.*
95. *Letters*, III, 163, Lady Louisa Stuart, 9/20/12, outlining this itinerary.
96. JGL, II, 231–2.
97. *Letters*, III, 163, as above. The fact that they stayed overnight at Bishop Auckland makes it obvious that they did not arrive at Rokeby till Sunday.
98. JGL, II, 232–3.
99. *Ibid.*
100. *Letters*, III, 165, James Ballantyne, 10/4?/12.
101. JGL, II, 233.
102. Ibid., 232. JGL says "about a week," but WS (*Letters*, III, 197, Southey, 11/26/12) says "three days," though perhaps he is un-

derstating it so that Southey's feelings should not be hurt.

103. *Letters*, III, 169–70, Morritt, 10/11/12.
104. *Ibid.*
105. *Ibid.*, 174, Joanna Baillie, 10/11/12; 186, Hartstonge, 10/29/12.
106. NLS MS, 1750, f. 130, WS to Wm. Erskine, 10/20/12.
107. *Letters*, III, 192, C. Rutherford, 11/3/12.
108. *Ibid.*, I, 421, James Ballantyne, (9/30/12, p.m. 10/2/12).
109. *Ibid.*, III, 166, James Ballantyne, 10/6/12; 168, fn. 2.
110. *Ibid.*, 166.
111. *Ibid.*, 167.
112. *Ibid.*, 168, James Ballantyne, 10/7/12.
113. *Ibid.*, 167, James Ballantyne, 10/6/12.
114. *Ibid.*, 168.
115. *Ibid.*, 164, James Ballantyne. (Here dated "Oct.," but I believe in Nov., probably 11/9, just before returning to Edinburgh from Abbotsford. In III, 165, WS discusses passages in Canto II, and that Canto was still being printed Oct. 29. See *Letters*, III, 183, to James Ballantyne.)
116. *Ibid.*, 177, James Ballantyne, 10/16/12.
117. *Ibid.*, 183–4, James Ballantyne, 10/28/12.
118. *Ibid.*, 178, James Ballantyne, 10/16/12.
119. *Ibid.*, 188, James Ballantyne, 11/?/12.
120. *Ibid.*, 189, James Ballantyne, 11/?/12.
121. *Ibid.*, 191, James Ballantyne, 11/3/12.
122. *Ibid.*, 186, Hartstonge, 10/29/12.
123. NLS MS, 1750, f. 13, WS to Wm. Erskine, 10/20/12.
124. *Letters*, III, 131, C. Rutherford (should be dated 10/22/12).
125. JGL, II, 238, Crabbe to WS, 10/13/12.
126. *Letters*, III, 181, Crabbe, 10/21/12.
127. *Ibid.*
128. *Ibid.*, 197–8, Southey, 11/26/12.
129. *Ibid.*, 201, Morritt, 11/29/12.
130. *Ibid.*, 189, James Ballantyne (here dated "Nov.," but clearly later

than the letter preceding—probably, therefore, early Dec.).
131. Gillies, "Recollections" (quoted by Pope-Hennessy, *Laird*, 139).
132. *Letters*, III, 190, James Ballantyne. (Also misdated "Nov." The fire to which WS refers as "last night's exhibition," took place in Dec.)
133. *Letters*, III, 205, Morritt, 12/10/12.
134. *Ibid.*, 190, James Ballantyne, 12/?/12.
135. *Ibid.*, 207, James Ballantyne, 12/31/12.
136. JGL, II, 249.
137. *Letters*, III, 212–4. WS sent off a gift copy of the quarto as early as 1/3/13, others on 1/6 or 1/7; but in writing to Morritt (*Letters*, III, 226) on 1/12/13, he says in a postscript that this is the second day of publication, which would make the publication date 1/10/13.

## Chapter 4

1. JGL, II, 248–9.
2. *Letters*, III, 226, Morritt, 1/12/13 says "2,250," but this is clearly a slip; earlier in the letter WS says "over 3,000").
3. *Letters*, III, 225.
4. Ballantyne, "Rambling Reminiscences," *Chambers's Edinburgh Journal*, 10/12/1843, 325, Mrs. Ballantyne does not specify the occasion, but the description is typical.
5. *Letters*, III, 225, Morritt, 1/12/13.
6. *Ibid.*, 213–25, *passim*.
7. *Ibid.*, 204, Duchess of Buccleuch, n.d, but wrongly placed in Dec.; must be Jan.
8. *Ibid.*, 225.
9. *Ibid.*, 213–25, *passim*.
10. *Ibid.*, 222–3, Joanna Baillie, 1/10/13.
11. *Ibid.*, 212, Lady Louisa Stuart, 1/3/13. Scott is quoting *Henry V*, II, 1.
12. *Ibid.*, 220–1, Ellis, 1/9/13. The printed text reads "son of Lancelot Gobbo," but the Morgan MS has "sire," as Grierson notes in *Letters*, XII, 339, fn. 1. Scott quoting *Hamlet*, III, 1, 125, and *Merchant of Venice*, II, 1, 16.
13. JGL, II, 254.

14. NLS MS, 3884, f. 26, Joanna Baillie to WS, 1/14/13.
15. Partington, *Post-Bag*, 95, Lady Charlotte Campbell to WS.
16. *Letters*, III, 218, Lady Abercorn, 1/8/13.
17. Partington, *Post-Bag*, 96, Clarke to WS, 2/5/13.
18. *Letters*, III, 236, Baillie, 3/13/13.
19. JGL, II, 257, fn. 2.
20. Pope-Hennessy, *Laird*, 141.
21. *Letters*, III, 222, Ellis, 1/9/13.
22. NLS MS, 742, f. 60, WS to Constable, 2/4/13.
23. *Letters*, VII, 465, Thos. Scott, 1/30/13.
24. JGL, II, 258. Grierson, in *Letters*, III, 212, fn. 1, says "a month," but aside from the reference in the letter to Lady Louisa Stuart, 1/3/13, below, which says the poem is not yet published, there is no further mention of it till March.
25. *Letters*, III, 212, Lady Louisa Stuart; *cf.* 255, Lady Abercorn, 4/22/13.
26. *Ibid.*, 293, Morritt, 7/13/13, and fn. 3, Jeffrey married Charlotte Wilkes, daughter of Charles Wilkes of New York, and niece of John Wilkes.
27. *Ibid.*, 212–3, fn. 1, Lady Louisa Stuart to WS, 4/22/13.
28. *Ibid.*, 262, Lady Louisa Stuart, 4/28/13.
29. *Poetical Works*, VII, 136, *Bridal;* also quoted by JGL, II, 258.
30. *Letters*, III, 237, Joanna Baillie, 3/21/13.
31. *Ibid.*, 240, Lady Abercorn, 3/23/13.
32. *Ibid.*, 252, Morritt, 4/9/13.
33. *Ibid.*, 263, Lady Louisa Stuart, 4/28/13.
34. *Ibid.*, 259, Henry Brevoort, 4/23/13, who was the guest and donor. One of the volumes is still in the Abbotsford Library.
35. *Letters*, III, 263–4, Sophia Scott, 5/3/13.
36. *Ibid.*
37. *Ibid.*, 311, Joanna Baillie, summer, 1813.
38. *Ibid.*, 253, Morritt, 4/9/13.
39. *Ibid.*, 262, Lady Louisa Stuart, 4/28/13.
40. JGL, II, 269, quoting Robert Cadell memorandum.

41. NLS MS, 861, f. 15, John Ballantyne to WS, 3/16/13.
42. *Ibid.*, f. 23, John Ballantyne to WS, 3/18/13.
43. *Ibid.*, f. 15, John Ballantyne to WS, 3/16/13.
44. *Ibid.*, f. 28, James Ballantyne to WS, 3/22/13.
45. *Ibid.*, f. 15, John Ballantyne to WS, 3/16/13.
46. *Ibid.*, f. 28, James Ballantyne to WS, 3/22/13.
47. *Ibid.*, f. 15, John Ballantyne to WS, 3/16/13.
48. *Ibid.*, James Ballantyne to WS at end of above.
49. *Ibid.*, f. 25, John Ballantyne to WS, 3/20/13.
50. *Ibid.*, f. 28, James Ballantyne to WS, 3/22/13.
51. *Ibid.*, f. 25, John Ballantyne to WS, 3/20/13.
52. *Ibid.*, f. 28, James Ballantyne to WS, 3/22/13.
53. *Ibid.*
54. *Ibid.*
55. *Ibid.*, f. 23, John Ballantyne to WS, 3/18/13.
56. *Ibid.*, f. 35, John Ballantyne to WS, 4/22/13.
57. *Ibid.*
58. *Letters*, III, 266, James Ballantyne, 5/4/13.
59. *Ibid.*, 267.
60. *Ibid.*, 266.
61. *Ibid.*, 264–5.
62. *Ibid.*, III, 266.
63. JGL, II, 269, quoting Cadell memorandum.
64. *Ibid.*
65. *Ibid.*, 270.
66. *Letters*, III, 271–2, John Ballantyne, 5/18/13 (complete in *Letters*, I, 422–4. See also I, 422–4, John Ballantyne, 5/19/13).
67. JGL, II, 14.
68. *Letters*, III, 267, memo following letter to James Ballantyne, 5/4/13, and *Letters*, I, 425–6, list attached to letter to John Ballantyne, 5/21/13.
69. *Letters*, I, 422, John Ballantyne, 5/19/13; 426, John Ballantyne, 5/21/13; 424, John Ballantyne, 5/21/13.
70. *Letters*, III, 272, Constable, 5/18/13.

71. *Ibid.*, I, 422, John Ballantyne, 5/19/13.
72. JGL, II, 270, fn. 1.
73. *Letters*, III, 265, James Ballantyne, 5/4/13.
74. *Ibid.*, I, 423, John Ballantyne, 5/19/13.
75. *Ibid.*, 423–4.
76. *Ibid.*, 426, John Ballantyne, 5/21/13.
77. *Ibid.*, 425.
78. *Ibid.*, 293, Morritt, 6/25/13.
79. *Ibid.*, I, 423, John Ballantyne, 5/19/13.
80. *Ibid.*, III, 269, Hartstonge, 5/10/13.
81. *Ibid.*, 294–5, Morritt, 6/25/13.
82. JGL, II, 275, quoting Terry, 6/20/13.
83. *Ibid.*, 274–5.
84. *Ibid.*, 274.
85. *Letters*, III, 290–1, Constable, 6/21/13.
86. *Ibid.*, 285, fn. 1.
87. *Ibid.*, 286, fn.
88. *Ibid.*, 286, Constable, 6/20/13.
89. *Ibid.*, 287, fn., Constable to Cadell, 6/21/13.
90. *Ibid.*, 286, fn., Cadell to Constable, 6/16/13.
91. *Ibid.*, 286–7, Constable, 6/20/13.
92. *Ibid.*, 287.
93. *Ibid.*, 289, Constable, 6/24/13.
95. *Ibid.*, 291, Constable, 6/25/13.
96. *Ibid.*, and fn. 1.
97. *Ibid.*, 298, Murray, 7/5/13.
98. *Ibid.*, 300, Morritt, 7/13/13.
99. JGL, II, 275. The nickname had been suggested by William Stewart Rose.
100. *Letters*, III, 297, Terry, 7/2/13.
101. *Ibid.*, 301, Morritt, 7/13/13.
102. *Ibid.*, 304, Lady Abercorn, 7/21/13.
103. *Ibid.*, 315, Morritt, 8/10/13.
104. *Ibid.*, 300, Morritt, 7/13/13, and fn. 2.
105. *Ibid.*, 298, Murray, 7/5/13.
106. *Ibid.*, I, 427, John Ballantyne, 7/24/13; 429, 7/25/13.
107. *Ibid.*, 427.
108. *Ibid.*, 429–30.
109. *Ibid.*, 430–1.
110. *Ibid.*, III, 318, Hartstonge, 8/21/13.
111. *Journal*, 219, 8/24/26.
112. *Ibid.*, 220, 8/25/26.
113. *Letters*, III, 356–7, Joanna Baillie, 9/21/13.
114. *Ibid.*, 356.
115. *Ibid.*, I, 432, John Ballantyne, 7/30/13.
116. *Ibid.*, 434, John Ballantyne, 8/1/13 (*not* 7/31/13).
117. *Ibid.*, 434, John Ballantyne, 7/30/13.
118. *Ibid.*, 8/1/13.
119. JGL, II, 281. JGL says WS cut short his visit to Drumlanrig and returned home for 2–3 days before going to Longtown. This is possible, but the correspondence doesn't mention it, and any such movements would draw the time very fine.
120. *Letters*, I, 435–6, John Ballantyne, 8/10/13.
121. *Ibid.*, III, 294, fn. 1, Morritt to WS, 6/29/13.
122. *Ibid.*, 314, fn. 2, Morritt to WS, 8/8/13. *Cf.* 314–5, Morritt, 8/10/13.
123. *Ibid.*, 318, Hartstonge, 8/21/13.
124. *Ibid.*, 316, John Ballantyne, 8/20/13.
125. *Ibid.*, I, 439, John Ballantyne, 8/20/13.
126. *Ibid.*, 440.
127. *Ibid.*, 439.
128. *Ibid.*, 441, John Ballantyne, 8/22/13; cf. *Letters*, III, 317, Hartstonge, 8/21/13.
129. ACLC, III, 18.
130. *Letters*, III, 319–20, Constable, 8/24/13.
131. *Ibid.*, 320.
132. *Ibid.*, 319.
133. *Ibid.*, 320.
134. ACLC, III, 21, Constable to WS, 8/24/13.
135. *Ibid.*, 22.
136. *Letters*, III, 321, James Ballantyne, 8/24/13; cf. *Letters*, XII, 488.
137. *Ibid.*, 322.
138. *Ibid.*, 325, Constable, 8/24/13; cf. III, 327, John Ballantyne, 8/24/13.
139. *Ibid.*, 323, fn. 1, Buccleuch to WS, 5/8/13.
140. *Ibid.*, 323, Buccleuch, 8/24/13.
141. *Ibid.*, 325, Constable, 8/24/13.
142. *Ibid.*, I, 442–6, John Ballantyne, 8/24, 26, 27/13.
143. *Ibid.*, 443.
144. *Ibid.*, 446.

115. *Letters*, III, 456–7, Morritt, 7/9/14.
116. JGL, II, 325, is wrong about the date of publication. *Letters*, III, 464, Hartstonge, 7/18/14, shows not yet published, though imminent.
117. *Letters*, III, 410, Hartstonge, 2/10/14.
118. *Ibid.*, 464–5, Hartstonge, 7/18/14.
119. JGL, II, 479.
120. *Letters*, III, 457, Morritt, 7/9/14.
121. *Ibid.*, 461, Constable, 7/10/14.

## Chapter 6

1. *Letters*, III, 464, Hartstonge, 7/18/14.
2. *Ibid.*, 477, Morritt, 7/28/14.
3. Scott's *Diary*, 7/29/14, quoted by JGL, II, 338–9.
4. NLS MS, 3885, f. 144, Buccleuch to WS, 7/27/14.
5. *Letters*, III, 458, Morritt, 7/9/14.
6. NLS MS, 3885, f. 144.
7. JGL, II, 474, fn. 1, Byron to Thos. Moore, 8/3/14.
8. *Ibid.*, 338–9.
9. NLS MS, 3831, Stevenson Reminiscences.
10. *Letters*, XII, 117, Charlotte Scott, 7/30/14.
11. NLS MS, 3831; JGL, II, 339, Scott's *Diary*, 8/30/14, and unpublished part from NLS MS, 1551, f. 63.
12. JGL, II, 339, and NLS MS, 1551, f. 63.
13. NLS MS, 3831.
14. JGL, II, 339–40 and NLS MS, 1551, f. 63; WS to Charlotte, 7/30/14 (XII, 118).
15. JGL, II, 340; NLS MS, 3831, Stevenson Reminiscences.
16. *Letters*, XII, 118, Charlotte, 7/30/14.
17. NLS MS, 3831, Stevenson Reminiscences.
18. JGL, II, 340, Scott's *Diary*, 7/30/14.
19. *Ibid.*; *Letters*, XII, 119, Charlotte, 7/31/14.
20. JGL, II, 341–2, Scott's *Diary*, 7/31/14; NLS MS, 1551, f. 165, WS to Charlotte, 8/1/14.
21. NLS MS, 1551, f. 165; JGL, II, 342–3.
22. *Letters*, XII, 122, Charlotte, 8/3/14.
23. JGL, II, 343, Scott's *Diary* 8/3/14.
24. *Letters*, XII, 122, Charlotte, 8/3/14.
25. JGL, II, 343, Scott's *Diary*, 8/3/14.
26. NLS MS, 3831.
27. JGL, II, 344, Scott's *Diary*, 8/4/14.
28. *Ibid.*, 346, Scott's *Diary*, 8/4/14.
29. *Ibid.*, 349–50, Scott's *Diary*, 8/5/14.
30. *Ibid.*, 350–1, Scott's *Diary*, 8/6/14.
31. *Ibid.*, 353.
32. *Ibid.*, 355.
33. *Letters*, III, 481–4, Buccleuch 8/8/14.
34. JGL, II, 364, Scott's *Diary*, 8/7/14.
35. *Ibid.*, 350, Scott's *Diary* 8/5/14; 363, Scott's *Diary*, 8/8/14; NLS MS, 3831, Stevenson Reminiscences.
36. *Ibid.*, 364, Scott's *Diary*, 8/8/14.
37. *Ibid.*, 364–6, Scott's *Diary*, 8/8–9/14.
38. *Ibid.*, 367, Scott's *Diary*, 8/9/14.
39. *Ibid.*, 368, Scott's *Diary*, 8/9/14.
40. *Ibid.*
41. *Ibid.*, 8/10/14.
42. *Letters*, XII, 126, Charlotte, 8/13/14.
43. JGL, II, 369, Scott's *Diary*, 8/10/14; 375, Scott's *Diary*, 8/10/14.
44. *Ibid.*, 369.
45. *Ibid.*, 372.
46. *Ibid.*, 375, Scott's *Diary*, 8/11/14.
47. *Ibid.*, 377.
48. *Ibid.*, 377–8.
49. *Ibid.*, 380, Scott's *Diary*, 8/12/14.
50. *Letters*, XII, 124, Charlotte, 8/13/14.
51. *Ibid.*, 127.
52. *Ibid.*, 126–7.
53. JGL, II, 384, Scott's *Diary*, 8/13/14.
54. *Ibid.*, 380–3, Scott's *Diary*, 8/12/14.
55. NLS MS, 3831, Stevenson Reminiscences. *Cf. The Pirate*, Advt. xxvii–xxix, and Pref. xxii.
56. NLS MS, 3831.
57. *Letters*, III, 484, Buccleuch, 8/13/14.
58. JGL, II, 360–1, Scott's *Diary*, 8/7/14.
59. *Letters*, III, 484.
60. JGL, II, 392–4, Scott's *Diary*, 8/16/14.
61. *Ibid.*, 397–8, Scott's *Diary*, 8/17/14.
62. *Ibid.*, 398.
63. *Ibid.*, 400.
64. *Ibid.*, 401, Scott's *Diary*, 8/18/14.
65. NLS MS, 3831, Stevenson Reminiscences.

66. JGL, II, 401, Scott's *Diary*, 8/18/14.
67. *Ibid.*, 402–5, Scott's *Diary*, 8/19/14.
68. *Ibid.*, 409–11, Scott's *Diary*, 8/20/14.
69. *Ibid.*, 412–3, Scott's *Diary*, 8/21/14.
70. *Ibid.*, 417, Scott's *Diary*, 8/22/14.
71. *Ibid.*, 418–9, Scott's *Diary*, 8/23/14.
72. WS, *Letters on Demonology and Witchcraft*, quoted by JGL, II, 419–20, fn.
73. *Letters*, X, 372, Miss Wagner, 2/7/28.
74. *Ibid.*, XII, 128, Charlotte, 8/24/14.
75. *Ibid.*, X, 373, Miss Wagner.
76. JGL, II, 423, Scott's *Diary*, 8/25/14.
77. *Ibid.*, 424–5, Scott's *Diary*, 8/25/14.
78. *Ibid.*, 338.
79. NLS MS, 3831, Stevenson Reminiscences.
80. JGL, II, 426–8, Scott's *Diary*, 8/25/14.
81. *Ibid.*, 429–30, Scott's *Diary*, 8/26/14. In *Letters*, III, 530, Southey, 12/27/14, WS says this mass murder had occurred 150 years ago.
82. JGL, II, 431–2, Scott's *Diary*, 8/27/14.
83. *Ibid.*, 435–6, Scott's *Diary*, 8/28/14.
84. *Ibid.*, 437, Scott's *Diary*, 8/29/14.
85. *Ibid.*, 338.
86. *Ibid.*, 437, Scott's *Diary*, 8/29/14; *Poetical Works*, X *Lord of Isles*, 148, fn. 2.
87. JGL, II, 437–8.
88. *Ibid.*, 438–9, Scott's *Diary*, 8/30/14.
89. NLS MS, 3831, Stevenson Reminiscences.
90. JGL, II, 440, Scott's *Diary*, 8/30/14.
91. NLS MS, 3831, Stevenson Reminiscences.
92. *Letters*, XII, Charlotte, 8/24/14.
93. JGL, II, 440, Scott's *Diary*, 8/31/14.
94. *Ibid.*, 442–3.
95. *Ibid.*, 444.
96. *Ibid.*, 444–50, Scott's *Diary*, 9/1/14.
97. NLS MS, 3831, Stevenson Reminiscences.

98. JGL, II, 451, Scott's *Diary*, 9/1/14.
99. *Letters*, XII, 131, Charlotte, 9/1/14.
100. JGL, II, 451, Scott's *Diary*, 9/2/14.
101. *Ibid.*, 453, Scott's *Diary*, 9/3/14.
102. *Ibid.*, 459, Scott's *Diary*, 9/16/14.
103. *Ibid.*, 455, Scott's *Diary*, 9/4/14.
104. *Letters*, III, 491–2, Buccleuch 9/8/14.
105. JGL, II, 471, Buccleuch to WS, 9/13/14.
106. *Ibid.*, 473, Buccleuch to WS, 9/13/14.
107. *Ibid.*, 455, Scott's *Diary*, 9/5/14.
108. *Ibid.*, 455–7.
109. *Ibid.*, 457–9.
110. *Ibid.*, 459, Scott's *Diary*, 9/6/14.
111. *Letters*, XII, 131, Charlotte, 9/6/14.
112. JGL, II, 460, Scott's *Diary*, 9/7/14.
113. *Ibid.*, 462, Scott's *Diary*, 9/8/14.
114. NLS MS, 3831.
115. JGL, II, 462, Scott's *Diary*, 9/8/14.
116. *Letters*, XII, 133, Charlotte, 9/8/14.

### Chapter 7

1. *Letters*, III, 461, Constable (7/16/14). The "2,000" here refers to the 2nd ed., not as fn. 1 interprets it, to the number of copies sold; the 1st ed. was only 1,000 copies. JGL, II, 479, below, is late by 2 weeks in saying this edition was "at least projected" by 7/24/14.
2. JGL, II, 479–80.
3. *Ibid.*, 481, Morritt to WS, 7/14/14.
4. *Ibid.*, 482, Morritt to WS (here dated 7/15/14, but should be 7/21/14).
5. Inglis-Jones, *The Great Maria*, 124.
6. Edgeworth, *Life and Letters*, 241.
7. *Ibid.*, 239.
8. *Ibid.*, 244.
9. *Waverley*, II, 366, ch. XLIII.
10. Edgeworth, *Life and Letters*, 244.
11. *Letters*, III, 517–8, James Ballantyne to M. Edgeworth, 11/10/14.
12. *Waverley*, Ed. Intro., xciii–xcvii.
13. *Ibid.*, xcii.
14. *Letters*, III, 479, Morritt, 7/28/14.

15. JGL, II, 483, Margaret Clephane to WS.
16. *Ibid.*, 482, Morritt to WS, 7/21/14.
17. *Letters*, III, 479, Morritt (p.m. 7/28/14). "Whistle it down the wind," etc.—see *Othello*, III, iii, 262, slightly modified.
18. *Letters*, III, 480, Morritt.
19. *Waverley*, Gen. Pref., xxv–xxvii.
20. *Ibid.*
21. *Ibid.*, xxix.
22. *Letters*, III, 541, James Ballantyne, (n.d., but in Dec. 1814).
23. *Waverley*, Pref., xxvi.
24. Huntington MS, WS to Thos. Scott, 12/9/14 (in *Huntington Library Quarterly*, II, 326–7; inaccurately printed in *Letters*, III, 502–3, and there erroneously dated Oct.).
25. *Huntington Library Quarterly*, II, 327.
26. In 1815 Tom seems to have been trying; see *Letters*, I, 494, John Ballantyne, 10?/27/15.
27. Ball, *SWS as a Critic*, 65–70.
28. JGL, II, 326.
29. Ball, *SWS as a Critic*, 67.
30. *Works of Swift*, X, 434, cited by Ball, *SWS as a Critic*, 67, fn. 2.
31. *Ibid.*, IV, 280, cited by Ball, *SWS as a Critic*, 67, fn. 2.
32. *Misc. Prose*, II *Life of Swift*, 119.
33. *Ibid.*, 61.
34. *Ibid.*, 60.
35. *Letters*, III, 498, Morritt, 9/14/14.
36. *Ibid.*, 476, Train, 7/28/14.
37. *Ibid.*, 573, Train, 11/7/14.
38. *Ibid.*, 519, fn. 1. Joseph Train to WS., n.d., but Train and JGL both say 11/18/14 (see JGL, II, 497, and Train's memo).
39. *Letters*, III, 519, Train, 11/22/14.
40. JGL, II, 498; Ball, *SWS as a Critic*, 154. Published in 2 vols., 8ᵛᵒ, but Ball erroneously dates it 1815. JGL is correct in saying Oct. 1814. See below.
41. Ball, *SWS as a Critic*, 163.
42. *Letters*, I, 467–8, John Ballantyne, 10/8/14; cf. *Letters*, III, 504, Constable, 10/9/14, saying "Somerville is completed and I presume delivered"; also, *ibid.*, 511, 10/22/14.
43. *Letters*, III, 518, Edgeworth, 11/10/14.
44. *Ibid.*, 514, Terry, 11/10/14.

45. *Ibid.*
46. *Ibid.*, 521, Lady Abercorn, 11/22/14.
47. *Ibid.*, 374, Byron, 11/6/13.
48. Byron, *Letters and Diaries* (Quennell, ed.), *Journal*, 11/17/13.
49. *Letters*, IV, 3, Lord Byron, which I agree with fn. 2. in dating autumn 1814, not Jan. 1815.
50. *Letters*, IV, 2, fn. 2.
51. James Ballantyne, *Recollections*, NLS MS, 921, f. 181, which also appears in JGL, II, 508, in a somewhat different form.
52. JGL, II, 509.
53. *Letters*, III, 490, James Ballantyne, 9/8/14.
54. *Ibid.*, 494, Constable, 9/17/14.
55. *Ibid.*, I, 458, John Ballantyne, 9/27/14.
56. *Ibid.*, 467–8, John Ballantyne, "Saturday Evening," which I believe 10/8/14, on basis of parallels to Constable 10/7/14 which also says that *Somerville* is completed.
57. ACLC, III, 73, Constable to Cadell, n.d. (Oct. 1814).
58. *Letters*, I, 464, John Ballantyne, 10/17/14.
59. NLS MS, 562, f. 26, James Ballantyne to WS, 10/23/14.
60. JGL, II, 504; cf. *Letters*, III, 505, fn. 1.
61. *Letters*, III, 506, John Ballantyne, 10/17/14.
62. *Ibid.*
63. *Ibid.*, I, 469–70, John Ballantyne, 10/21/14.
64. *Ibid.*, 473, John Ballantyne, n.d. (JGL, II, 503, dates it 10/14/14, but it is later than this in John's letter-book, and obviously later in fact).
65. *Ibid.*
66. JGL, II, 336.
67. *Ibid.*, 505.
68. *Ibid.*, 497.
69. *Poetical Works*, X, *Lord of Isles*, 196, V, xvii, 5–10.
70. *Ibid.*, 254, VI, xxiv, 31–7.
71. JGL, II, 497.
72. *Letters*, III, 528, Constable, 12/19/14.
73. *Ibid.*, 532, Constable, 12/25/14.
74. *Ibid.*, C. Erskine, 12/26/14.
75. *Ibid.*, IV, 12, Morritt, 1/19/15.
76. *Ibid.*
77. JGL, II, 491.

78. *Letters*, IV, 12–3, Morritt, 1/19/15.
79. *Ibid.*, 216–7, Terry, 4/18/16 and 217, fn. 1.
80. *Ibid.*, III, 276–8, Lady Abercorn, 5/21/13.
81. *Ibid.*, IV, 12–3, Morritt, 1/19/15; see also *Letters*, II, 411, Smith, 12/18/14, for origin of Meg Merrilies denouncing Ellangowan.
82. *Letters*, IV, 12–3, Berwick, 1/18/15.
83. JGL, II, 507–8. James Ballantyne's recollections agree in essence but are less vividly dramatic in language.
84. JGL, II, 507–8. Corrected verbally from James Ballantyne's memoir.
85. *Ibid.*, 507.
86. *Letters*, IV, 27, Lady Abercorn, 2/15/15.
87. *Ibid.*, 29, Maria Edgeworth, 2/17/15, replying to her letter of 2/11/15.
88. *Ibid.*, XII, 421–2, fn. 2. R. L. Edgeworth to WS, 2/11/15.
89. NLS MS, 2566, John Ballantyne's *Diary*, says WS finished the novel 1/19/15.
90. Bertram, *Memories*, 93.
91. *Ibid.*
92. Smiles, *Murray*, I, 433, ca. January, 1815.
93. JGL, II, 502.
94. *G. Mannering*, Intro., xviii.
95. *Ibid.*, xix.
96. *Ibid.*, xviii.
97. JGL, II, 512.
98. Bertram, *Memories*, 101.
99. *Ibid.*, 103–4.

## Chapter 8

1. Thorslev, *Byronic Hero*, 80–2, has a discussion of the literary archetypes included among the characters the *Gothic Villain* (Oswald), the *Man of Feeling* (Wilfrid), the *Child of Nature* (Redmond), the *Noble Outlaw* (Mortham, Bertram).
2. Cf. Grierson, *Scott*, 107.
3. *Poetical Works*, IX, 62, *Rokeby*, Canto I, xxiv.
4. *Ibid.*, 68, Canto I, xxx.
5. Grierson, *Scott*, 107.
6. *Poetical Works*, IX, 181, *Rokeby*, Canto IV.
7. *Ibid.*, 187.
8. *Letters*, V, 145, Edgeworth, 5/15/18.
9. *Poetical Works*, IX, 64, *Rokeby*, Canto I, xxvii.
10. Cf. Kroeber, *Romantic Narrative Art*, 176.
11. *Ibid.*, 175–7.
12. *Poetical Works*, IX, 35, Canto I, vii.
14. *Ibid.*, 47, Canto I, xv.
15. *Ibid.*, 50, Canto I, xvii.
16. *Ibid.*, 53, Canto I, xix.
17. *Ibid.*, 249, Canto V, xxxiv.
18. *Ibid.*, 250, Canto V, xxxv.
19. *Ibid.*, 252, Canto V, xxxvii.
20. *Ibid.*, 291, Canto VI, xxviii.
21. *Ibid.*, 293, Canto VI, xxx.
22. *Ibid.*, 296, Canto VI, xxxi.
23. *Ibid.*, 298, Canto VI, xxxii.
24. *Ibid.*, 299, Canto VI, xxxiv.
25. *Ibid.*, 141–4, Canto III, xvi–xviii; 155–6, III, xxviii; 222–4, xiii.
26. *Ibid.*, XI, 48, *Bridal*, Canto I, xvii.
27. *Ibid.*, 58, Canto II, ix.
28. *Ibid.*, 58–9, Canto II, x.
29. *Ibid.*, 71, Canto II, xxi.
30. *Ibid.*, 77, Canto II, xxvi.
31. *Ibid.*, 129, Canto III, xxxvi.
32. *Ibid.*, 130, Canto III, xxxviii.
33. *Ibid.*, 131, Canto III, xxxviii.
34. *Ibid.*, 132, Canto III, xxxix.
35. Cf. Kroeber's discussions, *Romantic Narrative Art*, 178–9.
36. *Poetical Works*, X, 36–7, *Lord of Isles*, Canto I, xi.
37. *Ibid.*, 47, Canto I, xxvi.
38. *Ibid.*, 47–8, Canto I, xxvii.
39. *Ibid.*, 33, Canto I, xi.
40. *Ibid.*, 70–1, Canto II, xiv.
41. *Ibid.*, 72, Canto II, xv.
42. *Ibid.*, 76, Canto II, xix.
43. *Ibid.*, 91–2, Canto II, xxxi–xxxii.
44. *Ibid.*, 98, Canto III, iii.
45. *Ibid.*, 99, Canto III, iv.
46. *Ibid.*, 119, Canto III, xxiii.
47. *Ibid.*, 170, Canto IV, xxvii.
48. *Ibid.*, 178, Canto V, ii.
49. *Ibid.*, 191, Canto V, xiii.
50. *Ibid.*, 206, Canto V, xxv.
51. *Ibid.*, 208, Canto V, xxvii.
52. *Ibid.*, 212, Canto V, xxxi.
53. *Ibid.*, 217, Canto V, xxxiv.
54. *Ibid.*, 230, Canto VI, vi–vii.
55. *Ibid.*, 232, Canto VI, ix.
56. *Ibid.*, 253–4, Canto VI, xxiv.
57. *Ibid.*, 260, Canto VI, xxix.
58. *Ibid.*, 139, Canto IV, iii.

## Chapter 9

1. NLS MS, 2566, John Ballantyne's *Diary*, 3/31/15. WS *had* expected to sail 4/1–4/15 but changed his plans. See *Letters*, I, 478, John Ballantyne, 3/17/15; 479, 3/21/15.
2. *Letters*, IV, 13, Morritt, 1/19/15.
3. *Ibid.*, 31–2, Maria Edgeworth, 2/17/15.
4. *Ibid.*, 42, Lady Abercorn, 4/11/15.
5. *Ibid.*, 76, Hartstonge, 7/6/15; though in IV, 46, Miss Clephane (4/11/15), he says the voyage took five days, which would have made the date of arrival 4/5 or 4/6. But inasmuch as to Hartstonge, WS specifically says that Ellis "died just two days after I reached town," and Ellis died 4/10/15, the correct date of arrival is probably 4/8.
6. JGL, II, 513.
7. *Letters*, IV, 76, and fn. 1.
8. NLS MS, 857, f. 1, WS to Mrs. Ellis, 4/13/15.
9. *Letters*, IV, 23–4, and fn. 2. JGL, II, 512, is wrong in saying "again"; see n. 11, below.
10. JGL, II, 514.
11. *Letters*, IV, 23, Joanna Baillie, 1/15/15.
12. JGL, II, 519–20.
13. The details about Carlton House in this and the next paragraph are from Bryant, *Elegance*, 112–3, based on Ackerman, Payne, etc., as noted in his fn. 1.
14. JGL, II, 520. The date on which this dinner took place is uncertain. *Letters*, I, 480, James Ballantyne, dated only "Sunday," says "I dined yesterday with the P.R." This could make the date 4/15, 4/22, or 4/29 —4/8, the date of Scott's arrival in London, is unlikely.
15. JGL, II, 522.
16. *Ibid.*, 520–1, although he does not give the name of the judge. In the 1st ed. JGL had identified him as Lord Braxfield, but when this was pointed out to him as an error, he removed the name from the 2nd ed.
17. JGL, II, 520–1.
18. *Letters*, IV, 52, Miss Clephane, 4/27/15. *Probably* Margaret Clephane, not only here, but through-

out the letters so addressed in this chapter.
19. NLS MS, 3831, Stevenson Reminiscences.
20. *Letters*, IV, 52, Miss Clephane, 4/27/15.
21. JGL, II, 522.
22. *Ibid.*, 520.
23. *Ibid.*, 522; *cf. Letters*, IV, 66, MacMahon, 5/23/15.
24. *Ibid.*, 522–3; *cf. Letters*, IV, 234–5, Morritt, 5/16/16; and 385, Morritt, 1/31/13.
25. JGL, II, 523. JGL quotes Ballantyne as saying "wild surprise," but this is surely a misreading for "mild."
26. JGL, II, 516; *cf.* Smiles, *Murray*, I, 257, 10/20/14.
27. *Letters*, XII, 424, Byron, erroneously dated 9/13/15; the contents of the letter shows that the two men had not yet met, so that it could not have been after Scott's return from Paris but must have been written immediately on his arrival in London in April.
28. JGL, II, 514.
29. *Ibid.*, 182.
30. *Ibid.*, 514–5.
31. Pearson, *Life and Personality*, 107.
32. JGL, II, 515.
33. *Ibid.*, 516, *Cf.* Scott's letter to Lord Byron, JGL, II, 518, n.d.; its wording is corrected from JGL on the authority of Dr. Corson. The gift was made in Apr. 1815, not, as Thos. Moore says, subsequently.
34. *Letters*, IV, 43–69.
35. *Ibid.*, IV, 43, Miss Clephane, 4/11/15.
36. *Ibid.*, 44, 47–8, fn. 1.
37. *Ibid.*, 48, Miss Clephane, 4/13/15.
38. *Ibid.*, 50, Miss Clephane, 4/21/15.
39. *Ibid.*, 64, Miss Clephane, 5/?/15.
40. *Ibid.*, 66.
41. *Ibid.*, 62, Miss Clephane, 5/13/15.
42. *Ibid.*, 64, Miss Clephane, 5/?/15.
43. *Ibid.*, 68, Miss Clephane, 6/6/15.
44. *Blackwood's Mag.*, Vol. 184, f. 625.
45. *Letters*, IV, 52. Miss Clephane, 4/24/15; 59, Miss Clephane, 5/4/15.
46. *Ibid.*, 57, Mackenzie, 4/29/15.
47. *Ibid.*, 68, Miss Clephane, 6/6/15.
48. *Ibid.*, 73, Rogers, 6/12/15.
49. *Chambers's Edin. Jo.*, 1/25/40, f. 2. Opie, "Recollections"; also in

*Life of Amelia Opie*, 176–7—though she erroneously dates the occasion in 1816, which is impossible, because WS was not in London in the latter year.

50. *Life of Amelia Opie*, f. 178.
51. *Letters*, IV, 61, Miss Clephane, 5/4/15.
52. *Ibid.*, 64, Miss Clephane, 6/6/15.
53. *Ibid.*, Murray, 6/10/15.
54. Bryant, *Elegance*, 214–5.
55. *Ibid.*, 217.
56. *Ibid.*, 250–1.
57. *Letters*, IV, 8, Terry—misdated 1/15/15; should be 7/15/15.
58. *Ibid.*, 74, Richardson, 7/15/15.
59. JGL, III, 5–6.
60. ACLC, III, 83, John Ballantyne to Constable & Co., 7/27/15.
61. NLS MS, 991, Bruce's *Diary*, and NLS MS, 875, Scott's *Diary*. Both say they left on Friday (7/28); Scott of Gala's published *Journal* (1842) says 7/27, which is followed by JGL, III, 14. I follow Bruce and WS as written at the time and as two-against-one testimony. Bruce was the son of George Bruce, a Deputy Clerk in the 1st Division with WS, and Laird of Longbee, which was 3 miles from Abbotsford.
62. NLS MS, 924, f. 34, Skene transcript of WS note to Ballantyne, 7/12/15.
63. Scott of Gala, *Journal*, though *he* gives the date as 7/27/15.
64. NLS MS, 991, Bruce's *Diary* 7/30–8/1/15.
65. NLS MS, 991, Bruce's *Diary* 8/2/15; also mentioned by Gala, quoted in JGL, III, 5.
66. JGL, III, 5.
67. NLS MS, 991, Bruce's *Diary*, 8/3/15; *Letters*, XII, 135, Charlotte, 8/3/15.
68. NLS MS, 991, Bruce's *Diary*, 8/8/15.
69. *Letters*, XII, 135–6.
70. *Ibid.*, 137.
71. *Ibid.*, 136.
72. Gala, *Journal*, 8/6; NLS MS, 991, Bruce's *Diary*, 8/6/15; WS *Journal*, 8/6.
73. WS *Journal*, 8/6; Gala, *Journal*, 8/6.
74. NLS MS, 991, Bruce's *Diary*, 8/7/15; Pearson, *Life and Personality*, 124.
75. NLS MS, 991, Bruce's *Diary*, 8/7/15.
76. *Letters*, XII, 138, Charlotte, 8/8/15. Adam was the son of Lord Chief Commissioner Adam.
77. NLS MS, 991, Bruce's *Diary*, 8/9/15.
78. Gala, *Journal*, 8/9/15, and Gordon, *Personal Memories*, II, 333–5.
79. *Letters*, IV, 79–80, Buccleuch, 8/11–2/15; XII, 139–40, Charlotte, 8/13/15.
80. *Ibid.*, 79.
81. Gordon, *Personal Memories*, II, 333–5.
82. *Letters*, IV, 82, Buccleuch, 8/11/15.
83. Gordon, *Personal Memories*, II, 335; also quoted by JGL, III, 9.
84. *Letters*, IV, 81, Buccleuch.
85. *Ibid.*, 84; XII, 141, Charlotte, 8/13/15; *Paul's Letters*, 185.
86. Lockhart, *Paul's Letters*, 196–7.
87. *Letters*, IV, 84–5, Buccleuch; *cf.* XII, 141.
88. Bryant, *Elegance*, 169–70.
89. NLS MS, 991, Bruce's *Diary*, 8/14/15.
90. Bryant, *Elegance*, 178.
91. *Ibid.*, 180–1.
92. Gala, *Journal*, 8/18/15; Bryant, *Elegance*, 169.
93. *Ibid.*, 254.
94. Bryant, *Elegance*, 170.
95. NLS MS, 991, Bruce's *Diary*. *Letters*, XII, 142, Charlotte, 8/15/15.
96. Gala, *Journal*, 8/14/15; Bryant, *Elegance*, 181.
97. *Letters*, XII, 142, Charlotte, 8/15/15.
98. Gala, *Journal*, 8/22/15.
99. NLS MS, 991, Bruce's *Diary*, 8/14/15.
100. Bryant, *Elegance*, 180.
101. NLS MS, 991, Bruce's *Diary*, 8/15/15.
102. *Letters*, XII, 143, Charlotte, 8/28/15.
103. *London Times*, 6/18/1934, quoted by Pearson, *Life and Personality*, 125.
104. Gala, *Journal*, 8/18/15.
105. *Letters*, XII, 143, fn. 1, quoting James Simpson, *Paris After Waterloo* (1853), 194.

106. Gala, *Journal*, 8/18/15.
107. JGL, III, 21; *cf. Letters*, XII, 145, Charlotte (*after* 8/18/15); Stevenson, NLS MS, 3831, says this interchange was not with the Czar but a *Prussian* general, and gives other variant details, but in this case JGL is more likely to have known the facts.
108. *Letters*, XII, 145–6, Charlotte.
109. JGL, III, 22.
110. Gala, *Journal*, 8/15/15; NLS MS, 991, Bruce's *Diary*, 8/15/15.
111. *Ibid.*, Scott of Gala, *Journal*, 8/28/15; NLS MS, 991, Bruce's *Diary*, 8/28/15.
112. Gala, *Journal*, 8/16- (or 17)/15.
113. *Ibid.*, (after 8/18/15).
114. *Ibid.*, 8/18/15.
115. *Ibid.*, after 8/18/15.
116. NLS MS, 991, Bruce's *Diary*, 8/19/15; Bryant, *Elegance*, 180.
117. Gala, *Journal*, 8/15/15.
118. NLS MS, 991, Bruce's *Diary*, 8/21/15; Gala, *Journal*, 8/18/15; Bruce, 8/16,18/15.
119. *Letters*, XII, 147, Charlotte (after 8/28/15).
120. *Ibid.*, 148, Charlotte.
121. NLS MS, 991, Bruce's *Diary*, 8/19/15, 8/16/15.
122. *Letters*, XII, 143, Charlotte, 8/28/15.
123. Gala, *Journal*, 8/29/15.
124. *Ibid.*, 8/27/15.
125. *Letters*, IV, 88, James Ballantyne, 8/30/15.
126. JGL, IV, 52.
127. Gala, *Journal*, 8/31/15.
128. *Letters*, IV, 95, Baillie (bet. 8/10 and 9/6/15).
129. Gala, *Journal*, 8/31/15.
130. *Letters*, IV, 96, Baillie.
131. WS, *Letters*, 316.
132. Gala, *Journal*, 9/1/15.
133. *Ibid.; cf. Letters*, IV, 168, Murray, 1/16/16.
134. Gala, *Journal*, 9/2/15.
135. *Ibid.*, after 9/2/15.
136. *Letters*, XI, 295, Lady Alvanley, 9/15/15; *cf.* 90, fn. 2, and JGL, III, 23–4, *Poetical Works*, XI, 295.
137. Gala, *Journal*, 9/8/15.
138. *Ibid.*, 9/1/15.
139. *Ibid.*, 9/8/15.
140. *Letters*, XII, 149, Charlotte, 9/6/15.

141. *Ibid.*, 148.
142. *Ibid.*, 150; Charlotte, 9/13/15; *cf.* Irving, 530–1.
143. *Letters*, XII, 149.
144. Gala, *Journal*, 9/9/15. But *cf. Letters*, IV, 126, Lady Compton, 11/12/15, where Scott says he improvised the line one night for Sophia.
145. Gala, *Journal;* also quoted in *Letters*, XII, 150–1, fn. 2.
146. *Letters*, XII, 150, Charlotte, 9/13/15.
147. Gala, *Journal*, n.d., but after 9/9/15.
148. *Ibid.*, n.d.; *Letters*, XII, 149, Charlotte, 9/13/15.

Chapter 10

1. Gala, *Journal*, 9/12/15; *Letters*, XII, 149–50, Charlotte, 9/13/15.
2. Gala, *Journal.*
3. *Letters*, XII, 150.
4. Gala, *Journal*, 9/13/15.
5. JGL, III, 24–5.
6. WS, *Journal*, 10–1, 11/23/25.
7. *Ibid.*, 52, 12/21/25; *cf.* JGL, II, 515.
8. Gala, *Journal*, 9/14/15. Mathews says 6 P.M. of same day they had had dined with Byron, but Gala definitely says 6 A.M.
9. Gala, *Journal*, 9/15/15.
10. *Ibid.*, 9/19/15.
11. *Letters*, IV, 99–101, Morritt, 10/2/15.
12. Gala, *Journal.*
13. *Letters*, IV, 101.
14. *Ibid.*
15. Gala, *Journal.*
16. Skene, quoted by JGL, III, 26; somewhat differently worded in *Memories*, 91.
17. JGL, III, 29.
18. NLS MS, 2566, John Ballantyne's *Diary*, 12/8/15.
19. JGL, III, 65.
20. *Letters*, IV, 87, James Ballantyne, 8/30/15.
21. *Ibid.*, 101–2, Morritt, 10/2/15. "The Dance of Death" was published in the *Edinburgh Annual Register* for 1815 and is included in *Poetical Works*, XI, 297–304.
22. *Letters*, IV, 6, Lady Abercorn, 1/10/15.
23. *Ibid.*, 105, James Ballantyne,

10/21/15, and NLS MS, 1750, f. 157, WS to Wm. Erskine, 10/27/15.

24. NLS MS, 863, f. 110, WS to James Ballantyne, 10/10/15.

25. JGL, III, 32–5.

26. *Ibid.*, 36.

27. *Letters*, I, 386, John Ballantyne, 10/9/15.

28. *Ibid.*, IV, 131, Constable, 11/21/15; *Trans. Edin. Bibliographical Soc.*, 1935–8, Ruff, *Bibliography*.

29. Gordon, *Personal Memories*, II, 325.

30. *Poetical Works*, XI, 226–7, Stanza XII, 30–8.

31. Quoted in "Waterloo," 283, fn. 1.

32. Gordon, *Personal Memories*, II, 327. These lines, however, are not in the version printed in later editions of the poem. Perhaps WS altered them in deference to criticisms by Wm. Erskine, alluded to in NLS MS, 1750, f. 156, WS to Erskine, Sept.– Oct. 1815.

33. John Ballantyne's *Diary*, 9/6/15, 12/8/15, 12/13/15. He took possession of the Stockbridge villa, according to the *Diary*, on 3/10/16.

34. *Letters*, IV, 119, Joanna Baillie, 11/7/15.

35. *Ibid.*, 111–2, Morritt, 11/2/15.

36. *Ibid.*, 119, Joanna Baillie, 11/7/15.

37. *Ibid.*, 127, Lady Abercorn, 11/12/15.

38. *Ibid.*, 119.

39. *Ibid.*, 131, fn. 1; *cf.* IV, 236, C. Erskine, 5/16/15, showing that it was not until this later date that WS completed paying the £400.

40. *Ibid.*, Mrs. Laidlaw, 11/20/15; Constable, 11/21/15.

41. *Ibid.*, 146, Morritt, 12/22/15.

42. *Ibid.*, 120, Joanna Baillie, 11/7/15.

43. *Ibid.*, 145, Morritt.

44. *Ibid.*, 127, Lady Compton, 11/12/15.

45. *Ibid.*, 166, C. Erskine, 1/12/16, shows that by this date WS did strike the bargain with Milne.

46. *Ibid.*, XII, 153, Charlotte, 11/11/15.

47. *Ibid.*, 153, fn. 2.

48. *Ibid.*, 154, Charlotte, 11/11/15.

49. Macfarlane, *Reminiscences*, 24.

50. NLS MS, 3836, WS to unknown correspondent, 10/26/15, says, "I shall pay off the Dr. this year."

51. Macfarlane, *Reminiscences*, 25.

52. *Letters*, I, 487, John Ballantyne, 10/17/15.

53. *Ibid.*, IV, 115, Constable, 11/3/15.

54. *Ibid.*, I, 487, John Ballantyne, 10/17/15; 489, John Ballantyne, "Sunday."

55. *Ibid.*, IV, 125, Lady Compton, 11/12/15. Dr. Corson, however, believes the four lines quoted were borrowed from an old Jacobite song.

56. JGL, III, 41–2.

57. *Ibid.*, 42–3.

58. *Ibid.*, 44–5.

59. *Letters*, IV, 144, Lady Compton, 12/12/15.

60. *Poetical Works*, XI, 312. Dr. Corson thinks these verses too were borrowed or adapted from an old Jacobite song.

61. JGL, III, 44.

62. *Letters*, IV, 142, Lady Compton, 12/12/15.

63. *Trans. Hawick Arch. Soc.*, Dec. 1871, 107.

64. JGL, III, 45.

65. *Letters*, IV, 143, Lady Compton, 12/12/15.

66. JGL, III, 231, fn. 1.

67. *Ibid.*, 56–7; *cf.* Hogg, *Domestic Manners.*

68. *Letters*, IV, 145, Morritt, 12/22/15.

69. *Ibid.*

70. *Ibid.*, 147, James Ballantyne, 12/29/15.

71. JGL, III, 53.

72. *Letters*, IV, 149, Murray, n.d.; JGL, III, 53.

73. *Glasgow Herald*, 9/3/1932, 11, correspondence of Scott and the Edgeworths.

74. *Letters*, IV, 129, Murray, 11/20/15.

75. *Ibid.*, 330, Miss Clephane, 12/26/16.

76. There are many letters devoted to Wm. Scott's problems in NLS MS, 2889. See f. 118, 2/21/16; f. 120, 2/24/16; f. 122, 2/29/16; f. 124, 3/3/16—all addressed to Wm. Scott.

77. *Letters*, IV, 166, C. Erskine, 1/12/16; 308, Lady Abercorn, 11/29/16.

78. *Ibid.*, 195, fn. 1; 194, fn. 1, Ferguson to WS, 3/4/16.

79. *Ibid.*, 194–6, Ferguson, 3/12/16.

80. *Ibid.*, 177, Miss Clephane, 2/10/16.

81. NLS MS, 852, f. 176, WS to Terry,

4/3/16; see *Poetical Works*, XI, 317-8, and fn. 1.

82. *Letters*, IV, 217-8, Terry, 4/18/16.
83. JGL, III, 53-4.
84. *Letters*, IV, 169, Terry, 1/26/16.
85. *Ibid.*, 217, fn. 1.
86. *Ibid.*, 162, fn. 1.
87. *Ibid.*, III, 515, Terry, 11/10/14.
88. *Ibid.*, IV, 162, Byron, 1/5/16. The play had its first night 5/9/16; see *Letters*, XII, 356, Maturin, 5/29/16, congratulating him on its success.
89. Partington, *Post-Bag*, 115-6, Joanna Baillie to WS, 2/26/16; also quoted in *Letters* IV, 202, fn. 1.
90. *Letters*, IV, 203, Joanna Baillie (early Apr. 1816). But the date should probably be Mar.; she replied in early Apr.
91. *Ibid.*, 244, fn. 1, Rogers to WS, 7/13/16.
92. *Ibid.*, 234, Morritt, 5/16/16.
93. *Ibid.*, 167, Murray, 1/19/16, and fn. 1. The review of the Culloden Papers appeared in the *Quarterly Review*, XXVII, for Oct. 1815 and is in *Misc. Prose*, XX, 1-93; the review of *Emma* in *Quarterly*, XXVIII, for Jan. 1816 but has never been collected.
94. *Letters*, IV, 177, Miss Clephane, 2/10/16; 259, fn. 3, lists WS's contributions to *Albyn's Anthology*. They are all collected in *Poetical Works*, XI, 915-27.
95. *Letters*, IV, 257, Constable, 6/18/16, and fn. 1.
96. NLS MS, 852, f. 176, WS to Terry, 4/9/16.
97. NLS MS, 862, f. 29, James Ballantyne to WS, 10/15/15.
98. *Ibid.*
99. Ballantyne Trustees *Reply*, 60-2, quoting WS to James Ballantyne, 11/5/15. The letter is also in *Letters*, I, 493, fn. 1.
100. *Letters*, IV, 157, James Ballantyne (early 1816).
101. NLS MS, 862, f. 29.
102. *Letters*, IV, 169, Terry, 1/26/16.
103. *Ibid.*, fn. 3.
104. *Ibid.*, 186, John Ballantyne, "Tuesday, March." Probably either 3/12 or 3/19/16.
105. JGL, III, 64.
106. *Letters*, IV, 218, Terry, 4/18/16, but previously mentioned to Joanna Baillie, *Letters*, IV, 206,

4/12/16. A note says the gift was made in Apr., but I believe it was in Mar. WS says he showed the animal to Mathews in Castle Street *before* coming to Abbotsford, and he was certainly there till Mar. 12 but probably not later than Mar. 31.

107. *Letters*, IV, 218, Terry, 4/18/16.
108. *Ibid.*, 206, Joanna Baillie.
109. *Ibid.*, 226, Hartstonge, 4/30/16.
110. *Ibid.*, 206.
111. *Ibid.*, 186, Morritt (Feb.-Mar. 1816).
112. *Ibid.*, 219, Terry, 4/18/16.
113. *Ibid.*, 230, Morritt. Here dated merely as "May," but I believe 4/19/16—see WS's announcement on 229 that "*The Antiquary* will be out in a fortnight or so." It was actually published 5/4/16.
114. NLS MS, 2889, f. 176, WS to Wm. Scott, 5/10/16, where he says the death occurred 5/9/16.
115. *Letters*, IV, 231, fn. 1, and *Letters*, VII, 445, Thos. Scott, 8/26/10.
116. Huntington MS, WS to Thos. Scott, 5/15/16. Also printed in *Huntington Library Quarterly*, II, 327-8, and inaccurately in *Letters*, IV, 231.
117. *Ibid.*
118. *Letters*, IV, 232, Morritt, 5/16/16.
119. *Ibid.*, 240-3, Thos. Scott, 5/29/16; VII, 481-3, Thos. Scott, 5/29/16, are both very much garbled as printed; I have corrected, where I quote them, from Huntington MS, which is accurately printed in *Huntington Library Quarterly*, II, 329.
120. *Letters*, IV, 233, fn. 2, Constable to WS, 5/4/16.
121. *Antiq.*, Intro., xxxiv.
122. *Letters*, IV, 233, Morritt, 5/16/16.

Chapter 11

1. *Antiq.*, I, vii, Advt.
2. *Waverley*, I, Ch. 1, 5.
3. *Ibid.*
4. Lukács, *Historical Novel*, 31.
5. *Ibid.*, 63.
6. *Ibid.*, 49.
7. *Ibid.*, 58.
8. Ferguson, *Essay*, 81, quoted by Forbes, "Rationalism."

9. *Waverley*, I, 113, Ch. VI, *Gen. Pref.*, xxiv.
10. *Letters*, III, 478, Morritt, 7/28/16, and fn. 1.
11. *Waverley*, I, 23, Ch. III, 33, Ch. V.
12. *Ibid.*, 20, Ch. III, 32, Ch. V.
13. *Ibid.*, II, 190, Ch. XXIII.
14. *Ibid.*, 239, Ch. XXX.
15. Tillyard, *Epic Strain*, 88.
16. *Waverley* II, 203, Ch. XXV.
17. *Ibid.*, I, 149, Ch. XVI.
18. *Ibid.*, II, 345, Ch. XII.
19. *Ibid.*, 256, Ch. XXXI.
20. Daiches, *Literary Essays*, 93.
21. *Waverley*, I, 239, Ch. XXV.
22. *Ibid.*, II, 326, Ch. XXXIX.
23. *Ibid.*, 327, Ch. XXXIX.
24. *Ibid.*, 338, Ch. XL.
25. *Ibid.*, 342–3, Ch. XL.
26. *Ibid.*, 200, Ch. XXV.
27. *Ibid.*, 199, Ch. XXV.
28. *Ibid.*, 200, Ch. XXV.
29. *Ibid.*, 201, Ch. XXV.
30. *Ibid.*, 308, Ch. XXXVII.
31. *Ibid.*, 357, Ch. XLII.
32. *Ibid.*, 352, Ch. II.
33. *Ibid.*, 150, Ch. XVIII.
34. Bagehot, *Literary Essays*, II, 56.
35. *Waverley*, II, 139–40, Ch. XVII.
36. *Ibid.*, 147, Ch. XVII.
37. Tillyard, *Epic Strain*, 83.
38. *Waverley*, II, 147, Ch. XVIII.
39. *Ibid.*, 150, Ch. XVIII.
40. Kroeber, *Romantic Narrative Art*, 169.
41. Hart, *Scott's Novels*, 24.
42. *G. Mannering*, Intro., I, xxxvi.
43. *Ibid.*, 53–4, Ch. VI.
44. *Ibid.*, 55, Ch. VI.
45. *Ibid.*, 71, Ch. VII.
46. *Ibid.*, 72, Ch. VII.
47. Tillyard, *Epic Strain*, 93.
48. *G. Mannering*, II, 204, Ch. XXIII.
49. *Ibid.*, 141, Ch. XII.
50. *Ibid.*, 246, Ch. XXI.
51. *Ibid.*, 263, Ch. XXII.
52. Buchan, *SWS*, 139.
53. *London Times Literary Supplement*, 4/15/1932, 630.
54. Welsh, *Hero*, 71, *passim*.
55. *G. Mannering*, II, 302, Ch. XXVI.
56. Buchan, *SWS*, 142.
57. *G. Mannering*, II, 283, Ch. XXIV.
58. *Antiq.*, I, 43, Ch. IV.
59. *Ibid.*, 49, Ch. IV.
60. Cf. Hart, *Scott's Novels*, 256: "Edie assesses a legendary past by the usefulness in the service of the present."
61. *Antiq.*, II, 210, Ch. XVII.
62. *Ibid.*, I, 155–6, Ch. XIII.
63. Austen, *Pride and Prejudice*, 177–8.
64. Virginia Woolf, quoted by J. A. Bramley, *Contemp. Rev.*, 193, ff. 149–53.
65. *Antiq.*, I, 90, Ch. VII.
66. *Ibid.*, II, 152–3, Ch. XIII.
67. *Ibid.*, 170, Ch. XIV.
68. *Ibid.*, 290, Ch. XXIII.

PART SIX

Chapter 1

1. ACLC, III, 85–6, Cadell to Constable, 10/11/15.
2. *Letters*, I, 493, John Ballantyne (Nov.–Dec. 1815).
3. *Ibid.*, 497, John Ballantyne, n.d.
4. JGL, III, 68.
5. Smiles, *Murray*, I, 457, James Ballantyne to Blackwood, 4/4/16; Oliphant, *Wm. Blackwood & Sons*, I, 57.
6. *Letters*, IV, 292, Lady Louisa Stuart, 11/14/16, and fn. 1.
7. Smiles, *Murray*, I, 457.
8. *Ibid.*
9. *Ibid.*, 462, Blackwood to Murray, n.d., but sometime after 6/21/16, probably in July.
10. Smiles, *Murray*, I, 457.
11. JGL, III, 68.
12. *Letters*, I, 497, John Ballantyne, 4/29/16.
13. Smiles, *Murray*, I, 457.
14. *Letters*, I, 497.
15. *Ibid.*, 498.
16. JGL, III, 69.
17. NLS MS, 3112, f. 165, John Ballantyne to Constable & Co., 5/11/16. On these proposals, cf. *Letters*, III, 509, Murray, 10/20/14; IV, 69, Murray, 6/10/15; 278, Constable, 10/10/16; 279, Constable, 10/26/16; 294, Lady Louisa Stuart, 11/14/16. Scott says this work had long since been written and merely needed revision, but it has never come to light. Possibly he used it later in his *Tables of a Grandfather*.
18. *Letters*, I, 476, John Ballantyne, 10/31/14, says "It is a sheet anchor," which implies that the *Regis-*

*ter* is at the least making some profit.

19. ACLC, III, 92, fn. 1, Cadell to Constable, 6/26/16.

20. Grierson, *Scott*, 138, fn. 1, Cadell to Constable, 12/3/16.

21. Smiles, *Murray*, I, 462, Blackwood to Murray, n.d., but, as noted, around July 1816. And WS himself had previously offered the *History* to Murray—see *Letters*, III, 509, Murray, 10/20/14; IV, 69, Murray, 6/10/15—although the texts do not indicate precisely whether Murray had accepted.

22. Smiles, *Murray*, I, 463.

23. *Ibid.*, 460.

24. *Letters*, IV, 183, Morritt (Feb.–Mar. 1816).

25. *Ibid.*, 269, Morritt, 8/26/16.

26. Bryant, *Elegance*, 366–7.

27. *Letters*, IV, 227, Morritt, 4/19?/16; cf. 213, Southey, 4/17/16.

28. *Ibid.*, 228.

29. *Ibid.*, 227.

30. *Ibid.*, 257, Constable, 6/18/16.

31. *Ibid.*, 189, Train, 3/7/16, in which WS tells Train he will be in from May to June, and fn. 1, Train's letter of 2/12/16.

32. NLS MS, 3277, f. 58 *et seq.*, Train's *Brief Sketch*.

33. *Ibid.* Some of this is also in JGL, II, 86, but with the dialogue more highly colored.

34. *Ibid.*

35. *Cf. Letters*, IV, 343, Lady Abercorn, 12/28/16.

36. *Letters*, IV, 263–4, Joanna Baillie, 7/12/16.

37. *Ibid.*, 268, Morritt, 8/21/16.

38. *Ibid.*, 267–8.

39. Train, *Brief Sketch;* also in JGL, III, 85.

40. Smiles, *Murray*, I, 466, Blackwood to Murray, 8/23/16.

41. NLS MS, 861, f. 38, James Ballantyne to Blackwood, 9/9/16.

42. JGL, III, 71; 72–3, fn. 1; quoting Blackwood to James Ballantyne, 10/5/16.

43. *Letters*, IV, 226, James Ballantyne, 10/3/16. JGL, III, 72, gives a melodramatically heightened version of this letter, but no MS source is known to exist: "I have received Blackwood's impudent proposal. G–d damn his soul! Tell him and

his coadjutor that I belong to the Black Hussars of literature, who neither give nor receive criticism. I'll be cursed but this is the most impudent proposal that was ever made."

44. JGL, III, 72, fn. 1; also quoted in *Letters*, IV, 276, fn. 1.

45. JGL, III, 72–3.

46. NLS MS, 2566, Glen MS, quoting WS, to unknown correspondent, 12/21/16.

47. Bryant, *Elegance*, 367.

48. *Letters*, IV, 227, Morritt, gives date as May, but I think 4/19/16.

49. *Letters*, IV, 265, Morritt, 8/21/16; 270, Morritt, 8/26/16, showing WS expected to meet Morritt at Jedburgh 9/15/16.

50. *Ibid.*, 295, Morritt, 11/22/16.

51. See Lockhart, *Letter to Adam Ferguson*, 56–62; cf. Wright, *Life*, 351, 373–6, and *Letters*, I, 509–12, James Ballantyne, 11/12/16.

52. Lockhart, *Letter to Adam Ferguson*, 57–8, quoting James Ballantype to WS, 10/25/16. The dates would be Monday, 10/21/16, and Wednesday, 10/23/16.

53. NLS MS, 861, f. 57, James Ballantyne to WS, 10/12/16.

54. Lockhart, *Letter to Adam Ferguson*, 59, quoting James Ballantyne to WS, 10/28/16; also *Letters*, I, 509, fn. 1.

55. NLS MS, 861, f. 70, John Ballantyne to WS.

56. *Letters*, I, 505, John Ballantyne, 10/26/16.

57. *Ibid.*, IV, 278, Constable, 10/10/16.

58. *Ibid.*, I, 506, John Ballantyne, 10/26/16, says WS will be finished by 11/2 or 11/3/16.

59. *Letters*, IV, 302, Joanna Baillie, 11/26/16; cf. 289, Terry, 11/12/16.

60. *Ibid.*, 286, Surtees, 11/12/16. The first part of the *History* was published in 1816.

61. *Letters*, IV, 289–90, Terry, 11/12/16.

62. *Ibid.*, 290, and fn. 1.

63. *Ibid.*, 289; cf 295, Morritt, 11/22/16.

64. *Ibid.*, 290.

65. *Ibid.*, 286.

66. *Ibid.*, 302. Dr. Corson writes me: "It is probably a myth that Scott got the Tolbooth stones from the

magistrates. He certainly had to pay for those to the demolition contractor."
67. *Ibid.*, 289.
68. *Ibid.*, 286.
69. *Ibid.*, 301; *cf.* 333, Terry, 12/28/16.
70. *Ibid.*, 296, Morritt, 11/22/16.
71. *Ibid.*, tells Morritt he expects publication by 11/29 or 11/30/16.
72. Grierson, *Scott*, 137, John Murray to Blackwood, 12/13/16.
73. *Letters*, IV, 296.
74. *Ibid.*, 288, Terry, 11/12/16.
75. *Ibid.*, 291-2, Lady Louisa Stuart, 11/14/16.
76. *Ibid.*, 296.
77. *Ibid.*, 288.
78. *Ibid.*, 293, Lady Louisa Stuart, 11/14/16.
79. *Ibid.*, 288, fn. 1, Terry to WS, 12/5/16.
80. *Ibid.*, 293, fn. 2, Lady Louisa Stuart to WS, 12/5/16.
81. *Ibid.*, 283, Lady Abercorn, 11/?/16.
82. *Ibid.*, 307, Lady Abercorn, 11/29/16.
83. *Ibid.*
84. *Ibid.*, 340, fn. 1, Lady Abercorn to WS, 12/7/16.
85. *Ibid.*, 340, Lady Abercorn, 12/28/16.
86. *Ibid.*, 345, fn. 1, Lady Louisa Stuart to WS, 1/11/17.
87. *Ibid.*, X, 172-3, fn. 2, Lady Louisa Stuart to WS, 3/1/27.
88. *Ibid.*, IV, 345, fn. 1.
89. JGL, III, 83.
90. Smiles, *Murray*, I, 469, Murray to WS, 12/14/16.
91. *Ibid.*

### Chapter 2

1. *Letters*, IV, 413, Morritt, 3/18/17.
2. *Ibid.*, 309, Buccleuch, 12/11/16.
3. Some of my treatment parallels that of Buchan, *SWS*, 167.
4. *Letters*, IV, 309-10.
5. *Ibid.*, 312, fn. 1, Buccleuch to WS, 12/13/16.
6. *Ibid.*, 312-4, Buccleuch, 12/14/16.
7. *Ibid.*, 318, Murray, 12/18/16; *cf.* 389, Murray, 2/9/17.
8. JGL, III, 82-3, fn. 1.
9. *Misc. Prose*, XIX, 1-86; *Quarterly Review*, Jan. '17.
10. *Letters*, IV, 381, Lady Louisa Stuart, 1/31/17, and 386, fn. 1.
11. *Misc. Prose*, XIX, 3-4.
12. *Ibid.*, 28.
13. *Letters*, IV, 319, Murray, 12/18/16; 366, Croker, 1/10/17; 377, Murray, 1/22/17.
14. *Ibid.*, 363-4, Murray, 1/10/17.
15. Huntington MS, printed in *Huntington Library Quarterly*, II, 341, WS to Croker (after 1/20/17).
16. *Letters*, IV, 363, fn. 1, Byron to Murray, 3/3/17; *cf.* Partington, *Post-Bag*, 124-5, Joanna Baillie to WS. The review appeared in the *Quarterly Review*, XVI, Oct. '16, and is collected in *Misc. Prose* IV, 351-99.
17. *Letters*, IV, 364, fn., Byron to Moore, 3/10/17.
18. *Poetical Works*, X, Intro., 9-10. JGL III, 88, says published "less than a month after the *Tales*," which would have been at the end of Dec. 1816; but *Letters*, IV, 381, Lady Louisa Stuart, 1/31/17, and 389, Morritt, 1/31/17, show that it had just appeared.
19. *Letters*, IV, 383, Morritt, 1/31/17.
20. *Poetical Works*, XI, *Harold the Dauntless*, 151, Canto I, 1, 5-10.
21. Perhaps both Byron's and Scott's poetical work were in this respect influenced by John Hookham Frere's *Whistlecraft*.
22. *Poetical Works*, XI, 352, "Search," I, 5-10.
23. *Ibid.*, 354-5, "Search," V, 1-4, 12-3, 5-6.
24. *Letters*, IV, 383, Morritt, 1/31/17.
25. *The Sale-Room* was published weekly between 1/4/17 and 7/12/17 and came to 28 numbers. *Cf.* JGL, III, 89, and *Ballantyne Press*, as well as Glen's comments in NLS MS, 2553, f. 259. *Letters*, I, 513, John Ballantyne, 12/26/16, shows that WS supplied the contents of Nos. 1, 2, and 3 as well, and that he suggested James Bayley as a contributor. See also John Ballantyne's letters to Bayley and WS about *The Sale-Room* and *Letters*, IV, 357, fn. 1. No. 4 contained John Ballantyne's "Fifteen Days in Paris."
26. NLS MS, 2566, John Ballantyne's *Diary*, 1/1/17, 1/20/17, 3/13/17.
27. *Letters*, IV, 498, Robert Johnstone, 4/21/17, and V, 484-5, fn. 2.

28. *Ibid.*, 513, John Ballantyne, 12/26/16.
29. *Ibid.*, 365, John Murray, 1/10/17.
30. *Ibid.*, 394-5, Joanna Baillie, 3/1/17.
31. *Ibid.*, 409, Joanna Baillie, 3/17/17.
32. *Ibid.*, 407-8; 396, Terry, 3/?/17.
33. *Ibid.*, 408; JGL, III, 99; *Fraser's Mag.*, 184, Gillies, "Recollections."
34. *Ibid.*, 413, Morritt, 3/18/17; 408.
35. *Fraser's Mag.*, 184, Gillies, "Recollections."
36. *Letters*, IV, 413.
37. *Ibid.*, 408.
38. *Ibid.*, 394, fn. 2.
39. *Ibid.*, 396, Terry, 3/?/17.
40. *Ibid.*, 408.
41. *Ibid.*, 418, Mrs. Clephane, 3/23/17.
42. *Ibid.*, 414, Morritt, 3/18/17.
43. *Ibid.*, 409.
44. *Ibid.*, 418; *cf.* 401, fn. 1.
45. *Ibid.*, 413, Morritt, 3/18/17.
46. *Ibid.*, 415, Terry, 3/22/17.
47. JGL, III, 107; *Poetical Works*, XI, 348.
48. *Letters*, IV, 403-6, Terry, 3/12/17.
49. *Ibid.*, 396-401, Terry, 3/?/17, and information supplied by Dr. Corson. Atkinson was also presently employed by Lord Montagu to rebuild Ditton.
50. *Letters*, IV, 421, Mrs. Clephane, 3/23/17.
51. NLS MS, 2889, f. 135, Charlotte to Wm. Scott, 3/20/17.
52. *Letters*, IV, 424, Terry, 3/29/17.
53. NLS MS, 3653, f. 53, WS to G.H. Gordon, 3/23/17.
54. *Letters*, IV, 526, James Ballantyne (dated "After March"; actually 4/13/17).
55. *Ibid.*, 327, Terry, 12/25/16; 439, Terry, 4/29/17.
56. *Ibid.*, 339, Terry 2/28/16.
57. JGL, III, 108-9.
58. *Letters*, IV, 427-8, Laidlaw, 4/5/17.
59. *Ibid.*, 237, C. Erskine, 5/16/17.
60. *Ibid.*, 326, Richardson, 12/23/16.
61. The new purchase had been in negotiation since the preceding spring. See NLS MS, 3836, f. 35, WS to C. Erskine, 5/26/16; MS, 3836, f. 36, WS to Usher, 12/4/16; *Letters*, IV, 324-5, C. Erskine, 12/21-5/16.
62. *Letters*, V, 152, Laidlaw, 5/19/18.
63. *Ibid.*, IV, 435, Ferguson, 4/24/17. Actually, Usher did not vacate and the Fergusons get in until a year later; see *Letters*, V, 151-2, Laidlaw, 5/19/18, and 152-3, Ferguson, 5/23/18.
64. *Letters*, IV, 388, Terry, 2/9/17.
65. *Ibid.*, 333, Terry, 12/28/16.
66. *Ibid.*, 334, 337.
67. *Ibid.*, 335.
68. *Ibid.*, 336-7.
69. *Ibid.*, 334-5.
70. *Ibid.*, 338.
71. *Ibid.*, 422, Terry, 3/28/17, and 439, Terry, 4/29/17.
72. *Ibid.*, 336.
73. *Ibid.*, 425, Terry, 3/29/17.
74. *Ibid.*, 436, Terry, 4/29/17.
75. *Ibid.*, 335, Terry, 12/28/16; 435-6, Terry.
76. *Ibid.*, 335.
77. *Ibid.*, 334. Dr. Corson notes that many of the plans so excitedly proposed in this paragraph were never carried out.
78. NLS MS, 852, f. 193, Terry, 4/12/17.
79. *Letters*, IV, 398, Terry, 3/?/17. Here, again, the notions in this letter differ from the final reality. The stone at Kaeside was graywacke, not whinstone, and Abbotsford has no rubble work.
80. *Letters*, IV, 399.
81. *Ibid.*, 446, Southey, 5/7/17.
82. *Ibid.*, 447-8.
83. *Ibid.*, 447.
84. *Ibid.*, 448.
85. *Ibid.*, 431, James Ballantyne, 4/16/17.
86. *Ibid.*, 430, fn. 2; 383, Morritt, 1/31/17.
87. *Ibid.*; Oliphant, I, 80.
88. Oliphant, *Wm. Blackwood and Sons*, I, 80, James Ballantyne to Blackwood, 4/7/17.
89. *Ibid.*, 81, Blackwood to James Ballantyne, 4/7/17.
90. *Ibid.*, James Ballantyne to Blackwood (Oliphant says "the same day," but misdated; probably 4/17/17. See *Letters*, IV, 430-1, below).
91. *Letters*, IV, 430-1, James Ballantyne, 4/16/17.
92. *Ibid.*, I, 514, John Ballantyne, 4/?/17.
93. *Ibid.*, John Ballantyne, 5/3/17.
94. *Ibid.*, 515.
95. JGL, III, 112-3.
96. *Ibid.*
97. *Ibid.*
98. *Ibid.*, 114.

99. *Ibid.*
100. *Letters*, I, 514, fn. 3, John Ballantyne to James Ballantyne, 5/6/17. If John's calculation is accurate, the profits must have been over £7,200.
101. Buchan, *SWS*, 169, and 169 fn.
102. *Fraser's Mag.*, Jan. 1836, Gillies, "Recollections," 104. Gillies erroneously dates 1818, but plainly at this time.
103. *Ibid.*
104. *Ibid.*
105. *Poetical Works*, XI, 336–7. The poem was composed in Aug. 1817.

Chapter 3

1. *Letters*, IV, 444, Southey, 5/7/17.
2. *Ibid.*, 493, Morritt, 8/11/17.
3. *Ibid.*, 455, Morritt, 5/27/17.
4. *Ibid.*, 494, Morritt.
5. *Ibid.*, 485, Jeffrey, 8/5/17.
6. *Ibid.*, 493–4.
7. *Ibid.*, 470, Buccleuch, 7/9/17; NLS MS, 3109, f. 87, Phillips, 7/29/17, says they left 7/12/17.
8. JGL, III, 124–5; *Family Letters*, 41, Sophia to Miss Millar, 8/3/17.
9. *Letters*, IV, 471–2, Buccleuch, 7/18/17. JGL dates this letter 7/30/17, but this is impossible. WS says (*Letters*, IV, 470) he expects to arrive at Drumlanrig on the evening of 7/18 or morning of 7/19; then (*Letters*, IV, 472) changes it to "this evening instead of last night as we had intended." This letter is therefore probably from Sanquhar around 7/18.
10. *Ibid.*, 474–8, Baillie, 7/24/17.
11. *Ibid.*, 481, Buccleuch, 7/30/17; 479, Donaldson, 7/27/17.
12. *Ibid.*, 464, Montagu, 6/8/17.
13. *Ibid.*, 489, Sharpe, 8/7/17.
14. *Ibid.*, 484, Wilkie, 8/2/17.
15. *Ibid.*, 480, Constable, 7/29/17.
16. *Ibid.*, 492, fn. 1, Constable to WS, 8/16/17.
17. *Ibid.*, 492, Constable, 8/10/17 and fn. 2.
18. *Ibid.*, 492, fn. 1; 502, Constable, 8/18/17.
19. *Ibid.*, III, 449, Hartstonge, 6/3/14; Dr. Corson, "The 'Border Antiquities,'" Edinburgh Univ., Lib., 24; *Misc. Prose*, VII, 1–139.
20. *Letters*, IV, 503, James Ballantyne, 8/28/17.
21. *Ibid.*, 499, James Ballantyne, 8/16/17; 492, fn. 1.
22. *Ibid.*, 492, fn. 1.
23. *Ibid.*, 499.
24. *Ibid.*, 489, Sharpe, 8/7/17.
25. *Ibid.*, 494, Morritt.
26. Bryant, *Elegance*, 347.
27. *Ibid.*, 341.
28. *Letters*, IV, 294–5.
29. *Ibid.*, 495–6. The allusion to "the sons of Zeruiah" is from II Samuel, 3:39.
30. *Family Letters*, 42, Sophia to Miss Millar, 8/3/17.
31. *Letters*, IV, 497, Johnston, 8/11/17.
32. *Ibid.*, 500, Johnston, 8/16/17.
33. *Ibid.*, 526, Terry, 9/26/17.
34. *Hawick Arch. Soc.*, Sess. 1932, 6th meeting, 9/13/1932, 28.
35. *R. Roy*, II, 63.
36. *Hawick Arch. Soc.*, 28.
37. *Letters*, IV, 497, Lady Byron, 8/14/17, shows that WS was expecting her; I agree with Grierson, *Scott*, 161–2, that the visit preceded Irving's.
38. *Letters*, IV, 522, Joanna Baillie, 9/26/17.
39. *Ibid.*, 513.
40. *Ibid.*, 523, fn. 1.
41. Irving, *Abbotsford*, 521–2. For date, see *Life and Letters of W.I.*, I, 285.
42. *Letters*, III, 259, Brevoort, 4/23/13.
43. Irving, *Abbotsford*, 523.
44. *Ibid.*, 522.
45. *Ibid.*, 523.
46. *Ibid.*, 524.
47. *Ibid.*, 526.
48. *Ibid.*, 525.
49. *Ibid.*, 528.
50. *Ibid.*, 530–1.
51. *Ibid.*, 533.
52. *Ibid.*, 534.
53. *Ibid.*, 534–6.
54. *Ibid.*, 536.
55. *Ibid.*, 538–9. Irving calls the dog "Finette," obviously a slip of memory, and also describes it as a spaniel; Fenella was a setter.
56. *Ibid.*, 540–1.
57. *Ibid.*, 545.
58. *Ibid.*, 549.
59. *Ibid.*, 542.
60. *Ibid.*, 554–5.
61. *Ibid.*, 558.
62. *Ibid.*, 561.

63. *Ibid.*, 549.
64. *Ibid.*, 563–4.
65. *Ibid.*, 566.
66. *Ibid.*, 567–8.
67. *Ibid.*, 568–70.
68. *Ibid.*, 571.
69. *Ibid.*, 572–3; *Life and Letters of W.I.*, I, 286.
70. *Letters*, IV, 506, Constable, 9/5/17.
71. *Ibid.*, 504, James Ballantyne, 9/?/17.
72. *Ibid.*, 508, James Ballantyne, 9/10/17; 519, Constable, 9/21/17.
73. JGL, III, 148–9 (in *Letters*, V, 280, John Ballantyne, misdated 1818; it refers to the arrangements for *Tales of My Landlord*, Second Series, and must therefore be Oct.–Nov. 1817).
74. *Ibid.*
75. *Letters*, I, 517, John Ballantyne, 9/10/17; 519, John Ballantyne, 5/16/17.
76. *Ibid.*, IV, 507, James Ballantyne, 9/10/17.
77. *Ibid.*, I, 516, John Ballantyne, 5/6/17.
78. *Ibid.*, IV, 510, James Ballantyne, 10/14/17; I, 519, John Ballantyne, 9/10/17; IV, 507.
79. *Ibid.*, IV, 510.
80. JGL, III, 149. He is mistaken, though, in depicting John Ballantyne as the agent; during the whole of this time, as Scott's letters make clear, John was in London, and James negotiated with Constable.
81. *Cf.* Wright, *Life*, 402–3.
82. JGL, III, 150.
83. ACLC, III, 98–9, Cadell to Constable, 1/22/18. Later, however, when JGL was writing his biography of Scott, Cadell told JGL there had geen a two-thirds loss. This statement may not be altogether reliable; after the Constable bankruptcy in 1826, Cadell was anxious to represent his former partner as a bad businessman who had ruined the firm by his extravagance and ill-judged bargains.
84. *Letters*, IV, 532, James Ballantyne, 9/30/17.
85. *Ibid.*, 512, James Ballantyne, 9/14/17.
86. *Ibid.*, 532.
87. *Ibid.*, 533.
88. *Ibid.*, V, 12, Constable, 11/10/17.
89. *Ibid.*, XII, 431, John Ballantyne, 11/14/17.
90. *Ibid.*, V, 13, Constable, 11/16/17.
91. ACLC, III, 103, fn., Cadell to Constable, n.d.
92. *Cf.* Grierson's discussion, *Scott*, 141–4.
93. *Ibid.*, 141.
94. ACLC, III, 105, Constable & Co. to WS, 11/12/17.
95. NLS MS, 322, Cadell to Constable, 11/28/17.
96. *Ibid.*, 11/24/17.
97. *Ibid.*, 3836, f. 80, WS to unknown correspondent, 10/9/17.
98. *Letters*, I, 522, John Ballantyne, 10/11/17.
99. *Ibid.*, IV, 542, Terry, 10/24/17.
100. *Ibid.*, V, 13, Constable, 11/10/17.
101. *Ibid.*, 3, Terry 10/29/17. Unlike some of Scott's other proposals for the house, all these plans *were* carried out.
102. JGL, III, 137.
103. Irving, *Abbotsford*, 574.
104. *Letters*, V, 13.
105. *Ibid.*, 23, Joanna Baillie, 12/12/17.
106. *Ibid.*, 29, Richardson, 12/13/17.
107. JGL, III, 147.
108. NLS MS, 1750, f. 180, WS to Wm. Erskine, 12/7/17.
109. *Letters*, V, 34, Buccleuch, 12/26/17.
110. *Letters*, V, 37, James Ballantyne; this quatrain-note is here dated 12/31/17, but JGL says, with much more likelihood, that it was around 12/21/17. *Rob Roy* was published 12/31/17, and some time would have been need for printing the last pages, binding, etc.
111. JGL, III, 180.
112. *Letters*, IV, 519, Constable, 9/21/17; 541, 10/11/17; 534, Mrs. Scott, 10/18/17.
113. *Ibid.*, 470, Buccleuch, 9/17/17.
114. *Ibid.*, 543, Johnstone, 10/27/17.
115. *Ibid.*, 4, Terry, 10/29/17.
116. *Ibid.*, Morritt, 1/14/18.

## Chapter 4

1. *B. Dwarf*, 203, Ch. II.
2. *Ibid.*
3. *Ibid.*, 204.
4. *Ibid.*
5. *Ibid.*, 247, Ch. VI.

6. *Ibid.*, 258–9, Ch. VII.
7. C. Keith, *Author of Waverley.*
8. *B. Dwarf*, 246, Ch. VI.
9. *Ibid.*, 289–90, Ch. X.
10. *Ibid.*, 270, Ch. VIII.
11. *Ibid.*, 237, Ch. V.
12. *Ibid.*, 209, Ch. III.
13. *Ibid.*, 229–30, Ch. IV.
14. *Ibid.*, 359, Ch. XVI.
15. *Ibid.*, 360, Ch. XVI.
16. *Ibid.*, 359, Ch. XVI.
17. *Ibid.*, 361, Ch. XVI.
18. *Ibid.*, 179, Ch. XVI, Hazlitt, quoted by Lang in Ed.'s Intro.
19. JGL, III, 84.
20. *B. Dwarf*, 332, Ch. XIII.
21. *Ibid.*, 335, Ch. XIV.
22. *Ibid.*, 298, Ch. X.
23. *Ibid.*, 357, Ch. XVI.
24. *Ibid.*, 368, Ch. XVII.
25. *Ibid.*, 369, Ch. XVII.
26. *Ibid.*, 260, Ch. VII.
27. *Ibid.*, 293–4, Ch. X.
28. *O. Mort.*, I, 84, Ch. VII.
29. *Ibid.*, 86, Ch. VII.
30. *Ibid.*, 87, Ch. VII.
31. *Ibid.*, 109, Ch. VII.
32. *Ibid.*, 73, Ch. VI.
33. *Ibid.*, 39–40, Ch. IV.
34. *Ibid.*, 70, Ch. VI.
35. *Ibid.*, 290–1, Ch. XXI.
36. *Ibid.*, 166, Ch. XII.
37. *Ibid.*, 172, Ch. XII.
38. *Ibid.*, II, 162, Ch. XIV.
39. *Ibid.*, I, 190–1, Ch. XIII.
40. *Ibid.*, II, 261, Ch. XXI.
41. *Ibid.*, 44, Ch. IV.
42. *Ibid.*, 151, Ch. XII.
43. *Ibid.*, 183, Ch. XV.
44. *Ibid.*, 183, Ch. XV.
45. *Ibid.*, 163, Ch. XIV.
46. See Rait, "WS and Thos. McCrie," 3–41.
47. *Ibid.*, 28.
48. Craig, *Scottish Literature*, 183–4, 187.
49. Rait, "WS and Thos. McCrie," 30.
50. *O. Mort.* I, 255–6, Ch. XVIII.
51. Craig, *Scottish Literature*, 187.
52. *O. Mort.*, II, 172, Ch. XIV.
53. *Ibid.*, I, 181, Ch. XIII.
54. Rait, "WS and Thos. McCrie," 20–1.
55. *Cf.* Tillyard, *Epic Strain*, 100; Daiches, *Literary Essays*, 57–8, the latter of whom thinks the structure bad.
56. Tillyard, *Epic Strain*, 99.

57. *R. Roy*, I, 9–10, Ch. I.
58. *Ibid.*, II, 286, Ch. XIV.
59. *Cf.* Davie, *Heyday*, 60–1.
60. *R. Roy*, II, 153, Ch. XI.
61. *Ibid.*, 157–8, Ch. XI.
62. *Ibid.*, 268, Ch. XVIII.
63. *Ibid.*, 270, Ch. XVIII.
64. *Ibid.*, 134, Ch. X.
65. *Ibid.*, 121, Ch. IX.
66. *Letters*, V, 50, Morritt, 1/14/18.
67. Buchan, *SWS*, 185.
68. *R. Roy*, II, 24, Ch. II.
69. *Ibid.*, 43, Ch. IV.
70. *Ibid.*, 34, Ch. III.
71. Buchan, *SWS*, 184.
72. Tillyard, *Epic Strain*, 104.
73. *R. Roy*, II, 243–4, Ch. XVI.
74. *Ibid.*
75. Diana, too, reveals a filial loyalty shown neither by Frank nor by Rashleigh and his oafish brothers. In a way, she is an example from which Frank learns, though not till much later does he know that the mysterious Vaughan who commands her obedience is her father.

Chapter 5

1. JGL, III, 148.
2. *Ibid.*
3. *Letters*, V, 43, Terry, 1/8/18.
4. *Ibid.*, 44; NLS MS, 2889, f. 752, WS to Wm. Scott, 1/2/18.
5. *Ibid.*, 58, Richardson, 1/16/18. The sawmill is at Huntly Burn and is still functioning.
6. *Letters*, V, 44–5, Buccleuch, 1/10/18. Mrs. Goldie's letter (Edin. U. Lib.) is postmarked 1/30/17.
7. *H. Mid.*, Intro., xxv–xxviii.
8. ACLC, III, 106–7, Cadell to Constable, 1/15/18.
9. *Ibid.*, 107, Cadell to Constable, 1/30/18.
10. *Letters*, V, 39, Laidlaw, 1/?/18.
11. *Ibid.*, 113, Southey, 3/23/18.
12. *Ibid.*, 73, Laidlaw, 2/?/18.
13. *Ibid.*, 39–40, 1/?/18.
14. *Ibid.*, 39–40. I have a MS letter NLS MS, 1750, f. 175) dated 11/22/17, which includes these words in a different context.
15. *Letters*, V, 61, Terry, 1/17/18.
16. *Ibid.*, 63, Terry, 1/23/18.
17. *Ibid.*, V, 65–6, Sanderson and Paterson, 1/30/18.
18. *Ibid.*, 69, Laidlaw, 2/?/18.

19. NLS MS, 969, f. 16, WS to Laidlaw, 1/21/18.
20. *Letters*, V, 72, Laidlaw, 2/?/18.
21. *Ibid.*, 69.
22. *Ibid.*, 73.
23. NLS MS, 969, f. 8, WS to Laidlaw, 3/4/18.
24. *Letters*, IV, 428, Laidlaw, 4/5/17.
25. *Huntington Library Quarterly*, 347, Laidlaw, 6/?/17. This letter, from a text manipulated by JGL, is in *Letters*, IV, 465, dated 6/16/17.
26. NLS MS, 969, f. 8, WS to Laidlaw, 7/?/17.
27. *Letters*, V, 70, fn. 1.
28. *Ibid.*, IV, 520, Blackwood, 9/21/17.
29. *Ibid.*, 520–1.
30. *Ibid.*, V, 5, Blackwood, 10/?/17.
31. *Ibid.*, 180, Blackwood (here dated 1818–9, but more likely 1817).
32. Lochhead, *Lockhart*, 27, 35–6.
33. *Ibid.*, 36.
34. *Ibid.*, 35, quoting from Oliphant.
35. JGL does not mention in his *Life of WS*, that he was one of the authors; he merely says "suspected."
36. "Chaldee MS," quoted by Lochhead, *Lockhart*, 37.
37. *Ibid.*, quoted by JGL, III, 165, fn. 1.
38. Ferrier, quoted by Daiches, *Literary Essays*, 124.
39. *Letters*, V, 6, Blackwood, 11/?/17, though *after* 11/14/17, when Scott visited Bowhill.
40. *Letters*, V, 208–9, Sharpe, 11/5/17 —not 1818.
41. *Ibid.*, 7, Blackwood.
42. *Ibid.*, 70–1, Laidlaw (2/?/17), but may be earlier.
43. Oliphant, *Wm. Blackwood and Sons*, I, 67, JGL to Williams, 2/21/18.
44. *Letters*, V, 48–9, Morritt, 1/14/18.
45. *Misc. Prose*, VII, 342–3, "Regalia."
46. *Letters*, IV, 372, Buccleuch, 1/14/17.
47. *Croker Papers*, I, 103, Croker to WS, 1/19/18. See also WS's correspondence with Croker on this subject in *Letters*, V, 123–6, 9/1/16; in *Huntington Library Quarterly*, 339–43, 1/11/17, after 1/20/17, 1/16/18; and *Letters*, V, 74, 2/11/18. Various omissions from the texts of *Letters* are in *HLQ*, 343–5. See also *Letters*, V, 51–3, Buccleuch, 1/14/18; 59–60,

1/17/18; and Buccleuch to WS in *HLQ*, 341, 1/20/17.
48. *Letters*, V, 74, Croker, 2/4/18.
49. *Misc Prose*, VII, 341; *Letters*, V, 49, Morritt, 1/14/18.
50. *Misc. Prose*, VII, 345.
51. *Ibid.*, 302, 306–7; *Letters*, V, 75, Croker, 2/7/18.
52. *Misc., Prose*, XII, 346–7. *Letters*, V, 278, Constable, 2/14/18: "The Commissioners adjourned to my house and got half *fou* to conclude the joyful occasion and wash the dust out of their throats."
53. JGL, III, 157–8.
54. *Misc. Prose*, VII, 347; *Letters*, V, 81–2, Henry Dundas, 2/14/18; 85, Lord Melville (2nd Viscount), 2/19/18; 157–8, Buccleuch, 5/25/18. But *cf. Letters*, 87, fn. 1.
55. *Letters*, V, 83–6.
56. *Ibid.*, 84–5, Lord Melville (2nd Viscount), 2/19/18.
57. *Ibid.*, 178, Buccleuch, 8/29/18. The amount of Ferguson's allowance was not confirmed till 4/16/21— see *Letters*, VI, 407, Ferguson.
58. JGL, III, 240, Lady Compton had heard of Scott's forthcoming honor by 11/17/18—see *Letters*, V, 211, fn. 1. As the end of this note implies, WS angled for the elevation a good deal more vigorously than he would say in letters to his friends. See also *Letters*, V, 87, fn. 1—Adams's account of the circumstances leading to the baronetcy.
59. ACLC, III, 107–8, Cadell to Constable, 2/6/18.
60. *Ibid.*, also, *Letters*, V, 55, Lady Louisa Stuart, 1/16/18.
61. *Letters*, V, 55–6; *cf.* also *Misc. Prose*, VII, 295–357.
62. *Letters*, V, 108–9, Murray, 3/23/18; 130, Murray, 4/26/18; 136, Murray, 5/4/18; 140, Murray, 5/15/18; 168, Murray, 7/17/18; 176, Murray, 8/22/18—the last enclosing the *Childe Harold* review.
63. *Ibid.*, 101, Constable, n.d., but after 3/9/18.
64. *Ibid.*, 100, Terry, 3/2/18; NLS MS, 1753, f. 217, WS to Terry, n.d., but late Feb.; NLS MS, 852, f. 259, WS 4/1/18.
65. Yale Univ. MS, WS to Bullock, 3/4/18.

66. NLS MS, 969, f. 70, WS to Laidlaw, 4/7/18.
67. *Letters*, V, 102, Hartstonge, to Terry, Mar. or Apr. 1818.
68. *Ibid.*, 110, Murray, 3/23/18.
69. *Ibid.*, 114, Southey, 3/23/18.
70. *Ibid.*, 110.
71. *Ibid.*, 115, Southey.
72. *Ibid.*, 115–6.
73. *Ibid.*, 116–7..
74. *Ibid.*, 121, Buccleuch, 4/24/18.
75. NLS MS, 2889, f. 156, WS to Wm. Scott, 4/11/18, saying she "arrived yesterday."
76. *Letters*, V, 133–4, Terry, 4/30/18.
77. *Ibid.*, 136–7, Terry, 5/4/18; *cf.* 138–9, Hartstonge, 5/13/18.
78. *Ibid.*, 133.
79. *Ibid.*, 136, Murray, 5/4/18; NLS MS, 3653, f. 168, Fordyce, 5/12/18.
80. JGL, III, 175.
81. *Letters*, V, 135, Terry, 4/30/18.
82. JGL, II, 332, places this episode in 1814, but that date is impossible. His host, Wm. Menzies, in a letter printed in the *Scotsman*, 11/11/1932, says he did not live in George Street until 1818. But the time could not have been much later than I am putting it, for before the end of May, JGL had met WS, and visited him in Castle Street and would therefore have known where he lived and whose hand it was that they had seen.
83. JGL, III, 181; Lochhead, *Lockhart*, 28; NLS MS, 3925, Lockhart,, probably to Blackwood, since it gives thanks for "Maga" (the nickname of *Blackwood's Magazine*), 4/24/18.
84. Lochhead, *Lockhart*, 4–11, 16–7, 22, 28.
85. Chaldee MS.
86. JGL, III, 181–2.
87. *Ibid.*, 183.
88. *Ibid.*, 184–5. JGL says, "regilt" and "a large proportion in blue morocco," but this is inaccurate—only a few; and only a few, furthermore, are "stamped," as JGL says, "with his device of the portcullis, and his motto."
90. *Letters*, V, 153–4, Buccleuch, 5/25/18. *Not* in Jan., as JGL says.
91. *Ibid.*, 145, Maria Edgeworth, 5/10–5/18.
92. *Ibid.*, 279, Heber, 4/27/18, and fn. 1.
93. *Ibid.*, 151–2, Laidlaw, 5/23/18. Usher moved out, and presumably Ferguson moved in, around 5/26–7/18.
94. *Ibid.*, 163–4, Terry, 6/17/18; 171, Terry, 7/25/18.
95. Inferrable from the fact that WS sent Terry proofs of the last volume on 7/10/18; see below. The printing and binding would take about ten days.
96. *Letters*, V, 169, Terry, 7/10/18.
97. Grierson, *Scott*, 165. The book was *not* published in June, as JGL says.
98. JGL, III, 198–9. Grierson says Anne coined "The Great Unknown." *Blackwood's* used it in Apr. and May 1818 (JGL, III, 81, 532).
99. *Ibid.*, 199.
100. *Ibid.*, 199–200.
101. *Ibid.*, 200.
102. *Ibid.*, 201.
103. *Ibid.*, 208–10. Quotes Lady Louisa's letter inaccurately; it is also in MacCunn, *Sir W's Friends*, 216. Later, the reviews were not so enthusiastic; *Blackwood's Mag.* damned it, and other reviews were highly critical.

Chapter 6

1. ACLC, III, 109, Constable to Cadell, 6/12/18.
2. *Ibid.*, 110.
3. *Ibid.*, Constable to Cadell, 6/15/18.
4. *Ibid.*, 111, Cadell to Constable, 8/10/18.
5. *Ibid.*, 112, Cadell to Constable, 11/9/18.
6. JGL, III, 201, 203.
7. *Letters*, I, 516, John Ballantyne, 9/6/17; IV, 498, James Ballantyne, 8/16/17.
8. *Ibid.*, IV, 505–6, James Ballantyne, 9/3/17.
9. *Ibid.*, 504, James Ballantyne, 9/?/17.
10. *Ibid.*, 519, Constable, 9/21/17.
11. NLS MS, 2566, John Ballantyne's *Diary*, 2/5/18.
12. JGL, III, 201–2.
13. *Ibid.*, 202–4.
14. *Ibid.*, 203.
15. *Ibid.*
16. *Ibid.*, 212.

17. *Letters*, V, 169, Terry, 7/11/18.
18. *Ibid.*, 174, Baillie, 7/?/18.
19. NLS MS, 863, f. 258, WS to Henderson and Curle, 7/24/18.
20. *Letters*, V, 171, Terry, 7/25/18.
21. *Ibid.*, 168, Murray, 7/17/18, saying he will send the review early next week.
22. *Ibid.*, 173, Joanna Baillie, 7/?/18.
23. *Ibid.*, 172, fn. 1, Baillie to WS, 7/6/18.
24. Everett, *Mt. Vernon Papers*, 123.
25. NLS MS, 3891, f. 41, Everett to WS, 3/28/20.
26. Everett, *Mt. Vernon Papers*, 135.
27. *Ibid.*, 139–40.
28. Fales MS, WS to Sir James Stuart, 8/17/18.
29. *Letters*, V, 183, Sir James Stuart, 9/5/18.
30. *Ibid.*, 177, Montagu, 8/17/18.
31. *Ibid.*, 178, Buccleuch, 8/29/18.
32. *Ibid.*, I, 529, John Ballantyne, 8/17/18.
33. NLS MS, 3653, WS to G. H. Gordon, 8/26/18; *Letters*, V, 178, Buccleuch, 8/29/18.
34. *Letters*, V, 186, James Ballantyne, 9/10/18.
35. ACLC, III, 111–2, Cadell to Constable, 9/6/18.
36. JGL, III, 215.
37. *Ibid.*, 216.
38. *Letters*, V, 171, Terry, 7/25/18.
39. *Ibid.*, 196–7, Terry, Sept.–Oct. '18.
40. *Ibid.*, 195, Lockhart, 9/24/18.
41. JGL, III, 216.
42. *Ibid.*, 217.
43. *Ibid.*, 217–8.
44. *Ibid.*, 219–20.
45. *Ibid.*, 220–1.
46. *Ibid.*, 221.
47. *Ibid.*, 222.
48. *Letters*, V, 201, John Ballantyne, 10/5/18.
49. JGL, III, 222–3.
50. *Ibid.*, 225.
51. *Ibid.*, 226.
52. *Ibid.*, 228–9.
53. *Ibid.*, 229–30.
54. *Ibid.*, 230.
55. *Ibid.*, 230–1.
56. *Letters*, V, 203, Lady Abercorn, 10/23/18. See V, 247, Mrs. Clephane, 12/3/18, for indication that Lord and Lady Compton had returned from Italy.
57. NLS MS, 3139, f. 3, WS to Blore,
 10/28/18; *Family Letters*, 48, Sophia to Miss Millar, 10/18/18.
58. *Letters*, V, 210, Morritt, 11/5/18.
59. NLS MS, 3134, f. 172, contract for *Provincial Antiquities*.
60. *Ibid.*, 3139, f. 3, WS to Blore.
61. ACLC, III, 114–5, John Ballantyne to Constable, 11/7/18; to WS, 11/7/18, and WS to John Ballantyne, in the same letter, accepting.
62. JGL, III, 249–50.
63. See n. 61, above; plus ACLC 115–6, John Ballantyne to Constable, 11/10/18, and Constable's acceptance 11/10/18. Actually Constable & Co. were to receive one third and John Ballantyne one sixth, but John sold his share to them; see ACLC, III, 111–8.
64. ACLC, III, 112–3, Cadell to Constable, 11/9/18.
65. *Letters*, V, 213–4, Montagu, 11/12/18.
66. *Ibid.*, 214.
67. *Ibid.*, 234, Montagu, 11/27/18.
68. *Ibid.*, 215–6, Buccleuch, 11/10/18.
69. *Ibid.*, 221, Buccleuch, n.d., but dated 11/20/18 by JGL.
70. *Ibid.*, 203–4, Lockhart, 10/29/18, and 204, fn. 1. WS's quotation is from Horace, *Odes*, I, 111, 9, and should "aes triplex circa pectixe erit."
71. *Letters*, V, 204–5.
72. *Ibid.*, 223, Buccleuch, n.d. JGL dates 11/20/18. JGL also says (III, 247) that WS contributed to Robert Jamieson's edition of *Burt's Letters from a Gentleman in the North of Scotland*, 2 vols., 1818, and (IV, 470) refers to this alleged contribution as an "article." Actually, WS did not write a line for this publication, though he did put in Jamieson's hands, as he wrote Constable (*Letters*, V, 274, 12/18/18), "two or three volumes of manuscript collections respecting the Highlands." WS was much annoyed to find his name used on the title page, and Constable saw that it was removed. See *Letters*, V, 276, fn. 1, Constable to WS, 12/17/18.
73. *Letters*, V, 211, fn. 1, Lady Compton to WS, 11/13/18.
74. *Ibid.*, 243, Lady Compton, 12/2/18.
75. *Ibid.*, 261, Morritt, 12/7/18.
76. JGL, III, 240, reverses the order,

but WS wrote Lady Compton about Lord Sidmouth's letter on 12/2/18, and to Morritt, 12/7/18, that the letter announcing Carpenter's death arrived on Saturday, 12/5/18.

77. *Letters*, V, 255, Mrs. Carpenter, 12/6/18.

78. N.Y.P.L., MS Division, has a Pearson sales catalog listing nine letters from Charlotte to Charles Carpenter. I have not been able to trace their present ownership.

79. *Letters*, V, 259, Morritt, 12/7/18.

80. *Ibid.*, 249, Ferguson, 12/5/18.

81. *Ibid.*, 257, Buccleuch, 12/7/18.

82. *Ibid.*, 260-1, Morritt, 12/7/18.

83. *Ibid.*, 237, Montagu, 11/30/18.

84. *Ibid.*, 234-5, Montagu, 11/27/18.

85. *Ibid.*, 228, Montagu, 11/21/18.

86. *Ibid.*, 238-9, Montagu, 12/1/18.

87. *Ibid.*, 253, fn. 1, Buccleuch to WS, 12/4/18.

88. *Ibid.*, Buccleuch, 12/5/18.

89. *Ibid.*, 265, Montagu, 12/8/18.

90. *Ibid.*, 276-7, fn. 2, Ferguson to WS, 12/30/18.

91. *Ibid.*, 268, Montagu, 12/8/18.

92. *Ibid.*, 276-7, fn. 2; JGL, III, 260.

93. *Ibid.*, 258, Buccleuch, 12/9/18.

94. *Ibid.*, 276-7, Ferguson, 12/31/18.

95. *Ibid.*, 247, Mrs. Clephane, 12/3/18.

96. *Ibid.*, 296, Richardson, here dated 1/18/19, but the NLS MS (3112, f. 171) is dated 1/12/18. Richardson's reply from London (*Letters*, V, 295, fn. 2) is dated 1/19/19.

97. *Letters*, V, 277, Ferguson, 12/31/18.

98. *Ibid.*, 287, Baillie, 1/1/19.

99. *Ibid.*, 295, fn. 2, Richardson to WS, 1/19/19.

100. *Ibid.*, 250, Buccleuch, 12/5/18.

101. *Ibid.*, 289, fn. 1.

102. *Ibid.*, 289, Melville, 1/14/19.

103. *Ibid.*, 291, Ferguson, 1/15/19.

104. *Ibid.*, 289. Rae was not made a Baron of Exchequer, but in the course of 1819 he did become Lord Advocate.

105. *Ibid.*, 291-2.

106. *Ibid.*, 292.


Chapter 7

1. NLS MS, 3109, f. 5, WS to Blore, 1/22/19.

2. Morgan MS, WS to Train, 1/16/19.

3. NLS MS, 1750, f. 210, WS to Laidlaw, 1/28/19.

4. *Letters*, V, 302, Montagu, 2/3/19.

5. NLS MS, 2289, f. 164, Wm. Scott to WS, 1/23/19; f. 165, WS to Wm. Scott, 1/28/19.

6. *Letters*, V, 294, Constable, 1/17/19.

7. *Ibid.*, 291, Ferguson, 1/15/19.

8. Berg, MS, Memorandum of Agreement, 2/2/19; *cf.* JGL, III, 249.

9. JGL, III, 248.

10. *Letters*, V, 303, Montagu, 2/3/19.

11. *Ibid.*, 318, Morritt, 3/2/19.

12. *Ibid.*, VI, 231, Thos. Scott, 7/23/20.

13. NLS MS, 2869, f. 169, WS to Wm. Scott, 3/2/19.

14. Dibdin, *Annals of the Edin. Stage*, 286-91, quoted in *Letters*, V, 315, fn. 2.

15. NLS MS, 1558, f. 159, Charlotte to JGL, n.d. The play ran uninterrupted for two months, an engagement unique for Edinburgh, and was played once a week long after that, to a total of 285 performances (JGL, III, 254, fn. 1).

16. JGL, III, 254.

17. *Letters*, V, 357-8, Baillie, 4/17/19.

18. *Ibid.*, 305-6, Mackay, n.d., but mid-Feb. 1819.

19. *Ibid.*, 306-7.

20. JGL, III, 261.

21. *Letters*, V, 336, fn. 2, Southey to WS, 3/11/19.

22. *Ibid.*, 339, Southey, 4/4/19, but continued to around 4/20/19.

23. JGL, III, 187-9.

24. *Peter's Letters*, quoted by Lochhead, 52.

25. Cockburn, *Memorials*, 230.

26. JGL, III, 190.

27. *Ibid.*, 191-2.

28. *Ibid.*, 194-6.

29. *Ibid.*, 196-7.

30. *Letters*, V, 313, fn. 1, Montagu to WS, 1/2/19; Buccleuch to WS, 1/22/19.

31. JGL, III, 260; partly quoted in *Letters*, V, 307-8, fn. 1.

32. *Letters*, V, 307-9, Buccleuch, 2/19/19.

33. *Ibid.*, 313, fn. 1, Buccleuch, 2/19/19.

34. *Ibid.*, 313, Montagu, 3/4/19.

35. *Ibid.*, 315.

36. *Ibid.*, 317.

37. *Ibid.*, 361, Terry, 4/18/19.

38. *Ibid.*, 315.
39. *Ibid.*, 317.
40. *Ibid.*, 319, Hartstonge, 3/14/19.
41. *Ibid.*, 335, Southey, 4/11/19.
41a. *Ibid.*, 319, Hartstonge.
42. *Ibid.*, 321, Lockhart, 3/23/19.
43. *Ibid.*, Hartstonge.
44. *Ibid.*, 321.
45. *Ibid.*, 325, Constable, 3/23/19.
46. *Ibid.*, 368, Buccleuch, 4/15/19.
47. *Family Letters*, 327, Sophia to Miss Millar, 3/26/19.
48. *Letters*, V, 324, Constable.
49. *Ibid.*, 326, Montagu, 3/25/19.
50. *Ibid.*, 328, Joanna Baillie, 3/26/19.
51. *Ibid.*, Hartstonge, 3/14/19.
52. *Ibid.*, 347, Buccleuch, 4/15/19.
53. Skene, *Memories*, 67–8.
54. *Ibid.*
55. *Letters*, V, 329, Morritt, 3/20/19, p.m. 3/30/19.
56. *Ibid.*, 355, Ferguson, 4/16/19.
57. *Ibid.*, 331, Lockhart, 4/1/19.
58. *Ibid.*, 329.
59. *Ibid.*, 333, Thomson (Apr. 1819).
60. NLS MS, Acc 2641, WS to James Ballantyne, 4/1/19.
61. *Letters*, V, 357, Baillie, 4/17/19.
62. *Ibid.*, 355, Ferguson, 4/16/19.
63. *Ibid.*, 361, Terry, 4/18/19.
64. *Ibid.*, 337, fn. 2.
65. *Ibid.*, 337, Southey, started 4/4/19, but continued over a week later; therefore, around 4/11–7/19.
66. *Letters*, V, 338.
67. *Ibid.*, but WS notes that he is resuming the letter ten days later still; therefore, around 4/27.
68. *Ibid.*, 347, Buccleuch, 4/15/19.
69. *Ibid.*, 366, R. Shortreed, 4/23/19.
70. *Ibid.*, 355, Ferguson, 4/16/19.
71. *Ibid.*, 348, Buccleuch, 4/15/19.
72. JGL, III, 279–80.
73. *Letters*, V, 341, Constable, 4/8/19 (complete in NLS MS, 742, f. 179).
74. *Ibid.*, 343, Constable, 4/11/19 (NLS MS, 742, f. 181).
75. JGL, III, 280. (But actually almost all the MS of the *Bride*, in the Signet Library, exists in WS's own hand, and G. H. Gordon says that he transcribed the *Legend* from WS's completed autograph. Portions of this autograph are in NLS and the University of Edinburgh Library. See Grierson, *Scott*, 173–4, and Laidlaw's and Gordon's testimony.)

76. *Letters*, VI, 88, James Ballantyne, 4/9/19.
77. *Ibid.*, V, 340–1, Southey (begun 4/6/19, but this part toward end of month).
78. *Ibid.*, 363, Terry, 4/18/19.
79. *Ibid.*, 364.
80. *Ibid.*, 363. WS wrote "You must be aware," but clearly meant "beware."
81. *Ibid.*, 351, Ferguson, 4/16/19.
82. *Ibid.*, 349, Buccleuch, 4/15/19.
83. *Ibid.*, 351.
84. JGL, III, 281, gives no date, but on 285 says that two days later they rode up the valley of the Ale on election business, which is referred to in Dalkeith MS, 5/4/19, as having been the previous day.
85. JGL, III, 282; cf. *Letters*, V, 388, Sharpe, 5/?/19. Skene, *Memories*, 70–1, tells the story differently and makes the poem a short ballad by Bürger.
86. JGL, III, 283.
87. *Ibid.*, 284–5.
88. NLS MS, 1750, f. 224, Montagu, 4/29/19.
89. Dalkieth MS, WS to Montagu, 5/2–4/19, partly in *Letters*, V, 374–5, though not the part here quoted.
90. Dalkeith MS.
91. *Ibid.*
92. *Letters*, V, 370, Montagu, 4/29/19; 375, 5/4/19.
93. *Ibid.*, 375, Montagu, 5/6/19.
94. *Ibid.*, 375–6.
95. *Misc. Prose*, IV, 297. It was done at the request of Lord Montagu; see *Letters*, V, 381, Montagu, 5/10/19.
96. Dalkeith MS, WS to Montagu, 5/10/19.
97. *Ibid.*, 5/15/19.
98. *Letters*, V, 392, John Ballantyne (here dated May–June, 1819, but has to be before 5/11, when WS left Abbotsford for Edinburgh).
99. *Letters*, V, 384, fn. 1.
100. *Ibid.*, 367, Constable, 4/26/19.
101. *Ibid.*, 372, Constable, 4/30/19.
102. *Ibid.*, 301, fn. 1.
103. Oliphant, *Wm. Blackwood and Sons*, I, 83, Blackwood to James Ballantyne, 5/6/19.
104. *Ibid.*, 84.
105. *Ibid.*, 85–6.

106. *Letters*, V, 380, James Ballantyne (after 5/6/19).
107. NLS MS, 742, f. 185, WS to Constable & Co., 5/27/19.
108. *Ibid.*, 188, WS to John Ballantyne, 6/?/19.
109. *Ibid.*, 190, memo from John Ballantyne, 6/?/19.
110. *Ibid.*, 191, memo of contract on *Ivanhoe*.
111. *Letters*, V, 454, John Ballantyne, 8/12/19.
112. *Ibid.*, 403–4, Constable, 7/4/19.
113. NLS MS, 742, f. 188, WS to John Ballantyne, 6/?/19.
114. *Letters*, V, 383, Montagu, 5/16/19.
115. *Ibid.*, 394, Ferguson, 6/3/19.
116. *Ibid.*, 377, Montagu, 5/6/19.
117. JGL, III, 292; NLS MS, 2889, f. 175, WS to Wm. Scott, 6/10/19.
118. *Letters*, V, 394, Ferguson, 6/3/19.
119. *Ibid.*, 385, Ferguson, 5/23/19.
120. *Ibid.*, 393, Ferguson, 6/3/19, saying his illness lasted eight days. Therefore it started about 5/25–6/19.
121. *Letters*, V, 385, Ferguson, 5/23/19.
122. *Letters*, V, 388, Sharpe, "Monday," 5/?/19.
123. *Ibid.*, 385.
124. JGL, III, 292.
125. *Ibid.*, 296.
126. *Ibid.*, 296–7.
127. NLS MS, 852, f. 225, WS to Terry, 6/27/19.
128. *Ibid.*, 2889, f. 175, WS to Wm. Scott, 6/10/19.
129. *Letters*, V, 395, Terry, 6/15/19.
130. JGL, III, 298. JGL does not say, and there is no evidence to show, whether the scene was before or after WS's removal to Abbotsford on 6/16/19. In view of JGL's report of the alleged deathbed words in 1832, this story, too, may be regarded with a certain dubiety.
131. *Letters*, V, 387–8, Sharpe, "Monday," 5/?/19.

## Chapter 8

1. The Porteous Riot was not fiction, of course, but a real historical event. It took place on 9/7/1336. See *H. Mid.*, I, 370–80, n. III.
2. *H.Mid.*, I, 70, Ch. V.
3. *Cf.* Pittock, *Essays in Criticism*, VII, 748.
4. *H.Mid.*, I, 91, Ch. VII.
5. *Ibid.*, 309, Ch. XX.
6. *Ibid.*, 65, Ch. V.
7. *Ibid.*, 307–8, Ch. XX.
8. *Ibid.*, 294–5, Ch. XIX.
9. Pritchett, *The Living Novel*, 64.
10. *Cf.* Van Ghent, *The English Novel*, 117–8, 121; Hart, *Scott's Novels*, 132–3.
11. *H.Mid.*, I, 50, Ch. X.
12. *Cf.* Hart, *Scott's Novels*, 133–4.
13. *H.Mid*, I, 140, Ch. X.
14. *Ibid.*, 142, Ch. X.
15. *Cf.* Hart, *Scott's Novels*, 133.
16. *H.Mid*, I, 341, Ch. XXIII.
17. Hart, *Scott's Novels*, 137.
18. *H.Mid.*, I, 346, Ch. XXIII.
19. Shaw, *Quintessence of Ibsenism*, in *Major Crit. Essays*, 117 n. Quoted by Fisher in *19th C. Fiction*, X, 111, fn. 3.
20. *H.Mid.*, I, 264, Ch. XVIII.
21. *Ibid.*, II, 2, Ch. I.
22. *Ibid.*, 39, Ch. III.
23. *Ibid.*, 41, Ch. III.
24. *Ibid.*, I, 245, Ch. XVII.
25. *Ibid.*, II, 6–7, Ch. I.
26. *Ibid.*, 199, Ch. XIII.
27. *Ibid.*, 200, Ch. XIII.
28. *Cf.* Van Ghent, *The English Novel*, 114–5, 120; Welsh, *Hero*, 133–4; Craig, *Scottish Literature*, 217; Mayhead, "Scott as Artist," 267, Fisher, "Providence, Fate." 105.
29. *Cf.* Hart, *Scott's Novels*, 133–4.
30. *H.Mid.*, II, 337, Ch. XXIV.
31. *Ibid.*, 365, Ch. XXVI.
32. *Ibid.*, 255, Ch. XVIII.
33. *Ibid.*, 333, Ch. XXIV.
34. *Ibid.*, 333, Ch. XXIV.
35. Lukács, *The Historical Novel*, 52.
36. *H.Mid.*, I, 15, Ch. I.
37. *London Mag.*, Jan. 1822.
38. *Cf.* Hart, *Scott's Novels*, 315–6.
39. *Bride*, I, 121, Ch. VIII.
40. *Cf.* Hart, *Scott's Novels*, 313.
41. *Bride*, I, 31, Ch. II.
42. *Contra* Gordon, *NCF*, 110–5.
43. *Bride*, I, 22, Ch. II.
44. *Ibid.*, 78, Ch. V.
45. *Ibid.*, 121, Ch. VIII.
46. *Ibid.*, 68, Ch. V.
47. *Ibid.*, 70, Ch. V.
48. *Cf.* Hart, *Scott's Novels*, 318, 321–2.

49. *Bride*, I, 38–9, Ch. III.
50. *Cf.* Hart, *Scott's Novels*, 331–2; Daiches, *Literary Essays*, 113–4; Gordon, *NCF*, 112, 117–8.
51. *Bride*, I, 193, Ch. XIV.
52. *Cf.* Gordon, *NCF*, 117–8.
53. *Bride*, I, 169–70, Ch. XII.
54. *Ibid.*, 227–8, Ch. XVII.
55. *Ibid.*, 228–9, Ch. XVII.
56. *Ibid.*, 253, Ch. XIX.
57. *Ibid.*, 256, Ch. XIX.
58. *Ibid.*, 258–9, Ch. XIX.
59. *Ibid.*, 260, Ch. XIX.
60. *Ibid.*, 267, Ch. XIX.
61. *Ibid.*, 276, Ch. XXI.
62. *Ibid.*, 37, Ch. III.
63. *Ibid.*, 234, Ch. XVIII.
64. *Ibid.*, 247, Ch. XVIII.
65. *Ibid.*, II, 34, Ch. II.
66. The *time* of the novel is just before the Union of 1707. (In thus dating it I agree with Hart, *Scott's Novels*, 322, and disagree with Gordon, *NCF*, 111, though there are anachronisms and ambiguities of evidence in the novel.)
67. *Bride*, II, 143, Ch. XIII.
68. *Ibid.*, 148–9, Ch. XIII.
69. See also, Buchan *SWS*, 193; Hart, *Scott's Novels*, 334.
70. See *Buchan*, SWS, 192–3.
71. *Nigel*, Intro. Epistle, xliv.
72. *Legend*, 25, Ch. III.
73. *Ibid.*, 26, Ch. III.
74. *Ibid.*, 26, Ch. III.
75. *Ibid.*, 36, Ch. IV.
76. *Ibid.*, 259, Ch. XX.
77. *Ibid.*, 164, Ch. XVIII.
78. *Ibid.*, 284, Ch. XXIII.
79. *Ibid.*, 45–6, Ch. IV.
80. *Ibid.*, 70, Ch. VI.
81. Lukács, *The Historical Novel*, 59.

Chapter 9

1. *Letters*, V, 395, Terry, 6/15/19.
2. *Family Letters*, 57, Sophia to Miss Millar, 6/14/19.
3. *Letters*, V, 397, Terry, 6/15/19. There is some confusion here; WS says "tomorrow," but he wrote Abel Moysey from Abbotsford on 6/15—possibly the evening of the same day he wrote Terry. Of course, he may have misdated one of these letters.
4. *Letters*, V, 399, John Ballantyne, 6/21/19.

5. Skene, *Memories*, 66.
6. JGL, III, 295.
7. *Ibid.*, quoting James Ballantyne memorandum.
8. *Letters*, V, 472–3, fn. 1, Lady Louisa Stuart to WS, 8/11/19.
9. Smith, Sydney, *Letters*, I, 328, Constable, 6/28/19. The critics, later, were more divided.
10. JGL, III, 299.
11. *Letters*, V, 473, fn. 1.
12. *Ibid.*, 402, Constable, 7/4/19.
13. ACLC, III, 127, John Ballantyne to Constable, 7/2/19.
14. *Letters*, VI, 4, James Ballantyne, 7/4/19—misdated "Nov.? 1819."
15. *Ibid.*, V, 402, Constable, 7/4/19.
16. JGL, III, 354; *cf. Ivanhoe*, I, xi, xli–lv.
17. NLS MS, 854, f. 255, WS to James Ballantyne, 7/17/19.
18. *Letters*, V, 426, John Ballantyne (but *before* July—not among the July letters as printed).
19. NLS MS, 854, f. 255.
20. *Ibid.*
21. *Letters*, V, 448, James Ballantyne, 8/4/19.
22. NLS MS, 742, f. 193, WS to Constable & Co., 7/2/19 (8/2/19).
23. *Letters*, V, 419, John Ballantyne, 7/19/19.
24. NLS MS, 1750, f. 238, WS to James Ballantyne, 7/19/19.
25. *Letters*, V, 423, James Ballantyne, 7/21–5/19.
26. *Ibid.*, 465, James Ballantyne, 8/19/19.
27. NLS MS, 1750, f. 21, WS to James Ballantyne, 8/?/19.
28. *Letters*, V, 474, Lady Louisa Stuart, 8/23/19.
29. *Ibid.*, 477, James Ballantyne, 8/25/19.
30. *Family Letters*, 59–60, Sophia to Miss Millar, 7/5/19.
31. *Letters*, V, 412–22, *passim* to various correspondents.
32. *Ibid.*, 442, John Ballantyne, 8/2/19; 468, Richardson, 8/22/19.
33. *Ibid.*, 408, Morritt, 7/8/19.
34. *Ibid.*, 405, Mrs. Clephane, 7/15?/19.
35. *Ibid.*, VI, 41, Walter, 12/3/19.
36. NLS MS, 1809, f. 183, WS to Mrs. Grahame, 7/16/19.
37. *Letters*, V, 436, Walter, 8/1/19.
38. *Ibid.*, 418, Walter, 7/19/19.

39. *Ibid.*, 416, John Ballantyne, 7/16/19.
40. *Ibid.*, 421, Hartstonge, 7/21/19.
41. *Ibid.*, 420, Maria Edgeworth, 7/20/19.
42. *Ibid.*, 416–7, John Ballantyne, 7/16/19.
43. *Ibid.*, 441, John Ballantyne, 8/2/19.
44. *Ibid.*, 427, John Ballantyne, 7/26/19.
45. *Ibid.*, 467, Richardson, 8/22/19.
46. *Ibid.*, 434, Walter, 8/1/19.
47. *Ibid.*, 449, Walter, 8/7/19.
48. *Ibid.*, 448, Walter, 8/7/19, noting that a letter from Walter dated 7/31/19 had arrived from Cork.
49. *Ibid.*, 435, Walter, 8/1/19.
50. *Ibid.*, 460, Walter, 8/13/19.
51. *Ibid.*, 467.
52. *Ibid.*, 480, Walter, 9/4/19.
53. *Ibid.*, 442–3, John Ballantyne 8/2/19.
54. *Ibid.*, 454, John Ballantyne, 8/12/19.
55. *Ibid.*, 445, John Ballantyne, 8/2/19.
56. *Ibid.*, 443–4, 454.
57. *Ibid.*, 443–4.
58. *Ibid.*, 454.
59. *Ibid.*, 463, John Ballantyne, 8/19/19.
60. *Ibid.*, 465, James Ballantyne, 8/20/19.
61. *Ibid.*, 463, fn. 1, John Ballantyne's *Diary*, 7/2/19, 8/19/19; *Letters*, V, 459, Walter, 8/13/19.
62. *Letters*, V, 439, James Ballantyne, 8/1/19 (p.m. 8/2).
63. *Ibid.*, 452, C. Rutherford, 8/11/19.
64. *Ibid.*, 483, Walter, 8/20/19.
65. *Ibid.*, 479, Mrs. Scott, "Saturday," 8/28/19, p.m. 8/30/19.
66. *Tait's Edin. Mag.*, X, 577 (Sept. 1843).
67. *Family Letters*, 61, Sophia to Miss Millar, 9/24/19.
68. *Letters*, V, 505, Montagu, 10/3/19.
69. *Ibid.*, 506, Montagu, 10/3/19.
70. *Ibid.*, 495, Montagu, 9/25/19.
71. *Ibid.*, 507.
72. *Ibid.*, 421, Hartstonge, 7/21/19.
73. NLS MS, 852, f. 225, WS to Terry, 6/27/19.
74. *Letters*, V, 396, fn. 2, Terry to WS, 6/7/19.
75. *Ibid.*, 396, Terry, 6/15/19.
76. *Ibid.*, 496–7, Walter, 9/27/19; *cf.* also 501, Terry, 9/28/19, and 503–4, Craig, Oct. 1819.
77. *Letters*, V, 479, Skene, "Sunday," 9/5/19 or 8/29/19? (NLS MS, 742, f. 195).
78. *Ibid.*, VI, 6, John Ballantyne, 11/8/19; *cf.* 11, Terry, 11//10/19.
79. JGL barely mentions the episode. For a full account, see *Scotsman*, 4/14/1933, W.N. Parker, "Pontefract Castle." The advertisements of the novel appeared on 10/17 and 10/22/19.
80. *Ibid.* Fearman's reply was published 10/28/19.
81. *Ibid.* The conversation with WS took place 11/26/19.
82. *Ibid.*, 11/3/19, 8/19/19.
83. NLS MS, 3112, f. 117, John Ballantyne to editor of *Blackwood's Mag.*, 11/15/19.
84. When Fearman published "Pontefract Castle" in 1820, however, it did fairly well; the following year he even brought out, in a so-called "Fifth Series of *Tales of My Landlord*, a novel entitled *The Fair Witch of Glas Lyn*, with a preface saying that he felt no need to recant.
85. *Ivanhoe*, Pref., xxxi.
86. *Ibid.*, Ded. Epistle, xlii–xlv.
87. *Letters*, VI, 17, Walter, 11/16/19.
88. *Ibid.*, 39, Walter, 12/3/19.
89. JGL, III, 353.
90. *Ivanhoe*, Intro., xx. The *Quarterly Review*, however, did not appear until Dec. 1821.
91. Smith, Sydney, *Letters*, I, 342, Constable, 12/15–25?/19.
92. *Ivanhoe*, Intro., xix–xx. Jeffrey added, however, some of his usual qualifications.
93. *Ibid.*, xvii–xxiii.
94. *Letters*, VI, 115–6, fn. 1, Lady Louisa Stuart to WS, 1/16/19. JGL mistakenly dates this letter Dec.
95. JGL, III, 354.
96. Yale U. Lib. MS, WS to Laidlaw, around 1/1/20.
97. Morgan MS, John Ballantyne, *Diary*, 12/22/19.
98. *Ibid.*, 12/31/19. Under this date John added an estimate of his own capital as now amounting to £5,000.
99. Bryant, *Elegance*, 380.
100. *Ibid.*, 383.
101. *Ibid.*, 384.
102. *Ibid.*, 385–6.

103. *Iibd.*, 387.
104. *Ibid.*, 385.
105. *Ibid.*, 387.
106. *Letters*, V, 467, Richardson, 8/22/19.
107. *Ibid.*, 483, Walter, 9/12/19.
108. *Ibid.*, 485, James Ballantyne, 9/12/19.
109. *Ibid.*, 485-6.
110. *Ibid.*, 484-5.
111. *Ibid.*, 487.
112. *Ibid.*, 488, James Ballantync, 9/?/19.
113. *Ibid.*, 485. Subsequently there was a letter in the *Edin. Weekly J.* defending the Manchester magistrates, signed "L.T." (Lawrence Templeton?), which was perhaps written by WS.
114. *Ibid.*, VI, 3, Lockhart, 10/17/19.
115. *Ibid.*, 8-9, Lockhart, 11/8/19.
116. *Ibid.*, 10.
117. *Ibid.*, 20, Irving, 11/17/19, corrected from Yale U. Lib. MS.
118. *Ibid.*, 44-5, fn. 2, Irving to WS, 11/20/19.
119. *Ibid.*, 23, fn. 1, Croker to Lockhart, 11/18/19 (*Croker Papers*, I, 126-7).
120. *Ibid.*, 24-5, Croker, 11/24/19.
121. *Ibid.*, 43, Croker, 12?/–/19.
122. *Ibid.*, 32, fn. 1.
123. JGL, III, 358.
124. Bryant, *Elegance*, 388-9.
125. *Letters*, VI, 39, Walter, 12/3/19.
126. *Ibid.*, 56, Morritt, 12/17/19.
127. *Ibid.*, 57-8, Morritt.
128. *Ibid.*, 61, Lord Melville (2nd Viscount), 12/19/19.
129. *Ibid.*, 62. *Cf.* also *Letters*, VI, 65-7, Laidlaw, 12/20/19; 70-2, Montagu, 12/21/19; and 64, fn. 1, 12/28/19, the formal offer to the Marquis of Lothian.
130. Bryant, *Elegance*, 389.
131. *Ibid.*, 386.
132. *Ibid.*, 389.
133. Smith, Sydney, *Letters*, I, 342, Constable, 12/25 or 12/15?/19.

#### Chapter 10

1. *Letters*, V, 509, Walter, 10/14/19.
2. *Ibid.*, VI, 50, Thos. Scott, 12/9/19.
3. *Ibid.*, 119, Lady Louisa Stuart (after 1/16/20).
4. *Ibid.*, 50-1, Walter, 12/17/19.
5. *Ibid.*, 51.
6. *Ibid.*, 52-3.
7. *Ibid.*, 55.
8. Skene, *Memories*, 77.
9. *Letters*, VI, 77-8, Walter, 12/28/19; NLS MS, 1566, f. 50, WS to Mrs. Curle, 12/24/19.
10. *Letters*, VI, 74-5 Thos. Scott, 12/23/19.
11. *Ibid.;* Skene, *Memories*, 77.
12. *Letters*, VI, 119.
13. JGL, III, 353.
14. *Letters*, VI, 80, Walter, 12/28/19.
15. *Ibid.*, 79.
16. *Ibid.*, 84, Lord Melville, 12/28/19, and fn. 1.
17. *Ibid.*, 81, Lord Melville.
18. *Ibid.*, 84.
19. *Ibid.*, 106, Croker, 1/2/20.
20. *Ibid.*, 109, Thos. Scott, 1/10/20.
21. *Ibid.*, 113, Lady Compton, 1/14/20.
22. *Ibid.*, 96, Joanna Baillie, 1/1/20.
23. *Ibid.*, 103, Montagu, 1/2/20.
24. *Ibid.*, 103-4.
25. *Ibid.*, 79, 96.
26. NLS MS, 2521, f. 159, WS to Croker, 1/10/20.
27. *Letters*, VI, 126, Montagu, 1/23/20.
28. *Ibid.*, 125, Montagu.
29. NLS MS, 1750, f. 259, Scott's "Broadside to the Volunteer," 2/8/20.
30. *Letters*, VI, 121, Walter, 1/17/20.
31. *Ibid.*, 122, Laidlaw, 1/19/20.
32. *Ibid.*, 127, Laidlaw, 1/25/20.
33. *Ibid.*, 109, Thos. Scott, 1/20/20.
34. NLS MS, 2521, f. 159, Croker, 1/10/20.
35. *Family Letters*, 72, Sophia to Miss Millar, 1/21/20.
36. NLS MS, 2521, f. 159.
37. Huntington MS, pub. in *Huntington Library Quarterly*, II, 349, WS to Croker, 1/22/20.
38. *Letters*, VI, 151, Lady Abercorn, 3/15/20.
39. *Family Letters*, 59-60, Sophia to Miss Millar, 7/5/19.
40. Lochhead, *Lockhart*, 69.
41. *Ibid.*
42. *Family Letters*, 74, Sophia to Miss Millar (Jan. 1820).
43. Lochhead, *Lockhart*, 70.
44. *Letters*, VI, 120, Walter, 1/17/20.
45. *Ibid.*, 188, Morritt, 5/19/20.
46. ACLC, III, 130, Constable to Cadell, 11/4/19.

47. JGL, III, 416–7. JGL says the novel was designed to introduce Queen Elizabeth "as a companion to the Mary Stuart of *The Abbot*," but the parallel is at least dubious. There is no certain proof that WS had this early indicated any intention of writing a sequel to *The Monastery* and introducing Mary as a character. *Letters*, VI, 111, Constable, 1/12/20, and Constable's footnote, however, show clearly that Constable had *already* made his suggestion.

48. Bryant, *Elegance*, 389.

49. *Letters*, VI, 128–9, Constable, 2/2/20; JGL, III, 367.

50. JGL, III, 361, says the middle of Feb., but *Letters*, VI, 131, Craig, 2/4/20, says WS will be at Abbotsford the following evening, and there is no evidence of his having gone there again later in the month.

51. JGL, III, 362.

52. *Ibid.*, 362–3. The details about John Ballantyne's coat are from *Tait's Edin. Mag.*, Sept. 1843, 478.

53. JGL, III, 363–4.

54. *Ibid.*, 365.

55. *Ibid.*, 366.

56. NLS MS, 3653, f. 170, WS to Walter, 2/12/20.

57. JGL, III, 370. Some biographers have written as if WS's decision was caused by the poor *reception* of *The Monastery*, but it quite evidently preceded public comment.

58. NLS MS, 3102, f. 170, WS to Constable, 2/17/20, accepting £350 for the future profits of *Tales of My Landlord; Letters*, VI, 145, Constable, 3/7/20, and *Letters*, V, 404, John Ballantyne (here erroneously dated 1819), all tying together a sequel to *The Monastery* with the sale of the copyrights.

59. *Letters*, V, 404, John Ballantyne, ca. Feb. 1820.

60. JGL, III, 416.

61. *Letters*, VI, 145, Constable, 3/17/20.

62. JGL, III, 409–10.

63. Adolphus, *Letters to Heber*, 13.

64. *Letters*, VI, 160, James Ballantyne, 3/28/20.

65. *Ibid.*, 28, fn. 1, Lady Abercorn to WS, 12/3/19.

66. *Ibid.*, 140, Morritt, 2/29/20.

67. *Ibid.*, 146, Rose, 3/10/20.

68. NLS MS, 2518, f. 117, Charles to Constable, n.d.

69. *Letters*, VI, 153, Arbuthnot, 3/17/20.

70. *Ibid.*, 188, Morritt, 5/19/20.

71. *Ibid.*, 157, Charlotte, 3/28/20.

72. *Croker Papers*, I, 154.

73. *Letters*, VI, 157.

74. *Ibid.*, 189.

75. *Ibid.*, 156–7, Charlotte.

76. *Ibid.*, 157.

77. *Ibid.*, 157, fn. 2; JGL follows WS in erroneously saying 4/2/20.

78. *Ibid.*, 168–9, Sophia, 4/2/20. WS erroneously writes 4/3/20.

79. Mathews, *Memories*, 57–8; JGL, V, 61, fn. 1, tells the same story, without quoting Tom.

80. *Letters*, VI, 162–4, Lockhart, 3/30/20.

81. *Ibid.*, 164.

82. *Ibid.*, 168, Sophia, 4/2–4/20.

83. *Ibid.*, 169.

84. *Ibid.*, 158, Constable, 3/28/20.

85. Leslie, *Memoirs*, I, 63; Irving, *Life and Letters*, I, 349, quotes a letter from Leslie, 4/9/20, which establishes the date of this party as 4/14/20.

86. Haydon, *Autobiography*, 354, *et seq.*, dates the dinner as 4/30/20, but his memory erred; WS had left London 4/24/20.

87. *Ibid.*

88. *Ibid.*

89. JGL, III, 373–4. *Letters*, VI, 173, Buchanan, 4/9/20, shows that sittings were then taking place. JGL, III, 371–2, is in error, however, in saying that during this visit Sir Thos. Lawrence began painting WS's portrait. This was not till the next year, 1821.

90. JGL, III, 374–6.

91. *Ibid.*, 376.

92. *Ibid.*

93. *Letters*, VI, 173, Buchanan, 4/9/20.

94. *Ibid.*, 188, Morritt, 5/19/20.

95. Lochhead, *Lockhart*, 71, Sophia to Lockhart, n.d.

96. *Ibid.*, 72, Lockhart to Sophia, n.d.

97. NLS MS, 1552, f. 13, Lockhart to Sophia, "Monday" (4/17/20 or 4/24/20).

98. *Letters*, VI, 174, Montagu, 4/10/20.

99. *Ibid.*, 161, Charles (misdated 3/28/20; should be 4/11/20); 167, Lady

Abercorn (misdated 4/1/20; should be 4/15/20).

100. *Letters*, VI, 178, Constable, 4/21/20.
101. *Ibid.*, 166–7, Lady Abercorn. There are two letters, both dated merely "Saturday," which are printed as 4/1/20, but the first is probably 4/8/20 and the second is placed by the visit to Woolwich and the approaching visit to Ditton as almost certainly 4/15/20. WS went to Ditton on Sunday, 4/16, stayed through Monday, 4/17, and returned to London on Tuesday, 4/18.
102. *Letters*, VI, 179, Sophia, 4/23/20.
103. *Ibid.*
104. *Ibid.*, 177, Lockhart, 4/18/20; 179, Sophia, 4/23/20.
105. *Ibid.*, 177–8, Constable, 4/21/20, and 177–8, fn. 2, quoting John Ballantyne's *Diary*.
106. Morgan MS, John Ballantyne's *Diary*, 4/28/20, quoted in *Letters*, VI, 178, fn.; but omitting the italics under the "not."
107. JGL, III, 384; *Scots Mag.*, May, 1820.
108. *Letters*, VI, 183, Lady Abercorn, 5/1/20.
109. Lochhead, *Lockhart*, 77.
110. *Letters*, VI, 183.

Chapter 11

1. NLS MS, 858, f. 24, WS to Mrs. Clephane, "Thursday evening." Docketed "Spring, 1820," probably May.
2. *Letters*, VI, 186, Lockhart, "Sunday" (5/7/20–p.m. 5/9/20).
3. *Ibid.*, 191, Scott of Gala, 5/20/20; JGL, III, 384–5; Skene, *Memories*, 85–6.
4. *Ibid.*, 195, Walter, 5/31/20.
5. *Ibid.*, 209, Walter, 6/17/20.
6. *Ibid.*, 196, Waltcr.
7. *Ibid.*, 215, Walter, 6/27/20.
8. *Ibid.*, 212, Richardson, 6/24/20.
9. *Ibid.*, 199, fn. 2.
10. *Ibid.*, 199–200, Lady Abercorn, 6/1/20.
11. *Ibid.*, 200, fn. 1, Lady Abercorn to WS, 6/10/20.
12. *Ibid.*, 199.
13. *Ibid.*, 217, Lady Abercorn, 7/1/20.
14. *Ibid.*, 252, Lady Abercorn, 8/2/20.

15. *Ibid.*, 194 fn. 1, Heber to WS, 5/24/20.
16. JGL, III, 386.
17. *Ibid.*, 208, Gordon, 6/12/20.
18. *Ibid.*, 197, fn. 2, quoting John Ballantyne's *Diary*.
19. *Ibid.*, 210–1, John Ballantyne, 6/18/20.
20. *Ibid.*, 229, Thos. Scott, 7/23/20.
21. *Ibid.*, 230–1.
22. *Ibid.*, 232.
23. *Ibid.*, 175, fn. 1.
24. *Ibid.*, 221, fn. 1, quoting Gordon, *Memoir of John Wilson*, I, 308–11.
25. *Ibid.*, 239, fn. 1, quoting Lockhart to WS, 7/20/20.
26. *Ibid.*, 220, Lord Provost—John Manderston, 7/8/20.
27. *Ibid.*, 227, Morritt (after 7/19/20).
28. *Ibid.*, 240, Lockhart, 7/25/20.
29. *Ibid.*, 242.
30. *Ibid.*, 243.
31. *Ibid.*, 247, fn. 1, Lockhart to WS, 7/25/20.
32. *Ibid.*, 248, fn., Wilson to WS, 7/29/20.
33. NLS MS, 3891, f. 120, Irving to WS, 8/13/20.
34. *Letters*, VI, 240, fn. 1, Lockhart to WS, 7/20/20.
35. *Ibid.*, 244, Lockhart, 7/25/20.
36. *Ibid.*, 250, James Ballantyne, 8?/?/20).
37. *Ibid.*, 251, James Ballantyne, 8/1/20.
38. *Ibid.*, 223, Constable & Co., misdated 7/10/20; should be 8/10, as is shown by the original NLS MS, 854, f. 205.
39. *Letters*, VI, 262, Constable, 8/20/20.
40. *Ibid.*, 225, Morritt (after 7/19/20).
41. *Ibid.*, 260, Walter, 8/15/20.
42. *Ibid.*, 240, fn. 1, Lockhart to WS, 7/20/20; 262, Constable, 8/20/20.
43. NLS MS, 852, f. 228, Terry (misdated 7/25/20; should be 8/25).
44. *Letters*, VI, 225, Morritt (after 7/19/20).
45. NLS MS, 852, f. 228.
46. *Letters*, VI, 286, Lady Abercorn, 10/26/20.
47. *Ibid.*, 225. JGL, III, 398–9, says that Wm. Allan was also there, but this may be an error: no letter mentions his presence.
48. JGL, III, 398–9.
49. *Ibid.*, 403–4.

50. *Ibid.*, 398–9.
51. *Ibid.*, 400.
52. *Ibid.*, 401.
53. *Ibid.*, 402.
54. *Ibid.*, 502–3.
55. *Letters*, VI, 265–6, Constable, 9/10/20.
56. *Ibid.*
57. *Ibid.*, 272, Constable, 10.
58. *Ibid.*, 262, fn. 3, Constable to WS, 9/4/20 (NLS MS, 791).
59. JGL, III, 410.
60. Adam, *Blair Adam Book*, quoted by JGL, III, 411.
61. *Letters*, VI, 309–10, fn. 1, Lady Louisa Stuart to WS, 12/4/20; also in Partington, *Post-Bag*, 146/7.
62. *Ibid.*
63. *Letters*, VI, 311, Lady Louisa Stuart, 12/14/20.
64. NLS MS, 3891, f. 128, Morritt to WS 9/12/20.
65. *Abbot*, Ed.'s Pref. xvi.
66. *Ibid.*, xvi–xviii.
67. *Ibid.*, xxviii–xix. But *Blackwood* here made a slip; it is Roland Graeme who changes the keys.
68. *Letters*, VI, 276, Walter (before 10/18/20).
69. *Ibid.*, 247, fn. 1, Lockhart to WS, 7/25/20.
70. Partington, *Post-Bag*, 142, Lockhart to WS (same letter as above).
71. JGL, III, 420. Cf. also Evans, *Lampeter*.
72. *Letters*, VI, 272, Constable, 10/6/20.
73. *Ibid.*, 273, fn. 1, Cadell to WS, 10/7/20.
74. *Ibid.*, 272–3, Cadell, 10/8/20.
75. Morgan MS, WS to C. Dumergue, 10/13/20.
76. *Letters*, VI, 277, Walter, 10/18/20.
77. *Ibid.*, 293, fn. 1, Williams to WS, 11/4/20.
78. *Ibid.*, 293–4, Charles, 11/14/20.
79. *Ibid.*
80. *Ibid.*, 265, Constable, 9/10/20.
81. NLS MS, 1750, f. 282, WS to Mrs. Clephane, 9/11/20.
82. *Letters*, VI, 285, Lady Abercorn, 10/26/20.
83. *Ibid.*, 269, Lady Compton (before 10/20/20); NLS MS, 1750, f. 285, WS to Lady Compton, 10/20/20.
84. *Letters*, VI, 306, Morritt, 12/8/20.
85. MLS MS, 1750, f. 285.

86. *Family Letters*, 78, Anne to Miss Millar, 11/4/20.
87. *Letters*, VI, 288, James Ballantyne, "Sunday," 11/5/20.
88. *Ibid.*, 265, Constable, 9/10/20.
89. *Ibid.*, 288–9, John Ballantyne, 11/9/20 and fn. 3.
90. *Ibid.*, 289.
91. *Ibid.*, 294, Charles, 11/14/20.
92. *Ibid.*, 295, Charles.
93. *Ibid.*, VII, 32, Charles, 11/20/20. JGL, III, 405, says there were often as many as 30–40 guests.
94. JGL, III, 405–6.
95. *Ibid.*, 406–7.
96. *Ibid.*, 407.

Chapter 12

1. *Letters*, VI, 291, Walter, 11/14/20.
2. *Ibid.*, 295, Charles, 11/14/20.
3. JGL, III, 433.
4. *Letters* VI, 306, James Ballantyne, "Wednesday" (mistakenly put in Nov.–Dec., 1820; WS was inducted as president on Tuesday, 1/16/21, and this letter was probably written the following day, 1/17/20).
5. *Letters*, VI, 364, Laidlaw (docketed 1/30/20 NLS MS, 976, f. 24 and 969, f. 32).
6. *Ibid.*, 306–7, Morritt, 12/8/20.
7. *Ibid.*, 305, James Ballantyne.
8. *Ibid.*, 307, Morritt.
9. *Ibid.*, 338, Montagu, 1/17/21.
10. *Ibid.*, 305, James Ballantyne.
11. Bryant, *Elegance*, 391.
12. *Ibid.*, 392.
13. *Letters*, I, 285, Ellis, 4/7/1800.
14. Bryant, *Elegance*, 393, 124.
15. *Letters*, VI, 215, Walter, 6/27/20.
16. *Ibid.*, 216, Montagu, 6/30/20.
17. *Ibid.*, 238, Thos. Scott, 7/23/20.
18. Creevey, *Papers*, I, 319.
19. Haydon, *Autobiography*, 386.
20. *Letters*, VI, 301–2, Montagu, 11/30/20.
21. *Ibid.*, 307–8, Morritt, 12/8/20. Cf. fn. 3, Morritt to WS 12/4?/20; cf. also, 309–16, Lady Louisa Stuart, 12/14/20; fn. 1, Lady Louisa to WS, 12/4/20.
22. Haydon, *Autobiography*, 387.
23. Cockburn, *Memorials*, 326.
24. *Letters*, VI, 336–7, Montagu, 1/17/20.
25. JGL, III, 435–6.
26. *Ken.*, Intro., xxv.

27. *Ibid.*

28. *Ibid.*, xxv–xxvi.

29. Partington, *Post-Bag*, 151–2, Morritt to WS, n.d.

30. *Ibid.*, 150–1, Mrs. Hughes to WS, 2/18/21.

31. *Ibid.*

32. *Letters*, VI, 385, fn. 2, Mrs. Hughes to WS, 3/15/21.

33. John Ballantyne, *Diary*, 1/1/21.

34. *Ibid.*, 1/3/21.

35. *Letters*, VI, 342, Croker, 1/25/21; 348–50, fn. 1. See also Lochhead, *Lockhart*, 82–3, and Lang, *Life of Lockhart*, I, 250–82.

36. *Letters*, VI, 348, fn. 1.

37. *Ibid.*, 349, fn.; 341, fn. 1, Croker to WS, 1/21/21.

38. *Ibid.*, 341, fn. 1.

39. *Ibid.*, 348, Walter, 2/4/21; 242, Croker, 1/25/21.

40. *Ibid.*, 341, fn. 1, Constable to Cadell, 1/28/21.

41. *Ibid.*, 367, Lockhart, 2/28/21.

42. *Ibid.*, 342, Croker, 1/25/21; cf. JGL, III, 437.

43. *Ibid.*, 351, Mrs. Carpenter, 2/5/21.

44. NLS MS, 1552, f. 21, Sophia to Lockhart, 1/21/21 (p.m. 1/22).

45. *Letters*, VI, 352, Mrs. Carpenter, 2/5/21.

46. NLS MS, 967, f. 27 (970, f. 28), WS to Laidlaw, 2/5/21; cf. also 1753, f. 52, WS to Mrs. Carpenter, 2/5/21.

47. *Letters*, VI, 354–5, Lockhart, 2/15/21, which says he began writing it three days ago and saw Christie the day before that; therefore he arrived at least 2/11/21.

48. *Ibid.*, 357, Sophia, 2/18/21.

49. *Ibid.*, 355, Lockhart, 2/15/21.

50. *Ibid.*, 349–50, fn. 1, John Scott's statements, 1/31/21, 2/2/21, from pamphlet in Edin. Univ. Lib.

51. *Ibid.*, 354, Lockhart, 2/15/21, showing that Christie consulted WS 2/11/21; *ibid.*, 359, fn. 1, Christie to WS, n.d., but around 2/19/21.

52. *Ibid.*, 349, fn. 1; 359–60, fn. 1.

53. *Ibid.*, 361, Lockhart, 2/20/21.

54. *Ibid.*, 363, Lockhart, 2/24/21; 366, Lockhart, 2/28/21.

55. *Ibid.*, 392, fn. 2, Christie to Lockhart, 4/14/21.

56. *Ibid.*, 363, Lockhart, 2/24/21.

57. *Ibid.*, 352, Mrs. Carpenter, 2/5/21.

58. *Ibid.*, 355, Lockhart, 12/17/21.

59. *Ibid.*, 356–7, Sophia, 2/18/21.

60. *Ibid.*, 379, Sophia, 3/14/21.

61. JGL, III, 376.

62. *Ibid.*, 371–2. But JGL has advanced the actual date by a year. *Letters*, VI, 368, Laidlaw, 2/28/21, and 372, Walter, 3/1/21, both show that the sittings to Lawrence are taking place in this year and are a *new* thing. Walter had been in London with his father in 1820, and if WS had begun sitting to Lawrence then, would not need such an explanation as the above letter gives him; and it is unlikely that WS would not have told Laidlaw in the previous year if the *command* had been given then. *Letters*, VI, 153–6, Charlotte, is misdated 3/20/21, as proved by the references to Mrs. Carpenter, who did not reach England till 1821.

63. *Letters*, VI, 368, Laidlaw, 2/28/21.

64. JGL, III, 372–3.

65. *Letters*, VI, 156, Charlotte, 3/20/21.

66. *Ibid.*, 380, Sophia, 3/14/21.

67. *Ibid.*, 357, Sophia, 2/18/21; NLS MS, 1750, f. 314, WS to Montagu, 2/14/21; *Letters*, VI, 356, Lockhart, 2/17/21; 359, Walter, 2/19/21; NLS MS, 1754, f. 96, WS to Heber, n.d. except "Thursday."

68. NLS MS, 853, f. 312, WS to Lady Davy, "Sunday night."

69. *Private Letters*, Grant Intro., 37.

70. NLS MS, 1750, f. 293, WS to Mrs. Carpenter, 2/25/21; *Letters*, VI, 154, Charlotte, 3/20/21.

71. *Letters*, VI, 375, Lockhart, 3/4/21.

72. *Ibid.*, 153, Charlotte.

73. *Ibid.*, 379, Sophia, 3/14/21.

74. *Ibid.*, 375–6, Montagu, 3/6/21; 377, Lockhart, 3/14/21; 379, Sophia, 3/14/21.

75. *Ibid.*, 375, Lockhart, 3/4/21.

76. *Ibid.*, 390, Walter, 3/27/21.

77. *Ibid.*, 382, Sophia, 3/19/21.

78. *Ibid.*, 155, Charlotte, 3/19/21.

79. NLS MS, 969, f. 41, Laidlaw (p.m. 3/19/21).

80. *Letters*, VI, 388, Walter, 3/27/21.

81. *Ibid.*, 370, Walter, 3/1/21.

82. *Ibid.*, 388, Walter, 3/27/21.

83. *Ibid.*, 370; 406, Walter, 4/6/21.

84. *Ibid.*, 388, Lockhart, 3/23/21; 407, Walter, 4/6/21; 410, Mrs. Carpenter, 4/13/21.

85. *Ibid.*, 380, Sophia, 3/14/21.
86. *Ibid.*, 409–10, Mrs. Carpenter; *cf.* 411, Montagu, 4/13/21; NLS MS, 2889, f. 179, WS to Wm. Scott, 4/11/21; 2889, f. 187, WS to Wm. Scott (n.d., but between 4/11 and 21/21); MS 3112, f. 178, WS to Pringle (dated only "Friday," but probably 4/13/21).
87. *Letters*, VI, 407, Ferguson, 4/6/21.
88. *Ibid.*, 424–5, Walter, 4/23/21.
89. *Ibid.*, 414, Montagu, 4/15/21.
90. *Ibid.*, 417, fn. 1, Sidmouth to WS, 4/15/21.
91. *Ibid.*, 397, fn. 1.
92. *Ibid.*, 397–405, Villiers, 4/7/21. WS's reasoning on the £100 stipend is not quite conclusive. Added to £5,000 a year it may not seem much, but added to £500 a year it represents a good deal.
93. *Ibid.*
94. *Ibid.*, 417, fn. 1, Sidmouth to WS, 4/15/21.
95. *Ibid.*, 418, Sidmouth, 4/20/21.
96. *Ibid.*, 417, fn. 1, Morritt to WS, n.d.
97. *Ibid.*, 479–80, Morritt, 6/16/21. The printed text says "our printed letters," but that is clearly a mis-reading.
98. *Ibid.*, 424, Walter, 4/23/21.
99. *Ibid.*, 425, Walter, 4/27/21.
100. *Ibid.*, 431, Sophia, 5/1/21.
101. *Ibid.*, 426, Walter, 4/27/21.
102. *Ibid.*, 431, Sophia.
103. *Ibid.*, 433–4, Walter, 5/1/21.
104. *Ibid.*, 437–9, Walter, 5/10/21.
105. *Ibid.*, 442–4, Walter, 5/15/21.
106. *Ibid.*, 450, Walter, 5/26/21.
107. *Ibid.*, 453, Walter, 5/26/21.
108. *Ibid.*, V, 368, fn. 2.
109. Morgan MS, John Ballantyne's *Diary*, 11/13/20.
110. NLS MS, 2566, f. 200.
111. The description is from JGL, III, 418, but the account of a visit there in the *autumn* of 1820 is a myth, since John Ballantyne did not decide on the place till 4/2/21.
112. *Letters*, V, 369, John Ballantyne, 4/28/21.
113. NLS MS, 2566, f. 202.
114. JGL, III, 459–60. But John Ballantyne had *not* been executing his will; he had done that on 2/17/21 (NLS MS, 2566, f. 208).
115. *Letters*, VI, 484, Walter, 6/27/21.
116. *Ibid.*, 477–8, Montagu, 6/16/21.
117. JGL, III, 460.

Chapter 13

1. *Ivan.*, I, 171–2, Ch. XIII.
2. *Ibid.*, II, 233, Ch. XV.
3. Rosenberg, *From Shylock*, 90, partly quoting James Duncan, *NCF*, IX, 298.
4. *Ivan.*, I, 95–6, Ch. VI.
5. *Ibid.*, 96–7, Ch. VI.
6. Rosenberg, *From Shylock*, 90.
7. *Ivan.*, II, 140, Ch. IX.
8. *Ibid.*, 281, Ch. XVII.
9. *Ibid.*, 287, Ch. XVIII.
10. *Ibid.*, 289, Ch. XVIII.
11. *Ibid.*, 103, Ch. VIII.
12. Rosenberg, *From Shylock*, 74.
13. *Ivan.*, I, 83, Ch. VII.
14. *Ibid.*, 85, Ch. VII.
15. *Ibid.*, 286, Ch. XXIII.
16. *Ibid.*, 289, Ch. XXIII.
17. *Ibid.*, II, 5, Ch. I.
18. Hart, *Scott's Novels*, 157.
19. Freeman, *Norman Conquest*, V, (1876), 839; App. n. III.
20. *Mon.*, I, Intro., xxi.
21. *Ibid.*, II, 203–4, Ch. XIV.
22. *Ibid.*, I, Lang's Intro., xv.
23. *Ivan.*, I, 24, Ch. II.
24. *Mon.*, II, 152, Ch. XI; 287, Ch. XX.
25. *Ibid.*, 161, Ch. XII.
26. There are chronological inconsistencies in both *The Monastery* and *The Abbot*. These especially affect the time supposed to have elapsed between the two novels; if Halkert was about ten years old when the battle of Pinkie was fought every year would have to count for two or three if he and Mary are to be almost middle-aged when *The Abbot* opens. In the same way the child Roland could hardly have reached sixteen when Mary of Scotland is imprisoned at Loch Leven. But the reader would have to sit down with a calendar of the historical events of more than a decade to be aware of these facts; we do not observe the condensation of time in reading the narrative.
27. Hart, *Scott's Novels*, 195.
28. *Abb.*, II, 32, Ch. II.
29. *Ibid.*, 41, Ch. II.
30. *Ibid.*, 42, Ch. II.
31. *Ibid.*, 43, Ch. II.

32. *Ibid.*, 75, Ch. V.
33. *Ibid.*, 81, Ch. V.
34. *Ibid.*, 129, Ch. VIII.
35. *Ibid.*, 76–7, Ch. IV.
36. *Ibid.*, 141–2, Ch. IX.
37. Buchan, *SWS*, 231.
38. *Ken.*, I, 261, Ch. XVI.
39. *Ibid.*, 262, Ch. XVI.
40. *Ibid.*, 266, Ch. XVI.

41. *Ibid.*, 276, Ch. XVI.
42. *Ibid.*, 278, Ch. XVI.
43. *Ibid.*, II, 264, Ch. XIX.
44. *Ibid.*, 291, Ch. XXI.
45. *Ibid.*, 51, Ch. IV.
46. *Ibid.*, I, 90, Ch. VI.
47. *Ibid.*, II, 66, Ch. V.
48. *Ibid.*, 128, Ch. IX.
49. Hart, *Scott's Novels*, 205.